THE OXFORD HAN]

# CONTINENTAL PHILOSOPHY

*The Oxford Handbook of Continental Philosophy* is the definitive guide to the major themes of the continental European tradition in philosophy in the nineteenth and twentieth centuries. Brian Leiter and Michael Rosen have assembled a stellar group of contributors who provide a thematic treatment of continental philosophy, treating its subject matter philosophically and not simply as a series of museum pieces from the history of ideas. The scope of the volume is broad, with discussions covering a wide range of philosophical movements including German Idealism, existentialism, phenomenology, Marxism, postmodernism, and critical theory, as well as thinkers like Hegel, Marx, Nietzsche, Freud, Heidegger, and Foucault. This *Handbook* will be an essential reference point for graduate students and professional academics working on continental philosophy, as well as those with an interest in European literature, the history of ideas, and cultural studies.

**Brian Leiter** is John P. Wilson Professor of Law and Director of the Center for Law, Philosophy, and Human Values at the University of Chicago.

**Michael Rosen** is Professor of Government at Harvard University.

# THE OXFORD HANDBOOK OF

# CONTINENTAL PHILOSOPHY

*Edited by*

BRIAN LEITER

*and*

MICHAEL ROSEN

OXFORD

UNIVERSITY PRESS

# OXFORD
UNIVERSITY PRESS

Great Clarendon Street, Oxford OX2 6DP

Oxford University Press is a department of the University of Oxford.
It furthers the University's objective of excellence in research, scholarship,
and education by publishing worldwide in

Oxford New York

Auckland Cape Town Dar es Salaam Hong Kong Karachi
Kuala Lumpur Madrid Melbourne Mexico City Nairobi
New Delhi Shanghai Taipei Toronto

With offices in

Argentina Austria Brazil Chile Czech Republic France Greece
Guatemala Hungary Italy Japan Poland Portugal Singapore
South Korea Switzerland Thailand Turkey Ukraine Vietnam

Oxford is a registered trade mark of Oxford University Press
in the UK and in certain other countries

Published in the United States
by Oxford University Press Inc., New York

British Library Cataloguing in Publication Data
Data available

Library of Congress Cataloging in Publication Data
Data available

Typeset by Laserwords Private Limited, Chennai, India
Printed in Great Britain
by
Biddles Ltd., King's Lynn, Norfolk

ISBN 978–0–19–923409–7 (hbk.); 978–0–19–957299–1 (pbk.)

1 3 5 7 9 10 8 6 4 2

# Acknowledgments

The editors are grateful to Carsten Korfmacher for his work on the bibliography and Jolyn Piercy for her invaluable assistance in preparing the manuscript for publication. We would also like to thank Peter Momtchiloff for the invitation to undertake this project and for his helpful advice and guidance throughout.

# CONTENTS

## PART II  REASON AND CONSCIOUSNESS

## PART III  HUMAN BEING

# Notes on Contributors

**Thomas Baldwin** is Professor of Philosophy at the University of York.

**Kenneth Baynes** is Professor of Philosophy at Syracuse University, NY.

**Frederick Beiser** is Professor of Philosophy at Syracuse University, NY.

**Jessica N. Berry** is Assistant Professor of Philosophy at Georgia State University.

**Alex Callinicos** is Professor of European Studies at King's College, London.

**Taylor Carman** is Professor of Philosophy at Barnard College and Columbia University.

**James Gordon Finlayson** is Senior Lecturer in Philosophy at the University of Sussex.

**Michael N. Forster** is Glen A. Lloyd Distinguished Service Professor of Philosophy at the University of Chicago.

**Paul Franks** holds the Grafstein Chair in Jewish Philosophy at the University of Toronto.

**Sebastian Gardner** is Professor of Philosophy at University College London.

**Maximilian de Gaynesford** is Professor of Philosophy at the University of Reading.

**Gary Gutting** is Professor of Philosophy at the University of Notre Dame.

**Brian Leiter** is Wilson Professor of Law and Director of the Center for Law, Philosophy, & Human Values at the University of Chicago.

**Stephen Mulhall** is Fellow and Tutor in Philosophy at New College, Oxford University.

**Herman Philipse** is Professor of Philosophy at the University of Utrecht.

**Peter Poellner**  is Reader in Philosophy at the University of Warwick.

**Michael Rosen**  is Professor of Government at Harvard University.

**Fred Rush**  is Associate Professor of Philosophy at the University of Notre Dame.

**Robert Stern**  is Professor of Philosophy at the University of Sheffield.

**Julian Young**  is Kenan Professor of Humanities at Wake Forest University.

# INTRODUCTION

## BRIAN LEITER AND MICHAEL ROSEN

SINCE the 1970s we have entered a 'Golden Age' for English-speaking scholarship on the so-called 'Continental' traditions of philosophy, meaning (primarily) philosophy after Kant in Germany and France in the nineteenth and twentieth centuries. Much of this work has been concerned to introduce and interpret the writings of major individual thinkers and to locate them within a conceptual framework that is familiar to those with a background in the mainstream of philosophy as conventionally taught in Anglophone departments.[1] At the same time, a hallmark of recent scholarly developments is the renewed appreciation for the sometimes distinctive historical and philosophical contexts in which Continental philosophy has been produced, allowing us to appreciate both where the Continental traditions depart from those familiar in the Anglophone world and to assess the philosophical merits of the distinctive philosophical positions developed.

This volume aims to give a representative sample of these important developments in philosophical scholarship, and, more importantly, to give a broad and inclusive *thematic* treatment of Continental philosophy, treating its subject matter *philosophically* and not simply as a series of museum pieces

[1] More recently a tendency has become noticeable, under the auspices of mostly French authors, for writing on Continental philosophy to appear in English that does not attempt to establish such connections but, rather, to detach itself entirely from what it takes to be the misguided rationalism of the mainstream philosophical enterprise. The approach of this volume is very different.

from the history of ideas. Each of the essays takes up a topic from within the field in such a way as to bring key ideas into focus and capture their distinctiveness as well as providing a critical assessment of their value.

Of course, the label 'Continental philosophy' is itself problematic—uninformative at best and misleading at worst. The geographic demarcation will not suffice, since Continental Europeans like Frege, Carnap, and the early Wittgenstein are routinely excluded while, on the other hand, there is a strong case on grounds of intellectual community for including within it some Anglo-American authors (for instance, Green, Bradley, and Royce). However, the most common alternative—'post-Kantian'—presents its own difficulties. After all, reactions to Kant, albeit to different aspects of his work, have been almost as important in determining the course of philosophy in Britain and America in the twentieth century as they were in Germany and France. Nor would 'post-Hegelian' be any better, for that would make no particular sense of the inclusion of Nietzsche or Husserl. Indeed, the problems and issues to which Husserl's early writings were a response (late nineteenth-century psychologism) were much more similar to those which moved Frege, the foundational figure of the 'analytic' tradition, than to those that motivated such paradigmatic 'Continental' figures as Marx or Nietzsche.

In the face of this, the difference between analytic and Continental philosophy is sometimes characterized by analytical philosophers as one of style: analytic philosophy is careful, rigorous, and clear; Continental philosophy is not. As far as clarity is concerned, things vary drastically from author to author. Schopenhauer and Nietzsche are gifted writers of German prose, while, to the extent that Habermas is, he certainly does not go out of his way to manifest it in most of his writing. But it would strain credibility to maintain that what marks out such distinguished analytical philosophers as Michael Dummett or John McDowell from their Continental brethren is their emphasis on 'clarity'.

As a first approximation, we might say that philosophy in Continental Europe in the nineteenth and twentieth centuries is best understood as a connected weave of traditions, some of which overlap, but no one of which dominates all the others. So, for example, German Idealism marks the immediate reception and criticism of Kant's philosophy in figures like Fichte, Schelling, and Hegel, who use a comprehensive conception of reason to provide connected answers to a broad range of questions of metaphysics, epistemology, and the theory of value. The breakdown of the German Idealist view was, in turn, of central importance in motivating Marx, Kierkegaard, Schopenhauer, and, more indirectly, Nietzsche.

The reactions against Hegel's Idealism in the decades after his death in 1831 were, in fact, manifold; they included: (1) the German Materialism of the 1850s and 1860s in writers like Büchner, Moleschott, Czolbe, and Vogt (though with resonances in better-known philosophical figures like Feuerbach, Schopenhauer, and Nietzsche), who took seriously the development of modern physiology, and advocated crude versions of mind–body identity theories and the replacement of philosophy by science; (2) Marx's own repudiation of the domain of philosophy as the attempt to establish doctrines in metaphysics and epistemology in favor of a political, critical, and scientistic conception of philosophical method; and (3) the emergence of neo-Kantian thought in the latter years of the nineteenth century (e.g. Lotze, Helmholtz, Fischer, Cohen, Windelband, and Rickert) as a response to the emergence of psychology as a scientific discipline by anchoring the Kantian idea of philosophy as a transcendental enterprise within a historically and empirically defensible account of human knowledge and action.

Most of the major twentieth-century developments in 'Continental' philosophy can, in turn, be seen as responses to one or more of the nineteenth-century philosophical currents. Inasmuch as there is a Marxist tradition in philosophy, for example, it is marked by a dissatisfaction with Marx's professed ideal of a scientific, historical approach to the study of society from which all philosophical questions have been purged, a dissatisfaction expressed in figures like Lukács, Gramsci, Adorno, Horkheimer, Marcuse, and, finally, Habermas, who returns Kantian-style questions about *justification* to center stage. (The analytical Marxists in Anglophone philosophy end up, arguably, with a similar dissatisfaction.) Modern Phenomenology arose, like neo-Kantianism, in reaction to the development of modern psychology, in particular the attempt to reduce issues regarding the nature of thought, meaning, and logic to questions to be answered by an empirical scientific investigation of the facts of mental life. (Frege, foundational figure of so-called 'analytic' philosophy, was responding, as noted earlier, to exactly the same tendencies.) In the hands of Heidegger, however, the tradition is importantly transformed, with a new emphasis on the relationship between structures of meaning and the lived experience of particular individuals that inspired the French Existentialists (like Camus and Sartre) in their belief in the priority of 'existence' over 'essence'.

Other important intellectual developments associated with Continental Europe in the twentieth century do not map neatly on to the story sketched so far. The philosophical tradition we associate with 'Hermeneutics', for example, which asserts the centrality and distinctiveness of interpretation for any understanding of language (and, hence, of human beings in whose lives language plays a constitutive role), intersects with both the German Idealist and the Phenomenological traditions and brings to them a distinctive set of issues regarding the relationship between language and thought, the nature of historical and social understanding, and the essential finitude of human understanding, issues that are manifest in hermeneutically minded writers from the eighteenth through the twentieth centuries, including, Herder, Schleiermacher, Dilthey, and Gadamer.

So, too, 'Structuralism' was a movement initially not in philosophy, but in linguistics and the social sciences—associated with figures like Saussure, Lévi-Strauss, Barthes, Althusser, and others—which placed emphasis on the explanatory autonomy of systems in contrast to psychological, historical, or teleological explanations. But once this idea was imported into philosophy and psychology itself (for instance, by Lacan and Foucault) the consequence took the form of the so-called 'death of the subject' out of which in turn the tendencies known as 'post-structuralism' and 'post-modernism' emerged (in figures like Derrida, Deleuze, and Foucault again). In its most radical forms—informed by Heidegger and one (contentious) reading of Nietzsche—post-structuralism is best understood as a modern form of skepticism, calling into question not just the possibility of objective truth but of determinate understanding.

In Part I ('Problems of Method'), contributors consider the methodological problem central to all philosophy since the scientific revolution, namely, its relation to the epistemic standards and methods of the natural sciences, on the one hand, and its connection to the historical and practical situation in which philosophy finds itself, on the other. Where most of the Continental traditions differ is in their *attitude* towards science and scientific methods. While forms of philosophical naturalism have been dominant in Anglophone philosophy, the vast majority of authors within the Continental traditions insist on the distinctiveness of philosophical methods and their priority to those of the natural sciences. (Materialism and Marxism are the most obvious dissenters on this score.) Contributors examine a variety of anti-naturalist philosophical postures in the Continental traditions: phenomenology (Taylor Carman), hermeneutics (Michael N. Forster), the centrality of aesthetic experience to philosophical knowledge (Sebastian Gardner), the constitutive role of history of philosophy to philosophy (Michael Rosen), historicism (Frederick Beiser), French skeptical themes in the history and philosophy of science (Gary

Gutting), and the connection between philosophy, especially in the Marxist traditions, and practice (Alex Callinicos).

In Part II ('Reason and Consciousness'), we consider some different ways in which Kant's Copernican revolution in philosophy—his claim that philosophical questions concern the relationship between the human mind and a reality which has been, in some partial sense, *produced* by the mind—lead to a reformulation and sometimes deflation of the classical questions of metaphysics and epistemology, with a particular emphasis on the relationship between theoretical and practical reason (and their limits), and between metaphysical and epistemological problems and the nature of selfhood and consciousness. In this regard, contributors examine the very idea of a *transcendental* philosophy (Paul Franks), the purported unity of theoretical and practical reason in Kant and later figures in German philosophy (Fred Rush), the project of 'overcoming epistemology' (Herman Philipse), the metaphysical problem of 'individuals' from Hegel onward (Robert Stern), and the reorientation of metaphysics and epistemology in phenomenology, especially Husserl's (Peter Poellner).

In Part III ('Human Being'), contributors take up a family of questions with which the Continental Traditions are most often associated. What is it to be a human being (a person, an embodied being, a social being)? What is the meaning of the human (individual, social) situation? What makes human lives morally worthy and what role should moral worthiness actually play in human life? From the fundamental 'existential' questions—the meaning of life (Julian Young), the role of the 'transcendent' (Stephen Mulhall), and the import of our bodily being (Maximilian de Gaynesford)—to the fundamental moral and political questions—the moral ideal of autonomy in human life (Kenneth Baynes), the influence of the Hellenic ideal of 'harmony' in social life ( Jessica Berry), the idea of a 'critical theory' of society (Gordon Finlayson), 'humanism' and the 'death of the subject' in ethical thought (Thomas Baldwin), and skepticism about morality and its value (Brian Leiter)—contributors here consider the ways in which Continental philosophers have tackled both perennial and distinctively post-Kantian philosophical questions about human life, its social and bodily nature, and its value and meaning.

# PART 1

---

# PROBLEMS
# OF METHOD

---

CHAPTER 1

# PHENOMENOLOGY AS RIGOROUS SCIENCE

## TAYLOR CARMAN

EDMUND HUSSERL, the founder of modern phenomenology, always insisted that philosophy is not just a scholarly discipline, but can and must aspire to the status of a 'strict' or 'rigorous science' (*strenge Wissenschaft*).[1] Heidegger, by contrast, began his winter lectures in 1929 by dismissing what he called the 'delusion' that philosophy was or could be either a discipline or a science as 'the most disastrous debasement of its innermost essence.'[2] What was all the fuss about?

---

[1] Husserl, 'Philosophie als strenge Wissenschaft,' *Aufsätze und Vorträge (1911–1921). Husserliana XXV*, ed. T. Nenon and H. R. Sepp, (Dordrecht: Martinus Nijhoff, 1987); 'Philosophy as Rigorous Science', trans. Q. Lauer, *Husserl: Shorter Works*, ed. P. McCormick and F. Elliston (Notre Dame: University of Notre Dame Press, 1981). Hereafter *AV/SW*.

[2] Heidegger, *Die Grundbegriffe der Metaphysik: Welt-Endlichkeit-Einsamkeit. Gesamtausgabe 29/30* (Frankfurt: Klostermann, 1983), 2; *The Fundamental Concepts of Metaphysics: World, Finitude, Solitude*, trans. W. McNeill and N. Walker (Bloomington: Indiana University Press, 1995). Hereafter *GM*, with page references to the German edition.

# 1. Discipline and Doctrine

To understand what Husserl had in mind, it is important to begin by remembering that the word *Wissenschaft* has a wider extension than the word 'science'. German distinguishes the *Naturwissenschaften* from the *Geisteswissenschaften*, or human sciences, which Husserl and Heidegger both believed could be perfectly 'rigorous' in their own way.[3] Speakers of English, by contrast, tend to draw a threefold distinction among the natural sciences, the social sciences, and the humanities. We happily apply the word 'science' to the natural or physical sciences, less so (or with less conviction) to the (so-called) social sciences, and not at all to the humanities. No one would call a classicist or a professor of literature a 'scientist', whereas in German *Wissenschaftler* can simply mean scholar or academic.

Philosophers, too, we say, are scholars and academics, not 'scientists.' Do philosophers nevertheless think of philosophy itself as a kind of science, or as aspiring to something like scientific rigor and respectability? Evidently so, though all efforts along these lines, including Husserl's, have thus far met with what can only be called abject failure. And yet, as we know, self-images, both positive and negative, can be resistant to countervailing evidence and argument, so perhaps it should come as no surprise that philosophers continue to go about their work as if it held out the promise of definitive results, widespread consensus, and unambiguous progress. Moreover, culturally speaking, affiliation with the problems and methods of the natural sciences is deeply ingrained in the self-conception of contemporary academic philosophers, just as affiliation with Catholic dogma was central to the self-understanding of Christian thinkers in the Middle Ages.

What did Husserl envision for philosophy in 1911, when he wrote his manifesto, 'Philosophy as Rigorous Science'? Roughly speaking, three things: (1) prior, foundational status vis-à-vis the empirical and deductive sciences, (2) systematic unity, and (3) positive 'doctrinal content' (*Lehrgehalt*) based on firmly established results. This concept of rigorous science stood opposed to the then popular idea that philosophy is essentially the expression of a cultural or intellectual 'worldview' (*Weltanschauung*), an idea Husserl attributed to the influence of Hegel and saw above all in the historicism of Wilhelm Dilthey.

---

[3] See Heidegger's remarks in 'The Age of the World Picture', *Holzwege* (Frankfurt: Klostermann, 1950; 6th, rev. edn. 1980), 77; *Off the Beaten Track*, trans. J. Young and K. Haynes (Cambridge: Cambridge University Press, 2002), 60.

Husserl dismissed *Weltanschauung* philosophy as failing to come to grips with the concept of science as absolute knowledge for its own sake: 'For modern consciousness, the ideas of culture (*Bildung*) or worldview and science ... have been sharply separated, and from now on they remain separated for all eternity' (*AV* 51/*SW* 191).

With respect to the first and possibly the second but not the third desideratum, philosophy as rigorous science stands opposed to *naturalism*, that is, the attempt to regard all phenomena as empirically given facts of nature. Psychologism, for example, is a form of naturalism with respect to consciousness, and Husserl began his *Logical Investigations* (1900/1) with a detailed critique of the fallacy of conflating the normativity and ideality of mental content, above all the cognitive content of logic and mathematics, with brute psychological facts. Indeed, what unites historicism and naturalism, Husserl argues, is their shared failure to distinguish facts from essences, hence their failure to recognize the way in which ideal logical and mathematical structures make reality, including psychological reality, intelligible: 'Naturalists and historicists ... both ... misconstrue ideas as facts and ... transform all reality, all life into an unintelligible, idealess jumble of "facts". The superstition of the fact is common to them all' (*AV* 56/*SW* 193).

In his 1919 'Recollections of Franz Brentano,' Husserl describes how his conception of philosophical scientificity had been initially inspired by his teacher: 'It was from his lectures that I first formed the conviction that gave me the courage to choose philosophy as my life's work, namely, that philosophy too is a field for serious work, that it too can and must be conducted in the spirit of a most rigorous science'(*AV* 305/*SW* 343). Husserl's conception of what rigorous scientific philosophy would require, however, soon departed from Brentano's. Of Brentano Husserl says,

Though deeply penetrating and often ingenious in intuitive analysis, he moved relatively quickly from intuition to theory ... He had little esteem for thinkers like Kant and the post-Kantian German idealists, for whom the value of original intuition and anticipatory presentiment was so much greater than that of logical method and scientific theory. That a philosophical thinker could be esteemed as great though all his theories taken strictly were unscientific ... Brentano would have scarcely conceded. ... Devoted to the austere ideal of rigorous philosophical science (represented for him by the exact natural sciences), he regarded the systems of German idealism as merely degenerate. Guided entirely by Brentano at the beginning, I myself later came to the view now shared by so many researchers intent on a rigorous scientific philosophy: that the idealistic systems ... must rather be seen as youthful and immature, but must also be valued to the utmost. Kant and the subsequent German idealists may have offered little that was satisfactory or tenable in the scientifically rigorous development of the problems that motivated them so powerfully. Yet anyone capable of really understanding and becoming acquainted with those problems in their intuitive content knows that entirely new and utterly radical dimensions of philosophical problems emerge in the idealistic systems, and that the final and highest goals of philosophy emerge only with the clarification and development of the methods characteristically demanded by them.   (*AV* 308–9/*SW* 344–5)

That same year, and in a similar vein, Husserl wrote, 'I speak of phenomenology as a mathematician speaks of mathematics: that it is a genuine science, forged out of clear evidence, a field of possible true and false propositions—he speaks this way in spite of all skeptics and confused philosophers, because he "sees" '[4] At least by 1919, then, Husserl was closer to the idealist tradition than Brentano ever was; moreover, it was precisely that tradition's emphasis on direct intuitive insight, as opposed to abstract analysis and theory construction, that informed his mature understanding of what true scientific rigor would mean for phenomenology.

Of course, just as there were deep and important differences between Kantian critical philosophy and the speculative systems that came after it, so too the differences between Kant and Husserl with regard to science and intuition are crucial as well as instructive. Near the beginning of 'Philosophy as Rigorous Science' Husserl writes, 'Kant was fond of saying that one could not learn philosophy, but only to philosophize. What is that but an admission of philosophy's unscientific character? As far as science, real science, extends, so far can one teach and learn, and this everywhere in the same sense' (*AV* 4/*SW* 166–7). Kant's remark occurs in the Architectonic chapter in the Doctrine of Method, near the end of the *Critique of Pure Reason*.[5] Earlier Kant distinguishes between a discipline (*Disziplin*), which corrects reason and is thus wholly negative, and a teaching or doctrine (*Belehrung*), which instructs and delivers positive content (A710/B738n). Mathematics has positive doctrinal content since reason can grasp synthetic a priori truths by pure intuition of formal spatial and temporal relations. Philosophy, by contrast, can have no such speculative or theoretical content of its own, since it deals only with concepts, not intuitions, and so cannot construct content

---

[4]  Letter to Arnold Metzger, *SW* 363.
[5]  *Kants Werke*, Akademie Textausgabe, iii and iv, ed. Königlich Preußische Akademie der Wissenschaften (Berlin: Walter de Gruyter, 1968). *Critique of Pure Reason*, ed. and trans. P. Guyer and A. W. Wood (Cambridge: Cambridge University Press, 1998). I quote the Guyer and Wood's translation, with very minor emendations.

beyond what is already contained in the concepts it considers: '*Philosophical* cognition is *rational cognition* from *concepts,* mathematical cognition that from the *construction* of concepts. But to *construct* a concept means to exhibit a priori the intuition corresponding to it. For the construction of a concept, therefore, a *nonempirical* intuition is required' (A713/B741).

For Kant, then, philosophical cognition, at least in its speculative or theoretical application, must be critical, not dogmatic; theoretical philosophy can only be a discipline, not a doctrine; it can be practiced, even mastered, but not acquired in the form of new information: 'all transcendental logic is in this respect nothing but a discipline' (A796/B824). 'Among all rational sciences (a priori), therefore, only mathematics can be learned, never philosophy (except historically); rather, as far as reason is concerned, one can at most only learn *to philosophize*' (A837/B865). Traditionally, in pursuing its systematic aims, philosophy has tended to swing like a pendulum between bold epistemic confidence and radical doubt; philosophers have proceeded, like Wolff or like Hume, 'either *dogmatically* or *skeptically*'. But both paths are dead ends, Kant claims to have shown, and 'The *critical* path alone is still open' (A856/B884).

In calling for a philosophy that could be learned in the form of a substantive doctrine, rather than merely mastered as a critical discipline, Husserl was in effect arguing that philosophy ought to be 'dogmatic' in the Kantian sense of the word. Philosophy must aspire not only to disciplinary rigor, but positive 'doctrinal content' (*Lehrgehalt*), as one finds in the empirical and deductive sciences. Such positive content, Husserl says, will not constitute 'a philosophical "system" in the traditional sense, like a Minerva springing forth complete and full-panoplied from the head of some creative genius, only in later times to be kept along with other such Minervas in the silent museum of history.' Instead, it will be 'a philosophical system of doctrine (*Lehrsystem*) that, after the enormous preparatory work of generations, genuinely commences from below with an indubitable foundation and rises up like any secure construction in which stone is set upon stone, each as solid as the next, in accordance with guiding insights' (*AV* 6/*SW* 167).

Kant regarded that philosophical goal as unrealizable in principle, at least for theoretical reason, which lacks the intellectual intuition necessary to supply knowledge beyond the bounds of experience, that is, beyond appearances to things in themselves. Husserl rejected Kant's distinction between phenomena and noumena; moreover, he believed that phenomenology could deliver rational synthetic insights based on what in *Logical Investigations* he calls 'categorial intuition,' and later in *Ideas I*, the 'intuition of essences' (*Wesenserschauung*).[6] Husserl's idea of philosophy as rigorous science, then, rests not just on his polemic against naturalism and historicism, but on a substantive epistemological theory of intellectual intuition. It was precisely that theory that Heidegger rejected, and with it Husserl's ambitious but forlorn conviction that transcendental phenomenology could play a vital role in laying the foundations for the sciences and expanding human knowledge.

## 2. INTUITION AND UNDERSTANDING

Essential to Husserl's conception of scientific phenomenological method is what he calls 'the principle of all principles,' namely, 'that every primordially presenting intuition (*Anschauung*) is a source of legitimacy for cognition, that everything that presents itself to us primordially in "intuition" (so to speak, in its incarnate actuality) is to be accepted simply as what it presents itself to be' (*Id I* 43).[7] This is because, for Husserl, 'immediate "seeing", not merely sensuous, experiential seeing, but seeing in general as primordially presenting consciousness of whatever kind, is the ultimate source of legitimacy of all rational assertions' (*Id I* 36). Husserl, that is, felt he could justify his own claims concerning the intentional structure of consciousness only by showing intuition itself to be a legitimate and legitimating source of philosophical evidence, capable of delivering general, intelligible contents, not just brute particulars. He therefore insisted that we enjoy not just sensuous, but also categorial, or logically structured, intuitions. The 'principle of all principles,' then, is a methodological application of the theory of categorial intuition, and what Husserl also later simply called the 'seeing' of essences. Categorial intuitions are intuitions satisfying or fulfilling attitudes whose contents include formal elements such as *is* and *not*, the logical connectives *if*, *then*, *and*, and

---

[6] Husserl, *Ideen zu einer reinen Phänomenologie und phänomenologischen Philosophie, Erstes Buch: Allgemeine Einführung in die reine Phänomenologie* (Tübingen: Niemeyer, 1913; 1993), 10 ff.; *Ideas Pertaining to a Pure Phenomenology and to a Phenomenological Philosophy. First Book*, trans. F. Kersten (The Hague: Nijhoff, 1983), 8 ff. Hereafter *Id I*, with page references to the German edition. By 'essence' (*Wesen*) Husserl does not mean the *defining* property of a thing, but *any* property or form understood as ideal or general, as opposed to real or particular.

[7] Heidegger refers explicitly to this passage some forty years later in *Zur Sache des Denkens* (Tübingen: Niemeyer, 1969), 69–70; *Time and Being*, trans. J. Stambaugh (New York: Harper & Row, 1972), 63.

*or*, and quantifiers like *all, some, many, few, a*, and *none*. Contrary to classical empiricism, such logical or conceptual content cannot be derived from sensations simply through processes of association and abstraction. Instead, we must have immediate intuitive insight into the logically structured states of affairs that render our higher-order judgments true or false.[8]

So, for example, we see objects (such as leaves) and their properties (such as green), but we also *see*— and not just metaphorically—that the leaf *is* (or *is not*) green. Similarly, without having to see the knife *and see* the fork (in two acts of seeing), we see the knife *and* the fork together on the table: we see their conjunction; we see the *and*. Similarly, we see that *if* the child pulls the cord, *then* the lamp will fall, or that *either* the child will tug on the cord *or* the lamp will *not* fall. When I look at the sky, I see the *manyness* of the stars or the *fewness* of the clouds without having to count them. Sartre makes the same point in *Being and Nothingness* when he says that whereas one *sees* that Pierre is *not* in the café, one at best idly judges, but does not literally see, that the Duke of Wellington and Paul Valéry are not.[9]

Is there such a thing as categorial intuition? The concept is easier to disparage than to refute, especially considering the implausible alternative of epistemically inert sense data disconnected from and radically heterogeneous with the conceptual contents of judgment.[10] More problematic than the idea of categorial intuition itself, however, is Husserl's insistence that it grounds our understanding of the world; that it is primitive, authoritative, and neither in need of nor susceptible to further critical analysis or genealogical scrutiny.

It is widely but wrongly assumed that Heidegger embraced the theory of categorial intuition, indeed that he simply took it for granted as licensing his own phenomenological claims in *Being and Time*. This is not so, though it is true that the theory made a powerful impression on him and inspired his effort to pursue the question of *being* by means of a phenomenology of everyday understanding. Heidegger, of course, was especially drawn to the account of 'the origin of the concept of being' in §44 of the Sixth of the *Logical Investigations*, in which Husserl argues that we have a direct intuition not just of sensible particulars, but of being (and nonbeing). No doubt Husserl's theory

[8] Husserl, *Logische Untersuchungen*, ii/2 (Tübingen: Niemeyer, 1921; 1980), §40; *Logical Investigations*, ii, trans. J. N. Findlay (London and New York: Routledge, 1970; 2001), §40.

[9] Sartre, *L'Être et le néant* (Paris: Éditions Gallimard, 1943), 43 ff.; *Being and Nothingness: An Essay on Phenomenological Ontology*, trans. H. Barnes (New York: Washington Square Press, 1966), 40 ff.

[10] For a recent influential anti-empiricist argument along these lines, see John McDowell, *Mind and World* (Cambridge, MA: Harvard University Press, 1994).

also appealed to Heidegger in offering an antidote to the intellectualism of neo-Kantian epistemology, according to which all objective experience must be mediated by judgment. Whatever attraction the theory held for Heidegger thus had less to do with its assertion of the primacy of intuition than with its claim that we have a prepredicative understanding of being, prior not just to reflection and introspection, but to all attitudes with fully propositional content.

If Heidegger ultimately rejected the theory of categorial intuition, then, it was not because he reverted to a sharp Kantian distinction between intuitions and concepts, but because he thought all forms of intuition, whether sensible or categorial, are derivative of a more basic form of intentionality that is *not* passive intuition or observation, but engaged practical agency, or 'understanding' (*Verstehen*). Heidegger's objection was thus not an objection to the notion that conceptual content can be apprehended in intuition prior to its articulation in an act of judgment, but rather to the idea that understanding must always be grounded in intuition, rather than vice versa. Husserl inherited the assumption of the primacy of intuition, whether sensible or categorial, from the epistemological tradition going back to Plato, and it was this assumption Heidegger emphatically rejected: 'Under the unbroken hegemony of traditional ontology, the genuine mode of registering what truly is has been decided in advance. It lies in *noein*, "intuition" in the widest sense, from which *dianoein*, "thinking" (*Denken*), is simply derived as a founded form.'[11]

The reduction of intentionality to intuition on the one hand and thought on the other is, according to Heidegger, part of a broader ontological assumption that entities can *be* only by being object-like or 'occurrent' (*vorhanden*), hence ideally accessible to theoretical attitudes such as observation and judgment. Husserlian phenomenology, notwithstanding its laudable injunction to return to a concrete description of phenomena, is yet another case of philosophical fixation on intuition, presence, and the temporal present:

> The thesis that all cognition has its goal in 'intuition' has the temporal meaning that all cognition is a making present (*Gegenwärtigen*). Whether every science, or even philosophical thought, aims at a making present shall remain undecided here.—Husserl uses the expression 'making present' (*Gegenwärtigen*) to characterize sense perception (*SZ* 363n.).

---

[11] Heidegger, *Sein und Zeit* (Tübingen: Niemeyer, 1927; 1979), 96. *Being and Time*, trans. J. Macquarrie and E. Robinson (New York: Harper & Row, 1962). Hereafter *SZ*, with page references to the German edition.

In *Being and Time* Heidegger attempts to supplant these long-standing epistemological and metaphysical prejudices, including those still at work in Husserl's phenomenology, with a *hermeneutical* account of understanding as situated projection into future—or more precisely, future-*constituting*—possibilities. Such an account is meant to reveal the untenability of the idea that understanding is grounded in thought and intuition directed exclusively to objects and objective states of affairs:

By showing how all sight is grounded primarily in understanding... we have robbed pure intuition of its privilege, which corresponds noetically to the privileging of the occurrent in traditional ontology. 'Intuition' and 'thought' are both derivatives of understanding, indeed rather remote ones. Even the phenomenological 'intuition of essences' (*Wesensschau*) is grounded in existential understanding.   (*SZ* 147)

The allusion to Husserl here is unmistakable, as is the implication that phenomenology cannot vindicate its scientific pretensions by appeal to any such notion of grounding and authoritative intuition. But again, the reason is not that Heidegger doubted that intuition can have categorial or conceptual content, but rather that he took conceptual content to be parasitic on the content of understanding, which is neither intuitive nor judgmental, but *projective* in character.


## 3. DESCRIPTION AND INTERPRETATION

What does Heidegger's rejection of Husserl's theory of intuition imply concerning the character and authority of phenomenological description? It is important to remember, first, that Husserl and Heidegger agree that phenomenology must be a qualitative and descriptive rather than a hypothetical or explanatory enterprise, let alone an exact science. But what is *description*? How do the relevant qualitative features of the world and ourselves manifest themselves? How are they available to us? Husserl, for his part, conceived of phenomenology on analogy with representation and taxonomy in natural sciences like botany. Geometry, for all its exactness, he says, lacks the resources for depicting qualities like ' "serrated", "notched", "lens-shaped", "umbellate", and the like' (*Id I* 138). Husserlian phenomenology thus aspires to a kind of 'systematic and eidetic morphology' of the structures and contents of consciousness (*Id I* 302).

Heidegger agrees that phenomenology must be descriptive rather than explanatory, but he is suspicious of what he calls 'the at bottom tautological expression "descriptive phenomenology".' Since there is no *other* kind of phenomenology, the qualifying adjective 'descriptive' is empty and misleading. Very probably with Husserl's gloss on the difference between exact and descriptive sciences in mind, Heidegger goes on to explain how he understands the descriptive aims of phenomenology: ' "Description" here does not mean a procedure in the manner of, say, botanical morphology' (*SZ* 35); rather, 'the meaning of phenomenological description as a method is *interpretation*'. For Heidegger, that is, 'The phenomenology of Dasein is a *hermeneutic*' (*SZ* 37).

Interpretation is not to be contrasted with description as such, then, but with a certain kind of description, one that purports to point us directly to some immediately given object, which we can simply *see* to be as the description says it is. A paradigm case might be, for example, calling the sky 'blue' or the grass 'green' and then pointing them out to someone and saying, 'See for yourself!' And in such mundane cases, hopefully, we can indeed simply see for ourselves.

Can the claims of phenomenology be vindicated in this way? If so, one is tempted to say, as some critics have, then surely the whole operation could be wrapped up pretty quickly and controversies settled once and for all. Why has this not happened? If Heidegger is right, the reason is that the kind of 'evidence' available to phenomenology is radically unlike the objects and states of affairs perceptually available to the empirical sciences and common sense and more like what is available to ethical interpretations of human conduct and aesthetic interpretations of works of art, namely, a certain way things have of *hanging together* and *making sense* in a context, under an aspect, which goes beyond anything we simply register or straightforwardly observe. As Heidegger says, 'Interpretation is never a presuppositionless apprehension of something pregiven' (*SZ* 150). The intelligibility underlying and legitimating the claims of phenomenology, then, reveals itself not to intuition, but to understanding and interpretation.

This is why, as early as 1920, in his 'Comments on Karl Jaspers's *Psychology of Worldviews*,' Heidegger expresses his distrust of blunt appeals to phenomenological intuition, in contrast to the always open-ended work of interpretation:

The path to the 'things themselves' under consideration in philosophy is a long one, so that the excessive liberties that certain phenomenologists have taken recently with insights into essences (*Wesenseinsichten*) appear in a highly dubious light, which hardly accords with the 'openness' and 'devotion' they preach.[12]

Intuition of essences, as Husserl describes it, can only look like a highly questionable shortcut in the ongoing effort of philosophical interpretation. Are such intuitions really as plainly manifest and self-evident as Husserl maintains? Are they not instead parasitic on prior interpretations that merely lend them the appearance of self-evidence? And what are the worldly phenomena themselves underlying those intuitions? Are they not phenomena we have already understood very differently than the intuitions now purport? In short, what understandings do our intuitions presuppose? There is arguably no such thing as getting back behind or around our presuppositions. Instead, what Heidegger calls the 'hermeneutic situation' in which fundamental ontology finds itself consists precisely in the presuppositions that always already situate such inquiry as a matter of principle (*SZ* 232).

And yet, if phenomenology must be hermeneutical in order to be descriptive in the right way, as Heidegger maintains, might it not still be 'scientific' in Husserl's sense? Heidegger's view about this seems to have oscillated during the decade of the 1920s. In his 1920–1 lectures on the phenomenology of religion he insists on a 'difference in principle between science and philosophy' and dismisses what he calls 'the prejudice of philosophy as a science'.[13] Similarly, in his 1923 Freiburg lectures on 'ontology' he cautions that the word should not be taken to mean a 'discipline, one belonging, for instance, within the field of inquiry of neo-scholasticism, or of phenomenological scholasticism and the directions of academic philosophy influenced by it'.[14]

However, during his five-year teaching stint at the University of Marburg, an untenured but prestigious appointment to which Husserl gave his enthusiastic support, Heidegger seems to have changed his tune. In his 1927 lecture on

---

[12] Heidegger, *Wegmarken. Gesamtausgabe* 9, ed. F-W. von Herrmann (Frankfurt: Klostermann, 1976), 5; *Pathmarks*, ed. W. McNeill (Cambridge: Cambridge University Press, 1998), 4. Hereafter *W/P*.

[13] Heidegger, *Phänomenologie des religiösen Lebens. Gesamtausgabe* 60, ed. M. Jung, T. Regehly, and C. Strube (Frankfurt: Klostermann, 1995), 3–4; *The Phenomenology of Religious Life*, trans. M. Fritsch and J. A. Gosett-Ferencei (Bloomington: Indiana University Press, 2004), 3–4.

[14] Heidegger, *Ontologie (Hermeneutik der Faktizität). Gesamtausgabe* 63, ed. K. Bröcker-Oltmanns (Frankfurt: Klostermann, 1988), 1; *Ontology—The Hermeneutics of Facticity*, trans. J. van Buren (Bloomington: Indiana University Press, 1999), 1. Interestingly, Heidegger's choice of words here echoes Dilthey's reference to Brentano's 'psychological scholasticism' and his observation that 'Husserl is the extreme instance of this.' See Dilthey, *The Formation of the Historical World in the Human Sciences. Selected Works*, iii, ed. R. Makkreel and F. Rodi (Princeton: Princeton University Press, 2002), 257.

'Phenomenology and Theology', for example, he glosses the relation between theology and philosophy as a '*relation of two sciences*': the former, a 'positive' science (a science of entities); the latter, '*the* science of being, the ontological science, philosophy'. Theology, he still insists, is 'therefore as such absolutely distinct from philosophy' (*W* 47–9/*P* 40–1). Similarly, in *Being and Time* itself Heidegger refers to fundamental ontology as 'a science *of being as such*' (*SZ* 230), and in the summer lectures of 1927 he seems to follow Husserl in dismissing *Weltanschauung* philosophy in order to affirm more emphatically the true 'scientific' character of philosophy. And yet, here again, he does so not exactly by endorsing Husserl's argument, but by casting doubt on the terms in which Husserl framed the issue:

The distinction between scientific philosophy and *Weltanschauung* philosophy is invalid . . . since the concept of a *Weltanschauung* philosophy is not even a coherent concept. . . . To anyone who has even the slightest understanding of the concept of philosophy and its history, the notion of a *Weltanschauung* philosophy is an oxymoron (*hölzeres Eisen*). If one of the terms of the distinction between scientific philosophy and *Weltanschauung* philosophy is a nonconcept, then the other must also be ill-defined. If one sees that *Weltanschauung* philosophy, if it is to be philosophy, is fundamentally impossible, then the distinguishing adjective 'scientific' is no longer needed to characterize philosophy. That it is that, lies in its concept.[15]

Like 'descriptive phenomenology,' then, the expression 'scientific philosophy' is inappropriate not because it's incorrect, but because it's redundant. Tellingly, in *Being and Time* Heidegger lodges the same objection to the expression 'philosophy of life' (*Lebensphilosophie*), since for him philosophy is *essentially* bound up with human being-in-the-world and cannot *not* be, so the term is vacuous (*SZ* 46). This observation should have led readers to doubt Heidegger's commitment to the programmatic intentions behind such labels, since evidently he regarded them all as at best empty and misleading.

It nevertheless may have come as a shock to anyone familiar with Heidegger's habit of echoing (or seeming to echo) Husserl's rhetoric of scientificity when, in his lectures of 1929–30, he dropped all ambiguity by explicitly repudiating the notion that philosophy was or could be anything like a science. That idea, he now says, is not merely empty or tautological, but fundamentally wrong. Heidegger opens his lectures with a rhetorical question:

---

[15] Heidegger, *Grundprobleme der Phänomenologie. Gesamtausgabe* 24. Marburg lectures, summer 1927, ed. F-W. von Herrmann (Frankfurt: Klostermann, 1975), 16; *The Basic Problems of Phenomenology*, trans. A. Hofstadter (Bloomington: Indiana University Press, 1982; rev. edn., 1988), 12.

'What if it were a *prejudice* that metaphysics is a fixed and secure discipline, and an *illusion* that philosophy is a science that can be taught and learned?' Having reiterated the familiar observation that modern philosophy has failed to establish any decisive results since its inception with Descartes, Heidegger asks,

Or is all this talk of philosophy being the absolute science a delusion? Not just because the individual or some school never achieves this end, but because positing the end is itself fundamentally an error and a misunderstanding of the innermost essence of philosophy. Philosophy as absolute science—a lofty, unsurpassable ideal. So it seems. And yet perhaps even judging philosophy according to the idea of science is the most disastrous debasement of its innermost essence. (*GM* 2)[16]

Heidegger still insists that 'the interpretation of philosophy as the propagation of a *Weltanschauung* involves the same mendacity as characterizing it as science.' In the end, he says, philosophy is '*determinable only in terms of itself and as itself*—comparable to nothing in terms of which it could be positively defined. In that case philosophy is something *original and autonomous (Eigenständiges)*, something *ultimate*' (*GM* 3). Philosophy, in any case, 'is something totally different from science' (*GM* 15), not just because it has failed to achieve definitive results, but because philosophical truth is different from and incommensurable with scientific, and particularly mathematical, truth:

We do not deny philosophy the character of absolute science because it has never yet attained it, but because this idea of the philosophical essence is attributed to philosophy on the basis of its ambiguity, and because this idea undermines the essence of philosophy at its core. . . . Although it objectively comprises a great wealth, mathematical knowledge is in itself, in terms of its content, the emptiest knowledge that can be conceived, and as such is at the same time the least binding for human beings. (*GM* 24–5)

Hence, for Heidegger, as for Kant before him, 'mathematical knowledge cannot be advanced as the ideal of philosophical knowledge' (*GM* 25).

By the winter semester of 1929/30, then, Heidegger had shed whatever remained of his lingering ambivalent loyalty to Husserl's vision of phenomenology as a rigorous and 'purely' descriptive scientific discipline.

---

[16] It is hard not to read the following caricature of academic philosophers as an allusion to Husserl and the technical jargon of phenomenology: 'And the teacher—what can he not prove, what a forest of concepts and terminology he moves about in, wielding some scientific apparatus, so that the poor listener is scared away. He enters in, as if with him philosophy has come to the world as absolute science for the first time' (*GM* 18).

The consistency that (re)emerged in Heidegger's view in 1929 was due in part, no doubt, to the professional and intellectual autonomy he now enjoyed, having taken over the chair in philosophy at Freiburg upon Husserl's retirement, and apparently having severed all personal and professional ties with his former friend and mentor. The truth is that the fervent antiscientism that surfaced in the 1929–30 lectures was the culmination of a sustained battle Heidegger had been fighting all along against Husserl's phenomenology, and indeed his entire conception of philosophy, throughout the 1920s.[17]

Heidegger was initially drawn to the theory of categorial intuition because it offered an alternative to Kantian intellectualism. But he rejected Husserl's assumption that understanding, which *projects* meaning beyond what is presently given, presupposes and must always appeal to intuition, which simply *presents* what is given as present. Heidegger's assertion of the priority of *understanding* to intuition—and of the *future* to the present—constitutes perhaps the deepest philosophical difference between his thought and Husserl's, and so too between the scientific ideal of pure description and the hermeneutic model of projective interpretation.

## 4. APPEARANCES AND PHENOMENA

Not surprisingly, then, Husserl and Heidegger turn out to have had radically different notions of what the *phenomena*, or the 'things themselves' are, to which phenomenology calls us to return. Remarking that the word 'phenomenon' is ambiguous 'between *appearing* and *that which appears*,' Husserl insists that the term be 'used primarily for the appearing itself, the subjective phenomenon,' that is, for the contents immanent in consciousness, not the objects transcendent to it.[18]

Heidegger, by contrast, initially treats the term 'phenomenon' as what he calls a 'formal indicator' referring simply to 'that which shows itself, the manifest' (*SZ* 28), a notion that 'has in the first instance nothing

[17] See my *Heidegger's Analytic: Interpretation, Discourse, and Authenticity in 'Being and Time'* (Cambridge: Cambridge University Press, 2003), 57–60.

[18] Husserl, *Die Idee der Phänomenologie: Fünf Vorlesungen*, ed. W. Biemel, 2nd edn., Husserliana II (The Hague: Nijhoff, 1950; rev. edn. 1973), 14; *The Idea of Phenomenology*, trans. W. P. Alston and G. Nakhnikian (The Hague: Nijhoff, 1973), 11.

whatever to do with what one calls "appearance", or indeed "mere appear-ance" ' (*SZ* 29).[19] Heidegger's point is that the phenomena of phenomenology are not 'appearances', if that term means something *indicating* or *referring to* something else, as for example, Husserl supposed, consciousness indicates or refers to its objects in the way linguistic expressions refer to theirs, by means of intervening descriptive, hence in principle explicable, semantic contents. For Heidegger, that is, the phenomenon of phenomenology is not what Husserl's calls 'the subjective phenomenon', namely the *immanent* content of consciousness standing in representational or referential relations to *transcendent* objects, which appear in or through it. Rather, a phenomenon is what 'appears' in the bland (nonrepresentational, nonreferential) sense of simply *showing up*, or *manifesting itself*. Heidegger thus refuses to define phenomenology from the outset in terms of its putative domain of application: 'The word only informs us of the *how* of the way of showing and treating *what* is to be dealt with in this science' (*SZ* 34–5); it does not yet specify the *what*, or subject matter, itself. Heidegger's deliberate redefinition of phenomenology is thus bound up with his repudiation of Husserl's representationalism, internalism, and mentalism.

In addition to the purely formal notion, Heidegger also offers a substantive, or what he calls the specifically 'phenomenological', concept of phenomena. Taken formally, a phenomenon is just anything that manifests itself, as opposed to appearing in or through some representational or referential intermediary. Substantively, however, not every aspect of what manifests itself is 'given' in the sense of being self-evident or fully open to intuitive inspection. Indeed, 'what is to become phenomenon can be hidden. And it is precisely because phenomena are first and for the most part *not* given that there is a need for phenomenology' (*SZ* 36). A phenomenon in the substantive phenomenological sense, then, is

something that first and for the most part precisely does *not* show itself, something that, in contrast to what first and for the most part shows itself, is *hidden*, but is at the same time something that essentially belongs to that which first and for the most part shows itself, and belongs to it in such a way as to constitute its meaning and ground.   (*SZ* 35)

The task of phenomenology is therefore not to give a 'purely' descriptive report of something self-evidently given, but rather to let the ordinarily

---

[19] By 'mere appearance' Heidegger means *phenomenon* in the Kantian sense, that is, the appearance of something that *never* shows itself, namely the thing in itself. That point is not directly relevant to Husserl, who rejected the phenomenon/noumenon distinction.

hidden aspects of what shows itself *show themselves*, or make themselves manifest. Moreover, since Heidegger interprets *logos* as a 'letting something be seen' (*SZ* 33), he takes the interpretive work of the phenomenologist to lie in *drawing out, evoking, and uncovering* what is covered up and buried over in what ordinarily shows itself in our everyday understanding.

## 5. Projection and Presentation

Why, then, according to Heidegger, can such an effort of hermeneutical uncovering never be rigorously scientific, in Husserl's sense? Because, in short, the *phenomena* of hermeneutical phenomenology are not objects or objective facts available to intuition and pure description, but rather aspects or conditions of intelligibility. They are not subjective conscious states, nor even, as Husserl would have it, objective essences of subjective conscious states, available to inner intuitive reflection on our own minds. They are hidden aspects of the ways in which things *show up* as making sense to us. Such aspects of intelligibility are not objects of intuition, but instead constitute an always transcendent horizon of understanding. The way something shows up as making sense, that is, consists in *how we are to* understand it, what *kind* of thing it is for us, how one *ought* to treat it, and so on. Such things are neither outwardly perceptible nor available to inner reflection, but go beyond any given objective or factual data. And where there can be no objective or factual data, there can be no empirical or intuitive inquiry, no fixed or enduring doctrine, no science. What is at stake in hermeneutical phenomenology, then, is neither *facts* nor essences regarded as objectively given data in intuition, but rather *norms* and conditions of understanding and interpretation.

Consider an analogy with textual interpretation, an analogy made at once obvious and inevitable by the hermeneutical model to which Heidegger appeals. When we interpret a text, we may be concerned with matters of fact about the letters or words on the page, original manuscripts or early editions, what the author was thinking, where or how or with whom he or she was living, and so on. And of course there can be (more or less) scientific inquiries into such matters of fact. Questions concerning the *meaning* or *significance* of the text, however, are questions of a radically different order. Crudely put, what is at stake in the interpretation of the text is nothing merely factual, but *normative*, not an *is* but an *ought*, namely *how to* understand the text, how it *ought* to be read. Hermeneutical questions, that is, cannot always be answered by appeal to facts, for what is often at issue in the interpretation of a text is not *how things are*, but rather, as Wittgenstein says, *how to go on*.

Does it make sense to talk about direct intuitive apprehension of a *norm* of this sort, that is, a way something *is to be done*? We rely freely on visual metaphors to describe both practical and theoretical insight, of course. Heidegger himself says, 'Dealing with things by using and handling them . . . is not blind, but has its own kind of sight (*Sichtart*), which he calls 'circumspection' (*Umsicht*)' (*SZ* 69). But ordinary locutions and metaphors like these leave entirely open whether the insight of circumspective intelligence is projective or intuitive, that is to say, whether it *anticipates* possibilities or merely *apprehends* actualities. To what degree is *seeing* my way out of an awkward conversation, or *seeing* how to repair a watch, like seeing the shape of a flower? Granted, there are borderline or hybrid cases: seeing how to get downtown by looking at a subway map involves both seeing the de facto layout of the lines and seeing *how* to get from here to there. But the borderline and hybrid cases just make the difference between projective understanding and passive perception that much clearer: seeing how to get out of debt is utterly unlike seeing the moon on the horizon.

Of course, what Heidegger says about practical understanding could also be said of disciplines involving deductive insight, as opposed to empirical intuition. Logic and mathematics are perfectly rigorous sciences, after all, even if it turns out that the kind of intelligence they require has more in common with the spontaneity of projective understanding than with the receptivity of sense perception. Suppose deductive insight is no more literally 'intuitive' than practical circumspection; surely logic and mathematics remain paradigms of rigorous scientific achievement nonetheless.

Two replies are open to Heidegger, one that he did make and another that he could have. First, as we have seen, Heidegger dismisses logical and mathematical knowledge as 'the emptiest knowledge that can be conceived, and as such . . . at the same time the least binding for human beings' (*GM* 25). This provocative remark raises deep issues about whether and how logical and mathematical norms are indeed 'binding' for us. A charitable reading might suggest that what Heidegger means is that such norms are not constraints on our freedom, since what they rule out is nothing one could knowingly want to think or assert. Indeed, what they prohibit is arguably precisely and only the kind of fallacies we already know to avoid and deny; it is not as if we are thwarted and barred from those fallacies because some obscure and arbitrary external authority forbids them. Similarly, in dismissing logical and mathematical knowledge as 'empty', Heidegger could be suggesting that, though formally valid, such disciplines do not strictly speaking supply us with *knowledge*, precisely because they are by definition indifferent with respect to all material content. These are not implausible claims, and if true, they do indeed distinguish phenomenology, which, after all, like the sciences, aspires to genuine cognitive constraint and content, from purely formal disciplines, which do not.

The second reply, of which Heidegger could have availed himself, though he did not, is to say that logic and mathematics are rigorous sciences not because they rest on passive intuitions of essences, as Husserl supposed, but simply because they have in fact achieved definitive and lasting results and established widespread and enduring consensus among knowledgeable experts. How they have done this, one might say, remains at some level an epistemological mystery. But they have done it, and their sheer success is arguably what vindicates their claim to scientific rigor. If philosophy enjoyed comparable success, it would hardly matter whether it did so by means of intuition or some other form of intelligence or insight. Platonism, after all—which is to say the assimilation of theoretical insight to visual perception—is a philosophical *interpretation* of the experience of understanding something by grasping it in an instant; it is not a condition or criterion that we know a priori scientific knowledge must satisfy.

It is important to remember, then, that Heidegger's argument against the scientificity of philosophy is at bottom an argument against Husserl's conception of what makes rigorous science possible, namely categorial intuition and the intuition of essences. If in principle, *pace* Husserl, rigorous science requires no such grounding in intuition, then arguments for and against the prospect of a scientific philosophy would have to proceed by appeal to some other criterion, for example rational systematic unity in the organization of knowledge as a whole.

# 6. Architectonic and Rhapsody

Systematic unity was the criterion of scientific knowledge for Kant and the German idealists, and Husserl too regarded it as a necessary though not a sufficient condition of rigorous science. According to Kant, 'systematic unity is that which first makes ordinary cognition into science, i.e. makes a system out of a mere aggregate . . . Under the government of reason our cognitions cannot at all constitute a rhapsody but must constitute a system' (A832/B860). What is a system? 'I understand by a system . . . the unity of the manifold cognitions under one idea. This is the rational concept of the form of a whole' (A832/B860). The organizing force of a single idea is what distinguishes a coherent body of scientific knowledge from a mere list or catalogue of facts and insights: 'The whole is therefore articulated (*articulatio*) and not heaped together (*coacervatio*)' (A833/B861). Scientific knowledge, that is, must exhibit not merely 'technical' but 'architectonic' unity:

What we call science . . . cannot arise technically, from the similarity of the manifold or the contingent use of cognition *in concreto* for all sorts of arbitrary external ends, but arises architectonically, for the sake of its affinity and its derivation from a single supreme and inner end, which first makes possible the whole.    (A833/B861)

More recently, owing to the unanticipated spectacular growth of human knowledge and the failure of attempts to impose any kind of overarching unity either across or within the sciences, defenders of the idea of scientific progress in philosophy have taken comfort in the truism that nothing succeeds like success. If, like logic and mathematics, philosophy can be shown to have achieved some firm results and won widespread consensus among leading experts in the field, then *how* it has managed to do this—by means of some special form of intuition or just ordinary intelligence, and whether systematically or rhapsodically and haphazardly—is less important than the sheer fact of success itself.

Thus, in 'The Age of Specialization,' the concluding epilogue of his recent two-volume history of twentieth-century analytic philosophy, Scott Soames argues that a kind of scientific progress has indeed occurred in philosophy since the 1970s, not because the discipline has at last become unified and systematic, but on the contrary precisely because it has splintered into small, conceptually isolated, hence potentially manageable, problem areas: 'Gone are the days of large, central figures, whose work is accessible and relevant to, as well as read by, nearly all analytic philosophers. Philosophy has become a highly organized discipline, done by specialists primarily for other specialists.'[20] Soames observes, 'the discipline itself—philosophy as a whole—has become an aggregate of related but semi-independent investigations, very much

---

[20] Soames, *Philosophical Analysis in the Twentieth Century*, ii: *The Age of Meaning* (Princeton: Princeton University Press, 2003), 463. Hereafter *PATC*.

like other academic disciplines' (*PATC* 467). This lack of systematic unity represents, for Soames, not a loss but a gain in scientific respectability. Nor is it a sociological accident extraneous to the problems themselves: 'what seems to be the fragmentation in philosophy found at the end of the twentieth century may be due to more than the institutional imperatives of specialization and professionalization. It may be inherent in the subject itself.'

More specifically, with respect to semantics, 'What we now see at the end of the century is ... the beginnings within the philosophy of logic and language of a less introspective, more theoretical and scientific, perspective on meaning' (*PATC* 476). What does this 'less introspective, more theoretical and scientific, perspective on meaning' amount to? Above all, abandonment of the idea of semantic incorrigibility, or what Soames calls the 'transparency of meaning', and with it the methodological notion that philosophy begins and ends with problems about language. From the new perspective, meaning is not immanent in the mind, but entangled in complex ways with the physical and social world:

Though facts about the meanings of our words and the information semantically encoded by our sentences are, from this perspective, real and important, we have no privileged epistemological access to them.

If this is right, it means that, as philosophers, we have no privileged and secure linguistic starting point, of the sort imagined by so many of our analytic predecessors. Meaning is neither the source of all philosophical problems, nor the key to solving them all.   (*PATC* 476)

The new perspective Soames describes may indeed reflect current prevailing opinion among contemporary professional philosophers of language. Interestingly, it also comes closer to the views of externalists like Heidegger, Gadamer, and Merleau-Ponty than to those of their internalist predecessors in the Continental tradition, above all Husserl.

But does the new perspective represent unambiguous rational progress and a 'more theoretical and scientific' approach to philosophy itself than, say, the logicism of Frege and Russell, the positivism of the Vienna Circle, the Oxford ordinary language philosophy of the 1950s, the naturalized epistemology of Quine, or for that matter the transcendental phenomenology of Husserl? Why should we not suppose, on the contrary, that the intellectual transformation Soames describes is just another drifting of philosophical opinion from one more or less compelling cluster of assumptions and arguments to another? Why suppose that today's professional philosophers have finally entered into genuinely scientific research, while yesterday's were still merely groping in the dark? Indeed, why not suppose that the disciplinary fragmentation Soames observes, far from representing an increase in scientific seriousness and theoretical progress, instead reflects a timid retreat from the kind of holistic vision that has inspired and sustained philosophical reflection from the profound musings of the Presocratics to the grand but failed programs of the twentieth century? Why, in short, should we believe that sheer technical specialization and intellectual compartmentalization, for all their professional comfort and emulation of scientific rigor, constitute philosophical virtues?

More precisely, if Soames believes that recent developments in the philosophy of language constitute a more scientific approach to philosophy, what are the criteria of that scientific status? What makes recent externalist theories of meaning and reference more rigorous than their predecessors, beyond the fact that many (though not all, perhaps not even most) experts have found them convincing? Were it true that new theoretical approaches had finally settled, or even just terminated, long-standing disputes about such things as meaning, reference, truth, and necessity, then one could perhaps argue plausibly that philosophy had indeed turned a corner and at long last inaugurated something like what Kuhn called 'normal science', that is, widespread consensus about the problems at hand and how to go about solving them. If, however, no such consensus has emerged in philosophy, then the new perspective in semantics is just what historicist and hermeneutical thinkers like Heidegger maintain all philosophical perspectives amount to, namely bold projective interpretations destined to remain as obscure and dubious as they are deep and stimulating.

CHAPTER 2

# HERMENEUTICS

## MICHAEL N. FORSTER

For the purpose of this chapter, 'hermeneutics' means the theory of interpretation, i.e. the theory of achieving an understanding of texts, utterances,
and so on (it does *not* mean a certain twentieth-century philosophical movement). Hermeneutics in this sense has a long history, reaching back at least
as far as ancient Greece. However, new focus was brought to bear on it in
the modern period, in the wake of the Reformation with its displacement
of responsibility for interpreting the Bible from the Church to individual
Christians generally. This new focus on hermeneutics occurred especially in
Germany.[1]

Two fairly common but competing pictures of the course of modern
hermeneutics in Germany are that it began with a fumbling germination
in the eighteenth century and then flowered in the systematic hermeneutics
of Friedrich Daniel Ernst Schleiermacher in the early nineteenth century,[2]
or that it began with a fumbling germination in the late eighteenth and
early nineteenth centuries and then eventually flowered in the philosophical
hermeneutics of Martin Heidegger and Hans-Georg Gadamer in the twentieth

---

[1] On the history of hermeneutics in general, and on the role of the Reformation in particular, see
W. Dilthey, 'Schleiermacher's Hermeneutical System in Relation to Earlier Protestant Hermeneutics'
(1860) and 'The Rise of Hermeneutics' (1900), both in W. Dilthey, *Hermeneutics and the Study of
History* (Princeton: Princeton University Press, 1996).

[2] This is roughly the view held by the German scholar of hermeneutics Manfred Frank, for example.

century (hence the very word 'hermeneutics' is today often treated as virtually synonymous with 'Gadamer's philosophy').[3]

I take both of these pictures to be deeply misguided (especially the latter). What I would like to substitute for them in the present essay is something more like the following picture. There has indeed been impressive progress in hermeneutics since the eighteenth century. However, this progress has consisted, not in the attainment of a hermeneutical system or a philosophical hermeneutics, but instead in the gradual accumulation of particular insights, both into the very nature of interpretation itself and into the scope and significance of interpretation. And the thinkers who have contributed most to this progress have not been the ones who are most likely to spring to mind at the mention of the word hermeneutics (e.g. Schleiermacher and Gadamer), but instead certain thinkers less commonly fêted in this connection (especially, Johann August Ernesti, Johann Gottfried Herder, Friedrich Schlegel, Wilhelm Dilthey, Friedrich Nietzsche, and more recently John Langshaw Austin and Quentin Skinner).

With a view to establishing this picture, this article will attempt to give a fairly comprehensive survey of the field of modern hermeneutics, focusing on the ideas of its most prominent representatives more or less in chronological sequence, and providing some critical assessment of them along the way.[4] The chapter will conclude with some suggestions for new horizons in hermeneutics.

* * *

A seminal figure in the development of modern hermeneutics in Germany was Johann August Ernesti (1707–81). Ernesti's *Institutio Interpretis Novi Testamenti* [*Instruction for the Interpreter of the New Testament*] of 1761 constitutes an important transition from a hermeneutics focused exclusively on the Bible towards a more general hermeneutics. The work was greatly respected by, and strongly influenced, important immediate successors in the German hermeneutical tradition such as Herder and Schleiermacher. It makes many points which can still be read with profit today.

---

[3]  This is roughly the view held by Gadamer himself, for example.

[4]  One of the more unusual and confusing features of modern hermeneutics lies in the fact that many of its most prominent thinkers tend to suppress rather than celebrate the intellectual influences on them. Accordingly, one of the tasks of this essay will be to try to bring some of these influences to light—in particular, Herder's influence on Schleiermacher, Nietzsche's on Freud, Nietzsche's on Gadamer, and Gadamer's on Derrida.

Ernesti in particular takes five vitally important steps in hermeneutics. First, he argues that the Bible must be interpreted in just the same way as any other text.[5] He does not follow through on this principle fully or consistently—for, while he does indeed forgo any reliance on a divine inspiration of the interpreter, he assumes that, as the word of God,[6] the Bible must be true and hence also self-consistent throughout,[7] which is not something that he would assume in connection with profane texts. However, Herder and Schleiermacher would soon go on to embrace this principle in a full and consistent way.

Second, Ernesti identifies the following twofold obstacle that he sees facing interpretation in many cases: (1) different languages possess markedly different conceptual resources;[8] and (2) a particular author's concepts often diverge significantly from those of his background language.[9] The conception that interpreters face such a twofold obstacle in many cases would subsequently be taken over by Herder and Schleiermacher, who would indeed make it even more fundamental to their theories. In particular, this conception is the source of an acute awareness which they both share of an ever-present danger in interpretation of falsely assimilating the concepts (and beliefs, etc.) expressed by a text to one's own, or to others with which one happens already to be especially familiar. And principle (2), specifically, also grounds an intuition which they both share that *linguistic* interpretation needs to be complemented by a side of interpretation that focuses on authorial *psychology*, namely in order to make it possible to penetrate authorial individuality in conceptualization.

Third, Ernesti argues that the *meaning* of words depends on *linguistic usage* (*usus loquendi*), so that interpretation is fundamentally a matter of determining the linguistic usage of words.[10] This is another vitally important move. It would eventually lead, in Herder, Johann Georg Hamann, and Schleiermacher, to a stronger version of the same thesis which grounded it in the further, revolutionary claim that it is true because meaning *is* word usage.[11] Ernesti's thesis also formed a sort of base line from which such successors would later

[5] *Ernesti's Institutes*, trans. C. H. Terrot, 2 vols. (Edinburgh: Thomas Clark, 1832–3), i. 30–2, 127. A step of this sort was also taken at around the same time by other progressive Bible scholars in Germany, such as Michaelis, Semler, and Wettstein.

[6] Ibid. ii. 1–4.    [7] Ibid. i. 36, 38.    [8] Ibid. i. 56–7.

[9] Ibid. i. 63–4. Ernesti identifies the language of the New Testament as a good example of this (cf. i. 121–3).

[10] Ibid. i. 27, 63.

[11] Ernesti did not himself go this far. Instead, he still conceived meaning, in continuity with the tradition of British empiricism (especially Locke), as a matter of a regular connection between words and *ideas* (see, for example, ibid. i. 15–17, 27).

set out to look for *additional* tasks that interpretation needs to accomplish (e.g. determining aspects of authorial psychology).

Fourth, Ernesti insists—in opposition to a tradition of exclusively text-focused reading of the Bible which was still alive in his day—[12] that interpretation must deploy a detailed knowledge of a text's historical, geographical, etc. context.[13] Subsequently, Herder, Schleiermacher, and August Boeckh would all take over this position in their hermeneutical theories.[14]

Fifth, Ernesti insists on various forms of holism in interpretation:[15] the parts of a text must be interpreted in light of the whole text;[16] and both of these in light of an author's broader corpus and other related texts.[17] Such holism is in particular necessary in order to acquire sufficient evidence to be able to pin down word usages, and hence meanings.[18] This principle of holism would subsequently be taken over and developed much further by successors such as Herder, Friedrich Ast, and Schleiermacher. Herder in particular would already place much greater emphasis on it,[19] and also expand it to include consideration of the author's whole historical context,[20] and of his whole psychology.[21] Such a principle of holism leads to the notorious problem of a 'hermeneutical circle' (later highlighted by Dilthey among others). For example, if interpreting parts of a text requires interpreting the whole of the text, then, given that interpreting the whole obviously also requires interpreting the parts, how can interpretation ever be achieved at all? Herder in the *Critical Forests*, and then following him Schleiermacher, already anticipate, and also develop a plausible solution to, that sort of problem: since understanding is not an all-or-nothing matter but instead something that comes in *degrees*, it is possible to interpret the parts of a text in sequence with some measure of adequacy, thereby achieve a measure of understanding of the whole text, then deploy that measure of understanding

[12]   See on this Dilthey, 'Schleiermacher's Hermeneutical System in Relation to Earlier Protestant Hermeneutics', 67, 73–4.

[13]   *Ernesti's Institutes*, i. 210, ii. 260–2. This move was again shared by other progressive Bible scholars in Germany from the period, for example Semler and Michaelis.

[14]   Hermeneutics threatened to go full circle on this issue in the first half of the twentieth century with the de-contextualizing position of the New Critics. But this particular piece of retrograde foolishness has mercifully receded into abeyance again.

[15]   This principle was not altogether new with Ernesti.

[16]   *Ernesti's Institutes*, i. 70–1.     [17]   Ibid. i. 74.     [18]   Ibid. i. 70–1.

[19]   See especially his early works on biblical interpretation and his *Critical Forests* (1769).

[20]   See especially his *This Too a Philosophy of History for the Formation of Humanity* (1774).

[21]   See especially his *On Thomas Abbt's Writings* (1768) and *On the Cognition and Sensation of the Human Soul* (1778).

of the whole text in order to refine one's understanding of the parts, thereby refining one's understanding of the whole text, and so on (in principle, indefinitely).

* * *

Another very important early contributor to the development of hermeneutics was the man already mentioned, Johann Gottfried Herder (1744–1803).[22] In addition to taking over and developing the five principles just described, Herder also made several further important moves.

Perhaps the most important of these was to set hermeneutics on the foundation of a new, and moreover arguably correct, philosophy of language. In particular, Herder grounded hermeneutics in the following three principles: (1) Meanings are—not, as many philosophers have supposed, referents, Platonic forms, empiricist ideas, or whatnot, but instead—word usages. (2) Because of this, all thought (as essentially articulated in terms of concepts or meanings) is essentially dependent on and bounded by the thinker's capacity for linguistic expression—i.e. a person can only think if he has a language and can only think what he can express linguistically. (3) Meanings are also essentially grounded in (perceptual and affective) sensations—either directly (as in the case of the 'in' of 'The dog is in the garden', for example) or via a sort of metaphorical extension (as in the case of the 'in' of 'Jones is in legal trouble', for example).[23] Principles (1) and (2) essentially established modern philosophy of language in one fell swoop, and would still be widely accepted by philosophers of language today. Principle (3) would meet with much more skepticism among contemporary philosophers of language, but may nonetheless very well be correct too (contrary to first appearances, it need not conflict with principle (1); and the widespread anti-psychologism concerning meaning due to Gottlob Frege and Ludwig Wittgenstein that is likely to make it seem dubious to philosophers of language today is arguably itself mistaken).

Now these three principles all carry very important consequences for inter-pretation. Principle (1) grounds at a deeper level Ernesti's thesis that it is

---

[22] Most, though not all, of Herder's works discussed in this article can be found in *Herder: Philosophical Writings*, trans. and ed. M. N. Forster (Cambridge: Cambridge University Press, 2002).

[23] Herder also in a way believes the converse: that the sensations of a mature human being are essentially grounded in meanings, and hence in language. This, together with his idea of metaphorical extensions, distinguishes his position in principle (3) from that of a traditional empiricist like Hume. I shall accordingly describe it as quasi-empiricist.

an essential task of interpretation to determine linguistic usage and hence meaning. Principle (2) implies not only that in order to access an author's thoughts an interpreter must explore the author's language, but also that there is no danger that an author's thoughts will transcend his capacity for linguistic expression. And the quasi-empiricist principle (3) implies that interpretation requires the interpreter to perform some sort of imaginative reproduction of an author's meaning-internal sensations (this is an important aspect of Herder's notorious thesis that interpretation requires *Einfühlung*, 'feeling one's way in').[24] Versions or variants of these three principles, and of their consequences for interpretation, would subsequently be taken over by Schleiermacher.[25]

But Herder also took further seminal steps in his theory of interpretation. One of these was to argue for the need to complement the focus on language which Ernesti had already championed with a focus on authorial *psychology*.[26] Herder has several reasons for making this move. A first is the idea just mentioned that interpretation requires an imaginative recapturing of certain authorial sensations. A second is the idea that recourse to authorial psychology is often necessary in order to resolve ambiguities in a text. A third is the idea that a focus on authorial psychology is an important means for penetrating an author's conceptual-linguistic individuality. Schleiermacher would subsequently take over Herder's principle of complementing linguistic with psychological interpretation, and especially the third of the rationales for doing so just mentioned (which he developed significantly). Indeed, one good way of characterizing the development of hermeneutics after Herder more generally is as a sort of progressive confirmation of his thesis that linguistic interpretation needs to be complemented with a focus on authorial psychology, a progressive confirmation taking the form of the identification of increasingly precise and additional reasons why that is so (examples of this trend are, besides Schleiermacher's

---

[24] For some further details concerning these three principles and their consequences for interpretation, see my 'Herder's Philosophy of Language, Interpretation, and Translation: Three Fundamental Principles', *The Review Metaphysics*, 56 (2002). For a discussion of the various aspects of Herder's multi-faceted concept of *Einfühlung*, see my *Herder: Philosophical Writings*, editor's introduction, pp. xvii–xviii.

[25] Schleiermacher's debt is most straightforward in connection with (1) and (2). His variant of (3) lies in his mature theory that concepts consist in empirical schemata, or rules for the production of images.

[26] See especially Herder's *On Thomas Abbt's Writings* and *On the Cognition and Sensation of the Human Soul*.

development of Herder's third rationale, a novel point of Schlegel's that a text will often express thoughts not explicitly in any of its parts but instead implicitly and holistically, and Austin and Skinner's novel assignment of an essential role in interpretation to the identification of illocutionary force).[27]

Herder also argues that interpretation, especially in its psychological aspect, requires the use of what he calls 'divination', by which he essentially means (not some sort of divinely guided insight or infallible intuition, but instead much more reasonably) a method of fallible and corrigible hypothesis based on but also going well beyond the relatively meager linguistic and other behavioral evidence available.[28] Schleiermacher would again subsequently take over this principle, similarly holding that a method of 'divination' predominates on the psychological side of interpretation, and similarly conceiving this as a method of fallible and corrigible hypothesis based on but also going well beyond the meager evidence available.[29]

Another of Herder's vital contributions to the theory of interpretation lies in his emphasis on the essential role played in interpreting a work by a correct identification of its *genre*, and on the difficulty of achieving such a correct identification in many cases. Herder conceives of a genre as consisting in a general purpose together with certain rules of composition which serve it.[30] He believes that identifying a work's genre correctly is crucial for interpreting it not only because identifying the genre is in itself partly constitutive of fully comprehending the work, but also because the genre often carries meanings which are not explicitly articulated in the work itself, and because a proper grasp of the genre is moreover essential for correctly interpreting many of the things which *are* explicitly articulated in the work. This much would probably have been broadly agreed to by several of Herder's forerunners in the theory of genre (for example, Aristotle and Herder's contemporary Gotthold Ephraim Lessing). But Herder adds an important new twist. Just as concepts often vary in subtle ways across historical periods and cultures,

---

[27] With a modicum of interpretive charity, Herder and Schleiermacher can indeed be seen as already hinting at these two additional rationales. For a little more discussion of this (focusing on Schleiermacher), see my 'Schleiermacher's Hermeneutics: Some Problems and Solutions', *The Harvard Review of Philosophy*, 13/1 (2005).

[28] See especially *On Thomas Abbt's Writings* and *On the Cognition and Sensation of the Human Soul*.

[29] As a clue to understanding Herder and Schleiermacher's conception of 'divination', it is more helpful to think of the French *deviner* (to guess, to conjecture) than of the Latin *divinus* (of a god, prophetic.)

[30] This conception arguably requires a little modification. For example, sometimes *multiple* purposes are constitutive of a genre.

and even between individuals within a single period and culture, thereby complicating the task of interpretation, in particular by creating ever-present temptations falsely to assimilate the concepts found to ones with which the interpreter is already familiar, so likewise the task of identifying a genre correctly is complicated by the fact that genres often vary in subtle ways across historical periods and cultures, and even between authors working within a single period and culture, indeed sometimes even between different relevant works by a single author,[31] so that interpreters face ever-present temptations falsely to assimilate an encountered genre to one that is already familiar.[32] In addition, Herder applies this whole position concerning genre not only to linguistic works but also to non-linguistic art.[33] Herder's insight into the vital role that identifying genre plays in interpretation and into the difficulty of accomplishing this properly would subsequently be taken over by Schlegel and Boeckh (by contrast, Schleiermacher emphasizes this much less).[34]

The points discussed so far have all been concerned with the question of the very nature of interpretation itself, but Herder also makes several important contributions in connection with the question of the scope and significance of interpretation. One contribution which straddles both questions concerns non-linguistic art (e.g. sculpture, painting, and instrumental music). Herder's views on this subject underwent a dramatic evolution early in his career. In the *Critical Forests* he was initially inclined to suppose that principles (1) and (2) in his philosophy of language precluded non-linguistic art expressing meanings and thoughts, and he therefore took the position that it did not. However, in the course of writing the work he came to recognize the (really rather obvious) fact that non-linguistic art often *does* express meanings and thoughts, and he came to realize that this is not inconsistent with principles

---

[31] For example, ancient Greek 'tragedy' is not really the same genre as Shakespearean 'tragedy', Shakespeare's 'tragedy' not quite the same genre as Jonson's 'tragedy', and indeed the genre of 'tragedy' even varies between some of Shakespeare's own 'tragic' works.

[32] See on this especially Herder's classic essay *Shakespeare* from 1773 (in its several drafts). Herder even countenances the possibility of a genre being found in just a single work by an author. That might seem incoherent at first sight, but it is in fact not. For, as Boeckh would later go on to point out explicitly, what is essential to a genre is not multiple instantia*tion*, but only multiple instantia*bility*.

[33] See, for example, his discussion of ancient Egyptian vs. ancient Greek portrait sculpture in *This Too a Philosophy of History for the Formation of Humanity*.

[34] Boeckh, who includes generic interpretation among the four basic types or aspects of interpretation which he distinguishes (along with historical, linguistic, and individual), seems to credit Schlegel as its real inventor. But Herder has a stronger claim to that title.

(1) and (2) after all, provided that the meanings and thoughts in question are ones which the artist possesses *in virtue of his linguistic capacity*. That was henceforth Herder's considered position. This position entailed two important consequences for interpretation: first, that non-linguistic art often requires interpretation, just as linguistic texts and discourse do (this constitutes a sort of broadening of the scope of interpretation); and second, that its interpretation needs to proceed via interpretation of the artist's language (this can be seen as a further insight concerning the very nature of interpretation itself). One of the most interesting and contested questions in modern hermeneutics is whether this position of Herder's is correct. For, while Herder's attribution of meanings and thoughts to non-linguistic art is beyond much dispute and has been accepted by most hermeneutic theorists since (for example, by Georg Wilhelm Friedrich Hegel, Dilthey, and Gadamer), his further thesis that such meanings and thoughts are always parasitic on the artist's linguistic capacity is far more controversial, and has been contradicted by several prominent theorists (including Hegel and Dilthey). I have argued elsewhere that this further Herderian thesis *is* in fact correct, however.[35]

Herder also effects another sort of broadening in the scope of interpretation. He recognizes that animals have mental lives even in the absence of any proper language, but he also holds, plausibly, that once language is acquired it transforms the character of a person's whole mental life, so that (for example) even his perceptual and affective sensations become implicitly linguistically articulated.[36] This position implies that any proper identification of a mature person's mental states requires interpretation of his language—an implication which constitutes a further sort of broadening of the scope of interpretation. Hegel would subsequently take over this whole position.[37] It also reappears in Heidegger's famous conception in *Being and Time* that *Dasein*, or Man, is of its/his very nature an interpretive being, a being possessed of an understanding of meanings, even for example in its/his perceptual sensations.[38]

---

[35] See my 'Gods, Animals, and Artists: Some Problem Cases in Herder's Philosophy of Language', *Inquiry*, 46 (2003); and 'Hegel and Some (Near) Contemporaries: Narrow or Broad Expressivism?', in W. Welsch and K. Vieweg (eds.), *Das Interesse des Denkens: Hegel aus heutiger Sicht* (Munich: Wilhelm Fink, 2003).

[36] See especially *Treatise on the Origin of Language* and *On the Cognition and Sensation of the Human Soul*.

[37] See, for example, G. W. F. Hegel, *Encyclopedia of the Philosophical Sciences*, paras. 2, 24 (Zusatz 1), and 462 (Zusatz), which argue that all human mental life is imbued with thought and that thought is impossible without language.

[38] See M. Heidegger, *Being and Time* (Oxford: Blackwell, 1978), paras. 31–4. Reading through *Being and Time*, one might initially wonder whether Heidegger conceives the understanding of meanings

These two steps of broadening the scope of interpretation begin an important trend in hermeneutics which continues after Herder. For example, Hegel not only follows these two steps (as already mentioned), but he also identifies a range of *socio-political institutions* which he calls 'Objective Spirit' as expressions of meanings and thoughts, and therefore as requiring interpretation, and he notes that human *actions*, since they essentially express human mental life (in particular, beliefs and desires), which is essentially imbued with meanings and thoughts, can only be properly understood with the aid of interpretation as well. Dilthey subsequently takes over this even broader conception of the role of interpretation from Hegel.[39] And as we shall see in the course of this article, further forms of broadening have occurred since Herder as well (for example, in connection with certain seemingly meaningless behaviors such as acts of forgetting and slips of the tongue, and in connection with animals).

In addition, Herder makes several seminal moves concerning the *significance* of interpretation. One of these lies in his assignment to interpretation of a central role in the discipline of history. He argues for this on the grounds that historians should focus less on the history of political and military events than they usually do, and instead more on the history of culture, where interpretation obviously plays a paramount role.[40] However, the sort of broadening of interpretation to cover human mental life generally, socio-political institutions, and actions which Herder himself began and Hegel extended further implies a central role for interpretation even in the historian's treatment of political and military events. And accordingly, Hegel would go on to assign interpretation a central role across the whole range of the historian's work, political and military as well as cultural. Subsequently, Dilthey would generalize this idea of the central role of interpretation in history, identifying interpretation as the central task not only of history but also of the human sciences more generally (as distinguished from the natural sciences, whose main task is rather causal explanation). He would thereby provide a plausible solution to two vexed questions concerning the human sciences: first, the

---

in question here essentially to involve language, for his opening discussion of the matter at paras. 31–2 focuses on understanding and meaning alone. However, he goes on at para. 34 to make it clear that language *is* essentially involved (and the later Heidegger is even more emphatic on this point).

[39] For a little more discussion of this whole subject, see my 'Hegel and Hermeneutics', in F. Beiser (ed.), *The Cambridge Companion to Hegel*, 2nd edn. (Cambridge: Cambridge University Press, forthcoming).

[40] For some details, see my *Herder: Philosophical Writings*, editor's introduction, pp. xxv–xxviii.

question of their appropriate method, and second, the question of how they can claim the status of genuine sciences. (On this more anon.)

Also, Herder introduces the vitally important insight that interpreting, or coming to a proper understanding of, (historical and cultural) others is essential for achieving a proper *self*-understanding. There are two main reasons for this, in his view. First, it is only by interpreting (historical and cultural) others and thereby arriving at a knowledge of the nature of their concepts, beliefs, etc. that one can come to see what is universal and what by contrast is distinctive in one's own concepts, beliefs, etc. Second, it is only by interpreting (historical) others who are one's forerunners in one's own cultural tradition that one can come to see how one's own concepts, beliefs, etc. arose over time, this insight in itself constituting an important contribution to their comprehension (this is Herder's justly famous 'genetic method'). This whole position has been central to much hermeneutically oriented thought since Herder. For example, it plays a vital role in Hegel, Friedrich Nietzsche, and Michel Foucault (all of whom are in particular strongly committed to enhancing our self-understanding by means of versions or variants of Herder's 'genetic method').

Herder also develops several further compelling ideas concerning the significance of accurate interpretation, especially in cases involving historical or cultural distance. One of these is the idea that (once we drop the naïve and narcissistic assumption that we represent a sort of historical and cultural pinnacle) it turns out that we have a lot to *learn* from the sources in question, for example in relation to ethical and aesthetic ideals.

Another is the idea that accurate interpretation of historical and especially cultural others is important for the ethical-political good of promoting intercultural respect: accurate interpretation of such others both expresses and encourages such respect, whereas sheer neglect or careless interpretation both expresses and encourages depreciation, and hence supports disrespectful treatment.

In sum, Herder makes a number of vitally important contributions to hermeneutics, both in connection with the very nature of interpretation and in connection with its scope and significance.

\* \* \*

One of the best-known theorists of hermeneutics is Friedrich Daniel Ernst Schleiermacher (1768–1834), who developed his views on the subject in lectures delivered during the first third of the nineteenth century.[41] Schleier-macher is indeed commonly regarded as the father of modern hermeneutics. I would suggest, however, that this title may more properly belong to one of his predecessors.

Like Herder, Schleiermacher grounds hermeneutics in a philosophy of language (one closely related and heavily indebted to Herder's)—in particular, doctrines that meaning consists in 'the unity of the word-sphere', that thought is identical with language (or inner language), and that meanings are constituted by empirical schemata, or rules for the production of images (à la Kant).

But Schleiermacher is especially famous for insisting on the following points: that hermeneutics should be a universal discipline, applicable to all types of interpretation alike; that, contrary to a common assumption that 'understanding occurs as a matter of course', in fact 'misunderstanding occurs as a matter of course, and so understanding must be willed and sought at every point'; that interpretation needs to complement a linguistic (or 'grammatical') focus with a psychological (or 'technical') focus; that while a 'comparative' (i.e. plain inductive) method should predominate on the linguistic side, a 'divinatory' (i.e. hypothetical) method should predominate on the psychological side; and that an interpreter ought to understand an author better than the author understood himself.[42]

I would suggest, though, that there has been a tendency to exaggerate Schleiermacher's importance for the development of hermeneutics, and that his contribution, while significant, was fairly modest.

To begin with the negative side of this assessment, when one views Schleiermacher's theory against the background of Ernesti and Herder's, it turns out that much of what is good in it is not new, much of what is new not good, and that it omits much that was good in the preceding theories.

## Much of what is good in it is not new

This applies to the philosophy of language on which Schleiermacher founds his theory of interpretation, which largely repeats Herder's. It also applies to Schleiermacher's complementing of linguistic with psychological

---

[41]  F. D. E. Schleiermacher, *Hermeneutics and Criticism* (Cambridge: Cambridge University Press, 1998), and *Hermeneutics: The Handwritten Manuscripts* (Atlanta, GA: Scholars Press, 1986).

[42]  These doctrines can all be found in the two works cited in the previous note.

interpretation, and even to his primary justification of this in terms of the need to penetrate authorial individuality in conceptualization—both moves which, as we saw, Herder had already made. It also applies to Schleiermacher's conception that the predominant method on the psychological side of interpretation should be 'divination', in the sense of fallible and corrigible hypothesis based on but also going well beyond the meager empirical evidence available—a conception which, as we saw, Herder had already introduced. And it also applies to Schleiermacher's insistence on various sorts of holism in interpretation, and to his conception that, contrary to first appearances, this does not make interpretation impossible because understanding comes in degrees and so can be achieved by means of a provisional understanding of parts which then affords a provisional understanding of a whole, which can then in turn be used to refine the understanding of the parts, and so on—an insistence and conception which, as we saw, Ernesti and especially Herder had already developed.

## Much of what is new in it is not good

This applies to Schleiermacher's modification of Herder's doctrine of thought's essential dependence on and boundedness by language into a doctrine of their outright identity (on reflection, this proves to be philosophically untenable). It also applies to Schleiermacher's modification of Herder's quasi-empiricism about meanings into an equation of meanings with empirical schemata à la Kant, for the sharply dualistic way in which Kant had conceived schemata as only contingently related to language leads to an inconsistency here with Schleiermacher's equation of meanings with rules of word usage, or 'the unity of the word-sphere'. It also applies to Schleiermacher's transformation of Ernesti and Herder's *empirically grounded rule of thumb* that authors *often* conceptualize in idiosyncratic ways into an *a priori principle allegedly grounded in the very nature of reason* that people *always* do so, so that *exact understanding of another person is never possible* (a principle which is implausible in its very a priori status, in its specific a priori argument concerning the nature of reason, and in that argument's highly counterintuitive implication that exact understanding of another is never possible). It also applies to Schleiermacher's novel specification of the central function of psychological interpretation as one of determining an author's 'seminal decision' (*Keimentschluß*) which unfolds itself into his whole work in a necessary manner (for how many works are actually written in such a way?). It also applies to Schleiermacher's restriction of the empirical evidence that can be adduced in order to arrive at an estimation of an author's psychology to *linguistic* evidence, rather than, as Herder had held, behavioral evidence more generally (for cannot non-linguistic behavior constitute just as valid and important evidence for relevant psychological traits as linguistic behavior?). Finally, it also applies to Schleiermacher's argument, contradicting Herder's predominant tendency in works such as *On Thomas Abbt's Writings* to treat interpretation as a science rather like the natural sciences, that due to the role of 'divination', or hypothesis, in interpretation, interpretation is not a science but an art (for have we not since Schleiermacher's day come to see hypothesis as a *paradigm* of natural scientific method?).

## It omits much that was good in the preceding theories

This arguably applies to Schleiermacher's omission of Herder's conception that *Einfühlung*, 'feeling one's way in', has an essential role to play in interpretation. It also applies to Schleiermacher's relative neglect, in comparison with Herder, of the importance to interpretation of determining *genre*, and of overcoming the serious obstacles that often stand in the way of doing so.

So what is Schleiermacher's real achievement in hermeneutics? I would suggest that it mainly consists of four things. First and foremost, he draws together in an orderly way many of the important ideas about interpretation that had already been developed by Ernesti and Herder (Herder in particular had left his own contributions to the subject scattered through a large number of works, moreover works largely devoted to other subjects). This process would subsequently be carried still further by Schleiermacher's pupil and follower August Boeckh (1785–1867) in his *Encyclopedia and Methodology of the Philological Sciences* (1877), which distinguishes four basic types or aspects of interpretation that need to be undertaken: historical, linguistic, individual (i.e. what Herder and Schleiermacher had called psychological), and generic.

Second, Schleiermacher's theory of the nature of meaning arguably takes one important step beyond Herder's, in that Schleiermacher introduces several forms of semantic holism (as distinct from—though no doubt also providing reasons for—interpretive holism): (1) a doctrine of 'the unity of the word sphere', which basically says that the several different usages and hence meanings which typically belong to a word (and which will be distinguished by any good dictionary entry) are essentially interdependent; (2) a doctrine that the usages and hence meanings of cognate words in a language are likewise essentially interdependent (this would apply both to morphologically evident cognates, for example 'to work', 'a worker', and 'a work' in English, and to morphologically non-evident ones, for example *physis* [nature] and *nomos* [custom] in Attic Greek); and (3) a doctrine that the distinctive *grammar* of a language is internal to the usages and hence meanings of the particular words in the language.[43] These several forms of semantic holism entail corresponding tasks for an interpreter (and furnish one specific rationale or set of rationales for holism in interpretation).

Third, as has already been mentioned, Schleiermacher embraces the project of a *universal* hermeneutics, a single theory of interpretation that will apply to all types of interpretation alike—as much to the interpretation of sacred works as to that of profane, as much to the interpretation of modern works as to that of ancient, as much to the interpretation of oral statements as to that of written, and so on. The conception of such a project already had precedents earlier in the hermeneutical tradition,[44] and Herder had recently in effect erased the sacred/profane and modern/ancient divisions in particular. But Schleiermacher's explicit commitment to this project still constitutes a significant contribution (and his idea of applying general hermeneutical principles to the interpretation of oral statements is perhaps especially noteworthy).

Fourth, Schleiermacher further develops Herder's idea that one reason why linguistic interpretation needs to be complemented with psychological interpretation is that the latter is required in order to penetrate authorial conceptual-linguistic individuality. Schleiermacher sees this, more specifically, as due to the fact that where an author's rules of word usage and hence meanings are idiosyncratic, rather than shared in common with a whole linguistic community, the relevant actual uses of a word which are available to serve the interpreter as his evidential basis for inferring to the rule of word usage that governs them will usually be poor in both number and

---

[43] Doctrine (1) is prominent in the hermeneutics lectures; doctrines (2) and (3) are especially prominent in Schleiermacher's essay 'On the Different Methods of Translation' (1813), in A. L. Willson (ed.), *German Romantic Criticism* (New York: Continuum, 1982). Note that Schlegel had already developed a version of doctrine (3) in his seminal work *On the Language and Wisdom of the Indians* (1808).

[44] See on this K. Vorländer, *Geschichte der Philosophie*, 3.1: *Die Philosophie in der ersten Hälfte des 19. Jahrhunderts* (Hamburg: Felix Meiner, 1975), 58–9.

contextual variety, so that the interpreter will need to have recourse to a further source of guidance, namely a general knowledge of the author's distinctive psychology.[45]

* * *

A figure of at least equal, and probably greater, importance for the development of hermeneutics is Friedrich Schlegel (1772–1829). During the late 1790s, the period when they both began working intensively on hermeneutics (and also translation theory), Schlegel and Schleiermacher were close friends, even sharing accommodation for a time, and there is a serious question as to which of them can claim the greater credit for the ideas which Schleiermacher eventually articulated in his hermeneutics lectures.[46] However, Schlegel's claim to importance in the development of hermeneutics does not, I think, turn mainly on that question. Rather, it rests on three contributions that he made which are not really found in Schleiermacher.

First, Schlegel makes the point that texts sometimes express meanings and thoughts, not explicitly in any of their parts, but instead through their parts and the way in which these are put together to form a whole.[47] Schlegel apparently believes that this feature is especially characteristic of ancient texts,[48] though not exclusive to them.[49] This point is correct and extremely important.[50] Consider, for example, *Iliad*, book 1. There Homer

---

[45] For further discussion of certain aspects of Schleiermacher's hermeneutical theory, see my 'Friedrich Daniel Ernst Schleiermacher' in *The Stanford Encyclopedia of Philosophy* (online), and 'Schleiermacher's Hermeneutics: Some Problems and Solutions'.

[46] Concerning this question, see J. Körner, Friedrich Schlegels "Philosophie der Philologie", *Logos*, 17 (1928), and H. Patsch, Friedrich Schlegels "Philosophie der Philologie" und Schleiermachers frühe Entwürfe zur Hermeneutik", *Zeitschrift für Theologie und Kirche*, 63 (1966).

[47] *Athenaeum Fragments* (1798–1800), in F. Schlegel, *Philosophical Fragments* (Minneapolis: University of Minnesota Press, 1991), 31: 'The teachings that a novel hopes to instill must be of the sort that can be communicated only as wholes, not demonstrated singly and not subject to exhaustive analysis' (cf. p. 64).

[48] Schlegel writes, quoting a famous fragment of Heraclitus: 'But Apollo, who neither speaks nor keeps silent but intimates, no longer is worshipped, and wherever a Muse shows herself, people immediately want to carry her off to be cross-examined' (ibid. 64).

[49] See Schlegel's reference to modern novels in the note before last.

[50] Note that it is a further question whether or not the meanings and thoughts involved *could* in principle have been linguistically expressed by the artist in the usual way. In the passage quoted a few notes back from *Athenaeum Fragments*, 31, Schlegel seems to commit himself to the position that they at least sometimes could not have been. But if so, then this is really a further thesis on Schlegel's part. Hence this point *need* not stand in conflict or tension with Herder's doctrines that meaning is word usage and that thought is essentially dependent on and bounded by language.

communicates something like the following message, not by means of explicitly stating it anywhere, but instead by means of artfully juxtaposing and
contrasting, on the one hand, the quarrel between the mortals Agamemnon
and short-lived Achilles (which Nestor attempts to mediate), with all its
grandeur, passion, and seriousness, and, on the other hand, the structurally
similar but parody-like quarrel between the immortals Zeus and Hera (which
Hephaistos attempts to mediate), with all its ultimate triviality and even
ludicrousness:

You may well have supposed that the immortality and the other apparent advantages
enjoyed by the gods would be a huge boon to any being who possessed them, raising
their lot far above that of mere mortals like us, as indeed the gods' traditional epithet
'blessed' implies, but in fact, if you think about it, since nothing would ever be
seriously at stake for such beings as it is for us mortals, their existence would be
reduced to a sort of unending triviality and meaninglessness, so that our lot is in a
very real sense the better one.[51]

Note that this point of Schlegel's provides an additional reason why, or sense
in which, Herder was correct in thinking that linguistic interpretation needs
to be complemented with psychological interpretation.

A second contribution of Schlegel's is as follows. Already before Schlegel,
Ernesti had allowed for the imputation of inconsistencies and other forms
of confusion to profane texts, and Herder had extended that principle to
sacred texts as well. Schlegel emphasizes and develops the principle still
more, not only stressing the importance of acknowledging the presence of
confusion in texts when it occurs, but also insisting that in such cases the
interpreter must seek to understand and explain it.[52] This principle is valid
and very important.[53] It is particularly valuable as a corrective to certain

---

[51] That this message is not merely being read in here but is indeed intended by the poet is confirmed
by a famous episode in the *Odyssey*, book 5 in which the fair nymph Calypso invites Odysseus to stay
with her as her consort and become immortal as she is, but he (the most intelligent man in all of
Homer, note!) declines the invitation, choosing instead to return to Ithaca and his aging wife Penelope
as a mere mortal and eventually to die.

[52] Schlegel writes in about 1797: 'In order to understand someone, one must first of all be
cleverer than he, then just as clever, and then also just as stupid. It is not enough that one
understand the actual sense of a confused work better than the author understood it. One must
also oneself be able to know, to *characterize*, and even *construe* the confusion even down to its very
principles' (*Kritische Friedrich-Schlegel-Ausgabe*, ed. E. Behler et al. (Munich: Schöningh, 1958– ),
xviii. 63).

[53] More questionable, though, is a philosophically ambitious general explanation which Schlegel
sometimes gives for the presence of, and consequent need to recognize, confusion in texts, namely
that this is due to the chaotic nature of the *reality* which texts aim to characterize: 'Is this infinite
world [of the texts of science and art] not formed by the understanding out of unintelligibility or

misguided ideas about the need for 'charity' in interpretation which have become widespread in recent Anglophone philosophy. Some recent theorists of hermeneutics who, by contrast, are in substantial and commendable agreement with Schlegel in insisting on a principle of this sort are Jacques Derrida and Skinner.[54]

A third important contribution of Schlegel's concerns the role of *unconscious* meanings and thoughts in texts, and hence in their interpretation. The general idea that unconscious mental processes occur already had a long history in German philosophy by Schlegel's day: it had been a commonplace among the Rationalists, Kant had been strongly committed to it, and so too had Herder, who had moreover discussed it in close connection with questions of interpretation in his *On the Cognition and Sensation of the Human Soul* (1778). However, it is above all Schlegel who develops this idea into a principle that the interpreter should penetrate beyond an author's conscious meanings and thoughts to include his unconscious ones as well: 'Every excellent work . . . aims at more than it knows';[55] 'In order to understand someone who only partially understands himself, you first have to understand him completely and better than he himself does.'[56] This is a very important idea.[57] It has been pursued further in the present century by Freud and his followers. However, their pursuit of it has perhaps done less to realize its full potential than to reveal its epistemological hazardousness, its encouragement of arbitrariness due to the fact that the appropriate criteria for imputing unconscious meanings

chaos?'; 'It is a high and perhaps the final step of intellectual formation to posit for oneself the sphere of unintelligibility and confusion. The understanding of chaos consists in recognizing it' ('Über die Unverständlichkeit', in *Athenaeum*, ed. A. W. Schlegel and F. Schlegel (1798–1800), iii/2. 350 f., 339).

[54] Derrida's commitment to such a principle will be discussed later in this chapter. For Skinner's, see his 'Meaning and Understanding in the History of Ideas', in J. Tully (ed.), *Meaning and Context: Quentin Skinner and his Critics* (Princeton: Princeton University Press, 1988).

[55] 'Über Goethes Meister' (1798), *Kritische Friedrich-Schlegel-Ausgabe*, ii. 140.

[56] *Athenaeum Fragments*, 81. Schleiermacher uses the formula of understanding an author better than he understands himself as well, but he means something much less ambitious by it—roughly, just that the sorts of rules of word usage and grammar which the native speaker of a language masters unconsciously should be known consciously by his interpreter—and is in general relatively hesitant to impute unconscious mental processes to people.

[57] Schlegel again has certain specific ways of developing it which are more questionable, though. In particular, he conceives this situation less as a matter of properties that belong to an author than as a matter of properties that belong to his text (a position which would no doubt find favor with recent French theorists of 'the death of the author', but perhaps not correctly), and that are moreover 'infinite' or divine in nature. (Concerning this aspect of Schlegel's position, see Patsch, 'Friedrich Schlegels 'Philosophie der Philologie' und Schleiermachers frühe Entwürfe zur Hermeneutik', 456–9.)

and thoughts are even less clear than those for imputing conscious ones.[58] Developing a proper methodology for, and application of, this aspect of interpretation arguably remains a work in progress.[59]

* * *

Another thinker who might be thought to have played an important role in the development of hermeneutics is Georg Wilhelm Friedrich Hegel (1770–1831). As in the case of Schleiermacher, however, the picture turns out to be equivocal.

Hegel can certainly claim considerable credit for taking over and further developing some of Herder's most important principles concerning the scope and significance of interpretation. As has already been mentioned: he takes over Herder's principles that non-linguistic art (architecture, sculpture, painting, instrumental music, etc.) often expresses meanings and thoughts, and hence stands in need of interpretation; and that the whole mental life of a mature human being is implicitly linguistically articulated, and hence stands in need of interpretation. He adds the principles that the socio-political institutions which he calls 'Objective Spirit' express meanings and thoughts and hence stand in need of interpretation, and that human actions, as expressions of a mature human being's mental life, do so too. And he accordingly espouses a richer version of Herder's principle that the central task of the discipline of history is an interpretive one. In addition, he adopts a form of Herder's principle that interpreting (historical and cultural) others is essential for a full *self*-understanding, both as making possible insight into what is distinctive and what universal in one's own outlook, and as enabling one to comprehend its historical emergence.

But Hegel might also be thought to have achieved important progress on the question of the very nature of interpretation itself. For he makes two moves in this area which sharply contradict previous theorists of hermeneutics and

---

[58] Derrida has aptly criticized certain Freudian readings of literature on the score of such arbitrariness. For a helpful discussion of these criticisms, see Matthew Sharpe's treatment in J. Reynolds and J. Roffe (eds.), *Understanding Derrida* (New York: Continuum, 2004), 67 ff.

[59] As in the case of Schlegel's first point, it might be thought that this third point violates or stands in tension with Herder's principles in the philosophy of language that meaning is word usage and that thought is essentially dependent on and bounded by language. However, once again this need not be the case. For it could be that the unconscious meanings and thoughts in question are always ones which an author has the linguistic capacity to express (as Lacan indeed seems to hold).

which have been extremely influential on subsequent theorists (especially Dilthey and Gadamer):

(1) Prior to Hegel hermeneutic theorists assumed that the meaning of a text or discourse was as objective a matter as any other, in particular that it was independent of whatever interpretations of the text or discourse might have taken place since—and that the interpreter's task was therefore to recapture such an original meaning, which in particular required resisting frequent temptations falsely to assimilate it to his own (or other more familiar) meanings and thoughts. Hegel often seems to hold otherwise, however, to *embrace* the assimilation of past meanings to one's own meanings and thoughts. And this Hegelian position has been warmly praised and imitated by Gadamer.[60]

(2) As we have seen, Herder had argued that the expression of meanings and thoughts by non-linguistic art is always in fact parasitic on the artist's capacity to express them linguistically. Hegel denies this, however—in particular arguing that ancient Egyptian architecture and ancient Greek sculpture already expressed meanings and thoughts (of a broadly religious nature) which were not yet linguistically expressible by the cultures in question.[61] This position of Hegel's was subsequently taken over by the later Dilthey (who, having begun his career more favorable to a position like Herder's, apparently absorbed this position of Hegel's while working on his classic study of the young Hegel, *Die Jugendgeschichte Hegels* [1905]).

Exciting as these two moves are, and influential as they have been, I strongly suspect that they are both errors. Having argued this case at some length elsewhere,[62] I shall confine myself here to a few brief remarks.

Concerning move (1), Hegel seems to rest his case for this on three main arguments:

(a) All past meanings and thoughts, when interpreted strictly, turn out to be implicitly self-contradictory, so that we may as well undertake to interpret them charitably as approximate expressions of self-consistent and true Hegelian meanings and thoughts instead.

---

[60] See H-G. Gadamer, *Truth and Method* (New York: Continuum, 2002), esp. 165–9. As Gadamer notes, Hegel holds this position in the 'Religion' chapter of his *Phenomenology of Spirit* (1807), for example.

[61] See especially *Hegel's Aesthetics*, trans. T. M. Knox (Oxford: Clarendon Press, 1975).

[62] See my 'Hegel and Hermeneutics' and 'Hegel and Some (Near) Contemporaries: Narrow or Broad Expressivism?'.

(b) All past meanings and thoughts can be seen to have been implicitly teleologically directed towards the achievement of Hegelian meanings and thoughts in the modern world.

(c) All mental conditions, including in particular all acts of meaning, are constituted by physical behavior (including linguistic behavior), but in an open-ended way such that it is always possible, at least as long as a person is alive, for his 'past' mental conditions, or acts of meaning, to be modified by his future behavior. Furthermore, meaning is essentially constituted by the linguistic behavior, not merely of an individual, but of a community or communal tradition to which he belongs. Putting these two principles together, it therefore seems that even the acts of meaning of a dead individual from the past are always in principle open to modification by a later communal tradition.

However, these arguments are problematic. Note, to begin with, that they seem to be inconsistent with each other. In particular, (c) seems to be inconsistent with both (a) and (b), for whereas (a) and (b) presuppose that there *is* such a thing as a determinate original meaning (the point being merely that it always turns out to be self-contradictory, and to be teleologically directed towards the achievement of another, consistent meaning), (c) implies that there is *not*.

But in addition, the arguments face separate problems. For one thing, it surely seems very unlikely in the end that all past (i.e. pre-Hegelian) meanings and thoughts really have been self-contradictory, or that they really have been teleologically directed towards the achievement of Hegelian meanings and thoughts, as (a) and (b) claim. For another thing, both the open-ended behaviorism and the social theory of meaning which serve as the premises in argument (c) turn out to be very dubious. They both conflict sharply with common-sense intuitions—in particular, the former with a common-sense intuition that mental conditions may occur which receive no behavioral manifestation at all, and with a common-sense intuition that, once a mental condition occurs, its character at the time to which we normally assign it is immutable whatever behavior may take place subsequently; the latter with a common-sense intuition that if, for example, a cosmic Robinson Crusoe, all alone in the universe, were to start using chalk marks in a systematic fashion on his cave wall to keep a record of his goats and their numbers, then those marks would have meaning. Moreover, the predecessor in the hermeneutical tradition with whom Hegel is most taking issue in (1), namely Herder, had already provided a plausible alternative theory of the nature of mental conditions, including acts of meaning, which, unlike Hegel's theory, can do justice to all of the common-sense intuitions just mentioned: mental conditions, including acts of meaning, are real 'forces' (*Kräfte*), in the sense of conditions of a subject that are apt to produce certain patterns of behavior though without being ontologically reducible to those patterns of behavior (hence the 'real')—or in other words, what a philosopher today might call real 'dispositions' to behavior.

Concerning move (2), Hegel's evidence for his thesis that certain forms of non-linguistic art express meanings and thoughts which are not yet linguistically articulable by the artist turns out to be dubious on closer inspection. In particular, while Hegel is clearly right to think that ancient Egyptian architecture expressed religious meanings and thoughts, his conviction that the architects or artists involved were not yet able to express these linguistically seems to be little more than an error due to the fact that he and his contemporaries are not yet able to identify any ancient Egyptian linguistic means for expressing them because Egyptian hieroglyphics have not yet been properly deciphered (Champollion only published his pathbreaking *Dictionnaire* and *Grammaire* in 1832, the year after Hegel's death).[63] And Hegel's conviction that Greek sculpture expressed meanings and thoughts which were not yet linguistically expressible flies in the face of a very plausible point which Herder had already made repeatedly: that the meanings and thoughts which it expressed were drawn from past poetry, myth, and legend (i.e. from linguistic sources).

In sum, while Hegel contributes significantly to the question of the scope and significance of interpretation, his more dramatic ideas concerning the very nature of interpretation itself arguably turn out to be misguided.

* * *

Another important theorist of hermeneutics is Wilhelm Dilthey (1833–1911). Like Hegel, Dilthey fails to make progress on the question of the nature of interpretation itself, but he does make a very important contribution to the understanding of its scope and significance.

---

[63] Hegel does mention Champollion's work in *The Philosophy of History*, but he presumably only knew his preliminary publications and those only cursorily.

Dilthey's interest in hermeneutics, especially in Schleiermacher's version of it, began early (his study *Schleiermacher's Hermeneutical System in Relation to Earlier Protestant Hermeneutics* is from 1860) and remained pronounced throughout his career (for example, his classic essay *The Rise of Hermeneutics* is from 1900).[64]

Ironically, though, his conceptions both of Schleiermacher's theory of interpretation and of the actual nature of interpretation turn out to be rather naïve and unsatisfactory.[65]

Instead, where Dilthey really comes into his own is in connection with the question of the *significance* of interpretation. He identifies interpretation as the central task of the human sciences—including not only history but also other disciplines such as literary studies, classical scholarship, anthropology, and art

---

[64] In the interim, he published the first volume of his *Das Leben Schleiermachers* in 1870, and continued working on volume 2 (eventually published after his death in 1922). This material contains further discussions of Schleiermacher's hermeneutics.

[65] For instance, his account of Schleiermacher's theory of interpretation and his own theory of interpretation tend to emphasize the psychological over the linguistic aspect of interpretation to a degree that is unfaithful both to Schleiermacher's theory and to the actual nature of interpretation. Again, Dilthey conceives the 'divinatory' method which according to Schleiermacher's theory predominates on the psychological side of interpretation as a sort of psychological self-projection by the interpreter onto the author or his text (see, for example, 'The Rise of Hermeneutics', 248–9)—a conception which, while not *entirely* without a textual basis in Schleiermacher (see *Hermeneutics and Criticism*, 92–3), fails to do justice to Schleiermacher's strong and proper emphasis, continuous with Herder's, on the need in interpretation to resist a pervasive temptation falsely to assimilate the concepts, beliefs, etc. expressed by texts (from the remote past, for example) to one's own (see ibid. 23). Again, Dilthey misconstrues Schleiermacher's theory as one that advocates omitting the consideration of historical context from interpretation ('Schleiermacher's Hermeneutical System in Relation to Earlier Protestant Hermeneutics', 217)—an extraordinary misunderstanding of Schleiermacher's principle that consideration of historical context should precede interpretation proper (see, for example, *Hermeneutics: The Handwritten Manuscripts*, 104), a principle whose real purport was in fact exactly the opposite, namely to emphasize that the consideration of historical context is a *conditio sine qua non* of any interpretation worthy of the name taking place at all. More promising-looking at first sight is the mature Dilthey's shift in his own theory of interpretation away from an exclusive focus on linguistic texts and discourse and towards a focus on a broader class of 'expressions' (see, for example, W. Dilthey, *The Formation of the Historical World in the Human Sciences* (Princeton: Princeton University Press, 2002), 168, 173, 230–1). However, the aspect of this shift that is clearly correct, namely its insistence that not only linguistic texts and discourse but also, for instance, architecture, sculpture, painting, and instrumental music express meanings and thoughts requiring interpretation, was not new, having already been emphasized by Herder and Hegel (as previously mentioned). And the aspect of it that is more novel, namely the claim, taken over from Hegel with slight modification (unlike Hegel, who focuses on architecture and sculpture in this connection, Dilthey especially focuses on instrumental music—see ibid. 245), that the additional forms of expression in question are in some cases autonomous of language, arguably turns out to be mistaken (for an argument to this effect, see my 'Hegel and Some (Near) Contemporaries: Narrow or Broad Expressivism').

history.[66] His rationale for this position has two sides—one negative, the other positive. Negatively, he is skeptical of alternative accounts of the main task of the human sciences which have been offered. In particular, he believes that the scope for *discovering causes and causal laws* in these disciplines is severely limited;[67] and he believes that grand systems which purport to *discover an overall meaning in history* (Hegel's system, for example) are little more than misguided after-echoes of a superseded religious outlook.[68] This leaves the task of interpretation as a sort of default. More positively, he emphasizes that the intellectual need for (interpretive) narration is more fundamental than that for (causal) explanation;[69] and he argues that the interpretive achievements of the disciplines in question can enrich our drab lives by acquainting us with types of mental experience that are very different from our own.[70] This whole rationale for regarding interpretation as the central task of the human sciences is heavily indebted to one that can already be found scattered through Herder's works.[71]

In addition, Dilthey holds—in sharp opposition to Schleiermacher's position that interpretation is not a science but an art—that this interpretive function warrants a claim that the disciplines in question have the status of genuine *sciences*, like the natural sciences. His line of thought here does not usually question Schleiermacher's position that the method of interpretation is sharply different from that of the natural sciences. Instead, it is usually that, *despite* that difference in method, interpretation can still claim the status of a science, namely for the following two reasons: (1) Its subject matter, the meaning of 'expressions', is as objective as that dealt with by the natural sciences (like almost everyone in his day, Dilthey takes this for granted).[72] (2) Due to the sorts of deep variations in concepts, beliefs, etc. between

[66] Over the course of his career he vacillates somewhat between assigning this role to interpretation/hermeneutics and assigning it to psychology. However, because of the prominence of psychology in his conception of interpretation itself, this is less of a vacillation than it may seem.

[67] See, for example, W. Dilthey, *Introduction to the Human Sciences* (Princeton: Princeton University Press, 1989), 88–9. Dilthey has a variety of specific reasons for this pessimism.

[68] See, for example, ibid. 145–7.

[69] See, for example, *Hermeneutics and the Study of History*, 261–2.

[70] See, for example, *Dilthey: Selected Writings*, ed. H. P. Rickman (Cambridge: Cambridge University Press, 1979), 228, 247, 257.

[71] Concerning this, see my *Herder: Philosophical Writings*, editor's introduction, pp. xxv–xxviii.

[72] *As* objective, note, not simply objective—for in his conception of the subject matters of both interpretation and the natural sciences Dilthey is strongly influenced by Kant's Copernican Revolution.

different historical periods, cultures, and even individuals that predecessors such as Herder and Schleiermacher had already emphasized, interpretation turns out to be a very *challenging task*, requiring very *rigorous methods*—just like natural science.[73] However, Dilthey also on occasion modifies this usual position, *downplaying* the difference in methods between interpretation and the natural sciences, in particular suggesting that induction and hypothesis are central to both[74]—a position which is arguably more correct, and which would furnish yet a *third* reason for according interpretation the status of science alongside the natural sciences.

\* \* \*

A further important development in hermeneutics that occurred during roughly the same period was the growth of what Paul Ricoeur has aptly called a 'hermeneutics of suspicion', exemplified by Karl Marx (1818–83), Friedrich Nietzsche (1844–1900), and Sigmund Freud (1856–1939).[75] This amounts to a project of *deepening* the task of interpretation in a certain way, adding new levels to it.

More precisely, the defining feature of a hermeneutics of suspicion is a thesis that the evident *surface* meanings and thoughts which a person expresses (and perhaps also certain aspects of his behavior which at first sight seem meaningless, for example bodily posture or slips of the tongue or pen) often serve as representative-but-masking proxies for *deeper* meanings and thoughts which are in some measure hidden (even from the person himself), which are quite different from and indeed often quite contrary to the surface meanings and thoughts involved, and which the person has some sort of motive for thus concealing (both from others and from himself). Three examples of such a position are Marx's theory that ideologies are rooted in class interests; Nietzsche's theory that

---

[73] Thus in his *Introduction to the Human Sciences* Dilthey's explicit aim is to provide a methodology for the 'Historical School' (including Herder, the Romantics, and Boeckh) which 'considered spiritual life as historical through and through' (p. 48). And in 'The Rise of Hermeneutics' he writes: 'Interpretation and its codification entered a new stage with the Renaissance. Because one was separated by language, living conditions, and nationality from classical and Christian antiquity, interpretation became even more than in ancient Rome a matter of transposing oneself into an alien spiritual life through linguistic, factual, and historical studies' (p. 242).

[74] See, for example, 'Schleiermacher's Hermeneutical System in Relation to Earlier Protestant Hermeneutics', 98, 158; 'The Rise of Hermeneutics', 253–7.

[75] P. Ricoeur, *Freud and Philosophy: An Essay on Interpretation* (New Haven and London: Yale University Press, 1970).

Christian morality, with its overt emphasis on such ideals as 'love' and 'turning the other cheek', is in fact motivated by hatred and *Ressentiment* (resentment); and Freud's theory that a broad range of both apparently meaningful and apparently meaningless behaviors express unconscious motives and meanings. What warrants classifying such theories as forms of *hermeneutics* is the fact that they offer not only deeper *explanations* of the surface meanings involved but deeper explanations in terms of underlying *meanings*.

These theories constitute a major development in the field of hermeneutics—indeed, one too large and important to be dealt with in any detail here. Accordingly, I shall confine myself to just a few remarks concerning them.

Marx's commitment to a hermeneutics of suspicion is perhaps the least obvious. For he usually casts his theory of ideology in terms of underlying *socio-economic contradictions*, or the underlying interests of *socio-economic classes*. However, even when so cast, the theory's reference to underlying *interests*—i.e. to something psychological and meaning-laden—provides at least some grounds for classifying it as a hermeneutics of suspicion. Moreover, since it seems plausible to say that class interests cannot coherently be conceived of as independent from the interests and motives of the individuals who compose the classes in question, the theory arguably also carries implications concerning the interests and motives of *individuals*.[76] And this points towards a level of the theory which makes it even more clearly a hermeneutics of suspicion.

Consider, for example, what for Marx is the very paradigm of an ideology, namely religious belief. Marx's full account of (Christian) religious belief seems to be roughly as follows: religious belief serves ruling class interests by defusing the dissatisfactions of the working class on whose oppression the ruling class depends; it does so, in particular, by (1) representing the working class's dissatisfactions in this world as natural and inevitable, part of the very order of things,[77] and (2) providing illusory compensations, namely in the form of fictitious satisfactions in a fictitious other world. It

---

[76] Cf. J-P. Sartre, *Search for a Method* (New York: Vintage, 1968), who argues persuasively that Marxism needs to bridge the gap between socio-economic classes and individuals, and that it should therefore call on auxiliary disciplines such as psychoanalysis in order to enable it to do so.

[77] This side of Marx's theory ultimately owes much to the 'Unhappy Consciousness' section of Hegel's *Phenomenology of Spirit*.

is surely an implication of this account of religious belief that a hermeneutics of suspicion applies at the level of (at least many) individual religious believers: that (at least in many cases) when members of the ruling class hold religious beliefs they do so in part from an underlying, unacknowledged, and rather contrary wish thereby to promote a mechanism which serves their own socio-economic interests at the expense of others'; and that (at least in many cases) when members of the working class hold religious beliefs they do so in part from an underlying, unacknowledged, and rather contrary wish thereby to see their own socio-economic dissatisfactions palliated.

Turning to Nietzsche, a preliminary point which should be noted is that there is a certain tension in Nietzsche's position on interpretation generally. His usual position, which reflects his own background as a classical philologist, is a fairly conventional assumption that texts mean certain things but not others, and that there is therefore a clear distinction between good and bad interpretation. This is the Nietzsche who in *The Antichrist* (1888) champions 'philology' in the sense of 'the art of reading well—of reading facts without falsifying them by interpretation, without losing caution, patience, delicacy, in the desire to understand',[78] claims such philology for himself and certain other people who stand opposed to Christianity,[79] but denies it to Christian theologians.[80] However, there are also certain strands in Nietzsche which seem to point towards a less conventional position—for example, his early hostility to careful philology as inimical to life in *On the Use and Disadvantage of History for Life* (1873), and his general perspectivist position that 'facts is precisely what there is not, only interpretations' (which presumably implies that in particular there are no facts about meanings).[81] In my view, Nietzsche's former position is his best one.[82]

Now to our main topic, Nietzsche's hermeneutics of suspicion. In works such as *The Gay Science* (1882) and *On the Genealogy of Morals* (1887) Nietzsche prominently develops all of the central theses of a hermeneutics of suspicion: that beneath a person's superficial conscious meanings (and other behaviors) there lie deeper unconscious meanings, that his superficial conscious meanings (and other behaviors) function as representative-but-masking

---

[78]  *The Portable Nietzsche*, ed. W. Kaufmann (New York: Penguin, 1976), 635.
[79]  Ibid. 600, 627–8.        [80]  Ibid. 635.
[81]  F. Nietzsche, *The Will to Power* (New York: Vintage, 1968), para. 481.
[82]  I shall not argue the case here, but for some hints as to why I find his latter position unattractive, see my criticisms of Gadamer later in this chapters.

proxies for those deeper unconscious meanings, that the latter are more-over typically contrary to the former, and that the person involved has motives for thus concealing or 'repressing' the latter (even from himself).[83]

Furthermore, Nietzsche applies this general model in some very plausible and interesting specific ways. For example, in *On the Genealogy of Morals* he argues that Jesus's explicit, conscious message of love in fact concealed and represented at a deeper, less conscious level a quite contrary motive of hatred and revenge (directed especially against an oppressing Greek and Roman imperial order) that he shared with his Jewish forebears and contemporaries—[84] a thesis which close scrutiny of the New Testament shows to be highly plausible.[85]

Finally, a few observations about Freud. As I have already implied, Freud's hypothesis of the unconscious, and even of unconscious meanings, was by no means new with him (nor, in fairness, did he claim that it was).[86] Indeed, as we just saw, even the additional features of his theory which turn it into a real hermeneutics of suspicion—his theses that superficial conscious meanings (and other behaviors) function as representative-but-masking proxies for those deeper unconscious meanings, that the latter are moreover typically contrary to the former, and that the person involved has motives for thus concealing or 'repressing' the latter—already had precedents in Nietzsche.[87] So Freud's claim to real importance in this area largely rests on the plausibility of his specific explanations (the worry, to put it pointedly, would be that he has merely added to a generic theory inherited from predecessors a lot of false specificity).

In that connection, the picture is in fact very mixed. Generally speaking, the more ambitious Freud's theory becomes, either in terms of the universality of its claims or in terms of their surprise, the less plausible it tends to be. For example, his position in *The Interpretation of Dreams* (1900) that *all* dreams

---

[83] See esp. F. Nietzsche, *The Gay Science* (New York: Vintage, 1974), paras. 333, 354; *On the Genealogy of Morals* (New York: Vintage, 1967), 57–8, 84–5.

[84] Ibid. 34–5.

[85] See, for example, Mark 7:27, where Jesus contrasts Jews and Greeks as children and dogs. As Nietzsche points out, Jesus' ideal of love can be plausibly seen as part of a broader systematic inversion of Greek and Roman values which he undertakes, for example in the Sermon on the Mount.

[86] For Freud's explicit recognition of forerunners, see for example S. Freud, *The Interpretation of Dreams* (New York: Avon, 1965), 650 ff.

[87] Freud does not acknowledge this intellectual debt to Nietzsche. However, it seems clear. Cf. the evident indebtedness of Freud's critique of morality in *Civilization and its Discontents* (1929) as aggression redirected against the self to Nietzsche's critique of morality in *On the Genealogy of Morals*.

are explicable in terms of wish-fulfillment seems very implausible indeed;[88] as does his similar position concerning *all* poetry in *The Relation of the Poet to Day-Dreaming* (1908); as does his position in *The Interpretation of Dreams* and elsewhere that an 'Oedipus Complex' plays a pervasive role in human psychology;[89] as does his position in *The Future of an Illusion* (1927) that all religion arises from an infantile longing for a protective father; as does his position in *Moses and Monotheism* (1939) that the Judeo-Christian tradition in particular arose out of, and replays, the trauma of a prehistorical murder of a 'primal father' by other male members of his tribe. By contrast, where Freud's theory becomes more flexible and intuitive in character—for example, in *The Psychopathology of Everyday Life* (1901), where his explanations of 'parapraxes' such as slips of the tongue or pen and acts of forgetting are quite various in nature, and usually quite intuitive (for instance, in terms of repressed sexual impulses and feelings of aggression)—they are proportionally more plausible.

So much for Freud's attempts to *deepen* interpretation in a hermeneutics of suspicion. Another aspect of Freud's position which deserves emphasis in connection with hermeneutics, though, is its plausible *broadening* of interpretation to include, not only phenomena which are usually seen as expressing meanings and thoughts and hence as interpretable (for example, literature), but also many phenomena which are not usually seen in that light at all (e.g. neurotic behaviors, parapraxes, and what we would today call body language), or which are at least usually seen as expressing meanings and thoughts only in an obvious and trivial way and hence as scarcely requiring or deserving interpretation (e.g. dreams and jokes).[90] This move significantly extends a broadening trend in hermeneutics which we have already encountered in such predecessors as Herder and Hegel.

---

[88] He does recognize the most obvious class of prima facie counter-examples: anxiety dreams. But his attempts to explain these in conformity with his theory—see *The Interpretation of Dreams*, 168 ff., 595–6—are unconvincing. And as Jonathan Lear has pointed out, he seems eventually to have conceded that such dreams constitute genuine exceptions (J. Lear, *Freud* (New York and London: Routledge, 2005), 110, 154 ff.). A less obvious, but perhaps no less important, class of prima facie counter-examples consists of what might be called neutral dreams: dreams which seem not to relate to wishes either positively or negatively.

[89] Cf. Lear, *Freud*, 180–3. Freud's theory of the 'Oedipus Complex' probably in the end tells us a lot more about Freud's own troubled relations with his parents than about the human condition generally.

[90] Concerning jokes, see Freud's *The Joke and its Relation to the Unconscious* (1905).

* * *

At this point in history, namely the early twentieth century, real progress in hermeneutics more or less comes to an end in Germany, and indeed in continental Europe as a whole, it seems to me (in keeping with a precipitous decline in the quality of German philosophy generally at the time). However, there are several further continental thinkers who are commonly *thought* to have made major contributions to the subject, including three who are bound together by ties both of influence and of shared views: Martin Heidegger (1889–1976), Hans-Georg Gadamer (1900–2002), and Jacques Derrida (1930–2004). One fundamental view which they all share, and which they can be commended for sharing, is a—probably correct—conviction, continuing Herder and Schleiermacher, that all meaning and thought are essentially dependent on language.

Martin Heidegger has had a strong influence on the course of hermeneutics in the twentieth century. But the value of his contributions to the subject has been greatly exaggerated, in my view.

One of Heidegger's key ideas, developed in *Being and Time* (1927), paragraphs 31–4, is that the understanding of meanings, and hence also the possession of language, are fundamental and pervasive modes of the existence of *Dasein*, or Man. However, as we have already seen, this (certainly very plausible and important) point essentially just repeats an insight originally developed by Herder in his *Treatise on the Origin of Language* and elsewhere, and then taken over by Hegel.

Another of Heidegger's key ideas, found in the same paragraphs of *Being and Time*, develops an aspect of that first idea in a more specific way: fundamental and pervasive in *Dasein*, or Man, is a sort of 'fore-understanding' (*Vorverständnis*) which essentially underpins explicit linguistic understanding, and which is involved for example even in cases of perceptual or active engagement with the world where explicit linguistic articulation is absent. Versions or variants of this idea have been fundamental to other twentieth-century German hermeneutical theories related to Heidegger's as well, in particular those of Rudolf Bultmann and Gadamer. Now it seems likely that this principle is correct in some form, and also important. In particular, as I hinted earlier, one should be skeptical about what is likely to be the main source of theoretical resistance to it, especially in the Anglophone world, namely a Fregean–Wittgensteinian tradition of anti-psychologism about meaning, which denies that psychological states or processes play any essential role in semantic understanding, on the grounds that semantic understanding instead consists purely in grasping a quasi-Platonic sense (Frege) or in possessing linguistic competence (later Wittgenstein).[91] However, Heidegger's principle is again much less original than it may seem. In particular, it is similar to Herder's quasi-empiricist principle in the philosophy of language (described earlier). Its claim to novelty as compared to Herder's principle rests mainly on two features: (1) Heidegger, and following him Gadamer, would be loath to equate fore-understanding with something as subjective as the possession of sensations, since it is an essential goal of their philosophies to overcome the subject–object dichotomy (in a *Dasein* or a 'Life World' that bridges or transcends it). (2) Heidegger, and following him Gadamer, would claim that fore-understanding is more fundamentally a matter of active engagement with the world than of theoretical contemplation of it, more fundamentally a matter of the world being 'ready-to-hand' (*zuhanden*) than of its being 'present-at-hand' (*vorhanden*)—which can seem to contrast sharply with Herder's conception in his *Treatise on the Origin of Language* that an attitude of theoretical detachment, which he calls 'awareness' (*Besonnenheit*) or 'reflection' (*Reflexion*), is fundamental to and distinctive of human language.[92] However, it is doubtful that these two features really constitute a major difference from and advance over Herder. Note to begin with that they would at least leave Heidegger and Gadamer's position belonging to the same general family as Herder's, constituting only a sort of family dispute within it. Moreover, feature (1) rests on a rather questionable philosophical theory. And feature (2) is arguably much closer to Herder's position than it may seem. For Herder's position in the *Treatise on the Origin of Language* in fact seems to be the very similar one that the detached 'awareness' or 'reflection' that is fundamental to and distinctive of human language emerges from a background of active engagement with the world which human beings share in common with the animals.

Finally, Heidegger is also famous for espousing a principle that, especially when interpreting philosophy, 'every interpretation must necessarily use violence'.[93] This principle hovers between two ideas, one of which is valid

---

[91] While the later Wittgenstein's arguments that psychological states and processes are never *sufficient* for semantic understanding are extremely strong, his arguments that they are never *necessary* are far weaker.

[92] See 'Treatise on the Origin of Language', in *Herder: Philosophical Writings*, esp. 87–9.

[93] M. Heidegger, *Kant and the Problem of Metaphysics* (1929; Bloomington: Indiana University Press, 1997), 141.

and important, the other of which is more questionable, but neither of which is original. One thing Heidegger has in mind here is a version of Schlegel's insight that a text often conveys meanings and thoughts which it does not express explicitly.[94] That is a valid and important point, but unoriginal. Another thing Heidegger has in mind, though, is something more like a principle that one should interpret texts in the light of what one takes to be the correct position on the issues with which it deals and as attempting to express that position, even if there is no real textual evidence that the author had the meanings or thoughts in question in mind, and indeed even if there is textual evidence that he did not. This idea is again unoriginal—in particular, versions of it can already be found in Kant,[95] and in Hegel (as discussed earlier). Concerning its value, much depends on exactly how it is conceived, and exactly how executed. Provided that it is not meant to exclude more textually faithful forms of interpretation, that the person who applies it is clear about what he is doing (both in general and at specific points in his interpretation), and makes this equally clear to his readers, and that the quality of his own opinions concerning the subject matter involved is sufficiently high to make the exercise worthwhile, then there is probably no harm in it, and there may even be a little good.[96] However, in practice these conditions are rarely met, and in particular it is far from clear that Heidegger himself meets them.

* * *

The most influential twentieth-century German theorist of hermeneutics, though, has been Heidegger's student Hans-Georg Gadamer. Gadamer's discussions of hermeneutics in *Truth and Method* (1960) and elsewhere are certainly learned and thoughtful, and can be read with profit. But what is distinctive in his position is, I think, misguided and indeed baneful.

Gadamer rejects the traditional assumption that texts have an original meaning which is independent of whatever interpretations of them may have occurred subsequently, and which it is the interpreter's task to recapture.

---

[94] See ibid. 140–1.

[95] For example, this is the force of Kant's famous remark in the *Critique of Pure Reason* concerning the interpretation of Plato that we often 'understand an author better than he has understood himself' (A314). (This slogan would subsequently be taken over by Schlegel and Schleiermacher, but in each case with a significant modification of its meaning.)

[96] For some similar thoughts delivered with greater enthusiasm, see R. B. Brandom, *Tales of the Mighty Dead* (Cambridge, MA: Harvard University Press, 2002), ch. 3.

Instead, Gadamer conceives meaning as something that only arises in the interaction between texts and an indefinitely expanding and changing interpretive tradition. Consequently, he denies that interpretation should seek to recapture a supposed original meaning, and instead holds that it must and should incorporate an orientation to distinctive features of the interpreter's own outlook and to the distinctive application which he envisages making of the text in question.

Despite the strong generic similarity between this position and the Hegelian one discussed earlier which Gadamer holds up as its inspiration, Gadamer's arguments for it are different from Hegel's.

A central part of Gadamer's case consists in a large family of urgings that we should assimilate interpretation, in the sense of achieving *understanding* of a text, discourse, etc., to various other sorts of activities from which, prima facie at least, and almost certainly also in fact, it is crucially different—in particular, *explicating* or *applying* a text, discourse, etc.; *translating* it into another language; *conversation* aimed at achieving agreement; *legal 'interpretation'*; and *re-presenting* a work of (theatrical or musical) art. These Gadamerian urgings hardly amount to an argument, however. Rather, they are just invitations to a nest of serious confusions, and should be firmly refused.

Gadamer does also offer several somewhat more substantial arguments, though, in particular the following four:

(a) Both in the case of linguistic and non-linguistic art and in the case of linguistic texts and discourse more generally, interpretations change over time, and these changing interpretations are internal to the meaning of the art, text, or discourse in question, so that there is after all no such thing as an original meaning independent of these changing interpretations.[97]

(b) The original meaning of artistic and linguistic expressions from the past is always strictly speaking unknowable by us owing to the essential role in all understanding of a historically specific form of 'fore-understanding' or 'prejudice' which one can never entirely escape.[98]

(c) The original meaning is something 'dead', something no longer of any possible interest to us.[99]

---

[97]  See, for example, Gadamer, *Truth and Method*, 339–40, 388.

[98]  See, for example, ibid. 246 ff., 293, 301–2, 265–307; also, H-G. Gadamer, *Gesammelte Werke* (Tübingen: J. C. B. Mohr [Paul Siebeck], 1990), ii. 475; viii. 377.

[99]  See, for example, *Truth and Method*, 167; *Gesammelte Werke*, viii. 377. Gadamer sometimes alludes in this connection to Nietzsche's famous argument along similar lines in *The Use and*

(d) *All* knowledge is historically relative, so interpretive knowledge is so in particular.[100]

But how convincing are these arguments? A first point to note is that arguments (a)–(c) seem to be inconsistent with each other: argument (a) says that there is no such thing as an 'original meaning', whereas arguments (b) and (c) say that there is (but that it is unknowable and 'dead'); argument (b) says that it is unknowable, whereas argument (c) implies that it is knowable (but 'dead', of no possible interest to us). However, since the arguments also face separate problems, I shall not here dwell further on this problem of their mutual inconsistency.

Argument (a) seems to be implicitly incoherent. Consider the case of texts, for example. To say that interpretations of a text change over time is presumably to say, roughly, that the author of the text meant such and such, that there then arose an interpretation A which meant something a bit different from that, that there then arose a further interpretation B which meant something a bit different again, and so on. In other words, the very notion of changing interpretations *presupposes* an original meaning (indeed, a whole *series* of original meanings, one belonging to the text, and then one belonging to each of its subsequent interpretations).[101] Moreover, as far as I can see, Gadamer has no real argument to begin with for his surely very counterintuitive claim that subsequent (re)interpretations are internal to an author's meaning. In particular, the mere facts (both emphasized by Gadamer in this connection) that (re)interpretations occur, and that authors often expect and even welcome this, by no means suffice to establish it.

---

*Disadvantage of History for Life* (see, for example, *Truth and Method*, 304; *Gesammelte Werke*, iv. 326; viii. 377). The debt to Nietzsche here is indeed probably a good deal greater than Gadamer lets on—being downplayed by him not so much from a wish to seem more original than he is (he is often generous in crediting influences, for example Hegel and Heidegger) but rather from embarrassment over Nietzsche's association with Nazism. (As we shall see, Derrida subsequently repays Gadamer for this obfuscation of an intellectual influence.)

[100]  See, for example, *Truth and Method*, 199–200, 230 ff. Here again there may well be a suppressed debt to Nietzsche, namely to his perspectivism. Anglophone interpreters have tended, misleadingly, to deny or downplay this relativistic aspect of Gadamer's position (see, for instance, several of the articles in R. J. Dostal (ed.), *The Cambridge Companion to Gadamer* (Cambridge: Cambridge University Press, 2002)).

[101]  Gadamer's strange suggestion at one point that the interpreter's contribution always gets reabsorbed into the meaning and so vanishes (*Truth and Method*, 473) is evidently a symptom of this incoherence in his position. What he is really trying to say here is that there both is and is not a reinterpretation involved, but he masks this contradiction from himself and his readers by casting it in the less transparently self-contradictory form of a process of precipitation followed by reabsorption.

Argument (b) runs into an epistemological problem. For if one were always locked into a modifying fore-understanding, then how could one even know that other perspectives undergoing modification existed?[102] Moreover, as I have argued elsewhere, this sort of epistemological problem eventually leads to a conceptual one as well: a problem about whether in that case it would even make *sense* to speak of such perspectives.[103] Furthermore, Gadamer's assumption that fore-understanding is internal to understanding and that it is always historically specific in an epistemically insurmountable way is very questionable to begin with. One objection to it which many Anglophone philosophers would be likely to find attractive is that the conception that fore-understanding is internal to understanding violates an anti-psychologistic insight about meaning and understanding which we owe to Frege and Wittgenstein. But, as I have already mentioned, such anti-psychologism seems quite dubious on reflection, so it is not on *this* ground that I would question Gadamer's assumption. Nor would I question its idea that fore-understandings are historically specific (that too seems true). Rather, I would suggest that what is really wrong with it is its implication that such historical specificity is epistemically insurmountable, that it is impossible to abstract from one's own specific fore-understanding and recapture the specific fore-understanding of a historical other. Indeed, I would suggest that Herder's conception that *Einfühlung* ('feeling one's way in') plays an essential role in the interpretation of texts from the past already quite properly pointed towards an ability which we possess to perform just this sort of imaginative feat, and towards the essential contribution that exercising this ability makes to our attainment of an exact understanding of past texts' original meanings.

Argument (c) is one of the weakest parts of Gadamer's case. Far from inevitably being 'dead', or of no possible interest to us, the original meanings of texts and discourse from the past, and also from contemporary others, can be of *great* interest to us, and for *many* different reasons (a number of which had already been pointed out by Gadamer's predecessors). One reason (which Herder and Dilthey had already pointed out) is simply that the

---

[102] In one formulation of his position which especially prompts this sort of objection, Gadamer writes that 'the discovery of the historical horizon is always already a fusion of horizons' (*Gesammelte Werke*, ii. 475). My brief statement of the objection here is meant to be suggestive rather than probative. For a fuller statement of an objection of this sort against a relevantly similar position of Wittgenstein's, see my *Wittgenstein on the Arbitrariness of Grammar* (Princeton: Princeton University Press, 2004), 168–72.

[103] See ibid., esp. 169–83. The argument is fairly complicated, so I shall not go into it here.

discovery of such meanings and of the views which they articulate satisfies our intellectual curiosity and enriches our experience. Another reason (again already important to Herder) is that it both expresses and promotes our respect and sympathy for others. Another reason (again already important to Herder) is that it promises to acquaint us with concepts, convictions, values, techniques, and so on which can help us to improve our own in various ways. Another reason (again already important to Herder) is that it makes an essential contribution to our *self*-understanding, both by enabling us to understand our own perspective in a comparative light and by enabling us to understand how it arose. And no doubt there are many further good reasons as well.[104]

Finally, argument (d) is unconvincing as well. One problem with it lies in the well-known fact that the thesis of relativism seems to run into problems of self-contradiction in connection with the awkward question of whether this thesis is *itself* of merely relative validity. Gadamer touches on this problem at various points, but his answers to it are naïve and unconvincing.[105] Another problem with the argument is that, contrary to Gadamer's wish to claim that meaning's relativity to interpretations makes it distinctive in comparison with other subject matters, such as those dealt with by the natural sciences, and consequently resistant to the sorts of methods which can legitimately be used in connection with these, in particular the 'positivist', or objectivity-presupposing, methods of the natural sciences, this argument would leave meaning *no less (if also no more) objective than anything else.*

In short, Gadamer fails to provide any good argument at all for his surely very counterintuitive position.[106] The position is therefore in all probability false. Moreover, if it *is* false, then it is so in a way which is likely to prove baneful for interpretive practice, in that it actively encourages (as allegedly inevitable

---

[104] Insofar as Nietzsche's case from *The Use and Disadvantage of History for Life* lies behind Gadamer's argument here, a full response would need to include some additional points (e.g. concerning the actual twentieth-century results of the attempt to enliven German culture by sacrificing scrupulous human science in favor of new mythologies).

[105] In one place (*Truth and Method*, 344) he concedes that a self-contradiction arises, but responds that this merely shows the weakness of the sort of 'reflection' that reveals this and objects to it! In another place he argues that the thesis of relativism is not 'propositional' but merely something of which one has 'consciousness', so that it and its own subject matter are 'not at all on the same logical level' (ibid. 448). But surely, the alleged circumstance that what is involved here is merely a consciousness that relativism is true, rather than, say, an explicit assertion that it is true, would not diminish either the fact or the unacceptability of the self-contradiction one whit.

[106] Despite widespread assumptions to the contrary. See, for example, recently R. B. Pippin, 'Gadamer's Hegel', in *The Cambridge Companion to Gadamer*, 236.

and hence appropriate) just the sort of assimilation in interpretation of the meanings and thoughts of (historical or cultural) others to the interpreter's own which it was one of the most important achievements of earlier theorists of hermeneutics such as Herder and Schleiermacher to identify as a constant temptation and to outlaw.[107]

* * *

Another twentieth-century continental figure who has been very influential in hermeneutics is the French philosopher Jacques Derrida.[108] However, here again performance falls short of promise.

Derrida encapsulates his theory of meaning and interpretation in such concepts as that of an open-ended 'iterability' (a word which he uses in the double sense of *other* and *again*) and 'différance' (a word which he uses in the double sense of *differing* and *deferring*).[109] In its synchronic aspect, this is largely just a cryptic way of repeating Saussure's point that meaning only arises through a system of linguistic oppositions.[110] In its diachronic aspect, it is largely just a cryptic way of repeating Gadamer's conception that meaning is something that only arises through an open-ended process of (re)interpretation.[111] Derrida provides even less of an argument for this surely

---

[107] It should be mentioned here that the later Heidegger's continued commitment to the principle of doing 'violence' to texts, Gadamer's denial to texts of an original meaning and consequent encouragement of interpretations which adapt them to the interpreter's own purposes, and also the similar position held by the deconstructionist Paul de Man have a much more sinister aspect as well. All of these men were Nazis or Nazi collaborators who had left a trail of embarrassing pronouncements behind them during the Nazi period. How convenient that they develop general methodologies of interpretation that warrant the reinterpretation of such pronouncements to their own current advantage and taste!

[108] One of Derrida's most explicit general discussions of interpretation is 'Structure, Sign, and Play in the Discourse of the Human Sciences', in J. Derrida, *Writing and Difference* (Chicago: University of Chicago Press, 1978), but many of his other works bear on this subject as well.

[109] For the concept of 'iterability', see especially the essay 'Signature, Event, Context', in J. Derrida, *Margins of Philosophy* (Chicago: University of Chicago Press, 1982). For the concept of 'différance', see especially the essay 'Différance', in the same volume and J. Derrida, *Of Grammatology* (Baltimore and London: Johns Hopkins University Press, 1974; corrected edn. 1997).

[110] See esp. *Writing and Difference*, 280.

[111] See esp. *Of Grammatology*, 66–7, 163, 296, 304, 311–14. There can be no doubt about the intellectual debt to Gadamer here: like Gadamer, Derrida stresses the open-endedness of this process (p. 163), takes the re-presentation of such things as theatrical works as a model (p. 304), even has a version of Gadamer's strange idea that the interpreter's contribution always gets reabsorbed into the meaning and so vanishes (pp. 313–14), and also in effect repeats Gadamer's sharp contrast between this whole model of interpretation and Romantic hermeneutics' allegedly misguided contrary conception of interpretation as the recapturing of an original meaning (*Writing and Difference*, 292). This raises an ugly question of plagiarism. For, to my knowledge, Derrida nowhere acknowledges

very counterintuitive conception than Gadamer does, however (and as we have seen, Gadamer's own arguments for it are woefully inadequate).[112]

Derrida also has a number of more interesting ideas about interpretation, though. One of these is a thesis that philosophical texts typically contain hidden contradictions, which interpretation should reveal (Derrida famously calls this revelation 'deconstruction', and practices it on many philosophers from the tradition, including for example Rousseau and Hegel).[113] This thesis is probably true of many texts, including philosophical ones, and is important. The thesis is not new; as we saw, Schlegel had already articulated it. But Derrida's commitment to it is at least superior to dubious contrary ideas about the need for interpretive 'charity', and in particular the need to avoid imputing logical inconsistencies to texts, which are currently widespread among Anglophone philosophers and historians of philosophy.[114]

Another interesting idea of Derrida's (shared with several other French theorists similarly influenced by structuralist linguistics, including Roland Barthes and Michel Foucault) concerns what is sometimes called the 'death

this intellectual debt to Gadamer. One might have been tempted to ascribe that sin of omission charitably to a political motive, namely aversion to Gadamer's conservatism and association with Nazism. However, this explanation seems implausible, given that Derrida is far from shy about giving credit to Heidegger, a figure who is even more conservative and tainted by Nazism.

[112] This state of affairs also carries negative consequences for Derrida's central thesis in *Of Grammatology* that *writing is primordial*. This thesis is far more ambitious than the sound and important point that the introduction of writing not only itself involved significant novelties, such as the spacing of words, but also thereby affected speech. And its greater ambition makes it prima facie absurd. How does Derrida propose to defuse this prima facie absurdity? One strategy to which he resorts is that of more or less completely redefining 'writing' (see, for example, pp. 54–5 on 'writing in the colloquial sense', 'a vulgar concept of writing' as contrasted with Derrida's 'reform[ed] ... concept of writing', which he sometimes calls arche-writing). But this strategy is altogether intellectually boring, rendering the thesis that writing is primordial merely a gratuitously confusing way of saying something quite different and much less surprising. However, a more sophisticated strategy to which Derrida sometimes appeals is rather to exploit Gadamer's theory about the nature of meaning and interpretation: since we end up in history with writing and speech influenced by writing, this retroactively becomes internal to the nature of all *earlier* language use as well (see esp. pp. 314–15). But if Gadamer's theory is mistaken, then even this more interesting of Derrida's two strategies for defending his prima facie absurd thesis that writing is primordial fails.

[113] For examples of this approach at work, see *Of Grammatology*, *Margins of Philosophy*, and *Writing and Difference*.

[114] Such ideas in the Anglophone tradition often stem in part from a sort of double error: a principle, espoused by many philosophers in one version or another (including Aristotle, Kant, the early Wittgenstein, and Quine), to the effect that it is impossible to think inconsistently; plus an inference from that principle to the inevitable erroneousness of imputing inconsistencies to texts. This is a double error, first, because the principle in question is mistaken (see on this my *Wittgenstein on the Arbitrariness of Grammar*, ch. 5), and second, because even if it were true, it would only plausibly apply to *explicit* inconsistencies, whereas the ones which need to be imputed to texts are normally *implicit* ones.

of the author', or in other words the alleged erroneousness of imputing what is expressed in a text to an individual author and his intentions.[115] This idea involves a huge exaggeration; much of what is expressed in texts *is* imputable to authors and their intentions. But it is at least useful as a counterweight to equally one-sided author-centered positions which ignore the large role played in texts by inherited linguistic conventions, borrowed formulas and tropes, and so on. Avoiding both the Scylla and the Charybdis here—or in other words, recognizing that texts involve a *synthesis* of 'universality' and 'individuality'—had in fact already been a driving and noteworthy ambition behind Schleiermacher's hermeneutical position.[116]

Finally, Derrida is also significant for espousing 'decentering' in interpretation. By this, he sometimes mainly means recognizing the (alleged) situation that there is never a discrete, pre-given meaning to interpret because of the sort of situation that Saussure and Gadamer had described.[117] But sometimes he rather means reading texts with a focus on aspects which the texts themselves present as only marginally important (e.g. aspects which carry an implicit political or social ideology).[118] Such readings can indeed on occasion be legitimate and illuminating.

* * *

A far more important contribution to the development of hermeneutics than any made by Heidegger, Gadamer, or Derrida is due to several recent theorists from the Anglophone world, especially John Langshaw Austin (1911–1960)[119] and Quentin Skinner (1941–present).[120] The contribution in question lies in their recognition of the central role that *illocutionary force* plays in texts and discourse, and in their interpretation.[121] This role

---

[115] See, for example, *Writing and Difference*, 226–7.

[116] See on this M. Frank, *Das individuelle Allgemeine* (Frankfurt am Main: Suhrkamp, 1985).

[117] See especially 'Structure, Sign, and Play in the Discourse of the Human Sciences'.

[118] Closely related to this strategy (or perhaps really just a special form of it) is Derrida's strategy in the interpretation of visual art of focusing on such seemingly marginal features of an artwork as the 'subjectile' (i.e. the material medium), the 'trait' (e.g. the brushstroke), and the 'parergon' (e.g. the frame, the title, or the signature). For a good account of this, see J. Wolfreys' discussion of Derrida's theory of art in *Understanding Derrida*, ch. 10.

[119] See J. L. Austin, *How to Do Things with Words* (1955; Cambridge, MA: Harvard University Press, 1975).

[120] See Skinner's essays in Tully (ed.), *Meaning and Context: Quentin Skinner and his Critics*.

[121] The division of labor here was roughly that Austin invented the concept of 'illocutionary force' and saw its relevance for interpretation in a general way, whereas Skinner then brought it to bear on the interpretation of historical texts in particular.

can be seen as a further form of vindication of Herder's basic intuition that linguistic interpretation needs to be complemented with psychological interpretation.

In order to see that interpretation requires the identification not only of linguistic meanings but also of something like illocutionary forces, consider the following example (loosely borrowed from Skinner). If I encounter a stranger by a frozen lake who says to me 'The ice is thin over there', I may understand the meaning of his words perfectly, and yet still not fully comprehend what he has said—for in order to do that I would in addition need to know whether he was simply informing me, warning me, joking (for example, by stating the obvious), threatening me (e.g. by alluding to the expression 'You're skating on thin ice'), or whatnot.

I say 'something like' illocutionary force because in order usefully to appeal to this concept originally introduced by Austin,[122] one probably needs to drop from it certain implications that he built into it. In particular, one probably needs to drop his restriction of it to cases where there are corresponding 'performatives' (it does not seem helpful to include here only such linguistic acts as promising, telling, and commanding, but to exclude such linguistic acts as joking and insinuating, simply on the grounds that one can promise, tell, and command by saying 'I promise', 'I tell [you]', and 'I command [you]' but one cannot joke by saying 'I joke' or insinuate by saying 'I insinuate').[123] And one probably also needs to drop his inclusion of 'uptake' by other people in his definition of an illocutionary act (there is indeed *a* sense of, for example, the verb 'to tell' in which it is a success word, so that one only tells someone if he actually hears and understands what one tells him, but there is surely also another and equally important sense of the verb in which one may tell someone even if he fails to hear and/or fails to understand).[124] The really crucial point is just that there are clearly aspects of any intelligible writing or discourse which are additional to its linguistic meaning, and which must be identified as well in order for full comprehension of the writing or discourse in question to occur (aspects which can at least be defined by

[122]  Austin, *How to Do Things with Words*.

[123]  For a similar point, cf. J. R. Searle, 'A Taxonomy of Illocutionary Acts', in his *Expression and Meaning: Studies in the Theory of Speech Acts* (Cambridge: Cambridge University Press, 1979), 7. It may not therefore after all be necessary to invoke additional categories such as Skinner's 'oblique strategies' in order to cover cases like irony which fail Austin's performative litmus test (in my broader sense of the term, these too can qualify as examples of illocutionary force).

[124]  For a similar point, cf. P. F. Strawson, 'Intention and Convention in Speech Acts', in his *Logico-linguistic Papers* (Bristol: Methuen, 1977), 156.

giving examples, such as the ones already mentioned in passing—informing, warning, etc.).

However, there are also some important further features of this situation which have been overlooked or even denied by the theorists mentioned and their followers, and which complicate the interpreter's task here still more. One of these is the fact that, despite Austin's and especially John Searle's resistance to the point,[125] but in accordance with a hint of Wittgenstein's,[126] the number of possible different illocutionary forces seems to be indefinitely large.[127] This raises the prospect, and the potential challenge, for an interpreter that he may on occasion encounter an illocutionary force with which he is unfamiliar, and which he therefore needs not merely to select correctly from a range of already understood types but to interpret in the first place in order for its selection to become possible.

A second further feature of the situation which complicates the interpreter's task is that in some cases the divergence of a newly encountered illocutionary force from any with which he is yet familiar may take the specific, subtle form of similarity to one with which he is already familiar but with significant differences (so that he might eventually be inclined to say, not that the alien people involved employ an entirely unfamiliar type of illocutionary force, but rather that they, for example, have a slightly difference practice and concept of 'assertion' than ours).[128] In its own way, this feature of the situation may be even more challenging for an interpreter than the former one, because it insidiously tempts him falsely to assimilate the illocutionary force in question to one with which he is already familiar.

These two additional challenges facing the interpreter in connection with illocutionary forces are precisely analogous to ones which Herder and Schleiermacher already identified as facing him in connection with *concepts* and *genres*.

\* \* \*

The points just made constitute a potential new horizon for hermeneutics. Let me conclude this essay by briefly mentioning two more.

---

[125] See Austin, *How to Do Things with Words*, and especially Searle, 'A Taxonomy of Illocutionary Acts'.

[126] L. Wittgenstein, *Philosophical Investigations* (1953; Oxford: Blackwell, 1998; 3rd edn. 2001), par. 23.

[127] For a defense of Wittgenstein's position on this subject against Searle's attack on it, see my 'A Wittgensteinian Anti-Platonism' (forthcoming).

[128] For an argument that this situation in fact occurs historically, see ibid., where I draw in this connection on some of my work in ancient philosophy concerned with the nature of Pyrrhonism.

The linguist Roman Jakobson has written that 'a faculty of speaking a given language implies a faculty of talking about this language . . . a "metalinguistic" operation'.[129] This is probably not *strictly* correct; in particular, 'implies' seems too strong a word, since one can at least coherently imagine forms of language-use which lack a metalinguistic component.[130] However, as an empirical matter language-use does usually include such a component. And this fact is important and interesting.

Discourse and texts often make *explicit* use of semantic terms: we talk or write about the specific meanings of words, about words being meaningful rather than meaningless, about words sharing the same meaning (being synonyms) rather than having different meanings, and so on. But this is only the explicit tip of a larger iceberg, for semantic concepts also play a large implicit role in the construction of discourse and texts, and (at the receiving end) in their interpretation. One example of this is the common occurrence of puns and other word-plays in texts such as Homer's *Odyssey* (with its famous 'Nobody' (*Outis*) episode, for instance) or Shakespeare's *Romeo and Juliet*. In order to compose such features of a text the author needs to think fairly consciously about the meanings of the words involved *as such*, and in order fully to understand him an interpreter needs to recapitulate those thoughts. Another example is texts governed by a strong aesthetic of avoiding unmotivated word-repetitions (Shakespeare's plays are again a case in point). In order to compose such a text, an author frequently needs to look for (near-)synonyms so as to avoid word-repetitions, and in order to interpret such a text accurately an interpreter needs to recognize that this is what is going on, and that, for instance, the author's shift in two adjacent lines from one word to another, nearly synonymous word therefore primarily has this sort of aesthetic significance rather than a semantic one. Another example is virtually any discourse or text which strives for a high degree of semantic or poetic precision (Shakespeare's plays are again a case in point). For this requires the author to reflect on and compare the semantic properties of various alternative words which are available to him, and full interpretation of such a text requires the interpreter to recapitulate those reflections and comparisons to a significant extent.

[129]  R. Jakobson, 'On Linguistic Aspects of Translation', in L. Venuti (ed.), *The Translation Studies Reader* (London and New York: Routledge, 2000), 115.
[130]  Think, for example, of some of the later Wittgenstein's primitive language-games in the *Philosophical Investigations* and elsewhere.

Now if there were just a *single* concept of meaning, meaningfulness/meaninglessness, sameness of meaning/difference of meaning, etc. common to all historical periods and cultures, then this situation would present only a modest challenge to an interpreter. But such concepts in fact vary significantly from period to period, culture to culture, and perhaps even individual to individual.[131] And this makes the situation a lot more challenging. For it raises the prospect that, in addition to the sort of first-order incommensurability between the explicit conceptual subject matter of a discourse or text and the closest concepts initially available to the interpreter which has been recognized as a major challenge for interpretation at least since Ernesti, there will also sometimes be a sort of hidden second-order incommensurability concerning the semantic concepts which implicitly articulate the discourse or text. Consequently, in order fully to understand the alien discourse or text in such cases, the interpreter will need (in addition to his other tasks) to recapture the author's distinctive semantic concepts and then construe the author's implicit (as well as explicit) deployments of them accordingly.

Another new (or at least fairly new) horizon for hermeneutics involves a further expansion of the *scope* of interpretation, beyond its traditional focus on human language-use. So far this article has been exclusively concerned with human beings. But what about animals? In recent years a wealth of fascinating research has been done into animal language-use, which turns out to be surprisingly extensive and sophisticated, both among certain animals in their natural state (for example, vervet monkeys with their differentiated alarm cries)[132] and among certain animals trained in language-use by human beings (for example, bonobo apes).[133] Philosophers have for the most part been slow and reluctant to recognize this situation, tending instead (in continuity with a long philosophical tradition that was originally rooted in religious assumptions) to look for reasons to deny that animal language is real language, or at least to claim that it is essentially different from human language.[134] However, the reasons they have produced have

---

[131] For an elaboration of this point, see my 'A Wittgensteinian Anti-Platonism', where I draw in this connection on some of my work in ancient philosophy concerned with Socrates.

[132] See D. L. Cheney and R. M. Seyfarth, *How Monkeys See the World* (Chicago: University of Chicago Press, 1990).

[133] See S. Savage-Rumbaugh, S. G. Shanker, and T. J. Taylor, *Apes, Language, and the Human Mind* (Oxford: Oxford University Press, 1998).

[134] Two examples of this attitude are Jonathan Bennett and Charles Taylor.

not been convincing (most of the criteria they have proposed in order to justify the discrimination turn out to be either arbitrary-looking or in fact satisfied by at least some animal language-use or in most cases both). We therefore probably need to recognize that some animals do indeed use language.[135] And that of course implies a corresponding task of *interpreting* it.[136]

In addition, reflection on the case of animals suggests the need for another sort of broadening of the scope of interpretation, as well as a modest modification in the very nature of interpretation. Animals' capacities for classifying perceptual experiences and for certain sorts of intellection (for instance, recognizing predators or prey) often far outstrip their capacities for linguistic expression (even when they do happen to use language), instead finding manifestation in other forms of behavior.[137] A similar point applies to human infants (as Jean Piaget and his followers have shown). We should arguably resist the temptation to describe such cases as ones of meaning or thinking, in the strict sense (hence avoiding conflict with Herder's first two principles in the philosophy of language). But, if so, then we at least need to acknowledge that they are very similar to meaning and thinking, and moreover that they constitute the evolutionary and individual foundations for these (we might therefore describe them as proto-meaning and proto-thinking). Accordingly, they also call for a type of *interpretation* (or if one prefers to reserve this term for the identification of meanings and thoughts proper, then 'interpretation') in many ways similar to that which we apply in connection with language. For example, if a certain animal's regular behavior of fleeing at the sight of predators provides evidence of its possession of some sort of proto-concept of a predator, then questions can be pursued concerning the more exact nature of that proto-concept, for instance concerning its exact extension (precisely which types of animals, or which types of animals in which types of situations, will provoke this

---

[135] For a little more discussion of this whole subject, see my 'Gods, Animals, and Artists: Some Problem Cases in Herder's Philosophy of Language'.

[136] Nor should it be assumed that the fact that animal language-use is going to be in some sense more 'primitive' than ours ensures that such a task will be an easy or trivial one. As can perhaps be seen from our experience in anthropology with attempting to interpret more 'primitive' language-use by other human beings, if anything the opposite may well turn out to be the case.

[137] For a broad-ranging and rich discussion of both linguistic and non-linguistic cases, see D. R. Griffin, *Animal Thinking* (Cambridge, MA: Harvard University Press, 1984), and *Animal Minds* (Chicago: University of Chicago Press, 2001).

flight response and which not?). And a similar point applies to human infants.

In sum, the development of hermeneutics—both as it concerns the nature of interpretation itself and as it concerns the scope and significance of interpretation—is still very much an ongoing process.

CHAPTER 3

.......................................................................................

# PHILOSOPHICAL AESTHETICISM

.......................................................................................

## SEBASTIAN GARDNER

THOUGH neither art nor affect had any importance in the original programme of analytic philosophy, in the course of its development Anglophone philosophy has incorporated both within its bounds: debates concerning the nature of aesthetic judgement, the representational, expressive, and other dimensions of works of art, the psychological role of emotion and its differentiation from other species of mental state, have become sophisticated and fine-grained. The approaches taken in analytic aesthetics and philosophy of mind remain, however, quite distinct from and largely at variance with the views of art and affect found in Continental European philosophy. There is, of course, no such thing as 'the' Continental view of art or of affect, and equally obviously, not all Continental philosophers concern themselves with either. Yet there is in philosophy after Kant a constant preoccupation with states of feeling and the meaning of art, and a marked tendency to claim for art and affect an extremely high philosophical importance, which goes well beyond the interest of early modern philosophy in passion and sentiment, and which has no analogue in analytic philosophy.

I am grateful to Brian Leiter for very helpful comments on an earlier draft of this essay, and to the Arts and Humanities Research Council and the Philosophy Department of University College London for research leave that enabled its completion.

A comprehensive survey of these developments would require a very great deal of space. What I aim to do here is to consider one strand in post-Kantian thinking about art and affect that is in my view especially important and distinctive. This is the view that art and affect are not merely central topics of philosophy, but must be included among the very *grounds* of philosophical thought. On the view to be examined, art and affect in certain of their forms are *philosophically cognitive*, and the task of philosophy is dependent, in some sense and at some level, upon their cognitive contribution. What this means more exactly will emerge in due course.

The historical origin of this outlook lies in early German Romanticism, and there is a loose sense in which all of its forms may be described as Romantic. It cannot, however, be identified with Romanticism *tout court*, because early German Romanticism incorporates specific metaphysical ideas which are rejected by later figures in the tradition that I am concerned with. Philosophical Aestheticism, as I will call the kind of outlook that I will be focusing on, is defined not by any specific philosophical doctrine but by the kind of *strategy* that it employs to establish the philosophically cognitive status of Aesthetic phenomena.[1] Section 1 describes and analyses this strategy, and Sections 2 and 3 examine some of its most striking historical instances. Section 4 looks briefly at two important historical critiques of Philosophical Aestheticism. Finally in Section 5 I will say something about the reasons we may be thought to have for taking Philosophical Aestheticism seriously.

# 1. The Strategy of Philosophical Aestheticism

1. If Aesthetic phenomena are to contribute to the task of philosophy, it is necessary that they should exhibit significant rationality. Whether ordinary, pre-philosophical consciousness supports this proposition is doubtful. Works

---

[1] I will use 'Aesthetic phenomena' as shorthand for 'works of art and/or states of feeling held to incorporate philosophical cognition'. This usage of 'aesthetic' harks back to the broader meaning that the term carried, reflecting its Greek root, in early modern philosophical discourse up to and including Kant, as concerning matters of feeling in general. The qualification 'Philosophical' distinguishes the position I am concerned with from aestheticism in the nineteenth-century sense of *l'art pour l'art*, with which there is no logical connection (on the contrary: if art is its own end, then no cognitive end may be attributed to it). Philosophical Aestheticism is also distinct from Kierkegaard's concept of the aesthetic as an existential orientation.

of art and states of affect may incorporate discursive, propositional elements, but what distinguishes them *as* instances of art and affect is something other than their discursive or propositional form, and moreover, something on account of which they are distanced from the states of belief and claims to knowledge which occupy philosophy's primary focus. Art and affect do not elude the net of rationalization altogether: some sort of rationality must be involved in responding to art and in states of full-fledged emotion, if not of mere feeling, since judgements of artistic worth are argued about and emotions are assessed for appropriateness. Perhaps, as some analytic philosophers have argued recently, art and affect assist cognition indirectly. But the fact remains that states of affect and works of art present themselves in the first instance, in contrast with other forms and objects of consciousness, as at least partially disconnected from reason, as distinct from cognition as ordinarily understood, and as standing only in a loose and indirect sense under the requirement of justification. Moreover, common-sense psychological lore affirms the assumption of seventeenth-century moral psychology that a deep problem is set by the susceptibility to passion at the root of human nature, the power of affect to pervert and override rational judgement.[2]

It does not follow that common sense endorses the strong, Platonic view that Aesthetic phenomena are necessarily and in all respects antagonists of reason—this requires additional metaphysical and epistemological assumptions. But it does give prima facie reason for doubting that art and affect have a proper place among the grounds of philosophical reflection. The most that can be claimed, it may be supposed, is that there is something right about the Romantic's endeavour to show that art and feeling have a proper place in human life, while the Aestheticist's attempt to give a more precise, philosophical form and meaning to this diffuse and nebulous idea must be rejected as ill-conceived.

If common sense fails to support, and to some extent resists, the idea that Aesthetic phenomena have inherent rationality, then two things are necessary. In the first place, the scope of the Aestheticist claim needs to be narrowed down: a distinction must be drawn between forms of affect that express practical, empirically derived motivation—what would traditionally be called passion—and those contemplative, disinterested forms of affect for which the Aestheticist claims philosophical significance. Second, because common sense does not provide Philosophical Aestheticism with a sufficient basis, an

---

[2]  See James, *Passion and Action*, 10 ff.

injection of philosophical theory is required: the Aestheticist must argue that, when the right philosophical assumptions are in place, the features of art and affect which may seem to show their irrelevance to the task of philosophy are converted into features that make them unique candidates for discharging it.

2. The question arises next whether anything general can be said about which kind or kinds of philosophical theory are capable of playing the relevant role. Historically, the association of Philosophical Aestheticism with the post-Kantian, transcendental tradition is very strong, but it should be asked if it is strictly necessary, and more specifically, whether Philosophical Aestheticism can make sense in the context of philosophical naturalism. What makes the latter question especially pertinent is the consideration that three figures who have made major contributions to the formation of a naturalistic world-view—namely Hume, Nietzsche, and Freud—regard affect (and, in Nietzsche's case, also art) as of outstanding philosophical importance.

It is no accident that naturalism in moral theory has frequently emphasized the role of affect, since states of feeling are obvious candidates for materials with which to construct naturalistic accounts of value. This means, in the first place, that the forms of affect most significant for naturalism are precisely those which Aestheticism puts to one side, the 'interested' ones which register the practical concerns of the empirical subject. More deeply, there is a crucial difference between the way in which affect figures for the naturalist and the way in which it does so for the Aestheticist. Naturalism explicates affective episodes, and aesthetic experiences, in terms of causal transactions between empirical objects and empirical subjects. The causality here, though it need not exclude relations of meaning, must be constrained in order for the analysis to qualify as interestingly naturalistic.[3] Now as argued above, the meaning which can be ascribed to affect on the basis of our ordinary conceptions of emotion and feeling does not support Aestheticism, and while any interesting naturalism is certain to go beyond common sense, it hardly seems possible that any naturalism that is serious about its commitment to continuity with the results and methods of natural science will be motivated to extend common sense in the direction proposed by the Aestheticist—that is, to treat art and affect as *media* of philosophical cognition. Philosophical

---

[3] Scheler, *The Nature of Sympathy*, p. xlix [*Wesen und Formen der Sympathie*, 14]: the 'higher' emotions, love and sympathy, 'can also be of significance, indeed crucial, interest to *metaphysics* . . . but only *if* it can be assumed that their manifestations are . . . incapable of further analysis in empirical or genetic terms'; they may then be considered 'functions of a special kind which bring us closer to the *very foundation of all things*'.

naturalism has already what it considers an adequate conception of the proper tool of philosophical cognition, viz. appropriately confirmed empirical theory. This allows art and affect to figure for the naturalist as objects of philosophical investigation, to compose or provide access to the data from which empirical theories are extrapolated, and thus also to furnish materials for the construction of psychological theories (of morality etc.) for which philosophical significance may be claimed. But it does not allow them to compose an autonomous cognitive resource. Hume's essay on taste and his theory of the passions are not the last word in naturalist analysis of art and affect, but they give a good idea of its general character: philosophical naturalism understands art and affect in psychological terms, and naturalistic psychology does not support the ascription to art and affect of the kind of trans-psychological meaning claimed by Aestheticism. (Nietzsche's relation to Aestheticism, however, requires further discussion, and I will return to it later.)

3. In order for art and affect to be argued up into a position within the core of philosophy, philosophy must first of all find itself in the situation of being unable to do something that it needs to do. In order for this to come about, two opposing vectors are required: on the one hand, a conception of the task of philosophy that is relatively demanding, and on the other, a theory explaining why the demand cannot be met without Aestheticist supplementation. Conceptions of philosophy that do not bind it in advance to a definite goal which there is no guarantee of its being able to achieve—for example, the relatively modest conception of philosophy as merely an adjunct to the natural and human sciences, responding to their difficulties as and when they occur, or as merely one participant in the conversation of mankind—will not be capable of generating the cognitive deficiency or shortfall, the vacant portion of philosophical space, required for the Aestheticist strategy to be set in motion.

The Aestheticist must, therefore, make it plausible that the deficiency is a consequence of some limiting feature inherent in the very nature of philosophy. Candidates for this feature, Aestheticists have argued, include the purely discursive character of philosophy's medium, and its commitment to a particular, bounded conception of explanation. Also required from the Aestheticist is an account of why art and affect, as opposed to some other non-discursive phenomenon, should be regarded as the appropriate means to compensate for the deficiency of philosophy, a point to which I will return shortly.

4. There are several respects in which the attempt to argue for Philosophical Aestheticism risks miscarrying. Analysis of the logical dangers to which the view is exposed reveals much about what constitutes it and distinguishes it from neighbouring philosophical positions, whilst also showing that successful execution of the Aestheticist strategy—far from being a quick and easy route to philosophical solutions—is a delicate matter.

The fundamental problem lies in the seemingly paradoxical claim of Philosophical Aestheticism that art and affect harbour a content which is philosophical yet inaccessible to philosophy. There are two levels of paradox here. First: If the content is inaccessible to philosophy, then how can it be a *philosophical* content? Second, even if this first paradox can be dissolved, the Aestheticist's claim appears to confute itself: If the Philosophical Aestheticist can access the content in question, how then can it be described as *inaccessible* to philosophy? It would seem that, in order to describe the content, the Aestheticist must express it, to do which is to incorporate it into philosophy.

In light of these puzzles, it is natural to wonder if Philosophical Aestheticism is not a confused attempt to formulate a really much plainer and more plausible (but less exciting) idea, namely that reflection on art and affect, as on many other things outside pure philosophy, can lead to philosophical insight. If so, then Philosophical Aestheticism conflates the occasioning cause of a cognition with the cognition itself, and it misattributes to art and affect a cognitive achievement that belongs properly to philosophy.

The apparent logical difficulties of Philosophical Aestheticism recall the more familiar and general paradox which is often alleged to surround claims for the existence of the ineffable or inexpressible: Philosophical Aestheticism wishes to locate philosophical content over the horizon of philosophical discourse, just as the ineffable is purportedly located over the semantic horizon. This suggests, however, a way in which the charge of contradictoriness can be dealt with, for there is nothing self-stultifying in asserting the existence of ineffable knowledge, nor in talking about it from certain angles: we can talk about what results when we attempt to express the ineffable and even evaluate these results in some respect. What we specifically cannot do with the ineffable is actually express it.[4] Similarly Philosophical Aestheticism can be restated so as to avoid incoherence. First, what makes the content ascribed by the Aestheticist to art and affect qualify as philosophical, is quite simply

---

[4] I follow Moore, *Points of View*, 155–6. Whether or not Moore's Wittgensteinian view that nonsense results from our attempts to express the ineffable, to say what can only be shown, would accommodate Philosophical Aestheticism, is a further matter.

the relation which it is revealed to have to philosophical needs once it has been taken up and deployed in philosophical reflection. Second, it does not follow from the Aestheticist's ascription of philosophical content to art and affect, that the ascription *expresses* the content in question. The relation is not so direct. What the Aestheticist does is identify the *conditions* under which the content is disclosed, without itself bringing it about that those conditions are realized: realization of the conditions for apprehension of the content is reserved for Aesthetic consciousness. The Aestheticist thus identifies a cognitive perspective in terms of how it is afforded, viz. Aesthetically, without actually expressing its contents. When the Aestheticist undertakes description of the content ascribed to art and affect, the relation between the two is like the relation between a poem and its paraphrase, or the relation between a proposition containing an indexical element thought *in situ* and the same proposition entertained unsituatedly, or the relation between a thought presented alongside its apodictic evidential basis and the same thought detached from it: the Aestheticist's claim is that the content is not truly thinkable, in its full significance, outside the Aesthetic context.

The appearance of paradox thus rests on an ambiguity between two different senses in which a content can be accessible (internal) to philosophy. The content ascribed to art and affect is *in*accessible, external to philosophy, in the sense that it cannot be grasped without occupying the requisite Aesthetic state of mind or perspective, in a way that is not required for philosophical cognition in general; yet it is accessible, internal to philosophy, in the sense that the content is disclosed to a state of mind or perspective the conditions for which can be stated philosophically. Philosophical Aestheticism, in describing the content of art and affect, does therefore make a claim to philosophical cognition, but this claim is distinct from the cognition that it ascribes to art and affect: it is cognition, one level up, *of the conditions* under which the latter is available.

There is a further point worth making here. The Aestheticist conception of art and affect as *perspectives* brings out the contrast with philosophical naturalism, for which they are instead empirical objects: whereas the naturalist looks *at* art and affect, the Aestheticist seeks to see things *by means of* them, regarding art and affect as extensions of our subjectivity, which raise it to a higher power.

5. Supposing that Philosophical Aestheticism escapes paradox, a further, no less substantial problem presents itself. Even if the Aestheticist claim

is coherent, can it be justified? There is a clear danger of dogmatism or arbitrariness. The epistemological worry is best illustrated in historical terms.

The neo-classical orthodoxy which dominated aesthetic theory up until the late eighteenth century—until the dawn of Romanticism—allocated to art a determinate place within an already complete intellectual edifice. Art was conceived as the imitation of nature, where 'nature' meant neither sensible appearance nor extended matter but the essential, underlying structure of the world, conceived as divine creation. 'Nature' was therefore, as well as being a metaphysical principle realized in all actual existence, also a norm, an objective principle of (moral) rightness, and in many contexts the term was used interchangeably with 'reason'. The correlated objectivist, neo-classical view of beauty as apprehension of the moral-rational order of things allowed works of art to be conceived as possessing truth simply on account of their exhibiting beauty. To the extent that art had a philosophical role, as distinct from a moral-didactic function, it was that of merely confirming or giving illustrative form to a philosophical outlook that had been arrived at independently.

Neo-classical formulae appear to us now to impose on art metaphysical conceptions which are alien to it: neo-classical aesthetics fails, it seems to us, to give art its proper due, instead reducing art to philosophy's looking-glass.[5] Philosophical Aestheticism must be able to meet the charge of similarly merely reading into art what it wishes to find there. It can do this by showing that the specific gap that it locates in discursive philosophical understanding is one which it is specifically appropriate for art and affect to fill—by revealing an affinity or congruence between the nature of art and affect and the philosophical content attributed to it. The Aestheticist must show therefore that distinguishing features of Aesthetic phenomena—their resistance to objectualization, their interstitial position on the borderline between sensation and thought, intuition and concept—suit them to the cognitive role ascribed to them. If the philosophical conceptions employed in the Aestheticist interpretation of art and affect are prompted by art and affect themselves—if there is an intelligible route from the Aesthetic to the philosophical conceptions employed in its interpretation—then Philosophical Aestheticism can rebut the charge of being arbitrary in the manner of neo-classicism: it can claim to have established an internal and reciprocal relation between philosophy on the one hand, and Aesthetic phenomena on the other.

---

[5]  On this theme, see Hilmer, 'Kunst als Spiegel der Philosophie'.

6. In view of the key role played by the appeal to privileged states of mind as conditions for the thinkability of the content ascribed to art and affect, Philosophical Aestheticism has something in common with mysticism. It is however important to locate Philosophical Aestheticism at the right point on the continuum of outlooks that may be brought under that heading. In the first place, Philosophical Aestheticism need not assert an *independent* non-discursive capacity for philosophical cognition that operates outside the context of philosophical reflection and that transcends altogether the cognitive capacities of ordinary, pre-philosophical consciousness: it may on the contrary argue for continuity between Aesthetic consciousness and discursive or ordinary consciousness. Two ways in which this can be done are the following. First, the relevant Aesthetic consciousness may be claimed to lie immanently in ordinary consciousness, contained in its deep background, Philosophical Aestheticism doing no more than to bring this implicit affective dimension to light. Second, insight into the philosophical content of art and affect may be held to depend upon a context of prior philosophical reflection. Thus in German Romantic speculation, the lacuna in philosophical understanding which Aesthetic insight is held to fill, is sometimes regarded as a 'presupposition' or 'postulate', that cannot be cognized determinately but which it can be shown to be necessary for us to think in an indeterminate form. The specific epistemological contribution of art and affect is then to give objective reality to the postulate, i.e. to show that it is not *merely* a postulate. On this account, art and affect are sub-adjacent to philosophical discourse: their contribution to philosophical cognition is not autonomous but depends upon, and can only occur within, a context of argument and reflection.[6]

It is clear from what has been said that the Aestheticist strategy cannot pretend to take the form of a strict proof. Making Aestheticism plausible involves a complex hermeneutical movement in which philosophical reason, dissatisfied with itself, looks outside to discover elements with the aid of which it can restore itself to equilibrium, and reaches a point where it recognizes that what it needs, but cannot generate from its own discursive resources, is presented in art and affect.[7]

---

[6] See the distinctions in Henrich, *Between Kant and Hegel*, 70–1.

[7] The connection of Philosophical Aestheticism with post-Kantian philosophy deserves brief comment. The relation is strictly contingent, in that nothing in the definition of Philosophical Aestheticism requires the philosophical knowledge claimed for the Aesthetic to be transcendental, and historically there have been theories, typically of a Neoplatonistic stamp, which reserve some portion of philosophical knowledge for states of higher feeling (Cambridge Platonism, Rousseau, Shaftesbury).

7. The history of post-Kantian attempts to interweave philosophy with art and affect encompasses, as noted earlier, a wide range of views. In order to be clear about which of these count as Aestheticist, two distinctions are important.

On the spectrum of different views of relation of art and affect to philosophy, Philosophical Aestheticism is flanked on each side by two other views, one weaker and one stronger. The weaker view, which may be called Aesthetic Parallelism, agrees that art and affect have cognitive import and are to be integrated with philosophy in a systematic fashion, but denies that there is any respect in which the Aesthetic should be accorded a cognitive facility which outstrips philosophy: it affirms only *parallels* between their respective contents. The extent of the parallel is left open: the Parallelist may hold either that Aesthetic cognition equals, or that it falls short of, philosophical cognition, but in either case the *dependence*, affirmed by the Aestheticist, of philosophy on Aesthetically grounded insight, is denied.

The stronger view, Aesthetic Subversivism, is an inversion of the Platonic view. Like Plato, it regards the relation of philosophy to art and affect as necessarily antagonistic, but it holds, against Plato, that the claims of philosophy are subverted, 'overthrown', by art and affect. Characteristically associated with Subversivism is the complaint that philosophy has sought, in the history of its theorizing about Aesthetic matters, to neutralize, disempower, or 'disenfranchise' art and affect.[8] Subversivism thus contradicts the positive, harmonious, reciprocal relation of philosophy to art and affect affirmed by Philosophical Aestheticism.

The distinction of Subversivism from Aestheticism is reflected in the account that each gives of how the limitations of philosophy come to be recognized. In the Aestheticist case, the limitations of philosophy are already in place—they have already been discerned and comprehended *by philosophy*—before art and affect make their appearance. On the Subversivist view, the limitations of philosophy must be shown *by art and affect* themselves. Subversivism

---

What distinguishes post-Kantian Philosophical Aestheticism is simply its greater methodological self-consciousness and theoretical intricacy, this being a direct consequence of its absorption of empiricist and Kantian lessons concerning the general epistemological difficulty attaching to metaphysical claims. Non-transcendental Philosophical Aestheticism belongs to a philosophical world in which the possibility of metaphysics and theology may be taken for granted and, though not for that reason lacking interest, belongs to a different story from that which this essay is concerned with.

[8] See Bernstein, *The Fate of Art*: 'Throughout its history philosophy attempted to tame art, to suppress its tendential protest to the reign of theory' (p. 12). Bernstein envisages art as the critique of philosophical cognition.

thus imposes a considerably heavier burden on art and affect than does Philosophical Aestheticism.

This difference is associated with another. The consequences for philosophy that are held to follow according to Subversivism are typically of a fairly extreme character: Aesthetic Subversivism, especially in French neo-structuralist philosophy, is associated with the promotion of radical skepticism, relativism, perspectivism, or anti-realism. Philosophical Aestheticism by contrast asserts only a limited aporia in philosophical reason, and does not pronounce a negative verdict on its general competence. For this reason Aestheticism does not encounter the difficulty for Subversivism that will be described later.

## 2. EARLY AESTHETICIST STRATEGIES: GERMAN ROMANTICISM

So far the characterization of Philosophical Aestheticism remains purely formal. In this section and the next, it will be seen in what ways the schema can be filled in.

That Philosophical Aestheticism should have emerged first in the post-Kantian period is, in view of what was said above, no accident. Kant's philosophy, under the interpretation and assessment which prevailed in the 1790s, furnished exactly the conditions described above. (1) Kant had argued conclusively, in the eyes of his most philosophically advanced readers, that there are a priori conditions on theoretical and practical cognition, the correct conception of which is found not in early modern rationalism but rather in Kant's transcendental theory of experience and metaphysics of morals. Also endorsed was (2) Kant's view that philosophy, as the expression of our highest cognitive ambition, is committed to seeking cognition of the (trans-empirical) unconditioned, and to achieving systematic form. This double demand would be met ideally by the foundation of philosophy on a single principle. Kant had not furnished this principle, but more immediately problematic was (3) Kant's restriction of claims to knowledge in the context of theoretical reason to the sphere of the (empirically) conditioned. Kant's claim that his Critical system, through its practical part, reconciled (2) and (3), was widely rejected—meaning that, if Kant's reasoning to (2) and (3) were correct, philosophy had shown itself to be incapable of meeting the demands that it rightly places on itself.

One response was provided by Fichte's *Wissenschaftslehre*, which offered the 'absolute I', the I that posits itself as absolute and the Not-I in opposition to itself, as a single principle that expresses the unconditioned and secures philosophical completeness. Early German Romanticism, inspired by Fichte's success in showing the potential for further development of Kantian thought, but dissatisfied with Fichte's claim to have located the required single principle, formulated itself at this point as an alternative. In this context there emerged over a short period of time an extraordinary number and variety of Aestheticist ideas.

1. Perception of Fichte's shortcomings, taken as symptomatic of the whole single-principle approach, was one element, to the fore in motivating early German Romantic Aestheticism, but in the background, and also of crucial importance, were the proto-Aestheticist ideas of F. H. Jacobi and Friedrich Schiller.

Shortly after the publication of the *Critique of Pure Reason*, but before its full effect had begun to be felt, Jacobi had succeeded in posing a radical question-mark over the ambition of systematic philosophy. Jacobi's *Concerning the Doctrine of Spinoza* (1785) belonged at one level to a local debate concerning the interpretation of Lessing's religious views, but its real message concerned an issue of maximal philosophical scope: the competence of human reason.[9] According to Jacobi, the consistent application of the principles of reasoning and explanation to which philosophy is committed by its very (systematic, rationalistic, concept-bound) conception of its task, has only one possible outcome: a metaphysics that denies the existence of God, individual personality, and human freedom. Spinoza's great achievement, Jacobi insisted, had been to demonstrate incontrovertibly these nihilistic entailments of philosophical reason.

The only means of avoiding this catastrophic outcome, Jacobi argued, is to embrace a non-systematic, non-rationalistic philosophy that, under the name of Hume and with appeal to his authority, firmly and aggressively subordinates philosophical reason to 'feeling' or 'faith', *Gefühl* or *Glaube*, a state of immediate assent to the directly given real existence of its object.[10] The broad sweep of Jacobian *Glaube* ranges from the objects of ordinary empirical knowledge to the supersensible being of God and our freedom. The ultimate ground of beliefs formed through *Gefühl* is, according to Jacobi, theistic: objects are given to us through what is in effect God's constant revelation. The

---

[9]  See Beiser, *The Fate of Reason*, ch. 2.
[10]  See Jacobi's summary account of what he means by *Gefühl*, in *David Hume on Faith*, Preface (1815), 563–4 [*David Hume über den Glauben*, Vorrede, 59–63].

dialogic character of cognition is, Jacobi holds, not excogitated by inference, but a further, internal component of the state of *Glaube* itself.

What Jacobi took to warrant this philosophical proposal, given his own admission of the logical unavoidability of 'Spinozism', was his claim to have shown, again through reflection on Spinoza, the incapacity of philosophy to ground its own basic principles: the possibility of knowledge of truth presupposes the unconditioned, but conceptuality is confined to the sphere of the conditioned. Connectedly Jacobi argued, with Kant and Fichte especially in mind, that the aconceptual, or trans-conceptual, character of all awareness of existence entails that the method of conceptual construction to which philosophical reason is confined leaves its results floating in logical space without existential validation. Thus, per Jacobi, we are forced to recognize the dependence of finite human reason on *Gefühl*, and while the adoption of Jacobi's point of view does require what he on one occasion calls a 'salto mortale',[11] it is not an instance of *credo quia absurdum*.[12]

Though Jacobi raised the philosophical prestige of affect, his position did little for art; indeed, if genuine cognition, belief with existential import, depends on felt divine revelation, it is not clear that artistic creation will do more than reflect the cognitive impotence of human subjectivity working under its own steam independently of God. Schiller, by contrast, in his *Letters on Aesthetic Education* (1794–5), presented a powerful case for art's pre-eminence, centred on the claim that it provides the unique means of resolving the problem facing Kantian philosophical reason. Schiller's view of the problem has some points of contact with Jacobi's—they share a dissatisfaction with the one-sidedness of *Aufklärung* ideals—but a much finer focus, and while Jacobi deployed affect to the end of undermining philosophical systems like Kant's, Schiller advanced the claims of art with a view to preserving and perfecting a modified Kantianism.

Whereas Kant's third *Critique* had merely differentiated the sphere of the aesthetic and explained its independence from theoretical and practical reason, thereby establishing a place for art, but without showing art to be strictly necessary for the human *telos*, Schiller contended that we are compelled to create art in order to solve a problem which is set for us by our metaphysical natures, and which is otherwise unsolvable.[13] The problem for Schiller is

---

[11]  *Concerning the Doctrine of Spinoza* (1785), 189 [*Ueber die Lehre des Spinoza*, 17].

[12]  For a short statement of Jacobi's position, see *Concerning the Doctrine of Spinoza* (1785), 230–4 [*Ueber die Lehre des Spinoza*, 162–72].

[13]  On the argument of the *Letters*, see Beiser, *Schiller as Philosopher*, ch. 4.

based on Kant's familiar dualism: human subjects are constituted of two heterogeneous elements or principles—the form drive, related to Reason and Freedom, and the material or sensuous drive, related to Nature. Schiller maintains that it is impossible for the two to cohabit, and for either to fulfil the purpose which is intrinsic to it, without the introduction of some third, mediating element which will not simply connect but actually comprehend the two drives. No such problem is recognized by Kant: on his account, once Critical philosophy has established a degree of coherence in reason, whereby the various spheres of its employment are coordinated with one another, there remains only the practical problem of achieving victory for duty over inclination, i.e. the problem of becoming morally good (and thereby acceding to the highest good, in which the claims of morality and happiness are harmonized). This neglects, on Schiller's account, a deeper, underlying problem of the metaphysical wholeness of human being, the solution to which is provided by a third drive, the 'play drive', which disentangles, reconciles, and facilitates the mutual enhancement of the otherwise antagonistic form and material drives, which it in some sense subsumes. The play drive is precipitated or activated in us by the experience of beautiful art, in which Freedom and Nature are apprehended as one, and its hypothetical historical and political realization is what would allow humanity to raise itself to a condition of individual and collective wholeness.[14]

Jacobi's and Schiller's ideas, for all of their appeal to dissatisfied post-Kantians, also exhibit weaknesses. In the case of Jacobi, these are clear: the cost of according total epistemic authority to *Gefühl* is to give up on the hope of being able to reply to the skeptic, or the naturalist, with something more than intensity of feeling. It is also to surrender all of the philosophical gains made by Kant, in particular regarding the concept of autonomy.

---

[14]  That Schiller succeeds in showing that the problem of deeper wholeness arises *within* Kant's own terms (or even takes himself to do so) is doubtful: his argument is rather that these terms must be *enlarged*. What Schiller shows convincingly is that the need for a higher degree of wholeness than Kant allows for is indicated in the light of (i) common-sense intuitions about human goodness (as located in the person as a whole, not merely in her capacity for practical judgement), (ii) historical and political knowledge (concerning the atomism and mechanization of modern social life and its correlative distortion of human personality, and the miscarriage of political reason evidenced in France's post-revolutionary Terror), and (iii) Kant's own conception of our reason as striving to absolute unity. Schiller believes also that aesthetic experience wakens us to this need. What then follows in terms of Schiller's argument with Kant, as I consider next, depends on whether orthodox Kantianism can meet the challenge set, and whether Schiller can complete the further (and philosophically harder) task of showing the *real possibility* of the wholeness he says we are in need of.

The weakness of Schiller's account is less obvious but more revealing of the specific direction pursued in German Romanticism. It lies essentially in Schiller's contradictory attempt to develop an Aestheticist position on foundations that stick closely to the letter of Kantian doctrine. The Aestheticist element in Schiller's theory consists in his claim that the Idea of a unity of freedom and nature is first given to us through Aesthetic experience and cannot be established through philosophical means in a form that makes it of real significance to us. The problem is that Schiller gives insufficient reason for thinking that this unity is not merely alluring, but also a rational possibility for us. Might not the Aesthetic unity of freedom and nature be a mirage, and its pursuit destructive? Kant will object that to grant nature a legitimacy equal to that of reason is simply to undermine morality. Schiller has something of an answer, in so far as he, first, attempts to show the inescapability of our need to achieve wholeness, to realize what he calls our infinite nature,[15] and second, sketches a transcendental argument designed to show that the third thing, beauty and the play-drive, is implied as a possibility if not an actuality by the conjunction of thought and feeling that we actually find within us.[16] Whether or not these parts of Schiller's theory (which make rather tendentious appeal to Fichte) are found convincing, there is a clear limit to what is achieved. The characterization of art in Schiller remains, so to speak, functional rather than cognitive: art projects an Idea of the unity of freedom and nature, and points us in its direction, such that, *if* we realize the Idea, then art will be describable as containing truth, in the weak sense of its having facilitated our realization of the Idea that it projects. But art does not give, in Kant's language, 'objective reality' to the Idea: Schiller does not show that the Idea of a higher unity possesses truth in a sense sufficient to warrant belief in its realizability.

Reflection on the imperfect Philosophical Aestheticism of Jacobi and Schiller yields the following formula, which governs German Romanticism: Aesthetic media can be claimed to yield access to the unconditioned, to the real existence of discursively inaccessible objects, and to the higher synthetic unity that is the proper telos of human development, but this claim must be, contra Jacobi, integrated with, rather than opposed to, systematic philosophy; in addition, the systematic philosophy in question must be one that departs further than

---

[15] Given in Letter 11, pp. 73–7 [*Briefe*, 341–4] in terms of a bifurcation in man's nature between his 'Personhood' and his 'Condition', with some anticipation in Letter 9, pp. 55–61 [*Briefe*, 332–6]; see also Letter 14, p. 95 [*Briefe*, 352–3].

[16] Letters 18–22, pp. 123–59 [*Briefe*, 365–83].

Schiller from the letter of Kantian doctrine—just as, the German Romantics appreciated, Fichte's *Wissenschaftslehre* had done.

2. The philosophical beginnings of German Romantic Aestheticism lie in early, unpublished reflections of Hölderlin and Novalis. A fragment of Hölderlin's, 'Judgement and Being', makes a deep and original criticism of Fichte, to the effect that the I by its very nature cannot be absolute and so is not fit to play the systemic role assigned to it by Fichte. Hölderlin's argument is, in rough summary: (1) In judgement, a separation is presupposed: a judgement can only be a joining together, an identity of things that are originally articulated as distinct, namely its subject- and predicate-terms. (2) This applies also to the self-relation, the self-consciousness exhibited in the pure 'I' which judges, 'I = I', 'I am self-identical'. It follows that (3) the pure 'I' is inhabited by a separation. (4) The proper criterion for absolute being, 'absolutes Seyn', is the Spinozistic one of essential oneness, a degree of unity that *precludes* the possibility of separation (immanent separability being a mark of conditionedness and hence non-absoluteness). It follows (5) that the 'I' is ruled out as a candidate for absolute being. Fichte has, therefore, in making the 'I' absolute, confused Being with identity. Thus, while the absolute—that unitary, unconditioned being which, playing the logical role of Spinoza's one substance, stands as the real ground of the epistemological, explanatory, conceptual, and ontological orders[17]—of course exists, it cannot be expressed in the form of a proposition about the I, nor about anything else: *no* proposition can express the absolute. A parallel line of thought appears in Novalis, who maintains *contra* Fichte that there must be a relation to an *independent* Not-I in order for the I to posit itself, and that when the I first posits itself, it does so *within* a 'sphere that encompasses' both I and Not-I and that therefore cannot be posited by the I.[18]

Such critique does not leave Fichte without room for manoeuvre, but it opens the door immediately to new possibilities. So long as the aspiration to grasp the absolute is not abandoned—and it remains axiomatic for the German Romantics that all philosophizing must 'end in an absolute ground'[19]

---

[17] The concept of the absolute was for the post-Kantian idealists not merely the name of a blank functional role within philosophical discourse: it could be known, so they argued, to have certain determinations, including infinite rationality and activity. These can be set aside, however, in the present context.

[18] *Fichte Studies*, no. 8, p. 7 [*Fichte-Studien*, 107–8]. For discussion of Hölderlin's and Novalis's critiques of Fichte, see Frank, *The Philosophical Foundations of Early German Romanticism*.

[19] *Fichte Studies*, no. 566, p. 167 [*Fichte-Studien*, 269].

or at any rate direct itself towards doing so—what is suggested is that our relation to the absolute must be construed in some new way, one that will count as relatively indirect from the standpoint of discursive reason. If the Fichtean absolute I is not philosophically the end of the story, then we must conceive of there existing some hinterland to Fichte's landscape: we must suppose that, at the point where the self relates to itself by positing itself, it does so against a background that contains some more basic, pre-individual ground. 'Judgement and Being' gives no hint as to what should be said about the connection, which of course must exist, between the self and absolute being, but the whole of Hölderlin's later theoretical and artistic development is in a sense guided by the task of binding them together. For both Hölderlin and Novalis, the primacy of being over consciousness can be grasped, as in Plato's allegory of the cave, on the model of a light in which consciousness beholds itself, flowing from a ground which consciousness cannot bend back to illuminate. The being that grounds consciousness, that reflection cannot represent, may however be presented through Aesthetic means:

Philosophy is originally a feeling. The philosophical sciences conceptualize the intuitions of this feeling...Thus philosophy always needs *something given*—it is *form*...Philosophy does not admit of construction. The borders of feeling are the borders of philosophy. Feeling cannot feel itself.[20]

The feeling Novalis speaks of is a feeling *of* the sphere that encompasses I and Not-I, of what Hölderlin calls absolute being.[21] From the premise that reflection is conditioned and bounded by feeling (all that philosophical reflection can do is *give form* to the material supplied by feeling), Novalis reaches the double conclusion that philosophy cannot be a pure, free reflective construction in the way that Fichte envisages his *Wissenschaftslehre* as being, and that (because feeling 'cannot feel itself') philosophy cannot complete its aim of closing the circle on itself.[22] Recognition that the aim of producing a complete, self-justifying philosophical system is strictly unfulfillable does not, however, mark the end of philosophical speculation. On the contrary, in the view of Novalis, and of his close philosophical associate Friedrich Schlegel, it provides it with a spur: philosophy will henceforth understand its task as one of infinite

---

[20] *Fichte Studies*, no. 15, p. 13 [*Fichte-Studien*, 113–14].

[21] Or 'Seyn, im einzigen Sinne des Worts', which is available to us only in Aesthetic form, as beauty: see *Hyperion* (Die vorletzte Fassung), Vorrede, 236–7.

[22] Novalis has a complex theory of why it should appear otherwise—of why reflection should appear to itself autonomous—in terms of an illusion of inverted order: see *Fichte Studies*, nos. 15–17, pp. 12–14 [*Fichte-Studien*, 111–15].

striving towards the systematic ideal and will stand alongside art's presentation of the discursively unpresentable, contributing to a comprehensive Aesthetic reinterpretation, or 'romanticization', of self and world. As Schlegel defines the new programme: 'Where philosophy stops, poetry has to begin'[23] — 'Whatever can be done while philosophy and poetry are separated, has been done and is achieved. So the time has come to unite the two.'[24]

3. The German Romantic integration of Aesthetic media into philosophical speculation has further rationales, in addition to the post-Fichtean motive of resolving the aporia in the *Wissenschaftslehre* and penetrating to the true ground of the I. One is the metaphysical organicism of the Romantics: the idea that the world as a whole and all of its elements have organic structure, which allows it to be held that works of art, on account of the way that the special interpenetration of parts and whole which they exhibit raises them to a higher unity, exhibit in microcosmic form, and thus furnish cognition of, the true shape of reality.[25]

Another, of fundamental importance on account of its methodological character and independence from any specific metaphysical doctrine, for which reason it recurs again and again in post-Kantian philosophy of art, is the theory of the identity of the transcendental with the Aesthetic point of view. The concept of the transcendental, which Kant had employed in a relatively narrow epistemological way, becomes greatly expanded in German Romantic usage.[26] Again the departure from Kant is grounded in a perceived deficiency of his system, this time in his alleged failure to explain how ascent can be made from the ordinary, pre-transcendental standpoint to the level of transcendental reflection. Here again the discursive shortfall meets with the German Romantic suggestion of Aesthetic compensation. The basic idea was first articulated by Fichte:

Perhaps one cannot express what fine art does in any better way than by saying that *it makes the transcendental point of view the ordinary point of view.*—The philosopher elevates himself and others to this point of view by means of work and in accordance with a rule. The beautiful spirit [*der schöne Geist*] occupied this viewpoint without thinking of it in any determinate manner; he is acquainted with no other viewpoint. He elevates those who open themselves to his influence to this same viewpoint, and he does that just as unnoticeably, so that they are not even aware of the transition.

---

[23]  Schlegel, 'Ideas', no. 48, p. 98 ['Ideen', 261].
[24]  Schlegel, 'Ideas', no. 108, p. 104 ['Ideen', 267].
[25]  Beiser explores this theme in detail in *The Romantic Imperative*.
[26]  'Transcendental is what is, should be, and can be, elevated', Schlegel, '*Athenaeum* Fragments', no. 388, p. 79 ['*Athenäums*-Fragmente', 237].

Let me make myself clearer: from the transcendental point of view, the world is something that is made; from the ordinary point of view, it is something that is given; from the aesthetic point of view, the world is given, but only under the aspect of how it was made.[27]

Fichte, as the quotation shows, envisages Aesthetic ascent to the transcendental as strictly inessential, since there is a 'rule' that the Fichtean philosopher can employ to elevate himself. Novalis and Schlegel by contrast treat the primary and central form of the transcendental viewpoint as intuitional rather than conceptual: on their view, Aesthetic media are what allow us to attain the transcendental, to enact in self-consciousness the shift from pre-Copernican to transcendental philosophy, and what provides assurance of the (peculiar) reality of the transcendental standpoint.

Just as Fichte's transcendental philosophy is anchored in moral freedom, and Schiller's philosophical writings have a moral-political purpose, so in German Romantic theory the significance of the Aesthetically induced transcendental standpoint is not exclusively or even primarily theoretical. The aporia in Fichte's philosophy, Hölderlin supposed, not only pertains to theoretical reason but amounts also to a practical or existential problem, which gives human life its basic form: because self-identity falls short of absolute being—because the self is essentially a unity, yet at the same time divided all the way down—self-consciousness as such is a problem for itself. Self-cognition of a theoretical and discursive sort does not allow the self to harmonize with itself, because it is premised on the distinction of subject and object, rendering it incapable of unifying the self's unity and multiplicity. A self-relation that achieves this unification is possible, however, in activity that has the form of poetic creation, in which the I steps outside itself.[28] The same pattern, of according privileged practical and axiological significance to the Aesthetic, is repeated in Novalis' visionary, transfigurative 'magical idealism',[29] and

---

[27]  Fichte, *The System of Ethics*, §31, p. 334 [*System der Sittenlehre*, 353–4]. The same idea is employed in Schopenhauer, *The World as Will and Representation*, vol. i. p. 173, §34, pp. 178–81, and §38, pp. 195–200 [*Die Welt als Wille und Vorstellung*, i. 204, 209–13, and 230–6]. Fichte and Schopenhauer count, in terms of the distinctions made earlier, as Aesthetic Parallelists. For an original contemporary Parallelist account of the transcendental significance of art, see Sacks, *Objectivity and Insight*, 320–1.

[28]  Hölderlin calls this the formation of a 'pure poetic I'; see 'Operations of Poetic Spirit', 72 and 72–3n. ['Über die Verfahrungsweise des poëtischen Geistes', 252–5]. Hölderlin's idea that the dynamic of human life can be grasped adequately only in Aesthetic form is pursued by Henrich in *Kunst und Leben*.

[29]  On which, see Beiser, *German Idealism*, pt. III, ch. 3.

in Schleiermacher's Romantic account of religion as proceeding from an intuition or feeling of the infinite.[30]

4. While Hölderlin and Novalis argue for a radical Aestheticist turn within philosophy, a more philosophically conservative form of Philosophical Aestheticism, which agrees on the limitations of Fichtean philosophy but holds complete systematicity to be still attainable, was developed by Schelling in Part Six of his *System of Transcendental Idealism*. If Schiller's ideal of a unity of freedom and nature overshoots what the Kantian system warrants, it at least makes it possible to ask what revision of Kantianism *would* be sufficient to support Schiller's ideal, and to attempt to innovate Kantian metaphysics accordingly. This in effect is what Schelling does, in what is perhaps the finest integration of the claims of philosophy and of art in modern philosophy. In place of annexing a strong Aesthetic claim to a philosophical structure that has been designed to show the self-sufficiency of discursive reason, Schelling designs a post-Kantian system in which epistemological and metaphysical needs find their consummation in Aesthetic consciousness.

The task that Schelling sets himself in the *System of Transcendental Idealism* is to put together Fichte's transcendental idealism, in a somewhat reworked form, with a philosophy of nature that, though remote from and opposed to any materialistic naturalism, regards nature in a realistic light and not as a mere counter-posit to the self-positing I. The result is a philosophical system with a remarkable, two-in-one structure. The key to the coherence of Schelling's double system lies in his innovation of the model that he took to be provided by Spinoza: just as Spinoza's One Substance is represented in terms of the two attributes of thought and extension, so we can, Schelling suggests, conceive a single philosophical system as composed from two sides, that of the subject and that of the object. The subjective side yields a Fichtean philosophy of freedom, the objective a philosophy of nature. As Schelling develops the two system-sides, they are discovered to interlock, each leading round to the starting-point of the other. The question arises nonetheless, what establishes the unity of the system as a whole—what shows the worlds of each system to be one and the same, the subjective and objective to be identical. Philosophy cannot supply a principle to perform this role: the highest principles that it can articulate are the self's freedom and nature's productivity, which constitute and so cannot overcome the subject–object division. Philosophy

---

[30]  See *On Religion*, esp. the Second Speech. Later this becomes a feeling of 'absolute dependence'; see *The Christian Faith*, Introduction, §4, pp. 12–18 [*Der christliche Glaube*, xiii/1. 32–40].

can do no more than postulate subject–object identity. This limit of discursive philosophy creates the context for Schelling's Aestheticism. The work of art, on Schelling's Romantic analysis, is an indissoluble unity of conscious and unconscious productive factors, of self and nature, freedom and necessity—a unity which, crucially, exists *as* such *for* the subject. Aesthetic intuition is thus what expresses subject–object identity and sets the seal of unity on Schelling's system.

Schelling's philosophy of art brings out well the way in which Aestheticism can avoid the paradox discussed earlier, by locating the Aesthetic's philosophically cognitive content in one sense inside and in another outside philosophy: the *concept* of the work of art, as Schelling analyses it, belongs to philosophical discourse, but what makes the concept more than an arbitrary discursive construction, and warrants the claim for its cognitive value, consists in an extra-conceptual, Aesthetic phenomenon. This is why Schelling describes the work of art as 'the only true and eternal organ and document of philosophy'.[31]

5. Though outside the orbit of German Romanticism, a brief comment is due on Nietzsche, whose relation to Philosophical Aestheticism is characteristically complex. Nietzsche's account of art and affect, although it includes many naturalistic elements, is not confined to the Humean schema described in Section 1. Though opposed to the post-Kantian idealist tradition, Nietzsche carries forward the Romantic theme of the involvement of art with fundamental questions of value, and *The Birth of Tragedy* presents what appears to be a hyper-Romantic case for regarding tragic art as a condition of possibility for genuine value. Nietzsche did not hold long to the view articulated in this early work, and in his later writings he rejects Romanticism in no uncertain terms, keenly aware of art's potential to serve the ascetic ideal.[32] And yet, even in the writings of his maturity Nietzsche supposes that Aesthetic notions hold their place within a post-metaphysical world-view, and indeed (in a way that is not typical of philosophical naturalists) that they are *necessary* if we are to orientate ourselves and flourish under modern conditions. In view of his generally skeptical stance, Nietzsche cannot be said to endorse squarely the Aestheticist claim that art is cognitive, and is better interpreted as upholding a non-cognitive analogue of Philosophical Aestheticism, in which art plays the trick of releasing us from the authority of a theoretical reason which has

---

[31]  *System of Transcendental Idealism (1800)*, 231 [*System des transcendentalen Idealismus*, 627].
[32]  *The Gay Science*, bk. 5, sect. 370, pp. 327–31 [*Die fröhliche Wissenschaft*, 301–4].

become incompatible with life.[33] Whether or not his position qualifies as Aesthetic Subversivism, as French neo-structuralist writing assumes, depends on how exactly the mechanism of release is understood and on more general issues in Nietzsche interpretation.

# 3. AESTHETICIST STRATEGIES IN TWENTIETH-CENTURY PHILOSOPHY

It may be asked how much, if anything, of Philosophical Aestheticism can survive the historical move away from classical German philosophy. That this is indeed possible is shown by Merleau-Ponty, Heidegger, and Adorno, all of whom take up Aestheticist positions. What they share, and what distinguishes them from the thinkers discussed in the previous section, is an intention to challenge, criticize, or revise ordinary, pre-philosophical self-understanding. So there is a shift in the goal of, and a new use for, the Aestheticist strategy: whereas Kant's early successors were seeking not to alter ordinary understanding but to embed it within systematic philosophy, and conscripted the Aesthetic to that end, the revisionary intentions of Merleau-Ponty, Heidegger, and Adorno mean that the Aesthetic is now set in opposition to ordinary self-understanding and to modes of philosophical thought that reflect and endorse what they consider its deficiencies.[34]

1. The philosophical positions which developed in the immediate post-Kantian context continue to conceive philosophy as, broadly speaking, a task of explanation, of uncovering the *grounds* of how things are and must be. Merleau-Ponty explicitly conceives philosophy instead as providing a special kind of *non*-explanatory description, which he calls 'giving voice to the

---

[33] The trans-cognitive or para-cognitive character of Nietzsche's view of what art achieves goes back to his famous, cryptic remark in *The Birth of Tragedy* that it is 'only as an *aesthetic phenomenon* that existence and the world are eternally *justified*' (sect. 5, p. 52) [*Die Geburt der Tragödie*, 43].

[34] Whether this different style of employment of Philosophical Aestheticism counts as progress depends, of course, on matters of general philosophical outlook; what deserves emphasis here is simply that Philosophical Aestheticism itself is able to stand both independently of the strong systematic ambition of classical German philosophy and as a resource for those who affirm that ambition. Thus, if one considers that twentieth-century transcendental philosophy ultimately leads back to, rather than leaving behind, the concerns that motivated classical German philosophy, and if one also does not accept Hegel's execution of the systematic project (discussed below), then by no means may the forms of Philosophical Aestheticism discussed in the previous section be regarded as surpassed.

experience of the world': 'phenomenological or existential philosophy assigns itself the task, not of explaining the world . . . but rather of formulating an experience of the world, a contact with the world which precedes all thought *about* the world.'[35]    This shift to a revelatory or expressive conception of philosophical cognition suggests immediately a convergence if not identity of aim with art, and a correlative conception of art as philosophically cognitive.

Merleau-Ponty's *Phenomenology of Perception* attempts to establish the existence of what Merleau-Ponty calls 'pre-objective' (also 'lived', 'unreflected') consciousness. At the pre-objective level there is, Merleau-Ponty claims, no distinction of subject and object: when the accretions of 'objective thought' are stripped away, we discover in perception an original point of connection between ourselves and the world that is completely unanalysable. Phenomenology can make us aware of this point and show that it is always presupposed in conceptual activity, but no philosophy can reach back by means of concepts to anything more primordial that might elucidate it. What is primarily revealed about the world from the pre-objective standpoint, according to Merleau-Ponty, is its indeterminacy: the world as perceived pre-objectively is not composed of distinct objects to which determinate characteristics can be assigned. The pre-objective is strictly ineffable, and because this is so, we cannot say how the objective, reflective conception of the world—to which Merleau-Ponty accords, of course, its own, relative validity—arises out of it, although we can know that it does so.

The path employed in the *Phenomenology* to establish these results consists in a critique of philosophical and psychological theories of perception, indicating their incoherences, explanatory failures, remoteness from phenomenological reality, antinomial structure, and so on. That this wholly negative procedure can never amount to *proof* of the reality of the pre-objective is a point acknowledged, indeed emphasized, by Merleau-Ponty. Art, however, in at least some of its forms, performs the same labour as the *Phenomenology*, employing positive and non-conceptual means. The artist whose expression of the passage from pre-objectivity to objectivity Merleau-Ponty regards as exemplary is Cézanne:

Cézanne did not think he had to choose between feeling and thought, between order and chaos. He did not want to separate the stable things which we see and the shifting way in which they appear [as do the Impressionists]; he wanted to depict matter as it takes on form, the birth of order through spontaneous organisation. He makes a basic

---

[35] 'Metaphysics and the Novel', 27–8 ['Le roman et la métaphysique', 54–5].

distinction not between 'the senses' and 'the understanding' [a distinction of objective thought] but rather between the spontaneous organisation of the things we perceive and the human organisation of ideas and sciences. We see things; we agree about them; we are anchored in them; and it is with 'nature' as our base that we construct our sciences. Cézanne wanted to paint this primordial world . . . He wished, as he said, to confront the sciences with the nature 'from which they came' . . . By remaining faithful to the phenomena in his investigations of perspective, Cézanne discovered what recent [Gestalt, phenomenological] psychologists have come to formulate: the lived perspective, that which we actually perceive, is not a geometric or photographic one . . . it is Cézanne's genius that when the over-all composition of the picture is seen globally . . . [we have] the impression of an emerging order, of an object in the act of appearing, organising itself before our eyes.[36]

The identification proposed by Fichte of the aesthetic standpoint with the transcendental is here clearly reaffirmed: in Cézanne we find, as Fichte put it, the world given under the aspect of how it is made.

2. The idea that the work of art is concerned with a transcendental process of world-constitution belongs also to Heidegger, though Heidegger arrives at it quite differently, and carries it a step further.

It is best to start with the sections of *Being and Time* in which Heidegger lays out the category of 'mood', *Stimmung*.[37] What is under consideration here is our affectivity, philosophical understanding of which has, he says, 'been able to make scarcely one forward step worthy of mention since Aristotle'.[38] This situation is not peculiar to affect, but a result of the general limitations of philosophical understanding since the Presocratics, which *Being and Time* diagnoses as consisting in the error of according priority to the mode of being of presence-at-hand (*Vorhandensein*), and which Heidegger's exposition of our properly fundamental mode of being-in-the-world aims to overcome.

Despite the obvious enormous differences from Kant, there is a good sense in which the Heidegger's inquiry into Dasein is transcendental: Heidegger aims to explicate how there comes to be a world for us in terms that refer to the necessary, non-empirical structures that compose us, the subjects for whom the world is. The differences from Kant, stated baldly, are these: Heidegger expressly refuses to allow transcendental reflection to fix in advance our understanding of 'object' and 'condition of possibility' in a way that would narrow the field of inquiry to what Kant calls *Erfahrung*, objective

---

[36] 'Cézanne's Doubt', 13–14 ['Le doute de Cézanne', 24–7].

[37] *Being and Time*, §§29–30, pp. 172–82 [*Sein und Zeit*, 178–89], and §68 (b), pp. 389–96 [*Sein und Zeit*, 449–57].

[38] *Being and Time*, 178 [*Sein und Zeit*, 185].

knowledge. Also and connectedly, Heidegger's transcendental inquiry aims to do something which Kant's does not do, namely to put in question, renew, and alter our grasp of the given. What causes Heidegger's transcendental analysis to reshape the field whose conditions of possibility it investigates is the fact that his primary interest lies, not in the constitution of human subjectivity, but in 'fundamental ontology': the question of Being which originally gives reason to make Dasein a theme of enquiry is a non-Kantian, supra-transcendental question, one which, if Heidegger is correct, neither ordinary, pre-philosophical consciousness nor philosophy hitherto has the resources to answer. This is why the transcendental enquiry into Dasein which sub-serves ontological inquiry into Being is bound to do more than revalidate the conceptions of ordinary consciousness: Heidegger needs to wring from ordinary consciousness, by means of transcendental analysis, an answer to a question which it does not even recognize.

Heidegger produces, accordingly, an account of affect which revises common-sense psychology. On Heidegger's view, the field of phenomena tax-onomized by common-sense psychology under the headings 'belief', 'desire', 'feeling', etc., cannot be accounted for without going back to more basic dimensions of Dasein. Dasein's 'being-there' comprises, Heidegger proposes, two basic structures: 'state-of-mind' (*Befindlichkeit*, Dasein's finding-itself-to-be some way or another) and 'understanding'. Mood is that which expresses *Befindlichkeit* in ordinary consciousness (in Heidegger's language: mood is the ontic phenomenon that expresses the ontological existentiale of *Befind-lichkeit*). Heidegger's revisions to the understanding of affect in common-sense psychology and its philosophical counterparts are several. (i) Mood carries a meaning which affective episodes, bound to particular entities in the world, cannot carry, but which they presuppose: mood registers (without repre-senting) the ontological dimension of Dasein. In mood Dasein is 'brought before its being as "there"', its own 'burdensome character', the fact that it is 'delivered over to the Being which, in existing, it has to be', the 'thrownness' (*Geworfenheit*) or '*facticity of its being delivered over*'.[39] Incorporated in this registering is a practical element: we turn 'towards or turn away' from that which mood discloses.[40] Mood is thus cognitive, though again, not in the manner of Kantian experience: in contradistinction to empirical cognition, mood is cognitive by virtue of its 'saying' something to us without offering us any object to grasp or proposition to entertain; it instead takes in all of the

---

[39] *Being and Time*, 173–4 [*Sein und Zeit*, 179–80].    [40] *Being and Time*, 174 [*Sein und Zeit*, 180].

world. (ii) Mood is necessary: Dasein cannot be 'free of' mood, even though its mood may be 'bare' and invisible to introspection. (iii) Since the registering of Dasein's facticity is sufficient for the phenomenon of mood, mood presupposes no beliefs or desires; these representational states arrive later in the day. Indeed, mood is required for cognition, since cognition presupposes the existentiale of 'understanding', and understanding 'always has its mood'.[41] (iv) Far from being logically secondary to emotion—a case of peculiarly vague emotion, or of emotion that has somehow lost track of its object—mood is the original, autonomous form of affect, which precedes and makes possible the affective episodes ascribed in common-sense psychology. It follows that affect in general has nothing to do originally or essentially with sensation, sensory affection, or corporeal conditions. Finally, (v) mood is a condition for practical orientation: it is what first discloses Dasein's being-in-the-world 'as a whole' and thereby 'makes it possible first of all to direct oneself towards something'.[42]

In arguing for this interpretation of mood as a transcendental condition (more accurately, as the ontic manifestation thereof) Heidegger appeals to those of its characteristic features which define it for (though without, he holds, allowing it to be rendered intelligible by) common-sense psychology: the way we slip from one mood to another, the way moods give themselves as independent of any 'why or wherefore', their fitful proneness to decay and to improve spontaneously, their enigmatic and inexorable quality, and so on. Heidegger's later intense preoccupation with art—in 'The origin of the work of art', with its famous accounts of van Gogh and of Greek temple architecture, and in the attention Heidegger gives to poetry, especially that of Hölderlin, from the late 1930s onwards—can be understood as an extension of his account of mood. In *Being and Time*, the conditions and structures that explicate there being a world for us are, as said above, 'subjective' in the sense that their description is a description of the mode of being of Dasein: though not themselves psychological, they show up at the 'ontic' level as elements of Dasein, in the way just described for mood. Heidegger's later thought may be regarded as providing a new locus for these conditions, which is in some degree outside Dasein (though not independent of it). Whereas, on the account given in *Being and Time*, mood is what most basically exposes Dasein to the ontological, in the later Heidegger this role is ascribed to works of art.

---

[41]  *Being and Time*, 182 [*Sein und Zeit*, 190].        [42]  *Being and Time*, 176 [*Sein und Zeit*, 182].

The Greek 'temple-work', Heidegger says,

opens up a world and at the same time sets this world back again on earth, which itself only thus emerges as native ground...To be a work means to set up a world...The work moves the earth itself into the Open region of a world and keeps it there...The setting up of a world and the setting forth of earth are two essential features in the work-being of the work.[43]

The distinction between 'world' and what Heidegger calls 'earth' replaces the traditional distinction of form and matter. The work of art makes both possible, and sets them in a relation of 'strife' or opposition to one another. This opening-up of world, and setting-forth of earth, is conceived by Heidegger as something that the work *itself* does, not as something done by the artist: 'in great art...the artist remains inconsequential as compared with the work, almost like a passageway that destroys itself in the creative process for the work to emerge'.[44] Nor does the work of art exist for the sake of its audience: our role is to 'preserve' the work, not in a material sense, but in the sense that we, by relinquishing our accustomed ties with the world, abide with the work in order to *let it be itself*; we enter into relation with the work, for the sake of the work.[45]

Heidegger's statements concerning the world-constitutive role of art invite the question whether they are to be read epistemologically (transcendentally) or ontologically: is the talk of the temple as 'setting up a world' talk of what it allows Dasein to cognize (relate to intentionally), or of an ontological operation? If there is one thing that is clear in the later Heidegger, however, it is that he—in this respect following the German idealists in their attempt to show the 'identity' or mutual implication of being and knowledge—wishes to overcome at the highest level of philosophical reflection the separation implied by this distinction, and that a merely epistemological (transcendental) reading of claims such as those that he makes about the Greek temple does not capture his meaning: 'The art work opens up in its own way the Being of beings. This opening up, i.e., this deconcealing, i.e., the truth of beings, happens in the work. In the art work, the truth of what is has set itself to work. Art is truth setting itself to work.'[46]   The temple therefore takes on the transcendental function of Dasein's mood, and with it, the ontological character of Dasein itself. Heidegger's conception is thus more radical than that of Merleau-Ponty, for whom art does no more than *represent* a transcendental process occurring

---

[43] 'The Origin of the Work of Art', 42–8 ['Der Ursprung der Kunstwerkes', 28–34].
[44] 'The Origin of the Work of Art', 40 ['Der Ursprung der Kunstwerkes', 26].
[45] 'The Origin of the Work of Art', 66–7 ['Der Ursprung der Kunstwerkes', 54–5].
[46] 'The Origin of the Work of Art', 39 ['Der Ursprung der Kunstwerkes', 25].

within individual subjectivity: in Heidegger the transcendental function is taken to be in some sense enacted *in* or *by* the work of art.[47] Consequently, with Heidegger art is raised to a still higher power than it enjoys in German idealist forms of Philosophical Aestheticism: art does not merely reveal metaphysical truths *about* the world, instead, or rather in addition, it contributes to (is part of) the world's coming-to-be. The philosophical truth that we glean *from* art is in fact the truth that art *is itself* truth, according to Heidegger's understanding of truth as *alethea*, a unitary disclosing and releasing-into-being of entities.

Heidegger's theory of art illustrates the general principle governing Aestheticist strategies, whereby the strength of the claim made on behalf of the Aesthetic is proportioned to the deficiency alleged in philosophy's ability to execute its task. In the present case, on account of the later Heidegger's assessment of the deep involvement of traditional philosophy with the danger posed by 'technology', the deficiency is considered extreme.

3. Adorno is of all philosophers the most explicitly and intensively concerned with the problem of truth in art, and he insists most strongly that the key to art's value lies in its claim to truth, while also thinking that the notion of art's truth is one of the most difficult to make sense of, and one of the most important problems that philosophy in general is faced with. Adorno's linkage of art and philosophical truth—enshrined in his central theoretical concept of art's 'truth-content'—constitutes a radically original version of the Aestheticist strategy. The term truth-content is meant to affirm the propriety of attributing truth-value to art while acknowledging that works of art themselves are not truth-bearers in an ordinary and straightforward sense: though not themselves true or false, they nevertheless *contain* truth. The truth-content of a work of art thus consists simply in the truth of whatever it is that the work says concerning the nature of the world in the most general and fundamental, hence philosophical, sense. The complexity lies in Adorno's complex account of *how* works of art possess truth-content.

In the first place, though committed to a constitutive connection of philosophical knowledge with social criticism, Adorno rejects vehemently the idea that the truth-content of art is something that can be determined on a theoretical, external basis—as for instance naive Marxist art criticism may impute truth to representational art on account of its social verisimilitude or didactic political potential. For Adorno the truth-content of art is aesthetically

---

[47]  In the full picture of the later Heidegger, 'language' takes on this role, but the connection with art is preserved through an identification of 'poetry' with ur-language.

realized in the *form* of the work, and it presupposes the work's autonomy. In part for this reason, on Adorno's account it is above all *music* that presses, in an exemplary pure form, a claim to truth, with which philosophy should concern itself. Despite the condition that music's truth-content be realized aesthetically—that it be something which one can either succeed in hearing musically or be said to be 'deaf to'[48] —it is not situated by Adorno at the level of the work's primary aesthetic appearance, where Schiller for example would locate it. On the contrary, this level of musical meaning is declared illusory:

The ideological element of music, its affirmative element, does not lie, as with other arts, in its specific content, or even in whether or not its form operates in terms of harmony. It lies merely in the fact that it is *a voice lifted up*, that it is music at all. Its language is magical in itself, and the transition to its isolated sphere has *a priori* a quality of transfiguration. The suspension of empirical reality and the forming of a second reality *sui generis* seem to say in advance: all is well. Its tone is by origin consoling, and to that origin it is bound. But that does not apply unambiguously to music's status as *truth*. . .[49]

Achieving the status of truth requires further moments, in which this first moment—called by Adorno 'aesthetic semblance', which he thinks belongs to the 'ideological', 'affirmative', transfigurative level at which we are told, falsely, that 'all is well'—is overcome.[50] The truth-content of art involves, Adorno supposes, a (non-sensuous, yet aesthetically realized) *operation on* aesthetic semblance, namely, a *negation* of the affirmation expressed in aesthetic semblance: we so to speak *hear* the music pass judgement on its own beauty, exposing it as untrue, as *not* reflecting how things truly are. This undoing of the message given out by aesthetic semblance is at the same time a criticism of the existing world order: 'Its depth is that of a judgement pronounced against the negative aspects of the existing world. The basis for judgement in music, as a cognitive force, is aesthetic form . . . In the cognitive act performed by art, the artistic form represents a criticism' of existing reality;[51] art negates 'the categorial determinations stamped on the empirical world'.[52] This idea is followed out in Adorno's brilliant, whether or not correct,

---

[48]  *Beethoven*, 171 [*Beethoven*, 246].        [49]  *Beethoven*, 6–7 [*Beethoven*, 25–6].

[50]  Art's truth-content is something that 'appears aesthetically', but that the work bears 'beyond aesthetic semblance': 'What is beyond the semblance of what appears is the aesthetic truth content: that aspect of semblance that is not semblance' (*Beethoven*, 172 [*Beethoven*, 247]).

[51]  *Philosophy of Modern Music*, 125 [*Philosophie der neuen Musik*, 119].

[52]  *Aesthetic Theory*, 5 [*Ästhetische Theorie*, 15]. Art 'seeks to aid the nonidentical', which is repressed by the compulsion to identity: see *Aesthetic Theory*, 4 [*Ästhetische Theorie*, 14].

interpretations of particular artists and works—his account, for instance, of the inexpressive fracturedness of Beethoven's late style and the calculated alienation of his *Missa Solemnis*,[53] and of how Schoenberg's negation of aesthetic semblance allows perception of 'untransfigured suffering'.[54] (Also illustratively relevant is the 'taking back' of Beethoven's Ninth by Adrian Leverkühn, the fictional composer in Thomas Mann's Adorno-influenced *Doctor Faustus*: after witnessing the death of a child, Leverkühn pronounces that the all-affirming humanistic Ninth *ought not to be*, and to this end composes his great '*Apocalypsis*'.)

Bound up with this second, negative moment is a third, positive moment: art's indication of the 'non-absolute aspect' of existing reality and of the 'possibility of reconciliation', and thus its articulation of 'authentic hope'.[55]

In describing truth-content as involving this complex conjunction of three moments—ideological-transfigurative, negative-critical, and hope-sponsoring—Adorno is in a sense simply taking seriously the common idea that musical structure is akin to argumentation. Regarding the 'how' of musical negation and affirmation, this remains ultimately ungraspable: while musicological analysis has a contribution to make, the means by which music negates and affirms cannot be spelled out—music has necessarily an 'enigmatic' quality and its enigma 'cannot be solved'.[56] To the extent that music's capacity to achieve judgemental import defies analysis, a limit is reached regarding what Adorno can say by way of explicating the concept of artistic truth-content in positive philosophical terms, indispensable though it remains for the theory of art. All that can be done at this point is to turn to concrete musical examples and their interpretation.

Adorno's reason for thinking that the negation of the world order and correlative articulation of authentic hope requires art and is unavailable in its full import outside it, lies in his general critical theory of reason as bound (by its conceptuality) to an instrumental, repressive, ideological function. This thesis plays in Adorno's Aestheticist strategy the role played in Merleau-Ponty by the critique of objective thought and in Heidegger by the critique

---

[53] *Beethoven*, 123–53 [*Beethoven*, 180–222].
[54] *Philosophy of Modern Music*, 29 ff. [*Philosophie der neuen Musik*, 34 ff.].
[55] *Beethoven*, 172 [*Beethoven*, 247]. The account given here is simplified, in so far as Adorno's account of music's truth-content is not uniform: what it amounts to exactly depends on which musical era (e.g. Beethoven or Schoenberg) is in question.
[56] *Aesthetic Theory*, 122 ff. [*Ästhetische Theorie*, 182 ff.].

of traditional ontology, of setting limits to what philosophy can achieve by discursive means and thereby preparing the context for Aesthetic insight. The element of 'authentic hope' that Adorno locates in the work's truth-content can have no discursive validation, for the reason that, on Adorno's account, no rational grounds can be given for anything but despair or melancholy.

Adorno's Aestheticist strategy both presupposes and subjects to critique the Philosophical Aestheticism of the German philosophical tradition. Schiller's claim that art aims at human emancipation, the Romantic programme of magical idealism, Hegel's claim that art realizes the Idea—all these ideas are accepted by Adorno, in the sense that, he agrees, they do indeed correspond to the telos which art, by virtue of its aesthetic semblance, projects. What sets Adorno apart from his predecessors is his conviction that the *realizability* of this telos, with its incorporated claim that suffering is redeemable, is, for us now, unintelligible. Hence the falsity of (idealist) philosophies of art that promise more than reality can deliver, and the predominantly negative character of the truth-content of art. Hence, also, Adorno's esotericism—the strong suggestion that the 'audibility' (visibility etc.) of the truth content of an artwork presupposes a philosophically informed consciousness, one that has passed through (and gone beyond) German idealism.[57]

4. That it should be possible for three philosophies as diverse and conflicting as those of Heidegger, Adorno and Merleau-Ponty nonetheless to concur in regarding art as, in Schelling's words, a 'document and organon' of philosophy, testifies to the appeal and versatility of the Aestheticist strategy.

Claims concerning the transcendence of philosophy by art and affect continue to be made in present-day Continental philosophy. They are of course not all of a piece, but typically they have an orientation which differs importantly from that of the three twentieth-century philosophers just discussed, and which reflects the influence of deconstruction. The radical critiques of rationality offered in deconstruction go beyond what is attempted in Merleau-Ponty, Heidegger, or Adorno, whose intention in criticizing objective thought, traditional ontology, and identity thinking, is to contest an entrenched philosophical paradigm, but not philosophical thought as such;

---

[57] Thus in some places Adorno suggests that the truth-content of art comes to light fully only through the mediation of philosophical commentary (which is not the same as saying that this commentary takes over its truth-content). It will be clear from what has been said that Adorno's form of Philosophical Aestheticism, to the extent that it may be estimated apart from his philosophy as a whole, is less epistemologically robust than those discussed earlier, in so far as the heavy burden that Adorno asks art to carry rests on super-fine conditions.

for which reason these thinkers, though relatively closer than the German Romantics to Aesthetic Subversivism, remain distinct from it.

In the hyper-critical context of deconstruction, it is not surprising that themes in philosophical Romanticism should have been picked up on,[58] but there is a deep difference of Philosophical Aestheticism from deconstruction which it is crucial to keep in view in order that the former should not be exposed to criticism drawn by the latter. Philosophical Aestheticism seeks to interpret in *philosophically coherent* terms the features of the Aesthetic that, the Platonist believes, make art indifferent or inimical to reason, and thereby to exhibit their true rationality; deconstructionist appropriations of art and affect insist, by contrast, in a Platonic way but to anti-Platonic ends, on the irreconcilable antagonism of reason and the Aesthetic. Deconstruction of this species therefore crosses the line between a *philosophically grounded* elevation of the Aesthetic designed to complement and extend philosophical reflection, such as Philosophical Aestheticism provides, to a *philosophically ungrounded* critique of philosophy from the standpoint of the Aesthetic.

When the Aesthetic is conscripted in opposition to philosophy in the deconstructionist manner, we have what was called earlier the Subversive view of the relation of art to philosophy. Such a view, where the Aesthetic is as if credited with a rationality, or 'logic', of its own, one that at no point joins up with ordinary or philosophical discursive reason, is hard to interpret. The problem lies in seeing how this Aesthetic (anti-)rationality can be recognized as such. If the opposition of the Aesthetic to philosophy is held to be total and unmediated, i.e. not an opposition that can be so much as *stated* within philosophy, but rather an opposition of philosophy to something which is absolutely 'other' to it, then it is not thinkable *as* an opposition. If on the other hand the opposition is philosophically mediated, then it seems that the moment which the Aesthetic is held to represent is really a further moment of philosophy. In the former case, the Aesthetic protest against philosophy seems mute and contentless; in the latter, the Aesthetic seems reduced to a mere cypher for discursive philosophical claims, i.e. it is instrumentalized in the very way that, Subversivists typically object, traditional, 'dogmatic' philosophy of art has done. The point to be grasped, in any case, is the logical distance of this scenario from that of Philosophical Aestheticism. The suspicion must be, furthermore, that Aesthetic strategies in deconstruction trade off the authority

---

[58] See Lacoue-Labarthe and Nancy, *The Literary Absolute*, for an example of deconstructionist reading of German Romanticism.

of the Aesthetic that philosophical Romanticism established historically, while undermining the qualified affirmation of philosophy's claim to systematic knowledge which was required to create that authority.[59]

# 4. Critics of Philosophical Aestheticism

Individual instances of Philosophical Aestheticism can, of course, be evaluated only in the context of the philosophical position to which they belong. As regards the strategy itself, the historical discussion in the last two sections bears out, I suggest, the contention in Section 1 that Philosophical Aestheticism is in principle coherent and defensible, within the context of a broadly transcendental, non-naturalistic conception of the task of philosophy, where understanding is sought of the world's non-empirical constitution or coming-to-be. Philosophical Aestheticism represents, I have also tried to suggest, the strongest claim that can be made coherently on behalf of the idea that the Aesthetic contributes to the task of philosophy; any stronger claim will either result in epistemological irresponsibility (Jacobi), or run into logical difficulty (Aesthetic Subversivism).

Two figures in the history of post-Kantian philosophy, Hegel and Sartre, are of particular interest from the point of view of arriving at a balanced critical assessment of Philosophical Aestheticism. It will be instructive to consider briefly their reasons for rejecting the notion that the Aesthetic enjoys cognitive privileges.

1. Hegel's relation to Philosophical Aestheticism is complex. On the one hand, Hegel appears to fall in line with his Romantic contemporaries when he includes art among the forms of 'absolute' spirit: by characterizing art as the realization of the Idea in sensuous form, a unity of form and content that may be taken as an expression of freedom and a presentation of the absolute, Hegel accepts the Romantic characterization of works of art as concerned with the relation, which it is the task of philosophy to grasp, of the finite to the infinite. What cancels the seeming consequent commitment to at least Aesthetic Parallelism, if not to Philosophical Aestheticism, is Hegel's crucial

---

[59] For an extended critique of what I have been calling Aesthetic Subversivism, see Megill, *Prophets of Extremity*.

historical qualification, that art is no longer 'the highest mode' of truth but has 'has lost for us genuine truth'.[60] Philosophical Aestheticism, on Hegel's account, is a misguided attempt to take up in contemporary philosophical self-consciousness an attitude which can be ascribed to historically earlier shapes of consciousness but which it is impossible for us to adopt in the present tense. Art has, Hegel accepts, served to project the unity of finite and infinite, but he denies that we now can regard a sensible appearance as incarnating the Idea. Art's loss of import leaves no cognitive deficit, however, because the need to which it once answered, philosophy shows, has been fulfilled. The Romantics' formulation of the concept of Aesthetic cognition comes too late, when there is nothing more for us to learn philosophically from art.

Hegel's grounds for maintaining this position derive from his broader opposition, spelled out in numerous contexts, to claims of feeling and immediacy.[61] Hegel grants that all productions of thought should, upon completion, become matters of feeling, as in the moral consciousness of a fully formed ethical agent. What he denies is that there can be more *original* content in feeling than in thought, in particular, elevated content of the sort claimed in Jacobi's theory of *Gefühl* and in Schleiermacher's account of religion. Hegel's argument is that feeling, because its form is that of mere immediacy, particularity, and subjectivity, is by its nature incapable of bearing the kind of universal content claimed by Romantics. Further, Hegel argues that if religion for instance is allowed to become a matter of feeling, then, absurdly, so may everything, and that in any case the pressure to ground belief on feeling dissolves when it is grasped that the limits of mere finite understanding are not those of philosophical reason. What Aestheticism mistakes for an original content of feeling is in fact, Hegel claims, a completed product of reason that has passed over into the form of feeling.[62]

---

[60] *Aesthetics: Lectures on Fine Art*, vol. i, Introduction, p. 103 and p. 11 [*Vorlesungen über die Ästhetik*, xiii. 140 and 24]. Hegel's well-known but enigmatic thesis that art is at an end, at least with respect to its highest vocation, is found at: pp. 9–11 [xiii. 21–5]; Introduction to Part 1, 'Position of art in relation to the finite world and to religion and philosophy', esp. pp. 101–3 [xiii. 138–41]; and 'The end of the romantic form of art', pp. 602–11 [xiv. 230–41].

[61] See *Philosophy of Mind*, §§446–8, pp. 192–8 [*Philosophie des Geistes*, 245–52]; 'Foreword to Hinrichs', 346 ff. ['Vorrede zu Hinrichs' Religionsphilosophie', 55 ff.]; and *Encyclopaedia Logic*, §§61–78, pp. 108–24, 'Third position of thought with respect to objectivity: immediate knowing' [*Logik*, 147–67].

[62] The tradition of criticism descending from Hegel, which includes Carl Schmitt and Georg Lukács, in which the Romantic emphasis on art and the affective is interpreted as irrationalist and an index of conceptual deficiency, is discussed in Bohrer, *Die Kritik der Romantik*, pt. II. A striking restatement,

2. Whereas Hegel treats Philosophical Aestheticism as a philosophical error, deriving from attachment to an inferior shape of rationality in the development of spirit, Sartre locates its origin in ordinary consciousness, in the a priori motivational dynamics of the individual subject. Discrediting the truth-claims of art and affect is a central motive of Sartre's early studies of emotion and imagination. Both of these modes of consciousness emerge from Sartre's analyses as, in effect, forms of self-deception. The essence of emotion consists, Sartre argues, in its phenomenological transformation of the subject's world, and the constant meaning of emotional transformations, he proposes, is to deny the existence or bury awareness of some respect in which the world poses a difficulty for the subject. The point of affect is to endow objects with qualities which reconfigure the world in such a way as to bring it into conformity with our wishes, 'as though the relations between things and their potentialities were not governed by deterministic processes but by magic'.[63] Imagination, similarly, presupposes a negation of reality: the act of imagination 'is a magical act. It is an incantation destined to make the object of one's thought, the thing one desires, appear in such a way that one can take possession of it.'[64] The impossibility of art's having cognitive significance follows directly: art presupposes imaginative consciousness, and so is premised on a rupture with the real world in favour of unrealities; because the work of art is 'an irreality',[65] so too are beauty and all the other qualities that art bestows on its objects—'the real is never beautiful'.[66] The concealed aspiration of art is to relocate subjectivity outside the world, to become God-like, in denial of one's project and radical freedom.[67] This holds, according to Sartre, for all of the arts that presuppose the 'poetic attitude', which include poetry, music, and painting; only prose literature, he argues, declines to exploit the unreal

and updating, of Hegel's anti-Romantic position is found in Pippin, 'What Was Abstract Art? (From Hegel's Point of View)'.

[63] *Sketch for a Theory of the Emotions*, 63 [*Esquisse d'une théorie des émotions*, 33]. *Being and Nothingness* shifts partially away from this standpoint, in so far as some instances of affective consciousness are interpreted, in line with Heidegger, as ontological cognitions: see pp. 29–33 [*L'être et le néant*, 64–9] and p. 464 [520] on anguish (which 'manifests our freedom to our consciousness'), and pp. 288–9 [335–6] on shame ('the original feeling of having my being *outside*, engaged in another being'). But the official line remains as it was in the *Sketch*: see pp. 444–5 [499–500], reaffirming the 'magical' nature of affect.

[64] *The Imaginary*, 125 [*L'Imaginaire*, 161].          [65] *The Imaginary*, 188 [*L'Imaginaire*, 239].

[66] *The Imaginary*, 193 [*L'Imaginaire*, 245].

[67] *What is Literature?*, 9–10 [*Qu'est ce que la littérature?*, 68–70]. See also however pp. 23–4 n. 4 [85–7 n. 4], where some trace of a different view is to be found. The theme of art's 'mystification' and 'transcendental' illusoriness—its being 'really a magical attempt to satisfy desire'—is resumed and elaborated in the *Notebooks for an Ethics*, 551–4 [*Cahiers pour une morale*, 566–70].

and expresses an existential stance consistent with human freedom. To set cognitive store by art, as Philosophical Aestheticism affirms that we should, is therefore to engage in an intentional falsification of reality and to negate human freedom.

3. The grounds on which Hegel and Sartre criticize Philosophical Aestheticism go back, in a sense, to Kant. Hegel's basic complaint is that Philosophical Aestheticism flouts the Kantian condition of conceptuality that cognition stands under, while Sartre's repudiation of art and affect as illusory modes of consciousness is a reaffirmation of the original, austere Kantian conception of the conditions for freedom, which Philosophical Aestheticism is viewed as undermining. Both are open to challenge. Hegel's objection of epistemological irresponsibility has force only against an Aestheticist position like Jacobi's, which makes *Gefühl* a general criterion of knowledge. The objection that Aestheticism evades the demands of conceptuality is not a straightforward matter, to be settled by a direct appeal to Kant's Transcendental Deduction. Hegel's own claim that philosophy has come to appreciate the comprehensiveness of conceptuality in a sense that leaves no shortfall in the power of philosophical discourse to express truth, for which art or anything else would be required to compensate, requires that this comprehensiveness be demonstrated; to that extent, his criticism of Philosophical Aestheticism presupposes his *Logic*. Sartre's anti-Aestheticism, for its part, promises to return us to the much-criticized Kantian dualism of freedom and nature. For as long as a question-mark hangs over the alternatives, the Aesthetic turn in post-Kantian philosophy may be claimed to hold its own.

4. Criticism of a different sort, taking the form of a charge of conceptual or logical confusion, has come from aestheticians with an analytic orientation. Thus, in a detailed critical study of the German aesthetic tradition, it has been claimed by Jean-Marie Schaeffer that the distortions (as he sees them) of the 'speculative theory of Art' are founded on a '*category error*', compounded by a decision to 'sacralize' profane reality,[68] much as, very much earlier, I. A. Richards had argued that 'Revelation Doctrines' of literary art are rooted in a confusion of referential and emotive language use.[69] The weakness of such external criticism lies in the difficulty it faces in demonstrating non-circularly the methodological failing it alleges in Philosophical Aestheticism and its tendency simply to disregard the motivation Aestheticism lays claim to. For

---

[68]  *Art of the Modern Age*, 64; see also pp. 12–13, 273.
[69]  *The Principles of Literary Criticism*, chs. 32–5.

example, Schaeffer's claim that the speculative theory errs in so far as it 'treats art as a specific ontic domain *by virtue of its value*'[70] hardly succeeds in showing a confusion unless a negative thesis concerning the ontological non-significance of value is assumed;[71] the alleged mere 'decision to sacralize' is, from another angle, an axiological discovery. Similar remarks—to the effect that what presents itself as a logical criticism turns really on disputed matters of doctrine—apply to Richards' (undisguised) reliance on the assumption that knowledge is necessarily discursive, indeed coextensive with natural science.[72]

## 5. THE CONTEMPORARY PERSUASIVENESS OF PHILOSOPHICAL AESTHETICISM

In view of the remoteness of the philosophical preconditions of Philosophical Aestheticism from the basic, predominantly naturalistic working assumptions of much current Anglophone philosophy, it is appropriate to raise the question of the strength of its claim to attention outside the sphere of Continental philosophy.

In the first instance it is clear that there can be no question of undermining or weakening, let alone refuting, the naturalistic outlook which stands opposed to Philosophical Aestheticism through a direct appeal to the phenomena—any description of the phenomena substantial enough to count as 'evidence' against naturalism will be gravely tendentious. However, this still leaves another task in view, namely to show that Philosophical Aestheticism has plausibility from the standpoint of one whose philosophical commitments are (to the extent that this is possible) neutral as between naturalism and transcendentalism,[73] and on this score there are various things to be said, centred on two connected

---

[70] *Art of the Modern Age*, 64.

[71] Genette, in *The Aesthetic Relation*, Introduction, approves Schaeffer's conclusions, adding that the speculative theory mistakes the proper function of aesthetics, which 'is not called upon either to justify or excoriate the aesthetic relation; its function is, if possible, to define, describe, and analyze it' (p. 5)—a thesis which again circumscribes philosophy of art in a way unacceptable to Philosophical Aestheticism.

[72] Further criticism of Philosophical Aestheticism may be found in Geuss, *Outside Ethics*, essays 11–12. Geuss presents his negative verdict regarding what he calls 'Romantic common sense' in company with a strongly anti-realist, Nietzschean view of value, and to that degree his criticisms are external to the transcendental programme.

[73] This is perhaps how Gadamer's project in *Truth and Method*, pt. I, 'The question of truth as it emerges in the experience of art', should be understood, i.e. as arguing from the experience of art to

ideas: that there is a natural route to be plotted from the pre-philosophical interior of aesthetic experience towards transcendentalism, and that, unless art is thought about in a transcendental light, the value which we ascribe to it cannot be fully accounted for. I will begin with the second.

1. Appeals to 'our' conception of the value of art encounter inevitably the initial complication that no view of art which is free of the rich and complex cumulative history of reflection on art, a history which exhibits (if we take the full span from classical times to contemporary post-modernism) much greater diversity than reflection on moral matters, can be pinned on a would-be naïve, pre-philosophical natural consciousness. Nor even should it be supposed that there is any unitary view of art that we can collectively self-ascribe—most probably the 'folk' view of art of late modernity is fragmented and inconsistent.[74] Yet, allowing that the ideas of 'common sense' concerning art's value are infected by Romanticism (just as they are by scientism, a reminder that the difficulty affects all sides), there is overwhelming evidence that the idea that art is a privileged source of the deepest and most important truths represents at least *one*, central and abiding component of the folk understanding of art in late modernity.[75] Our practice of setting a special kind of value on the experience of art, and our attribution to it of an elevated spiritual authority, which would have appeared bizarre and irrational to many earlier ages, is not self-justifying and prima facie makes no sense if art is cognitively impotent. This is Adorno's deep insight: that in so far as engagement with art is distinguished from consumption or entertainment, it is impossible to take works of art in any other way than as saying *how things are*; cognitivity, though not among the manifest primary characteristics on the basis of which entities are distinguished as works of art, is a necessary,

---

the *possibility* of a kind or mode of truth which falls outside the scope of natural science, although Gadamer also allows himself to be read more ambitiously (and less plausibly) as attempting to *overturn* natural science's claim to a monopoly on truth by an appeal to art.

[74] For which reason the Hegelian objection that Philosophical Aestheticism is at odds with modernity as such expresses at most a half-truth: see, e.g. Bürger, *Zur Kritik der idealistischen Ästhetik*, esp. pp. 17–25 and 87–90, and Genette, *The Aesthetic Relation*, 4. This criticism is especially weak when unsupported by a comprehensive theory of modernity such as Hegel himself offers.

[75] 'A painting is a statement of the artist's notions of reality in the terms of plastic speech. In that sense the painter must be likened to the philosopher rather than to the scientist' (Rothko, *The Artist's Reality*, 22). Illustrations from the writings of artists and critics could be multiplied indefinitely. Distinguished expressions of the idea include Fry's statement of the 'metaphysical hypothesis' regarding the significance of 'significant form' in chapter 3 of *Art*, Sullivan's description of our expectation regarding art's relation to reality in *Beethoven*, bk. I, ch. 1, and Steiner's evocation of the experience of literary meaning in *Real Presences*.

teleological condition on artistic *validity*; the experience of beauty impresses us as having *importance*, and this claim cannot be got to stand without ascribing to beauty the import of an act of judgement. Approximately the same thought was articulated by Schiller in a letter to Goethe deploring the return to a neo-classical aesthetics:

I think that recent analysts, in their struggle to separate out the concept of beauty and present it in a certain purity, have almost hollowed it out and turned it into an empty sound, and that the opposition between the beautiful and the true or correct has been taken much too far . . . I should like somebody to venture to dismiss from circulation the concept and even the word beauty, to which all those false notions are attached inseparably, and, as is proper, to set up in its place truth in the fullest sense of the word.[76]

This then raises the questions: can art's claim to truth be understood in naturalistic terms (or can it be redeemed only through transcendentalism or some other 'metaphysical' position)? And, if naturalism cannot underwrite art's claim to truth, can it nevertheless offer an adequate account of the value of art?

While there is no space here for a proper discussion, some brief points may be made suggesting that a detailed examination of naturalistic aesthetics is likely to return a negative answer to both questions. To the extent that we take our bearings from the results of analytic aesthetics—which, to be sure, is not as such committed to philosophical naturalism, but with which, as indicated previously, it typically shares the presently relevant assumptions—there are good grounds for doubting that any reconstruction of artistic truth which grants it more than an incidental connection with the value of art can emerge.[77] The tendency of empirically orientated inquiry is to locate artistic 'truth' at the level of sense rather than reference, i.e. in the presentational or 'illustrative' power of art (art makes vivid, gives a feeling of actuality, represents things in emotion-arousing ways, etc.), or to identify art-based cognition with interpersonal tourism (fictional art allows us to take up foreign points of view), and neither of these functions is in any way unique to art, or cannot be performed just as well or better by historical and biographical writing, documentary film-making, face-to-face conversation, etc. This is furthermore a conclusion that analytic aestheticians themselves have come to: John Passmore, pursuing the question whether we have grounds for taking art as seriously as we do and considering cognitivity as a candidate, concludes

---

[76]  Letter to Goethe, Jena 7 July 1797, in *Briefe 1796–98*, no. 104, p. 98.
[77]  For a recent attempt to make the connection more than incidental, see Young, *Art and Knowledge*.

that little more can be said than that art may focus attention in ways that prove cognitively fruitful, while Jerome Stolnitz emphasizes the embarrassing banality of the propositionally articulated 'truths' that literary works of art may be said to communicate.[78] The likely result of empiricist aesthetics, therefore, is that talk of 'artistic truth' either falls away, or reduces to the sincerity or self-expressive achievement of the artist, or serves as an infelicitous way of referring to the formal unity or some other non-cognitive merit of the artwork.

If so, naturalistically orientated aesthetics, to the extent that it accepts the challenge of accounting for the value of art in general (a question which for a long time, precisely on account of its historical association with 'metaphysical' systems, remained off the agenda of analytic aesthetics), is bound to interpret the value of art apart from any idea of a cognitive vocation. While here again no survey of the field is possible, it is fair to say that the basic thrust of analytic accounts of art's value has been, unsurprisingly, towards a broadly affective, Humean view.[79] The point to make accordingly is that dissatisfaction with such accounts—which revise the ordinary understanding of aesthetic experience by, among other things, making the aesthetic subject's mental state bear the value that the subject herself ascribes to the aesthetic object—is the systematic as well as historical starting point of anti-empiricist, transcendental theories of the aesthetic.[80]

2. The second idea which, I said, can be pursued in support of Philosophical Aestheticism is that aesthetic experience tends by nature towards transcendentalism.

It is generally agreed that aesthetic experience exhibits the following characteristics: (i) *Rupture with the attitude ordinarily entertained towards the world*, leading traditional theorists to posit a special kind of 'disinterestedness', 'aesthetic attitude', 'psychic distance', etc., as the mark of the aesthetic. (ii) *Apprehension of distinctive unity*, in the sense that the aesthetic object is experienced as exhibiting a special kind of wholeness, naturally glossed in 'organic' terms, whereby whole and parts stand in a relation of mutual explanation and exist for the sake of one another. (iii) *Fusion of fact and value*, in the sense that the aesthetic object is experienced as saturated with value, and value is

---

[78] Passmore, *Serious Art*, chs. 6–7, and Stolnitz, 'On the Cognitive Triviality of Art'.

[79] For an exceptionally thorough statement of a naturalistic conception of aesthetic value, see Railton, 'Aesthetic Value'.

[80] It is also to be observed that, the more naturalistic theories of the aesthetic fill themselves out in the attempt to do art full justice, the weaker their naturalistic commitment becomes: Dewey's endeavour in *Art and Experience* to forge a conception of 'experience' adequate to elucidate aesthetic value, for example, moves in the direction of German idealism.

accordingly experienced as 'real', 'present', 'immediately given', etc.; value figures phenomenologically in aesthetic experience as a kind of object, as part of what-is-experienced, not merely an attribute of the subjective upshot that results from the encounter with the object.

Now while the existence of experience which is taken to have these properties is by no means inconsistent with naturalism—empirical-psychological, evolutionary, etc., explanations of the human organism's disposition to *represent* certain objects in the aesthetic way are entirely possible—the point to be emphasized is that the structure of the experience is itself *non-naturalistic*: when objects are experienced aesthetically, they are experienced in a way that differs from and is inconsistent with the naturalistic way in which empirical objects are (centrally, if not exhaustively) ordinarily experienced. Though aesthetic experience does not involve the application of a conceptual scheme, if a conceptual scheme were to be articulated on its behalf, it would not be naturalistic: the 'implicit conceptual scheme' of aesthetic experience would correspond to a world governed by final not efficient causality, in which the distinction of empirical from evaluative properties, the realism of the natural attitude, and empirical determinacy itself are all broken down, and to whose contents the subject is related as something other than a further, causally enmeshed empirical item. As Schiller formulates this idea more specifically in his *Letters*, artistic form is autonomy, the freedom which cannot be found in nature.[81] At the same time, the non-naturalistic form or 'conceptual scheme' of aesthetic experience is proto-transcendental—the 'invitation in art' so often spoken of is, among other things, an invitation to transcendental philosophy. Hence the suggestion of Fichte (and Schopenhauer) that the aesthetic and transcendental standpoints are not simply analogous, but that aesthetic experience is itself an _instance_ of taking the transcendental turn, an intuitive enactment or phenomenological realization of the conceptual shift from pre-Copernican philosophy and common-sense realism to the plane of transcendental reflection.[82]

There is a further and important connection with the earlier idea that truth is a condition on artistic value. The developments in transcendental philosophy

---

[81]   And Adorno: 'Music recognises no natural law; therefore, all psychology of music is questionable' (*Philosophy of Modern Music*, 32 [*Philosophie der neuen Musik*, 37]).

[82]   Closely connected is the way in which the experience of art resists explanation in terms of the schemata of common-sense psychology—aesthetic response is not a case of coming to believe, desire-satisfaction, perception, emotional reaction, symbol comprehension, etc.; responses that can be explained on these familiar patterns belong, for all the good reasons given by Collingwood, to the sphere of craft and not art. Hence the standard resort to the catch-all category of 'imagination'.

after Kant that ascribe philosophical significance to the Aesthetic involve a reaction against the sharp differentiation of modes of validity (theoretical-cognitive, practico-moral, aesthetic) that results from Kant's *Critiques*, in favour of the idea that these are but different 'moments' of a single, unified, underlying mode of validity. Now this pursuit of 'higher unity of reason' again receives a warrant from the interior perspective of aesthetic experience, which as it were—that is, in so far as we again speak on its behalf—denies the absoluteness of Kant's differentiation by affirming the identity of the True, the Good, and the Beautiful: the integrity and comprehensiveness of aesthetic experience resists the idea that truth is irrelevant to and can be disentwined from a supposedly 'purely aesthetic', non-cognitive mode of validity. (For which reason post-Kantian idealists were drawn to the idea that the aesthetic is not just one member-branch of human reason, but that it is, or anticipates, *the* point in human reason at which *all* of its branches are united.) In this light, an explanation of the aesthetic in naturalistic terms will be necessarily, once again, a sideways-on explaining *away*, which imputes error to the consciousness it explains.

That there are limits to what naturalism can make of art, and that there is an elective affinity of aesthetic experience with transcendental reflection, is not sufficient to justify Philosophical Aestheticism, since Aesthetic Parallelism is equally consistent with those conclusions. It does, however, take us to the point where the Aestheticist strategy can begin to be argued for.[83]

## References

ADORNO, THEODOR W., *Aesthetic Theory*, trans. and ed. R. Hullot-Kentor (London: Athlone Press, 1997) [*Ästhetische Theorie, Gesammelte Schriften*, vii, ed. Gretel Adorno and Rolf Tiedemann (Suhrkamp: Frankfurt am Main, 1970)].

—— *Beethoven: The Philosophy of Music: Fragments and Texts*, trans. Edmund Jephcott, ed. Rolf Tiedemann [*Beethoven: Philosophie der Musik: Fragmente und Texte*, in *Nachgelassene Schriften*, ed. Theodor W. Adorno Archiv, Abt. 1, Bd. i, (ed.) Rolf Tiedemann (Frankfurt am Main: Suhrkamp, 1970)].

[83] For further discussion of the figures and themes discussed in this chapter, in addition to works already referred to, see the following: Bowie, *Aesthetics and Subjectivity* and *Romanticism and Critical Theory*; Crowther, *Art and Embodiment*; Eldridge, *The Persistence of Romanticism*; Geuss, 'Art and Theodicy'; Hammermeister, *The German Aesthetic Tradition*; Redding, *The Logic of Affect*; and Zuidervaart, *Artistic Truth*.

—— *Philosophy of Modern Music*, trans. Anne G. Mitchell and Wesley V. Blomster (New York: Continuum, 2003) [*Philosophie der neuen Musik*, rev. edn. (Frankfurt am Main: Europäische Verlagsanstalt, 1958)].

BEISER, FREDERICK C., *The Fate of Reason: German Philosophy from Kant to Fichte* (Cambridge, Mass.: Harvard University Press, 1987).

—— *German Idealism: The Struggle against Subjectivism, 1781–1801* (Cambridge, Mass.: Harvard University Press, 2002).

—— *The Romantic Imperative: The Concept of Early German Romanticism* (Cambridge, Mass.: Harvard University Press, 2003).

—— *Schiller as Philosopher: A Re-Examination* (Oxford: Clarendon Press, 2005).

BERNSTEIN, J. M., *The Fate of Art: Aesthetic Alienation from Kant to Derrida and Adorno* (Cambridge: Polity, 1992).

BOHRER, KARL HEINZ, *Die Kritik der Romantik* (Frankfurt am Main: Suhrkamp, 1989).

BOWIE, ANDREW, *Aesthetics and Subjectivity: From Kant to Nietzsche* (Manchester: Manchester University Press, 1990).

—— *Romanticism and Critical Theory: The Philosophy of German Literary Theory* (Manchester: Manchester University Press, 1990).

BUBNER, RÜDIGER, *Ästhetische Erfahrung* (Frankfurt am Main: Suhrkamp, 1989).

CROWTHER, PAUL, *Art and Embodiment: From Aesthetics to Self-Consciousness* (Oxford: Clarendon Press, 1993).

BÜRGER, PETER, *Zur Kritik der idealistischen Ästhetik* (Frankfurt am Main: Suhrkamp, 1983).

DEWEY, JOHN, *Art as Experience* (New York: Minton, Balch & Co., 1934).

ELDRIDGE, RICHARD, *The Persistence of Romanticism: Essays in Philosophy and Literature* (Cambridge: Cambridge University Press, 2001).

FICHTE, J. G., *The System of Ethics*, ed. Daniel Breazeale and Günter Zöller (Cambridge: Cambridge University Press, 2005) [*Das System der Sittenlehre nach den Prinzipien der Wissenschaftslehre* (1798), in *Johann Gottlieb Fichtes sämmtliche Werke*, (ed.) Immanuel Hermann Fichte (Berlin: Walter de Gruyter, 1971), iv. 1–365].

FRANK, MANFRED, *The Philosophical Foundations of Early German Romanticism*, trans. Elizabeth Millán-Zaibert (Albany, NY: State University of New York Press, 2004) ['*Unendliche Annäherung': Die Anfänge der philosophischen Frühromantik* (Frankfurt am Main: Suhrkamp, 1997), pt. III].

GADAMER, HANS-GEORG, *Truth and Method*, 2nd rev. English edn., trans. Joel Weinsheimer and Donald G. Marshall (London: Sheed & Ward, 1993) [*Wahrheit und Methode: Grundzüge einer philosophischen Hermeneutik*, 6. Auflage, in *Gesammelte Werke*, i (Tübingen: Mohr, 1990)].

GENETTE, GÉRARD, *The Aesthetic Relation*, trans. G. M. Goshgarian (Ithaca, NY: Cornell University Press, 1999) [*L'Oeuvre de l'art. La relation esthétique* (Paris: Seuil, 1996)].

GEUSS, RAYMOND, 'Art and Theodicy', in *Morality, Culture, and History: Essays on German Philosophy* (Cambridge: Cambridge University Press, 1999), 78–115.

—— *Outside Ethics* (Princeton: Princeton University Press, 2005).

Hammermeister, Kai, *The German Aesthetic Tradition* (Cambridge: Cambridge University Press, 2002).

Hegel, Georg Wilhelm Friedrich, *Aesthetics: Lectures on Fine Art*, 2 vols., trans. T. M. Knox (Oxford: Clarendon Press, 1975) [*Vorlesungen über die Ästhetik* (1823, 1826, 1828–9), in *Werke. Auf der Grundlage der Werke von 1832–1845 neu edierte Ausgabe*, (ed.) Eva Moldenhauer and Karl Markus Michel (Frankfurt am Main: Suhrkamp, 1979) (Theorie-Werkausgabe), vols. xiii–xv].

—— *The Encyclopedia Logic: Part 1 of the Encyclopaedia of Philosophical Sciences*, trans. T. F. Geraets, W. A. Suchting, and H. S. Harris (Indianapolis: Hackett, 1991) [*Die Wissenschaft der Logik* (1830), in *Werke. Auf der Grundlage der Werke von 1832–1845 neu edierte Ausgabe*, (ed.) Eva Moldenhauer and Karl Markus Michel (Frankfurt am Main: Suhrkamp, 1979) (Theorie-Werkausgabe), vol. vii].

—— 'Foreword to Hinrichs' *Religion in its Inner Relation to Science*', in *Miscellaneous Writings of G. W. F. Hegel*, (ed.) Jon Stewart (Evanston, Ill.: Northwestern University Press, 2002) ['Vorrede zu Hinrichs' Religionsphilosophie' (1822), in *Werke. Auf der Grundlage der Werke von 1832–1845 neu edierte Ausgabe*, (ed.) Eva Moldenhauer and Karl Markus Michel (Frankfurt am Main: Suhrkamp, 1979) (Theorie-Werkausgabe), ii. 41–66].

—— *Philosophy of Mind: Being Part Three of the Encyclopaedia of Philosophical Sciences* (1830), trans. William Wallace (Oxford: Clarendon Press, 1971) [*Die Philosophie des Geistes*, in *Werke. Auf der Grundlage der Werke von 1832–1845 neu edierte Ausgabe*, (ed.) Eva Moldenhauer and Karl Markus Michel (Frankfurt am Main: Suhrkamp, 1979) (Theorie-Werkausgabe), vol. x].

Heidegger, Martin, *Being and Time*, trans. John Macquarrie and Edward Robinson (Oxford: Basil Blackwell, 1978) [*Sein und Zeit* (1927), in *Gesamtausgabe* (Frankfurt am Main: Klostermann, 1975– ), Abt. 1, Bd. 2, ed. Friedrich-Wilhelm von Herrmann (1977)].

—— 'The Origin of the Work of Art', trans. Albert Hofstadter, in *Poetry, Language, Thought* (New York: Harper & Row, 1971), 15–87 ['Der Ursprung der Kunstwerkes' (1935–1936), in *Gesamtausgabe* (Frankfurt am Main: Klostermann, 1975– ), Abt. 1, Bd. 5, *Holzwege*, (ed.) Friedrich-Wilhelm von Herrmann (1977), 1–74].

Henrich, Dieter, *Versuch über Kunst und Leben: Subjektivität—Weltverstehen—Kunst* (München: Hanser, 2001).

—— *Between Kant and Hegel: Lectures on German Idealism*, (ed.) David S. Pacini (Cambridge, Mass.: Harvard University Press, 2003).

Hilmer, Brigitte, 'Kunst als Spiegel der Philosophie', in Andrea Kern and Ruth Sonderegger (eds.), *Falsche Gegensätze: Zeitgenössische Positionen zur philosophischen Ästhetik* (Suhrkamp: Frankfurt am Main, 2002).

Hölderlin, Friedrich, *Hyperion* (Die vorletzte Fassung) (1796), in *Sämtliche Werke: Große Stuttgarter Ausgabe*, iii, (ed.) Friedrich Beißner (Stuttgart: Kohlhammer, 1957), 235–52.

—— 'Operations of Poetic Spirit', in *Essays and Letters on Theory*, trans. and ed. Thomas Pfau (Albany: State University of New York Press, 1988) ['Über die Verfahrungsweise des poëtischen Geistes' (1800), in *Sämtliche Werke: Große*

*Stuttgarter Ausgabe*, Bd. 4, 1e Hälfte, ed. Friedrich Beißner (Stuttgart: Kohlhammer, 1961), 241–65].

JACOBI, FRIEDRICH HEINRICH, *Concerning the Doctrine of Spinoza in Letters to Herr Moses Mendelssohn* (1785), in *The Main Philosophical Writings and the Novel* Allwill, trans. George di Giovanni (Montreal and Kingston: McGill-Queen's University Press, 1994), 173–251 [*Ueber die Lehre des Spinoza, in Briefen an den Herrn Moses Mendelssohn* (Breslau: Gottl. Löwe, 1785)].

—— *David Hume on Faith, or Idealism and Realism, A Dialogue: Preface and also Introduction to the Author's Collected Philosophical Works* (1815), in *The Main Philosophical Writings and the Novel* Allwill, trans. George di Giovanni (Montreal and Kingston: McGill-Queen's University Press, 1994), 537–90 [*David Hume über den Glauben, oder Idealismus und Realismus: Ein Gespräch. Vorrede, zugleich Einleitung in des Verfassers sämmtlichte philosophische Schriften*, in *Werke*, ed. Friedrich Roth and Friedrich Köppen, ii (Leipzig: Gerhard Fleischer, 1815; reprod. Darmstadt: Wissenschaftliche Buchgesellschaft, 1976), 3–123].

JAMES, SUSAN, *Passion and Action: The Emotions in Seventeenth-Century Philosophy* (Oxford: Oxford University Press, 1997).

LACOUE-LABARTHE, Philippe, and Jean-Luc Nancy, *The Literary Absolute: The Theory of Literature in German Romanticism*, trans. Philip Barnard and Cheryl Lester (Albany, NY: State University of New York Press, 1988).

MEGILL, ALLAN, *Prophets of Extremity: Nietzsche, Heidegger, Foucault, Derrida* (Berkeley: University of California Press, 1985).

MERLEAU-PONTY, Maurice, 'Cézanne's Doubt', in *Sense and Non-Sense*, trans. Hubert L. Dreyfus and Patricia Allen Dreyfus (Evanston, Ill.: Northwestern University Press, 1964) ['Le doute de Cézanne', in *Sens et non-sens* (Paris: Nagel, 1948), 15–49].

—— 'Metaphysics and the Novel', in *Sense and Non-Sense*, trans. Hubert L. Dreyfus and Patricia Allen Dreyfus (Evanston, Ill.: Northwestern University Press, 1964) ['Le roman et la métaphysique', in *Sens et non-sens* (Paris: Nagel, 1948), 51–81]

MOORE, A. W., *Points of View* (Oxford: Clarendon Press, 1997).

NIETZSCHE, FRIEDRICH, *The Birth of Tragedy out of the Spirit of Music and The Case of Wagner*, trans. Walter Kaufmann (New York: Vintage Books, 1967) [*Die Geburt der Tragödie. Oder: Griechenthum und Pessimismus*, in *Werke: kritische Gesamtausgabe*, ed. Giorgio Colli und Mazzino Montinari, Abt. 3, Bd. 1 (Berlin: de Gruyter, 1972)].

—— *The Gay Science*, trans. Walter Kaufmann (New York: Vintage, 1974) [*Die fröhliche Wissenschaft*, in *Werke: kritische Gesamtausgabe*, ed. Giorgio Colli und Mazzino Montinari, Abt. 5, Bd. 2 (Berlin: de Gruyter, 1973)].

NOVALIS, *Fichte Studies*, ed. Jane Kneller (Cambridge: Cambridge University Press, 2003) [*Fichte-Studien*, in *Schriften*, ii, *Das philosophische Werke I*, (ed.) Richard Samuel, Hans-Joaquim Mähl, and Gerhard Schulz (Stuttgart: Kohlhammer, 1981)].

PASSMORE, JOHN, *Serious Art: A Study of the Concept in all the Major Arts* (London: Duckworth, 1991).

Pippin, Robert, 'What Was Abstract Art? (From Hegel's Point of View)', in *The Persistence of Subjectivity: On the Kantian Aftermath* (Cambridge: Cambridge University Press, 2005), 279–306.

Railton, Peter, 'Aesthetic Value, Moral Value, and the Ambitions of Naturalism', in *Facts, Values, Norms: Essays towards a Morality of Consequence* (Cambridge: Cambridge University Press, 2003), 85–130.

Redding, Paul, *The Logic of Affect* (Ithaca, NY: Cornell University Press, 1999).

Richards, I. A., *The Principles of Literary Criticism*, 2nd edn. (London: Routledge & Kegan Paul, 1926).

Rothko, Mark, *The Artist's Reality: Philosophies of Art*, (ed.) Christopher Rothko (New Haven, Conn.: Yale University Press, 2004).

Sacks, Mark, *Objectivity and Insight* (Oxford: Clarendon Press, 2000).

Sartre, Jean-Paul, *Being and Nothingness: An Essay of Phenomenological Ontology* (London: Methuen, 1957) [*L'être et le néant. Essai d'ontologie phénoménologique* (Paris: Gallimard, 1943)].

—— *The Imaginary: A Phenomenological Psychology of the Imagination*, trans. Jonathan Webber (London: Routledge, 2004) [*L'Imaginaire: psychologie phénoménologique de l'imagination* (Paris: Gallimard, 1940)].

—— *Notebooks for an Ethics*, trans. David Pellauer (Chicago: University of Chicago Press, 1992) [*Cahiers pour une morale* (1947–8) (Paris: Gallimard, 1983)].

—— *Sketch for a Theory of the Emotions*, trans. Philip Mairet (London: Methuen, 1962) [*Esquisse d'une théorie des émotions* (Paris: Hermann, 1939)].

—— *What is Literature?*, trans. Bernard Frechtman (London: Methuen, 1986) [*Qu'est ce que la littérature?*, Situations 2 (Paris: Gallimard, 1948)].

Schaeffer, Jean-Marie, *Art of the Modern Age: Philosophy of Art from Kant to Heidegger*, trans. Steven Rendall (Princeton, NJ: Princeton University Press, 2000) [*L'art de l'âge moderne* (Paris: Gallimard, 1992)].

Scheler, Max, *The Nature of Sympathy*, trans. Peter Heath (London: Routledge & Kegan Paul, 1979) [*Wesen und Formen der Sympathie*, 6. Auflage, in *Gesammelte Werke*, vii, (ed.) Manfred S. Frings (Bern and München: Francke, 1973)].

Schelling, F. W. J., *System of Transcendental Idealism* (1800), trans. Peter Heath (Charlottesville: University Press of Virginia, 1978) [*System des transcendentalen Idealismus*, in *Schellings Werke. Nach der Originalausgabe in neuer Anordung*, ed. Manfred Schröter (München: Beck, 1927–), ii. 327–634].

Schiller, Friedrich, *Briefe, 1796–98*, *Schillers Werke: Nationalausgabe*, xxix, (ed.) Norbert Oellers and Fritjhof Stock (Weimar: Böhlaus, 1977).

—— *On the Aesthetic Education of Man: In a Series of Letters*, trans. Elizabeth M. Wilkinson and L. A. Willoughby (Oxford: Clarendon Press, 1982) [*Über die ästhetische Erziehung des Menschen in einer Reihe von Briefen* (1793–5), in *Schillers Werke: Nationalausgabe*, xx (Philosophische Schriften, Teil 1), (ed.) Benno von Wiese and Helmut Koopmann (Weimar: Böhlaus, 1962), 309–412].

SCHLEGEL, FRIEDRICH, '*Athenaeum* Fragments', in *Philosophical Fragments*, trans. Peter Firchow (Minneapolis: University of Minnesota Press, 1991) ['*Athenäums-Fragmente*', in *Kritische Friedrich-Schlegel-Ausgabe*, (ed.) Ernst Behler et al. (Paderborn: Schöningh, 1958–  ), ii ed. Hans Eichner (1967), 165–255].

—— 'Ideas', in *Philosophical Fragments*, trans. Peter Firchow (Minneapolis: University of Minnesota Press, 1991) ['Ideen', in *Kritische Friedrich-Schlegel-Ausgabe*, (ed.) Ernst Behler et al. (Paderborn: Schöningh, 1958–  ), ii, (ed.) Hans Eichner (1967), 256–72].

SCHLEIERMACHER, FRIEDRICH DANIEL ERNST, *The Christian Faith*, ed. H. R. Mackintosh and J. S. Stewart (Continuum/T. & T. Clark: London, 1999) [*Der christliche Glaube nach den Grundsätzen der evangelischen Kirche im Zusammenhange dargestellt*, 2nd edn. (1830), in *Kritische Gesamtausgabe*, Abt. I, Bd. 13, Teilbde. 1–2, ed. Rolf Schäfer (Berlin: de Gruyter, 2003)].

—— *On Religion: Speeches to its Cultural Despisers*, trans. and ed. Richard Crouter (Cambridge: Cambridge University Press, 1996) [*Über die Religion: Reden an die Gebildeten unter ihren Verächtern* (1799), in *Kritische Gesamtausgabe*, Abt. I, Bd. 2, ed. Günter Meckenstock (Berlin: de Gruyter, 1984)].

SCHOPENHAUER, ARTHUR, *The World as Will and Representation*, i, trans. E. F. J. Payne (New York: Dover, 1969) [*Die Welt als Wille und Vorstellung* (1st edn. 1819, 2nd edn. 1844), vol. i, in *Sämtliche Werke. Neu bearbeitet*, ed. Arthur Hübscher, vol. ii (Wiesbaden: Brockhaus, 1949).]

STEINER, GEORGE, *Real Presences: Is There Anything in What We Say?* (London: Faber & Faber, 1989).

STOLNITZ, JEROME, 'On the Cognitive Triviality of Art', *British Journal of Aesthetics* 32 (1992), 191–200.

SULLIVAN, J. W. N., *Beethoven: His Spiritual Development* (London: Jonathan Cape, 1927).

YOUNG, JAMES O., *Art and Knowledge* (London: Routledge, 2001).

ZUIDERVAART, LAMBERT, *Artistic Truth: Aesthetics, Discourse, and Imaginative Disclosure* (Cambridge: Cambridge University Press, 2004).

# CHAPTER 4

## THE HISTORY OF PHILOSOPHY AS PHILOSOPHY

### MICHAEL ROSEN

IN the late 1970s a number of Anglo-American philosophers set out to read Hans-Georg Gadamer's *Truth and Method*, believing (rightly) that it contained material that was relevant to contemporary debates regarding the rule-governed nature of language. What they found there was surprising. The book opens with a long discussion (it lasts for nearly a hundred pages) of the history of a series of concepts—of taste, genius, 'common sense', judgement, *Bildung*, among others. The discussion is obviously erudite, but what relevance might such an investigation of the history of ideas have to substantive questions about the nature of language? Gadamer does not spell out the connection—at least, not in terms that the analytical philosophers would have found useful—so let me explain it briefly here.

The object of Gadamer's book is to argue that philosophy and the human sciences (the *Geisteswissenschaften*) are distinct from the natural and mathematical sciences, and that they have their own, no less valid, methodological approach.[1] How, though, is he to argue this? It would be quixotic to hope that he could challenge the claim that the standards and methods derived from the natural sciences are of unrestricted scope with arguments that will meet those very standards. Instead, Gadamer claims that the conception of the human sciences that he favours forms part of a tradition, one which, although it has become obscured, is alive and open to recovery. Such a presentation of his case might well be dismissed as merely rhetorical when judged against the standards set by the natural sciences. However, Gadamer tries to meet this objection historically, by showing that ideas such as the inferiority of rhetoric to proof themselves have a history. To identify such a tradition is, of course, not to give an argument in its favour with the compulsive force of a scientific demonstration, but that is, if we follow Gadamer, not a decisive objection: there is no alternative for him but to practise what he preaches. The only argument available to convince others that historical argument is a valid philosophical method is itself historical.[2]

Until recently, a historical approach to philosophy like Gadamer's has been very unusual in the English-speaking world, although it is one of Continental philosophy's (in particular, German philosophy's) most marked features. The purpose of this chapter is to outline the origins of the idea that history can enter into the method of philosophy, while at the same time to analyse the forms that the idea has taken—and might take—in practice. I shall focus on the four thinkers who were most influential in developing the historical conceptions of philosophy that we find in the Continental tradition, Hegel, Marx, Nietzsche, and Heidegger, before evaluating what this might mean for the practice of philosophy and discussing their legacy.

# I. Hegel

Unsurprisingly, we start with Hegel. Hegel was the first philosopher to identify the history of philosophy as a philosophical problem: how, Hegel asks, can

---

[1] 'The following investigation starts with the resistance within modern science against the universal claim of scientific method. It is concerned to seek that experience of truth that transcends the sphere of the control of scientific method wherever it is to be found, and to inquire into its legitimacy' (Hans-Georg Gadamer, *Truth and Method* (New York: Continuum, 1975), p. xii).

[2] The idea that we could find an Archimedean point from which to found philosophy is, Gadamer admits, unfulfilled. 'But is the discourse with the whole of the philosophical tradition in which we stand, and which we, as philosophers, are, purposeless? Do we need to justify what has always supported us?' (*Truth and Method*, p. xxiv).

philosophy be both historical and rational?[3] Moreover, the solution that he proposes to that problem is one that integrates the history of philosophy within philosophy itself. As we shall see, however, Hegel's integration of philosophy and its history depends on his very particular claims about the nature of philosophy.

If the subject matter of philosophy—the objects into which it inquires—is timeless (as Hegel says) the most natural inference from the diverse history of philosophy is that its many attempts to get to know the nature of those objects have proved fruitless and that the history of philosophy is a history of failure.[4] The existence of a multiplicity of philosophical systems, each claiming exclusive correctness, invites the thought that none of them are:

The whole of the history of philosophy becomes a battlefield covered with the bones of the dead; it is a kingdom not merely formed of dead and lifeless individuals, but of refuted and spiritually dead systems, since each has killed and buried the other.[5]

Hegel sets out to counter this view. His own way of reconciling the apparently contradictory history of philosophy with the idea that philosophy is nonetheless a rational enterprise depends upon his belief in the complex nature of

[3] The subject for discussion here is Hegel's view of the history of philosophy, but it would be impossible to detach it entirely from his philosophical view of history, particularly since the historical approach to philosophy has been interwoven with what is called 'Geschichtsphilosophie'. The latter term has an elastic meaning (see the article 'Geschichtsphilosophie', in J. W. Ritter (ed.), Historisches Wörterbuch der Philosophie (Basel: Schwabe, 1971)) but, in general, it has signified an approach to history that sees history as having a systematic structure, governed by changing ideas or conceptions of reality. Geschichtsphilosophie antedates Hegel, although he gave it a very powerful impulse. Likewise, the Kantian idea that the history of philosophy represents a rational development from dogmatism, through scepticism, to criticism gave the impulse to several systematic histories of philosophy that preceded Hegel but did not raise the philosophical problem that troubled Hegel, since they were written under the assumption that Kant was right and his predecessors wrong (for instance, Tiedemann and Tenemann, of whom Hegel remarks that, in Tenemann's opinion, all the philosophers of the past share the same defect: that they are not Kantians).

[4] If we now take it for granted that science is marked by a history of theoretical revolution then this is a sign of how much we live in a post-Hegelian world. Hegel, himself, however, asserts a very different view of the history of the natural sciences: science, he believes, involves the progressive accumulation of a body of permanent knowledge: 'The other sciences, indeed, have also according to their content a history. A part of that contains alterations and the abandonment of propositions which were formerly held valid. But a great, perhaps the greater, part of that content is of a kind that has proved permanent, so that what has come about that is new was not an alteration of earlier acquisitions, but an addition to and increase of them. These sciences progress through a process of juxtaposition. It is true that in botany, mineralogy, and so on, much is corrected in the course of progress, but by far the greatest part remains stationary and is enriched but not altered by what is added afresh. With a science like mathematics, history has, in the main, only the pleasing task of recording further additions. Thus to take an example, elementary geometry as it was created by Euclid may from that time on be regarded as having no further history' (Vorlesungen über die Geschichte der Philosophie, I, Werke, xviii. 27).

[5] Vorlesungen über die Geschichte der Philosophie, I, Werke, xviii. 35

truth. 'The true', as he famously says, 'is the whole. The whole, however, is merely the essential nature reaching its completeness through the process of its own development.'[6] Any separate part of the truth—any particular claim or assertion taken on its own—is incomplete; no part, however, is unnecessary. For Hegel, philosophical truth is articulated in two ways: synchronically, as it were—that is, in the exposition of philosophy as it is now known to be in the form of a speculative system; and diachronically—the history of philosophy through time shows the structure that truth will have when the historical process by which it comes to be has been completed.[7] Since 'the sequence in the systems of philosophy in history is similar to the sequence in the logical deduction of the notion—determinations in the Idea', it follows that 'the study of the history of philosophy is the study of philosophy itself; indeed, it can be nothing else'.[8]

But a further claim also plays a very important role in Hegel's account of the history of philosophy: namely, the idea that each stage of society is held together by a single principle, one that finds its expression in all areas of culture.[9] This principle is articulated with especial clarity in the discipline of philosophy, Hegel maintains, and for this reason the history of philosophy has pre-eminence in the history of *Geist* (that collective mind in which we all, as individuals, participate whether we recognize it or not). Philosophy is,

[6] *Phänomenologie des Geistes*, ed. J. Hoffmeister (Hamburg: Meiner, 1952), 21.

[7] 'Philosophy is system in development; the history of philosophy likewise. . . . The one kind of progression which represents the deduction of the forms, the necessity thought out and recognized, of the determinations, is the business of philosophy; and because it is the pure Idea which is in question and not yet its mere particularized form as nature and as mind, that representation is, in the main, the business of logical philosophy. But the other method, which represents the part played by the history of philosophy, shows the different stages and moments in development in time, in manner of occurrence, in particular places, in particular people or political circumstances, the complications arising thus, and, in short, it shows us the empirical form' (*Vorlesungen über die Geschichte der Philosophie*, I, *Werke*, xviii. 47–8).

[8] *Vorlesungen über die Geschichte der Philosophie*, I, *Werke*, xviii. 49.

[9] 'The particular form of a philosophy is thus contemporaneous with a particular constitution of the people amongst whom it makes its appearance, with their institutions and forms of government, their morality, their social life and the capabilities, customs and enjoyments of the same; it is so with their attempts and achievements in art and science, with their religions, warfares, and external relationships, likewise with the decadence of the states in which this particular principle and form had maintained its supremacy, and with the origination and progress of new states in which a higher principle finds its manifestation and development. Mind (*Geist*) in each case has elaborated and expanded in the whole domain of its manifold nature the principle of the particular stage of self-consciousness to which it has attained. Thus the mind of a people in its richness is an organization, and, like a cathedral, is divided into numerous vaults, passages, pillars, and vestibules, all of which have proceeded out of one whole and are directed to one end. Philosophy is one form of these many aspects' (*Vorlesungen über die Geschichte der Philosophie*, I, *Werke*, xviii. 73).

Hegel says, 'the fullest blossom, the notion of Geist in its entire form, the consciousness and spiritual essence of all things, the Geist of the time as Geist present in itself'.[10]

Plainly, such ambitious claims were far from being accepted by the majority of Hegel's successors. So it may seem strange to assert that Hegel's history of philosophy established the groundwork for the way in which the relationship between history and philosophy has been conceived in the Continental tradition. Hegel's importance for the historical approach to philosophy does not lie in these idealist theses themselves, however, but in a particular consequence that he drew from them. This is the idea that we should look at philosophy as embodying unacknowledged presuppositions that are to be understood historically. At every point in history a certain tacitly accepted conception of the nature of mind, world, and human agency ('the principle of the particular stage of self-consciousness which [Geist] has attained.'[11]) lies behind and conditions the explicit arguments that philosophers make. The proper task of the history of philosophy is to reveal the connection between the two. For an example of what this meant for Hegel we may look at what he has to say about Kant's theoretical philosophy.

In the Lectures on the History of Philosophy, as well as in other writings, Hegel argues that Kant's epistemology contains a fundamental circularity. Kant sets out to assess our 'faculty for knowledge' (Erkenntnisvermögen), and yet, Hegel objects, such an investigation presupposes that we are already in possession of the ability to know. Otherwise, how would we have the capacity to carry the epistemological investigation out? Thus Kant, according to Hegel, is assuming the validity of what he is putting into question.

To investigate the faculty of knowledge means to know it. The requirement then is this: we should know the faculty of knowledge before we know; it is the old story of wanting to swim before one goes in the water. The investigation of the faculties of knowledge is itself knowing, so it cannot reach what it aims at because it is there already—it cannot come to itself because it is already with itself (bei sich).[12]

Kant, says Hegel, starts out from the same point of view as Hume: that whatever general qualities there are in our experience—both its conceptual and its spatio-temporal character—are not to be found in what is given to us through the senses but are added by the mind itself. As Hegel remarks

---

[10]  Vorlesungen über die Geschichte der Philosophie, I, Werke, xviii.
[11]  Ibid. I, Werke, xviii. 74.
[12]  Ibid. III, Werke, xx. 333–4.

in another famous image, 'Matters are represented as follows: there are things in themselves out there, but without space and time; now there comes consciousness with time and space in it already as the possibility of consciousness, just as it has mouth and teeth and so on as the conditions for eating. The things that are eaten don't have mouth and teeth and just as eating affects things so consciousness affects them with space and time.'[13] In consequence, Kantianism, for Hegel, faces two (obviously connected) problems. First, it represents the process by which spatio-temporal experience comes to be the way it is (is 'synthesized', in Kant's terminology) as if it were analogous to a material or physical process. But this is flatly contradictory. Physical processes take place in time. How can there be a process by which time itself is 'added' to experience? Second, it presupposes that the philosopher is in possession of a privileged vantage point—a kind of 'sideways view'—by which to explain and assess that process when, in fact, it is the announced task of the Kantian philosophy to put knowledge-claims to the test.

Similar objections have often been made by other critics of Kant.[14] What concerns Hegel, however, is not just the inconsistencies in Kant that he diagnoses here but their source, and this leads him to ask a more basic question. Why, he asks, does Kant presuppose that the object of philosophy should be to assess the subjective apparatus that each individual brings to the task of knowing the world in the first place? The reason, he answers, is that this is the inevitable consequence of Kant's individualistic starting point: the assumption that all that is given to us are appearances and that 'such determinations as universality and necessity are not located in perception . . . and have another source; this source is the subject, me in my self-consciousness'.[15] It is symptomatic, Hegel asserts, of Kant's limited conception of the nature of *Geist* that it should presume a separation between the knowing subject and the nature of things as they really are. From this assumption, the fundamental difficulties in Kant's position arise as necessary consequences. This subjective starting point—'the Enlightenment made method', as Hegel calls it[16]—underlies Kant's philosophy. But it is not an assumption peculiar to Kant. On the contrary, it is one that he shares with

---

[13] *Vorlesungen über die Geschichte der Philosophie*, III, *Werke*, xx. 341.

[14] Criticisms of the mysterious quasi-psychology of the idea of synthesis have been made by many philosophers in the analytic tradition, most notably P. F. Strawson, in *The Bounds of Sense* (London: Methuen, 1966).

[15] Ibid. III, *Werke*, xx. 333.

[16] Ibid.

those empiricist philosophers (chiefly, Hume) whose scepticism he aimed to refute. Once it is assumed that the general character of experience is introduced by the mind, the only hope for the possibility of philosophical knowledge is to undertake a self-examination of the knowing subject.

Hegel's strategy for the understanding of philosophy is exemplary for much of what would come later. Instead of looking at a philosophical dispute (in this case, that between Kant and Hume) in the terms in which the participants understood it—as a fundamental clash regarding the possibility of a priori knowledge—Hegel points towards a presupposition that the two disputants held in common. In fact, his strategy closely resembles that which was pioneered by Kant himself in the 'Antinomy of Pure Reason' in the *Critique of Pure Reason*. There, Kant took pairs of apparently compelling philosophical arguments with logically incompatible conclusions and pointed out that they shared a common premise: the belief that concepts can be extended beyond the limits of experience to apply to reality as a whole. Once that premise was given up, neither argument would be forceful, Kant maintained. Hegel (although he has no sympathy for the particular arguments of the Antinomy) is trying to make a similar move in a historical context: the subjective starting point in philosophy leads, inevitably, either to scepticism (Hume) or an implausible transcendental psychology (Kant). The solution is to give up that presupposition. Such presuppositions are rooted, Hegel believes, outside philosophy (at least, outside philosophy narrowly conceived as an academic discipline). They are part of the wider way in which mind and its relation to the world is conceived and realized in practice at a certain time—the 'principle' of a 'particular stage of *Geist*', as Hegel puts it.

Thus philosophy, for Hegel, 'points beyond itself', in the sense that its disputes, which are incapable of resolution in the terms within which the participants themselves conduct them, must be referred back to a historical understanding, from which standpoint the dispute will be not so much resolved as dissolved.

## II. MARX AND MARXISM

Since Marx rejected Hegel's idealism, it is not surprising that his understanding of the history of philosophy was also quite different. While Hegel interprets all areas of culture as expressions of a single underlying ideal principle, Marx asserts the primacy of economic life (the 'material base') in determining the culture and ideas of a society. Thus, Marx writes, it is necessary, 'in contrast to German philosophy, which descends from heaven to earth . . . to ascend from earth to heaven'.[17] Marx's metaphor is deliberately chosen: in Marx's view, philosophy is no more than a disguised form of religion—a socially produced illusion which in point of fact has no independent rational history.[18] In direct contrast to Hegel, for whom the problem was 'how could philosophy be both rational and have a history?', what is significant for Marx is how the illusory belief in the history of philosophy as an independently rational discipline should have come about and how that illusion might be dispelled.

According to the view that he presents in *The German Ideology*, the reason for the presumption of the independence of philosophy is that society has reached a stage at which it has established a division between material and mental labour.[19] In consequence,

consciousness *can* really flatter itself that it is something other than consciousness of existing practice, that it *really* represents something without representing something real; from now on consciousness is in a position to emancipate itself from the world and to proceed to the formation of 'pure' theory, theology, philosophy, ethics, etc.[20]

It is not simply that different ideas are caused by the different social circumstances that give rise to them. Beyond that, they also *resemble, reflect, correspond to, are images of*, or *express* (Marx uses a variety of different terms) those circumstances. Marx famously writes that 'in all ideology men and their circumstances appear upside-down as in a *camera obscura*'[21] and, slightly later, that:

It is self-evident, moreover, that 'spectres', 'bonds', 'the higher being', 'concept', 'scruple' are merely the idealistic spiritual expression, the conception apparently of

---

[17] 'That is to say, we do not set out from what men say, imagine, conceive, nor from men as narrated, thought of, imagined, conceived, in order to arrive at men in the flesh. We set out from real, active men, and on the basis of their real life-process we demonstrate the development of the ideological reflexes and echoes of this life-process. The phantoms formed in the human brain are also, necessarily, sublimates of their material life process, which is empirically verifiable and bound to material premises' (K. Marx and F. Engels, *The German Ideology*, ed. C. J. Arthur (London: Lawrence & Wishart, 1970), 47).

[18] 'Morality, religion, metaphysics, all the rest of ideology and their corresponding forms of consciousness . . . have no history, no development; but men, developing their material production and their material intercourse, alter, along with this their real existence, their thinking and the products of their thinking' (*The German Ideology*, 47).

[19] For a more detailed account of Marx's theory of ideology (of which his remarks on philosophy form a part) see M. Rosen, *On Voluntary Servitude: False Consciousness and the Theory of Ideology* (Cambridge: Polity Press, 1996), ch. 6.

[20] *The German Ideology*, 52.      [21] Ibid. 47.

the isolated individual, the image of very empirical fetters and limitations, within which the mode of production of life and the forms of intercourse coupled with it move.[22]

Philosophy is thus a kind of 'transfigured representation' of society; in the context of philosophy ideas which are in fact expressions of existing social reality are falsely taken to be pure or of independent validity. Philosophy is a product of a society in which unequal social relations require a spurious justification. Philosophy helps to provide that justification by representing those social relations as if they were independent and so (we may infer this next step although Marx does not state it explicitly) encourages the belief that they are justified—or, at the least, inevitable. It is the task of the new approach to history that Marx champions to reconnect ideas to society and so to dispel the illusions of philosophy:

Where speculation ends—in real life—there real, positive science begins: the representation of the practical activity, of the practical process of development of men. Empty talk about consciousness ceases, and real knowledge has to take its place. When reality is depicted, philosophy as an independent branch of knowledge loses its medium of existence.[23]

It is notable that the quotation above is ambiguous. On one reading, Marx is saying, apparently, that philosophy is without any cognitive value whatsoever. From which it would follow that the history of philosophy can be no more than a kind of diagnostic sociology—and indeed a great deal of Marxist writing on the history of philosophy has represented not so much the integration of the history of philosophy into philosophy as the dissolution of philosophy into its history. On the other hand, one might read the passage to see Marx as disparaging not philosophy *as such* but only philosophy that purports to be 'an independent branch of knowledge'. Seen in this way, the distance between Marx and Hegel is less than it at first appeared to be: in connecting philosophy back into a wider context—revealing the unacknowledged presuppositions that sustain it—the illusion behind the idea of philosophy qua discipline with an independent rational history can be overcome without denying that philosophy contains any elements of value whatsoever.

In *Ludwig Feuerbach and the End of Classical German Philosophy*,[24] Engels, Marx's close collaborator, appears to be taking this view when he takes up

---

[22] *The German Ideology*, 52.    [23] Ibid. 48.
[24] 'Ludwig Feuerbach and the End of Classical German Philosophy', in Marx and Engels, *Selected Works* (Moscow: Progress Publishers, 1970), vol. 3, pp. 335–76.

a famous distinction originally made by Marx himself between the positive worth of Hegel's dialectical method and the illusory Idealistic system within which that method is to be found. Hegel, according to Engels, recognized that reality is in process and that, in consequence, all purportedly timeless truths are in fact provisional and relative, but he betrayed his own discovery by presuming that a philosophical system within which all these different perspectives are included will constitute a final, absolute truth. Thus, for Engels, Hegel's philosophy contains real insights while at the same time concealing and mystifying them by its drive to set itself up as an independent system of absolute, once-and-for-all-truth. The valuable elements of Hegel's philosophy would be redeemed, when taken out of their original, philosophical context and made part of the new science of 'dialectical materialism'.

Despite the fact that he had written a doctorate on the subject, Marx in his mature years had no interest in the history of philosophy and Engels's remarks on the history of philosophy were sketchy, to say the least. That an understanding of the history of philosophy that was something other than reductive historical sociology emerged in the Marxist tradition is due above all to the inspiration of a work written forty years after Marx's death: Georg Lukács's *History and Class Consciousness*.[25] *History and Class Consciousness* was far from being intended as a work in the history of philosophy—Lukács's principal objective was to intervene on behalf of his own conception of Leninism in the debates then taking place within the Marxist movement. But his book proved exceptionally influential for those Marxist and neo-Marxist intellectuals who were disturbed that, apparently, Marxism reduced ideas to nothing more than epiphenomenal offshoots of economic life.[26]

Lukács and his successors are often described as 'Marxist-Hegelians' and, from the point of view of the history of philosophy, this label is appropriate, since Lukács' position comes close to that which we have attributed to Hegel. Where Hegel sees philosophy as expressing the stage arrived at by *Geist* in

---

[25] G. Lukács, *Geschichte und Klassenbewusstsein* (1923), *History and Class Consciousness* (London: Merlin Press, 1971).

[26] Lukács' influence was less within the official Communist movement of which he himself remained (if sometimes precariously) a part than amongst dissident Marxists such as the Frankfurt School, Leszek Kolakowski, and the Praxis Group. The most extensive analysis of the history of philosophy from a broadly Lukácsian standpoint can be found in the writings of the French philosopher Lucien Goldmann, in particular, in his *Introduction à la philosophie de Kant* (1948) ((Paris: Gallimard, 1967) translated as *Immanuel Kant* (London: New Left Books, 1971) ) and *Le Dieu caché*, a study of Pascal (Paris: Gallimard, 1955) translated as *The Hidden God* (London: Routledge & Kegan Paul, 1964) ). Goldmann brings together Lukács' approach with the claim to relate individual authors to the 'world vision' (*Weltanschauung*) in which they participate (*The Hidden God*, 14–15).

the course of its historical self-articulation, so Lukács sees it as the intellectual expression of a wider social process. Marxism, for Lukács, is the theoretical articulation of a revolutionary *praxis* whose ultimate goal is the self-realization of the proletariat:[27]'the identical subject-object of history whose praxis will change reality.'[28] Thus, although philosophy has no independent rational history, it is generated by a process that underlies the whole of social reality and that, since it leads through the conflicts and exploitation of class society to a higher form of human social existence, is ultimately rational. The similarity to Hegel is clear. While Hegel asserts that the common source that holds together the different areas of culture is that each is an expression of the stage of development reached by *Geist*, Lukács argues that cultures are to be understood from the standpoint of the process of self-realization of humanity as a practical, collective agent.

*History and Class Consciousness* contrasts Marxism's 'dialectical' under-standing of reality with the 'reification' (*Verdinglichung*) characteristic of bourgeois thought that separates knowledge of the world from engagement with it. Reification runs through bourgeois society and conditions philo-sophical understanding: 'Modern critical philosophy springs from the reified structure of consciousness,' Lukács writes.[29] Reification leads to what he claims to be the most significant background assumption of modern philosophy, namely, 'the equation which appears naïve and dogmatic even in the most 'critical' philosophers, of formal, mathematical, rational knowledge both with knowledge in general and with 'our' knowledge.'[30] This assumption (which is, of course, exactly the same one argued against by Gadamer in *Truth and Method*) has many consequences. It makes it impossible, in Lukács' opinion, for bourgeois philosophy to achieve a 'standpoint of totality' and thus creates the Kantian problem of the 'thing in itself'—the idea that corresponds to a residual point of completion 'outside' the Kantian system that that system nevertheless requires.

The Lukácsian approach has characteristic strengths and weaknesses. One strength is certainly that (like Hegel) Lukács draws attention to the perva-siveness in Western philosophy of the tendency to conceive reality exclusively in mathematical-scientific terms and to think of the self as a kind of blank,

---

[27] 'The essence of the method of historical materialism is inseparable from the "practical and critical" activity of the proletariat: both are aspects of the same process of social evolution. So, too, the knowledge of reality provided by the dialectical method is likewise inseparable from the class standpoint of the proletariat' (*History and Class Consciousness*, 20–1).

[28] Ibid. 197.    [29] Ibid. 110–11.    [30] Ibid. 112.

passive perceiver. Another is that, whereas the functionalism of a 'base-and-superstructure' theory of ideology asserts that a set of ideas is present because it helps to preserve a social structure without explaining how or why this should be so, Lukács relates philosophical ideas and social life in a way that helps to make the connection between them intelligible (thus the reification that is common to both economic and intellectual life limits human beings both practically, in terms of their social relations with one another, and theoretically, in their ability to conceive of reality in anything other than an impoverished way). There are, however, difficulties. Lukács' account of the history of philosophy is strongly teleological. Just as, for Hegel, all past philosophies are only imperfect anticipations of what is fully articulated in his own fully developed speculative philosophy, so the Lukácsian sees the history of philosophy as just a series of unsuccessful efforts towards the final consummation of philosophy in Marxian dialectical thought. Moreover, what precisely such dialectical thought consists in remains very sketchily characterized: Lukács does not explain in any detail what it might be to understand reality from the 'standpoint of totality' beyond gesturing to a kind of romantic ideal of organic plenitude that is denied to those who remain limited by the separation between subject and object characteristic of 'bourgeois' thought. Finally, the notion of a 'collective subject'—although Lukács argues that it is compatible with materialism—seems to commit Marxism to the existence of a supra-individual entity that is both ontologically dubious and epistemologically obscure.

For one strand of Marxist thought, philosophy is to be contrasted with science—either natural science or the science of society, Marxism. For the 'Hegelian Marxists', on the other hand, the scientific status of Marxism lies in its incorporation of the heritage of philosophy within itself. Philosophy is, Marxism in all its variants agrees, an activity that has become frozen and alien, cut off from the real activity that is its true source. To comprehend the development of philosophy we must seek its centre elsewhere, in the development of economic life and in the relations of class power that sustain it. It is this, not rationality, that moves history forward.

## III. Nietzsche

Admirers of Nietzsche may be shocked to see him described as a founding father of a historical approach to philosophy. Did not Nietzsche polemicize fiercely against historicism? Was his adoption of the method of 'genealogy' not intended as a counter to the teleological developmentalism so prevalent in his own day? My claim, however, is that Nietzsche adopted his own distinctive historical approach to the understanding of philosophy—one that was indeed very different from that of the historicists and Hegelians (to say nothing of the Darwinists and progressive socialists) of the time. For Nietzsche, like Marx, the idea of philosophy as a discipline with no connection to the broader flow of human life and passion is an abstract fiction, but this is not to deny that the history of philosophy is governed by the search for truth. On the contrary, it is the motivation behind the search for truth that Nietzsche seeks to diagnose and to show how, when pushed to its limits, it leads to the dissolution of philosophy.

To explain Nietzsche's position, I propose to concentrate on his first published book, *The Birth of Tragedy*. *The Birth of Tragedy* is often misunderstood. Readers—perhaps reasonably enough, given its title—think of *The Birth of Tragedy* as essentially a discussion of the culture of the pre-Socratic Greeks and of the place of tragic drama within that culture. They see Nietzsche as analysing Greek culture in terms of a bipolar structure—the contrast between the Apollonian and the Dionysiac—and of seeking to present tragedy as a synthesis between elements representing both poles. Now this is accurate, so far as it goes, but it leaves out of account what is, to my mind, the most significant dimension of the book. For Nietzsche does not confine himself to the *birth* of tragedy in the time of the Greeks; he develops (in outline, at least) a picture of the way in which the tragic culture of the Greeks came to an end, of the successor culture that led to that end, and, finally, of how, in Nietzsche's view, that successor culture has now come to an end in its turn. To do this, Nietzsche develops an account of culture that is not so much bipolar as triangular: as well as Dionysianism and Apollonianism there is a third form to be analysed: Socratism. It is Nietzsche's account of the end of Socratism that will concern us here.

To see the relationship between these three psychic structures, we must first understand the common problem that, Nietzsche asserts, all cultures face. Every society must deal with the problem: how can human beings come to terms with the fact of death and suffering? Nietzsche suggests that there have been two dominant answers to that problem: either to try to escape from suffering or to see it as having a meaning. Dionysianism and Apollonianism are different versions of the former strategy. Where the Dionysian escapes from suffering by losing himself in a kind of frenzied ecstasy—through the intoxication of wine, drugs, or sexual desire—the Apollonian seeks escape through a vision of happiness and beauty—'the separate art-worlds of *dreams* and *intoxication*'.[31] Thus the Greek gods are not principally benevolent organizers of the world in the interests of human beings—they are frequently indifferent to human beings or even malevolent towards them. Yet they still give men something valuable: a vision of a dream-world of beauty inhabited by beings who do not know suffering in the way that humans do. ('Thus do the gods justify the life of man: they themselves live it—the only satisfactory theodicy. Existence under the bright sunshine of such gods is regarded as desirable in itself . . .')[32] Tragedy took its power from a composite of Dionysian and Apollonian elements.

This essentially *aesthetic* response to suffering, characteristic of the early Greeks, was displaced by another attitude: instead of escaping from suffering, the Greeks of the Socratic era set out to justify it by reason. The term 'justification' here is broad. One way of justifying suffering is to show that it is deserved—why suffering serves the ends of justice. It can be justified too, however, by being shown to be *necessary*, that there is a reason for it. Thus the world-view of scientific materialism, with its closed, deterministic account of reality is, for Nietzsche, also a variant of the justificatory enterprise. For Socratism, the gods are no longer the happy, capricious beings who treat humans 'as flies to wanton boys' but become increasingly the rational guardians of a moral order who dispense suffering as a deserved punishment for transgression. The two enterprises—showing the world as *good* and showing the world as having a systematic order—originally go together. They are both part of the attempt to find a reason for everything. To deal with suffering, human beings strive to act rightly (to be virtuous) and to gain insight into the order of things (aspire to knowledge). At Socratism's apogee, in the philosophy of Plato, knowledge and virtue are identified. It is easy enough to see how the drive for knowledge can offer a solution to the problem of suffering when it is joined to the belief that the world is under the auspices of a benevolent and omnipotent being (as is the case, of course, in the great monotheistic religions). But Nietzsche extends the force of Socratism beyond explicit religious belief. The search for knowledge carries its own consolation to the extent that it allows the sufferer to identify himself with the majesty and inexorable power of an impersonal world-order (the

---

[31]   *The Birth of Tragedy*, trans. Walter Kaufmann (New York: Vintage Books, 1967), §1.
[32]   Ibid. §3.

example here being Stoicism). Socratism is, Nietzsche says, *optimistic*, in the technical (Schopenhauerian) sense of representing the world as intrinsically good, as containing within itself an intelligible, rational structure. ('Consider the consequences of the Socratic maxims: "Virtue is knowledge; man sins only from ignorance; he who is virtuous is happy." In these three basic forms of optimism lies the death of tragedy.')[33]

Socratism is the driving force behind Western civilization ('the influence of Socrates, down to the present moment and even into all future time, has spread over posterity like a shadow that keeps growing against the evening sun'),[34] carried, of course, by Christianity, and philosophy is its bearer. The Christian religion, committed to understanding the world as the product of an omniscient, omnipotent, and benevolent Deity, is essentially a religion of reason—God creates, rewards, and punishes for good reasons. Yet in the end reason has proved to be a weapon against Christianity. The philosophy of the Enlightenment pushed the requirement that all beliefs should be justified to the point that it challenged the belief in God himself. But the process of Socratism does not stop even there. Finally, Socratism turns upon itself.

The picture that Nietzsche paints is this. The Socratic impulse is a drive to find reasons, to stand on firm foundations and to know the world as it really is. Yet this desire to believe only what is justified calls into question the very possibility of such a foundation: philosophy has advanced to the point that it is no longer possible to believe rationally that our beliefs about the world correspond to a unique, determinate reality to which our senses give us access. The most recent philosophers—Nietzsche is thinking here of Kant and Schopenhauer—have shown that the idea of access to a world of things in themselves is itself a consoling myth.

... great men, universally gifted, have contrived, with an incredible amount of thought, to make use of the paraphernalia of science itself, to point out the limits and the relativity of knowledge generally, and thus to deny decisively the claim of science to universal validity and universal aims. And their demonstration diagnosed for the first time the illusory notion which pretends to be able to fathom the innermost essence of things with the aid of causality. The extraordinary courage and wisdom of Kant and Schopenhauer have succeeded in gaining the most difficult victory, the victory over the optimism concealed in our culture. While this optimism, resting on apparently unobjectionable *aeternae veritates*, had believed that all the riddles of the universe could be known and fathomed, and had treated space, time, and causality as entirely unconditional laws of the most universal validity, Kant showed that these

---

[33] *The Birth of Tragedy*, §14.     [34] Ibid. §15.

really served only to elevate the mere phenomenon, the work of *maya*, to the position of the sole and highest reality, as if it were the innermost and true essence of things, thus making impossible any knowledge of this essence or, in Schopenhauer's words, lulling the dreamer still more soundly asleep.[35]

Socratism has pushed itself to the point that it has undermined its own *raison d'être*. What lies beyond it? At this stage of his career still heavily under the influence of Wagner, Nietzsche speculates that a new mythology will revive under the auspices of German music and that there will be a *rebirth* of tragedy. Later, Nietzsche would see himself as the protagonist of a higher, post-rational kind of human being.[36]

It is common to see the development of philosophy as part of humanity's transition from a mythical world-view to a rational one—the passage from *mythos* to *logos*—and, on one level, Nietzsche endorses this: philosophy is a rational enterprise with a continuing, coherent focus, the drive towards grounded knowledge, and it is indeed the enemy of mythical belief-systems. The picture of philosophy that Nietzsche creates is one of a rational enterprise carried forward by the force of its own internal impetus—it is not as if it were the 'reflex and echo' (to use Marx's phrase) of a process that has its real force elsewhere—but it is an enterprise that is unaware of itself for it treats rationality as a self-evident, unmotivated good that requires no further justification or explanation. For Nietzsche we need to look beyond philosophy in order to understand the non-rational sources of the appeal of rationality itself. What human needs does this drive to find reasons for things satisfy? In this way, Nietzsche calls the philosophical enterprise into question, not by rejecting the search for grounded knowledge (indeed, he identifies himself with this project) but by asking what *motives* lie behind that search: what emotional and spiritual needs do human beings hope to satisfy by its means? The ability to see the world as intelligible and orderly helps to reconcile human beings to suffering, but there is more to the drive to truth than this alone. There is weakness, inasmuch as human beings wish to abdicate responsibility for their beliefs (they would like to see them as 'rationally mandatory'), but there is also honour and integrity in the refusal to allow oneself to practise deceit on oneself. At one time the drive for rational knowledge fulfilled the

---

[35] Ibid. §18.

[36] 'There are cases of individual success constantly appearing in the most various parts of the earth and from the most various cultures in which a *higher type* does manifest itself: something which in relation to collective mankind is a sort of superman' (*The Anti-Christ* (Harmondsworth: Penguin, 1968), §4).

need to see the world as justified; now it has turned against it. Those who continue the enterprise of philosophy in rejecting groundless beliefs (among whom Nietzsche includes himself)[37] must give up the consolations of belief in an objective world-order.

Nietzsche offers a radical and original way of looking at philosophy. As with Hegel, Nietzsche's starting point is an antinomy within philosophy. In this case it is the tension between the search to find a foundation for our beliefs (and its negative corollary, the rejection of those beliefs that are without foundation) and the discovery that emerges at the end of that search: that our belief in an objective world lacks foundation. This antinomy cannot be resolved within philosophy itself. Instead, we must look at the motive behind that search for foundations—the Socratic impulse. It is here that philosophy points beyond itself to history.


# IV. Heidegger

Adorno once remarked that while Heidegger talks a lot about historicity, he has little to say about history. There is some point to the jibe but, in fact, Heidegger's work does contain an extremely important historical dimension, although it is presented extremely abstractly.[38] To appreciate the place of history in Heidegger's conception of philosophy, we must look briefly

---

[37] 'The great majority of people does not consider it contemptible to believe this or that and to live accordingly, without first having given themselves an account of the final and most certain reasons pro and con, and without even troubling themselves about such reasons afterward: the most gifted men and the noblest women still belong to this "great majority." But what is goodheartedness, refinement or genius to me, when the person who has these virtues tolerates slack feelings in his faith and judgements and when he does not account the desire for certainty as his inmost craving and deepest distress—as that which separates the higher human beings from the lower' (The Gay Science, trans. Walter Kaufmann (New York: Vintage, 1974), §2).

[38] Being and Time was first published in 1927, by which time, under the influence of Dilthey, in particular, the historical approach to the study of philosophy was firmly established in Germany. The philosophical movement within which Heidegger's thought is grounded—phenomenology—was, however, strongly anti-historical and Heidegger was the first to take it in a historical direction.

In the Crisis of the European Sciences and Phenomenology, Edmund Husserl, Heidegger's teacher and the founder of the phenomenological movement, tries to show how his conception of phenomenology has its roots in the European tradition of philosophy and resolves the issues besetting that tradition. Whether the Crisis is an attempt to pursue philosophy historically or to put the emergence of an unhistorical attitude to philosophy into a historical context will not be discussed here. It should be noted, however, that the Crisis was written by Husserl after the appearance of Heidegger's Being and Time and may reasonably be seen as to a large extent a response to it.

at Heidegger's overall project in *Being and Time*. The book actually opens
with a historical assertion: the question of the meaning of Being, Heidegger writes in the book's very first sentence, 'has today been forgotten.'[39]
It is, Heidegger claims, a significant historical fact that the question of the
meaning of Being—the basic question of ontology—has been systematically
obscured, one that has had important consequences, both for philosophy and
for Western society more broadly. Ontology, properly understood, constitutes the distinctive subject matter of philosophy, he believes. For traditional
philosophy, ontology was the study of what there is. The sort of questions
it addressed were 'are there universals?', 'are numbers real?', and so on.
In modern philosophy, ontology has been seen as a branch of philosophy
subordinate to epistemology—how could we settle questions about what
there is without having previously settled the question of what we can
know and how we can know it? Heidegger, however, so far from accepting
ontology's subordinate role, asserts that ontology is 'more primordial' than
the empirical sciences themselves.[40] Since the time of Plato and Aristotle,
he argues, philosophers have approached the ontological question as if it
were a form of the question: what sorts of things are there? Thus, whatever things philosophers have come up with as ultimately real—substances,
matter, atoms, events, universals, modes, entities, categories, classes, even
consciousness, representations, or ideas—are tacitly assumed to have this
positive, thing-like nature. Even if, like Plato's Ideas, the entities in question
are supposed to be outside time, they are conceived of as being in some
way 'present'.[41]

A grasp of the 'Being of what there is' (*das Sein des Seienden*) is sedimented,
Heidegger claims, in our language and is implicit in the attitudes we take
up towards the world. And yet philosophical understanding is made difficult
because this 'ontological' comprehension has been consistently misconstrued.
A kind of preconception has become overlaid on the understanding of
Being, and Being is thereby made into something objectified and thing-like.
Being is understood in the mode of what Heidegger calls 'presence-at-
hand' (*Vorhandenheit*). This is what makes the task of renewing ontology so
pressing:

---

[39]  M. Heidegger, *Being and Time*, trans. J. Macquarrie and E. Robinson (Oxford: Basil Blackwell, 1967), 21.

[40]  Ibid. 31.

[41]  'Entities are grasped in their Being as 'presence'; this means that they are understood with regard to a definite mode of time—the 'Present'' (ibid. 47).

The very fact that we already live in an understanding of Being and that the meaning of Being is still veiled in darkness proves that it is necessary in principle to raise this question again.[42]

The history of Western philosophy—of Western thought in general—lies under the shadow of this great mistake. It is not just a mistake on the part of philosophers but expresses something fundamental about the nature of Western culture (in particular, its domination by a scientific, technocratic way of life). *Dasein*, says Heidegger, is 'fallen' (*Verfallen*) and 'at the same time has fallen prey to its more or less explicitly grasped tradition'.[43] It is a tradition that keeps *Dasein* in what Heidegger calls a 'deficient mode' of Being.[44] All the central concepts of modern philosophy—consciousness, the subject, reason, *Geist*, and so on—are infected with the prejudices inherited from Greek ontology.[45] Conventional understandings of the history of philosophy (inspired, whether consciously or not, by Kant) represent the development of philosophy in the early modern period as a radical break with what had preceded it, marked by the emergence of epistemology as the starting point for philosophy. Heidegger, however, argues that, appearances to the contrary, it is what modern philosophy continues from the earlier metaphysical tradition (namely, the ontological understanding of reality in terms of *Vorhandenheit*) that is the most important key to understanding it. In articulating this view, *Being and Time* makes a number of highly original and thought-provoking claims about the history of philosophy.[46] Such historical interpretations are not merely incidental to the main task of *Being and Time*.[47] They are part of Heidegger's project to try to 'destroy' the traditional ontology and thereby

---

[42] 'Entities are grasped in their Being as "presence"; this means that they are understood with regard to a definite mode of time—the "Present" ' 23.

[43] Ibid. 42.

[44] 'When tradition thus becomes master, it does so in such a way that what it "transmits" is made so inaccessible, proximally and for the most part, that it rather becomes concealed' (ibid. 43).

[45] 'The categorical content of the traditional ontology has been carried over to these entities' (ibid. 44).

[46] And, of course, a great proportion of Heidegger's writing subsequent to *Being and Time* was devoted to interrogations of the history of philosophy.

[47] It is significant that the never-written Part II of *Being and Time* was to be essentially historical, at least in its framework of interrogation. As announced in the Introduction to *Being and Time* as published, Part II 'has three divisions. 1. Kant's doctrine of schematism and time, as a preliminary stage in a problematic of Temporality; 2. the ontological foundation of Descartes' "*cogito sum*", and how the medieval ontology has been taken over into the "*res cogitans*"; 3. Aristotle's essay on time, as providing a way of discriminating the phenomenal basis and the limits of ancient ontology' (ibid. 64).

allow *Dasein* to grasp its own history in a free and transparent way.[48] For Heidegger, as for Hegel, philosophy is an exercise in self-understanding, but it is an understanding that has become blocked to the point that the very need for it has become obscured. History plays an essential role in uncovering and enabling that understanding.

Of *Being and Time*'s historical discussions, perhaps the most celebrated is to be found in §43 where Heidegger takes issue with Kant's 'Refutation of Idealism'. For Kant, it was a 'scandal' that philosophy had hitherto been unable to give a proof of the existence of things outside ourselves and the 'Refutation of Idealism' was supposed to provide one. Heidegger's quarrel is not so much with the substance of Kant's argument as with its presupposition. The object of Kant's proof is to show a necessary connection between the possibility of self-conscious experience and the existence of a world of objects. This would seem to imply the rejection of 'the Cartesian approach of positing a subject one can come across in isolation'.[49] But this appearance, says Heidegger, is deceptive, for the way in which the subject is conceived still continues the Cartesian tradition of thinking of consciousness in the mode of *Vorhandenheit*. Thus Kant reaches an anti-Cartesian conclusion from a Cartesian starting point: 'even if the ontical priority of the isolated subject and inner experience should be given up, Descartes' position would still be retained ontologically.'[50] It is, in fact, the Cartesian starting point that generates the problem in the first place and the real 'scandal of philosophy' is not that we still await a proof of the existence of the external world 'but that such proofs are expected and attempted again and again':[51]

Such expectations, aims and demands arise from an ontologically inadequate way of starting with *something* of such a character that independently *of it* and 'outside' *of it* a 'world' is to be proved as present-at-hand. It is not that the proofs are inadequate, but that the kind of Being of the entity which does the proving and makes requests for proofs has *not been made definite enough*. ... If Dasein is understood correctly, it defies such proofs, because, in its Being, it already *is* what subsequent proofs deem necessary to demonstrate for it.[52]

---

[48] 'If the question of Being is to have its own history made transparent, then this hardened tradition must be loosened up, and the concealments which it has brought about must be dissolved. We must understand this task as one in which by taking *the question of Being as our clue*, we are to *destroy* the traditional content of ancient ontology until we arrive at those primordial experiences in which we achieved our first ways of determining the nature of Being—the ways which have guided us ever since' (*Being and Time*, 44).

[49] Ibid. 248.      [50] Ibid.      [51] Ibid. 249.      [52] Ibid.

For Heidegger, the impasses of philosophy—in this case, the repeated attempts to find a proof of the existence of the external world—are not to be resolved by finding a new proof. What is necessary is to reinterpret what is at issue in terms of a superior ontological understanding, at which stage the problem itself can be dissolved because its starting point has lost its apparent self-evidence. Such an understanding is not simply the product of the application of the internal logic of philosophy: the dominant tradition in philosophy is characterized by an inauthentic understanding of Being that obscures rather than reveals ontology. To improve our ontological understanding we must look beyond the philosophical tradition as it has come down to us—either by looking outside the domain of philosophy altogether or by drawing on philosophical thinking which escapes the dominance of misleading inherited preconceptions.[53]

# V. History and the Practice of Philosophy

Hegel, Marx, Nietzsche, and Heidegger view philosophy as a discipline that points beyond itself, but they do so in very different ways. For Hegel, the history of philosophy represents a history of rational progress, but that rationality only becomes fully accessible when the history of philosophy is integrated within the wider history of the coming-to-be of *Geist*. For Marx, the representation of philosophy as having an independent history is an ideological fraud: philosophy must be deciphered in relation to the social forces that give rise to it and the interests that it advances. Nietzsche endorses the view of the history of philosophy as a history of rational progress, inasmuch as the development of philosophy is motivated by the drive to believe only that which can be firmly grounded, but he looks beyond philosophy to ask what motivates us to pursue such an enterprise (and what will be the consequences when its self-undermining nature becomes apparent). For Nietzsche, the view of philosophy as driven by non-rational motivations does not compete with the account of it as rational; it encompasses it. Finally, Heidegger sees both philosophy (and culture more widely) as the site of contending historical traditions. To overcome the inauthentic understanding of Being that has

---

[53] Hence Heidegger's interest in the poetry of Hölderlin and the Presocratic Greek philosophers.

come to dominate philosophy, we should uncover its historical origins and use that knowledge to reinterpret our comprehension of philosophy and of human culture more broadly.

But where does the existence of a connection between philosophy and history leave the understanding of philosophy as a rational discipline? Does a historical approach to philosophy lead to relativism? The suspicion that it does is, surely, one reason why philosophers in the analytical tradition often react so allergically to the suggestion that there is a substantive connection between philosophy and its history. To address this very important issue it is necessary first to say something more precise about what it would mean to see philosophy as a discipline with a rational history.

Let us start with the following suggestion:

(1) A discipline is rational if it follows a rational procedure, and

(2) A procedure is rational if each step within it is taken for a reason.

This suggestion is plainly insufficient as it stands. We act for all sorts of reasons, some of them highly disreputable (vanity, jealousy, and so on). Actions performed for those kinds of reason are clearly not the constituents of a rational procedure. We must therefore require that the steps in the procedure are taken for a good reason. What, then, is a good reason? At a minimum, good reasons are reasons that are appropriately directed towards the procedure in question. This is a necessary but not a sufficient condition, however. Many procedures that are marked by the fact that individual participants act for what look like very good reasons are, when viewed overall, hardly rational—arms races, for example. So let me make a further suggestion:

(3) A good reason is one which is designed to advance the goal of the procedure, and

(4) actually does advance that goal. [54]

Thus, to take a simple example, in the game of noughts and crosses (tic-tac-toe) each player has the goal of completing a line of three characters before her opponent. The rational player will endeavour to complete lines herself

---

[54] Must the end of a rational procedure itself be a rational one or could there be a rational procedure with a pointless or reprehensible end? I am inclined to think that the answer to this is 'yes'—that coaching football players (rationally preparing people to pursue an activity that is neither rationally required nor rationally prohibited) can be a rational procedure. Indeed, I imagine that a training school for torturers might count as following a rational procedure, however despicable the end promoted by it.

and will block situations where her opponent already has two characters in a line. Let us call a procedure *fully endogenously rational* where:

(5)  Each step taken is taken for a good reason (in the sense just defined), and

(6)  the step is the unique one that best advances the procedure's goal.

The idea of a fully endogenously rational procedure expresses a very strong conception of rationality: it identifies at each point what counts as a rational step and defines rational behaviour in relation to that. Fully endogenously rational procedures are very rare—even noughts and crosses does not prescribe a unique best move at each stage. In those more common cases where no single move is rationally mandatory, however, a further question of motive arises: why did the agent choose the particular one of the available rational moves that he did? At this point, other factors can enter into the explanation (emotional, aesthetic, or historical reasons, for example) without compromising the claim that the move was rational.

Moreover, the notion of a good reason as one that advances the goal of the procedure in question is frequently too demanding. Chess is commonly (and with justification) assumed to be a paradigm of a rational procedure, but chess is so complicated that in most situations even the greatest experts (and most sophisticated computers) do not know for sure that a particular move is a good one (let alone, a fortiori, whether it is the best one available). Some chess moves are bad, as it turns out, but still rational. We do not say that a weak player is necessarily irrational. But where does limited skill end and irrationality begin? So, in the case of chess and other very complex procedures (like philosophy), rather than tying the notion of acting for a good reason to making a good move, a better conception of a good reason would be that:

(7)  A move made for a good reason is one that responds appropriately to the state of the procedure at the time that the move is made (in the case of chess, to the state of the board).

This conception of what it is to act for a good reason is weaker and its boundaries are less well defined. Inevitably, there is a shading as we pass from moves that are clearly rational to those that are clearly not. What counts as an 'appropriate' response to the state of the procedure cannot be sharply delineated. Since there is only rarely a determinate and determinable 'best move', the scope for wider explanations is further increased: factors other than rational ones internal to the procedure can play a role without giving up the idea that the player is playing rationally. Some chess players (even the greatest) are especially aggressive, others cautious, and so on.

Turning now to philosophy, we see that it is even further away from full endogenous rationality for it differs from chess in two important and closely connected ways. First, there is no clear agreement about what the goal of philosophy is. Philosophers may say, perhaps, that the goal of philosophy is the pursuit of truth, but evidently they disagree about what particular region or kind of truth philosophy aims at (indeed, many of them disagree quite fundamentally about what truth is). Moreover, there is no agreement about what constitutes the proper procedure of philosophy—what are the 'rules of the game'. Philosophy, it may be said, seeks to proceed on the basis of good arguments, but as soon as we ask what constitutes a good argument the disagreements begin. To tie the notion of philosophical rationality to the idea that a rational procedure is one whose moves advance towards a given goal would presume that we know what that goal is and can judge what takes us nearer to it. Although many contemporary philosophers write as if they stood at the end of philosophical history, the fact is that much of what has been most highly esteemed in philosophy has consisted in challenges to received ideas of what the proper goals of the subject or its methods are (certainly this was true of all four philosophers whom we have discussed so far) and there is every reason, surely, to believe that this will continue in future.

To give a brief example of the way in which controversy about method stands at the heart of philosophy, consider the following. One response made to Kant's Critical Philosophy in the period immediately after its appearance was a Humean one. Kant's challenge to Hume, it was argued, amounted to no more than a *petitio principi*—that his argument depends upon the principle of sufficient reason, which is precisely what Hume denies. This was the position of 'Aenesidemus' (Gottlob Ernst Schulze) who had a great impact on Fichte, amongst others.[55] But Fichte, instead of trying to meet Aenesidemus' argument in its own terms, developed his own, even more ambitious, conception of transcendental philosophy—a very puzzling response, one might think. The move is a rational one, however, if we see it from the point of view of Fichte's conception of philosophical method. For Fichte, the principle of sufficient

---

[55] See Paul Franks, 'Transcendental Arguments, Reason and Scepticism: Contemporary Debates and the Origins of Post-Kantianism', in R. Stern (ed.), *Transcendental Arguments: Problems and Prospects* (Oxford: Oxford University Press, 1999), 111–45 (p. 133).

reason required a ground for everything—a 'ground of grounds' (the so-called *Grundsatz*). In asserting the priority of this requirement for philosophical method Fichte believed that he was continuing and strengthening Kant's position in a way that would make it immune to sceptical challenges such as that of Aenesidemus—even if Aenesidemus himself would not have accepted that conception of philosophical method. Thus Fichte's apparently strange move can be seen as rational, even if not rationally mandatory, and there is an important historical question to be asked: why did just this aspect of philosophical method come to seem compelling—not just to Fichte, but to the German Idealist movement that he thereby brought into being—at just this time?[56]

To return now to the question whether acknowledging a historical dimension to philosophy compromises its claim to rationality, the answer clearly depends both on how we conceive of philosophical rationality and on what form such a historical dimension might take. Hegel, for example, thinks of rationality in the last analysis as something like what I have called full endogenous rationality. But such rationality is only available from the comprehensive vantage point of *Geist* as the self-realization of reason; the rationality of philosophy, its pre-eminence in the history of *Geist* notwithstanding, is deficient until completed by this wider, historical perspective. But that is something that few nowadays would find plausible; if philosophy has a rational history then not in that strong sense. Marx, as we have seen, vigorously rejects the claim that philosophy has a rational history at all. But on the more modest conception that philosophy is rational inasmuch as philosophers respond to one another by moves that count as reasonable responses to the state of the discipline as they find it, there need be no conflict between the rationality of philosophy and the idea that the history of philosophy makes a positive contribution to philosophical practice.

Philosophical arguments, even if they can be expressed deductively (and this is something that many philosophers in the Continental tradition would dispute), are enthymematic: that is to say, they are valid, but with respect to premises that are not explicitly stated. The business of philosophy, then, consists in large part in identifying, attributing, and challenging such premises. Yet how are we to do so? It is here that history can play its role. Hegel attributes the premise that what is given to us through the senses contains no general

---

[56] See Michael Rosen, 'From Kant to Fichte: A Reply to Franks', in Stern (ed.), *Transcendental Arguments*, pp. 147–54.

or essential elements to both Kant and Hume, from which it follows that, if our experience has a necessary structure, then it is one that must have been introduced by us ourselves. This is a premise that Kant and Hume would not have been reluctant to acknowledge; it is, indeed, something that they took for granted. Why, then, should we follow Hegel in rejecting it? That it leads to philosophical difficulties is not enough: perhaps there are other ways to deal with those difficulties or—if the premise is compelling enough—perhaps we just have to live with them. As Mill points out in *Utilitarianism*, however, even if a philosophical question is not susceptible of proof, we do not have to depend on 'blind impulse or arbitrary choice': 'Considerations may be presented capable of determining the intellect either to give or withhold its assent to the doctrine.'[57] Now many things might make a philosophical doctrine more or less appealing to the intellect, but one might be to ask ourselves how we judge it when we see it, not as presented to us in isolation for intuitive approval or rejection, but as part of a wider view of and attitude towards the world. And this is just what Hegel's presentation of Kant and Hume's assumptions about the nature of what is given to the senses as part of the Enlightenment world-view aims to do. We see those assumptions as optional, not mandatory, and are more or less attracted to them according to how we feel about the world-view of which they are a part. Explicit proof, we might say, to the extent that it plays a role in philosophy, has to depend on persuasion to sustain its premises.

I have referred to the 'assumptions' and 'presuppositions' behind philosophical doctrines in order to emphasize the continuity between the kind of argument favoured by the historically minded philosophers and what is commonly regarded as philosophical argument in contemporary Anglo-American philosophy, but such terms are potentially misleading to the extent that they suggest that what these philosophers are concerned to bring to our attention is a set of propositions necessary to complete otherwise incomplete deductive arguments. This is to present things in a way that neither Hegel, Heidegger, nor many other practitioners of philosophy in the Continental tradition would have accepted, for they had in many cases a very different conception of meaning and truth. Hegel has a conception of philosophical reasoning that goes beyond the deductive: both the 'background assumptions' of philosophy and its 'foreground' arguments attain truth by being integrated into a more comprehensive discourse,

---

[57] J. S. Mill, *Utilitarianism* (London: Fontana, 1962), 255.

while Heidegger sees the persuasive activity of philosophical history as part of an interpretative process that is directed towards truth (although to a different conception of truth than that of truth as correspondence to a domain of mind-independent facts). Truth, for Heidegger, is paradigmatically *aletheia*, a kind of insightful illumination that is more likely to be found in art and poetry than in the forensic reason-giving characteristic of proof and demonstration. For Heidegger, the hermeneutic activity of ontological comprehension (following through Heidegger's reinterpretation of the categories of philosophy and the course of its history) is a particular way of accessing truth. Historical interpretation operates by means of procedures quite unlike the systematic way of dealing with truth-claims made by science, mathematics, or even just ordinary, everyday propositions, but truth nonetheless.

Whether we follow Hegel and Heidegger here or not, it seems clear that part of the point of a historical approach to philosophy is to indicate features of the background to explicit exercises in philosophical reasoning that are more than just unasserted propositions. A better term for the object of interpretation might be 'picture', in the sense of referring to a composite that may well include attitudes as well as beliefs. Locating such attitudes and beliefs historically and representing them as part of a form of life is an important part of the way that we may try to advocate or criticize them. Such a conception of the place of philosophy is less ambitious than that which Hegel or Heidegger would have wished for. But whether we think that historical reinterpretation generates a higher form of truth or not, what the historical practitioner is aiming for is to invite us to reassess attitudes and beliefs by articulating the way that they are rooted as a 'form of life'.

At this stage, we may bring in Nietzsche and Marx. For Marx and Nietzsche, the principal task of the history of philosophy is to connect philosophy back to its motivation or sociological roots: to look at it from the point of view of the interests that it serves. To think that such considerations have a role to play in the arguments of philosophy is often condemned as fallacious—indeed, it even has a name: *the genetic fallacy*. To commit the genetic fallacy is to think that the validity of a belief is determined by its origins. And certainly, there is no logical reason why a belief cannot be true just because it helps to console us in the face of our own mortality or because it serves the interests of the ruling class. But we are not dealing here with deductive proof; though pointing out the discreditable origins of a belief or its consoling function does not, strictly speaking, refute that belief, it may play a role (and a very reasonable one at that) in helping to change our mind about it when the grounds for or against it are not independently conclusive.

In summary, we can identify four central elements in the use of the history of philosophy as part of philosophy:

(1) The philosophical use of the history of philosophy looks at philosophical arguments—both past and contemporary—from the point of view of the assumptions and attitudes that inform them.

(2) Inasmuch as those assumptions are taken for granted, either because thinkers are not aware of them at all or because, if they are aware of them, they take them to be self-evident, history is a way of calling them into question.

(3) The aim of historical interpretation is persuasive, rather than demonstrative in the sense of giving an argument that must be compelling to all rational beings who understand it.

(4) The historical interpretation does not aim simply to uncover presuppositions but to connect them: to depict them as part of an intellectual or social context within which the reader can be persuaded to see them as less or more attractive, as the case may be.

# VI. LEGACIES

Variations of this conception of philosophy have been so successful in Continental philosophy (in France and Italy as well as in Germany) that it would be as difficult to enumerate its adherents as it would be to identify all the contemporary Anglo-American philosophers who use the tools of formal logic as a means of philosophical analysis. It is possible, however, to indicate briefly some of the most important.

The historical approach to philosophy reached a first heyday in Germany at the turn of the twentieth century with Dilthey's *Die Typen der Weltanschauung und ihre Ausbildung in den metaphysischen Systemen* (1911).[58] The Marburg School neo-Kantians and Husserl's phenomenology, in reasserting the principled differences between 'genetic' and 'transcendental' questions against 'historicism', represented something of a move in the other direction, but it

---

[58] Translated as *Types of Worldview and their Development in Metaphysical Systems*, in *Dilthey's Philosophy of Existence* (New York: Bookman Associates, 1957).

was one that would prove temporary—the historical approach to philosophy was reasserted strongly within each tradition by Ernst Cassirer and Heidegger, respectively. Marxism, as it moved into the academy in Germany in the 1920s and 1930s, did so very largely under the auspices of Lukács, with the result that Marxist writing on the history of philosophy began to appear that did more than treat philosophical ideas as a mere offshoot of an underlying economic 'base'. Horkheimer and Adorno's *Dialektik der Aufklärung*,[59] for example, interprets philosophy historically by seeing it as part of a single, continuing project, the domination of nature. For Horkheimer and Adorno, the Enlightenment conceptions of theory that underpin philosophical system-building are products of an instrumental conception of reason that have become hypostatized and mistaken for the ultimate structure of reality—a process that they trace back to the mythical need to see the order of the world as repeating itself eternally and inevitably.

In France, the historical approach to philosophy developed to some extent independently, through the influence of Bergson and Bachelard, but it was certainly reinforced by the transmission of Hegelian and Heideggerian ideas by Alexandre Kojève in the 1930s. Although 'historicism' was to become a term of abuse in post-war France with the development of structuralism, the pre-eminence of the historical approach to philosophy was actually strengthened by the work of Althusser and Foucault, historicism's main avowed enemies. Althusser's entire *oeuvre* was an exercise in a very particular kind of historical interpretation, aiming to release the 'scientific' character of past historical texts (above all, those of Marx), while Foucault, no less sceptical than Marx himself about philosophy's claims to cognitive value, endeavoured to situate philosophical systems within a framework of historically variable structural *epistemes* that ran through different societies at different periods. The development of 'post-structuralism' in the work of Derrida and Deleuze was equally historical. For both authors the practice of philosophy was principally a process of textual reinterpretation. For Deleuze, the canonical account of the history of philosophy depicts it as a history of debate about the nature of reason, stretching from Plato to Hegel. His aim was to oppose that account with a different narrative, bringing to the forefront those thinkers from Epicurus to Spinoza and Nietzsche whose conception of philosophy was the place of man in nature rather than the character of reason and logic.

---

[59] M. Horkheimer and T. W. Adorno, *Dialektik der Aufklärung* (Amsterdam, 1947; Frankfurt, 1969), trans. E. Jephcott (Stanford: Stanford University Press, 2002).

Derrida's interpretation of texts is framed by a grandly conceived account of the domination of Western thought by what he terms 'logocentrism'.

Returning to Gadamer, their German near-contemporary, we find that Gadamer's position is very similar to Heidegger's—hardly surprising, given that he was Heidegger's pupil and close disciple. For Heidegger, the point of the history of philosophy is to revive our ontological understanding by a critical engagement with the dominant tradition that now obscures it. For Gadamer likewise there are two traditions: a limited one which identifies truth with the 'methodical knowledge' of the natural sciences and another, richer tradition 'which corresponds to the whole of our hermeneutic experience'.[60] Gadamer thinks that historical narrative gives us access to truth—but it is access to truth of a different kind from the truth to be found in the natural sciences. So Gadamer's 'history of ideas' is not just a preliminary to philosophical practice but a form of philosophical argument itself.

Gadamer's argument from tradition (like Heidegger's) is conservative or restorative, in the sense that it aims to persuade the reader to reconnect with an older and more satisfying (as they believe, truer) way of understanding and thinking about the world by bringing this earlier tradition to light and placing it in contrast with currently dominant ways of thinking. The position is not without political significance. Those ways of thinking are dominant in philosophy just because they are dominant in modern society. Thus to criticize them is, at the same time, to criticize society. We should not, however, assume that an argument from tradition is necessarily conservative in its political implications: an important theme of radical political thought has often been the need to restore (but in a new and better form) those human values that have been lost with the development of modernity (thus, for Lukács, the overcoming under communism of the reification characteristic of societies based upon commodity production will be at the same time a restoration of values that have become lost).

One effect of the great influence of Heidegger in post-war Germany was to produce a confluence between philosophy, literary history, and the history of ideas. Gadamer helped to found the journal *Archiv für Begriffsgeschichte* and he participated, with historians such as Reinhart Koselleck and literary historians such as Peter Szondi, in the research group *Poetik und Hermeneutik* that produced a series of important interdisciplinary publications. Of the contributors to this strand, the most original and significant was the

---

[60] Gadamer, *Truth and Method*, p. xiii.

historian of ideas Hans Blumenberg. Blumenberg's vast and hugely learned output cannot easily be summarized. It includes a synoptic account, heavily influenced by Nietzsche, of the history of Western thought as a struggle on the part of a monotheistic culture to come to terms with the problem of evil and the ever-present threat of gnosticism.[61] Of particular interest to philosophers are Blumenberg's explanations of how the vocabulary of philosophy incorporates a history of metaphor (often now forgotten) within its vocabulary.[62]

A forward-looking application of Heidegger's approach to philosophical history is to be found in the work of the German philosopher Ernst Tugendhat (a colleague of Gadamer's at the University of Heidelberg), particularly in his *Vorlesungen zur Einführung in die sprachanalytische Philosophie*.[63] Tugendhat's—at first sight very surprising—thesis is that it is analytical philosophy of language that best draws the consequences of Heidegger's criticism of the philosophical tradition. The outline of the argument is as follows. Tugendhat starts from Heidegger's claim regarding the domination of philosophy by received ontological conceptions, in particular, the understanding of Being in the mode of *Vorhandenheit* (presence-at-hand). Traditional philosophy, on this view, is dominated by a conception of reality as something composed of positive or quasi-positive elements and characteristically gives an account of thinking about them as a kind of mental pointing. This conception Tugendhat calls 'object theory'. For object theory, mental contents that cannot be directly pointed to (e.g. non-existent things) are mysterious and a source of paradox. It is the virtue of analytical philosophy, however, that it recognizes that thinking and knowing are not a kind of seeing (*noein*) but are propositional attitudes (*legein*). In this way, analytical philosophy can give an account of meaning in language without having to invoke the strange intermediary world of 'ideas' or 'intentional objects' that the philosophy of consciousness (*Bewusstseinsphilosophie*) uses to deal with such problematic entities and which brings with it the problem of the existence of the external world and the threat of scepticism. Heideggerian history of philosophy is thus reinterpreted to yield a progressive message: by giving a truth-conditional

---

[61] See in particular *Die Legitimität der Neuzeit* (Frankfurt: Suhrkamp, 1966), translated as *The Legitimacy of the Modern Age* (Cambridge, MA: MIT Press, 1985).

[62] See, for instance, 'Das Licht als Metapher der Wahrheit', *Studium Generale* 10 (1957), 432–54.

[63] Ernst Tugendhat, *Vorlesungen zur Einführung in die sprachanalytische Philosophie* (Frankfurt: Suhrkamp, 1976), translated as *Traditional and Analytical Philosophy* (Cambridge: Cambridge University Press, 1982).

account of the structure of propositions, analytical philosophy escapes from the antinomies that continue to dog philosophy on the Continent.

In closing, I should like to note that the historical approach to philosophy has been used in some of the most important and interesting philosophical writings in English of the last twenty-five years, particularly in moral and political philosophy. Alasdair MacIntyre's *After Virtue*,[64] for example, depicts our thinking about the self in terms of two competing poles: a self reduced, in tendency at least, to a disengaged nodal point suitable to a disenchanted, naturalistic conception of reality, on the one hand, and a richer, historically embedded, narrative self on the other. Like Gadamer, MacIntyre faces the problem of how to oppose a conception of rationality modelled on the natural sciences in ways that will be persuasive to those who take it for granted. As he writes, 'Arguments in philosophy rarely take the form of proofs; and the most successful arguments on topics central to philosophy never do. (The ideal of *proof* is a relatively barren one in philosophy.)'[65] Like Gadamer, MacIntyre articulates his narrative, historical conception of rationality by means of a historical argument—in this case, an examination of the way in which the moral language of the West has changed.

Charles Taylor in his many writings, above all in his monumental *Sources of the Self*,[66] also tries to reconnect modern moral philosophy to the wider outlooks that it embodies (and thus to make it amenable to a kind of criticism that points beyond its boundaries). However, as Taylor recognizes somewhat ruefully, much of modern philosophy has 'made it a point of honour not to admit to any such outlook'.[67] Nevertheless, for Taylor,

... there is one great recourse here and that is history ... In understanding our differences from the ancients, we have a better idea what our assimilation of their paradigms of self-rule actually amount to for us; and in looking more closely at the 'traditions' which our Enlightenment thought supposedly repudiated, and at the forms that repudiation took, we may come to see the differences between the two opposed terms in a new light, and consequently to take a new view on contemporary philosophy.[68]

Similar ideas are to be found in Edward Craig's *The Mind of God and the Works of Man*.[69] 'Philosophical thought', Craig writes, 'has always had the function of articulating certain very general pictures of the real, even if there

---

[64] Alasdair MacIntyre, *After Virtue* (London: Duckworth, 1981).      [65] Ibid. 241–2.
[66] Charles Taylor, *Sources of the Self* (Cambridge: Cambridge University Press, 1989).
[67] Ibid. 103.      [68] Ibid. 103–4.
[69] Edward Craig, *The Mind of God and the Works of Man* (Oxford: Oxford University Press, 1986).

have been times, like our own, that have denied it'.[70] Although professional philosophy is written as if the metaphysical views that it advocates were 'solidly established by arguments starting from a neutral position', the fact is, according to Craig, that this is never true: 'On the contrary, it is repeatedly found that content smuggled in from the *Weltbild* itself is somehow assisting the passage to the conclusion.'[71] Hence the need for a historical perspective by which such *Weltbilder* are identified and their role made explicit.

Not all applications of the historical approach to philosophy are aimed at the revival of past traditions. On the contrary, a number of historically inspired works of philosophy aim in the opposite direction: to show the presence of older (usually, theologically inspired) ways of thinking within supposedly modern and secular bodies of thought and to argue that they represent an unacknowledged and debilitating hangover within them which we would be better off without. We might call this approach 'emancipatory' or 'icono-clastic'. Two justly celebrated examples are Bernard Williams's attack on the presence of theologically inspired conceptions of obligation and responsibility in supposedly secular moral systems in *Ethics and the Limits of Philosophy*[72] and Richard Rorty's attempt to show how far modern analytical philosophy is limited by continuing to embody the assumptions of the early modern conception of epistemology as we find it in Descartes, Locke, and Kant.[73]

All of these important and deservedly influential works have been written in the belief that history has an important role to play in philosophy, particularly so where there is methodological conflict within the discipline—and that such conflict is endemic except in those rare times when the discipline has sunk back into no more than a bogus imitation of the natural sciences. The fact that they have appeared in English suggests something both about the way that the discipline of philosophy is now developing in the Anglo-Saxon countries and of what it stands to gain by engagement with the Continental tradition.

---

[70] Edward Craig, 2.    [71] Ibid. 3.

[72] Bernard Williams, *Ethics and the Limits of Philosophy* (London: Fontana, 1985).

[73] Richard Rorty, *Philosophy and the Mirror of Nature* (Princeton: Princeton University Press, 1979). My own work—for example, the books *Hegel's Dialectic and its Criticism* (Cambridge: Cambridge University Press, 1982) and *On Voluntary Servitude: False Consciousness and the Theory of Ideology Hegel's Dialectic and its Criticism* (Cambridge: Cambridge University Press, 1982), *On Voluntary Servitude* (Cambridge: Polity Press, 1996)—also falls into this category. In the former I argue that the continued presence of ideas such as 'reflection' and 'mediation' that play a role within Hegel's Absolute Idealism are used out of context in Adorno's 'negative dialectic', and undermine its claim to be a form of materialist philosophy. In *On Voluntary Servitude*, I explore the roots in earlier, providential views of history and society of the beliefs that sustained the theory of ideology, hoping thereby to make the theory more open to criticism. See esp. ch. 1.

CHAPTER 5

# HISTORICISM

## FREDERICK BEISER

## 1. BASIC MEANING

In 1936, in the nostalgic preface to his magisterial *Die Entstehung des Historismus*, Friedrich Meinecke wrote that historicism was 'one of the greatest intellectual revolutions that Western thought has experienced'.[1] There was perhaps a whiff of hyperbole in Meinecke's remark. It was also a bit self-serving, since he was trained in the historicist tradition and became one of its leading spokesmen. Still, there can be no doubt that historicism was one of the most important intellectual movements of the nineteenth century. For better or worse, it had an enormous impact on nineteenth- and twentieth-century philosophy. Almost all German philosophy in the late nineteenth and early twentieth century—whether Dilthey's hermeneutics, Windelband's and Rickert's neo-Kantianism, Husserl's phenomenology or Heidegger's existentialism—grew out of a reaction to historicism.[2]

What was historicism? It is not easy to say. The term 'historicism' has meant many things to many people, and it has been defined by conflicting doctrines.

---

[1] Friedrich Meinecke, *Die Entstehung des Historismus* (Munich: Oldenbourg, 1965), 1 (vol. iii of *Werke*, ed. Hans Herzfeld, Carl Hinrichs and Walther Hofer).

[2] On the importance of historicism for these thinkers, see Charles Bambach, *Heidegger, Dilthey, and the Crisis of Historicism* (Ithaca: Cornell University Press, 1995).

We can avoid some of the controversy, and give the term at least a working definition, if we define historicism not as a doctrine but as a programme. This programme, which began in the middle of the eighteenth century and extended throughout most of the nineteenth century, had a simple but ambitious goal: to legitimate history as a science. The historicists wanted history to enjoy the same status and prestige as the natural sciences; but they claimed that it had its own goals, methods, and standards of knowledge, which were unlike those of the natural sciences. Just what these methods and goals should be was a matter of dispute; but it was generally agreed that they were not reducible to those of the natural sciences, and that they should be distinct from those of metaphysics.

The historicist's goal was sometimes expressed as a demand for autonomy: history should be self-governing, following its own rules and standards; it should not tolerate interference from the outside, whether it came from political and religious authority or some other discipline.[3] The danger of interference first came from metaphysics, from the grand idealist systems of Fichte, Schelling, and Hegel, which threatened to make history the mere handmaiden of philosophy. After the decline of idealism in the 1840s, this danger came from positivism, which made the standards and methods of the natural sciences definitive for all intellectual life. Historicism therefore had to fight two consecutive battles: first, prior to the 1840s, against metaphysics; and then, after the 1840s, against positivism.

Who were the historicists? If we define historicism by this programme, it is easy to identify them. The leading historicists of the nineteenth century, the proper age of historicism, were Barthold Georg Niebuhr (1776–1831), Leopold von Ranke (1795–1886), Johann Gustav Droysen (1838–1908), Wilhelm Dilthey (1833–1911), Jacob Burckhardt (1818–97), and the founders of the historical school of law, Friedrich Savigny (1779–1861) and Karl Friedrich Eichhorn (1781–1854). The main historicists of the eighteenth century, who first formulated its programme, were J. A. Chladenius (1710–59), Christoph Gatterer (1727–99), and Jacob Wegelin (1721–91). There were also several godfathers of historicism, thinkers who, although they did not

---

[3] See, for example, Ranke, 'Idee der Universalhistorie' (1831–2), in *Vorlesungens-Einleitung: Aus Werk und Nachlass*, ed. Walther Fuchs and Theodor Schieder (Munich: Oldenbourg, 1975), iv. 74, 76; and Droysen, *Historik: Vorlesungen über Enzyklopädie und Methodologie der Geschichte*, ed. Rudolf Hübner (Munich: Oldenbourg, 1937), pp. 3–4; and Dilthey, *Einleitung in die Geisteswissenschaften*, in *Gesammelte Schriften*, ed. Bernhard Groethuysen (Göttingen: Vandenhoeck & Ruprecht, 1966), vol. i, pp. xv–xvii.

explicitly advance its agenda, were crucial in forming its methods and outlook. They were Johann Georg Hamann (1730–88), Johann Gottfried Herder (1744–1803), Wilhelm von Humboldt (1767–1835), Justus Möser (1720–94), and A. W. Rehberg (1757–1836).

What about Hegel and Marx? Were they not historicists too? For many scholars Hegel and Marx are indeed the paradigms of historicism. After all, they shared the historicist agenda: they wanted history to be a science, and they too were opposed to naturalism (at least in the positivist sense). However, it is important to recognize that most of the leading historicists were highly critical of Hegel and Marx, whose philosophy of history they found too metaphysical. Ranke, Droysen, Burckhardt, and Dilthey rejected all philosophy of history, whether Hegelian or Marxist, because they believed it to be too speculative, transcending the limits of experience definitive of all proper science. In their early years, they saw Hegel as their main enemy, and they believed that history could become a science only by getting away from the embrace of Hegelianism; it was only later that the enemy became Comte and the positivists.[4] So, for all their importance for historicism, Hegel and Marx fell outside the historicist movement proper.

Although we cannot define historicism by a specific doctrine, a definite *Weltanschauung*, we can attribute a few basic principles to it. These principles are inherent in its very programme, implied by its attempt to make history a science; they are part of the historicist's conception of the methods, standards, and goals of historical knowledge. Corresponding to their belief in the autonomy of historical knowledge, the historicists affirmed the autonomy of the historical world. According to this principle, everything that happens in history must be explained within history and according to specifically historical methods. This principle excludes two alternatives: *metaphysics*, i.e. explaining actions by goals outside history, such as the ends of providence; and *naturalism*, i.e. explaining historical actions as part of nature and according to the methods of the natural sciences. Historicism is therefore the counterpart of naturalism: just as naturalism holds that every event in nature is explicable according to the methods of natural science, so historicism

---

[4]  It is worth noting, however, that both Dilthey and Droysen had great debts to Hegel, which they acknowledged in their later years. Their chief debt was to Hegel's concept of objective spirit, i.e. the doctrine that the characteristic embodiment of mind is in social and political institutions. Droysen was a close student of Hegel, attending many of his lectures in Berlin; and Dilthey's *Die Jugendgeschichte Hegels, Gesammelte Schriften* Band IV, was crucial for the revival of Hegelianism in the early twentieth century.

holds that everything that happens in history is explicable according to the methods of history. Both naturalism and historicism reject appeals to the transcendent and supernatural, i.e. attempts to explain something in nature or history by something *outside* the realm of nature of history. But, for the historicist, nature and history are not the same. Although history might fall within nature, it is not reducible to it. The historicists deny that we can understand the characteristic qualities of historical events in naturalistic terms, i.e., according to the laws of cause and effect that hold sway over the physical world. They were not *metaphysical* dualists: they did not affirm the distinction between the mental and physical; and they indeed insisted that the mental and physical sides of humanity are inseparable. They were, however, *methodological* dualists: they held that the methods of history are distinct from those of the natural sciences. Although these methods do not reveal a distinct realm of substances, inaccessible to natural science, they at least did explain *aspects* of human action that are not reducible to naturalistic forms of explanation.

Another fundamental historicist principle is that everything in the human world—the state, society, morality, literature, science—is part of history. This principle seems trivial—obviously human actions take place in time—but the historicists gave it a deeper meaning. It meant, first, that all human values and institutions change, so that nothing in the human world is eternal. This point is directed against our natural tendency to eternalize our values and institutions, as if they were true for humanity in general and held for all time; the historicists remind us that all values and institutions are the product of time and place, and that they too will disappear into history. It meant, second, that everything in the human world has to be understood within its specific social-historical context. The historicists stress the radical *context-dependency* of all social-historical phenomena, i.e. they hold that they do not exist apart from their specific context, such that they would change their identity in a different context. This point is directed against our natural tendency to hypostasize social-historical phenomena, as if they have an identity independent of their context; the historicist teaches that the more concrete we become, i.e. the more we individuate our object, the more we find that its identity depends on its context.

The autonomy of the social-historical world, and the complete historicization of the human world, are the two fundamental principles of historicism. In one form or another, they would be explicitly affirmed, or implicitly assumed, by all the major historicists, including Hegel, Marx, and the German idealists.

Further generalizations, though, are hazardous. The more principles we add, the more detail we provide, the more likely we are to forfeit the claim to generality. To illustrate just how perilous, consider the following example. One might think that the objectivity of historical knowledge was a central historicist principle. After all, the historicists were claiming scientific status for their discipline, and objective knowledge is one of the chief characteristics of science. But the possibility of objective historical knowledge was one of the most contentious issues within historicist circles. While Ranke and his school insisted upon such knowledge, Droysen and the Prussian historians hotly contested its possibility, demanding that the historian should write from his own moral and political standpoint.[5] Both Ranke and Droysen were historicists insofar as they defended the scientific status of history, and the two principles of the autonomy of history and the historicization of the human world. However, they had radically different views about what scientific knowledge should be. Any adequate definition of historicism must be general enough to accommodate differences of this kind.

## 2. HISTORY AS SCIENCE

The historicist agenda to make history a science was a reaction against an old and powerful legacy. From antiquity, history had suffered from an acute inferiority complex, a severe problem of legitimation. It did not seem to deserve the title of science, which had been bestowed on philosophy and mathematics. Since science demands universal and necessary knowledge, and since history deals only with particular and contingent events, history cannot realize the kind of knowledge required by science. On these grounds Aristotle placed history below even poetry as a form of knowledge.[6] Whereas the historian could only say what a particular person did at a particular time, the poet at least could inform us about something more universal: what a certain *kind* of person would do under a certain *kind* of circumstances.

---

[5]  Ranke famously declared his ideal of objectivity when wrote that the historian should simply state 'how something actually happened'. See the preface to his *Geschichte der romanischen und germanischen Völker von 1494 bis 1535*, in *Sämtliche Werke* (Leipzig: Duncker & Humblot, 1868–90), XXX–XXXIV, p. vii. Droysen famously countered in his *Historik* that Ranke's ideal of objectivity was only fit for eunuchs. See his *Historik*, p. 287.

[6]  *Poetics* 1451ª36 and *Metaphysics* A981ª.

The stigma against history endured well into the age of Enlightenment. The ancient distinction between history and science was revived by the rationalist epistemology of Leibniz and Wolff, which kept the historian firmly chained in the depths of Plato's cave. True to the ancient paradigm, Leibniz and Wolff taught that science demands universality and necessity, while history dwells only in the realm of particularity and contingency.[7] Common historical knowledge is the lowest grade of knowledge, Wolff once wrote, because it depends on the senses and gives us no insight into the reasons for things.[8] There seemed to be a gulf, then, between the realms of science and history. Thus Lessing, who was raised in the rationalist tradition, would later famously write of 'that broad and ugly ditch' between the historical and the rational. 'Contingent truths of history can never become the proof of necessary truths of reason.'[9]

The attempt to legitimate history as a science began already in the middle of the eighteenth century. Such thinkers as J. A. Chladenius, Christoph Gatterer, and Jacob Wegelin,[10] who had all been schooled in the Leibnizian-Wolffian tradition, became disgruntled with its narrow rationalism, not least because it denied scientific status to history. Although they recognized that history could not achieve the demonstrative certainty of mathematics, they insisted that it is still a specific form of knowledge in its own right. They accepted the rationalist doctrine that there is a fundamental difference in kind between history and the natural sciences, which employed the mathematical method and the mechanical paradigm of explanation. They did not agree, however, that *all* knowledge demands universality and necessity, or that the *only* form of science is mathematical. In their view, history had its own special standards and methods of knowledge, which are no less demanding and exacting than those of the natural sciences. While the methodology of the natural sciences is mechanical and mathematical, the methodology of history is holistic and interpretative. The natural scientist attempts to discover through reason laws that hold in all times and places, whereas the historian attempts to fathom

[7] See Leibniz, *Novus methodus discendae docendaeque jurisprudentiae* §32, in *Sämtliche Schriften und Briefe*, ed. Prussian Academy of Sciences (Darmstadt: Reichl, 1930) VI/1, 284; and Wolff, *Philosophia rationalis sive logica* §7, in *Gesammelte Werke*, ed. J. Ecole et al. (Hildesheim: Olms, 1968), II/1, 3.

[8] Wolff, *Philosophia rationalis* §22, *Werke* II/1, 10.

[9] Lessing, 'Beweis des Geistes und der Kraft', in *Werke und Briefe* (Frankfurt: Deutsche Klassiker Verlag, 1989), viii. 441.

[10] On these thinkers and their role in the development of historicism, see Peter Hanns Reill, *The German Enlightenment and Rise of Historicism* (Berkeley: University of California Press, 1975), 100–26.

through intuition the unique and individual. It was the task of science to know the individual and unique as much as the universal and the uniform.

The rise of German idealism toward the end of the eighteenth century begins a very different chapter in the attempt to legitimate history as a science. Fichte, Schelling, and Hegel adopted a very different strategy from that of Chladenius, Gatterer, and Wegelin. Attempting to leap Lessing's ugly ditch, they argued that it is possible to determine the general laws of history on the basis of reason itself. While Fichte, Schelling, and Hegel agree that there are fundamental differences between the standards and methods of history and those of the natural sciences, they reject the Leibnizian–Wolffian doctrine that reason has no place in history. Reason can discover universal and necessary laws in history just as it does in nature, although these laws are not mechanical and mathematical but teleological and interpretative. Hence Fichte, Schelling, and Hegel formulate a philosophy of history that attempts to determine nothing less the general purpose of world history itself. They see history as the fulfillment of a plan, as the realization of an idea, as if it were a novel or drama.

Although the German idealists did much to advance the cause of history, their conception of historical method was not shared by the historicists. Already in the 1820s in Berlin, there were constant skirmishes between 'the historical' and 'philosophical' party, i.e. between Niebuhr, Ranke, and Savigny on the one hand, and Hegel and his school on the other hand.[11] The tension between them had much to do with historical methodology. The philosophical school had used a dialectical logic to develop a teleological conception of world history, whereas the historical school stressed the importance of following a strictly empirical method and doubted the validity of all teleology. The historians accused the philosophical school of reviving the old methodology of scholasticism, which was completely at odds with the empirical procedure of all science. With hindsight, the affinities between these parties seems much greater than their differences—they all agreed on the fundamental principles of historicism and the importance of making history a science. But, as in politics, so in academia: the finer the differences, the more heated the quarrels.

Eventually, the battle was decided in favor of the historicists. With the decline of Hegelianism in the 1840s, a reaction set in against all speculative philosophy, whose methods were regarded as too systematic, too

---

[11]  For a valuable account of these skirmishes, see Ernst Simon, 'Ranke und Hegel', in *Beiheft der Historischen Zeitschrift* 15 (Munich: Oldenbourg, 1928), 16–119.

deductive, and too a priori for reliable and rigorous empirical science.[12] Eager to continue the legacy of Niebuhr, Savigny, and Ranke, the new genera-tion of historicists—Droysen, Dilthey, and Burckhardt—maintained the old hostility against speculative philosophy. Following their predecessors, they allied themselves with the empirical scientists in stressing the importance of piecemeal empirical investigation and the need to bracket all metaphysi-cal assumptions. They likened the philosophy of history to the now utterly discredited speculative *Naturphilosophie*. Droysen, Dilthey, and Burckhardt rejected the generalizing a priori approach of the philosophy of history, which they held to be inappropriate for the individuality of historical phenomena. Since each culture or age is unique, they argued, it is impossible to make reliable generalizations that hold for all cultures and ages. If we treat each culture and age as an end in itself, as proper history demands, we cannot see it simply as a stage in the development of reason or the idea. Hence the new generation of historicists reaffirmed the traditional dualism between history and reason, and they returned to the earlier tradition of Chladenius, Gatterer, and Wegelin. Like their forbears, they affirmed that history is radi-cally contingent and particular, and that it cannot achieve the universal and necessary laws that hold in the natural sciences. Nevertheless, they continued to believe that history could still be a science because it has its own standards and methods, which are no less empirical than those of the natural sciences. The most rigorous and systematic efforts to formulate these standards and methods appears in the work of Droysen and Dilthey in the late nineteenth century.[13]

The decline of idealism in the 1840s had eliminated one foe of the historicists. But there soon arose an even greater one, who gave the historicist agenda relevance and urgency throughout most of the nineteenth century. In 1844, in the second edition of his *Die Welt als Wille und Vorstellung*, Schopenhauer added a section on history that attacked the very possibility of

---

[12] On this reaction, see Herbert Schnädelbach, *Philosophy in Germany, 1831–1933* (Cambridge: Cambridge University Press, 1984), 66–108.

[13] The crucial works are Droysen's *Historik* and Dilthey's *Einleitung in die Geisteswissenschaften*. It is noteworthy, however, that these works had no major impact in the nineteenth century because they were either unpublished or incomplete. Droysen's *Historik*, which is based on lectures given from 1857 to 1883, was not published until 1937 (see above n. 3). It was known only in the form of a brief compendium, *Grundriss der Historik*, which was published by Droysen himself in 1868. Dilthey's *Einleitung* was incomplete. The first volume appeared in 1883; but the planned second volume, which was to treat the philosophical foundations of the social-historical sciences, was never completed. All that remains is a mass of fragments, which are in volumes vii and xix of the *Gesammelte Schriften*.

history as a science.[14] Schopenhauer's attack is interesting from an historical standpoint because it goes back to the ancient tradition the historicist had struggled against all along. Schopenhauer reaffirmed the classical rationalist ideal of science and noted how history falls far short of that ideal. Since history deals with the individual, and since science demands universal and necessary knowledge, a science of history is a contradiction in terms. All historical knowledge, Schopenhauer further contended, is conditioned by the standpoint of the spectator and lacks the objectivity required for science. Schopenhauer's critique simply reinstated the old ideal of science against which historicism rebelled; yet his attack was still effective because of the growing influence of his philosophy after the middle of the century.[15] It was the predecessor of Nietzsche's later attack upon 'historical culture' in the second of his *Unzeitgemässe Betrachtungen*.[16]

## 3. Historical and Philosophical Significance

So far it might seem as if historicism concerns little more than the methodology of history, and more specifically the question whether history has its own standards and methods apart from the natural sciences. But such an impression is misleading. Although historicism indeed began as a response to this issue, it would be a serious mistake to limit its significance to a matter of historical methodology alone. The implications of historicism for epistemology, ethics, and politics are as deep as they are wide.

One of the most important results of the debate about historical method is that it soon evolved into the broader question about the standards and methods for the study of society and culture in general. For most German thinkers of the eighteenth and nineteenth centuries, history was the paradigm for all the social sciences or human studies. If its methods were distinct from the natural sciences, the same case could be made for other social and cultural sciences. So the question of historical method raised the more general

---

[14] Schopenhauer, 'Ueber Geschichte', Kapitel 38 in *Die Welt als Wille und Vorstellung, Sämtliche Werke* (Frankfurt: Insel, 1968), ii. 563–73.

[15] Schnädelbach, *Philosophy in Germany*, 60.

[16] Nietzsche, *Sämtliche Werke, Kritische Studienausgabe*, ed. G. Colli and M. Montinari (Berlin: de Gruyter, 1980), i. 248–334.

problem of the philosophical foundations of all social and cultural studies, and whether their methods are fundamentally different in kind from those of the natural sciences. This problem was first generalized by Dilthey, who, in his *Einleitung in die Geisteswissenschaften* of 1883, asked about the foundation for the '*Geisteswissenschaften*', i.e. for what might be loosely translated as the human studies or sciences. Among these sciences Dilthey gave pride of place to history; but he also explicitly included economics, law, literature, and aesthetics.

The implications of historicism go much further. Seen from a broad historical perspective, historicism questioned the enduring search in Western philosophy to find *transcendent* justifications for social, political, and moral values, i.e. the endeavor to give these values support or sanction outside or beyond their own specific social and cultural context. Such justifications could be straightforwardly religious, viz. divine providence; or they could be secular, viz. natural law or human reason. In either case, historicism threw into question the validity of all such justifications.

The historical significance of historicism is best measured by its *break* with the Enlightenment, which had dominated European intellectual life during the eighteenth century. The star of historicism rose as that of the Enlightenment fell. Historicism was not the only intellectual current to attack the Enlightenment; but it was the most effective. The skeptical and religious attacks on the Enlightenment were sporadic and fleeting; but the criticisms of historicism were persistent and enduring, their effects lasting well into the nineteenth century. While the religious attacks seemed dated by the progress of the sciences, historicist criticism was more troubling because it seemed to come from the advance of the sciences.

From the perspective of historicism, the general problem with the Enlightenment is that it remained, in spite of itself, too deeply indebted to the legacy of the Middle Ages, which it pretended to overcome. The theology of the Middle Ages had always required a transcendent sanction for all social, political, and moral values. Although the Enlightenment removed the religious trappings of such a transcendent sanction, it continued to seek it in more worldly terms, whether that was natural law, the social contract, a universal human reason, or a constant human nature. All these concepts seemed to promise a validity beyond the flux of history, a sanction transcending the concrete context of culture, politics, and society. All the thinkers of the Enlightenment—the French *philosophes*, the German *Aufklärer*, or the English free-thinkers—wanted to find some eternal and universal Archimedean standpoint by which they could judge all specific societies, states, and cultures. One of the most profound implications of historicism is that there can be no such standpoint.

For many contemporary historians, to claim that the historical and philosophical significance of historicism rests upon its break with the Enlightenment is to propagate an old myth. These scholars have argued that historicism arose from historiographic traditions within the Enlightenment, and they have shown how many of the methods and standards of knowledge of the later historicists were already apparent in eighteenth-century writers firmly within the Enlightenment tradition.[17] The main target of their criticism has been Meinecke, who had constantly opposed historicism to the Enlightenment. They have rejected Meinecke's paradigm as simplistic and misleading, and they have advocated instead seeing a continuum rather than a break between historicism and the Enlightenment. At the risk of appearing a spoilsport and fuddy-duddy, I would like to question whether these scholars have advanced the discussion at all. They have criticized Meinecke for a point he would never have questioned, and that he indeed went to great pains to demonstrate: that historicism has its roots in the historiography of the Enlightenment. They have also ignored the testimony of the historicists, who themselves opposed their doctrines to the Enlightenment; while their views are not necessarily infallible, they show that the opposition is not anachronistic. Finally, they have also confused matters of history with logic: because historicism grew out of the Enlightenment, it scarcely follows that it accepts the fundamental values and principles of the Enlightenment. The evidence is overwhelming that the leading historicists did break, explicitly and self-consciously, with some of fundamental principles of the Enlightenment.

Since the historical and philosophical significance of historicism rests upon its break with the Enlightenment, and since recent scholarship has neglected or disputed this break, it is worthwhile to examine it in a little detail. Let us consider two fundamental articles of faith of the Enlightenment and see how historicism explicitly questioned or implicitly undermined them.

A fundamental article of faith for the Enlightenment was its belief in natural law, i.e. that there are universal moral standards that apply to all cultures and epochs. These standards were regarded as 'natural' because they are based upon a universal human nature, or the ends of nature itself, and because

---

[17] See, for example, Reill, *The German Enlightenment and the Rise of Historicism*, 2–3; Friedrich Jaeger and Jörn Rüsen, *Geschichte des Historismus* (Munich: Beck, 1992), 10–11; and Herbert Schnädelbach, *Geschichtsphilosophie nach Hegel* (Freiburg: Alber, 1974), 27–8.

they do not rest on the positive laws and traditions established in a specific state. The natural law tradition therefore assumed that there was not only a uniform human nature throughout the flux of history, but also that there was a universal human reason that would endorse the same moral values for all epochs and cultures.

It is telling that the leading nineteenth-century historicists—Ranke, Droysen, Dilthey, Burckhardt, and Savigny—self-consciously and explicitly rejected the natural law tradition. They believed that this tradition had illegitimately universalized the values of eighteenth-century Europe as if they held for all epochs and cultures, and that it had illicitly legislated moral and political values for all cultures, irrespective of their specific circumstances, traditions, and ways of life. To know the values of a culture or epoch, they argued, it is necessary to study it from within, to examine how these values have evolved from its history and circumstances; it is impossible to judge what its values ought to be from some standpoint outside it, as if, regardless of circumstance and tradition, there were one set of values for all peoples. The more we examine values historically, the historicists argued, the more we see that their purpose and meaning depends entirely on their specific context, on their precise role in a social-historical whole. Since these contexts are unique and incommensurable, so are the values within them; it therefore becomes impossible to make generalizations about what values everyone ought to have, regardless of social and historical context.

Another fundamental article of faith of the Enlightenment was its belief in the value of criticism, i.e. that we should examine all our beliefs according to reason, accepting or rejecting them strictly according to the evidence for them. Hence the Enlightenment made thinking for oneself, intellectual autonomy, into its primary intellectual virtue.

Well before the French Revolution, some of the first thinkers in the historicist tradition began to question the Enlightenment demand for rational belief. Herder and Möser, for example, asked whether the demand for radical criticism simply missed the point. Although many of our beliefs would perhaps prove to be prejudices when examined strictly according to the evidence for them, they were still crucial for life and action. They were important not only to motivate the individual, but also to create social solidarity and political stability. We should value our beliefs not so much according to the evidence, they suggested, but more according to the role they play in moral and political life. Hence the young Herder noted that many of our beliefs, though perhaps fictions, are still necessary to make a people happy and to give their life cohesion and meaning.[18] And Möser was convinced that illusion is crucial to the fabric of social and political life. He thought that it was fine that we used our reason to see through these illusions; but he insisted all the same that that was no reason to reject them. 'The English', he once wrote, 'distinguish their king from common mortals, and dress him with the most magnificent splendor, but they know well that he is a human being just like everyone else.'[19] What Herder and Möser argued in the eighteenth century would eventually become a leitmotif of the historicist tradition.

# 4. THE PROBLEM OF RELATIVISM

In the late nineteenth and early twentieth centuries 'historicism' became a term of abuse because it was often equated with relativism, i.e. the doctrine that moral and political values have no universal validity but are valid only for the specific epoch and culture in which they originate. The term acquired these connotations chiefly among the opponents of the historicists, especially Husserl and the neo-Kantians, Windelband and Rickert.[20] It is noteworthy, however, that no historicist regarded himself as a relativist, and all were eager to avoid any such accusation. One looks in vain for a relativist among the ranks of the historicists—though the alarmist rhetoric is such that one expects them to lurk around every street corner.

On the face of it, the equation of historicism with relativism is understandable. It seemed the straightforward implication of some common historicist doctrines. One of these doctrines was the historicist rejection of the natural law tradition, and the insistence that one determine the laws and policies of a state from its specific circumstances and traditions. The historicists had argued that these laws and policies cannot be determined from outside according to some supra-historical standpoint, but only from inside according to local conditions and history. Since local conditions and histories differ, the historicist

---

[18] Herder, *Auch eine Philosophie der Geschichte der Menschheit*, in *Sämtliche Werke*, ed. Bernard Suphan (Berlin: Weidmann, 1891), v. 510.

[19] Möser, 'Wer die Kunst verstand, verriet den Meister nicht', in *Sämtliche Werke: Historisch-kritische Ausgabe*, ed. Akademie der Wissenschaften zu Göttingen (Osnabrück: Wenner, 1944–95), x. 204–5.

[20] See, for example, Husserl, 'Philosophie als strenge Wissenschaft', *Logos* I (1910/11), 323; and Windelband, 'Kritische oder Genetische Methode?', in *Präludien: Aufsätze und Reden zur Philosophie und ihrer Geschichte* (Tübingen: Mohr, 1921), ii. 132; and Rickert, *Die Probleme der Geschichtsphilosophie* (Heidelberg: Carl Winter, 1924), 129.

would have to accept different, even conflicting, laws and policies for different states.

It is questionable, however, that this doctrine implies a complete relativism. Although *specific* laws and policies will differ, they could still be variations upon more general principles. This was indeed the position of many historicists, viz. Herder, Rehberg, Dilthey, Droysen, and Burckhardt, who, despite their emphasis on historical change and variation, continued to believe in universal moral principles and the uniformity of human nature. It is also important to note the precise purport of their critique of the natural law tradition. The historicist's critique of the natural law tradition was not a rejection of universal principles as such but only of their blind and dogmatic application. While the historicists affirmed the validity of universal principles, they insisted that they had to be applied differently to different circumstances; general principles took on different specific forms according to local traditions and cultures.

Another historicist theme that seemed to imply relativism was its critique of the pragmatic history of the Enlightenment. Pragmatic history would examine the past for the sake of moral instruction, and it was therefore committed to making moral judgments on past actions and cultures. The historicists rejected pragmatic history, however, because it judged the past by the standards of the present; it was guilty of 'ethnocentrism', i.e. assuming that the values of one's own culture are valid for all others. While the pragmatic historians would pretend to judge the past according to the standards of a universal reason, they were really judging them according to the prejudices and conventions of their own age; their apparently 'natural' or universal principles were really only an illicit generalization from the values of their own culture, which were those of eighteenth-century Europe. For the historicists, the paradigm case of such a fallacy was Voltaire's judgment upon the Middle Ages in his *Siècle de Louis XIV*, which condemned the monks and saints basically because they did not have the values and views of late seventeenth-century French courtiers.

Here, too, however, it is questionable that this historicist theme implies a radical relativism. The historicist need not claim that *all* judgments on the past are ethnocentric, only that *some* of them are, and that we have to be careful to note the difference. The principle that we should not judge the past in terms of the present is indeed a moral principle itself. The whole issue was put nicely in a late lecture by the ageing Ranke. While Ranke insisted that the historian should attempt to be objective and impartial, rising above all partisan disputes, he readily acknowledged that the historian had a moral principle all his own: the attempt to do justice to all moral and religious existence.[21]

The question remains, however, how the historicists could justify their moral principles. Granted that they wanted to affirm their universal validity, how could they defend them, especially in the face of historical change and variability? But it was precisely in this regard that historicism falters. Having rejected the natural law tradition, the ball was now in the historicists' court; it was up to them to develop an alternative justification of the principles of morality. But few of them answered this question directly. We must remember that most historicists were practicing historians rather than philosophers. Their philosophical interests were largely limited to the problems of historical knowledge, and they devoted little attention to ethics as such. Their belief in moral principles seemed to rest, for the most part, in their faith in a constant and uniform human nature; but it is difficult to see how this concept could be anything more than an empty abstraction after one subtracts all the concrete differences between people in history. They were not willing to accept Hegel's solution to the problem: that all the different epochs of world history are attempts to realize a single universal goal. They rejected this solution as too speculative. Since they insisted on empirical standards of proof, they doubted the possibility of finding sufficient evidence to determine the laws for *world* history. What, then, is left? Ranke and Droysen had an answer, though they admitted it was a personal one: Christian faith.[22] Both of them affirmed a belief in providence, that God directs history for the good, though all we ever have is a glimpse into his mysterious ways. But this answer was likely to satisfy only the Christian faithful. For anyone else, the historicists had left a moral vacuum, a problem with no solution. Although they were not guilty of affirming relativism, they had no explanation for how the belief in a universal morality could be combined with their general principles.

The historicist most troubled by the problem of relativism was also the most philosophical among them: Dilthey. He made the problem the central subject of a late manuscript, 'Das geschichtliche Bewusstsein und die Weltanschauung.'[23] The task of the manuscript was to resolve the 'antinomy between the

---

[21] See 'Einleitung zu einer Vorlesung über Neuere Geschichte', 1859–1861, in *Aus Werk und Nachlass*, iv. 295.

[22] See Ranke's 'Idee der Universalhistorie', *Aus Werk und Nachlass*, iv. 77, 83; and Droysen's early essay 'Theologie der Geschichte', in *Historik*, 369–85.

[23] *Gesammelte Schriften*, viii. 3–71.

claim of every worldview to universal validity with historical consciousness'. The problem, as Dilthey formulated it, is that each metaphysics or worldview makes a claim to universal validity; it attempts to resolve in a systematic manner through reason 'the life or world puzzle'. But 'the historical consciousness' shows that each worldview is the product of specific historical circumstances. This suggests that its validity is also limited to these circumstances: 'What is conditioned by historical relations is also relative in its validity.'[24] 'World history as world judgment shows each metaphysical system to be relative, transitory, perishable.'[25] How is it possible to escape this antinomy? Dilthey's solution is to resolve it within the realm of historical consciousness. If history causes the wound, so it will heal it.[26] The more we examine the development of the various kinds of worldviews in history, he argues, the more we see that each expresses one and the same life under different circumstances. Each is true because it sees one side of the universe; it is one perspective upon it; but each is one-sided and has to be supplemented by others to get the whole truth.[27] There is no contradiction between them as long as we recognize that each is valid only from its perspective.

Dilthey's solution was as problematic as it was sketchy. By granting each worldview only a relative validity from its historical perspective, Dilthey had clearly forfeited the claim to universal validity that it was his intention to preserve. It was precisely this aspect of his historicism that would become the target of neo-Kantian criticism. *Pace* Dilthey, Windelband and Rickert argued that the only way to avoid such relativism is to leave the historical realm entirely and enter into the domain of the transcendental.[28] They insisted that it is necessary to distinguish two questions, which had been utterly confused by Dilthey. One is the *quid facti?* or genetic question, which concerns the *origin* of our knowledge; the other is the *quid juris?* or critical question, which concerns the *validity* of knowledge. When Dilthey reasoned that 'what is conditioned by historical relations is limited in its validity' he was guilty of a non sequitur, which came precisely from confusing these two questions. Whenever we deal with the question of validity, Rickert and Windelband argued, we are no longer concerned with history at all but are concerned with matters of evidence and purely logical relations. Responding to these criticisms, Dilthey countered that

---

[24] *Gesammelte Schriften*, viii. 6.
[25] Ibid. viii. 12.    [26] Ibid. viii. 10, 12, 222.    [27] Ibid. viii. 8, 12, 222.
[28] See Windelband, 'Kritische und Genetische Methode?' and 'Normen und Naturgesetze', in *Präludien*, ii. 59–98, 99–135; and Rickert, *Kulturwissenschaft und Naturwissenschaft* (Tübingen: Mohr, 1921), 12–20.

the transcendental realm of the neo-Kantians was a fiction, an hypostasis, and that it is impossible to distinguish between the critical and genetic questions. The quarrel between Dilthey and the neo-Kantians, which we cannot pursue further here, was one of the most fruitful and fateful in the development of early twentieth-century philosophy.[29]

# 5. THE CRISES OF HISTORICISM

In the first decades of the twentieth century, scholars in Germany began to write about a 'crisis of historicism'. They developed this concept to explain the puzzling collapse of historicism as an intellectual movement. Historicism had been one of the most powerful intellectual movements in nineteenth-century Germany; but toward the end of the century it seemed to have exhausted itself, to have lost all confidence in itself; and, after World War I, it was only a matter of writing its epitaph. What happened? What led to the collapse of one of the most important and influential intellectual movements of the modern era? There are many accounts of the crisis of historicism; and because they differ so much, it is more accurate to talk about 'crises' in the plural. Here all that we can do is take note of some of these accounts.

According to one popular theory,[30] the crisis of historicism came from the relativism implicit in the historicist approach to human values. If values are the product of a specific social and historical context, and if these contexts are unique, individual, and incommensurable, it appears as if there are no universal human values, and as if they cannot have any transcendent sanction beyond their own immediate context. Since historicism was regarded as relativist in its implications, it was taken to be a major source of nihilism, the feeling of the meaninglessness of life made popular by Nietzsche.

According to another theory, the crisis of historicism had its roots in Schopenhauer's and Nietzsche's attack upon the values and culture behind historicism.[31] Although Schopenhauer's critique did little more than reinstate

---

[29] For more details about this debate, see Michael Ermath, *Wilhelm Dilthey: The Critique of Historical Reason* (Chicago: University of Chicago Press, 1978), 186–97.

[30] This account of the crisis came from Troeltsch. See his 'Die Krise des Historismus', *Die neue Rundschau* 33 (1922), 572–90. This article is an epitome of his massive *Der Historismus und seine Probleme* (Tübingen: Mohr, 1922).

[31] See Schnädelbach, *Philosophy in Germany*, 62–4.

the old objection against history as a science, it was still effective because of the growing influence of his philosophy after the middle of the century.[32] While Nietzsche's work sparked little immediate reaction, it became more influential in time and weighed heavily with the post-war generation.

According to yet another theory,[33] the crisis of historicism began in the 1890s with the publication of Karl Lamprecht's *Deutsche Geschichte* (1891), which advanced a conception of history based on the natural sciences. Lamprecht believed that history should determine general laws of cause and effect just like the natural sciences. In defending his methodology, Lamprecht launched an attack on the methods of the most important historians of the Wilhelmine era (Friedrich Meinecke, Max Delbrück, Otto Hintze, Max Lenz, Hermann Oncken, Georg von Below), who had grown up in the historicist tradition. The result was an acrimonious debate between Lamprecht and Below, the so-called *Lamprecht-Streit*, about historical method. While this debate shed more heat than light, and while it certainly did not topple historicist hegemony, it did force historicists to think more critically about their own methodology. The ultimate effect of the debate was Windelband's and Rickert's attempt to formulate the methods of historical study and their differences from the natural sciences.[34]

Still another theory of the crisis of historicism associates it with the collapse in attempts to find meaning, structure and progress in history.[35] The chief cause of this collapse came from the aftermath of the Great War, the widespread sense that millions of young lives were sacrificed for a lost cause and no apparent reason. Although the historicists were skeptical that historical research would ever vindicate the claims of universal history, they never lost their faith in progress and providence. Some of the leading German historicists—Troeltsch and Meinecke—were liberal nationalists who believed firmly in the values of a strong central German state, which could direct history down the path toward greater freedom, equality, and welfare.

---

[32] See Schnädelbach, *Philosophy in Germany*, 60. Both Troeltsch and Dilthey testify to the influence of Schopenhauer's critique. See Troeltsch, 'Krise', 583, and Dilthey, *Das Wesen der Philosophie*, in *Gesammelte Schriften*, v. 371/

[33] See Jaeger and Rüsen, *Geschichte des Historismus*, 141–6.

[34] On Windelband and Rickert, see Bambach, *Heidegger, Dilthey and the Crisis of Historicism*, 57–126; Iggers, *German Conception of History*, 147–59; and Jaeger and Rüsen, *Geschichte des Historismus*, 151–6.

[35] See, for example, Bambach, *Heidegger, Dilthey and the Crisis of Historicism*, 1–20; Georg G. Iggers, *The German Conception of History* (Middletown, CN: Wesleyan University Press, 1968), 128–9; and Meinecke, 'Von der Krisis des Historismus', in *Werke* iv. 200–1.

The actual conduct of the war by the German state, however, completely undermined their faith. Rather than leading the German nation toward more freedom and happiness, the German state slaughtered an entire generation for a bankrupt cause.

According to one final theory,[36] the crisis of historicism came from its own inner contradictions, more specifically from the conflict between its ideal of objective knowledge and its own belief in the powerful conditioning forces of history. Some historicists assumed an ideal of objective knowledge, as if the historian could somehow stand above the flux of history and determine the pure truth independent of all values and preconceptions. Yet historicism itself shows such an ideal of knowledge to be utterly naive. The tension is obvious: if all human standpoints are subject to historical and cultural conditioning, how does the historian write an objective and impartial history? His own standpoint should be subject to the conditions of his own culture and epoch, so that the historian too is caught in the web of his own relativism.

Which of these accounts is correct? All of them and none. All of them because they all point to real problems in the historicist tradition; none of them because they cannot explain the disappearance of the historicist tradition. Behind all accounts of the crisis of historicism there was the tacit assumption that historicism disappeared because of some deep tragic flaw or some inherent contradiction. There is, however, a much simpler explanation. Here we only need to recall the original project of historicism: to make history a science. In attempting to achieve this goal the historicists were remarkably successful. At least they made history into a recognized academic subject taught in all the universities and having the same prestige as the natural sciences. Skeptics only need to consider the remarkable rise of history as an academic discipline in Germany since the movement began in the middle of the eighteenth century.[37] So the reason for historicism's demise is simple: having achieved what it set out to do, historicism did not need to exist anymore. Historicism was not an abject failure, but an astonishing success. Since it continues to exercise such enormous influence, it never really died at all.

[36]  Thus Iggers, *German Conception of History*, 124, 133, 141, 143.
[37]  On the development of the institutional substructure of historicism, see Konrad Jarausch, 'The Institutionalization of History in 18th-Century Germany', in Hans Erich Bödeker et al. (eds.), *Aufklärung und Geschichte* (Göttingen, Vandanhoeck & Ruprecht, 1986), 25–48.

# 6. The Study of Historicism

Anyone who embarks upon the study of historicism should be wary: he enters an intellectual minefield. The very word 'historicism' poses dangers. One of these is anachronism. 'Historicism' became common as an historiographic term to refer to a specific intellectual tradition only in the 1930s after the publication of Friedrich Meinecke's *Die Entstehung des Historismus*. Following Dilthey's lead,[38] Meinecke traced the origins of historicism to such eighteenth-century writers as Montesquieu, Herder, Möser, and Goethe. He saw the pinnacle of the historicist tradition in his teacher, Leopold von Ranke. It is noteworthy, however, that none of these thinkers would have referred to themselves as historicists; it is likely that few of them ever heard the word. When Dilthey was called an 'historicist' by one of his critics, he brusquely rejected the label, because of its relativist and nihilist associations.[39]

Another danger behind the term 'historicism' is that it has acquired opposing meanings because it has been used to refer to diametrically opposed views of history. According to one view, the purpose of history is to know the general laws or ends of history; its aim is to find the system or unity behind the chaos of the past. According to the other view, the purpose of history is to know the individual, to plumb the depths of the unique and singular, through exacting detailed research; it rejects the possibility of discovering general laws or ends of history. While these laws or ends might exist, it is impossible for us to know them through empirical research. The first view appears in late Herder and the German idealists, who developed a systematic philosophy of history; the latter view surfaces in Ranke, Droysen, Dilthey, and Burckhardt, who rejected the very possibility of a systematic philosophy of history and who stressed the importance of historical individuality. Both views have been called 'historicist' because they stress the importance of history for the understanding of human life and action, and because they claim that the methods and standards of historical knowledge are distinct from those of the natural sciences. Despite their shared principles, these traditions were frequently at odds with one another. Hence Droysen, Ranke, Dilthey, and Burckhardt were deeply hostile to Fichte's and Hegel's philosophy of history,

---

[38]  See Dilthey, 'Das Achtzehnte Jahrhundert und die Geschichtliche Welt', in *Gesammelte Schriften*, iii. 209–68. Dilthey did not use the term 'historicism'.

[39]  See Walter Biemel, 'Der Briefwechsel Dilthey-Husserl', *Man and World* 1 (1968), 434.

which, they claimed, forced the richness and detail of history into a conceptual straitjacket.

The history of the word 'historicism' (*Historismus*), only the barest outlines of which can be recounted here, reflects some of these confusions.[40] The common claim that it first had a pejorative meaning is false. It appears as early as the late eighteenth century in the writings of the German romantics, who used it in a neutral sense. In 1797 Friedrich Schlegel used 'historicism' to refer to a philosophy that stresses the importance of history; a little later the same usage resurfaces in Novalis's notebooks.[41] The term came into wider use by the middle of the nineteenth century in the wake of Hegelianism. It is noteworthy that already by then the word was used in both senses noted above. Thus in 1847 C. J. Braniss championed an 'historicism' that attempts to discover the general laws of history; he contrasted 'historicism' with 'naturalism': while naturalism attempts to explain all of reality, including history, according to natural laws, historicism tries to explain all of reality, including nature, according to historical laws.[42] However, in 1852, Carl Prantl wrote of a 'true historicism' that recognizes concrete historical individuality, which he opposed to a speculative philosophy of history that attempts to formulate general laws.[43] By mid-century the most common use of the term was to refer to the methods of the historical school of law. It was only toward the end of the century that the term acquired its derogatory sense when two political economists, Carl Menger and Eugen Dühring, described 'historicism' as the undue neglect of theory for the sake of history. Only after World War I did 'historicism' become a widely discussed and controversial concept. It was Ernst Troeltsch who made the term notorious by writing about 'the crisis of historicism'.[44] He defined historicism as 'the historicizing of our entire knowing and experiencing of the spiritual world, as it has taken place in the course of the nineteenth century'.[45] In 1932 Karl Heussi noted three different

[40]  On the early use of the term, see the article in *Historisches Wörterbuch der Philosophie* (Stuttgart: Schwabe & Co., 1974), iii. 1141–7; Erich Rothacker, 'Historismus', in *Schmollers Jahrbuch* 62 (1938), 388–99, and 'Das Wort 'Historismus'', *Zeitschrift für deutsche Wortforschung* 16 (1960), 3–6; and the article 'Historicism' in *Dictionary of the History of Ideas* (New York: Scribner, 1973), ii. 456–64.

[41]  See Friedrich Schlegel, *Fragmente zur Poesie und Literatur, Kritische Ausgabe*, ed. Hans Eichner (Paderborn: Schöningh, 1981), XVIII, 91, 481; and Novalis, *Das Allgemeine Brouillon #927*, in *Werke, Tagebücher und Briefe*, ed. Hans-Jachim Mähl and Richard Samuel (Munich: Hanser, 1978), ii. 688.

[42]  Christian Johann Braniss, *Die wissenschaftliche Aufgabe der Gegenwart als leitende Idee im akademischen Studium* (Breslau: Gosohorsky, 1848), 113–38.

[43]  Carl Prantl, *Die gegenwärtige Aufgabe der Philosophie* (Munich: Akademie der Wissenschaften, 1852), 19, 31, 38.

[44]  See the sources cited in n. 30, above.    [45]  Troeltsch, 'Krisis', 573.

senses of the term 'historicism' common in German intellectual discourse: (1) the specialized study of history for its own sake, regardless of practical needs; (2) any attempt to take history beyond its appropriate bounds within the general realm of intellectual discourse; and (3) a neutral historical sense to refer to a specific intellectual movement in the nineteenth century.[46] It was the third and more neutral sense that eventually prevailed and still persists today.

Apart from the pitfalls surrounding the term 'historicism', there are other serious problems confronting the student of historicism. Not the least of these is that the subject is so controversial. The controversies are many, but the major one concerns the very concept of historicism itself. There is a longstanding contradiction corresponding to the opposing uses of the term noted above. The contradiction reflects a cultural and linguistic divide, since one concept of historicism is prevalent in the Anglophone world, the other in the Germanic world. The meaning of historicism in the contemporary Anglophone world has been largely set by Karl Popper's *The Poverty of Historicism*. Popper defined historicism as 'an approach to the social sciences which assumes that *historical prediction* is their principal aim, and which assumes that this aim is attainable by discovering the 'rhythms' or the 'patterns', the 'laws' or the 'trends' that underlie the evolution of history'.[47] Attacking any attempt to determine laws or trends of history, Popper advocated an approach that would value the singular, unique, and specific: 'I wish to defend the view, so often attacked as old-fashioned by historicists, that *history is characterized by its interest in actual, singular, or specific events, rather than in laws or generalizations.*'[48] It is Popper's usage that has been enshrined in dictionaries and drilled into the minds of Anglophone social scientists.[49]

The main problem with Popper's concept of historicism is that it is too narrow; it applies to only one phase or branch of the historicist tradition. As we have just seen, the term 'historicism' has also been used to refer to an intellectual movement that *criticized* the attempt to establish general laws of history, and which emphasized the *singularity* of historical events. Ironically, many classical nineteenth-century 'historicists' would have rejected what Popper called historicism, and they would have done so on Popperian grounds!

---

[46]   Karl Heussi, *Die Krisis des Historismus* (Tübingen: Mohr, 1932), 6–15.
[47]   Karl Popper, *The Poverty of Historicism* (London: Routledge & Kegan Paul, 1957), 3.
[48]   Ibid. 143.
[49]   See, for example, the definitions of 'historicism' in *The Oxford Concise Dictionary* (Oxford: Clarendon Press, 1964), 472, and in the *Oxford Dictionary of Philosophy* (Oxford: Oxford University Press, 1994), 174.

For this tradition, Popper's diatribe against the philosophy of history would have been a tired old refrain. Of course, Sir Karl, like Humpty Dumpty, has the right to make words mean what he wants them to mean; but the baronial manner in which he made use of this privilege, and his enormous influence in the Anglophone world, has only led to misunderstanding. After Popper 'refuted' historicism, people believed that another tradition, unfortunately using the same name, had been dead and buried.

The concept of historicism in the Germanic world has largely been formed by Meinecke's *Die Entstehung des Historismus*.[50] Meinecke famously declared that historicism was 'nothing more than the application of the new principles of life, which were discovered in the great German movement from Leibniz to Goethe, to historical life'.[51] There were two such principles: individuality and development. The principle of individuality means that historical events, actions, or personalities should be studied in all their particularity and for their own sake. Following in the tradition of Ranke, Meinecke held that history is unlike the natural sciences because its characteristic aim is to individuate and differentiate particular events, actions, and personalities. The principle of development states that all human activities and institutions change and evolve in history, and that they should be understood within a process of development. Besides these principles, Meinecke would often stress a third characteristic of historicism: irrationalism. He called historicism irrationalist because the individual, which is the specific object of historical investigation, is ineffable. The fundamental dictum of the historicist, Meinecke said, is *individuum est ineffabile*. While the historian would indeed attempt to describe the individual, he would also acknowledge that none of his descriptions would ever exhaust it; there remained something to the individual that would forever elude analysis and explanation. This third principle was Meinecke's guarantee of historical autonomy, the independence of history from philosophy and the natural sciences. The ineffability of the particular meant that the object of history is *sui generis*, that it would never disappear in a welter of philosophical concepts or natural laws.

Meinecke's concept of historicism is no less problematic than Popper's. For one thing, the concepts of individuality and development are either

---

[50]  See, for example, Jaeger and Rüsen, *Geschichte des Historismus*, 7–8; Schnädelbach, *Geschichtsphilosophie*, 19; and Iggers, *German Conception of History*, 3–28. Iggers limits the term to the idiographic tradition, though he also claims, somewhat inconsistently, that the unity of the historicist tradition rests upon its origins in German idealism.

[51]  Meinecke, *Entstehung*, 2.

ambiguous or vague. The concept of individuality is ambiguous: it might be a particular, but it also might be an irreducible whole, of which many particulars are parts. Meinecke shifts constantly between these senses, not a little to the confusion of his readers, who first think that the subject of history is individual human beings, only to find that it is also states, cultures, and epochs. The concept of development is vague. When finally pushed to define it in his later years, Meinecke gave it a remarkably Hegelian flavor.[52] He explained that development is more than the self-conscious and voluntary actions of individuals; it also involves the tendencies and directions of history as a whole, of which individuals are only parts. Development is indeed the realization of 'the special spirit' of an epoch. But if this is what development means, it is far from clear that it would be affirmed by all historicists, some of whom denied that history is more than the actions of particular individuals, and most of whom denied that it is possible to know general developments or tendencies.

There are two further difficulties with Meinecke's concept. First, it is an error to characterize historicism as irrationalist, either by intention or by implication. Meinecke neglected the attempt in the historicist tradition to develop alternative models of explanation to those of the natural sciences, specifically the central role of hermeneutics in the work of Boeckh, Droysen, and Dilthey. The hermeneutical tradition attempts to avoid the dilemma between irrationalism and naturalistic explanation by forming another paradigm of understanding from the interpretation of texts. Second, Meinecke's central thesis that the historicist tradition simply applies the concepts of life to the historical world is a mistake. Droysen and Dilthey explicitly rejected the application of organic concepts to history on the grounds that it could not explain what is characteristic of history. Following Hegel, they made a sharp distinction between the realm of life and that of history. History was the realm of spirit, which is not simply life but the self-awareness of life. For Droysen and Dilthey, the organic still belongs to the domain of nature, which is not yet history. The source of both Meinecke's mistakes is all too easy to see: he made Ranke, his teacher, into the paradigm of historicism. The principles of individuality and development apply perfectly to Ranke; but Ranke does not define historicism.

It should be clear from this brief survey that the study of historicism is a risky undertaking. I have tried to point out some of the worst pitfalls. But I

---

[52] Meinecke clarified his use of the term in his important essay, 'Ein Wort über geschichtliche Entwicklung', in *Zur Theorie und Philosophie der Geschichte* (Stuttgart: Koehler, 1965), 102–16.

hope it is also clear that the study of historicism, in the Germanic as well as the Anglophone world, is still in its infancy. A proper history of historicism, as Meinecke himself would readily concede, has never been written. So, ultimately, at least for the properly prepared and warned student, the study of historicism presents more opportunities than pitfalls.

# CHAPTER 6

# WHAT HAVE WE BEEN MISSING?

## SCIENCE AND PHILOSOPHY IN TWENTIETH-CENTURY FRENCH THOUGHT

GARY GUTTING

## I. INTRODUCTION: PHILOSOPHY vs. SCIENCE

WHAT we now call 'philosophy of science' developed in the nineteenth century from continuations of and reactions to Kant's critical philosophy. The project arose from modern science's challenge to the cognitive authority of traditional philosophy. Galileo, Descartes, and Newton no doubt thought of themselves as philosophers, answering fundamental questions about the nature of planetary and terrestrial motions that had been central for 'natural philosophy' since

Plato and Aristotle. It gradually became apparent, however, that the empirical methods of the new natural philosophy were quite different from the a priori methods of traditional philosophy; and the question gradually arose of what, if anything, there remained for philosophy in the traditional sense to do. Kant placed this question at the center of philosophical thinking, where it has remained ever since.

Philosophical discussions of science have, after Kant, displayed three fundamental attitudes toward scientific knowledge. The empiricist or, more precisely, the *positivist attitude*, sees science as the sole ultimate cognitive authority. The only role for philosophy is as a reflection on science that clarifies its conclusions and makes explicit its methods. (On some views, even this philosophical reflection is a part of empirical science, perhaps a division of psychology.) The *critical attitude*, deriving from Kant's own work, accepts science as the only first-order knowledge, but preserves for philosophy a distinctive domain of truth: that concerning the necessary conditions for the possibility of scientific knowledge. Here the idea is that justifying philosophical truths requires presupposing the validity of science, but these truths themselves (unlike those of positivist philosophy of science) constitute a domain of 'transcendental' truth that is of a different order from that of science. Finally, what I will call the *ontological attitude* maintains the traditional view of philosophy as ultimate cognitive authority, asserting that there are philosophical truths entirely independent of science and even cognitively superior to scientific truths. This superiority is variously located in philosophy's more general, more fundamental, or more concrete vision of reality, of which science is just one subordinate part and in terms of which it must be understood.

These three attitudes define, in particular, the main directions in French philosophy of science during the twentieth century. The positivist attitude is typically found among reflective scientists and philosophers deeply involved in science. The most famous proponents in France were Henri Poincaré, Pierre Duhem, and Émile Meyerson, founders not only of French philosophy of science but also of what developed into the dominant Anglo-American direction in philosophy of science. However, during the first two decades of the twentieth-century, positivism in France was overshadowed by a revival of Kantian thinking, most prominently in the work of Lachelier, Boutroux, and Brunschvicg. This neo-Kantian turn took the specific form of philosophy of science in the work of Gaston Bachelard and his successor, Georges

Canguilhem, and was extended and transformed in a distinctly maverick way by Michel Foucault.[1] The ontological attitude arose first in Bergson and, later, was revived in a distinctive way in existential phenomenology, particularly by Maurice Merleau-Ponty.

After its beginnings, French philosophy of science developed in essential separation from work elsewhere—particularly, from the philosophy of science dominant in the United States and Britain. Precisely because of this causal independence, French work is extremely valuable for anyone seeking a critical perspective on Anglo-American philosophy of science. First, even from their positivist outset, the French avoided the naïve forms of empiricism and foundationalism too often found in Anglophone philosophy of science. Also from the outset, they saw the philosophy of science as inseparable from its history and, well before the Kuhnian revolution, developed deep and subtle perspectives on science as an essentially historical enterprise. Most important, whereas philosophy of science in English-speaking countries has almost always proceeded on the positivist assumption that science provides the only substantive knowledge of the natural world, French work has most often proceeded from what I am calling the critical and the ontological attitudes.

The positivist strand of French philosophy of science, particularly the work of Poincaré and Duhem, has been a significant presence in the history of Anglo-American philosophy of science and has, to an important extent, been assimilated into its thinking. I will, therefore, focus rather on the critical and the ontological strands. Through fairly detailed discussion of two examples, I will show how attention to French philosophy of science can enrich our thinking about science. The first example uses the critical approach of Bachelard and Canguilhem to restore intellectual energy to the debates over issues raised by Kuhn's *The Structure of Scientific Revolutions*. The second example uses the ontological approach of Bergson and Merleau-Ponty to engage the issue, little discussed by Anglo-American philosophers of science, of the alleged need to supplement science with a distinctive domain of philosophical knowledge. In both cases, I hope to show that the French tradition of philosophy of science fruitfully supplements and challenges current Anglophone discussions of science.

---

[1]  For a treatment of Foucault in relation to the Bachelard–Canguilhem 'network', see my *Michel Foucault's Archaeology of Scientific Reason* (Cambridge: Cambridge University Press, 1989).

# II. The Critical Attitude
## and the Kuhnian Problematic

By the 'Kuhnian problematic' I mean the set of issues bequeathed by Kuhn's *The Structure of Scientific Revolutions* concerning the progress of science, the ontological significance of scientific theories, and the rationality of scientific judgments. Long before Kuhn's book, French philosophers of science taking the critical attitude had been discussing these issues as they arise for a historicist conception of science. As a result, French thinkers typically saw the Anglophone furor over the 'Kuhnian revolution' as old news, which they had recognized and fruitfully assimilated long before.[2] This Gallic self-congratulation was not entirely justified, since the work of Kuhn's 'precursors' had not decisively dealt with many of the problems raised by Anglo-American discussions of science as an historical entity. But it is also true that post-Kuhnian discussions of these issues have been unproductive for a long time, with many philosophers of science simply moving on to new topics. The French treatment of these issues suggests ways of reanimating the Kuhnian discussion.

Foucault, commenting on the philosophical world in which he was educated, pointed out that there had long been a basic split in French thought between a 'philosophy of experience, of meaning, of the subject and a philosophy of knowledge [*savoir*], of rationality, and of the concept'.[3] In Foucault's student days, the 'philosophy of experience' was, of course, existential phenomenology (although Bergson's philosophy was an earlier major example). The 'philosophy of the concept' was historically tied to the French tradition, ultimately traceable to Comte, of the history and philosophy of science. In the latter half of the twentieth century, this tradition was primarily represented by Gaston Bachelard and Georges Canguilhem, Bachelard's successor at the Sorbonne. Although their work was scarcely known outside of France, Bachelard and Canguilhem were major influences on several generations of French philosophy students, and their 'philosophy of the concept' remained a significant alternative to existential philosophy.

---

[2] When George Steiner criticized Foucault for (in *The Order of Things*) not mentioning Kuhn, Foucault responded that he had instead cited a thinker who had anticipated Kuhn, Georges Canguilhem ('Foucault responds 2', *Diacritics*, 1/2 (Winter 1971), 60).

[3] Michel Foucault, 'Life: Experience and Science', in *The Essential Works of Michel Foucault, 1954–1984*, ii: *Aesthetics, Method, and Epistemology* (Harmondsworth: Penguin, 1998), 466.

Indeed, but for the contingencies of World War II, there might well have been a 'conceptual' appropriation of Husserl to rival Sartre's and Merleau-Ponty's 'experiential' readings. Jean Cavaillès (1903–44), writing in the 1940s, had offered a brilliant formal reading of Husserl that moved his thought away from its Heideggerian future and back toward its origins in logic and the philosophy of mathematics. Unfortunately, Cavaillès, who was one of the founders of the French Resistance, was captured by the Germans and executed. His 'rationalist' development of phenomenology was continued by, for example, Suzanne Bachelard (the daughter of Gaston Bachelard) and by the Belgian Jean Ladrière. But the existentialized Husserl remained dominant.

As a result, the philosophy of the concept was developed in a non-Husserlian direction by Bachelard and then by Canguilhem. Canguilhem's work is deeply Bachelardian, although his approach is more that of a philosophical historian than of, like Bachelard, a historically sensitive philosopher. Moreover, Canguilhem worked almost entirely on the biological and medical sciences, whereas Bachelard focused on physics and chemistry. I will sketch the relevant features of Bachelard's and Canguilhem's critical philosophy of science as a basis for showing their significance for the Kuhnian problematic.

## Gaston Bachelard

Bachelard's work was deeply rooted in Léon Brunschvicg's idealist histories of science, but with a sharper focus on the recent history of physics and a much more ambivalent attitude toward idealism. He also differed from Brunschvicg (and most other philosophers of science) in his insistence on radical discontinuities in the history of science. More than thirty years before Kuhn's work on scientific revolutions, Bachelard presented the history of physics as a series of epistemic 'breaks' in which one conception of nature was replaced by a radically different conception. He also pointed to an initial fundamental break that initiated a scientific account of the world in opposition to accounts (such as Aristotle's) derived from common-sense categories.

Bachelard thought philosophers needed to pay particular attention to radical changes in science since philosophy must always 'go to the school of the sciences': its project is precisely that of developing new philosophical conceptions corresponding to each new stage of scientific achievement. He was particularly concerned that, in the wake of the relativistic and quantum revolutions, philosophers no longer employ the Cartesian and

Kantian concepts that formulated a philosophy appropriate to Galilean and Newtonian science. Such outdated concepts are now what Bachelard called *epistemological obstacles* to our understanding of nature, and he worked to develop a philosophical standpoint that mirrored the new mode of thinking. He sought, for example, a 'non-Cartesian epistemology' (parallel to 'non-Euclidean geometry') that rejected the Cartesian foundationalist privileging of immediate experience. Also, although he maintained a Kantian active role for the mind, he moved to an epistemology that was non-Kantian in its rejection of essentially Newtonian categories such as substance and causality.[4]

Bachelard did not, however, think that his emphasis on breaks and discontinuity was inconsistent with scientific progress. Despite the conceptual and methodological breaks from one scientific worldview to another, there is still progress in the sense that some specific achievements are preserved within later science. So, for example, just as the Euclidean claim that all triangles have 180 degrees as the sum of their interior angles remains true of a special class of triangles ('Euclidean triangles') in Riemannian geometry, so the concepts of Newtonian mass remain valid in limit cases of relativity theory. Even a notion such as that of specific heat, which Joseph Black introduced as part of the now thoroughly outdated caloric theory, has maintained a role in contemporary chemistry parallel to the one it played in Black's work.

I have already mentioned Bachelard's ambivalence regarding idealism. He emphatically rejects a 'realism' that privileges 'the prolix richness of the individual sensation' over what it sees as 'the systematic impoverishment of abstractive thought'.[5] Against this sort of common-sense or empiricist realism he asserts the concrete ontological primacy of theoretical entities. His critique of such realism, however, amounts to what current analytic philosophers of science call 'scientific realism'.

On the other hand, unlike many philosophers of science, Bachelard does not think that his 'realistic' view of theoretical entities implies, in the manner of traditional metaphysical realism, that the objects of scientific knowledge are entirely mind-independent. He remains a rationalist in his insistence on both the mind's active construction of scientific concepts with which we describe

---

[4] At the same time, Bachelard recognized the essential role even of outdated common-sense and scientific images in human experience. He offered what he called a 'psychoanalysis' of certain images (such as earth, air, fire, and water), which presented them not only as obstacles to epistemological progress but also as perennial positive factors in poetic experience and expression. See, for example, *The Psychoanalysis of Fire*, trans. G. C. Waterston (New York: Orion, 1969).

[5] *La Valeur inductive de la relativité* (Paris: Vrin, 1929), 206.

reality and on the richness and specificity of these concepts in contrast to the vagueness and generality of sensations. But Bachelard also rejects the idealistic assertion that the world is constituted by pure thought. Truth is not the mind's creation, but the result of the mind's 'revision' (*rectification*) via scientific concepts of a world that is already there. His rationalism is, he says, 'applied': the mind does not create objects *ex nihilo* but rather applies concepts to pre-given objects. The point, however, is muddled by Bachelard's insistence that objects are not pre-given in any absolute sense; what is given at any point has been the outcome of previous applications of concepts. As a result, although Bachelard intends applied rationalism as a way between the unacceptable extremes of idealism and realism, his refusal to accept objects that exist independent of our conceptions seems to force him back to something very much like Brunschvicg's idealism.

Whatever its difficulties with idealism, Bachelard's applied rationalism provides, as I shall argue below, a starting point for fruitful thought about the ontological issues raised by Kuhn. Bachelard's view is also important because of its emphasis on the central role of scientific instrumentation in the constitution of the physical world. Anticipating the work of Ian Hacking, he says that instruments are 'theories materialized' and that concepts are scientific only to the extent that they are 'realized' through 'techniques of realization'.[6] Rather than Husserl's phenomenological description of the mind's constitution of the objects of ordinary experience we need, according to Bachelard, a 'phenomeno-technics' that will describe the constitution of scientific objects by instrumental technology.

## Georges Canguilhem

Canguilhem's most important methodological contribution is his distinction between concepts and theories. Philosophers of science have often regarded concepts as functions of theories and derived their meaning from the roles they play in theoretical explanations of observed phenomena. For example, 'mass' as employed by Newton and by Einstein express fundamentally different concepts because they operate in fundamentally different physical theories. This follows, however, only on the assumption that the interpretation of a phenomenon via a given set of concepts is equivalent to explaining the phenomenon in terms

---

[6] *The New Scientific Spirit*, trans. A. Goldhammer (Boston: Beacon Press, 1984), 16.

of a particular theoretical framework. Canguilhem, by contrast, asserts an essential distinction between the conceptual interpretation of phenomena and their theoretical explanation. A set of concepts gives a preliminary description of a phenomenon, which in turn provides the basis for questions about how to explain it. There will be very different theories—even though they are all formulated from the same set of concepts—providing competing answers to these questions. Galileo, for example, introduced a new conception of the motion of falling bodies that replaced the Aristotelian conception. Galileo, Descartes, and Newton all accepted this new conception in their work on falling bodies but used it to articulate very different theories of motion, thereby illustrating what Canguilhem calls the 'theoretical polyvalence' of Galileo's concepts. Canguilhem himself wrote a number of impressive histories of concepts (e.g. of reflex movement) that have persisted through a diverse series of theoretical formulations.[7]

The distinction between concepts and theories led Canguilhem to important deviations from Bachelard's view of science. For example, Canguilhem understood epistemological breaks as instances of conceptual rather than theoretical innovation. As a result, even radical theoretical changes may not effect epistemological breaks on the conceptual level. Correspondingly, Canguilhem refined Bachelard's notion of an epistemological obstacle, emphasizing that a conceptualization that is an epistemological obstacle in one theoretical context may be a creative breakthrough in another.

Canguilhem's adjustments of the notions of epistemological breaks and obstacles also weakens Bachelard's sharp distinction between science and non-science. Science is still understood as the intellectual project that overcomes epistemological obstacles and produces epistemological breaks. But to the extent that Canguilhem made the notions of obstacle and of break ambivalent, the notion of science becomes less well defined. Canguilhem is, accordingly, more hesitant than Bachelard to conclude that, in a given context, a given idea or approach is 'more scientific' than another.

Canguilhem also moves beyond Bachelard in his account of scientific rationality and objectivity, an account based on Canguilhem's extensive philosophico-historical treatment of norms. Having eschewed the absolute certitudes of Cartesian epistemology as well as the 'egocentric predicament' of modern philosophy, Bachelard was committed to grounding the objectivity of science in social norms. What we need, he said, is not the isolated *cogito*

---

[7]  For example, *La Formation du concept de reflex au XVIIe et XVIII siècle*, 2nd edn. (Paris: Vrin, 1977).

but the social *cogitamus*, which will take us from the subjectivity of the merely psychological to the objectivity of the epistemological. Unfortunately, Bachelard had very little to say about the nature of social norms and how they can function to guarantee rationality and objectivity.

Canguilhem offers a much more detailed treatment, rooted in his analysis of biological norms.[8] He notes that, in contrast to modern physics, which has no room for a distinction between normal and pathological states, modern biology, for all its rejection of teleology, requires a distinction between states that enhance the functioning of organisms and states that impede it: a distinction between health and disease. Canguilhem acknowledges that biological norms are not objective in any scientific sense. Physiology can describe the states that we call 'normal' or 'pathological', but their status precisely as normative comes not from the physiological description but from the meaning they have for the organism. Biological norms are, accordingly, subjective in the sense that their status as norms derives from the very organism to which they apply. On the other hand, 'subjective' does not here mean 'based in individual idiosyncrasy', since the 'subject' from which the norms derive is the biological nature of the organism in question. Even though biological norms are not independent of the needs and orientations of the organisms they govern, the relevant needs and orientations are those of the biological species as such.

Canguilhem further notes that there are important similarities between societies and organisms that allow social norms to have the same sort of necessity as biological norms. This is so, however, only for so-called traditional societies, where there is a set of norms that define the essential nature and purpose of the society. Modern societies have no such intrinsic finality and are defined by nothing more than the incontestability of any claims about what should be their fundamental direction. Nor does Canguilhem think that a merely de facto consensus among its members would legitimate norms for a modern society. As we will see below, he criticizes Kuhn for, as Canguilhem sees it, trying to derive norms from a contingent, merely psychological agreement that can have no regulative force. Similarly, Canguilhem criticizes Bachelard,[9] who, he says, poses but does not solve the problem of finding a middle ground between basing scientific norms on Cartesian foundations and reducing them to mere descriptions of empirical psychology. But Canguilhem himself also

---

[8] *On the Normal and the Pathological*, trans. C. R. Fawcett (Dordrecht: Reidel, 1978).
[9] *Etudes d'histoire et de philosophie des sciences*, 5th edn. (Paris: Vrin, 1983), 204–6.

fails to solve this problem and, despite the subtlety of his analysis, norms for him remain without a philosophical basis. Nevertheless, as we shall see, Canguilhem's approach can be developed into an effective response to Kuhn's problem of scientific rationality.

## Bachelard, Canguilhem, and the Kuhnian Problematic

### Progress and ontology

Like Bachelard and Canguilhem, Kuhn sees science as an essentially historical process that involves fundamental discontinuities ('revolutions') that raise serious questions about its linear progress (and, correspondingly, ontological significance) and rationality. One standard response to such questions is that science progresses in that later theories are typically closer to the truth than earlier ones. But Kuhn rejects such a notion of scientific progress because he finds no sense in the claim that a given scientific paradigm is true (or truer than another). His distrust of truth has two sources. First, Kuhn thinks competing paradigms assign different meanings to basic scientific terms: Newtonian and Einsteinian statements about mass, for example, only apparently conflict with one another and cannot be said to compete as assertions of truth. (This is one major context in which Kuhn talks of incommensurability.) Second, Kuhn thinks that truth implies correspondence between thought and reality and that there is no way around the 'vexing problems' raised by the idea of correspondence: 'There is, I think, no theory-independent way to reconstruct phrases like "really there"; the notion of a match between the ontology of a theory and its "real" counterpart now seems to me illusive in principle.'[10]

Having excluded truth, Kuhn turns to puzzle-solving for an explanation of scientific progress, now understood as a new paradigm's ability to answer questions (how to do certain calculations, how to explain certain experiments, etc.) that previous paradigms could not. Rival paradigms, however, disagree about which puzzles need solving and what counts as a solution. Galileo pointed to the superiority of his mechanics for the mathematical calculation of the rates at which heavy bodies fall to earth, but Aristotelians saw such calculation as marginal to the central issue, which Galileo ignored, of explaining why heavy bodies fall to earth. Even given agreement on a set of problems and criteria for solving them, there remains the intractable difficulty

---

[10] *The Structure of Scientific Revolutions*, 2nd edn. (Chicago: University of Chicago Press, 1970), 'Postscript', 206.

of assessing the relative puzzle-solving power of rival paradigms. There is no way of rationally counting the number of puzzles a paradigm solves, and, even if there were, there would remain the difficulty of judging whether some puzzles are more important to solve than others. Puzzle-solving seems quite incapable of providing an adequate account of scientific progress.

The Bachelard–Canguilhem tradition of critical philosophy of science provides a very helpful perspective on Kuhn's problem. Whereas Kuhn sees the discontinuity of science—apparent in the incommensurability of successive theories—as an insuperable obstacle to progress toward truth, Bachelard suggests that, despite fundamental discontinuities, some scientific achievements attain a perennial status: 'One may smile at the dogmatism of a rationalist philosopher who writes "forever" regarding a scholastic truth. But there are concepts so indispensable in scientific culture that we cannot conceive being led to abandon them.'[11] Not that the concepts in question are unaltered as science progresses. But a condition on the progress of science is that the concepts be reformulated so that they—and truths expressed in their terms—are preserved in subsequent accounts. So, for example, Black's concept of specific heat, although initially formulated in terms of caloric theory, has reappeared in Newtonian and then quantum accounts of heat.

Bachelard's approach here is reinforced by Canguilhem's distinction of concept and theory. For Kuhn the meanings of terms in rival paradigms are incommensurable because he thinks concepts vary with their use in different theoretical contexts. But Canguilhem shows that the same concept can occur in quite different theoretical contexts; for example, the concept of a reflex action in an organism was first introduced by Thomas Willis in the context of a vitalistic theory based on traditional ideas of the animal soul. Later, however, this same concept was employed in the mechanistic theories of Descartes and his followers. Concepts bridge the discontinuity between successive paradigms and support the persistence of truths from theory to theory and, therefore, the progressive increase of persisting truths over time.

The resulting picture of scientific progress is not a naïve positivist one of the linear accumulation of truths within a single standpoint that defines an unchanging 'scientific view' of the world. As in Kuhn's account, the dominant standpoint at one time may be later rejected as erroneous. The history of science is a history of error as well as of truth. But progress still occurs because each successive scientific standpoint (corresponding to a Kuhnian paradigm) represents a more general perspective from which previous perspectives can be assessed and, to the extent that they remain valid, incorporated in the current formulation.[12]

But what of Kuhn's second reason for distrusting the idea of truth: its apparent connection with an untenable notion of correspondence? One obvious solution would be to reject the realism of the correspondence theory of truth in favor of idealism. This seems to have had a certain resonance for Kuhn, who often claims that, after a scientific revolution, scientists 'live in a different world'. As Paul Hoyningen-Huene makes particularly clear,[13] Kuhn is thereby committed to a view of the scientific mind as somehow constituting the phenomenal world. Kuhn, however, like most Anglophone philosophers of science, regarded idealism as a threat rather than a resource and took pains to reconcile his view with a core of realism about scientific theories. Similarly, Bachelard, despite the influence of Brunschvicg and the idealistic tendencies of his own thought, struggled to maintain a realistic view of science. Some reflection on this struggle will help us with Kuhn's problem of the ontological significance of science.

Bachelard calls his position an 'applied rationalism'. The rationalism lies in its recognition, shared with Kuhn, that the mind constitutes the concepts with which science describes the world. This rationalism is 'applied' because this constitution does not literally create the scientific world; rather, it works with (is applied to) objects that exist prior to and independent of the mind and its concepts. Bachelard sees applied rationalism as a way between traditional idealism and realism, accepting idealism's active role of the mind as well as realism's independent existence of the object.

Bachelard's applied rationalism may seem merely to evade the basic onto-logical issue. He tries to maintain realism by saying that any scientific concept is applied to an object that exists independent of that application. But his accommodation with idealism requires that the object pre-existing the appli-cation of a given concept was nonetheless constituted by previous applications of other concepts. Unless there is an unintelligible infinite regress of applica-tions and objects, there must be an initial object that is the starting point of our knowledge. This object is either entirely constituted by the mind—which

---

[12]  A similar approach to scientific progress can be developed from Wilfrid Sellars' view of meaning. See Gary Gutting, 'Conceptual Structures and Scientific Change', *Studies in History and Philosophy of Science*, 4 (1973), 209–30.

[13]  *Reconstructing Scientific Revolutions* (Chicago: University of Chicago Press, 1993), ch. 3.

amounts to an implausible idealism—or it is a conceptually inaccessible thing-in-itself—which amounts to an implausible realism.

The above objection, however, takes applied rationalism as a full-blooded alternative to traditional idealism and realism. It assumes that applied rationalism offers a new solution to the traditional metaphysical problem of the ultimate nature of reality in its relation to mind. Bachelard may well have seen his view in this way. But we can rather take applied rationalism as a refusal to take sides in the traditional metaphysical dispute. The idea would be to maintain a healthy skepticism about the deep global issues posed by this dispute and limit ourselves to merely local or regional claims about the nature of specific scientific objects. (This would, moreover, fit very well with Bachelard's insistence that there is no monolithic conception of scientific rationality, merely diverse 'regions of rationality'.)[14] For each case, applied rationalism says that the given object is constituted in a distinctive way by the mind's creative conceptualization, but that this constitution applies to an object existing prior to that constitution. In each case, it is the task of a philosophically reflective history of science to sort out what is given and what is constituted. As Bachelard suggests, one theme of such a history of modern physical science will surely be the role of instruments in the constitution of scientific objects. But applied rationalism, as I suggest we interpret it, avoids taking any position on the question of the ultimate relation of the mind and the world of objects. In this way, Bachelard can assert a sophisticated scientific realism (sophisticated in its accommodation with key idealist themes) and at the same time avoid taking a position on the question of metaphysical realism. Exactly the same line can be taken toward the Kuhnian ontological problematic. We can maintain a realism about scientific objects (and the truth of assertions about them) while maintaining a healthy metaphysical skepticism about the 'vexing problems' of the correspondence theory of truth.

## Rationality

The Bachelard–Canguilhem approach also suggests a fruitful way of dealing with the Kuhnian problem of scientific rationality. Although he vigorously denied it, many readers thought Kuhn rejected the rationality of science, at least implicitly, because he located the cognitive authority of science in

---

[14]   *Le Rationalisme appliqué* (Paris: Presses Universitaires de France), 1949), ch. 7.

the consensus of the scientific community. Canguilhem agrees with many Anglophone critics when he accuses Kuhn of abandoning rationality for merely shared opinions. The point is this. By accepting the judgment of the scientific community as the ultimate justification of scientific claims, Kuhn makes reason-giving nothing more than a social practice. But surely I can have perfectly good reasons for believing something that everyone else thinks is false or unjustified. Why should enough recalcitrant Athenians put Socrates in the wrong? Kuhn seems to erase the boundary between objective knowledge and subjective opinion. His doctrine of incommensurability rejects any objective, community-independent epistemic ground (e.g. a neutral observation language or a priori methodological rules) that we can use to resolve scientific disagreements and leaves him only a contingent, merely intersubjective agreement among scientists.

The problem becomes particularly clear when we reflect on Kuhn's distinction of normal and abnormal science. Normal science occurs when scientists sufficiently agree on fundamentals to allow the evaluation of contested claims by shared standards. They can then engage in the behavioral equivalent of the discourse that would be possible if there were standards of rationality independent of their judgments. Although Kuhn denies that there are any such standards, in normal science the agreement of investigators allows them to proceed as if there were. Abnormal science arises when someone, for whatever reason, speaks in a manner counter to the consensus of normal science (as when a Galileo says that the earth is not at rest). According to Kuhn, this typically is a response to a perceived 'crisis' in the paradigm guiding normal science. If the community ultimately decides that there is no crisis, the abnormal approach is ignored. But the community may come to share the innovator's sense of crisis and even eventually pick up the new approach. The result is a radical change to a new paradigm, and the innovator is hailed as a revolutionary genius. But, on Kuhn's account, all that has actually happened is that the community has accepted new discursive standards. Given this, critics ask how Kuhn can preserve any meaningful epistemological distinction between objective knowledge and subjective belief. Scientists know that the earth moves relative to the sun; but for Kuhn this seems to mean merely that all members of the relevant scientific community agree that the earth moves. Group consensus—driven by what Lakatos called 'mob psychology'—has become the only standard of knowledge.

To sharpen the objection—and develop possible responses to it—we need to reflect on the distinction between 'objective' and 'subjective'. The distinction can be taken in various ways. Sometimes 'subjective' refers to what is a matter of individual preference and 'objective' to what is generally accepted. In this sense, 'Chateau Lafite-Rothschild is Bordeaux wine' is objective, whereas 'Chateau Lafite-Rothschild 1945 was the best Bordeaux of the twentieth century' is subjective. Kuhn obviously does not make knowledge subjective in this sense. The consensus of a scientific, literary, or political community is not a matter of personal opinion. It is objective at least in the sense of being intersubjective. In other cases, 'subjective' refers to what is a matter of judgment rather than what can be unequivocally demonstrated. Kuhnian consensus is subjective in this sense, but then so is virtually all our knowledge outside of the most rigorous mathematical demonstrations. (Even mathematical demonstrations involve ineliminable acts of judgment regarding, for example, the applicability of a general principle to a particular case.) So Kuhn's view is not damagingly subjective in either of these two senses.

A third sense of the distinction takes 'subjective' to mean 'how things appear to us' as opposed to 'how things really are'. In these terms, if knowledge is nothing more than group consensus, then it expresses only how things seem to us, which may well not be how they really are. This poses no problem for Kuhn if it means only that there is a difference between *how things appear to us* (that is, how they appear in first impressions, before serious inquiry) and *how things appear after the fullest possible scrutiny*. On this reading of the appearance-reality distinction, Kuhnian knowledge is obviously objective, since scientific consensus results from the most thorough investigation and discussion. On the other hand, the appearance-reality distinction can also be taken as between *how things are described by our most careful and thorough inquiries* and *how things are just in themselves, entirely apart from how we describe them*. But then the objection presupposes the metaphysical realism that our discussion above showed that we can dispense with. The conclusion seems to be that Kuhn can deploy an intelligible sense of scientific objectivity. Even so, however, it does not follow that Kuhn has an answer to the Socrates-versus-the-Athenians objection. A consensus derived from the sustained investigations of a trained group of inquirers may still be wrong, and a maverick who rejects it may be right. Is there any way to do justice to this point without introducing the metaphysical realism Kuhn rejects?

It is at this point that the Bachelard–Canguilhem tradition once again becomes relevant to the Kuhnian problematic. Where Kuhn speaks of consensus as the ultimate epistemological category in our understanding of science,

Bachelard and, especially, Canguilhem speak of norms. These are, of course, social norms, ultimately constituted by the practices of the groups that follow them. But there is a crucial distinction between social practice and group consensus. As Canguilhem emphasizes, the fact that a norm has no objective reality outside the group it regulates does not entail that it expresses the mere opinions or whims of the group (and much less of individuals within it). Just as biological norms are rooted in the organic reality of organisms they regulate, so social norms derive from the 'social reality' of the groups for which they are valid. Belonging to a community means coming under the norms that constitute that community, but not every opinion shared by all or most members of a community expresses a communal norm. It is even, in fact, quite possible for a single individual to be in accord with a community's norms when the rest of the community is not. I could, for example, be the only person who pronounces my name correctly or who knows that the twenty-first century did not begin until 2001. Of course, enough changes in the views and practices of the members of a community will eventually lead to changes in its norms, since norms have no ultimate basis outside the community itself. But this does not mean that norms are changeable at the whim of a group, even if the group includes everyone. Even if we all say something different, we may not all be able to believe it or be able to reflect it in our practices.

To avoid confusion here we need to reflect carefully on the relation between consensus and reason-giving (justification). Consensus is closely tied to reason-giving in both origin and outcome. Like any social practice, reason-giving proceeds from an intersubjective acceptance of a set of norms; and it tends toward agreement on claims that have been justified by the practice. We can all too easily collapse these two points into the misleading claim that consensus is what justifies a proposition. This, however, is true only in a very indirect sense. At some point, further demands for justification of the norms governing our reason-giving no longer make sense; and we can do no more that point out that these are the norms we accept (as Wittgenstein emphasizes in *On Certainty*). But such acceptance is by no means an optional choice by individuals. It is the outcome of the deep-rooted and complex process whereby they have become reason-givers. In Canguilhem's terms, this is the process that forms a community as a social reality. Conversely, consensus is (when things go right) the outcome of successful reason-giving: the process of discussing the evidence, presenting arguments, answering objections leads to widespread agreement on what to believe. Consensus about norms, then, is the ultimate source of the practice of reason-giving, and consensus about specific beliefs is the appropriate outcome of the practice.

None of this, however, implies that all our beliefs are justified only to the extent that we agree on them. This is why Canguilhem objects to Kuhn's focus on consensus rather than norms. As he reads Kuhn, 'A paradigm is the result of a choice by those who use it. The normal is what is common, over a given period, to a collectivity of specialists in a university or other academic institution. We think we are dealing with concepts of a philosophical critique, only to find ourselves on the level of social psychology.'[15] Canguilhem may not be entirely justified in forcing on Kuhn a purely psychological reading of consensus, but he is right in suggesting that Kuhn needs to make a clearer distinction between the roles of norms and of individual and group judgments governed by norms. Given such a distinction, we can see that an individual might have good reasons to believe that everyone else in the community is ignorant of, misinterpreting, or simply incapable of understanding the relevant community norms appropriate for evaluating a given claim. Perhaps, for example, the rest of the community has lost the ability to understand the millennial significance of the fact that there is no year zero. In such a case, the individual will be justified against everyone else——not necessarily *sub specie aeternitatis* but in light of his superior understanding of norms implicit in his community's practices.

There are special cases in which consensus is the direct source of justification. When astrophysicists accept the existence of black holes, their justification is a complicated body of evidence and arguments based on it, not the fact that they agree that black holes exist. But non-experts who accept the results of astrophysics on authority may justify their belief in black holes by the consensus of astrophysicists. This, however, is a derivative sort of justification that does not define the nature of the practice.

Rethinking Kuhn's position from the Bachelard–Canguilhem perspective, then, there is no need to assimilate rational justification to voluntary consensus, as though norms of belief depended on the majority vote at the next epistemic town-meeting. There is no need to formulate the idea that reason-giving is a social practice in this decisionistic way. Admitting that rationality is ultimately a matter of sharing a practice rather than, say, attaining self-evident insights does not make the routine results of ordinary epistemic deliberations a matter of arbitrary choice. Thomas McCarthy has rightly maintained that

---

[15] *Idéologie et rationalité* (Paris: Vrin, 1977), 232.

'"our" culture is shot through with transcultural notions of validity'. As he says, our actual practices of justification 'involve constructing arguments that claim to be universally valid', not appealing to our agreement on a given claim. 'In general, it is not because we agree that we hold a claim to be valid; rather, we agree because we have grounds for granting its validity.'[16] But Kuhn can accept this point even while giving epistemic priority to the judgment of the scientific community. The issue is not about the content of the norms involved in our practice of justification, but only about the ultimate basis of these norms. To say that there is nothing underlying these norms other than the practices they define is not to make the practices irrational. It is merely to reject an indefensible philosophical interpretation of what a practice is.

## III. THE ONTOLOGICAL ATTITUDE AND PHILOSOPHY IN A WORLD OF SCIENCE

There have been many vehicles for staking out the domain of philosophy, from Descartes' dualism through the positivist's analytic–synthetic distinction. But one of the most persistently attractive has been the claim that philosophy can and should root itself in an experience with an *immediacy* or *concreteness* that escapes the abstractions required for successful empirical science. The precision required for rigorously testing hypotheses requires us, it is said, to ignore certain aspects of our experience that are not open to scientific (e.g. quantitative) formulation. The claim (or hope), however, is that philosophy is capable of giving us an epistemically adequate access to the experience that science must ignore.

This appeal to a distinctive realm of philosophical experience is prominent among French philosophers of science who adopt what I am calling the ontological attitude. Two of the most powerful and instructive views are those developed by Henri Bergson and Maurice Merleau-Ponty. In what follows, I will sketch their critiques of the limitations of scientific knowledge, their consequent conceptions of philosophy as a distinctive epistemic domain, and their ultimate disagreement about the nature of concrete experience.

---

[16] Thomas McCarthy, 'Philosophy and Social Practice: Richard Rorty's "New Pragmatism"', in McCarthy, *Ideals and Illusions* (Cambridge, MA: The MIT Press, 1991), 17, 19.

These disagreements will lead to my own concluding reflections on science, philosophy, and experience.

## Bergson and the experience of duration

In contrast to his friend, Léon Brunschvicg—and, more generally, the neo-Kantian tradition dominant in the early years of the century—Bergson rejected the idea that science was the unique source of our knowledge of nature. Kant, on Bergson's reading (*Creative Evolution* [CE], 387–90),[17] starts from the early modern rationalist vision of a world made intelligible by the power of God's mind, but asks why this intelligibility cannot be due to the human rather than the divine mind. Even more important, Kant goes on to make a distinction between the forms and the material of knowledge, a distinction no doubt tied to the fact that the human mind does not have the creative power of the divine. The crucial question for Bergson concerns the status of this 'matter' from which the objects of knowledge are constituted. For Kant, it is merely the vehicle for the mind's structuring of the world by the imposition of its forms. But, according to Bergson, this neglects the possibility, opened up in principle by Kant's approach, that this matter of knowledge is something with significance in its own right, beyond what it is given by the forms of the intellect. Kant, unfortunately, uncritically assumed that knowledge could only be scientific knowledge; given this, since the realm of science is defined by intellectual forms, there could be no knowledge beyond these forms (no 'extra-intellectual' knowledge).

But, according to Bergson, this assumption ignores the obvious limitations (incompleteness) of scientific knowledge, particularly as we move from the inanimate through the vital to the psychological. If we avoid Kant's mistake, we will recognize 'a supra-intellectual intuition' of reality that gives us knowledge of reality in itself, not just the phenomenal constructions of the intellect. For Bergson, the object of this intuition is the duration (lived time, *la durée*) that science excludes from its purview but which is in fact the 'richer' whole from which scientific objects are abstracted. Kant's idealistic successors (Fichte, Hegel) recognized the need to find intuitive knowledge beyond the forms of the intellect that would put us in contact with reality in itself. But they wrongly sought this in a *non-temporal* intuition, which is really just a reformulation

---

[17]  *Creative Evolution*, trans. Arthur Mitchell (New York: Modern Library, 1944).

of the pre-Kantian mechanism of Spinoza and Leibniz in mentalistic terms. Abandoning these intellectual constructions for the concreteness of experience brings us back to duration.

Science's abstraction from the concreteness of duration results in what Bergson calls its 'cinematographical method' (CE, 357), whereby science views reality not as a continuous flux (the duration that it in fact is) but as a series of instantaneous 'snapshots' extracted from this flux. In terms of a simple but, for Bergson, fundamental example, science derives from the mindset that makes Zeno's paradoxes both inevitable and unsolvable. Such a view is essential for science, given its goal of controlling nature for the sake of more effective action in the world. For, Bergson maintains, action is concerned only with getting from a starting point to an end-point and has no concern with whatever may exist between the two. The practical (instrumental) nature of science leads to its abstraction from the reality of duration, and a full philosophical account of the world *in concreto* must restore what science omits. Indeed, the heart of Bergson's philosophical effort was to show, for a succession of key philosophical questions—freedom, the mind–body relation, the nature of existence, the truth of religion—how answering them requires supplementing the abstractions of science with the intuition of duration.

Bergson develops the notion of duration and its significance for philosophy through his account of intelligence, instinct, and intuition. As we have seen, the intellectual categories of science are not adequate to the concreteness of our immediate experience of lived duration. Intellect, although it is biologically the distinctive human trait, is a limited instrument of knowledge, formed to deal only with inert matter, and has 'a natural inability to comprehend life' (CE, 182, emphasis omitted). But humans can overcome the limitations of the intellect, for we are, biologically, creatures of instinct as well as of intellect; and instinct is directed to the singular, concrete object, and hence to time as duration. Ordinarily, of course, instinct lacks the distance from objects needed for theoretical knowledge of them; its access to duration remains an unreflective sympathy that goes no further than an implicit know-how. But, according to Bergson, it is possible for instinct to become disengaged, for it to 'become disinterested, self-conscious, capable of reflecting on its object' (CE, 194). Instinct then becomes intuition, the privileged vehicle for philosophical knowledge of duration.

Bergson thinks that the possibility of something like intuition is apparent from the reality of aesthetic experience, which grasps the temporal unity of individual objects in a way that normal, spatialized perception does not.

Philosophical intuition is the basis of an 'inquiry turned in the same direction as art, which would take life in *general* for its object' (CE, 194). The turn toward generality derives, according to Bergson, from intelligence itself. 'Without intelligence, [intuition] would have remained in the form of instinct, riveted to the special object of its practical interest' (CE, 195). Philosophy is born from a fundamental cooperation between two complementary powers: 'There are things that intelligence alone is able to seek, but which, by itself, it will never find. These things instinct alone could find; but it will never seek them' (CE, 167, emphasis omitted). Intuition is precisely instinct directed toward the intellect's goal of general, theoretical knowledge. The object of intuition so understood is precisely duration.

As opposed to instinct, intuition does involve knowledge of duration, but this knowledge cannot be expressed in conceptual or theoretical terms. It seems to exist simply as an awareness of the limitations of all concepts and theories. We should not expect, therefore, any explicit articulation of the philosopher's intuitive knowledge of duration; such knowledge can never be incorporated into the realm of thought. But this knowledge does enable us to see the points at which various modes of thought become inadequate, and hence to avoid intellectual paradoxes that would otherwise lead us to deny fundamental realities such as freedom, life, morality, and God.

## Merleau-Ponty and the Phenomenal Field

In France, as in the German-speaking world, philosophy between the two world wars saw a strong reaction against neo-Kantianism. But, whereas the German reaction went in both an existential-phenomenological (Heideggerian) and a positivist direction, in France there was no parallel to the rise of logical positivism, for two reasons. First, the spirit of positivism in France (which, after all, had been born there with Comte) had for a long time been channeled out of philosophy and into the social sciences. Second, most of the promising French philosophers of logic and mathematics—Louis Courturat, Jean Nicod, Jacques Herbrand, and Jean Cavaillès—who might well have developed along something like positivist lines, died at an early age.

Even the considerable French interest in Husserl shied away from the epistemological, particularly foundationalist, themes that might have led to something similar to what became positivist philosophy of science. What energized French existentialism was rather Husserl's emphasis on concrete experience. His foundationalist *Cartesian Meditations* (given as lectures at the Sorbonne in 1929) were an unfortunate choice for a French audience and were not well received.

Nonetheless, the young French philosophers of the 1930s and 1940s who were seeking a philosophy grounded in the immediacy of experience turned not to Bergson but to Husserl, who was his exact contemporary. Merleau-Ponty himself comments on this neglect of Bergson in an essay commemorating Bergson's centenary.

If we had been careful readers of Bergson, and if more thought had been given to him, we would have been drawn to a much more concrete philosophy, a philosophy much less reflexive than Brunschvicg's. But since Bergson was hardly read by my contemporaries, it is certain that we had to wait for the philosophies of existence in order to be able to learn much of what he would have been able to teach us. It is quite certain—as we realize more and more today—that Bergson, had we read him carefully, would have taught us things that ten or fifteen years later we believed to be discoveries made by the philosophy of existence itself.[18]

One reason Merleau-Ponty and his friends such as Jean-Paul Sartre did not take Bergson seriously may have been his association with conservative, religious thought. By the 1930s, his radical metaphysics had been appropriated by vapid 'spiritualist' thinkers and his last book, *Two Sources of Religion and Morality* (1932), showed his increasing affinity for Catholicism. From one point of view, the entire story is summed up in Père Sertillanges' remark that the Church would never have put Bergson's books on the Index in 1913 had it realized how his thought would look by 1934.[19]

But the rejection of Bergson was also on philosophical grounds. Merleau-Ponty's treatments of him in *The Phenomenology of Perception* (and his lectures on Bergson a few years later) are clearly the products of a 'careful reading' and raise serious philosophical objections. At the same time, there are interesting grounds for a Bergsonian critique of phenomenology. For a generation that sought a philosophy grounded in immediate experience, Bergson was a potentially viable alternative to Husserl. To understand the philosophical reasons behind Merleau-Ponty's preference for Husserl, we need to take a quick look at Merleau-Ponty's development of a phenomenological philosophy.

The domain of phenomenological inquiry is what Merleau-Ponty calls the 'phenomenal field', roughly, our immediate experience as we actually

[18] 'The Philosophy of Existence', in *Texts and Other Dialogues*, ed. Hugh J. Silverman and James Barry, Jr. (Atlantic Highlands, NJ: Humanities Press, 1991), 132.

[19] L. Kolakowski, *Bergson* (Oxford: Oxford University Press, 1985), 94.

live it through, as opposed to scientific, philosophical, and even common-sense reconstructions of that experience. Merleau-Ponty particularly insists on the inadequacy of both science and traditional philosophical reflection for providing an accurate and complete description of this field.

According to Merleau-Ponty, the basic problem with a scientific approach is that the deployment of its rigorously empirical and quantitative methodology requires regarding the contents of the phenomenal field as fully determinate and totally objective; that is, in no way dependent on our experience of them. Science must conceive of its objects in a way that allows them to be understood entirely in terms of ideal mathematical constructs. This means that science understands everything, including not only inanimate but also living, feeling, and thinking bodies, as nothing more than a set of physical elements connected by causal relations. As a result, even the human body becomes pure exteriority, a mere collection of parts outside of parts, interacting with one another according to scientific laws. On this view, genuine subjectivity is simply eliminated, something that Merleau-Ponty regards as an obvious travesty of our experience of the phenomenal field. This is the motivation behind his dramatic statement that phenomenology's 'return to the "things themselves" . . . is from the start a rejection of science' (*The Phenomenology of Perception* [PP], viii). He also thinks he can show that the purely scientific account fails systematically when it is applied to particular physiological and psychological data, when, for example, we try to understand sense perception in terms of sensations produced by the brain's interaction with the world. The general problem in any such application is that the phenomenal field involves irreducible meanings (significations) that cannot be dealt with in objective causal terms. Science cannot, for example, explain why (to take an example from Max Scheler) 'the light of a candle changes its appearance for a child when, after a burn, it stops attracting the child's hand and becomes literally repulsive' (PP, 52).

Rationalist and idealist philosophers have opposed the scientific reduction of the phenomenal field and agreed with Merleau-Ponty that the phenomenal field is prior to the objective world of science, which represents an abstraction from it. In Merleau-Ponty's view, their mistake (and even, in some texts, Husserl's) is in going on to subordinate the phenomenal field to a domain of transcendental subjectivity, a separate and entirely 'inner' world accessible only via special acts of introspection or intuition. This domain is said to provide a privileged reflective standpoint from which we can, in principle, have completely explicit knowledge of the phenomenal field, by understanding how its meanings are constituted by the transcendental ego.

Despite their differences, the empiricist (scientistic) and rationalist (intellectualistic) approaches are, according to Merleau-Ponty, grounded in a common desire to make our fundamental experience of the world entirely explicit and disengaged. The world must be the pure object of either an autonomous subjectivity or an autonomous scientific method. The mistake in both cases is to think that there can ever be total disengagement from the phenomenal field. Both scientific objectification and philosophical reflection are themselves rooted in and ultimately inseparable from the lived world. To overcome the mistake, we must realize that there is no going beyond the phenomenal field, neither below it via an empiricist reduction nor above it by idealistic constitution. We must remain on the concrete level of existential phenomenology.

The key to avoiding empiricist and idealist errors is to maintain a proper appreciation of the central place of the *body* in our experience. The body is not an object on a par with other objects. As *my* body it is the ineradicable locus of experience, the standpoint from which I must perceive the world. This is apparent from the perspectival nature—both spatially and temporally—of perception. We experience an object as situated in a surrounding world and hence as having different perspectives from different positions. In this sense, an object, far from being seen from nowhere (as empiricism and idealism would suggest), is in fact seen from *everywhere*. But among all these perspectives, that from here—i.e. from the perceiving body—is privileged. My gaze actually presents only those aspects of the object that are apparent from here (that is, given in a full perceptual synthesis); all other perspectives are indefinite and only presumptive.

The body is privileged with regard not only to perspective but also to all other perceived meanings, such as color or tactile sensation. How I experience, say, a pin prick depends not only on the pin but also on the internal disposition of the body that is being pricked. 'The function of the organism in receiving stimuli is, so to speak, to "conceive" of a certain form of excitation' (PP, 75). There is a 'constitution' of the objects of my experience, but it is through a pre-conceptual structuring provided by my body.

This structuring is accessible only through the phenomenal field, the domain of phenomenological description, which thus provides a locus for situating the truths pointed to by both traditional philosophical reflection and scientific explanation. But this 'synthesis' of science and philosophy requires recognizing that neither traditional philosophical reflection nor empirical science provides an adequate account of our immediate experience; for that we must look to phenomenological description.

## What Do We Experience? Merleau-Ponty vs. Bergson

Bergson and Merleau-Ponty both see science as a 'thin' form of knowledge in comparison to the 'thickness' of experience. But they have different views of just what experience involves. Merleau-Ponty notes that Bergson 'shows in a profound way that science should be considered not only with respect to its completed formulas but also with an eye to the margin of indetermination which separates these formulas from the data to be explained'. He further comments that metaphysics, for Bergson, 'would then be the deliberate exploration of this world prior to the object to which science refers'. Up to this point, he has no quarrel with Bergson: 'In all these respects it seems to us that Bergson has perfectly defined the metaphysical approach to the world.'[20] But he remains dubious of Bergsonian intuition. His doubts can be cast in the form of a dilemma. On the one hand, Bergson's intuition may be taken as pretending to 'the absolute observer's viewpoint' that would 'transcend the world'. If so, 'Bergson is not fully aware of his own presuppositions and of that simple fact that all we live is lived against the background of the world.' If, on the other hand, Bergson in fact avoids this illusion of transcendence and 'his philosophy is finally to be understood as a philosophy of immanence', then 'he may be reproached with having described the human world only in its most general structures (e.g. duration, openness to the future); his work lacks a picture of human history which would give a content to these intuitions, which paradoxically remain very general'.[21]

In developing this second horn of his dilemma, Merleau-Ponty objects not merely to the generality of Bergson's account but to its rejection of certain essential structures of lived experience. Bergson rightly rejects the scientific view of reality as a mere 'multiplicity of things externally juxtaposed'. But his alternative to this view is a 'multiplicity of fusion and interpenetration'. Bergson's duration swallows up objects, along with the space and time in which they exist, into an amorphous unity: 'He proceeds by way of dilution,

---

[20] 'The Metaphysical in Man', in *Sense and Non-Sense*, trans. Hubert L. Dreyfus and Patricia Allen Dreyfus (Evanston, IL: Northwestern University Press, 1964), 97 n. 15.
[21] Ibid.

speaking of consciousness as a liquid in which instants and positions dissolve.' Bergson's mistake is to 'seek a solution in ambiguity'.[22] Merleau-Ponty maintains that 'space, motion and time cannot be elucidated by discovering an "inner" layer of experience in which their multiplicity is erased and *really* abolished.' The problem with Bergson's intuition is that it purports to be a purely internal experience, prior to any division between subject and object. Evoking Kant, Merleau-Ponty argues that 'external experience is essential to internal experience', that there is an implicit separation of subject and object, of consciousness and world, in even our most immediate experience (PP, 276, n. 1).

Merleau-Ponty makes the same point in terms of the central Bergsonian notion of time. As Bergson describes it, duration is a concrete unity in which what the intellect distinguishes as past, present, and future are all dissolved. Consciousness, as Bergson's famous metaphor has it, is a snowball rolling down a hill, bringing the whole of time into a homogeneous unity. There is, according to him, a principle of continuity whereby 'the past still belongs to the present and the present already to the past'. But then, Merleau-Ponty argues, 'there is no longer any past or present'. 'If consciousness snowballs upon itself, it is, like the snowball and everything else, wholly in the present' and the structures of temporality (past, present, and future) lose all meaning (PP, 276, n. 1; for the snowball image, see CE, 4).

To sum up: Merleau-Ponty maintains that, if Bergson is offering a description of our actual lived experience in the world, then the description is inaccurate because it dissolves into a unified flux structural elements (past, present; subject, object) that need to be differentiated for our experience to have any meaning at all. The only alternative would be for Bergson to maintain that he has gone beyond our lived experience and attained a transcendent, absolute standpoint that yields metaphysical truth beyond what is available to lived experience.

Bergson would not be without response to this critique. For one thing, he is entirely aware of the level of description at which Merleau-Ponty's phenomenology operates. It is, indeed, the level at which Bergson himself operates in the beginning of his second book *Matter and Memory* (1896),[23] where, as Merleau-Ponty himself puts it, he offers 'an astonishing description of perceived being'. Indeed, Merleau-Ponty goes on to say:

---

[22]  Although, of course, in another sense, Merleau-Ponty's is a 'philosophy of ambiguity'.
[23]  *Matter and Memory*, trans. N. M. Paul and W. S. Winter (New York: Zone Books, 1988).

Never before had anyone established this circuit between being and myself which is such that being exists 'for me,' the spectator, but which is also such that the spectator exists 'for being.' Never had the brute being of the perceived world been so described. By unveiling it according to duration as it comes to be, Bergson regains at the heart of man a pre-Socratic and 'prehuman' meaning of the world.[24]

But Bergson himself, at least by the time he wrote *Creative Evolution* (1907), regarded this sort of description of perception as less than ultimate. The problem is that perception itself is structured by our practical activity in the world and is, therefore, informed by the categories appropriate for action. As we noted earlier, these categories replace the continuity of life with the more practically effective discontinuities of spatial and temporal moments and separately existing bodies. There is, of course, a continuum from the full abstraction of mathematicized science, which maximizes discreteness and intellectual structure, to the philosophical intuition of pure duration, which, if only for brief moments, unites us with the full concreteness of the temporal flux. Merleau-Ponty's descriptions in *Phenomenology of Perception*, like Bergson's similar descriptions in *Matter and Memory*, allow us to avoid certain puzzles and confusions resulting from the extreme abstractions of science (e.g. intractable forms of the mind–body problem). But they themselves, Bergson would maintain, are still significantly imbued with intellectualist categories. The very phenomenological project of *description* requires general categories that distort the lived experience of pure duration.

We see, then, that although Bergson and Merleau-Ponty agree on the fact that scientific knowledge is incomplete because it abstracts from the full concreteness of lived experience, they disagree on the proper philosophical characterization of that experience. Nor, of course is this sort of disagreement limited to these two philosophers. To Bergson's duration and Merleau-Ponty's phenomenal field we may add not only Heideggerian and Sartrean versions of phenomenology but also, in quite different veins, the classical sense-data account of Hume and the positivists, Reid's common-sense realism, and even the pantheistic sensibility of certain mystics.

It might be maintained that these diverse accounts merely show the difficulty of discovering what in fact is given in immediate experience and should spur us to more penetrating efforts to get the description right. But can we in fact even imagine carrying out such a project? Recent philosophy on both sides

---

[24] 'Bergson in the Making', in *Signs*, trans. Richard McCleary (Evanston: Northwestern University Press, 1964), 185.

of the Atlantic has shown that there is no such thing as interpretation-free observation; historico-philosophical analyses such as those of Kuhn and of Foucault strongly suggest the contingent nature of all substantive interpretative categories. If there are any unsurpassable limits on experience, they are not likely to take us beyond those of logical and common-sense banalities. If so, there is no point in trying to adjudicate the dispute between Bergson and Merleau-Ponty. The lesson of the confrontation I have evoked is that experiential immediacy is a well from which many buckets may draw. The 'immediate givens of consciousness' (to echo the title of Bergson's first book) are an irrefutable and inevitable starting point of any inquiry. But while the sheer experience itself is certainly given, no non-trivial preferred description or interpretation of it is. Experience can be read in many different ways, each with its own plausibility, self-consistency, and limitations. Some of these readings may be mutually incompatible, but many are literally consistent, tensions arising only when we ask which is the most comprehensive or most concrete. It is these latter questions I suggest we eschew, at least in their general form. On the whole, questions of superiority make sense only given a specific context, perspective, or purpose. Experience as such is no doubt an absolute, but there is nothing absolute that follows from it.

What, then, can we conclude about the status of philosophy and of science as ways of knowing? Scientific methods can, of course, be applied in one way or another to any subject matter at all. But there is no guarantee that these methods (essentially, the rigorous intersubjective testing of precisely formulated hypotheses) will tell us everything we want to know about a given subject. This is particularly true of experience, the first-person awareness that is our constant and immediate mode of encountering the world and, especially, ourselves. So far, at least, our scientific accounts have always left out something of this awareness; they do not, in Einstein's phrase, give us 'the taste of the soup'. It is, however, easy to conclude too much from this fact. It does not, for example, follow that there is another realm of things outside of those treated by science; for example, spiritual substances such as souls. Nor does it follow that the entire domain of consciousness could never be entirely understood in terms of strictly empirical scientific categories. Nonetheless, immediate experience cannot be ignored. Science must ultimately come to terms with it, and we cannot imagine our lives not centering on it. This is sufficient to justify the projects of philosophers such as Bergson and Merleau-Ponty.

But there is no basis for assuming, as do Bergson and Merleau-Ponty (along with many other philosophers), that any one description or account of immediate experience is uniquely correct. This may be true of scientific accounts of the 'external' world (though the point is controversial even there); but there is good reason to think that, for a domain as complex and elusive as experience, no one formulation will be comprehensively and exhaustively adequate. In appreciating and evaluating the great philosophies of experience, we should rather think of each as a particular vocabulary, with its own strengths and limitations, which we can expect to be of varying values for different purposes. In this regard, I would suggest, philosophies are like novels: not alternative absolutes among which we must choose the 'right one' but different perspectival visions (perhaps complementary, but perhaps incompatible or even incommensurable), all of which have their relative values and uses.

In thinking about the relative significance of science and philosophy, it is crucial to avoid not only the well-known fallacy of scientism but also the much less noted fallacy of what I will call *philosophism*. Scientism illegitimately infers from the success of science in knowing certain aspects of reality to its ability to know anything, in any domain. Philosophism is the corresponding error of arguing from the inability of science to know certain sorts of truth (regarding, e.g. ethics, religion, or subjective experience) to the ability of philosophy to achieve such knowledge. Bergson and Merleau-Ponty make effective cases against scientism by showing that science has succeeded precisely by excluding from its purview certain domains of truth. But it does not follow that there is some non-scientific, philosophical method (Bergsonian intuition, phenomenological description) that knows this truth. The proper conclusion from the cognitive failure of science in a given domain may be skepticism about our ability to know that domain. My own conclusions about the prospects of philosophical cognition are not skeptical. But I would suggest that there is hyperbole in the claim of any philosophical method to have a privileged insight into the deliverances of experience.

Nonetheless, the immediacy of experience is the primary source for philosophers' development of overall 'pictures' of human existence. The philosophical instinct has long been to insist that we need to establish just one comprehensive picture as uniquely preferable, something I think we are very unlikely to do. But our inability to establish the unique privilege of a general picture does not imply that we have no need to develop such pictures and maintain them through precise theoretical formulations. A first and crucial point is that general pictures are essential elements of human culture. We have an ineradicable cosmic urge to act out of a comprehensive understanding of our situation. Even a view that is skeptical about substantive grand narratives deploys this very skepticism as a general vision of the human predicament. Further, individuals and even entire cultures can face destruction through persistent adherence to a failing picture. The people perish not only when there is no vision but also when their vision no longer provides effective responses to the exigencies of life. When a dominant picture fails, we need others to replace it. It follows that the creation of alternative pictures—a primary achievement of philosophy—is culturally vital.

But a picture has no value for us unless we perceive it as a live option. There are, of course, many merely affective reasons why certain pictures remain dead for us. But, at some level, intelligence is always a factor in our lives and the viability of a general picture will always importantly depend on whether we see it as coherent and plausible. We therefore need formulations of our guiding visions that make them intellectually respectable, even if they do not vindicate them over all rivals. This is the positive function of philosophy, and carrying it out requires passionate and meticulous attention to the concreteness of lived experience. Here, I conclude, we find the true value of both Bergson's and Merleau-Ponty's efforts to develop a philosophy of experience.[25]

[25] Portions of this essay have employed (often with revisions) material from my *French Philosophy in the Twentieth Century* (Cambridge: Cambridge University Press, 2001) and my 'Thomas Kuhn and French Philosophy of Science', in Thomas Nickles (ed.), *Thomas Kuhn* (Cambridge: Cambridge University Press, 2003). My thanks to Brian Leiter for helpful comments on an earlier draft.

CHAPTER 7

# MARXISM AND THE STATUS OF CRITIQUE

## ALEX CALLINICOS

MARXISM has always had a complex, not to say conflicted, relationship with philosophy, whose ultimate source derives from uncertainty and indeed ambivalence about its own status as a form of theoretical discourse. Marx himself was indubitably a philosophical child of German classical idealism: his conceptual vocabulary and intellectual preoccupations are unintelligible outside the whole complex movement from Kant to Hegel. But the painful process through which Marx, alongside Engels, worked through left Hegelianism and began to develop a distinctively different theoretical project pulled in two conflicting directions.[1] This project involved, of course, the two collaborators' political judgement that communism, which they identified with the struggle of the working class to liberate itself from its plight in capitalist society, represented the only acceptable solution to the conflicts of European modernity in the era following the French Revolution. But Marx and Engels

---

[1] Three relevant French studies of Marx's early development are G. Labica, *Marxism and the Status of Philosophy* (Brighton, 1980); E. Renault, *Marx et l'idée de critique* (Paris, 1995); and S. Kouvelakis, *Philosophy and Revolution* (London, 2003).

did not see communism primarily as an ideology or a moral and political doctrine, but rather as a historical process arising from the material and social conditions of capitalist society but tending towards a radically different form of society based on the sovereignty of those whom Marx in *Capital* calls the 'associated producers'.

'We call communism the *real* movement which abolishes the existing state of things,' Marx and Engels declare in *The German Ideology*.[2] Accordingly this text, written in the mid-1840s, develops the first outline of Marx's theory of history, according to which (as he more concisely stated it in the 1859 Preface to *A Contribution to the Critique of Political Economy*) systemic social transformations are a consequence of the tendency of the productive forces to come into conflict with the prevailing social relations of production. The transition from capitalism to communism therefore will develop as a result of the economic crises that are the specific form taken by this conflict under capitalism and of the class struggles between capital and labour that these crises will intensify.[3] But where did this leave the philosophical tradition, critical engagement with which had allowed Marx to develop this theory of history and the political project that was (for him at least) indissociably connected? Marx himself famously wrote in the eleventh 'Thesis on Feuerbach': 'The philosophers have only *interpreted* the world in various ways; the point is to *change* it.'[4]

Marx's own writings suggest two different ways in which to take this altered view of the relationship between theory and practice. The first was to radicalize the tendency implicit in Feuerbach's critique of Hegel (even if Feuerbach himself hesitated about taking this step): that is, to give up the most basic move made by German classical idealism—the constitutive role assigned to a subject (whether Kant's transcendental unity of apperception or Hegel's Absolute Idea) conceived as distinct from the flow of sense-impressions—for some version of naturalistic positivism. In Marx this solution is most evident in those passages in *The German Ideology* where philosophy is denied any cognitive status at all (most disparagingly when it is compared to masturbation) compared to the scientific study of the 'real material conditions' of individuals' existence.[5] Maybe the same kind of thinking also helps to motivate Marx's

---

[2]  K. Marx and F. Engels, *Collected Works*, 50 vols. (London, 1975– ), v. 49.

[3]  See above all G. A. Cohen, *Karl Marx's Theory of History*, 2nd edn. (Oxford, 2000).

[4]  Marx and Engels, *Collected Works*, v. 5.

[5]  Ibid. v. 236. The stress on individuals in *The German Ideology*, not repeated in later texts, reflects the pressure Marx and Engels felt from Max Stirner's anarcho-individualism in *The Ego and its Own*,

refusal to acknowledge any normative dimension to his critique of capitalist exploitation and his espousal of a relativist metaethics in which values and norms belong to the prevailing ideology in the mode of production in question.[6] The naturalistic-positivist conception of the relationship between theory and practice was, however, much more fully developed by the Marxists of the Second International (1889–1914)—most notably Karl Kautsky and Georgi Plekhanov—who tended to conceive the triumph of socialism as the inevitable product of an historical process governed by the same evolutionary laws (which they typically took from Lamarck rather than Darwin) as those at work in nature. Engels's discovery of 'laws of the dialectic' common to the physical and social worlds offered doctrinal warrant for this naturalistic strain of Marxism (even though Engels himself conceived these laws in a relatively loose and open way that he thought offered a way of avoiding both the physicalist materialism of Büchner, Moleschott, and Vogt, and the teleological speculations of Romantic *Naturphilosophie*).[7]

But there was another strain in Marx's thought, even if it went more or less underground for more than thirty years after his death in 1883. In the *Economic and Philosophical Manuscripts of 1844*, written before *The German Ideology*, Marx used his first reading of classical political economy to develop a philosophical anthropology in which transformative social labour is conceived both as what makes humans distinctively human and as what workers lose control of under capitalism when they sell their labour-power to their employer. This anthropology resurfaces in the massive cycle of manuscripts—the *Grundrisse*, the 1859 *Contribution*, the *Economic Manuscript of 1861–63*, and finally the three volumes of *Capital*—through which Marx sought (unsuccessfully) in the decade 1857–67 to bring his critique of political economy to completion. In the first place, production, the anchor of social life, is conceived as the interaction between humankind and nature mediated by labour, through which humans cooperate socially to transform their physical environment and thereby to meet their needs. Secondly, the capitalist mode of production is regulated by what Marx calls the law of value—the mechanism

---

a philosophical bombshell directed at Feuerbachian humanism. The naturalistic materialism they expound in response is one of the main themes explored by Jacques Derrida in *Spectres of Marx* (New York, 1994).

[6] See especially N. Geras, 'The Controversy about Marx and Justice', *New Left Review*, I/100 (1985), and S. Lukes, *Marxism and Morality* (Oxford, 1985).

[7] See A. Callinicos, 'Marxism and Anarchism', in T. Baldwin (ed.), *The Cambridge History of Philosophy, 1870–1945* (Cambridge, 2003).

thanks to which commodities tend to exchange in proportion to the socially necessary labour-time required to produce them. Marx inherited the labour theory of value from Ricardo, but he gave it a much broader social and historical meaning than it had enjoyed in classical political economy. In particular he argues that it is through competition among autonomous but interdependent producers that the immense variety of different productive activities that make up a modern industrial economy are reduced to so many units of abstract social labour. The value of commodities is thus less some physically ascertainable sum of labour than a social norm imposed on producers through their own competitive interactions. Finally, Marx argues that the governing role of social labour in a capitalist economy is systematically occulted by the very workings of that economy. The most celebrated instance of this process is commodity fetishism: the imperative inherent in the nature of a capitalist economy for the products of social labour to be exchanged as commodities on the market leads to an inversion, in which social relations among human beings take on the form of the autonomous and apparently natural relations among these products. But the entire argument of *Capital* painstakingly reconstructs the process through which the law of value—as well as what it allows us to perceive, namely the exploitation of workers through the extraction of surplus-value—is progressively concealed, by the circulation of commodities, by the competitive struggles of rival capitalists to maximize their profits, and by the distribution of surplus-value among different kinds of capital—for example productive capital invested directly in the exploitation of workers and money capital active in financial markets—as well as among landowners claiming rent.[8]

The conceptual construction of *Capital* pulls away from the naturalistic positivism of the Second International. In the first place, Marx continues in *Capital* and his drafts to describe his enterprise as scientific, but the investigation of 'material conditions of existence' proves to be much more complex and problematic than it appeared to be in *The German Ideology*. The way in which capitalist society tends to conceal its inner mechanisms requires its scientific study rigorously to distinguish between what Marx usually calls essence and appearance. Both in *Capital* and in the portion of the *1861–3 Manuscripts* published as *Theories of Surplus Value*, he praises Smith and

---

[8] The best commentary on these aspects of *Capital* remains I. I. Rubin, *Essays on Marx's Theory of Value* (Detroit, 1972), but see A. Saad-Filho, *The Value of Marx* (London, 2002) for a state-of-the-art discussion.

Ricardo for penetrating the surface appearance of capitalist society and coming to some understanding of its real workings; 'vulgar political economy'—by which is meant the ancestors of the neo-classical orthodoxy that dominates contemporary academic economics—is by contrast relentlessly denounced for merely transcribing how the market seems to work to those engaged in it. Marx is careful to stress that the founders of modern physics also distinguished between how the world seems and how it really works, but the failure of vulgar political economy is more than that of not matching up to the demands of theoretical explanation *tout court*. Simply uncritically to describe the appearances of capitalist society is *apologetic*—that is, it is a form of ideology, inasmuch as, for example, it takes at face value the apparent equality between market actors, ignoring the real inequality in access to productive resources that underlies the seemingly innocent exchange between capital and wage-labour. But this rebounds on the status of Marx's own undertaking. For it indicates that he is doing something different from or more than what, say, Galileo or Darwin undertook: he is, not simply, like them, offering an explanatory theory that seeks to identify the mechanisms underlying and responsible for certain phenomena or processes, but is also providing a critique of other, false theories that, in concealing or misrepresenting the nature of these mechanisms, suppress the fact that the phenomena under examination are part of an unjust social reality. Marx implicitly concedes the point in titling or subtitling all his major economic texts 'Critique of Political Economy': he is engaging in the critique of bourgeois ideology as well as the formulation of scientific theories of the usual explanatory kind.[9]

But what does 'critique' mean here? Recall that Marx denies that his critique of capitalist exploitation appeals to any normative principles: it is a sign of the tensions in his position that, in order to present his views in the previous paragraph, I had in fact to misrepresent them by referring to 'an unjust social reality'. Marx's resistance to the moral condemnation of capitalism has exceptionally complex theoretical sources: one, very different from the naturalistic positivism referred to above, is provided by Hegel's

---

[9]  Good discussions of this dimension of Marx's thought include J. Rancière, 'Le Concept de critique et la critique de l'économie politique dès les *Manuscrits de 1844* au *Capital*', in L. Althusser et al. (eds.), *Lire le Capital*, 4 vols. (Paris, 1973); N. Geras, 'Essence and Appearance: Aspects of Fetishism in Marx's *Capital*', *New Left Review*, I/65 (1970); Renault, *Marx et l'idée de critique*; M. Rosen, *On Voluntary Servitude* (Cambridge, 1996), ch. 6; and H-G. Backhaus, 'Some Aspect of Marx's Concept of Critique in the Context of his Economic-Philosophical Theory', in W. Bonefeld and K. Psychopedis (eds.), *Human Dignity* (Aldershot, 2005). An English translation of Rancière's essay has been published in a useful selection of articles on related issues: A. Rattansi (ed.), *Ideology, Method and Marx* (London, 1989).

critique of Kantian transcendental philosophy. Kant's analysis of morality as irreducible to the 'pathological' processes governing empirical human nature and constituted by universal moral laws capable of being adopted by a community of autonomous subjects is for Hegel one instance of the fundamental flaw in Kant's thought, the systematic separation of form and content that reduces the transcendental subject to an empty shape disjoined from the natural world and from human history. Hegel believes himself capable of closing the gap between form and content because he has developed the dialectical intuitions of earlier philosophers into the doctrine of determinate negation, according to which the tension inherent in every concept (and hence in the world itself, since it is through concepts that the world achieves form) does not destroy the concept, but replaces it with a newer more inclusive concept that incorporates all the content exposed through its earlier contradictory development. Hegel's *Logic*, and the model that it offers of a form of science that does not simply transcribe sense-appearances but captures its object through the progressive construction of an articulated system of categories, evidently influenced Marx's method in *Capital*. But Hegel is able to pull off the process of sustained reconciliation of opposites—for example, of theoretical and practical reason—because of the implicit teleology that binds his categories together and that makes each stage in the dialectic a step closer to the self-realization of the Absolute Spirit that is identical with the process itself. Underlying the debates among Marxist philosophers about whether and if so how materialistically to appropriate the Hegelian dialectic is the problem of whether, once one has dropped the Absolute and the teleology that sustains it, one is entitled to the reconciling and incorporating power that Hegel claims for his method. The naturalistic-positivist take on Marxism offered by, for example, Kautsky did offer an alternative teleology in the idea of an evolutionary process driven by the imperative of adapting societies to their environment. But the result is less the transcendence of oppositions such as that between value and fact but rather the reduction of the former to the latter.[10]

---

[10]  Michael Rosen offers a definitive discussion of the philosophical issues in *Hegel's Dialectic and its Criticism* (Cambridge, 1982). The best treatments of Marx's method in *Capital* include E. V. Ilienkov, *The Dialectics of the Abstract and the Concrete in Marx's* Capital (Moscow, 1982); R. Rosdolsky, *The Making of Marx's* Capital (London, 1977); G. Duménil, *Le Concept de loi économique dans* Le Capital (Paris, 1978); J. Bidet, *Que faire du* Capital?, 2nd edn. (Paris, 2000); and E. Dussel, *Towards an Unknown Marx* (London, 2001). Demonstrating that the conceptual structure of *Capital* is identical to that of Hegel's *Logic* is currently popular among Marxist philosophers—see, for example, T. Smith, *The Logic of Marx's* Capital (Albany, 1990), C. J. Arthur, *The New Dialectic and Marx's* Capital (Leiden,

But, secondly, who is the subject of critique? In whose name is it conducted? Conceiving value as abstract social labour implies that the working class is more than the sum of the deprivations and exclusions to which it is subjected. In *Capital* Volume I and the so-called Sixth Chapter on 'The Results of the Immediate Production Process' that he dropped from the published version, Marx conceptualizes capitalist production as the contradictory relationship between a capital driven by the imperatives of competitive accumulation and a working class that is progressively transformed by the increasingly complex and socialized character of the labour process into a 'collective worker' capable of taking control of the economy and inaugurating a communist society. This distinctive sociology of class dovetailed in with the political stress that Marx and Engels laid, for example, in their role within the First International (1864–76) and in advising the leaders of German Social Democracy, on the working class as, not an inert suffering mass, but the agent of its own emancipation, schooled by its daily conflicts with capital into a subject capable of assuming sovereign power. Such a stress on revolutionary class subjectivity sat ill with the political gradualism that prevailed in the Second International, though the dissident voices—whether representatives of anarcho-syndicalism such as Georges Sorel or more orthodox Marxists like Rosa Luxemburg—remained relatively muted until the First World War and the Russian Revolution of October 1917 blew the international labour movement apart.[11]

# Lukács's Revolution

It was in this context that Georg Lukács effectively inaugurated Marxist philosophy as a distinct intellectual discipline by publishing *History and Class Consciousness* in 1923. But although this collection of essays was an immensely partisan work, in which a sophisticated aesthetic philosopher intimate with the leading figures in German social theory justified the political choice he had made to rally to the Bolshevik cause, this is not the main

2002), and, for a more sceptical view, A. Callinicos, 'Against the New Dialectic', *Historical Materialism*, 13/2 (2005).

[11]  The most gifted Austro-Marxist theorists did address both these issues, essentially by seeking to incorporate Marxist social theory within a modified version of Kantian critical philosophy: see T. Bottomore and P. Goode (eds.), *Austro-Marxism* (Oxford, 1978) and my brief discussion in 'Marxism and Anarchism'.

reason why *History and Class Consciousness* remains such a compelling work. Its brilliance lies in the rigour and *élan* with which Lukács cuts the Gordian knot, resolving the tensions we have been surveying by embracing Marx's Hegelian heritage with enthusiasm. In the central essay of *History and Class Consciousness*, 'Reification and the Consciousness of the Proletariat', Lukács radicalizes and historicizes Hegel's critique of Kantian formalism. Surveying the 'antinomies of bourgeois thought' from Descartes to Dilthey, he situates them within the logic of capitalist society, and more specifically within the comprehensive commodification of social life inherent in this logic. Lukács here develops Marx's theory of commodity fetishism, arguing that commodification implies a process of *reification* in which, in the one hand, social relations are fragmented through the progressive specialization of productive activity, and, on the other, the mediation of interactions by market exchanges promotes the reduction of social processes to natural objects, eternal and unamenable to change. The scission that Max Weber identifies in *Economy and Society* between formal and substantive rationality, and the implication that modern reason allows human beings to ascertain the most effective means of achieving their goals, but not to identify what these goals should be, is an instance of the *irrationality* of capitalism as a distinctive social form, where individual parts of society may be purposively regulated, but the whole remains beyond either comprehension or control. The same unattainability of a rational totality also, according to Lukács, structures post-Cartesian philosophy: the great merit of Hegel is to have grasped the problem, but his own solution—the reconciliation of subject and object in Absolute Spirit—maintains the separation that Hegel himself denounces between thought and history since it is achieved through the retrospective contemplation of the process by philosophy. It is only in Marxism that these antinomies—including that between fact and value, with which Lukács had struggled in his pre-Marxist philosophical writings—are definitively resolved by comprehensively demolishing the oppositions between thought and the world and subject and object. The proletariat is 'the identical subject-object of history': its reduction to an object, that is, the transformation of labour-power into a commodity, is the presupposition of the commodification and reification with which bourgeois thought has struggled unavailingly because it takes for granted the legitimacy and perpetuity of capitalist society. It is therefore only by assuming the class perspective of the proletariat (which may well not be the same as the actual class consciousness of the proletarians themselves) that capitalism becomes an intelligible object—or rather a totality structured by the exploitation of wage-labour, the pivot on which the entire society rests. But this rational understanding is precisely not $\theta\varepsilon\omega\rho\iota\alpha$—it is not the detached contemplation of the totality. It is only through active engagement in the class struggle that, on the one hand, Marxist theory can obtain a real grasp of the contradictions of capitalist society, and, on the other hand, workers forge themselves into the self-conscious collective subject that, as long as bourgeois normality prevails, they are only *in potentia*. The privileged locus for the further development of the critique that Marx inaugurated is therefore a revolutionary party on the Bolshevik model that can mediate between the theoretical understanding of capitalism and the practice of class struggle.[12]

Lukács intended his *tour de force* as a philosophical counterpart to the political break that Lenin and the infant Communist International were making with the timid reformism into which European social democracy had (they believed) degenerated: just as socialist political practice needed to be reoriented around the theme of 'the actuality of the revolution', so the naturalistic positivism of the Second International had to be replaced by a theory of class subjectivity.[13] But, instead of being welcomed, *History and Class Consciousness* was comprehensively denounced by the leadership of the Third International. In large part this reflected the process of 'Bolsheviza-tion' through which the Communist parties were increasingly transformed into disciplined instruments of Soviet foreign policy. But the dogmatic and unthinking character of the predominant Communist reaction to *History and Class Consciousness* should not be allowed to conceal the presence of more substantive issues. The most obvious problems were those implied in the com-mon charge of idealism: by so thoroughly historicizing the dialectic Lukács seemed to rule out the possibility of it having any extension to the physical world. More seriously perhaps for anyone as concerned as Lukács was with squaring his interpretation of Marx with the latter's theory of history (*History and Class Consciousness* is distinguished, among other things, for being the first close philosophical reading of *Capital*), it is hard to reconcile the idea of

---

[12]  See M. Merleau-Ponty, *The Adventures of the Dialectic* (London, 1974), ch. 2; G. Stedman-Jones, 'The Marxism of the Early Lukács', *New Left Review*, I/70 (1971); M. Löwy, *Georg Lukács: From Romanticism to Bolshevism* (London, 1979); A. Arato and P. Breines, *The Young Lukács and the Origins of Western Marxism* (London, 1979); J. Rees, *The Algebra of Revolution* (London, 1998), esp. ch. 5, the Introduction and Postface, respectively by John Rees and Slavoj Žižek to G. Lukács, *A Defence of 'History and Class Consciousness'* (London, 2000), and A. Callinicos, 'Western Marxism and Ideology Critique', in Baldwin (ed.), *The Cambridge History of Philosophy, 1870–1945*.

[13]  The actuality of the revolution is the organizing theme of Lukács's *Lenin* (London, 1970).

the proletariat as the identical subject-object of history with Marx's narrative of successive modes of production rising and falling in response to conflicts between the forces and relations of production. It was difficulties of this nature that led Lukács, after drafting a robust defence of his book, later to embrace a much more objectivist interpretation of the dialectic that (in particular after he read the *1844 Manuscripts* prior to their publication in 1932) focused, not on the dynamics of class subjectivity, but instead on the interaction between labour and nature.[14] Implicit in these difficulties but arguably more interesting from a longer-term perspective is the fact that Lukács sought in *History and Class Consciousness* philosophically to ground a revolutionary interpretation of Marxism through a theory of absolute subjectivity at precisely the historical moment when Western philosophers began seriously to interrogate the category of the subject—first in all the twists and turns of Heidegger's writings, and then, of course, with the gradual emergence of anti-humanism as one of the dominant themes of French thought after 1945. One way of thinking about the subsequent development of Marxist philosophy (and later of increasingly more explicitly 'post-Marxist' critical theory) is to see it as a succession of attempts to address an agenda largely inherited from Lukács by seeking to disengage the critique of capitalism that Marx inaugurated from any theory of subjectivity. The early Frankfurt School, Althusser, and Habermas all offer examples of this kind of attempt.

## Beyond the Subject: Adorno, Althusser, and Habermas

Lukács's use of the idea of commodity fetishism as the organizing metaphor for any attempt to understand capitalist society is enormously influential on the central figures in the Frankfurt School, Theodor Adorno and Max Horkheimer. What, by contrast, they find very hard to swallow is the conception of the proletariat as the identical subject-object of capitalist society. Initially this scepticism is motivated by fairly straightforward political and sociological reasons—on the one hand, the defeat of the revolutionary wave

---

[14]  Thus compare Lukács, *Defence of 'History and Class Consciousness'*, drafted in the mid-1920s but only published nearly thirty years after Lukács's death, with, for example, Lukács, *The Young Hegel* (London, 1975), written in 1938 and published after the war.

after the First World War and the subsequent victories of Fascism and National Socialism, and, on the other, the evidence that the Frankfurt School's empirical studies (particular after their flight into American exile) provided that the processes of commodification that Lukács had highlighted were fragmenting class consciousness and therefore systematically preventing the Western proletariat from constituting itself as a self-conscious collective subject. But the radicalization of Horkheimer's and Adorno's critique of 'late capitalism' in *Dialectic of Enlightenment* (1947) entails an increasingly philosophical suspicion of the category of the subject itself. Reification is henceforth conceived in transhistorical terms as the consequence of humankind's drive to dominate nature: class exploitation, while still condemned, is thereby reduced to an instance of a much broader pattern of subjugation. Within this framework reason itself appears to be necessarily instrumental, a tool in the effort to render the physical world fungible and controllable. Adorno's philosophical master-work, *Negative Dialectics* (1966), denounces the very idea of the constitutive subject at the heart of classical German idealism as a philosophical rationalization of the urge by a humankind divorced from nature to dominate and consume it. He does not therefore dismiss the concept of the subject as altogether worthless—the ideal of individual autonomy articulated by classical liberalism during the early phase of bourgeois society did provide a refuge, however privileged and problematic, from the processes of commodification. But, with the onset of the 'totally administered society' whose triumph in more subtle forms than those offered by Nazism was secured by the victory of liberal democracy in the Second World War, that refuge is invaded and conquered. Particularly through the operations of the culture industry symbolized by Hollywood, the individual subject is broken open and subject to the direct and unmediated imperatives of capital accumulation and mass consumption. Amid this almost comprehensive disaster, the thought of Hegel and Marx, for all their limitations, retain their uses for critical thought. In particular, the subsumption of individual existence under the categories of the *Logic* mirrors how the law of value reduces particular human activities into units of abstract social labour—Adorno continues to affirm the actuality of Marx's critique of political economy, for example, criticizing Lukács's concept of reification for idealism, even though the collective subject whom that critique was intended to help constitute has long ago succumbed to the very processes revealed by *Capital*. [15]

---

[15]  See Rolf Wiggershaus's monumental study, *The Frankfurt School* (Cambridge, MA, 1994).

It is to the Frankfurt School that we owe the expression 'critical theory', initially as an academically acceptable synonym for Marxism, but increasingly as a name for the pursuit of at least aspects of Marx's project beyond the confines of orthodox Marxism. But the obvious problem—thematized extensively by Jürgen Habermas, widely seen as Horkheimer's and Adorno's philosophical heir—was what kind of status they provided for critique itself. Marx and Lukács had given it a definite social location: it is only from the vantage point of the proletariat that capitalist society, with all its injustices and dysfunctions, becomes intelligible as a totality. For Horkheimer and Adorno the atomization and incorporation of the working class by late capitalism meant that this kind of class perspective offered no sort of critical leverage. Karl Mannheim, also influenced by Lukács, proposed the 'free-floating intelligentsia' as the social vehicle for rational insight into capitalist modernity, but Adorno dismissed this as implying too reconciling a vision of contemporary society. The problem was, however, more than sociological or political. If reason itself is implicated in the domination not simply of exploited and oppressed humans, but of nature itself, how could it provide the means to illuminate and criticize this domination? How was critical theory itself possible? Adorno, a much more sophisticated philosopher than Horkheimer, circled round this problem for decades. His answer seemed to be that critical theory could evoke the sheer suffering inflicted on humans and animals alike by the totally administered society, notably by philosophical reflection on the high Modernist works of art whose dissonant structures alluded to this suffering and thereby, by negation, implied the possibility of a Utopian reconciliation of humankind and nature. But, even if coherent, this solution offered no direction for the kind of programme of research that, for example, the Frankfurt School itself had pursued in the 1930s and 1940s, and no route to anything resembling a serious politics (even though large numbers of German students in the late 1960s, to Horkheimer's dismay and Adorno's embarrassment, used their books to justify rebelling against capitalism).[16]

An alternative strategy for Marxist philosophy was, while trying not to lapse back into naturalistic positivism, to break altogether with Hegel and indeed

---

[16]  See T. W. Adorno and H. Marcuse, 'Correspondence on the German Student Movement' (1969), *New Left Review*, I/233 (1999), and, for the diagnosis of the dilemmas of the early Frankfurt School offered by their successors, J. Habermas, *The Theory of Communicative Action*, i (London, 1984), ch. 4; A. Wellmer, 'Truth, Semblance and Reconciliation', *Telos*, 62 (1984–5); and A. Honneth, *The Critique of Power* (Cambridge, MA, 1991), pt. I.

with the idea of constitutive subjectivity. The most influential exponent of this strategy was Louis Althusser. Althusser went through his own ultra-Hegelian phase in the late 1940s and early 1950s when, along with many other young intellectuals, he rallied to the French Communist Party.[17] But the books for which he is most famous—*For Marx* and the collective work *Reading Capital*, both published in 1965—espoused an avowedly anti-Hegelian Marxism. Althusser—in the late 1960s and early 1970s identified with Maoist dissidents within French Communism—presented this as a 'return to Marx', but in fact what he and his collaborators offered was a highly controversial reconstruction resting on three main elements. In the first place, a 'symptomatic reading' of Marx's writings, modelled on Freud's interpretations of dreams and parapraxes as the distorted fulfilment of repressed desires, reveals an 'epistemological break' dividing the young Marx, whose thought is impregnated with Hegelianism and humanism, from mature scientific works such as *Capital*. This reading of Marx implies that the fundamental difference in problematic—the implicit system of questions organizing a theory—that separated him from Hegel made all the attempts from Engels onwards to distinguish Hegel's dialectical method from his idealist system essays in self-deception. Replotting Marx's trajectory in this fashion implied, secondly, a very different conception of science from that to be found in the Frankfurt School, early or late. Horkheimer, Adorno, and Habermas all conceive science as a form of instrumental rationality, constitutively tied to the practical imperative of mastering nature to meet human needs. For Althusser, by contrast, science is characterized above all by its *autonomy*, its distance from everyday activities and concerns. This view reflects the influence of the French 'epistemological' tradition in the philosophy of science, and in particular of his teacher Gaston Bachelard, who argues that a science is formed by breaking with sense-experience and folk beliefs and developing an internally powered dynamic of conceptual refinement and reconfiguration. Althusser tries to incorporate this conception of science into Marxism by, on the one hand, presenting theory as a distinct social practice governed by its own special protocols, and, on the other, reinterpreting the rupture through which a science is constituted as a break with ideology (conceived along roughly Marxist lines as the imaginary relationship that social actors have with their actual relationship to their conditions of existence). Finally,

---

[17] L. Althusser, *The Spectre of Hegel*, ed. F. Matheron (London, 1997) and Y. Moulier Boutang, *Louis Althusser: Une biographie*, i (Paris, 1992).

this theory of science is conceived as a specification of a larger reinterpretation of Marx's theory of history. The main thought here is that the forces and relations of production (under the influence of the Chinese Cultural Revolution Althusser gives primacy to the latter) must be understood as structures irreducible to the relations among the persons taking part in them. History is 'a process without a subject or goals'. Individuals are transformed into subjects through ideology, which 'interpellates' them, summoning them to perform the role required of them as 'supports' of the prevailing relations of production.[18]

The rereading of Marxism offered by Althusser and those influenced by him (most notably the state theorist Nicos Poulantzas) had a major impact on the renaissance of Marxism produced by the upheavals of 1968 and after. Its main philosophical thrust made it part of the broader phenomenon of French anti-humanism that, as it took shape in the course of the 1960s, threw up the names 'structuralism' and then 'poststructuralism'. As philosophy tutor at the École Normale Supérieure in Paris, Althusser taught Foucault and was a colleague and friend of Derrida's: at the height of his fame he positively revelled in the notoriety his anti-humanist reading of Marx attained.[19] But whereas the influence of Derrida and Foucault expanded enormously in subsequent decades, Althusser's vanished almost as quickly as it had emerged. In part this was for reasons of external history: he was the most spectacular victim of the profound crisis that overwhelmed European Marxism in the late 1970s, as it became clear that the revolutionary hopes raised by 1968 would not be fulfilled (Althusser's personal fall was, of course, greatly accelerated in October 1980, when he murdered his wife during one of the depressions from which he had suffered since his teens).[20] But it was also that the contradictions in his theoretical project rapidly became visible. Two are worth mentioning here. First, the autonomization of theory he attempted sat ill with the Marxist framework in which he incorporated it. For one thing, if (as he argues) every science has its own internal criteria of validity, how to distinguish it from a theoretically elaborated ideology? For another, the reconceptualization of the social totality as a plurality of autonomous practices seemed all too liable to

[18] The fullest account of Althusser's theory of ideology is to be found *Sur la reproduction* (Paris, 1995), a posthumously published text from which the celebrated essay 'Ideology and the Ideological State Apparatuses', first published in English in Althusser, *Lenin and Philosophy and Other Essays* (London, 1971), was extracted.

[19] L. Althusser, *The Humanist Controversy and Other Essays*, ed. F. Matheron and G. M. Goshgarian (London, 2003).

[20] See Althusser's autobiographies in *The Future Lasts a Long Time* (London, 1993).

collapse into more mainstream ideas of society as a contingent collection of different factors. In both these respects—that is, the tendencies to blur the distinction between science and ideology and to disaggregate the social into a play of difference—Althusser pointed in the direction that poststructuralism took, notably in Foucault's writings on 'power-knowledge' in the mid-1970s. The second major difficulty is, however, common to both Althusser and Foucault: in what sense can a consistent anti-humanism coherently claim to be engaging in critique? The logic of both Althusser's theory of ideology and texts of Foucault's such as *Discipline and Punish* and '*Society Must be Defended*' is to treat individual subjects as having no identity independent of the relations of domination that they are constructed within and in order to perpetuate. But—as was most forcefully expressed by the great English Marxist historian Edward Thompson in his polemic against Althusser—if that's how things are, what is the point of resisting these relations in practice and of criticizing them in theory? Though it would be misleading to bracket Althusser and Foucault with the naturalistic positivism of the Second International, they too resist introducing any normative dimension from which to motivate social critique—and, consistent in their anti-humanism, they disdain the evocation of sheer brute suffering that informs Horkheimer's and Adorno's philippics against late capitalism.[21]

Habermas and his co-thinkers never showed much more than contemptuous incomprehension for Althusser's enterprise.[22] But Habermas's own project is best understood as a response to the same set of problems that had motivated Althusser. Like the anti-humanists of Paris, Habermas rejects 'the philosophy of consciousness'. This philosophy informs classical Marxism, whose 'production paradigm' posits a monologic relationship between a collective human subject and a nature conceived as the former's passive object. The aporias of the early Frankfurt School stem ultimately from Horkheimer's and Adorno's failure to break with this conceptual framework, even though they increasingly saw the historical process thus understood not as, say, Kautsky perceived it, as the progressive conquest of nature by rationally organized humanity, but as the destruction of reason. But the conclusion of Habermas's critique of

---

[21]  E. P. Thompson, *The Poverty of Theory and Other Essays* (London, 1978). See also P. Anderson, *Arguments within Western Marxism* (London, 1980); E. Balibar, *Ecrits pour Althusser* (Paris, 1991); A. Callinicos, *Althusser's Marxism* (London, 1976); G. Elliott, *Althusser: The Detour of Theory* (London, 1987); G. Elliott (ed.), *Althusser: A Critical Reader* (Oxford, 1994); E. A. Kaplan and M. Sprinker (eds.), *The Althusserian Legacy* (London, 1993); P. Raymond (ed.), *Althusser philosophe* (Paris, 1997).

[22]  See, for example, A. Honneth, 'History and Interaction', in Elliott (ed.), *Althusser*.

classical Marxism is not the straightforward abandonment of the concept of the constitutive subject, but rather its transformation into a communicative theory of *inter*subjectivity. On this account, communication implicitly oriented towards the goal of achieving uncoerced agreement between speaker and hearer is the paradigm of all human action. Social theory, consequently, must start from the dialogic relationship among a plurality of interacting and communicating persons, not the monologic subject–object relationship that is the basis of Marx's anthropology. This does not imply a Romantic rejection of instrumental rationality, which has its place when humans seek to understand and control nature in order to meet their needs. But it must be seen as one specific and limited form of a much broader rationality that is fundamentally communicative. Correlatively, the development of modernity involves crucially a process of differentiation in which specific forms of rationality (instrumental, aesthetic–practical, moral–political) articulate themselves as the presuppositions of distinct discourses each governed by its own protocols. The peculiar imperatives of instrumental rationality further produce the separation from the lifeworld of implicit pre-understandings presupposed by every communicative act of the economy and polity as autonomous subsystems each regulated by its own medium—respectively, money and power. Society as a decentred system is thus not, as Althusser claimed, a constant in human history conceived as 'a process without a subject', but an achievement of modernity. And Habermas does see modernity as an achievement—'an incomplete project' threatened, not by the differentiation that is required for the rational development of humankind, but by the tendency of the subsystems to colonize the lifeworld, in the way in which, as he sought to show in his first major work, the public sphere of rational and critical debate that developed in early bourgeois society in the eighteenth and nineteenth centuries was penetrated and increasingly dominated by the imperatives of commodified mass consumption.[23]  These trends do not, however, lead Habermas to despair of modernity: his view is the one he attributes to Adorno—'he remains true to the idea that there is no cure for the wounds of Enlightenment other than the radicalized Enlightenment itself.'[24]  Communicative action, institutionalized in modern liberal democracy and its legal systems, has the capacity to rein in unrestrained instrumental rationality. Habermas cites the examples of the success of the post-war welfare state in regulating capitalism

---

[23]  J. Habermas, *The Structural Transformation of the Public Sphere* (Cambridge, MA, 1989).
[24]  Habermas, *Autonomy and Solidarity* (London, 1992), 155.

and thereby avoiding its worst excesses and the emergence of forms of global governance that in his view represent faltering steps towards Kant's idea of a world confederation with sufficient power and authority to prevent war.[25]

One of the principal motivations behind Habermas's entire philosophical enterprise is to provide a defensible basis for the kind of critique that Marx inaugurated.[26] His mature theory of communicative action is supposed, among other things, to offer the reconciliation between scientific and normative discourses that Marx and his successors had failed to give. But it is never clear quite how this is meant to happen. Habermas displays a degree of hesitation about the status of critical theory itself. In *Knowledge and Human Interests* (1968) the idea of the 'knowledge-constitutive interest' presupposed by each kind of discourse bears a strong resemblance to Kant's concept of the transcendental conditions of experience. Partly to avoid any implication of constitutive subjectivity, Habermas in his later writings treats the presuppositions of communicative action as counterfactual commitments implicit in every speech act. But this (as he sees it) pragmatist strategy is in tension with his desire to show how the idea of communicative action can justify, not a specific set of values or duties, but at least the normative framework of modern liberal democracies. For example, Habermas writes: 'Communicatively acting individuals are thus subject to "must" of a weak transcendental necessity, but this does not mean that they already encounter the prescriptive "must" of a rule of action.'[27] The content of this 'weak transcendental necessity' is primarily procedural: the institutions of liberal democracy should as far as possible have the open, dialogic structure required by the implicit commitment of communicative action towards uncoerced consensus. But the apparently purely procedural character of communicative rationality makes Habermas vulnerable to the charge that he is retreating into the kind of formalism for which Hegel criticized Kant, as well as to Davidson's deconstruction of the distinction between conceptual scheme and substantive judgement.[28] Moreover, particularly in his theory

---

[25] The most important expositions of Habermas's developed views are *The Theory of Communicative Action*, i (London, 1984), and ii (Cambridge, 1987); *The Philosophical Discourse of Modernity* (Cambridge, 1987); and *Between Facts and Norms* (Cambridge, 1996). Axel Honneth offers a version of Habermas's theory of modernity that grounds it, not in communicative action, but in the struggle for recognition that binds together human actors: see *The Critique of Power* and *The Struggle for Recognition* (Cambridge, 1996).

[26] See especially *Knowledge and Human Interests* (London, 1972).

[27] Habermas, *Between Facts and Norms*, 4.

[28] D. Davidson, 'On the Very Idea of a Conceptual Scheme', in id., *Inquiries into Truth and Interpretation* (Oxford, 1984).

of law and democracy, Habermas's pragmatism, and the influence of the normative functionalism of Durkheim and Talcott Parsons encourage him to conceive communicative action as the source of social integration, leading to a constant slide from the epistemic validity (*Gültigkeit*) of norms to their social acceptance (*Geltung*). Habermas's attempt to integrate critical theory and functionalist sociology therefore threatens to abolish to the distance from existing social reality that seems to be a necessary condition of critique performing its role.[29]

# CONTEMPORARY MARXISM AND POST-MARXISM

With Habermas we step definitively beyond the boundaries of orthodox Marxism into the world of post-Marxism—that is, of the cluster of projects that seek to continue Marx's critique while rejecting many of his most important substantive claims and often also the method through which he arrived at them.[30] A variety of strategies have been pursued by contemporary theorists unconvinced by Habermas's attempted reconstruction of historical materialism. What is intriguing is how often these strategies replicate or reactivate some of the tendencies to be found in the more classical Marxist debates surveyed above.[31] The naturalistic positivism of the Second International has remained deeply unattractive to later generations. Attaching this label to the school of Analytical Marxists that briefly flourished in the 1980s, as many more orthodox critics polemically tended to, failed to capture the concerns and methods of this group. Nevertheless, in one respect Analytical Marxism did resemble the most intellectually creative group of Second International Marxists, the Austro-Marxists. The latter tended to accept Kant's distinction between theoretical and practical reason: thus, in his preface to *Finance Capital*, Rudolf Hilferding famously argues that it is perfectly possible to accept Marx's theory

---

[29] See A. Callinicos, *Against Postmodernism* (Cambridge, 1989), ch. 4, and *The Resources of Critique* (Cambridge, 2006), § 1.1, and P. Anderson, *Spectrum* (London, 2005), chs. 5 and 7.

[30] Ernest Laclau and Chantal Mouffe adopted the label 'Post-Marxism' in *Hegemony and Socialist Strategy* (London, 1985), but compare Jon Elster's concluding remarks in *Making Sense of Marx* (Cambridge, 1985) and Jacques Bidet's ambitious attempt to develop a theory of modernity to rival Habermas's in *Théorie générale* (Paris, 1999).

[31] This section deals largely with authors discussed in much more detail in *The Resources of Critique*.

of capitalism but not to follow him in seeking this system's overthrow. Turning to Analytical Marxism, we see, in the first place, the effort to develop defensible restatements of Marxist theory, most notably in G. A. Cohen's *Karl Marx's Theory of History* (1978). In principle, conceptual reconstruction of this kind was no different from what Althusser and his collaborators had undertaken a decade or two before, though the Analytical Marxists' reliance on analytical philosophy and Anglophone social science as their main source of intellectual style and paradigms did set them apart from earlier Marxist philosophers. But, secondly, Analytical Marxism increasingly took rights—and the rest of the apparatus of normative discourse—seriously. John Roemer's *A General Theory of Exploitation and Class* (1982) provided the bridge between the two forms of inquiry, since it offered a critical reconstruction of Marx's theory of exploitation, which its author had regarded as belonging firmly in the domain of explanatory theory, but Roemer's restatement of which moved discussion of exploitation into the terrain of the egalitarian conceptions of justice developed by John Rawls and his interlocutors. Cohen's and Roemer's main theoretical preoccupations subsequently came to focus on issues in normative political philosophy—a shift that the former argued was justified both by the inadequacies of Marxist social theory and by the incoherence of the Hegelian dialectic, which purported to transcend the opposition between theoretical and practical reason. This movement from clarifying the nature of Marxism as an explanatory theory to exploring normative problems in a philosophical space developed by egalitarian liberalism may in a certain sense have been made possible by the Althusserian critique of Hegelian Marxism: quite against Althusser's own intentions, once the illusion was removed that the secret of the dialectic was to be found in Hegel, sooner or later Marxist philosophers would have to shake off orthodoxy and ask themselves what place ethical and moral considerations should play in socialist thought. In the case of Analytical Marxism, the pursuit of these questions involved the abandonment of the kind of explanatory social theory more traditionally undertaken by Marxists, though there does not seem to be any reason to think that the two kinds of inquiry are inherently incompatible—a point to which I return below.[32]

---

[32] See especially G. A. Cohen, *Self-Ownership, Freedom, and Equality* (Cambridge, 1995) and *If You're an Egalitarian, How Come You're So Rich?* (Cambridge, MA, 2000); M. Roberts, *Analytical Marxism: A Critique* (London, 1996), and A. Callinicos, 'Introduction: Analytical Marxism', in id. (ed.), *Marxist Theory* (Oxford, 1989), and 'Having Your Cake and Eating It', *Historical Materialism*, 9 (2001).

A second direction taken by contemporary critical theory has involved resort to a version of naturalism very different from the kind of social Lamarckianism favoured, for example, by Kautsky. The most celebrated recent work of Marxist theory is undoubtedly Michael Hardt and Antonio Negri's *Empire* (2000). This book is best known for the thesis that contemporary capitalism involves a new form of transnational network power that has rendered imperialism, with its antagonisms among rival national centres, obsolete and required the emergence of a novel kind of sovereignty, Empire, which recognizes no limit to its dominion. Challenging Empire is a new form of class subjectivity, multitude, in which all those dominated by capital converge in resistance to it. *Empire*'s critique of more traditional Marxist theories of capitalism and class has aroused immense debate. Often obscured in these arguments is Hardt and Negri's reliance on the vitalist ontology originally developed by Gilles Deleuze, most notably in *Mille plateaux* (1980, written in collaboration with Félix Guattari). For Deleuze, Life is to be understood less as the kind of organic force at the centre of Bergson's philosophy than as an anarchic tendency to subvert all hierarchies and stratifications, and to decentre all relations of domination. The significance of Empire for Hardt and Negri is that it is the variant of capitalism in which the subversive potential of Life is most fully realized, notably through the decentring of power-relations implied by the increasing reliance on network forms of organization the economy, the military, and elsewhere. But this potentially liberating attainment reflects the growing dependence of an increasingly parasitic capital on the creativity of the multitude. This creativity can no longer be understood within the framework of Marxian value theory, for the new network capitalism systematically demolishes the barriers between work and the rest of human life, promoting the development of what Hardt and Negri call 'biopolitical production': with the decline of manual labour and the growth of the service sector, it is now Life itself that is exploited by capital rather than the purposive activity of transforming nature with which Marx identified labour. Consequently the multitude represents, within the limits of capitalist class relations, the triumph of the inherent productivity of Life.[33]

---

[33] Hardt's and Negri's vitalist presuppositions are most evident in *Empire* (Cambridge, MA, 2000), chs. 4.1 and 4.2. See also A. Negri, *Le Pouvoir constituant* (Paris, 1997), ch. 7; M. Hardt and A. Negri, *Multitude* (New York, 2004); and P. Virno, *The Grammar of the Multitude* (New York, 2004). Critical responses to *Empire* are collected in G. Balakrishnan (ed.), *Debating 'Empire'* (London, 2003) and P. A. Passavant and J. Dean (eds.), *Empire's New Clothes* (New York, 2004).

Hardt and Negri undeniably offer answers of a kind to the two questions that, as I noted above, are posed by Marx's critique of political economy, namely the status of this critique and its subject. But their philosophical presuppositions are radically different from the Hegelian heritage out of which Marx developed his critique. As a philosophical reference point Hegel is replaced by Spinoza—a step that Althusser and his collaborators had already taken when seeking to formulate an anti-Hegelian, anti-humanist Marxism.[34] Negri's project is similarly anti-Hegelian: 'That Marx was Hegelian has never seemed to me the case: on the sole condition of reading Marx and Hegel.'[35] His reading of Spinoza is heavily influenced by that of Deleuze, for whom the concept of God as immanent cause implies a non-hierarchical conception of being, what he calls 'the principle of an equality of being', according to which all entities are equally valid expressions of the divine substance.[36] Deleuze's conception of the 'plane of immanence', where entities are related to each other laterally and hierarchies of any kind are temporary and liable to subversion, is an important source of the idea of Empire as a transnational network. One attraction of this kind of Spinozist Marxism for anti-humanists is that it is incompatible with any conception of subjectivity as constitutive. Hardt and Negri call the multitude 'an active social subject, which acts on the basis of what singularities share in common', but how these singularities somehow spontaneously converge to form a subject is one of the great mysteries of *Empire*.[37] Hardt and Negri's break with the idea of constitutive subjectivity is, however, more apparent than real: the multitude may be little more than a placeholder for the trans-individual creative impulses of Life, but what is Life itself as they conceive it but a subjectivized nature? The general refusal of serious Marxist philosophers since the collapse of the Second International to countenance any kind of naturalistic conception of the unity of the social and physical worlds may well have ossified into a dogma demanding critical re-examination. But to treat nature as a projection of the political desire for egalitarian and domination-free social relations, as Hardt and Negri do, following Deleuze, is simply to foreclose serious discussion of what a non-positivist and non-reductionist naturalism might look like.[38]

---

[34]  See, for example, P. Macherey, *Hegel ou Spinoza?* (Paris, 1979).

[35]  A. Negri, *Marx Beyond Marx* (South Hadley, MA, 1984), 57.

[36]  G. Deleuze, *Spinoza et le problème d'expression* (Paris, 1968), 157. Negri's own study of Spinoza concentrates on his political thought: *The Savage Anomaly* (Minneapolis, 1991).

[37]  Hardt and Negri, *Multitude*, 100; see E. Laclau, 'Can Immanence Explain Social Struggles?', in Passavant and Dean (eds.), *Empire's New Clothes*.

[38]  See Callinicos, *Resources of Critique*, esp. chs. 4–6. John Holloway has formulated a version of Marxism whose political conclusions are quite similar to those of Hardt and Negri, but whose

Another influential strand in contemporary post-Marxist thought pursues a philosophical strategy radically opposed to that developed by Hardt and Negri. For the latter the capacity to criticize and transform existing social reality is a consequence of what they call, in the famous concluding paragraph of *Empire*, 'the joy of being'—of the plenitude of Life.[39] For Alain Badiou, by contrast, a subject capable of bearing witness—in Badiou's special vocabulary, being faithful to—innovation proceeds through a subtraction, a radical break from the normal course of being. Influenced in his youth by both Sartre and Althusser, Badiou swims against the anti-humanist stream in the emphasis he places on developing a theory of subjectivity that does not focus, as, say, Althusser and Foucault do, on how individual persons are formed by and in relations of domination. But he does not thereby return to a version of the idea of constitutive subjectivity. For one thing, not all persons are subjects. On the contrary, subjects emerge from an exceptional constellation of circumstances. Badiou, particularly in his major philosophical work, *L'Etre et l'événement* (1988), seeks to theorize the event—conceived not as one mere occurrence among many, but as a singularity, something unique and exceptional. The subject, defined by its fidelity to such an event, is therefore 'rare and heroic'.[40] For another, subjects emerge from trans-individual processes. But Badiou conceives these processes in a manner radically different from the decentring flux of Life celebrated by Deleuze and Negri. Ontology, he claims, recapitulates the main proofs in set theory. The complexities of Badiou's interpretation of mathematical logic in *L'Etre et l'événement* are far too great to consider here, but it is perhaps worth underlining that it implies, compared to the luxuriant extravagances of Deleuze's metaphysics, an austere ontology whose content is established through the conceptual clarification of the nature of number. What this analysis reveals that being consists of situations in each of which the

philosophical foundations are provided, not by Spinoza and Deleuze (or Spinoza read through Deleuze), but by a development of the early Frankfurt School, and in particular of Adorno's negative dialectic, very different from that offered by Habermas: see especially John Holloway, *Change the World Without Taking Power* (London, 2002).

[39] Hardt and Negri, *Empire*, 413.

[40] A. Badiou, *Saint Paul* (Paris, 1997), 7. Badiou's theory of subjectivity is the most important articulation of a preoccupation in contemporary Continental philosophy with the exceptional: thus among leading deconstructionists, the idea of the event (conceived as Badiou does as a break with normality) is powerfully influenced by Carl Schmitt's theory of the political sovereign as the instance of state power that has the authority to declare a state of emergency (or state of exception, *Ausnahmezustand*) and suspend the constitution: see C. Schmitt, *Political Theology* (Cambridge, MA, 1985); J. Derrida, *Politics of Friendship* (London, 1997); and G. Agamben, *Homo Sacer* (Stanford, 1998) and *State of Exception* (Chicago, 2005).

multiple (conceived as a set) is unified into a structure—'counted-as-one', as Badiou puts it, as *a* situation. The fact that every situation is a result of this operation of 'counting-as-one' implies that lying beyond the situation but presupposed by it is what Badiou calls 'inconsistent multiplicity', or the void—the condition of indifference that being possesses when it does not belong to a situation. This void haunts every situation, threatening to subvert it—a danger that is warded off through the reduplication of the structure that defines the situation in a 'metastructure', the state of the situation that, like the political state in classical Marxism, seeks to give the situation a unity that it inherently lacks. But the void can still make itself felt through an event—that is, through a singular occurrence that, in a random and unpredictable fashion, transcends the situation, but that is made possible by elements of the situation (what Badiou calls the 'eventual site') that somehow manage to avoid inclusion in the metastructure, in the constraining unity imposed by the state. An event thus bears an ambiguous relationship to the situation—Badiou, drawing on set theory, describes it as an element of the situation that is not included in it—that places it '*on the edge of the void*'. The occurrence of an event is thus not self-evident: to become visible it requires an 'interpreting intervention' that retroactively identifies it as both a break from and an element of the situation. Badiou calls such interventions 'generic procedures' through which truths emerge. It is through fidelity to a specific 'truth-event' that a subject is formed: 'A subject is not a result, any more than it is an origin. It is the *local* status of the procedure, an exceptional configuration of the situation.'[41]

This is hardly the most perspicuous of philosophical schemes. It may therefore be helpful to consider some of the illustrations Badiou gives. One of the more remarkable is provided by his little book on St Paul. Badiou portrays him as 'a thinker-poet of the event', who sought to universalize Christianity by dissociating it from both Jewish law and Greek metaphysics and stripping it down to the 'pure event' of the Resurrection. For Badiou, Paul's role in the debate over whether gentile converts to Christianity should have to conform to the Jewish law by becoming circumcised exemplifies the relationship between an event and its eventual site. Paul recognized that, if Judaism was the site of the 'Christ-Event', the event nevertheless transcended its site. By becoming the apostle to the gentiles and preaching a 'New Law'

---

[41] A. Badiou, *L'Etre et l'événement* (Paris, 1988), 195, 430. Badiou distinguishes four kinds of generic procedure—art, science, love, and philosophy. Peter Hallward was written an excellent and exhaustive introduction to Badiou's philosophy in general and to *L'Etre et l'événement* in particular: *Badiou: A Subject to Truth* (Minneapolis, 2003).

in which the gift of divine grace is offered to all, Paul became 'one of the very first theoreticians of the universal'.[42] The emphasis laid here on the universal should serve as a signal that there is a political dimension to Badiou's theory of subjectivity. The French Revolution of 1789 and the Russian Revolution of 1917 are paradigm cases of political events. Badiou, one of the most prominent and polemical French exponents of Maoism in the decade after 1968, remains, despite his subsequent renunciation of Marxism, among those 'faithful to the event of October 1917'.[43] This naturally poses the question of how one identifies events worthy of such fidelity. That October 1917 should belong in this category is, of course, deeply controversial, but—to take an easier case—what about those who wish to remain faithful to the National Socialist 'revolution' in Germany? Badiou's answer is that genuine events have universal addressees, which Nazism plainly did not.[44] But the feeling that this is an arbitrary stipulation is reinforced when one considers that Badiou's account of the universal both gives it a strongly normative content and ascribes to it the same properties—in particular, that of being exceptional—that he discovers in events themselves.[45] This apparent circularity underlines the impression that Badiou has constructed an elaborate ontology in order to theorize the stance of active political commitment that he developed in his Maoist days (and seeks to continue in the post-Marxist *groupuscule* enigmatically entitled the Organisation politique) but that this ontology lacks the substantive content needed make such a practice plausible. One can understand why Badiou's great philosophical antagonist Deleuze should accuse him of Kantian formalism.[46]

Meanwhile, another major figure on the French intellectual scene, Pierre Bourdieu, developed in the last years of his life a version of Hegel's conception of the universal class, that is, of the class for whom 'the private interest is

[42]  Badiou, *Saint Paul*, 5, 47, 116.       [43]  id., *D'un désastre obscur* (Paris, 1998), 7.

[44]  id., *Ethics* (London, 2001), ch. 4.

[45]  id., 'Eight Theses on the Universal', in id., *Theoretical Writings*, trans. and ed. R. Brassier and A. Toscano (London, 2004).

[46]  Badiou reports this criticism, apparently made frequently in the correspondence that took place between the two philosophers not long before Deleuze's suicide in 1995, in *Deleuze* (Minneapolis, 2000), 76, 99. Apart from Hallward's detailed treatment, other critical discussions of Badiou include D. Bensaïd, *Resistances* (Paris, 2001), ch. II.2; Callinicos, *Resources of Critique*, ch. 3; S. Kouvelakis, 'La Politique dans ses limites, or les paradoxes de Alain Badiou', *Actuel Marx*, 28 (2000); J.-J. Lecercle, 'Cantor, Lacan, Mao, Beckett, *même combat*: The Philosophy of Alain Badiou', *Radical Philosophy*, 93 (1999); and S. Žižek, *The Ticklish Subject* (London, 1999), ch. 3. One of the main influences on Badiou is Jacques Lacan's interpretation of psychoanalysis: though Slavoj Žižek has played a major role in making Badiou's thought more accessible in the English-speaking world, he also criticizes him for being insufficiently Lacanian.

satisfied through working for the universal'.[47] Hegel of course identified the state bureaucracy with this class; Marx later gave the concept a very different inflection when he claimed that the universal class is the proletariat, 'a class with *radical chains*', which has 'a universal character by its universal suffering and claims no *particular right* because *no particular wrong* but *wrong generally* is perpetrated against it'.[48] In the decade before his death in 2002—a decade in which he became a leading spokesperson for the movement for another globalization, Bourdieu identified yet another avatar of the universal class—the intellectuals who, in a distinctively French tradition initiated by Zola during the Dreyfus affair, by virtue of their authority in the specific cultural field in which they work, assert the interests of the universal in the larger society. If this all sounds very French (Bourdieu cites Sartre and Foucault as exemplars of this syndrome, but in the 1990s he himself took on a similar role), Bourdieu offers a distinctive, essentially sociological explanation of why intellectuals should have 'a *particular interest in the universal*'.[49] His larger theory of social structure identifies the latter with fields each of which is constituted by a struggle for recognition driven by competition for some particular scarce resource—what he calls symbolic capital. In the case of the sciences (which should be understood in the broad sense of *Wissenschaft*, systematic knowledge), the struggle for prestige and advancement encourages researchers to reach results that can be validated by intersubjectively shared standards that define what counts as 'objectivity' and 'truth' in the specific discipline in question. In the particular case of the scientific field, then, competition gives actors a social interest in advancing objective knowledge. We have here then 'a historical place where transhistorical truths are produced'.[50]

This intriguing argument, which bears a striking resemblance to Adam Smith's metaphor of the hidden hand through which the pursuit of private interest produces optimal results for the general welfare, invites various questions. For one thing, Bourdieu endorses an anti-realist epistemology according to which '[t]his objective reality to which everyone else tacitly or explicitly refers is ultimately no more than what the researchers engaged in the field at a given moment agree to consider as such.' It is at the very least doubtful

---

[47] G. W. F. Hegel, *Elements of the Philosophy of Right* (Cambridge, 1991), § 205, p. 237.

[48] Marx and Engels, *Collected Works*, iii. 186.

[49] P. Bourdieu, *Pascalian Meditations* (Cambridge, 2000), 123. Bourdieu seems first to have developed his theory of the intellectual in *The Rules of Art* (Cambridge, 1996).

[50] Bourdieu, *Science de la science et réflexivité* (Paris, 2001), 136.

whether making the real a matter of intersubjective agreement can provide Bourdieu with a strong enough basis to allow him to achieve his avowed objective of renouncing 'the absolutism of classical objectivism without falling into relativism'.[51] Moreover, even if he were to have a sufficiently robust conception of scientific objectivity, much further argument would be required to connect it with the distinctively normative universal principles that are surely at stake when intellectuals—and not only intellectuals—engage in politics. For all that, Bourdieu's theory of the intellectual intriguingly revives the idea that we find, not just in Marx but also in Lukács, that access to the universal (however conceived) depends not, as is commonly thought in a tradition that must ultimately be traced back to Plato and Aristotle, on achieving impartiality, that is on detaching oneself from the diurnal struggle between antagonistic social interests, but rather on finding the particular, necessarily partial social location that provides its occupants with a vantage point from which to understand and transform the whole. A similar thought is present in the efforts of Badiou and those influenced by him to continue with Marx's conception of the proletariat as the universal class while seeking to disentangle what they regard as the paradigm of a political subject from any more empirical and sociological analysis of where (if anywhere) the working class is to be found today.[52]

# MOVING ON

What is striking about this survey of contemporary versions of critical theory, whether Marxist or post-Marxist, is the extent to which, despite the progress that many would think was achieved by the anti-humanist critique of the 'philosophy of consciousness', the tensions and questions that emerged as Marx sought to define the nature of his project continue to be active. There is, to begin with, the problem of how to address the idea of constitutive subjectivity first developed by Kant. Arguably this idea is still active in some

---

[51] Bourdieu, *Pascalian Meditations*, 113, 120.

[52] See, for example, Žižek, 'Georg Lukács as the Philosopher of Leninism', in Lukács, *A Defence of 'History and Class Consciousness'*, and Kouvelakis, *Philosophy and Revolution*. For further discussion of Bourdieu on intellectuals see A. Callinicos, 'Social Theory Put to the Test of Practice: Pierre Bourdieu and Anthony Giddens', *New Left Review*, I/236 (1999); 'Pierre Bourdieu and the Universal Class', forthcoming in a collection of essays on Bourdieu edited by Jim Wolfreys; and *The Resources of Critique*, §2.2. See also Jeremy Lane's admirable *Pierre Bourdieu: A Critical Introduction* (London, 2000).

contemporary post-Marxist philosophers—albeit in forms very different from both Kant's transcendental philosophy and each other: Habermas and Badiou might be considered as examples of this kind of position. Then there is the question of how to situate oneself in relation to Hegel's critique of Kantian formalism. One very distinguished contemporary Marxist, Fredric Jameson, unapologetically pursues a version of Hegelian Marxism sufficiently catholic to accommodate both Lukács and Althusser and to interpret postmodernism as a symptom of the advent of global capitalism.[53] But if one renounces Hegel's absolute idealism, how to do so without falling victim to all the polarities that he promised to transcend and reconcile? The naturalistic positivism of the Second International remains an awful warning of the fate to which would-be materialist appropriations of the dialectic can succumb. Hardt and Negri have sought to use Spinoza and Deleuze to develop an anti-Hegelian and non-positivistic naturalism, but at the price of relying on a vitalist ontology that is implausible in its own right and that undermines the account they offer of contemporary capitalism and the forms of resistance to it.

How might one attempt to continue Marx's critique while avoiding these pitfalls?[54] One strategy has been developed independently, and in different modes by Terry Eagleton and me (though what follows is my own version).[55] This strategy involves a return to Marx's philosophical anthropology—the acknowledgement, in other words, that Marx's theory of history requires a broader conception of human nature. This conception, while drawing from Marx himself a view of human beings as active social producers, could also find support in some versions of evolutionary biology (perhaps not surprisingly, since contemporary left-wing Darwinians tend also to be influenced by Marx).[56] Based on this conception of human nature one could then move upstream, seeking to ground the constants of human nature in

[53]  See especially F. Jameson, *The Political Unconscious* (London, 1981), *Late Marxism* (London, 1990), *Postmodernism, or the Cultural Logic of Late Capitalism* (London, 1991), and *The Cultural Turn* (London, 1998).

[54]  There are, of course, other contemporary attempts to continue Marxism philosophically than the strategy sketched out in these concluding paragraphs. One of the most interesting is Daniel Bensaïd's resort to Benjamin and Derrida to help develop a non-determinist version of historical materialism: see, for example, *Resistances, Le discordance des temps* (Paris, 1995), *Marx for Our Times* (London, 2002), and *Un monde à changer* (Paris, 2003).

[55]  For example, T. Eagleton, *The Ideology of the Aesthetic* (Oxford, 1990), *Marx and Freedom* (London, 1997), *Sweet Violence* (Oxford, 2002), and *After Theory* (London, 2003); A. Callinicos, *Making History*, 2nd edn. (Leiden, 2004), *Theories and Narratives* (Cambridge, 1995), and *The Resources of Critique*, esp. pt. II.

[56]  For example, R. Levins and R. Lewontin, *The Dialectical Biologist* (Cambridge, MA, 1985); E. Sober, *The Nature of Selection*, 2nd edn. (Chicago, 1993); and S. Rose, *Lifelines* (London, 1998).

a non-reductive naturalism. Critical to any such move is the thought that different levels of being each have their own specific properties (rather than being intermingled on the Deleuzian 'plane of immanence' or somehow deduced from the basic properties of matter). One way of elaborating on this thought might be to draw on the idea, developed in the school of 'critical realism' founded by the radical philosopher of science Roy Bhaskar, that the world consists of nested clusters of interacting mechanisms and of the events to which these mechanisms and their interactions give rise.[57] An attraction of critical realism is that it conceives the real as stratified: the generative mechanisms that are, according to Bhaskar, the bearers of causal powers are as it were arranged into layers each of which is emergent from but irreducible to a more 'basic' layer. Marx's model of science of *Capital* implies some such layering: the successive introduction of more complex categories as his reconstruction of the capitalist mode of production proceeds is intended at once to capture the specific character of each determination and to account for that determination by locating its role within the larger capitalist totality. But, on a broader scale, setting Marxist social theory within a critical realist ontology would make it possible to treat humans as continuous with the rest of nature without denying them the specific properties (most importantly intentionality and agency) on which post-Marxist theorists such as Habermas who are influenced by the hermeneutic tradition have rightly laid stress.

One could also move downstream from a restatement of Marx's anthropology to acknowledge what he consistently refused to recognize, namely that any critique of capitalism necessarily has a normative dimension. This avowal of what might seem to be the obvious could have more productive consequences than the ontological undergirding towards which I have just gestured, though the two moves are connected: a recognition of the finite character of human existence consequent on our dependence on nature is, for Eagleton, the key to an understanding of why morality is inescapable. 'It is the mortal, fragile, suffering, ecstatic, needy, dependent, desirous, compassionate body which furnishes the basis of all moral thought', he writes.[58] But explicitly acknowledging its normative commitments might also allow Marxism to engage with the most interesting strain in contemporary political philosophy, the egalitarian

---

[57]  R. Bhaskar, *A Realist Theory of Science*, 2nd edn. (Hassocks, 1978) and *The Possibility of Naturalism* (Brighton, 1979); and A. Collier, *Critical Realism* (London, 1994).

[58]  Eagleton, *After Theory*, 155.

liberal tradition whose main reference point is, of course, Rawls's *A Theory of Justice*. Now, as we have seen, leading Analytical Marxists have taken on the Rawlsian enterprise, but in doing so have abandoned the terrain traditionally occupied by Marxist social theory. It is no disparagement of the valuable work that Cohen and Roemer have undertaken in normative political philosophy to say that in making this choice they have turned up the chance to pursue the potentially more fundamental reorientation that would have involved a much more direct mutual interrogation of Marxism and egalitarian liberalism, perhaps strengthening both. One reason why such a project failed to emerge from Analytical Marxism is the contempt that practitioners of this approach displayed towards Marxist economic theory—a stance with which it would be easier to sympathize had they themselves produced anything to compare with the wealth of radical political economy published by more orthodox Marxists in recent years.[59] It is only fair to add that dialogue between Marxism and egalitarian liberalism has not been exactly helped by the former's hostility to any version of liberal thought, an attitude given canonical sanction by Marx's disparagement of John Stuart Mill.[60]

This is, however, intellectual history, not philosophy. The fact that Marxist social theory has failed so far to engage in any real depth with egalitarian liberalism is no reason why this should continue to be the case.[61] An incentive to do so is provided by a potential convergence in practical concerns. Plainly any attempt to continue the Marxist critique of political economy today is likely to pay particular attention to the mechanisms responsible for the enormous poverty and inequality that exist on a global scale and have, in part because of the efforts of the anti-globalization movement, begun to register even in official politics. Global inequality and poverty are also one of the main preoccupations of the cosmopolitan wing of egalitarian liberalism, which has sought both to bring out the scale of contemporary inequalities and the suffering they cause and to argue that these violate universally valid principles of justice.[62] This offers a potential meeting ground on which normative critique and Marxism's more explanatory focus could begin to engage directly with one another around issues that are of pressing political

---

[59] See, for more on this topic, A. Callinicos, 'G. A. Cohen and the Critique of Political Economy', *Science and Society*, 70 (2006).

[60] K. Marx, *Capital*, i (Harmondsworth, 1976), 652–4.

[61] For some first faltering steps at a dialogue, see A. Callinicos, *Equality* (Cambridge, 2000) and *The Resources of Critique*, ch. 7.

[62] See, for example, T. W. Pogge, *World Poverty and Human Rights* (Cambridge, 2002); id. (ed.), *Global Justice* (Oxford, 2001); and B. Barry, *Why Social Justice Matters* (Cambridge, 2005).

concern.[63] Of course, this strategy leaves unresolved many questions, most obviously that of the subject of critique: Hardt's and Negri's concept of the multitude may have renewed discussion of the revolutionary subject, but they certainly haven't concluded it, if indeed any conclusion is available. Nevertheless there does seem to be a way of at once carrying on and renewing Marx's critique.

[63] The recent work of David Harvey is notable for the effort it makes to bring together the explanatory and the normative: see, for example, *A Short History of Neo-liberalism* (Oxford, 2005).

# PART II

REASON
AND
CONSCIOUSNESS

# CHAPTER 8

# SERPENTINE NATURALISM AND PROTEAN NIHILISM

## TRANSCENDENTAL PHILOSOPHY IN ANTHROPOLOGICAL POST-KANTIANISM, GERMAN IDEALISM, AND NEO-KANTIANISM

### PAUL FRANKS

So massive has Kant's impact been that numerous traditions of Continental philosophy define themselves either as his rightful heirs or as his true foes. One way to claim Kant's heritage is to emulate him by calling one's philosophy *transcendental*, while denying some competing view's right to the term. But it is no easier to adjudicate disputes about what Kant means by 'transcendental' than it is to settle the meaning and significance of his philosophical revolution.

Instead of endorsing a particular interpretation, I will show how Kant uses the term in response to problems raised by naturalism for the possibility of metaphysics, and how his usage gives rise to several possible continuations. Then I will examine the contests over the transcendental between two major Continental traditions—German Idealism and anti-psychologistic Neo-Kantianism—and two more naturalistic post-Kantian traditions. These disputes are haunted, I will argue, by problems raised at the inception of transcendental philosophy: the irrefutability of naturalist skepticism and the protean character of nihilism.

## 1. KANT AND THE TRANSCENDENTAL

Kant did not invent the term 'transcendental'. He wrested it from the grip of a tradition that he had come to think was dead.

In the thirteenth century, Christian philosophers in the West first confronted Aristotle's *Metaphysics*, along with an Arabic commentary literature.[1] Like the Muslims and Jews who preceded them, they were impelled to ask *what metaphysics was*. It clearly included the science of the divine being or theology—a term that Aristotle himself sometimes used—but also much more. Ibn Sina, the great commentator, had himself been helped by al-Farabi to give the answer that metaphysics was the science of being qua being—that is, the science of that which pertains to every being just insofar as it is a being. But it was unclear that there could be such a science, what its content could be, and how it would be related to theology. Responding to these problems, Western philosophers developed various theories of what they came to call *the transcendentals*. These were maximally general predicables—the determinations ascribable to every being just in virtue of its being a being at all—and, at

I gratefully acknowledge conversations with Robert Gibbs, Klaus Jahn, Hindy Najman, Lydia Patton, Martin Pickavé, Carolyn Richardson, Michael Rosen, Fred Rush, Mark Wrathall, and Günther Zöller. Translations are mine unless otherwise stated.

[1] In what follows, I draw on the following works: Jan A. Aertsen, 'The Medieval Doctrine of the Transcendentals: The Current State of Research', *Bulletin de Philosophie médiévale* 33 (1991), 130–47; Jan A. Aertsen, *Medieval Philosophy and the Transcendentals: The Case of Thomas Aquinas* (Leiden: Brill, 1996); Jan A. Aertsen, 'Transzendental, II', in Joachim Ritter and Karlfried Gründer, eds., *Historisches Wörterbuch der Philosophie*, x (Darmstadt: Wissenschaftliche Buchgesellschaft, 1998), 1360–5. Martin Pickavé kindly pointed me to this literature.

the same time, the first concepts of the understanding, whose proper function was to know being qua being. Transcendentals were convertible—that is, equivalent, in some sense—to being itself, and were therefore supposed to pertain not only to finite beings but also—again, in some sense, and there were many proposals—to God as the infinite being.

In the version of this tradition received by Kant, metaphysics was divided into *general metaphysics*—the science of being qua being—and *special metaphysics*—which comprised the three sciences of the supersensible beings: theology, psychology, and cosmology. Being qua being was thought to be both convertible with every maximally general predicable, and the proper object of the understanding. So general metaphysics was at once both what had recently come to be called *ontology* and what would come, in the wake of Kant, to be called *epistemology*. Since the thirteenth century, philosophers had formulated increasingly elevated conceptions of the transcendentals, and Kant followed Francisco Suarez in taking the highest conception to be that of *the thing or object in general*, a conception applied not only to actual and possible, but also to impossible things. Thus Kant wrote, in his copy of Alexander Baumgarten's *Metaphysica*, the textbook for his lectures on metaphysics, 'A *science of things in general* actually abstracts from all differences and determinations of things as objects, and thus deals merely with pure reason: *transcendental philosophy*.'[2]

But it was precisely metaphysics in this sense that Kant came to reject—after decades of unrequited love—as doomed to failure. He came to think that *pure reason*—that is, reason employed without any assistance from the senses whatsoever—is utterly incapable of knowing anything at all. All human knowledge must involve the senses. This alone would hardly have been novel. But Kant also argued that human sensibility can receive input only from objects with spatio-temporal form, and that this form cannot pertain to things in general. So he reached the truly novel conclusion that human knowledge is limited to appearances or objects as they appear to us humans, as opposed to things in general or as they are in themselves. If things in general are unknowable, then so are the transcendentals. In that case, as Kant saw with admirable clarity, the idea of a metaphysical science—the idea that had captivated Aristotle, then Muslim and Jewish philosophers since the tenth century and Christian philosophers since the thirteenth—was an idle dream. Philosophy needed a new aspiration.

---

[2] Immanuel Kant, *Gesammelte Schriften*, ed. Deutsche Akademie der Wissenschaften (Berlin: de Gruyter, 1900– ), xviii. 100, R5129. Hereafter Kant, *Schriften* (1900– ).

It is therefore striking that, in his groundbreaking *Critique of Pure Reason*, Kant appropriates the term 'transcendental' on behalf of the new discipline with which he wants to replace the old metaphysics. Introducing his novel use of the term, he writes: 'I call all cognition *transcendental* that is occupied not so much with objects but with our manner of cognition of objects insofar as this is to be possible a priori.'[3] It should be kept in mind, as we consider this formulation, that what is at stake in the question of what counts as transcendental is not only the interpretation of Kant, but also the right to claim his inheritance in the event that one disagrees with him. And disagreement somewhere—whether on some purely philosophical point or because of subsequent developments in mathematics, physics, or some other discipline—is all but inevitable.

## 2. TRANSCENDENTAL, A PRIORI, AND METAPHYSICAL

The new transcendental philosophy will be concerned with 'our manner of cognition of objects insofar as this is to be possible a priori'. But what is the a priori? Some have thought that the priority at stake must be in some sense developmental, so that Kant's conception of a priori representations is closely related to the early modern rationalists' conception of innate ideas. Others distinguish the a priori from the innate, explaining the former in conflicting ways.

It is all too easy to lose sight of the fact that transcendental philosophy is concerned with a priori modes of cognition of objects, not because we happen to have such modes of cognition and need a theory of them as much as we need a theory of anything else, but rather *because these are problematic in a particularly pressing way*. As we will see, how one understands the a priori depends on how one understands the problem motivating interest in it.

Kant says that he was awoken from his 'dogmatic slumber' by Hume's skepticism about causation, and that it was the generalization of this skepticism

---

[3] Immanuel Kant, *Critique of Pure Reason* [1781/1787], B25, in Kant, *Schriften* (1900– ). Hereafter Kant, *Critique of Pure Reason* [1781/1787] (1900– ). Translations are from Immanuel Kant, *Critique of Pure Reason*, trans. Paul Guyer and Allen W. Wood (Cambridge: Cambridge University Press, 1999). On the difference between A and B formulations, see Norbert Hinske, *Kants Weg zur Transzendentalphilosophie* (Stuttgart: Kohlhammer, 1970), 37–9.

that led him to what he called 'the general problem of pure reason': the problem of the possibility of synthetic a priori judgments.[4]

What concerns us here is the problem *as it motivates transcendental* philosophy, so we can set aside the question whether Kant interprets Hume correctly and even whether Hume is a skeptic at all. The skepticism of primary interest to Kant is not, like the skepticism of Descartes' *Meditations*, antecedent, but rather consequent: it arises not prior but posterior to an investigation of our cognitive capacity. Whereas antecedent skepticism is concerned to show that we can use our reason to attain knowledge, consequent skepticism of the relevant kind arises after we have successfully done so. After our success in attaining knowledge of that which is other than our cognitive capacity, we turn this capacity on itself, in order to develop a 'science of man', and we find, to our dismay, that this reflection undermines the very knowledge which we thought we had attained. *At the moment of its success, when human reason turns inward and reflects on itself, it undermines itself.*

To use Kant's favourite Humean example, 'There is no difficulty about how, by means of experience, I can go beyond the concepts that I possess so far', and there is no difficulty about how I can reach greater clarity about the relations of my concepts by means of reason alone.[5] 'But we also believe ourselves to be able to go beyond our concepts a priori and to amplify our cognition.' Thus, if we observe an event, we believe ourselves able to infer the occurrence of some prior event that caused it. But here lies a difficulty. How can we amplify our cognition, without any help from the senses by which we learn about the world beyond the mind? If we try to find some prior principle from which our right to causal inference may itself be inferred, we will succeed in discovering only principles whose justification depends once again on causal inference. Any attempt at an inferential justification of causal inference begs the question. But this seems to undermine all the cognition of nature which we initially thought we had achieved, since this cognition essentially involves causal inference, and causal inference now seems to lack justification. Thus Hume 'held all of [reason's] supposedly a priori principles to be merely imagined, and found that they are nothing but a custom arising from experience and its laws, thus are merely empirical, i.e., intrinsically contingent rules to which we ascribe a supposed necessity and universality'. Hence, 'according to his inferences everything that we call metaphysics would come down to a mere delusion of

---

[4] Kant, *Critique of Pure Reason* [1781/1787] (1900– ), B19.      [5] Ibid., A764/B792.

an alleged insight of reason into that which has in fact merely been borrowed from experience and has from habit taken on the appearance of necessity; an assertion, destructive of all pure philosophy'.[6]

Humean skepticism, as Kant understands it, primarily threatens meta-physics, which is supposed to be a purely rational science. But in so doing it questions science in general—not only natural science, which involves causal inference and indeed has an a priori part, but also mathematics, which involves more than the inspection of relations among concepts. This generalization of the problem is the key to its solution. For Kant's confidence in pure mathematics and pure natural science exceeds his confidence in the skeptical line of thought traced above. So he is sure that there must be something wrong with that piece of reasoning, and he knows where to look in order to locate the error. The new transcendental philosophy will first generalize Humean skepticism as much as possible, thus achieving a systematic inventory of all inferential principles of the pertinent kind, which Kant calls synthetic a priori. Then, diagnosing what is wrong with Humean skepticism, it will proceed to explain how our actual synthetic a priori cognition is possible, and to trace the limits of what we can know by means of pure reason, hence the limits of what we can know at all.

This will show decisively what is wrong with traditional metaphysics, which will be replaced by a transcendental philosophy concerned with cognition, not with objects, foregoing 'the proud title of an ontology'.[7] But does this mean that only epistemology should be pursued, not ontology in any sense whatsoever? Or, since Kant argues that the conditions of knowledge are constitutive of the objects available to us, does it mean that transcendental philosophy would be ontology in a new sense—the science of the maximally general determinations, not of things in general, but of phenomenal objects?[8] If so, would transcendental philosophy be the ontology of a subset of the totality of objects, or rather the ontology of the only objects, properly speaking?

Moreover, in addition to his pejorative use of the term 'metaphysical' and his use of it for the subject matter of rational belief, Kant sometimes uses the term positively within the successor version of general metaphysics mapped out in the Analytic of the first Critique. He distinguishes, for example, between

---

[6] Kant, *Critique of Pure Reason* [1781/1787] (1900– ), B20.    [7] Ibid., A247/B303.
[8] See ibid., A111. Cf. A158/B197: 'The conditions of the possibility of experience in general are at the same time conditions of the possibility of the objects of experience.'

arguments establishing the a priori status of some representation, which he calls *metaphysical expositions or deductions*, and arguments establishing the foundational status of some a priori representation for a mode of a priori cognition, which he calls *transcendental expositions or deductions*.[9] He also refers to the system founded through transcendental philosophy as consisting of the metaphysical foundations of physics and morals.[10] Is this merely an unfortunate choice of terminology? Or the symptom of a metaphysical residue from which transcendental philosophy needs to be cleansed? Alternatively, could transcendental philosophy be the renewal rather than the end of general metaphysics?

Whatever Kant's own answers may have been, his successors would have to answer for themselves, not only in their interpretations of Kant, but also in their own work, to the extent that it laid claim to the title of transcendental philosophy.[11]

# 3. Transcendental Method

In the passage where he introduces his novel use of the term 'transcendental', Kant says nothing about *how* the new transcendental philosophy is to study 'our manner of cognition . . . a priori'. But elsewhere he describes the *Critique* as 'a treatise on the method, not the system of the science itself'.[12]

A crossroads lies here. If you think that what leads to skepticism is some *contingent* feature of the natural sciences of Hume's day, or of Hume's extension of them to the human mind, then you will seek to develop a better science of the human mind, whose claim to designation as transcendental will

---

[9] Kant introduces the distinction in the B version of the Transcendental Aesthetic. In B he also adds the designation 'metaphysical deduction' to the argument preceding the transcendental deduction. See Kant, *Critique of Pure Reason* [1781/1787] (1900– ), B159.

[10] See ibid., A841/B869. See also *Metaphysical Foundations of Natural Science* [1786], in Kant, *Schriften* (1900– ), iv. 469–70, 478, translated in Immanuel Kant, *Theoretical Philosophy after 1781*, trans. Michael Friedman, Gary Hatfield, Henry Allison and Peter Heath; ed. Henry Allison and Peter Heath (Cambridge: Cambridge University Press, 2002). Both transcendental philosophy and metaphysics concern a priori principles, but the former involves only pure concepts, such as the concept of nature in general, whereas the latter also involves the empirical concept of some kind of sensible thing, such as the concept of matter. See, however, B3, where Kant says that 'Every alteration has its cause' is impure, though it is deduced within transcendental philosophy, not metaphysics.

[11] On Kant's own conception of philosophy, see Eckart Förster, 'Kant's Notion of Philosophy', Monist 72 (April 1989) 285–304.

[12] Kant, *Critique of Pure Reason* [1781/1787] (1900– ), Bxxii.

depend on its a priori subject matter, not its distinctive method. However, if you think that skepticism is the *inevitable* result of employing *any*
method of natural science for philosophical purposes, then you will seek to
develop a distinctively philosophical method as essential to transcendental
philosophy.

# 4. TRANSCENDENTAL AND EMPIRICAL

In addition to distinguishing between a priori and empirical or a posteri-
ori representations, Kant distinguishes between two *uses* of either kind of
representation. They can be used either transcendentally—with reference
to 'all objects in general'—or empirically—with reference to 'objects of
experience'.[13]

Consequently, some important terms are subject to 'unavoidable ambiguity', since their meaning depends on whether they are used transcendentally or
empirically in some particular context.[14] For example, the contrasting terms
'outside us/real' and 'inside us/ideal' can be used *either* transcendentally—to
draw a distinction between things in general as they are in themselves, independently of human sensibility, and things as they appear to us by means of the
universal forms of human sensibility—*or* empirically—to draw a distinction
between objects of experience as they are in themselves, such as rain, and
'mere appearances', such as a rainbow.[15]

Hence, as Kant uses the terms, whether someone is a transcendental realist
or a transcendental idealist about X depends on whether she thinks that X
is independent of or dependent upon the universal forms of human sensibility—namely, space and time. However, whether someone is an empirical
realist or an empirical idealist about X depends on whether she thinks that
X is independent of or dependent upon the conditions and/or position of
some particular sensing subject. Thus, when Kant characterizes his position
as *transcendental idealism*, he means that he considers all the objects of
human knowledge to be spatio-temporal and hence dependent on the forms
of human sensibility. This position must be distinguished from *empirical*

---

[13]  Kant, *Critique of Pure Reason* [1781/1787] (1900– ), B80. As Kant uses the term, 'objects of
experience' are not merely causes of sensation, as in the empiricist tradition that has dominated much
Anglophone philosophy, but rather objects of empirical *knowledge*.

[14]  Kant, *Critique of Pure Reason* [1781/1787] (1900– ), A373.    [15]  Ibid., A45.

*idealism*: the view that all objects of experience depend on features of some particular sensing subject. Indeed, Kant argues that *only* the transcendental idealist can consistently affirm empirical realism: the view that some objects of experience—namely, objects in space—are independent of the features of any particular sensing subject.[16] For the transcendental realist is prepared to count as genuine objects of knowledge only things wholly independent of human sensibility, and this is a standard that the objects accessible to human beings cannot meet.

In other words, much of what Kant says is, on his own account, riddled with ambiguities that can be disentangled only by someone who has mastered Kant's own subtle distinctions. This has led to much confusion and to another crossroads. Many ascribe to Kant what he would call empirical idealism—either because they misunderstand him, or because they think him wrong to distinguish between transcendental and empirical uses of representations and words. Others think that transcendental philosophy is intelligible only to someone who occupies an appropriate *standpoint*, distinct and in some sense opposed to the empirical standpoint pertinent to ordinary life, natural science, and non-transcendental philosophy.

## 5. Transcendental and Human

The new transcendental philosophy is to deal with the conditions of the possibility of '*our* manner of cognition'. Kant's use of the first-person plural signifies the crucial importance of *humankind*—*our* kind—for his project. Indeed, transcendental idealism involves a double reference to the human: it deals with *human knowledge*, which it limits to objects dependent on the forms of *human sensibility*—that is, forms that are *brute* rather than rational, since no reason can be given why they are so and not otherwise.

Since human understanding is nothing other than finite and object-constitutive reason, and since even *finite* reason can have only rational forms, it follows that human understanding and human sensibility are importantly distinct. Most post-Kantians are dissatisfied with the resulting duality of sensibility and understanding. But the grounds of their dissatisfaction vary. So, accordingly, do their revisions of Kant.

---

[16]  Ibid., A371–2.

Others accept that there are brute facts about human capacities, taking this to be a revolutionary discovery of Kant's about human finitude. However, they disagree with Kant about the proper method for identifying these brute facts, and perhaps also about what these facts are.

Transcendental philosophy also involves humanity in a third way that became clearer only as Kant discovered that he needed to write not only the *Critique of Pure Reason*, but also the *Critique of Practical Reason*, and later also the *Critique of Judgment*, neither of which he had originally thought possible. Namely, transcendental philosophy is to be an account of the necessary conditions, not only of human knowledge, but also of human morality and of an ultimate state of the world—the highest good—in which nature would be so arranged that happiness would be proportional to human virtue. So transcendental philosophy does not only take a *theoretical* interest in humanity as essentially involved in its domain of study. It also takes a *practical* interest in humanity as intrinsically valuable.

# 6. ANTHROPOLOGICAL POST-KANTIANISM AND THE FACTS OF CONSCIOUSNESS

In its first decade, Kant's transcendental philosophy must already confront two fateful problems. One is the irrefutability of naturalistic skepticism by transcendental philosophy, a point made most forcefully by Salomon Maimon. A putative refutation will consist of a supposedly undeniable premise and an argument that this premise necessarily entails the validity of some synthetic a priori principle. To remove the sting, only the transcendental *interpretation* of the argument need be contested. The naturalist may concede the premise's undeniability and the conclusion's inexorability, while explaining both as results of non-truth-tracking psychological mechanisms, hence as failing to resolve the question of justification. Consequently, transcendental philosophy can only beg the question, or argue in a circle, against naturalistic skepticism. Universal agreement is unattainable here. Like Adam after the fall, the transcendental philosopher will tread upon the head of the naturalistic serpent, but his heel will always be bitten in return.[17]

---

[17] Salomon Maimon, *Streifereien im Gebiete der Philosophie* [1793], reprinted in *Gesammelte Werke*, ed. V. Verra, 7 vols. (Hildesheim: Olms, 1975–6; repr. 2000), iv. 80, based on Genesis 3:15. See Paul

A second problem is raised by Friedrich Heinrich Jacobi. For Jacobi, the problem with Humean naturalism is that it leads to what he calls *nihilism*: it abolishes our ordinary sense of ourselves and of external objects as given individuals, and it thereby undermines the conditions of its own possibility. Moreover, this is the inevitable outcome of *any* attempt to provide inferential justifications for convictions that are ordinarily basic. *All* philosophical reflection is self-undermining, and novel versions that employ non-naturalistic methods will only give rise to new, non-naturalistic modes of nihilism. Like Proteus, nihilism responds to interrogation by shifting shape.[18] The solution is to refuse skeptical questions altogether, reaffirming instead 'the natural faith of reason' in what is ordinarily basic.[19]

Each of two opposing parties in Kant's early reception can be seen as adjusting Kantianism in light of the problems raised by Maimon and Jacobi. On one side lie those I call the anthropological post-Kantians. For them, skepticism is irrefutable and nihilism protean, but naturalism leads to skepticism only on the basis of inappropriate expectations for naturalistic human science. A rigorous psychology or anthropology should be modeled on natural science, while acknowledging that its subject-matter is in some ways *sui generis*. It will be transcendental in virtue, not of its distinctive method, but of its distinctive conclusions, which include insights into the synthetic a priori status of certain principles.

Thus, according to Jakob Friedrich Fries, Kant correctly identifies the transcendental subject matter of philosophy, which aspires to 'cognition of the possibility and applicability of a priori cognitions'.[20] But Kant errs in thinking that the achievement of transcendental cognition also involves a distinctively transcendental, a priori method. Fries calls this error 'the transcendental prejudice', which consists in the assumption that deduction must consist in

---

W. Franks, *All or Nothing: Systematicity, Transcendental Arguments, and Skepticism in German Idealism* (Cambridge, MA: Harvard University Press, 2005), 176–200. Hereafter Franks, *All or Nothing* (2005).

[18] Friedrich Heinrich Jacobi, *Werke* [1812–25], eds. J. F. Köppen and C. J. Roth (Leipzig: Fleischer; repr. Darmstadt: Wissenschaftliche Buchgesellschaft, 1968), xi. 14. Hereafter Jacobi, *Werke* [1812–25] (1968). Friedrich Heinrich Jacobi, *The Main Philosophical Writings and the Novel 'AllWill'*, trans. and ed. George di Giovanni (Montreal: McGill-Queens University Press, 1994), 542. Hereafter Jacobi, *Main Writings* (1994).

[19] Jacobi, *Werke* [1812–25] (1968), xi. 37; *Main Writings* (1994), 552. See Franks, *All or Nothing* (2005), 154–74.

[20] Jakob Friedrich Fries, *Neue oder anthropologische Kritik der Vernunft*. Text of the 1828–31 2nd edn, revising the 1807 edition. Reprinted in *Sämtliche Schriften*, 1, 3 vols., ed. Gert König and Lutz Geldsetzer (Aalen: scientia Verlag, 1967), i. 28. Hereafter Fries, *Neue oder anthropologische Kritik der Vernunft* [1807] (1967).

inferential proof (*Beweis*). This leads Kant to develop inferential deductions of synthetic a priori principles from the actuality of the experience they enable, which cannot escape from a 'logical *circle* in the *proofs*'.[21] Kant's error is in fact an instance of a still more widespread confusion that Fries calls 'the rationalist prejudice': the assumption that *all justification is inferential*. This has misled philosophers into thinking that every science must take the form of Euclidean geometry, and that all the sciences must form a hierarchy, in which the basic principle of each lower science is provable within a higher science, and in which philosophy must be the highest science of all.[22] Humean skepticism arises, on Fries' view, from the same prejudice, plus the insight that the principle of causality cannot be inferentially proven. Instead of seeking a novel method for the inferential proof of synthetic a priori principles, the transcendental philosopher should abandon the underlying prejudice.[23]

Here Fries is adopting—as he explicitly acknowledges—Jacobi's view that justification consists in the immediate perception of the evident as evident.[24] Inferential proof can at most ground that which is not perceived as evident in that which is so perceived. Consequently, the conversion of all justification into inferential proof would in fact amount to the annihilation of justification.

However, while Jacobi sees himself as propounding a 'non-philosophy', Fries intends to reconstruct Kant's philosophy, by acknowledging that what Kant calls transcendental cognition is 'really psychological or, better, anthropological cognition', and by developing an appropriate method *that makes no pretension whatsoever to justificatory force*.[25] This is analogous to the method of the natural sciences. Thus Fries writes:

one has also cast on my philosophical deductions the aspersion of circular proof, but they are not circular, for they are not proof at all. They belong rather to a theory of these cognitions, and the analogous situation is manifest without any difficulty in all inductions in physics. For example, from individual facts I discern the phenomena of electricity, and lead them back to their universal laws; then I assume these laws as principles of a theory of electricity, and explain from them once again those facts with which I began. Only once my reasoning goes, in preparatory fashion, along the

---

[21]   Fries, *Neue oder anthropologische Kritik der Vernunft* [1807] (1967), i. 25.
[22]   Ibid., 21–5.        [23]   Ibid., 27.
[24]   Jakob Friedrich Fries, *Knowledge, Belief, and Aesthetic Sense* [1805], trans. Kent Richter, ed. Frederick Gregory (Köln: Dinter, 1989), 30. Hereafter Fries, *Knowledge* [1805] (1989).
[25]   Fries, *Neue oder anthropologische Kritik der Vernunft* [1807] (1967), i. 29.

regressive path, does it subsequently go along the progressive path of the system. In an entirely analogous way, we proceed from the observation of our cognition, showing thereby how human cognition is created, elevating ourselves to a theory of the same, showing which principles, according to this theory, must lie in our cognition, and now deriving once again the individual cognitions and judgments from these principles.[26]

The 'individual facts' with which Fries begins are what he and others call 'facts of consciousness' (*Tatsachen der Bewusstsein*), such as its unity. These are doubly universal: they concern the content or structure of any state of consciousness whatsoever; second, they are recognizable as true by anybody who merely reflects on her own conscious states and acts. We may say, then, that Fries replaces Kant's metaphysical expositions and deductions with *inductive identifications* of the facts of consciousness, and he replaces Kant's transcendental expositions and deductions with *explanations* of these facts in terms of a priori principles. Since the identified facts are universally accessible, and since the a priori principles are supposed to be explanatory in a sense by anyone who grasps natural scientific methods, Friesian transcendental philosophy aspires to universal agreement. Naturalistic skeptics are not to be refuted but should be diagnosed as victims of their own 'rationalist prejudice'.

Friesian philosophy is neither empirical nor metaphysical in the methodological sense that it does not seek to justify a priori cognitions by appealing either to empirical perception or to inferential proof. It is also substantively non-metaphysical, according to Fries, because it deals, not with questions of 'transcendental truth' or mind-independent actuality, but only with the coherence of our representations.[27] Ontological claims about the maximally general properties of beings are really transcendental claims about the workings of our minds. The same applies to claims apparently about the traditional subject matter of special metaphysics. Fries ascribes to us a capacity that he calls *Ahndung*—an untranslatable term best rendered as 'intimation'—by which we perceive the functional organization of particular organisms and of the world as a whole, and on this basis he develops a basically Kantian moral theology.[28] Here too he follows Jacobi, who thinks that we humans can

---

[26] Ibid. 26.

[27] Ibid. 343, 346–52; *Knowledge*, [1805] (1989), 31; Jakob Friedrich Fries, *Wissen, Glaube und Ahndung* [1805], reprinted in *Sämtliche Schriften*, i/3, ed. Gert König and Lutz Geldsetzer (Aalen: Scientia Verlag, 1968), 30. Hereafter Fries, *Wissen* [1805] (1968).

[28] Fries, *Wissen* [1805] (1968), 258–327; *Knowledge* [1805] (1989), 95–157.

immediately perceive not only the sensibly evident, but also the supersensibly evident.[29] For Fries, however, the upshot must be regarded once again as transcendental insight into the human mind, not metaphysical insight into things in themselves.

There are two general problems with anthropological post-Kantianism. First, at worst Fries concedes empirical idealism to skepticism, and at best he offers only a *diagnosis* of skepticism, but telling patients a diagnosis does not cure them—even if the diagnosis is correct. Fries inherits this problem from Jacobi, but he makes it worse. For, if we *could* take Jacobi's advice and refuse philosophical reflection, we would avoid skeptical doubt. However, if we follow Fries and *adjust* our reflection, it is unclear how we can free ourselves from the demand for justification. Second, Fries seems wholly unguarded against Maimon's persistently skeptical naturalist, who will try to undermine our ordinary convictions by explaining *both* what Fries regards as facts of consciousness, such as its unity, *and* the explicability of these facts in terms of a priori principles, as resulting from psychological mechanisms that, on reflection, we have no reason to trust.

# 7. German Idealism and the Facts of Reason

The German Idealists are convinced by Jacobi, not only that every justification must in some way involve immediacy, but also that naturalistic reflection undermines our self-understanding in ways that cannot be limited, as Hume had thought, to the study. Someone who comes to think, for example, that naturalistic reflection undermines her understanding of herself as a free agent capable of rational choice, may find it difficult to achieve the level of conviction necessary for the formation of epistemically and ethically virtuous dispositions. A culture to which undermining reflection of this sort becomes essential may render those who are brought up within it all but incapable of resolute, hence of virtuous, action.

They are also convinced by Jacobi that formal logical inference is an inadequate model for philosophy, and that Spinoza discovered the true structure of ultimate justification. Such justification must have two features.

---

[29] See, e.g. Jacobi, *Werke* [1812–25] (1968), xi. 9; *Main Writings* (1994), 540.

First, it must be *holistic*, taking the form of a system in which every finite element is what it is in virtue of its role within the whole. Second, it must be *monistic*, so that the whole is constituted as a whole—not a mere aggregate—by a single, immanent, absolute, and infinite first principle.[30]

This leads the German Idealists to some fundamental revisions of Kant, whom they initially and mistakenly assume to share their conception of systematicity. As Kant had recognized and as Jacobi had pointed out, Kant's views on space and time render empirical reality holistic. However, in part because this holism is incompatible with what Kant takes to be an indispensable component of any absolutely rational ontology—namely, the existence of individual entities with some non-relational properties—Kant also thinks that space and time cannot be absolutely rational and are therefore brute features of human sensibility.[31] Consequently, Kant's holism is not monistic.

On the other hand, Kant sounds like a monist when he is discussing the metaphysical deduction of the categories, which he says must be exhaustively identified through '*connection in a system* . . . that is to be grasped and determined under one idea, the completeness and articulation of which system can at the same time yield a touchstone of the correctness and genuineness of all the pieces of cognition fitting into it'.[32] The list of categories must be deduced from an idea of the whole into which they fit, hence 'in accordance with a principle'.[33]

However, the German Idealists—like many other readers of the *Critique* until quite recently—are disappointed by Kant's execution of this deduction. As a 'transcendental clue' to 'transcendental logic'—the logic of inferences that are objectively valid, tracing rational relations as they are actualized in the world—Kant employs 'general logic', which is the logic of inferences that are entirely formal and abstract from all relation to actuality. But, since the more abstract logic must be derivative from the less abstract logic, and not vice-versa, it is hard to see how Kant's procedure can work. To be sure, Kant also says that, 'since the time of Aristotle [general logic] has not had to go a single step backwards . . . [and] until now it has also been unable to take a single step

---

[30] The interpretation of German idealism as holistic and monistic is elaborated in Franks, *All or Nothing* (2005), 84–108. 'Monism' is sometimes used differently, for example when Stern (1990), 19, denies that Hegel holds the monistic view that reality is homogeneous and unanalyzable.

[31] See, e.g. Kant, *Critique of Pure Reason* [1781/1787] (1900– ), B66–8.

[32] Ibid., A64–5/B89–90.    [33] Ibid., A67/B92.

forward, and therefore seems to all appearance to be finished and complete.'[34] But, even if one accepted Kant's depiction, which historians of logic would surely contest, this stasis could be taken as a sign, not of completion, but of paralysis. Joachim Jungius had pointed out in the seventeenth century that, in its existing state, logic could not explain inferences essentially involving relations, and a crucial step in Kant's rejection of traditional metaphysics had been his realization that there was a fundamental distinction between 'logical' relations and 'real' relations such as spatio-temporal difference and causality.[35] Should not transcendental logic be deduced from its principle *independently* of general logic? Should general logic not be *reformed* on this new basis?

All this suggests the project of revising Kant's metaphysical deduction in order to achieve a more compelling derivation, meeting the standards of Spinoza's holistic monism, and deriving not only the categories, which would provide the basis for an improved general logic, but also space and time as forms of sensibility, which will no longer be brute facts about human beings and the objects of human knowledge.

Reinhold, the first to attempt this project, intends the first principle, from which the metaphysical deduction is to proceed, also to articulate *the* fact of consciousness, maximally universal both in its validity and in its accessibility on reflection. But, to make a long story short, Reinhold is forced to choose between universal validity and universal accessibility.[36] A general feature of conscious states may be readily accessible, but the complexity of the life of the mind is such that no one feature seems to be discernible in every such state. Moreover, a holistic monist must seek a principle that constitutes the whole as a whole rather than a mere aggregate, and a feature that is discernible within each part *taken on its own* can provide the basis only for an aggregate of parts that share a common property.

Accordingly, some of Reinhold's students abandon the project of improving Kant's metaphysical deduction and satisfy themselves with some version of anthropological post-Kantianism. But Reinhold's successor at Jena, Fichte, undertakes instead to revise Reinhold's project, seeking a first principle fit for

---

[34] Kant, *Critique of Pure Reason* [1781/1787] (1900– ), Bviii.
[35] On Jungius, see G. H. R. Parkinson, ed., *Leibniz: Logical Papers* (Oxford: Clarendon Press, 1966), p. xix. On real relations, see, e.g. 'Attempt to introduce the concept of negative magnitudes into philosophy' [1763], in Kant, *Schriften* (1900– ), ii. 167–204; Immanuel Kant, *Theoretical Philosophy, 1755–1770*, trans. David Walford with Ralf Meerbote (Cambridge: Cambridge University Press, 1992), 207–41.
[36] Franks, *All or Nothing* (2005), 211–37.

holistic monism, even if—as he eventually realizes—that principle is not universally accessible to anyone who merely reflects on his or her conscious states.

Thus Fichte criticizes *any* version of transcendental philosophy that regresses from the facts of consciousness:

Reinhold . . . with a sense of what is truly philosophical, starts with facts in order to ascend to the foundation of these facts . . . Reinhold's procedure would be the reverse of the *Wissenschaftslehre*, if only such a reversal were possible, and if only one were able, by ascending from what is founded to its foundation, to arrive at an ultimate foundation. But this series is endless.[37]

If one starts from facts—that is, from what someone occupying the empirical standpoint of ordinary life and natural science can be guaranteed to affirm on reflection—and one then regresses to the necessary conditions for the possibility of these facts, one will succeed only in discovering conditions that are discernible from the empirical standpoint, and one will never manage to find a foundation for empirical reality as a whole, which would require one to take up an entirely different—transcendental—standpoint.

Fichte thinks that there is hope for Reinhold, who is looking for the right thing in the wrong place. But he sees no hope at all for Carl Christian Erhard Schmid, a Jena Kantian, a proto-Friesian who appeals to 'facts of consciousness' 'in order to descend to the consequences of these facts—in order to arrange them and to argue about them in various ways'. In a notorious 'act of annihilation', following some exchanges in print and a couple of years as colleagues at Jena, Fichte declares Schmid to be 'null and void as far as I am concerned', wholly incapable of either doing or judging transcendental philosophy:

If it is a painting which is supposed to be evaluated, one listens to the opinion of people who can see. However bad a painting may be, I do not think that it should be criticized by people who are blind from birth.[38]

Schelling later endorses this analogy between transcendental philosophy and art, though he distinguishes between creativity, which requires a special gift in both cases, and appreciation, which does not.

---

[37] Johann Gottlieb Fichte, *Sämmtliche Werke* [1845–6], ed. Immanuel Hermann Fichte (Berlin: Veit; repr. Hamburg: Meiner, 1971), ii. 455. Hereafter Fichte, *Werke* [1845–6] (1971). Johann Gottlieb Fichte, *Early Philosophical Writings*, trans. and ed. Daniel Breazeale (Ithaca, NY: Cornell University Press, 1988), 333–4. Hereafter Fichte, *Early Writings* (1988).

[38] Fichte, *Werke* [1845–6] (1971), ii. 456–7; *Early Writings* (1988), 334–5. For Fichte's quarrel with Schmid, who was teaching Kantianism at Jena before Reinhold, see Breazeale in Fichte, *Early Writings* (1988), 307–15. Fries published in Schmid's journal.

If transcendental philosophy does not start with facts of consciousness, how can it avoid begging the question against Humean naturalism and perhaps vicious circularity? German Idealists find a model in Kant's *Critique of Practical Reason*. After a long attempt to find a deduction of the moral law's validity from the actuality of our freedom, Kant acknowledges, first, that our freedom as theoretical knowers lacks any implication for morality, and, second, that while our freedom as practical agents has moral implications, there is a circle here: 'freedom and unconditional practical law reciprocally imply one another.'[39] Instead of giving up altogether, however, Kant seems to regard the circle as virtuous, and he proceeds to reverse direction, deducing the actuality of freedom from the validity of the moral law. The strategy depends on an epistemic asymmetry.

While I cannot become immediately aware of my own freedom as a capacity to act independently of any causal determinant, I can become immediately aware that I am obligated to act by the moral law. I thereby become mediately aware that I am free to act on the basis of the moral law, hence that I am free.[40]

To make this vivid, Kant introduces what he calls an 'experience'—better, an *experiment*— that 'confirms this order of concepts in us':

Suppose someone asserts of his lustful inclination that, when the desired object and the opportunity are present, it is quite irresistible to him; ask him whether, if a gallows were erected in front of the house where he finds this opportunity and he would be hanged on it immediately after gratifying his lust, he would not then control his inclination. One need not conjecture very long what he would reply. But ask him whether, if his prince demanded, on pain of the same immediate execution, that he give false testimony against an honorable man whom the prince would like to destroy under a plausible pretext, he would consider it possible to overcome his love of life, however great it may be. He would perhaps not venture to assert whether he would do it or not, but he must admit without hesitation that it would be possible for him. He judges, therefore, that he can do something because he is aware that he ought to do it and cognizes freedom within him, which, without the moral law, would have remained unknown to him.[41]

The first question is intended to elicit from me the acknowledgment that my 'love of life' outweighs any particular desire I may have. The underlying idea

<hr />

[39]  Immanuel Kant, *Critique of Practical Reason* [1788], in Kant, *Schriften* (1900– ), v. 29. Hereafter Kant, *Critique of Practical Reason* [1788] (1900– ). Translations are from Immanuel Kant, *Practical Philosophy*, ed. Mary J Gregor (Cambridge: Cambridge University Press, 1996).

[40]  Kant, *Critique of Practical Reason* [1788] (1900– ), v. 4n. On what follows, see Franks, *All or Nothing* (2005), 278–98.

[41]  Kant, *Critique of Practical Reason* [1788] (1900– ), v. 30.

is of course that I cannot satisfy any desire once I am dead. Kant's second question is intended to elicit from me the acknowledgment that the moral law outweighs my 'love of life' itself, since there are circumstances in which I recognize that, were I to act to save my life, I would be doing something morally wrong.

It is not merely that I am supposed to *infer* from my obligation to my *capacity*, on the principle that 'ought implies can'. Rather, my awareness of moral obligation manifests itself as a feeling of respect for the moral law, a feeling that I am at once both humiliated—as a finite being, who has sensuous desires that can give rise to reasons for immoral action—and elevated—as a rational being, who acknowledges the incommensurability between these reasons and the moral law in a case of conflict between them. This feeling of respect is an *actualization* of my freedom, in which I as rational being affect myself as finite being with sensuous desires.[42]

After Kant has thus deduced the actuality of freedom, he proceeds to derive the conditions for its full actualization in an autonomous life.[43] Such a life is motivated by the moral law and oriented by hope for the attainment of the highest good: a state of the world in which happiness is proportional to virtue. The conditions in question are the existence of God and the immortality of the soul, which Kant calls 'the postulates of pure practical reason'. One point to note is that Kant here reintroduces the three topics of special metaphysics—the intelligible world, God, and the soul—not as topics for science or theory, but rather as matters for the 'rational faith' of a practical agent. Another is that the postulates are progressively derived from a single, absolute first principle. Properly speaking, then, the derivation of the postulates is not a transcendental but rather a metaphysical deduction. Indeed, since the feeling of respect is an effect of reason, which here determines sensibility, this metaphysical deduction pre-empts the need for a transcendental deduction by overcoming the duality of principle and sensibility to which transcendental deductions are supposed to respond. Furthermore, the postulates are not conditions for the possibility of freedom and morality in the sense that they enable us to understand *how* what they condition is possible. At the end of the *Groundwork*, Kant says that we cannot comprehend the possibility of freedom. At best, we can comprehend its incomprehensibility.[44] The *Critique of Practical Reason*

---

[42] Ibid., 72–89.    [43] Ibid., 110–46.

[44] Immanuel Kant, *Groundwork of the Metaphysics of Morals* [1785], in Kant, *Schriften* (1900– ), iv. 463.

does not change this situation, but adds a demonstration of the *actuality* of freedom, an account of what is involved in the full actualization of freedom within an autonomous life, and a derivation of the conditions necessary for the leading of such a life.

What is important for present purposes is not the details of Kant's attempted deduction, but the deductive strategy: (a) one undertakes or undergoes an experiment in which one subjects oneself to a conflict (b) which leads to a transformation in one's self-understanding, such that one recognizes oneself as who one has been all along, (c) which in turn amounts to the acknowledgment of a single, absolute first principle of reason, and (d) to the assumption of a standpoint other than the empirical standpoint of ordinary and scientific cognition, (e) a standpoint from which it is possible to carry out (f) a progressive derivation of necessary conditions for the actualization of the first principle, conditions that are intimately related to the topics of traditional special metaphysics.

German Idealists may be seen as attempting a family of deductions with just these features. Unlike Kant, however, their goal is to deduce the actuality of pure reason *in general*, both practical and theoretical. Consequently, their various deductions aspire to ground transcendental cognition, not mere rational faith.

For Fichte, the ultimate goal of transcendental philosophy is to derive, from the principle whose actuality is recognized in the fact of reason, the necessary conditions for the actualization of reason within an individual, autonomous, human life. Despite some important modifications with respect to the character of moral judgment, Fichte remains close to Kant insofar as autonomy is for him a matter of living according to the moral law, which outweighs any sensuous desire and constitutes something like a rational sensibility. However, this does not mean that Fichte begins his derivation from the moral law, which would make it impossible to derive the principles of theoretical cognition. To be sure, the acknowledgment of the moral law as supreme principle of reason is essential for the assumption of the transcendental standpoint, because, on Fichte's view, acknowledgement of the moral law as supreme is acknowledgment of its supremacy in *every* part of one's life, which includes one's pursuit of theoretical knowledge and hence one's philosophizing. Moral autonomy thus represents *the starting point of the transcendental philosopher*. But it is not therefore the starting point of *the system of transcendental philosophy*, though its derivation is to be the system's *culmination*.

The assumption of the requisite standpoint requires not only moral development but also aesthetic cultivation.[45] Someone who is morally autonomous but aesthetically undeveloped will not be able to see *how* the moral law can be the supreme principle in one's philosophizing. For aesthetic appreciation involves viewing artworks as if they were artificial worlds, and the ultimate artwork would therefore be the actual world, created in such a way as to accord with the demands of morality. Taking such a condition of the world as her ideal, the transcendental philosopher investigates the necessary conditions for the maximal approximation to this goal, which is possible only if the world is already in some sense constituted by freedom. Consequently, the starting point of the system must be, not the moral law, but rather a more original principle that is the condition both for the moral law and for the world that manifests itself to both theoretical and practical sensibility.

By 1796, Fichte comes to think that prior to the fact of autonomous reason is the fact of *heteronomous* reason, which Fichte calls the *summons*.[46] Fichte's thought is that a finite rational agent can first come to recognize himself as such only through the awareness of a conflict between what he wants to do and what someone else wants him to do. Through the other's recognition of him as a rational agent, he recognizes himself as a rational agent with his own individual will and freedom to choose. In this 'fact' is disclosed the possibility of heteronomous or impure practical reason, which takes sensuous desires—one's own but also those of others—as normative. At the same time, since—as Fichte argues—the summons can occur only through the reciprocal recognition of two embodied beings who recognize each other as animated organisms, the natural world as the arena of desire-formation and intersubjective interaction is also disclosed. However, in the summons the finite rational agent also discovers a limit: namely, though he can choose how to respond to the summons issued by the other, he cannot help but choose since, once he recognizes the summons, whatever he does will count as a response to it—no matter whether he refuses or ignores the other's desire. There is thus not only an individual will to respond as one chooses, but also an absolute will to responsiveness. In Fichte's view, this absolute will, implicit in the summons and thus in heteronomous rationality, is the transcendental ground of the moral law. For one lives autonomously, precisely when one takes

---

[45]  See Franks, *All or Nothing* (2005), 332–3.
[46]  For the summons as a fact, see Fichte, *Werke* [1845–6] (1971), iii. 35, 51; and Johann Gottlieb Fichte, *Foundations of Natural Right* [1796–7], trans. Michael Baur, ed. Frederick Neuhouser (Cambridge: Cambridge University Press, 2000), 34, 48.

as one's highest norm the explicit and absolute principle of responsiveness to reason as such.

The fact of heteronomous reason is a precondition for rational agency in general, while the fact of autonomous reason is a precondition for leading a moral life. Both are preconditions for philosophy, in addition to aesthetic cultivation. However, another precondition, according to Fichte, is the absence of miseducation. Too specialized an education, common in modernity due to a highly advanced division of labour, can inhibit aesthetic cultivation, and this could take the form either of preventing one from employing one's faculties in the unified way required for appreciating beauty, or of preventing one from extending this unified approach outside the designated realm of aesthetics—say, to philosophy.[47] Fichte is not committed, then, to the view that someone like Schmid, whom he regards as philosophy-blind, is immoral in his practical life. The problem could lie in Schmid's lack of aesthetic cultivation, or in an education that has fragmented his mind.

All of this pertains to the transcendental philosopher's starting point. The starting point of the system of transcendental philosophy itself, however, consists in a re-enactment of the genesis of rational agency. In the mature 1796–9 version of Fichte's Jena *Wissenschaftslehre*, this proceeds as follows. First, we are summoned by another to think from the standpoint we have assumed, hence to seek a formulation of the absolute and immanent principle from which the facts of consciousness are ultimately to be derived. This other is a teacher—perhaps Fichte himself, in proper or textual persona. As we clarify the character of consciousness within the context of this summons, we descend to 'the deepest point' of the system, the point at which the principle is formulated in the most primordial way. Here the summons is understood as the fact of both heteronomous and autonomous reason. From this point, we should ascend, deriving the necessary forms of both theoretical and practical reason. Thus the starting point of the system is a reflective re-enactment of the starting point of rational agency, which is clarified as such, not at the outset, but rather at the mid-point of transcendental philosophy.

In 1799, Kant finally repudiated both Reinhold and Fichte, who had clearly departed from Kant's own views in their quest for a holistic monist system.[48] By 1801, however, Schelling—until now Fichte's junior partner—and

---

[47]  See Franks, *All or Nothing* (2005), 332–2.
[48]  Kant, *Schriften* (1900– ), xii. 370–1; Immanuel Kant, *Correspondence*, trans. Arnulf Zweig (Cambridge: Cambridge University Press, 1999), 559–60.

Hegel—first appearing on the philosophical scene as Schelling's junior partner—have come to think that transcendental philosophy, as Fichte conceives
it, is insufficient to constitute the philosophical system. In addition to Fichtean
transcendental philosophy, there must also be a *philosophy of nature* to which
no lesser status is accorded. Like the attributes of thought and extension
in Spinoza's *Ethics*, the philosophy of mind and the philosophy of nature
are mutually irreducible, yet manifestations of the absolute principle nonetheless.[49]

One way to understand this is to note that, despite all Fichte's efforts,
the success of his ambitious project would still leave Humean naturalism,
radicalized by Maimon, intact. As long as natural psychology or anthropology
are required to account for acknowledgments of normative principles and of
inferences in terms of mechanisms whose explanation involves no notion of
validity whatsoever, the naturalistic serpent can still bite the transcendental
philosopher's heel. And this remains the case: while Fichte derives some
principles constitutive of organic and inorganic nature, he does so only insofar
as the natural world provides the background and the instruments for rational
action. Only the human world, not the natural world, can be said to incarnate
reason. Consequently, naturalistic thinking remains unaccommodating to
rational agency. If Fichte overcomes Humean naturalism, it is not by refuting
it, but rather by finding himself both morally obligated and theoretically able
to think non-naturalistically.

One can therefore see the attraction of a more direct approach, in which one
seeks to understand nature in general as the incarnation of reason—so that
even inorganic nature is, in a phrase drawn by Hegel from Schelling, 'petrified
intelligence'—with the consequence that no natural scientific explanation is
adequate unless it can be placed within a framework that renders rational
agency intelligible.[50] This would *denaturalize natural science itself*, showing
that, when modern science is properly considered, reason does not in the end
undermine itself in reflection. The fact of reason pertinent to the philosophy
of nature as conceived by Schelling and Hegel is an engagement with nature as
holistically intelligible, for which aesthetic appreciation is still more important
than for Fichte. The model here is not only Kant's conjunction of aesthetics

[49]  On Schelling's development, see Frederick Beiser, *German Idealism: The Struggle Against Subjectivism* (Cambridge, MA: Harvard University Press, 2002), 483–550.
[50]  Georg Wilhelm Friedrich Hegel, *Enzyklopädie der philosophischen Wissenschaften im Grundrisse*
[1830], in Georg Wilhelm Friedrich Hegel, *Werke in 20 Bänden* (Frankfurt am Main: Suhrkamp, 1971),
ix. addition to section 24. *Werke in 20 Bänden* hereafter Hegel, *Werke* (1971).

and teleology in his *Critique of Judgment*, but also Goethe, whose ability to see the *Urpflanze*—the original plant in the sense of 'the inner essence' of the plant—in the apparent morphological variety of plant parts is intimately connected with his poetic genius. In the late eighteenth and early nineteenth centuries, this approach attained definite results, such as Goethe's discovery of the intermaxillary bone. It seemed promising, not only for the life sciences, which seemed resistant to Newtonian methods, but for physics itself. The project of making physics more like morphology, instead of making biology more like physics, had genuine appeal.

It is not enough, however, to put the philosophy of nature on a par with philosophy of spirit or mind. How could someone committed to Holistic Monism be content with *two* foundational sciences of philosophy? There must also be, as Schelling and Hegel come to think, a *third*, still more foundational science that shows the underlying identity of nature and mind, demonstrating the necessity with which the immanent and absolute principle gives rise to their apparent duality. Such a science will not, however, be a self-standing foundation on which to build with security. Rather, it will be an expression in the most primordial terms of the absolute and immanent first principle, which must also express itself as both nature and mind, and must do so indeed in that order, so that mind is its highest expression. In this respect, Schelling and Hegel are far from Spinozism and closer to Fichte, for whom—as we have seen—transcendental philosophy constitutes a circle in which the principles both make possible and are justified by means of an actual experience or experiment.

For Schelling around 1800, philosophy culminates in aesthetics, since 'Philosophy in its totality becomes truly objective only in art.'[51] This suggests that aesthetic cultivation is the primary aspect of the relevant fact of reason, which explains why, if some lack the gifts required for philosophy, this should disturb us no more than the small number of people who have what it takes to be artists. To Hegel, however, as to Fichte, this seems incompatible with philosophy's status as the highest expression of our self-knowledge as *rational* agents, and with philosophy's aspiration to *science*. Thus Hegel distinguishes

---

[51] Friedrich Wilhelm Josef Schelling, *Vorlesungen über die Methode des akademischen Studiums* [1803], in Friedrich Wilhelm Josef Schelling, *Werke*, ed. Karl Friedrich August Schelling, 2nd edn, reorganized by Manfred Schröter (Munich: Beck, 1958; first published in 1927), i/3. 306; Friedrich Wilhelm Josef Schelling, *On University Studies* [1803], trans. E. S. Morgan, ed. Norbert Guterman (Athens, OH: Ohio University Press, 1966), 79. *Werke* hereafter Schelling, *Werke* (1958).

himself implicitly from Schelling by emphasizing the role of *religion* in the conflict through which the standpoint of the system is assumed.[52] For religion is the concern of an entire people, not an elite. Hegel has in mind Protestantism, whose origination he barely distinguishes from the advent of modernity itself.

By the time he writes the *Phenomenology of Spirit*, which marks—or at least effects—a break from Schelling, Hegel has developed this view into a striking alternative to Fichte's and Schelling's versions of the fact of reason.[53] They conceive this fact as undergone by an *individual*. But Hegel now thinks of it as a *generation's* experience of reason in the *history* that culminates in the present they are living. On this view, 'we' are all capable of assuming the standpoint from which to grasp the system, just as Fichte thinks. But this is not because of a universal property or capacity that we all possess as rational agents. Rather it is because, thanks to the history that has brought us to this moment, we already implicitly occupy the requisite standpoint, though only a few have become aware of this. Through an explicit re-enactment—or 'recollection'—of our own history, which includes much from Fichte and Schelling but much more besides, drawn from the history of culture in the broadest sense, we can become aware of our own standpoint and proceed to the foundational science and thence to the philosophies of nature and mind. Hegel calls this foundational science *logic*, by which he means the truly philosophical self-understanding of reason from which not only the *logoi* of nature and mind, but also the technical discipline of general logic, is derivative.

Clearly, Schelling and Hegel agree with Fichte that an adequate response to Humean naturalism, and to the more general problem of whether modern reason undermines itself through reflection, demands a philosophical method quite different from the methods of modern natural science. But the extension of this method by Schelling and Hegel to a philosophy of nature that challenges naturalism in its heartland raises the question whether they can avoid undermining the very methods through which natural science achieves its successes in the first place.

---

[52] Georg Wilhelm Friedrich Hegel, [*Differenz des Fichteschen und Schellingschen Systems der Philosophie*] [1801], in Hegel, *Werke* (1971), iv. 75–6; Georg Wilhelm Friedrich Hegel, *The Difference between Fichte's and Schelling's Systems of Philosophy*, trans. Walter Cerf and H. S. Harris (Albany, NY: SUNY Press, 1977), 171–2.

[53] See Georg Wilhelm Friedrich Hegel, *Phänomenologie des Geistes* [1807], in Hegel, *Werke* (1971), iii. 31–4; Georg Wilhelm Friedrich Hegel, *Phenomenology of Spirit*, trans. A. V. Miller (Oxford: Oxford University Press, 1977), secs. 28–9.

Fichte contends in correspondence with Schelling that the latter's philosophy is now metaphysical rather than transcendental, since philosophy ceases to be transcendental when it investigates necessary conditions that the transcendental I can no longer self-ascribe. Consequently, philosophy of nature cannot portray nature as self-constructing, and cannot be on a par with philosophy of mind.[54] To Schelling, however, this limitation is unacceptable. Since Fichte leaves nature and the natural sciences as they are, he fails to pre-empt naturalism. But, if Fichte fails to do that, then he has not succeeded—not *fully*, anyway— in leaving the empirical standpoint.[55]

Yet Schelling does not extend the term 'transcendental philosophy' to philosophy of nature. Instead, he restricts it to philosophy of mind. In 1801, Hegel goes farther, drawing a fresh distinction that will soon supersede that between transcendental and empirical. [56] *Reflective* thinking cannot help but think of identity as excluding difference. Consequently, it is inadequate for the articulation of a Holistic Monism that regards finite beings, in all their variety, as identical with the absolute and immanent first principle. Such a system can be articulated only through *speculative* thinking, which employs a notion of identity as enabling and indeed requiring difference. Thus Fichte's transcendental philosophy, which fails to see the identity in the difference between mind and nature, is reflective, while Schelling's *System of Transcendental Idealism* is genuinely speculative, as is his philosophy of nature and, of course, the foundational philosophy underlying the two. It is a small step from this to Schelling's and Hegel's abandonment of the term 'transcendental', which they finally concede to the reflective philosophies of Kant and Fichte. As speculative philosophy, German Idealism speaks ontologically once more: it considers 'what everything is in itself'.[57]

Kant, Fichte, and Fries could have agreed that Schelling and Hegel regress to pre-Kantian metaphysics. Worse than the rationalists, however, what they say from their standpoint is neither universally intelligible nor supported by

[54] Fichte to Schelling, 15 November 1800; Jochen Schulte-Sasse, ed., *Theory as Practice: An Anthology of German Romantic Writings* (Minneapolis: University of Minnesota Press, 1997), 74. Hereafter Schulte-Sasse, *Anthology* (1997).

[55] Schelling to Fichte, 19 November 1800; Schulte-Sasse, *Anthology* (1997), 75.

[56] See Klaus Düsing, 'Spekulation und Reflexion. Zur Zusammenarbeit Schellings und Hegels in Jena', *Hegel-Studien* 5 (1969), 95–128.

[57] Schelling, [*Fernere Darstellungen aus der System der Philosophie*] [1802], in *Werke* (1958), i/4. 396; Friedrich Wilhelm Josef Schelling, 'Further Presentations from the System of Philosophy (1802)', trans. Michael G. Vater, *Philosophical Forum* 32/4 (2001), 373–97, 388. German Idealists claim to know the in-itself, but reject characterization of it as a *thing*.

recognizable reasons. Moreover, as Jacobi is only the first to argue, it is unclear how a Holistic Monist system, construing both nature and mind as a whole, can make room for individuals and thereby avoid nihilism.[58]

# 8. Psycho-Physiological Neo-Kantianism and the Facts in Perception

Variations on this first contest over Kant's legacy have been played several times, and continue to be played today. An important case is the emergence in the mid-nineteenth century, during and after German Idealism's decline, of a new version of anthropological post-Kantianism. This leads in turn to a renewal of the German Idealist critique of anthropological post-Kantianism as failing to assume the transcendental standpoint, now launched as an attack on what came to be called *psychologism*. The Neo-Kantian attackers, however, want at the same time to avoid what they regard as the German Idealist lapse into metaphysics.[59]

Definitive of Neo-Kantianism is the call for a return from German Idealism to a more—though not wholly—Kantian approach. Such calls become audible in the first third of the nineteenth century, from Fries along with some whom he influences, such as Friedrich Ernst Beneke, and also from some who are closer to late Fichte than to Hegel, such as Christian Weisse. An important role is played by a number of figures with serious philosophical interests who, having studied medicine, make major contributions to the burgeoning field of physiology, notably Hermann Helmholtz and Hermann Lotze.

---

[58] Jacobi first deploys the nihilism charge against Fichte in 1799, but it continues his criticism of Spinoza and Kant, and is later pressed against Schelling. See Franks, *All or Nothing* (2005), 170–2. On the centrality of this objection to criticism of Hegelianism in the 1840s, see Warren Breckman, *Marx, the Young Hegelians, and the Origins of Radical Social Theory* (Cambridge: Cambridge University Press, 1999). See Stern's contribution to this volume for an exploration of Hegel's response to the criticism.

[59] Both Cohen and Windelband published early writings in the journal of Moritz Lazarus and Hajim Steinthal, dedicated to the project of *Völkerpsychologie*, a social psychology drawing on philology as well as individual psychology. This was not intended to be a natural science, and both Cohen and Windelband remained indebted to its cultural and historical approach. The question whether such a project is psychologistic, and in general what role non-psychologistic psychology should play in philosophy, remains crucial for Neo-Kantianism.

Helmholtz's call is significant because it comes from a cutting-edge natural scientist, already famous for his contribution to the law of the conservation of energy. Neo-Kantianism comes to be seen as the philosophy of the natural scientists themselves, whose achievements contrast with the decline of German Idealism after Hegel's sudden death in 1831. Yet Helmholtz is not interested in Kant's transcendental method and believes, like Fries, that he can reach a revised version of Kant's transcendental results by empirical methods. However, Helmholtz is not close to Jacobi and does not look to the commonsensical facts of consciousness. Instead, he looks to what he calls 'the facts in perception': the facts in *perception* and not consciousness, because it is possible to apply the Newtonian method—a careful mix of experimentation and theory-formation, with the aim of formulating exact and universal laws—to the interface between the mental and the physical; the facts *in* and not merely *of* perception, because perception is sometimes illusory, and common-sense reflection may turn out to be no more reliable when measured against the standard of a theory accounting for both veridical and illusory perception. Whereas Fries employs in his anthropology an *analogue* of the natural scientific method, Helmholtz aspires to employ *exactly* the same method in his study of man as physicists use to study the world. As we shall see, however, this yields a less than fully satisfying response to the problem of Humean naturalism, to which transcendental philosophy is in the first place a response.

I call the Neo-Kantianism represented by Helmholtz *psycho-physiological* because of this focus on perception as the interface between the psychic and the physical—which, in the human case, has come to be called the physiological. Indeed, a major controversy between what came to be the Helmholtz and Hering schools, lasting from the 1860s until its dissipation in the 1920s, concerns the competing claims of psychology and physiology to explain characteristics of sense perception, especially vision.[60] Notwithstanding his contributions to sense physiology, Helmholtz is committed to maximizing the role of psychological explanation, while Karl Ewald Konstantin Hering takes the opposite approach. Helmholtz characterizes the debate as between his own *empiricism* and Hering's *nativism*, but this is on the assumption that the physical capacities of human beings are invariant and unacquired, whereas psychic capacities can be acquired and may vary.[61]

---

[60]  Gary Hatfield, *The Natural and Normative: theories of Spatial Perception from Kant to Helmholtz* (Cambridge, MA: MIT Press, 1990), 182. Hereafter Hatfield, *Natural* (1990).

[61]  Hatfield, *Natural* (1990), 193, gives an insightful summation: 'Helmholtz's arguments against nativism failed on all counts to provide conclusive arguments against his opponents. He was generally

In any event, Helmholtz's characterization is misleading, because the debate is not about whether physiological nativism is acceptable in general. Helmholtz's view also includes some nativism, and indeed he thinks that it is just here that his views accord with Kant's. Thus he thinks that Kant's central insight is confirmed by the law of specific nerve energies, discovered by his teacher, the physiologist Johannes Peter Müller. This law states that, however one stimulates a specific nerve, only sensations appropriate to the pertinent sense modality will result, so that physically indistinguishable stimulations of two different nerves can produce radically different sensations.[62] Müller infers that, 'What comes to consciousness through the senses is immediately only the properties and states of our nerves. But representation and judgment are ready to interpret the processes produced in our nerves by external causes as properties and alterations of bodies outside us.'[63] According to Helmholtz, this is equivalent to the core of transcendental idealism: the thesis that 'the quality of our sensation . . . can pass for a sign—but not for an image' of 'the peculiarity of the external influences stimulating it'.[64] Thus Helmholtz rejects what Fries calls the 'transcendental truth' to which pre-Kantian metaphysics had aspired, in favour of what Helmholtz calls 'practical truth'. Though Müller had not considered himself as a Kantian, Helmholtz thinks that Müller's law shows that:

our physiological make-up incorporates a pure form of intuition, insofar as the qualities of sensation are concerned. Kant, however, went further. He claimed that, not only the qualities of sense experience, but also space and time are determined by the nature of our faculty of intuition, since we cannot perceive anything in the external world which does not occur at some time and in some place and since temporal location is also a characteristic of all subjective experience. Kant therefore called time the a priori and necessary transcendental form of the inner, and space

prepared to admit that the empirical data were equivocal; his argument that empirism is simpler was subject to being turned around and urged by a nativist [who could claim to appeal only to structures also admitted by Helmholtz, whereas he had also to invoke a complicated process of learning through experiments of innervation]; and his claim that nativism is incapable of explaining the origin of our capacity for spatial perception failed to take into account the possibility of Darwinian interpretation of nativism [i.e. of sense physiology as acquired at the species-level through evolution].'

[62] Johann Peter Müller, *Zur vergleichenden Physiologie des Gesichtssinnes des Menschen und der Thiere* (Lepizig: Cnobloch, 1826), pp. xii–xiii.

[63] Johann Peter Müller, *Handbuch des Physiologie des Menschen*, 2 vols. (Coblenz: Hölscher, 1834–40), ii. 249.

[64] Hermann von Helmholtz, *Vorträge und Reden* (Braunschweig: Vieweg, 1896), ii. 222. Hereafter Helmholtz, *Vorträge* (1896). Hermann von Helmholtz, *Selected Writings*, ed. Russell Kahl (Middletown CT: Wesleyan University Press, (1971). Hereafter Helmholtz *Selected Writing's* (1971).

the corresponding form of the outer, intuition. Further, Kant considered that spatial characteristics belong no more to the world of reality (the *Dinge an sich*) than the colours we see belong to external objects. On the contrary, according to him, space is carried to objects by our eyes.[65]

Indeed, Kant is right to say that space is the transcendental form of outer intuition. Sensations change as a result of either change in their causes or human movements, and the latter occur through 'the innervation of our motor nerves'. By experimenting with these innervations, which we cannot directly feel, we come to distinguish between outer sensations, which these innervations can alter immediately, and inner sensations, along with mental states generally, which they cannot. 'If we use the term *spatial* to designate those relations which we can alter directly by our volition but whose nature may still remain conceptually unknown to us,' then, 'space, charged with the qualities of our sensations of movement, will appear to us as that through which we move or that about which we gaze. In this sense spatial intuition is a subjective form of intuition, just as the qualities of sensation (red, sweet, cold) are.'[66]

As this comparison of space with sensible qualities betrays, the argument is not Kantian but is instead a materialist version of Berkeley's extension to primary qualities of arguments for the subjectivity of secondary qualities. The underlying principle is that qualities knowable only through human interaction with the external world are not—or, at any rate, cannot be known to be—qualities of what Helmholtz calls 'the actual': the mind-independent world of things in themselves.

However, we can know 'the real', which is to say, the lawlike in the phenomena, which is the proper topic of natural science. Metaphysics, as a science of the actual, is therefore entirely impossible. This extends also, Helmholtz thinks, to the new metaphysics that Kant hoped to found. In other words, *transcendental philosophy in Kant's sense, as a new version of metaphysics, is impossible as well*. The mathematics and physiology of Kant's day had misled him into thinking that the transcendental form of outer intuition is sufficiently determinate to include Euclid's postulate of the parallels. Without this understandable error, Kant would never have thought that the a priori principles of the understanding were sufficiently determinate to ground Newtonian mechanics. Thanks to Gauss, Riemann, and Lobachevsky, we are now familiar with non-Euclidean geometry and,

---

[65]  Helmholtz, *Vörtrage* (1896), ii. 223; *Science and Culture* (1995), 348.
[66]  Helmholtz, *Vorträge and Reden* (1896), 224; *Selected Writings* (1971), 374.

thanks to his own work on the physiology of vision, Helmholtz believes that the human senses could operate in a non-Euclidean world. Scientific advances have shown, then, that the parallel postulate is *not*, as Kant thought, a fact in perception.

Helmholtz understands the *transcendental* form of a human capacity to consist in the capacity's *invariant* features. The underlying reason—about which he is not himself altogether clear—why he wants to minimize the role of physiological explanation in the account of perception is methodological: invariants are limits of explanation, and a maximally explanatory account has a minimal number of invariants.[67]

Though he does not address the question explicitly in quite this way, it would seem that Helmholtz has two views about how to establish an invariant feature, one appropriate for the forms of sensibility, the other for the forms of understanding. In the case of sensibility, invariants are to be identified neither through Friesian empirical deduction—that is, inductive reflection on ordinary consciousness—nor through metaphysical deduction—that is, German Idealist derivation from an absolute principle—but rather through what we may call *natural scientific deduction*. Since our sensory representations are signs, and only 'practical truth' is at stake, Helmholtz sees no need for a transcendental deduction to show the validity of the form of the senses. Both the metaphysical thesis that the world is a dream and the thesis that it is ultimately real are equally indemonstrable and irrefutable.

Helmholtz revises the Kantian account of understanding, like that of sensibility, in an empiricist direction. Following Mill, he reduces deduction to induction and induction to association. This yields an account that is supposed to cover not only the activities of concept-formation, judgment, and inference that Kant ascribed to the understanding, but also the 'unconscious inferences' by means of which Helmholtz wants to explain those features of outer sense that he believes Kant to have mistakenly considered given in a priori intuition. However, a Kantian residue remains. For we could not carry out inductive inferences, or in general refer our perceptions to natural objects, which we regard as their causes, without presupposing the law of causation or sufficient reason. Consequently, there can be no empirical or natural scientific deduction of causality, which is 'a law of our thinking

---

[67]  As Hering points out, this suggests that Helmholtz neglects the possibility that what is invariant at the individual level is variable at the species level, and hence susceptible to evolutionary explanation. See Hatfield, *Natural* (1990).

which is prior to all experience'. [68] Apparently Helmholtz does not consider viable any Friesian empirical deduction, which renounces all interest in justification and therefore considers circularity a non-issue. Perhaps this is because, as Helmholtz explicitly acknowledges, if the law of causation were considered empirical, this would compromise some of his most cherished arguments—notably his argument against Müller's own vitalism, in the service of which he developed the law of the conservation of energy. For if the law of causation is empirical, then its universality cannot be assumed, and there may be regions where it is not valid, which is just what the vitalists claim about life.

Helmholtz offers the consideration that:

the law of causation bears on its face the character of a purely logical law, chiefly because the conclusions derived from it do not concern actual experience, but its interpretation. Hence it cannot be refuted by any possible experience. For if we founder anywhere in applying the law of causation, we do not conclude that it is false, but simply that we do not yet completely understand the complex of causes mutually interacting in the given phenomenon.[69]

But, though the law of causation cannot be refuted, it cannot be proven either. So this hardly counts against the vitalists and others who question its apriority.

Lacking any project of transcendental deduction, Helmholtz can conclude only that:

the law of sufficient reason is nothing more than the *urge* (*Trieb*) of our understanding to bring all our perceptions under its own control. It is not a law of nature. Our intellect is the faculty of forming general conceptions. It has nothing to do with our sense perceptions and experiences, unless it is able to form general conceptions or laws. These laws are then objectified and designated as causes. But if it is found that the natural phenomena are to be subsumed under a definite causal connection, this is certainly an objectively valid fact, and corresponds to special objective relations between natural phenomena, which we express in our thinking as being their causal connection, simply because we do not know how else to express it.

Just as it is the characteristic function of the eye to have light-sensations, so that we can see the world only as a *luminous phenomenon*, so likewise it is the characteristic function of the understanding to form general conceptions, that is, to search for

---

[68] Hermann von Helmholtz, *Handbuch der physiologischen Optik* (Leipzig: Voss, 1850–67), iii. 453. Hereafter Helmholtz, *Handbuch* (1850–67). Hermann von Helmholtz, *Helmholtz's Treatise on Physiological Optics*, trans. James P. Southall (Menasha, WI: Optical Society of America, 1924–5; repr. Bristol: Thoemmes, 2000), ii. 32. Hereafter Helmholtz, *Treatise* [1850–67] (2000).

[69] Helmholtz, *Handbuch* (1850–67), iii. 454; *Treatise* [1850–67] (2000), ii. 33.

causes; and hence it can *conceive* of the world only as being *causal* connection. We have other organs besides the eye for comprehending the external world, and thus we can feel or smell many things that we cannot see. Besides our understanding there is no equally systematized faculty, at any rate for comprehending the external world. Thus, if we are unable to *conceive* a thing, we are unable to imagine it existing.[70]

In other words, the law of causation is objectively valid, not because it is a law of nature, as Kant argues, but because it is an *urge* of *our* nature. It is not even a *law* of human nature since we need not apply it universally, as Helmholtz has already admitted. Still, we cannot dispense entirely with causation. If one is worried by Humean naturalism, then indispensability—which Hume already acknowledges—will hardly alleviate one's concern. At best, Helmholtz's Neo-Kantianism leaves us with a metaphysical agnosticism that neither decisively undermines nor vindicates our pre-reflective presuppositions: we cannot know the properties or even the existence of the actual, but we also cannot know that it does not exist or does not have any of the properties we ascribe to it, so nobody can prove that we are wrong to assume that the actual exists as cause of our perceptions. Here Helmholtz cannot help sounding like Jacobi: 'Only one piece of advice is valid here: trust and act (*Vertraue und handle*)!'[71]

From a strictly Kantian viewpoint, Helmholtz's philosophy avoids the German Idealist regression to metaphysics only by regressing to British empiricism—to updated versions of Berkeleyan phenomenalism and Humean associationism. But this is, in its own way, no less problematic, and in this respect Helmholtz is representative of a range of mid-nineteenth-century Neo-Kantians.

Among these, an important figure is Kuno Fischer, a student of Lotze.[72] He differs from Helmholtz in at least two significant ways: he is closer to Jacobi than to Mill, regarding transcendental principles as immediate or self-evident; and he views transcendental idealism more as an analytic truth following from the self-evidently subjective character of consciousness, than as an empirical truth following from the significatory character of the sense-organs. Yet Fischer shares important features with Helmholtz too: a desire to avoid the supposed excesses of German Idealist claims about the transcendental or speculative standpoint; lack of interest in Kant's detailed strategies for transcendentally

---

[70] Helmholtz, *Handbuch* (1850–67), iii. 455; *Treatise* [1850–67] (2000), ii. 34–5.

[71] Helmholtz, *Vörtrage* (1896), ii. 244; *Science and Culture* (1995), 363.

[72] See Kuno Fischer, *system der Logik und der Metaphysik oder Wissenschaftslehre* [1865], 2nd edn (Frankfurt am Main: Minerva, 1983).

deducing synthetic a priori principles; and a conflation of—or at least an inability to distinguish clearly between—Kant's transcendental idealism and Berkeley's empirical idealism.

The weakness of this sort of Neo-Kantianism, both as appropriation of Kant and as philosophical position, is brought out by the Trendelenburg–Fischer debate, which begins in 1865 with Fischer's attempt to respond to Trendelenburg's criticism of Kant.[73] Trendelenburg had argued that Kant's arguments in the Transcendental Aesthetic for the subjective or transcendentally ideal character of space failed to exclude the so-called 'neglected alternative' that space was *also* objective or transcendentally real—which was Trendelenburg's preferred Aristotelian position. Since Fischer thinks that exclusive transcendental ideality follows self-evidently from the subjective character of consciousness, he cannot see that there is a neglected alternative. He can only repeat or paraphrase Kant's words.

Trendelenburg's point can be made against Helmholtz too. Transcendental idealism is supposed by Kant to be both incompatible with transcendental realism and uniquely compatible with empirical realism. But if transcendental idealism means only that the objects of human perception have invariant features explainable in terms of human nature—regardless of whether these are attributable to human physiology or to what we humans all perceive as self-evident—then neither consequence follows. The spatiality of things in themselves is not excluded and, as we saw in Helmholtz's case, no vindication of categories such as causation is forthcoming against naturalistic skepticism.

# 9. Anti-Psychologistic Neo-Kantianism, the Fact of Science, and the Normal Human Being

But a better Kant interpretation would be insufficient to overcome the impasse. For it is no longer possible to assume with Kant that syllogistic logic can serve

---

[73] See K. C. Köhnke, *Entstehung und Aufstieg des Neukantianismus: Die deutsche Universitätsphilosophie zwischen Idealismus und Positivismus* (Frankfurt am Main: Suhrkamp, 1986); partially translated by R. J. Hollingdale as *The Rise of Neo-Kantianism: German Academic Philosophy between Idealism and Positivism* (Cambridge: Cambridge University Press, 1991). See also Christopher Adair-Toteff, 'The Neo-Kantian Raum Controversy', *British Journal of the History of Philosophy*, 22 (1994): 131–48.

as 'transcendental clue' to transcendental logic; that Euclidean geometry secures the connection between mathematics and its application to sensible objects; and that we need not worry about the exciting but troubling prospect of extending Newtonian physics to blades of grass and even to the human sense-organs. What is needed is a clear diagnosis of what is wrong with both the empirical and the metaphysical, as the Scylla and Charybdis between which transcendental philosophy must steer, as well as a transcendental programme that is viable in light of post-Kantian developments in mathematics and natural science.

The basic terms of the diagnosis are given by Fischer's teacher, Lotze, while Trendelenburg's student, Hermann Cohen, is the first to develop an alternative Kant-interpretation, along with the programme of what comes to be called the Marburg school. Before long, Fischer's student Wilhelm Windelband develops the distinct programme of the Southwest German (Baden or Heidelberg) School.

Lotze insists on the distinction between *the eternal validity of ideas*, such as the laws of logic, and *the temporal actuality of beings*. If Aristotle is the first to endanger Plato's insight, by construing ideas as beings, then the most recent is 'the latest phase of German philosophy', which sets on the throne the Absolute Idea as a being.[74] The target is surely Hegel's statement that, 'What is rational is actual, and what is actual is rational.'[75] Lotze's distinction enables the formulation of a thought attributable to both Cohen and Windelband: metaphysical philosophies—including pre-Kantian and German Idealist versions—conflate actuality with rational validity, while empirical philosophies—including anthropological and psycho-physiological versions of Kantianism—conflate validity with actuality. The late nineteenth- and early twentieth-century Neo-Kantian schools are formed in opposition to this second error, which—drawing on Hegel's criticism of Kant and Fichte, and Erdmann's Hegelian criticism of the Friesian philosopher Beneke—they call *psychologism*.[76] By this they do not mean only the fallacious attempt to

[74] Rudolf Hermann Lotze, *Logik* (Leipzig: Hirzel, 1874), 507. Trans. Bernard Bosanquet as *Logic* (Oxford: Clarendon Press, 1884).

[75] Georg Wilhelm Friedrich Hegel, *Grundlinien der Philosophie des Rechts* [1821], in Hegel, *Werke* (1971), vii. 24; Georg Wilhelm Friedrich Hegel, *Elements of the Philosophy of Right*, trans. H. B. Nisbet, ed. Allen W. Wood (Cambridge: Cambridge University Press, 1991), 20.

[76] The term seems to have been used first by Johann Eduard Erdmann, *History of Philosophy* [originally published in 1866 as *Die Deutsche Philosophie seit Hegels Tod*], iii, trans. Williston S. Hough (London: Swan Sonnenschein, 1890), 38. The context was Erdmann's criticism of Beneke, in whose forced departure from the University of Berlin Hegel had apparently been

justify a putatively eternal truth on the basis of a claim about temporal actuality. As we have seen, neither Fries nor Helmholtz makes this move. Psychologism is, rather, the attempt to attain transcendental cognition through a method appropriate for empirical psychology, and the charge is that *it fails to so much as clearly conceive transcendental principles*. That Fries, Helmholtz, and Fischer cannot adequately distinguish Kant's transcendental idealism from Berkeley's phenomenalism is no accident, but a consequence of their attempt to grasp transcendental philosophy without transcendental method.

At least two opposing morals might be drawn from this diagnosis, leading in distinct yet Fichtean directions. One is that a properly transcendental philosophy must find a way in which the gap between the valid and the actual can be *overcome without conflation*. Cohen believes that Kant finds just such a non-conflationary overcoming in the construction of geometric figures in pure intuition, where a method *constitutes* the *real* object of a science, thus illuminating *actual* sensible particulars without annihilating them; that Kant attempts to interpret Newtonian physics as involving a similarly constructive method; and that this attempt may now be completed thanks to post-Kantian developments in mathematics.[77] Another moral, drawn by Windelband, is that a properly transcendental philosophy must regard us as obliged by valid norms to *idealize* the actual, without ever overcoming the gap between our constructions and the objects to which they are ultimately supposed to answer.

The Marburg programme is rooted in a reading of the Analytic of Principles in Kant's first *Critique*. It is close to Fichte's second Jena *Wissenschaftslehre*, which involves object-constitution without identifying nature and mind—except that Marburgers focus on mathematical and natural science whereas Fichte focuses on norm-governed intersubjective interactions. The Southwest German Neo-Kantian programme appropriates Kant's account of

involved. Hegel's criticism of the tendency to 'psychological idealism' in the reflective philosophies of Kant and Fichte may provide some precedent. See Georg Wilhelm Friedrich Hegel, *Glauben und Wissen* [1802], in Hegel, *Werke* (1971), i. 303, 305, 307; Georg Wilhelm Friedrich Hegel, *Faith and Knowledge*, trans. Walter Cerf and H. S. Harris (Albany, NY: SUNY Press, 1977), 75–7. Wilhelm Windelband, *Geschichte der neueren Philosophie* (Leipzig: Breitkopf & Härtel, 1880), 386–97 extends the term to others whose method is not transcendental, e.g. Fries and Krug.

[77] See Hermann Cohen, *Das Prinzip der Infinitesimalmethode und seine Geschichte* [1883] in *Werke*, v, ed. Helmut Holzhey (Hildesheim: Olms, 1984). Hereafter Cohen, *Prinzip* [1883] (1984). Cohen argues for the particular significance of the work of Augustin Cournot. For a helpful account, see Lydia Patton, 'Hermann Cohen's History and Philosophy of Science' (unpublished dissertation, Montreal: McGill University, 2004).

concept-formation and reflective judgment as regulated by ideals that cannot be empirically instantiated. With its construal of the theoretical as infinite striving, hence as in some sense practical, it is close to Fichte's first Jena *Wissenschaftslehre*.[78]

Cohen's view is intimately intertwined with his ground-breaking Kant-interpretation. For him, the problem motivating transcendental philosophy is first and foremost the problem of understanding how eternally valid truths have come to be known in a particular time—how the modern scientific revolution is possible—and how to effect an equivalent revolution in philosophical reflection on modern science. Experience is *scientific* experience and the starting point of transcendental philosophy is 'the fact of science'—which is to say, *the temporal actuality or event of our knowledge of the eternally valid laws of nature*.[79] But many pitfalls must be avoided, and Cohen reads the *Critique* as a complex and gradual—if not altogether successful—attempt to bring us safely to the transcendental standpoint.

The acknowledgment of the fact of science is a crucial but initial step, which already involves a move beyond empiricism to the distinction between the *temporal beginning* of experience—a proper topic for psychology's developmental explanations—and the *origin* of experience in eternally valid principles.[80] A second step is taken in the Aesthetic's metaphysical exposition and the Analytic's metaphysical deduction: here *facts of consciousness* are adduced to show that space, time, and the categories are a priori in the sense that they are invariants of human sensibility and understanding; consequently, they have no temporal development and signify *limits* for psychology.[81]

This metaphysical conception of the a priori is, however, still preliminary and hence open to misunderstanding.[82] Psycho-physiological Neo-Kantians

---

[78]    The primacy of the practical in Southwest German Neo-Kantianism should be understood as the primacy of value, which manifests itself pre-eminently in ethics, but is essential to cognition as well. See Heinrich Rickert, 'Zwei Wege der Erkenntnistheorie', *Kant Studien* 14 (1909): 169–228, 215–16. Hereafter Rickert, *Zwei Wege* (1909).

[79]    Hermann Cohen, *Kants Theorie der Erfahrung*, [1918] in *Werke*, 1.1–2., ed. Helmut Holzkey (Hildesheim: Olms, 1989), 41: 'The fact of science is the basic assumption from which philosophy proceeds and without which it cannot begin.' Hereafter Cohen, *Kants Theorie* [1918] (1989). This was Cohen's breakthrough work, the first edition of which was published in 1881, with revised editions in 1885, 1918 and 1925.

[80]    See Cohen, *Kants Theorie* [1918] (1989), 176, on the beginning of the B edition of *Critique of Pure Reason*.

[81]    Cohen, *Kants Theorie* [1918] (1989), 261: 'It is the methodical character of psychology to be developmental history.' Hence its interest in eliminating putatively innate ideas (p. 98).

[82]    Cohen, *Kants Theorie* [1918] (1989), 140: 'That investigation of the facts of consciousness in cognition, which establishes the elements of consciousness as having to be recognized as inaccessible to

are stuck at this stage, interpreting the transcendental as the limit of psychology, without passing beyond psychology to another method.

German Idealists are also stuck here. They see that transcendental philosophy cannot begin with facts of consciousness if it is to leave the empirical standpoint. But they make everything depend on a metaphysical deduction from a single absolute principle, and they inevitably conceive this principle as an absolute and mind-like being developing in its own fictitious or actual temporality, which means that they have rendered psychology cosmic, instead of escaping it altogether.[83]

Thus a third step is required: a transcendental exposition or deduction in which a regress is carried out from the fact of some mathematical or natural science to the methodical construction of its objects. Here, for the first time, the a priori is construed transcendentally—as the valid and non-actual principle of methodical object-synthesis—hence in no way as a being, and thus Trendelenburg's 'neglected alternative'—which accords to the a priori both mental and extra-mental being—is at last excluded.[84]

On Cohen's reading, the arguments Kant designated metaphysical and transcendental are not supposed to be complementary, as is usually thought. Instead, the metaphysical prepares the way for the transcendental, which corrects and completes it. Similarly, the Aesthetic as a whole, with its suggestion that sensibility is distinct from understanding, prepares the way for the Analytic, which corrects and completes its predecessor. The distinctions between the matter and form of sensibility, and between sensibility and understanding, are not distinctions between psychological components or faculties, but are rather reflective distinctions between aspects of scientific, reality-constituting method. Thus, for Marburg Neo-Kantianism, transcendental logic becomes *transcendental methodology*. Only thus emerges the *transcendental method* that makes systematic philosophy possible at last.[85]

---

psychological analysis—which is to say, *a priori*—elements of consciousness, Kant calls a "metaphysical exposition". And this is a necessary precondition of the transcendental.'

[83]  See Cohen, *Kants Theorie* [1918] (1989), 749 on Reinhold; 739 on Fichte, who 'set the agenda for all his successors' (750); and 754–5 on Schelling and Hegel. Cohen's attitude to the Spinozistic argument motivating German Idealist systematization deserves discussion elsewhere, along with his own conception of systematicity.

[84]  See Cohen, *Kants Theorie* [1918] (1989), 214–16.

[85]  See, e.g. Cohen, *Kants Theorie* [1918] (1989), 143: 'The bearers of the *a priori* in the Kantian theoretical construction—*space and time*, also the *categories*—are to be understood as methods, not as forms of mind.'

Southwest German Neo-Kantianism does not focus, like its Marburg counterpart, on mathematical and natural science. For Windelband, the problem
motivating transcendental philosophy is put in general terms ultimately drawn
from Jacobi: all proof, whether deductive or inductive, presupposes indemonstrable axioms perceived as self-evident, and *the problem of philosophy is the
validity of axioms*, a problem that psychology, as a *genetic* science concerned
with temporal development, cannot address.[86] For him, there is no equivalent
to the *fact* of science, no event in which the eternally valid is deployed to constitute the object of knowledge. Like the Marburgers, however—and explicitly
following Fichte—he does not consider facts of consciousness adequate as
a starting point for transcendental philosophy. Such a fact is merely actual,
hence 'brute', and vulnerable to all of Locke's objections against nativism.[87]
Instead, he begins with 'an ideal of the normal human being'—with 'faith' in
the absolute validity of the *end* or regulative ideal of the species of experience
in question, which may but need not be scientific.[88] For natural or nomo-
thetic science, the end is the determination of absolutely valid law, while for
historical or idiographic science, it is the determination of absolutely valid
individuality.[89] For ethics, the end is absolutely valid goodness; for aesthetics,
absolutely valid beauty. In each case, the end is an absolute *value*, and there
is no prospect of refuting a naturalistic skeptic who does not acknowledge
the end.[90]

Assuming the appropriate end, the transcendental philosopher considers
which norms must be acknowledged if this ideal is to be pursued. To be sure,
however, the ideal cannot be actualized, and the real object, instead of being
constructed, remains forever a transcendent standard. For the actual is, in
the formulation of Windelband's student, Heinrich Rickert, a 'heterogeneous
continuum' that can be grasped only through an acknowledgment of norms

---

[86] Wilhelm Windelband, *Präludien* [1883], 3rd enlarged edn (Tübingen: Mohr, 1907), 327.
Hereafter Windelband, *Präludien* [1883] (1907).

[87] Windelband, *Präludien* [1883] (1907), 333: 'If 'validity' is to be understood factually (*im Sinne
des Tatsächlichen*), meaning that something is acknowledged or is the factically determining principle,
then the axioms are 'valid' only for individuals and occasionally, but neither for all nor forever.' See
Windelband, *Präludien* [1883] (1907), 337 for reference to 'the brutal fact' (*brutale Tatsache*).

[88] Windelband, *Präludien* [1883] (1907), 342.

[89] See Windelband's 1894 rectoral address, 'Geschichte und Naturwissenschaft', published in
subsequent editions of Windelband, *Präludien* (1907), and further developed in Heinrich Rickert, *Die
Grenzen der naturwissenschaftlichen Begriffsbildung*, 1st edn (Tübingen: Mohr, 1896–1902); 5th edn
(Tübingen: Mohr, 1929). Hereafter Rickert, *Die Grenzen* (1929). Trans. Guy Oakes as *The Limits of
Concept Formation in Natural Science* (Cambridge: Cambridge University Press, 1986).

[90] Windelband, *Präludien* [1883] (1907), 342–3.

necessarily involving an element of subjective choice. For example, one may choose to *homogenize* the continuum, treating, say, a diamond as an object of natural science, or one may choose to render the heterogeneous *discrete*, treating it as an historical individual. One cannot choose both at once. Nor, since actuality as such cannot be known, can one refrain from choosing.[91]

The unavoidability—if not of evaluation then—of free reference to values constitutes, on this view, the core of transcendental idealism.[92] It also excludes Trendelenburg's 'neglected alternative', which would ascribe the same properties *both* to what depends on the subject's free value-references *and* to value-reference-independent actuality. Southwest German Neo-Kantianism treats the distinction between nature and mind methodologically rather than metaphysically, but it is not merely a broader version of its Marburg counterpart, because it views transcendental logic fundamentally as *transcendental axiology*.[93]

The differences between the two schools are such that each must see the other as inadequately transcendental or residually metaphysical. To Southwest German Neo-Kantians, Marburgers are essentially Hegelians who confine their identity philosophy to mathematical and natural science and thereby make matters worse rather than better, since they relegate non-scientific experience to the realm of the irrational. To Marburgers, Southwest German Neo-Kantians are essentially Fichteans who are vulnerable to Hegel's criticism: they are subjectivists who cannot see how to overcome duality and therefore cannot understand science.

Nevertheless, both schools consider themselves engaged in *epistemology*, and this is central to their self-understanding as transcendental philosophers who are neither empirical like the anthropologists or psycho-physiologists, nor metaphysical like the German Idealists. Consequently, a break seems to occur when, shortly before the First World War, both Kant-interpretation and post-Kantian philosophy break a taboo by acknowledging their proximity

---

[91]  See Rickert, *Zwei Wege* (1909); *Die Grenzen* (1929), 36–7.

[92]  Rickert believes that history necessarily involves value-reference but not evaluation, and can thus be objective. See Heinrich Rickert, *Kulturwissenschaft und Naturwissenschaft*, 6th and 7th edns (Tübingen: Mohr, 1926), 88–9.

[93]  Cohen's system does extend his version of transcendental philosophy beyond science to ethics, aesthetics, and religion, but his conception of systematicity is neither derivational like the German Idealist conception, nor axiological like the Southwestern, but rather, like Kant's, teleological, and the telos is essentially ethical.

to German Idealism, and then, in the 1920s, take an explicitly ontological or metaphysical turn.[94]

But there is recognizable continuity. First, proximity to German Idealism is discernible from the start, at least in retrospect. Second, while Kant's transcendental philosophy is clearly intended to replace metaphysics as a purely rational science of beings in general and of supersensible beings, it is arguable that transcendental philosophy is the ontology of phenomena, that Kant retains a non-scientific thinking of supersensible beings, and even that the former needs the latter. Moreover, if one overcomes a supposed duality of sensibility and understanding in Kant, as both German Idealism and Marburg Neo-Kantianism do, then this excludes a two-world interpretation of transcendental idealism. But, if transcendental philosophy is the ontology of the phenomenal world, which is the only world there is, then transcendental philosophy is ontology in the only sense there is. Heidegger's distinction between the ontic and the ontological is a recognizable successor to the distinction between the empirical and the transcendental.[95]

One feature of Neo-Kantianism's proximity to German Idealism is its dependence on *history*. Consider, first, that the starting points of Neo-Kantianism—the fact of science and the value of absolute validity—are unacceptable to Humean naturalists. The question arises once again how transcendental philosophy can avoid begging the question. It is unclear what Southwest German Neo-Kantians can say to improve the situation. But Cohen can respond in a way reminiscent of Hegel. The fact of reason for Hegel, I argued earlier, is the advent of the present moment, which is a 'birth-time' for philosophy and society—the age of Kant and the French Revolution—and we already occupy the standpoint required for systematic philosophy, as we can come to see by recollecting the history that has brought us here. For Cohen, the fact of reason is the advent of the present moment as the age of accomplished and still advancing mathematical physics, and what is needed

---

[94] On the former, see Wilhelm Windelband, *Die Erneuerung des Hegelianismus. Sitzungsberichte der Heidelberger Akademie der Wissenschaften. Philosophisch-Historische Klasse* (Heidelberg: Winter, 1910). On the latter, see Gottfried Martin, 'Die deutsche ontologische Kant-Interpretation', in *Gesammelte Adhandlungen. Kant-Studien Ergänzungshefte* 81 (1961), 104–9. Roughly contemporaneously, others with roots in Marburg or Berlin Neo-Kantianism are taking a turn towards the empirical. They will come to be called logical positivists or empiricists. For a helpful account, see Michael Friedman, *A Parting of the Ways: Carnap, Cassirer, Heidegger* (Chicago: Open Court, 1999).

[95] See, e.g. William Blattner, *Heidegger's Temporal Idealism* (Cambridge: Cambridge University Press, 1999).

is a recollection of the history of science and philosophy. Laws are eternally valid, but the reason that discloses these laws has a history, which consists of successive concept-formations and a priori syntheses, each responding to problems confronted and raised by its predecessors. Cohen's conception of logic as methodology and of the idea as hypothesis both indicate the centrality of history to transcendental philosophy as he understands it. Appeal to the fact of science is therefore not dogmatic, but must rest on a painstaking history of modern philosophy and science.[96]

Southwest German Neo-Kantianism also depends on history. From an ideal end there is no route whatsoever to subordinate norms without information about the capacities and limitations of concrete people and the practices whereby they pursue the end. So transcendental philosophy needs 'the facts of psychology and history', not 'as grounds of validity for norms', but 'as the objects through which it completes its philosophical examination and reflection'.[97] Here lie the seeds of the Southwest German Neo-Kantian preoccupation with the scientific status of history, and of the increasingly intimate relationship between this Neo-Kantian school and Husserl's phenomenology, which takes its own transcendental turn and seems to promise a transcendental psychology that will enable transcendental axiology to specify determinate norms without compromising itself by becoming empirical.[98]

But what if the laws central to Marburg and the absolutely valid norms central to Southwest German Neo-Kantianism turn out to be—if not temporal in the way that natural beings are, nevertheless and in their own way—historical? The eternality of laws and norms is equivalent to the eternality of *humanity*, which transcendental philosophy has traditionally not only affirmed but also valued. What if humanity itself is a historically specific development whose value may not be unquestioningly assumed?

The first question lies at the heart of Heidegger's development from Neo-Kantianism, whose transcendental approach presupposes the ahistoricity of validity, to a fundamental ontology that thematizes the historicity of *Dasein*, including the historicity of philosophy itself. Later he comes to think, not only that philosophy is historically situated, but also that there are multiple, conflicting understandings of being. So fundamental ontology, which would

---

[96] On the relationship between transcendental philosophy and the history of philosophy and science, see especially Cohen, *Einleitung mit kritischem Nachtrag zur neunten Auflage der Geschichte des Materialismus von Friedrich Albert Lange in dritter, erweiterter Auflage* (Leipzig: Friedrich Brandstetter, 1914).

[97] Windelband, *Präludien* [1883] (1907), 349.    [98] See, e.g. Rickert, *Zwei Wege* (1909).

articulate primordial temporality as the unified ground of historicity, is no less flawed than the project of a unified transcendental philosophy.[99] The second question distinguishes Heidegger's later thinking—and, indeed, much post-Heideggerian philosophy—from that of late Neo-Kantians such as Ernst Cassirer. Notwithstanding his thematization of historicity and dimensions of life prior to natural and mathematical science, Cassirer remains a humanist.[100]

Here it becomes clear that nihilism has changed shapes again. Thanks in part to the development of philology and historiography during the nineteenth century, transcendental philosophy must now confront *historicism*. Though non-naturalist, historicism threatens to undermine our conviction in the validity of laws and norms, and the value of humanity. For it suggests that not merely our theoretical and practical presuppositions, but also laws, norms, and humanity themselves, have histories, and that these histories cannot be understood teleologically as culminating in the present moment.

# 10. CONCLUSION

'Transcendental' has been a contested term since Kant used it to designate the discipline he was proposing as a successor to traditional metaphysics. So intimately tied to the complexities and shifts of Kant's thinking is his usage of the term that, even if there were an agreed characterization of the essence of Kant's transcendental philosophy, it would be unreasonable to expect consensus about applying the term to post-Kantian philosophers. For these are bound to think that continuing Kant's project requires differing from him somewhere, not least because of post-Kantian developments in mathematics, the natural sciences, and the human sciences.

Contests over what counts as transcendental are therefore partly political. One reason why Schelling and Hegel abandoned their claim to the term in 1801 was that Kant's 1799 repudiation of Fichte, along with their own departure from Fichte in a still more radical direction, made it unprofitable to emphasize their continuity with Kant. But later interpreters have argued

---

[99] Here I am indebted to forthcoming work by Mark Wrathall.

[100] See the 1929 Cassirer–Heidegger debate at Davos in Martin Heidegger, *Kant und das problem der Metaphysik*, 5th enlarged edn (Frankfurt am Main: Klostermann, 1991), app. IV. Trans. Richard Taft as *Kant and the Problem of Metaphysics*, 5th enlarged edn (Bloomington, IN: Indiana University Press, 1997).

that it still makes sense to see Hegel as a transcendental philosopher, and this argument is worthwhile when continuity with Kant is a mark of philosophical respectability—as it has been in recent Anglo-American philosophy.[101] Similarly, though Heidegger was never enthusiastic about calling himself a transcendental philosopher, which would have tied him to a crumbling establishment, nevertheless a case can be—and has been—made for interpreting fundamental ontology in transcendental terms. The case is harder to make for his later work, which grapples with historicism and questions the traditional humanism of transcendental philosophy. But an intimate relation to Kant and post-Kantianism continues to make the issue worth raising there too.

I have argued that some crucial developments in transcendental philosophy since Kant may be fruitfully understood in light of two early challenges entered by Maimon and Jacobi, and I have traced these developments to one point where the continental and analytic traditions, both emerging from Neo-Kantianism, self-consciously divide. On the Continental side lies a non-naturalist tradition that attends to historicity and the human sciences, questioning the traditional humanism of transcendental philosophy. On the analytic side, which I have not discussed here, logical empiricism begins as a non-naturalist tradition attending to the mathematical and natural sciences with the help of modern logic, while questioning transcendental philosophy's traditional commitment to a priori synthesis. Too often, Continental thinkers have left themselves unguarded against sophisticated naturalisms, while analytic thinkers have neglected non-naturalistic nihilisms, rendering each tradition superficial in the eyes of the other. The vicissitudes of the transcendental in the nineteenth century remind us how demanding and yet how important it is to struggle with *both* naturalism *and* nihilism, anticipating that the former will bite back and that the latter will shift shapes, yet again.

---

[101] See, e.g. Robert Pippin, *Hegel's Idealism: The Satisfactions of Self-Consciousness* (Cambridge: Cambridge University Press, 1989).

# CHAPTER 9

# DIALECTIC, VALUE OBJECTIVITY, AND THE UNITY OF REASON

## FRED RUSH

WITH advances in science from the Enlightenment onwards the explanatory role of theological concepts has receded. As a result, the idea that human reason unproblematically tracks objective basic features of the world was put in question. More and more, objectivity was sought in terms of the structure of reason itself, now understood as a 'subjective' faculty whose relationship with the world was not a given. But how can the structure of a human, 'subjective' faculty account for the objectivity of its claims about the world, or, more specifically, for the objectivity of value judgments?

There are many ways to chart responses to this question in post-Kantian European philosophy. I will emphasize a way to view these responses that is, I believe, neglected. I begin by setting out Kant's views on the dialectic of reason and the related concept of reflective judgment. I then show how two main strands of German philosophy in the nineteenth century develop those doctrines in different directions. On the one hand, German Idealism develops dialectic in a way that minimizes the necessity for the kind of rational presupposition that is indicative of Kantian reflective judgment. Idealism does this in the service of constructing more and more 'scientific' philosophical systems that ground objectivity of claims and theories in terms of necessity. On the other hand, German Romanticism embraces the idea of reflective judgment and the idea of an 'Absolute' that is beyond human comprehension, arguing that objectivity cannot be grounded in the idea of a total, all-encompassing system of thought. I then treat two major twentieth-century representatives of these approaches: Adorno and Habermas, who stand in the same sort of proximity to one another that German idealism and romanticism did before. I focus on Adorno's idea of negative dialectic and Habermas' arguments for dialectical intersubjectivity as a basis for value objectivity.

## KANT'S CONCEPT OF DIALECTICAL REASON

Kant distinguishes sharply between what he calls understanding (*Verstand*) and reason (*Vernunft*). Understanding is, for Kant, the capacity to think singular representations presented in intuition under general representations, or concepts. Knowledge (*Erkenntnis*) is the outcome of deploying concepts in ways that track the base features of experience, as those features are governed by what Kant takes to be basic forms of judgment and a basic set of pure a priori concepts he calls 'categories'. Experience of objects (*Erfahrung*) is possible only by exercising the understanding to conceptualize what is given in intuition. The experience of the self is no exception to this general rule.

Unlike the understanding, reason does not take singular representations as its proximal objects. Its point of application is experience that is already conceptually articulated according to the laws of the understanding. In what Kant calls its 'theoretical' employment, reason is a faculty of pure inferential thought.[1] While the understanding, Kant says, is 'nothing but' a faculty of judgment, or of the synthesis of intuition under concepts, reason's task is to link these judgments inferentially. Reason in and of itself, however, is insensitive to whether the judgments it links together have intuition-based content, i.e.

---

[1] Kant defines 'reason' in a number of ways. Perhaps the most inclusive definition is that it is the faculty of 'logical deduction', by which Kant means mediate inference (A299/B355-6; A303/B360). When Kant speaks of 'rational inference' (*Vernunftschluß*) he means just this sort of inference.

refer to real states of affairs. Reason in its 'pure', theoretical employment can overstep the bounds of possible experience—i.e. the permissible limits of the understanding—without compromising its own native function. What is more, Kant thinks that reason has a built-in and ineradicable propensity to do just that, which he calls 'dialectic' or 'dialectical'.[2] Writing of the fallacious metaphysical conclusions that result from such overreaching, he claims:

> These conclusions . . . are not fictitious, nor have they arisen fortuitously, but have sprung from the very nature of reason as such. They are sophistications not of men, but of reason itself. Even the wisest of men cannot free himself from them. After long effort, he perhaps succeeds in guarding himself from actual error, but he will never be able to free himself from the illusion which unceasingly mocks and torments him. (A339/B397)[3]

The mechanism by which this overstepping occurs is a rational operation that moves from conclusions to premises. Kant calls this procedure 'dialectic syllogistic', although it is not, strictly speaking, syllogistic nor even inferential.[4] The ideas of reason are outcomes of this procedure. 'Dialectic' can also mean the study (by reason) of this propensity and of its results.

Dialectical reasoning takes the following form according to Kant. Given a state, event, or concept, reason construes it as a link in a chain of like states, events, or concepts and seeks its antecedent, toward the overall goal of stating, as Kant puts it, 'the totality of its conditions' (A322/B379). That is, reason takes a state of affairs, constructs a premise based on it, and then searches for a yet more general premise from which it may be derived as a conclusion. In doing so, the true statement becomes situated in an explanatory nexus constituted by the premises so established; through dialectical syllogism, one systematically relates truths that one already has with truths yet to be established. Such a process is unending in principle and, thus, the system it produces is open; reason will always inquire into the antecedent of a purported first premise. In the face of never being able to reach a premise that it will accept as unconditioned, reason substitutes for a real end to the sequence a merely conceptual one. This is what Kant calls an 'ideal', the representation of which

---

[2] There is also an architectonic sense of the term 'dialectic' in Kant that is involved in a rather complex set of distinctions he makes between types and branches of logic. These are largely of only academic interest. See Allison (1983: 123 f.) for a synopsis.

[3] The same point is made in a slightly different way when Kant insists that the doctrines criticized in the Dialectic of the first *Critique* are fallacies of a *faculty* of thought—i.e. of a cardinal and fundamental capacity to think. A341/B399; A570/B598.

[4] A333/B390.

is an idea. Any purported object an idea might take as a referent would itself have to be unconditioned and there can be no unconditioned objects of which we can have knowledge. Concepts of reason thus afford an ideal, systematic totality to representations. Because of this *merely* conceptual status one may not infer from the idea of such a totality to its reality. Dialectical error ensues when the ideal order is taken as real—when a conceptual scheme unanchored in sensibility is projected onto nature (echoes of Hume). It is just this sort of error that Kant thinks is the daily bread of 'dogmatic' metaphysics. The fact that deploying ideas as if they were concepts of the understanding leads to massive philosophical error does not disqualify the ideas of reason from all theoretical employment. Reason may utilize ideas as representations of goals set for scientific enquiry or even for more basic cognitive pursuits such as the construction of empirical concepts. Kant goes even farther than this; he thinks the assumption of certain ideal principles necessary for cognitive purposes.[5] But the point remains that pure reason can have no constitutive role in the possibility of first-order objective experience.

Kant was not the first philosopher in the modern period to have deployed the concept of dialectic, nor was he the first to contrast it with a procedure called 'analytic'. The concept of dialectic relevant to Kant can trace a pedigree back to Aristotle's definition of dialectic as probable, not demonstrative, reasoning.[6] This meaning of the term persisted through the medieval period on into modern university philosophy, where logic handbooks typically glossed dialectic as the science of subjective probability.[7] Kant is careful to warn against understanding the force of dialectic in this way (A293/B349), but the idea that dialectic is a form of reasoning that begins from possible premises remains important for him. Kant is not interested in questions of the nature of statistical inference or of empirical subjective probability as such. Rather the history of thought about dialectic suggests to him three aspects of rational inference as a focus for his own concept of dialectic. The first of these takes off from the idea that such inferences are *subjective* in the sense that they register something about the subjects who make them. For Kant,

---

[5]  See Guyer (1990), cf. Rush (2000).

[6]  Aristotle defines dialectic as deduction 'from what is acceptable'. *Top.* 100ᵃ30–1; see also 104ᵃ9–16.

[7]  It is likely that the proximate influence on Kant's division of logic into analytic and dialectical components was J. G. Darjes's *Introductio in artem inueniendi*, a copy of which (with copious marginalia) Kant had in his library. See especially *Praecognoscendorum* VI. § 212. What must have seemed most interesting to Kant about this division is that it was an example that logic could be a *Methodenlehre* as well as system of demonstrative proof. This would have contradicted the standard Wolffian treatment.

this will ultimately find expression in his claim that dialectical inference or judgment, when well-founded, will express conditions necessary for judgment generally, but cannot guarantee objective reference for the judgment. Second, the idea that such inferences involve merely probable premises is translated into the thought that dialectical judgment involves theoretical or practical posits that, while perhaps transcendentally necessary and a priori, cannot be known to be true. This is Kant's idea of a regulative principle that has a necessarily speculative content.[8] And third, it occurs to Kant that just this sort of demonstration might have uses in accounting for the normativity of some types of value judgments, since they cannot be grounded in a strict epistemic or classically metaphysical way. In fact, Aristotle held that ethical judgment was 'dialectical' in just this sense and established the first distinction between theoretical and practical reason on that basis.[9]

It is this 'positive' role of dialectical reason that forms one part of the basis for Kant's account of the intersubjective validity of value judgments. Reason in its regulative (i.e. 'positive dialectical') mode has three areas of application: (1) *theoretical*—regulative reason must posit certain goals and final entities in order to make maximally rational the inherently totalizing activity of conceptual thought; (2) *ethical*—reason in its pure employment has a constitutive role to play in morality and certain of the structures motivationally necessary for empirical moral agents may have an explicitly regulative cast; (3) *aesthetical*—regulative reason under the rubric of 'reflective judgment' provides the key to understanding how judgments of beauty can be intersubjectively valid even though they are not strictly speaking objective judgments.

Of the two areas I have not discussed, (2) and (3), in many ways (3) is the most interesting subject for two reasons. First, it is the analysis of the role of reflective judgment in aesthetic experience that causes Kant to specify more than he has previously the idea that even pre-conceptual mental life aims towards totality. Second, Kant claims that it is the analysis of reflective judgment in aesthetics and in the explanation of organic life that allows one to see most precisely how nature and moral freedom are properly thought of as related to one another.

But let's begin with (2): the moral case. Reason has a practical employment in which precisely those elements that preclude it from having unrestricted

---

[8]  Cf. Aristotle, *Top.* 104$^b$1−105$^a$9 on the nature of a dialectical 'problem'.
[9]  See, e.g. Aristotle, *EN* 1094$^b$11−27.

theoretical application qualify it for the realm of moral action. For Kant, rational creatures are ultimately able to conceive of themselves *as rational* only by thinking of themselves as standing outside causal determination. While one surely would be able to consider oneself empirically rational according to one's setting of ends in virtue of representing aims, Kant is of the view that, in the final analysis, the idea of rational agency and responsibility require more. They mandate the idea of being initiating causes, not merely that of being caused causes of actions. This requirement is especially significant in value judgment, where the relation between empirical nature and freedom is pointed. In order that ascription of moral praise or blame be justified, moral subjects must be viewed as first causes and not merely as effects in a causal sequence. If one were merely another link in a causal chain leading up to a particular action that were a candidate for a moral ascription, and if the ascription were proper to the extent that it redounds to an author of the act in question, then if there were no initial (i.e. rational) causation in the actor, the ascription would be either free-floating or would have to be traced *ad infinitum* backwards in the line of causes of which the act in question was only a single link. In either case, the idea of moral agency evaporates without the idea of freedom. Kant never proves (and after chapter 3 of his *Groundwork*, never attempts to prove) that we are free in this sense. But he does take himself to have proven that, *if* one wants to conceive of oneself as a being to whom moral predicates are applicable, one must assume that one is free. The first *Critique*'s doctrine of pure reason leaves room for just this assumption, for one can think that one is free without logical contradiction: there is nothing about the character of experience that could confirm or disconfirm the assumption. As necessary as Kant thinks the assumption is for moral discourse, in the end it is important to keep in mind that the assumption secures whatever universality and objectivity it does for moral judgment in terms that are scripted according to discursive human limitations. It is because of the nature of discursive judgment that the assumption is in place. As with the theoretical employment of reason and the understanding, objectivity is circumscribed by judgment.

The role for positive dialectic *cum* regulative principles in aesthetic experience ((3) above) brings one back to the question of the empirical reach of understanding and reason. Kant claims that certain types of intuition-based experience are unintelligible unless one posits an order to nature that is not the product of our subjective contribution to it (i.e. in virtue of the categories, etc.). The two main sorts of experience he is concerned to vindicate regulatively are the experience of beauty and the experience of organisms.[10] Both these experiences are structured in terms that require application to them of the concept of final cause. Both beautiful things and organisms are structured such that their parts and wholes are holistically related: the parts are only parts in virtue of their functional role in the whole and the whole is only the whole of its parts. If one were to deploy the concept of relation of part to whole that is available on the basis of the first *Critique*, the organization of such things would be inexplicable, since the idea of relation there is specified exclusively in terms of efficient cause. Of course, Kant *might* have solved the problem of the experience of beauty and organic objects by including final cause as a thirteenth category (or teleological judgment as one of the primary judgment forms). But this would have been, to his mind, to throw the critical baby out with the regulative bath water. It would have reintroduced into the base structure of the critical philosophy the very elements of high rationalism that he was so intent on superseding. The very distinction between negative and positive dialectic would vanish.

How is this supposed to work specifically? I shall discuss the case of beauty as paradigmatic, although some adjustments would have to be made for the case of organisms. Kant believes that the only way to make sense of the experience of beauty is to draw upon the idea of spontaneous agency that is closest to us, i.e. our own. The structure of beautiful things cannot be due to our cognitive apparatus (limited as it is to thought in terms of efficient causation) and can only be accounted for if we add to our arsenal of critical concepts the idea of 'purposiveness without a purpose' (*zweckmäßigkeit ohne Zweck*).[11] We think of the order of such things as if they were products of a will and the only will that could create such products would be God's. As Kant often intimates, this assumption holds out a very nice picture for finite, human intellects. Not only are we able to understand such things under the standing hypothesis of purposiveness, but we are also enabled thereby to gain a needed general perspective on what it is to be a finite agent in the world. Kant's thought is this: to judge a thing as having a systematic coherence that exceeds what transcendental constitutive epistemic constraints can guarantee is to view its form as not being grounded in (our) concepts. This permits the thought that the world so structured is a place that is made

---

[10] I shall not discuss the experience of sublimity because it introduces complications that are not directly germane to the topic of this chapter.

[11] *Critique of Judgment*, § 12, AA 5: 222, see also § 17, AA 5: 236.

amenable to our basic receptivity, the very receptivity that is at the base of our conceptual orientation in the world. To put the point in a slightly more technical Kantian way, a superabundance of order intelligible as order only against the background of assuming a creative intelligence as a cause of the order displays the world as made for our basic synthesizing intelligence. In this way Kant transfers theodicy from the sphere of rational proof to the realm of regulatively determined aesthetics.

There are two important consequences of this revolutionary move. The first involves the normative status of aesthetic judgment. Because they are not based on a concept of how a thing ought to be (or ought to be thought of as being), reflective aesthetic judgments cannot be objectively valid. Yet, they are intersubjectively valid. This can be so because Kant identifies a non-conceptual state that they are based upon—i.e. the imaginative activity of ranging over a manifold of intuition without ever having to settle on one way to construct it—that is common to all discursive creatures. Provided that one is in a frame of mind that Kant thinks allows for this non-conceptual imaginative free-ranging, a beautiful object will support this activity and judgments that are based in it. Because the activity in question is unconscious, it is available consciously only as a feeling, a feeling with a source entirely in the workings of mind. It is not going too far to say that we take pleasure in our agency as such in these circumstances—and this is a feeling all can enjoy in principle.

The second result of Kant's account of dialectic cum reflective judgment relates even more directly to the main theme of this essay: the issue of the unity of reason. As we saw, theoretical reason is limited by self-critique to its operation on the deliverances of the understanding, if epistemic warrant is of concern. Otherwise, its only positive application is methodological. In this sense, epistemic agency is not fundamentally disjoint from nature. Nature just is, Kant writes, the 'sum total of phenomena',[12] and that is just to say coextensive with all possible true deployments of concepts. Nature is, in this way, encompassed by human cognitive lawfulness. On the practical side, however, where pure reason does have constitutive employment, nature is conceived of as problematic for human agency. To be morally free is to act from duty alone and that means to act in a way that, potentially at least, disregards the way the empirical world determines one's inclinations. Since humans are both empirical and rational beings according to Kant moral

---

[12] 'By nature in the empirical sense we understand the connection of appearances...' (A 216/B 263). Contrast this with Kant's definition of 'world' as the totality of what exists.

action can bring with it extreme tension within subjects concerning how the diametrically opposed elements of their subjectivity belong together. Kant thinks that in all cases of such conflict the right thing to do is to distance oneself from one's inclinations in order to act rationally. If one has a properly developed sense of how ingrained one's empirical nature is, then, this sort of activity can seem alienating. Now, Kant is not insensitive to how rigoristic his concept of a unified agent was bound to seem and took steps to blunt its impact. One of Kant's main strategies is to introduce several 'bridging principles' into his moral theory that serve to bring empirical and rational subjectivity, and thus theoretical and practical rationality, closer. Some of these principles or concepts are clearly regulative, e.g. the concept of the *summum bonum* and the role of the concepts of heaven and of God in moral motivation.[13] Kant sees his analysis of positive dialectic cum regulative reason as tailor-made for an even better fit between theoretical and practical reason and it is easy to see why. Reflective judgment narrows the 'great gulf' (*große Kluft*) between freedom and nature, as Kant puts it.[14] It is the component of Kant's system that unifies reason by unifying the field of its application—the world as it must be for judgment to take hold in it. The main idea here is that judging reflectively, especially with regard to beauty, requires one to disregard, distance, or otherwise put out of play the 'interests' one might have in the object in question, including any interest in categorizing it or otherwise seeing it as fitting in with other experiences one might have. This brings aesthetic response very close to ethical response in that both require that judgment not be based on empirical interest. Yet, unlike moral judgment, aesthetic reflective judgment does not require the empirical to be treated as quite so potentially alien. The principle governing aesthetic judgment is 'purposiveness without a purpose'. Kant holds that this principle requires one to assume that nature is *in itself* prestructured for one's cognitive benefit. This means that the experience of beauty is one had against the background assumption that the exercise of human freedom and empirical necessitation are not mutually inimical. Put in Kantian vernacular, the unity of reason is the demand of reason relative to the power of judgment as it generally spans both the theoretical and practical contexts. But any unity that reason can postulate on its own behalf must be critical, i.e. it must be, in the end, an indemonstrable

---

[13] See Wood (1970: 69 ff.) and Engstrom (1988), (1992).

[14] *AA* 5:176–8, 20:246–7. The geological metaphor is no throw-away. It underscores Kant's claim that the division between reason and nature can never be closed and can only be bridged by a human artifact.

unity.[15] It is a problematic referent to a thought one must think in order to give a fully rational account of one's place in the world. Approaches to the problem of the unity of reason and its relation to value-objectivity in the two centuries following Kant largely divide on this question of rational purchase. And this amounts to two views on the relation of dialectic to reason in post-Kantian European philosophy: one that stresses the positive capacity of dialectic to achieve 'rational closure' and one that credits more the critical or 'negative' aspect of dialectic and denies that such closure is possible.[16]

## IDENTITY IN DIFFERENCE — FICHTE, SCHELLING, AND HEGEL

For Kant the expanding ambit of empirical science applies pressure to the idea of moral freedom. He responds to this threat by a stratagem of 'divide and conquer'. If moral and aesthetic judgment can be shown to be qualitatively different from empirical judgment, perhaps one can establish that moral and aesthetic judgments have their own normative criteria and their own claim to objectivity. But the cost of this sort of approach is to install the idea of a subject compartmentalized into rational and empirical aspects at the very core of one's analysis of agency. This was widely seen by later idealists to be unacceptable. German idealism from Fichte to Hegel consists in a set of 'improvements' on Kant in hopes of solving the problem of the unity of reason and the objectivity of judgment. The basic theoretical move in such accounts can be stated quite simply: reconceive the base structure of theoretical agency in practical terms so that practical agency is built into the idea of agency in general, prior to or coeval with theoretical judgment. The guiding thread to the different approaches of Fichte, Schelling, and Hegel is their development of the ideas of dialectic and of 'identity in difference' as means to that end. Their contributions to the history of the interconnected concepts of dialectic, objectivity, and unity of reason place them firmly in the camp that disputes the Kantian approach to human finitude and, with it, the continued importance

[15]  *Critique of Judgment*, § 57 (Zweite Bemerkung), *AA* 5: 346.

[16]  Discussion of the advent of dialectic often focuses on its roots in Kantian antinomial form. This is no doubt crucial but I shall not discuss it here. Adequate attention to this other (and complementary) way to conceive of the genesis of post-Kantian dialectic requires detailed analysis of the different argument forms of the individual Antinomies that I cannot go into here.

of something like regulative reason. Their view of what dialectic consists in will involve nothing less than a reconceptualization of the structure of rationality as a whole. 'Reason' as it is allegedly unified in later German idealism is not Kant's 'reason' at all.

The phrase 'identity in difference' is, to say the least, not self-explicating. It is perhaps best to approach understanding it by first considering the aims of German idealist philosophy more generally. If Kant is correct, human agency is defined by a potential tension between the kind of relation one feels towards one's empirical existence and one's ethical and aesthetical selves. Qua empirical being I orient myself fundamentally in the world in terms of my knowledge of it and other aspects of my empirical being in the world—e.g. feelings, emotions, other preintentional or subpersonal states—do not have orientational status for me. What I mean by this is that feelings, etc. that are not subject to further conceptualization have no normative force for Kant. They *are* 'meaningful' in a thin sense for him but their meaning cannot by itself anchor any orientation that would be available to one *as* an orientation. It is this 'as' that is crucial. This structure is replicated in Kant's ethical and aesthetic theories in slightly different terms, as we saw. In both spheres the onus is placed squarely on a constitutive tension between the empirical and practical selves. Two ways to alleviate this tension suggested themselves to Kant's successors within idealism. Fichte takes his lead from Kant's practical philosophy and Schelling mines Kant's views on aesthetic and teleological judgment.

A. Fichte's main treatment of the issue of the unity of reason, its relation to his concept of dialectic, and the objectivity of value is his *Foundation of the Entire Wissenschaftslehre* (1794/5). Fichte's methodology and form of argument can be forbiddingly abstruse and unforgivingly arid. The particular context in which Fichte writes is one that is not especially known for lapidary expression, to say the least. But even amongst his peers in the unstylish philosophy of the period—Kant, Hegel, etc.—Fichte is exceptionally dense and plodding. Nevertheless, it is possible to pare down the excess of material somewhat to arrive at a reasonably clear picture of what he intends and why the result of that intention is important.

Like Kant, Fichte conceives of philosophy transcendentally. Given a particular agreed-upon 'fact', the *Wissenschaftslehre* argues to a set of necessary conditions that support the possibility of the fact in question. In Kant, concepts like 'experience' and 'morality' name such facts. Fichte holds that the facts from which Kant begins are not considered deeply enough. Indeed, in some of his moods, Fichte does not think that Kant has identified the right facts at all. For him, Kant's transcendental philosophy begins a level above the facts, belatedly allowing an entry point for skepticism into even transcendental philosophy. What deeper-level facts are there for Fichte, from which transcendental philosophy makes the right start? The deeper-level facts as Fichte understands them are really just one fact. And this fact forms the basis for the first principle of his philosophical system from which all other principles are 'deduced'. Following Reinhold's lead Fichte construes the first principle of philosophy to be a *fact of consciousness*. It is what it is necessary to posit if consciousness of objects in even a minimal sense is to be so much as possible. Fichte is philosophically regressing to the conditions for the possibility of intentionality and this project, at least arguably, does operate at a deeper level than Kant's concern with 'knowledge'. In any event, the result of Fichte's transcendental procedure, the soundness of which need not concern us here, is the proposition that 'the I posits itself'.[17] 'Positing' (*setzen*) for Fichte simply means 'to be aware of' and does not implicate any explicit assertion or even reflective awareness. So, one can substitute for Fichte's first principle the proposition 'the I is aware of itself'. But what *is* this 'I'? Just here is Fichte's great innovation. Fichte realizes that he cannot construe the I substantially (for Kantian reasons), not even as a proper object of consciousness. He cannot do this because the possibility of object-consciousness is supposed to be the explanandum of the procedure he is undertaking, not its explanans. So, Fichte characterizes the I as *nothing but* its activity in self-positing. In other words, the I is both the activity and the product of itself. The idea that an activity can be a product of itself is not exactly intuitive, to say the least, but it is not unprecedented in philosophy either. Rigorous modern concepts of substance, e.g. in Spinoza and Leibniz, require related ideas of self-actuality. But Fichte has taken the Copernican turn away from such concepts and seeks to accommodate them in a relatively Kantian register. He does this, he believes, by characterizing the first principle also as a *Tathandlung*.[18] This word is often translated into English as 'fact/act', in order to track the two ordinary German component terms out of which the concept is fashioned: 'Tat' ('fact') and 'Handlung' ('act', 'action'). This translation is not incorrect but it can obscure an important dimension of the concept for Fichte. 'Tat' is a substantivation from the verb 'tun' ('to do'). The English 'fact' has a similar structure, although only in its etymological history (from Latin 'factum'). So, even though the

---

[17] *SK* 97; *SW* 1: 96.    [18] Ibid. For Fichte's first use of this term, see *EPW* 63–4; *SW* 1: 8.

resonance might still be caught in the English 'fact', the better translation of the term might be 'deed' or 'act'. Why is this important? It is important because a *factum* for Fichte—as opposed to Kant, I would argue[19]—is expressly not a *given* thing. This puts the emphasis of the term in the right way for Fichte, for what *Tathandlung* is supposed to indicate is the nature of the I viewed in terms of two of its aspects: from the side of 'practice' or 'becoming' the I is self-activity and from the side of 'theory' or 'being' it is self-product. In other words, Fichte is importing into his theory of subjectivity a monist idea central to Spinoza's *Deus sive Natura*, the name of the one substance that can be characterized along two dimensions according to its attributes: extension (nature) and thought (God).[20] So, while Fichte adamantly denies that the self-positing I is a thing or substance, something like the dual-aspect theory of Spinoza's account of substance is quite helpful in sorting out how the self-positing I can be both activity and product of that activity.

But Fichte does not always maintain the transcendental mode; he often slips into a more phenomenological way of speaking about the first principle that stresses the psychology or experience of the self-positing I. One can have no experience as of one's self-positing; because it is supposed to ground the possibility of any intentional state, even a reflexive one, the self-positing must be 'unconscious' in some sense, if one holds that all consciousness, or at least all object-consciousness, is intentional. Fichte puts the phenomenological point in terms of the idea of self-presence: the subject has immediate, intuitive basal relation to itself. Such 'intellectual intuition' is inferred, i.e. it is not itself a conscious mode of access of an empirical subject to itself.[21]

The I's self-positing is only possible, however, if one introduces another structure at this unconscious level: the I's positing of itself *as limited*.[22] This follows because in order for the I to posit itself, it must contrast itself (again, implicitly) with something else, minimally specified at this transcendental level as 'not-I'. And because the limit in question must function as a real contrast to the I's initial posit of merely itself (and not just as a barrier that the I creates) the not-I must carry the force of making the I finite. Fichte specifies this force as that of a 'check' (*Anstoß*).[23] Both these posits are only

---

[19] Here I disagree with Franks (2005: 278–9).

[20] Spinoza holds of course that substance has infinite attributes and that extension and thought are just the two of which humans are able to conceive.

[21] *FTP* 110–18; *WLnm* 29–33. See also *SK* 38–9; *SW* 1: 463–4.    [22] *SK* 108; *SW* 1:108.

[23] *SK* 189–92; *SW* 1: 209–14. If one were looking for a metaphorical way to capture the effect of the check visually, a camera dissolve in film might be apt.

separated for purposes of analysis; Fichte holds that they are part of a single synthetic process—one cannot have one without the other This is Fichte's core account of agency. The activity of empirical agents is grounded in that of a transcendental subject or 'I' that is characterized by what Fichte famously calls 'striving' (*Streben*).[24] The I's impetus towards positing itself 'absolutely' is deflected back upon itself by the bare constraint of the check and finite limitation is just this deflecting back. Accordingly, within the I one finds two essential components that are dialectically interlocked: (a) a striving for infinity and unconditioned agency and (b) the check of that striving in terms of conditioned finitude. Neither component is possible without the other and it is only when they are considered together that one has a viable account of freedom according to Fichte. And it is in this form that the motto 'identity in difference' has application to Fichte. One is only free to the extent that one is limited in various ways. The experience of freedom is not transcending finite constraints, it operates within such constraints. The I *is* the I only to the extent that it distinguishes itself from something it is not. And in this act of distinguishing the not-I is 'identical' with the absolute I, in the sense that its being the not-I depends upon being posited *in* the I.

For Fichte, then, theoretical and practical reason are one from the outset. The same transcendental structures that underwrite theoretical objects also generate freedom. To be able to have conscious experience of objects is predicated on a free act of the subject, the freedom of which cannot be proved; it is a presupposed, necessary condition on the possibility of being a subject. This is why Fichte states in the introduction to his later *Wissenschaftslehre nova methodo* (1797) that one cannot address epistemic or moral skeptical challenge by counterargument from shared premises. One either starts with the I (i.e. with an assumption of freedom) and is an 'idealist' or one begins with the concept of a thing wholly apart from subjects (i.e. with the assumption of determinism) and is a dogmatist. Fichte thinks that coherent systems can be achieved under either assumption—one can be Spinoza or Fichte—and where one begins is a matter of choice or perhaps even character.[25] In this way, Fichte believes that he has achieved a unified account of objectivity across the theoretical and practical spheres. The normativity of ethical judgment is based on the idea that the objective structure of nature, as the product of the interaction of empirical subjectivity and worldly inputs is not, as Kant would have it, only problematically amenable to ethical spontaneity. This is brought

---

[24] *SK* 231–9; *SW* 1: 261–71.     [25] *FTP* 12 ff.; *SW* 1: 429 ff.

out most clearly in Fichte's *System of Ethics according to the Principles of the Wissenschaftslehre* (1798). There Fichte claims that an 'embodied will' with 'efficacy' (*Wirksamkeit*), i.e. a will that is freely active (within the limits of finitude) in the world, is a necessary result of the doctrine of the posits. His argument for this claim is not easy to follow, and quite probably is neither valid nor sound. But the main point seems to be that the I's reciprocal, limiting relation to the not-I shows that the I must also posit its causal efficiency (i.e. freedom) in the world. In this way, Fichte generates a kind of moral realism within his rather 'existentialist' variant of idealism. Values and things are on a similar footing when it comes to their objectivity and, so, the normativity of ethical and aesthetic judgment is not a special problem for him.

It is often thought, rightly or wrongly, that Fichte's views place too much emphasis on subjectivity and undervalue 'really real' features of the world, i.e. what features there are prescinding from subjective contributions to it. Although Fichte's idealist successors had a rather crude version of this objection—recent Fichte research has refined this understanding—that sentiment is likely to persist, for Fichte does offer an account of unified reason by arguing that the world is unified in subjectivity. His gambit is to push world-structure deeper into subjective constitution and it is in virtue of this that he can deny Kant's claim for the necessity of regulative principles. It is true that something like regulative reason is at work in Fichte's idea of striving but the massive redeployment of the claims of rationalism through the arsenal of reflective judgment is entirely missing.

B. Schelling approaches the problem of the unity of reason from what is, in many ways, a more Kantian perspective. While Fichte attempts to build into the idea of agency in general a moral component by reinterpreting the idea of a *Faktum der Vernunft*, Schelling latches onto Kant's own offer of a bridge over the 'gulf' separating determination and freedom: his theory of aesthetic and teleological reflective judgment. This strategy is entirely in keeping with a very general tendency on the part of Schelling to be suspicious of the Fichtean project of generating real constraints on the world wholly from an analysis of the conditions on subjectivity. Schelling is much more concerned to give an account of subjectivity emerging from non subjective nature, albeit from nature conceived in a radically non-Newtonian, vitalistic way. In other words, Schelling hopes to advance an account for the dialectical unity of reason and of objectivity that situates reason in developmental terms within a natural, evolutionary process.[26] Human subjectivity and the kind of rationality inherent in it is a result of this process and not its ground. Schelling most likely takes this initial orientation under the influence of the poet-philosopher Friedrich Hölderlin, who held that the basic philosophical principle was Being (*Seyn*)—an undifferentiable unity from which subjects and objects first emerge. But, whatever its origin, Schelling's views diverge from Fichte's, then, almost immediately on the issue of the primacy of subjectivity to philosophical analysis. Where Fichte rests, Schelling presses further, asking after the very origin of human subjects in the non-human.[27]

In what is often considered his first mature work (Schelling was a philosophical prodigy, whose *Naturphilosophie* (1797) was published when he was 22 years old), *The System of Transcendental Idealism* (1800), Schelling sees the key to advancing such an evolutionary account in a reintroduction of teleology into the Kantian framework. Because his early transcendental idealist project culminates in an I that can come to offer a transcendental account of its own origin in non-human nature, Schelling conceives of dialectic diachronically, i.e. as a historically unfolding process. Although one might differ on whether it is Herder or Reinhold who first holds that history is, in some sense, central to philosophical explication, it is surely Schelling who first implemented the idea that dialectic must be historical.[28] Urged on by advances in the biological sciences, Schelling is willing to argue for a constitutive philosophical role for the idea that nature is teleologically organized, not so much in the classical conception, i.e. organized in terms of God's purposes, but rather in terms of an internal algorithm that works in terms of nature realizing itself in producing individuals of a 'highest' type, i.e. the type that can reflect that very structure of nature intellectually. When one rids the position of its divinizing

---

[26] By 'evolutionary process' here I do not mean, of course, anything Darwinian.

[27] One can see this approach as early as Schelling's essays 'Of the I as the Principle of Philosophy, or on the Unconditional in Human Knowledge' and 'Philosophical Letters on Dogmatism and Criticism' (both 1795); Schelling (1980: 63 ff., 156 ff.); *FSW* 1: 73 ff., 205 ff.. Schelling's criticisms of Fichte in these essays are essentially the same ones that Hegel will later deploy across the board against the whole range of 'subjective idealism'—e.g. the claim that Fichte's concept of dialectic is 'one-sided' (over-emphasizing one component in the dialectical relation and thereby skewing the reciprocity that is supposed to characterize dialectical components).

[28] Although Kant has various interesting and suggestive things to say about the historical progression of reason in his political and historical essays from the late 1780s and 1790s, he does not display the overarching confidence of a Schelling or Hegel that reason evolves through history according to an internal mechanism geared towards maximizing its self-awareness. Yovel (1980) is to my knowledge the strongest statement that Kant entertains something like a teleological conception of the progress of philosophy that ends in his own critical thought.

romantic trappings, the 1800 *System* argues for a series of transcendental conditions on the possibility of subjectivity emerging *at all*. What Schelling calls the 'Absolute I' is in fact not a subject in any ordinary sense, but rather an entire process of self-differentiation and reunification within nature. At the earliest stages of development, this process produces material objects that are 'unconscious'.[29] Consciousness is introduced generally into the scheme with the advent of organisms and self-consciousness with that of humans. Within the category of self-consciousness the *conatus* towards self-explication of nature from within is continued in the dialectical development of more and more adequate conceptions or 'world-views' in terms of which general understandings of the nature of the world and of humans in it are articulated. In the penultimate sections of the book, another cue from Kant's third *Critique* is taken, this time in terms of art. Schelling is committed to the proposition that, although philosophy can render systematically a transcendental account of the origin of the division of the world into subjects and objects, one can never, even at the loftiest station of humanity, experience the ground for 'Being' directly *and* reflectively.[30] Schelling takes quite seriously Kant's suggestion that the artistic genius is a 'favorite of nature' ('ein Günstling der Natur') and is gifted thereby with a capacity to make objects of tremendous complexity and unified structure without conscious attention to rules. In truth, Kant's own idea of genius, at least as it manifests itself in what he calls 'fine art' (which is correlative with 'beautiful art'), is fairly middle of the road. For Kant holds that 'taste' must 'clip the wings' of genius in order that structured objects be made at all. Nonetheless, Schelling cleaves to the more Germanic, *Sturm und Drang* element of Kant's view that emphasizes an independence from constraint that yet ends up in objects that track our affective responsiveness to nature by tapping into those aspects of our own cognitive constitutions that are necessary for appreciating nature at all. This idea, that the structures of nature can be on offer without the intercession of theory and that objects can be made that, so to speak, 'house' this fact, is extremely suggestive to Schelling. Because it is an inherently reflective enterprise, philosophy cannot provide an experience of the Absolute that contains the root of subjectivity,

---

[29]  What Schelling means by nature being 'unconscious' is twofold. First, this specification of degree (*Grad*) of nature is not conscious at all, i.e. there are no conscious things produced by nature *at this level*. Second, if one views nature as a whole as having some kind of agency because of its teleological structure, then one might also claim that, relative to that agency, nature is an 'I' whose products (thus far) cannot register matters consciously and thus that nature is, as a whole (thus far) unconscious—i.e. it cannot be conscious or, more to the point, conscious of itself, because its products are not.

[30]  *STI* 219 ff.; *FSW* 2: 612 ff.

as well as that of the non-subjective differentiation from which subjectivity emerges. Art, however, can provide non-discursive access to this Absolute because it calls upon a dialectical mix of conscious and unconscious forces in its production and appreciation. The artist is certainly conscious, and highly so, in terms of the production of the work. But, qua product, the work is inhabited by unconscious, genius-expressive being that is not captured in terms of descrying a prior plan or structure. Moreover, Schelling holds that art escapes the principle of sufficient reason that binds theoretical reflection on nature and shows, rather than states, the unity of efficient and final causes.[31]

Although Schelling's 1800 *System* may seem somewhat antiquated nowadays it would be churlish to withhold admiration for his achievement. Its main contribution to the debate on the relation of the three terms that I have been discussing—dialectic, the unity of reason, and value objectivity—is clearly his emphasis on the historicized teleology of reason. This view will have a determining effect on Hegel's version of the 'identity in difference' formula. Perhaps no less influential is the idea that one must approach such a teleological account of the development of reason naturalistically (albeit still surrounded by the transcendental nimbus). Last, the idea that intuitive cognition of art 'fuses' reason in its practical and theoretical aspects is a core romantic idea and one that occasions some of Hegel's most important reactions to early idealism, although, as I shall discuss below, it is not one that was uniformly accepted in German Romanticism.

C. Hegel attempts to marry Schelling's emphasis on the historical teleology of reason and on a more robust role for the concept of nature in idealism to what he takes to be a more adequate concept of dialectic. What is inadequate from Hegel's point of view about both Fichte's and Schelling's concepts of nature is that they both make final appeal to a non-discursive access of the subject to the source for the initial division between subject and object that is constitutive of subjectivity as it is conceived in post-Kantian German idealism. Hegel rightly sees this sort of appeal as a threat to the project of 'improving' Kant's philosophy by further systematization of it. Of course, it might be so improved if Kant's analysis of the conditions for experience could be pushed back to issues of conditions upon object-consciousness in the mode of Fichte and Schelling, even if an ultimate principle unifying reason and experience

---

[31] Schelling's severe later reaction to Hegel's version of idealist dialectic, which is so important for Kierkegaard and existentialism more generally, takes this naturalism in a realist direction. Cf. Schopenhauer and the early Nietzsche on this point.

were still wanting (or even beyond hope). But Hegel is right to insist that this (relatively) modest proposal for systematicity was not the avowed goal of idealism. Hegel's project is to provide an account of the dialectical development of the unity of reason that demonstrates that evaluative claims are essentially on a par with other sorts of claims that are generally thought to be more unproblematically objective. He does this by proposing an account of dialectic that denies that final appeal must be made to non-discursivity and replaces the idea of discursive, representational limitation of knowing agents with the doctrine of what Hegel calls the 'speculative proposition' (*spekulativer Satz*).

Hegel's concept of dialectic helps itself to three orienting devices that post-Kantian idealist thinking on the unity of reason provides. The first of these is Fichte's methodology of solving the question of the relation of theoretical and practical agency and knowledge by building practical freedom into theoretical agency. The second inheritance comes directly from Schelling: the idea that reason emerges from nature and structurally develops over time, i.e. that dialectic is 'historical'. The third strand of German thought crucial to Hegel is non-Kantian. This is a network of ideas one finds in Herder's philosophical anthropology involving how one is to think of 'history' in the relevant sense. Hegel was very impressed with Herder's views that: (1) human concepts and affect are continuous, i.e. that there is no bright-line distinction between (a) reflective and (b) non-reflective orientations in the world; (2) that (a) and (b) are causally interdependent, i.e. belief is often determined by conative content and vice versa; (3) that individual beliefs, affects, dispositions, etc. are the result of holistically structured processes that operate largely unconsciously and at levels of great base generality in cultures; and (4) that these cultures must be seen in their historical contexts, i.e. that the base-level meanings that constitute the background against which local conceptual and affective contexts are to be interpreted are products of historical developments. Herder's own version of these ideas tended to slide uncomfortably between a more or less Kantian idea of universal reason (albeit historically articulated) and the much more arresting idea that the cultural constitution of *Weltanschauungen* was so complete and, at least in principle, historically particularized that something like radically different and perhaps even incommensurable sets of concepts could develop.

Hegel's dual allegiances to a historical yet essentialist account of the unity of reason and value objectivity made the concept of historicity at the same time enticing and unbearable. The enticing part is the idea that reason develops in terms of an internal dynamic that is realized in various interlocked general world-views that are embedded in full-blown forms of life. But history itself is, according to Hegel, determined at a basic level by an internal logic and this means that not only is reason historical, but also that history is rational. This latter claim is what Hegel the essentialist is interested in establishing. If he can establish this claim, he will show that his version of dialectic and his account of the unity of reason and its connection to value objectivity will be, as a theoretical matter, systematic and, as a practical matter, communally realized in ways that prior idealist accounts were not. The unbearable part is the contingency and potential relativism that the category of 'the historical' brings in train. Thus Hegel is very concerned to criticize versions of historicism that he contends are not essentialist enough, e.g. those of Herder or Friedrich Schlegel. For Hegel the unity of reason must be the unity of *one concept* of reason and not an aggregation of plural, yet unified forms of rationality that are irreducible to one another. And because value objectivity for Hegel is based in this sort of invariant unity, the objectivity of values will be invariant as well.

This gives one the basic building-blocks of Hegelian dialectic, at least in the form present in the *Phenomenology of Spirit* (1807). Hegel claims that objectivity of values is not different in kind from the objectivity of factual statements and believes that one can make good on this claim if one correctly understands the role of philosophical analysis vis-à-vis pre-philosophical experience. Standard foundationalist accounts of the grounds for beliefs, concepts, theories, etc. trace experience back to fundamental constituents that are well-formed and perhaps even defined antecedently to any role they might have in the experience that they purportedly ground. Hegel completely rejects this approach to philosophical systematics. In many ways his answer to establishing the objectivity of values—by dialectically moving away from this version of a foundationalism built upon definition of key terms, concepts, or ontological elements—is an extension of the reactions to late-modern foundationalism found in Kant, Fichte, and Schelling. The unifying concept here would be that of a transcendental response to the business of giving philosophical foundations (and the perennial *bête noire* of that enterprise, skepticism). But the sense in which Kant's, Fichte's, and Schelling's own philosophical systems are transcendental varies in important respects with each of them and changes, in some cases, even within the work of a single philosopher, depending on period (e.g. the Fichte of the 1794 versus the Fichte of 1804). But Hegel's methodology is not a mere embellishment of transcendental philosophy, no matter how much current Hegel scholarship wants to interpret it in this way.

One useful way to begin to comprehend Hegel's dialectical innovation begins with understanding what the term 'phenomenology' means to him. This is important because one of the primary uses of dialectic relating to the project of establishing value objectivity is present in the *Phenomenology*.[32] The term 'phenomenology' has its modern origin with the mathematician J. H. Lambert, all but forgotten with the exception of his correspondence with Kant. Kant contemplated use of the term in his pre-critical period to denote a science of the principles (and limitations) of sensibility, as distinguished from those of the faculty of concepts. At that time in Kant's career, he has, so to speak, only one-half of the apparatus of his critical philosophy in view. Kant's use of the term is mentioned in a letter to Lambert that was enclosed in a copy of Kant's *Inaugural Dissertation* (1770).[33] The *Dissertation*, it is well known, argues that knowledge based in sense experience was limited to phenomena, while still allowing a place for noumenal knowledge through concepts. A 'phenomenology' for Kant, then, has the standard Kantian critical implication of an account of the importance of limitation in assessing a faculty of thought that might also, if Kant had developed this idea more in his pre-critical period, have led him to propose a dialectic of sorts as a component of that analysis. I have mentioned Kant's passing use of the term because it illuminates Hegel's understanding of it. Kant saw critical philosophy as a necessary first stage in the re-establishment of a better metaphysics. Hegel also treats phenomenology as a precondition for substantive philosophy that is metaphysical. What will count as 'metaphysical' for Hegel will be radically different from what Kant would count as properly metaphysical, given Hegel's Kant-like claim to have provided a much more illuminating specification of the initial structure within which philosophy is to be done. In Hegel's view the subject matter of phenomenology is limited. The pertinent limitation in Hegel's case is not one that rests on a distinction between phenomena and noumena—Hegel thinks that one of the results of his phenomenology is that this distinction will be seen as ultimately untenable. Rather, phenomenology

---

[32] I am simplifying here for ease of exposition. The relation between the different fora in which Hegel deploys his version of dialectical reason is contested. It seems certain that Hegel gave systematic precedence to the dialectic of his *Wissenschaft der Logik* (1812). But recognizing that fact settles very little with regard to the question of the precise relation of various portrayals of dialectic across the Hegelian corpus. I can't even begin to sort out that question here.

[33] Letter of 2 Sept. 1770, *AA* 10: 96–9; Kant (1967: 58–60).

has to do with the dialectical instantiations of what Hegel takes to be the basic constituents of thought in limited, lived forms of theoretical interchange with the world.[34]

It is often thought that Hegel's systematic philosophy is deeply revisionist and, given its neologistic and overtly reconstructive cast, one can see why that is so. But Hegelian dialectic or, more precisely, what knowledge results from dialectic is based in the assumption that dialectic is a matter of elucidating knowledge that is already present pre-philosophically. To know the objective and final features of value for Hegel is just to take part in a complex procedure of elucidating them, the very same procedure through which the values are constituted as objective and objectively binding. There is a sense in which Hegel thinks that this knowledge is always 'there', even in radically underdeveloped forms of human participation in this process. But it is especially present, he thinks, in the historical epoch in which he is writing. So, in its deepest structure Hegelian dialectic operates to *extrapolate* tacit knowledge and not to fix the meanings or values of the central terms in which philosophy is done antecedent to philosophical analysis. The way this extrapolation proceeds is by means of internal critique, where particular 'forms' or 'shapes' of 'consciousness' (viz. more or less comprehensive world-views) generate both claims about the ultimate structure of the world and criteria against which these claims are measured and in terms of which they shall finally fail. Forms of consciousness are forms of what Hegel calls 'spirit' (*Geist*). It is difficult, and perhaps even improper, to be too exacting when talking about the scope of this term—after all, the last thing Hegel wants to suggest is that there is a definition of spirit in any traditional sense. Spirit is the whole of social reality as that reality is reflected in the constituents of that reality. So, to say that spirit progresses through various shapes of consciousness through internal critique is to say that (a) human social reality has various forms through which it passes, (b) in virtue of questioning the implicit commitments, (c) to a more or less global set of beliefs, attitudes, and desires, (d) that are meant to render the world finally meaningful as those implicit commitments are made to become more explicit, (e) by the very act of generalizing the structure.[35] Note that I have stressed conative as well as cognitive factors here; Hegel is quite insistent that thinking of shapes of consciousness as disembodied, sheer representational bodies of propositions or theories under some other kind of description would be quite wrong. Shapes of consciousness are *lived* ways of giving meaning to the world.

---

[34]  See *PhS* 29; *HW* 3: 48–9.    [35]  *PhS* 21; *HW* 3: 38–9.

Hegel insists that the structure just outlined is closed and complete and that the conceptions analyzed in it are rendered objective through that completion.[36] Hegel claims that the series of forms of consciousness interlock in such a way that they are both strictly and immediately sequential (i.e. one form follows upon another with 'necessity' and without 'gaps') and that the series ends in virtue of exhausting itself (i.e. that there is an exhaustive way to show that all but one understanding of the roles of fundamental philosophical concepts can be ruled out as only partially and inadequately true).[37] This is to say that spirit is autotelic. What Hegel calls the 'absolute standpoint' is just the maximal point of elucidation via extrapolation, at which point the complete series of forms has been passed through.

For Hegel, individual agents act ethically, politically, and aesthetically in virtue of their participation in forms of life in which those types of values figure. Although there are ways to twist Hegel's ethical theory into a form of autonomy theory by reinterpreting autonomy as a form of Hegelian autotelos, such reinterpretations are in constant danger of losing what is revolutionary in Hegel's theory. For it is much more plausible to think of Hegelian ethics along heteronomous lines. Not only the binding nature of ethical norms but also their objectivity depends, Hegel holds, on shifting the emphasis away from individual human agency as the unique and basic source of ethical value towards the idea of collective agency—expressed in concrete communal ways of life—that is the basis from which norms, ethical and otherwise, issue. Now, the idea of what community expresses these norms in a fully objective way is quite different from the idea of community common to early modern atomistic ethical and political theory one finds at home in Hobbes, Locke, or even Rousseau and Kant.[38] Communities where the full objectivity of norms is instantiated are ones in which the constituents of the community 'recognize' one another primarily in terms of an ability to 'identify' with the community (and the social structures of what Hegel calls, in later writings, 'objective spirit'). 'Recognize' (*anerkennen*), here, is a term of art for Hegel.[39]

---

[36] *PhS* 485 f.; *HW* 3: 582 f.      [37] *PhS* 486 f.; *HW* 3: 584 f.

[38] I use the qualification 'fully objective' here to honor Hegel's claim that even relatively underdeveloped forms of consciousness express and are organized in terms of norms that are partly objective from the point of view of the final Hegelian specification of objectivity. Of course, those norms will also appear fully objective from within the form of consciousness in question, that is, until they are no longer adequate to the advancing tacit sense of freedom of *Geist*.

[39] Wildt (1982) is an excellent treatment of this concept.

I 'recognize' another, in the relevant sense, if I 'see myself in another'. That only happens if I have advanced enough in my conception of what is essential to humans qua humans to view what would be, under an inadequate conception of the same, quite different (i.e. you are *you* and I am *I*) as 'the same'. And we are 'the same', in the relevant sense, because our being human involves, and in some sense depends on, the capacity to have ethical and political structures that are fully satisfactory to your deepest need to 'be at home' (*zu Hause sein*) or 'reconciled' (*versöhnt*) with the world.[40] To put the point in a somewhat simplified way, recognizing myself in the other, whether it is another person or the community, or the state, etc., is a matter of seeing the other as a way of expressing what I am at my deepest as a member of the human community.

Let's gather the strands of the analysis. Final objectivity of value (as well as of all else) is established by the dialectical exhaustion of holistically complete and sequentially more adequate whole conceptions of how humans (must) conceive of themselves as being in 'the world', where 'the world' is not just the totality of physical objects but also the world of social fact, the world of art, etc. To reach this final standpoint is no more (and no less) than to be able to survey the series of dialectical progression up to that point as a whole and as exhausting the possibilities. This exhaustivity claim leaves no theoretical role for regulative reason that asymptotically approximates to a limit. The very category of merely regulative reason is anathema to Hegel; it is a theoretical admission that some requirements of reason, amongst them the requirement that its practical and theoretical employment be unified in one ultimately indivisible rational faculty, cannot be *demonstrated* rationally but must be, instead, merely posited or presupposed. In Hegel's estimation, Schelling and Fichte are just as much at fault as is Kant; they can only offer what Hegel calls 'bad' infinities, i.e. accounts of rationality and objectivity that establish only an asymptotic approach to a limit of absolute knowledge. As we saw earlier, this is tantamount to an admission that regulative reason, and with it, open dialectic, still has a place in systematic philosophy. Because Hegel denies this at all cost, his teleological and metaphysical version of dialectic is the apex of the first strand of descent from Kant's account of dialectical reason and regulative judgment with which I began.

---

[40] Hardimon (1994) is a very useful analysis of this concept in Hegel and, especially, of its political implications.

# OBJECTIVITY AND VALUES IN GERMAN ROMANTICISM

There were forms of Kantianism that were not as obsessed with issues of systematicity and completeness as was post-Kantian idealism. Prominent among these is the early German romanticism of Hölderlin, Novalis, and Friedrich Schlegel.[41] For them the unity of reason remains an ideal, the regulative use of reason retains importance, and dialectic is seen as an uncompletable project. Moreover, the fact that it is uncompletable is the nub of the significance of dialectic according to the romantics. Grasping the orientation of one's life in terms of being a finite project of unending completion or, alternatively, as constituted by a fundamental tension between striving for the Absolute and being finite, is just what it is to be human. The objectivity of values is accommodated to this general picture of being human. As was the case with the systematic idealists, the romantics developed these ideas against the background of questioning philosophical foundationalism.

The fundamental point of reference here is Fichte's 1794/5 system. The early romantics agree that philosophical reflection requires one to posit an undifferentiated ground condition that is itself unconditioned, from which subjectivity (i.e. the very distinction between subject and object, as that distinction figures even implicitly in basal cognitive states) originates. They also agree with Fichte that such a state cannot itself be reflective (on pains of either infinite regress or vicious circularity, since the possibility of reflection, as a state that requires such differentiation, is precisely at issue). They also concede that, in some sense, the state must be pre-intentional and, thus, 'unconscious'. But where they disagree with Fichte is in what all of this portends for foundationalism at the heart of the idealist project of better unifying Kantian practical and theoretical reason by means of a positive account of dialectics. As we saw, one can interpret Fichte in two ways on this point. The traditional interpretation is that Fichte forwards a

---

[41] I shall not treat Hölderlin here. This is a major omission and, in a way, is indefensible. Because Hölderlin shares common philosophical roots with Hegel (and Schelling) it is his form of open dialectic that is the best counterpart to the more 'realistic' idealists. Novalis and Schlegel are more concerned with Fichte. Any monograph-length study of the fate of reflective judgment in nineteenth- and twentieth-century German philosophy could not omit him (nor Schiller, Schleiermacher, the Southwest neo-Kantians, etc.). Still, attention to Hölderlin would require a detailed analysis of at least some of his poetic output and I cannot hope to do that here.

kind of intellectual intuition as a quasi-cognitive faculty which can ground intentionality (or at least object-consciousness) in such a way as to make that ground systematically available as a foundation. A second way to understand Fichte's foundationalism is transcendental: Fichte does not think that intellectual intuition is an experience that a subject 'has', but rather that its existence must be posited in order to account for intentionality and in order to satisfy reason's demand for foundations. On this second view, however, the sense of unifying foundationalism does not really move much beyond Kant and seems belied by the way Fichte claims his own project to be revolutionary. Moreover, it still leaves in place the idea that the fundamental state from which the subject/object distinction in all of its applications arises is one of a *self-relation* (*Selbstbeziehung*). If one credits the first interpretation, the romantic criticism of it becomes simple: there is no basis for the claim that such a relationship of intellectual intuition can afford the sort of foundation that Fichte's system requires. If one takes the second, transcendental tack the romantic criticism strikes even deeper. For here it is the very idea that self-relation is an appropriate way to think of the sought-after unity. Thinking rigorously about unity requires a thoroughgoing ontological monism, i.e. that what exists is basically just one thing that has no separable parts that can stand in relations to one another. The only appropriate idea of unity here is one of what Novalis calls 'absolute identity' or what one might call 'self-same' identity: an identity that is only inadequately captured in any relational notion, even the logical relation of identity (i.e. A = A).[42] What is left for the early romantics is to fall back upon Kant's doctrine of regulative reason and a view of the dialectic and unity of reason compatible with it. Novalis and Schlegel have different versions of this general idea.

It is Novalis who pressed criticisms of Fichte most vigorously. He attempts to capture the idea of a constitutive tension in subjectivity in his idea of 'romanticization' (*Romantisierung*).[43] Romanticizing is a procedure with two aspects, each one corresponding to one element in what Novalis thinks is the essential tension inherent in living a life. On the one hand, the commonplace or ordinary is made to be seen as extraordinary, even supernatural. Novalis

---

[42]  See *Fichte-Studien* 1.1, FS 3–5; NS II, 104–5; cf. ibid. 1.1 28, 247, FS 20–3, 84–5; NS II, 122–4, 186–7. Of course ascription of the property of not being differentiated to the ground is illicit, since the ground might be differentiated, but not in a way that is available to human cognition. At best, one might claim the ground not to be differenti*able* (i.e. by 'us'). This important distinction is not generally observed in the debates of the period.

[43]  NS 6: 545.

calls this part of the romanticizing procedure 'potentializing', and says that it contrasts the ordinary with the 'infinite'. This requires one to treat the objects of the world as *problematically given*, by showing what they 'are not'—taking them out of the context in which they can appear to be normal. On the other hand, romanticizing the world also involves treating the infinite, mysterious, or extraordinary as ordinary. In this way, the fact that objects have the meaning that they have defeasibly must be admitted into one's present understanding of them. Combining the two aspects of the one operation, Novalis thinks that life is characterized by a tension between endorsing the way of life that one finds oneself in and endorsing it critically, i.e. in the face of its acknowledged inability to get at things as they are: full stop. And again, the question of the objectivity of values hangs on that of unending dialectic, that the Absolute for Novalis is an ideal structure relative to the ability of discursive subjects to know it. Values will be objective as they are situated in forms of life that support them generally with concrete practices, beliefs, and affects. Although Novalis tends to slip back into a kind of universalistic ethics of affect based on a kind of nostalgia for medieval uniformity in the mysteries of religion, the writings most proximate to his criticism of Fichte support a nascent pluralism.

This pluralism, however, is seen to best effect in Schlegel's concept of irony. Beginning from the same critique of Fichtean foundationalism, Schlegel accentuates how the plurality of ways to make the world consistent with the doctrine of the Absolute present in early Jena romanticism is registered from within single, particular ways to take the world. In terms that may or may not have been influential on Hegel, Schlegel emphasizes the holistic and yet partial nature of *Weltanschauungen* and their interlocking, dialectical relations to one another. According to Schlegel any philosophically self-aware form of consciousness will view itself in a bifurcated way. As an inhabitant of a perspective that largely determines one's self-understandings one must *affirm* their point of view. Schlegel treats this affirmation as one of the two components of irony. But, Schlegel thinks, if one reflects with sufficient acumen, one will also recognize that there are other possible ways that the world may be like for others, situated in perspectives that are, to varying degrees, different from one's own. For the romantics this is the same as saying that there are any number of ways to express the Absolute by representing the world as being a certain way. If one is conscious of this fact, then, although one cannot help but affirm the customs and principles governing one's perspective, one must register *within one's perspective* the fact that, qua a perspective, that perspective is but one of many attempts to express the Absolute. Schlegel thinks, therefore, that a critical cognitive stance balances *distancing* from a perspective against affirmation of it, and this is the second element in irony. Irony thus involves an acute and circumspect awareness of one's own perspective *as a perspective* that is simultaneously an affirmation and critical distancing from the perspective in question. Or, put another way, irony is the acknowledgement that perspectives are *partial*, in both senses of the word—we who share them are partial to them, yet should recognize that they are but partial representations of the world.[44]

Art, and especially the sort of poetry and fragmentary philosophical writing that Schlegel favors, is the most adequate vehicle for this ironic form of life because art by its very nature is interpretively 'open', i.e. interpretation or description cannot exhaustively render an artwork's content. Schlegel is here not advocating non-systematicity, but rather a novel idea of a 'system of fragments' or a dialectically open-ended system according to which world-views or perspectives are juxtaposed and perhaps even entered into, which thereby establish ironic contrast with the beliefs and truths of their contrasting perspectives. The Jena romantic doctrine of *Symphilosophie*, developed jointly by Schlegel and Novalis (and including, at times, Schleiermacher as well), is just this notion of overlapping and non-reductive sharing of views. The romantic idea of an ethical or political community is based in this idea. Such a community is not created and held together ethically by reflectively endorsed principles; ethical principles are but shorthand and ultimately defeasible ways of rendering lived commitments that are sensitive to cultural and historical change. Hegel claimed that Jena romanticism ends up in wanton relativity and is a form of ironic *Besserwisserei* or, even *menefregismo*.[45] This is still the view of a majority of commentators.[46]

If one takes the views of the romantic writers considered here in hand, a common picture on the relation of the unity or reason, dialectic, and value

---

[44] Schlegel tends to express the tension inherent in irony in at least three different ways. Perhaps the most famous characterization involves the idea that the ironist oscillates between self-creation (*Selbstschöpfung*) and self-annihilation (*Selbstvernichtung*). *Athenäum-Fragmente* 51, SPF 24; KFSA 2: 172; cf. *Philosophische Lehrjahre*, Beilage I, i.13; I, vi; I, l. A slight variant that is more explicitly Fichtean identifies three elements, adding self-limitation (*Selbstbeschränkung*) as a median term. *Lyceum-Fragmente* 37, SPF 4; KFSA 2: 150. A third way in which Schlegel expresses the point, and one that brings the metaphysics of it to the foreground, is that irony allows an intimation of the Absolute, or 'chaos'. *Ideen* 69, SPF 100; KFSA 2: 263.

[45] Roughly, 'screw-you-ism'.

[46] See, e.g. Kierkegaard [1841] (1989), Lukács (1962), Eldridge (1997), Berlin (1999). For an alternative to this received view, see Rush (2006).

objectivity emerges. Dialectic is seen as a 'negative' or pure eristic process that elucidates the tension between finitude and the Absolute inherent in human nature. As such it is uncompletable—it neither starts from certain beginnings (Fichte), nor can it be brought to teleological conclusion through exhaustive elimination (Hegel). Any unity of reason is local and provisional, even if empirically widespread, and the final unity of reason is 'ideal'. It is housed in the idea of the Absolute that one is constrained to posit by the dialectical need of reason for such an ideal. But the ideal and the unity can never be known as such. Finally, values are 'objective' only if the relevant idea of objectivity can be made compatible with romantic pluralism. Objectivity will here be a matter of overlapping consensus, which is to say a looser form of intersubjectivity than one finds in Hegel.

The move from strict lawlike understanding of value objectivity on the order of Kant to value objectivity based on purportedly necessary features of intersubjective activity is of crucial importance in linking the nineteenth-century concern with dialectic to its twentieth-century successors. There are, of course, many versions of this idea, some extending to the more teleological views of Hegel and some favoring the more empirical, contingency-forgiving proposals of the German romantics. In the concluding two sections of this chapter, I shall turn to two twentieth-century representatives of these strands: Adorno and Habermas.

## ADORNO ON NEGATIVE DIALECTIC AND VALUE OBJECTIVITY

Hegel's autotelic form of dialectic and the value objectivity that follows from it is a projection of his overwhelming need to show that 'the rational is actual'.[47] Adorno's idea of dialectic is informed by his conviction that 'the whole is the false'[48] or that the world is, to refer back to a Kantian idea, *radically evil*.[49] There is no getting around this claim as a starting point for understanding Adorno's views; it is certainly not something he argues for. It is built upon a

---

[47] *PR* 20; *HW* 7: 24. Hegel does not mean here that the status quo is what is rational. He wants to convey that reason is actualizing itself in the present. Still, he did think that he had discovered the fully adequate philosophical framework within which to understand that process. It is in this sense that Hegel is a quietist.

[48] *MM^E* 50; *MM*, in *AGS* 4: 55.      [49] *AA* 6: 19–53.

thoroughgoing negative view of the accessibility to humankind of anything like the Absolute, if what is meant by that is a secure ethical-political form of life in which human agents can experience continuously 'the Good'. Adorno inherits the metaphysical basis for this view from his friend Walter Benjamin, but transfers many of these views into a Hegelian dialectical register completely foreign to Benjamin.

Dialectic is a form of critical resistance for Adorno. It is precisely *not* a phenomenological project bent on elucidating given forms of life that are already, unbeknownst to one, free. To believe that one can achieve such an elucidation of a final form of rationality is to succumb to yet another form of dialectical illusion. Reductions of experience to what can be grasped by technological modes of thought are the main temptations to embrace the illusion in its many forms. 'Technological thought' for Adorno is quite an abstract and general category. It is, at a very basic conceptual level, characterized by what Adorno calls 'identity thinking', which is in the service of 'instrumental reasoning'. Under modern conditions, Adorno holds that conceptual thought tends to assimilate particulars (i.e. items thought under the concept at hand) so strongly that any differences that they might have, and thus all properties that mark them off as the individual things that they are, are effaced.[50] There are various strengths to the charge in Adorno, but the main point is that this sort of thorough assimilation under a concept treats what is conceptualized as having significance only in terms of the characteristics it shares with other things.[51] Moreover, concepts for Adorno are not inert theoretical items; they are ways of action in the world and, in a world given over to prediction and control of nature and other people, concepts will have at least part of their content in virtue of the guiding interests of that form of life. Identity thinking is part and parcel of a more general orientation in the world that revels in the status quo by reducing difference and, thus, hamstrings attempts to imagine other ways of treating things. Crucially, identity thinking distorts knowledge of the nature of the dialectical relation between theoretical and practical reasoning.

Identity thinking seeps down into all areas of experience, value theory not excepted. Modern society is characterized by inadequate concepts of freedom

---

[50] Adorno does not limit the claim to the modern historical period; instrumental reasoning (and one presumes, identity thinking) is also present in the ancient world. See *DA* 50–87; *DE* 35–62 ('Excursus I'). 'Enlightenment', that is, for Adorno is not a historical category; rather, it is a socially formed kind of thinking.

[51] See Früchtl (1986) for an analysis of the all-important concept of *mimēsis* in this connection.

built around misleading views on the nature of the ultimate bearers of value—various strains of high individualism, in which subjects are treated as essentially separate, atomic centers of value. Adorno is especially concerned to challenge the interpretations that liberal political theory places upon freedom. Classically, such theories embrace 'negative' concepts of liberty—i.e. the freedom to be let alone, so long as one's being let alone does not impinge on the like right of another. This concept of freedom seamlessly realizes itself, or is realized, in capitalism. But Adorno is also suspicious of versions of self-actualization theories that base themselves on various 'positive' concepts of liberty (e.g. Kantian autonomy, Hegelian republicanism).[52] All 'traditional'[53] political theories share the claim to be in a position to identify a final form of 'the Good' that political life must express and propagate. In Hegel one finds this sort of claim made against a very strenuous ontological backdrop. (After all, what Hegel calls 'the Concept' is precisely not some representational item that reflects the world. It is rather an entity that *is* the basic structure of the world. If one can specify the ultimate structure of *that*, then one is *living in* it.) According to Adorno, less metaphysically committed forms of neo-Kantianism and 'scientific' or 'vulgar' forms of Marxism are similarly marred by the overly optimistic or 'imperialistic' idea that such basic end forms can be known. For Adorno the idea of one, final resting place for spirit from which one can, assuming philosophical perspicuity, survey the form that a finally good society must take is a version of what his friend and sometime co-author Max Horkheimer called 'transfiguration' (*Verklärung*). Transfiguration takes suffering as its object and holds out affirmatively the idea (or reality) of a place in which suffering no longer obtains, typically in 'another world'. This 'other world' is classically perhaps, the heaven of many religions, more subtly the *summum bonum* and idea of heaven of Kant, and even more 'realistically' Hegel's claim that spirit has, in fact, arrived at its highest vocation, the specifics, to be sure, to be filled in later. Suffering, or at least suffering as a modern fact, is ineluctable for Adorno—again, an inheritance from Schopenhauer and Nietzsche.[54] The quasi-religious idea of reconciliation of humanity with itself can only be for him what Kant would have called a regulative ideal. But even

---

[52] The distinction between 'negative' and 'positive' concepts of freedom is, of course, Isaiah Berlin's. The *locus classicus* is Berlin (1969).

[53] 'Traditional' is an adjective that some members of the early Frankfurt School deploy to contrast in specific ways their own 'critical' social thought with most competing strands of early twentieth-century epistemology and social theory. Horkheimer (1972); see also Rush (2004).

[54] Schopenhauer is especially important for Horkheimer. See Horkheimer (1967). Schopenhauer is of course *sensu stricto* a 'transfigurer' in Adorno and Horkheimer's way of thinking.

this category is too freighted with optimism for Adorno; the Kantian idea of a regulative ideal (and its counterpart, the German romantic idea of asymptotic approximation to 'the Absolute') is overtly progressive. Adorno certainly allows that there *might be* progress and even that there *has been* and *is* progress in various features of political and social reality. But there often *is not* progress and there *need not be* any; following a set of precepts that promise progress in any way that would diminish the requirement that the social theorist always be skeptical of any purportedly stable political state is dangerous. Such a state of reconciliation is neither attainable nor is it subject to a guaranteed progressive approach.[55] For Adorno dialectical reason is emphatically uncompletable and negative.[56]

This unrelenting negativity goes hand in glove with Adorno's views on the practice of social science as a form of investigation in which practice and theory intertwine. Adorno treats societies as holistic systems. He extends the thought present in Hegel and, especially, Marx, that many of the connections between elements of society are hidden in such a way that the ordinary theories produced by such social wholes for the purpose of reflecting upon that structure cannot penetrate the social whole sufficiently to lay bare the connections. And it is the occluded connections that are the most important, since they involve those aspects of the social life that are free from determination by the status quo and, thus, that may be the rough material for different ways of thinking about at least some parts of social life. This is one reason why the early Frankfurt School, again following the lead of Benjamin, stresses the study of cultural marginalia.

If one steps back sufficiently, negative dialectic is quite similar to the open, interpretation-based, dialectic of Schlegel's irony.[57] To summarize: negative dialectics is an open, non-teleological form of dialectical analysis in which various components of society that are accepted on a superficial level are shown internally to be unstable. Showing this establishes grounds for excluding portions of the social self-understanding in question from being fully rational, although it may be quite difficult to determine which elements in which combination are so excluded. Part of this procedure also generates a more 'positive' result, as it did in Hegel. For, showing the status quo to be rationally wanting in some important respects is also to

---

[55] *ND*, in *AGS* 6: 155; *AT* 135 f.; *ÄT*, in *AGS* 7: 204 f.

[56] *ND*, in *AGS* 6: 161 f. The question of whether negative dialectics can claim a Hegelian provenance at all is trenchantly discussed in Rosen (1982: 159 f.).

[57] See *AGS* 1: 334; see also Geuss (2005: 122 and n. 32).

be able to imagine ways of being social, political, artistic, etc. that are not this way. For Hegel, there are no gaps in this process; successful dialectical criticism in itself yields an incrementally superior dialectically positive result in the form of a successor form of consciousness. For Adorno, however, that is not the case. Negative dialectic does not yield as positive recommendation for a successor for the status quo over and above the daimonic and emphatic 'not *that*'. Critical theory has done its job when a section of society is revealed to be non-rational by its own lights and when certain phenomena that are problematically included in the status quo are placed in a light where they *might be* usefully considered as spurs to imagine other ways of being. All of this is extremely minimal for Adorno; there is nothing here of Marcuse's 1960s turn to hedonistic utopianism.

How might one assess the question of the unity of reason in light of negative dialectics? Although the term 'reason' has undergone a fundamental materialist shift for Adorno away from the idealistic account of Hegel, the question of the unity of reason is still pertinent if adjusted in terms of the shift. Here the component terms are 'theory' and 'practice', which are meant to capture a less abstract and more labor-oriented understanding of these aspects of rationality. The first of these terms corresponds to the human product or production of reflective modes of life, in which (among other things) humans can purchase an understanding of their activity at a remove. For Adorno this component is the main bearer of critique, although it would be wrong to insist that theory and practice are ever hermetically sealed off from one another for him. The second, practical, component has to do with action in the concrete cases in social life. Theory in its various instances guides action in this sense, but not always—it is an intellectualist distortion to see reason, and especially reason in its more instrumentalist forms, as necessary, even implicitly, to action. Adorno's 'hope', if that is not too strong a word, is that critique of standing regimes of interaction between theory and practice will yield starts for better interactions of the same. There is nothing that guarantees this, however, and much in late capitalism, Adorno thinks, to caution against best expectation. Theory and practice *pace* Hegel can never be shown to coincide and thus there is no demonstrable unity of reason in the sense pertinent to Adorno.[58] At best there are non-final partial unities. And, to the extent that objectivity of value judgments depends on the unity of reason to transfer over

---

[58] Often Adorno forwards the stronger claim that there can *never* be coincidence of theory and practice (and not just that such a coincidence can never be demonstrated).

warrant from one component of reason to the other ('Fichte's gambit'), then there is no objectivity of such judgments.

Does this mean that Adorno gives up on objectivity in the spheres of ethics, politics, and aesthetics? Yes and no. From its earliest days, critical theory struggled with the question of the objectivity of the judgments of social theory. Generally, critical theorists were firmly in the camp that treated such judgments as 'scientific' by making a distinction between the methodology appropriate to the 'natural sciences' (*Naturwissenschaften*) and the methodology appropriate to the 'human sciences' (*Geisteswissenschaften*), of which critical theory is a member.[59] The kind of objectivity relevant to the former fields (i.e. based in 'truth' and having the form of 'strict' laws) is not applicable in the latter.[60] So, if by 'objectivity' of values one means the sort of objectivity physical laws have, there is no objectivity of values. At most there is intersubjective validity relative to the particular dialectical array of practice and theory in question, together with whatever critical potential can be unearthed by immanent critique. But if one means by 'objectivity' just *that* and allows that normative force attaches first, foremost, and fully to values qua particularistic, then there are ethical and other standards available.

# Habermas and the Return to Transcendental Philosophy

Adorno's neo-romantic, negative variant of Marxist-Kantianism is almost entirely reversed by a return to the more transcendental extrapolation of Kant in Habermas' work of the 1980s and after. Whereas first-generation critical theorists pursued critique by making problematic any final unity of reason and thus gave up on the idea of a strictly 'true' or 'objective' account of social value, Habermas beats a path back to pre-Marxist German philosophy and, specifically, to the Fichtean program of arguing for a unity of practical and

---

[59] Horkheimer viewed critical theory as a new, synthetic discipline that would replace philosophy (and other social sciences). See *BPSS* 8–9; *HGS* 3: 28–9.

[60] I simplify here for purposes of exposition. Some critical theorists toyed with the idea that there was not a strict separation between the natural and human sciences and, in a reversal of positivist reduction, claimed that, for example, physics, or at least the philosophy of the physical sciences, was at base just as interpretive as the social sciences. See Rush (2004: 14, 21–2).

theoretical reason by construing the latter as dependent on, or even as a part of, the former.[61]

Habermas' main work prior to the 1980s, *Knowledge and Human Interests* (1968), is a sustained attempt to re-found critical theory on a transcendental basis via an umbrella category of reason that Habermas calls 'cognitive interests'. This category is deployed expressly to forge new connections between knowledge and action that are sundered in modern society. Habermas' view here is that instrumental ends-oriented rationality and communicative and rationality-coordinating practice are undercut and deformed by ideological features that result from the hegemony of technological reason and late-capitalist economic domination in ways that do not obviously show up linguistically (and thus cannot be corrected in ways internal to the status quo of communicative practice). Critical theory is supposed to deliver emancipation in the form of *knowledge*, so that the ideological features can be recognized as such and corrected. Habermas came to abandon this version of the role of communicative rationality in freedom because of a dilemma contained in the particular formulation it receives in *Knowledge and Human Interests*. Habermas' account of reason's ability to turn critically and decisively upon the ideological deformation of the linkage between theoretical (i.e. ends-rational) and practical (i.e. communicative) reason involved strong evolutionary claims about reason's ability to distance itself from its instrumental function. Habermas interpreted this social evolution in a way that could seem, on the one hand, quite naturalistic yet, on the other, universalistic and transcendental. In truth, this tracks two ways to understand Marx's concept of the 'natural self-formation' (*Naturwüchsigkeit*) of humanity through social labor.[62] Habermas interprets this idea as a transcendental enabling condition on more 'advanced' forms of human rationality. That would mean that the concept would be 'derived' by a regressive argument running from a purported fact to the necessary conditions for the fact's possibility. But Habermas nearly always hedges his Kantian commitments, and not only on account of its 'philosophy of the subject', sometimes calling such conditions 'quasi-transcendental' (this way of speaking persists in his later work as well).[63] The reason for hesitation is that Habermas is also very drawn to a much more materialistic and classically Marxist way of speaking of the self-formation as both historically contingent and naturalized. But this cannot deliver the sort of normativity in the

---

[61] See *KHI* 205 ff.; *EI* 253 ff.    [62] See *KHI* 28; *EI* 39–40.
[63] See *PT* 139–46; *NmD* 179–86.

form of universal law that Habermas has always thought is necessary to give critical theory. For this undermines the idea that critical theory is a kind of knowledge, at least as 'knowledge' is usually understood in other philosophical contexts. All of this causes Habermas to shift from the epistemic program of *Knowledge and Human Interests* to an approach that directly bases critical social philosophy on certain allegedly universal features of linguistic agency.

What should not be lost in the complexity of this change in emphasis is that it is *only* a change in emphasis. That is, Habermas never gives up the idea that it is a necessary condition upon a critical theory to provide its pronouncements with a fixed, universal normative status. And the shift in question does not change the fact that Habermas is concerned to solve the problem of the relation of technical reason and argumentative rationality, which is the problem of the unity of theoretical and practical reason in a different guise. And the move to linguistic agency is his way of addressing the issue of what sort of dialectic of reason is appropriate to understanding the nature of that relation.

Habermas offers a typology of action that breaks down into two main categories that more or less track the bifurcated account of reason in his earlier work. Ends-rational action comprises both instrumental reason proper (end-rationality directed towards physical objects) and what Habermas calls 'strategic' action (ends-rationality as applied to human beings).[64] Both species of purposive action have as their proper criteria technical notions of efficiency, predictive power, etc. Contrasted with both species of purposive action is communicative action and it is here that analytic speech act theory (married to Hegel's account of mutual recognition) has force for him. More precisely, speech act theory has application in understanding a specifically modern sort of communicative action in terms of procedural intersubjective action.[65] Habermas identifies three sorts of 'validity claims' involved in modern communicative action: those involving truth (Austin's constative meaning), those involving right (Habermas calls these 'regulative'), and those having to do with expressivity (where truthfulness in display of a subjective state is important).[66] The most interesting contrast here is between strategic purposive action and regulative communicative action. Although Habermas tends to juxtapose these categories rather severely in his exposition, he claims that strategic action is 'parasitic on' its communicative counterpart.[67]

---

[64] i.e. both instrumental and strategic action would be examples of 'instrumental reason' in Horkheimer and Adorno's sense.

[65] *TCA* 1: 67 ff.; *TkH* 1: 103 ff.    [66] *TCA* 1: 75 ff.; *TkH* 1: 114 ff.

[67] *TCA* 1: 192, 287; *TkH* 1: 269–70, 386–7.

The question of the relation between theory and practice in Habermas, as was the case with Adorno, will not turn on conceiving of thought and action as two fundamentally separate categories. Rather, the division will have meaning within the sociological category of action itself. There are two possibilities. One might think that the issue of the relation between theoretical and practical reason drives Habermas' division between purposive and communicative action and that Habermas' claim that the former is dependent upon the latter is an attempt to argue for a kind of Fichtean unity in terms of communicativity. That would sit well with his linguistic turn of course, but Habermas is never very clear about the sense of dependency here and so the sense in which there might be 'unity' between the two categories of action must remain imprecise. In any event, it does not seem that the objectivity of the sort of claims forwarded by instrumental or strategic action depend on interpretation, which Habermas holds is the stock-in-trade of communicative action. Alternatively, one might suppose that the theory-practice schism is present within the category of communicative action itself. Here the contrast would be between constative and regulative claims. These two species of communicative action track the activities of giving and expecting reasons in support of, respectively, factual and normative claims in order to reach understanding and are thus unified under the idea of communicative, reason-giving action.[68]

Now, what Habermas understands to be the communicative force of language goes beyond mere understanding of the communication, or even convincing someone by what one has said. Both of those states of affairs can obtain where the communication in question is rhetorical or even coercive. To 'communicate' in the sense in which Habermas is emphatically interested is to 'reach an understanding'—i.e. *Verständigung*, not just *Verstehen*—and to do so in order to coordinate action consensually.[69] Communication is thus a question of dialogue and interpretation. This is a matter of bridging

---

[68] Habermas exempts aesthetic valuation from consideration among the truly normative categories of action. *TCA* 1: 10; *TkH* 1: 28. This has its roots, again, in a kind of Kantianism, and Habermas sometimes attributes to aesthetic judgment the capacity to work at the margins of or in the life-world background of truly normative sets of factual and ethical claims in order to see them better as part of a whole normative structure. But Habermas is even less forgiving than Kant's own views in that regard, denying aesthetic evaluation any true normative character. Habermas' exclusion of aesthetics and art from his account of critical valuation is very significant; it is a radical departure from earlier Frankfurt School treatments. Habermas' most significant discussion of aesthetics is 'Bewußtmachende oder rettende Kritik—die Aktualität Walter Benjamins', in *PPP*[E] 129–64; *PPP* 336–76.

[69] *TCA* 1: 94–102; *TkH* 1:141–51.

understanding to the end of agreeing on a description of a particular normatively charged situation at issue. In order for this to take place, agents
must be able both (a) to identify what particular speech act category (e.g.
constative, regulative, etc.) is in force and (b) to be competent to evaluate
actions of others and oneself in the terms proper to that category.[70] In such
an exchange the speaker must be able to appeal to norms that are then open
to her audience's 'yes/no' judgment.[71] Accordingly, a speech act situation
structured so that 'communication' is of the essence is a process of holding
oneself open to another's reasons and to giving reasons that can be tested
should dispute arise. This means that knowledge about the criteria for such
testing must be at least implicitly available to competent communicative
agents. In the categories that are structured in truly normative ways, agents
orient their action in terms of rational, intersubjective consensus. This is what
Habermas terms 'discourse'.[72] To sum up: intersubjectivity in the normative
sphere is anchored in a purportedly core property of argumentative speech,
i.e. it transcends merely subjective points of view and causes speakers to enter
into a process of mutual rational recognition aimed generally at achieving
normative results that are universalizable.[73]

But what about historical examples of the great variety of norms that have
been thought to be legitimated? Habermas' answer is that such variety is either
a product of ideology or a lack of 'social evolution'. Either way, Habermas
argues that there are blocks to 'good argumentation' at work, i.e. systematic
impediments to (full) exercises of communicative capacity. This takes us to the
heart of Habermas' views on value objectivity and its relation to dialectic (i.e.
mutual recognition cum speech act theory). For here the question of whether
discourse is 'free' or 'uncoerced' becomes especially pertinent. Habermas
holds that the freedom of communicative action is governed by a meta-norm
that he terms the 'ideal speech situation', in which communicative interchange
would be absolutely unforced.[74] The agreement that would be reached at the

---

[70] *TCA* 1: 69 f., 287; *TkH* 1: 105, 386–7. There might be, of course, several overlapping categories
in play at any one time.

[71] *FN* 119; *FG* 152. Habermas seems to think that it is not enough merely to recognize an utterance
as a candidate for a 'yes/no' answer in order to treat it as a reason. One must actually take a position
on the character of the claim in those terms. While understanding qua *Verständigung* might require
this, it is clear that run-of-the-mill understanding qua *Verstehen* (which is, after all, all that speech acts
require) does not. Habermas is unclear on whether he takes the requirement to attach to both senses
of 'understanding' or merely the more Hegelian one.

[72] *TCA* 1: 23 ff.; *TkH* 1: 45 ff.      [73] *MC* 43 ff.; *MkH* 53 ff. Cf. *TCA* 1: 11 ff.; *TkH* 1: 29 ff.

[74] *MC* 87–8; *MkH* 98.

end of such a process in which there has been maximal freedom would be objective and have universal binding force.

Communicative action theory and the discourse ethics that is based on it have inspired many responses, from fawning approval to withering criticism. I would like to close by discussing one set of responses that bear directly on the question of where Habermas stands in terms of the conceptual history of value objectivity I have charted. Hidebound ethical or political universalists will not accept Habermas' coherentist appeal to intersubjectivity as a basis for objectivity, for all the classical reasons. They will, in essence, lump Habermas in with 'historicists'—i.e. many of those whom Habermas himself is concerned to criticize. Habermas no doubt will view such objections as based in acquiescence with a technological paradigm of social theory. But it is clear from his writings that he keenly feels the bite of such resistance and is always finding new ways to shore up intersubjectivity as a real source for value objectivity. Still, it is far from clear that Habermas has progressed beyond a problem that bedeviled even his earlier attempts at turning the ethics clock back to moral laws. There is no magical incantation that, once intoned, changes subjectivity into intersubjectivity so that intersubjectivity becomes something more than inter-*subjectivity*. That is, not unless one's mantra is something like Hegelian absolutism.[75]

Now, it can seem that the ideal status of the communication situation might allow Habermas to deflect some of this criticism. Intersubjective agreement under increasingly free conditions will not yield *strict* universality, but that is because the project of ever-increasing intersubjective agreement is one of *convergence* on what is objective. Indeed, idealization might be seen as a step in the direction of the reflective judgment-open dialectical strand of thought that I have been contrasting to the universalism that stems from systematic German idealism. Of course, this is not the Absolute of the Jena romantics, nor is it Adorno's negative dialectics, since a brand of ideal knowledge is still on offer here. Still, Habermas' views on the unity of reason and dialectical agency are perhaps not as unitary as Hegel's, although, again, this has been contested.[76]

Far from assuaging critics, this emphasis on idealization can serve to drive criticism deeper into Habermas' account. The main point here involves the twin grand assumptions that force or power (1) is the sort of thing that corrodes ethically desirable communicative exchange and (2) is the sort of

---

[75] See Theunissen (1969), § IV.     [76] See Benhabib (1986: 330).

thing that one can (and should) eliminate from communicative situations. Although Habermas does not precisely follow Kant in thinking that empirical interest as such is an ethically suspect category, his view is decidedly Kantian in that it requires that free moral and political exchange abstract from argumentative interests in order to arrive at universalizable moral precepts. To anyone impressed by a line of thought running from Pascal to Nietzsche and through Freud, Adorno, and Foucault, this requirement is bound to seem Panglossian. Force need not be thought to be spectacularly coercive and it is far from certain that it is something that is less than constitutive of any communicative situation. The response that Habermas is concerned with idealized conditions does not address this concern at all, as it is sometimes thought to. The point is not merely that force is difficult to root out and that all we can hope to do is do a better job of it; the point is rather that the job itself doesn't make any sense.[77] The coercion/non-coercion distinction has been quite pliable, historically speaking. What exempts Habermas' own view on the matter on this count? It is useless to argue for a value in approximating ideal circumstances where what is idealized is not factually stable in any increment, not to mention to import that into a non-ideal speech situation in a way that would have a structuring effect on it.[78] For someone persuaded of what one might call the 'ineffability of force', one might as well idealize away oxygen in a discussion of how mammals survive under earthlike conditions.

Habermas' reformulation of the classic problem of the unity of reason, and of the role of dialectic in its solution, is a mixed bag. On the one hand, the solution attempts a marriage of intersubjective agreement as a basis of normativity with an idealized role for universality that replicates many of the same problems that beset systematic idealist approaches to the problem. Chief among these is the insistence on ethical univocity at all costs. On the other hand, Habermas' treatment of the issue is sensitive to *de facto* pluralism in world-views. He attempts to accommodate this by emphasizing that the constraints are procedural and radically underdetermine what particular ethical regimens would result from discourse. Oddly, although Habermas disallows aesthetic evaluation true normative status, the combination of intersubjectivity and

---

[77] Geuss (1981: 66–7) and Bernstein (1995: 214 f.). make this point in different ways. Cf. arguments against Rawls' 'original position' found in contemporary 'communitarianism'. For Habermas' treatment of communitarian, see *EzD* 119 *passim; JA* 19 *passim* and *EzD* 119 ff.

[78] Here I differ from the excellent Benhabib (1986: 285, 314–15) and Chambers (1996: 132–3). Cf. Habermas' (2001) appeal to Kantian regulative principles.

universality is a vestige of the dialectic-reflective judgment paradigm that begins in Kant's third *Critique*.

In an essay devoted specifically to the theme of the unity of reason, Habermas admits that communicative action theory and discourse ethics might be seen to court transcendental illusion.[79] He believes communicative action theory can proof itself against the danger. Habermas' views on force may suggest otherwise. If Kant, the Jena romantics, and Adorno are correct, philosophical illusion—transcendental or not—is not something one just shuts down once and for all. The idea that it is so is no less an illusion.[80]

# CONCLUSION

I have argued that there is an interesting thought present in both the Jena romantics and Adorno that stems from the side of Kant's thought that puts in fine balance (1) human cognitive limitation and (2) the ineluctable human need and propensity to think in terms that exceed those limitations. This Kantian inheritance stands in contrast with the project, represented in German idealism as well as in Habermas, of seeking a foundation for value objectivity in universalistic claims about the nature of reason.

Metaphysical versions of universalism, especially in value theory, presuppose either overt or covert theological beliefs that are not apt to command common assent nowadays. Some of the main alternatives to theologically grounding objectivity and reason have been different forms of transcendental argumentation. Transcendental argumentation also typically seeks to establish objective grounding in strictly universal terms. But transcendental argumentation always relies on alleged 'facts' as premises, which facts are subject to contest, and, often, on stipulations about the nature of reason that are just as tendentious.

There is presently a division in Continental philosophy on the question of whether value objectivity needs to be secured by way of invariant norms. Much

[79] *PT* 143; *PmD* 182–3.

[80] Thanks to Karl Ameriks, Paul Franks, and Michael Rosen for their very helpful comments. I undertook much of the initial work on the concept of dialectic incorporated in this essay when I was visiting Cambridge University in 1998 and I would like to thank Raymond Geuss and the Faculty of Philosophy for their hospitality and support. Brian Leiter and Michael Rosen's invitation to contribute to this volume has allowed me to revisit this topic in a sustained way and I am grateful to them for this opportunity.

recent French philosophy is of the view that objectivity cannot have such a basis, if the notion of objectivity has any useful role to play at all. Some recent German philosophers have, cautiously, taken on board aspects of this French approach (e.g. Manfred Frank, Axel Honneth, and Christoph Menke). But there is also continued fealty to more classical Kantianism in Germany, as well as a resurgence of interest in Kantian accounts of normativity in France (e.g. Luc Ferry, Alain Renault). Viewing the thought of the Jena romantics and Adorno in terms of their special inheritance from Kant may help to dispel the misconception that *all* Kant-inspired philosophy must stand in opposition to those strands in European thought descending from Nietzsche that also stress the ultimate contingency of value systems. This may not offer in itself a solution to these debates, but it may usefully complicate what is now an oversimplified picture of the options.

# Works Cited

## Abbreviations Used for Primary Sources

*Adorno*

| | |
|---|---|
| *AGS* | *Gesammelte Schriften*, ed. R. Tiedemann (Frankfurt/M: Suhrkamp, 1970– ) |
| *AT* | *Aesthetic Theory*, trans. and ed. R. Hullot-Kentor (Minneapolis: University of Minnesota Press, 1997) |
| *ÄT* | *Ästhetische Theorie* (Frankfurt/M: Suhrkamp, 1970) |
| *DA* | *Die Dialektik der Aufklärung* (Frankfurt/M: Fischer, 1969 [1944/7]) [with M. Horkheimer] |
| *DE* | *Dialectic of Enlightenment*, trans. E. Jephcott and ed. G. Schmid Noerr (Stanford: Stanford University Press, 2002) [with M. Horkheimer] |
| *MM* | *Minima Moralia* (Frankfurt/M: Suhrkamp, 1951) |
| *MM^E* | *Minima Moralia*, trans. E. F. N. Jephcott (London: Verso, 1974) |
| *ND* | *Negative Dialektik* (Frankfurt/M: Suhrkamp, 1966) |

*Aristotle*

EN       *Ethica Nichomachea*, ed. L. Bywater (Oxford: Oxford
         Classical Texts, 1986 [1894])

Top.      *Topica et Sophistici Elenchi*, ed. W. D. Ross (Oxford:
         Oxford Classical Texts, 1958)


*Fichte*

EPW      *Fichte: Early Philosophical Writings*, ed. and trans.
         D. Breazeale (Ithaca, NY: Cornell University Press, 1988)

FGA       *Gesamtausgabe*, ed. R. Lauth, H. Jacobs, and H. Gliwitsky
         (Stuttgart: Frommann-Holzboog, 1964–  )

FTP       *Foundations of Transcendental Philosophy:*
         *(Wissenschaftslehre) nova methodo* (1796/99), ed. and
         trans. D. Breazeale (Ithaca, NY: Cornell University Press,
         1992)

SK        *The Science of Knowledge*, ed. and trans. P. Heath and
         J. Lachs (Cambridge: Cambridge University Press, 1982)

SW        *Sämmtliche Werke*, ed. I. H. Fichte (Berlin: de Gruyter,
         1971)

WLnm      *Wissenschaftslehre nova methodo*, ed. E. Fuchs (Hamburg:
         Meiner, 1982)


*Habermas*

EI        *Erkenntnis und Interesse* (Frankfurt/M: Suhrkamp, 1968)

EzD       *Erläuterungen zur Diskursethik* (Frankfurt/M: Suhrkamp,
         1991)

FG        *Faktizität und Geltung* (Frankfurt/M: Suhrkamp, 1992)

FN        *Between Facts and Norms*, trans. W. Rehg (Cambridge,
         MA: MIT Press, 1998)

JA        *Justification and Application*, trans. C. Cronin
         (Cambridge, MA: MIT Press, 1997)

KHI       *Knowledge and Human Interests*, trans. J. Shapiro
         (Boston: Beacon, 1971)

MC        *Moral Consciousness and Communicative Action*, trans.
         C. Lenhardt and S. W. Nicholsen (Cambridge, MA: MIT
         Press, 1990)

| | |
|---|---|
| *MkH* | *Moralbewußtsein und kommunikatives Handeln* (Frankfurt/M: Suhrkamp, 1983) |
| *NmD* | *Nachmetaphysiches Denken. Philosophische Aufsätze* (Frankfurt/M: Suhrkamp, 1988) |
| *PPP* | *Philosophisch-politische Profile* (Frankfurt/M: Suhrkamp, 1981) |
| *PPP*[E] | *Philosophical-Political Profiles*, trans. F. Lawrence (Cambridge, MA: MIT Press, 1983) |
| *PT* | *Postmetaphysical Thinking*, trans. W. M. Hohengarten (Cambridge, MA: MIT Press, 1992) |
| *TCA* | *The Theory of Communicative Action*, trans. T. McCarthy (Boston: Beacon Press, 1984) |
| *TkH* | *Theorie des kommunikativen Handelns* (Frankfurt/M: Suhrkamp, 1981). |

*Hegel*

| | |
|---|---|
| *HW* | *Werke in zwanzig Bänden*, ed E. Moldenhauer and K. M. Michel (Frankfurt/M: Suhrkamp, 1971–  ) |
| *PhS* | *Phenomenology of Spirit*, trans. A. V. Miller (Oxford: Oxford University Press, 1977) |
| *PR* | *Elements of the Philosophy of Right*, ed. A. Wood and trans. H. B. Nisbet (Cambridge: Cambridge University Press, 1991) |

*Horkheimer*

| | |
|---|---|
| *BPSS* | *Between Philosophy and Social Science: Selected Early Writings*, trans. G. F. Hunter, M. Kramer, and J. Torpey (Cambridge, MA: MIT Press, 1993) |
| *HGS* | *Gesammelte Schriften*, ed. G. Schmid-Noerr and A. Schmidt (Frankfurt/M: Fischer, 1987–  ) |

*Kant*

| | |
|---|---|
| *AA* | *Gesammelte Schriften*, ed. Berlin Akademie der Wissenschaften (Berlin: de Gruyter, 1902–) |
| *A/B* | *Kritik der reinen Vernunft*, vol. 3 in *AA* [A = 1781; B = 1787 ed.] |

*Novalis (Friedrich von Hardenberg)*

| | |
|---|---|
| FS | *Fichte Studies*, ed. and trans. J. Kneller (Cambridge and New York: Cambridge University Press, 2003) |
| NS | *Schriften*, ed. P. Kluckhorn and R. Samuel (Stuttgart: Kohlhammer, 1960– ) |

*Schelling*

| | |
|---|---|
| FSW | *Werke*, ed. M. Schröter (Munich: Beck, 1927) |
| STI | *System of Transcendental Idealism* (1800), trans. P. Heath (Charlottesville: University of Virginia Press, 1978) |

*Schlegel*

| | |
|---|---|
| KFSA | *Kritische Friedrich-Schlegel-Ausgabe*, ed. E. Behler (Paderborn: Schöningh, 1958– ) |
| SPF | *Philosophical Fragments*, trans. P. Firchow (Minneapolis: University of Minnesota Press, 1991) |

## Other Sources

### References

Allison, H. (1983), *Kant's Transcendental Idealism* (New Haven: Yale University Press).

Benhabib, S. (1986), *Critique, Norm, Utopia: A Study of the Foundations of Critical Theory* (New York: Columbia University Press).

Bennett, J. (1974), *Kant's Dialectic* (Cambridge: Cambridge University Press).

Berlin, I. (1969), 'Two Concepts of Liberty', in *Four Essays on Liberty* (Oxford: Oxford University Press), 118–72.

—— (1999), *The Roots of Romanticism* (Princeton: Princeton University Press).

Bernstein, J. M. (1995), *Recovering Ethical Life: Jürgen Habermas and the Future of Critical Theory* (London: Routledge).

Chambers, S. (1996), *Reasonable Democracy: Jürgen Habermas and the Politics of Discourse* (Ithaca, NY: Cornell University Press).

Darjes, J. G. (1747), *Introductio in artem inueniendi, seu logicam theoretico-practicam, qua analytica atque dialectia in usum et issu auditorum suorum methodo iis commoda proponitum* (Jena).

ELDRIDGE, R. (1997), *Leading a Human Life: Wittgenstein, Intentionality, and Romanticism* (Chicago: University of Chicago Press).

ENGSTROM, S. (1988), 'Conditioned Autonomy', *Philosophy and Phenomenological Research* 58: 435–53.

——(1992), 'The Concept of the Highest God in Kant's Moral Philosophy', *Philosophy and Phenomenological Research* 52: 747–80.

FRANKS, P. (2005), *All or Nothing: Systematicity, Transcendental Arguments, and Skepticism in German Idealism* (Cambridge, MA: Harvard University Press).

FRÜCHTL, J. (1986), *Mimesis. Konstellation des Zentralbegriffs bei Adorno* (Wurzburg: Königshaus & Neumann).

GEUSS, R. (1981), *The Idea of a Critical Theory: Habermas and the Frankfurt School* (Cambridge: Cambridge University Press).

—— (2005), 'Suffering and Knowledge in Adorno', in *Outside Ethics* (Princeton: Princeton University Press), 111–30.

GUYER, P. (1990), 'Reason and Reflective Judgment: Kant on the Significance of Systematicity', *Noûs* 24: 17–44.

HABERMAS, J. (2001), 'From Kant's "Ideas" of Pure Reason to the "Idealizing" Presuppositions of Communicative Action', in W. Rehg and J. Bohman (eds.), *Pluralism and the Pragmatic Turn: The Transformation of Critical Theory* (Cambridge, MA: MIT Press), 11–39.

HARDIMON, M. (1994), *Hegel's Social Philosophy: The Project of Reconciliation* (Cambridge: Cambridge University Press).

HORKHEIMER, M. (1967), 'Die Aktualität Schopenhauers', in *Zur Kritik der instrumentalen Vernunft* (Frankfurt/M: Fischer), 248–68.

—— (1972), 'Traditional and Critical Theory', in *Critical Theory: Selected Writings of Max Horkheimer*, trans. M. O'Connell et al. (New York: Continuum), 188–243.

KANT, I. (1967), *Philosophical Correspondence, 1759–99*, ed. and trans. A. Zweig (Chicago: University of Chicago Press).

KIERKEGAARD, S. (1989) [1841], *The Concept of Irony*, trans. and ed. H. Hong and E. Hong (Princeton: Princeton University Press).

LUKÁCS, G. (1962), *Die Zerstörung der Vernunft* (Neuwied: Luchterhand).

ROSEN, M. (1982), *Hegel's Dialectic and its Criticism* (Cambridge: Cambridge University Press).

RUSH, F. (2000), 'Reason and Regulation in Kant', *Review of Metaphysics* 53: 837–62.

—— (2003), 'Romanticism and Benjamin's Critical Epistemology', in B. Hanssen and A. Benjamin (eds.), *Walter Benjamin and Romanticism* (London and New York: Continuum, 2003), 123–36.

—— (2004), 'Conceptual Foundations of Early Critical Theory', in F. Rush (ed.), *The Cambridge Companion to Critical Theory* (Cambridge and New York: Cambridge University Press, 2004), 6–39.

—— (2005), 'Mikroanalyse, Genealogie, Konstellationsforschung', in M. Mulsow and M. Stamm (eds.), *Konstellationsforschung* (Frankfurt/M: Suhrkamp), 149–72.

—— (2006), 'Irony and Romantic Subjectivity', in N. Kompridis (ed.), *Philosophical Romanticism* (London: Routledge), 173–95.

SCHELLING, F. W. J. (1980), *The Unconditional in Human Knowledge: Four Early Essays, 1794–1796*, ed. and trans. F. Marti (Lewisburg, PA: Bucknell University Press).

THEUNISSEN, M. (1969), *Gesellschaft und Geschichte: Zur Kritik der kritischen Theorie* (Berlin: de Gruyter).

WILDT, A. (1982), *Autonomie und Anerkennung: Hegels Moralitätskritik im Lichte seiner Fichte-Rezeption* (Stuttgart: Klett-Cotta).

WOLFF, M. (1981), *Der Begriff des Widerspruchs: Eine Studie zur Dialektik Kants und Hegels* (Königstein: Hain).

WOOD, A. (1970), *Kant's Moral Religion* (Ithaca, NY: Cornell University Press).

YOVEL, Y. (1980), *Kant and the Philosophy of History* (Princeton: Princeton University Press).

# CHAPTER 10

## OVERCOMING EPISTEMOLOGY

### HERMAN PHILIPSE

The idea of 'overcoming epistemology' is a recurrent theme in the philosophy of the last two centuries, and it means many different things. At the beginning of this period, Georg Wilhelm Friedrich Hegel rejected the Kantian prescription that metaphysics should be preceded by a critical investigation of our epistemic faculties. In the introduction to his *Phenomenology of Spirit* (*Phänomenologie des Geistes*, 1807) he argued that the idea of a preliminary critique of reason presupposes that the knowing subject is separated from its metaphysical object, that is, from absolute spirit as it is in itself. But if one engages in the intellectual journey of discovery described in the *Phenomenology*, one will gradually become aware that the knowing subject is an integral part of the absolute and divine spirit, which embraces everything, so that the Kantian assumption is mistaken. At the end of the *Phenomenology* the reader will have reached the absolute point of view, from which he can engage in the sublime dialectics of divine *Logic*.

Another example of a philosopher who aimed at overcoming epistemology is Willard Van Orman Quine. For Quine, the paradigm of philosophical epistemology was provided by Rudolf Carnap, who in his early book *The Logical Structure of the World* (*Der logische Aufbau der Welt*, 1928) set himself the task of showing by means of conceptual analysis that our knowledge of the 'external world' can be considered as a logical construction out of, and can therefore be reduced to, elementary experiences as basic elements. From a logical point of view, Quine rejected Carnap's conceptual reductionism, insisting on semantic holism, and as an adherent of the behaviourism developed by Watson and Skinner he could not endorse Carnap's mentalist basis for the reconstruction of knowledge. For these and other reasons, Quine argued in his celebrated essay 'Epistemology Naturalized' (1969) that an a priori epistemology, which produces the ultimate justification for scientific claims about the external world, should be ruled out. Epistemology had to be 'naturalized' in the sense that it should become 'a chapter of psychology and hence of natural science'.[1]

The point of juxtaposing philosophers as different as Hegel and Quine in this context is to show that the theme of overcoming epistemology admits of variations. Not only was the philosophical epistemology that had to be superseded rather different in these two cases, as different as Kant's transcendentalism and Carnap's early sensationalist reductionism. The philosophical positions by which epistemology was meant to be surmounted were widely divergent as well, and, indeed, mutually exclusive. No supporter of Quinean naturalism will regard the spiritualist absolutism of someone like Hegel as even a possible candidate for serious philosophical consideration.

As a consequence of this diversity, the theme of overcoming epistemology in the philosophy of the nineteenth and twentieth centuries is in fact a family of related themes, and the first question that we should raise whenever this theme emerges in the works of a philosopher is: what exactly does it mean? Which is in each case the epistemology that is supposed to be overcome by repudiating its very problems, and what are the philosophical assumptions that allegedly justify the rejection of that type of epistemology? This first set of questions belongs to the history of philosophy and we might call it the *quaestio facti*. However, there is a second set of questions to be answered,

---

[1] W. V. Quine, *Ontological Relativity and Other Essays* (New York: Columbia University Press, 1969), 83. Quine's holism figures as an important premise in his argument, but one should note that Quinean holism is much more radical than that of Duhem, for example. Whereas Duhem's holism was merely concerned with the testing of scientific theories, which may posit theoretical entities such as atoms, Quine concludes from his stimulus-behaviourism that *all* objects are posits, even chairs, tables, and trees, so that all meaning and language should be regarded as holistic, with the exception of the stimulus-meaning of observation sentences. As a consequence, the label of the 'Quine—Duhem thesis' is a misnomer.

questions that are properly philosophical. How successful were the attempts to overcome epistemology? Did these attempts diagnose correctly the defects of the respective epistemologies that allegedly merited rejection, and were these epistemologies replaced by a viable philosophical view? Let us refer to questions of this second type as the *quaestio iuris*.

With regard to Hegel's attempt to overcome epistemology, most contemporary philosophers will answer the *quaestio iuris* in the negative. After all, Hegel's diagnosis of Kantian epistemology can be convincing only from the point of view of Hegel's own theologico-philosophical position of absolute idealism, which is a heavy metaphysical price to pay. Moreover, Hegel did not provide us with sufficient reasons for thinking that absolute idealism is true, or indeed, that it makes sense. Edmund Husserl, who is one of the main protagonists in this essay, ironically observed in 1911 that Hegel's claim to have erected a 'scientific' system in philosophy could not be substantiated without a preliminary 'critique of reason'.[2] Without any doubt, Quine's naturalization of epistemology conforms better to the philosophical tastes of our times than Hegel's philosophy of absolute spirit.

Yet it is not at all clear that Quine's attempt to overcome traditional epistemology by naturalizing it was more successful than Hegel's venture. According to Quine, philosophical epistemology had to be replaced by a scientific investigation of the 'physical human subject'. In his conception of naturalized epistemology, '[t]his human subject is accorded a certain experimentally controlled input—certain patterns of irradiation in assorted frequencies, for instance—and in the fullness of time the subject delivers as output a description of the three-dimensional external world and its history.' Quine continued this celebrated passage as follows: '[t]he relation between the meager input and the torrential output is a relation that we are prompted to study for somewhat the same reasons that always prompted epistemology: namely, in order to see how evidence relates to theory, and in what ways one's theory of nature transcends any available evidence.'[3] Unfortunately, the Quinean conception of naturalized epistemology as stated in these quotes seems to be incoherent in some crucial respects.

Although natural science is able to detect and measure an input of patterns of irradiation at the surface of our retinas, for example, it cannot detect or

---

[2] Edmund Husserl, 'Philosophie als strenge Wissenschaft', *Logos* 1 (1910–11), 292: 'Wiewohl auch Hegel auf die absolute Gültigkeit seiner Methode und Lehre besteht, so fehlt seinem System die philosophische Wissenschaftlichkeit allererst ermöglichende Vernunftkritik.'

[3] Quine, *Ontological Relativity*, 83.

measure the output of the knowing subject if this output is characterized as 'a description'. At best, natural science can detect and measure patterns of noises, but doing so will not tell us what the knowing subject thinks or knows, unless one interprets these noises as meaningful utterances, which then fall outside of the province of natural science.[4] Furthermore, it is unclear in what sense one can say that the input of the human subject is 'meagre' and the output 'torrential', if the input consists of patterns of irradiation and the output is a pattern of noises. How can one compare such patterns in a non-arbitrary manner? Suppose that the knowing subject looks at its environment and shuts up. Should we then say that the input is torrential and the output zero? Clearly, this input—output relation, if conceived of in purely physical or behaviourist terms, has no relevance to the traditional epistemological problem of the ways in which one's 'theory of nature transcends any available evidence'.[5]

One may conclude that although overcoming epistemology has been an aspiration of both so-called 'continental' and so-called 'analytical' philosophers, successfully overcoming epistemology is more difficult than is often thought. In this essay, I shall focus mainly on two attempts to overcome epistemology, those of Edmund Husserl and Martin Heidegger, and I shall try to answer both the *quaestio facti* and the *quaestio iuris* with regard to their endeavours. Before doing so, however, I shall have to explain why philosophers in the twentieth century thought it important to overcome or repudiate epistemology in the first place. As we shall see, one reason was that according to many authors at the end of the nineteenth century a specific type of epistemology had gained the status of 'first philosophy', that is, of the foundational discipline of philosophy and the sciences. When it turned out that there was no prospect of providing a satisfactory solution to the problems of this foundational discipline, although these problems had emerged already during the scientific revolution, philosophers started to deconstruct the problems of epistemology, and to argue that they had to be overcome or dissolved in one way or another. This happened not only on the Continent of Europe, where Husserl, Heidegger, Carnap, and Merleau-Ponty are the main protagonists in this tale, but also in Britain and the United States. A great

---

[4] Jaegwon Kim has argued that we cannot intelligibly interpret this 'output' as expressing beliefs unless we assume that the subject is rational in some minimal sense, so that belief attribution requires belief evaluation. See his essay 'What is 'Naturalized Epistemology'?', in *Supervenience and Mind: Selected Philosophical Essays* (Cambridge: Cambridge University Press, 1993).

[5] Cf. for a conceptual critique of Quine's epistemological project: P. M. S. Hacker, 'Passing by the Naturalistic Turn: On Quine's Cul-de-sac', *Philosophy* 81 (2006), 231–53.

many authors, such as Ryle, Austin, the later Wittgenstein, Quine, and Rorty, have attempted to overcome epistemology in different manners.[6]

# 1. Epistemology

The term 'epistemology' is used to refer to at least four very different sets of disciplines or problems, which may be interrelated in numerous ways. In a first sense, 'epistemology' denotes (a) normative methodologies for obtaining knowledge, which focus on various methods of forming and justifying our beliefs. In this first sense, Karl Popper's falsificationism or Bayesian confirmation theory are epistemologies of scientific knowledge at a high level of abstraction. Secondly, the term 'epistemology' might refer to (b) all empirical investigations of animal and human knowledge in disciplines such as cognitive biology, cognitive psychology, artificial intelligence, the history of science, cultural anthropology, etc. Sometimes the Quinean expression 'naturalized epistemology' is used for (b), but this is confusing, because many empirical disciplines that investigate knowledge, such as the history of science or applied rational decision theory, do not belong to the natural sciences.[7]

In a third sense, 'epistemology' stands for (c) a philosophical analysis of our concept of knowledge and of related concepts such as belief, memory, and consciousness. In this area, different approaches are possible. According to one approach, which has been popular from Plato and Aristotle to Edmund Gettier and Robert Nozick, the philosopher should come up with a list of necessary conditions for attributing (propositional) knowledge, which, taken together, are sufficient for knowledge. Controversies such as that between externalism and internalism, or between contextualism and invariantism, are usually fought out within the framework of this approach. According to some philosophers, however, it is not at all clear that all nouns and verbs of our language are used in such an 'essentialist' manner. Instead of searching for a set of necessary and sufficient conditions for speaking of 'knowledge', the

---

[6] Cf. on Rorty's attempt to overcome epistemology in *Philosophy and the Mirror of Nature* (Princeton: Princeton University Press, 1979) my article 'Towards a Postmodern Conception of Metaphysics: On the Genealogy and Successor Disciplines of Modern Philosophy' (*Metaphilosophy* 25 (1994), 1–44), in which I develop some of the ideas mentioned in this essay.

[7] Cf. for an attempt to disambiguate the expression 'naturalized epistemology' Susan Haack, *Evidence and Inquiry* (Oxford: Blackwell, 1993), ch. 6: 'Naturalism Disambiguated'.

epistemologist should rather pay attention to the different ways in which this term is actually used and to its intricate relations to other uses of language. Assessing (a), (b), and (c), we may conclude that in principle they all are legitimate endeavours, which do not call for any philosophical 'overcoming', although (a) and (b) are more important for the welfare of humanity than (c).

There is yet a fourth use of the term 'epistemology', however, and it was mostly epistemology in this fourth sense that philosophers wanted to 'overcome' in the twentieth century: epistemology as (d) the attempt to solve the so-called problem of the external world, an attempt that was often linked to the idea that there are a priori 'limits' to human knowledge. This problem emerged during the scientific revolution, primarily in the writings of Descartes, and various solutions were given to it by Descartes, Leibniz, Locke, Berkeley, Hume, and Kant. During post-Kantian German idealism, the problem disappeared from the centre of the philosophical stage, and Hegel also rejected the Kantian version of epistemology in sense (d). Let us label epistemology in this latter sense 'external world epistemology'.

When German philosophers sobered up from absolute idealism around 1850, they turned primarily to epistemology in sense (b). Philosophers such as J. F. Fries and Leonard Nelson argued that Kantian epistemology had to be reinterpreted as a part of empirical psychology, and the gradual emancipation of psychology from philosophy convinced many authors that the traditional philosophical problems of epistemology, such as (d), had to be solved by empirical psychologists, using the methods of natural science. This 'naturalization' of epistemology had already been defended by Schopenhauer and it became a dominant conception during the second half of the nineteenth century owing to the writings of F. E. Beneke, John Stuart Mill, Hermann von Helmholtz, William James, Wilhelm Wundt, and of Carl Stumpf, one of Husserl's teachers.

However, at the end of the nineteenth century, an increasing number of philosophers argued against 'psychologism' or 'naturalism' in epistemology and defended the view that epistemology in sense (d) is the fundamental philosophical discipline, which should be a 'presuppositionless science' (*voraussetzungslose Wissenschaft*). Eduard von Hartmann wrote in 1907, for example, that it is the primary task of philosophy 'to examine the presuppositions that all sciences (*Wissenschaften*) use uncritically, that is to say the assumption that it is possible to acquire knowledge which transcends immediate experience, and to investigate the conditions upon which this possibility depends. Conceived in this manner, philosophy is epistemology or philosophia prima, or theory of science (*Wissenschaftslehre*).'[8]

In other words, epistemology as the discipline (d) that is concerned with the problem of the external world is 'first philosophy', and it is fundamental to all empirical sciences including psychology, because they all presuppose that knowledge of the external world is possible. It was this conception of first philosophy as epistemology that Edmund Husserl initially endorsed, and which both Husserl and Heidegger wanted to overcome by transcendental phenomenology or by the fundamental ontology of *Dasein*, respectively. Since external world epistemology was conceived of as the fundamental philosophical discipline, overcoming epistemology required a radical shift in the very conception of philosophy itself.

## 2. CORPUSCULAR PHILOSOPHY AND THE PROBLEM OF THE EXTERNAL WORLD

In order to understand adequately the philosophical revolutions against epistemology staged by Husserl and Heidegger, some further stage-setting is necessary. In particular, two questions have to be answered. First, why did the sceptical 'problem of the external world' arise precisely at the time of the scientific revolution, when scientists so greatly enlarged our knowledge of this external world? How are we to explain historically the astonishing fact of intellectual history that the splendid advances in astronomy and physics by philosopher-scientists such as Kepler, Galileo, Descartes, Boyle, and Newton were accompanied by sceptical questions concerning the very possibility of such knowledge? Secondly, how was it possible that the sceptical problem of the external world, which was raised by Descartes as a mere methodological device in his attempt to establish indubitable first principles of his new physics, acquired the prestigious position of 'first philosophy' at the end of

---

[8] Eduard von Hartmann, *System der Philosophie im Grundriß 1: Grundriß der Erkenntnislehre* (Bad Sachsa im Harz: Hermann Haacke Verlagsbuchhandlung, 1907), 12, my translation. The German text reads: 'die Voraussetzungen zu prüfen, deren alle Wissenschaften sich kritiklos bedienen, also die Möglichkeit einer die unmittelbare Erfahrung überschreitenden Erkenntnis und die Bedingungen zu untersuchen, von denen diese Möglichkeit abhängt. So verstanden ist die Philosophie Erkenntnistheorie oder philosophia prima, oder auch Wissenschaftslehre.'

the nineteenth century? For surely, it was metaphysics and not epistemology that was considered as 'first philosophy' in the tradition from Aristotle to Descartes and beyond.

As an answer to the first of these questions I shall endorse and defend the bold thesis that it was precisely the corpuscular conception of matter, which served as a philosophical underpinning of the new physics, that implied the sceptical problem of the external world. In this section, I shall try to substantiate this thesis by a rather schematic rational reconstruction of the arguments advanced by the philosophers of the scientific revolution from Descartes to Kant, without going into the details of their writings. In a letter to Mersenne of 11 October 1638, Descartes criticized Galileo, saying that the latter had 'built without foundations' (*il a bâti sans fondement*). What was lacking in Galileo, Descartes argued, was a correct conception of material nature that could provide the first principles and causes in physical explanations. For most scientist-philosophers of the scientific revolution, this general conception was some version of the corpuscular philosophy, either atomism or Descartes' mathematical version, which identified material substance with three-dimensional space (*res extensa*), denied the possibility of a vacuum, and held that matter can be divided indefinitely.

One good reason for accepting the corpuscular theory of matter was that it could provide non-circular explanations of empirical phenomena such as heat, sounds, smells, liquidity, and colours, which were lacking in Aristotelian physics. If one asked the Aristotelian physicist why wine is a liquid, for example, he would answer that wine consists largely of the element water, and that the element water is constituted by the essential properties 'cold' and 'wet'. But since 'wetness' is just another word for liquidity, such explanations are circular, the reason being that the theoretical terms ('wet') of the explanans are not really different from the empirical terms ('liquid'), by means of which the explanandum is described. A corpuscular philosopher such as Descartes could explain the different states of water, gaseous, liquid, and solid, in terms of the geometrical shapes of the particles constituting water and the kinetic interactions between these particles. Although in the seventeenth century most of these explanations were speculative, such as Descartes' explanation of colours in terms of the different angular velocities of light particles, there also was some empirical confirmation of the corpuscular philosophy.[9] If one hits a nail with a hammer, for example, the nail will be hot. Assuming that

---

[9]  For Descartes' physics of colour, cf. *La Dioptrique*, Discours premier.

the impact of motion can produce other motions only, this phenomenon confirms the theory that heat as it exists in matter is nothing but an agitation of its small particles, which we call hot if it is greater than normal.[10]

Paradoxically, this new corpuscular theory of matter evoked the sceptical doubts concerning the very existence of matter that much later were labelled 'the problem of the external world'. We may reconstruct the argument leading up to this problem of the external world in the following eight steps. First (1), it was argued that the determinate properties of empirical explananda such as colour, heat, odours, and sounds should not be ascribed to the imperceptibly small particles that are stipulated in their theoretical explanations, on pain of the explanations becoming as circular as Aristotle's explanations had been. In Lockean terminology, 'secondary qualities' are not qualities of the constitutive particles of matter. From this legitimate first premise it seemed to follow, however, that (2) qualities such as colour or heat as they are commonly understood cannot be attributed to the macroscopic objects that consist of these particles either. For how could the purely geometrical or mechanical composition of macroscopic bodies out of particles yield something radically new, such as colour? As Descartes argued, for example, the geometrical composition of macroscopic bodies out of particles that merely have geometrical properties can yield new geometrical properties only.

This second step has embarrassing implications, since secondary qualities such as colour and heat were the macroscopic explananda that the corpuscular physics was supposed to account for in the first place. If these qualities cannot be attributed to matter, the corpuscular philosophy threatens to lose its *raison d'être*. In other words, this second step raised the problem of the ontological status of secondary qualities, which was resolved as follows. As far as material objects are concerned, (3) secondary qualities are physical properties that can be described adequately in the theoretical terms of physics, that is, in terms of 'primary qualities'. For example, sounds as they exist in the material world are nothing but vibrations in the air, and heat is nothing but an (accelerated) movement of constituent particles. However, since the sounds, colours, and other secondary qualities are not *perceived as* vibrations and the like, we must further assume that (4) secondary qualities-as-we-perceive-them are in some sense 'subjective' or 'perceiver-dependent'. Obliterating

---

[10]  Cf. Descartes, *Principia philosophiae*, IV, §29; Locke, *An Essay concerning Human Understanding*, II, viii, §21.

conceptual distinctions such as the difference between feeling hot and feeling that something is hot, the philosophers of the scientific revolution assimilated these subjective secondary qualities to 'sensations'.

The fourth step created two further difficulties. First of all, if secondary qualities-as-we-perceive-them, such as colours, cannot exist in matter, these 'sensations' cannot be material modifications of the perceiving organism either, as Galileo supposed.[11] Hence, (5) they have to be non-material modifications of something and, since they are essentially objects of perceptual awareness, they were supposed to be 'mental' or 'in the mind' in some sense. We might call this conclusion the 'principle of immanence', which implied or presupposed some sort of dualism between matter and the mental. But as soon as (5) is endorsed, there is yet another difficulty. Typically, sensations proper are felt at bodily locations, for it is my back that itches or my toe that aches. But if colours-as-perceived are assimilated to sensations, we should at least admit that these visual sensations are not felt in the eye, and that sounds are not experienced as sensations in the ear. This is why (6) the perception of secondary qualities cannot merely consist in our having the relevant 'sensations'. Somehow, we also have to postulate a projective mental mechanism, which explains that we perceive colours, for example, as qualities of material objects in the 'external' world.

Although the term 'projection' became popular in the nineteenth century only, the conception of a projective theory of perception was already present in the writings of authors of the seventeenth century such as Descartes, who held that apart from our having visual sensations, the psychology of visual perception also involves a 'judgement'.[12] The motivation for developing the projective theory of perception sprang from the problems about secondary qualities that I have just sketched. But as soon as the theory was in place, it seemed plausible to generalize it to the perception of primary qualities such as spatial shapes, particularly to those philosophers who denied an ontological difference between primary and secondary qualities. Sensations of shapes were distinguished from material shapes by implicitly applying the rules of perspective, and it was often said that whereas the sensations or ideas

---

[11] Galileo, *The Assayer* (1623), excerpt translated and reproduced in A. C. Danto and S. Morgenbesser (eds.), *Philosophy of Science* (Cleveland and New York: Meridian Books, 1960), 28.

[12] In Germany, the most influential writers defending a projective theory of perception or of 'the world' were J. Müller (*Handbuch der Physiologie des Menschen*, 2 vols. (Koblenz: Hölscher, 1840), ii. 337) and K. Bisch-Reichenwald Aars (*Zur psychologischen Analyse der Welt* (Leipzig: Johann Ambrosius Barth, 1900)). The majority of psychologists endorsed such a theory, including Freud.

of secondary qualities do not resemble secondary qualities as they exist in material reality, the ideas of primary qualities such as shapes do resemble the material properties to which they correspond.[13]

The resulting 'representational' theory of perception implies (7) that there are three sets of problems for further research. First, the physics of perception should study the causal material processes that produce the proximal stimuli of perception in our perceptual organs, and the material processes in the body that pass on these stimuli to the brain. Second, the psychology of perception investigates the ranges of perceptual sensations, the projective mental mechanisms which account for the fact that we attribute the content of these sensations, such as colours-as-perceived, to material objects, and the unifying mental mechanisms which account for the fact that we attribute various properties perceived by means of different sense organs to one and the same material object in the world. And third, there is the puzzling problem of how mental mechanisms and sensations are related to our body, to the brain and the central nervous system in particular. We might designate the first set of problems as 'the causal problem' and the second set as 'the constitutive problem', for the second set is concerned with the question of how the world-as-we-perceive-it is constituted out of the raw material of our sensations. The third set does not need a new label, for it is the familiar mind—body problem.

Clearly this philosophy of perception, which was motivated by the corpuscular theory of matter, implied (8) sceptical questions about the very existence of matter. The reason is that the perceptually constituted world is qualitatively different from the physical world, which, supposedly, contains the causal processes that indirectly occasion the occurrence of sensations 'in the mind'. While perceiving, we are not aware of these causal processes. What is worse, the corpuscular philosophy implies that in perception we are not aware of the material world as it really is in itself, for what we are aware of is the perceived or 'phenomenal' world that is subjectively constituted out of the mental stuff of our sensations. But if that is the case, what reasons do we have to assume that the real physical world exists at all? Once this sceptical worry was raised, it was not put to rest again easily, and neither Descartes' assurance that the physical world really exists because God does not deceive us, nor Berkeley's view that only the subjective world of sensations exists because God is very well able to cause ideas in our minds without the cumbersome intermediary of matter, nor Hume's

---

[13]  Cf. Locke, *An Essay concerning Human Understanding*, II, viii, §15.

exasperated conclusion that we should accept the existence of the material world on blind faith because no sound inductive argument can support it, was able to convince the philosophical community. This is why, in Kant's terminology, the problem of the external world amounted to a 'scandal of philosophy'.[14]

If this reconstruction of the rise of external world epistemology is correct, we may say that the deepest philosophical assumption motivating the sceptical problem of the external world is the thesis that what elementary particle physics says about the world is *incompatible* with many of our everyday perceptual claims, or in the terminology of Wilfrid Sellars, that the scientific image is incompatible with the manifest image.[15] Let us call this assumption the 'incompatibility thesis'. It is important to identify this assumption, because we may expect that no attempt to overcome epistemology in sense (d) will succeed as long as this assumption is not fundamentally questioned. I shall argue below that neither Husserl nor Heidegger really challenged it. Clearly, Quine did not challenge the incompatibility thesis either. He endorsed it for logical and other reasons, and as a result he tried to eliminate from his picture of reality everything that belongs to the manifest image but does not fit into the scientific image, such as colours and consciousness.[16] However, because in his behaviourist naturalization of the problem of the external world Quine retained the very structure of this problem (a human subject 'posits' bodies and 'projects' his view of the world from his data, which are now defined as stimulations of sensory receptors and not as sensations), even though that structure does not make sense within a behaviourist and physicalist framework (what can it mean to say of a physical system that it 'posits' bodies, and in which sense are stimulations 'data' or 'evidence'?), his project of a naturalized epistemology lacked conceptual coherence.[17]

---

[14]  Kant, *Kritik der reinen Vernunft*, B xxxix, footnote.

[15]  W. Sellars, 'Philosophy and the Scientific Image of Man', in W. Sellars, *Science, Perception, and Reality* (London: Routledge & Kegan Paul, 1963). Cf. Descartes, *Le Monde*, ch. 1.

[16]  It should be noted, however, that in his later works, Quine acknowledged both the irreducibility and the indispensability of intensional idioms such as 'A believes that p'. As a result, he moved from the eliminative materialism of *Word and Object* (Cambridge, MA: MIT Press, 1960) to the Davidsonian 'linguistic dualism of anomalous monism' in later writings such as *Pursuit of Truth* (Cambridge, MA: Harvard University Press, 1990), 72. Yet Quine argued that 'there is good reason not to try to weave it [i.e. intensional discourse, HP] into our scientific theory of the world to make a more comprehensive system', since '[w]ithout it science can enjoy the crystalline purity of *extensionality*' (*Pursuit of Truth*, 71). Cf. for an analysis of this development: David Woodruff Smith, 'How to Husserl a Quine—and a Heidegger, too', *Synthese* 98 (1994), 153–73.

[17]  As Quine himself said, his naturalized epistemology is a 'physical mimicry of phenomenalistic epistemology'. Cf. W. V. Quine, *From Stimulus to Science* (Cambridge, MA: Harvard University Press, 1995), 19.

# 3. EXTERNAL WORLD EPISTEMOLOGY
## AS FIRST PHILOSOPHY: FROM
## DESCARTES TO KANT

Let us now turn to the second question that has to be answered in order to complete the stage-setting for Husserl's and Heidegger's projects of overcoming epistemology. How did external world epistemology rise to the position of first philosophy at the end of the nineteenth century, so that overcoming it required a revolution regarding the very idea of philosophy? In the Aristotelian tradition, it is not external world epistemology but general metaphysics (*metaphysica generalis*) that occupies the position of first philosophy. The idea of scientific knowledge (*episteme*) as explained in Aristotle's *Posterior Analytics* implied that, since scientific theories ideally are axiomatic-deductive systems, there must be first principles of the sciences that cannot be supported further by (deductive) arguments. All sciences of reality have some of these first principles in common, and the sum of such common principles is the content of metaphysics or first philosophy, which is a foundational conception of reality as a whole. This global view of science and metaphysics, which we may call Aristotelian or classical foundationalism, was inherited by Descartes, Hobbes, Locke, Kant, and most other philosophers of the scientific revolution.[18] But if initially first philosophy was metaphysics and not external world epistemology, why did the latter topic replace metaphysics as the foundational discipline at the end of the nineteenth century? In order to simplify the complex historical answer that this question deserves, I shall focus on Descartes and Kant only, a thorough knowledge of whose works is essential for understanding Husserl's and Heidegger's attempts to overcome epistemology.

In outline, the answer to this second preliminary question is as follows. External world epistemology could move to the centre stage of philosophy because it played a role in solving another epistemological problem, which is inherent in classical foundationalism. Whereas this role was still somewhat marginal in Descartes' case, it became central because of Kant's Copernican revolution. The problem to which I am referring is the epistemological

---

[18]   Because Descartes accepted only a small number of first principles of physics, he soon realized that physical explanations of specific empirical phenomena cannot be deduced from his first principles, so that he had to introduce the notion of a hypothesis. Cf. *Les principes de la philosophie*, pt. iv, §§204–6.

problem of the first principles, which each variety of foundationalism has to solve. If there is a distinction between derived and basic knowledge, a foundationalist epistemology must give an account both of the logical form of the derivations and of the manner in which basic knowledge is acquired and justified. In classical or Aristotelian foundationalism, the latter issue is particularly difficult, because Aristotle thought that all scientific knowledge is necessarily true. This requirement may be unproblematic in the case of mathematics, but Aristotle also endorsed it for the empirical sciences of nature. Accordingly, he required of the first principles of the empirical sciences that (x) they are necessarily true, that (y) they are logically universal, and that (z) they can be justified on the basis of sense perception. Let us call the issue as to how knowledge of such first principles can be acquired and justified the problem of (e) classical first principles epistemology. At first sight, this problem of classical first principles epistemology may seem to be insoluble. How can one reconcile requirements (x), (y), and (z), which seem to define an inconsistent set?

It was within the framework of the conception of metaphysics as first philosophy that Descartes raised his sceptical doubts regarding the existence of the material world. As he explained in the letter to Picot that served as an introduction to the French edition of his *Principles of Philosophy* of 1647, Descartes endorsed the Aristotelian idea that metaphysics is concerned with the first principles of knowledge, from which all other knowledge can be derived, and which are 'so clear and self-evident that the human mind cannot doubt their truth'.[19] What he rejected were both the particular first principles that Aristotle had proposed and Aristotle's solution to (e) the epistemological problem of the first principles.

According to Aristotle, we are able to know necessarily true and universal first principles of an empirical science such as physics by intuitive induction on the basis of repeated sense perceptions. This epistemological doctrine presupposes the Aristotelian ontology of hylomorphism, according to which each particular that we can perceive by the senses consists of a universal essence particularized by individuating matter. Aristotelian induction is 'intuitive' because according to Aristotle we can absorb the universal essence of particulars in our soul after having perceived some of these particulars by the senses, and this absorption enables us to know necessary truths about

---

[19] Descartes, 'Lettre de l'auteur à celui qui a traduit le livre laquelle peut ici servir de préface', *Les principes de la philosophie*, AT ix. 2.

all particulars that share a specific essence.[20] Since during the scientific revolution Aristotelian hylomorphism had been replaced by the corpuscular philosophy, Aristotle's solution to the epistemological problem of the first principles of physics was not available any more. This is why Descartes had to propose a new method for establishing the first principles of metaphysics and physics.

Two elements of this new Cartesian method are relevant here: Descartes' methodical doubt and his criterion of truth. Often, historians of modern philosophy tell us that the 'quest for certainty' in epistemology started with Descartes, but this is misleading. Descartes derived the idea that first principles had to be indubitable from classical foundationalism, in particular from the Aristotelian requirement (x) that they must be necessarily true, and he argued that we can establish the indubitability of a principle only by methodically doubting everything and then seeing whether anything is left as indubitable. Since the epistemological reasons for doubting our convictions methodically may be flimsy or 'hyperbolic', Descartes could advance a far-fetched argument as the third and most pervasive reason for doubt in his first *Meditation*:

And yet firmly rooted in my mind is the long-standing belief that there is an omnipotent God who made me the kind of creature that I am. How do I know that he has not brought it about that there is no earth, no sky, no extended thing, no shape, no size, no place, while at the same time ensuring that all these things appear to me to exist just as they do now?[21]

Of course, Descartes never genuinely doubted the existence of the material world. He argued in his fourth and sixth *Meditations* that it is incoherent to suppose that God can deceive us, so that the existence of the material world is beyond reasonable doubt. And yet, doubting the existence of the external world methodically had more than a merely instrumental value for Descartes in establishing indubitable first principles, because it allegedly showed that we can conceive of the mental without matter, so that, in principle, the mental can exist without matter in a purely spiritual afterlife. As we will see, Husserl's thought experiment of the 'destruction of the world' (*Weltvernichtung*) in §49 of his *Ideas* I (1913) had a similar function, although Husserl did not use the argument of a deceiving God.

---

[20]  Aristotle, *Posterior Analytics*, B, ch. 19.
[21]  Descartes, *Meditationes de prima philosophia*, first meditation (AT vii. 21), quoted from Descartes, *Selected Philosophical Writings*, ii, trans. John Cottingham et al. (Cambridge: Cambridge University Press, 1988), 78. It should be noted that the representational theory of perception is a necessary condition for the logical possibility of this sceptical thought-experiment.

Having established the indubitability of self-consciousness as a first principle in his second *Meditation*, Descartes proceeded to solve problem (e) of the first principles by means of a criterion of truth. Rejecting the third Aristotelian requirement (z) for the first principles of physics, Descartes argued that these principles can be justified a priori in the same way as the principles of mathematics by their 'clarity and distinctness'.[22] However, the assumption that 'clarity and distinctness' can function as a criterion of truth for the principles of physics is not obvious, since even if these principles would have the alleged self-evidence traditionally attributed to mathematical axioms, it is unclear how this self-evidence can guarantee that they are true of an independently existing physical reality. Descartes attempted to validate his criterion of truth in *Meditations* 3 and 4 by arguing that God exists and that He is not a deceiver. In particular, Descartes assumed that elementary a priori knowledge of nature is innate, and that God, by creating clear and distinct ideas in our minds in conformity with the fundamental structures of matter, guarantees the truth of the first principles of Cartesian physics. We may conclude that external world epistemology (d) played a limited role in Descartes' attempt to solve (e) the epistemological problem of the first principles. As I said before, this role became a major one because of Kant's Copernican revolution.

In the prologue to the second edition of his *Critique of Pure Reason*, Kant argued that disciplines such as logic, mathematics, and physics had gained the 'secure path of a science' by what he called a 'revolution in their way of thinking'.[23] Likewise, Kant suggested, first philosophy in the sense of general metaphysics would be able to become an established scientific discipline by a revolution in its way of thinking, and he aimed at accomplishing this revolution in his first *Critique*. Kant referred to his revolution in metaphysics as the Copernican revolution, and he described it as the assumption that the objects of knowledge conform to our knowledge of them instead of the other way around. Why did Kant think that such a Copernican revolution was necessary? What did it amount to? And why was one of its results that the issue of the first principles of physics became so intimately intertwined with the traditional problem of the external world that during the second half of the nineteenth century the issue of the external world could usurp the position

[22] Descartes rejects requirement (z) in the second half of the second *Meditation* (the analysis of the piece of wax).
[23] *Kritik der reinen Vernunft*, B vii–xii. In his essay in the present volume, Taylor Carman elucidates the semantic differences between the German word 'Wissenschaft' and 'science' in English.

of first philosophy? In the remainder of this section, I shall briefly sketch the answers to these three questions.

The Copernican revolution was Kant's solution to (e) the classical epistemological problem of the first principles, and it was necessary because the earlier solutions of Descartes and Hume had failed miserably. Descartes' rationalist solution was unsatisfactory for a number of reasons. Leibniz correctly observed that the criterion of 'clarity and distinctness' is itself not clear and distinct, so that it does not satisfy its own demands, and we cannot be sure that we apply it correctly. Also, Descartes' validation of the criterion is circular, as Arnauld argued in his objections to the *Meditations*, because in order to be justified in accepting the premises for Descartes' proof of the existence of God, by which the criterion is validated, we should have validated the criterion already.[24] Finally, some direct deductive consequences of the principles of Cartesian physics were refuted by empirical research during the second half of the seventeenth century. For example, Blaise Pascal argued that we have to accept the existence of the void in nature in order to account for Toricelli's results, although the Cartesian principle that matter is nothing but *res extensa* logically excludes that there be empty space. And whereas Descartes held on the basis of his principles of physics that the propagation of light is instantaneous, Rømer discovered in 1676 by observing an eclipse of a satellite of Jupiter that light has a finite speed. Surely, if the principles of Cartesian physics can be refuted by empirical research, it cannot be the case that a veracious god guarantees their necessary truth.

As a consequence, Hume followed Newton in repudiating Descartes' rationalist solution to the epistemological problem of the first principles. Like Newton, he held that the general first principles of physics are inferred from observations of particular phenomena by induction. Given the rejection of knowable Aristotelian essences during the scientific revolution, this meant that he had to abandon the requirement (x) of necessary truth. In Hume's hands the notion of induction was transformed from Aristotelian intuitive induction

---

[24] Descartes tried to escape from the objection of begging the question by limiting the scope of his systematic doubt, for example to our *memory* of clear and distinct proofs (AT vii. 245, cf. 140), or to our *trust* that, if we intuit something clearly and distinctly, it cannot be rendered dubious afterwards by sceptical arguments (AT vii. 141). However, from this it would follow that Descartes does not intend to validate his criterion of truth in its *actual* applications. Yet this is necessary, for it is not self-evident that proposed principles of physics are true of an extramental reality if only they are clear and distinct. I disagree, then, with Anthony Kenny when he writes that 'the simple intuition by itself provides both psychologically and logically the best grounds for accepting its truth'. Cf. A. Kenny, *Descartes: A Study of his Philosophy* (New York: Random House, 1968), 194.

into enumerative induction, and we cannot justify apodictically the universal principles of physics by enumerative induction based on the perception of particular instances.[25] Hume also argued that the necessity of universal causal laws is projected into nature by the mental habits of association. However, since Hume did not unambiguously repudiate the traditional conception of science, he became a sceptic about scientific knowledge.

For Kant such a Humean scepticism was unacceptable, because Newtonian mechanics was generally considered as a successful scientific discipline, an instance of *scientia* and not of *opinion*. Hence, Kant accepted the challenge of showing that some fundamental principles of Newtonian physics satisfy all three requirements of scientific principles in Aristotle's sense: they are (x) necessarily true, they are (y) logically universal, and they are (z) in some sense inherent in sense experience. But how can this be the case? In other words, Kant argued that the principles of physics are 'synthetic a priori judgements' and he tried to explain how this is possible.

At first sight it may seem that by formulating problem (e) of classical first-principle epistemology in his technical terminology as the question 'How are synthetic a priori judgements possible?', Kant dropped requirement (z). For although he used (x) necessary truth and (y) logical universality as criteria for assessing a judgement as a priori, he defined the notion of an a priori judgement as a judgement that epistemologically speaking is independent from all experience.[26] Yet, according to Kant's transcendental theory, it is experience that triggers our synthetic a priori knowledge of necessary structures, because these structures are 'conditions for the possibility of experience'.

Of course the principles of physics are not only a priori. They also must be synthetic in Kant's technical sense of containing information about the world. Accordingly, Kant's transcendental question of how synthetic a priori judgements are possible in fact consists of two separate issues: (1) how can we know the principles of physics a priori, that is, independently of experience, and (2) how can we explain that these a priori principles are synthetic in the sense of containing information about the world?

Kant's originality lies entirely in his answer to the second question of correspondence. Although he avoided the terminology of innateness, his answer to the first question was not essentially different from that of Descartes: we can have a priori knowledge because this knowledge is somehow already present in the knowing subject independently of experience. If we express

---

[25]  Of course, Hume had many precursors at this point.    [26]  *Kritik der reinen Vernunft*, B 2–3.

Kant's view of the knowing subject in the terminology of modern cognitive science, we might say that according to Kant there are modules of information-processing in the knowing subject that yield the knowledge of geometry, arithmetic, and the principles of physics, no matter what specific input is fed into these modules. But if this is so, how can such a priori knowledge also be synthetic, that is, how can it contain information about the material world? The Cartesian answer to this second question of correspondence, which referred to God's creation of innate knowledge in our minds in conformity with the essential structures of matter, was not available to Kant, who rejected the arguments for God's existence. How could one explain that innate knowledge is necessarily true of the material world?

It is at this point that Kant merged the problem of the external world with the problem of the first principles. As we saw in section 2 above, the problem of the external world as it arose during the scientific revolution in fact consists of two separate problems, the causal and the constitutive problem. The causal problem is the question of how we can justify the view that our perceptual 'sensations' are really caused by a material world that exists in itself, independently of the perceiving subject. The constitutive problem is at least as pressing: how is the world-as-we-perceive-it constituted out of the raw material of our perceptual sensations? It is this second issue that Kant used in order to solve the problem of the first principles. If we assume that the epistemic modules in the knowing subject that yield a priori knowledge of mathematics and physics also process the information that is contained in the sensations produced by external stimuli of our senses, it follows that the world-as-we-perceive it will conform to the a priori knowledge of mathematics and of the principles of physics, so that this knowledge is also synthetic. This view is Kant's Copernican revolution in metaphysics, according to which the objects of empirical knowledge are constituted by the workings of the very same epistemic modules that also produce synthetic a priori knowledge.

The Copernican revolution in metaphysics had a number of interesting corollaries. The first is that it forges an intimate connection between external world epistemology (d) and first principles epistemology (e). If the epistemic modules in the knowing subject that enable us to know a priori the synthetic principles of natural science also process our perceptual sensations in the constitution of the phenomenal world, the solution to the epistemological problem of the first principles of physics is part and parcel of the solution to the epistemological problem of constitution, which was one of the two problems covered by the label of (d) external world epistemology.

A second corollary is surprising given the genesis of the problem of the external world in the seventeenth century. Whereas for authors such as Descartes the subjectively constituted phenomenal world is the world of (Aristotelian) common sense, whereas the real material world is the world as described by corpuscular physics, it follows from the Copernican revolution that our physical knowledge applies to the subjectively constituted phenomenal world only, because it is this world which is constituted by the a priori principles of physics. Kant welcomed this corollary, because it enabled him to provide an even-handed solution to the problem of science and religion, which had become pressing at the end of the eighteenth century. According to Kant, both religion and science have one advantage and one disadvantage. The advantage of science is that it is able to acquire real knowledge (*episteme*), but its disadvantage is that it is concerned with the phenomenal world only. Religion cannot aspire to knowledge, because its claims cannot be substantiated by scientific research, but this disadvantage is compensated for by the blessing that it is concerned with the world as it really is (*an sich*). By relegating science and religion to different domains, the phenomenal world and the noumenal world, Kant ensured that they could never clash, and he solved the traditional problem of freedom and physical determinism in a similar manner. Both Husserl and Heidegger endorsed the Kantian idea that religion is deeper than science, because the latter is concerned with a phenomenal reality only.

If science is about the phenomenal world, the Cartesian distinction between science and common sense cannot be accounted for by the distinction between the real world in itself and the subjectively constituted phenomenal world, as it was in Descartes' conception. Indeed, if one wants to make the former distinction at all, the line has to be drawn within the phenomenal world. This third corollary of Kant's transcendental theory was developed explicitly by Husserl in *Ideas* I (*Ideen* I, 1913), by Heidegger in *Being and Time* (*Sein und Zeit*, 1927), and by Merleau-Ponty in *The Phenomenology of Perception* (*La phénoménologie de la perception*, 1945). All these authors distinguished between on the one hand a meaningful life-world (*Lebenswelt*, Husserl), or world of everyday life (*Welt der Alltäglichkeit*, Heidegger), or lived world (*monde vécu*, Merleau-Ponty), and on the other hand the world-as-physics-sees-it, and they argued that this latter world of science is some kind of secondary constitution on the basis of the life-world, instead of being an external cause of sensations in the perceiving subject. Although only Husserl followed Kant in underpinning his conception of the life-world by a version of transcendental idealism, all three authors were followers of Kant in that they relegated science to a secondary place within their *Weltanschauung* as a whole. If they were realists of some kind, they were not scientific realists like Descartes or Brentano.

We may wonder, finally, what happened to the other problem that sailed under the flag of external world scepticism, the causal problem of accounting for our sensations by a causal hypothesis. Clearly, for Kant and his followers, solving the causal problem was not necessary for laying the foundations of physics, because this latter task had become intertwined with the problem of constitution. If there still was some external world that was causally responsible for the presence of sensations in us, it was not the world of physics. This situation explains the surprising fate of the causal problem in Husserl, for example. Since solving it was not necessary for laying the foundations of natural science, it could be 'overcome'. As we shall see, this Husserlian enterprise of overcoming epistemology (d) by transcendental phenomenology was in fact nothing but a deconstruction of the causal problem in order to focus exclusively on the problems of constitution.

The deconstruction of the causal problem started with Kant himself. The German philosopher Friedrich Heinrich Jacobi (1743–1819) correctly observed that without the assumption of realism one could not construct the Kantian system, whereas with the assumption of (transcendental) realism one could not dwell in it.[27] On the one hand, Kant needed the causal and projective theory of perception developed during the scientific revolution in order to stage his Copernican revolution. He had to assume that perceptual sensations are caused in the perceiving subject by external stimulation of the senses, and the Kantian terminology of *affizieren* is incomprehensible without this causal assumption.[28] But on the other hand Kant's Copernican revolution implied that categories such as causality or substance could be legitimately applied within the phenomenal world only, and not to the relation between the world in itself and our perceptual sensations (where 'our' refers to the transcendental subject). As one of the first critics of Kant, Jacobi drew attention to this contradiction concerning the 'thing in itself' (*Ding an sich*) in transcendental philosophy. The problem of the thing in itself

---

[27] Jacobi, *Friedrich Heinrich Jacobi's Werke*, ii: *David Hume über den Glauben oder Idealismus und Realismus. Ein Gespräch*, ed. Friedrich Roth (Leipzig: Gerhard Fleischer d. Jüng, 1815), 'Beylage über den transscendentalen Idealismus', p. 304.

[28] Kant, *Kritik der reinen Vernunft*, B 93: 'Alle Anschauungen, als sinnlich, beruhen auf Affektionen'; cf. B 33, 75, 129, 309.

was aggravated by the fact that Kant included so much in the transcendental modules that constitute the phenomenal world: not only categories such as substance and causality, but also the 'forms of intuition' (*Anschauungsformen*) of space and time. This implies that we cannot even apply temporal or spatial determinations to the world as it is in itself, so that we cannot legitimately say anything whatsoever about it.

If, as Kant himself admitted, we can have no conception of the thing in itself, how could he claim to have removed the 'scandal of philosophy'?[29] If we look somewhat closer at the argument of Kant's 'refutation of idealism', according to which our temporal self-awareness presupposes our (immediate) awareness of continuing things in the spatial world, we see that this proof of the existence of the external world is concerned with the phenomenal world only, and not with the world as it is in itself.[30] In other words, what Kant refutes is merely what he calls psychological idealism, and this is what he announced in his preface to the second edition of the first *Critique*.[31] To put this result in my terminology, Kant shifted the focus of the problem of the external world from the causal problem to the problem of constitution, because it was this latter problem only that his transcendental philosophy was able to solve. As we will see, Husserl's 'overcoming of epistemology' consists essentially in a repetition of the Kantian move at a somewhat higher level of sophistication.

Globally speaking, one might say that in the course of nineteenth-century German philosophy, the Kantian problem of the thing in itself (*Ding an sich*) gave rise to two opposite types of reactions. German Idealists concluded that if Kant had to assume a thing in itself that was not accessible to empirical science, it had to be accessible to some higher form of cognition in order to make sense at all, that is, to a new idealist metaphysics of reason (*Vernunft*), which identified the thing in itself with the divine (Hegel) or with an irrational will to live (Schopenhauer), or with a will to power (Nietzsche). But since such (theologico-)metaphysical speculations about the world in itself could not be controlled by the apparatus of a preliminary critique of reason or

---

[29]  *Kritik der reinen Vernunft*, B 329: 'von diesem [i.e. the thing in itself] haben wir *keinen* Begriff'. Cf. on the 'scandal of philosophy' KdrV, B xxxix, footnote: 'so bleibt es immer ein Skandal der Philosophie und allgemeinen Menschenvernunft, das Dasein der Dinge außer uns (von denen wir doch den ganzen Stoff zu Erkenntnissen selbst für unseren inneren Sinn her haben) bloß auf *Glauben* annehmen zu müssen, und, wenn es jemand einfällt es zu bezweifeln, ihm keinen genugtuenden Beweis entgegenstellen zu können.'

[30]  *Kritik der reinen Vernunft*, B 274 ff.: 'Widerlegung des Idealismus.'

[31]  Ibid., B xxxix, footnote: 'eine neue Widerlegung des psychologischen *Idealismus*.'

by any other decent methodology, they evoked disgust with philosophy in the scientific community. This explains the strength of the second reaction: to naturalize Kant's transcendental philosophy, and to embrace some form of hypothetical scientific realism, which postulates that the world in itself structurally resembles our phenomenal world and that it is accessible to scientific research. Around 1850, naturalism had become a dominating fashion in European epistemology, which was reinforced by the emancipation of empirical psychology from philosophy. Apart from psychological varieties of naturalism in epistemology, there were around the turn of the century versions of naturalism influenced by contemporary Darwinism, such as Nietzsche's Darwinian fragmentation of Kantian epistemology, and attempts by sociologists such as Émile Durkheim to explain the grip of the Kantian categories on our minds by sociological mechanisms.[32]

# 4. Husserl: From Epistemological Naturalism to Transcendental Phenomenology

Edmund Husserl (1859–1938) was educated as a mathematician in Berlin by celebrities such as Kronecker and Weierstrass, but he switched to philosophy after having met Franz Brentano during a visit to Vienna in 1884. His original training inspired him with a lifelong ambition to turn philosophy into a 'rigorous science' (*strenge Wissenschaft*). Whereas initially it seemed to Husserl that this ambition could be satisfied by philosophical naturalism à la Brentano, he later argued that a transcendental revolution à la Kant was necessary to turn philosophy into a strictly scientific (*wissenschaftlich*) foundational discipline, which it had pretended to be since Plato and Aristotle. At the end of his life he claimed in a messianic mood that his transcendental phenomenology could save European civilization from a crisis provoked by positivist and anti-foundationalist interpretations of science.[33]

---

[32] Cf. the introduction to Émile Durkheim, *Les Formes élémentaires de la vie religieuse* (1912; 5th edn., Paris: Presses Universitaires de France, 2003), 18–28.

[33] Cf. Husserl, *Die Krisis der europäischen Wissenschaften und die transzendentale Phänomenologie* (*Husserliana*, vi).

In both phases of his philosophical career, the naturalist and the transcendental ones, Husserl argued that 'phenomenology' is the foundational discipline or first philosophy, which is able so solve all epistemological problems, but his conception of phenomenology changed drastically quite a number of times, in particular between *Logical Investigations* of 1900/1 (*Logische Untersuchungen*) and *Ideas* I of 1913 (*Ideen zu einer reinen Phänomenologie und phänomenologischen Philosophie*, erstes Buch). What was Husserl's original naturalist conception of philosophy and epistemology? Why did he reject this conception between 1901 and 1913 in favour of a turn to transcendental idealism? And how did he manage to overcome external world epistemology by transcendental phenomenology? These are the questions that have to be answered in the present section.

Following Brentano's lead, Husserl identified phenomenology initially with descriptive psychology. Brentano had argued in *Psychology from the Empirical Point of View* (*Psychologie vom empirischen Standpunkt*, 1874) that the new scientific discipline of 'explanatory' psychology (*erklärende Psychologie*), which aims at providing physiological and other scientific explanations of mental phenomena, must be preceded by a descriptive investigation of mental phenomena, which distinguishes them clearly from physical phenomena and provides a detailed classification of the mental phenomena that psychology is supposed to explain. Inspired by the British empiricist tradition of Locke, Hume, and John Stuart Mill, Brentano argued that such a preliminary descriptive psychology (*beschreibende Psychologie*) or phenomenology also has a foundational function for ethics and mathematics. By elucidating the basic concepts of mathematics, which allegedly are 'abstracted' from mental phenomena, descriptive psychology can render self-evident the a priori mathematical axioms that are postulated by mathematicians for their deductive derivations of theorems. In other words, descriptive psychology was conceived of as the foundational discipline for mathematics, in particular for the theory of numbers, because it studies the phenomena from which mathematical concepts are abstracted.

It was this conception of phenomenology that Husserl endorsed in his first book *Philosophy of Arithmetic* (*Philosophie der Arithmetik*) of 1891.[34] If numbers can be conceived of as properties of sets, the question arises as to what binds together into a set the entities that are the members of that set. Husserl argued that this binding link consists of a special kind of

---

[34] *Husserliana*, xii.

intentional mental act, the 'collecting act' expressed in the conjunction 'and'. He also held that concepts of specific numbers are abstracted from, and can be elucidated by reflecting upon, such collecting mental acts. Since this intuitive elucidation of number concepts by descriptive psychology is possible for very small positive numbers only, Husserl's phenomenological foundation of arithmetic immediately led to another question: how can we justify all other mathematical concepts and operations, such as those of large numbers or of the number zero, which are 'merely symbolical' in the sense that they cannot be elucidated by phenomenological reflection or intuition?

Although Frege in his trenchant review of *Philosophy of Arithmetic* partly overlooked and partly misunderstood the subtleties of descriptive psychology—he did not even mention the crucial concept of intentionality, which Husserl took over from Brentano—he raised pertinent objections that may have triggered Husserl's first transformation of Brentano's phenomenology in *Logical Investigations*.[35] Did Husserl's account of arithmetic not threaten the objectivity of mathematics, since numbers allegedly consist in mental acts of collecting, whereas both Frege and Husserl assumed that mental acts are accessible by reflection only to the person who performs them? In his caustic critique of Husserl's psychological account of numbers, Frege wrote that by reading Husserl's book, he could measure 'the extent of the havoc wreaked upon logic by the intrusion of psychology into this domain', and he argued that the objectivity of mathematics could only be understood by postulating numbers as entities that exist independently of human thought.[36] But this mathematical Platonism raises other perennial problems: how can humans who exist in space and time have knowledge of the objective entities of mathematics, which allegedly exist 'outside' of space and time? Similar questions can be raised when in the wake of Bolzano one posits objective propositional contents (*Sätze an sich*) as the objects of logic.

It is typical for the difference between Frege, who primarily was a mathematical logician, and Husserl, who primarily was a philosophical mind, that these 'crucial doubts as to how the objectivity of mathematics and of all scientific disciplines can be reconciled with a psychological account of logic' drove Husserl to 'general critical reflections upon . . . the relation between the subjectivity of knowing and the objectivity of the content of knowledge'.[37]

---

[35] Husserl refers to Frege in a note to §45 of his *Prolegomena zur reinen Logik*.
[36] G. Frege, 'Rezension von E. G. Husserl, *Philosophie der Arithmetik. I*', *Zeitschrift für Philosophie und philosophische Kritik* 103 (1894), 313–32.
[37] Husserl, *Logische Untersuchungen, Vorwort* 1900 (my translation).

Husserl's epistemological ruminations on logic were published in 1900/1 as *Logical Investigations* (*Logische Untersuchungen*) in two volumes: a long introductory volume (1900) and a second volume containing six loosely connected investigations (1901).[38]

In the first volume, called *Prolegomena to Pure Logic*, Husserl staged the most extensive attack ever written on what he called 'psychologism' in logic. Surprisingly, he defined psychologism quite narrowly as the view that the laws of logic and mathematics are a subset of contingent psychological laws of thinking, a view he had never adhered to himself, since he had been a follower of Hume and Brentano rather than of John Stuart Mill. Husserl argued that psychologism in this empiricist sense implies scepticism, for if the laws of logic are a subset of empirical psychological laws, one actually performed formal fallacy would refute the relevant law of logic. Husserl now held that the objectivity of knowledge can be rescued only if we accept Platonism in logic and mathematics (cf. the second investigation). It should be stressed, however, that Husserl's Platonism differs from Plato's Platonism. The difference may be explained by the fact that Plato developed his Platonism initially in order to account for the objectivity of geometry, while Husserl focused on arithmetic and logic. Whereas for Plato ideal objects are 'more perfect' than their mundane instances, just as a geometrical circle is said to be perfectly circular in contradistinction to round material objects, such a difference of 'perfection' does not make sense for numbers, so Husserl denied it.[39]

Contrarily to what one might expect, the acceptance of Platonism in the philosophy of logic and mathematics did not convince Husserl that he had to abandon phenomenology as a foundational discipline. On the contrary, the introduction of Platonism triggered a first fundamental transformation of phenomenology or descriptive psychology into what Husserl later called an 'eidetic' discipline (*eidos* = platonic entity). In *Logical Investigations*, Husserl conceived of platonic entities primarily as a-temporal and non-spatial 'ideal essences' or 'ideal species' (types) of tokens that might exist in the spatio-temporal world. Platonic numbers, for example, are types or ideal species of equinumerous collections of entities that may be in space and time, such as the set of my fingers. In order to get acquainted with these platonic objects or types,

---

[38]   Page references to the first edition of 1900–1 (Halle a. S.: Max Niemeyer), are labelled as LU A and to the second edition of 1913/21 as LU B.

[39]   Cf. *Logische Untersuchungen*, vol. ii, first investigation, §32.

Husserl argued, we have to perceive (or imagine) some of their instances or tokens, and then to perform an 'idealizing abstraction' or *Wesenserschauung*, which he later called the 'eidetic reduction'. If the tokens are mental, the perception required for *Wesensschau* is a psychological or phenomenological reflection.

For example, Husserl thought in 1900/1 that the 'ideal science' of 'pure logic' is an investigation of the forms of platonic propositions (*Sätze an sich*), which are types of tokens that consist in the mental contents of psychological acts of judging, so that we can only get to know these platonic propositions by first reflecting on our mental acts of judging and then performing *Wesensschau*. This is one reason why, in spite of Husserl's Platonism, logic should still be founded by descriptive psychology or phenomenology, and why phenomenology can be an eidetic discipline, which yields a priori truths. Since Husserl generalized his notion of ideal essences, he came to the conclusion that we might intuit ideal essences or ideal types of *any* token whatsoever, so that *Wesensschau* permits us to acquire synthetic a priori knowledge of any domain of objects. Husserl's early followers in Munich or Göttingen were delighted by this generalized essentialism, because it enabled them to argue against logical positivists that an a priori foundation of all empirical sciences was possible after all, and this was also Husserl's later conviction. Each empirical discipline should be founded by an a priori 'eidetic regional ontology', Husserl argued in 1913, and Heidegger still endorsed this view in *Being and Time* of 1927.[40]

These notions of eidetic reduction and of a priori regional ontologies do not yet explain why Husserl held in 1913 that a completely novel descriptive discipline called 'transcendental phenomenology' is the foundational science (*Wissenschaft*) *par excellence*, a first philosophy that is even foundational with respect to eidetic regional ontologies. On the contrary, it seems that Husserl's essentialism would relegate a more modest place to eidetic phenomenology: as a regional ontology of empirical psychology. How could Husserl transform phenomenology in the sense of an eidetic descriptive psychology into transcendental phenomenology? In order to understand this transformation, we have to zoom in on Husserl's notion of intentionality and on his philosophy of perception. Let me start, however, with a final observation on Husserl's philosophy of arithmetic and logic of 1900/1.

In the first volume of *Logical Investigations* of 1900, Husserl still held that concepts of numbers are abstracted by an 'idealizing abstraction' from

---

[40]  Cf. Husserl, *Ideen* I, § §1–17 (*Husserliana*, iii/1); Heidegger, *Sein und Zeit*, §3.

mental acts of collecting or counting.[41] The only difference with regard to *Philosophy of Arithmetic* of 1891 consisted in a new theory of abstraction. Abstraction was now conceived of as *Wesensschau* or eidetic intuition, and not as a mere concentration of attention on some aspects of the perceived token, as Husserl thought in 1891. This change in the theory of abstraction apparently sufficed to guarantee the objectivity of mathematics, at least if ideal essences are intersubjectively accessible. But in the second volume of 1901 (sixth investigation), Husserl argued that the 'origin' (*Ursprung*) of the abstraction of the concepts of number has to be different from the origin of the abstraction of the concept of counting, since these concepts are distinct. In other words, number-tokens are not mental acts of counting but objective sets of entities, whereas what binds together these entities is not a mental act but an objective 'categorial form', which is neither mental nor physical. The same holds, Husserl now thought, for the concepts of logical constants such as the copula 'is' or the conjunction 'and', since he assumed that all elements of language have a referential function. They too are abstracted from categorial copulative or conjunctive forms that hold between objects or between states of affairs. What are these categorial forms and how do they arise? Surely, if they are neither mental nor material, they cannot be accounted for by the sciences of nature.[42] And if they are not mental, why should it still be phenomenology that studies them?

Husserl's answer to these questions is as follows. The objective categorial forms, the ideal types of which are studied by logic and mathematics, are indeed objective, but they do not belong to the natural world. Rather, they are free formations of empirical contents that can be accounted for by a phenomenological analysis of consciousness, because they are 'constituted' by a special type of intentional mental act, which Husserl calls 'categorial intuition'. Categorial intuitions are 'founded' acts in Husserl's technical sense that they essentially cannot exist without other mental phenomena, such as acts of sensory perception or of imagination (cf. third investigation). With regard to each mental act, we should distinguish between its strictly psychological or 'really' (*reell*) immanent content, as Husserl calls it, and its

---

[41] LU A, I, §46, pp. 170–1: 'Die Zahl Fünf ist nicht meine oder irgend jemandes Anderen Zählung der Fünf, es ist auch nicht meine oder eines Anderen Vorstellung der Fünf. In letzterer Hinsicht ist sie möglicher *Gegenstand* von Vorstellungsacten, in ersterer ist sie die ideale *Species*, die in gewissen Zählungsacten ihre concreten *Einzelfälle* hat—ähnlich wie etwa die Farbenspecies Roth in Acten des Rothempfindens' (the italics are Husserl's; this passage has been changed in the second edition).

[42] *Logische Untersuchungen*, ii, sixth investigation, §§40–66.

'intentional' content or intentional object, and Husserl holds that intentional objects are constituted by 'objectifying' interpretations or apperceptions of other contents. For example, a set consisting of empirical objects a, b, and c, is constituted by first perceiving these objects and then performing a collecting mental act that constitutes the categorial object {a *and* b *and* c}.

This analysis of intentionality, which was a modification of Brentano's original account, triggered a second major revolution in the notion of phenomenology, which Husserl explained more thoroughly in five lectures of 1907 published posthumously under the title *The Idea of Phenomenology* (*Die Idee der Phänomenologie*).[43] Husserl now conceived of phenomenology as 'correlational analysis', that is, as an analysis of intentional objects-as-constituted-in-mental-acts and of mental acts-as-constituting-intentional objects. Like Kant, whose theoretical works he studied thoroughly at this time, Husserl claimed that the epistemological mysteries of the relation between the knowing subject and the known object could all be resolved by an analysis of the constitution of objects in a network of constituting mental acts, such as the constitution of categorial entities like sets by founded acts of categorial intuition. In other words, even external world epistemology should adopt the methods of phenomenology, and focus on the act—object correlation by means of an 'epistemological reduction'. Because 'higher' mental acts, such as acts of categorial perception, are founded upon basic mental acts, such as acts of sensory perception, it is to Husserl's analysis of sensory perception that we should turn in order to understand his basic solution to the epistemological problem of the relation between the knowing subject and the object known.

Many commentators have concluded from Husserl's celebrated appendix on image- and sign-theories of perception in the fifth investigation that in *Logical Investigations* Husserl was a naive realist with regard to sensory perception.[44] But such an interpretation is mistaken and it overlooks Husserl's theory of perception and his phenomenological stance. What Husserl argues in the appendix is that theories of perception which claim that 'in' consciousness there is a sign or an image of an 'external' object, fly in the face of a phenomenological analysis of the constitution of signs or images. In order to interpret a given object, such as a name printed on paper or a painting on canvas, as a sign or an image of something else, we first have to perceive

---

[43]  *Die Idee der Phänomenologie, Husserliana,* ii.
[44]  *Logische Untersuchungen,* ii, fifth investigation, 'Beilage zu den Paragraphen 11 und 20'.

this object (the printed name, the painting) by an act of sensory perception. In other words, consciousness of signs or images is 'founded' (in Husserl's technical sense) on other mental acts such as acts of sensory perception, so that interpreting sensory perception in terms of signs or images would result in an infinite regress.[45] Whereas in sensory perception the perceived object is 'bodily given' as 'the object itself', the sign or image is interpreted as a sign or image 'of something else', and this is due to a mental act of 'apperception' or interpretation *sui generis*. Husserl stresses that if it exists, the intentional object of a sensory perception is identical with the real and 'external' object perceived, and that it is absurd (*widersinnig*) to distinguish between these two.

Although these phenomenological observations sound like naive realism, such a realism was not Husserl's view in the *Logical Investigations* of 1900/1. This is shown both by Husserl's phenomenological analysis of sensory perception and by his division of labour between phenomenology and explanatory psychology. Like the philosophers of the scientific revolution and their nineteenth-century successors such as von Helmholtz and Brentano, Husserl adhered to a projective theory of perception. Mental acts of sensory perception, Husserl argued in his sixth *Logical Investigation*, consist of a number of different ingredients. The two most important ingredients are a series of perceptual sensations (*Empfindungen*) such as colour- or sound-sensations, which according to Husserl are non-intentional 'really immanent' mental contents, and an 'objectifying interpretation' or 'apperception' of these immanent contents, which accounts for the fact that an object appears to us, such as an inkpot, for example. In other words, this inkpot as an object that appears perceptually to us is constituted by an objectifying interpretation of sensations which are really immanent in consciousness.[46] In the first edition of *Logical Investigations*, Husserl even draws the conclusion that the inkpot that we perceive is constituted out of 'the same stuff' as our subjective sensations, although of course we should not say with Berkeley that properties of appearing physical objects *are* sensations, because sensations are elements of the stream of consciousness, whereas properties of appearing objects are not. Husserl also says that the inkpot which we perceive belongs to the *phenomenal world* (*erscheinende Welt*).[47]

---

[45] Husserl added this latter argument in the second edition of *Logische Untersuchungen* (1913).

[46] 6th *Logische Untersuchung*, §6.

[47] Ibid., Beilage, §5 (LU A II, pp. 706–7): 'Man mag mit Recht sagen, daß die Dinge der *erscheinenden* Welt nach allen ihren Beschaffenheiten aus demselben Stoff constituirt sind, den wir als

This view conforms to the tradition of representational theories of perception, which goes back to the seventeenth century (cf. section 2, above). In mental acts of perception, a phenomenal world is constituted, but this phenomenal world is not identical with the real physical world, which causes sensations in consciousness by impinging upon our senses. Of course the sceptical question whether such a real physical world exists cannot be answered by phenomenology, which merely studies descriptively our mental life in correlation with the objects constituted by intentional acts. At best, it can be answered by explanatory psychology, as naturalist epistemologists claimed, or perhaps by metaphysics. However, since Husserl held in 1901 that epistemology should be a presuppositionless discipline, which restricts its investigations to the phenomenological domain of Cartesian certainty, he was landed in an epistemological impasse with regard to the causal problem of the external world. This impasse was to be resolved by Husserl's transcendental revolution against naturalism and by his deconstruction of the causal problem.

In an important essay of 1911 called 'Philosophy as a rigorous science' (*Philosophie als strenge Wissenschaft*), Husserl argued that philosophical naturalism is shipwrecked by two crucial problems. First, naturalizing the ideas and norms of mathematics or logic has the sceptical implications which Husserl exposed in his *Prolegomena* to *Logical Investigations*. Second, naturalizing consciousness leads to a paradox in external world epistemology, which was typical for Brentano and perhaps also for Husserl's own position in *Logical Investigations*. All scientific disciplines, including psychology, are naive concerning the existence of the natural world, of which they investigate different aspects. Psychology holds, for example, that mental phenomena occur in (e.g. pain) or are activities of (e.g. perception) humans and other animals, and depend causally on physical processes in human or animal bodies. However, external world epistemology raises sceptical questions with regard to the very existence of material bodies in general: how can we justify the assumption that our perceptual sensations are caused by a material world 'in itself', which exists independently of consciousness? Clearly, such sceptical questions can be answered neither by phenomenology in the sense of a descriptive eidetic psychology, nor by explanatory psychology, as Brentano had thought, since explanatory psychology already presupposes that the mental depends upon

Empfinduungen zum Bewußtseinsinhalt rechnen' etc. This passage has been changed in the second edition.

the physical: 'all psychological determinations are *eo ipso* psychophysical'. In other words, naturalized epistemology presupposes what it has to vindicate, so that it moves in a logical circle.

It follows that if phenomenology aims at solving the problems of external world epistemology, it should be a 'presuppositionless' discipline which 'brackets' all implicit assumptions as to the existence of a mind-independent world. But such 'bracketing' (*Einklammerung*) or this phenomenological *epoche*, as Husserl came to call it, necessitates a third and last transformation of the very notion of phenomenology, if at least phenomenology should be able to solve, or to overcome, the problems of epistemology. This third transformation is the transcendental revolution which Husserl tried to explain in the 'Phenomenological Fundamental Meditation' (*Die phänomenologische Fundamentalbetrachtung*) of *Ideas* I, published in 1913. Because his pupils could not follow him, he attempted to elucidate the transcendental turn again and again in all his later books by sketching different 'roads' to transcendental phenomenology.

Husserl's argument in the *Fundamental Meditation* starts with a description of what he calls our 'natural attitude'. Living in this natural attitude, we never question the existence of a mind-independent world, which we perceive and in which we move and act as embodied beings. But Husserl claims that we may change our natural attitude drastically by reflecting upon, instead of enacting, the implicit 'general thesis' that a mind-independent world exists. Performing such a 'phenomenological reduction' we come to reflect upon the manner in which the intentional objects of our mental acts are constituted in consciousness, such as material bodies in our life-world, other minds and intersubjectivity, categorial entities such as sets-as-tokens, the theoretical entities postulated by physics, social institutions, and the platonic entities of arithmetic, logic, or geometry. Distinguishing between the objects of higher or 'founded' constitutions, such as sets or objects of theoretical physics, and the objects of basic constitutions, such as the material things in our life-world or our own stream of consciousness, Husserl focuses upon the latter, and argues that there is a crucial difference between the manner in which our own mental life is 'given' to us and the manner in which material bodies are given to us in sensory perception.

If we feel pain, for example, the phenomenon of pain is given to us adequately in the sense that the pain is nothing more than what we in fact feel. Expressed in Husserl's phenomenological jargon, there are no 'transcending apperceptions', which posit more than we are aware of, so that it does not make sense to doubt the existence of such a mental phenomenon.[48] With regard to material bodies, including our own body, the situation is very different. They are always perceived from a certain point of view, in 'adumbrations' (*Abschattungen*) so to say, and it is a priori clear that we can never have a complete series of adumbrations of one particular material object. This means that the perception of a material body typically is a temporal series of perceptions, merged into each other by a unifying apperception, which always transcends what is perceptually given, because infinitely many more perceptions of the same object are possible in principle. As a result, we may always doubt to some extent the existence of a material body, because we can imagine at any moment that in the future the series of perceptions of this body becomes incoherent or even chaotic, so that no material body can be constituted any more. Husserl concludes in a Cartesian manner that our own mental life is given to us with absolute certainty, whereas the existence of bodies and other 'external' entities always remains hypothetical.[49]

Since in *Ideas* I Husserl identifies the adumbrations of material bodies with the sensations or 'hyletic data' of the theory of perception he held in *Logical Investigations*, his analysis of sense perception implies the thought-experiment of the destruction of the world (*Weltvernichtung*), which he explains in section 49. The stream of sensations in our consciousness might be such that no unifying perceptual constitution of bodies is possible at all. In such a case, our stream of consciousness would exist, although the (phenomenal) material world would not. This eidetic possibility proves, according to Husserl, that consciousness is ontologically independent from matter, because something of type A is ontologically dependent ('founded') upon something else of type B only if, essentially, an A cannot exist without a B.[50] In other words, consciousness is a substance in the Cartesian sense that 'nulla "re" indiget ad existendum', whereas the material world, including our own body, is an intentional correlate of consciousness, which essentially depends upon it,

---

[48] Of course, this is not entirely correct, because we feel pain in a part of our body, so that, living in the natural attitude, we interpret our pains by a 'transcending apperception' which posits our body. But in phenomenological reflection, we 'bracket' this transcending apperception.

[49] This sense of 'hypothetical', in which the existence of bodies given in perception always remains hypothetical, differs from the sense in which a 'thing in itself', posited as the cause of our sensations, would be hypothetical.

[50] One might object that our conscious life depends upon bodily processes, and that this dependence cannot be accounted for by an analysis of sensory perception. Although Husserl acknowledges these two ways in which conscious life is 'interwoven' (*Verflechtung; Ideen* I, §39) with the material world, he seems to reduce the dependence of consciousness on an animal body to the sensory perception of our own body.

because it is constituted by conferring an objective sense or 'noema' on a series of 'really immanent' sensations.

According to Husserl, this idealist conclusion not only refutes the naturalist interpretation of consciousness as essentially depending upon a body. It also necessitates a transcendental reinterpretation of the stream of consciousness in which the external world is constituted. Of course, psychological idealism would be absurd, because according to psychology our mental phenomena depend causally and ontologically upon bodily processes, so that they must be part and parcel of the constituted world. That is to say, psychological idealism is landed in what Husserl later called the 'paradox of human subjectivity', according to which the entire world is constituted by one of its minute mental parts.

The solution to this paradox is a 'transcendental reduction' of consciousness, which reinterprets it as a fundamental transcendental region, by which everything else is constituted, including our own psychological consciousness. Like Kant's Copernican revolution, Husserl's transcendental turn implied a distinction between the transcendental subject, which constitutes the phenomenal world by its transcending apperceptions, and psychological or empirical subjects, which are dependent parts or aspects of animal bodies in this phenomenal world. Like Kant, Husserl combined transcendental idealism with empirical or psychological realism. But since Husserl as the founder of the phenomenological school had to compete with the neo-Kantians as rival philosophical schools, he insisted on differences between his and Kant's transcendental philosophy, five of which are important here.

First, whereas Kant developed his transcendental philosophy by constructing 'transcendental arguments', which merely *postulate* mental mechanisms in the transcendental subject in order to explain the possibility of synthetic a priori judgements, Husserl claimed that his transcendental reduction opens up the 'field' of transcendental consciousness to a specific type of empirical investigation, so that the transcendental structures are 'really given' in phenomenological reflection, instead of merely postulated.[51] This gave transcendental phenomenology a clear Cartesian advantage of evidence and certainty over neo-Kantianism, so Husserl argued.

Second, such an empirically transcendental investigation could yield synthetic a priori results if one also performed the eidetic reduction and described the essences of the constituting activities of our transcendental ego. Kant had failed to discover this eidetic reduction, so that he lacked a reliable method for

---

[51] Cf. *Ideen* I, §24.

discovering the essence of transcendental structures and the a priori principles of the empirical sciences.

Third, since Kant did not have at his disposal the notion of intentionality, he confused the 'real' contents of consciousness with its 'intentional' contents, or, in other words, what is part of the stream of consciousness (sensations, intentional mental acts) with intentional objects constituted by consciousness. As a consequence, neo-Kantians could not develop what Husserl called a correlational analysis (*Korrelationsanalyse*), whereas it is only such an analysis that is able to solve the problems concerning the relation between the knowing subject and the known object. For example, Husserl argued that in order to discover in what 'sense' numbers or the objects of geometry exist, in contradistinction to the 'sense' in which material objects exist, we have to study phenomenologically the different 'noetic—noematic correlations' between such objects and the complex interweavings of their constituting mental acts.

One will object to Husserl at this point that phenomenology can only solve the problems of *constitution* with regard to the phenomenal world, but not the *causal* problem of the external world, which is concerned with the relation between the world in itself (*Ding an sich*) and the sensations in transcendental consciousness. As we have seen, the problem of the 'thing in itself' led to a paradox in Kant's transcendental philosophy, and there is a similar paradox in Husserl's phenomenology. On the one hand, Husserl claimed that phenomenology could solve all epistemological problems, whereas on the other hand, the causal problem is not accessible to his correlational analysis of constitution. Like Fichte and many neo-Kantians, Husserl aimed at overcoming or deconstructing radically the causal problem of the external world, and this is the fourth difference between Husserl's transcendental phenomenology and Kant's own version of transcendental philosophy.

Already in *Logical Investigations*, Husserl reinterpreted the notion of a thing-in-itself, arguing that all legitimate epistemological concepts have to be constructed on the basis of phenomenological analysis. The thing-in-itself in this new sense is the intentional object of a perception in which no transcending apperception remains perceptually unfulfilled. In the case of a physical object, such an 'adequate' perception would imply an infinite series of adumbrations, so that perceiving a thing-in-itself in this case is an unattainable 'ideal in the Kantian sense'. But, as Husserl observes in §15b of the sixth investigation, this thing in itself is not 'totally different' from the phenomenal thing that appears to us, for it is the limiting idea of that very same thing as adequately perceived.[52] Similarly, Husserl defined the world in itself à la Peirce as the intentional correlate of the ideal community of scientists, that is, of the community of scientists that possesses complete knowledge.[53] In *Ideas* I, this phenomenological notion of a thing in itself is taken to be the only legitimate notion. As a consequence, the causal problem of whether the sensations in transcendental consciousness are caused by an independently existing thing in itself cannot be formulated any more, and the phenomenal world is the only world there is. As Husserl now says, the Kantian notion of a thing in itself is an absurdity, or a 'mythical conception'.[54] It follows that the causal problem of the external world is a pseudo-problem, so that external world epistemology in the sense of the causal problem has been overcome or deconstructed.

As Husserl stressed in *Ideas* I and ever after, the mysteries of the subject—object relation can only be clarified by transcendental phenomenology, which studies the constitution of objects by transcendental consciousness. Since the constitution of objects of sensory perception is an objectifying interpretation of immanent sensations, these objects are 'senses' or 'noemata' projected by transcendental consciousness, so that the world is ontologically dependent on transcendental consciousness.[55] Of course, this 'transcendental idealism' also holds for objects of higher constitutions, such as the theoretical entities of physics or the objects of mathematics, since all higher constitutions depend upon the basic constitution of the 'life-world'. Accordingly, Husserl's transcendental revolution is not only a reinterpretation of consciousness as transcendental consciousness; it is also an ontological reinterpretation of the natural world, which now turns out to be an intentional correlate of transcendental consciousness, depending ontologically upon the latter. Whereas according to naturalism, psychological consciousness ontologically depends upon material bodies, the transcendental reduction radically reverses this relation and reinterprets its terms.[56] As Husserl stressed in *Cartesian Meditations* of 1931, 'Only those who misunderstand the most profound sense of the intentional method or of the transcendental reduction or even of both, may want to separate phenomenology from transcendental idealism.'[57]

---

[52]  This is §14b in the second edition; cf. §§37 and 65.

[53]  LU A II, fifth investigation, §7, p. 337: 'die Welt der (ideal vollendeten) Wissenschaft, die Welt an sich' (§7 has been deleted in the second edition).

[54]  *Ideen* I, §52; cf. *Die Krisis*, §30, and *Husserliana*, vii. 274.

[55]  Cf. *Ideen* I, §§47–55.      [56]  Ibid. 30–2.

[57]  *Cartesianische Meditationen, Husserliana* I, 2nd edn., p. 119. I have elaborated this interpretation in 'Transcendental Idealism', in Barry Smith and David Woodruff Smith (eds.), *The Cambridge Companion to Husserl* (Cambridge: Cambridge University Press, 1995), 239–322. Cf. for more

By eliminating the causal problem of the external world, Husserl was able to avoid the contradictions implicit in the Kantian conception of a *Ding an sich*. Yet Husserl thought that there remains a deep question concerning perceptual sensations at the transcendental level, which the eidetic constitution analysis of phenomenology is unable to answer. How should we explain the contingent fact that the transcendental stream of sensations is not completely chaotic, but allows for the constitution of an ordered empirical world? There seems to be an immanent teleology here, which cries out for an explanation. Husserl speculated that the coherence of the transcendental stream of consciousness should be explained by a 'theological principle', that is, a God, who is neither a mundane entity in the world nor completely immanent in transcendental consciousness. In an appendix to section 51 of *Ideas* I, Husserl suggests that although God cannot be causally responsible for the sensations in transcendental consciousness, His 'transcendence' must be accessible to intuition and to theoretical reason. This is a fifth major difference between Husserl and Kant. As against Kant, Husserl rehabilitated the idea of a theoretical metaphysics of God, based upon a transcendental version of Berkeley's argument from design. Whereas he treated the theme of a theist metaphysics discreetly, Husserl's later messianic vision of phenomenology as the saviour of western civilization cannot be fully understood without taking into account the fact that for Husserl transcendental idealism gave access to God and to a new transcendental notion of immortality.[58]

## 5. HEIDEGGER: FROM EPISTEMOLOGY TO FUNDAMENTAL ONTOLOGY

No continental philosopher of the twentieth century launched a more radical attack on external world epistemology than Martin Heidegger in *Being and Time*. In section 43a Heidegger paraphrased Kant's dictum according to which 'it always remains a scandal to philosophy and to human reason in general that the existence of things outside us ... must be accepted merely on *faith*

---

references to Husserl's works: Vittorio de Palma, 'Ist Husserls Phänomenologie ein transzendentaler Idealismus?', *Husserl Studies* 21 (2005), 183–206.

[58] For Husserl's proof of the temporal infinity of the transcendental stream of consciousness, cf. *Ideen* I, §81: 'Aber der Erlebnisstrom kann nicht anfangen und enden.'

and that if anyone thinks it good to doubt their existence, we are unable to counter his doubts by any satisfactory proof.'[59] Heidegger wrote instead:

The 'scandal of philosophy' is not that this proof has yet to be given, *but that such proofs are expected and attempted again and again.* Such expectations, aims, and demands arise from an ontologically inadequate way of starting with *that entity* independently *of which* and 'outside' *of which* a 'world' is to be proved as present.[60]

Heidegger claimed that the problem of the external world arises from an inadequate ontological conception of the human subject and of the world in which human beings live. However, if external world epistemology is based upon mistaken ontological conceptions, epistemology cannot be 'first philosophy', as many philosophers around 1900 had thought. Ontological issues must be more fundamental, and Heidegger argued that a 'fundamental ontology' was needed, which raises what he called 'the question of being', or the question in which sense entities may be said to exist.[61] A more adequate ontological analysis of human existence and of the world in which humans live will bring to light, so Heidegger thought, that the questions whether a world exists and whether we can prove that it does, are *meaningless* if raised by human beings who live in the world.[62]

This conclusion that the traditional problem of the external world is *meaningless* had already been stated by Husserl and it was also argued for by Rudolf Carnap in his *Pseudoproblems in Philosophy* (*Scheinprobleme in der Philosophie*) of 1928. Compared to Heidegger's analysis, however, Husserl's and Carnap's attempts to overcome traditional epistemology were superficial. Carnap eliminated the problem of the external world from a scientific and empiricist perspective. In 1928 he argued that statements can only be meaningful in the sense of having a factual content if experiential conditions can be specified under which they can be called true and conditions under which they can be called false. Since such experiential conditions cannot be

---

[59] *Kritik der reinen Vernunft*, B xxxix.

[60] *Sein und Zeit* (Halle a. S.: Max Niemeyer Verlag, 1927), 205: 'Der 'Skandal der Philosophie' besteht nicht darin, daß dieser Beweis bislang noch aussteht, sondern *darin, daß solche Beweise immer wieder erwartet und versucht werden.* Dergleichen Erwartungen, Absichten und Forderungen erwachsen einer ontologisch unzureichenden Ansetzung *dessen, davon* unabhängig und 'außerhalb' eine 'Welt' als vorhandene bewiesen werden soll' (Heidegger's italics).

[61] Cf. for an analysis of the different meanings of Heidegger's question of being Herman Philipse, *Heidegger's Philosophy of Being: A Critical Interpretation* (Princeton: Princeton University Press, 1998).

[62] *Sein und Zeit*, 202: 'Die Frage, ob überhaupt eine Welt sei und ob deren Sein bewiesen werden könne, ist als Frage, die das *Dasein* als In-der-Welt-sein stellt – und wer anders sollte sie stellen? – ohne Sinn' (Heidegger's italics).

indicated in the case of the problem of the external world, this problem is empirically meaningless, and its traditional solutions such as idealism or realism lack factual content.[63] However, Carnap did not criticize the traditional physicalist conception of the world or the representational theory of perception, which produce the inescapable urge to raise the problem of the external world again and again. For this reason, his empiricist dismissal of the problem remains unsatisfactory.

Husserl probed deeper than Carnap. Like Heidegger, he held that the problem of the external world is due to a mistaken ontological interpretation of the knowing subject and its objects. Husserl argued that if we reinterpret the knowing subject as transcendental consciousness and the world as its intentional correlate or noema, the causal problem becomes meaningless, whereas all problems of constitution can be solved by transcendental phenomenology. But, as Heidegger correctly observed, the account of the 'natural attitude' with which Husserl started his argument for transcendental idealism was still contaminated by the theoretical ontology of the scientific revolution, and his transcendental idealism was not essentially different from Kant's. If we really want to develop a natural conception of ourselves and the world, Heidegger thought, we should reject the representational theory of perception and we should also reject the idea that at the deepest level of analysis the subject is related to the world primarily by perception, as Husserl had assumed. A conception of ourselves and of the world is needed which is really 'natural', that is, adequate to the mode of existence of human beings, or *Dasein*, as Heidegger called it. Since Heidegger held that such a natural conception of human life had not been developed in the philosophical tradition from Aristotle to Kant and beyond, he wanted to stage an ontological revolution in our self-conception and the concomitant conception of the world, focusing upon the crucial notion of temporality.

This revolutionary ambition explains the original set-up of Heidegger's most important book, *Being and Time*. As he explains in section 8, the book had to consist of two parts, each comprising three divisions (*Abschnitte*): a first, constructive part in which the new ontology of *Dasein* and its temporality

---

[63] Carnap's dismissal of the problem of the external world as a pseudo-problem survived his liberalization of the empirical meaning criterion in his later works. In 'Empiricism, Semantics, and Ontology' of 1950, Carnap argued that the problem is an illegitimate confusion between empirical questions of existence internal to a linguistic framework and external questions about the pragmatic efficiency of a linguistic framework. Cf. Rudolf Carnap, *Meaning and Necessity*, 2nd edn. (Chicago: University of Chicago Press, 1956), Supplement A.

is developed, and a second, destructive part in which the traditional ontologies of Kant, Descartes, and Aristotle are critically analysed. In 1927, Heidegger published as *Sein und Zeit* merely one-third of the work as originally planned, that is, the first two divisions of Part One on the ontological analysis of *Dasein*. The remaining four divisions never appeared, although one can reconstruct their contents from Heidegger's lectures and from other publications such as his book on Kant of 1929. Here, I focus on the published part of *Being and Time*.

Whereas Descartes' ontology had been inspired primarily by his physics, Heidegger argued that in order to develop an adequate ontology of human *Dasein* one should not be influenced by scientific conceptions. Instead, one should try to explicate everyday human self-understanding by an interpretative method called 'hermeneutic phenomenology', and replace the traditional categories of philosophy by new concepts that capture structural features of human existence, so-called 'existentialia'. In a preparatory analysis of *Dasein* (first division), Heidegger sketched the basic structure of human existence, called being-in-the-world, and in the second division he developed its temporal dimension, a clear awareness of which he saw as a prerequisite for raising 'the question of being' properly, probably in a religious sense.[64] In order to understand why Heidegger held that the epistemological problem of the external world is meaningless, we do not need to go into the details of his ontological analysis of *Dasein*, which are intricate and not always easy to understand. It will suffice to explain briefly Heidegger's idea that human existence essentially is existence-in-the-world.

If in circumstances of everyday life we try to explain to someone else (or to ourselves) who we are, we will say things such as that we are born in a specific city or country, that our parents were Mr and Mrs so-and-so, that we went to a particular school or university, that we live at some determinate place, or that we have some specific job. This means that our everyday self-conception inevitably refers to 'the world', that is, to places, institutions, other people, and so on. However, if this is the case, it is logically impossible that we ourselves exist and are truly who we are whereas the world does not exist, so that the epistemological question of the existence of the external world cannot be raised

---

[64] Cf. Herman Philipse, 'Heidegger's Grand (Pascalian) Strategy: On the Problem of Reinterpreting the Existentialia', in *Metaphysics: The Proceedings of the Twentieth World Congress of Philosophy*, ii (Bowling Green, KV: Philosophy Documentation Center, 1999). Cf. also my 'Heideggers philosophisch-religiöse (pascalsche) Strategie. Über das Problem der Umdeutung der Existenzialien', *Zeitschrift für philosophische Forschung* 57 (December 2003), 571–88.

by us as 'beings-in-the-world'. This is what Heidegger argues in section 43a of *Being and Time*. It should be stressed that the world about which Heidegger speaks here is not at all the world as elementary particle physics conceives it. Rather, the world in which human beings live is a meaningful horizon of human dwellings and landscapes, of institutions and of human history.

When we compare Carnap's and Heidegger's attempts to overcome epistemology, we might say that their perspectives are diametrically opposite. Whereas Carnap attempted to overcome epistemology from an empiricist and scientific perspective, Heidegger opted for the perspective of everyday human existence. Although both Carnap and Heidegger came to the conclusion that the problem of the external world is meaningless, their arguments turn out to be completely different. In choosing the perspective of 'everydayness', Heidegger's approach rather resembles that of G. E. Moore in his papers 'A Defence of Common Sense' (1925) and 'Proof of the External World' (1939). But whereas Moore argued from the perspective of common sense that a proof of the external world is trivial and easy—it would suffice to hold up one's hands and point to each of them saying 'Here is one hand'—Heidegger held that from a similar perspective such proofs are nonsensical, as is the demand that they should be given at all. In this respect, Heidegger's analysis should be preferred to that of Moore, and it coheres with Wittgenstein's criticisms of Moore in *On Certainty*.[65]

However, both Heidegger's and Moore's views on the problem of the external world are open to a similar objection of an *ignoratio elenchi*. If my analysis of the origin of the problem in section 2, above, is correct, the problem of the external world did not arise from an everyday perspective. Rather, it was triggered by a scientific analysis of the structure of matter and of sense perception. This was also the view of Bertrand Russell, who wrote in *An Inquiry into Meaning and Truth* of 1940:

The observer, when he seems to himself to be observing a stone, is really, if physics is to be believed, observing the effects of the stone upon himself. Thus science seems to be at war with itself: when it most means to be objective, it finds itself plunged into subjectivity against its will. Naive realism leads to physics, and physics, if true,

---

[65] In another essay, 'Certainty', Moore suggests a somewhat different strategy. He accepts the second premiss (2) of sceptical arguments having the following structure: (1) I cannot know that H (a sceptical hypothesis, e.g. that I am dreaming, or a brain-in-a-vat) is false; (2) if I do not know that H is false, I do not know that I am now standing up, or have hands; so (3) I do not know that I am now standing up, or have hands. Moore then claims that we are much more certain of the falsity of (3) than of the truth of (1), so that, using (2) and assuming the falsity of (3), we should conclude that (1) is false. In this strategy, no 'proof' of the falsity of (3) is required.

shows that naive realism is false. Therefore, naive realism, if true, is false; therefore it is false.[66]

If the problem of the external world arises from a scientific point of view only, and not within the perspective of common sense or of 'everydayness', arguing that the problem is easy to solve or even meaningless from this latter perspective will not help much to 'overcome' it.

Whereas G. E. Moore had no answer to this objection, Heidegger developed an astute strategy for countering it. In a Kantian manner, he claimed in section 69b of *Being and Time* that a scientific discipline such as physics is possible only on the basis of an a priori conceptual framework (*Entwurf*), which is projected by *Dasein* onto nature. It is in the light of such a 'projected mathematical conception of nature' only that the physicist is able to discover 'facts' and to confirm his theories. Furthermore, Heidegger attempted to demonstrate, but did not quite succeed in showing, that this projected transcendental framework of natural science is secondary in relation to the world of everyday *Dasein*, not only secondary in the historical sense that came later, but also ontologically speaking. For example, he wrote in italics that the world of everyday life is the world-*as-it-is-in-itself* (*an sich*), in which the things we encounter have the mode of being of 'readiness-to-hand' (*Zuhandenheit*).[67] The fact that we also adopt the scientific perspective, within which objects appear as meaningless things that are merely present (*Vorhanden*), would be because of a *deficiency* in our practical dealings with things.[68] Furthermore, the scientific transcendental framework is based on (*fundiert in*) our primary dwelling in the world, and it passes over (*überspringt*) the fundamental phenomenon of the world.[69] If the scientific image of the world is taken as fundamental, this must be because of some sort of self-alienation of *Dasein* that Heidegger calls *Dasein*'s falling (*Verfallen*). It follows that if the problem of the external world is raised only within the transcendental framework of natural science, raising it is itself a symptom of *Verfallen* or self-alienation. This is what Heidegger argues in section 43a of *Being and Time*:

The 'problem of reality' in the sense of the question whether there is an external world and whether the existence of such a world can be proved, turns out to be an impossible problem, not because its consequences lead to inextricable impasses, but because the very entity which serves as its theme is one which, as it were, repudiates any such

---

[66]  B. Russell, *An Inquiry into Meaning and Truth* (Harmondsworth: Penguin Books, 1962), 13.
[67]  *Sein und Zeit*, §§15, 18, 23, 26, 43b; pp. 71, 87, 88, 106, 118, 209.
[68]  Ibid., §13, p. 61.       [69]  Ibid., §§14, 21, 43.

formulation of the question. Our task is not to prove that an 'external world' is present or to show how it is present, but to point out why *Dasein*, as Being-in-the-world, has the tendency to bury the 'external world' in nullity 'epistemologically' before going on to prove it. The cause of this lies in *Dasein*'s falling . . . [70]

As we see now, Heidegger's strategy of overcoming epistemology was inextricably bound up with an ontological depreciation of natural science. Indeed, from his youth as a Catholic student onwards, Heidegger criticized the movements of 'modernism' or 'naturalism', according to which the ontology of man and world should be based upon the latest scientific theories. Science is perfectly all right within its own sphere, Heidegger argued. But ontologically speaking, scientific research has no access to *Dasein* and world as they are in themselves. That is the domain of hermeneutic phenomenology, transcendental philosophy, and of religion.

# 6. Conclusion: How Should Epistemology be Overcome?

In this essay I have focused mainly on the *quaestiones facti* of why external world epistemology arose during the scientific revolution, how it could attain the status of first philosophy around 1900, and how Husserl and Heidegger attempted to overcome this type of epistemology during the first half of the twentieth century. But the reconstruction of these historical developments in Continental philosophy also enables us to answer the *quaestio iuris* whether Husserl and Heidegger have succeeded in overcoming epistemology.

Like Kant's attempt to remove 'the scandal of philosophy', Husserl's and Heidegger's strategies of overcoming epistemology turn out to depend on an ontological depreciation of natural science. The scientific analysis of matter and perception, which triggered the problem of the external world during the scientific revolution, is now said to presuppose a subsidiary transcendental framework that is projected by a transcendental subject (Husserl) or by *Dasein* in the world (Heidegger). Both Husserl and Heidegger conclude that the causal problem of the external world is meaningless at the deepest ontological level. We have also seen that eliminating external world epistemology by such

---

[70] *Sein und Zeit*, §43a, p. 206 (my translation).

a transcendental turn and the concomitant ontological depreciation of science presupposed (e) the classical problem of first principles epistemology, at least in Kant's case, to which the transcendental turn was a solution. If this analysis is correct, Husserl's and Heidegger's attempts to overcome epistemology are confronted by two massive objections.

First, the scientific revolutions of general relativity and quantum mechanics during the first quarter of the twentieth century have sufficiently disconfirmed classical foundationalism, so that the classical problem of first principles has to be rejected. As the logical positivists argued, these revolutions show that even the most fundamental principles of general scientific theories cannot be demonstrated apodictically, but will always remain hypothetical to some extent, however well confirmed they are by experience. It follows that philosophy cannot be a foundational discipline, establishing the fundamental principles of the sciences by a metaphysics of nature or by eidetic regional ontologies, which are founded in their turn upon a transcendental philosophy (Kant, Husserl) or a fundamental ontology of *Dasein* (Heidegger). The first principles of the sciences are taken care of by empirical science itself. Although Heidegger in *Being and Time* took notice of scientific revolutions, he did not yet abandon the idea of a foundational role for philosophy.[71] From our perspective of eighty years after 1927, the foundationalist presumptions of Husserl and the early Heidegger have to be rejected because of these developments in the philosophy of science. The same holds for Husserl's essentialism, which Heidegger implicitly endorsed in *Being and Time*, and which cannot withstand the criticisms by philosophers such as Popper and Wittgenstein.

Second, given the spectacular advances of scientific research in the twentieth century and the concomitant 'consilience of inductions', we cannot but accept a naturalist *Weltanschauung*, which regards human consciousness and culture as a late and very local product of cosmic evolution. In other words, the ontological depreciation of science, which was essential in Husserl's and Heidegger's attempts to overcome epistemology, is a price that for good reasons most contemporary philosophers do not want to pay.

It follows that neither Husserl's nor Heidegger's strategy for overcoming external world epistemology will help us with regard to the recent naturalistic guise that the sceptical problem of the external world has adopted: the

---

[71] Cf. my *Heidegger's Philosophy of Being*, 36–41, for an analysis of Heidegger's views on this point.

hypothesis of a brain-in-a-vat.[72] Husserl's strategy is even less promising than Heidegger's, because it endorses the principle of immanence, according to which secondary qualities-as-we-perceive-them are sensations immanent in consciousness, or 'qualia', as they are now called, an assumption that is crucial to the thought-experiment of a brain-in-a-vat as well. To this extent, Husserl's transcendental revolution still depends upon the naturalist assumptions that he rejects (cf. section 2).

Although Heidegger repudiated the representational theory of perception, he still endorsed the deepest presupposition of external world epistemology: the incompatibility thesis. He held that the scientific view of the world (*Vorhandenheit*) cannot be true of the world as it is in itself, which, Heidegger claimed, is the world of everyday life (*Zuhandenheit*). It is this assumption that the 'scientific image' is incompatible with the 'manifest image' which should be questioned if one wants to overcome radically external world epistemology.

A first attempt to do so is to be found in the fifth chapter of *Dilemmas* by Gilbert Ryle, but Ryle's analysis is not convincing.[73] What should be shown by meticulous conceptual analysis is that scientific accounts of matter and perception do not refute the perceptual judgements of everyday life, according to which things in our environment are red or blue and cold or warm, so that there is no need to introject these qualities into the mind as 'sensations' or 'qualia'.[74] Conversely, if one holds that this cannot be shown, one should conclude that external world epistemology cannot be overcome, and that its central problem is perfectly legitimate, although the history of modern philosophy teaches us by a pessimistic induction that probably it is insoluble.[75]

---

[72] Cf. Duncan Pritchard, 'Recent Work on Radical Skepticism', *American Philosophical Quarterly* 39 (2002), 215–57 for an overview.

[73] Gilbert Ryle, *Dilemmas: The Tarner Lectures* (Cambridge: Cambridge University Press, 1954), lecture V on 'The world of science and the everyday world'. Cf. for my critique of Ryle's argument: Herman Philipse, 'What is a Natural Conception of the World?', *International Journal of Philosophical Studies* 9 (2001), 385–99.

[74] Cf. M. R. Bennett and P. M. S. Hacker, *Philosophical Foundations of Neuroscience* (Oxford: Blackwell, 2003). Cf. also P. M. S. Hacker, *Appearance and Reality* (Oxford: Blackwell, 1987).

[75] I am grateful to Victor Gijsbers, Peter Hacker, Carlo Ierna, Rosja Mastop, Fred Muller, Eric Schliesser, and to the editors of this volume for comments on a first draft of this chapter.

# CHAPTER 11

# INDIVIDUAL EXISTENCE AND THE PHILOSOPHY OF DIFFERENCE

## ROBERT STERN

I⊤ is a commonplace to say that it is hard to understand the trajectory of 'continental' philosophy without coming to terms with the influence of Hegel. It might be thought that this is because Hegel led those who came after him in a new direction, which can only be followed by going 'via' his work, and in part this is true. But the opposite is also true: namely, that Hegel represents for many 'continental' thinkers not a *break* with the mainstream of philosophical thinking, but a *continuation* of it, so that unless one has some insight into Hegelian philosophy, one will not be able to see how through their engagement with Hegel, many continental philosophers are engaged with certain perennial philosophical questions—questions that are often of concern to 'analytic' philosophers as well. Hegel should therefore not just be seen as a 'parting of the ways' between 'continental' and 'analytic' philosophy, but as a bridge between them too, as many continental thinkers have come to address the traditional problems of philosophy through their encounters with Hegel, in a way that is hard to see if he is left out of the picture, as most 'analytic' discussions of these problems tend to do.

One such traditional question is *the problem of individuality*. This problem concerns the question of what makes something an individual, as a unified entity distinct from other individuals. As we shall see, this problem has its roots in the history of philosophy, from Plato onwards, and is a problem with several dimensions, as it raises concerns not only in metaphysics, but also in epistemology and ethics. Recognizing its importance, Hegel made the issue central to his philosophical system, and offered what he took to be a satisfactory solution to it, using the idea of the 'concrete universal'. However, from Schelling, Feuerbach, and Kierkegaard onwards, dissatisfaction with this solution has been central to 'continental' thought, the objection being that Hegel's solution fails to do justice to the real uniqueness of individuals, where our incapacity to capture that uniqueness in conceptual terms is seen as a crucial limitation on the Hegelian approach, and on the approach of the philosophical tradition more generally. A recent and sophisticated expression of this dissatisfaction can be found in the work of Gilles Deleuze, whose position we will examine in some detail, in order to see whether his 'philosophy of difference' offers a distinctive way out of the difficulties that the problem of individuality poses for us.

# 1. The Problem of Individuality

We can begin by looking in more detail at the problem, and exploring its ramifications.

At an intuitive level, it seems commonsensical to hold that the world around us contains individual entities which (a) are unified conjunctions of properties, (b) are distinct from all other entities, (c) belong to a type or class of relevantly similar entities which has or can have several members, (d) instantiate properties that can be instantiated by other individuals, (e) remain the same over time and various alterations, and (f) have properties but are not properties of anything else. Thus Fido the dog has numerous properties belonging to him (being brown, hairy, lazy, four-legged, and so on) that belong together as *his* properties, while Fido himself is distinct from Rex and all other dogs. At the same time, Fido is one amongst others of the doggy kind, and he is also one amongst others who are brown, lazy, and so on (who may or may not also be dogs: Rex is also brown, while Harry the boy is also lazy).

Now, this common-sense metaphysical position can of course be challenged from the outside, for example by science or theology. But it also has certain internal difficulties, as some of these views seem to be in tension with one another. Two areas of tension will concern us here. The first is that, on the one hand, how are we able to do justice to the apparent similarity or sameness between things in terms of their properties and the kind to which they belong ((d) and (c) above), while on the other hand acknowledging their individuality, both as being distinct from other things ((b) above), and as being unified ((a) above)? And the second tension is this: how are we to account for the way in which one entity forms a unified individual, when it exemplifies a plurality of properties? Let us call the first issue *the problem of individuation* (what makes A distinct from other things?), and the second *the problem of indivisibility* (what makes A a single unified thing?). The real difficulty here (which constitutes *the problem of individuality* as a whole) is that what may look like a good answer to one of these problems leaves us in a poor position to answer the other, so what we want is a position that would properly deal with *both*.

Thus, in relation to the problem of indivisibility, a traditional answer has been that the properties of an individual entity are held together by some sort of underlying substratum, in which the properties inhere. However, substratum theories are then criticized on the grounds that they seem unknowable (what Locke called 'a supposed, I know not what, to support those *Ideas*, we call Accidents'),[1] while also leading to the problem of individuation: for if each substance is in itself propertyless, what can distinguish one substratum from another? Reacting against the substratum view, philosophers have therefore adopted instead what are known as bundle theories: individual entities are collections of properties tied together by the relations between those properties, rather than any underlying substratum.[2] However, a difficulty for the bundle

---

[1] John Locke, *An Essay Concerning Human Understanding*, ed. P. H. Nidditch (Oxford: Oxford University Press, 1975), bk. II, ch. XXIII, §15, p. 305.

[2] Cf. David Hume, *A Treatise of Human Nature*, 2nd edn., ed. L. A. Selby-Bigge and P. H. Nidditch (Oxford: Oxford University Press, 1978), bk. I, pt. I, §VI, p. 16: '[N]one will assert, that substance is either a colour, or a sound, or a taste... We have therefore no idea of substance, distinct from that of a collection of particular qualities, nor have we any other meaning when we either talk or reason concerning it.'

theory is the problem of individuation: if individuals are nothing more than bundles of properties, it follows that to be distinct from one another, two individuals must differ in their properties—but couldn't there be individuals who have exactly the same properties, which are nonetheless distinct? Couldn't Fido have an identical twin, while for all that each is a different individual? To deny that this is possible, one would have to be committed to an implausibly strong version of Leibniz's principle of the identity of indiscernibles, which would rule this out. The bundle theorist might counter this difficulty by appealing to what are sometimes called 'impure' properties (such as being identical with oneself, or being in a specific spatio-temporal location), where including such properties in the bundle would make Leibniz's principle more plausible, perhaps even trivial—but to have such properties (it might be felt), a thing must *already be* an individual, so this cannot explain or constitute its individuality.

Another response might be for the bundle theorist to query the conception of properties on which the problem arises: for, if we conceive of properties not as universals (which can be instantiated by more than one thing, so that Fido and his twin can both be brown at the same time), but as what are usually called *tropes* (which are *particulars*, so that Fido and his twin each have their distinct trope of brown), then the difficulty disappears, as the bundle that constitutes the individual is made up of properties that are *themselves* particulars (so that the brown property Fido possesses could not be possessed by his twin, though of course he could possess one exactly similar to it).

Now, as a form of nominalism, trope versions of the bundle theory have been attacked on that score. But they have also been criticized as not really solving the problem of individuation: for, if this does not now arise at the level of individual entities, it may still seem to arise at the level of individual properties, namely, what makes Fido's brownness numerically distinct from his twin's? A natural answer might be, because $brown_1$ belongs to Fido, and $brown_2$ belongs to his twin. But, if Fido and his twin are nothing but bundles of properties, and we are explaining the individuality of each bundle through the particularity of the properties that constitute the bundle, how can we explain the particularity of a property by appealing to the fact that they belong to different bundles—isn't this hopelessly circular? Moreover, the trope theorist cannot appeal to space–time location to determine the identity and diversity of properties, because he must allow such properties to exist 'compresently', that is, at the *same* spatio-temporal location (in the way that Fido's hairiness and four-leggedness do, to the extent that his legs are hairy).[3]

A natural way to respond to these difficulties is to look for a position that relies on more than just the properties of the individual (such as brownness or hairiness) to differentiate it, but in a way that does not go back to the earlier substratum model, with its mysterious 'I know not what'. One such response is to argue that what grounds the distinctness of an individual is not the particularity of its properties (as on the trope theory), or the characterless substratum in which they inhere (as on the substratum theory), but the *substance* universal that the individual exemplifies, where the substance universal is the kind to which the individual as a whole belongs (such as 'dog', 'human being', 'rose', and so on) rather than the property the individual may have qua member of that kind (such as being a brown dog, a white dog, a black dog, or whatever). The idea here, then, is that substance universals are *intrinsically individuative*: it is by virtue of exemplifying the kind 'dog' that Fido is distinct from his twin, even if they have all their ('pure') property universals in common, because qua dog, Fido is a different individual from all members of the same kind. This appeal to substance-universals can therefore be presented as a way out of the difficulties of the bundle and substratum approaches to the problem of individuation:

Kinds are universals whose instantiations are numerically different; but the instantiations of a substance-kind just are the various substances which belong to or fall under it. Thus, there is no need either to deny what is obvious—that it is possible for different objects to be indiscernible with respect to their pure universals [which is the problem for the bundle theory] or to appeal to bare substrata in explaining how this is possible [as on the substratum theory]. Indiscernible substances agree in their substance-kinds; but for two or more objects to agree in a substance-kind is *eo ipso* for them to be numerically different. Substance-kinds of and by themselves diversify their members, so that in being given substance-kinds we are thereby given universals that guarantee the diversification of the objects which exemplify them.[4]

---

[3] For this and related problems for the trope view, see E. J. Lowe, 'Form Without Matter', in David S. Oderberg (ed.), *Form and Matter: Themes in Contemporary Metaphysics* (Oxford: Blackwell, 1999), 1–21, 17–20.

[4] Michael J. Loux, *Substance and Attribute: A Study in Ontology* (Dordrecht: D. Reidel, 1978), 163–4. Cf. also Michael J. Loux, *Metaphysics: A Contemporary Introduction* (London: Routledge, 1998), 117–27, and 'Beyond Substrata and Bundles: A Prolegomenon to a Substance Ontology', in Stephen Laurence and Cynthia Macdonald (eds.), *Contemporary Readings in the Foundations of Metaphysics* (Oxford: Blackwell, 1998), 233–47, esp. pp. 242–5. A similar view is defended by E. J. Lowe: see 'Form without Matter', 12–13, and *Kinds of Being: A Study of Individuation, Identity and the Logic of Sortal Terms* (Oxford: Blackwell, 1989), 11: 'the notions of *individual* (or particular)

The substance-kind theory (as I will label it) may therefore seem to show a way out of the problem of individuation. It may also seem to show a way out of the problem of indivisibility, for the claim is also that (like the substratum view) we can think of properties as inhering in something while (as on the bundle theory) refusing to treat this underlying subject as a bare particular: rather, the properties inhere in the individual qua member of the kind, not as an indeterminate substratum, so that it is as a dog that Fido is brown, lazy, and so on, where it is his dogginess that unifies these properties in him as an individual.

It may be felt, however, that there is something rather mysterious about this substance-kind theory. For, if the substance-kind is a universal that members of the kind all exemplify, then how can this differentiate the individuals, when as a universal it is the same in each? As an instantiation of a substance-kind, isn't there still a question of what makes a substance of that kind the particular individual it is, if the kind is common to other individuals of the same type? If, on the other hand, this is accounted for on the ground that the substance-kind is instantiated in the individual not as a universal, but as a particular, then this is to opt for a trope-like view of substance-kinds: but as with the trope view of properties, don't we then need some explanation of what makes Fido's exemplification of dogginess distinct from his twin's? To say that it *just is* distinct is not to solve the problem of individuation, but to repeat it.

At this point, it may then be tempting to think we must return to something like a substratum view, as offering some grounding for the difference between individuals. One such view is the traditional position of hylomorphism, which treats individuals as the particular individuals they are in virtue of a combination of the stuff (*hyle*) of which they are made, and the form or nature or essence (*morphe*) imposed upon it, where the matter is then seen as providing a principle of individuation for the individual entity that exemplifies the universal type: what makes Fido and his twin distinct is that the form 'dog' is exemplified in different parcels of matter or stuff.[5] However, if we are

---

and *sort* (or kind) are, very arguably, interdependent and mutually irreducible. Individuals are only recognizable as *individuals of a sort*, while sorts are only intelligible as *sorts of individuals*'.

[5] Cf. Aristotle, *Metaphysics*, 1034$^a$5–7: 'And when we have the whole, such and such a form in this flesh and in these bones, this is Callias or Socrates; and they are different in virtue of their matter (for that is different), but the same in form; for their form is indivisible'. This may suggest that the theory for which Aristotle is the main ancestor is hylomorphism, but in fact some support in Aristotle can be found for most of the positions we have discussed. For an interesting discussion of Aristotle that relates to the themes of this essay, see Theodor W. Adorno, *Metaphysik: Begriff und Probleme*, ed. Rolf Tidemann (Frankfurt: Suhrkamp, 1998); translated as *Metaphysics: Concepts and Problems* by Edmund Jephcott (Cambridge: Polity Press, 2000).

obliged to think of matter as formless in itself, how can this be a source of individuality in a thing?

Another attempt to account for individuality is proposed by those who hold that individuals have a unique feature which is the basis for their difference from other things, usually termed 'thisness' or *haecceitas*, which is a non-qualitative property responsible for individuation (as opposed to 'whatness' or *quidditas*, which are the properties the thing can share with other things, such as brownness, laziness, etc.). Like the substratum theory, the haecceity theory therefore introduces something over and above the qualitative properties of a thing to serve as its individuator, but unlike the substratum theory, it treats this 'thisness' as a non-qualitative part of the bundle that constitutes the thing, rather than as a substratum *underlying* its properties. The difficulty with this view, however, is that any such 'thisness' looks as mysterious as the substratum it partially resembles, in not really *explaining* individuation, but just marking the phenomenon we want explained.

We thus seem to face a fundamental tension on how to approach the problem of individuality. On the one hand, we can try to deal with the problem in a qualitative way, arguing that individuals are nothing over and above the properties and substance universals that constitute them: but then we face the difficulty of explaining the unity of individuals, and that it always seems possible that another individual might exist that shares the same properties, in such a way as to show that they are not really individuative. On the other hand, we can add something further to this qualitative view of individuals; but this additional feature (such as a substratum, or haecceity) seems to involve a problematic ontological commitment that it would be good to be without. The difficulties faced here run like a thread through the history of philosophy from at least Plato onwards.

## 2. Hegel and the 'Concrete Universal'

Having sketched the problem of individuality, and some of the various attempted solutions it has given rise to, I now want to explore the way in which the problem figures in Hegel's thought. Broadly speaking, as we shall see, Hegel wanted to follow a qualitative way out of the difficulty, while his subsequent opponents argued that this was an inadequate response, and so turned to non-qualitative solutions.

At first sight, it may seem surprising to claim that a concern with such traditional philosophical issues forms part of the Hegelian system, because Kant is widely believed to have shown that such metaphysical concerns can be traced back to nothing more than the 'natural illusions' of reason; so further speculation on such matters might be expected to seem futile to a post-Kantian philosopher such as Hegel. However, in fact if anything the Kantian revolution in philosophy had the opposite effect: for, to Hegel, it appeared that Kant had shown how much our view of the world depends on the fundamental concepts (or categories) we bring to it, so that unless we reflect deeply on the kinds of metaphysics implicitly presupposed by these categories, we can never hope to arrive at a satisfactory picture of reality, making metaphysical speculation seem of more vital significance than ever:

metaphysics is nothing but the range of universal thought-determinations, and is as it were the diamond-net into which we bring everything in order to make it intelligible. Every cultured consciousness has its metaphysics, its instinctive way of thinking. This is the absolute power within us, and we shall only master it if we make it the object of our knowledge. Philosophy in general, as philosophy, has different categories from those of ordinary consciousness. All cultural change reduces itself to a difference of categories. All revolutions, whether in the sciences or world history, occur merely because spirit has changed its categories in order to understand and examine what belongs to it, in order to possess and grasp itself in a truer, deeper, more intimate and unified manner.[6]

Hegel thus believed that 'to him who looks at the world rationally, the world looks rationally back; the two exist in a reciprocal relationship',[7] in the sense that only if we come to the world with the right metaphysical framework will we be able to make the world seem a rationally intelligible place, and that continuing metaphysical puzzles are evidence of our failure to achieve this.

Of all such puzzles, Hegel took the problem of the relation between individuals and universals to be the most fundamental, because on this question so much of our view of epistemology, ethics, political philosophy, aesthetics, and much else depends. To take an example: in one of his discussions of the

---

[6] G. W. F. Hegel, *Enzyklopädie der philosophischen Wissenschaften, Zweiter Teil: Die Naturphilosophie*, §246 Zusatz, in *Werke in zwanzig Bänden, Theorie Werkausgabe*, ed. Eva Moldenhauer and Karl Markus Michel (Frankfurt: Suhrkamp, 1969–71), ix. 20–1; translated as *Hegel's Philosophy of Nature* [= pt.2 of the *Encyclopaedia of the Philosophical Sciences*] by Michael John Petry, 3 vols. (London: George Allen & Unwin, 1970), i. 202.

[7] Ibid., *Vorlesungen über die Philosophie der Geschichte*, in *Werke*, xii. 23; translated as *Lectures on the Philosophy of World History: Introduction*, by H. B. Nisbet (Cambridge: Cambridge University Press, 1975), 29.

struggle for recognition, which precedes the famous 'master–slave' dialectic, Hegel presents a fundamental difficulty we face in our social interaction as the clash between realizing that we are one amongst others who in some sense are the same as us, with the feeling that we are also unique and so fundamentally distinct:

In this determination lies the tremendous contradiction that, on the one hand, the 'I' is wholly universal, absolutely pervasive, and interrupted by no limit, is the universal essence common to all men, the two mutually related selves therefore constituting one identity, constituting, so to speak, one light; and yet, on the other hand, they are also two selves rigidly and unyieldingly confronting each other, each existing as a reflection-into-self, as absolutely distinct from and impenetrable by the other.[8]

Here, then, the problem of individuality takes a socio-political form, as we attempt to come to terms with our sense of both identity with and difference from one another. The fundamental nature of this problem meant that Hegel therefore felt obliged to deal with it, and thus address the views of the tradition on this question.

As I understand it, there are two strands to Hegel's discussion of the problem, one negative and critical of certain ways of approaching the difficulty, the other positive and constructive, in attempting a solution. The negative discussion comes largely in the opening sections of the *Phenomenology of Spirit*, where Hegel takes as his target two prominent non-qualitative ways of thinking about individuality (the haecceity theory and the substratum theory), while he is also critical of one form of qualitative approach (the bundle theory). In his positive account, Hegel offers a version of substance-kind theory, which is defended largely in Book III of his *Logic*.

The first part of Hegel's negative discussion comes in the section on 'sense-certainty' at the beginning of the *Phenomenology*. As in the *Phenomenology* in general, Hegel's aim here is to present an 'immanent critique' of a position taken by consciousness: that is, he wants to show that a certain view of the world which consciousness adopts is internally incoherent or unstable. The view taken by sense-certainty which concerns him is that the

---

[8] Ibid., *Enzyklopädie der philosophischen Wissenschaften, Dritter Teil: Die Philosophie des Geistes,* §430 Zusatz, in *Werke*, x. 219; translated as *Philosophy of Mind: Being Part Three of the Encyclopaedia of the Philosophical Sciences*, by William Wallace and A. V. Miller (Oxford: Oxford University Press, 1971), 170–1. Cf. also G. W. F. Hegel, *Enzyklopädie der philosophischen Wissenschaften, Erster Teil: Die Wissenschaft der Logik*, §163 Zusatz, in *Werke*, viii. 311–13; translated as *The Encyclopaedia Logic: Part 1 of the Encyclopaedia of the Philosophical Sciences*, by T. F. Geraets, W. A. Suchting, and H. S. Harris (Indianapolis: Hackett, 1991), 240–1.

best way to gain knowledge of the world is to experience it directly or intuitively, without applying concepts to such intuitions, for fear that this distorts our knowledge or makes it more abstract. The claim of sense-certainty is, then, that the 'richest' and 'truest' knowledge comes from 'immediate' rather than 'mediated' knowledge, which involves '*apprehension*' rather than '*comprehension*'.[9] This conception of knowledge is made plausible for sense-certainty by a certain ontological view underlying it, namely, that because it does not use concepts but just intuits, it is able to grasp a thing *as an individual*, without any abstraction from its unique specificity or pure particularity, so that for sense-certainty, 'the existence of *external* objects, which can be more precisely defined as *actual*, absolutely *singular, wholly personal, individual* things, each of them absolutely unlike anything else' had 'absolutely certainty and truth'.[10] In claiming that each individual has a unique nature which is subject to direct intuition, sense-certainty resembles the haecceity theory, where this unique nature cannot be grasped conceptually, for all concepts are general and so only apply to universal and shareable characteristics of the thing:

Consciousness, for its part, is in this certainty only as a pure 'I'; or I am in it only as a pure 'This', and the object similarly only as a pure 'This'. I, *this* particular I, am certain of *this* particular thing, not because I, *qua* consciousness, in knowing it have developed myself or thought about it in various ways; and also not because *the thing* of which I am certain, in virtue of a host of distinct qualities, would be in its own self a rich complex of connections, or related in various ways to other things. Neither of these has anything to do with the truth of sense-certainty: here neither I nor the thing has the significance of a complex process of mediation; the 'I' does not have the significance of a manifold imagining or thinking; nor does the 'thing' signify something that has a host of qualities. On the contrary, the thing *is*, and it *is*, merely because it *is*. It *is*; this is the essential point for sense-knowledge, and this pure *being*, or this simple immediacy, constitutes its *truth*. Similarly, certainty as a *connection* is an *immediate* pure connection: consciousness is 'I', nothing more, a pure 'This'; the singular consciousness knows a pure 'This', or the single item.[11]

In so far as sense-certainty maintains that the being of the object it knows is constituted by its unique individuality in this way (its 'thisness' or haecceity), sense-certainty naturally also holds that knowledge also needs to be aconceptual, and that such knowledge is the 'richest' and 'truest': for (it claims) if we

---

[9]  G. W. F. Hegel, *Phänomenologie des Geistes*, in *Werke*, iii. 82; translated as *Hegel's Phenomenology of Spirit*, by A. V. Miller (Oxford: Oxford University Press, 1977), 58.
[10]  Hegel, *Phänomenologie*, 91; *Phenomenology*, 66.          [11]  Ibid., 82–3; *Phenomenology*, 58–9.

bring in concepts, we bring in general terms that take us away from things in their singularity.

Hegel now goes on to show, however, that this position is unstable, for it turns out that the 'thisness' which sense-certainty attributes to individuals is completely indeterminate, and thus far from being specific to each entity; it is in fact entirely general—to the extent that sense-certainty grasps what it means by 'this', *everything* possesses it. Because 'thisness' is conceived as a non-qualitative property, it cannot be described; but because it cannot be described, there is no feature by which the 'thisness' of Fido can be distinguished from the 'thisness' of his twin, or of any other object—so 'thisness' is utterly general or universal:

> If they actually wanted to *say* 'this' bit of paper which they mean, if they wanted to *say* it, then this is impossible, because the sensuous This that is meant *cannot be reached* by language, which belongs to consciousness, i.e. to that which is inherently universal. In the actual attempt to say it, it would therefore crumble away; those who started to describe it would not be able to complete the description, but would be compelled to leave it to others, who would themselves finally have to admit to speaking about something which *is not*. They certainly mean, then, *this* bit of paper here which is quite different from the bit mentioned above; but they say 'actual *things*', 'external or *sensuous objects*', 'absolutely *singular entities*' and so on; i.e. they say of them only what is *universal*. Consequently, what is called the unutterable is nothing else than the untrue, the irrational, what is merely meant [but is not actually expressed].[12]

Hegel's discussion of sense-certainty, therefore, can be interpreted as a critique of one prominent approach to the problem of individuality, where this is attributed to some unique 'thisness' belonging to the individual, rather than constructed through the qualitative features of the individual which it may share with others.

Having come to see that it cannot coherently think of individuality in terms of some sort of unique individuating essence, the presentation of consciousness in the *Phenomenology* moves on to the next level of *perception*, where consciousness is now ready to conceive of individuals as being constituted by properties, and so treats each individual as a bundle of universals at a spatio-temporal location, which Hegel terms an 'Also'.[13] However, consciousness

---

[12]  Ibid., 91–2; *Phenomenology*, 66.

[13]  Ibid., 95; *Phenomenology*, 68–9; translation modified: 'This abstract universal medium, which can be called simply "thinghood" or "pure essence", is nothing else than what Here and Now have proved themselves to be, viz. a *simple togetherness* of a plurality; but the many are, *in their determinateness*, simple universals themselves. This salt is a simple Here, and at the same time manifold; it is white and *also* tart, *also* cubical in shape, of a specific weight, etc. All these many properties are in a single simple

then finds that this bundle view of the object is unstable and so moves to the opposite view, which takes the individual to be a 'One', and thus a unified substratum over and above its properties.[14] Hegel therefore presents consciousness as playing out a familiar dialectic between bundle and substratum views, and oscillating from the one to the other: on the one hand, the bundle view makes it hard to explain why we think of properties as inhering in an individual, whereby different instances of these properties are distinct from one another; on the other hand, the substratum view leads us to a characterless 'One' underlying the 'Also'. Locked in this dialectic, consciousness cannot find a satisfactory way of dealing with the problem of individuality, as it turns from one standpoint to the other.

Hegel's diagnosis of what has gone wrong here, and thus the basis for his positive solution to the problem, is hinted at at the end of the 'Perception' section of the *Phenomenology*, where he comments that while perception involves universality, 'it is only a *sensuous universality*',[15] so that the properties perception attributes to the individual are just sensible properties, such as 'white', 'tart', 'cubical in shape', and so on. The difficulty with such properties is that they appear to be merely properties or accidents *of* the individual, so that the individual *itself* is treated as something underlying them, which leads us to the substratum view. What we need, then, is a conception of universality which is more than just a 'sensuous universality', where the universal which the individual exemplifies is constitutive of it in some way, and so underlies

"Here", in which, therefore, they interpenetrate; none has a different Here from the others, but each is everywhere, in the same Here in which the others are. And, at the same time, without being separated by different Heres, they do not affect each other in this interpenetration. The whiteness does not affect the cubical shape, and neither affects the tart taste, etc.; on the contrary, since each is itself a simple relating of self to self it leaves the others alone, and is connected with them only by the indifferent Also. This Also is thus the pure universal itself, or the medium, the "thinghood", which holds them together in this way.'

[14] Hegel, *Phänomenologie*, p. 95–6; *Phenomenology*, 69: 'In the relationship which has thus emerged it is only the character of positive universality that is at first observed and developed; but a further side presents itself, which must also be taken into consideration. To wit, if the many determinate properties were strictly indifferent to one another, if they were simply and solely self-related, they would not be determinate; for they are only determinate in so far as they *differentiate* themselves from one another, and *relate* themselves *to others* as to their opposites. Yet, as thus opposed to one another they cannot be together in the simple unity of their medium, which is just as essential to them as negation; the differentiation of the properties, in so far as it is not an indifferent differentiation but is exclusive, each property negating the others, thus falls outside of this simple medium; and the medium, therefore, is not merely an Also, an indifferent unity, but a One as well, a unity which *excludes* an other. The One is the *moment of negation*; it is itself quite simply a relation of self to self and it excludes an other; and it is that by which "thinghood" is determined as a Thing.'

[15] Ibid., 105; *Phenomenology*, 77.

its accidental properties; in this way, the individual is viewed as neither a bundle of diverse property-universals, not a bare propertyless substratum, but as constituted by a *substance*-universal (such as 'man', or 'horse', or 'dog') that characterizes it as a unified individual, to which diverse properties belong.

Hegel puts forward a substance-universal theory of this kind in Book III of the *Logic*, where he introduces his distinction between abstract and concrete universality. What this distinction amounts to can be seen by looking at the examples Hegel gives of each kind of universal, particularly as these are presented in his discussion of the hierarchy of judgements and syllogisms. At the most basic level of the qualitative judgement and the qualitative syllogism, the universal is an accidental property of an individual, which fails to differentiate it from other individuals:

When we say: 'This rose is red,' the copula 'is' implies that subject and predicate agree with one another. But, of course, the rose, being something concrete, is not merely red; on the contrary, it also has a scent, a definite form, and all manner of other features, which are not contained within the predicate 'red'. On the other hand, this predicate, being something abstractly universal, does not belong merely to this subject. For there are other flowers, too, and other objects altogether that are also red.[16]

Thus, with a universal like 'red', there is a clear distinction we can draw between the universal and the individual that possesses that property, and that universal and the other properties it possesses. At the next level, in the judgement and syllogism of reflection, we get a closer interrelation: for here we predicate properties of individuals which we take to belong to other individuals of the same kind, where being of this kind then comes to be seen as *essential* to the individual, and where some properties are seen as essential to any member of the kind. Thus, in the case of a judgement like 'All men are mortal', we treat being a man as an essential property of each individual man, and not a mere feature that these individuals happen to have in common, such as possessing earlobes.[17] Here, then, we get a closer interconnection between the universal and the individual, in so far as the universal is now seen as

[16] Hegel, *Enzyklopädie Logik*, §172 Zusatz, p. 324; *Encyclopaedia Logic*, 250. Cf. also G. W. F. Hegel, *Wissenschaft der Logik*, in *Werke*, vi. 300; translated as *Hegel's Science of Logic*, by A. V. Miller (London: George Allen & Unwin, 1977), 621: 'When one understands by the universal, what is *common* to several individuals, one is starting from the *indifferent* subsistence of these individuals and confounding the immediacy of *being* with the determination of the Notion. The lowest conception one can have of the universal in its connexion with the individual is this external relation of it as merely a *common element*.'

[17] Cf. *Enzyklopädie Logik*, §175 Zusatz, p. 327; *Encyclopaedia Logic*, 253.

an essential property of the individual; and we also have a closer connection between the universal and the particular properties that make something an individual, because it is only qua individual of a certain *kind* that the individual has these properties, and not as a 'bare' individual:

[I]t would not make sense to assume that Caius might perhaps be brave, learned, etc., and yet not be a man. The single human is what he is in particular, only insofar as he is, first of all, human as such, and within the universal; and this universal is not just something over and above the other abstract qualities or mere determinations of reflection, but is rather what permeates and includes within itself everything particular.[18]

This then leads to the judgement and syllogism of necessity, where the particular properties that distinguish one individual from another (e.g. this straight line from this curved line) are seen as different manifestations of a shared substance universal (linearity) by virtue of being different particularizations of the way that universal can be (lines are either straight or curved). So, not only do we see how universality is essential to particularity (Caius can only be a particular individual if he is a man); we also see how particularity is essential to universality (Caius cannot be a 'man in general', but must be a determinate example of a man, whose differences from other men nonetheless does not prevent him exemplifying the same universal 'man').[19] At this point, Hegel says, the universal as it is now envisaged is truly concrete, in the following respects:

- it is not merely a property, in the sense of being a way an individual may be: rather, it is *what* the individual *is*, in so far as that individual is an instance of

---

[18] *Enzyklopädie Logik*, §175 Zusatz, p. 327; *Encyclopaedia Logic*, 253, translation modified. Cf. also *Wissenschaft der Logik*, in *Werke*, v. 26; *Science of Logic*, 36–7: '[E]ach human being though infinitely unique is so primarily because he is a *man*, and each individual is such an individual primarily because it is an animal: if this is true, then it would be impossible to say what such an individual could still be if this foundation were removed, no matter how richly endowed the individual might be with other predicates, if, that is, this foundation can equally be called a predicate like the others.'

[19] Cf. *Enzyklopädie Logik*, §24 Zusatz, p. 82; *Encyclopaedia Logic*, 56–7: [I]n speaking of a definite animal, we say that it is [an] "animal." "Animal as such" cannot be pointed out; only a definite animal can ever be pointed at. "The animal" does not exist; on the contrary, this expression refers to the universal nature of single animals, and each existing animal is something that is much more concretely determinate, something particularised. But "to be animal," the kind considered as the universal, pertains to the determinate animal and constitutes its determinate essentiality. If we were to deprive a dog of its animality we could not say what it is. Things as such have a persisting, inner nature, and an external thereness. They live and die, come to be and pass away; their essentiality, their universality, is the kind, and this cannot be interpreted merely as something held in common.' Cf. also Hegel, *Vorlesungen über die Philosophie des Geschichte*, 38; *Lectures on the Philosophy of World History*, 72: 'For the individual *exists* as a determinate being, unlike man in general who has no existence as such.'

that kind of thing; it is therefore a substance universal (e.g. 'man' or 'rose') and not a property universal (e.g. 'red' or 'tall')[20]

- it supports generic propositions, such as statements of natural law ('human beings are rational agents') and normative statements ('because this person is irrational, he is a poor example of a human being'); these are therefore to be distinguished from universally quantified statements ('all human beings are rational'), which tell us about the shared characteristics of a group of individuals, rather than the characteristics of the kind to which the individuals belong
- it can be exemplified in individuals which have different properties, so that there need be nothing *further* in common between these individuals than the fact they exemplify the same concrete universal (the way in which one individual is a man may be different from the way in which another individual is a man)

We can now see what Hegel means by his claim that 'the *abstract* universal . . . is opposed to the particular and the individual',[21] while the concrete universal is not. A rose is not an individual rose by virtue of exemplifying the abstract universal 'red', whereas it is an individual rose by virtue of exemplifying the concrete universal 'rose'—so the latter is dialectically related to individuality in the way the former is not; and it exemplifies the abstract universal 'red' in the same way as other red things, whereas it exemplifies the concrete universal 'rose' differently from other roses, in so far as some roses are scented and others are not, some are evergreen and others are not, etc.—so the latter is dialectically related to particularity in the way the former is not. Thus, whereas it may appear that we can conceive of 'red' in abstraction from individuality and particularity, we cannot conceive of 'rose' in this manner, so that this kind of universality involves the other 'moments' of particularity and individuality in the way that an abstract universal does not.

Taken in this way, Hegel's position can be viewed as a distinctive contribution to the metaphysical discussion concerning universals, in the tradition of substance-universal accounts. The trouble with abstract universals like 'red', Hegel argues, is that instances of such universals are not individuals in themselves, so that individuals are reduced to 'bundles' of such universals, while difficulties in individuating these bundles leads to the 'substratum'

---

[20] Cf. Hegel, *Enzyklopädie: Die Philosophie des Geistes*, §456 Zusatz, p. 266; *Philosophy of Mind*, 209, where Hegel distinguishes the genus as a concrete universal, from the particular properties of the individual: 'This common element is either any one *particular* side of the object raised to the form of universality, such as, for example, in the rose, the red colour; or the *concrete universal*, the genus, for example, in the rose, the plant.'

[21] Hegel, *Wissenschaft der Logik*, in *Werke*, vi. 275; *Science of Logic*, 602.

view of objects: but because this substratum is 'bare' (i.e. propertyless), it is hard to see how it can do the individuating job required of it. However, if we recognize that there are also concrete universals like 'man', we will avoid these problems: for, while instances of 'red' are not individuals, instances of substance universals like 'man' are; but for this to be the case, it must be possible to exemplify a universal like 'man' in many different ways, such that each of us can be a man uniquely, in a way that constitutes our individuality. Hegel thus offers a way of solving the problem of individuation, without appealing to any of the 'non-qualitative' solutions we have discussed, such as haecceity theory, substratum theory, or trope theory: while there is nothing more to the individual than the universals it exemplifies, those universals are a combination of property and substance universals, so that it is qua man that I have the particular set of properties that make me into an individual, not qua a bare 'this'. Unless we recognize Hegel's way of drawing a distinction between abstract and concrete universals, this way of solving the problem is something we will miss.

Hegel's doctrine of the concrete universal may therefore be summarized as follows. The individual is no more than an instantiation of universals (there are no 'bare' individuals). But the universals that constitute the individual are not just property universals, as these just tell us what attributes the individual has, not what the individual *is* (so the 'bundle view' is false). However, the substance universals which constitute the nature of the individual qua individual do not exist in the abstract, but only as particularized through property universals, and thus as instantiated in the form of individuals (so Platonism is false). So, starting from any one of the categories of the Concept (universality, particularity, individuality), this category can only be made intelligible in the light of the other two: individuality is constituted by the particularized substance universal (as an individual, I am a man with a determinate set of properties that distinguish me from other men); the substance universal exists only in individuals, through its particularization (the universal 'man' exists *in rebus*, as instantiated in *different* men); and particularity is the differentiation of a substance universal, whereby it constitutes an individual (it is qua man that I have the properties which distinguish me from other men). It is the dialectical interconnection between the three categories which Hegel thinks is needed if we are to have an adequate solution to the problem of individuality, of the sort that is required.

# 3. The Existential Protest

Hegel's doctrine of the 'concrete universal' thus offers a subtle and in many ways appealing approach to the problem of individuality, in trying to account for the singularity of the individual on the one hand, while avoiding the obscurities of substratum or haecceity theories on the other. However, as we saw in the opening section, such theories appeal to those who feel that no qualitative approach (such as Hegel's) can really do justice to the individuality of an object.

In Hegel's case, this worry may be pressed as follows. On Hegel's version of the substance-kind theory, as we have seen, an individual is viewed as a particularized substance-universal; that is, Fido qua individual is an instantiation of the substance-kind 'dog', but in a particular way, so that as a dog, Fido is distinct from Rex. Hegel is therefore suggesting that what individuates Fido is not *just* that he instantiates the substance-universal, as on the 'classical' substance-kind theory introduced in the first section—for that gives rise to the question of how this could be so, as Fido and Rex are both dogs, and so both exemplify the *same* universal. Rather, Hegel is claiming that what differentiates Fido and Rex is that they have distinct ways of being dogs—Fido is one colour, Rex another, and so on, so that in each of them the substance-universal is 'particularized' in a different manner.[22] Now, one question this approach raises is that if Fido and Rex exemplify dogginess differently, how can we say that they exemplify dogginess as a *universal*, which is supposed to be the *same* in each of its instances? Hegel's response would seem to be that this is just what is distinctive of a *concrete* as opposed to an *abstract* universal: whereas a red rose and a red ball may both be red in the same manner, individuals who are dogs will each be so in different ways. Another question is this: if we are relying on the different properties of Fido and Rex to account for the fact that they are different individuals qua dogs, doesn't this in effect lead us back to the problems of the bundle view? For, it is surely possible that two dogs could have the same particularizing qualities (of laziness, brownness, etc.), so what could then make them distinct? If the reply is, 'they are distinct qua dogs, even if their properties are the same', we are back with

---

[22] Cf. again Hegel, *Enzyklopädie Logik*, §24 Zusatz, p. 82; *Encyclopaedia Logic*, 56: ' "The animal" does not exist; on the contrary, this expression refers to the universal nature of single animals, and each existing animal is something that is much more concretely determinate, something particularised.'

the 'classical' substance-kind theory, which claims that substance-universals are intrinsically individuative: but how? Hegel's doctrine of particularization seemed to make this less mysterious; but if that means that two dogs can only be distinct if they have different properties, that would appear to mean that, like Leibniz, Hegel must deny that two things could ever be qualitatively identical—but then what individuative work is the substance-universal doing, if what makes Fido and Rex distinct are their respective properties?[23]

To his subsequent critics, it appeared that Hegel had been led to this impasse because the nature of his philosophical project made it impossible for him to leave room for the unique specificity of the individual: for, as they understood that project, Hegel was an idealistic rationalist, who wanted to show that the fundamental nature of the world is accessible to thought, and who could therefore not acknowledge anything in the 'that' over and above the 'what', for otherwise the existence of a thing would be determined by something unconceptualizable. One of the first to criticize Hegel in these terms was F. W. J. Schelling, who in his later years argued that Hegel had failed to see that 'We live in this determinate world, not in an abstract or universal world that we so much enjoy deluding ourselves with by holding fast to the most *universal* properties of things, without penetrating to their actual relationships.'[24] As a result of this error, Schelling argued, Hegel had propounded what he characterized as a *negative* philosophy, which is confined to a world of concepts and essences, and neglects the facticity of *existence*, with its fundamental contingency and singularity.

---

[23] Cf. Hegel's discussion of Leibniz in the *Science of Logic*, where Hegel endorses the Leibnizian position, but just argues that it has not been properly proved: 'Ordinary thinking is struck by the proposition that no two things are like each other—as in the story of how Leibniz propounded it at court and caused the ladies to look at the leaves of trees to see whether they could find two alike. Happy times for metaphysics when it was the occupation of courtiers and the testing of its propositions called for no more exertion than to compare leaves!... The law of diversity... asserts that things are different from one another through unlikeness, that the determination of unlikeness belongs to them just as much as that of likeness, for determinate difference is constituted only by both together. // Now this proposition that unlikeness must be predicated of all things, surely stands in need of proof; it cannot be set up as an immediate proposition, for even in the ordinary mode of cognition a proof is demanded of the combination of different determinations in a synthetic proposition, or else the indication of a third term in which they are mediated. This proof would have to exhibit the passage of identity into difference, and then the passage of this into determinate difference, into unlikeness. But as a rule this is not done' (Hegel, *Wissenschaft der Logik*, in *Werke*, vi. 53–4; *Science of Logic*, 422–3).

[24] F. W. J. Schelling, *Die Philosophie der Offenbarung Zweiter Teil*, in *Sämmtliche Werke*, ed. K. F. A. Schelling, 14 vols. (Stuttgart and Augsburg: J. G. Cotta, 1856–61; reprinted Darmstadt: Wissenschaftliche Buchgesellschaft, 1974–6), xiv. 332.

Moreover, Hegel's critics did not only set out to explore the inadequacy of Hegel's own position: they also tried to show that his arguments against the alternative views were unfounded. Thus, both Ludwig Feuerbach and Søren Kierkegaard offered criticisms of Hegel's treatment of sense-certainty, arguing that his attempts to refute the insights of this position were unsuccessful and begged the question against it. On their view, Hegel's central claim was that while sense-certainty holds that each individual has the unique property of being 'this', which is meant to belong just to the particular individual, in fact *everything* has this property; for, when we come to say anything about it, there is nothing we can do to characterize the 'thisness' belonging to Fido, or indeed any other individual, so it appears to be an entirely *general* property, and thus universal. It therefore seemed to be crucial to his argument that Hegel made the demand that sense-certainty should be able to respond to the question 'What is the *This*?', when he then stated that this question could not be satisfactorily answered, except in the most general terms:

It is as a universal too that we *utter* what the sensuous [content] is. What we say is: 'This', i.e. the *universal* This; or, 'it is', i.e. *Being in general*. Of course, we do not *envisage* the universal This or Being in general, but we *utter* the universal; in other words, we do not strictly say what in this sense-certainty we *mean* to say. But language, as we see, is the more truthful; in it, we ourselves directly refute what we *mean* to say, and since the universal is the true [content] of sense-certainty and language expresses this true [content] alone, it is just not possible for us ever to say, or express in words, a sensuous being that we *mean* . . . When Science is faced with the demand—as if it were an acid test it could not pass—that it should deduce, construct, find *a priori*, or however it is put, something called 'this thing' or 'this one man', it is reasonable that the demand should *say* which 'this thing', or which 'this particular man' is *meant*; but it is impossible to say this.[25]

To his critics, however, the question this passage raises is whether Hegel is right to ask sense-certainty to respond to this demand 'What is *This*?', and whether in so doing he is proceeding *immanently*, examining sense-certainty in its own terms. For, they argued, language is inherently *conceptual*, so that if we are asked to *say* something about the 'This', we will find we cannot characterize it in descriptive terms, and so will appear to be saying that the 'This' is abstract and empty, a mere 'Being in general' that belongs to everything equally. But why should sense-certainty treat the 'This' as if it were linguistically expressible rather than ineffable, something *beyond* the

---

[25] Hegel, *Phänomenologie*, 85–7; *Phenomenology*, 60–2.

conceptuality of language? After all, isn't that what sense-certainty claims about it in the first place: that it can be *ap*prehended but not *com*prehended? So, by setting his question as a test that sense-certainty must pass, isn't Hegel in fact begging the question against it, and so not proceeding 'immanently' in the way he claims?

In his essay 'Towards a Critique of Hegel's Philosophy' (1839), Feuerbach presents this objection as follows, quoting Hegel's remark about 'Language being the more truthful' which we have cited above:

> But is this a dialectical [i.e. properly immanent] refutation of the reality of sensuous consciousness? Is it thereby proved that the general is the real? It may well be for someone who is certain in advance that the general is the real, but not for sensuous consciousness or for those who occupy its standpoint and will have to be convinced first of the unreality of sensuous being and the reality of thought...Here, language is irrelevant. The reality of sensuous and particular being is a truth that carries the seal of our blood. The commandment that prevails in the sphere of the senses is: an eye for an eye and a tooth for a tooth. Enough of words: come down to the real things! *Show* me what you are talking about! To sensuous consciousness it is precisely language that is unreal, nothing. How can it regard itself, therefore, as refuted if it is pointed out that a particular entity cannot be expressed in language? Sensuous consciousness sees precisely in this a refutation of language but not a refutation of sensuous certainty...[The *Phenomenology*] begins, as mentioned already, not with the 'other-being' of thought, but with the *idea of the 'other-being' of thought*. Given this, thought is naturally certain of its victory over its adversary in advance. Hence, the humour with which thought pulls the leg of sensuous consciousness. But this also goes to show that thought has not been able to refute its adversary.[26]

Feuerbach thus tries to turn the tables on Hegel's argument from language: rather than the ineffability of the 'This' showing it to be an empty abstraction, it rather shows the limitations on what language can express, namely the uniqueness of the individual, so that while Hegel refutes '"this-being," *haecceitas*' as an '*idea*',[27] something that can be conceptualized, he does not refute it as a *fact*, as the 'other-being' of thought. For Feuerbach, therefore, there is no reason to take Hegel's arguments against the haecceity theory with any great seriousness, in so far as he himself failed to take that position seriously.

---

[26] Ludwig Feuerbach, 'Zur Kritik der Hegelschen Philosophie', in *Gesammelte Werke*, ed. Werner Schuffenhauer, ix (*Kleinere Schriften II (1839–1846)*, 43–5; translated as The *Fiery Brook: Selected Writings of Ludwig Feuerbach*, by Zawar Hanfi (Garden City: Doubleday, 1972), 77–9; reprinted in Robert Stern (ed.), *G. W. F. Hegel: Critical Assessments*, 4 vols. (London: Routledge, 1993), i. 117–18.

[27] Feuerbach, 'Zur Kritik', 45; *The Fiery Brook*, 79; *Critical Assessments*, i. 118.

In a similar manner, what Kierkegaard finds striking in Hegel's discussion of sense-certainty is not that it provides a refutation of the immediacy of sense-certainty, but that it points up a tension between that immediacy and the mediacy of language, as sense-certainty struggles to put into words the nature of its unmediated encounter with the individual:

What, then, is immediacy? It is reality itself (*Realitet*). What is mediacy? It is the word. How does the one cancel the other? By giving expression to it, for that which is given expression is always *presupposed*.

Immediacy is reality; language is ideality; consciousness is contradiction (*Modsigelse*). The moment I make a statement about reality, contradiction is present, for what I say is ideality.[28]

In an alternative formulation, Kierkegaard makes the issue even clearer: 'Intrinsically there is already a contradiction between reality and ideality; the one provides the particular defined in time and space, the other the universal'.[29] For Kierkegaard, Hegel is to be criticized as seeming to want to overcome this contradiction, but in a way that favours ideality over reality, the universal over the particular, and it is this then that makes him think he can get beyond sense-certainty, whereas in fact it merely raises problems for him that his subsequent account of the 'concrete universal' fails to solve, concerning the 'contradiction between reality and ideality'.

We have seen, therefore, how there is an important strand of nineteenth-century 'continental' thought—out of which different forms of existentialism, materialism, critical theory, and empiricism were to develop—that emerges as a reaction against Hegel's approach to the problem of universality. Turning now to the twentieth century, we will consider how this question plays a role in the thought of Gilles Deleuze, who offers a particularly sophisticated treatment of the issue.

---

[28] Søren Kierkegaard, *Papirer*, ed. P. A. Heiberg, V. Kuhr, and E. Torstling (Copenhagen: Gyldendal, 1909–48), IV B1: 146; translated as *Johannes Climacus, or De Omnibus Dubitandum Est*, in *Philosophical Fragments and Johannes Climacus, Philosophical Writings*, vii, ed. and trans. Howard V. Hong and Edna H. Hong (Princeton: Princeton University Press, 1985), 167–8. Cf. also a draft of this passage (*Papirer* IV B 14: 6; translated Hong and Hong, p. 255): '[I]t is language that cancels immediacy; if man could not talk he would remain in the immediate. This could be expressed, he [Johannes Climacus] thought, by saying that the immediate is reality, language is ideality, since by speaking I produce the contradiction. When I seek to express sense perception in this way, the contradiction is present, for what I say is something different from what I want to say. I cannot express reality in language, because I use ideality to characterize it, which is a contradiction, an untruth.'
[29] *Papirer* IV B 10: 7; translated Hong and Hong, p. 257.

# 4. INDIVIDUALITY AND DIFFERENCE

Deleuze approaches the problem of individuality from the perspective of what is known as his 'philosophy of difference'. This perspective is captured in the following passage from one of his major works, *Difference and Repetition*:

That identity not be first, that it exist as a principle but as a second principle, as a principle *become*; that it revolve around the Different; such would be the nature of the Copernican revolution which opens up the possibility of difference having its own concept, rather than being maintained under the domination of a concept in general already understood as identical.[30]

For Deleuze, Hegel is typical of a thinker who does not give difference 'its own concept', because for Hegel when something is an individual and so distinct from anything else, it is not distinct 'immediately' or 'in itself', but distinct from things that are of the same kind as itself, by virtue of properties that set these identical things apart from one another. Thus, Deleuze takes Hegel to put identity prior to difference, because he holds that while the difference between things makes them individuals, their difference is grounded in an underlying identity: Fido and Rex are distinct in the properties they possess, but they only possess those properties qua dogs, which is a substance universal they both share. In this respect, he argues, Hegel puts identity first and difference second, whereas Deleuze wants to put them the other way round.[31]

Deleuze makes clear that he sees the need for his 'Copernican revolution' in order to overturn a certain 'image of thought',[32] which in part arises from treating as essential to individuals what they have in common, in the manner of Plato's Forms. The danger with this view, as Deleuze sees it, is its essential conservatism: thought will attempt to assimilate all individuals into a general type, and thereby exclude or devalue their difference or singularity, as when we speak of a 'common sense' that is supposed to be shared by everyone, but which in fact imposes a false consensus on the minority; or think of the individual as the less than perfect instantiation of the kind to which

---

[30] Gilles Deleuze, *Différence et Répétition* (Paris: Presses Universitaires de France, 1968), 59; translated as *Difference and Repetition* by Paul Patton (London: Athlone Press, 1994), 40–1.

[31] For helpful general discussions of Deleuze's critique of Hegel, see Bruce Baugh, *French Hegel: From Surrealism to Postmodernism* (New York and London: Routledge, 2003), 147–56, and Catherine Malabou, 'Who's Afraid of Hegelian Wolves?', in Paul Patton (ed.), *Deleuze: A Critical Reader* (Oxford: Blackwell, 1996).

[32] Cf. Deleuze, *Différence et Répétition*, ch. III, and pp. xvi–xvii of the English translation.

it belongs.[33] Deleuze believes he can bring out what is wrong with Hegel's conception of individuation, whereby Socrates is treated as a variant on a kind, rather than something fundamentally new, unique, original, something which thought cannot assimilate as a 'reproduction' of what it has already encountered (as another man, like Callicles or Caius).[34]

Thus, in order to turn the Hegelian picture on its head, Deleuze sets out to challenge it as a solution to the problem of individuation. First, he argues that Hegel cannot account for *difference*, because he must do so in terms of the concepts that the individual exemplifies, which are always general and can therefore be shared by other individuals; and second, he argues that Hegel cannot account for *repetition*, because he must think of this as two (or more) individuals exemplifying the same concept at different places and/or times, which is to misrepresent the phenomenon of repetition, which involves one individual repeating another *individual* as such, rather than exemplifying the same properties *as* another individual.

Deleuze urges the problem of difference against Hegel by arguing that, like Leibniz, Hegel must find himself committed to an implausibly strong version of the principle of the identity of indiscernibles. In Leibniz's case, he finds himself obliged to argue that no two things can be the same with respect to just their non-relational or intrinsic properties, because when God decides to bring an individual thing into existence, what makes it an individual thing different from anything else cannot be its relation to other things, as these relations do not obtain until *after* God's creative act. Leibniz is therefore forced to argue that two leaves must differ from each other not just because

[33] Cf. also Adorno, *Metaphysik*, 125–6; *Metaphysics*, 79: 'It might be said with some exaggeration that matter is the *principium individuationis* in Aristotle, and not, as we are inclined to think, form, which is that which determines a particular thing as particular. For him, however, individuation itself is founded precisely on this particularization—the lack of identity, or full identity, of an existent thing with its form. Individuation thus becomes something negative in Aristotle. And that, too, is a basic thesis of all western metaphysics, as it reappears in Kant, where cognition is equated with the determining of an object in its generality and necessity, and as you find it worked to its extreme in Hegel, where only the universal manifesting itself through individuation is the substantial—whereas anything which lies outside the identification with the universal principle is regarded as absolutely insignificant, ephemeral and unimportant'.

[34] Theodor W. Adorno, *Negative Dialektik* (Frankfurt: Suhrkamp, 1966), 175; translated as *Negative Dialectics*, by E. B. Ashton (London: Routledge, 1973), 173: 'The concept of the particular is always its negation at the same time; it cuts short what the particular is and what nonetheless cannot be directly named, and it replaces this with identity . . . The idealist will not see that, however devoid of qualities "something" may be, this is no reason yet to call it "nothing." Hegel is constantly forced to shadow-box because he shrinks from his own conception: from the dialectics of the particular, which destroyed the primacy of identity and thus, consistently, idealism itself.'

they differ in their relational properties (e.g. in their age, or their spatial properties), but in their intrinsic properties (e.g. their colour or shape). Now, Deleuze suggests that Hegel must also be committed to a view that is implausibly strong in the same way: for, on Hegel's view, individuation is the result of the particularization of the substance-universal; but no individual has its relational properties qua instantiation of a kind, or its spatial and temporal properties either, if these are thought of in a non-relational way (as in Kant's example of left and right hands);[35] so that on this view these properties cannot be what distinguishes one individual from anything else. For example, while being a certain colour or shape is part of what it is for Fido to be a dog, it is arguable that being here or being born when he was is not an aspect of his dogginess in the same way. But if this is so on the Hegelian view, where it is only qua dog that Fido is an individual, and none of these relational properties or spatio-temporal properties are parts of his dogginess, then isn't the Hegelian therefore required to hold (like Leibniz) that each individual must differ with respect to its *intrinsic* qualities only, where (as with Leibniz) this seems implausible? Deleuze argues, therefore, that what makes an individual *this* individual can be nothing to do with its nature qua member of a kind, which is what he means when he says that difference need not be anything to do with *conceptual* difference: for example, two hands can be identical qua hands, but still be different, where the non-conceptual difference between them (for example, one being the left hand and the other the right) is not grounded in this identity, as it is a difference that is not an aspect of 'being a hand', while nonetheless making them distinct. Deleuze thus argues that while Hegel may have thought that he had a better way of establishing Leibniz's principle than looking to see if in fact two things sharing the same intrinsic properties could be found, his position is equally unsatisfactory:

is every difference indeed intrinsic and conceptual in the last instance? Hegel ridiculed Leibniz for having invited the court ladies to undertake experimental metaphysics while walking in the gardens, to see whether two leaves of a tree could not have the same concept.[36] Replace the court ladies by forensic scientists: no two grains of

---

[35] Cf. Immanuel Kant, 'Von dem ersten Grunde der Unterschiedes der Gegenden im Raume', in *Immanuel Kant's gesammelte Schriften*, 29 vols., Akademie edn., Deutsche Akademie der Wissenschaften (Berlin: Walter de Gruyter, 1902– ), ii. 375–83, 381–2; translated as 'Concerning the Ultimate Ground of the Differentiation of Regions in Space', in *Theoretical Philosophy, 1755–1770*, trans. David Walford (Cambridge: Cambridge University Press, 1992), 361–72, 370.

[36] Cf. G. W. Leibniz to Samuel Clarke, fourth letter, 2 June 1716, §4; G. W. Leibniz to the Electress Sophia, 31 October 1705.

dust are absolutely identical, no two hands have the same distinctive points, no two typewriters have the same strike, no two revolvers score their bullets in the same manner. ... Why, however, do we feel that the problem is not properly defined so long as we look for the criterion of a *principium individuationis* in the facts? It is because a difference can be internal, yet not conceptual (as the paradox of symmetrical objects shows).[37]

Deleuze thus concludes: 'Perhaps the mistake of the philosophy of difference, from Aristotle to Hegel via Leibniz, lay in confusing the concept of difference with merely conceptual difference, in remaining content to inscribe difference in the concept in general'[38]—which I take to mean, that because these philosophers have taken the individuality of a thing to be determined by how it differs from other things of the same kind, any non-conceptual basis of difference has been treated as extrinsic to it qua individual, and so has been lost as a ground for individuation, where this can be a basis for difference which is not related to any identity it has with other individuals of the same kind (Fido may differ from Rex in colour qua dog, but his spatial difference from Rex has nothing to do with his dogginess and so is a difference that cannot be 'inscribed in the concept in general').

As well as claiming that Hegel cannot account for difference in this way, Deleuze also argues that he cannot account for the nature of *repetition*. A natural way to think of repetition, and one that may easily seem to follow from the Hegelian picture, is as follows: $B$ is a repetition of $A$ when $B$ has all the same properties as $A$. So, for example, $Fido_1$ is brown, hairy, lazy, etc., and $Fido_2$ is just the same, so $Fido_2$ is a repetition of $Fido_1$. However, the question Deleuze asks is: why doesn't this just make $Fido_1$ and $Fido_2$ different instances of the same *type*, rather than what we were after, namely a way of seeing $Fido_2$ as a repetition of $Fido_1$ qua individual? What has gone wrong, according to Deleuze, is that each individual is seen as an instance of a general kind, whereas the phenomenon of repetition involves the repetition of an *individual*, not merely the instantiation of the same type one more time. Thus, for example, suppose an artist wants to repeat a pattern he has already drawn, or a performance that has already happened—he wants to repeat *this* pattern or *this* performance, not to do something of the same *type* as what has occurred before. But, Deleuze argues, the Hegelian picture has no room for

---

[37] Deleuze, *Différence et Répétition*, 39; *Difference and Repetition*, 26.

[38] *Différence et Répétition*, 41; *Difference and Repetition*, 27. Cf. also *Différence et Répétition*, 20–4; *Difference and Repetition*, 11–14.

this distinction between repetition and generality, because the individual is never anything more than an instance of a type, so that another individual identical to the first is just another instance, not a repetition of the individual qua individual:

To repeat is to behave in a certain manner, but in relation to something unique or singular which has no equal or equivalent. And perhaps this repetition at the level of an external conduct echoes, for its own part, a more secret vibration which animates it, a more profound, internal repetition within the singular. This is the apparent paradox of festivals: they repeat an 'unrepeatable'. They do not add a second and a third time to the first, but carry the first time to the 'nth' power. With respect to this power, repetition interiorizes and therefore reverses itself: as Péguy says, it is not Federation Day which commemorates or represents the fall of the Bastille, but the fall of the Bastille which celebrates and repeats in advance all the Federation Days; or Monet's first water lily which repeats all the others. Generality, as generality of the particular, thus stands opposed to repetition as universality of the singular. The repetition of a work of art is like a singularity without concept... If repetition exists, it expresses at once a singularity opposed to the general, a universality opposed to the particular, a distinctive opposed to the ordinary, an instantaneity opposed to variation and an eternity opposed to permanence. In every respect, repetition is a transgression. It puts law into question, it denounces its nominal or general character in favour of a more profound and more artistic reality.[39]

Deleuze therefore sees in repetition a deep challenge to the Hegelian position, and its account of individuation and individuality.

Having identified these two problems for Hegel, Deleuze makes clear what he sees as the underlying difficulty: that because Hegel adopts a 'philosophy

---

[39] *Différence et Répétition*, 7–9; *Difference and Repetition*, 1–3. Cf. *Différence et Répétition*, 36; *Difference and Repetition*, 23: 'We are right to speak of repetition when we find ourselves confronted by identical elements with exactly the same concept. However, we must distinguish between these discrete elements, these repeated objects, and a secret subject, the real subject of repetition, which repeats itself through them. Repetition must be understood as pronominal; we must find the Self of repetition, the singularity within that which repeats. For there is no repetition without a repeater, nothing repeated without a repetitious soul'; and Gilles Deleuze, 'La conception de la différence chez Bergson', *Les études bergsoniennes*, 4 (1956), 77–112, 104; translated as 'Bergson's Conception of Difference' by Melissa McMahon, in John Mullarkey (ed.), *The New Bergson* (Manchester: Manchester University Press, 1999), 42–65, 58: 'Repetition does indeed form objective kinds, but these kinds are not in themselves general ideas, because they do not envelop a plurality of objects which resemble each other, but only present us the particularity of an object which repeats itself in an identical way'. In focusing on repetition as a central issue, Deleuze was picking up on critical insights he found in Nietzsche and Kierkegaard: cf. *Différence et Répétition*, 12–13; *Difference and Repetition*, 5: 'There is a force common to Kierkegaard and Nietzsche... What separates them is considerable, evident and well-known. But nothing can hide this prodigious encounter in relation to a philosophy of repetition: *they oppose repetition to all forms of generality*.'

of identity', he treats the differences between things as beginning with an underlying identity; but differentiation conceived of in this manner can never go far enough: no matter how many properties are added to the universal 'dog', Fido's individuality must remain elusive, for these properties can always be shared with another individual, and thus all we reach is the 'infima species' or lowest species, rather than the individual as such:

The individual is neither a qualification nor a partition, neither an organisation nor a determination of species. The individual is no more an *infima species* than it is composed of parts. Qualitative or extensive interpretations of individuation remain incapable of providing reasons why a quality ceases to be general, or why a synthesis of extensity begins here and finishes there. The determination of qualities and species presupposes individuals to be qualified, while extensive parts are relative to an individual rather than the reverse . . . Because there are individuals of different species and individuals of the same species, there is a tendency to believe that individuation is a continuation of the determination of species, albeit of a different kind and proceeding by different means. In fact any confusion between the two processes, any reduction of individuation to a limit or complication of differenciation, compromises the whole of the philosophy of difference.[40]

Given this sort of view, it is therefore not surprising to find that Deleuze is drawn to something like a haecceity conception of individuality, as a way of securing his claim 'that individuation precedes differenciation in principle, that every differenciation presupposes a prior intense field of individuation'.[41] Deleuze accepts that individuality conceived of in this way is ineffable, as something that 'rises to the surface yet assumes neither form nor figure. It is there staring at us, but without eyes';[42] but he resists the Hegelian suggestion that this leaves us in 'the night in which all cows are black', where no individual is distinguishable from any other: 'how differenciated and differenciating is this blackness, even though these differences remain unidentified and barely or non-individuated'.[43] In *A Thousand Plateaus*, Deleuze and his co-author Felix Guattari characterize this 'prior intense field of individuation' as the singularity of spatio-temporal relations, where they treat times and places as having a haecceity, rather than individuals as such, and argue that the former are prior to the latter, where individuals should therefore be seen more as 'events' than as 'subjects',

[40]  Deleuze, *Différence et Répétition*, 318; *Difference and Repetition*, 247.    [41]  Ibid.
[42]  Ibid., 197; *Difference and Repetition*, 152.
[43]  Ibid., 355; *Difference and Repetition*, 277. The reference to 'the night in which all cows are black' is to Hegel's well-known criticism of what he saw as Schelling's monistic conception of the Absolute: see Hegel, *Phänomenologie*, 22; *Phenomenology*, 9.

in opposition to the traditional metaphysics of individuation that we have been considering.[44]

We have seen, then, how in common with many post-Hegelian thinkers, Deleuze believes that his attempt to construct a 'philosophy of difference' must take him away from Hegel, and into a 'generalized anti-Hegelianism' summarized in the slogan: 'We propose to think difference in itself independently of the forms of representation which reduce it to the Same.'[45] To Deleuze, Hegel's commitment to this reductionism is clearly evident from the role Hegel (like Aristotle) gives to the substance-universal: for if it is only qua dogs that Fido and Rex can be said to be particularized into individuals, doesn't this show that, for Hegel, difference is only allowed to exist in terms of an underlying identity belonging to the generic concept?

However, is Deleuze too quick to set up his 'philosophy of difference' as a challenge to Hegel here in the way he does? Does he overlook the complexities of Hegel's doctrine of the 'concrete universal'? This could perhaps be argued by looking at a passage from Deleuze himself, which comes from an early discussion of Bergson:

In some essential pages dedicated to Ravaisson,[46] Bergson explains that there are two ways of determining what colours have in common. *Either* one extracts the abstract and general idea of colour, extracted 'by taking away from red what makes it red, from blue what makes it blue, from green what makes it green': one then ends up with a concept which is a genre, with several objects that have the same concept. There is a duality of concept and object, and the relation of the object to the concept is one of subsumption. One thus stops at spatial distinctions, at a state of difference exterior to the thing. *Or*, one passes the colours through a converging lens which directs them on to a single point: what we obtain, in this case, is a 'pure white light', which 'brought out the differences between the tints'. In this case the different colours are no longer *under* a concept, but the nuances or degrees of the concept itself, degrees of difference itself and not differences of degree. The relation is no longer one of subsumption, but participation. White light is still a universal, but a concrete universal, which enables us to understand the particular because it is itself at the extreme of the particular. Just as things have become nuances or degrees of the concept, the concept itself has become the thing. It is a universal thing, we could say, since the objects are sketched

---

[44]  Cf. Gilles Deleuze and Felix Guattari, *Capitalisme et schizophrenie tome 2: Mille plateaux* (Paris: Éditions de Minuit, 1980); translated as *A Thousand Plateaus: Capitalism and Schizophrenia* by Brian Massumi (London: Athlone Press, 1987), 260–3.

[45]  Deleuze, *Difference and Repetition*, p. xix.

[46]  This is a reference to Bergson's 'La vie et l'oeuvre de Ravaisson', in *La pensée et le mouvant* (Paris: Librairie Félix Alcan, 1934), 281–322, 287–9; translated as 'The Life and Works of Ravaisson', in Henri Bergson. *The Creative Mind: An Introduction to Metaphysics*, trans. Mabelle L. Andison (New York: Philosophical Library, 1946), 225.

therein as so many degrees, but a concrete thing, not a kind or a generality. Strictly speaking there are no longer several objects with the same concept, as the concept is identical to the thing itself, it is the difference between the objects related to it, not their resemblance. Such is internal difference: the concept become concept of difference.[47]

In treating Bergson as an ally here, Deleuze offers no acknowledgement that the very idea of a concrete universal has an Hegelian provenance, and that in adopting it, Hegel intended to make just the points that Deleuze follows Bergson in making here; and yet, Deleuze does seem to accept that if we think of the universal in concrete terms, 'the concept [has] become concept of difference'. If this can be allowed, then given Hegel's own account of the concrete universal, Deleuze's claim that Hegel reduces difference to identity could perhaps be resisted in the same way:

When people speak of the Concept, they ordinarily have only abstract universality in mind, and consequently the Concept is usually also defined as a general notion. We speak in this way of the 'concept' of colour, or of a plant, or of an animal, and so on; and these concepts are supposed to arise by omitting the particularities through which the various colours, plants, animals, etc., are distinguished from one another, and holding fast to what they have in common. This is the way in which the understanding apprehends the Concept, and the feeling that such concepts are hollow and empty, that they are mere schemata and shadows, is justified. What is universal about the Concept is indeed not just something common against which the particular stands on its own; instead the universal is what particularises (specifies) itself, remaining at home with itself in its other, in unclouded clarity.[48]

Just as Deleuze finds attractive in Bergson's position the idea that the concept of colour cannot be thought of as something in abstraction from the particular colours, so Hegel emphasizes that these 'particularities' cannot be 'omitted'; and as a result, like Bergson on Deleuze's reading, Hegel claims that the universal is not just something individuals have in common prior to what makes them distinct as individuals, so that he would agree that 'the different colours are no longer *under* a concept' (in a Platonic manner), but 'the nuances or degrees of the concept itself'. On these grounds, it could be argued, it makes no more sense in Hegel's case than it does in Bergson's to claim that

---

[47] Deleuze, 'La conception de la différence chez Bergson', 98–9; 'Bergson's Conception of Difference', 54.

[48] Hegel, *Enzyklopädie Logik*, §164 Zusatz, pp. 311–12; *Encyclopaedia Logic*, §163, p. 240. For a further attempt to bring out these aspects of Hegel's position, see Robert Stern, 'Hegel, British Idealism, and the Curious Case of the Concrete Universal', *British Journal for the History of Philosophy*, 15 (2007), 115–53.

identity is *prior to* difference, in so far as the latter can equally be said to be required for the former.

Of course, even if it can be claimed that Hegel's conception of the 'concrete universal' is closer to Deleuze's philosophy of difference than Deleuze was prepared to allow, this does not show that either position is unproblematic or indeed yet free of apparent incoherence: for each, as we have seen, tries to strike a balance between different competing pressures when it comes to thinking of the problem of individuality. But we have seen how fundamental this problem has become within the 'continental' tradition, and how the complex approaches offered to it reflect the real difficulties it gives rise to, not only in metaphysics, but in ethics, political philosophy, and 'philosophies of life'.[49]

---

[49] A version of this essay was presented to a Departmental seminar at the University of Warwick, and I am grateful to members of the audience for comments on that occasion. I am also grateful for comments from Keith Ansell-Pearson and Alison Stone.

# CHAPTER 12

# CONSCIOUSNESS IN THE WORLD

## HUSSERLIAN PHENOMENOLOGY AND EXTERNALISM

### PETER POELLNER

## 1. INTRODUCTION

DURING the last two decades, talk about 'phenomenology' has proliferated in some quarters of analytic philosophy. Often the expression has been used as a portmanteau term for the conscious 'what-it-is-likeness' of experience (or its phenomenal contents), without much attention to, or interest in, the structural articulations of this what-it-is-likeness. But it is precisely the analysis of these structures that has been the central concern of phenomenology, understood as the distinctive philosophical tradition that was inaugurated by Edmund Husserl, and subsequently continued and modified by philosophers like Jean-Paul Sartre, Maurice Merleau-Ponty, and the early (pre–1930) Martin Heidegger, to name but the most eminent figures. Phenomenology in this second, technical, sense has also received increasing attention in analytic circles in recent years, largely for two reasons. First, the work of the later, 'existential' phenomenologists has been found helpful in elucidating the fundamental constitutive role played in conscious intentionality by embodied practical comportment, in particular by skilled bodily action.[1] Secondly, Husserl's classical phenomenology has been recognized as anticipating the thought, influentially articulated in Gareth Evans's *The Varieties of Reference*, that the contents of personal-level intentionality are not exhaustively analysable by way of the analysis of their linguistic expression; and in particular, that the contents of perception play a foundational role, although they do not have the structure of fully linguistically articulable propositions.[2]

Yet, while Heidegger's (and Merleau-Ponty's) versions of phenomenology may be suggestive, their work is often also seen, not entirely without reason, as not very hospitable to some of the fine-grained distinctions relevant to a philosophical analysis of intentional content. Husserl, by contrast, certainly does offer an extremely nuanced conceptual arsenal in this respect, but his approach is often thought to be irremediably compromised by two problematic, and related, methodological commitments: (1) a form of 'Cartesian' content internalism, according to which a subject can have thoughts about itself and the world without having any warranted *beliefs* about a world of real external (spatial) objects; (2) the idea that conscious thought about the world is at the basic level epistemically indirect, involving mediating entities of some kind, such as Fregean senses.[3]

I shall offer an alternative interpretation of Husserl which rejects both of these exegetical claims. This will require some detailed attention to a central, much-debated, indeed notorious, methodological technique of his: the so-called phenomenological (or transcendental) reduction. My argument will be that, properly understood, it entails neither (1) nor (2). According to the interpretation offered here, Husserl's classical phenomenology is an

---

[1] Particularly influential here has been Hubert Dreyfus, *Being-in-the-World: A Commentary on Heidegger's 'Being and Time', Division 1*.

[2] For a conceptualist version of this claim, see John McDowell, *Mind and World*. Husserl's anticipation of this general type of approach was made more widely known in an analytic context by Michael Dummett's *Origins of Analytical Philosophy*, a study whose interpretation of Husserl suffers, however, from a number of misunderstandings and from its exclusive focus on the early *Logical Investigations*.

[3] For an influential interpretation of Husserl's theory of intentionality as involving a commitment to such Fregean mediating entities, see David Woodruff Smith and Ronald McIntyre, *Husserl and Intentionality*.

externalist philosophy of conscious intentionality, according to which the logically basic level of world-representation is to be found in direct *perception*, the contents of which are, in principle, not fully linguistically encodable. Moreover, Husserl holds that the perceptual representation of a world is only possible for an embodied subject that is capable of self-movement and bodily action. Husserl's account of intentionality thus anticipates, and in some respects provides a more fundamental analysis of, the idea of extra-linguistic ground-level components of conscious intentional content that we find in contemporary philosophy of thought. On the other hand, it is also much closer to the later, 'existential' accounts of embodied intentionality than is often recognized, especially in the Anglophone reception of his work. Indeed it could be argued to capture most (although not all) of what is right in the early Heidegger's emphasis on practical comportment, while avoiding some of its problems.

The argument of this essay is primarily about substantive philosophical issues, with current debates in view, rather than about interpretive matters.[4] While the basis of the interpretation offered is of course in Husserl's own texts, where I have had to choose between either pursuing exegetical disputes, or the philosophical development or discussion of a position found or suggested in the texts, I have opted for the latter. The structure of the essay is as follows. Section 2 briefly introduces the mature Husserl's philosophical project—the putatively foundational, 'transcendental' explication of the constitutive conditions of a subject's being able to represent a world at all—and Husserl's fundamental methodological principle—the idea that the claims of phenomenology are to be based on what is 'self-given' in experience. The central Sections 3 and 4 of the essay will address and defend the most controversial, and most often misinterpreted, aspects of Husserl's phenomenological approach: the suspension of (certain types of) 'theory', and what he sometimes refers to as the 'bracketing' of beliefs about the real world. In the concluding Section 5, I shall offer some brief reflections on how Husserl's phenomenological (in a quasi-Kantian sense, 'empirical') externalist realism relates to stronger, metaphysical claims. This will also indicate the shape of an answer to the question why, for Husserl and the philosophical tradition inaugurated by him, phenomenology, rather than metaphysics or the epistemology of the actual world, is 'first philosophy'.

---

[4]  For a more extensive discussion of the interpretive issues, see Zahavi, 'Husserl's Noema and the Internalism-Externalism Debate'.

# 2. HUSSERL'S AIMS: EXPLICATING THE CONDITIONS OF REPRESENTATION AND SUBJECTIVITY

For Husserl, the fundamental issue of philosophy, as he comes to conceive of it with increasing clarity in his middle period and later writings from 1907 onwards, is a transcendental inquiry into the question of how it is possible that a world should be representable by a subject:

> Elucidating in their entirety the interwoven [*Ineinander*] achievements of consciousness which lead to the constitution of a possible world—a possible world: this means that what is at issue is the essential form of world in general and not just our factual, actual world—this is the comprehensive task of constitutive phenomenology.   (*EJ*, §11, p. 50/50)[5]

'Constitution', here as elsewhere in Husserl, must of course not be understood as 'creation' but as 'constitution-for-experience', that is, as roughly synonymous with 'manifestation to consciousness'. His question thus is about what is *constitutively* required for a world to be experiencable by someone at all, and about the necessary structures of this 'constitution'. Husserl never argues in detail for the claim that the representation of objects necessarily requires consciousness, but from the outset seems to regard it as self-evident that the relation of representation, in any sense that might be relevant to a transcendental investigation into the conditions of the possibility of there being a world for a subject, is essentially a matter of intentional experiences ('acts') in which objects 'appear' to a consciousness (see, e.g. *LI* 5, §8, II/1, p. 362/II, p. 93). And by 'consciousness' he means what is sometimes referred to as 'phenomenal consciousness', involving various phenomenal, experienced properties, a certain 'what-it-is-likeness'. The task of phenomenology consists in an explication of the actual complexity of this what-it-is-likeness.[6]

---

[5] This and all subsequent translations from Husserl are mine. Husserl's conception of philosophy contrasts markedly with much of the mainstream of modern philosophy since Descartes, where either metaphysical questions ('how do our subjective representations relate to what there really is?'), or questions of factual epistemology ('how can we attain knowledge of the actual world?'), have tended to be taken to be fundamental. It is not my intention here to provide a defence of the motivations for the philosophical reorientation, the 'phenomenological turn' initiated by Husserl, but some suggestions on this score will be made in the conclusion.

[6] One of the many important distinctions here—emphasized by Husserl but often conflated in contemporary discussions—is the distinction between the phenomenal properties of *experiences* and

Many contemporary philosophers of mind would argue that the conditions minimally required for an information-processing system to count as representational do not include phenomenal consciousness.[7] But it is doubtful whether Husserl would want to contest, and he certainly does not *need* to deny, that functional analogues of conscious representation can be defined over sets of subpersonal states. His question is not whether something sharing some or many of the features of our everyday concept of representation is usefully applicable to certain sorts of non-conscious information-processing. His central point should rather be taken to be that whether this is so or not, without evidences presenting themselves phenomenally to our consciousness, 'there would be *for us*...no real and no ideal world. Both of these exist *for us* thanks to evidence or the presumption of being able to make evident and to repeat acquired evidence' (*CM*, §27, p. 96/60).[8] 'Objects exist *for us* and are *for us* what they are only as objects of actual or possible consciousness' (*CM*, §30, p. 99/65; all emphases mine). His thought here is that there could be no personal-level representations, no *world for a subject*, without this world manifesting itself in or to phenomenal consciousness. Whether this thesis can be vindicated depends in part on what is implied by the phrase 'for a subject'. One reasonably uncontroversial interpretation of this would be to say that the content of an informational state is available to the subject being in that state just in case the subject is in fact able to use this content in rationalizing his or her actions and judgements. This condition on personal-level representational content comes fairly close to what Ned Block calls a representational content's being *access-conscious*.[9] Yet, according to

those which *objects* appear as having when experienced (e.g. the red surface colour of a tomato). As Michael Martin notes, a great deal of qualia talk in current debates equivocates on these different meanings of 'what it is like'. See Martin, 'Setting Things before the Mind', 158–66.

[7] One illuminating account of subpersonal representation is J. L. Bermúdez's, according to which states of an information-processing system can count as representational if they satisfy the conditions of (a) plasticity and flexibility in relation to environmental stimuli, (b) cognitive integration with other states of the system, (c) compositional structure, and (d) possession of correctness conditions defined in terms of proper or improper functioning. None of these conditions require the presence of phenomenal consciousness. (J. L. Bermúdez, 'Nonconceptual Content: From Perceptual Experience to Subpersonal Computational States', 333–67.)

[8] 'Evidence' (*Evidenz*) is a technical term in Husserl, signifying, in the wider sense relevant in the above citation, the direct presentation or 'self-givenness' of the intentional object in experience (see *EJ*, §4). An item X is directly presented (self-given) in consciousness just in case there is no conscious epistemic intermediary representing or standing for X. Husserl also calls direct presentation 'originary'.

[9] Ned Block, 'On a Confusion about a Function of Consciousness', 227–47. The analogy is not precise, however, since Block also allows contents to be access-conscious in circumstances where the subjects 'entertaining' them possess no concepts relevant for using the contents in inference (p. 246).

Block, it is conceptually possible that a content should be access-conscious, being poised for use as a premise in reasoning and for the rational control of actions, without being phenomenally conscious. It is precisely this conceptual possibility which Husserl denies. Block illustrates his anti-phenomenological point by the following thought-experiment (p. 233). Imagine a subject that is like what a blindsight subject claims to be, having no phenomenal consciousness at all of parts of his visual field. Yet, unlike a real blindsighter, he can not only make correct guesses, when prompted, about what is in the occluded part of his visual field, when given the choice among a limited number of relatively simple alternatives. Rather, this 'superblindsighter' can prompt himself at will to make correct 'guesses' about what is in his blind field about a wide range of objects. 'Visual information from his blind field simply pops into his thoughts' (ibid.). According to Block, this would be a case of access-consciousness without phenomenal consciousness. However, the crucial question to ask here is whether the superblindsighter could come to regard his (*de facto* correct) guesses as *reasons* for belief or action. It seems that, while he would have a method of acquiring information that was in fact reliable, he would have no grounds recognizable by him to regard it as such. But information that is not recognizable by me as a reason cannot be a reason *for me*. As far as the superblindsighter is concerned, the correctness of his guesses is no different from a bizarre fluke.[10] But even to say this is to help oneself to the idea that he has a way of finding out that his guesses have been correct. But how should he establish *this* without some further information that is *not* phenomenally unconscious to him? Only if at least some of his representations are phenomenally conscious can he recognize the correctness of his guesses and, as a consequence, inferentially come to regard them as reasons for belief. Thus, access consciousness cannot generally be independent of phenomenal consciousness, if we want to hold on to the idea that, for something to qualify as a subject's reason for judgements and other actions, it has to be in principle available to, and therefore recognizable by, the subject. Without phenomenal consciousness, nothing can constitute a reason *for* a subject. And this is precisely *one* part of Husserl's point in the following passage:

Direct 'seeing', not only sensory seeing of spatio-temporal particulars, but seeing quite generally understood as consciousness that presents something originarily [i.e.

---

[10] Similar arguments can be found in Lowe, 'Experience and its Objects', 90–5, and Eilan, 'Perceptual Intentionality. Attention and Consciousness', 182–4.

directly] in whatever way, is the ultimate source of justification for all rational assertions. . . . It would be incoherent, when answering the question 'why?', to give no weight to the response 'I am seeing it'.    (*Id 1*, §19, pp. 36/36–7)

This passage also alludes to a related methodological commitment of Husserl's, which he sometimes calls his 'principle of principles': the phenomenological investigation of a subject matter requires that the latter be made directly ('originarily') present in experience (e.g. LI, Introduction, §2; *Id 1*, §24). The aspiration expressed in his slogan 'back to the things themselves' is that the philosopher qua phenomenologist should confine herself to explicating descriptively what has thus been perceived or otherwise directly given to the investigator in its phenomenal character. Husserl's thought here is that anything that is *constitutive* for world-manifestation would have to be accessible in direct experience.

In fact, his 'principle of principles' is even more restrictive. The position he eventually adopts is that phenomenological claims are to be exclusively about what has been, and can again be, self-given with 'apodictic' evidence, i.e. effectively about what is presented as indubitable or certain, such that any subsequent falsification is inconceivable to the investigator, or to any subject having a type-identical presentation, at the time of having it (*CM*, §§6–7). It is clear that Husserl's motivation for this exceedingly demanding conception of phenomenological investigation is the classical foundationalist aspiration to provide philosophy with a set of basic non-inferential propositions that are known with certainty to be true—this is at least part of the import of his claim that phenomenology is to provide an 'absolute' starting point for philosophical inquiry (*Id 1*, §§46, 50; *CM*, §§3–6).[11]

What sort of items can be apodictically self-given, according to Husserl? In his later work, he recognizes that no categorical predicative judgement about contingent matters (e.g. about some particular experience or object-appearance) can plausibly claim such apodicticity: 'in unqualifiedly apodictic evidence, self-explication brings out only the universal structural forms'

---

[11]  Cf. Tugendhat, *Der Wahrheitsbegriff bei Husserl und Heidegger*, 194–5. Some commentators have denied that this Cartesian theme continues to motivate Husserl in his final period, since it does not appear prominently in his last work, the *Crisis* (1936). (See Kern, *Husserl und Kant: Eine Untersuchung über Husserls Verhältnis zu Kant und zum Neukantianismus*, 236. Also Carr, 'The "Fifth Meditation" and Husserl's Cartesianism', 14–15.) But the emphatic presence of the Cartesian requirement of indubitability from the middle period *Ideas I* (1913) to the late *Cartesian Meditations* (1929) seems to me to tell against such interpretations. In fact, even in *Crisis*, while the theme is indeed no longer prominent, Husserl still insists on the apodicticity of phenomenological claims. See *Crisis*, §15, p. 73/72.

(*CM*, §46 p. 133/103). And it is only these 'universal structural forms' that phenomenology is ultimately concerned with; all its truths are to be necessary truths about 'eidetic' states of affairs, intuited 'originarily' on the basis of actual or possible particulars—self-given or imagined—serving as illustrations of them (cf. *Crisis*, §§50–1; on imaginative illustration, see *Id 1*, §70).[12]

The problems with the exorbitant demand for absolute certainty are familiar and need not be rehearsed here. To mention but one obvious difficulty: how could I even have indubitable and persisting knowledge of the *meanings* of the words I have used to explicate the phenomena? Husserl himself in later writings comes close to recognizing the futility of the aspiration towards contentful (non-formal) apodictic truths. For he concedes that it is possible to be deceived in thinking that an evidence is genuinely apodictic (*FTL*, §58), a concession which would seem to render the appeal to apodicticity otiose. Arguably, nothing of significance is lost to phenomenology if it contents itself with claiming, for most of its results, an epistemic distinction less ambitious than apodicticity. This does not imply that Husserl's 'principle of principles' is nugatory, but that the philosophically fruitful thought behind it (or behind a modified version of it) may be different from his own explicit justification of it. As in other contexts also, his actual *practice* is often more persuasive than his second-order reflective characterization of it. I suggest that the only aspect of his fundamental principle that is essential to this practice is this:

---

[12]  These general structures also include the formal properties of objects qua objects, which ultimately ground the basic truths of logic. I shall not discuss in detail Husserl's view that not only particulars, but also general features and structures, such as sensory properties and relations, or categorial properties, can be perceived on the basis of the presence of particulars exemplifying or instantiating them. Similarly, I shall not discuss his later methodological development of this idea—the so-called *eidetic reduction* (see *Id 1*, §§65–70; *Crisis*, §52). What is important in our context is only Husserl's demand that the outcome of phenomenological reflection on the basis of particulars should be appropriately universalized. Phenomenological claims should not concern, say, the structure of *this* temporal object, but the necessary structure of all temporal objects qua temporal objects. The details of this process of intuition-based universalization ('ideation'), which he analyses differently at different stages of his career (*LI 2*, §§1–4, and *EJ*, §§87–8), and indeed differently for different types of universals (*EJ*, §64d), need not concern us here. Let me just briefly remark that the tenet that there can be an 'intuition'—a perception—of universals on the basis of particulars exemplifying them is originally developed by him as the only plausible answer to questions such as: what is it we do when we judge, on the basis of current experience, that *a* is red, or square, or smaller than *b*? His answer is that we express our noticing of a general feature, a *way of being* or universal, which is such that the very same universal can also be exemplified by indefinitely many other particulars. Husserl's theory of a perception of properties and categorial structures is not without difficulties, although Husserlians would argue that this holds for any theory in this area and that greater problems are in store for rival theories which seek to dispense with such a notion. For a perceptive independent defence of the core Husserlian position, see T. L. S. Sprigge, *Facts, Words and Beliefs*, ch. 2.

phenomenological constitutive analysis should aim at a description of the essential intrinsic phenomenal features and structures of the conditions of world-manifestation on the basis of 'intuitively fulfilled' (re-)presentations of them.[13] Such intuitive fulfilment, which should strive for as much relevant detail as possible, may involve perceptions or imaginative representations of exemplifications of these features, or, in the case of subjective experiential characters of conscious episodes (their 'noetic' features), 'living through' (*erleben*) or simulating them (see note 53 below). What justifies this modified Husserlian methodological requirement of 'intuitive fulfilment' is the compelling thought that no descriptive account of the essential *phenomenal* structures of the constitutive conditions of world-manifestation can be well-grounded unless it has a basis, ultimately, in such suitably direct experience.

# 3. The Phenomenological Reduction: A Story of Misunderstandings

Among the methodological devices of Husserlian phenomenology, the one which undoubtedly has attracted most criticism, even among the first generation of his students, is the so-called phenomenological (or 'transcendental') reduction. Husserl developed this procedure in lectures from 1907 onwards and it finds its first canonical statement in *Ideas I*:

Everything belonging to the natural world that comes experientially to consciousness prior to all thinking . . . has the character: 'there', 'actually occurring' [*vorhanden*]—a character which essentially permits an explicit (predicative) existential judgement based upon it . . . This general thesis that pertains to the essence of the natural attitude we put out of action; we place in brackets all and everything that it

---

[13] 'Intrinsic' is intended to contrast with 'extrinsic', not with 'conceptually non-relational'. *Being loved by y* is an extrinsic property of x, but *being in love with y* is an intrinsic (albeit conceptually relational) property of x. The demand that phenomenology should offer elucidations of the intrinsic features of its target objects makes for an obvious contrast with *functionalist* theories, which provide characterizations of their objects in terms of their functional role. While no actual entity can have a functional role without having some *in principle* 'intuitable' intrinsic properties, functionalist analysis abstracts from the latter. Such abstraction is, for Husserl, legitimate in the context of natural science (*Crisis*, §9a, p. 23/26; §34d), whose central aim is prediction. But it is unacceptable in a discipline which, like phenomenology, aims to offer a *fundamental* account of the constitutive conditions of world-manifestation.

embraces ontically,...I practise the 'phenomenological' $\varepsilon\pi o\chi\eta$, which disallows any judgement about spatio-temporal existence. Thus I suspend [*schalte aus*] all the sciences relating to this natural world...I make absolutely no use of its valid claims...consciousness has in itself its own being, which in its absolutely own essence is not affected by the phenomenological suspension. Thus it remains as 'phenomenological residuum'...    (*Id 1*, §§31–2, pp. 53/57–8, 56–7/61, 59/65)

And thus we ask quite generally, keeping in mind these suspensions, what is 'inherent' in the whole 'reduced' phenomenon. Well then, what is inherent in a perception is also this, that it has a noematic sense, its 'perceived as such': 'this blossoming tree there in space'—understood with the quotation marks—that is, the correlate essentially pertaining to the phenomenologically reduced perception. ... The 'bracketing' which has been applied to the perception prevents any judgement about the perceived reality...But it does not prevent a judgement that the perception is consciousness as *of* a reality (whose thesis must now not be 'gone along with', however); and it does not prevent a description of this perceptually appearing 'reality as such', with the specific modes in which it is conscious, e.g. ...appearing in this or that orientation, etc. ...we must now take care not to attribute anything to the experience than what is essentially contained in it, and to 'attribute' this to it just as it actually is 'inherent' in it.    (*Id 1*, §90, pp. 187–8/220–1)

The two central methodological demands expressed in these passages are that the philosopher qua phenomenologist must

(1)  give faithful explicative analyses of the experiences under investigation *and* of their objects just as they are experienced, without recourse to *scientific-theoretical* interpretations, and

(2)  suspend any 'judgement about spatio-temporal existence'.

(1) will turn out to be relatively straightforward and I shall therefore address this demand first. The idea runs like a red thread through Husserl's writings that phenomenology must be 'presuppositionless' in not using any premises, and not relying even implicitly on assumptions from scientific, metaphysical, or common-sense 'theories' (see, e.g. LI, Introduction, §7; *EJ*; §10). Its motivation is twofold. First, there is the problematic 'Cartesian' motif we have already encountered: no such theoretical claims can claim apodictic status. Husserl's second motivation for the demand for theoretical abstemiousness is, however, independent of, and more compelling than, his commitment to a Cartesian ideal of knowledge. Scientific and metaphysical theories are intended as explanations of the phenomena of our everyday life-world. Their explanatory power in part depends on correct descriptions of these phenomena—a theory putatively explaining a phenomenon that has been significantly misdescribed is not an explanation of that phenomenon

at all. But any 'theoretical' assumptions entering into the description of phenomena themselves are liable to promote such erroneous descriptive characterization of the explananda. For example, the idea, shared by common sense and the physical cognitive sciences, that consciousness of objective properties of the world depends upon causal impacts which instances of these properties, or causal powers associated with them, have upon the organism's peripheral nerve endings, creates a theoretical pressure to construe properties for which no appropriate causal role or mechanism can be found—such as the Lockean secondary properties, or value properties—as 'subjective' in the sense of 'intramental' (non-world-involving), and their instances as analogous to sensations or raw, non-intentional 'qualia'. But this construal, hardly less widespread today than in the days of Locke, necessitates a radical misdescription of the very phenomena allegedly explained by the theory:

It is a bad legacy of the psychological tradition since Locke that the sensible qualities of the bodies genuinely experienced in our everyday perceptible environment . . . , which are perceived as in the bodies themselves, are continually conflated with . . . 'sense data' [a conflation which results in] the fundamentally mistaken view . . . that what is immediately given are 'sense data'. (*Crisis*, §9b, pp. 27–28n./30n.)

This example illustrates one potentially critical dimension of phenomenology as conceived by Husserl: no theory that is incompatible with a correct description of the phenomena can be adequate as an *explanation* of those phenomena. A necessary condition upon theoretical adequacy is that a theory should 'save the phenomena'.

The demand that the phenomenologist must aim to describe the 'given as it is given', purified of any theoretical prejudgements, does *not* commit Husserl to a version of what Sellars called the 'myth of the given'—the thought that epistemic justification has its foundation in pre-theoretical, in the sense of *non-conceptualized*, data or impressions.[14] On the contrary, phenomenological analysis shows that such data are not discretely present in normal, attentionally focused experience at all:

The world in which we live and . . . out of which everything that can become a substrate of possible judgements affects us, is always already pre-given as pervaded by sedimentations of logical accomplishments; it is never given otherwise than as a world in which we or others, whose experiential acquisitions we take over through

---

[14] See W. Sellars, 'Empiricism and the Philosophy of Mind', esp. pp. 164–96.

communication, learning, tradition, have been logically active in judgements and cognitions.   (*EJ*, §10, p. 39/42)

Every object of simple (*schlicht*) conscious awareness, e.g. of sense perception, is necessarily presented as exemplifying a 'generality of a determinate type. Its appearance awakens protentional anticipations regarding its being thus-and-so' (*EJ*, §22, p. 114/105). Husserl's reasons for this claim are extremely perceptive, but a discussion of them will have to wait for another occasion. The important point in the present context is that he agrees with Kant that any completely non-conceptual experience is not experience of *objects* at all and hence cannot be cognitive (representational), although it may well contribute to cognitive states by guiding or motivating practical comportment (see pp. 429–30, 439–41). But what, then, does Husserl's distinction between 'theoretical interpretation' and 'describing the given just as it is given' come to? The passage just cited provides a clue to the answer. Some conceptualizations of objects, events, or persons in our environment have the character of what he calls 'sedimented' 'familiarities' for us (*EJ*, §10, p. 39/42; §22, p. 114/105); this means, for one thing, that those items are perceived by us *non-inferentially* under the aspects registered through the concepts in question. Having received the appropriate training and cultural immersion, one can non-inferentially recognize, for example, certain bodily movements as expressions of anger. To say that this conceptualization is 'sedimented' in a subject's very perception of another's behaviour is to say, first, that the applicability of the concept is not consciously inferred from the applicability of other concepts. The subject does not reason: this person is knitting his brow, clenching his fist, and stamping his foot; such behaviours are normally signs of anger; therefore this person is (probably) angry. Rather, 'being angry' is a *basic* perceptual concept (for this subject and in this situation). Secondly, the conceptualization 'this person is angry' is 'sedimented' in that it is *involuntary* rather than the result of an active decision, or even of reflective deliberation, on the part of the subject. So, when Husserl calls for a 'theory-free' description of what is given as it is given, he means by this a description of it as it non-inferentially, involuntarily, and pre-deliberatively presents itself to us.

(2) The second essential component of the phenomenological reduction as Husserl conceives it is the suspension of 'any judgement about spatio-temporal existence'. I shall again postpone the question of the motivation for this requirement and shall first try to elucidate what it actually commits its practitioners to. Phenomenology is to describe consciousness and its objects

just as they are presented to consciousness without entering into any commitments about the existence of *either* the states of consciousness described (*Id 1*, §33, p. 57/63) or any of their objects. The 'phenomenological residuum' that is claimed to remain after this 'bracketing' of existential commitments Husserl sometimes calls 'transcendental consciousness', and the task of phenomenology as envisaged by him is the investigation of its structures. This investigation he also refers to as *phenomenological* (or transcendental) *reflection*. What is distinctive of such 'reflection'? Ordinary ('natural' or 'psychological') reflection is defined by Husserl as an attending to ('thematizing') the experiential quality (the 'noetic moment') of some current intentional experience. Consider the experience expressed by the following sentence:

I am imagining Odysseus's coming on shore in Ithaca.

Psychological reflection on this experience involves attending to one's current *imagining* (rather than perceiving, wishing for, regretting, remembering, etc.) the state of affairs which is its intentional object and which happens in this case to be a fictional object.[15] Transcendental reflection, unlike such natural reflection, abstains from any theoretical or existential commitments concerning what is being reflected upon. Moreover, again unlike natural reflection, its focus is not necessarily on what is intra-psychic, subjective, or 'inner'—i.e. it is *not* originally 'introspective'—for transcendental reflection involves a thematizing not only of the subjective, noetic moment of a current experience but, *necessarily prior* to this, of its noematic component, that is, the intentional *object* just as it is experienced (*Crisis*, §§50, 51).[16] Through transcendental reflection and the faithful description of what is revealed in it, the phenomenological investigator is said to acquire a knowledge of consciousness and its objects qua appearances, that is, of their actually experienced phenomenal character, whatever the metaphysical significance

---

[15] Cf. *Id 1*, §38. For an account of Husserl's wide concept of object, which applies indifferently to actual or fictional states of affairs, material objects, phantoms, properties, and indirectly presented experiences, see below.

[16] On the extended sense of 'reflection', which includes the thematizing of noemata and noematic senses ('the object as it is intended') and, founded upon this, of their essential properties, see e.g. *Id 2*, §4, p. 5/7; *Crisis*, §41. (For more on Husserl's concept of noematic sense, see n. 49 and 50.) Neither the 'object as intended' in an intentional experience, nor its essence, are *reell* contained in the experience, i.e. they are in one sense 'transcendent' of, rather than 'immanent' in, the experience. See *Id 1*, §38, p. 68/79; *Id 1*, §97, p. 202/237. In later writings Husserl tends to stress that the most comprehensive thematic focus of transcendental reflection is on the *relations* between the structures of the object as it is given and the structures of conscious subjectivity which are necessary for the object thus to manifest itself. See *Crisis*, §§41, 51, 53; pp. 155/152, 177/174, 182/179.

of these appearances may be. It thus seems that Husserl believes that a reflective, conceptualized self-consciousness, terminating in the acquisition of various true beliefs about the subject's 'pure', that is, metaphysically uninterpreted, experiences and their conscious contents is possible without committing the investigator to any beliefs about the existence of a physical or otherwise 'external' world. Many critics of the transcendental reduction therefore tend to charge Husserl with subscribing to a version of 'Cartesian' content internalism, according to which the contents of (self-) consciousness are in principle independent of consciousness's being embedded in a world of real spatial objects. To give just two recent examples of this criticism, Mark Rowlands says that

for Husserl, it is possible to make the transcendental role of experience into an empirical item . . . he does believe that consciousness—experience in both empirical and transcendental roles—is *logically* prior to the physical world. Consequently, he also believes that an investigation of the structure of consciousness is *methodologically* prior to an investigation of the physical world. [17]

Similarly, Thomas Baldwin asserts:

Husserl . . . requires that [the philosopher] should not think of himself and his thoughts as elements within the natural world at all. He is not to suppose that his thoughts are the thoughts of a human being, located in objective time and space and standing in causal relations with other physical objects . . . It is this thesis, that there is a domain of pure consciousness . . . not conceptually dependent upon the natural world, which is distinctive of Husserl's phenomenology.[18]

I believe that these familiar, indeed orthodox, interpretations of the phenomenological reduction as implying a form of Cartesian content internalism or methodological solipsism are mistaken. My qualified defence of it as, in its essentials, unobjectionable from a moderate externalist perspective, and indeed as potentially fruitful, will proceed in three stages. First (i), I shall show that most of Husserl's more problematic formulations in this context allow for a philosophically less contentious reading; secondly (ii), I shall argue that the results of Husserl's own first-order analyses of the contents of intentional experiences and their 'order of foundation' actually *commit* him to a type of content externalism; thirdly, I shall suggest (in Section 4) that the phenomenological reduction is not only philosophically unexceptional, but that it is a useful methodological device.

[17]  Mark Rowlands, *Externalism*, 60–1.
[18]  Thomas Baldwin, 'Phenomenology, Solipsism and Egocentric Thought', 28–9.

## (i)  Another Look at the Textual Evidence

There are formulations by Husserl which prima facie support the interpretation of his position as a form of content internalism according to which, as Descartes suggests in his First Meditation, a finite subject can in principle have thoughts, including reflective thoughts about its own consciousness, even if it neither has well-grounded beliefs about a world of spatial objects causally affecting it nor is actually embedded in such a world. These potentially misleading formulations are mostly found in *Ideas I*, rather than in the later detailed discussions of the transcendental reduction in *Erste Philosophie* and *Crisis*. In *Ideas I* Husserl says, for instance, that as phenomenologists 'we keep our gaze fixed on the sphere of consciousness and what we find immanently in it' (*Id 1*, §33, p. 59/65). 'Pure consciousness in its absolute intrinsic being . . . remains as the 'phenomenological residuum' we were looking for; it remains although we have 'suspended' [*ausgeschaltet*] the entire world with all its material objects, living organisms, humans, ourselves included' (*Id 1*, §50, p. 94/113). In this last sentence, the method of phenomenological reduction seems to be fused, in a deeply problematic way, with Husserl's advocacy, in *Ideas I* and subsequently, of a metaphysics of transcendental idealism, according to which consciousness has 'absolute being', while the physical world exists only relative to consciousness of it. Apparently continuous with this metaphysical view, in a notorious passage, he claims that even if there was no world of relatively persisting and re-identifiable spatial things representable by a consciousness, this consciousness could still continue to exist ('albeit necessarily in a modified way'), for transcendental consciousness is

a nexus of absolute being into which nothing can penetrate and out of which nothing can slip; which has no spatio-temporal exteriority and which is not situated within a spatio-temporal context, which can neither be causally affected by any thing nor affect any thing—provided that causality here is understood in the normal sense of natural causality, as a relation of dependence between [spatio-temporal] realities. (*Id 1*, §49, p. 93/112)

Let me take the three centrally problematic points in these formulations in turn. First, there is the idea that phenomenology focuses exclusively on what is 'immanent' in consciousness. In Husserl's terminology, 'immanence' in the strict sense names the relation between a reflected-upon experience (*Erlebnis*) and an experience of reflecting upon that experience, for example the relation that obtains between a pain I am feeling and my *attending* to this pain (cf. *Id 1*, §38, pp. 68–9/79–80). The pain, as it is now thematically experienced by virtue of my reflection upon it, is 'fused' with this attending to it, such that it—this very pain—could not continue to appear as it does without this act of reflection. The pain is, in this 'objectified' mode of presentation, 'really contained within' (*reell beschlossen*) the act of reflection and does not, in this objectified form, exist outside or beyond ('transcend') the reflection. Clearly most of the objects of phenomenological analysis are not 'immanent in consciousness' in *this* sense. For most types of object (e.g. physical things), the noematic 'object as experienced' is 'transcendent' relative to any individual experience of it (*Id 1*, §76, p. 142/171–2; §97, p. 202/237), and the universal phenomenal properties and structures which are the ultimate objects of phenomenological study are necessarily thus transcendent (see also note 16 above). As Husserl puts it, they are transcendent objects within 'immanence' (*CM*, §47). A phenomenal item's being 'immanent' to consciousness here has the much looser sense of 'manifesting itself in its constitutive phenomenal properties to the investigating consciousness'. And Husserl's dictum that phenomenology proceeds 'immanently' then amounts, *not* to some kind of methodological introspectionism, but to nothing more controversial than the idea that phenomenology is to limit its investigations to what shows up within the first-personal perspective of the investigator's (transcendentally 'purified') consciousness in an appropriately 'intuitively fulfilled' manner. This idea by itself is only 'internalist' in an invidious Cartesian sense on the phenomenologically unwarranted *theoretical* assumption, which Husserl has precisely asked us to leave aside (see above), that the intuitively accessible, phenomenal properties of objects are merely intramental effects of those objects and thus ontologically distinct from them.

Much more questionable is Husserl's conflation in some places of the requirements of the reduction with the idealist thesis that consciousness has 'absolute being', since it cannot be dependent on any objects absolutely external to it, actual objects being only conceivable as relative to some actually existing consciousness.[19] To be sure, this idealist thesis *by itself* does not, *pace* Baldwin ('Phenomenology', 30), make Husserl a content internalist, since it may well turn out that for Husserl, as for Kant, conceptualized contents of consciousness and self-consciousness are only possible for a subject that has good reasons for thinking of itself as embedded in a world of real objects *empirically* external

---

[19] Herman Philipse has argued that idealist metaphysical commitments are already present in *Logical Investigations*, despite that work's avowed metaphysical neutrality('Transcendental Idealism', esp. 272–8).

to it.[20] But it is still clear that Husserl, by his own requirement of ontological presuppositionlessness, is not entitled to metaphysical characterizations of the results of the reduction, such as we find in his talk about transcendental consciousness being a region of ontologically 'absolute being' (*Id 1*, §49, p. 92/110). While there is nothing illicit about a phenomenologist *also* doing metaphysics, any metaphysical claims, by Husserl's own injunctions, should be *posterior to* the use of the method of the reduction, and the latter must therefore be logically independent of them. Husserl, *on his own terms*, is at the fundamental level of his philosophical inquiry barred from a *metaphysical* reading of his assertion that the transcendental consciousness yielded by the reduction is 'a nexus of absolute being … which can neither be causally affected by any thing nor affect any thing' (*Id 1*, §49, p. 93/112). What he is entitled to is only an *epistemological* variant on this, to the effect that in the phenomenological attitude produced through the method of transcendental reduction, consciousness and its phenomenal objects are only *considered* as correlates, and the question of whether *this entire correlation* or nexus is an effect of causes that are ontologically independent of consciousness altogether, *cannot yet arise*—for this metaphysical causal question is, as it were, downstream from the transcendental constitutive questions with which phenomenology at the basic level concerns itself. Husserl's articulation of this point in *Crisis* serves as a useful corrective to the occasionally misleading formulations in *Ideas I*:

Obviously what is required first of all is the *epoché* with respect to all objective sciences. This doesn't simply mean abstracting from them … Rather, what is meant is an *epoché* of … the critical stance in which we are interested in their truth or falsity … (*Crisis*, §35, p. 138/135)

[T]he exclusive and persisting direction of our interest lies in *how* … the world gets constituted for us …    (§38, p. 147/144)

Through the radical *epoché* every interest in the reality or unreality of the world is … put out of play. And in the pure correlationist attitude created by it, the world … itself becomes something subjective in a special sense.    (§53, p. 182/179)

While the idealist elements in some of Husserl's descriptions of the reduction are thus easily excised without significant loss, there remains his notorious

---

[20]  In fact, such an empirical (or phenomenal) externalism is precisely the view Husserl holds (see below). An object is externally real in the relevant sense just in case it is veridically perceivable as having spatial and properties causal powers.

claim that consciousness could exist even if the world of physical objects were 'annihilated' (*Id 1*, §49, pp. 91–2/109–10). But there is no need to take his point here to be any stronger than that it is *conceptually* possible for there to be some kind of rhapsodic phenomenal consciousness even in the absence of a world empirically external to it. His qualification that such a consciousness would be 'necessarily modified', 'soul-less', and 'non-personal' (*Id 1*, §54, p. 105/127) may be taken as signalling his sympathy with the Kantian thought that such a consciousness would not have the resources to entertain conceptual, objectifying representations of anything at all, including itself.

## (ii) Husserl's Commitment to Content Externalism

I maintained earlier that many of Husserl's own positions in fact commit him to a moderate version of content externalism. It is now time to make good this claim. As understood here, such an externalism about the contents of thoughts of certain types is the view that thoughts of these types—for example thoughts about physical objects, or thoughts about oneself or one's experiences—are necessarily unavailable to a finite subject unless the subject is situated in a world of spatial objects causally affecting it and has well-grounded beliefs about that world. In this sort of externalism, the necessity operator is interpreted in terms of a stronger-than-nomological, ultimately conceptual necessity. It is difficult to see how such a thesis could be vindicated unless thoughts of the relevant types are necessarily dependent upon—are 'founded upon', in Husserl's terminology—thoughts about such external objects, and if, furthermore, the fundamental thoughts of the latter type are *co-constituted* by items which we have good reasons to regard as real external objects.[21] In the kind of externalism I have in mind, the fundamental type of thought about

---

[21] Note that the above formulation deliberately falls short of saying that the fundamental thoughts apparently about the external world are co-constituted by *external objects*, or that external objects necessarily *enter into* these thoughts themselves. Such formulations seem too ambitious, although they are found frequently in the externalist literature (see, e.g. Campbell, *Reference and Consciousness*, 116–20). It would be surprising if scepticism about the particular constituents (as opposed to the general existence) of the external world could be refuted simply by reflection on what is entailed by the concept of thought, or of thought about particulars. For Husserl, it is not a priori impossible that the particular contents of all our past and present demonstrative thoughts subsequently turned out not to have been real external objects, but elements of a highly coherent and complex illusion—a scenario sometimes entertained in dystopian science fiction. If such a state of affairs actually obtained, the identity of our current demonstrative thoughts would be different from what we now take them

external objects is often considered to be perceptual demonstrative thought, for example the thought expressed by 'this is spherical', entertained about an object singled out perceptually by the subject from the ambient array. The demonstrative 'this' here expresses an incomplete sense, which is completed by the item pointed to *itself*, that is, in this instance, by a particular spherical object in the thinker's environment as this is perceptually available to him. Thus the phenomenal object pointed to can be said to be itself a constituent of the thought expressed by 'this is spherical' on that occasion. If (a) perceptual thoughts are best analysed as object-involving in this sense, and if (b) they constitute a fundamental class of thoughts about external objects, without which such thoughts would not be possible at all, and if (c) other kinds of thoughts are in turn necessarily dependent on thoughts which we have good reasons to take to be about real external objects, then, granted other Husserlian premises, this entails content externalism as articulated above.[22]

It is clear, albeit not often remarked upon, that the mature Husserl subscribes to all these propositions. With respect to (a), it is one of Husserl's fundamental claims that all genuinely perceptual presentations present their objects directly, rather than through epistemically mediating items. Indeed, for him this is definitionally true, since he defines (genuine) perception as the (usually only partial or aspectual) *self-givenness* of the phenomenal object (*LI* 6, §§23, 45). True thoughts articulating the content of ordinary sensory perceptions are for him genuinely perceptual thoughts in this sense. If they did not present their objects in an epistemically direct way, they would have to do so either via signs (symbols) that were, at some stage, arbitrarily chosen to stand for these objects, or via 'images' or 'pictures' (*Bilder*) taken as resembling their objects.[23] But nothing can function as a sign or as a pictorial representation of an object for me unless it is taken (*aufgefasst*) or used as such (*sich seiner*

---

to be. They would not be thoughts co-constituted by real external objects but by non-real, quasi-hallucinatory objects. But the actual obtaining of such a scenario, for which there is no evidence, is only coherently conceivable if the real (not merely logical) possibility of a future disconfirmation of our current perceptual beliefs by veridical external perceptions has been provided for, however currently unavailable such veridical perceptions may be. If such disconfirmation of current perceptual beliefs by future experience were not really possible, the idea that all our current perceptions are non-veridical would be 'counter-sensical' (*widersinnig*). What is thus, according to Husserl, a priori impossible is the sheer non-existence of a real external world, although its future 'annihilation' is certainly conceivable.

[22]  The additional premises are: there can only be illusory perceptions or hallucinations concerning an apparent external world if veridical external perceptions are really possible (see n. 21); and, necessarily, some perceptions as of external objects are belief-involving (see n. 31).

[23]  Some interpreters maintain that Husserl recognizes a further kind of indirect representation, namely representation by way of mediating 'abstract' (ideal) entities, analogous to Fregean senses.

*bedient*) by me (*LI* 5, appendix to §§11 and 20, II/1, pp. 421–5/II, pp. 125–8). Husserl insists that what is characteristic of the articulated content of ordinary sense perception is precisely that it is *not* taken in this way, and that it is, on the contrary, sharply distinguished from the awareness or conscious use of something as a sign or as a representational image (see below).

If genuine perception is defined as the mode of intentional consciousness which presents its object without epistemic intermediaries, this entails that its content is most adequately expressed by the use of demonstrative expressions like 'this'. Although Husserl only explicitly acknowledges this consequence in later writings, he already articulates the reasons for it in *Logical Investigations*. In the perceptual use of demonstratives, only 'the actual circumstances of utterance' *themselves* suffice to give the expression a determinate sense (*LI 1*, §26, II/1, p. 81/I, p. 218), for demonstratives, unlike non-indexical symbols, here necessarily refer to the object 'directly (that is, without any attributive mediation)' (*LI* 6, §5, II/2, p. 19/II, p. 198). The last point implies that no image, sense datum, or other representational item can stand for the object in perceptual demonstrative thought, for if it did, the reference to the object would *have* to be 'attributively mediated', for example through a definite description like 'the F-thing causing this sense datum'. Phenomenologically, perceptual demonstrative thoughts establish a direct contact with the object referred to, and *this is why* 'without the perception . . . the pointing would be empty, without determinate differentiation, *in concreto* not even possible' (*LI* 6, §5, II/2 pp. 18–19/II p. 198).[24] In successful sense perception, then,

---

Indeed, according to this reading, for Husserl *all* representations are epistemically mediated in this way. I believe that this interpretation is erroneous. For further discussion of it, see n. 50.

[24] In *Logical Investigations*, the point that complete demonstrative senses involve the objects referred to themselves is obscured by, and indeed in tension with, the idea of sense data (later called *hyle*) which are supposedly *reell* immanent in intentional experiences and, while not themselves being intentional objects, allegedly serve as 'representative contents' necessary for reference to the perceptual object (see also *Id 1*, §85). This idea of psychically immanent sense data is one of the philosophically most problematic aspects of Husserl's early and middle-period thinking. The kind of considerations that he thinks require such non-intentional sense data in fact only point to variations in the way a perceived *object* may *appear* which are neither variations in the perceived object nor variations in the 'intentional essence' of the experience (e.g. the appearance of the surface colour of an object may vary depending on the lighting conditions, without either the object having changed or the subject changing his perceptual belief regarding the object's colour; see *Id 2*, §15c, p. 41; and §18a, pp. 57–9). For criticisms of Husserl's conception of non-intentional hyletic data, see Gurwitsch, *The Field of Consciousness*, 265–73; and Drummond, *Husserlian Intentionality and Non-foundational Realism*, 63–70, 144–6. Immanent hyletic data are abandoned in Husserl's later thought from around 1928, which in this regard squares more easily with the theory of perceptual demonstratives sketched in *Logical Investigations* (see Sokolowski, *The Formation of Husserl's Concept of Constitution*, 177–80,

we make precisely such direct contact with worldly objects, so that it makes no sense to speak of the content of sense perception as we actually enjoy it without adverting to the worldly objects presumptively presented in it.

What is it that establishes this contact? To put the question slightly differently: what *enables* the expression 'this', in its perceptual demonstrative use, to refer to some worldly object without 'attributive mediation'? Husserl's answer is that what establishes referential contact with a perceptually presented item, and what therefore essentially underpins the knowledgeable use of demonstrative signs, is conscious perceptual *attention* (*EJ*, §§17–18; *Id 1*, §§35, 37). In accordance with his 'principle of principles', the relevant notion of attention can of course not be merely a functionalist one, along the lines of 'whatever selects items of information from the perceptual field for further cognitive processing at the personal level'[25] but must itself be cashed in phenomenological terms—as a structure of experience. While I cannot go into the details of Husserl's extensive phenomenological analysis of selective perceptual attention here, let me briefly mention three of its features that are central in the present context. First, selective attention is a focussing of consciousness upon some part of a pre-attentive perceptual field. Pre-attentive or 'background' consciousness is not simply a 'chaos of sensations', but rather presents a field which has a phenomenal structure or contour—there are, among other features, *qualitative contrasts* in it, our pre-attentional consciousness of which may make us 'turn towards' them (*zuwenden*)—i.e. they draw our attention to them (*EJ*, §16). Thus, the 'passively pre-given' perceptual field is neither completely devoid of conscious intentionality, nor is it 'inner', unlike its deeply problematic counterpart in Husserl's

204–11). In Husserl's most detailed later account of perceptual content, in *Experience and Judgement*, psychically immanent hyletic data have been replaced by a noematic, consistently non-immanentist, account of 'the given' (*EJ*, §§16–17).

[25] The adoption of such a broad functionalist conception of attention is one problem with John Campbell's original development of the Husserlian-sounding thesis that we should be 'taking demonstrative reference to be a phenomenon of attention' (Campbell, 'Sense, Reference and Selective Attention', 73). If we mean by attention nothing more specific than 'selection of information for further processing' (p. 57), the claim becomes virtually vacuous. However, the notion of attention in play in Campbell's later *Reference and Consciousness* does seem to be a phenomenological notion and his argument in that work is to that extent analogous to Husserl's, although the latter would no doubt object to its particular way of linking intentional, personal-level, and subpersonal levels of description. For example, Campbell's claim (p. 28) that through conscious attention *we* select unconscious information-processing routines would be unacceptable to Husserl. While conscious attention supervenes on whatever causes such procedures to come into operation, what *we* select by means of attention is not *them* but some aspect of the environment being attended to.

earlier account of intentionality, namely 'hyletic data' or 'sensation' (*EJ*, §13, p. 64/62). Rather, the pre-attentive perceptual field is simply some part of the (phenomenal) *world* as it affects us prior to our taking notice of it. Thus what is essential to the phenomenon of attention is a *foreground–background* structure of consciousness.[26] Secondly, attention is an *activity* of the subject. It is, as Husserl puts it partly by invoking Kantian terminology, the most basic form of ego-activity, spontaneity at work within receptivity (*EJ*, §17). Thirdly, through the activity of attention the ego consciously directs itself towards (*zuwendet*) and thematizes some part or aspect of the passively pre-given perceptual field, thereby making it possible for *objects* to become 'constituted' for—i.e. to be consciously representable by—it. Selective attention is thus a necessary, albeit not sufficient, condition for the individuation of intentional objects.[27]

But is Husserl right to claim that when an object is directly presented ('self-given'), as in sense perception, the object itself enters into the content of the intentional experience? Might not the content of, for example, the sensory perception of a particular object be *both* epistemically direct *and* adequately characterizable without adverting to a relation, attentional or otherwise, to that very object itself? An opponent might argue that the correct way to articulate the content of the direct perception of a particular is not, say, 'this is spherical', but: 'there is now one object straight in front of me which is spherical.' While this still contains occasion-dependent components, the object itself is characterized entirely in general terms, involving a numerical property, an ontological category (*object*), a relational property (*straight in front of x*), and a perceptible intrinsic property (*spherical*). But we must ask: how are these *general* contents, which supposedly supply the object-constituting components of the perception, supposed to be grasped, if perception is to be a *direct* presentation of a particular object? If they themselves were grasped indirectly, for example through linguistic symbols, they obviously would not be suitable as essential core-constituents of *perceptual* content in Husserl's sense at all, since the object would then not be

---

[26] For the use of unthematic (background) consciousness, or pre-attentive conscious processing, in empirical cognitive psychology, see e.g. Neisser, *Cognitive Psychology*, ch. 4.

[27] Could someone not demonstratively identify an object without conscious attention? Sean Kelly suggests that a blindsighter might gradually learn through feedback that her guesses about her environment are generally reliable and that these guesses might then count as knowledge ('Reference and Attention', 283–4). Husserl would of course respond that such inference-based knowledge would not be *perceptual* and could not possibly be our fundamental way of knowledgeably individuating objects.

*self*-given through these general contents. So, for this account as an account of genuinely perceptual content even to get off the ground, the general contents would *themselves* have to be perceived.[28] But, leaving aside the objection that such a perception would also not be appropriately expressed (as proposed) by an existentially quantified proposition, Husserl insists, very plausibly, that *if* universals such as sensory properties are perceptible, they are so only in intentional experiences which are 'founded on' the simultaneous intuitive presence, in perception or imagination, of actual or possible particulars exemplifying them (*LI 2*, §§1–4; *EJ*, §§87–8). If a perception of general contents is possible, it therefore *presupposes* an intuitive acquaintance with particulars, and it thus cannot itself be our basic mode of access to such particulars. Consequently, if the direct perception of external objects were to be analysed in this manner, it could not be our *fundamental* way of consciously representing external particulars.

However, as against this latter idea, Husserl also concurs with (b): direct, perceptual presentations of external objects *are* fundamental such that, necessarily, thoughts about external particulars would not be available at all without them. This is a thought that is familiar from current discussions of the foundational role of perception for conscious representation of a spatio-temporal world. For example, Bill Brewer has argued, developing a point originally made by P. F. Strawson, that without perceptual demonstrative thought that picks out environmental objects directly, there could be no thoughts about particulars at all. For the only form of linguistic reference to particulars that is not straightforwardly dependent on perceptual demonstratives is pure definite descriptions. But for any true pure definite description, no matter how complex, it is conceivable that it should be satisfied by more than one thing. It is conceptually and epistemically possible that there should be a twin world symmetrical with this world in which every particular is duplicated down to the minutest detail. But if it is thus possible, for any pure definite description applying to a particular, and for all the subject can tell, that the description should be satisfied by more than one particular, then such

---

[28] It might be objected here that what is needed is not that the general properties in question *themselves* are perceived, but only that *exemplifications* or instances of them are. However, the perception of a property-exemplification is not a representation of a *general* content at all. The form of such a perception is that of a perception as of a particular: '*this* is an instance of sphericalness.' But if the point of the objection is merely that we should articulate the content of ordinary sense perception along the lines of 'there is one exemplification of sphericalness straight in front of me', then the criticisms made above in the text have not been addressed at all.

descriptions cannot be a rational subject's fundamental way of referring to any one particular at all, even if the possibility of global duplication *fails* to be actualized.[29]

While the Strawson–Brewer thought experiment shows *that* pure definite descriptions cannot play a foundational role in thought about particulars, it does not *explain* why this should be so. Now, the later Husserl reaches the same conclusion,[30] but by a quite different route which does explain why perceptions of particulars with object-involving contents are constitutively fundamental for any thought about a real external world. Husserl's reflections illuminate what it is about conscious, personal-level thought that makes such perceptions necessarily basic, and other forms of representation, such as definite descriptions, asymmetrically dependent upon them. His point of departure is that all personal-level representation of objects requires a vehicle or bearer with phenomenal properties (*LI* 6, §§25, 26, 58). We can classify different generic ways of consciously relating in thought to objects, in terms of their types of vehicles. There are, Husserl argues, three such possible generic ways. We may, first, have objects directly, perceptually, presented to us such that, when we take the contents of these presentations at face value, we take the object to be *itself* present, without any epistemic intermediary we are taking as standing for it or representing it—in these cases, the object itself is the vehicle of thought. As we have seen, sense perception presents spatial objects in precisely this way, albeit necessarily incompletely. Secondly, we may represent an object by way of other objects we interpret as representations of it, without taking them, 'pre-theoretically' (in the sense defined earlier), as resembling it. This is 'empty', signitive, or symbolic representation, a class which includes all fully linguistically encoded representations. Thirdly, there are representations on the basis of pre-theoretically recognized relevant *similarities* of some representative item distinct from the object represented with that object. The two more specific types of representation by similarity that are important here are imaginative or 'fantasy' representation (*phantasiemäßig*), and pictorial or 'image' representation (*bildlich*).

---

[29] Brewer, *Perception and Reason*, 25–48. Cf. P. F. Strawson, *Individuals*, ch. 1.1, and Quinton, *The Nature of Things*, ch. 1.

[30] While in *Logical Investigations* he holds—inconsistently, one may well think—that demonstrative and other indexical contents are in principle, albeit not for us, replaceable by 'objective senses' (*LI 1*, §28), this view is unequivocally abandoned in his later writings: 'all judging about particular individuals (*individuelle Diesheiten*) [is] to a greater or lesser extent bound to the situation where they are directly experienced (*Erfahrung*). This is mostly indicated also linguistically, by the use of demonstratives or other expressions with "occasion-dependent" (*okkasionell*) meanings' (*EJ*, §80, p. 384/319).

With respect to our question regarding external, spatial objects that are 'transcendent' to any one intentional experience representing them, Husserl now claims that the two generic types of *indirect* representation of such objects cannot be autonomous, but that they are essentially dependent on the availability of direct, perceptual representations of what we must believe, and have good reasons to believe, to be such objects.[31] This implies that we could not even *think* about such objects without standing in appropriately direct perceptual relations with items we reasonably take to be such objects. And if this is the case, the phenomenological reduction cannot coherently require us to give up all beliefs that such direct perceptual relations in fact obtain. Without endorsing some such beliefs, the phenomenologist could not coherently investigate any thoughts or representations about external spatial objects at all. This would, at the very least, severely curtail the range of possible phenomenological inquiry and would arguably (see below) render it impossible *tout court*.

In what way are 'indirect' representations, such as fully encoded (i.e. non-indexical) linguistic representations of particular spatial objects, necessarily dependent on perceptions? It is the essence of an object-referring symbol that it stands for something else not identical with it, yet *not* by virtue of being taken to be relevantly similar to it. To grasp the sense of such a symbol is, in part, to grasp what it stands for. Such a grasp necessitates knowing what would render a categorical assertion deploying the symbol true, what would conclusively verify it. And knowing *this* requires, for a basic class of cases including representations of external objects,[32] being able to encounter or to envisage the verifying object(s) or state(s) of affairs in an 'intuitively fulfilled' way (*CM*, §24, p. 93/58), which in most cases is possible only incompletely (e.g. '*x* is a house') or by way of analogies ('Napoleon crowned himself

---

[31] Husserl plausibly maintains that the most fundamental kinds of perceptual representation include a doxic component: a *non-reflective*, and in this sense 'passive', *taking* the object to be as it perceptually appears to be. This 'passive primordial belief' (*passive Urdoxa*) or 'simple certainty' (*EJ*, §21d) may subsequently become modified or neutralized through the experience of conflict or discrepancy among the contents of one's perceptual experiences (e.g. in perceptual illusions, such as the Müller–Lyer illusion). But his point is that (a) any such modification or questioning of one's perceptions essentially presupposes the occurrence of *other* perceptual experiences with the 'thetic' character he calls *Urdoxa*; and that (b) not all perceptual experiences could simultaneously be devoid of this non-reflective, unquestioning, belief character, or have it cancelled or reflectively suspended. The very possibility of questioning some of my perceptions requires others that remain unquestioned at the time. See *EJ*, §§7–10.

[32] For the argument to show that the basic class cannot consist exclusively of 'inner' items (mental states), see below.

Emperor'). Symbolic representation is thus only *intelligible* in relation to intuitively fulfilled representations, such as perceptions and imaginations. While it is a moot point whether *all* object-referring symbols need to be cashable in perceptual or imaginative-analogizing ways, if a core repertoire of such symbols were not intuitively fulfillable, then we could not understand anything *as* a symbolic representation at all.

What about imagination (*Phantasie*)? Might it be conceptually possible to entertain thoughts about external objects utilizing, in addition to symbolic representations, only *phantasiemäßige* images? A phenomenological analysis of imagination shows that this is not possible. Husserl argues that imagination is closely analogous to 'thetic' or 'positing', i.e. belief-involving, 'presentifi-cations' (*Vergegenwärtigungen*), of which imagistic memory is a paradigm case. But just as the thetic component in sense perception is neutralized in the awareness of something *as* a perceptual illusion, so imagining is a form of presentifying something absent where the belief component of episodic memory is lacking (*Id 1*, §111). While in imagistic memory I recollect not just some past event, but also *witnessing* that event, in imagination I imagine some intentional object 'as if' it were seen, or believed, or desired (in the light of some belief), etc., from the conscious perspective of some, perhaps indeterminate, subject. Thus there is in imagination a 'reference' to, and dependence on, other, and ultimately on 'thetic' modes of conscious representation, such as sense perception or pictorially fulfilled belief (although this dependence may be indirect, as when I imagine someone else imagining being present at the battle of Salamis). Moreover, it is *constitutive* of imagination that the 'images' it involves should be *experienced as clashing* with perceptual representations, and thus as 'occluding... something in reality' (*HUA 23*, appendix 51, p. 485). Yet this occlusion is only ever incomplete and the perceptual world clashing with the imagined contents nevertheless remains 'continually present' to consciousness, it only 'nearly disappears' and remains poised *aktuell* to impinge upon me as soon as my imaginative activity slack-ens. Wherever this *experienced* conflict with current perceptual experience is lacking, we are no longer dealing with *Phantasie*, but with hallucination (*HUA 23*, §20, pp. 42–3). But even ignoring these points, fantasy images could not possibly suffice to give appropriate intuitive fulfilment to verbal thoughts about real particulars. What individuates a real particular is its objective spatio-temporal position (*EJ*, §40, p. 203/173; §91, p. 430/355). An imagined material object or state of affairs involving such objects has as such not even a determinate position in objective time (*EJ*, §39, p. 197/169) without which localization in objective space is not possible (*EJ*, §38, p. 191/164–5). Thus 'fantasy' images cannot individuate real particulars: 'here there is no possibility for speaking of several [qualitatively identical] objects or of the same singular object merely repeatedly represented' (*EJ*, §39, p. 197/169).

If symbolic, including linguistic, representation and imagination do not suffice to enable thoughts about real external particulars, might we improve the situation by adding *picture-like* representation? According to indirect realism as classically stated by Locke, ordinary sense perception is of this kind.[33] We have already seen that Husserl rejects indirect realism as an account of our actual sensory awareness of the world. But is it not at least *conceivable* that our fundamental mode of thought about external objects should be *bildlich*? No, for it is constitutive for pictorial (as opposed to imaginative) representation that some features *of a perceived object* are taken as representing another object distinct from it by virtue of resemblance, as we can see paradigmatically in painting or in film images. If one construed the foundational perception as *itself* pictorial, this would lead to an infinite regress (*LI 5*, appendix to §§11 and 20, II/1, p. 423/II, p. 126). Moreover, every conscious taking or using an item as a pictorial image (without which it could not *be* such an image at all) necessarily involves an awareness of a discrepancy between the space occupied by the physical thing that functions as the bearer of the representation, and the quasi-space within the representation (*HUA 23*, no. 1, §14, esp. pp. 32–3). Thus, like imaginative representation of spatial particulars, pictorial representation of them is essentially dependent upon direct perceptual representation. And since not all of a subject's perceptual experiences could be devoid of the doxic character of non-reflective belief, which simply takes the object to be as it perceptually appears to be, it follows that there could be no thoughts about real, external, spatial things without beliefs that there are such things.

It might be objected that the argument just given leaves open the possibility that the directly perceived objects serving as the bearers of the pictorial representation might have quite different properties from those of the objects represented (as they do to some extent in the Lockean version of indirect realism), and thus pictorial thoughts about a world of external objects might still be possible without having perceptually based beliefs about many, or

---

[33] John Locke, *An Essay Concerning Human Understanding*, Book II, ch. 8, esp. sections 8, 15, 16.

perhaps any, of the fundamental properties of those objects. However, an item can only function as the bearer of pictorial representations if it allows for the exemplification of properties that are appropriately similar to those of the target objects. Therefore no perceptual item can successfully serve as a *Bild* of causally effective, relatively persisting, three-dimensional spatial things without itself exemplifying persistence and causal efficacy, and having spatial features. The phenomenological reduction therefore cannot, on Husserl's own terms, require the philosopher to regard all perception-based beliefs about real spatial objects as dispensable, and it consequently cannot coherently be intended as a 'Cartesian', internalist manoeuvre. We should therefore take Husserl seriously when he says:

It is a matter of course, presupposed by all scientific thought *and all philosophical questions*, that the world exists . . . Objective science also only poses its questions on the basis of this world that always exists in advance, in pre-scientific life. Science presupposes the world's being, just like all *praxis* does.    (*Crisis*, §28, pp. 112–13/110; emphasis mine)

Could the phenomenological philosopher even thematize *herself* qua subject of experience ('transcendental' or otherwise), or her experiences and their structures, without remaining committed to beliefs about a real external world? Husserl explicitly denies this: 'Reality and subjectivity . . . essentially require each other' (*Id 2*, §30b, p. 64/69). 'Real' objects, in Husserl's terminology, are objects having a non-egocentric spatio-temporal location and causal properties (*Id 2*, §15, esp. pp. 41–5/44–9). Thinking of oneself as a subject, or having the concept of an experience, is only possible on the basis of warranted beliefs about a real, external world in this sense (*Id 2*, §47, p. 170/179). Even in an early text like *Logical Investigations*, where some of the issues relevant here are obscured by his implausible assumption of *reell* immanent sense data, Husserl says unequivocally that 'all act-characters are ultimately founded on external sensory contents' (*LI 6*, §58, II/2 pp. 179–80/II p. 304; see also *EJ*, §29, p. 153/139). A subject cannot entertain contents of empirical reflection ('inner objects') at all without having had intentional experiences in which some item has been presented as empirically external in the Kantian sense, that is, as having spatial (and causal) properties.[34] Why should this be so? From the many scattered considerations

---

[34] For Kant's conception of empirically external object as essentially spatial, see *Critique of Pure Reason*, esp. A23/B37–B30/B45, and A367–A380.

offered by Husserl in support of this view, I here want to reconstruct two lines of argument.

First, thinking of myself as a subject of intentional experiences implies the ability to think about intentional experiences as such. But I evidently cannot think about experiences *as* intentional experiences without being able to distinguish them from that which they are experiences *of*—from their conscious ('intentional') objects. But what is it to think of something as an *object* of consciousness? We can paraphrase Husserl's conception of an intentional object as follows:

**Intentional Object (Def.):** X is a conscious, or intentional, object for a subject S at time t just in case (a) S at t is conscious of X through an experience $E_1$, and (b) S at t has the ability become conscious of X again, without modifying it, in other experiences $E_2$, $E_3$, ..., differing in respect of their qualitative (noetic) moments, and (c) S at t has the ability to become thus conscious of X *as the same* across these different experiences of it (see esp. *EJ*, §13; also *HUA 26*, pp. 49–53, pp. 62–9).

Consciously represented physical things, phantoms, fictional individuals, properties, states of affairs, and experiences as thought about, all fall under this broad Husserlian understanding of objecthood. Being able to represent an item as identically the same across different experiences of it is essential to the concept of an object of consciousness. Representing something as an object therefore necessarily involves the ability to represent it as actually or potentially *absent*—as not currently 'self-given' in, for example, sense perception. The thought here is that, if I could *only* become conscious of X when actually perceiving it, I would not yet have 'objectified' it, for I would not be able to *re-cognize* it, on later perceptual encounters with it, as the same X that was perceived earlier. But the very possibility of thinking of a particular item as currently absent, as not directly intuited, in turn requires a capacity to think of it as being *somewhere else* in time or space.[35] It thus requires more than the egocentric, or *purely* perspectival, conception of time and space which is characteristic of sense perception, in which items are given as (implicitly)

---

[35] There are of course representations of absent intentional objects which do not represent them as being in another spatio-temporal location. I can imagine or entertain verbal thoughts about, say, unicorns. But, as we saw, Husserl plausibly holds that any such 'non-thetic' representations are possible only on the basis of there being a class of perceptual representations at least some of the contents of which must be 'passively' taken at face value, as really being thus-and-so (*EJ*, §§7–10). Hence the very concept of an intentional object is tied to that of 'thetic' perception.

relative to the subject—as 'now' or 'earlier' (*Time*, A, §§10, 17), or as 'here', 'in front', 'to the left', 'up', and so forth (*Id 2*, §§41a, 42).[36] What is needed for the conscious representation of an object is thus a non-egocentric, and in this (weak) sense objective, conception of time and space which allows the subject to think about an item as *retaining its own position* in time or space even when it is not currently perceived or experienced by the subject. It is its occupying such a position that individuates an item as a particular (*EJ*, §91, p. 430/355; §43b, p. 219/186). But the idea of an item as itself occupying a determinate spatio-temporal position in a non-egocentric, objective, frame of reference implies the notion of its having *causal properties*. Only in so far it has dispositions causally to affect and be affected by other items external to it can it actually 'fill' or 'occupy' its *own* spatio-temporal position. It is such causal properties that essentially distinguish a real external thing from a spatial phantom (*Id 2*, §15b-c, pp. 36–45/39–48). While there are meaningful questions about spatial phantoms which allow for true or false answers (*Id 2*, §15b, p. 36/39), such appearances have no objective (non-egocentric) spatial location, and even the ascription to them of a position in objective time *presupposes* their being conceived as occurring in some subject's experiential history. Hence they cannot be part of the constitutive story explicating the conditions that make the conception of such a subject and its experiences possible in the first place.

Husserl now argues that a subject's conception of an intentional object as *real*—as having causal properties—essentially requires thinking of it as potentially *interacting with the subject*. This in turn is conditional upon the subject's being able to think of *itself* as a real object—to objectify itself as 'the point of intersection of real causalities' (*Id 2*, §18, pp. 62–5/67–70). This 'intersection' is experienced paradigmatically in *perceptions* as of particulars which normally, unless there are special reasons to the contrary, are, and must be, taken (*aufgefasst*) by the subject as a being-affected by the object (*LI 5*, §27, II/1 pp. 442–3/II pp. 137–8; *EJ*, §§7, 17), and in spontaneous, self-moving *action*—as Husserl puts it: in the experience of the 'I do' (*Id 2*, §18, p. 58/63; §15, p. 39/42; §38).

What are the reasons behind Husserl's claim that only a worldly, 'mundane' subject—a subject that represents itself (objectifies itself) as a *part* of the real world and as interacting with it—can have a conception of such a

---

[36]  Apparently monadic egocentric manners of presentation—e.g. 'x is to the right'—are implicitly relational. Cf. Campbell, 'Joint Attention and the First Person', 128–31.

world at all? It seems clear that it is motivated by an application of his view that a conception of any property that is constitutively fundamental for the conscious representation of a world—such as the property *being a cause*—presupposes an acquaintance or imaginative quasi-acquaintance with something exemplifying the property. If one holds the view, for which there are strong independent reasons, that the concept of causality is not just that of functional co-variation, but that something like the idea of *efficacy* or causal power is needed to capture the priority of the cause relative to the effect, then Husserl's claim about the necessary self-mundanization of the subject follows, assuming that he *also* holds that the concept of efficacy or causal power is only 'intuitively fulfillable' in a subject's purposive action on an environment offering resistances to it. There are passages suggesting such a view, although Husserl untypically gives us little detail in this regard:

*Impact and pressure* cannot strictly be *seen*, one can only see the spatial and *gestalt* processes accompanying it. Even through mere touching one cannot experience *pressure, traction, or resistance*. One has to 'tense the muscles', 'press against it', etc. (*Id 2*, §15, p. 39/42)[37]

As this passage indicates, Husserl takes the subject's agency that is implicated in any representation as of real spatial objects as requiring a *phenomenal body*, experienced and conceived of as having causal powers: 'The lived body on the other hand cannot be lacking. Even a ghost necessarily has a ghost's body' (*Id 2*, §21, p. 94/100). We get a clearer picture of what this experience of the causal power of the body involves if we turn to Husserl's second line of argument for the necessary embodiment of subjects. It begins by unfolding the implications of the perspectival character of spatial phenomenal objects. A spatial object cannot even in principle be directly presented to a possible perceiver all at once, but only through profiles which include 'adumbrations' (*Abschattungen*) indicating to the perceiver, sometimes quite indeterminately, the object's other profiles not currently sensorily given—e.g. the back of a house one is currently perceiving (*Id 1*, §§41–42; *EJ*, §§8, 20, 83a). It is only because my perception of the front of the house includes such 'horizonal' characteristics that I can take myself to be perceiving (rather than inferring the presence of) the *house* as opposed to a mere façade. What Husserl calls the

---

[37] Versions of the view adumbrated here were developed in detail by some of Husserl's contemporaries, most influentially by Dilthey and Scheler. (Somewhat earlier, it can also be found in Nietzsche.) See Dilthey, 'Beiträge zur Lösung der Frage vom Ursprung unseres Glaubens an die Realität der Aussenwelt', 90–138; and Scheler, *Erkenntnis und Arbeit*, esp. pp. 237–50.

inner perceptual horizon of an object is to be understood in terms of mostly unthematic, implicit, anticipations (protentions), aroused by adumbrations in what is sensorily given, concerning sides or aspects of the object which are currently not thus given.[38] Husserl now argues that the possibility of perceiving different profiles or sides of a spatial object as sides of the *same* particular object, and therefore the possibility of taking a spatial object to *have* currently unperceived sides—without which one could not take it to be a spatial object at all—is conditional upon the possibility of having an awareness of oneself as *moving through* space so as to perceive different profiles of the object in continuous succession (e.g. when walking around the house). But a consciousness of myself as moving through space and thereby potentially gaining perceptual purchase on different parts of objective space (as opposed to the contents of my egocentric space changing) necessitates some system of subjective indices which allow a conscious registering of my movements (*Id 2*, §§18a, 38). Anticipating Gibson's 'ecological' theory of perception, Husserl thus arrives at the idea that spatial perception requires the processing of information not just about the subject's environment, but also and correlatively about the subject itself.[39] In order for this information to be available *to* the subject, it needs, of course, to be consciously registered. Husserl

---

[38] The concept of *horizonal* givenness ('appresentation') is one of Husserl's most important contributions to the analysis of intentionality. In its application to perception, it is the idea that the content of any perceptual experience necessarily includes more than what is explicitly presented in it (*CM*, §§19–20). Horizonal appresentation is *sui generis*. It must not be confused with imaginative representation. I do not *imagine* the back of the house when I perceive it *as* having a back while looking at its front (*TS*, §18). But it is also quite wrong to think of the Husserlian horizon as a *hypothesis* or a *belief* about something not sensorily given in an experience (*pace* Kelly, 'Seeing Things in Merleau-Ponty', 79–80). For one thing, if horizonal characteristics were hypothesized, they would not be part of the *perceptual* content (in Husserl's sense), and if they were not, one could not ever non-inferentially perceive any particular object, temporal or spatial, at all. But Husserl is emphatic that we do genuinely perceive houses, books, or melodies (e.g. *LI* 6, §47; *EJ*, §22; *Time*, A, §16). Secondly, a hypothesis about a sensorily absent profile would be a predicative judgement, an instance of 'categorial synthesis'. One of Husserl's basic claims is that categorial synthesis presupposes 'simple' (*schlicht*), non-categorial, sensory syntheses—as when I successively see different sides of a house as sides of the same object when walking round it (*LI* 6, §46). But such continuous sensory synthesis, according to Husserl, is itself only possible because each individual perceptual experience of the object includes horizonal anticipations (*CM*, §19). The latter therefore cannot have a predicative, categorial structure. It follows that they also cannot be explicit, propositionally structured expectations. They are implicit 'passive protentions', the presence of most of which necessarily becomes explicit only subsequently, for example when they are being disappointed (when what was originally seen as a house on inspection turns out not to have a back because it was only a stage prop).

[39] Cf. Gibson, *The Ecological Approach to Visual Perception*. It should be stressed that Husserl is not claiming that the subject's awareness of bodily self-movement is *sufficient* for her grasping the idea of a non-egocentric space through which she is moving.

calls these necessary subjective indices of self-movement 'kinaestheses'. In the case of human subjects, they include such things as the proprioceptive awareness of our eye movements, or the feelings we have of our muscles, joints, and tendons when walking. But they also include experiences *of acting* which, Husserl insists rightly, distinguish voluntary bodily actions from passive or reflex movements potentially involving the same proprioceptive sensations (*Id 2*, §41–2, pp. 159–61/166–9).[40] These systems of kinaestheses are what Husserl calls the 'lived body from within' (*Innenleib*). His claim, then, is that any representation of particular spatial objects by a subject implies the subject's practical grasp of possible self-movements which would make available different profiles of the object in a continuous sensory synthesis. But for *this* to be possible, there have to be functional correlations between the subject's systems of kinaesthesis and the sets of object profiles potentially encounterable. I cannot rationally take myself to have actively moved around a house and now to be perceiving the back of it, unless I have experienced, or believe I have experienced, an ordered series of appropriate kinaestheses in correlation with successive object profiles.[41]

Now since, as we saw above, a conception of myself as interacting with real spatial objects requires me also to *objectify* myself—to think of myself qua causal agent as a spatial object—it is necessary that the kinaestheses

[40]  While for Husserl intentional bodily action essentially involves experiences of acting, it is false to claim, as Hubert Dreyfus does, that this commits him to the idea that such action is characterized by a Jamesian 'feeling of effort', or that when engaged in such action the subject thematically represents her own intentions (see Dreyfus, *Being-in-the-World*, 54–9). Presumably even John Searle, whom Dreyfus rather freely interprets as holding a Husserlian theory of action, and who believes that the content of intentional action includes a reference to the respective intention-in-action itself (cf. John Searle, *Intentionality*, 83–98), would not say that there is a *consciously* explicit self-reference of this kind in all intentional action (cf. *Intentionality*, 92). But whatever Searle's view may be, Husserl is absolutely clear that the kinaestheses are, in normal skilled action, *unthematic*—they are given in the mode of *background* consciousness (*EJ*, §19, p. 89/84). Consequently, *pace* Dreyfus, the experience of acting cannot by Husserl's lights be an *object* of consciousness in such standard skilled actions. While Dreyfus paints something of a caricature of Husserl, there are genuine, and important, differences on this issue between Husserl's actual position and Dreyfus's Heidegger: (1) Husserl insists that there are unthematic experiences of acting which distinguish absorbed active self-movement from passive or reflex behaviour (see Poellner, 'Non-conceptual Content, Experience and the Self', 48–51, for a defence of this claim). (2) For Husserl, any absorbed skilled use and awareness of equipment in terms of its instrumental features (its 'available' or 'practical' characteristics; cf. *EJ*, §14, p. 68/65–6) presupposes a prior thematic acquaintance with it, or with items of its type, in terms of some of its non-instrumental sensible features (see *Id 1*, §37; *Id 2*, §4, p. 10/12; §8; *EJ*, §18). If he is right on this, it follows that 'absorbed coping with equipment' in Dreyfus's sense cannot be the fundamental form of conscious intentionality

[41]  For detailed discussion, see Drummond, 'On Seeing *a* Material Thing *in* Space', 19–32. Also Claesges, *Edmund Husserls Theorie der Raumkonstitution*.

which comprise my subjective self-movement should be ascribable by myself to this spatial object. Thus, for Husserl, the possibility of a consciousness as of real spatial objects necessitates a *twofold* bodily self-consciousness. I need to experience myself kinaesthetically as *Innenleib*, but also to be able to think of these kinaestheses as pertaining to, and *located in*, a physical object. It thus emerges that, for Husserl, possession of the very concept of a subject of experience ultimately involves a self-conception as an embodied spatial agent in interaction with real spatial objects.[42] To put it differently: the ego, considered in its transcendental role in the phenomenological reduction, must *eo ipso* be considered as *necessarily* 'objectifying itself' as an embodied being *within* the phenomenal world (*Crisis*, §54b): 'Clearly it belongs to the essence of the world that is transcendentally constituted in me ... that it is, by virtue of essential necessity, also a world of humans [i.e. of socialized embodied beings]' (*CM*, §56; p. 158/130).

How plausible are these Husserlian transcendental-phenomenological claims? It should be uncontentious that the subject of consciousness is not thinkable without reference to its intentional experiences, and the latter cannot be individuated without reference to their contents. And it is indeed difficult to see how a subject should be able to objectify itself as an entity which, through having experiences, is enabled to interact with the world, without thinking of both itself and the world in something closely analogous to spatial concepts.[43] Husserl is clearly also correct in insisting that a subject can have no such self-conception without conceptualizing itself as a source of *agency*.

---

[42] David Bell, who claims that the Husserl of *Ideas I* operates with a conception of a disembodied transcendental subject, interprets his analysis of bodily intentionality as marking a significant departure from this earlier putative Cartesianism (*Husserl*, 207–14 and 250, n. 8). However, the textual facts are not easily squared with this line of interpretation. Husserl offers his first and most detailed description of the necessarily body-involving nature of spatial perception in the lectures on *Ding und Raum* in 1907. Similar analyses are also prominent in the material that was used for *Ideas II*, dating mainly from 1912–15. It is just not credible that Husserl simply should not have noticed the incompatibility of these thoughts in his lectures and manuscripts with the conception of a disembodied subject which is said to figure, more or less simultaneously, in *Ideas I* (1913). A more plausible interpretive strategy is surely to relinquish the conventional reading of Husserl as having been a Cartesian in the relevant sense at the time of *Ideas I*. In fact, even in that text Husserl states that the concept of a soul is 'founded on', i.e. necessarily dependent upon, the concept of a real object (*Id 1*, §17).

[43] What is the force of 'closely analogous' here? It is intended to exclude, for one thing, Strawson's conception of a universe of purely temporal, auditory, objects (P. F. Strawson, *Individuals*, ch. 2). It is difficult to attach any clear sense to, say, the supposition of a subject objectifying itself by thinking of itself as being, or being somehow united with, such a purely temporal object, and to its thus being enabled to think of itself as interacting with other real, but similarly purely temporal, subjects.

What is more problematic, however, is his 'absent profiles' argument for the thesis that such a self-conception ultimately depends on the possibility of bodily, kinaesthetically indicated, self-movement. Why should a subject only be able to think of, or perceive, an object as having other, currently unperceived, aspects which could be perceived from other perspectives, if it can also understand itself, practically or otherwise, as potentially *moving* to take up those other perspectives? This does not seem to be an a priori truth. There might conceivably be subjects who, while embodied, are paralysed from birth and cannot experience or think of themselves as actively moving through space at all, and who might yet take their surrounding world to consist of spatial particulars with aspects unperceived by them, but perceivable from somewhere else.[44] After all, in the parallel temporal case, we can uncontroversially think of events having objective *temporal* properties (e.g. Napoleon studying his maps for one hour on the eve of the battle of Jena) which we can neither directly witness, nor gain any clear conception of what it would be to 'move ourselves' to a temporal position from which we could witness them.[45] The claim about the role of bodily self-movement thus seems to be one instance where Husserl does not so much analyse the constitutive conditions for *any* subject's having representations of a certain (here: spatial) type, but rather the way in which certain kinds of subjects, namely humans, in fact represent the world thus. Husserl's claims to the contrary notwithstanding, this is arguably not part of a transcendental story valid with 'strict universality', but of a phenomenology of the specifically *human* world.[46]

---

[44] Cf. G. Strawson, *Mental Reality*, ch. 9. Alva Noë's *Action in Perception* is a sustained recent defence of the essentially Husserlian thesis that 'a perceiver's ability to perceive is constituted (in part) by sensorimotor knowledge, i.e. by a practical grasp of the way sensory stimulation varies as the perceiver moves' (p. 12; also p. 95). But Noë's arguments do not substantiate such a strong constitutive claim since they tend to rely on empirical hypotheses about the cognitive abilities and limitations of specifically human or animal perceivers (the phenomenon of sensory fatigue, among others, pp. 13–15). Even if one accepts that a grasp of the possibility of *movement* is essential for perceiving a spatial object as having aspects currently occluded or outwith focal attention, why should this have to include *self*-movement, rather than merely movement of the *object* (e.g. pp. 87–90)? An additional argument would be needed to show that an understanding of object-movement necessitates a grasp of possible self-movement.

[45] Kant suggested influentially that objective time determinations of this kind depend on representations of spatial objects (*Critique of Pure Reason*, B 274–B279). But I cannot see that his point, if accepted, does anything to undermine the temporal case as a counter-example against Husserl's transcendental claim about the necessity of bodily self-movement for the representation of spatial particulars.

[46] Cf. A. D. Smith, *Husserl and the 'Cartesian Meditations'*, 121–5.

Despite the failure of the 'absent profiles' argument *qua* transcendental proof, Husserl's central point about the necessary twofold bodily self-presentation of the subject as kinaesthetically experienced *Innenleib* and as a spatial object in which the kinaestheses are located may still be vindicated if it can be shown that the very idea of an *interaction* with the physical world requires not only the subject's self-conceptualization as object, but also her non-conceptual kinaesthetic self-awareness as *Innenleib*. As we have seen, Husserl broaches this thought (*Id 2*, §15, 39/42), but he does not develop it.

# 4. An Alternative Interpretation of the Phenomenological Reduction

It should be clear from the arguments so far that the phenomenological reduction is not the misguided methodological device of a Cartesian content internalist. We should take seriously Husserl's consistent protestations that what comes (logically) first in the phenomenologist's investigations, having performed the reduction, is the 'simply [i.e. pre-categorially] given life-world' (*Crisis*, §50, p. 175/172), that in the phenomenological attitude this life-world 'remains in its own essence what it previously was' (*Crisis*, §50, p.177/174), and that in the attitude shift of the *epoché* the philosopher 'loses nothing of its [the natural world's] being and its objective truths, and indeed none of the mental acquisitions of his life in the world' (*Crisis*, §41, pp. 154–5/152; cf. *Id 1*, §§50, 88).

But if the phenomenological reduction is not a Cartesian manoeuvre, what is it and what does it *positively* do? Some formulations suggest that what the reduction makes possible is a conscious reference to—as Husserl would say, a thematizing of—the *sense* or mode of presentation in which a given object is presented. Any intentional object involving an actual or possible particular, with whatever 'noetic' quality it is presented in an intentional episode (whether it is imagined, perceived, judged, desired, etc.), is necessarily presented under some aspect or mode of presentation, *as* such-and-such, or from such-and-such a point of view. Husserl calls this mode of presentation of the object the *sense* (*Sinn*) of the intentional experience in question. Thus he can speak, for instance, not only of the sense of a linguistic presentation such as a sentence token, but also of the sense of a perception (*Wahrnehmungssinn*). Indeed, given the basic role of perceptual representation, this is a logically more fundamental application of the concept of *Sinn* than its application to language. The *sense* of the perception of an apple tree in bloom in the garden is, in a minimal interpretation, *the tree just as it is perceived*, that is, from a certain angle, distance, with a certain seen shape, a certain apparent play upon its leaves of light and shade, and so forth (*Id 1*, §88). Husserl sometimes characterizes the phenomenological reduction is essentially no more than an unprejudiced, 'theory'-free thematization of—an attending to—the sense of an intentional experience, the way in which whatever is presented becomes conscious in it (ibid.). What the phenomenologist should investigate is the 'sense' of both the noetic (experiential) and the noematic (intentional content) components of intentional life, and their essential correlations (cf. *Crisis*, §50). But while this formulation is in some respects correct, there are pitfalls here. To begin with, the notion of sense is originally introduced by Husserl to capture the aspectual mode of givenness of intentional objects (*LI 1*, §§12–15). This notion therefore applies naturally to the noematic component of intentional experiences, but not to the noetic, experiential component. Husserl, despite some prevarications, ultimately believes that the noetic moment of an intentional experience (its being a perceiving, desiring, etc.) is itself not an intentional *object* of consciousness in its fundamental mode of presentation, namely when the experience is actually pre-reflectively 'lived through' (*erlebt*) (*Id 1*, §38, p. 67/78; §45; *Time*, A, appendices 6, 9, 12).[47] If the phenomenologist is to describe faithfully 'what is given as it is given', she must take appropriate account of this *pre-objective* aspect of experience as it is actually lived. She thus needs a notion of sense which is broader than Husserl's official definition of it, one which does not tie it quite so directly to the concept of an intentional object—she needs to understand 'sense' roughly as the experienced phenomenal character of whatever may be present to consciousness, whether that is an intentional object or not.

Secondly, the phenomenological thematization of *Sinn* should not be understood as analogous to the Fregean change of the reference of an expression when it occurs in quotation marks or in oblique contexts. In such

---

[47] This was clearly recognized by some early readers of Husserl, but not by others. For an insightful interpretation, see J-P. Sartre, *The Transcendence of the Ego*, 41–5. An influential early misunderstanding of Husserl as holding that experiences, when 'lived through', are immanent objects, is found in M. Heidegger, *History of the Concept of Time*, 102–7. Among those who have followed Heidegger on this point is Tugendhat (*Der Wahrheitsbegriff bei Husserl und Heidegger*, 208–11). For criticisms of this reading, see Zahavi, *Self-Awareness and Alterity*, 67–82; and Poellner 'Non-conceptual Content, Experience and the Self', 45–56.

contexts, the expression refers not to its normal referent, but to its normal *Sinn*, which for Frege is an ideal ('abstract'), self-subsisting, non-spatio-temporal entity ontologically distinct from its referent.[48] I suggest that Husserl's talk about sense cannot at the fundamental level (and indeed not at *any* level) be understood in this Fregean manner. Leaving aside other problems with the Fregean approach for the moment (but see note 50 below), it is clear that if interpreted in this way, Husserl's phenomenological reduction would, even in its initial move, 'lose the world' of particulars, and the phenomenologist would not actually make direct evidential contact with the spatio-temporal world at all. But it is clear that the move towards the consideration of essences or other universals (the 'eidetic' reduction) is for Husserl a 'founded' accomplishment, *presupposing* the transcendental reduction made possible by the *epoché* and quite distinct from it (cf. *HUA* 24 p. 224; also *Crisis* §52, p. 181/178), and moreover presupposing the phenomenologist's continuing to have some exemplifying or instantiating *particular* intuitively or imitatively present to her.[49] Husserl, unlike Frege, is precisely *not* a Platonist, for he does not believe that universal (ideal) items, whether they be sensory properties, categorial features, or objectified concepts, can in principle be directly encountered or 'grasped' by themselves (rather than perceived *in* and *through* actual or imagined particulars exemplifying or instantiating them).[50]

---

[48] G. Frege, 'The Thought', 307–8. For an interpretation of Husserl along these lines, see David Bell, *Husserl*, 184–8.

[49] Although Husserl's conception of the details of the process of eidetic intuition—the perception of universals—changes significantly from the early *Logical Investigations* (see *LI 2*, §§1–4) to the late *Experience and Judgement* (*EJ*, §§87–8), what remains constant is the claim that any such perception presupposes the continued intuitive (or imitative) presence of particulars exemplifying (or instantiating) the relevant universals during this process. With respect to concepts and propositionally structured senses, the matter is complicated by the fact that he recognizes, after *Logical Investigations*, that our 'grasping' of these is not adequately understood as the *exemplification* of an ideal *object* (*EJ*, §64d). But this does not mean that he subsequently holds that when I understand a declarative sentence, I somehow directly latch onto a non-spatio-temporal ideal object—a Fregean sense. Rather, Husserl now recognizes the implications of his view that grasping a signitively presented (e.g. verbally articulated) sense is a conscious *ability*. Grasping the sense here essentially involves an awareness of my ability either to verify the sentence or at least to envisage the circumstances that *would* verify it (*CM*, §24). As Gianfranco Soldati has argued, this view is already clearly present in the doctrine of 'meaning fulfilment' in *Logical Investigations*, but is incompatible with Husserl's official doctrine in that text, according to which the grasping of linguistic meanings is an exemplification of meaning-species (Soldati, *Bedeutung und psychischer Gehalt*, esp. pp. 183–207). Soldati suggests that Husserl should more consistently have spoken of understanding a linguistic meaning as the *instantiation* of an ability, rather than the *exemplification* of a property (p. 185). I have followed this terminological proposal.

[50] For Husserl's explicit rejection of Platonism, see e.g. *EJ*, §82. David Bell cites as the main evidence for a Fregean reading of Husserl the latter's observation that the tree as perceived (the 'perceptual

So if talk of the phenomenological reduction as essentially an attending to the 'sense' or mode of presentation of conscious experiences or their contents is potentially misleading, can we do better? We should take our lead here from Husserl's insistence that the reduction involves an investigation of the world

sense'), unlike the tree itself, 'cannot burn away; it has no chemical elements, no forces, no real [i.e. causal] properties' (*Id 1*, §89, cited in Bell, *Husserl*, 188). But this remark, which is in fact the only explicit textual evidence apparently supporting the Fregean interpretation, allows for less recondite alternative readings. For if the transcendental reduction requires a suspension of judgement about the ontological status of any sample objects examined by the phenomenologist, then it follows that the object presented *cannot*, in the phenomenological attitude, be *considered* to have chemical elements or forces, even if it in fact does—and that is precisely Husserl's point in this passage. For all the phenomenologist knows or cares, the sample tree might be a *hallucinated* tree, and although it is certainly presented *as* a particular, it makes no sense to say of a hallucinated tree that it burns away, or has chemical elements, or has forces.

A few more words on Fregean readings of Husserl are in order here, since these are widespread in Anglophone Husserl scholarship (although much less so among continental interpreters). These readings originated in Dagfinn Føllesdal's influential paper 'Husserl's Notion of the Noema' and have found perhaps their most elaborate development in D. W. Smith and R. McIntyre, *Husserl and Intentionality*. Smith and McIntyre argue that the later (post-*Logical Investigations*) Husserl holds a 'mediator' theory of sense which is designed to explain how intentional experiences can be contentful even when their purported object does not exist (as in hallucination). According to Smith and McIntyre, Husserl attempts to solve this problem by assuming a 'common element' in veridical perception and hallucination, which he calls the *noematic sense* of the perception. This noematic sense is, they argue, closely analogous to Frege's linguistic senses: it is an 'abstract', ideal, non-spatio-temporal *entity* distinct from the object, is essentially expressible in language (p. 107, but see pp. 216–19), and is 'entertained' in intentional experiences. In the case of successful reference, this ideal entity mediates reference to the object, while ensuring the contentfulness of thought even when there is no object. I want to mention just two fundamental problems with this interpretation. First, in the basic perceptual case, it commits Husserl to the deeply implausible view that the existence-independence of intentional relations requires a *common ontological element*, an entity, shared between situations of successful perceptual reference and situations where there is no, or no relevant, real object. But Husserl nowhere says that he holds such a view and in fact his explicit discussions of this issue sketch a quite different, disjunctivist position, *denying* the 'common element' claim (*LI 5*, appendix to §§11 and 20, II/1, p. 425/II, pp. 126–7; *Id 1*, §90; for a detailed account of Husserl's disjunctivism, see A. D. Smith, 'Husserl and Externalism'). Secondly, in the case of both perception and non-perceptual judgement, Husserl is emphatic that, *pace* Frege, understanding a sense, as opposed to thinking *about* it, is *not* a 'grasping' of it as an object, propositional or otherwise (*FTL*, §42a). Smith and McIntyre seem to acknowledge this (e.g. pp. 80–1). According to them, a Husserlian noematic sense is an 'abstract' entity, distinct from the intentional object, by virtue of which an intentional experience is directed to the object (if there is one), but which is itself not only unthematic, but *unconscious* in the act (pp. 119–25). Noematic senses only become conscious in phenomenological reflection (pp. 106, 122). But here Smith and McIntyre seem simply to abandon phenomenology altogether in favour of what Husserl would surely call 'theory'. To explain the constitutive phenomenological structure of conscious 'acts' by recourse to entities which can *in principle* not be consciously given in the act *itself* seems a clear breach of Husserl's 'principle of principles'. But it is not difficult to see why they are forced into adopting this un-phenomenological position. For according to Husserl, whether early or late, any intuitively fulfilled (non-empty) consciousness of ideal (*irreal*), non-spatio-temporal items is founded on the consciousness of particulars, involves spontaneity, and is necessarily a thematic consciousness of higher-order intentional *objects* (*LI 2*, §1; *EJ*, §§63, 81b). Since he explicitly denies *itself* 'just as it was previously for me and as it still is' (*Crisis*, §41, p. 155/152), and not of some item ontologically distinct from it, but that it investigates *this very world* with a 'special habitualized direction of our interest' distinct from the interests of the 'natural attitude' (*Crisis*, §35, p. 139/136). The *epoché* consists in the philosophizing subject's adopting a different *attitude* to the world and its denizens, rather than disclosing or thematizing a different *set of objects*. In the natural attitude as understood by Husserl we are interested in the truth-values of our representations of the world. It matters to us whether our perceptions are veridical, whether our judgements are true, whether our pre-reflective evaluative responses and our emotions are adequate or appropriate to whatever elicits them (*Crisis*, §§40–1, pp. 152–5/149–52). By contrast, in the attitude of phenomenological investigation we are, for the duration of that investigation, not concerned with the truth-value, or with the appropriateness to their objects, of our sample representations. It is *irrelevant* to us whether the representations we are using to elucidate, say, the essential structural components of the perception of spatial objects are veridical perceptions or whether they are hallucinations, for in so far as the phenomenal character of a hallucination is indistinguishable from that of a corresponding veridical perception, and indeed is ultimately parasitical on the character of veridical perception, it can serve the phenomenologist just as well.[51] Similarly, if the phenomenologist is investigating the structure of value and evaluative representation, he 'brackets' or suspends his 'natural' interest in whether his samples satisfy whatever normative constraints he may, in his everyday 'natural' life, think appropriate to evaluative representations. In the phenomenological attitude,

just as the perceiving is correlated with the perceived as such, in a sense which rules out the question after the reality of what is perceived, so the valuing is correlated with what is valued as such, and again in such a way that the being of the value (of the

that senses are intentional objects for us when we understand them, this leaves Smith and McIntyre only the appeal to unconsciously grasped idealities. But this appeal makes the understanding of sense entirely mysterious, even more so than does Frege's theory of a 'third realm' (for criticism of the latter, see e.g. Dummett, 'Frege's Myth of the Third Realm'). There is no need to attribute to Husserl a theory that is both implausible and profoundly at odds with his central methodological commitments. For an alternative interpretation of perceptual noematic sense, see Drummond, *Husserlian Intentionality and Non-foundational Realism*, ch. 6.

[51] The example of hallucination is also used by Edith Stein, Husserl's assistant and doctoral student, to illustrate the shift of perspective essential to the reduction. See her *Zum Problem der Einfühlung*, §1. On the subjective indistinguishability of perception and hallucination, see *HUA 23*, no. 1, §20, pp. 42–3). On the conceptual dependence of the content of hallucination on the content of perception, see also n. 21, and Soteriou, 'The Subjective View of Experience and its Objective Commitments'.

valued thing *and* of its actually being valuable) remains out of question.    (*Id 1*, §95, p. 198/232)

Any interest in being, reality, or non-being of the world, that is, any theoretical interest directed at knowledge of the world, but also any practical interest in an ordinary sense . . . is barred to us. . . . How could we make perception and what is perceived . . . , also art, science, philosophy, into our transcendental themes without experiencing them through samples . . . ? . . . In a certain manner the philosopher in the *epoché* also has to 'live through naturally' natural life . . . . Every kind of *praxis* is really or empathetically [*im Nachverstehen*] lived through by the phenomenologist. . . . [But] through the radical *epoché* any interest in the reality or unreality of the world (in all modalities, including possibility, conceivability, or decidability of such matters) has been put out of play.    (*Crisis*, §§52–3; pp. 178–82/175–9)

The phenomenologists temporarily suspends his interest in the truth value or veridicality of the sample representations used in his inquiry, *not* in order to turn away from the actual world (ibid., pp. 178–9/175–6), but in order to understand *it* more adequately qua phenomenon, focusing exclusively on the details of how it is presented to consciousness.[52] This is a quite different operation from the 'neutrality modification' whereby a content that was previously judged or asserted is now merely entertained (*Id 1*, §31, p. 55/60). If the phenomenologist wants to investigate the *noetic* component of intentional experiences, for example what it is to *perceive* an object, he needs to present to himself, or at least to simulate, also the 'thetic' character of (in this case) perception—the element of belief or conviction normally involved in it—yet somehow *also* not *go along* with it: to 'put it out of action' (ibid.). An empirical analogue to the cognitive attitude Husserl has in mind here, taking again the specific example of perceptual experience, would be a subject's *attending* to his own tendency to be perceptually taken in by a perceptual illusion (e.g. the spikes of a fast-turning wheel stubbornly seeming to stand still) while also, in this empirical case due to countervailing knowledge, not 'going along' with his tendency to believe the appearances.[53]

---

[52]  On this point, see especially Merleau-Ponty, 'Phenomenology and the Sciences of Man', 41–95.
[53]  It is therefore misleading when Heidegger in his 1925 Marburg lectures famously and influentially criticizes Husserl for asking the phenomenologist to 'abstract from the reality of consciousness'. As Heidegger understands Husserl, in the attitude of the reduction 'the real experience . . . is not *posited* and *experienced* as real' (*History of the Concept of Time*, §12, p. 109, my emphasis). This formulation blurs a distinction Husserl would insist on. If the focus of the inquiry is, as in Heidegger's objection, on the experience itself (the 'noetic moment'), it is indeed incumbent on the phenomenologist to *experience* for herself whatever features are essential to experiences as they are lived through, including whatever it is that makes them seem actual to the subject (cf. *Crisis*, §52, cited above). But

When the phenomenologist investigates the *noematic* side of intentional experience—for example what it is for an object to be presented as *valuable*, or simply as a *real spatial object*—the reduction commits her to an attitude which is indifferent to whether the sample instances through which she conducts her analysis are *really* valuable, or are veridically perceived spatial objects (as opposed to hallucinated ones). In the latter, perceptual example, such indifference implies suspending any belief that the sample, such as Husserl's apparent apple tree in the garden (*Id 1*, §88), is a *real* apple tree, for this does not matter for the purpose of the phenomenological analysis. It is only in this sense that the tree becomes a 'phenomenon', is not *taken as* a spatio-temporal reality (*Id 1*, §49, p. 93/112), and is consequently not *considered* as a node of real natural forces causally affecting the subject (*Id 1*, §88, p. 182/215).

Contrary to widely held opinion, then, Husserl's transcendental reduction does *not* require an abandoning the world in favour of some Cartesian

---

Husserl claims, *contra* Heidegger, that this is possible *without* what Heidegger here calls 'positing' the experience—more precisely, without 'going along' with it, that is, without unqualifiedly 'living through' it. Whether he is right on this is itself a matter for substantial phenomenological investigation, but it is far from obvious, as Heidegger takes it to be, that Husserl is precluded from thematizing the being of pre-reflective consciousness merely on account of the phenomenological reduction. Heidegger's objections in §§10–11 of *History of the Concept of Time* do, however, pinpoint a problematic area in Husserl's account, from which much of subsequent phenomenology, including Heidegger's, Sartre's, and Merleau-Ponty's work, takes its departure. Husserl recognizes that intentional experiences (noeses) are, when normally and non-reflectively lived through (*erlebt*), *conscious*, but not as intentional *objects*. But if this is so, they cannot be presented without distortion or modification—i.e. not as what they phenomenologically are—in *reflection*, including phenomenological reflection, *if* all reflection objectifies. Now Husserl's predominant official view is indeed that reflection makes intentional experiences into objects (*Id 1*, §38). But he is also alive to the problems that arise from this view if experiences are necessarily non-object-like in their primary and fundamental manner of presentation: 'Anger may quickly dissipate through reflection, and modify its content . . . To study it reflectively in its originarity is to study a dissipating anger; which is certainly not pointless, but perhaps is not what was supposed to be studied' (*Id 1*, §70, p. 130/158). One solution to this inconsistency in Husserl's account would be to abandon his 'official' claim that all reflection objectifies. Dan Zahavi has interpreted some intriguing manuscript remarks by Husserl to suggest such a modified view of reflection as not necessarily objectifying the experiences reflected upon (*Self-Awareness and Alterity*, 181–94). A further and distinct issue arising from Husserl's account of pre-reflective experience is whether it is possible in all cases, even in principle, to give 'faithful' linguistic expression (*Id 1*, §24) to what is experienced just as it is experienced, if all linguistic encoding, by virtue of being conceptual, necessarily objectifies (*EJ*, §13, pp. 62–3/60–1). If a pre-reflective experience (*Erlebnis*) is indeed necessarily non-object-like, then it follows that it cannot even in principle be *described* 'just as it is given'. Phenomenological language therefore in this case has to resort to metaphor (as Husserl avowedly does in his talk of pre-reflective consciousness as a 'flow'; *Time*, A, §36) which, in conjunction with negative characterizations, can do no more than point the reader to *re-living* or re-actualizing for herself what is being thus inadequately described (cf. *EJ*, §43b, p. 218/185; *Crisis*, §52, p. 180/176–7).

'immanent'—empirically subjective—sphere of consciousness, nor does it by itself (i.e. without the *distinct* 'eidetic' reduction) purport to disclose a set of ideal, non-spatio-temporal objects. What it does involve is, rather, (a) the temporary suspension of interest in the truth, veridicality, or correctness of the representations of particular samples it investigates, and (b) an attention to these samples that is purified of 'theoretical assumptions' in the sense elucidated earlier, with the ultimate aim of disclosing their general phenomenal structures or properties. In some passages Husserl does indeed go further and suggests not only that the actual being or non-being of the world and its denizens is of no interest in the phenomenological attitude, but that from a philosophical, reflective perspective, its non-being is conceivable (*Id 1*, §46). But, rightly understood, these remarks are also compatible with his content externalism. We saw that for conceptualized self-consciousness to be possible, we must have well-confirmed beliefs about a world of real spatial objects, and also that it is not possible, when in the natural attitude, *globally* to suspend our pre-reflective beliefs (*Urdoxa*) in the veridicality of our perceptions. But even in the natural attitude the *specific* contents of our beliefs, both common-sense and scientific, about the real world are in each individual case defeasible, although what is *not* defeasible is the general belief that there is an empirically real world. Secondly, Husserl maintains, like Hume, that a complete breakdown of the specific regularities of experience that have so far governed and indeed constituted the phenomenal world for us is conceivable; although, *contra* Hume, he seems to think that the thoroughgoing 'consonance' (*Einstimmigkeit*) of past experience does provide rational grounds for dismissing this theoretical possibility as unlikely to be actualized (ibid.). This implies that while the veridicality of *all* the specific contents of our past and present perceptual beliefs *can* globally and intelligibly be doubted at the philosophical reflective level (although not at the immersed level of the natural attitude), such doubts are rationally unmotivated (*EJ*, §78, pp. 370–1/306–7).

I have argued that Husserl's method of transcendental reduction is misunderstood when interpreted as a form of Cartesianism in a philosophically objectionable sense, and that, on the contrary, Husserl is committed to an externalist theory of intentionality. But while the arguments offered here may have shown the reduction to be philosophically undamaging, we may still ask: what *positive* contribution does the reduction make to philosophical understanding? For Husserl, its crucial contribution lies in making it possible to understand explicitly or transparently *how* the world is constituted in—how it can manifest itself to—consciousness in the natural attitude. It is only through adopting the stance of the phenomenological reduction—even if only intermittently and for short periods of time—that the natural attitude itself and its objects become adequately transparent to the subject. Its achievement is thus ultimately to make possible the self-explication of subjectivity and its necessary correlate, the world as it shows up for the subject. The reason why the natural attitude cannot itself achieve such self-transparency is that it is, as Husserl defines it, necessarily concerned with the *objects* of consciousness (*Crisis*, §§38, 40). In ordinary sense perception we are focused on some part of the perceptual environment, in everyday linguistic judgements we are interested in the states of affairs they represent and whether they represent them truthfully, in everyday evaluation we are concerned about whatever it is that we value. But this very focus on the objects *precludes* any explicit understanding of the aspectual modes of presentation which are necessary for these objects to manifest themselves as they do to consciousness. This is so for two reasons. First, because a simultaneous thematizing of the objects and of the ways in which they are consciously presented would involve a bifurcation of thematic interest in a single intentional experience or project which would be tantamount to a self-division of the subject:[54] I cannot simultaneously focus on, say, answering the question whether a current experience as of an apple tree is veridical—a project which might involve various tests to confirm the experience—*and* on answering the question of what in the experience makes it the case that the apparent tree can appear to me as a spatial object at all, for the attempt to answer the latter question forces me into an entirely different direction of investigation. For Husserl, the importance of this realization and of its implications for philosophical method can hardly be overestimated, although it has only been inadequately recognized in the philosophical tradition. Secondly, and just as importantly, many intentional comportments in the natural attitude involve 'senses' (i.e. conscious aspects or 'moments') which are *implicit*, that is unthematic, if the comportment is to be what it is—think of the bodily self-awareness involved

---

[54] This argument is premised on Husserl's claim—which I cannot defend here—that on one (abstract) level of subjectivity, which he calls the transcendental ego, the subject at any moment *is* (or 'lives in') the conscious activity of being engaged with some thematic object or other (*Id 2*, §§22–6; *EJ*, §19, p. 90/84–5). This is Husserl's phenomenological recasting of Kant's notion of transcendental subjectivity (*Critique of Pure Reason*, esp. B157–B159). A thematic engagement in two different cognitive projects simultaneously is therefore incompatible with what Kant would have called the transcendental unity of apperception. For a detailed argument to this effect, see O'Shaughnessy, *The Will*, vol. ii, esp. pp. 22–38.

in skiing down a slope, or of the phenomenon of self-deception. One of the central tasks of phenomenology as Husserl conceives it is the *explication of what is implicit* in the life of (necessarily embodied) consciousness (*CM*, §20, esp. pp. 83–5/46–8).[55] But any such explication obviously requires a certain stepping back from those 'absorbed comportments' while yet also retaining a grip on what is presented in them as it is presented. Husserl himself sometimes describes this mode of attention to the manner of givenness of experience and its intentional contents as 'disinterested' (*CM*, §15, p. 73/35) and thus aligns it with a traditional characterization of aesthetic experience—a faithful attention to what is given as it is given, engaged in 'for its own sake', but contributing to the ultimate goal of 'authenticity' in Husserl's sense: the self-clarification of the subject and of its correlative phenomenal world.

# 5. Conclusion

The aim of this essay has been to show that Husserl's often misunderstood methodological theses do not stand in the way of a serious engagement with his substantive first-order analyses and claims. In particular, they do not commit the phenomenologist to Cartesian content internalism, but explicitly recognize the necessarily embodied nature of potentially self-conscious finite subjectivity, and the fundamental importance of agency for subjecthood. But there is surely an as yet unaddressed basic question invited by Husserl's phenomenological project and the conception of philosophy associated with it. Why, you may ask, should we be prepared to follow Husserl in considering the investigation of the structures involved in the conscious manifestation of the world to subjectivity to be the fundamental philosophical issue? From a more traditional, epistemologically or metaphysically motivated, perspective, the central question would instead appear to be how these putatively correlative structures of subjectivity and phenomenal worldhood

---

[55] This implies that, while Husserlian phenomenology aims at descriptive, rather than causally explanatory, truths, it has rather more than the modest ambition, often associated with the later Wittgenstein, of merely providing a transparent overview of what we knew already before we started doing philosophy. Rather, the insights of phenomenology are often striking and new, for it sees as one of its main tasks the explication of what is only implicitly conscious in the 'natural attitude'. On some aspects of Husserl's account of implicit conscious contents, see Poellner, 'Non-Conceptual Content, Experience and the Self'.

relate to the 'world as it is in itself'. After all, with respect to the subject's relation to the world, all that Husserl's transcendental efforts, if successful, have shown is that a potentially self-conscious finite subject has to have, and to be able to think of itself as having, a body with phenomenal properties, experienced and conceived as having causal powers, located in an environment of other such bodies. It does not tell us how all these *phenomenal* objects and features relate to a metaphysically accurate account of the real world, or indeed to scientific accounts of subjectivity in terms of computational or neurophysiological properties. To be sure, Husserl *also* gives us a (transcendental idealist) metaphysics, but I have argued that this is in principle separable from the phenomenological analyses which make up the great bulk of his work. Husserl's metaphysics is, both in principle and in terms of the actual thematic focus exhibited by the overwhelming majority of his writings, evidently extraneous to his main philosophical preoccupations. Irrespective of his later self-interpretation as, ultimately, also a metaphysician, the actual prevailing emphases of his work consign metaphysics to the margins, and his practice is therefore in this respect comparable to what we find in central texts of existential phenomenology, such as Heidegger's *Being and Time* and Sartre's *Being and Nothingness*. How might one justify this 'phenomenological turn'—the shift of philosophical orientation from issues of factual epistemology ('what can we know about the actual world?') and from metaphysics to, ultimately, a phenomenology of the human world? The issue becomes particularly pressing if one regards Husserl's own explicit aim—the provision of an apodictic foundation for objective science, including the empirical sciences—to be neither particularly compelling nor attainable.

In order to understand the deeper reasons why phenomenology came to dominate much of twentieth-century continental European philosophy, quite independently of what Husserl's own explicit motivations may have been, it is crucial to bear in mind that it is not in competition with a scientific understanding of the physical correlates of consciousness. While Husserl resists the conflation of empirically 'genetic' (i.e. causal) questions with constitutive questions, this does not impugn the legitimacy of the former in their own domains. For example, when we try to cure a person's depression, the best and most useful kind of account of this person's condition may sometimes be one couched, not in terms of phenomenal consciousness and conscious motivating reasons, but in terms of a deficiency of neurotransmitters like serotonin or catecholamine in the brain. In other cases, neurophysiological accounts and psychological theories making use of phenomenological concepts may usefully complement each other. The general point here is that the application in empirical psychology, or indeed in everyday 'folk psychology', of concepts developed in a transcendental-phenomenological context does not conflict with scientific neurophysiological explanations of mental phenomena just in case the phenomenal properties adverted to in the former kinds of explanation are strongly supervenient on (i.e. co-variant with) scientific properties simultaneously exemplified.[56] And there is absolutely nothing in Husserl's phenomenology that commits him to denying strong supervenience of phenomenal on scientific properties at the empirical ('natural') level of inquiry.

What does, however, *de facto* cease to be of focal concern to philosophy influenced by the phenomenological turn initiated by Husserl, are purely theoretical questions, pertaining neither to phenomenology nor to science, that continue to dominate much of analytic philosophy—questions about what might *metaphysically explain* such supervenience relations. The philosophical reasons which render this relative indifference to such traditional metaphysical questions most compelling can arguably not be found in Husserl, nor in the Heidegger of *Being and Time*, but in the work of Nietzsche, and they lie beyond the scope of this essay.[57] Consonant with these, and whatever Husserl's own explicit motivations may have been, one of the most fruitful ways of understanding the broader significance of the phenomenological turn he inaugurated may, in the end, have been expressed by the existentialist Albert Camus in *The Myth of Sisyphus*. According to Husserl, as Camus understood him:

thinking is not unifying or making the appearance familiar under the guise of a great principle. Thinking is learning all over again to see, directing one's consciousness, making of every image a privileged place. In other words, phenomenology declines to explain the world. ... [From this] apparent modesty of thought that limits itself to describing what it declines to explain ... results paradoxically a profound enrichment of experience and the rebirth of the world in its prolixity ... It affirms solely that without any unifying principle, thought can still take delight in describing and understanding every aspect of experience [58]

---

[56]  The notion of strong supervenience alluded to here is Kim's. If A and B are families of properties, then A strongly supervenes on B just in case, necessarily, for each x and each property F in A, if x has F, then there is a property G in B such that x has G and, necessarily, if any y has G, then it has F. (Kim, *Supervenience and Mind*, 65.)

[57]  I have attempted to reconstruct these reasons in 'Affect, Value and Objectivity', esp. Section 5.

[58]  Camus, *The Myth of Sisyphus*, 44–5.

# ABBREVIATIONS AND EDITIONS
## OF HUSSERL'S WORKS USED

Translations from Husserl's writings are mine. Where page references to Husserl's writings are given in the essay, the first of these in each case refers to the German edition cited below. In those cases where there is also an English edition, a second page reference, separated from the first by a slash, refers to this edition, details of which are given below next to the German edition.

| | |
|---|---|
| *CM* | *Cartesianische Meditationen*, ed. E. Ströker (Hamburg: Felix Meiner, 1995). **English edition:** *Cartesian Meditations*, trans. D. Cairns (The Hague: Martinus Nijhoff, 1977) |
| *Crisis* | *Die Krisis der europäischen Wissenschaften und die transzendentale Phänomenologie*, ed. W. Biemel, 2nd edn. (The Hague: Martinus Nijhoff, 1962). **English edition:** *The Crisis of European Sciences and Transcendental Phenomenology*, trans. D. Carr (Evanston: Northwestern University Press, 1970) |
| *EJ* | *Erfahrung und Urteil*, ed. L. Landgrebe (Hamburg: Felix Meiner, 1985). **English edition:** *Experience and Judgement*, trans. J. S. Churchill and K. Ameriks (Evanston: Northwestern University Press, 1973) |
| *FTL* | *Formale und transzendentale Logik* (Tübingen: Max Niemeyer, 1981). **English edition:** *Formal and Transcendental Logic*, trans. D. Cairns (The Hague: Martinus Nijhoff, 1969) |
| *HUA 8* | *Erste Philosophie (1923–1924). Zweiter Teil: Theorie der phänomenologischen Reduktion*, ed. R. Boehm (The Hague: Martinus Nijhoff, 1959). (Husserliana, vol. 8) |
| *HUA 23* | *Phantasie, Bildbewusstsein, Erinnerung*, ed E. Marbach (The Hague: Martinus Nijhoff, 1980). (Husserliana, vol. 23) |
| *HUA 24* | *Einleitung in die Logik und Erkenntnistheorie. Vorlesungen 1906/07*, ed. U. Melle (Dordrecht: Martinus Nijhoff, 1984). (Husserliana, vol. 24) |
| *HUA 26* | *Vorlesungen über Bedeutungslehre. Sommersemester 1908*, ed. U. Panzer (Dordrecht: Martinus Nijhoff, 1987). (Husserliana, vol. 26) |
| *Id 1* | *Ideen zu einer reinen Phänomenologie und phänomenologischen Philosophie, Erstes Buch* (Tübingen: Max Niemeyer, 1980). |

English edition: *Ideas Pertaining to a Pure Phenomenology and a Phenomenological Philosophy, First Book*, trans. F. Kersten (Dordrecht: Kluwer, 1982).

*Id 2*    *Ideen zu einer reinen Phänomenologie und phänomenologischen Philosophie, Zweites Buch*, ed. M. Biemel (The Hague: Martinus Nijhoff, 1952). **English edition:** *Ideas Pertaining to a Pure Phenomenology and a Phenomenological Philosophy, Second Book*, trans. R. Rojcewicz and A. Schuwer (Dordrecht: Kluwer, 1989).

*LI 1–6*    *Logische Untersuchungen* (Tübingen: Max Niemeyer, 1980). **English edition:** *Logical Investigations*, trans. J. N. Findlay, 2 vols. (London: Routledge, 2001).

*Time*    *Zur Phänomenologie des inneren Zeitbewusstseins (1893–1917)*, ed. R. Boehm (The Hague: Martinus Nijhoff, 1966). **English edition:** *On the Phenomenology of the Consciousness of Internal Time (1893–1917)*, trans. J. B. Brough (Dordrecht: Kluwer, 1990).

*TS*    *Ding und Raum. Vorlesungen 1907*, ed. U. Claesges (The Hague: Martinus Nijhoff, 1973). **English edition:** *Thing and Space: Lectures of 1907*, trans. R. Rojcewicz (Dordrecht: Kluwer, 1997).

## BIBLIOGRAPHY OF OTHER WORKS CITED

BALDWIN, T., 'Phenomenology, Solipsism and Egocentric Thought', *Proceedings of the Aristotelian Society*, supp. vol. 62 (1988), 27–44.

BELL, D., *Husserl* (London: Routledge, 1990).

BERMÚDEZ, J. L., 'Nonconceptual Content: From Perceptual Experience to Subpersonal Computational States', *Mind and Language* 10 (1995), 333–67.

BLOCK, N., 'On a Confusion about a Function of Consciousness', *Behavioral and Brain Sciences* 18 (1995), 227–47.

BREWER, B., *Perception and Reason* (Oxford: Clarendon Press, 1999).

CAMPBELL, J., 'Sense, Reference and Selective Attention', *Proceedings of the Aristotelian Society*, supp. vol. 71 (1997), 55–74.

—— 'Joint Attention and the First Person', in A. O'Hear (ed.), *Current Issues in Philosophy of Mind* (Cambridge: Cambridge University Press, 1998).

——, *Reference and Consciousness* (Oxford: Clarendon Press, 2002).

CAMUS, A., *The Myth of Sisyphus* (Harmondsworth: Penguin, 1975).

CARR, D., 'The "Fifth Meditation" and Husserl's Cartesianism', *Philosophy and Phenomenological Research* 34 (1973–4), 14–15.

CLAESGES, U., *Edmund Husserls Theorie der Raumkonstitution* (The Hague: Martinus Nijhoff, 1964).

DILTHEY, W., 'Beiträge zur Lösung der Frage vom Ursprung unseres Glaubens an die Realität der Aussenwelt', in *Gesammelte Schriften* (Leipzig: Teubner, 1923), v. 90–138.

DREYFUS, H., *Being-in-the-World: A Commentary on Heidegger's 'Being and Time', Division I* (Cambridge, MA: MIT Press, 1991).

DRUMMOND, J. J., 'On Seeing *a* Material Thing *in* Space', *Philosophy and Phenomenological Research* 40 (1979–80), 19–32.

—— *Husserlian Intentionality and Non-foundational Realism: Noema and Object* (Dordrecht: Kluwer, 1990).

DUMMETT, M., 'Frege's Myth of the Third Realm', in *Frege and Other Philosophers* (Oxford: Clarendon Press, 1991).

—— *Origins of Analytical Philosophy* (London: Duckworth, 1993).

EILAN, N., 'Perceptual Intentionality. Attention and Consciousness', in A. O'Hear (ed.), *Current Issues in Philosophy of Mind* (Cambridge: Cambridge University Press, 1998).

EVANS, G., *The Varieties of Reference* (Oxford: Clarendon Press, 1982).

FØLLESDAL, D., 'Husserl's Notion of the Noema', *Journal of Philosophy* 66 (1969), 680–7.

FREGE, G., 'The Thought', *Mind* 65 (1956), 289–311.

GIBSON, J. J., *The Ecological Approach to Visual Perception* (Hillsdale, NJ: Lawrence Erlbaum, 1979).

GURWITSCH, A., *The Field of Consciousness* (Pittsburgh: Duquesne University Press, 1964).

HEIDEGGER, M., *Being and Time* (Oxford: Blackwell, 1962).

—— *History of the Concept of Time* (Bloomington and Indianapolis: Indiana University Press, 1985).

KANT, I., *Critique of Pure Reason* (London: Macmillan, 1950).

KELLY, S. D., 'Reference and Attention: A Difficult Connection', *Philosophical Studies* 120 (2004), 277–86.

KELLY, S. D., 'Seeing Things in Merleau-Ponty', in T. Carman and M. B. N. Hansen (eds) *The Cambridge Companion to Merleau-Ponty* (Cambridge: Cambridge University Press, 2005).

KERN, I., *Husserl und Kant: Eine Untersuchung über Husserls Verhältnis zu Kant und zum Neukantianismus* (The Hague: Martinus Nijhoff, 1964).

KIM, J., *Supervenience and Mind* (Cambridge: Cambridge University Press, 1993).

LOCKE, J., *An Essay Concerning Human Understanding* (Oxford: Oxford University Press, 1975).

LOWE, E. J., 'Experience and its Objects', in T. Crane (ed.) *The Contents of Experience* (Cambridge: Cambridge University Press, 1992).

McDowell, J., *Mind and World* (Cambridge, MA: Harvard University Press, 1994).

Martin, M. G. F., 'Setting Things before the Mind', in A. O'Hear (ed.), *Current Issues in Philosophy of Mind* (Cambridge: Cambridge University Press, 1998).

Merleau-Ponty, M., 'Phenomenology and the Sciences of Man', in *The Primacy of Perception* (Evanston: Northwestern University Press).

Mulligan, K., and Smith, B., 'A Husserlian Theory of Indexicality', *Grazer Philosophische Studien* 28 (1986), 133–63.

Neisser, U, *Cognitive Psychology* (New York: Appleton-Century-Crofts, 1967).

Noë, A., *Action in Perception* (Cambridge, MA: MIT Press, 2004).

O'Shaughnessy, B., *The Will: A Dual Aspect Theory*, 2 vols. (Cambridge: Cambridge University Press, 1980).

Philipse, H., 'The Problem of Occasional Expressions in Edmund Husserl's *Logical Investigations*', *Journal of the British Society for Phenomenology* 13 (1982), 168–85.

——, 'Transcendental Idealism', in B. Smith and D. Woodruff Smith (eds.), *The Cambridge Companion to Husserl* (Cambridge: Cambridge University Press, 1995).

Poellner, P., 'Non-conceptual Content, Experience and the Self', *Journal of Consciousness Studies* 10/2 (2003), 32–57.

—— 'Self-Deception, Consciousness and Value: The Nietzschean Contribution', *Journal of Consciousness Studies* 11/10–11 (2004), 44–65.

—— 'Affect, Value and Objectivity', in B. Leiter and N. Sinhababu (eds.), *Nietzsche and Morality* (Oxford: Oxford University Press, 2007).

Quinton, A., *The Nature of Things* (London: Routledge & Kegan Paul, 1973).

Rowlands, M., *Externalism* (Chesham: Acumen, 2003).

Sartre, J.-P., *The Transcendence of the Ego* (New York: Octagon Books, 1972).

—— *Being and Nothingness* (London: Routledge, 2003).

Scheler, M., *Erkenntnis und Arbeit* (Frankfurt am Main: Vittorio Klostermann, 1977).

Searle, J., *Intentionality* (Cambridge: Cambridge University Pres, 1983).

Sellars, W., 'Empiricism and the Philosophy of Mind', in *Science, Perception and Reality* (London: Routledge, 1963).

Smith, A. D., *Husserl and the 'Cartesian Meditations'* (London: Routledge, 2003).

—— 'Husserl and Externalism', *Synthese* (forthcoming).

Smith, D. W., and McIntyre, R., *Husserl and Intentionality* (Dordrecht: Reidel, 1982).

Sokolowski, R., *The Formation of Husserl's Concept of Constitution* (The Hague: Martinus Nijhoff, 1970).

Soldati, G., *Bedeutung und psychischer Gehalt: Zur sprachanalytischen Kritik von Husserls früher Phänomenologie* (Paderborn: Ferdinand Schöningh, 1994).

Soteriou, M., 'The Subjective View of Experience and its Objective Commitments', *Proceedings of the Aristotelian Society* 105 (2005), 177–90.

Sprigge, T. L. S., *Facts, Words and Beliefs* (London: Routledge, 1970).

STEIN, E., *Zum Problem der Einfühlung* (Munich: Kaffke, 1980).

STRAWSON, G., *Mental Reality* (Cambridge, MA: MIT Press, 1994).

STRAWSON, P. F., *Individuals* (London: Methuen, 1959).

TUGENDHAT, E., *Der Wahrheitsbegriff bei Husserl und Heidegger* (Berlin: de Gruyter, 1970).

ZAHAVI, D., *Self-Awareness and Alterity* (Evanston: Northwestern University Press, 1999).

—— 'Husserl's Noema and the Internalism-Externalism Debate', *Inquiry* 47 (2004), 42–66.

# PART III

## HUMAN BEING

# CHAPTER 13

# NIHILISM AND THE MEANING OF LIFE

## JULIAN YOUNG

NIETZSCHE's 1882 announcement of the 'death of God' is more complex than it seems. For a start, when the 'madman' appears in the late nineteenth-century 'market-place' it is filled with educated positivists who have long ago ceased to 'believe in God' and so laugh at his self-importance. But the *news* the madman brings is neither that 'God is dead' not that 'we [men of science] are his murderers'. It is, rather, that the death of God—the transformation of the West from a religious into a secular culture—is no laughing matter.

As representatives of *Wissenschaft* in general, of a 'science' which includes not only Darwin but also nineteenth-century biblical deconstructionists such as David Strauss and Nietzsche himself, Nietzsche picks on Copernicus and Galileo as God's murderers:

What were we doing when we unchained this earth from its sun? Where is it moving to now? Away from all [e.g. Plato's] suns? Are we not continually falling? And backwards, sidewards, forwards, in all directions? Is there still and up and down? Aren't we straying as through an infinite nothing? (GS 125)[1]

---

[1] For a list of abbreviations used in this essay see its final page.

Nietzsche's point is that the medieval world-view, taken over from Plato and modified by Christian theology, was not merely an astronomy and a physics. It was, rather, a completely integrated account of astronomy, physics, metaphysics, and the meaning of life. When the medieval farmer looked up into the night sky from his place on earth, the centre of the cosmos, he simply *saw* the light of heaven shining down through the openings in the 'dome of the heavens' ('stars' as we call them). And so he *knew* the meaning of life. He knew that the purpose, task, or goal of his and every human life was, by living in Christian virtue, to achieve the everlasting, heavenly bliss promised to us in God's sacrifice of himself as man. So the Copernican Revolution in science was in fact much more than that. For in changing our astronomy it also, as the madman observes, robbed life of its 'direction'; of its '*sens*' which, in French, means both 'direction' and 'meaning'.

*This* is the news that has not yet reached the laughing positivists. 'This tremendous event is still on its way . . . the light of the stars is still on its way . . . deeds need time even after they are done to be seen and heard' (GS 125). The *Wissenschaft* of Western modernity has destroyed religion. What nineteenth-century positivism did not realize, however, was that the inevitable consequence of this would be the onset of 'nihilism', the conviction that our lives are meaningless.

A hundred and twenty-five years on, we ought to be able to answer two questions about Nietzsche's prediction. Was he right in anticipating that God's death would lead to nihilism? And if he was, does it matter?

\* \* \*

As with Nietzsche, a decisive role in George Eliot's loss of faith was played by David Strauss's deconstruction of the authority of the Bible in his *Life of Jesus* (1835–6).[2] Eliot, however, thought that though intelligent people could no longer believe in arrival in a supernatural heaven as the meaning of life, they could still believe in the ideal of Christian virtue as its meaning. Eliot, believed, in other words, that Christian morality, previously the *means* to the attainment of the goal of the Christian life, could and should now stand on its own feet as *itself* life's ultimate goal.

Nietzsche attacks Eliot (though it is doubtful he ever read her):

G. *Eliot*. They are rid of the Christian God and now believe all the more firmly that they must cling to Christian morality. This is an English consistency: we do

---

[2]  As Marian Evans, Eliot made what remains the only English translation of the work.

not wish to hold it against little moralistic females à la Eliot. In England one must rehabilitate oneself after every little emancipation from theology by showing in a veritably awe-inspiring manner what a moral fanatic one is.   (TI IX 5)

What, in Nietzsche's view, makes Eliot intellectually 'little' is her failure to realize that

Christianity is a system, a *whole* view of things thought out together. By breaking one main concept out of it one breaks the whole . . . . Christian morality is a command: its origin is transcendent; it is beyond all criticism, all right to criticism; it has truth only if God is the truth—it stands and falls with faith in God.   (ibid.)

For all the ignorance contained in his abuse of a one of the supreme minds of his century, Nietzsche has a point here: if you do away with the authorizer of Christian values you are left with *mere* values, free-floating and with no visible means of support.

Heidegger makes a related point. 'No one', he says, 'dies for mere values' (QCT, p. 142). Values 'devoid of background' (ibid.), values that fail to be grounded in a total understanding of reality—'ought's that fail to be grounded in 'is's—lack authority and cannot generate genuine commitment.

If so, then the fact that suicide bombers *do* die for their values suggests that they are not *mere* values. Our reaction to terrorism is complex. We experience horror, and revulsion. But typically, I think, we also experience a kind of *bafflement*. What makes the suicide bomber the representative of an alien 'otherness' is that we find it very hard to imagine any 'cause' for which we would volunteer ourselves for certain death.

This, however, was not always the case. Five hundred and seventy-eight Harvard men (who could easily have avoided the war by pulling rank) volunteered to fight against slavery in the American Civil War, and as late as 1914 the flower of both the British and German intelligentsia rushed to die on the killing fields of Flanders.

Historical epochs are, of course, never homogeneous. As well as the contemporary, they contain anticipations of the future and relics of the past. Western people still sometimes sacrifice themselves for 'God and freedom' (though not, if they can help it, in Iraq). Yet to the extent to which we are baffled by the phenomenon of suicide bombing, to the extent to which we have the sense of confronting a pre-modern cast of mind, what is revealed is how lightly our 'values' sit upon us; the fact that they no longer possess the power to commit which they possessed in the past and which Islamic values still possess today.

Nietzsche (and, of course, Dostoyevsky) was, then, I suggest, right to predict that Western values, uprooted by Western science from their metaphysical foundations, would slowly lose their power to commit, their power to provide direction and meaning to our lives. He was right, that is, to predict, the arrival of nihilism.

# CAMUS

My second question was: does nihilism, as Nietzsche supposed, matter? Though it might seem almost true by definition that it does, one brave and important thinker who denies this is Albert Camus.

*The Myth of Sisyphus* was written in German-occupied Paris in 1940 and, on the face of it, casts an extraordinary light on the life of its author, who was, at the time, risking his life in the French Resistance. Its famous opening lines hold that: 'There is but one truly serious philosophical problem and that is suicide. Judging whether life is or is not worth living amounts to answering the fundamental question of philosophy' (MS, p. 11).

To say that the question of whether life is worth living is a *problem* is to say that something at least *threatens* a negative answer. The threat, according to Camus, comes from 'the absurd'. This, he says, threatens suicide because it produces a feeling of 'nausea' (MS, p. 21), a world-'weariness' (MS, p. 19), a 'longing for death' (MS, p. 14).

What is 'the absurd'? To live in absurdity is, says Camus, to live in a world in which 'belie[f] in God' is no longer possible (MS, p. 7). Since, however, utopian Marxism, with its promise of 'a miraculous event at the end of time', is essentially 'religious in nature' (MS, pp. 188–9), the impossibility of 'belief in God' includes, for Camus, the impossibility of belief in Marxism. So to live in an absurd universe is to live with a post-Marxist, as well as post-Christian, understanding of things.

Essentially, then, the absurd is the death of God (together with, as Nietzsche calls them, his 'shadows').[3] This, Camus claims, threatens suicide because if

---

[3] This is a simplification. What Camus actually says is that the absurd is 'born of the confrontation between human need [for meaning] and the unreasonable silence of the world' (MS, p. 32). It consists, in other words, in a *discrepancy*, of large—'absurd'—proportions, between what we need and what reality provides. As his discussion proceeds, however, the need tends to drop out of the picture, so that the 'absurdity' of the universe comes to consist *simply* in its Godlessness. The two-place mutates into a one-place predicate.

God is dead it seems that there is no 'meaning of life' (MS, p. 12), no longer any 'great idea that transcends [life] . . . and gives it meaning' (MS, p. 15). And if life is meaningless, one is tempted to think, it is not worth living. One might as well, in other words, commit suicide.

The task Camus sets himself, however, is to show that, even in an absurd universe, 'suicide is not legitimate' (MS, p. 7). It is not legitimate because, even in God's absence, life is still worth—indeed splendidly worth—living.

\* \* \*

On the face of things, there are two possible strategies one might adopt in order to show this to be the case.

First, one might seek to attack the inference from the death of God to the death of meaning. One might set out to show that even in the absence of God (and his shadows), life—or, at the very least, *my* life—can still have a meaning. Introducing a more refined use of 'nihilism' than we have so far adopted, we might seek to show that the death of God does not entail nihilism *about meaning*.

Alternatively, while accepting that the death of God *is* the death of meaning, one might seek to show that life can still be worth living even in its absence. The death of meaning, one might argue, does not entail the death of life's value, does not entail nihilism *about life's worth*. Life can be both meaningless and wonderful.

The crucial fact about Camus is that he adopts the *second*, heroic, strategy. With clear eyes, and with an intellectual courage matching the physical courage of his life in the Resistance, he asserts that 'Hitherto . . . people have played on words and pretended to believe that refusing to grant a meaning to life necessarily leads to declaring that it is not worth living. In truth, there is no necessary common measure [no necessary connection] between these two judgments' (MS, p. 15). Not only does the death of meaning fail to entail the death of life's worth, it actually, Camus asserts, increases it: 'life will be lived all the better if it has no meaning' (MS, p. 53).

Camus develops his argument by painting a portrait of 'the absurd man': an heroic figure who recognizes the absurdity of the universe but lives, nonetheless, a life that, in both his and our eyes, is splendidly worthwhile. What Camus offers, in other words, is a 'role model', an exemplary figure who shows us what it is to live well in an absurd universe.

\* \* \*

Camus' absurd hero is distinguished by a gargantuan appetite, a limitless lust for experience. His life is marked by the fact that he 'expends' himself in a life devoted to, by all normal standards, 'excess' (MS, p. 78).[4] What counts is 'quantity not quality'. The life of the absurd hero is governed by an 'ethics of quantity' (MS, p. 69). Camus offers three paradigms of such a hero: Don Juan, 'the actor', and the friends of his Algerian boyhood.

Even though signally unsuccessful in Mozart's opera, Don Juan is, by repute, a man who seduces more women in an evening than most men manage in a lifetime. He does not fall in love or engage in improving conversation, but makes the same speech to every woman he meets, since 'to anyone who seeks mere quantity in his joys, the only thing that matters is efficiency' (MS, p. 68). When all that matters is conquest, in other words, it is foolish to depart from the tried and true.

'The actor' is a marked by a similar lust for experience. As a stage actor, 'for three hours' Iago, for three hours Gloucester, is a 'mime of the ephemeral' (MS, p. 74), so one who lives like an actor is devoted to 'dispersion', lives through a 'heretical multiplicity of souls' (MS, p. 78).

The third paradigm of the absurd hero is offered, not in *The Myth* itself but in a series of lyrically nostalgic essays written a few years either side of *The Myth*, and published together with it in the standard English translation: 'Summer in Algiers', 'The Minotaur', and 'Helen's Exile'.

Writing out of the northern greyness of a Paris winter, Camus recalls the band of 'brothers' with whom he spent his youth on the sun-drenched beaches of his Algerian homeland. What characterizes these wondrous beings is a 'magnificent vocation for facile joys' (MS, p. 132); the simple joys of just 'being there' such as sauntering along the boulevard in shiny new shoes and admiring 'cool-legged' girls. In a land where 'every summer morning seems to be the first in the world' and 'each twilight seems to be the last' (MS, p. 160), in a land where people are not 'nudists' (those 'tedious protestants of the flesh'), but are simply 'comfortable in the sunlight', in a land where one says not 'go for' but rather 'indulge in' a swim (MS, p. 129), one cannot fail to 'participate in [the] . . . dialogue of stone and flesh in tune with the seasons' (MS, p. 130). In a land where a thirty-year-old workman has already 'played all the cards in his hand' (MS, p. 132), one has no time to devote oneself to any 'purpose' (MS, p. 142). Realizing that, as we say, 'life is not a rehearsal',

---

[4] This again is a simplification of Camus' discussion. For as well as heroic 'excess' he also offers heroic 'revolt', the latter personified in the figure of the eponymous Sisyphus. See, further, n. 7 below.

one lives with 'a haste to live that borders on waste' (MS, p. 132). Life, that is to say, is 'not to be built up but burned up' (MS, P. 133).

Reflecting on this southern dream, Camus concludes that his boyhood friends at once 'repeat the gestures of the athletes of Delos' (MS, p. 129) and, he hopes, 'are modelling the image of a culture in which the image of man will at last find its true likeness' (MS, p. 133). In a word, what these models of splendid living in the midst of absurdity tell us is that we are to return to the 'insolence and *naïveté*' (MS, p. 129) of the Greeks.[5]

Two questions need to be raised at this point. First, in what sense, exactly, is meaning excluded from the lives of Camus' absurd heroes? And second, on what grounds is it excluded?

A meaning of life is I suggested, a defining purpose, aim, or goal. But, of course, all of Camus' heroes have at least short-term goals—food shelter, warmth—for otherwise they would die. And, in fact, they also have long-term, even life-defining, goals: the Don wishes to seduce as many women as possible (and then some), the actor to live as many lives as possible, and the surfer friends of Camus' youth to spend as much time on the beach chasing girls and as little in the classroom as possible. So the question becomes pressing as to the sense in which meaning is excluded from the life of the absurd hero.

Camus says, to repeat: 'Life is not to be built up but burned up. Stopping to think and becoming better are out of the question' (MS, p. 133). What this excludes is the life of self-improvement, the life guided by the goal of approximating, ever more closely, to an ideal conception of the self. What it excludes, to use a slightly ponderous phrase, is *life as a project of self-development*.

The second question was: *why* is life as a project of self-development (for remainder of this essay I will understand 'meaning' in this way) excluded? Why are 'men with a purpose' confined to the cold grey cities of northern Europe and excluded from the southern joys of the Algerian beach (MS, p. 142)?

Camus' argument consists in a contrast between the absurd hero and what he calls 'everyday man'. The latter lives with 'aims', 'weighs up his chances . . . counts on "some day", his retirement, the labour of his sons' (MS, p. 56). He lives, as we say, 'in the future'. The absurd hero, on the other hand, lives in complete 'indifference' to the future (and the past), living instead 'in

---

[5] One feels, I think, that Camus' boyhood friends are somehow more attractive than either the Don or the 'actor'. I shall try to explain why this is so towards the end of this essay.

he present and the succession of presents' (MS, p. 62). To him, as we saw, every morning is 'the first in the world' and every twilight 'the last'. So the argument is that to live with a project of self-development is to rob oneself of the present. And since all joy happens in the present, so to live is to rob oneself of life's joys.

The principle strategic role of this argument is to support the claim that 'life will be lived *all the better* if it has no meaning' (my emphasis). Camus wants to reaffirm the Nietzschean point that by making the supernatural the locus of all value, Christianity 'de-divinized' natural life, turned it into an joyless waiting room we are forced to inhabit while waiting for the non-existent Godot, waiting for the train to carry us to our 'true' (but non-existent) destination. A similar point is made in Ian McEwen's novel, *Black Dogs*. The life of Bernard, one of its two central characters, is defined by communism, by total commitment to the class struggle and to the coming into being of the final 'brotherhood of man'. But the very totality of this commitment robs him of the joys, insights, and sensitivities accessible only to those who inhabit the present.

In fact, however, Camus' argument hits a great deal more than its primary target. For if sound, it shows not merely that we should avoid projects of self-development grounded in grand, world-historical narratives such as those of Christianity and utopian Marxism, but rather that we should avoid projects of self-development *überhaupt*. That it is the—not necessarily Christian—'everyday man' who is criticized shows that the destruction of, as we may call them, 'personal' as well as 'universal' meanings is what Camus intends.

\* \* \*

The irony is, however, that while the 'everyday man' of the early twentieth century may have still been committed to projects of self-development—the phrase itself has a slightly Victorian ring to it—the everyday man of the early twenty-first century, when not a work-weary node in the global cybernetwork, increasingly matches up to Camus' requirement of living without (either universal or personal) meaning. As German sociologists have been telling us for some time, what we increasingly inhabit is an *Erlebnisgesellschaft*, a society given over, precisely, to the 'experiences'—thrills—of the present, whether these be the product of recreational drugs, sex, techno music, bungee jumping, or the Sunday 'hit' of evangelical Christianity. Reduced to its basics, Camus' account of the worthwhile life in an absurd universe amounts to something very simple: St Paul's 'if the dead do not rise let us eat and drink [and be merry] for tomorrow we die' (1 Corinthians 15:32). But increasingly, this is the way we *do* live. So if Camus is right as to how to live well in a post-death-of-God world then the (at least leisure-time) life of meaning-less (post)modernity is just fine.

* * *

In fact, however, Camus' argument is open to serious criticism. The first point which needs to be made is that to *have* a goal is not the same as being *obsessed* by it. One may conceive one's life as a journey towards a destination and yet be relaxed enough about one's goal to allow oneself genuine freedom to enjoy the sights one passes on the way. (The businessman may be in the foreign city to conclude an important deal yet genuinely enjoy being a tourist as well.) Indeed it is usually part of a sensible strategy for achieving a goal that one does allow oneself a relaxed attitude to it: since stress is counterproductive, generous amounts of stress-relief ought usually to be budgeted into a successful strategy for achieving the goal.

Camus is certainly right to point out that loss of the present represents a serious *trap* that one can easily fall into. As Schopenhauer wisely observes, purposeful people are prone to live 'in the expectation of better things' so that 'the present is accepted only for the time being, is set at naught, and looked upon merely as the path to the goal'. The result, Schopenhauer continues, is that when, at the end of their lives, goal-obsessed people look back, they find that: 'they have lived throughout *ad interim*; they will be surprised to see that the very thing they allowed to slip by unappreciated and unenjoyed was just their life, precisely that in the expectation of which they had lived.'[6] Possession of a life-defining goal creates the *danger* that we will find ourselves robbed of the present. But a danger is not an inevitability, indeed Camus' signposting of the trap makes it less likely we will fall into it.

A second point against Camus' argument is that the possession of a future goal is often the *precondition* of present pleasure. One cannot enjoy the slow emergence into intelligibility of the hieroglyphs on the French wine label unless one is in the process of learning French, one cannot enjoy beating

---

[6] *Parerga and Paralipomena*, 2 vols., trans. E. F. J. Payne (Oxford: Clarendon Press, 1974), ii. 285–6.

yesterday's mark on the bench-press unless one has the goal of increasing one's muscular strength.

* * *

Against Camus, I have argued so far that a goal-defined life does not *have* to be one of joyless drudgery, that goal-directedness, project-possession, meaning, *can* belong to a life worth living. Now, however, I want to argue the stronger point that it *must*.

Nietzsche observes (an observation to which I shall shortly return), that life is '*essentially*' the 'will to power', the will, that is, to 'grow' (BGE 259). At least part of what this means is that human beings are *essentially* project-needing beings, beings who need to experience their lives as continual 'growth'. This, I think, helps pinpoint something that is seriously wrong with the lives of Camus' absurd heroes.

What is wrong is that they are completely *static*. The Don learns nothing from his seductions, nothing carried over from one to the next. Like his speeches, every encounter is just like its predecessor, merely another entry in Leporello's 'List' aria. Similarly, 'the actor' (a poststructuralist as well as a Camusian hero), since he is a mere *sequence* of 'souls', has no sense of a continuing self and, a fortiori, no sense of a developing self. And the friends of Camus' youth are so laid back that they do not even try to become better surfers. 'Stopping to think and becoming better' are, remember, 'out of the question'. Camus is quite explicit as to the static character of his heroes' lives. Of the Don he says that, like his speeches, 'he will not change'. 'Only in novels does one change one's condition or become better' (MS, p. 69). But if this is right what it means, ultimately, is that the life of Camus absurd hero is actually one of deadly tedium, a life, in the end, of *boredom*. (Weirdly, Camus seems to concede this by making Sisyphus—who is condemned for all eternity to push a rock to the top of his mountain whence it promptly rolls to the bottom again—also an absurd hero.)[7] But a life of boredom cannot be one that is worth living.

I suggested earlier, that Camus' defence of the life of 'absurd man' amounts to a defence of what is, increasingly, the character of contemporary Western

---

[7] Camus tries to justify Sisyphus' life by glorifying it as a life of heroic, teeth-gritting 'revolt' against fate. For a rejection of his argument see my *The Death of God and the Meaning of Life* (London: Routledge, 2003), 164–6.

humanity. If, however, the above critique is correct then it points to what is wrong with Western postmodernity: in so far as it is an *Erlebnisgesellschaft*, a society of cheap, sensual thrills, its underlying, fundamental mood, its *Grundstimmung*, to borrow a term from Hölderlin, is one of boredom—or 'depression' as we would likely call it these days. From this perspective, recreational sex, drugs, and Christianity appear not so much as the joys of the good life but rather as desperate, ever more futile, attempts to escape the tedium of postmodernity.

# NIETZSCHE

Earlier, I distinguished two strategies for discovering a worthwhile life in a Godless universe: the heroic strategy of denying that the death of meaning entails the death of life's worth, and the less heroic, but intuitively more plausible, strategy of denying that the death of God entails the death of meaning. What we have seen in the examination of Camus is the failure of the first strategy. So if we are to overcome 'nausea' and 'world-weariness' we need to turn to the second.

Traditional meanings of life, whether Christian or Marxist, are marked by two features: they are, as already noted, *universal*—what makes life meaningful for me is exactly what makes it meaningful for you—and they are *discovered* rather than created. In a Christian cosmos, that is to say, we do not *choose* the meaning of our lives. Rather, we are simply *born into* a situation in which people are sorted into the saved and damned, and into a powerful desire to be numbered among the former rather than the latter. As with our height, gender, and race, the meaning of our life belongs to our 'facticity'.

What the death of God (and his shadows) might seem to entail is that a life-meaning possessing these two features is no longer available. Still, one might be moved to reflect, that there is no *universal* meaning does not preclude my having my own *personal meaning*—that *life* has no meaning does not preclude *my life* from having a meaning—and that there is no ready-made meaning waiting to be discovered does not entail that meaning cannot be *created*. So, granting the point that we are essentially meaning-seeking beings, one might be led to the conclusion that what we need to do in order to live worthwhile lives is to *create our own individual meaning* by choosing to dedicate ourselves—or, better, choosing to *be*—a certain project of self-development. These reflections bring us to the works of Friedrich Nietzsche.

* * *

Nietzsche quips: 'If we have our own *why* of life, we shall get along with almost any *how*. Man does not strive for pleasure; only the Englishman does that' (TI I 12). The point here is essentially the same as that made elsewhere in terms of the fundamental status of the will to 'power' or 'growth'. What we need in our lives is not 'pleasure'—only the English utilitarian (and Camus) regard that as the *summum bonum*—but rather meaning. If we have a 'why' we are here, a project of self-development, then we can live satisfying lives. 'My suffering . . . does it matter . . . am I concerned with happiness?' Zarathustra asks at the very end of his journey. And replies: 'I am concerned with my work.'

Yet for Nietzsche, as much as for Camus, we inhabit an absurd universe: 'the total character of the world is . . . to all eternity chaos—in the sense not of a lack of [causal] necessity but of lack of order, arrangement, form, beauty, wisdom, and whatever other names there are for our aesthetic anthropomorphisms' (GS 109). This repeats the 'madman's' observation that we post-Copernicans live in a 'directionless' universe, that no world-historical meaning is given to us, any longer, as part of our facticity. So, Nietzsche seems to conclude, we must each of us construct our own meaning.[8]

We must, he says, become the 'hero' of our lives. To do this, of course, we need first of all to *see* the hero we are to be, 'see . . . the hero that is concealed in everyday characters' (GS 78). And to do this we must make use of the techniques of artists. Everyday existence is 'nothing but foreground' (ibid.), a mass of meaningless details. As Nietzschean self-creators, we must achieve aesthetic 'distance' from our lives so that they appear to us 'simplified and transfigured' (ibid.).[9] By recessing some details into shadow and bringing

---

[8] I actually believe that, on the best reading, this is *not* Nietzsche's conclusion: that what he really holds, with early Heidegger (to whom I shall turn shortly), that meaning *is* part of our facticity, put there by the community into which we are born. (See my *Nietzsche's Philosophy of Religion* (Cambridge: Cambridge University Press, 2006), *passim*.) Nonetheless, the reading I am about to sketch (substantially that presented in Alexander Nehamas's influential *Nietzsche: Life as Literature* (Cambridge, MA: Harvard University Press, 1985)) is (a) a plausible account of *The Gay Science*, (b) historically important as a principal inspiration for both Sartrean existentialism and French poststructualism, and (c) philosophically important as a repository of important truths (as well as important falsehoods.)

[9] Of course, some works of literature deliberately eschew the clear and simple lines that Nietzsche is talking about here. Implicit in this remark is his lifelong classicism, his insistence that all good art

others forward into sunlight, we create—as if producing a well-constructed novel—a coherent narrative of our life to date, a narrative which tells us the outline of its proper continuation into the future.

Thus—an illustration simplified to the point of banality—consider Gauguin. A successful stockbroker, Gauguin lives, with wife and children, the comfortable life of the Parisian *haut bourgeoisie*. Though outwardly successful he is, we may imagine, inwardly miserable. He feels his life to be confused and meaningless. Taking Nietzsche's advice, perhaps on his first trip to Tahiti, he gains 'distance' from his life and attempts to grasp, in simple and coherent outline, the totality of the narrative he is in the middle of living. There are two stories (actually, of course, many more) he can decide to adopt.

His first story is that he is a person possessed of both a shrewd grasp of financial markets and the moral responsibility to provide for his family who is making himself miserable with unrealistic yearnings for the life of a painter, a life for which, in the opinion of the admired Paul Cézanne, he has no talent. The outcome of this story is that (like the future Duke of Wellington breaking his violin over his knee on joining the army) he must burn his brushes.

According to the second story, however, Gauguin is a painter of genius with a burning social message who is making himself miserable doing work he abhors out of a sense of responsibility to a wife he does not love, a sense of responsibility which is really nothing more than cowardice in the face of bourgeois opinion. The outcome of this story is that he must abandon job, wife, and children and depart to Tahiti for ever.

Notice two things about the moment of decision—the *Grenzsituation*—in which 'Gauguin' finds himself. First, each story tells him the meaning of his life—loving father and husband on the one hand, painter and messianic social critic on the other. Second, which story he adopts is entirely *up to him*. His moment of decision really is a moment of *decision*.

Nietzsche's talk of 'seeing' the hero in everyday characters might mislead on this point. But that he is in fact using 'see' in the same way as it is used when we speak of 'seeing' the duck in the ambiguous picture—a seeing which does not preclude someone else seeing a rabbit—is indicated by the demand that we be 'creators' of ourselves, that we become beings who are 'new, unique, incomparable, who give themselves laws, who create themselves' (GS 335).

* * *

is 'classical' art. See my *Nietzsche's Philosophy of Art* (Cambridge: Cambridge University Press, 1992), 78–81, 86–7, 141–4.

Self-creation cannot be God-like since it is limited by facticity. If I live in the twelfth century I cannot create myself as an astronaut. If I am five foot six I cannot become a professional basketball player. Within these limits, however, there are many, in fact indefinitely many, identities I may construct for myself. So the question is: how should I choose among the plethora of possibilities?

What is crucial, Nietzsche observes, is that whoever we choose to be should be someone we 'esteem' (GS 78), 'desire' (GS 290), are 'well-disposed' (GS 341)—indeed passionately well-disposed—towards. It is perfectly possible to use one's 'artistic' intelligence to construe one's life as that of a victim. Or as a life of bourgeois boredom, a life 'measured out with teaspoons' (T. S. Eliot). On such paths, however, lie depression and despair. So the hero of our lives must be a 'hero' not only in the sense of 'central character' but in the sense, too, of being someone we admire.

As mentioned earlier, Nietzsche views the will to continual 'power' or 'growth' as intrinsic to human nature. And since growth must always have a specific direction, must be growth towards a specific goal, at least part of what he is saying is that human beings require ongoing projects: that a sense of continual 'self-overcoming', of 'continual ascent as on stairs' (GS 288) is essential to a flourishing life.

Without a sense of ongoing ascent, life will be (leaving aside the continual *descent* of the depressed) the static, boring life of Camus' Don Juan. Ascent, Nietzsche holds, is the essence of a life to which one can be 'well-disposed'. How is one to achieve this?

By, he says, using one's artistic skill in 'interpreting and arranging events' to uncover in them a 'personal providence'. We need, he says, to reach a 'high point' where we can see

how palpably always everything that happens to us turns out for the best. Every day and every hour, life seems to have no other wish than to prove this proposition again and again. Whatever it is, bad weather or good, the loss of a friend, sickness, slander, the failure of some letter to arrive, the spraining of an ankle, a glance into a shop, a counter-argument, the opening of a book, a dream a fraud—either immediately or very soon after it proves to be something that 'must not be missing'; it has a profound significance and use precisely for *us*.   (GS 277)

What Nietzsche is suggesting here is the idea of scripting one's life as a *Bildungsroman*—a novel (*Roman*) of 'education' (*Bildung*) in the widest possible sense of the word: a history of progress from immaturity through, as we call them, 'learning experiences', towards maturity, a narrative of self-development, of an ever-ascending 'learning curve'.

Notice that '*Bildung*', here, really means (and sounds) the same as 'building': 'education' is 'building up' the life of a person. Nietzsche's view directly, and it seems to me correctly, contradicts Camus' claim that 'life is not to be built up but burned up'.

* * *

So has Nietzsche then provided the answer to the problem of living a flourishing life in an absurd universe, a universe that is in his sense 'chaos'? As I observed (in footnote 8 above), the foregoing reading of Nietzsche represents the birth of (at least Sartre's version of) Existentialism, the birth of the idea of 'existence before essence'; of the idea that we are born 'essence'- or identity-free and have then to choose who we are to be. A way, therefore, of answering the question about Nietzsche is to examine the further development of the idea of self-creation in the Existentialism of Jean-Paul Sartre.

# SARTRE

In essence, the 600-odd pages of *Being and Nothingness* (published in German-occupied Paris in 1943) boil down to two tasks. The first is to establish that we are radically free, freedom representing the principle dividing line between *être-pour-soi*, 'being-for-itself' (persons), and *être-en-soi*, 'being-in-itself' (things). The 'radical' character of Sartrean freedom can be grasped by contrasting it with what might be called 'Bush-freedom'—the freedom to do what you want provided that what you want is controlled by big business. The essence of the freedom Sartre affirms is that we are free not only to do what we want but also to determine what it is that we want. Sartre's second, and by far the most space-consuming, task is to work out the consequences of radical freedom.

Sartre acknowledges the inescapability of facticity. There are a huge number of facts about ourselves—cultural facts such as the historical epoch to which we belong and biological facts such as our genetic inheritance—that we can do nothing about. A thesis he calls 'psychological determinism' (BN, p. 31) holds that how one acts is completely determined by one's facticity. Who I am, my 'essence', is inevitably and unalterably determined by my past. Nature and nurture determines me to be unalterably the kind of person that I am. '*Wesen ist was gewesen ist'* (BN, p. 35), 'essence is what has been'. Sartre repeatedly uses this quotation from Hegel to sum up the thesis of psychological determinism.

Psychological determinism denies Sartre's fundamental distinction between the 'for-itself' and the 'in-itself'. It sees no ontological difference between a person and a rock. Each has an 'essence' that is determined by the total set of facts about the world at the moment of its coming into being and which, in conjunction with current circumstances, completely determines how it behaves.

Sartre holds psychological determinism to be absolutely false. His argument for this is what is sometimes called the 'feeling of freedom' argument: that we are free is simply an immediate and indisputable fact of self-consciousness, more certain than anything else. Hiking along a mountain path I look over the edge to the sheer drop below and simply *know* that, if I chose, I *could* throw myself to my death. The weird anxiety of the feeling is generated precisely by its being a confrontation with the uncanniness of absolute freedom (BN, p. 31).

Another way Sartre has of making the same point concerns the phenomenon of 'questioning' (BN, pp. 33–4). Descartes held that though most of our powers are limited, in one respect they match the unlimited power of God: my power to withhold assent from propositions that are open to doubt is absolutely unlimited. Nothing can force me to believe that $2 + 2 = 5$. Similarly, given that it is absolutely certain, nothing can force me to withhold assent from '$2 + 2 = 4$'.

Loyal to his Cartesian ancestry, Sartre thinks of the self in exactly the same way. What I, this present being, am is nothing but freedom, nothing but the power of assent and dissent. What I am, in particular, is the power of assent to or dissent from my past self, the self established by my facticity. I am the power either to choose that self to be my present self or to reject it in favour of something else. I am, Sartre says (with the Teutonic convolution the French take to be necessary to authentic philosophizing), 'the permanent possibility of negating what I am in the form of having been' (BN, p. 439). Radical freedom is the power, overnight, as it were, to trade in an old identity and be 'reborn' as a fundamentally new person.[10]

It might be objected that the 'feeling of freedom' could be illusory. That after a few drinks one *feels* one is saying something terribly profound does

---

[10]  The figure of 'the actor' seems to commit Camus, too, to belief in radical freedom. Other such believers are: poststructualists and people on death row who, having been 'reborn', feel themselves no longer answerable for their crimes.

not mean that one is. That people on certain drugs *feel* they can fly does not mean that they can; in fact science tells us quite certainly that they cannot. It is important to note, however, that *Being and Nothingness* is subtitled 'An Essay on Phenomenological Ontology'. Since 'phenomenology' is essentially a matter of acute, presupposition-less description, this amounts to the claim that, in the language of P. F. Strawson, *Being and Nothingness* is an essay in 'descriptive metaphysics'. Sartre's point, I think, is that scientific representations of the world are irrelevant to his interests. His concern is to describe the everyday world in which we live and move and have our human being, and to that world—the 'life-world', in Gadamer's language—the 'for-itself'/'in-itself' distinction is fundamental.

In sum, then, from the point of view of the life-world, though I am born into an 'essence' I can, at this very moment, choose to 'negate' it and replace it with another one. Since to refuse to choose a new identity is to endorse the existing one, the only choice I cannot make is the choice not to choose. Freedom is inescapable (BN, p. 439), a point to which I shall return.

\* \* \*

I have been talking about 'essences' but Sartre also has a more precise way of talking. Choosing one's identity is, for him, choosing one's 'fundamental project' (BN, pp. 565, 479–80), that is, choosing the project which makes sense of all one's lesser projects. This idea is essentially equivalent to Nietzsche's idea of 'choosing the hero' of one's life, which makes clear the fundamental continuity between the two philosophies.

Sartre often puts the point in terms of 'values'. One's fundamental project is one's fundamental value. If, for example, one's fundamental self-description is 'the communist' then one's most basic value is social equality.

\* \* \*

At first sight, Sartre's affirmation of our radical freedom for self-creation—our ability to transmute from Saul to Paul and back again—looks exhilarating, as indeed it was received in the aftermath of the Second World War. After Auschwitz, precisely what we seemed to need was a philosophy that allowed us to be 'born again' after the disasters wrought by out parents' generation.

Yet, carefully read, Sartre himself does not regard radical freedom as exhilarating at all. Far from a blessing, it is, he says darkly, something to which we are 'condemned' (BN, p. 439). Far from being something we celebrate it causes us, he says, 'anguish' (BN, p. 29), an anguish which we seek to cover over by indulging in 'bad faith' (*mauvaise foi*).

Bad faith is attempted self-deception. In it, we seek to convince ourselves that we are part of the causal order in the same way that an ink bottle or a rock is. We attempt to deny our essence-free existence, to convince ourselves that our existence *is* our essence in just the way it is for a rock. What we engage in, in other words, is a wilful 'category mistake': we seek to transfer ourselves from the category of the 'for-itself' to that of the 'in-itself'. We seek, says Sartre, the 'impenetrability and infinite density' of a mere thing (BN, p. 566). In his novel *The Age of Reason*, his hero, Daniel, 'wishes to be a pederast as an oak tree is an oak tree'.

Sartre's famous example of this attempt to transform oneself into a thing is the Paris waiter (BN, pp. 59–60), whose waiterly gestures (one thinks here, perhaps, of the mime of Marcel Marceau) are always perfect, indeed too perfect, an exaggeration which endows them with a robotic quality—which is just what the waiter seeks to convince himself that he is.

But why should we do this? What is it about freedom that causes us anguish and so launches us into the (ultimately futile) attempt to deny it? Sartre's answer is that since my own free choice is the 'unique foundation of values', it follows that 'nothing justifies me in adopting this or that particular value, or this or that particular scale of values. As a being by whom values exist, I am unjustifiable. My freedom is anguished at being the foundation of values while itself without foundation' (BN, p. 38).

Normally, says Sartre, my existence is one of engagement. I am fully and busily engaged in activities shaped by my fundamental project, the result of which is that my life is, or at any rate seems, meaningful. Alarm clocks, traffic lights, even tax forms show up as meaningful things demanding 'urgent' attention because they show up *within* my fundamental project. But sometimes engagement breaks down. I 'disengage' from the world (BN, p. 39). Now I look at my fundamental project from *without*. And what I realize is that my free choice of that project is utterly without foundation. So I see that I—this tiny pinpoint of Cartesian consciousness, naked save for the power of choice—am the 'foundationless foundation' of my project, that I create myself, in a certain sense, '*ex nihilo*' (BN, p. 33).

Realizing this, I realize, says Sartre, that that my choice of values is 'beyond all reasons', is, that is, 'gratuitous' (BN, p. 479). And realizing this, I realize 'the *absurdity* of my choice and consequently of my being' (BN, p. 480).

What does 'absurd' mean here? Not what it means in Camus, but rather 'a feeling of unjustifiability' (BN, p. 480).[11] I realize that whatever choice I have made is no more justified—or unjustified—than any alternative choice. Suppose, for example, that I am fighting for the French communists against the Nazi occupiers, and that committing myself to communism and to opposing fascism is a life-defining, fundamental choice. Suppose however that the fascist has made a similar act of fundamental choice. How can I show that *my* choice is the right one and not his?

For Sartre, there is no way I can do this. When it comes down to *fundamental* choices there is no way of showing that one is any better than another, and so no way of showing that it *matters* which choice I make. In other words it does *not* matter, any more than it matters whether I walk on the left or right of the pavement (sidewalk) or whether I drink Pepsi or Coke.

So what is 'absurd' about our lives is that we take so seriously something that does not and cannot matter. We are clowns, our lives tragic comedies. Viewed with the insight of disengagement, we are people who devote absolute seriousness and concentration to, as it were, never walking on the cracks in the pavement.

But exactly what is it about the ridiculousness of human being that causes 'anguish'? It is the fact that once we have seen the absurdity of our fundamental projects we cannot, in our heart of hearts, take them seriously any more. We can no longer, that is, find ourselves genuinely *committed* to them. And if one is not committed to a goal then one does not really *have* that goal. Confrontations with the absurd, that is to say, plunge our lives into meaninglessness, frustrate our fundamental need for meaning.

The concrete form taken by this frustration is paralysis of action. Since action requires a purpose it follows that if our lives have no purpose we cannot act. We are reduced to Hamlet-like indecision or are at best 'going through the motions'. Sartre explores this problem in the novels that make up the *Paths of Liberty* quartet written during the same period as *Being and Nothingness*. The only way Sartre's characters can act—get married, join the communist party, die a soldier's heroic death, stab a knife into the back of one's hand—is via the *act gratuit*— the spur-of-the-moment action performed without reason since it is known that there are no reasons.

\* \* \*

[11]  But since, as I shall shortly suggest, the absence of God is the *source* of this feeling, the two uses of 'absurd' are not unrelated.

Sartre's Existentialism is a philosophy of bereavement. It yearns for a command from God in which to ground one's freedom. But where God should be there is only an absence. So Sartre's philosophy ends in nihilism, nihilism about life's meaning and so about its value. If God is dead then all things are permitted—and so worthless. The only way to avoid anguish is through the repression that is 'bad faith', and even then one cannot really succeed since, as Sartre says, to evade something you have to know that it is there (BN, p. 43).

Yet, as observed, Sartre's Existentialism is simply Nietzschean self-creation thought through to its ultimate conclusion. It is self-creationism shooting itself in the back. What this shows is, *not* that the idea of our need for a life-defining project is defective, but rather that, as in the Christian era, meaning must be something we *discover* as part of our facticity and so do not have to *choose*. For Sartre is, it seems to me, right: if—*if*—our lives must be based on ungrounded choice then they *are* meaningless and so not worth living. This insight, I believe, plays a crucial role in the early[12] philosophy of Martin Heidegger.

# EARLY HEIDEGGER

A prominent theme which links Nietzsche, Camus, Sartre, and Heidegger together, and often underlies their co-classification as 'Existentialists', is that of the 'outsider': all of them valorize, both morally and cognitively, the heroic individual who stands outside the conventionalities of bourgeois existence. In *Being and Time* the valorizing term is 'authentic'; *eigentlich*, literally 'ownly'.

Mostly, says Heidegger, our existence is *in*authentic. Mostly, we succumb to the 'dictatorship of *das Man*' ('the One' or 'the They'), the pressure to conform to public opinion. Mostly, 'we take pleasure and enjoy ourselves as *one* takes pleasure; we read, see and judge about literature and art as *one* sees and judges; likewise, we shrink back from the "great mass" as *one* shrinks back; we find shocking what one finds shocking' (BT 126–7).

Why, Heidegger asks, to we do this? Why do we so powerfully exhibit what Nietzsche calls the 'herd' mentality? Why do we allow ourselves to be driven by the 'One-self' rather than the 'I-self'? Why do we evade our 'ownliness'?

---

[12]  By 'early' I mean the philosophy of *Being and Time*. Some scholars would refer to this as the philosophy of Heidegger's 'middle' period.

Without conformity, of course, there could be neither language nor society. And without language there could be no thought. Conformity is a necessity of human existence. But conform*ism* is not. Indeed, if Nietzsche is right, the non-conformism of the 'free spirit' is an absolute necessity, since it is a condition of the social group's being able to adapt to ever-changing circumstances. So why is it so difficult to become a non-conformist?

Heidegger's startling answer is: death, 'the nothing'. Individuals die. But the One lives on. So to the extent that I think of myself *as* the One I transcend the mortality which is the penalty of individuality[13] and so seem to evade the object of my most primal 'anxiety'.

If evasion of death is the source of inauthenticity, facing up to death — *Vorlaufen*, 'anticipation', literally, 'running forward into' — is the key to becoming authentic (BT, sections 52–3). Heidegger says that facing up to death 'wrenches Dasein [a person] away from the One'. It does this because, in 'anticipation', one realizes that 'all being-with-others will fail us when [death] . . . is the issue' (BT 263).

What Heidegger is suggesting, here, is that inauthentic life is a kind of strategy or device for evading the annihilating nothingness that is death. But, as with Sartre's 'bad faith', it involves, of course, self-deception.[14] Vivid confrontations with one's own mortality, grasping the 'mineness' (*Jemeinigkeit*) of death, reveal the deception for what it is. In 'anticipation', says Heidegger, Dasein is 'individualized down to itself' (BT 263). Understanding that entry into death is something I do alone, I attain a vivid grasp of my own individuality. I understand that my choices (even the choice to be a conformist, Sartre might interject) have to be made by *me myself*. I become (in my own, rather than Heidegger's, language) autonomous.

'Anticipation', however, achieves a further effect. Grasping one's finitude, says Heidegger, liberates one from 'lostness in those possibilities [of self-definition] which may accidentally thrust themselves upon one', liberates one

---

[13] 'Penalty' is the term used by Anaximander in the oldest known fragment of Western philosophy: 'Whence things have their coming into being there they must also perish according to necessity; for they must pay a penalty and be judged for their injustice, according to the ordinance of time.' Heidegger's thought is deeply influenced by this aphorism, which he discusses at length in 'Anaximander's Saying' (OBT, pp. 242–81).

[14] 'Inauthenticity' and 'bad faith' are, it seems to me, essentially the same phenomenon. The divergence between Heidegger and Sartre lies in the fact that while the former identifies evasion of death as its source the latter identifies evasion of freedom. Given, however, that both speak of 'the nothing' as that which is being evaded, the divergence is not, perhaps, as great as might appear.

'in such a way that one can authentically understand and choose among the factical possibilities lying ahead of . . . [death]' (BT 264).

Part of the thought here is that grasping that death is inevitable, but even more importantly that it may happen *at any moment*, makes me realize that there is no time to lose, makes it *urgent* to cut out 'accidental' trivia and pare my life down to its absolute essentials. But to do that, of course, I have to know *what are* those essentials. Yet this is delivered by 'anticipation' too. 'Running forward' in imagination to its end, Heidegger says, I grasp my life as a 'totality' (BT 232). As in the imminent-car-crash experience, encounters with death place 'one's whole life' before one's eyes. I shall call this second effect of *Vorlaufen* 'focus'.

Authenticity is, then, autonomy plus focus. Better, it is *focused autonomy*. To live such a life is to live a life that is intense, passionate, urgent, and committed. It is to live a life, in other words, that is intensely *meaningful*. Authenticity is early Heidegger's account of what it is to live a meaningful life.

\* \* \*

Early Heidegger is, as he acknowledges (BT 396), deeply indebted to Nietzsche. For focus is just what Nietzsche calls being the 'hero' of one's life, and autonomy is what he calls being a 'free spirit', one of those beings who are 'new, unique, incomparable, who *give themselves* laws' (GS 335, my emphasis) rather than taking them from the 'herd'. To Nietzsche's discussion of self-creation Heidegger adds the important observation that 'anticipation' is the path to grasping the 'hero' of your life. Even this, however, is partially anticipated by Nietzsche, who observes that, for all its failings, it has to be conceded to Christianity that, with its notion of sin and final judgment, it at least taught man to see himself 'as something past and [therefore] whole' (GS 78).

But if this is so, must it not follow that Heidegger's account of the meaningful life is afflicted by exactly the same fatal flaw that is revealed in Nietzsche's account by Sartre's taking it to its logical, self-immolating, conclusion? Does not, that is, liberation from 'the dictatorship of the One' leave me in the position of having to make an ungrounded *choice* of my life-focus and so render my life ultimately 'absurd' and so meaningless? This suspicion is what underlies the frequent accusation that *Being and Time* propounds a 'decisionist' philosophy, a philosophy which requires us to make an heroic but ungrounded act of life-defining commitment (Sartre's *act gratuit*), and as such helps explain Heidegger's commitment to Nazism. Decisionism means, it is claimed, that any commitment is as good as any other, so that what is really culpable about Heidegger's philosophy is that it failed to provide him with the 'moral resources'[15] for opposing Nazism.

In fact, however, this criticism of *Being and Time* could only be made by someone who had not read the work to its conclusion. For towards the end Heidegger—noting that, as explained prior to section 74, authenticity (focused autonomy) remains a purely formal concept—explicitly raises the question of content. 'From whence', he asks, can authentic Dasein 'draw those possibilities on which it factically projects itself?' (BT 383). And he answers—*not* 'from ungrounded choice', but rather—'from heritage' (BT, sections 74–5).

* * *

Unlike, say, the U.S. constitution, heritage—the fundamental values or ethical tradition of a culture—is not primarily contained in any written code. Rather—here Heidegger acknowledges his debt to Nietzsche's *On the Uses and Disadvantages of History for Life* (BT 396)—it is embodied in exemplary, 'hero' figures whose lives belong to the collective memory of a culture and are preserved in the myths, folk-tales, artworks, and sacred texts that are handed down from generation to generation. These figures—very crudely, 'role models'—show us the outline of what it is to live the kind of life to which authentic Dasein will commit itself.

Heidegger's, for present purposes, crucial thought is that *heritage is not something we choose*. Rather we are born into it. As we grow to adulthood within particular cultural practices and a particular language, we find ourselves *already* living our lives in the sight of a particular pantheon of 'heroes' or, as one might also put it, 'gods'.

The values personified by our gods, Heidegger emphasizes, *all belong to one's authentic self*. One is who one is, in large part, because one has grown to adulthood within a particular culture. The commitments of heritage, he holds, are *one's own* fundamental commitments. It follows that authenticity, and in particular autonomy, is acting out of the values of heritage. *Being true to heritage is being true to one's own, deepest self*.

---

[15] The 'decisionism' critique was first articulated by Karl Löwith in 1939, but has been repeated many times since. For a detailed discussion see my *Heidegger, Philosophy, Nazism* (Cambridge: Cambridge University Press, 1997), ch. 3.

Heritage determines the kind of life to which authentic Dasein commits itself in the following way. I find myself in a particular facticity. This is partially determined by my personal strengths and weaknesses and partly by the historical 'situation' (BT 300) in which I find myself. The latter consists in the gap between the ideals of heritage on the one hand and the values endorsed by the current 'One' on the other. (Since ideals are just that there will always be such a gap—of greater or lesser size.) So let us suppose that I discover, say, a particular talent for writing and that what strikes me is the gap between fundamental Western values of equality and the currently disadvantaged situation of women. My authentic life will then become that of a feminist journalist.

Notice that while Nietzsche sometimes *talks* of 'seeing', of discovering, 'the hero concealed in everyday characters' Heidegger really *means* it. The meaning of one's life appears not through self-creation but through *receptivity*. In freeing oneself from the blinkers imposed by the One, one becomes 'unclosed',[16] receptive to the gap between the true gods of heritage and the false, or at least compromised, gods worshipped by current public opinion.

* * *

It seems, then, that the problem of the 'absurd', Sartrean nihilism, has finally disappeared. We should indeed, as Nietzsche suggests, live our lives with the economy and clarity of a well-constructed artwork. But the fundamental goal around which that artwork is to be constructed is not to be created in an act of (groundless, and so self-undermining) choice, but is to be discovered, rather, in heritage.

And yet doubts remain. Sartre observes, correctly, that Heidegger's notion of heritage is really a notion of *place* (BN, pp. 489–96). My heritage is the natural-cultural place within which, according to Heidegger, I become myself. It follows that a way of putting Heidegger's view of the self is to say that, at the deepest level, *I am my place*. Heidegger thinks that there can be no question of *my* not choosing my 'place' since anyone who chose another 'place' would not be *me*. And so there can be no question of my choosing my 'place', either. My

---

[16] Heidegger introduces the term 'resoluteness', *Entschlossenheit*, to refer to the fully developed concept of authenticity. But sometimes he hyphenates it, *Ent-schlossenheit* (BT 300), the effect of which is to indicate that the essence of 'resoluteness' is 'un-closedness'. This emphasis on receptivity as the precondition of authentic action is the ancestor of Heidegger's later concept of *Gelassenheit*, 'releasement', which will shortly be discussed.

heritage is simply my 'here I stand: I can do not other'. In fact, however, this 'social constructivist' view of the self sounds more convincing than it really is.

＊ ＊ ＊

One line of attack might proceed along the following lines. Suppose, one might suggest, I go and live in Iran and come to believe in a hierarchical, sexually differentiated society. Suppose, that is, that, as a Western woman who has converted to Islam, I come to believe that Western notions of sexual equality are actually immoral. The constructivist might want to defend his thesis by speaking of this as a kind of 'rebirth', the replacement of one person by another. In reality, however, the objection might conclude, this 'rebirth' is only metaphorical, since continuity of memory and character is preserved. Hence heritage is actually not inescapable in the way Heidegger suggests. One may change one's heritage yet remain the same person.

As stated, however, this line of criticism is inadequate. For the constructivist can reply by suggesting that one can only (non-absurdly) prefer Islamic to Western values on the basis of some already possessed, deeper set of values against which the latter are judged and found wanting. So, actually, the above case just reduces to a critique of the current Western 'One' on the basis of fundamental heritage. The imagined 'taking of the hijab' actually expresses the conviction that the deepest values of the West are better embodied in current Islam than in the current condition of the West.

Consider, however, another case. This differs from the first in that, rather than choosing to become a Muslim I develop the capacity to *view things from an Islamic perspective* from time to time, as well as from the Western perspective. The result of this is the realization that my morality hitherto, like all moralities, is 'just a perspective'. And the result of that is ethical paralysis, an encounter with the Sartrean 'absurd'.

This is what Nietzsche calls the 'disadvantage', the disastrous effect of 'history'—i.e. knowledge of past and alien cultures—on life. Through the indiscriminate accumulation of facts, Western (post)modernity, he suggests, has become a mere 'encyclopaedia' of other cultures (UM II. 4), a 'fairground motley'[17] of confused and different styles (UM I. 1). We have become so 'tolerant', so 'multicultural', that we have lost the self-confidence necessary to concerted action. An excess of 'history', says Nietzsche, breeds 'cynicism'

---

[17] This, of course, is why, in *Thus Spoke Zarathustra*, the town that is the object of Zarathustra's scorn and love is called 'the *Motley* Cow'.

and 'senility', stifles the 'fire of youth' (UM II. 9). Information-overload deconstructs, defuses, the power to act.

This, it seems to me, is what is really wrong with social constructivism. What it actually represents is not the truth about the nature of the self but at best a pious hope. Though at some times and places the self really is a social construction this is by no means universally the case. In particular, it is not the case in our Western postmodernity. What social constructivism fails to accommodate is the 'placelessness' of postmodernity, what later Heidegger calls our 'homelessness'.

* * *

According to the Nietzsche–Sartre view that we have examined, the meaning of life is a matter of individual 'creation'. This view, we have seen, runs aground on the shores of 'the absurd' and reduces to nihilism. Initially, early Heidegger's appeal to communal heritage as the source of meaning seemed to promise an alternative to this path of thinking. This alternative, however, now shows itself to be illusory since, along with social constructivism in general, early Heidegger's view of the self as constructed by its society, and thereby endowed with a meaning of life, is not universally true. In particular, is not true now.

This, however, does not mean that the *strategy* pursued by early Heidegger is mistaken. Quite plainly, in fact, it is correct. If absurdity and nihilism are to be avoided we *must* once again be able to find a meaning which belongs to our facticity, a meaning that is waiting to be discovered and so does not have to be the object of groundless choice. At this point we may usefully turn to Heidegger's later (post-*Being and Time*) philosophy.

# LATER HEIDEGGER

Later Heidegger's starting point is a reflection on the contrast between (partially mythologized) ancient technology and modern technology. Compare and contrast: the ancient wooden bridge (QCT, p. 16) which allows the river to remain a river with the modern hydro-electric dam which turns it into a reservoir; or the ancient peasant farmer who sows just those seeds appropriate to the local soil, climate, and season with modernity's 'mechanized food industry' (ibid.) which uses glasshouses, artificial fertilizers, genetic modification, and EU subsidies to force the land to produce whatever the 'consumer' demands; or compare the eleventh-century Japanese gardener who, advised by the *Sakutei-ki*, 'listen[s] to the request made by the land' with the modern property 'developer' who fells the forest and concretes over the land where it once was. Contrasts such as these suggest that modern technology constitutes a 'Copernican Revolution' in something quite close to Kant's sense of the term. Ancient technology seems to have accommodated itself to *nature's* designs. It allowed itself to be limited by those designs, and sometimes to have put itself at nature's disposal by allowing them to complete themselves through its activity, as when the ancient gardener 'brings forth' (QCT, pp. 6–9) the design 'requested' by the land. Modern technology, on the other hand, demands and compels nature to accommodate itself to *human* designs. Whereas ancient technologists saw themselves as the conservers and facilitators of nature's self-expression, modern technologists regard themselves as its masters and conquerors.

Why did this come to pass? Because, says Heidegger, while the ancients experienced the visible world as the self-expression of a divinity—Sophocles refers to Earth as 'the most sublime of the gods'—to modernity, nature is mere 'resource' (QCT, p. 23), human nature counting as 'human resource' (PLT, p. 111). To modernity, nature is mere raw material, 'ready-to-hand' for human exploitation. It has become nothing but a 'gigantic gasoline station' (D, p. 50).

The crucial difference between the world of the ancients and that of modernity is (to hyphenate Max Weber's term) *Ent-zauberung*, dis-enchantment. The ancients treated the world with the awe and reverence appropriate to a divinity. But for us, who no longer experience the sacredness of things, there is nothing to limit the 'unconditional self-assertion' (PLT, p. 111) of the technological will.

But is not the 'disenchantment' of reality simply the inevitable result of the advance of knowledge, of the replacement of superstition by science? Not so, Heidegger replies. Rather, the opposite. Modernity's experience, its 'disclosure', of the world as 'resource', represents an advance, not into enlightenment, but into blindness.

Heidegger argues this in a way that is indebted to Nietzsche's 'perspectivism' and, more remotely, to Spinoza's 'aspectism'. Truth about the world, he says, is always relative to a perspective, a 'horizon' of disclosure (D, p. 63). This is not relativism about truth but rather anti-totalitarianism, a rejection of what Heidegger calls 'metaphysics'. Many of our beliefs about the world are *true*—unqualifiedly so. But their totality can never amount to *all* the truth there is since 'disclosure' is simultaneously 'concealment'. The world-disclosure that is quantum mechanics conceals the disclosure that is everyday common sense and vice versa. This means that to every world-disclosure 'belongs...a reservoir of the not-yet-uncovered, the ununcovered in the sense of concealment' (PLT, p. 60). So, to deploy a metaphor Heidegger borrows from Rilke, reality resembles the moon in that concealed behind its lighted side is a—in fact infinite—darkness (PLT, p. 124). Modernity's claim to have colonized the totality of truth is thus not merely arrogant but also—arrogance's usual companion—stupid. It resembles the child's belief that the moon is a flat, illuminated disk.

The point, then, is that 'truth', disclosure, our world, is 'awesome' (PLT, p. 68), 'sublime' in more traditional language. It is, moreover, something gifted to us rather than something we create. Truth, that is to say, happens in language, and language is something we have to have *before* we can think and experience, before we can create anything. So we are constrained to regard our life-world as something gifted to us by an inexhaustible and infinitely awesome 'mystery' (P, p. 148). The ancients, in particular the Greeks, are not, therefore, to be patronized. Far from being lost in primitive superstition, they actually possessed a deep 'insight into that which is' (QCT, p. 46). Intuitively and poetically, they had a profound understanding of the nature of truth and reality—of 'Being', as Heidegger prefers to put it. The progressive 'disenchantment' of our world is a march, not into enlightenment, but into ignorance and illusion.[18]

From this Heidegger concludes that the reverence towards Being embodied in ancient technological practices is in fact the *correct* stance towards the world. A word he uses for the ancient combination of conservation and facilitation is 'guardianship' (PLT, p. 184). Another word is *Gelassenheit* (D, *passim*) which, deriving its meanings from *lassen*, to let or allow, is intended to suggest the notion of 'letting be' in the sense of conserving, 'letting be' in the sense of 'allowing what is coming to arrive', as well as 'equanimity' (the 'letting go' of anxiety) which is the everyday meaning of the word.

Heidegger emphasizes that *Gelassenheit*, 'releasement' in the standard English translation, is not passivity. Rather, it is *receptivity*, a receptivity to, for

---

[18] This is all very sketchy. For a full discussion of Heidegger's account of truth and reality see the first chapter of my *Heidegger's Later Philosophy* (Cambridge: Cambridge University Press, 2002).

example, 'the request made by the land', which is the precondition of ancient technological practice.[19]

Guardianship, i.e. *Gelassenheit*, is later Heidegger's account of the meaning of life. If we are to flourish as excellent human beings, if we are to dwell in insight rather than illusion, if we are to achieve 'equanimity' and dwell in harmony with our environment, then we will become 'guardians of Being' (which includes, importantly, human being)—in whatever way, of course, is appropriate to our own particular facticity.

* * *

The thing to notice about Heidegger's later philosophy is how much it represents a retrieval of traditional thinking. Nietzsche's claim that 'the total character of the world is to all eternity chaos', that any provision of 'order' is a mere 'aesthetic anthropomorphism', epitomizes the outlook of postmodernity. Later Heidegger, however, returns us to an order in the human being's relation to Being as a whole, an order which at once provides us with a cosmological homeland—allows us, as he puts it, to 'dwell'—and determines the task and meaning of our life.

Heidegger calls this task and meaning the human 'essence' (QCT, p. 28; P, p. 257). This indicates two things. First, that the task of guardianship or *Gelassenheit* is something we find ourselves *already* possessing simply in virtue of being *human* beings. For present purposes, what is important about this is that it represents a return to *discovered* meaning—it returns meaning to our facticity—and so avoids the problem of absurdity that afflicts all accounts of meaning as *chosen*. And second, it indicates that, if later Heidegger is right, meaning is neither merely personal, as in the Nietzsche–Sartre account, nor confined to specific communities, as in early Heidegger, but is, rather, universal. In later Heidegger, therefore, we are returned to a meaning of life which, in two important respects, resembles that which defined the Christian era.

Let me pursue further, for a moment, this return to tradition. Heidegger rejects many times the God of traditional Christianity—'the God of the philosophers' or 'the God of the theologians'—as an anthropomorphic

---

[19] Though they lack the readiness for action that is part of *Gelassenheit*, Camus' boyhood friends, in their integration into the 'dialogue of stone and flesh in tune with the seasons' have something *gelassen* about them. This, I think, is what differentiates them from Camus' Don Juan who, in his lust for conquest and exploitation, is, in fact, a paradigm of the modern 'technologist'.

diminution of the 'mystery', and so majesty, of the divine. Yet the ethics of guardianship, of, in the broadest sense of the term, 'caring-for' (*Schonen*[20]) (PLT, p. 149), is rather clearly a return to Christian *caritas*, to Jesus' highest commandment, that of love. It is a return, however, that is all the better for being purged of human chauvinism, of the view that only humans count as proper objects of love.

Nietzsche held Christianity to be a massive aberration—a two-millennia interruption—that obliterated the true, that is, Greek, essence of Western culture. Heidegger shows us, however, how to accept much of Nietzsche's critique of Christianity together with his reverence for the Greeks, but yet combine with it the core of Christian ethics. While Nietzsche *rejects* Christianity in favour of the Greeks Heidegger *synthesizes* the Greek with the Christian. In this respect Heidegger's later philosophy (to which the present author counts himself a subscriber) represents a deeper thinking than that of Nietzsche, a thinking in which Christian ethics—that is to say, a Christian account of the meaning of life—reappears. It reappears, however, not in the free-floating way Nietzsche criticizes in George Eliot, but rather as grounded, once again, in the fundamental character of reality.

# ABBREVIATIONS

## Camus

MS       *The Myth of Sisyphus*, trans. J. O'Brian (Harmondsworth: Penguin, 1975)

## Heidegger

BT       *Being and Time* trans. J. Macquarrie and E. Robinson (Oxford: Blackwell, 1978). (Page references are to the pagination of the seventh German edition given in the margins of this translation.)

D        *Discourse on Thinking* trans. J. M. Anderson and E. H. Freund (San Francisco: Harper & Row, 1971)

---

[20] 'Sparing and preserving' in the standard English translation.

OBT      *Off the Beaten Track*, trans. J. Young and K. Haynes (Cambridge: Cambridge University Press, 2002)

P        *Pathmarks*, ed. W. McNeill (Cambridge: Cambridge University Press, 1998)

PLT      *Poetry, Language, Thought*, trans. A. Hofstadter (New York: Harper & Row, 1971)

QCT      *The Question concerning Technology and Other Essays*, trans. W. Lovitt (New York: Harper & Row, 1971)

## Nietzsche

(All Nietzsche references are to sections and sub-sections, not pages.)

BGE      *Beyond Good and Evil* trans. J. Norman (Cambridge: Cambridge University Press, 2002)

GS       *The Gay Science*, trans. J. Naukhoff (Cambridge: Cambridge University Press, 2001)

TI       *Twilight of the Idols and The Anti-Christ*, trans. R. Hollingdale (Harmondsworth: Penguin, 1968)

UM       *Untimely Meditations*, ed. D. Breazeale, trans. R. Hollingdale (Cambridge: Cambridge University Press, 1997)

## Sartre

BN       *Being and Nothingness*, trans. H. E. Barnes (New York: Philosophical Library, 1956)

# CHAPTER 14

# 'THE PRESENTATION OF THE INFINITE IN THE FINITE'

## THE PLACE OF GOD IN POST-KANTIAN PHILOSOPHY

STEPHEN MULHALL

THE struggle to cognize and articulate the 'transcendent'—that which exceeds the realm of human experience and empirical knowledge, the unconditioned or Absolute—is a recurring theme in philosophy from Plato onwards; and given the degree to which the history of philosophy in the West is informed by Christian preconceptions and concerns, it is not surprising to learn that few of the many complex and influential variations upon this theme to be found in philosophy's past avoid confronting the discipline with fundamental questions concerning religion—with the object, and hence the nature, of religious faith, but also with the proper relationship between the claims of faith and those of (let's say) reason. It is with this aspect of the concept of 'transcendence', as it finds expression and elaboration in the work of certain so-called 'Continental' philosophers, that I shall be primarily concerned in this essay.

It has often been pointed out that the division, or rather the complex of interlocking and cross-cutting divisions, between philosophy as practised in the Anglo-American mainstream and its counterparts in French and German culture can be understood as originating in very different ways of inheriting Kant. Against this background, it seems worth exploring the possibility that certain limitations or constraints in the way in which Anglo-American philosophers typically engage with religion come more clearly into focus if we conceive of that engagement as predicated on the implicit assumption that Kant's Enlightenment settlement with faith succeeded in putting God in general, and the Christian God in particular, definitively in His place.

Such is certainly the received opinion in analytical philosophy of religion concerning Kant's refutation of the ontological argument. This short passage in the Dialectic of the *Critique of Pure Reason*[1] has now attained canonical status, as an exemplary dissection of the fundamental confusion inherent in the suggestion that merely grasping the idea of a being than whom nothing greater can be conceived suffices to show that denying its real existence would be a contradiction. For, Kant tells us,

*'Being'* is obviously not a real predicate; that is, it is not a concept of something which could be added to the concept of a thing. It is merely the positing of a thing, or of certain determinations, as existing in themselves. . . . If, now, we take the subject (God) with all its predicates . . . and say 'God is' or 'There is a God', we attach no new predicate to the concept of God, but only posit the subject in itself with all its predicates, and indeed posit it as being an *object* that stands in relation to my *concept* . . . Whatever, therefore, and however much, our concept of an object may contain, we must go outside it, if we are to ascribe existence to the object.   (CPR, A599–601/B627–9)

Kant's confrontation with God in the person of Christ takes place in the *Groundwork of the Metaphysics of Morals*;[2] and although it is not, perhaps, as famous as the refutation just cited, it is—in its own way—as exemplary a

---

[1] *Critique of Pure Reason*, trans. N. Kemp-Smith (London: Macmillan, 1929)—hereafter CPR.
[2] *Groundwork of the Metaphysics of Morals* trans. H. J. Paton, under the title *The Moral Law* (London: Hutchinson, 1948)—hereafter G.

statement of core Enlightenment assumptions about the autonomous authority of rational animals. At the beginning of chapter 2, Kant warns us that

we cannot do morality a worse service than by seeking to derive it from examples.
Every example of it presented to me must first be judged by moral principles in order
to decide if it is fit to serve as an original example—that is, as a model: it can in
no way supply the prime source for the concept of morality. Even the Holy One of
the gospel must first be compared with our ideal of moral perfection before we can
recognize him to be such.   (G, p. 73)

On one perfectly natural reading of these texts, Kant is placing a substantial
question-mark over God's existence or reality. On the one hand, in so far as
any genuinely existential question is assumed to be synthetic, and hence a
matter of going beyond the concept to investigate whether or not anything
corresponds to it in the realm of experience, then belief in God's existence must
either wait (as it typically does not—recall the advocates of the ontological
proof) upon the acquisition of appropriate empirical evidence, or else it must
amount to the illicit positing of the existence of something transcendent, some
thing projected as existing beyond the limits of intelligible employment of
any concept of a thing (of a possible object) whatever. On the other hand,
in so far as Christianity claims that God, in the person of Christ, did take on
worldly existence, he could have no spiritual authority over us; even a divine
exemplar of how to live could not, and should not, be acknowledged as such
except when underwritten by the exercise of our own reason.

Kant's overall settlement with the Christian God is, of course, far more
complex and multifaceted than has so far been suggested. It includes, for
example, his argument in the second *Critique* that we must postulate God's
existence in order to make moral sense of the non-coincidence of virtue
and happiness in our worldly existence. It also stretches to encompass a
discussion of radical evil and original sinfulness in *Religion within the Bounds
of Reason Alone*. But such complexities tend not to play much of a role in
the composition of the Kant familiar to analytical philosophy of religion.
That more or less imaginary figure is one who conceives of God as either
not to be met with or not to be acknowledged within the realm of possible
experience; he is either a figment of reason—a projection of our concept of a
being beyond the domain of its intelligible employment—or simply one man
amongst other men, a human instance of no particular moral authority.

Perhaps most fatefully for his analytical successors, Kant's construction
of this dilemma for faith seems to work by driving a wedge between God's
existence and His moral being. The architecture of his critical thinking

appears to presuppose that the question of God's status as the *ens realissimum* (the absolutely necessary being), and that of his status as moral source and exemplar (the absolutely Good), must be assigned to essentially autonomous spheres of investigation, with the ontological question being handled not only independently of, but also prior to, the spiritual one. Kant knows in advance what kind of thing an ontological question is: it has to do with whether or not to a given concept there corresponds an object, by which he understands an actual or possible object of experience, a spatio-temporal entity. The natural world is the field of existence, the realm of contingent fact, the objective correlate of essentially finite knowledge. This world is empirically real, but transcendentally ideal; that in relation to which the empirically real world counts as phenomenal, as a mere appearance, is the noumenal realm—the domain of the thing-in-itself, which (since it transcends all possible experience) is labelled 'X'. It is the essentially unknowable ground of nature, a something about which nothing can be experienced, thought, or said, which hence amounts to nothing whatever (except as the bare marker of our finitude as knowers, our ultimate cognitive dependence upon the brute givenness of something to know). Spiritual questions, by contrast, have to do with the rational animal's internal battle for authority over itself, with its status as the self-originating source of moral worth within and against nature. In so far as it is part of nature, it resists and opposes reason as categorically or absolutely demanding; and in so far as it is rational, it instantiates value of a kind that utterly transcends the sublime extremes of natural power and extent.

However, this aspect of Kant's Enlightenment respect for the dignity of distinct facets of human concern, and hence of distinct cultural dispensations, amounts to a failure to respect what is distinctive about Christianity as a form of faith—its Incarnational (and hence Trinitarian) emphasis, and its corresponding sense that everything we can learn about God must either be learned or radically reconceived through the fact of Christ, the God-man, and his exemplary mode of existence. For Christianity, in other words, Christ *is* the presentation of the infinite in the finite; he is not a finite messenger or natural proxy for an essentially transcendent Being, but rather transcendence incarnate. The fact of his existence tells us that God's transcendence is such that it is not only able but willing—even that it deeply desires—fully to inhabit finitude. And this utterly changes our sense of what transcendence (hence finitude, and hence moral existence) might be.

For the Kant inherited by analytic philosophy of religion, God's transcendence confirms the utter heterogeneity of the infinite and the finite. The transcendent cannot be modelled on or otherwise understood in the terms appropriate to the finite realm, on pain of incoherence; it can do no more than provide an underpinning for the rational animal's moral sense of itself, and even then only in so far as that animal's rationality licenses it to do so. For Christianity, an encounter with the Word made flesh redefines the kind of moral sense we can make (and fail to make) to ourselves, and recalibrates our conception of the absolutely unconditioned so that it appears as finitude's most intimate Other. And one way of understanding the significance of some of the most influential figures in the French and German post-Kantian philosophical traditions is to interpret them as finding that Christianity's conception of these matters may contain more philosophical insight than Kant's.

# 1. The (Non-)Existence of the Christian God: Kant, Nietzsche, Kierkegaard

Kierkegaard and Nietzsche might not be thought to have much in common; but each, from his very different perspective on the human value of Christianity, develops a critical engagement with Christian faith which rejects every central assumption of what is usually regarded as the Kantian settlement with God. Take, for example, Kant's attempted refutation of the ontological argument, and the casually revealing way in which that refutation—aiming to convince us that, with respect to 'conceptual content', the real contains no more than the merely possible—pivots around a comparison between belief in the existence of God and belief in the existence of a pile of coins:

A hundred real thalers do not contain the least coin more than a hundred possible thalers. For as the latter signify the concept, and the former the object and the positing of the concept, should the former contain more than the latter, my concept would not, in that case, express the whole object, and would not therefore be an adequate concept of it. My financial position is, however, affected very differently by a hundred real thalers than it is by the mere concept of them . . . For the object, as it actually exists, is not analytically contained in my concept, but is added to my concept . . . synthetically; and yet the conceived hundred thalers are not themselves in the least increased through thus acquiring existence outside my concept.   (CPR, A599/B627)

And when concluding his argument, Kant picks up the same figurative thread: 'We can no more extend our stock of [theoretical] insight by mere ideas, than a merchant can better his position by adding a few noughts to his cash account' (CPR, A602/B630). This conjunction of God and Mammon destabilizes Kant's analysis in a number of ways. Even if we set aside the factual point that adding a few noughts to one's account seems to be a very effective way of bettering one's financial position in the world of transnational capitalism, it is hard to ignore how deeply this example of the thalers resonates with some of the most famous of Christian parables. In comparing heavenly to earthly treasure, but taking the latter as the former's best measure, Kant precisely inverts the point of Christ's urging us to store up the heavenly kind as incomparably more valuable than its earthly counterpart, and entirely overlooks the fact that Christ's concern with what we regard as treasure is ultimately a concern with the orientation of our heart; for Kant, belief in God is rather a putative theoretical insight, a more or less prudent epistemological investment. And his concern that the reality of this treasure should not outrun or exceed our concept of it recalls another parabolic instance of unproductive financial operations in the gospels, where talents rather than thalers are the unit of currency; but in Christ's version of the tale, the servant who buries his master's talents is banished for his fearful prudence, whereas those who take a risk with their capital do something pleasing in their master's sight.

However, the truly fateful point about this analogy in the present context is that it uses a particular kind of physical object to model the mode of existence belonging to God; and Kant's response to the ontological argument is pervasively shaped by his sense that this is the only possible way of modeling divine existence. About existence claims with respect to physical objects, everything that Kant argues in his refutation is correct. In so far as we claim to believe in the existence of a particular (kind of) spatio-temporal entity, we commit ourselves to the existence of some thing that corresponds to our concept of it; and we can, accordingly, justify that claim only by investigating the field of possible objects of experience, and hence by going outside the concept in search of the facts of the relevant matter. Such existential claims, if true, are contingently true; they might have been otherwise—hence nothing in our concept of a physical object can determine a priori whether or not there exists anything in the world corresponding to it.

But the nerve of the ontological argument is to be found in its reminder that the Christian conception of God is of a being whose existence is necessary; to think that God might conceivably not have existed is to fail to understand the kind of being God is, and hence to fail to understand what belief in God amounts to. To this, the Kantian might respond by offering the following summary of the believer's claim: if God exists, then he exists necessarily. But this takes away with its antecedent what it claims to give in its consequent. If God's existence is necessary, then there is and can be no 'if' about it; the antecedent clause treats God's existence as a possibility rather than a necessity, which is the very thing its consequent clause denies.

What follows immediately from the reminder that God's existence is necessary is the recognition that belief in God is not and could not be belief in the existence of a spatio-temporal entity; what the ontological argument makes manifest is that God is not an object or being at all—he is not a possible object of experience. Indeed, from a religious point of view, to view God as an entity is not simply a conceptual error; it is a form of idolatry, of the kind exemplified when the Israelites set up a golden calf (another manifestation of Mammon) to worship on the slopes of Mount Sinai. To treat any part of God's creation as if it were (a fitting representative of) the Creator is to blaspheme—to misplace one's heart as well as one's head.

Is God, then, better understood as an impossible object of experience—an entity or being who resides outside the realm of possible experience? This seems to be a concession that Kant is prepared to offer towards the end of his discussion:

Whatever, therefore, and however much, our concept of an object may contain, we must go outside it, if we are to ascribe existence to the object. In the case of objects of the senses, this takes place through their connection with some one of our perceptions... But in dealing with objects of pure thought, we have no means whatever of knowing their existence, since it would have to be known in a completely *a priori* manner. Our consciousness of all existence... belongs exclusively to the unity of experience; any [alleged] existence outside this field, while not indeed such as we can declare to be absolutely impossible, is of the nature of an assumption which we can never be in a position to justify.   (CPR, A601/B629)

Everything turns on the particular weight we assign to Kant's talk of an 'assumption' we might make about the existence of an 'object of thought'. On one natural way of taking these remarks, Kant accepts that we can intelligibly make assumptions about objects of thought as existing outside the unified field of experience; we simply cannot ever claim to know whether or not there are such objects. But to talk of such objects as located outside the phenomenal realm, and of their existence as something we might assume or posit, is implicitly to treat objects of thought in the (spatial and hypothetical) terms appropriate to objects of experience, and hence it amounts not to a transcendence but to a furtherance of the idolatrous attempt to model God's existence on that of a physical object. Here, however, the idolatrous impulse risks all-but-explicitly subverting itself; for if objects of thought lie beyond the field of experience, they lie beyond such determinations as spatio-temporal location, and it is unclear what content is left to our concept of an object in the absence of such determinations.

The situation is rather like that with respect to Descartes' concept of 'immaterial substance'; such content as the concept possesses depends upon it retaining its connection with our familiar concept of material substance despite Descartes' overt attempt to deny that connection. What, after all, is left of the concept of a substance if we deny its materiality, and everything that flows from that determination? The adjective in this phrase does not so much modify the noun as deprive it of sense.

The parallel difficulty in Kant's case is obvious. If one drops the familiar concept of physical objects as our model for objects of thought, then our concept of an object here has no content whatever; it can signify nothing other than the notion that our thought about such 'objects' is not empty—that it picks something out, without picking out any particular thing (no particular phenomenal thing, and no particular noumenal thing either). That is the conclusion to which the logic of Kant's own thought directs us, with its restriction of conceptual content to the domain of possible experience; and it might be argued on a more charitable reading of the passage quoted above, that this is the conclusion pointed at in Kant's emphasis on the fact that, with objects of thought, we have 'no means whatever' of knowing of their existence. It is also, of course, the conclusion to which the ontological argument directs us, with its message that the nature of God is such that his existence simply cannot be an open question, and hence must not be modelled on any modes of existence that leave that question open. How that existence should be understood, and hence how a belief in that existence should be conceived, will then itself appear as an open question, and one of real philosophical importance.

The exercise of further interpretative charity on Kant's behalf might even present this as the underlying lesson of his biblically resonant choice of comparison in his refutation of the ontological argument. For in so far as this Anselmian line of reasoning is advanced (as Kant plainly thinks it is advanced by Descartes and Leibniz) as an argument delivering a theoretical insight, then its point is as comprehensively and idolatrously misconceived as it is by those who respond critically to it in the same terms. It is not only unbelievers who are prone to model heavenly treasure rather too closely on earthly treasure;

and one way of helping them to see that this is what they are doing is to make it explicit on their behalf, in the hope that they might thereby be brought to question the orientation of their hearts, and perhaps to see that it is in this dimension of finite human life—the realm of value rather than that of empirical knowledge—that we will find the true significance of the concept of divine transcendence.

It is on this central point that Nietzsche and Kierkegaard find themselves in agreement, and hence in a position to shed some light. Nietzsche's madman, as presented in the *Gay Science*,[3] for example, finds that the atheists he encounters in the marketplace have a confidence in their own beliefs about God's non-existence that betray a remarkably similar set of ontological assumptions about the divine:

Haven't you heard of that madman who in the bright morning lit a lantern and ran around the marketplace crying incessantly 'I'm looking for God! I'm looking for God!' Since many of those who did not believe in God were standing around together just then, he caused great laughter. Has he been lost, then? asked one. Did he lose his way like a child? asked another. Or is he hiding? Is he afraid of us? Has he gone to sea? Emigrated?—Thus they shouted and laughed, one interrupting the other. The madman jumped into their midst and pierced them with his eyes. 'Where is God?' he cried; 'I'll tell you! *We have killed him*—you and I! We are all his murderers. But how did we do this? How were we able to drink up the sea? Who gave us the sponge to wipe away the entire horizon? What were we doing when we unchained this earth from its sun? Where is it moving to now? Where are we moving to? Away from all suns? Are we not continually falling? And backwards, sideways, forwards, in all directions? Is there still an up and down? Aren't we straying as through an infinite nothing?    (GS, section 125)

The weightlessness of marketplace atheism is made manifest in its proponents' over-determined, gleeful comparisons of God with a lost or hiding child, a sailor and an emigrant. All insist on modelling God's absence on the absence of a human being, and hence on understanding the Creator on the model of his creatures; more specifically, they picture divine absence as an essentially spatial confusion, seclusion, or withdrawal, quite as if God could and should be sought in the nooks and crannies of the natural world—in which case, of course, a lantern might indeed prove useful. But the madman lights his lantern in broad daylight, as if to enact the futility of this picture of divine presence and absence. And in a similar way, his response to the atheists begins

---

[3] *The Gay Science*, ed. B. Williams, trans. J. Nauckhoff (Cambridge: Cambridge University Press, 2001)—hereafter GS.

by picking up their misconception, but ends by developing it in ways that reveal its flaws.

The atheists' mocking comparison of God with a frightened child expresses their conviction that if God were real, then he would have had the kind of reality appropriate to that of one of his creatures—if not exactly that of a natural entity, then certainly that of a supernatural one (an entity just like a natural one, only located outside space and time). Their atheism is the enlightened recognition that no such being exists, or indeed ever existed; it is the transcendence of an illusion. The madman picks up their comparison, only to subvert it; God's absence is indeed comparable to that of a human being, but to that of a dead—more specifically, a murdered—one; perceiving and affirming God's non-existence is not a discovery but a deed, and a bloody, terrifying one at that. The atheists think of this perception and affirmation as bloodless because they think of ideas (particularly ideas they hold to be mistaken or cognitively erroneous) as bloodless; the madman rather regards the idea of God as a living thing, a real presence woven into the living tissue of our culture, our responses, our most intimate self-understanding. His destruction is therefore a radical act of violence, not only against him but against ourselves. Hence the madman insistently compares God's death to the wiping away of our horizon, the swallowing up of an ocean, a complete loss of spatial orientation; he is not one entity amongst or above others within such frames of reference, but rather a frame of reference in himself—the means by which humans might plot their course through life, and hence might come to define themselves as on track or not, at home or lost. God is not one more, perhaps unusually heavenly, body, but rather that in relation to which voyagers orient themselves; hence to unchain this earth from its sun is utterly to disorient its inhabitants.

Furthermore, the madman's desire to picture this disorientation as the aftermath of a murder, as the death of god at our human hands, unavoidably echoes Christianity's own conception of what is central to the frame of reference whose loss engenders such disorientation; to be unchained from Christianity's sun is to be no longer oriented by the Son—by Christ understood as God-made-man. And the central lesson or moral of Christ's life is his death at our hands—the fact that fully divine humanity lives out an existence of self-denial and self-sacrifice even unto death on a cross, hence that absolute goodness in human form will incite absolute hatred and must not reiterate it, must absorb it without passing it on, even when the cost of so doing is (apparently) everything. For the madman, then, the question of belief in

God is no merely theoretical or cognitive matter—a dispute about what to count amongst our inventory of existing things which may have evaluative consequences but is itself evaluatively neutral, and as such to be settled prior to any question that might arise concerning the validity of religious values. To take responsibility for denying that God exists is essentially to reject the Christian way of evaluating existence—a particular way of seeing or finding meaning in our lives and in the world.

Nietzsche's views about the prospective costs and benefits of losing or transcending the Christian orientation may differ significantly from those of Kierkegaard; but that what is at stake *is* a matter of orientation, of the acknowledgement or denial of a frame of reference or horizon of significance capable of informing the course of a human life, is a perception to which Kierkegaard's main philosophical pseudonym, Johannes Climacus, devotes his exceedingly long and involved *Concluding Unscientific Postscript*.[4]

The first part of this book generates an argument precisely parallel to our earlier claim that comprehending the existence and nature of God in terms whose primary application is to physical objects results only in logical and spiritual confusions; but Climacus' argument does so in a more specific form, one appropriate to his unremitting acknowledgement of the internal relation within Christianity between belief in God and belief in Christ. In other words, it focuses on analogous misunderstandings of the seemingly historical claims upon which Christianity distinctively rests—claims about Christ's birth, life, and death.

It certainly seems reasonable to assume that the validity of the Christian Church's claims about Christ's existence, about the origin and unbroken tradition of the Church itself, and about the accumulation of divinely inspired testimony over the years—and hence the validity of Christian teaching itself—should ultimately be settled by the deliverances of the usual procedures for assessing historical hypotheses. In this case, these would presumably include the results of investigations by Bible scholars, archaeologists, and Church historians. But Climacus' view is that this chain of apparently innocuous assumptions leads to a set of ludicrous conclusions. It implies, for example, that an individual's decision about becoming a Christian will in effect be taken by someone else—by whichever scholar is taken to be the most reliable in this field; that that individual will be forced to alter her religious beliefs, or at least

---

[4] *Concluding Unscientific Postscript*, trans. H. V. Hong and E. H. Hong (Princeton: Princeton University Press, 1992)—hereafter CUP.

the degree of her conviction in them, as the scholarly consensus changes; and that, for as long as the scholars fail to establish a consensus, she must suspend judgement, unable for much if not all of her life to determine what she should believe about Christ, and hence about Christianity.

Climacus sums up by saying that 'with regard to the historical, the greatest certainty attainable is only an *approximation*' (CUP, p. 23). His point is not that there is no such thing as certainty with respect to historical claims. Imagine that the veracity of most of the Gospel narratives *had* been established with genuine certainty, by the standards appropriate to the discipline of biblical scholarship; would a wavering believer in the Incarnation (the fully divine authority of a particular, fully human being) have been brought thereby one step closer to faith? Would the most exacting scholarly demonstration of the falsity of the Gospel accounts entail that Christ did not exist, and hence compel the religious believer (on pain of irrationality) to relinquish his belief in the Incarnation? For Climacus, the kind of certainty that is in play when historical claims are in question is significantly different from the kind that is at stake with respect to faith.

For him, affirmations of religious belief are not of the same epistemic species as affirmations of historical beliefs, or indeed of empirical beliefs more generally. If we nonetheless attempt to model the former on the latter, then it will seem impossible to take religious believers seriously as rational evaluators, since they patently do not in general adjust their commitments according to the fluctuating state of the empirical evidence, and in fact maintain a degree of commitment that no amount of empirical evidence could license. But for Climacus, it is not the behaviour of the religious believers that is ludicrous; it is the terms in which philosophers are attempting to understand them. What the undeniable lack of correspondence between the commitments of the religious believer and the supposedly pertinent historical evidence reveals is that that historical evidence is not in fact pertinent (or rather, not pertinent in the same way)—that religious beliefs do not have an empirical basis in this sense. In short, the evidence for religious beliefs, the doubts to which they may be subject, and the certainty they may command are not species of empirical evidence, empirical doubts, and empirical certainty.

Climacus will go on to characterize religious beliefs as subjective rather than objective. He does not mean by this that their purported truth is relative to the subject or simply a matter of subjective preference; he means that they primarily concern the subject who affirms them—they are to be incorporated into the life of that subject, given subjective reality by being made manifest in an essentially practical and personal way as she responds to the choices with which her existence necessarily confronts her and lives out those choices. Without ever relinquishing any claim to objectivity (for they certainly claim to articulate a requirement that really does apply to all), the fact that they are articulated in the form of a requirement—that they impose a demand on those who affirm them to give a certain shape or form to their lives—is essential to their nature. Hence, the distinctive historicality of Christian faith has to be understood in terms that acknowledge two things: that the Christian truth is both way and life; and that the truth of Christianity lies not in any message Christ brings (which might in principle be detached from his person and evaluated for its validity), but is rather embodied in the fact and mode of his existence. Genuinely to affirm that Christ *is* the Way, the Truth, and the Life—which means, genuinely struggling to realize that affirmation in her own existence—is in fact how the Christian believer gives expression to the historicality of Christianity; it is what that historicality amounts to.

## 2. RELATING TO THE ABSOLUTE (LY GOOD): KIERKEGAARD

Before we can see in more detail exactly how this historicality finds existential expression, we must first explore the existential significance of religious belief as Climacus understands it in the absence of its distinctively Christian inflection. Once again, however, it would be easy to misunderstand Climacus' specification of why and how we should relate ourselves to God in just the terms that he is ultimately concerned to subvert. For he famously appears to argue that only a religious answer to the question of how to live can properly satisfy us, on grounds that presuppose that God is a being whose nature locates him beyond the finite, empirical world.

The argument seems to take the following form. Since the nature of human existence is such that individuals necessarily and constantly confront the question of how to live, they must employ some standard or value by reference to which they might make that choice. And in so far as it is intended to govern every such choice, that standard confers significance on the whole life that these moments make up; the life which grows from a series of choices made by reference to the same standard will necessarily manifest an underlying unity.

Hence our original question might be reformulated as follows: what standard is capable of giving meaning to our life as a whole?

Suppose we aim at a specific goal or achievement—the pursuit of power or wealth, or the development of a talent. Since such goals have significance only in so far as the person concerned desires them, what gives meaning to her life is in reality her wants and dispositions. But such dispositions can alter, and even if they don't, they might have been otherwise; so staking my life on a desire I merely happen to have would amount to staking it on a sheer accident, and thereby to depriving it of any meaning. Furthermore, since I always have more than one desire, when I do act in accordance with one as opposed to another of my desires, I am in effect choosing between them; so the true foundation of my existence is not whatever desires I happen to have but rather my capacity to choose between them.

Can we avoid this difficulty, as well as the threat of self-deception, by explicitly grounding our lives on our capacity to choose—by, for example, relating to our sexual desires by choosing an unconditional commitment to marriage, or choosing to view a talent as a vocation? We can thereby choose not to permit changes in our desires or in the circumstances of their implementation to alter the shape of our lives; we simply will to maintain their unity and integrity regardless of fluctuations in the intensity of our wants, and thereby create a self for ourselves from ourselves. However, this way of insulating ourselves from contingency presupposes an understanding of the human will as the source of life's meaning; but that capacity is still part of the person's life, and so a part of that which has to be given meaning as a whole, and no part can give meaning to the whole of which it is a part. With respect to it, as with respect to any given desire or disposition, we can still ask: what justifies the choice of the capacity to choose as the basis of one's life? What confers meaning upon it?

The true nature of our difficulty is now evident; the question existence sets us is not answerable in terms of anything *in* that existence, because life cannot determine its own significance in terms of (some element of) itself. It follows that meaning can only be given to one's life as a whole by relating it to something outside it; for it is only to something outside it that my life can be related *as a whole*. Only such a standard could give a genuinely unconditional answer to the question of the meaning of one's life. And the only candidate for this role—the absolutely Good, standing utterly outside the realm of contingency and finitude, our non-finite or transcendent Other—of which we have any conception is God. We can relate properly to each moment of our existence only by relating our lives as a whole to God.

Whatever one's sense of the merits of this argument, it is hard to avoid seeing it as presupposing that God is an entity of a distinctive kind—one which is supposedly absolutely other than any finite thing, but nevertheless something to which we can and must relate ourselves, something lying beyond the finite, and hence a supernatural or transcendent thing of some kind (however strange). And Climacus' specification of what might be involved in relating oneself unswervingly or unconditionally to God might seem to confirm this suspicion. For he tells us that establishing such a relation requires us 'simultaneously to relate oneself absolutely to one's absolute telos and relatively to relative ends' (CUP, 387); and this seems to suggest that we are here talking about two distinct, and hence independently specifiable, relations to different things—one to the Absolute or God, the other to essentially finite or contingent goals and preoccupations—and that establishing the religiously correct relation to finite matters is a correlate or consequence of establishing the religiously correct relation to an infinite being.

However, Climacus' way of glossing these formulations completely under-cuts this appearance. For he restricts himself to defining the God-relation by contrast with its non-religious counterparts. They amount to various modes of relating absolutely to what is relatively good—that is, to treating some particular contingent, changeable thing (such as money, power, or talent) as always to be preferred whenever their pursuit comes into conflict with other goods. Hence, we learn by contrast what is involved in relating to such goods relatively; it means treating no such good as absolutely valuable in the above sense, but rather regarding them all as possessed of real but finite and relative value, hence as never amounting to something always to be preferred over anything and everything else. To adopt such an attitude to all the ends of finitude is not a consequence of treating one's relation to the Absolute as being of absolute importance, not a supplement to or fall-out from one's relation to God; to relate relatively to relative goods just *is* to relate absolutely to the Absolutely Good. The two relations are simultaneous not because the one causes or brings about the other, but because they are two different ways of describing one and the same relation to one's existence; in so far as one treats every worldly value as non-absolute, then to precisely that extent one is relating to God as the only absolute value.

To live out a relation to God understood as the absolutely Good is not, then, to establish and maintain a relation to some supernatural or transcendent entity in addition to establishing and maintaining a relation to natural entities; it is to live a certain kind of (intra)worldly existence. Climacus' vision of the God-relation requires no substantial characterization of God (for Climacus, the absolute Good 'can be defined only by the mode in which it is acquired'; CUP, 427), and no substantial characterization of what adopting an absolute relation to God might be that goes beyond characterizing what it is to relate non-absolutely to the non-absolute. In short, his vision of religious belief, and hence of the transcendent, is exhaustively specified in terms of a certain kind of relation to finitude; and that relation is itself specified in terms of a form of human life that gives a subjective existential reality to a certain way of valuing finite goods and goals.

According to Climacus, the key characteristics of a form of life that relates itself to the transcendent, and hence the distinguishing marks of the transcendent as it presents itself in the immanent, are: renunciation, suffering, and guilt. Since the individual will naturally tend to begin by relating absolutely to relative goods, she will naturally find herself having to renounce those relative goods if she is to make any space at all in her life for God. This does not mean denying that such goods are of any worth—nothing in creation can be entirely worthless from the perspective of its Creator; it means establishing a sense of their worth that duly reflects their essential contingency. It is not utterly unimportant that one's desires be satisfied or one's talents be given the opportunity to develop; but there is a difference between taking pleasure in a good meal or a professional accolade, and being prepared to disregard all other claims or sources of value in their name. For the religious believer no such relative good is in that sense absolute; and that means that the believer will be prepared to suffer the loss of any such good without feeling that their existence has lost its ground.

Guilt is a further mark of the religious life, and it sharply distinguishes the believer's conception of her own ethical status from that of secular moral agents. On Climacus' view, non-religious ethics demands that we measure our actions against moral standards, and hence it allows for the fact that we can fail to meet those standards; but it sees us as capable, in our autonomy, of adequately responding to such faults—for if we sincerely repent of them, and perhaps atone for them, then we master them (even entirely eliminate them) through the exercise of our will, and nothing in principle prevents us from resolving successfully never to fail again. In other words, secular ethics conceives of the individual's ethical failings as essentially accidental modifications of a nature capable of guiltless integrity.

From the point of view of religion, such a conception of the self is (not a consequence of but rather) a criterion for our failing to relate absolutely to the absolute good. For in the context of such a relation, the most minimal particle of guilt removes or distances us absolutely from the goodness to which we are striving to relate ourselves, revealing a possibility in us that is absolutely absent from God, and thus signifying a difference of essence between us. Furthermore this absolute standard is meant to apply to every moment of our lives, to our lives taken as a whole; and as essentially temporal beings, even the most immediate and thoroughgoing attempt on our part to realize that standard in our lives will necessarily fail to reach back beyond its own point of origin. To become aware of the demands of the good is not to enact them, but it is to become aware that one is not at present enacting them; and that failure of enactment will always be irredeemable. The temporal structure of human existence thus makes us essentially guilty, essentially incapable of bringing our lives as a whole into relation to the good; guilt is not an occasional, aberrant state that leaves the attainability of moral perfection unquestioned, but an essential (dis)qualification of our nature.

The religious conception of guilt thus characterizes human beings and God as absolutely different from one another in moral terms; in relation to God, human beings are as nothing, ethically speaking. Living out such a relation thus amounts to acknowledging oneself as nothing—living a life of moral self-abnegation. In part this is already implicit in the other marks of the God-relation, since relativizing one's relation to relative goods means not only renouncing the goods but also renouncing the self in so far as it desires them. By renouncing the absolute value we attach in secular ethical mode to our capacity for making autonomous choices, we renounce our will and the ego of which it is the expression as the ground or source of our life's meaning—we renounce another, related aspect of the self. In short, in dying to immediacy, dying to the world's absolute valuation of its relative goods (including the human will), one is asked to die to the self.

Once again, this does not mean regarding oneself as of no value whatever. This would amount to denying the value of God's creation, and the practice of self-denial would exact no price (no suffering and renunciation worthy of the name) if we believed that what we renounced was utterly worthless. Take the gospel injunction to love one's neighbour as oneself; this formulation does not deny but rather depends upon the fact that we love ourselves. It does not ask us to dismiss ourselves as utterly worthless—to regard ourselves as if we had no rights or moral status to which others have a duty to respond, or to feel that we have no claim upon the affections of those we love. It rather asks us to be prepared to renounce those claims—to relate to them not as absolute but as relative goods. This might mean being prepared to treat those others to whom we stand in such supposedly reciprocal relationships (our relatives, friends, spouses) as they deserve to be treated even when they do not reciprocate, to go beyond what they could reasonably demand or expect of us in the terms such relationships articulate, and to respect and exceed those demands and expectations in the way we treat those who stand in no particular relationship to us, or perhaps only one of enmity or foreignness—those who are simply our fellow human beings, our neighbours. If the believer places no a priori limits on her responses to her neighbour's claims on her, if she does not demand reciprocation or consideration from her, if she does not resent ingratitude, deceit, or betrayal, then her love of her neighbour is independent of the way things happen to go in the world, unchanging and hence immune from defeat. In thereby becoming responsive to her neighbour not because of who or what she is but solely because she *is*, because of her sheer, contingent existence, the believer at once allows the other to displace herself in her scheme of things, dies to the claims of the self and relates herself to God.

It is not hard, then, to see why Climacus characterizes the God-relation as paradoxical or absurd; but it is important to recognize that this is not a logical or conceptual, but rather a moral or spiritual, paradox. The difficulty in living out a God-relation is not that of understanding how a finite being could relate itself to one that is infinite, as if religious belief is demanding primarily because it requires one not only to comprehend but to realize a relationship between two entities whose natures are categorically distinct and in fact entirely heterogeneous. This is a way of interpreting the difficulty that would certainly appeal to philosophers; but Climacus is inclined to suspect that it is also a way of covering over or distracting ourselves from the real difficulty—that of actually trying to live a life of dying to the self, of finding it not only spiritually intelligible but spiritually required that one should go beyond those conceptions of the inherent dignity and absolute worth of the autonomous individual which are so fundamental to our sense of what morality is, to be prepared to suspend and disregard their pertinence in our own case in certain circumstances. For Climacus suspects them of giving expression to a deep human need to see oneself as the centre of the universe, as the sole and ultimate source of moral value, even when this means refusing to respond to others when they are simply, sheerly, in need (in a way that is not articulable in terms of rights and reasonable expectations).

# 3. RELATING TO THE INCARNATE
## ABSOLUTE: KIERKEGAARD

Climacus' account of the distinctiveness of a Christian form of religious life turns on the way it intensifies or redoubles the paradoxicality of the God-relation. For to conceive the God-relation as a relation to Christ is to reconceive the object of the individual's paradoxical relation to the eternal in paradoxical terms. The Christian doctrine of the Incarnation entails that believers relate themselves to the absolute by relating themselves to a particular, fully human individual; it thus redefines the absolute as the absolute-made-flesh. This means that we not only can but must relate absolutely to one finite being—or rather, relate absolutely to a being understood as both finite and absolute. But if this is not to collapse into the idolatrous absolutizing of a relative good that Climacus has previously condemned as a regression from any genuine God-relation, how exactly are we to understand what a Christ-relation might amount to? For Climacus, this question may overtly be addressed by specifying what the nature of Christ tells us about the nature of God, but its true answer resides in his specification of what might count as an existential realization of a relationship to Christ. In other words, the underlying question is: in what form of finite human life might the substance of such a relationship to transcendence incarnate make itself manifest?

We just saw that the paradoxicality of the God-relation makes itself manifest in a life of dying to the self—a life of renunciation, suffering, and guilt. To claim that Christ is paradoxicality incarnate therefore implies that the inner nature of the absolute is similarly self-sacrificial. The Christian God is a God of renunciation and suffering, one whose very nature is to sacrifice himself for others out of love; hence, for Christians, self-sacrifice is not a further regrettable reflection of the infinite difference between their finite nature and that of eternity, a mark of the nothingness of humanity, but rather a participation in or imitation of the divine nature. To die to the self is to share in the mode of being of the divine; and every aspect of our conception of the divine must be inflected by that perception. For example, God understood as Creator is not a wielder of supernatural power, but a sufferer of self-abnegation or kenosis; divine creation is a ceding or emptying out of his own power to make way for that of nature, a continual negation of himself in order to facilitate and maintain the existence of the world and us within it. And of course, this is precisely the conception of love as kenosis to which Christ's life gives perfect expression—both in the extremity of divine self-abasement that is the act of incarnation itself, and in the pattern of redemptive self-emptying within Christ's life that finds its climax in his Passion and death (a sacrificing of himself that incorporates the experience of God-forsakenness, and thus incorporates a mode of self-sacrifice that reveals a certain non-self-identity within the Trinitarian life of God).

What such claims amount to in existential terms is the following. On the one hand, Christian forms of life do not reject or modify the distinguishing marks of the God-relation—Christ's way, as exemplified in his life, is also the way of renunciation, suffering and self-sacrifice. But on the other, the fact of his existence as God-man at once intensifies and entirely revalues this practice of dying to the self. It intensifies it by substituting for an understanding of ourselves as guilty an understanding of ourselves as originally sinful. For if Christ *is* the truth as well as the way and the life, then without his incarnation we would have been absolutely deprived of the truth—not only ignorant of it (since ignorance is an accidental attribute of a being essentially capable of knowledge), but lacking the condition for the possibility of understanding it. Since truth-seeking is what characterizes us as human, we cannot have been created lacking that capacity; but since God would not have deprived us of it, and no contingent event can deprive us of an essential qualification of our nature, we must have deprived ourselves of this condition.

In other words, where the God-relation requires that we think of ourselves as essentially in the wrong in relation to God, the Christ-relation further requires that we hold ourselves responsible for our essentially guilty state (rather than viewing it as a simple consequence of our finitude and God's infinitude), and as completely incapable of overcoming our sinfulness and its consequences on our own. But the very same event that reveals us to ourselves as definitively oriented away from the truth, hence as not even aware that this is the truth of our present state, and as nevertheless entirely responsible for existing in untruth, is also what holds out the possibility of being redeemed from this state. For the truth of our condition can be disclosed only through a relation to Christ, and a Christ-relation just *is* a relation to the truth; hence to establish it is to begin to live once again in the truth, and thereby to realize a reintegration of our fallen nature, a rebirth.

Living a Christ-like life will certainly involve dying to the self, and indeed will demand a certain intensification of that practice, since it will include living out an understanding of ourselves as the ultimate ground for our own sinful nature, as born sinners before any particular sinful deed. But since Christ's own life shows not only that finitude is fully capable of accommodating the absolute, but that the fullest expression of the absolute-in-finitude is a fully human life like Christ's, then this self-denying form of human life must be seen not as a wholly external imposition upon rational animals whose nature is essentially other, and certainly not as a punishment that the infinite exacts from the finite simply because of its finitude; dying to the self must rather be seen as the fullest expression of our humanity. Precisely because the Christ-relation is a relation to transcendence incarnate, it challenges us to see self-abnegation not as an expression of human alienation from finitude, but rather as the realization of the truth of our own essentially finite nature, and hence of the truth of finitude as such. In other words, dying to the self is not only the truth of God's nature; it makes manifest and affirms the true nature of the self and of nature as a whole. The realization of transcendence within finitude, whether in Christ or in human lives patterned after his, is the realization of the true meaning and significance of finitude (of the Being of all beings as created, as sustained through—and hence expressive of—kenotic love).

The world of the believer in God and the world of the believer in Christ are thus not exactly different in any particular respect—they present no distinguishing existential marks, since regarding our state as originally sinful is best understood not as denying that it is one of guilt but rather as taking responsibility for it. However, the self-denying orientation that the believer in God lives out in the mood or key of infinite resignation is realized by the Christian as joyful affirmation; and hence each can be said to inhabit an utterly different world (just as Wittgenstein tells us in the *Tractatus* that the world of the happy man is utterly different from the world of the unhappy man, even though they may be indistinguishable with respect to both content and form).

In the more specific terms of our discussion, we might say that both religious and specifically Christian understandings of the infinite accept that its nature or reality can find expression only in relation to finitude. Both deny that this relation is to be understood as holding between two distinct kinds or domains of entity (say, between the natural and the supernatural); rather, it holds within finitude, finding expression in a distinctive relation between human beings and the empirical world they experience and inhabit. However, whereas religious belief in general specifies a certain self-denying form of human life as the existential realization of (a relation to) the infinite understood as the absolute other of finitude, the Christian inflection of religious belief further specifies that same form of human life as the existential realization of (a relation to) the infinite understood as the truth of finitude—as its fulfilment and affirmation. On either account of the matter, the difficulty of presenting or realizing the infinite in the finite is not that of relating heterogeneous kinds of phenomena, or of making sense of a connection between concepts apparently defined as one another's negations; it is a matter of moral or spiritual practice—of giving existential reality to an understanding of self and world that renders their significance essentially non-absolute.

## 4. ABSOLUTELY PARADOXICAL FINITUDE: KIERKEGAARD, HEIDEGGER, SARTRE

One way of articulating Climacus' conception of the Christian God would be to say that absence is the mode of his presence. First, he is not an entity; hence he is not to be found within the world, and not to be found outside it either. Second, the finite world taken as a whole manifests his presence in so far as its reality results from God's loving self-withdrawal; the creator is completely and fully present in his creation, just in so far as its presence excludes his. Third, divine life is made fully real in a form of finite human life to the extent to which that form of life realizes a conception of finitude as non-absolute, as a domain in which the absolutely valuable—that on which one might unconditionally found a meaningful life—is not to be found. Fourth, any form of human life that fully realizes such a conception of absolute value as absolutely absent from the world will incite and achieve its own annihilation; the world will not only fail to comprehend it and reject it—it will hate it, crucify it, and murder it. Fifth, since such self-denying forms of life provide the orientation through which the true nature of finitude (as contingent, dependent, non-self-sufficient) finds full expression and proper acknowledgement, then to relate to the absolute, to realize the divine life in oneself, just *is* to make finitude real to and in oneself as what it truly is.

One might then say: for Climacus, the relation to God through which humanity fulfils its nature is a relation to nothing. God's nature is specified by negation: we are not told what he is but rather what he is not (any kind of entity); and we are told what it is to relate to him partly by specifying what it is to fail to relate to him (i.e. by relating absolutely to relative goods), and partly by specifying a certain kind of relation to what he is not (i.e. that of relating non-absolutely to relative goods). To grasp the infinite is certainly to grasp that it is not finite; but it is also to grasp that one grasps the infinite only by achieving a certain grasp of finitude. In other words, for Climacus, the Christian God both is and is not something entirely heterogeneous to finitude; to relate to him is to relate to nothing but finitude, to nothing other than finitude, to finitude understood in its relation to nothingness or nullity (i.e. in its utter contingency, the non-necessity of its presence, its content, and its form). And since the human individual is herself finite, then achieving a God-relation amounts to fulfilling her nature as finite precisely because it means realizing her own internal relation to nothing, to nullity or negation.

These ways of formulating Climacus' conception are designed to bring out the breadth of the field that his work clears for the analyses of finitude that are so strongly associated with the existential phenomenologies of Heidegger and Sartre. One might say that, whereas Climacus' approach begins from the infinite or transcendent, and finds that an adequate grasp of that concept can be achieved only by making manifest the ways in which it can (fail to) be realized in forms of finite human life, Heidegger and Sartre begin from the side of the finite human subject, and find that an adequate grasp of its finitude can be achieved only by making manifest the ways in which it can (fail to) acknowledge its relation to the infinite or transcendent, understood as that which it is not, its nullity or negation. For Climacus, the only adequate presentation of the infinite is in or through the finite; for Heidegger and Sartre, the only adequate presentation of the finite is against the background of the infinite.

For the Heidegger of *Being and Time*,[5] the primary structure of the human mode of being (of what he calls 'Dasein') that embodies this internal relation to nullity is our mortality—our Being-towards-death. He begins by stressing that Dasein relates to its death not as an actuality (since when Dasein is actually dead, it is no longer there to relate to anything) but as a possibility—as its ownmost, non-relational and not-to-be-outstripped possibility. It is that possibility in which what is at issue is nothing less than the entirety of our worldly existence; it impends at every moment of that existence, since each such moment might be our last; and in relating to it, all our relations to other human beings are undone—no one can die my death for me.

And yet, if death cannot conceivably be made actual by the Dasein whose possibility it is, then it cannot really be one of its existential possibilities

---

[5] *Being and Time*, trans. J. MacQuarrie and E. Robinson (Oxford: Blackwell, 1962).

(just like drinking a cup of coffee or becoming a police officer); it is rather an existential impossibility, an impossible possibility. It is a contradiction in existential terms, a standing rebuff to our attempts to make sense of it, to grasp what it means to say (as we must say, on pain of denying our finitude) that our life has an end, that we are mortal.

Heidegger's response is, in effect, that if death is essentially or necessarily resistant to any existential understanding of it, we must incorporate that resistance as fully as possible into our attempt to understand it (otherwise, we will simply be failing to grasp death as death). By thinking of it not as a peculiar existential possibility but rather as an ontological structure of Dasein—an aspect of that which makes Dasein the kind of being it is—Heidegger permits himself to claim that our relation to death not only can but can only be manifest in the relation we establish to any and every genuine possibility of our Being. Precisely because death is an ungraspable but undeniable aspect of every moment of Dasein's existence, Dasein can only relate to it in its relation to what *is* graspable in our existence. Death is that ungraspable condition in relation to which specific features of the existential terrain disclose themselves, a self-concealing condition for Dasein's capacity to grasp things (including itself) as they really are.

For Heidegger, then, death is a phenomenon of life; it shows up only in and through life, in and through that which it threatens to render impossible. Life is the proxy through which death's resistance to Dasein's grasp is over-come only through its rigorous acknowledgement. It is *life*—finite human existence—that is our ownmost, non-relational, not-to-be-outstripped pos-sibility. There is no moment of such an existence in which Dasein's Being is not at stake, in which determining the nature and form of its existence matters to it, and not just from moment to moment but as a totality of such moments—as a whole. Its life is its own to live, or to disown; it makes a claim that cannot be sloughed off onto others. And in so far as its life is fated to be utterly nullified by death, Dasein must acknowledge its utter non-necessity—the non-necessity of our birth, of the actual course of our life, of its continuation from one moment to the next. Authen-tic Being-towards-death—taking responsibility for one's existence, leading a life that is genuinely one's own—is thus a matter of living in a way that does not treat the merely possible or actual or conditionally necessary as beyond any question or alteration. It means stripping out false neces-sities—becoming properly attuned to the real modalities of finite human existence.

Heidegger goes on to argue that Dasein's internal relation to negation or nullity makes itself manifest in other ways, in any proper understanding of the temporality of our existence, characterized as what he calls 'thrown projection'. As temporal beings, every moment of our existence confronts us with the question of how to go on, offering us a range of existential possibilities, from which we must choose (stay in bed, or have breakfast? Watch morning television, or go to the library?), and hence revealing the present moment of choice as the result of a past choice with whose consequences we must now engage. But when we actualize (or project upon) one such possibility, we reject or negate the others, and we negate our favoured option qua possibility; all choices in this sense annihilate that which made them choices in the first place. And since any such choice is a projection out of a situation whose structure must be accepted as given, the past choices which partly determined it being now beyond our ability to revise, we find that the ground of our projection lies outside ourselves—we lack power or authority over it, and hence over ourselves, from the ground up. A thrown projective existence is thus inherently both negating and negated—a nullifying power that is itself nullified by its inherent situatedness in space and time. Heidegger labels this ontological structure of Dasein as our Being-Guilty, which he summarizes as our 'null Being-the-basis of a nullity'.

Heidegger earlier calls Dasein's existence 'uncanny'—literally, being not-at-home in the world. This may seem inconsistent with his most famous initial characterization of Dasein as 'Being-in-the-world'. But uncanniness is simply the *way* in which Dasein exists in the world: it registers the fact that Dasein is not only not identical with the world it inhabits, it is not identical with itself either. For the actualized existential possibility that constitutes its present, and declares its ground in the unalterable past, might nonetheless have been otherwise, and can be modified or negated by the choice it presently confronts. In other words, Dasein is never entirely exhausted by or coincident with what it presently is; its existential potentialities should never be conflated with its specific *existentiell* actuality, any more than its inherent worldliness entails that it must maintain the particular worldly situation in which it finds itself—although, of course, we find it very tempting to do so (given the relief it provides from the task of taking responsibility for how we live). Indeed, doing just that is how Heidegger defines inauthenticity in human life, the condition he thinks most of us inhabit most of the time.

At its most general, then, the way in which human individuality is always marked by negation lies in the fact that Dasein is both non-self-sufficient and non-self-identical. On the one hand, its worldly, temporal existence relates it necessarily to an independently existing world and an already determined past; on the other it is always capable of being more or other than it is and has been, always transcending its actual substance and circumstances, and thus essentially not what it actually is, hence existing primarily in relation to what it is not yet (both its unactualized possibilities and its death). Human finitude can thus be fully understood only in relation to nullity, negation, and nothingness, and can be fulfilled only by living out that self-understanding.

The absent presence of Kierkegaard in Heidegger's thought is hard to miss here. But neither is it much of a leap from this conception of human finitude as inherently uncanny to Sartre's famous specification of the for-itself (his favoured term for human existence) as the mode of being 'that is what it is not, and is not what it is'. Indeed, much of Sartre's detailed initial explanations of this formulation in *Being and Nothingness*[6] essentially go over the Heideggerian ground we have just examined—a fact that neither author seemed willing to acknowledge. But in the present context, I would like to conclude our investigation of the immanence of the transcendent by dwelling on one specific strand of Sartre's further characterizations of the for-itself—that which links his treatment of desire with that of human relations to other human beings.

Sartre takes it that a for-itself can exercise freedom in its life only in so far as it is capable of evaluating the options it chooses between; in choosing one option as against others, it reveals that it prefers whatever that option makes available—that it desires or wants those things more than others. This in turn reveals that the for-itself's subjection to desire is an aspect of its finitude, since to desire something is to make manifest that one lacks something that one would prefer to have; it therefore declares that the for-itself is not self-sufficient, that in so far as it exists as desiring it relates to itself as not-having, as incomplete.

Since the for-itself is embodied, it necessarily participates in the natural world; but it does so as dependent on that world for the satisfaction of its desires, for sustenance, for the bare necessities of its continued existence. This is one respect in which it is—its existence necessarily realizes itself in relation to—what it is not; the world external to its body is not a part of that body, but it is that without which its bodily existence would cease. Hence the for-itself relates to that world negatingly: as the subject of desire, it must incorporate,

---

[6] *Being and Nothingness*, trans. H. Barnes (London: Methuen, 1958).

absorb into itself, cancel as independent existences, whatever elements of the world it desires, and must thereby make what is not itself a part of itself.

This arduous, even dangerous, process of relating oneself negatingly to the world is also endless—not because any given desire is essentially unsatisfiable, but rather because no satisfaction of any given desire or set of desires (however complete) could relieve a finite being from desire as such. Hence, on Sartre's view, to exist as a desirous being is necessarily to secrete the desire not to be a desirous being—not to be in this respect what one is. But not all ways of not being a desirous being would satisfy this particular desire: certainly not becoming a corpse, or in any other way transforming one's mode of being from that of the for-itself to that of the in-itself (the mode of material reality, mere substance, or objecthood), because there would then be no consciousness around to appreciate its own freedom from desire. The for-itself rather desires to lose this desire-related qualification of its mode of being whilst retaining its essential nature as for-itself: it desires, as Sartre has it, to be a for-itself-in-itself—to attain a mode of being in which freedom combines with freedom from dependency, in which we achieve absolute self-sufficiency without sacrificing our awareness of the world and ourselves.

On Sartre's analysis, however, the absolute self-sufficiency of the in-itself is an aspect of its self-identity, its pure coincidence with itself—of the fact that its underlying essence completely determines and is fully manifest in the content and form of its existence. And this is precisely what distinguishes the in-itself from the for-itself, which can be free only in so far as it fails to coincide with itself, is essentially not identical with, or exhaustively expressed by, what it presently is. In short, this desire has an incoherent object, one whose very nature would require the combining of the incombinable; the for-itself's subjection to this desire thus amounts to its desiring at once to be and not to be what it is not—to be and not to be its absolute negation. It is, therefore, exactly the kind of desire that one might expect to find harboured by a being characterized as being what it is not and not being what it is. It is, in fact, the purest possible expression or realization of the for-itself's essentially negating or nullifying relation to itself—it is, one might say, the ultimate fulfilment of the for-itself's nature in the mode of desire.

But of course, the incoherent object of this self-contradictory desire precisely answers to the traditional monotheistic conception of God as the perfect being, hence one who sees and knows everything and seeks only the good, whilst incorporating all reality, containing and coinciding with all that is—the *ens realissimum*. This God is both for-itself and in-itself, a synthesis of the two unsynthesizable modes into which Being is always already divided. On the one hand, then, Sartre's position amounts to a radical critique of religious belief, since it identifies the object of religious belief as an incoherent fantasy. On the other, he thinks that the for-itself cannot fully realize itself in the mode of desire except in so far as it subjects itself to the impossible desire to participate in the divine life, to relate itself negatingly to God understood as at once its absolute other and its absolute telos.

This strikingly Kierkegaardian sense of a God-relation as at the heart of the for-itself's self-negating ontological structures is further developed in Sartre's discussion of the for-itself's relations to other for-itselfs. Sartre famously thinks of such relations as tending towards irreconcilable conflict. He conceives of one for-itself's recognition of another for-itself as requiring that it acknowledge that other as another embodied center of consciousness; and that entails the realization that there is another point of view on the world from which the original for-itself is encountered primarily as visible within that world—as one more object within it. This other consciousness therefore objectifies the for-itself in a way which at once threatens its negating relation to its own body (the for-itself is necessarily embodied, but it is not identical with its body), its non-identity with its present mode of existence (for the other for-itself, I *am* the waiter in his café), and its conception of own consciousness as a point of view on the world from which everything is visible and to which everything (including the embodied, active other for-itself) is subordinated.

Together with this conception of the other's gaze as hostile, however, comes a conception of it as greatly to be desired—and for exactly the reasons that make it threatening. For what the other appears to present is the possibility of a point-of-view on the original for-itself from which it can be taken up as a whole, as a finite totality, without in principle denying its nature as for-itself. The other, so conceived, could both acknowledge the original as another for-itself and do so from a point-of-view from which that original can be acknowledged completely—in a way that no for-itself can do from the inside, since it will always have to do so *from* the very point-of-view that must be included within the survey, and hence will always exceed its own grasp. Hence, the original's relation to that other would be one through which it could relate to itself as both wholly for-itself and wholly in-itself—as at once essentially not identical with itself and essentially self-coincidental.

This is Sartre's diagnosis of the myth or ideology of human romantic love; and of course he regards it as doomed from the outset, since the perspective of the other can only survey the original for-itself as a whole in so far as it reduces it to an embodied agent, a characterization of it that it must exceed or transcend if it is a for-itself at all, which exists as a negating relation to its own body and actions. But once again, he does not think that diagnosing this myth of the other as an incoherent fantasy will make us any less attached to it; on the contrary, he sees it as the intersubjective inflection of the very desire he initially identified in the realm of the for-itself's relation to the in-itself—the desire to relate oneself to an essentially divine perspective from which one might simultaneously be both for-itself and in-itself. What the irruption of others into that realm effects is the displacement of this fantasy from the beyond of finitude to a certain kind of creature encountered within finitude; it engenders the human incarnation of that impossible object of desire. The other both is and is not God-made-man.

Sartre's account therefore suggests that the for-itself's ways of relating to others cannot ever be disentangled from an essentially Christian conception of a look that is complete, loving, and liberating, and hence that the Christian conception of the God-relation will haunt our conception of our lives with others for as long as we continue to exist in the mode of the for-itself. The endlessly renewed attempt to realize a relation to ourselves, to finite others, and to finite phenomena more generally which will deliver the existential substance of the Christian relation to the absolute is, one might say, an ineliminable expression of our finitude. Sartre cannot conceive of a mode of conscious and self-conscious finite freedom that would not be marked by this search; and hence any account of human finitude that omitted it would deprive itself of any claim properly to acknowledge that finitude.

Nietzsche might see Sartre's indebtedness here as an indication of the stupefying extent to which Christian slave morality is capable of perpetuating itself beyond any rejection, however explicit and radical, of the terms of religious faith. Kierkegaard might rather see it as confirming that it is only within the terms provided by Christianity that a proper acknowledgement of the truth of finitude can be achieved. Both, however, agree that this aspect of our concept of the transcendent must be understood as only presentable through, indeed as always already immanent in, our conception of that which it transcends—the realm of finite human existence.

# CHAPTER 15

# BEING AT HOME

## HUMAN BEINGS AND HUMAN BODIES

### MAXIMILIAN DE GAYNESFORD

die findigen Tiere merken es schon, daß wir nicht sehr verläßlich zu Haus sind in der gedeuteten Welt.

R. M. Rilke, *The First Duino Elegy*, lines 11–13[1]

## I. BEING AT HOME IN THE WORLD

BEING human and engaging in philosophy are interdependent if not identical; this is a central tenet of Continental thought. In one direction, to engage in philosophy is to think about what it is to be human. Kant bequeathed this view to his successors when he claimed that philosophy could be reduced to what he called anthropology: the study of what it is to be human. In the other direction, the conviction that being human is to engage in philosophy has been expressed in various ways, from Hegel to Heidegger. The central insight here is that humans share a characteristic and peculiar form of being, one that

---

[1] Even the canny animals now know: we are not particularly at home in the interpreted world.

is both able and constrained to question that being. The deepest expression of this tenet, as it operates in both directions in Continental philosophy, is to be found in the writings of Heidegger, and specifically the anthropology of *Being and Time* and other works of the same period (1927–30).[2] So it is on these writings that we shall focus below.

Since Continental thinkers treat being human and engaging in philosophy as one, there can be no full account of their views on either which does not incorporate a full account of the other. This is an impossible task in an essay of this sort. But one theme in particular has stimulated the major figures in this tradition to some of their most valuable work. And by noting its features and development at the hands of various thinkers, we can obtain an overview of the larger subject.

The theme in question was voiced by Novalis in the immediate post-Kant period. He described the philosophy with which human beings cannot but engage as homesickness, the expression of the 'urge to be everywhere at home'.[3] After many complex inflexions, the theme is nevertheless still recognizable at the other end of the era under examination when Adorno argued 'Today, it is part of morality not to be at home in one's home'.[4] In between, those philosophers who thought about what it is to be human found the struggle with two questions particularly compelling: (a) the theoretical issue: *what* it is for humans to be 'at home' in the world, and (b) the practical issue: *how* human beings are to be made 'at home' in the world. Answers to the first question were correctly taken to ground answers to the second, so we shall mainly be interested in the theoretical issue in what follows.

Primary significance in answering (a) is given by Continental philosophers to the fact that human beings are bodily beings; this is in notable contrast, at least until recently, with the analytic tradition. It is being a corporeal object of a certain sort that both conditions and enables human beings to relate to the world in ways that reveal a preparedness to act in it and on it, and to respond differentially to what it is likely to throw up. And since this is precisely what it is for humans to be 'at home' in the world, accounting for our bodily being becomes essential to answering (a).

---

[2] Heidegger, *Being and Time*, trans. John Macquarrie and Edward Robinson (Oxford: Blackwell, 1962). I shall refer to this work henceforth as 'BT'.

[3] Novalis, *Philosophical Writings*, trans. and ed. Margaret Mahony Stoljar (Albany: State University of New York Press, 1997), 131, 135.

[4] Theodor Adorno, *Minima Moralia*, trans. E. F. N. Jephcott (London: New Left Books, 1974), §18, p. 39.

Phenomenology offers one set of characteristic approaches to the everyday ways in which we are in the world. It takes as its starting point the fact that human beings are privileged beings in a disclosed world, and then attempts to understand how this fact manifests itself in our ability to acquire powers which can be exercised in various situations, given the opportunity; our tendency to become accustomed or used to things, familiar with them, experienced in certain ways, and thus in control, skilled, knowledgeable, proficient, secure, composed, confident, sure—in other words 'at home' in the world.

Various significant complicating factors have been noted by the Continental tradition as regards (a). One was fully recognized within phenomenological accounts and especially Sartre: that no matter how significant bodies are to our way of being in the world, it is not as bodies showing suitably human behaviour that we tend to relate to each other, but as conscious and concernful human beings. Another was inherited from Kant and considerably sharpened by Schopenhauer: the difficulty of identifying the item to which the contents of one's inner consciousness or awareness refer with the bodily presence, the human being one is.[5]

A third complication finds expression in Husserl's distinction between *Leib* (the animated flesh of an animal or human being) and *Körper* (mere inanimate physical matter).[6] The clearest formulation of these issues is to be found in Merleau-Ponty's *Phenomenology of Perception*. Since one's body is 'a nexus of living meanings, not the law for a certain number of covariant forms', it cannot be just 'one more among external objects'; indeed, it is not a 'physical object' at all, in the sense of something reducible to the subject matter of science.[7] It is more like a work of art, Merleau-Ponty suggests, consciously applying to the *body* the tradition's earlier attempts to aestheticize the *self* (under the influence particularly of Schopenhauer, Kierkegaard, and Nietzsche). His discussion has been deeply influential in Continental thought and has begun to exert itself on analytic philosophy. So it is on this out of all the complicating factors in relation to (a) that we shall focus.

Once we have some idea of *what* it is for humans to be 'at home' in the world, we can ask *how* they are to be made 'at home' there. Although, again,

---

[5] I discuss this issue elsewhere: 'Kant and Strawson on the First Person', in Hans-Johann Glock (ed.), *Strawson and Kant* (Oxford: Oxford University Press, 2003), 155–67.

[6] E. Husserl, *Ideas pertaining to a Pure Phenomenology and to a Phenomenological Philosophy, Second Book: Studies in the Phenomenology of Constitution*, trans. R. Rojcewicz and A. Schuwer (Dordrecht, Kluwer Academic Publishers, 1989). See Editors' Introduction, p. xiv.

[7] *Phenomenology of Perception*, trans. C. Smith (Bury St Edmunds: Routledge & Kegan Paul Ltd, 1962), 73, 93, 151–2, 174. Henceforth, I shall refer to this work as 'PP'.

each writer gives the fact of our bodily being central place, philosophers in the Continental tradition vary greatly in their response to this question (i.e. to (b)).

Some agree with Novalis: there is a kind of paradox at the heart of what it is to be human; the urge to be at home in the world will never abate but will also never be satisfied; it is a 'logical illness'. One explanation for this is provided by those Continental philosophers who have argued that a precondition for describing the world as containing human beings at all is the existence of intrinsically alienating methods of organizing and thus subjecting entities. So the very notion of being humanly at home is contradictory.

Thus Foucault emphasized ways in which human beings are individuated as 'subjects', items which are *subjected*. For methods of individuating entities depend on the existence of principles of individuation and opportunities for their application. And Foucault focused on various different such principles and opportunities—those for deciding who is or is not rational, guilty, safe for society, worthy of the interest of the social sciences, worthy of 'care', and so on.[8] But these differences are not deep. What matters is what is true for each: that, in the very process of becoming a 'subject' or counting as such, a human being is made the victim of various types of violence, repression, and/or political ordering.

In a similar way, Deleuze and Guattari regard an 'organism' as that which is *organized*. The principles of individuation on which the process depends are, for Deleuze and Guattari, directly related to theology: 'The judgement of God, the system of the judgement of God, the theological system, is precisely the operation of He who makes an organism, an organization of organs called the organism.'[9] By 'organs', they mean objects that perform specific functions in relation to desire, its production and transference. An infant's eye or mouth counts as such, for example, in desire-producing connection with its mother's breast.[10] Thus a single organized collection of organs might, but need not, map onto a single corporeal object—such as a human or animal body.[11]

---

[8] See, in particular, M. Foucault, *Madness and Civilisation*, trans. R. Howard (New York: Random House, 1965); *The Order of Things* (London: Tavistock Publications, 1970); *Discipline and Punish*, trans. A. Sheridan (Harmondsworth: Penguin, 1975); *The Care of the Self: The History of Sexuality*, iii, trans. R. Hurley (New York: Pantheon, 1988).

[9] Gilles Deleuze and Félix Guattari, *A Thousand Plateaus: Capitalism and Schizophrenia*, trans. Brian Massumi (London: The Athlone Press, 1988), 158.

[10] See Eugene W. Holland, *Deleuze and Guattari's 'Anti-Oedipus': Introduction to Schizoanalysis* (London: Routledge, 1999), 26.

[11] I criticize these views elsewhere: 'Bodily Organs and Organisation', in M. Bryden (ed.), *Deleuze and Religion* (London: Routledge, 2001), 87–98.

Some Continental philosophers have taken the diametrically opposed view, denying that the very notion of being humanly at home is inherently contradictory. Heidegger in *Being and Time*, for example, considers the urge to be at home a symptom of illness rather than the illness itself. He argues that, given what it is to be human, we are already 'at home' in the world. It is philosophy (or at least false ways of engaging with the subject) which keeps us from appreciating this fact by misleading us into experiencing an urge to satisfy what is already satisfied. Once we appreciate what being human is, the urge itself should abate.

A third option is taken by those like Marx in his 1844 manuscripts on alienation, who consciously focused historically located features Hegel had applied to humanity as a whole onto conditions of individuals, and thereby found the means to reject the first option as too quietist and the second as too optimistic.[12] Given the ways in which human beings are systematically alienated by various social and economic forces, they will not be made 'at home' in the world by mere philosophizing; structural change of various kinds is necessary, brought about by various means. And this is not simply because such forces distance us from other human beings, from our own labours, activities, and desires, but because they alienate us from own bodies.

There are complicating features as regards (b). First, philosophers who claim that we are already at home in the world, or at least that it is possible for us to be at home there given structural change, do not argue that we necessarily are or will be comfortable with it, at ease, relaxed, calm, or free from anxiety. Indeed Heidegger and others stress the extent to which we, precisely because of our humanity, are constantly disquieted by the world in the various ways it has of disclosing our finitude to us. This is one of the main differences between human beings and non-human animals, a sub-issue in Continental thought.[13] The crucial point here is that being at home in the world is not the same as being at peace with it. One's ways of dealing competently with any situation of threat, for example, require renouncing ease, relaxation, and comfort (being at peace) while retaining confidence, skill, and a sure manner (being at home).

Second, philosophers like Adorno (in the phrase quoted above) insist that the nature of human beings and the present state of the world are such as to

---

[12] Karl Marx, *Selected Writings*, ed. D. McLellan (Oxford: Oxford University Press, 1977), 75–88.

[13] I discuss the issue as it relates specifically to Continental authors (it has usually been of greater concern to analytic philosophers) in 'Humanism, Reflective Capacities, and Prejudice', in M. Qizilbash (ed.), *Impurity, Authenticity and Humanity* (Oxford: Arthur Rowe Ltd., 1996), 109–16.

undercut previous responses to questions (a) and (b). It is not so difficult to be at home in the world as others suggest, but being at home there is also not so easy to justify morally as others assume.

# II. HEIDEGGERIAN ANTHROPOLOGY

Heidegger's starting point was Kant. In the *First Critique*, Kant had reflected on what he called 'the field of philosophy', remarking that the whole interest of his reason, both speculative and practical, was focused on three questions, namely, 'What can I know? What ought I to do? What may I hope?'[14] But the *Logic* (1800) records a development in his view. This text has been regarded as an application of his general position to a particular topic. And, indeed, it grounds an account of general logic as the study of what it is legitimate to say on the principles and constraints of transcendental apperception. But when it appears that Kant will merely repeat his earlier statement about the fundamentals of philosophy, he adds a fourth fundamental question: 'What is it to be human?' More striking still, Kant then claims that the first three questions can be *reduced* to the fourth.[15] Thus Kant makes anthropology the foundation of philosophy, or at least that part of it encompassed by 'the whole interest of his reason': roughly metaphysics and epistemology, aesthetics, practical philosophy, and religious speculation.

Heidegger digs deeper even than Kant, though at Kant's prompting. Before we can ask 'what is it to be human?' we have to know what would be a suitable stance from which to ask that question. And it was with the search for such a stance that Heidegger identified the most fundamental impulse to philosophize. Call this the quest for an anthropological stance.

Heidegger came to his own views on what it is to be human by distinguishing himself from what he calls by turns 'traditional anthropology', 'traditional metaphysics', and 'traditional ontology'. The relationship of Heideggerian anthropology with traditional anthropology is complicated by the fact that he does not differ from it so little as to be said to have 'corrected' it nor so much that he can be said to have 'replaced' it. We can say instead that Heidegger

---

[14] *Critique of Pure Reason*, trans. Norman Kemp Smith, 2nd impression (London: Macmillan, 1933), A 804, B 832 f.

[15] 'Im Grunde konnte man aber alles dieses zur Anthropologie rechnen, weil sich die drei ersten Fragen auf die letzte beziehen' (*Kants Werke*, ix (Berlin, 1968), 25).

'relieves' traditional anthropology.[16] For he attempts to arouse the question of the meaning of Being from the discourse of traditional anthropology where it is hidden and unexplored. He raises it as a problem and explores it. He provides a new terminology so that the expression of what it is to be human is not compromised by the indeterminate nature of the usual terms to be found in traditional metaphysics. Finally, he provides his own formulation of an anthropological stance to maintain the question of the meaning of being as a question. In what follows I intend to go beyond this description of Heidegger's relieving strategy in order to investigate the use to which Heidegger puts it. This will entail showing how Heidegger's basic terms engage with the kind of being that we call being-human and relieve the question of the meaning of being from traditional anthropology. The argument will conclude with a description of Heidegger's own stance.[17]

Heidegger gives the term 'anthropology' several interlocking meanings depending on the nuance with which he intends it to be interpreted. For example, in *Kant and the Problem of Metaphysics* (henceforth 'K'), he writes:

Today, then, anthropology is no longer just the name for a discipline, nor has it been such for some time. Instead the word describes a fundamental tendency of humanity's contemporary position with regard to itself and to the totality of human beings. (K, 143)

There are four ways in which this statement performs what I describe as Heidegger's 'relief' of anthropology. First, anthropology is generally described as the science of human beings, or, more specifically, the subjection of human beings as human beings to questioning. The idea that anthropology is 'a fundamental *tendency* of humanity's contemporary position with respect to itself' makes anthropology stand out from what might be understood by the phrase 'humanity's contemporary position'. It is, or might have been, possible for human beings to take up a position with respect to themselves which is not of this contemporary tendency. Second, anthropology is described as

---

[16] The term was suggested to me because of the likeness between Heidegger's strategy and that employed by Hegel in his notion of *Aufhebung*. *Aufhebung* is successfully translated as 'relief' into English (and French: 'relève'), witness Alan Bass's translation of 'Tympan' by J. Derrida in *Margins of Philosophy* (1982). But I justify my use of the term on the basis of the correspondence between its ordinary meanings and my analysis of Heideggerian strategy rather than on any internal connections between relief, *Aufhebung*, Hegel, and Heidegger.

[17] Heidegger described his own ideas on these matters, in conscious imitation of Kant, as 'Heidegger's Anthropology' (*Kant and the Problem of Metaphysics*, passim).

a 'fundamental tendency of humanity's *contemporary* position with respect to itself'. This implies that within the 'today' there are other tendencies and opportunities perhaps equally fundamental in the subjection of man to questioning. Anthropology occupies a major but not necessarily dominant and certainly not exclusive position in epistemology. Third, anthropology is the name of a discipline which is structured in order to subject 'humanity's position with respect to itself' to questioning and it can therefore be distinguished from that position. In order to regard a position one must be detached from it. Fourth, and crucially, Heidegger argues in the most prominent aspect of these two sentences that the word 'anthropology' also describes the detached position itself. There is that about the position from which human beings reflect upon themselves which is itself humanity's position with respect to itself. This fourth movement is reminiscent of Hegel's description of philosophy as the self-consciousness of the age.

Thus, in the fourth sense of this passage, anthropology is identified with humanity's position. Heidegger argues that anthropology cannot be distinguished from humanity's position either by describing it as a contingent position to be discovered by synchronic and diachronic analysis or by using it as a critique of humanity's position. The first three movements displace what Heidegger means by anthropology from humanity's position while the fourth replaces anthropology in that position. This fourth returning movement does not neglect or cancel the displacing movements of the first three: the act of replacing something entails repeating in reverse the movements by which that thing was displaced. These four movements constitute the relief of anthropology from the position of human beings. Anthropology is raised over that position (as a tendency, as a contemporary position, and as a discipline) in order to examine it. At the same time it is said to contain and support that position. This preliminary relief of humanity's position prefigures the movements by which, in its turn, traditional anthropology is relieved by Heideggerian anthropology.

Heidegger relieves anthropology in the following manner. He argues that traditional anthropology has attempted to determine the essence of humanity as an entity but has allowed the question of the meaning of our being to remain hidden. This has come about through the pernicious influence of Greek philosophy and Christian theology over the development of traditional anthropology (cf. BT 45–50). In defining man as *zōon logon echon* Greek philosophy presented man as an animal endowed with reason. This leaves the kind of being which belongs to the animal-human (prior to the acquisition of reason) entirely unexplored, thus giving the impression that it is self-evident. In defining humanity as made in the image and likeness of God, Christian theology condemned human beings to believing that, to be the kind of being they 'truly' are, they must transcend themselves. The position one has to reach if one is to fulfil that expectation, which is also, paradoxically, one's definition, is that of the Godhead.

This position, if it is a position, is obscure and undetermined. Thus traditional anthropology fails to get beyond the preliminary exploration of humanity as a combination of body, soul, and spirit because it fails to get to grips with the kind of being humans are before they are endowed with reason and before they receive the call to transcend themselves.[18] An example Heidegger often uses of the way that traditional anthropology has influenced thinking about being to the detriment of philosophy is that of Descartes and the Cogito (e.g. BT 22–5; 40–6; 89–101). Descartes takes *Cogito ergo Sum* to be the point of departure in philosophy but then proceeds to attend solely to the *cogitare* of the *ego*. Heidegger on the other hand claims to raise the ontological question of the being of the *sum*. In doing so, he analyses what he calls the 'phenomenal content of *Dasein*'.

Heidegger prosecutes his relief by pointing out ontological questions that traditional anthropology ignores, by bringing them into prominence and thus examining them, and by providing an alternative understanding of anthropology which is intended to prevent those questions from returning to the obscurity in which he found them.

In what follows, I shall keep to the Heideggerian strategy of relief and therefore to this threefold structure. I shall examine Heidegger's phenomenological method in order to give an account of the way he finds and uncovers the question about the meaning of being. Then I shall discuss the way in which Heidegger examines this question and elucidates some of his basic terms. With this background in place, I will describe Heidegger's anthropology, the most significant feature of which is this: that it is designed to contain the question of the meaning of being in such a way as continually to impress upon us that the meaning of being *is* a question. This will involve examining the foundation of Kant's anthropology with which Heidegger's alternative can usefully be contrasted.

---

[18] Heidegger's relationship to Greek and Christian thought is more complicated than BT 45–50 suggests. As we shall find, the notion of 'discourse' to which he is committed is close to the logos with which the *zoon* is endowed.

# III. The Phenomenal Content of *Dasein*

What is it to ask 'What is the question of the meaning of being?'? It is with this inquiry into the anthropological stance that Heidegger begins *Being and Time*, and it might appropriately introduce our examination of anthropology ((BT 1–4)).

Heidegger treats the question of the meaning of being as a 'hidden' question. It is hidden both from and by the investigations of being that began with Plato and Aristotle (BT 1–3). Heidegger argues that Plato's open-ended inquiry into the meaning of being was replaced almost immediately with a dogmatic approach to his ideas that continues to characterize traditional metaphysics. This dogmatism canonized what were meant to be the tentative suggestions of Plato and Aristotle so that they appeared to be, and were treated as, statements of the truth of the matter (BT 3–4).

The question of the meaning of being is hidden *from* this heritage for the following reason. When the Greeks described being as 'the most universal concept', as 'indefinable' and as 'self-evident' they were getting into position to raise the question of its meaning. They were conscious that the meaning of being was still hidden from them and that, as these notions were so vague, their investigations had not yet begun. The question of the meaning of being is hidden *by* this heritage because the following generations mistook such manoeuvring for solid truths to be unpacked. They exhausted themselves in the unpacking and in the illusion that they were facing 'the meaning of being'. What in fact they were facing were the rather haphazard and flawed attempts of Plato and Aristotle to get into a position from which to question the meaning of being.

Heidegger sets out therefore to recover the initial spirit with which the Greeks first began to ask *how* to approach the meaning of being before ever they reached any conclusions as to how it *should* be tackled (BT 5). *Being and Time* is the record of his attempts, before ever investigating the meaning of being itself, to find the proper position and the proper approach with which to raise the question of the meaning of being.[19]

Let us allow for the sake of argument that Heidegger is correct in his historical analysis and that traditional anthropology simply reflects a series of

---

[19] This project, notoriously, was never completed in either *Being and Time* or in the works which cluster about it even as Heidegger conceived the project. The third Division of Part One and the entirety of Part Two in *Being and Time* never appeared.

unimaginative footnotes to Plato and Aristotle on the question of being. This will allow us to withdraw the object of our enquiry to Plato and Aristotle. Heidegger however wishes us to ignore Plato and Aristotle also in order to face the question of the meaning of being *tabula rasa*. If, he argues, we confront the question properly, we must do so intimately and without the observations of Plato and Aristotle.[20] His methodology is designed to give us access 'to the things themselves' mediated through his own phenomenological observations and interpretations.

The notion of intimacy upon which Heidegger bases his philosophical method he refers to as 'existential understanding' (BT 12–13). This understanding, he claims, allows us to grasp the question of the meaning of being 'from within' (BT 13). It causes us to be dissatisfied with an understanding that would grasp only the objective features of the structure of existence, and indeed with any approach that is not directed 'to the things themselves' (cf. BT 34). Heidegger argues therefore for the existence of an a priori familiarity or intimacy with the world.[21] This a priori familiarity is the condition for the possibility of 'discovering' phenomena in the world.[22] It is possible to provide a 'logos' for phenomena because, as beings ourselves, there is a transparency about our relationship with other beings (*Durchsichtigkeit*; BT 186–7). We are in significant ways transparent to them and they to us. This a priori privilege of transparency can only be endangered if we do not 'thrust aside' the temptation to *interpret* being (cf. BT 96). That is: in everyday life we grasp being familiarly; in order to interpret being we must set about grasping it 'objectively'; and this is to step away from the primary locus of being and experience. Traditional metaphysics presumes that this step gets us into a position to 'see' being more deeply: Heidegger argues that the opposite is the case and that this step 'de-familiarizes' us and removes us from the meaning of being (BT 5–6).

[20] 'the meaning of being must already be available to us in some way. As we have intimated, we always conduct our activities in an understanding of being' (BT 5).

[21] '. . . we must lay bare a fundamental structure in *Dasein* being-in-the-world. In the interpretation of *Dasein* this structure is something 'a priori' (BT 41). See also BT 44, 45, 53.

[22] This notion of intimacy which provides the basis of Heidegger's phenomenological method startlingly denies that various familiar metaphysical problems are in fact problems. Scepticism about the external world and the Subjective/Objective distinction for example swiftly disappear if he is correct. My purpose here, somewhat conservatively, is not to justify Heidegger's argument, nor to elaborate on the myriad implications of his claims but simply to remain focused on one aspect of his argument. The question of *how* knowledge claims can be made in relation to the world is an epistemological question. My purpose is to illustrate how, given Heidegger's answer to this, his epistemology affects claims about what it is to be human. This is to remain focused on the anthropological question.

Phenomenology seeks to remain faithful to the explication of our familiar hold on life (BT 27–39). It refuses to be drawn into a 'theorizing' about the world which distances the objects of that world, externalizes them, and thereby falsifies any reading it tries to make of that world (BT 35). A proper reading must remain true to the transparency of entities and phenomena. Since the existential-ontological foundation of language is discourse (BT 161), a reflexivity involving language and phenomena occurs. Phenomena do not show themselves unless through a discourse that is faithful to the intimacy that exists between entities (BT 32–4).[23] Phenomenology, as the science of the being of entities, is therefore a kind of ontology (cf. BT 61). It is distinct (relieved) from other kinds of ontology in the way that it allows an entity to be seen from itself rather than from a theoretical and manufactured objective distance.[24] Heidegger uses *entity* to apply to anything that is, in any sense or way whatsoever.[25] The *being* of an entity applies to the most general way in which an entity is (deriving from *Sein*). Thus, to translate Heidegger's definition of phenomenology given above, the proper discourse for dealing with the general way in which anything is, is relieved ontology. Other approaches to ontology, in not speaking from or through the position of what it is to be, fail to grasp the question about the meaning of being and thus fall into an improper or false discourse on this subject ('anthropologism', we might call it). The proper discourse takes account of the prior intimacy of the being of entities, what Heidegger calls *Phenomenal Content* (*der phänomenale Bestand*) and is thus aptly named phenomenology (BT passim; see p. 351 fn. 1).

Heidegger's faithfulness to the task of providing a *logos* which would retain phenomenal content leads him to diverge from Husserl's phenomenology in a way that is crucial to his relief of anthropology.[26] The divergence occurs on the question of what it is to be human. Heidegger felt that on this question Husserl held on to the last vestiges of false ontology by speaking of the 'pure' ego and of the 'subject'. Husserl describes the subject as having private

---

[23] 'Rede', a crucial piece of Heideggerian terminology which can also be translated as 'talk' but for which no truly appropriate English equivalent exists, cf. BT 203 fn. 1.

[24] Heidegger reminds the reader somewhat sternly to '*keep in mind*' that 'the expression "phenomenon" signifies *that which shows itself in itself*, the manifest' (BT 28; his emphasis).

[25] Or rather, Heidegger speaks of 'Seiendes' ('something which is') which his translators refer to as 'entities'. They justify this at BT, p. 22 fn. 1.

[26] See Heidegger's own footnote to Chapter One, Division One. Husserl is commended for having 'given us the necessary [phenomenological] tools', but Heidegger seems also to be directing at his old teacher the comment 'But . . . a priori research requires that the *phenomenal basis be properly prepared*' (my emphasis).

intentional experiences, a description which Heidegger argued detached the self from the world, obscured its relationship with other entities, and left it somewhat alone in its own 'sphere'.[27] In *Being and Time*, Heidegger speaks generally of the misinterpretation of the being that we are as human beings by the use of the term 'Subject' (e.g. BT 317–23). The use of the term, he argues, perpetuates the notion of a *Hypokeimenon*, something that 'underlies' our being, that is hidden from other entities and provides a dull private sphere in which generally we are (BT 34, 46). We cannot use the term 'sub-ject' therefore without reneging on the a priori familiarity with the world which is the condition for the possibility of our way of being.[28] Heidegger invents his own term therefore for our way of being; namely, *Dasein. Dasein* he describes as 'This entity which each of us is himself and which includes inquiring as one of the possibilities of its being' (BT 27).

We will investigate *Dasein* more closely in what follows. For the moment it is enough to be clear about why Heidegger sees the need for a 'relieved' discourse on the kind of being that we are. There are many ways for an entity to 'be'. Heidegger makes our ordinary everyday condition of being his focal point (*Alltäglichkeit*; see BT 69). Traditional metaphysics is perverse, he argues, because it deals with human beings as if their most natural way to be is to be distanced from the world, to hold theories about it rather than to live in it. The idiosyncratic term '*Dasein*' is meant to mark the way in which the being that we are is always situated (*da*), that it does not need to reflect knowingly on existence in order to be (*sein*).[29]

There are several ways in which our natural conception of the world is hidden (covered) from a conception of it based on theory. An analysis of the way in which the meaning of being is covered by traditional discourse indicates the places where and the manner by which it is to be relieved from that discourse. There is firstly that about our being which is neither known nor unknown because it has never been discovered. Second, there is that about our being which has been discovered in the past but which has been forgotten, allowed to deteriorate and to fall back into a position where it needs once more to be discovered. Third, there is that about our being which is

[27] Cf. *The Basic Problems of Phenomenology* (1927), trans. A. Hofstadter (1982), 64 and 160.

[28] 'No matter how vigorous', Heidegger adds, 'one's ontical protestations against the "soul substance" or the "reification of consciousness"' (BT 46).

[29] 'We must rather choose such a way of access and such a kind of interpretation that this entity can show itself in itself and from itself. And this means that it is to be shown as it is proximally and for the most part-in its average everydayness' (BT 16).

preserved in traditional metaphysics as a mere semblance of the phenomena which once were discovered (BT 34–9). An example of something covered in the first way would be the notion of everydayness, the central place of which in any account of ontology needs to be discovered, Heidegger argues. An example of the second category might be the characterizations of being by Plato and Aristotle, the descriptive value of which have deteriorated owing to their treatment as pieces of dogma. An example of the third category might be the notion of the subject which contains enough half-truths about the being that we are to convince the unwary that it represents the whole truth.

It is from the third position in particular that Heidegger relieves his ontology. He does this, as we have begun to indicate, by a phenomenological approach to the everyday ways in which we are in the world. Such an approach can adequately position itself in relation to being in order to ask of it its meaning. To answer the question raised at the beginning of this section, what Heidegger sees in the question 'what is it to ask "what is the question of the meaning of being"?' is nothing other than the whole point and justification of the philosophical enterprise. Phenomenology stands or falls on whether it places us in the position to ask of being its meaning. The a priori familiarity on which it rests is left unexamined by Heidegger. *How* we are in the world is of the greatest moment to him, but *that* we are, *that Dasein* is an enlightened entity in a disclosed world, is not, at least philosophically. In the beginning, according to Heidegger, there was *this* fact. And as human beings engaged in questioning the meaning of being, we have only to provide an authentic logos for it.

# IV. BEING-IN-THE-WORLD

When Heidegger speaks of *Dasein*, he means to make us aware of two things in particular: (a) the nature of a being one of whose modes of being it is to inquire, and (b) the proximity in that entity of situation (*da*) and being (*Sein*). As regards (a), there are many ways, Heidegger argues, in which an entity can be. 'Being lies in the fact that something is, and in its being as it is; in reality; in presence-at-hand; in subsistence; in validity; in *Dasein*; in the "there is"' (BT 7). Why then does he choose to focus on *Dasein*? To raise the question of the meaning of being adequately, Heidegger must 'make an entity—the inquirer—transparent in his own being'. *Dasein* is that entity whose mode of being it is to inquire (BT 7). Thus *Dasein* is the focus of Heidegger's inquiry. Turning to (b), the compound of an adverb of place (*da*) and the verb 'to be' (*sein*) in '*Dasein*' is intended to make the point that our way of being is nothing other than the disclosedness to us of our whereabouts. Heidegger describes *Dasein* as always already 'being-in-the-world' (*In-der-Welt-sein*; see BT 52–63).

The notion of being-in-the-world is of crucial importance for Heidegger's anthropological stance. It is as a consequence of this notion that Heidegger accounts for a characteristic feature of being-human: that, being-human, we tend to relate to others as conscious and concern-ful human beings and not as bodies showing suitably human behaviour.[30]

What, then, does Heidegger mean by 'being-in-the-world'? He attempts to convey by this phrase that interpenetration of being and world which allows us to speak of '*Dasein*' whose being belongs to its situation and whose situation belongs to its being.[31] The terms of this definition can be clarified by examining an example of being-in-the-world, the example of being-employed.

When the kind of being that we are encounters other entities in the world such as physical objects, it is in order often enough to employ those entities towards some end or other. Thus the entity is present as an *instrument* (*Zeug*). Heidegger describes what he means by 'the world' in this case as the whole system of significations which are present to *Dasein* as its instruments while *Dasein* is in the mode of being-employed.[32] To explain: *Dasein* understands an entity as instrumental to its ends and projects. These instruments in their turn and by the way in which they are used reveal depths about those ends and projects which aid *Dasein*'s self-understanding. The world is 'there' as a totality of involvements; being is 'there' (*Dasein*) as the one so involved; thus being and world are, in and through the nature of instrumentality, represented as mutually interpenetrating. An entity 'comes into focus' for *Dasein* as an instrument and *Dasein* understands its own purposes through employing that instrument the functioning of which allows it to be further revealed to *Dasein*.

---

[30] This is one of the points at which the Heidegger of 1927–30 appears closest to the Wittgenstein of the 1940s; in particular the remarks collected as *Zettel*.

[31] 'The compound expression "Being-in-the-World" indicates in the very way we have coined it, that it stands for a unitary phenomenon. This primary datum must be seen as a whole' (BT 53). See also *The Basic Problems of Phenomenology*, trans. Hofstadter, 297.

[32] Heidegger notes that the meaning of his term 'world' when he uses it in this manner as 'the world of everyday *Dasein*' is close to the reference of 'environment' (BT 66).

Thus *Dasein* and world are indistinguishable in the one employment, *Dasein* in its mode of being employed and the world as the system of involvements assigned for that purpose.[33]

The interpenetration of being and world is effected through the possibility of *Dasein*'s a priori familiarity with the world. This familiarity with the world allows *Dasein* to be unreflective in being-employed. It is this half-conscious state of being-in the world which interests Heidegger. It is the ordinary background out of which a great deal of human life is made up. Granted, being-in-the-world can stand out from the world in various ways and for various reasons, often enough to theorize about it (BT 60–2). But this is exceptional. I cannot remember putting on my shirt this morning and I have every reason to believe that I was acting unreflectively in-the-world. A great part of our lives is spent in just such an interpenetration of being and situation. If we are to question being, Heidegger argues, we must in the first instance take account of being-in-the-world.[34]

It should be clear that by 'being-in-the-world' Heidegger does not mean us to understand that one mode of *Dasein*'s being is to be contained spatially within a certain physical environment.[35] Nor does he mean us to understand that there are two entities, Being and World. The assumption that experience consists of a subject bringing concepts to bear on a physical environment and that being and world are two entities (in Heidegger's use of the terms) dominates traditional metaphysics (BT 60). It gives rise to the idea that there are specific moves to be made if the subject is to get into position to deal with the world of objects. If being is distinct from world, it must force a connection with that world. The character of that connection will depend on the way one understands the ontological configuration of those entities and on how one sees the physical environment as constraining their relationship. If we do not need to get into position in the first place then we have no reason to develop, for example, the finer points of empiricist or rationalist doctrine in this manner. Heidegger describes the possibility of being-in-the-world in such a way as to relieve traditional metaphysics of the need to connect being with world. His argument can be reduced to the claim that *Dasein* 'is' rather than

---

[33]  See Heidegger's analysis of hammering as an example of this mode of being, BT 69.

[34]  'Being-in is not a "property" which *Dasein* sometimes has and sometimes does not have, and without which it could be just as well as it could with it. It is not the case that man "is" and then has, by way of an extra, a relationship-of-being towards the "world"' (BT 57).

[35]  The world is not Descartes' 'Res extensa'. See Heidegger's criticism of the Cartesian ontology of the world at BT 89–101.

that *Dasein* 'has' access to its world.[36] Heidegger gives three ways in which the proper description (logos) of experience can be relieved from traditional metaphysical assumptions about the involvement of subjects within the world.

First, traditional metaphysics describes a person as only contingently connected to their environment. The connection rests on the slender and intermittent possibility of entertaining beliefs about that environment. Scepticism about the very existence of that environment is thus made possible and even compelling. Heidegger argues that, through employment, instrumentality, and the a priori disclosedness of self and world, *Dasein* is always already *attuned* to its situation.[37] The system of instrumental entities which is the world reveals itself according to the way *Dasein* is 'disposed' to them. Because there is no encounter with the world prior to *Dasein*'s disposition towards it, there is no need nor room to allow for anything resembling a 'connection' between being and world.

Secondly, traditional metaphysics tends to describe language as interposing itself between subject and world. The manner in which it interposes itself is of course a matter of much debate, but *that* it does, Heidegger argues, is accepted as a matter of course. Discourse, in the way that Heidegger uses the term, is the articulation of the situation in which *Dasein* finds itself.[38] Traditional metaphysics understands discourse as existing independently of the world. If *Dasein* 'is its world existingly' (BT 364), then the articulation of that world in which *Dasein* finds itself must *be* the world (BT 161–2). *Dasein* does not need to find a position from which to make sense independently of what is encountered since the articulation of *Dasein*'s situation *is Dasein*'s mode of being. Heidegger's argument puns provocatively on the word 'articulate'.[39] The world is 'articulated' both as the functioning instrument of *Dasein*'s purposes and as that situation in which *Dasein* finds itself articulate.

---

[36] At one point Heidegger states clearly, 'If no *Dasein* exists, no world is "there" either' (BT 365).

[37] 'Gestimmtsein'. 'In a state-of-mind *Dasein* is always brought before itself, and has always found itself, not in the sense of coming across itself by perceiving itself, but in the sense of finding itself in the mood that it has' (BT 135).

[38] Heidegger admits that, if *logos* (as in '*zoon logon echon*') is taken to mean 'discourse', then his definition of *Dasein* as that being essentially *determined* by its potentiality for discourse is close to a refined interpretation of the Greek position (BT 25, 165).

[39] Although one cannot assume that this is the case. The two meanings of the word *can* be distinguished in German by using 'gliedern' instead of 'artikulieren' and on occasion Heidegger uses this alternative. (See BT 195 fn. 1.) But since in German the words are almost synonymous and one can 'hear' both meanings in both words, this is surely a quibble.

Thirdly, traditional metaphysics describes projects in such a way as to distinguish the action from the goal to which that action is directed. This alienation can yield at best a fragmented and synoptic self-awareness. By employing entities as instruments-towards-ends, Heidegger counters, *Dasein* is always already engaged in and understanding itself through its ends. *Dasein* is a *projected*-being pressing forward into possibilities (*Entwurf*; see BT 145). The world is a system of instruments *for a purpose*. The purposiveness of the world and *Dasein*'s mode of being-projected meet indistinguishably in the single phenomenon of being-in-the-world.[40]

The sum of these three arguments is that the world of *Dasein* is a 'with-world' (*Mitwelt*; see BT 118). Through being familiar a priori with the world we are familiar also with the being of others who share this familiarity. Thus our being-in the world is articulated as a being-with others. Our familiarity with the being of others in turn articulates for us our being in the world.[41] Being a 'being-in-the-world', *Dasein* is also 'being-with' (*Mitdasein*). Thus Heidegger appears to claim to have found a priori evidence against the possibility of scepticism about Other Minds. It would appear that it makes little sense to Heidegger to doubt that a being whom we recognized as a being-with is a human being. We should however be wary of imagining that in the concept of *Mitdasein* alone we have come upon Heidegger's response. The deduction of 'Being-with' from 'Being-in' is not compelling unless we can see Heidegger's notion of the *Mitdasein* as part of and in some sense indistinguishable from the whole concept of being-in-the-world. There is nothing in the idea of Being-in for example which rules out the possibility of a work-world, fully equipped with objects encountered as instruments, that is inhabited by a single *Dasein* and which therefore excludes *Mitdasein*.[42]

Through an analysis of being-in-the-world Heidegger seeks imaginatively to redescribe our experience in order to avoid the methods of haphazard and unreflective beholding-from-a-distance to which traditional metaphysics commits itself by its radical distinction of being and situation.[43]

---

[40] 'An entity whose kind of being is the essential projection of being-in-the-world has an understanding of being, and has this as constitutive for its being' (BT 147).

[41] 'because *Dasein*'s being is being-with, its understanding of being already implies the understanding of others' (BT 123).

[42] It will not be clear how Heidegger would have used *Mitdasein* for the Other Minds case until the whole tenor of his distinction between the human, the non-human, and the infra-human is examined.

[43] 'The idea of grasping and explicating phenomena in a way which is "original" and "intuitive" is directly opposed to the naivety of a haphazard, "immediate", and unreflective beholding' (BT 36).

The 'wherein' of an act of understanding which assigns or refers itself is that for which one lets entities be encountered in the kind of being that belongs to involvements; and this 'wherein' is the phenomenon of the world'. (BT 86)

Traditional metaphysics requires relief precisely when it begins to theorize about 'the kind of being that belongs to involvements' (BT 21). It does so especially by creating the notion of a subject distinct from its objective engagements.[44] This splits the phenomenon of being-in-the-world into 'objects'—be they physical objects or goals—and a subject who needs to secure for itself a position from which to relate to those objects (BT 132). Subjective discourse—the logos founded upon the notion of a subject—cannot help therefore but 'split the phenomenon'.

What then is the relation of being-in-the-world to anthropology? We are concerned to raise the question of the meaning of being. The discourse or 'logos' in which this question is raised is anthropology. An improper or false discourse on this subject, 'anthropologism', is one that cannot raise the question meaningfully. Any interpretation of the ontological configuration of being and world which 'splits the phenomenon' of everyday experience cannot raise that question meaningfully because it is untrue to that phenomenon. The subjective discourse favoured by traditional metaphysics grounds itself in just such a splitting of the phenomenon.[45] Therefore that discourse is founded on anthropologism. The Heideggerian analysis of 'being-in-the-world' relieves this discourse by substituting for it a *logos* in which being and situation interpenetrate. Accordingly we have in an analysis of being-in-the-world the foundation of an anthropology as a Heideggerian would relieve it.[46]

# V. Heidegger and Kant

In his Introduction to Part Four of *Kant and the Problem of Metaphysics*, Heidegger meditates on his construction of an anthropology with regard to

---

[44] Whereas 'By its very nature, *Dasein* brings its "there" along with it. If it lacks its "there", it is not factically the entity which is essentially *Dasein*; indeed, it is not this entity at all. *Dasein is its Disclosedness* (Das *Dasein* ist seine Erschlossenheit)' (BT 133; Heidegger's emphasis).

[45] 'What is decisive for ontology is to prevent the splitting of the phenomenon—in other words, to hold its positive phenomenal content secure' (BT 132; my emphasis).

[46] One of the professed aims of *Being and Time* is 'to provide some of the pieces' in the construction of 'a complete ontology of *Dasein*, which assuredly must be constructed if anything like a "philosophical" anthropology is to have a philosophically adequate basis' (BT 17).

Kantian anthropology which could be described as a 'relief' of Kant. The strategy of relief presumes that it is impossible to start afresh and Heidegger declares that he must first 'make sure of what constitutes the authentic outcome of the earlier, in this case the Kantian, ground-laying' (K, 139). Even after correction, the original ground-laying is 'preserved in its capacity as a problem' (K, 139). It is in fact the 'problem' which constructs the original ground-laying which makes it possible to elevate oneself above the original ground-laying and to question it.

By the retrieval of a basic problem, we understand the opening-up of its original, long-concealed possibilities, through the working-out of which it is transformed. (K, 139)

Heidegger begins his dialogue with Kantian anthropology with Kant's claim in the *Logic* that the question 'what is it to be human?' is basic to philosophy.[47] The project of laying the foundation of philosophy in anthropology Heidegger views as justified. But much rests on that laying of the foundation and he takes up this point in his *Kant and the Problem of Metaphysics*. He claims in that work, in ways that need not concern us, that the Kantian Subject fails to free itself from the ontological undetermination characteristic of the ontologies which Kant was attempting to criticize.[48] Kant failed to raise the question of the meaning of being and thus failed to provide an adequate stance for anthropology.

Heidegger's starting point is, appropriately enough, to ask a question:

How must this fourth question [i.e. 'what is it to be human?'] itself be asked so that it can take up and bear each of the three questions ['What can I know? What ought I to do? What may I hope?'] unified within it?' (K 147)

Heidegger is entirely in agreement with Kant that philosophy is rooted in 'humanity'. Kant's fourth question must however take account of Heidegger's relief of 'humanity' in *Dasein*. For Heidegger, then, the problem of the laying of the foundation of metaphysics is rooted in the question of *Dasein* (K 157) and most especially in the mode of *Dasein*'s being which he refers to as its attitude towards finitude. He argues at one point that 'More primordial than humanity is the finitude of the *Dasein* in it' (K 156).

---

[47] 'Im Grunde konnte man aber alles dieses zur Anthropologie rechnen, weil sich die drei ersten Fragen auf die letzte beziehen' (*Kants Werke*, ix (Berlin, 1968), 25).

[48] 'With the revelation of the subjectivity of the subject, Kant recoiled from the ground which he himself had established' (*Kant and the Problem of Metaphysics*, trans. J. S. Churchill (1962), 221).

What Heidegger means by 'finitude' can be readily seen if we use the passage from Kant's *Logic* as an example. Whoever asks 'What can I know? What ought I to do? What may I hope?' betrays his own finitude. It is not according to the essence of an immortal or all-powerful entity to be able to pose the question 'What can I do?' because it would make no sense for it to ask 'What can I *not* do?' Therefore whoever can ask the three fundamental philosophical questions shows herself to be fundamentally orientated towards that which is contained within the fourth question (K 147). Heidegger argues therefore that what to Kant was a radical reduction (of philosophy to anthropology) is the obvious fact of the matter. For if we take up an appropriate (anthropological) stance to the being that we are, we will notice that being and its limitations are an *issue* for *Dasein*.[49]

The philosophical questions surrounding metaphysics, morality, and religion spring from being-as-issue. When Heidegger says therefore that '*Dasein*'s being is not to be deduced from the idea of man' (BT 182), what does he mean in this context? There is that about the phenomenal content of the being that we are which sees being itself as an issue in the specific sense that it has an attitude towards its limitations. The interpretation of being and situation in the one term '*Dasein*' reflects the way in which such limitations and the anxiety attendant on them *are* our being. The term 'humanity' cannot bear this conjunction within its terms of signification. One would have to *predicate* of humanity that a particular specimen of the genus was anxious.[50] This would be to split the phenomenon of being-in-the-world:

Self and world belong together in the single entity *Dasein*. Self and world are not two entities like subject and object or like I and you; rather self and world are the basic determination of *Dasein* itself in the unity of the structure of being-in-the-world.[51]

In so far as one cannot use the term 'humanity' and avoid splitting the phenomenon of self and world, one cannot use it either to express the way of being of an entity who wishes to engage in an examination of its limitations.[52]

---

[49] Recall that Heidegger defines *Dasein* as 'This entity which each of us is himself and which includes enquiring as one of the possibilities of its being' (BT 27).

[50] As to predication, recall that Heidegger argues 'It is not the case that man "is" and then has, by way of an extra, a relationship-of-being towards the "world"' (BT 57).

[51] *The Basic Problems of Phenomenology*, trans. Hofstadter, 297.

[52] Heidegger's argument here depends heavily on Max Scheler (to whose memory *Kant and the Problem of Metaphysics* was dedicated) and his analysis of the essential difficulties facing the attempt to attain 'a unitary idea of man'. See *Kant and the Problem of Metaphysics*, trans. J. S. Churchill (1962), 216–17.

Philosophy is not the product of an entity for whom being is not an issue. If philosophy claims therefore to have solved the meaning of being or to have made it self-evident or unproblematic, it has engaged in self-undermining logical absurdity.

So Heidegger works outwards, from laying the foundation of anthropology by preserving the phenomenal content of *Dasein*, to speaking of philosophy. By contrast, Kant approached the same matter from the opposite direction; he reduced philosophy to anthropology where Heidegger relieves philosophy through the relief of the anthropological stance. But the relief of philosophy, Heidegger makes very clear, is not to be understood as the 'settling' or the 'establishment' of the meaning of being. There is no relief in that sense for *Dasein* faced with the disclosedness of its being as finitude. Thus at the same time that he argues that an anthropology which is based upon a genuine interrogation of the finitude in being-human is the only possible basis for philosophy, he is aware that no anthropology can entirely avoid the risk of concealing from itself that being-human is always already a question.[53] It is anthropologism to ignore 'the necessity of developing the question concerning human beings first and foremost as a question, with a view towards a laying of the ground for metaphysics' (K 149).

The value and strength of Heidegger's anthropology depends upon the accuracy with which its underpinnings deal with the phenomenal content of *Dasein* as a questioning being-in-the-world. Heideggerian anthropology defines itself as a discourse that is relieved from traditional anthropology. It is relieved because, unlike traditional anthropology, it is true to the phenomenal content of *Dasein*. It is crucial to Heidegger's anthropology that being remains an issue for *Dasein* in its attitude towards its finitude. It does not give in to the temptation to imagine that philosophy can dissolve/analyse the question of the meaning of being. There would be no questions to *raise* were there not prior to those questions an anxiety about being. To deny that being-human is to question and to be called into question is to hide that anxiety and to 'cover' the ontological configuration which gives rise to it. Therefore it is Heidegger's design in his anthropology to maintain at the heart of discourse the phenomenal content of being-as-issue. This is the 'preserving' aspect of a relief which Heidegger describes in a passage in the *Kant and the Problem of*

---

[53] '*Dasein*'s kind of being demands that any ontological interpretation which sets itself the goal of exhibiting the phenomena in their primordiality should capture the being of this entity *in spite of this entity's own tendency to cover things up*' (BT 359; my emphasis).

*Metaphysics*: 'To preserve a problem means to free and keep watch over those inner forces which make it possible, on the basis of its essence, as a problem' (K 139).

Heidegger's anthropology is a stance that self-consciously guards against the temptation towards anthropologism. It claims to be the stance from which it is possible to judge the truth and falsity of claims about what it is to be human. In the next section, we shall examine an argument that would undermine that stance.

# VI. MERLEAU-PONTY ON HUMAN BODIES

The influence of Maurice Merleau-Ponty on current philosophical and broadly psychological approaches to bodily awareness and self-awareness is great and continues deservedly to grow.[54] Part One of his *Phenomenology of Perception* has provided many, in the analytical tradition also, with particularly keen insights. In this section, we shall examine a central theme to be found there: that one's body cannot be considered an object among others in the world. If this claim is true, of course, then much that we assume is rendered false. And one of the casualties would be Heidegger's distinctive approach to anthropology. For his stance depends on the claim that the body associated with *Dasein* is one among other such in the world.

Merleau-Ponty's argument may be reconstructed as follows so as to bring out its main elements.

First, he establishes a basic claim (PP 67–72):

(1) To be an object among other objects in the world, an entity must be perceptible as just such an object.

He then claims that 'the body is the vehicle of being in the world' (PP 82), that 'the body is our general medium for having a world' (PP 146), and, consequently, that

---

[54] I have discussed a representative collection of recent philosophical and psychological work (J. L. Bermúdez, A. Marcel, and N. Eilan (eds.), *The Body and the Self* (Cambridge, MA: MIT Press, 1995)) which places Merleau-Ponty's writings explicitly in the centre of various concerns, in 'Critical Notice', *Ratio* 10 (1997), 91–6.

(2) My body is the means by which I perceive objects in the world.

At this point, Merleau-Ponty introduces a new thought: 'What prevents [the body] ever being an object, ever being "completely constituted" is that it is that by which there are objects' (PP 93). Together with (2), this leads him to claim that,

(3) In so far as it is that by which objects are perceived, my body is not itself perceptible as an object among others in the world.

So, he concludes, 'the body therefore is not one more among external objects with the peculiarity of always being there' (PP 93). In other words,

(4) My body is not an object among others in the world.

Merleau-Ponty's argument shares a similar form to other arguments which draw a distinct conclusion. These distinct conclusions are variations on a Humean theme: that, in introspection, one is not aware of the self as a genuine object.

Thus Hume concluded that the self is a mere collection of different perceptions.[55] Kant argued that the *I* of apperception cannot *know* itself as an object in the world, and so cannot *be* such an object.[56] Schopenhauer claimed that the 'subject of representations' cannot, by definition, become the object of any pure representation, and so cannot be an object in the empirical world.[57] And Wittgenstein famously asked, expecting the answer 'nowhere', 'Where *in* the world is a metaphysical subject to be found?'[58]

Merleau-Ponty's claim is different. He is free to accept that there may be something which would count as purely perceptually identifying an object of perception as the subject of that perception. For what Merleau-Ponty denies is that there is anything which would count as purely perceptually identifying an object of perception as that which provides for, or may be identified with, that perception.

---

[55] *A Treatise of Human Nature*, ed. L. A. Selby-Bigge and P. H. Nidditch (Oxford: Oxford University Press, 1978), 1739, 252.

[56] A 107; B 158.

[57] *The World as Will and Representation*, trans. E. F. J. Payne, 2 vols. (New York: Dover, 1966), ii. 273–8.

[58] *Tractatus Logico-philosophicus*, trans. D. F. Pears and B. F. McGuinness (London: Routledge & Kegan Paul, 1961), p. 57.

The important differences are these. First, it is the body, rather than the *I*, person, or subject, about which the claim is made. So, for all that the argument (1)–(4) shows, the *I*, person, or subject *might* be an object in the world. It is just that, if it is, it cannot be identified with the body. Second, Merleau-Ponty's conclusion concerns what kind of thing the body is, not what kind of thing the referent of *I* must be if first-personal statements are to be possible.

Given these departures from familiar arguments, (1)–(4) needs careful contextualization. Merleau-Ponty describes his approach as 'phenomenological': an a priori inquiry into human beings and their world as they appear to consciousness, i.e. as they are, or can be, experienced. Phenomenology treats the world as 'always "already there" before reflection begins' (PP vii). The world 'is not what I think, but what I live through. I am open to the world, I have no doubt that I am in communication with it, but I do not possess it; it is inexhaustible' (PP xvii). Consequently, Merleau-Ponty does not regard the world as 'an *object* such that I have in my possession the law of its making; it is the natural setting of, and field for, all my thoughts and all my explicit perceptions' (PP xi; my italics).

Considerations about what it is to be in the world lead naturally to a discussion of the body; for, according to Merleau-Ponty, it is my body which 'opens me out upon the world and places me in a situation there' (PP 165). Moreover, being a body 'is to be tied to a certain world' so 'our body is not primarily *in* space: it is of it' (PP 148). Given that the world is not possessed as an object, and that 'being' a body 'is our general medium for having a world' (PP 146), Merleau-Ponty concludes: 'the body therefore is not one more among external objects' (PP 93).

Given this special background, we might wonder whether (4) denies anything we are so far committed to—whether it talks past our current concerns. I suspect it does. By denying that one's body is an 'object', Merleau-Ponty means to deny that the body can be reduced to a 'scientific object' (PP 174): something which 'acknowledges between its parts, or between itself and other objects external and mechanical relationships in the sense of motion received or transmitted' (PP 73). But it is apparently at least as an object in *this* sense that one is allegedly aware of the body one is by, for example, pressing one's fingers down onto a key-pad while typing. So there is a case to be answered.

# VII. The Problem with Merleau-Ponty on Human Bodies

I have described Merleau-Ponty's position in some detail because, while I disagree with his conclusion, it is based on premises that are close to an account of direct bodily identification which I have argued is plausible.[59]

The distinction can briefly be summarized before the event by reference to the formal presentation of Merleau-Ponty's argument (1)–(4). I regard (2) as basically correct: my body *is* the means by which I perceive the world. But it is false to claim, with (3) and (4), that my body is not a perceptible object among others in the world. The reason why (2) does not lead to this conclusion is that Merleau-Ponty's argument is invalid; (2) only leads to (3)–(4) if a hidden premise is introduced, and we should reject that premise as false.

We may expose what is wrong with Merleau-Ponty's argument by looking carefully at various steps in his argument. Consider, first, his premise (2):

(2) My body is the means by which I perceive objects in the world.

This is not implausible. Perceiving an object's shape is to perceive its various parts as standing in various spatial relations to one's body;[60] and the possibility of *that* kind of perception depends on a primary, direct awareness of one's own body. Thus body-provided awareness is basic to perceptual awareness of the world and of objects as such. That is one reason for agreeing that my body is the means by which I perceive the world.

So we might accept (2). On the other hand, it is false to claim, with (3) and (4), that my body is not a perceptible object among others in the world. The reason why (2) does not lead to this conclusion is that Merleau-Ponty's argument is invalid; (2) only leads to (3)–(4) if a hidden premise is introduced, and we should reject that premise as false.

Say, then, that (2) is true; this leads us to (3):

(3) In so far as it is that by which objects are perceived, my body is not perceptible as an object among others in the world

---

[59] I have discussed these matters elsewhere: (a) 'Bodily Organs and Organisation'; (b) 'Kant and Strawson on the First Person'; (c) 'On referring to Oneself', *Theoria* 70 (2004), 121–61.

[60] e.g. Gareth Evans, *Collected Papers*, ed. A. Phillips (Oxford: Oxford University Press, 1985), 388–90.

Why should Merleau-Ponty suppose (2) implies that my body is not a perceptible object among others in the world (i.e. (3))?

The intuition driving the step appears to be this. If my body is the means by which I perceive the world, then perceiving something as an object just is bringing body-provided awareness to bear on it. This presumably applies to perceiving the body as an object also. But the body cannot be grasped as an object *of* body-provided awareness if it is the body which *provides for* that awareness. For we may bring into being the kind of intelligibility proper to identifying an entity as an object. But this is only because we have, in so doing and by definition, exercised body-provided awareness ('the body is our general medium for having a world' (PP 146)). And to grasp the body providing for *that* awareness as an object, we must bring deeper possibilities of intelligibility into being-possibilities which are in turn made actual by deeper and as-yet-ungrasped features of the body. And so on in infinite regress.

In short, if it is possible to be aware of some act or feature of the body as the act or feature of an object, the possibility must be underwritten by an as-yet-ungrasped exercise of body-provided awareness. So no such awareness can amount to awareness of the body as a whole as an object. And if there is no such ungrasped prior exercise, then there can be no such awareness of the body-as-object either.

That this is the kind of hidden premise linking (2) and (3) which Merleau-Ponty has in mind is suggested by the following passage:

I observe external objects with my body, I handle them, examine them, walk round them, but my body itself is a thing which I do not observe: in order to do so, I should need the use of a second body which itself would be observable. (PP 91)

So the thought licensing the step from (2) to (3) is this: something (i.e. the body) cannot be the object of an awareness for which it provides.

This claim requires further examination:

*Nothing can be the object of an awareness for which it provides.*

This thought is false—something *can* be the object of an awareness for which it provides. The brain, for example, can become the object of study by the concept-using entity whose activity it provides for; and even though visual experience is provided by the workings of the optic nerves, those nerves can themselves be seen.

Furthermore, what is true about Merleau-Ponty's comments concerning observation of 'external objects' may be applied to observation of my own body. I may 'handle it', 'examine' it, and 'observe' it using all of my senses. I cannot, of course, 'walk round' my body. But then I cannot walk round many objects that I may nevertheless be said to observe—the sun and other heavenly bodies, for example.

It may be true that I have no 'point of view' on my body that is itself distinct from or independent of my body. But this does not undermine my ability to perceive it as a genuine object—i.e. as something capable of occupying space, of moving, of being publicly observable and by more than one sensory modality, of being located in its entirety at no more than one place at one time, of being internally causally connected over time, of being the common cause of many phenomena, and of existing unperceived.

There is, admittedly, another possible way to read the hidden premise if we are prepared to alter (2) somewhat: something (i.e. the body) cannot be the object of an awareness with which it must be *identified*. And this claim still fits Merleau-Ponty's remark about the need for a second body: how could the body be fully grasped as an object of our awareness, if it is also to be *identified* with that awareness, without the body being the perceptual object of another body, and so in infinite regress? But this reading of the premise surrenders the notion of body-provided awareness to absurdity. We cannot *identify* the body with body-provided awareness any more than we can *identify* visual experience with the optic nerves. Having a body may be necessary for accrediting an entity with awareness of objects as objects; but it is not sufficient. (Merleau-Ponty himself recognizes this point in his discussion of Schneider, a patient with only residual kinaesthetic and proprioceptive capacities (PP 103–36).) Yet it would have to be both necessary and sufficient if an identity claim is to be made.

So, we may conclude that we have good reason to accept certain of Merleau-Ponty's claims: specifically, that if one's body is an object among others in the world, it must be perceptible as such; and, moreover, that one's body is not only perceptible, but one's means of perceiving objects in the world. We may, however, reject his conclusion: that one's body is not an object among others in the world. That is because we can affirm what seems commonsensical: that one's body is perceptible as such an object. And this preserves a vital feature of Continental approaches to being human, in particular one that is lodged in Heidegger's account of anthropology.[61]

---

[61] I am most grateful to audiences at Pittsburgh, Auckland, Oxford, and Richmond, Virginia for discussion of the arguments contained here.

## CHAPTER 16

# FREEDOM AS AUTONOMY

## KENNETH BAYNES

THE interpretation of individual freedom as autonomy or 'self-governance' has a long tradition reaching back at least to early modern natural law theory and, before that, the Stoic tradition of the Graeco-Roman period (Schneewind). However, in the modern era, and especially in the thought of Rousseau and Kant, the idea of autonomy became a central category through which the individual's relation to the world, to others, and to his own inner self or motivational structure was reconceived. It could safely be said that the interpretation of individual freedom as a form of 'self-governance' produced a 'Copernican revolution' in practical philosophy at least as significant as Kant's critical philosophy was for modern epistemology. Moreover, despite the fact that today the ideal of autonomy has many critics, much of the contemporary literature is best read as contributing to a refinement of that ideal rather than as a rejection of it. Modern attempts to understand freedom as autonomy produced a wave of philosophical reflection whose effects can be seen in Romanticism, in the nineteenth-century reactions of Kierkegaard and Nietzsche, in the existentialist movement, and in the various contemporary attempts to refine, extend, and appropriate this radical ideal.

'Autonomy' (*auto-nomos*) initially arose as a political ideal within the ancient city-state of Athens and the thought that there might be a deep structural analogy between the city-state (*polis*) and soul (*psyche*) is a prominent feature of Plato's *Republic*. However, Plato did not seriously entertain the idea of self-governance as a model for the self and the *Republic* is generally understood as a criticism of democracy or political autonomy. Still, later reflection on the idea of freedom as a form of self-governance highlighted features and paradoxes common to both the political and the individual context—for example, in the idea of an original founding (who is the 'people' that gives itself law?) and parallel concerns about the status of the self who governs in individual self-rule. As importantly, it noted the ways in which one form of autonomy (say, personal or individual autonomy) might depend on the presence of other forms (civic and political autonomy). In the end, if the idea of freedom as autonomy is to remain attractive it will not be as a single ideal (the self determining itself), but rather as a constellation of related ideals that depend in various ways on one another. Even the idea of individual or personal autonomy has several dimensions and includes not only the capacity for self-rule but also capacities for self-discovery and self-definition (Meyers 1989). As importantly, as Rousseau and Hegel argue, personal autonomy is neither especially appealing nor realizable in isolation from other forms of autonomy. Rather, the effective pursuit of personal autonomy requires forms of legal, political, and moral autonomy as well.

# 1. ROUSSEAU

Jean-Jacques Rousseau (1712–78) is the source of most modern and contemporary discussions of autonomy. Freedom (or liberty) is a fundamental human interest—'To renounce one's freedom is to renounce one's quality as a man' (*Social Contract* [*SC*], I.4, p. 45)—yet, as importantly, this freedom is for the most part conceived positively, as self-rule or self-mastery, rather than negatively, as the absence of interference by others: What Rousseau calls 'moral freedom'—'which alone makes man truly the master of himself'—is defined as 'obedience to the law one has prescribed to oneself' (*SC*, I.8, p. 54; see also *Emile*, V. 445). In a concise formulation Rousseau says, 'Liberty consists less in doing one's will than in not being subject to someone else's; it further consists in not subjecting someone else's will to ours' ('Eighth Letter from the Mountain', 260–1). At the core of this conception are two controversial ideas: that (moral) freedom is only possible under (self-imposed) laws rather than in the absence of law, and that the project of self-rule cannot be secured individually, but requires forms of mutual recognition in which no person's will is arbitrarily subjected to the will of another. Though all recognize that autonomy is a central theme for Rousseau, his commentators otherwise widely disagree about the significance and even coherence of that idea: Some read him as a harsh critic of the inevitable vices and dangers of social life, others as a champion of a genuine democracy in contrast to its distorted forms, and still others as a 'collectivist' and precursor of totalitarianism. There are certainly tensions in his various writings as well as passages that are difficult to interpret—as when he infamously remarks that he who resists the 'general will' must be 'forced to be free' (SC, I.7). However, Rousseau insisted on the essential unity of his work and interpretive charity demands that we at least begin by taking him at his word.

The *Social Contract* (1762) opens with the remarkable line, 'Man is born free, and everywhere he is in chains.' Somewhat disingenuously (since it was a central topic of his two earlier *Discourses*) Rousseau claims not to know how this condition came about. However, he does claim to know what could set things right. The 'fundamental problem' of the *Social Contract* can be easily stated: 'to find a form of association that will defend and protect the person and goods of each associate with the full common force, and by means of which each one, uniting with all, nevertheless obey only himself and remain as free as before' (SC, I.6, pp. 49–50). For Rousseau the only association that meets this requirement is an association in which individuals jointly relinquish their natural liberty and form a new political body. What distinguishes this association from all others is that it is based on the creation of a new 'artificial' political sovereign who is the source of all law and whose will (the 'general will') is the final word on matters of common concern (including, for the most part, what will count as common concern). Since, per the terms of the original contract, each member becomes an inseparable and equal part of the new political body, no one is subordinated to the will of another. More importantly, however, though the parties to the contract relinquish their 'natural liberty'—their ability to think and act according to their own discretion—according to Rousseau they acquire in exchange a far greater 'civil' and 'moral' freedom—obedience to self-imposed law (SC, I.8). Further, or so Rousseau claims, the political sovereign is in a position to protect each from a freedom-diminishing dependence on another (Neuhouser). Of course, this new freedom does not do away with all social dependence; nor does it restore all his former natural liberty. Rather, it transforms his social dependence so that he is no longer subject to the arbitrary will of another. As importantly, it assumes a political equality that makes possible mutual recognition of individual status and worth so that individuals need not plunge into unending competition for esteem and recognition. Still, if, as he claims, the contract leaves the individual freer than he was in the state of nature, Rousseau must clarify the character of this newly found freedom. Even more controversially, Rousseau states that if an individual citizen finds his own will at variance with the general will he must conclude that he is mistaken, and should the individual refuse to obey the general will Rousseau infamously replies that he may be compelled to do so, 'which means nothing other than that he shall be forced to be free' (*SC*, I.7). This formulation, it must be conceded, has at least an air of paradox.

It is thus not difficult to see why many find in Rousseau's argument a profound sleight of hand whereby an individual's natural liberty is exchanged for a form of collective rule that is a form of freedom in name only. This is in effect the conclusion of Berlin's influential essay, 'Two Concepts of Liberty', in which he claims that the concept of positive liberty (or 'self-rule') is especially vulnerable to semantic manipulation and, as a result, real coercion and loss of liberty (Berlin). The criticism is often coupled with the claim that at least some of Rousseau's difficulty is the result of the extreme opposition he sets up between the freedom and goodness of the individual in the state of nature and the oppressive character of life in society. However, this objection moves too quickly and does not do justice to Rousseau's efforts to come to grips with the complex relationship between individual freedom and social dependence. On the one hand, it does not take seriously enough Rousseau's critique of 'discretionary liberty' or the freedom to do what one wants. For Rousseau, this form of liberty taken alone leads to slavery and dependence. An individual's preferences are to a large extent a function of the social institutions and relations in which he lives. The transformation (described in the *Discourse on Inequality*) of our natural *amour de soi* (self-love) into an 'inflamed' *amour-propre* (usually translated as selfishness or vanity) in society carries with it an aggressive and unending competition for goods, status, and distinction as each strives to improve his standing relative to others. The result, according to Rousseau, is that in society the individual lives wholly 'always outside himself' and becomes entirely dependent on the opinions of others (*Discourse*, 187). In such a condition, the individual can hardly be considered free even if technically his negative or 'discretionary' liberty remains untouched since he lacks the ability to distinguish true from false needs or discern positive virtues from their opposites. The individual is at this point not unlike the situation of the tyrant in Plato's *Republic* who is dependent on the opinion and will of others and utterly lacks capacity for discernment with respect to his own aims and desires. A critique of Rousseau must take seriously this account of the condition of individuals in society.

An alternative response to the concerns raised by Rousseau's remark that 'one must be forced to be free' and, more generally, to the stark opposition he presents between the citizen (*citoyen*) and the individual in modern society (as bourgeois) pursues two lines of interpretation. First, though 'man is naturally good, and it is solely by [our] institutions that men become wicked' (*Lettres a Malesherbes*, cited in Cohen 1997: 102), Rousseau did not think that social life must be necessarily or inevitably corrupting. Equally important, the account of 'inflamed' *amour-propre* and the competition to which it gives rise does not mean that *amour-propre* is in sharp conflict with *amour de soi* or that Rousseau viewed it only negatively. On the contrary, Rousseau's considered view seems to have been that, given the right conditions, *amour-propre* could play a positive role in promoting social relations based on equality and mutual respect. Rather than a negative force, *amour-propre* is neutral in content and, again under the right conditions, could help secure enabling social bonds (*Emile*, IV.235; and Dent 2005: 105).

The second line in an alternative reading of Rousseau focuses attention on the 'right conditions' required for the development of individual autonomy in the context of social dependency. A full account requires a more careful analysis of the argument of the *Social Contract* than can be provided here, but a few general observations are in order. Rousseau did not think that just any political association could constitute itself as a political sovereign whose legislative judgments would express the 'general will'. On the one hand, Rousseau listed a number of social conditions that must be present, including general peace and stability, adequate resources, appropriate size, and relative equality of wealth. As importantly, Rousseau noted several epistemic or cognitive conditions that had to be satisfied if the opinion of the sovereign was to express the 'general will'. In particular, the members of the legislative assembly must be adequately informed in their deliberations, free to form their own opinions about the issue before the assembly, and committed to finding the common good. Further, the legislative assembly itself had to be free of factions or political parties (see *SC*, II.3). This all suggests that Rousseau's position demands a greater role for the rule of law and guarantee of civil liberties (thus enabling each member to form his own opinion) than is often assumed and that his notion of autonomy or self-rule is not expressed only in the idea of political autonomy (each member's equal voice in the legislative power) but includes dimensions of legal and civil liberty as well (see Neuhouser 1993). And, most importantly for our own purposes, it suggests that individual autonomy (self-rule) cannot be understood or realized without attention to other dimensions of autonomy. Rousseau's considered view seems to be that given human nature—or, given fundamental human interests (including an interest in liberty), autonomy can only be realized under some fairly demanding social and political conditions (Cohen 1986).

Despite this more sympathetic reading of Rousseau's views on autonomy, it might be claimed that difficult questions still remain. In particular, if autonomy involves forms of social recognition that in turn require, to put it mildly, rather demanding social conditions, doesn't this render Rousseau's account rather unattractive? Further, if individuals have become so corrupted and alienated by social conditions, what hope for reform can there be? Finally, doesn't this interpretation render Rousseau's account utopian in just the way that his critics have found so dangerous? Rousseau in fact seems to have been alert to these difficulties—and it is for this reason that his texts continue to be intriguing. For example, after having set out the demanding terms of the social contract mentioned above, Rousseau continues: 'How will a blind multitude, which often does not know what it wills because it rarely knows what is good for it, carry out an undertaking as great, as difficult, as a system of legislation?' (SC, II.6, p. 68). In sum, if the terms of the social contract require civic dispositions that themselves presuppose a society based on the contract, doesn't this produce an unhappy regress? Rousseau's response is to introduce the semi-divine Lawgiver whose distinguishing features include 'a superior intelligence who saw all of man's passions and experienced none of them, who had no relation to our nature yet knew it thoroughly, whose happiness was independent of us and who was nevertheless willing to care for ours' (II.7, p. 68). This Lawgiver is not a legislator who enacts positive law—that is a task reserved to the political sovereign—rather the figure refers to someone who through inspiration, example, and persuasion is able to bring about the civic dispositions and cultural mores that would support such law. Interestingly enough, a similar characterization is given of the tutor in *Emile*. There are many different readings of Rousseau at this point, including those claiming that he is a precursor of totalitarianism. However, far from appealing to the need for an historical (or ahistorical!) figure that would grant individuals their autonomy from on high, Rousseau is acknowledging the real challenge that his social conception of autonomy presents. Whether or not Rousseau believed in an actual state of nature, any return or access to it is forever cut off. Thus, if individuals are to extract themselves from their condition of slavery and alienation, it can only be through a kind of 'bootstrapping' process in which they attempt to design institutions that will allow for maximal self-rule (the absence of subordination to the will of another) while acknowledging the inevitability of social dependence. As Rousseau puts it in a relevant remark in *Emile*, 'One must use a great deal of art to prevent social man from being totally artificial' (IV. 317). Given the great extent to which individual aims and desires are shaped by social relationships and social conditions, the project of autonomy, if not short-circuited by appeal to limited forms of 'negative liberty', requires that greater attention be given to the complex ways that the various forms of subordination and domination (including cultural and political, as well as legal and economic) shape not only real opportunities (however these are measured) but subjective or psychological motivations and aspirations as well. It might fairly be argued that Rousseau placed too much faith in the ability of specifically political institutions to identify and overcome these forms of domination, but he is nevertheless the first to have been alert to the depth and complexity of such forms of domination. Further, contrary to the charge of collectivism or worse, Rousseau seems to have been aware of the importance of distinguishing between civil, legal, and political dimensions of autonomy, while also realizing that their complex interrelations needed to be kept in view. In sum, then, if freedom is conceived as autonomy—rather than a limited form of 'negative liberty'—the various dimensions of legal, political, civil, and personal autonomy must be considered, as well as the complex ways that they can impact on one another. This insight is one of the great legacies of Rousseau's reflections on autonomy.

## 2. KANT AND HEGEL

A conception of freedom as autonomy is also central to the practical philosophy of Immanuel Kant (1724–1804). However, despite his acknowledged indebtedness to Rousseau, Kant's primary concern is not how autonomy can be reconciled with social dependence. Rather, for Kant autonomy—'the property of the will by which it is a law to itself (independently of any property of the objects of volition)' (*Groundwork*, 440)—is primarily understood as the will's freedom or independence from domination by inclination or desire and then secondarily as independence from domination by others (Guyer 2003). In addition to this focus on the relation of the will to its ends or objects, Kant is also primarily (though not exclusively) concerned with moral autonomy in contrast to other forms of autonomy (personal, legal, political, etc.). Kant's categorical imperative ('Act only on that maxim [subjective principle of action] which you can at the same time will as a universal law') is introduced as an *a priori* principle of practical reason that can serve as the supreme principle or criterion for determining morally right action. Thus Kant develops the notion of autonomy in ways quite different from Rousseau. However, as others have pointed out, there remain nonetheless deep affinities in their thought (Cassirer 1970).

Kant's best-known discussion of autonomy is in the *Groundwork for the Metaphysics of Morals* (1785) where he argues that the 'supreme principle' of morality can be derived from the idea of practical reason or free agency. Briefly and schematically, Kant argues in this text that rational action or 'acting for a reason' (in contrast to causal necessitation) is only possible insofar as we are free or at least regard ourselves as free—in his phrase, 'act under the idea of freedom' (448). Freedom, however, does not mean arbitrary choice but rather the capacity to act from laws or principles that the agent proscribes or legislates to himself. Yet, Kant continues, the idea of acting from self-proscribed laws just is what moral action amounts to (as evidenced in the formulation of the categorical imperative above). Any other moral criterion—such as the promotion of general happiness—runs afoul of the unconditional respect that, according to Kant, we ascribe to moral agents on the basis of their capacity to will or 'set ends'. Though Kant's argument in this text can certainly be challenged at many levels—he himself later dismissed his supposed derivation of morality from our capacity for free agency or rational action as a failure (*Critique of Practical Reason*, 5:47)—there is no doubt that Kant located an understanding of freedom as autonomy at the basis of his conception of morality (Henrich 1994). Indeed, it is not misleading to describe his theory as a conception of morality as freedom (or autonomy) (Allison 1990).

One of the main difficulties emerging from Kant's account of autonomy in the *Groundwork* is that it was difficult to see how a person could be held responsible or accountable for an immoral act. If moral action is too closely identified with autonomous action, then it would seem that an immoral act for Kant must be heteronomous. But a heteronomous act, for Kant, is one for

*[handwritten annotation]* heteronomous morality is also known as moral relativism
autonomous morality is also known as moral relativism.

which the agent could not be blamed since he would not be acting for a reason or voluntarily but rather would simply be causally responding to his strongest incentive or desire. Kant also seems to have been aware of this difficulty and, at least by the time of *Religion within the Limits of Pure Reason* (1793), he distinguished between two conceptions of autonomy. According to the first conception, *Willkür* or the capacity for choice, an agent is autonomous (and hence responsible or accountable) if she acts on the basis of considerations that she 'incorporates' into her maxims or adopts as a reason for action. Thus, even this notion of *Willkür* already points to the agent's capacity for self-legislation or self-governance. However, according to the second conception of autonomy, *Wille*, an agent is only fully autonomous when the reasons for which she acts are ones that can be willed as universal laws or, in other words, are ones that survive testing by the categorical imperative (Nell 1975). This distinction between two forms of autonomy enables Kant to respond to the charge that agents can only be held responsible for moral actions. It also has the important additional consequence that it enables Kant (or a Kantian) to distinguish between moral autonomy and personal or individual autonomy in ways that have become important in more recent discussions of autonomy. An agent can be individually autonomous—act in ways for which she is accountable and which she may 'endorse' given her 'higher-order' aims and desires—even though she may fail to be fully morally autonomous—that is, the maxim of her action may not be one that can pass the categorical imperative test. It also enables Kant to distinguish between agency-autonomy (or minimal conditions for responsibility) and more demanding forms of autonomy (see section 4 below). Of course, distinguishing in this way between *Willkür* and *Wille* may mean that it will be even more difficult for Kant to show that the 'supreme principle' of morality can be derived from, or is even implicit in, the idea of agency-autonomy or rational agency *simpliciter*.

Kant's conception of morality as autonomy encounters other difficulties as well. First, given the close connection between freedom and morality on this view, it is hard to see why, from the agent's perspective, an individual should ever choose to act immorally. If in acting morally an individual expresses his autonomy or capacity for self-governance most fully why should he ever choose to act otherwise? In one form, of course, this is a version of the problem of evil but the common response that genuine freedom of choice requires the real possibility of evil is not readily available to Kant. This is because, as I mentioned above, freedom is not simply the capacity for arbitrary choice but rather the capacity to act on the basis of reasons the agent adopts and if that capacity is most fully realized when the reasons are universalizable Kant, it would seem, is hard pressed to explain why an individual should choose against such reasons. Surprisingly, Kant's response to this difficulty is in many respects close to Rousseau's. Evil, he argues, is not the result of an arbitrary individual decision but rather is much more inscrutable and seems to have its roots not in the individual but rather in the history of the species as a whole (*Religion*, 21). The principle of self-love (or what Rousseau called *amour-propre*) which, to be sure, an individual must also adopt or incorporate into his maxim if he is to be held responsible, competes with the principle of morality (or full autonomy) and Kant seems to have believed that it becomes a more compelling force in the emergence of civilized society with its emphasis on social distinction and the competition for goods and esteem. Thus, like Rousseau, Kant locates the failure to act morally not immediately in the individual will, but (at least in part) in society. However, perhaps more optimistically than Rousseau, Kant seems also to have held that such social competition—or what Kant called 'unsocial sociability'—might also serve as the occasion for the development of more widespread moral conduct and character (see 'Idea for a Universal History', 44–5; 'Perpetual Peace', 108–9; 'Theory and Practice', 90—all in *KPW*). Such a view of the more or less inscrutable origins of a predisposition for evil in social history also may have helped Kant in his insistence upon the absolute goodness of autonomy (*Wille*) even though individuals might use their autonomy (*Willkür*) for ignoble ends.

Another difficulty for Kant's conception of autonomy concerns his account of fully autonomous or moral action. According to the *Groundwork*, to act morally the motive or reason for the agent's action must be duty alone or 'duty for duty's sake' (see 398, and Herman 1981). Any other motive for moral action—such as the satisfaction that one might derive from doing what morality demands—tends to corrupt the moral worth of action and, it seems, should therefore be shunned. This has seemed to many to be an extremely demanding conception of morality—one, in fact, that exceeds normal human capacities—and, in an example made famous by Bernard Williams, requires 'one thought too many' (Williams 1981: 18). In the sort of example Williams has in mind, the beloved about to go down with a sinking ship does not wish to be saved by his lover because she has determined that it is both permissible and indeed a morally worthy act if done for the sake of duty alone. He wants his lover to save him *because* she loves him. Several discussions of this example by Kantians have attempted to make Kant's account of morality seem more attractive, some of which are more compelling than others. It must nonetheless be conceded that Kant's account of morality (and hence fully autonomous conduct) does make greater demands on individuals than do more popular accounts of morality. However, this only counts decisively against Kant's view if the demands of morality can be shown either to be humanly impossible or so to alter other centrally important interpersonal relations that it becomes unreasonable to expect general compliance. The verdict on that question, I think, is still out.

A final issue concerning Kant's account of moral autonomy concerns its relation to the other forms of autonomy noted in our discussion of Rousseau. As I mentioned above, the distinction between *Willkür* and *Wille* creates room for a notion of individual or personal autonomy that was not especially emphasized by Kant. Indeed, the further idea that quite different maxims might be morally permissible—that is, might equally pass the categorical imperative test—suggests greater room for pluralism than is usually associated with Kantian morality. More generally, Kant's distinction between the right and the good and his refusal to make the former dependent on the latter also opens the way for greater plurality at the level of personal autonomy or individual conceptions of the good life. However, the relation between moral autonomy and political autonomy (and hence the relation between morality and politics) in Kant's thought is also more complex than generally assumed. At least in his more popular reception, Kant (in contrast to Rousseau) did not maintain that the only possible reconciliation of individual autonomy and social dependence required political institutions based on popular sovereignty. Rather, he advocated a republican form of government (that is, one based on the separation of powers and rule of law, including guarantee of basic liberal rights: see 'Perpetual Peace', 100–1). Thus, in contrast to Rousseau who allowed for a more dynamic relation between public and private autonomy—or the rights of the ancients and the rights of the moderns—Kant apparently gives priority to the rights of the moderns by constraining democratic rule in connection with a morally specified set of natural rights. However, this interpretation of the relation between morality and politics has not gone unchallenged and some recent interpretations of Kant's political thought have sought to interpret the role of autonomy in a more dialectical manner—that is, in a way that (like Rousseau) allows for a more dynamic interplay between political and individual autonomy (Maus 2002 and Habermas 1996). However, it must also be conceded that Kant paid less attention to the multiple forms of autonomy (and the distinct forms of social recognition required for them) than did Rousseau before him or Hegel after him.

It is widely supposed that G. W. F. Hegel (1770–1831) introduced a novel and distinct conception of freedom, motivated in large part by his dissatisfaction with Kant's account and shaped in important ways by his own doctrine of speculative or absolute idealism. Hegel refers to his conception as 'absolute freedom'—in contrast to relative, partial, or dependent forms—or 'concrete freedom'—in contrast to the abstract or formal freedom primarily associated with Kant and Fichte—and, perhaps most enigmatically yet most importantly, he describes freedom as 'being at home with oneself in another' (*Logic*, §24A and *PR*, §7A). This last formulation, which Hegel also equates with the more familiar experiences of love and friendship, suggests for him both a unity of independence and dependence (or constraint) and an identity of indeterminacy (or universality) and determinacy (see *PR* §258A). Freedom as 'being at home with oneself in another' expresses, in short, Hegel's recognition of—and eventual response to—the problem of freedom formulated by Rousseau: namely, how is it that a person can be autonomous despite his inevitable dependence on others? Hegel's originality lies not in the fact that he proposed an alternative conception of freedom but in the fact that he distinguished among several elements in this general conception—including an important distinction between self-realization (or personal freedom) and self-determination (or moral autonomy, more narrowly conceived)—and argued that each element (and thus the general conception) requires distinct 'forms of recognition' embodied in social institutions and practices. In fact, Hegel accepts much in Kant's account of freedom as autonomy outlined above. In particular, he agrees that acting for a reason is a normative status rather than a causal psychological condition. He also agrees that to be accountable or responsible as an agent one must act for reasons that she in some sense 'endorses' (and that can thus be attributed to her) and hence that a fully autonomous person is one whose life is rationally self-governed (*PR*, §4 and 7). Rather, Hegel's disagreements with Kant have more to do with his view about how rational self-governance might be achieved and the overly abstract conception of moral autonomy connected with that view.

In a difficult and compact section of the *Phenomenology of Spirit* entitled 'The Moral Worldview' Hegel presents a series of sometimes puzzling criticisms of Kant's moral philosophy, several of which are later repeated in the *Philosophy of Right* in support of his claim that morality must be superseded by *Sittlichkeit* or ethical life. The best-known of these criticisms is the so-called 'emptiness charge' whose significance is still contested in the secondary literature. Some interpretations focus on Hegel's description of the CI-test as exclusively a test for logical contradictions and dismiss it as a caricature; while others focus on the motivational problems surrounding the idea of acting from duty for duty's sake (Wood 1990). However, there is a version of this charge that has, I think, not been sufficiently considered in the literature. This is Hegel's claim that, conceived as a general rule of action, the CI-test cannot by itself yield any determinate duties. Or, put slightly differently, that acting for a reason understood as 'acting under a rule' is not sufficient to determine the moral status of a particular act. On Kant's normative account of acting for reasons, there will always be a gap between the rule and the act such that the same act could be 'subsumed' under different rules and/or different acts could fall under the same rule (*Phenomenology*, §605 and 626). This is because the selection of an act-description is, according to Hegel, not exclusively an individual affair. Understood in this way, Hegel's emptiness charge anticipates the discussion about rule-following inspired by Wittgenstein's remarks and Kripke's later interpretation. It is not possible to identify privately the rule under which one acts or, indeed, meaningfully to claim that one is even acting *for* a reason. If one responds that the relevant act-description for testing is simply the maxim subjectively identified by the agent, this leads directly to Hegel's worries about an appeal to conscience in which any act can be rationalized and/or to what Hegel calls the 'beautiful soul' that finds itself unable to act for fear of tainting its pure intention (compare Nell 1975: 32 and *Phenomenology*, §632).

Similarly, if one considers Kant's account of full autonomy—the moral or rational self legislating a (universal) rule or law for itself—related difficulties in connection with the idea of rule-following arise. Is the idea of an agent imposing a rule on him- or herself any more coherent than the idea of following a rule alone? Doesn't a rule have to have a certain independence from my own will in order to bind my will? And if rules are thus independent doesn't that constitute a form of heteronomy? Kant attempted to address these concerns by sharply distinguishing between full moral autonomy (*Wille*) and my own particular endorsement of it and characterizing the former in terms of the pure form of all rational willing. But Hegel did not consider this to be a particularly promising strategy.

Hegel's own attempt to close the (normative) 'gap' between reason (as rule) and act, or to show how one can be constrained by norms yet remain autonomous, is to be found in his notion of recognition (*Anerkennung*) which is raised explicitly, though not for the first time, at the end of the section on

'The Moral Worldview' (*Phenomenology*, p. 408). Hegel's extension of Kant's insight that freedom is a normative status—specifically, acting from rules the agent gives to herself—is found in his claim that this sort of freedom is also a social status, that one cannot act 'under a rule' 'alone', and that individual freedom (as he develops it most notably in the master/slave dialectic) requires mutual or reciprocal recognition. Hegel's response to the emptiness charge and thus to the indeterminacy that haunts morality is, in short, to 'go social'.

Two points should be noted about Hegel's social or recognitional account of autonomy. First, freedom, for Hegel, is not only a normative status—it is also, for that reason, a social status. A person cannot 'act for a reason' 'privately'. To act 'under a rule' or 'for a reason' is fundamentally to be accountable or 'answerable' to others; it requires being recognized or treated as a 'reason-giver' by other 'reason-givers' or to be located, as Wilfred Sellars put it, within the 'space of reasons'. Secondly, Hegel maintains that 'concrete freedom' requires not just any social form of recognition, but rather a differentiated account of distinct yet mutually supporting forms of recognition. Such an account would also show how, without appeal to an independently given order, these forms of recognition, taken together, are rational to the extent that they serve to unite or combine what Hegel calls the subjective and objective aspects of freedom (*PR*, §258). These two aspects correspond roughly to Kant's distinction between *Willkür* and *Wille*—that is, the need for the subject to 'incorporate' a rule of action into his maxim, to pursue his own good, or to satisfy what Hegel calls the 'right of subjectivity or particularity' and the requirement that the action conform to the 'right of objectivity' or satisfy the demand of reason or the requirement of public or intersubjective validation (see *PR*, §132A). The *Philosophy of Right* can instructively be read as an argument for the forms of recognition required for realizing these two interdependent aspects of autonomy.

The main contours of Hegel's argument for this alternative conception of autonomy can be briefly summarized: 'Abstract Right', the first section of the *Philosophy of Right*, introduces the most formal and minimal mode of recognition. The social status mutually attributed to members is that of legal persons with basic rights, including the right to own property and form contracts. However, this relatively simple form of recognition, which brackets all subjective motives and intentions of actors, is incomplete and unstable without the introduction of further, distinctively moral concepts (*PR*, §141). In particular, the appearance of crime in the community is described as a conflict between the 'particular' will of the individual and the 'universal' will of the community and its punishment points to the need for an 'impartial' judge. An impartial judge, however, implies the idea of a will in which particularity and universality are united or what Hegel calls a 'moral will'.

The section on 'Morality', by far the most difficult, covers a range of phenomena but its central theme is the development of an account of the moral will (Kant's full autonomy) that begins roughly with Kant's notion of *Willkür* or the idea that a person is only responsible for an action if she can recognize it as her own. Hegel refers to this as the right of subjectivity or subjective insight (*PR*, §132). However, as he argued in the *Phenomenology*, even this form of freedom (what finally takes shape as self-realization) requires yet finds itself in conflict with forms of recognition that also require treating others (and oneself) as 'self-determining', that is, as subjects who are not only free to pursue their own good but also 'rational' in the sense that their action-plans should also conform to the 'general will', be universal or, in Hegel's phrase, satisfy the equal 'right of objectivity' (132A). The moral will is thus inherently unstable and indeterminate and, as Hegel illustrates in particular in connection with the collision between welfare and right, gives rise to distinctively modern forms of ethical tragedy: Tragic conflicts are not simply the result of fate in the classical sense, but are an inevitable consequence of tensions within the modern conception of freedom or autonomy itself—conflicts, in short, between self-realization and self-determination.

The third and final section, 'Sittlichkeit', outlines the differentiated forms of recognition that are required to deal with indeterminacy and to mediate these conflicting aspects of the moral will (subjectivity and objectivity). The forms of recognition in the family, civil society, and a constitutional state serve to 'concretize' or make determinate the moral will and thereby mitigate (at least partially) tragic conflict. It is for this reason that Hegel claims that freedom or autonomy is finally realized or actualized in the state (*PR*, §257, §260). Much of the continuing debate regarding the 'transition' or '*Aufhebung*' from morality to *Sittlichkeit* concerns whether it leaves morality behind in favor of something else or whether it provides the conditions under which morality, at least in a limited form, can be realized (Siep 1983). However, details aside, it should be relatively clear that what Hegel presents is not a radical alternative to Kant's conception of freedom as autonomy, but rather a more developed account of the specific forms of recognition (and their corresponding social institutions) required to realize his notion of rational self-governance.

# 3. NIETZSCHE, SARTRE, AND HEIDEGGER

It might seem strange to turn next to Friedrich Nietzsche (1844–1900) for an interpretation of freedom as autonomy. Nietzsche denies that individuals possess a 'free will' and he is equally dismissive of the idea of the self as a subject or unified center of agency. It seems, then, that his philosophy leaves no room for a conception of autonomy. Further, Nietzsche is even more vehement in denying that a universal morality (such as Kant's) could have anything to do with autonomy (*Anti-Christ*, 11). Kantian morality—like its Christian predecessor—represents a form of heteronomy in which the individual is made subordinate to the will of others. Yet, despite these views, Nietzsche does not simply dismiss the idea of freedom as autonomy (or 'self-mastery'); rather, in critically examining the idea of a self that gives itself 'laws', he pushes both terms in the idea of 'self-rule' to their extremes. Autonomy, for Nietzsche, is ultimately not a form of 'self-governance' in any straightforward sense and certainly not a subordination of the self to universal laws. Rather, it is a process of disciplined self-experimentation in which the individual imposes stylistic unity or form upon himself in an unending process of self-creation and self-definition. In fact, however paradoxically, in the most demanding exercise of 'self-overcoming'—the willing of the eternal return of the same—the individual does not strive to rule or master himself, but rather wills his own dispersal into the world from which he emerged and of which he is a part. Thus, without wholly rejecting a notion of freedom as autonomy, Nietzsche exposes both its unseemly origins in history and its paradoxical limits.

*On The Genealogy of Morals* (1887) is a sustained attack on the popular conception of morality and agency and Kant's attempt to give that conception a rational grounding. The popular conception holds that individuals are morally accountable agents who can be praised or blamed for their conduct to the extent that it issues from their own free choice. Moreover, on this conception, moral conscience is a natural and relatively accurate guide for determining right action and, via experiences of guilt, curbing violations of the moral code. Kant's moral philosophy, as we have seen, attempts to justify this popular conception of morality and, through the categorical imperative, provide a criterion for moral conscience when it is corrupted or led astray (*Groundwork*, 390).

Nietzsche challenges both the popular conception and the Kantian justification. Conscience, Nietzsche argues, is not the natural voice of moral duty;

rather it is the product of a long (and largely contingent) process of social evolution. It reflects the triumph of the contrast between good and evil over the contrast between good and bad, and, in connection with a long slave revolt against the nobility, the imposition of a 'herd morality' by the masses on the stronger class (*GM*, I.11 and 16; see also *Human*, §45, and *Gay Science*, I.117). Similarly, popular belief in a free will arose in connection with a practice of punishment that demands that the punished accept responsibility for his deed. The free or sovereign agent then is not a distinct subject existing prior to its action; it is rather a fictitious idea postulated at the end of a 'long chain of events' to serve certain social demands.

For just as the popular mind separates the lightning from its flash and takes the latter for an *action*, for the operation of a subject called lightning, so popular morality also separates strength from expressions of strength, as if there were a neutral substratum behind the strong man, which was *free* to express strength or not to do so. But there is no such substratum; there is no 'being' behind the doing, effecting, becoming; 'the doer' is merely a fiction added to the deed—the deed is everything. (*GM* I.13, see also *GM* II.2 and *BGE* I.19)

Still, much like Marx's own appreciation of the truly revolutionary character of the bourgeoisie—before whom 'all that is solid melts into air'—Nietzsche's critique of the 'sovereign individual' contains an element of admiration as well. One passage is worth quoting at length:

If we place ourselves at the end of this tremendous process, where the tree at last brings forth fruit, where society and the morality of custom at last reveal what they have simply been the means to: then we discover that the ripest fruit is the sovereign individual, like only to himself, liberated again from morality of custom, autonomous and supramoral (for autonomous and moral are mutually exclusive), in short the man who has his own independent, protracted will and the right to make promises. . . . (*GM* II.2)

It is not possible simply to dismiss this passage as a case of irony; Nietzsche's praise of the 'strong' or 'healthy' will and, more generally, the 'free spirit' suggest otherwise (*GS*, §347; *EH*, 'Human', sec. 1; see White 1997).

Nietzsche is even more ruthless in his rejection of Kant's claim that a universal and impersonal principle can be derived from this fiction of a rational agent (a 'doer'):

What? You admire the categorical imperative within you? This 'firmness' of your so-called moral judgment? This 'unconditional' feeling that 'here everyone must judge as I do'? Rather admire your selfishness at this point. And the blindness, pettiness, and frugality of your selfishness. For it is selfish to experience one's own judgment as a universal law; and this selfishness is blind, petty, and frugal because it betrays that you have not yet discovered yourself nor created for yourself an ideal of you own, your very own—for that could never be somebody else's and much less that of all, all! (*GS*, §335)

The details of his Kant interpretation can be disputed, but Nietzsche's objection to the claim that a principle of universalizability can be derived from free agency is one he repeats (see *AC*, §11) and one that others have made as well. For Nietzsche every action is unique and not identical with any other, so there cannot be a general rule for all action. Moreover, to assume that such a rule exists, or to suppose that one acts rightly (and thus for Kant most freely) only when one acts from such a rule, is to deny what is most unique and distinctive about humans—namely the capacity for self-definition or self-creation. The passage from *The Gay Science* continues: 'We, however, *want to become those we are*—human beings who are new, unique, incomparable, who give themselves laws, who create themselves.'

This last sentence points again to an important ambivalence in Nietzsche's assessment of Kant. On the one hand, Kant's idea of an impersonal moral-ity—the categorical imperative—continues to reflect a Christian asceticism that retreats from life to an abstract (and false) universality. Further, it allows him to reintroduce, now as practical postulates, all that he had rejected in his critique of metaphysics—God, the soul, freedom, and immortality (GS, §335). Yet, Nietzsche also acknowledges that Kant's 'Copernican revolution' was an expression of (at least Kant's own?) freedom: 'Yet it had been his strength and cleverness that had broken open the [metaphysical, ascetic] cage' (*GS*, §335). Curiously, in the same passage, Nietzsche states that to be self-creators and 'to become who we are' we need also to become 'physicists'. His point seems to be that autonomy does not lead us away from the world (into abstract metaphysics) but more deeply into the world and to a more honest assessment of our natural origins.

Thus despite his criticisms of popular morality and Kant, it is difficult to read Nietzsche as abandoning any conception of agency or entirely rejecting autonomy as an ideal (Janaway 1991). On the contrary, some conception of agency seems indispensable to his (positive) account of the 'free spirit', expressed in ideas of the will to power, the Overman, and the eternal return of the same. Nietzsche's criticisms are rather directed against the idea that there is a pre-given, deeper, or even 'rational' self that should be allowed to express itself (perhaps in opposition to competing natural impulses) and the idea that autonomy is acting under general rules that this truer self gives to itself. Autonomy is better conceived in terms of the work of a creative artist who, often as the result of great discipline and effort, fashions from what she has a new work of art and even a new set of terms or criteria by which it is to be judged.

How is this idea of creative self-experimentation related to Nietzsche's injunction, 'become who you are' (GS, §§270 and 335)? Though there is some tension between these two ideas, the latter demand should not be seen as presupposing a potential waiting to unfold—like the potential of an acorn to become an oak tree. Nietzsche rejects that view of the self. On the other hand, Nietzsche did not think that we could create ourselves *ex nihilo* and, more importantly, he did not think we were free to become whatever we might choose. Rather, he saw in the widespread desire to become other than what we are an expression of the ascetic denial of life and opposed to it his doctrine of *amor fati* or love of one's fate. 'My formula for greatness in a human being is *amor fati*: that one wants nothing to be different, not forward, not backward, not in all eternity' (EH, 'Why I am So Clever', 10). Indeed, it is in connection with this idea that the ethical significance of Nietzsche's views on eternal recurrence become clear:

The greatest weight. What, if some day or night a demon were to steal after you into our loneliest loneliness and say to you: 'This life as you now live it and have lived it, you will have to live once more and innumerable times more; and there will be nothing new in it, but every pain and every joy and every thought and sight and everything unutterably small or great in your lie will have to return to you, all in the same succession and sequence—even this spider and this moonlight between the trees, and even this moment and I myself. The eternal hourglass of existence is turned upside down again and again, and you with it, speck of dust!'

Would you not throw yourself down and gnash your teeth and curse the demon who spoke thus? Or have you once experienced a tremendous moment when you would have answered him: 'You are a god and never have I heard anything more divine.' If this thought gained possession of you, it would change you as you are or perhaps crush you. The question in each and every thing, 'Do you desire this once more and innumerable times more?' would lie upon your actions as the greatest weight. Or how well disposed would you have to become to yourself and to life to crave nothing more fervently than this ultimate eternal confirmation and seal? (GS, §341)

As others have noted, the doctrine of eternal recurrence is Nietzsche's alternative to Kant's categorical imperative (Welshon 2004). We are to ask ourselves not whether the maxim of our action is universalizable, but whether we could will that our action, with all that led up to it and all that follows from it, be just as it is eternally and without regret. Understood in connection with *amor fati* and eternal recurrence, the injunction to 'become who you are' does not conflict with his idea of self-creation. Rather, it reflects his view of what it means to be life-affirming. For Nietzsche, autonomy does not mean the freedom to become whatever we want (and, to repeat, popularly understood to mean, 'anything but what I am now!'); rather, it means a playful (if nonetheless serious and disciplined) experimentation with what nature or fate has given us. Autonomy so conceived is a long way from Kant's notion of morality as freedom and from Rousseau's conception of the free republican citizen. It is rather an ideal of personal autonomy paradoxically poised between radical self-creation and a playful abandonment or dispersal ('self-overcoming') of the individual in the world—or, in more Nietzschean terms, between Apollonian mastery and Dionysian dispossession (White). As we shall see, the tensions and limits in Nietzsche's conception of individual autonomy reappear in later continental European thought. In particular, in the writings of Sartre and Heidegger one can also find the same ambivalent relationship to the Kantian tradition and attempts to radicalize it. In both, we see an attempt to formulate a conception of personal autonomy in isolation from forms of moral and political autonomy. However, despite their important contribution to an ideal of personal autonomy, these authors underscore as well the difficulty of formulating an attractive conception of individual autonomy in isolation from these other forms and apart from the structures of recognition that sustain them.

In *Being and Nothingness* (1943) and 'Existentialism is a Humanism' (1946) Jean-Paul Sartre (1905–80) defends a conception of freedom as autonomy that is in some respects close to Kant's conception of agency-autonomy (or *Willkür*) but quite different in others. Like Kant, freedom is a condition (or status) more or less naturally assigned to an individual. At least in Sartre's earlier period, it is not a condition that depends at all on one's social circumstance. Rather, though we find ourselves simply 'thrown' into the world, any and every response to that world (including indifference) counts as a free choice. 'Man is condemned to be free' (*BN*, 707) is Sartre's more dramatic version of the Kantian claim that freedom is a 'fact' (*Faktum*) known by all finite rational beings. It is not up to us whether to regard ourselves as free; but, for Sartre, everything else about our existence is a matter of choice ('Existentialism', 41). Moreover, this freedom is radical in a twofold sense: Choice is not constrained by any prior conception of human nature, so that you are only free to the extent that you choose in accordance with that conception—that is, 'existence precedes essence'. And, second, the responsibility that follows from any and every decision is absolute. We are, Sartre says, responsible not only for actions that are in some relevant sense our own but also for the entire world. There are no unintended 'accidents' or 'unforeseen consequences' on the basis of which we might excuse ourselves. Even if my country goes to war it is 'my war' and simply 'for lack of getting out of it—Sartre suggests, for example, by suicide—I have *chosen* it' (*BN*, 708). This is a far more demanding notion of responsibility than Kant's and more demanding even than the utilitarian view of 'negative responsibility' (criticized by Bernard Williams) according to which all that matters for establishing responsibility is whether our action can make a difference (Williams and Smart 1973). Or, one might say that for Sartre radical freedom entails that the entire world into which you have been thrown *is* your 'ground-project' and thus you are completely responsible for it. Even the person who is in a situation of 'bad faith'—someone, that is, who denies his responsibility for a situation—is in that situation because he has 'put himself' there.

Somewhat surprisingly, Sartre also attempts to derive a moral obligation from this idea of radical freedom. On the one hand, there are no binding values apart from those that I as an individual create through my choice. However, for Sartre, this conception of freedom does not produce a condition of licence or indifference to others. In a manner reminiscent of Kant, Sartre claims that

I can take freedom as my goal only if I take that of others as a goal as well. Consequently, when, in all honesty, I've recognized that man is a being in whom existence precedes essence, that he is a free being who, in various circumstances, can want only his freedom, I have at the same time recognized that I can want only the freedom of others. ('Existentialism', 58)

In fact, Sartre defends an ethics that is even more stringent than Kant's. For Kant, not all universalizable maxims establish obligations or prohibitions; most establish permissions. Yet, Sartre's reasoning seems only to have obligations in mind:

If existence precedes essence, and if we grant that we exist and fashion our image at one and the same time, the image is valid for everybody and for our whole age. Thus, our responsibility is much greater than we might have supposed, because it involves all mankind. ... For every man, everything happens as if all mankind had its eyes fixed on him and were guiding itself by what he does. ('Existentialism', 37 and 39)

Sartre's conception of autonomy is thus in significant ways more radical than Kant's. And, if his arguments are valid, it leads to an ethics that is both more demanding and more stringent than Kant's. It is also, arguably, more individualistic. Whereas Kant held that reasoning was something that depended on the presence of other agents and thus that freedom, to the extent that it is a fact of reason, is also a status that depends on the recognition of others, Sartre claims that 'freedom as the definition of man does not depend on others' ('Existentialism', 58). In this sense, he is more Cartesian than Kantian—that is, freedom is an individual conscious phenomenon rather than a normative status or standing.

In his later writings, however, Sartre came to have some reservations about the radical freedom he advocated in the 1940s and 1950s. In an interview with the *New Left Review* in 1969 Sartre described as 'incredible' his earlier remark that 'Whatever the circumstances, and wherever the site, a man is always free to be a traitor or not' and suggested that it must have been due to the particular circumstances of the Resistance he was in at the time (Sartre 1979: 34). The change in his thinking was most likely owing to a greater appreciation for the role of society and socialization in shaping individuals and, more specifically, the result of his attempt to integrate the insights of Marxism with his existentialism. In the *Critique of Dialectical Reason* (1960) he writes,

there can be no doubt that one *makes oneself* a bourgeois. . . . But in order to make oneself bourgeois, one must be bourgeois. . . . Individuals find an existence already sketched out for them at birth; they 'have their position in life and their personal development assigned to them by their class' (Marx). What is assigned to them is . . . a fundamental attitude, as well as a determinate provision of material and intellectual tools; it is a strictly limited field of possibilities. (231–2)

Yet, even if one is not completely free to choose who one is, even if who we are is to a large extent the product of environmental circumstance and social position, we are nonetheless, according to Sartre, always responsible for what one *makes* of oneself: 'For I believe that a man can always make something out of what is made of him. This is the limit I would today accord to freedom: the small movement which makes of a totally conditioned social being someone who does not render back completely what his conditioning has given him. Which makes of Genet a poet when he had been rigorously conditioned to be a thief' (Sartre 1979: 35). Among other things, one can discern in this passage a shift in Sartre from something like freedom as an irrevocable and totalizing condition to an understanding of freedom as a limited achievement under constraints. A person is autonomous to the extent that he or she is able to find (or establish) some reconciliation or harmony between what he is and what he can become. Such reconciliation does not mean acquiescence, but it does mean acknowledgement of the fact that we are not free to make of ourselves whatever we choose. More importantly, however, even this notion of autonomy as a limited achievement under constraints is not exclusively an individual affair, for it depends on the forms of recognition that others sustain as well. Although some commentators have suggested that Sartre made some gestures toward such a social conception of freedom—autonomy as '*mitsein*' (being with another)—this is not a theme to which Sartre gave any sustained attention in his published work. For that reason, Sartre's account is ultimately not an intersubjective or recognitional model like that found in Rousseau or Hegel.

In *Being and Time* (1927) Martin Heidegger (1889–1976) developed a notion of radical freedom or 'resoluteness' (*Entschlossenheit*) similar to Sartre's view in *Being and Nothingness*. Of course, this is not surprising since Sartre's own position is much indebted to Heidegger's work. The similarities are often overlooked, however, not only because Heidegger denied that he was an existentialist, but also because Heidegger's principal aim in that work is to move beyond a basic Cartesian ontology that sharply contrasts the 'for-itself' and the 'in-itself' in favor of a novel inquiry into the 'meaning of Being'. Nonetheless, Heidegger's *Dasein* (human being) is also an entity that finds itself 'thrown' into the world and knows itself not through an infallible act of introspection but 'always already' in the midst of an environment (*Umwelt*) toward which it has a wide range of moods, understandings, and expectations. The transition from the question of (the meaning of) being to the 'existential analytic of *Dasein*'—that is, the clarification of the ways of *Dasein*'s 'being-in-the world'—is based on Heidegger's somewhat controversial claim that an answer to the former can only be acquired through an analysis of the latter since *Dasein* is unique in that 'in its very Being, that Being is an issue for it' (§2). Whatever the merit of this claim, Heidegger proceeds to an analysis of *Dasein* and the now familiar characterizations of 'being toward Death', care, anxiety, etc. For our own purposes, what is important is that *Dasein* is also fundamentally confronted with the authenticity of its mode of existence. According to Heidegger, most of us live our lives without asking about its meaning. We pass our lives as part of an anonymous crowd—'the One' or 'they' (*Das Man*)—and rarely if ever question the norms and practices into which we are socialized. It is often only in the individual's confrontation with his own mortality that the question of the meaning of his existence and whether he chooses to live authentically is raised. However, the difficulties posed by this idea of authentic choice can be seen in the following passage:

With *Dasein*'s lostness in the 'they', that factical potentiality-for-Being which is closest to it (the tasks, rules, and standards, the urgency and extent, of concernful and solicitous Being-in-the-world) has already been decided upon. The 'they' has always kept *Dasein* from taking hold of these possibilities of Being. The 'they' even hides the manner in which it has tacitly relieved *Dasein* of the burden of explicitly choosing these possibilities. It remains indefinite who has 'really' done the choosing. So *Dasein* makes no choices, gets carried along by the nobody, and thus ensnares itself in inauthenticity.

This process can be reversed only if *Dasein* specifically brings itself back to itself from its lostness in the 'they'. But this bringing-back must have that kind of Being by the neglect of which *Dasein* has lost itself in inauthenticity. When *Dasein* thus brings itself back from the 'they', the they-self is modified in an existentiell manner so that it becomes authentic Being-one's-Self. This must be accomplished by making up for not choosing. But 'making up' for not choosing signifies choosing to make this choice—deciding for a potentiality-for-Being, and making this decision from one's own self. In choosing to make this choice, *Dasein* makes possible, first and foremost, its authentic potentiality-for-Being (*BT*, 312–13).

Two comments on this passage are in order. First, this characterization of authentic choice (autonomy) is merely formal and does not impose any substantive constraints on choice. In this sense, it seems that one could even authentically choose to live inauthentically, to remain carried along by *das Man*. Although one might question whether this is a genuine option for Heidegger, his stated position is clear: 'But on what basis does *Dasein* disclose itself in resoluteness? On what is it to resolve? Only the resolution itself can give the answer' (BT, 345). In response to Heidegger's call for resolute choice, it is reported that his students joked, 'We are resolute, we only don't know what for' (Lowith 1994: 30 and Tugendhat 1986: 207). In other words, it seems that there are no other constraints on authentic choice than resoluteness itself.

Second, while Heidegger is clear that authenticity requires resolute choice and suggests that inauthenticity is rather something that happens to *Dasein*— '*Dasein* makes no choices, gets carried along by the nobody, and thus ensnares itself in inauthenticity'—the danger of an infinite regress is close at hand. If the decision for authenticity must be 'from one's own self' it would seem that this self must already be authentic for otherwise it would not be one's *own* self who has decided. Yet for this prior self to be authentic, it too must result from a resolute decision, etc. If, on the other hand, it is not one's *own* self that chooses, if one is 'ensnared' in the One, it is not clear how any particular decision, no matter how resolute, could bring about a condition of authenticity. That is, unless individuals possess a basic agency-autonomy or capacity for (authentic) choice (even in their inauthenticity) it is not clear how any particular decision, no matter how 'resolute', transforms their mode of existence into an authentic one. (Charles Guignon, in responding to this difficulty, suggests that Heidegger distinguishes between the authentic Self (as the capacity for authentic choice) and 'authentic being-one's-Self' (as the specific modification or *existentiell* that an individual chooses (Guignon 2004). Although his suggestion addresses the problem, it is less obvious that it is Heidegger's own position.)

For reasons that are still debated, in writings that begin not too long after the publication of *Being and Time* Heidegger distanced himself from his earlier position. Heidegger himself suggested that that work remained too entangled in the metaphysical tradition he sought to overcome. In particular, he thought that the prominent position assigned to *Dasein* contributed to an understanding of it that was still too 'subjectivistic' and still too close to a view of the self as a self-determining agent or will (see Olafson 1987: 155 f., 169). In his 'Letter on Humanism' (1947), which is partly a response to Sartre, Heidegger (1977) denied that he was existentialist or an atheist. More importantly, he also claimed that the discussion in *Being and Time* was misleading in that it suggested that *Dasein* had some responsibility or control over the fate of either Being or beings. 'Man is not the lord of beings. Man is the shepherd of Being' (221). 'Man does not decide whether and how beings appear' (210); rather, 'he gains the essential poverty of the shepherd, whose dignity consists in being called by Being itself into the preservation of Being's truth. The call comes as the throw from which the thrownness of Da-sein derives' (221–3). These passages and many others similar to them after Heidegger's *Kehre* or turn are difficult to understand. However, the general point seems to be that Heidegger did not believe that he had moved sufficiently beyond a metaphysics in which a knowing and acting subject strives to master a world standing over against it. Heidegger maintains that it is this metaphysics of the subject (epitomized in Nietzsche's will to power) that is at the basis of the technological world-picture that has so captivated the modern age ('Question'). In this period Heidegger goes so far as to suggest that freedom is not a property of man at all; rather, it is the 'letting be' of Being that makes possible its disclosure or truth (*aletheia*) to *Dasein* ('Question', 330 and 'Essence', 127). *Dasein* is the site of an event (*Ereignis*) that happens; not the locus of reflective choice, however constrained that choice might be by temporal, social, or bodily circumstances. It is not hard to see in this contrast between *Dasein*'s resoluteness in *Being and Time* and Heidegger's discussion of human freedom after the *Kehre* something like the polarity we observed in Nietzsche's account of the Overman and eternal recurrence—that is, the contrast between a radical freedom in which one is responsible for one's entire destiny and a notion of self-dispossession in which the individual will merges with the world, the eternal recurrence, or the destiny of Being. Indeed, there is some evidence that Heidegger was aware of this parallel himself, sometimes reading Nietzsche's Overman as the 'civil servant of technology' and hence the final shape of a metaphysics of will to power and, at other times, interpreting it as the true 'shepherd of Being' (see Haar 1996). Thus, also like Nietzsche, Heidegger's reflections on the authentic self point to the opposing extremes of a self-*definition* as pure assertion and calculability—or a 'self-preservation without a self' (Horkheimer 1947, p.128)—and a self-*discovery* in which the self is dispersed in or returned to the world from which it arose. In both cases, they also highlight the difficulty of conceptualizing individual autonomy (or authenticity) in isolation from other forms of autonomy and their corresponding forms of recognition.

# 4. SOME CONTEMPORARY DEVELOPMENTS

Contemporary work on autonomy has tended to focus on personal (or individual) autonomy rather than its other forms. This is the result of the influential work of Harry Frankfurt, Gerald Dworkin, Charles Taylor, and others who, by introducing a hierarchical or 'split-level' conception, offered a new approach to the topic of personal autonomy (see Christman 1989 and Taylor 1995). Roughly speaking, on this approach, a person acts autonomously if her 'higher-order desires' stand in an appropriate relation to her 'lower-order' or ground-floor desires (the desires that are effective in action). Different hierarchical accounts then characterize this appropriate relation differently—as one of reflective endorsement, 'whole-hearted identification'', integration, etc. Other proposals have suggested that such 'structural' accounts are inadequate since they do not consider the way in which the agent acquired the preferred motivational structure. Thus, it has been argued that even if a person identifies with her ground-floor desires in the appropriate manner, if the identification came about in a way that disrupts certain basic cognitive or other competences (irrational means, self-deception, etc.) then she may fail to act autonomously (Christman 1991). Further, particularly in connection with some recent feminist approaches, it has also been suggested that hierarchical accounts fail to meet our intuitions about personal autonomy if they do not include various substantive constraints on preference-formation as well (Stoljar 2002). Accordingly, we can distinguish broadly between procedural and substantive accounts of individual autonomy. Further distinctions can then be made, within procedural accounts, between structural and historical views and, within substantive accounts, between those that propose substantive constraints (Stoljar 2002) and those that propose specific substantive norms that must be part of the content of the autonomous agents motivational structure (Wolf 2005).

However, a survey of the literature reveals not only that there are many competing conceptions of personal autonomy but also that there is a variety of motivations for their introduction. This creates a serious challenge since if we are to assess competing conceptions it is important to ask what purpose or role the proposed account is intended to serve. Sometimes a conception of autonomy is introduced as an ideal of human flourishing or a description of when a person can be said to be 'leading a life of her own'. Other accounts are introduced in connection with a specification of the conditions of moral responsibility or accountability. Still other accounts seek to specify something like the necessary and/or sufficient conditions of basic agency. In this last context, one sometimes finds the term 'agency autonomy' or 'rational agency' or even 'ultra-minimal personal autonomy', where the idea is that someone who lacks autonomy in the specified sense is then not properly an agent and her behavior not fully an action (Gaus 2005: 295). Further, some accounts associate autonomy with a capacity or set of capacities, while others refer to the actual performance of individuals, raising the question of whether a person can have a capacity for autonomy even though he fails to exercise it on a particular occasion. Finally, some accounts of autonomy treat it primarily as a psychological phenomenon, while others refer to it as a normative authority, status, or right that individuals might claim for themselves or be granted by others. It is unlikely that any single conception can serve all of these demands and thus the question, 'How can any of my actions genuinely be my own?' (Benson 2005)—initially seemingly straightforward—cannot be answered without first specifying the purposes for which we seek an account. In fact, it is not uncommon to see in the literature a shift from one role or purpose to the other.

In this final section, I will consider this difficulty in connection with some recent proposals for relational or recognitional accounts of (personal) autonomy (see Mackenzie and Stoljar 2000, and Christman and Anderson 2005). These accounts are primarily presented as ideals of human flourishing or living a life that is one's own in an important sense, but this is not consistently the case, and so it is important to ask again what role the account is intended to play. Paul Benson, to cite one example, links his relational account to the conditions of moral responsibility, whereas Joel Anderson and Axel Honneth (2005) present their account not only as a view of human flourishing but also as a basis for claims to a revised account of social justice. Finally, some relational accounts seem primarily aimed at criticizing dimensions of autonomy they believe have been neglected in more traditional or 'individualistic' accounts (without otherwise specifying the proposed aim of the alternative account) (Barclay 2000). In all these accounts, there is certainly an air of paradox to the claim that a person can be living a life of his or her *own* only if he or she stands in certain kinds of social relations with others—though, as we have seen, it is an idea that goes back at least to Rousseau and Hegel.

Among relational or recognitional accounts, I call those accounts 'weakly' recognitional that emphasize the importance of various social relations for the development and exercise of autonomy, and those accounts 'strongly' recognitional that also include relational or recognitional elements within the conception of autonomy or make these elements 'constitutive' for autonomy (see also Benson 2005: 119). Thus, as others have noted, many traditional philosophical accounts of individual autonomy are at least *weakly* recognitional—indeed, it is hard to see how any plausible account could deny the developmental role social relations can play (see Friedman 1997 and Barclay 2000). However, *strongly* recognitional accounts are both more controversial and more difficult to characterize. Some take their cue from various 'communitarian' insights (Taylor, MacIntyre, and Sandel, discussed critically in Barclay 2000); others do not (Habermas 1992, Pettit and Smith 1996, Benson 2000).

In the remainder of this essay, I will focus on *strongly* recognitional models and consider two different (non-communitarian) approaches. The first model construes autonomy in terms of something like the bare or minimal conditions of agency or rational agency. This approach can be found in Jürgen Habermas's *Theory of Communicative Action*, where he contrasts the idea of purposive or instrumental action with a model of action defined in terms of the actor's readiness to give reasons for his action when called upon to do so (or what he calls 'communicative action') (Habermas 1984: 286). This idea of communicative action implies a fairly minimal notion of agency-autonomy (the capacity to justify or give reasons) and yet is also clearly *strongly* recognitional since justification is always justification to others. Moreover, in other writings, Habermas appeals to this minimal notion of communicative autonomy in the derivation of the basic moral principle of his discourse ethics (Habermas 1990: ch. 3) and in his argument for a basic principle of political legitimacy (Habermas 1996: 445). In each case, the strategy is to begin with a fairly minimal conception of rational agency in order to bootstrap from it to more demanding normative principles and richer notions of autonomy (e.g., moral, political, and personal). It is, of course, a controversial approach, with similarities to Kant's attempt to derive a moral principle from the idea of agency-autonomy or rational action *simpliciter*.

The second recognitional model is more robust in character and is presented in the context of a general ideal of human flourishing. For example, Anderson and Honneth write:

> The key initial insight of social or relational accounts of autonomy is that full auton-omy—the real and effective capacity to develop and pursue one's own conception of a worthwhile life—is achievable only under socially supportive conditions. It is an impressive accomplishment that, on the path from helpless infancy to mature autonomy, we come to be able to trust our own feelings and intuitions, to stand up for what we believe in, and to consider our projects and accomplishments worthwhile. (2005: 130)

Initially, it might seem that their account is only *weakly* recognitional, since the passage stresses the social conditions 'supportive' for autonomy. However, it is clear that their account is also intended to be *strongly* recognitional. Under the rubrics of 'self-trust', 'self-respect", and 'self-esteem', they then go on to describe a 'recognitional infrastructure' (133) that is required not only for the acquisition of a set of competences, but is also central to those competences.

> Self trust, self-respect, and self-esteem are thus neither purely beliefs about oneself nor emotional states, but are emergent properties of a dynamic process in which individuals come to experience themselves as having a certain status, be it an object of concern, a responsible agent, a valued contributor to shared projects, or what have

you. One's relationship to oneself, then, is not a matter of a solitary ego reflecting on itself, but is the result of an ongoing intersubjective process, in which one's attitude toward oneself emerges in one's encounter with an other's attitude toward oneself. (131)

A striking feature of this account is how far it extends beyond specifying minimal conditions of agency. The ideal of individual autonomy involves a wide range of capacities, including not only the 'capability to stand up in public without shame' but also an 'openness to both a multiplicity of internal voices and a variety of communicative relations to [one's inner life]' and a 'semantic-symbolic environment' that allows for rich self-interpretations and the formation of meaningful life-projects. Thus, what Anderson and Honneth have in view are not the basic conditions of agency but an ideal of human flourishing that most of us, even if we are fortunate, are only likely to realize to a limited degree.

Yet, it is relatively easy to slide from one model to the other. Anderson and Honneth, for example, suggest that their conception of autonomy provides the basis for a revised conception of social justice, implying that someone who lacks the requisite 'recognitional infrastructure' can claim a violation of their legitimate rights. As such, they intend it to play a role often reserved for the more limited concept of agency-autonomy. Similarly, Habermas does not always restrict himself to a characterization of minimal conditions of rational agency but also goes on to propose a 'communication-theoretic' model of a post-conventional ego-identity (in Habermas 1992). But, whatever the merits of the more robust account, it carries with it significant burdens as well. In particular, making conditions of individual autonomy in the more robust sense a matter of political or social justice raises concerns about perfectionism and the introduction of one favored conception of the good life as a measure of political legitimacy. As Anderson and Honneth maintain, the notion of autonomy includes not only 'self-respect' (connected to a citizen's political or legal status) but self-trust (developed via intimate relationships) and self-esteem (connected to cultural and social recognition) as well. As such, as they also acknowledge, the demand for autonomy entails a shift from a procedural theory of justice to a more substantive (or perfectionist) account. However, this observation leads us back to the question of the purpose or motivation for introducing an account of autonomy. We cannot settle the question of whether we have the right or even the best account of autonomy apart from an answer to the prior question of the role the account is intended to serve.

In a related discussion John Christman considers the contribution of various relational conceptions of autonomy, particularly by feminist theorists (2004). Christman is more explicit than most about the role his preferred (procedural and anti-perfectionist) conception of autonomy is to play in the context of a defense of liberalism and thus about his criterion for an acceptable account. His reservation concerning at least some relational conceptions of autonomy is that they will thwart that political role. In a criticism of Marina Oshana's relational account of autonomy (1998), which holds that a person who 'freely' endorses what are otherwise judged to be oppressive social norms may not be autonomous, he concludes: 'to say that she is not autonomous implies that she does not enjoy the status marker of an independent citizen whose perspective and value orientation get a hearing in the democratic processes that constitute legitimate social policy' (157). But Christman's remarks also reveal at least three distinct roles for a conception of autonomy: Oshana's view (which is presented as an ideal of human flourishing, and is substantive in character), an account of the basis of the respect that citizens owe one another as members of a common polity (and thus limits potentially paternalistic policies), and a conception of human agency *simpliciter* that might be appealed to in the justification of political institutions. Christman is especially concerned that adopting a conception designed with the first role in mind (as Oshana does) will open the door to paternalistic measures that the second role seeks to forestall:

Liberation from oppression must be undertaken within a normative framework that leaves the most room for disparate voices, even those who endorse traditional and authoritarian value systems, for it must be accepted, in principle at least, that many women and marginalized people will embrace traditional conceptions of social life and cultural roles that offend western, liberal ideals of individual self-sufficiency. While some version of that ideal is certainly worth defending, it is dangerous to couch that defense in the definition of the autonomous person. (Christman 2004: 152)

Christman goes on to argue that accounts of autonomy that include recognitional elements in their definition—and hence are 'strongly' recognitional in my sense—are invariably 'substantive' or not 'content-neutral' and are, as a result, objectionable. Thus, his explicit aim is to find a model of autonomy that can be used to defend liberal institutions and he argues that a procedural account offers a better candidate for that role.

Paul Benson offers another example (2005). His essay begins with the question, 'How can any of my actions genuinely be my own?' and he states that he is interested in clarifying 'the difference between merely intentional action and action that is, in the fullest sense, the agent's own' (101). He continues from there to criticize various hierarchical accounts of autonomy on the grounds that they do not do justice to certain intuitions we have. In particular, he argues that hierarchical accounts are both too demanding (since I can be autonomous even when I fail to identify in the relevant sense) and not sufficient (since I can have the relevant identification, yet still fail to be autonomous). For the latter, Benson offers the example of the 'gaslighted woman' (from the film, *Gaslight*). Although the gaslighted woman satisfies conditions for autonomy in procedural, hierarchical accounts (such as Christman's), Benson maintains she is not autonomous since she lacks a sense of self-worth that would allow her to make use of the reflective capacities she otherwise has. Benson goes on to propose his own recognitional account and concludes with some suggestions as to how his account might offer a better defense of liberalism than more individualistic alternatives. The difficulty, once again, is that during the course of the essay Benson moves from agency-autonomy, to something like what it means for a person to 'lead a life of her own', to some (admittedly brief) remarks about how his alternative conception of autonomy might serve as a defense and/or revision in liberal political theory.

One final example of a recognitional account helps to underscore the concerns that have been raised. Rainer Forst (2005) identifies five notions of autonomy and then pursues a slightly different strategy than the two mentioned above—Habermas and Anderson/Honneth. Forst begins with a notion of political liberty (or autonomy) and moves from there to the question of what additional forms of autonomy are required for its effective exercise. He writes:

The concept of political liberty is comprised of those conceptions of autonomy that persons as citizens of a law-governed political community must reciprocally and generally grant and guarantee each other—which means that political liberty includes all those liberties that citizens as autonomous freedom-grantors and freedom-users can justifiably claim from each other (or, negatively, that they cannot reasonably deny each other) and for the realization of which they are mutually responsible. To spell this out, five different conceptions of individual autonomy have to be distinguished: moral, ethical, legal, political and social autonomy. All of these play a certain role in the concept of political liberty, yet none of them should become—as is so often the case—paramount and dominant at the expense of the others. (Forst 2005: 229)

This approach does not attempt to derive moral or political norms from a minimal notion of (communicative) agency (as Habermas does), but neither does it begin with a more robust conception of personal autonomy (or human flourishing) that is in turn used as a criterion of political justice. Rather, it is arguably closer to Hegel's approach in the *Philosophy of Right* which, as we saw, begins with a notion of the legal person and argues, via a kind of regressive argument, that the ideas of moral agency and a complex ethical (*sittliche*) self must be introduced to explain even the notion of a legal person. Thus, in contrast to the first two models, we have a proposal for a third strongly recognitional account: namely, the conception of autonomy that is central to a person's status as a citizen or member of a political community in which she is the author of the laws under which she lives and so is, in this sense, self-governing.

Thus, as the recent literature illustrates, it is difficult to discuss personal autonomy in isolation from other forms of autonomy (legal, political, moral) and increasingly necessary to specify the purpose the proposed account is intended to serve. It is more difficult, however, to identify which particular approach to personal autonomy is likely to be most promising. Accounts that focus on minimal (and formal) features of agency-autonomy, especially if they are introduced for the further purpose of specifying basic moral or political principles (e.g. Kant, Habermas, Christman) run the risk of overlooking or obscuring other dimensions that our intuitions or considered judgments about autonomy support. On the other hand, accounts of personal autonomy that present a more robust account of human flourishing, or 'leading a life of one's own', risk being unsuitable for that normative purpose because they incorporate features that not all citizens (in political evaluation) or all moral agents (in moral evaluation) could reasonably be expected to endorse (Benson 2000, 2005). Of course, it is also possible that our assumptions about even basic or minimal conditions of rational agency will change as we acquire a better understanding of the various material, psychological, and social conditions necessary for effective 'self-governance'. That, it seems, is exactly the 'challenge' many recent conceptions of (personal) autonomy present to more traditional defenses of liberalism. In that sense, the debate about personal autonomy—including its value and its constitutive features—can on occasion also lead us to modify our understanding of other forms of autonomy as well. Indeed, that seems to be one important role the ideal can perform in the context of social criticism (see Mackenzie and Stoljar 2000).

This essay has attempted to show that the idea of freedom as autonomy has had (and continues to have) an enormous influence on our understanding of modern life and its institutions and practices—indeed, it is central to our conception of what it is to *be* modern (Pippin 1999). However, I have also attempted to show that autonomy is not a single or unitary ideal; rather it contains a variety of distinct dimensions, including moral, political, legal, and personal autonomy. More importantly, I have also attempted to show that these various dimensions are for the most part ones that cannot be realized separately. Rather, attempts to realize one dimension challenge our understanding of the others. Thus, Nietzsche's views on self-experimentation and self-overcoming challenge our understanding of moral autonomy, Hegel's reflections on the practice of moral autonomy point to the need for forms of autonomy found in other institutions (e.g. legal, political, personal), and further reflections on moral autonomy modify our views about the respect and toleration we should have for the choices and lifestyles of others. Autonomy, then, is an 'unfinished project' in which its various dimensions continuously challenge others and prompt us constantly to reconsider what it means to be 'self-governing'.

## References

ALLISON, HENRY (1990), *Kant's Theory of Freedom* (New York: Cambridge University Press).

ANDERSON, JOEL and HONNETH, AXEL (2005), 'Autonomy, Vulnerability, Recognition and Justice', in Christman and Anderson, 127–49.

BARCLAY, LINDA (2000), 'Autonomy and the Social Self', in Mackenzie and Stoljar, pp. 52–71.

BENSON, PAUL (2000), 'Feeling Crazy: Self-Worth and the Social Character of Responsibility', in Mackenzie and Stoljar, 72–93.

—— (2005), 'Taking Ownership: Authority and Voice in Autonomous Agency', in Christman and Anderson, 101–26.

BERLIN, ISAIAH (1969), 'Two Concepts of Liberty', in *Four Essays on Liberty* (New York: Oxford University Press).

CASSIRER, ERNST (1970), *Rousseau, Kant and Goethe* (Princeton: Princeton University Press).

CHRISTMAN, JOHN (ed.) (1989), *The Inner Citadel: Essays on Individual Autonomy* (New York: Oxford University Press).

—— (1991) 'Autonomy and Personal History', *Canadian Journal of Philosophy* 21: 1–24.

—— (2004), 'Relational Autonomy, Liberal Individualism, and the Social Constitution of Selves', *Philosophical Studies* 117: 143–64.

CHRISTMAN, JOHN and JOEL ANDERSON (eds.) (2005), *Autonomy and the Challenge of Liberalism* (New York: Cambridge University Press).

COHEN, JOSHUA (1986), 'Reflection on Rousseau: Autonomy and Democracy', *Philosophy and Public Affairs* 15: 275–97.

—— (1997), 'The Natural Goodness of Humanity', in A. Reath, et al. (eds.), *Reclaiming the History of Ethics* (New York: Cambridge University Press), 102–39.

DENT, NICHOLAS (2005), *Rousseau* (London: Routledge).

FORST, RAINER (2005), 'Political Liberty: Integrating Five Conceptions of Autonomy', in Christman and Anderson, 226–41.

FRIEDMAN, MARILYN (1997). 'Autonomy and Social Relationships', in Diana Meyers (eds.), *Feminists Rethink the Self* (Boulder, CO: Westview Press).

GAUS, GERALD (2005) 'The Place of Autonomy within Liberalism', in Christman and Anderson, 272–89.

GUIGNON, CHARLES (2004) 'Becoming a Self: The Role of Authenticity in *Being and Time*', in C. Guignon (eds.), *The Existentialists* (Rowman & Littlefield).

GUYER, PAUL (2003) 'Kant on the Theory and Practice of Autonomy', *Social Philosophy and Policy*: 70–98.

HAAR, MICHEL (1996) 'Critical Remarks on the Heideggerian reading of Nietzsche', in C. Macann (ed.), *Critical Heidegger* (London: Routledge).

HABERMAS, JÜRGEN (1984) *The Theory of Communicative Action*, trans. Thomas McCarthy (Boston: Beacon Press).

—— (1990) *Moral Consciousness and Communicative Action*, trans. Christian Lenhardt and Shierry Weber Nicholsen (Cambridge, MA: MIT Press).

—— (1992). *Post-Metaphysical Thinking* (Cambridge, MA: MIT Press).

—— (1996) *Between Facts and Norms*, trans. William Rehg (Cambridge, MA: MIT Press).

HEGEL, G. W. F. (1975) *Hegel's Logic* [*Logic*], trans. William Wallace (Oxford: Clarendon Press).

—— (1977) *Phenomenology of Spirit*, trans. A. V. Miller (Oxford: Oxford University Press).

—— (1991) *Elements of the Philosophy of Right* [*PR*], ed. Allen W. Wood, trans. H. B. Nisbet (Cambridge: Cambridge University Press).

HEIDEGGER, MARTIN (1927) *Sein und Zeit* [*BT*], trans. as *Being and Time* by John Macquarrie and Edward Robinson (Oxford: Basil Blackwell, 1978).

—— (1977) 'Letter on Humanism', 'The Question Concerning Technology', and 'The Essence of Truth' all in *Basic Writings*, ed. David Farrell Krell (New York: HarperCollins).

HENRICH, DIETER (1994) *The Unity of Reason* (Cambridge, MA: Harvard University Press).

HERMAN, BARBARA (1981) 'On the Value of Acting from the Motive of Duty', *Philosophical Review* 90: 351–82.

HORKHEIMER, MAX (1947) *The Eclipse of Reason* (New York: Oxford University Press).

JANAWAY, CHRISTOPHER (1991) 'Nietzsche, the Self, and Schopenhauer', in K. Ansell-Pearson (ed.), *Nietzsche and Modern German Thought* (London: Routledge).

KANT, IMMANUEL, [*KPW*] (1970) *Kant's Political Writings* New York: Cambridge University Press.

KANT, I. (1960) *Religion within the Limits of Reason Alone* (New York: Harper & Row).

—— [*PP*] (1996) *Practical Philosophy*, ed. and trans. M. J. Gregor with introduction by A. W. Wood (Cambridge: Cambridge University Press).

LOWITH, KARL (1994) *My Life in Germany before and after 1933* (Urbana: University of Illinois Press).

MACKENZIE, CATRIONA and STOLJAR, NATALIE (2000) *Relational Autonomy: Feminist Perspectives on Autonomy, Agency and the Social Self* (New York: Oxford University Press).

MAUS, INGEBORG (2002) 'Liberties and Popular Sovereignty: On Habermas's Reconstruction of the System of Rights', in R. von Schomberg and K. Baynes (eds.), *Discourse and Democracy* (Albany: SUNY Press).

MEYERS, DIANA (1989) *Self, Society and Personal Choice* (New York: Columbia University Press).

NELL [O'NEILL], ONORA (1975) *Acting on Principle* (New York: Columbia University Press).

NEUHOUSER, FREDERICK (1993) 'Freedom, Dependence and the General Will', *The Philosophical Review* 102: 363–95.

NIETZSCHE, FRIEDRICH (1967) *On the Genealogy of Morals* [*GM*] *and Ecce Homo* [*EH*], trans. Walter Kaufmann (New York: Vintage).

—— (1968) *Twilight of the Idols and The Anti-Christ* [*AC*], trans. R. J. Hollingdale (New York: Penguin).

—— (1973) *Beyond Good and Evil* [*BGE*], trans. R. J. Hollingdale (New York: Penguin).

—— (1974) *The Gay Science* [*GS*], trans. Walter Kaufmann (New York: Vintage).

—— (1984) *Human, All Too Human*, trans. Marion Faber and Stephen Lehman (Lincoln, NB: University of Nebraska Press).

OLAFSON, FREDERICK (1987) *Heidegger and the Philosophy of Mind* (New Haven: Yale University Press).

OSHANA, MARINA (1998) 'Personal Autonomy and Society', *The Journal of Social Philosophy* 29: 81–102.

PETTIT, PHILIP and SMITH, MICHAEL (1996) 'Freedom in Belief and Desire', *Journal of Philosophy* 93: 429–49.

PIPPIN, ROBERT (1999) *Modernism as a Philosophical Problem* (2nd edn. (New York: Blackwell).

ROUSSEAU, JEAN-JACQUES (1979) *Emile*, trans. Alan Bloom (New York: Basic Books).

—— (1990) 'Eighth Letter from the Mountain', in *Collected Writings of Rousseau*, ix, ed. Roger Masters and Christopher Kelly (Hanover, PA: University Press of New England).

—— (1997a) *The Discourses and Other Early Political Writings*, ed. Victor Gourevitch (New York: Cambridge University Press).

—— (1997b) *The Social Contract and Other Later Political Writings*, ed. Victor Gourevitch (New York: Cambridge University Press).

SARTRE, JEAN-PAUL (1943) *L'Être et le Néant. Essai d'ontologie phénoménologique* (Paris: Gallimard); trans. H. E. Barnes, *Being and Nothingness: An Essay of Phenomenological Ontology* (New York: Philosophical Library, 1956; London: Methuen, 1957). [*BN*]

—— (1946) *L'Existentialisme est un humanisme* (Paris: Nagel). 'Existentialism is a Humanism', in *Essays in Existentialism* (Secaucus, NJ: The Citadel Press, 1965), 31–62.

—— (1960) *Critique de la raison dialectique, précédé de Questions de methode, I, Théorie des ensembles pratiques* (Paris: Gallimard; repr. in new annotated edn., 1985); first essay trans. H. E. Barnes, *Search for a Method* (New York: Knopf, 1963); main text trans. A. Sheridan-Smith and ed. J. Rée, *Critique of Dialectical Reason* (London: New Left Books, 1976, and Atlantic Highlands, NJ: Humanities Press, 1976).

—— (1979) 'The Itinerary of a Thought', in *Between Existentialism and Marxism* (New York: Morrow Quill), 33–64.

SCHNEEWIND, JEROME (1998) *The Invention of Autonomy* (Cambridge: Cambridge University Press).

SIEP, LUDWIG (1983) 'The "Aufhebung" of Morality in Ethical Life', in L. Stepelevich and D. Lamb (eds.), *Hegel's Philosophy of Action* (New Jersey: Humanities Press).

STOLJAR, NATALIE (2000) 'Autonomy and the Feminist Intuition', in Mackenzie and Stoljar, 94–111.

TAYLOR, JAMES STACEY (ed.) (2005) *Personal Autonomy* (New York: Cambridge University Press).

TUGENDHAT, ERNST (1986) *Self-Consciousness and Self-Determination* (Cambridge, MA: MIT Press).

WELSHON, REX (2004) *The Philosophy of Nietzsche* (Montreal: McGill-Queen's University Press).

WHITE, RICHARD (1997) *Nietzsche and the Problem of Sovereignty* (Urbana: University of Illinois Press).

WILLIAMS, BERNARD (1981) *Moral Luck* (New York: Cambridge University Press).

—— and SMART, J. J. C. (1973) *Utilitarianism: For and Against* (New York: Cambridge University Press).

WOLF, SUSAN (1995) 'Freedom within Reason', in Taylor (2005).

WOOD, ALLEN (1990) *Hegel's Ethical Thought* (New York: Cambridge University Press).

# CHAPTER 17

## THE LEGACY OF HELLENIC HARMONY

### JESSICA N. BERRY

Jeder sei auf seine Art ein Grieche, aber er sei's.

(Goethe)[1]

THE intellectual history of Germany in the late eighteenth and nineteenth centuries is sometimes compared to the philosophical achievement of Athens at the very height of the classical age. Both were tremendously fruitful periods, which saw the birth of revolutionary philosophical systems that inspired a fantastic intellectual commerce among new and rival schools of thought. The plenitude of references to Greek mythology in literary works from Goethe and Lessing to Schiller, Novalis, and Hölderlin; the burgeoning interest in classical philology and the translation and transmission of works of antiquity, as in Mendelssohn's liberal translation and reading of Plato's *Phaedo*; and the growing interest in the history of skepticism in ancient Greece, as in Schulze's

---

[1] 'Everyone should be a Greek, in his own way.' Johann Wolfgang Goethe, *Gedankenausgabe der Werke, Briefe und Gespräche*, 24 vols., ed. Ernst Beutler (Zurich, 1948–54); xiii. 846. Cited by volume number and page.

attack on the Kantian system, which he published under the pseudonym 'Aenesidemus'; all are instances of a widespread preoccupation with Hellenic thought and culture that persisted, as we see in the work of Nietzsche and Heidegger, throughout the nineteenth and into the twentieth century. The intellectual associations and even close friendships enjoyed by many seminal thinkers during this time make it a relatively easy matter to trace the transmission of this enthusiasm from one figure or group to another. But the question remains how exactly it began, and why it took such firm hold as to persist for over a century. What is the philosophical significance of the Germans' longstanding affair with Hellenic culture?

# I. Winckelmann and *Gräkomanie*

The answers to these questions must begin in an unlikely place, since the founding father of the German Classicism that would so significantly influence philosophy in that country was not himself a philosopher, but a critic and historian of art, Johann Joachim Winckelmann (1717–68). Curiously, Winckelmann never set foot in the country whose legacy he was to establish so determinedly for his successors. Growing up in a small village in Prussia, Winckelmann developed what can only be described as a personal obsession with ancient Greek thought and culture. While Latin was still the dominant language of scholarly inquiry, and the teaching of Greek confined almost exclusively to what was necessary for the study of the New Testament, Winckelmann went to lengths to learn the Greek language and then occupied the majority of his few spare hours away from tutoring with Homer, Plato, and Sophocles and other Greek playwrights. During that time, his enthusiasm for Greek art was unflagging, in spite of the fact that his exposure to it was limited to the generally poor engravings and antique gems in circulation at the time, and to some quite inferior copies of sculpture in a private collection in Dresden.[2] He was middle-aged before he took the opportunity to travel

---

[2] For a lively account of Winckelmann's early life and education, including his knowledge of Greek artifacts, see Henry C. Hatfield's *Winckelmann and his German Critics* (New York: King's Crown Press, 1943) and his *Aesthetic Paganism in German Literature* (Cambridge, MA: Harvard University Press, 1964), esp. 5–23. Hatfield does not hesitate to characterize Winckelmann as 'the most renowned German between Leibniz and Goethe', except for Frederick II of Prussia (p. 8). For a more poetic but still very informative intellectual biography of Winckelmann, see also E. M. Butler, *The Tyranny of*

beyond the boundaries of his homeland, and even then he went no further south than Rome. The fruit of that journey, however, was Winckelmann's explosively popular pamphlet, *Reflections on the Imitation of Greek Works in Painting and Sculpture* (1755),[3] which made Winckelmann a legend in his own time and became one of the forces that turned the intellectual tide in Germany toward Greece.

In light of his somewhat accidental road to scholarship and his lack of formal philosophical training, the origins of the German obsession over Hellas in Winckelmann's work must, from a philosophical standpoint, make that obsession look equally accidental. Winckelmann was surely not the first European to notice the Greeks and to become involved in the cultural history of antiquity—he was only the most popular. The circulation of a few small cultural artifacts, especially gems, was already in vogue, and the excavations at Herculaneum in 1738 and at Pompeii in 1748 were beginning to arouse the interest of the academic world in classical antiquity. Indeed, there was a rising tide of interest in ancient artifacts in eighteenth-century Germany, which Winckelmann did not initiate, but only rode. Winckelmann was an eloquent and impassioned writer who animated his vision of Hellas in a way that captured the general interest and became a genuine sensation. However, in order to explain the philosophical relevance of this picture, and how an aesthetic trend ultimately became an active force in German philosophy, we clearly need to look beyond his sparkling prose and his scholarly thoroughness. In fact, we need to look beyond Winckelmann's popular pamphlet to the much longer and more exhaustive historical study to which it led, Winckelmann's four-volume magnum opus, *A History of the Art of Antiquity* (1764).[4]

For art historians, the significance of Winckelmann's masterwork is readily appreciated; it still enjoys a reputation as one of the seminal texts in the discipline. For one thing, it was for its time and for years afterward the most comprehensive synthesis of knowledge about art in the ancient world. Winckelmann marked out four periods in this history, into which works were

---

*Greece over Germany*, 2nd edn. (Boston: Beacon Press, 1958; originally published 1935 by Cambridge University Press).

[3] Johann Joachim Winckelmann, *Reflections on the Imitation of Greek Works in Painting and Sculpture*, trans. Elfriede Heyer and Roger C. Norton (LaSalle: Open Court, 1987). First published in 1755 as *Gedanken über die Nachahmung der griechischen Werke in der Malerei und Bildhauerkunst. Kleine Schriften. Vorreden. Entwürfe* (Berlin, 1968).

[4] Johann Joachim Winckelmann, *History of Ancient Art*, 4 vols., trans. Alexander Gode (New York: Frederick Ungar Publishing Co., 1968). First published as *Geschichte der Kunst des Alterthums* (Dresden, 1764).

slotted: an archaic era of relatively primitive pictorial representation, followed by an early classical phase of austere work and a later classical phase in which the beauty of Greek art reached its peak in more elaborate works, and finally a long era of mere imitation and decline.[5] Not long after the publication of the *History*, this schema had become commonplace—so much so that Winckelmann was no longer recognized as having invented it, when it was recognized as having been invented at all, that is, and not taken as some sort of eternal verity.[6]

But the real innovation of Winckelmann's study, and the beginning of its interest beyond the purview of antiquarians, was historiographical. The mid-eighteenth century saw the dawn of historicism as a phenomenon in the German academy.[7] Anticipating this movement, Winckelmann clearly expressed the desire to elevate the history of art, heretofore a somewhat dry fact-gathering enterprise with narrow appeal, to the level of a science. To realize this goal, he recognized that art history would need to develop its own methodological program, and his work can easily be read as a manifesto for this cause. Winckelmann's approach to this project is especially interesting for the light it sheds on a larger struggle in this period, between an essentially rationalist approach to history, in which the historian's task is to uncover the universal or necessary truths underlying historical change, and an empiricist approach, one that looks suspiciously on a priori methods and adopts a more scientifically naturalistic approach, deriving its accounts inductively from the empirical data.

Winckelmann, who betrays no awareness of a methodological tension in his own work, employed both deductive and inductive strategies in order to develop an historical and theoretical framework for the presentation of the facts—one that would not just give an encyclopedic chronology of art in antiquity, but would make *sense* of this history by demonstrating how and why one stylistic period arose from another, organically, and necessarily, in a rationally discernible pattern of rise and decline. The Preface to his *History of Art* opens with the programmatic declaration that, 'The History of Ancient Art which I have undertaken to write is not a mere

---

[5]  See book VIII, vol. iii of the *History*, 'The Rise and Fall of Greek Art', which devotes a chapter to each stage.

[6]  Alex Potts, *Flesh and the Ideal: Winckelmann and the Origins of Art History* (New Haven: Yale University Press, 1994), 15. In addition to giving perhaps the best in-depth analysis of Winckelmann's methodology and scholarship, Potts also clarifies its importance and impact on Winckelmann's contemporaries.

[7]  See Frederick Beiser's chapter on 'Historicism' in this volume.

chronicle of epochs, and of the changes which occurred within them. I use the term History in the more extended signification which it has in the Greek language; *and it is my intention to present a system*.'[8] Foreshadowing Hegel's view of history, one of Winckelmann's most deeply held convictions, almost an article of faith with him, was that the history of art and the societies that produce it unfolds according to an internal logical principle, initially hidden but discernible through careful observation. The *History*, curiously, embraced the methodological commitments of scientific naturalism at the same time as it retained all the Enlightenment confidence in the power of reason: that reason can discover the necessary and law-like principles governing the unfolding of history because that unfolding is itself a rational process. Look rationally at history, and history looks rationally back.

On Winckelmann's account, the works produced during the late classical period, the penultimate period of his four (during the fourth and fifth centuries BCE, or what Nietzsche would later describe as the 'tragic age' of the Greeks), achieved the highest ideal of beauty and refinement. The formula of the Greek aesthetic ideal most associated with Winckelmann's legacy belongs to this account: *'noble simplicity and quiet grandeur'*. The slogan, which appeared in the earlier *Reflections on the Imitation of Greek Works*, was oft-repeated, and his choice of illustration for it became legendary:

The general and most distinctive characteristics of the Greek masterpieces are, finally, a noble simplicity [*edle Einfalt*] and quiet grandeur [*stille Größe*], both in posture and expression. Just as the depths of the sea always remain calm however much the surface may rage, so does the expression of the figures of the Greeks reveal a great and composed soul even in the midst of passion.

Such a soul is reflected in the face of Laocoon—and not in the face alone—despite his violent suffering. ... The physical pain and the nobility of soul are distributed with equal strength over the entire body and are, as it were, held in balance with one another. Laocoon suffers, but he suffers like Sophocles' Philoctetes; his pain touches our very souls, but we wish that we could bear misery like this great man.[9]

---

[8]  Winckelmann, *History*, 3 (emphasis added).
[9]  Winckelmann, *Reflections*, 33–5. The *Laocoon* group, perhaps made by Agesander, Atheodoros, and Polydoros of Rhodes in the first century BCE, represents in marble the priest Laocoon as he struggles to free himself and his two sons from two enormous snakes. Such was Laocoon's punishment by the gods for his having urged the Trojans not to admit the Greeks' wooden horse into their city; his warning, of course, went unheeded. A reference to the work can be found in Pliny the Elder's *Natural History*; Winckelmann clearly agrees with his assessment of the *Laocoon* group as 'a work superior to all the pictures and bronzes of the world' (Book 36).

As 'the demonstration of Polyclitus' rules, the perfect rules of art',[10] the *Laocoon* group is plausible; alongside the *Apollo Belvedere*, which Winckelmann also praised highly, it has long been one of the most admired statues of antiquity. Nevertheless, on the face of it, nothing seems more inappropriate as a paradigm of 'noble simplicity and quiet grandeur', or as an emblem of tranquility, harmony, and wholeness, than the contorted bodies depicted in the *Laocoon* group—a work more neatly captured in Winckelmann's passing reference to the subject's 'violent suffering'. In reflecting upon *Laocoon*, Winckelmann found the virtues of the Homeric hero embodied together with those of the Stoic sage; the question of the tension between the passion of the former and the placidity of the latter he never raised. This is no gross oversight, however. Rather, this unresolved tension and other ironic tensions in Winckelmann's account are more the fruit of his tenacious commitment to the theoretical foundations of his historical narrative and his willingness to make the empirical account subservient to it.

The guiding principle in the case of *Laocoon* and other Greek statuary is that, in Winckelmann's view, works of the highest aesthetic order were representations of the highest order of beauty in life; the Greeks had realized a level of perfection in human subjectivity such that any accurate representation of a human being in sculpture could not but project this perfection as aesthetic beauty. In forming his notion of the ideal human being, Winckelmann was in many ways a product of his own time—an era of tremendous social and cultural upheaval, in which the success of the Enlightenment seriously threatened the stability of institutions both political and religious upon which daily life seemed to depend. Motifs of 'fragmentation' in modern life and 'disharmony' within the self were becoming nearly ubiquitous in literary and philosophical discourse. The Hellenic individual as conceived by Winckelmann, by contrast, demonstrated two characteristics in which its perfection consisted and that were therefore worthy of emulation.

First, Winckelmann observed a *unity* or *wholeness* that he and his successors found lacking in modern individuals. He advocated the study and contemplation, even the imitation, of ancient works for just this reason: 'The concepts of unity and completeness in the nature of antiquity', he predicted, 'will purify and make more meaningful the concepts of those things that are divided in our nature.'[11] His assessment of the art of antiquity in terms of 'unity' and 'purity' sharply reflected his intense hatred of the busyness of modern

---

[10]   Ibid. 5.        [11]   Ibid. 21.

baroque, distaste for which grew out of the way in which art seemed to imitate life in the eighteenth century. His notion of Hellenic harmony appealed nostalgically to others as a palliative for the modern condition, testament to the possibility of an alternative to life in what Friedrich Schiller (1759–1805) would call 'the noisy market-place of our century'[12] in which individuals are not only psychically fragmented, but also feel themselves mere 'fragments' of a longed-for whole.[13] The divisive tendencies of modernity were already a popular theme in Continental thought. Winckelmann was the first, but far from the last thinker clearly to press the Greek ideal, as an *aesthetic* ideal, into the service of improving it.

The second salient characteristic Winckelmann observed in the beautiful figures of Greek statuary, in addition to their unity and wholeness, was their embodiment of *freedom*. According to Winckelmann, it was not just that social and political freedom, and perhaps a modicum of luxury, were necessary conditions for artists to produce great art; Winckelmann took that to be true, but even by his time this sociological observation was a commonplace. More than that, the Greeks' singularly beautiful and graceful representation of individual figures would not have been possible, he argued, if the artistic individuals doing the representing and the subjects *being represented* did not themselves embody ideal freedom: 'The independence of the Greeks is to be regarded as the most prominent of the causes, originating in its constitution and government, of its superiority in art.'[14] On one level, Winckelmann's acknowledgment of Hellenic freedom resonates with a more general contemporary trend: in the years leading up to the French Revolution, thinkers throughout continental Europe were preoccupied with the central questions of political philosophy—statecraft, political and cultural identity, and the specification of the good for human beings both individually and socially. Rousseau's reflections on human nature raised serious concerns about the direction in which modern society, science, and Enlightenment principles would lead; specifically, not toward human freedom, but farther from it. On another level, however, it is crucial to note that although Winckelmann here identifies the government of the Greeks as the originating *cause* of their freedom and independence, he is for the purposes of his analysis more interested in exploring the *effects* of these political conditions on the

---

[12] Friedrich Schiller, *On the Aesthetic Education of Man*, trans. E. M. Wilkinson and L. A. Willoughby (Oxford: Clarendon Press, 1982), 2: 7. Cited by letter number and page.
[13] Schiller, *Letters* 6: 33–5.     [14] Winckelmann, *History*, 179.

minds of Greek citizens and how these effects contribute to the uniquely beautiful art the Greeks were capable of producing: 'The thoughts of the whole people rose higher with freedom, just as a noble branch rises from a sound stock. ... The freedom which gave birth to great events, political changes, and jealousy among the Greeks, planted, as it were in the very production of these effects, the germ of noble and elevated sentiments.'[15] Winckelmann's concern is with the subjective experience of freedom, with freedom as a state of consciousness occupied by a particular sort of subject. The concept of freedom in Winckelmann's *History* is the complement of his concept of unity and harmony, and it has far less to do with the larger political and civic questions than with the characteristics embodied in the ideal individual.

Winckelmann's portrait of the Hellenic individual offered to thinkers at this time a compelling reason to believe (or an account they were all too ready to accept, at any rate) that this ideal had at one time been realized. In this way, Winckelmann's thorough and persuasive history made its indelible mark on the minds of his contemporaries: His Hellas and the ideal it represented were taken not as a mere *illustration* of the modern desire for wholeness and freedom, but as *evidence* that human beings had at one time, long before the Enlightenment, been nothing less than the flesh-and-blood embodiment of all its own aspirations. Thus Winckelmann would declare of his contemporary Germany that: 'The only way for us to become great or, if this be possible, inimitable, is to imitate the ancients.'[16] In his view, 'imitation' would demand not slavish copying, but an attempt to uncover the basic aesthetic principles at work so that they could be put to use in the service of a cultural revolution—a sentiment eagerly taken up, developed, and even radicalized in early German Romanticism (*Frühromantik*). Clearly, he suspected or at least hoped that the causal relation he posited between a great people and great art held in both directions, so that in adopting the artistic methods and principles of the Greeks, the modern European could be transformed into a stronger, healthier, and more superior spirit. From the publication of Winckelmann's *History*

---

[15] Winckelmann, *History*, 182–3. See also Potts (*Flesh and the Ideal*, 55), who argues eloquently for this point: 'But in the final analysis, Winckelmann's emphasis on the experience of freedom ... links him more with notions of freedom current in German idealist philosophy than it does with the conceptions of political liberty that seized the imagination of the French revolutionaries. ... Indeed Winckelmann's understanding of freedom has little of the civic public dimension already evident in the more progressive writing of his immediate French contemporaries, who held up antiquity as the model for an art based on republican liberty.'

[16] Winckelmann, *Reflections*, 5.

forward, the historical truth and the value of this harmonious ideal were all but unchallenged. His declaration, moreover, was received as an imperative, and it soon sparked a heated debate among some of the greatest literary and philosophical minds of the time about the best means of achieving such a goal, and about whether such a goal was in principle achievable at all in an entirely different historical period and cultural climate.

What makes this conversation significant for the development of philosophy in Germany is how the debate over the possibility of recovering the freedom and wholeness of the Greeks dovetailed with, and became polarized around, a debate of much broader scope at the end of the Enlightenment and on the eve of Kant's Copernican Revolution—the debate over the viability and the promise of a systematic philosophy grounded upon unshakeable first principles. Again reflecting one of the peculiar tensions in Winckelmann's work, arguments on both sides of the debate about the resurrection of the Hellenic ideal seemed to be contained in his *History*. On the one hand, in the theoretical framework Winckelmann developed for the presentation of his history he suggested strongly that (1) cultural greatness is achieved via the greatness or eminence of its individual subjects; (2) such greatness arrives at a certain, perhaps predictable point along an arc between the rise and decline of a culture; (3) the shape of that arc is itself a function of a quasi-teleological process underlying which are foundational first principles concerning the consciousness of individual subjects; and (4) the rational reconstruction of these principles should yield insight into the conditions for recovering the ideal the moderns sought.

This line of thinking appealed strongly to Goethe and Schiller, the central figures associated with Weimar Classicism, who devoted themselves to the project of cultural reform. But this argument, like Winckelmann's periodization of antiquity and many other features of his *History*, also expanded gradually beyond the provenance of art historians, cultural critics, and literary figures, until a version of it came to characterize the attitude of rational optimism embraced by those who were critical of Kant but nevertheless committed to the notion of first principles in philosophy—notably, the German Idealists Johann Gottlieb Fichte (1762–1814), Friedrich Wilhelm Joseph von Schelling (1775–1854), and Georg Wilhelm Friedrich Hegel (1770–1831). These thinkers embraced the Hellenic ideal very much according to Goethe's dictum, that is, each in his own way; but in every case, that Hellenic model guided and informed either the methods or the results of the philosophical system being developed. As Hegel observed in his *History of Philosophy*, the

Greeks are at home in the world as the moderns are not: 'Higher, freer philo-
sophic science, and the beauty of untrammeled art, together with the taste
and love of them, we know to have had their root in Greek life and to have
derived from them their spirit. If we were permitted to have an aspiration, it
would be for such a land and such conditions.'[17].

On the other side of the debate about the recovery of the Greek ideal,
Winckelmann, by grounding his interpretations of Greek works on his
knowledge of the political history and literary culture of the Hellenic world,
acquired though long familiarity with ancient texts, gave this ideal a heretofore
unrecognized historical specificity. At the close of his chapter addressing the
causes of aesthetic greatness among the Greeks, Winckelmann concludes,
'Such were the advantages which Greece had over other nations in art, *and
only such a soil could produce fruits so splendid.*'[18] This specificity, ironically,
made the Greek ideal singularly unfit as a model for emulation and undermined
the very notion of imitation Winckelmann was advocating, inspiring a deep
pessimism among those who were committed to the ideality of Winckelmann's
model. This pessimism found its most poignant expression in literary works
like Schiller's *The Gods of Greece*, and in the poetry of Hölderlin. Galvanized
by a negative reaction to Kant's critical philosophy, suspicious not only
of the viability of the project to discover 'first principles' but even of the
desirability of rehabilitating metaphysics, and influenced to varying degrees
by an empiricism that had its roots in Hume's work, those associated with
German Romanticism embraced the factual side of Winckelmann's *History*,
especially the suggestion that the Greek ideal was the product of a nexus of
causes utterly peculiar to its time.

## II. THE WINCKELMANNITES: LESSING, HERDER, GOETHE, AND SCHILLER

Many of Winckelmann's successors took issue with the details of his interpretation of *Laocoon*, and in fact his *History* was corrected on numerous
points of fact by fellow critics and historians; but these disagreements tended

---

[17] G. W. F. Hegel, *History of Philosophy*, 'i,' trans. E. S. Haldane (New York: Humanities Press, 1955), 'i,' §§187–8'; p. 150'

[18] Winckelmann, *History*, 189 (emphasis added).

to leave the substance of Winckelmann's discovery of 'noble simplicity and quiet grandeur' and his overall vision of antiquity largely intact. The spirit of Winckelmann's work had won the day; his *Gräkomanie* had taken firm hold. One of the first enthusiastic followers of Winckelmann's work was Gotthold Lessing (1729–81). He replied to Winckelmann with his own *Laocoon: An Essay on the Limits of Painting and Poetry* (1766). This famous investigation of aesthetic principles, which presents the struggle between poetry and the plastic arts in order to resolve the dispute in favor of poetry, is oriented entirely *contra* Winckelmann: it opens with an extended quote from *Reflections on the Imitation of Greek Works*, and its efforts are oriented toward systematically countering Winckelmann's thesis. Lessing's treatise, however, did more to enhance the visibility and tighten the grip of Winckelmann's view on the popular imagination than it did to overturn his interpretation. Thereafter, Winckelmann's remarks on the 'noble simplicity and quiet grandeur' of the sculpture were repeated verbatim and critically engaged not only by Lessing, but also by Herder, Goethe, Schiller, and later Schlegel and Hölderlin, among others.

Johann Friedrich Herder (1744–1803) in particular, an enthusiastic scholar of Greek texts and already an admirer of Winckelmann's work (he would author a monograph on Winckelmann in 1778), soon weighed in on Winckelmann's side of the argument with his own *Sylvae Criticae* (1769), a reply to Lessing's *Laocoon*. He attacked Lessing's assertion of the superiority of literature over the plastic arts, targeting especially his analyses of Homer; but his defense of Winckelmann's reading of the *Laocoon* group drew that interpretation to a pessimistic conclusion. While Winckelmann and Lessing had both delivered an imperative to imitate the Greeks in art, Herder's was the first explicitly pessimistic response, an attempt to show that this could not be done. A virulent opponent of supernaturalism in explanation, Herder concentrated on the empirical character and historical specificity of Winckelmann's account and agreed that Hellenic individuals could never have sprung from modern soil. His works on classical themes are a eulogy to the greatness of a lost world, a pessimistic motif that would echo for the next century and a half in Germany.

In Strasbourg in 1771, Herder befriended the young Johann Wolfgang Goethe (1749–1832) and became, along with Lessing, one of the most prominent influences on his work. Like them, Goethe steeped himself in Winckelmann's thought and personality: his *History of Art* was reportedly 'never out of Goethe's hands' during Goethe's own travels in Rome,[19] and Goethe attended fervently to his letters and other essays. By 1798, Goethe had begun to work on Winckelmann as a critic, introducing his own *Propylaea* with an essay on *Laocoon* in which he attempted to vindicate Winckelmann's interpretation, and he later authored a still-admired essay on Winckelmann.[20] Lessing's work had certainly aided in the popularization of Winckelmann's picture of Greece, but it was Goethe's passionate animation of that picture and his dedication to the mission of resurrecting the Greece Winckelmann imagined that guaranteed it for posterity.

It is in Goethe's masterful literary corpus that we find the most vibrant expression of Germany's growing obsession with Hellenistic culture and its promise of noble simplicity and quiet grandeur. His early lyric works, many written under the influence of Herder, quite liberally combine images from Greek mythology and epic poems as ornamentation. But Winckelmann's aesthetic agenda would soon begin to inform and organize these references, to give them purpose. In a letter of 1770, Goethe relates a valuable lesson taught him by his drawing teacher Friedrich Oeser, a committed Winckelmannite: 'His instruction will affect my whole life. He taught me that the ideal of beauty was simplicity and tranquility.'[21] Goethe's young Werther, a sufferer as much from the apparently meaningless turmoil of modern life as from unhappy love, like Goethe himself finds comfort in the contemplation of Homer—Goethe's principle guide to Hellenism for many years. Goethe's later *Hermann and Dorothea* was the result of his quite serious determination to become the Homer of his day, to revive the spirit of the Homeric epics in German verse. In the works of his most pronounced 'Classical' period, Goethe takes up such ancient mythological and literary themes as the human struggle with fate and tragedy in *Iphigenia in Tauris*.

Goethe fell so much under the sway of Greek thought that Friedrich Schiller, with whom Goethe came to be great friends, and who knew Goethe's mind so intimately as to describe Goethe to himself in a famous letter of 23 August 1794, characterized Goethe as a Greek born out of his time and recognized immediately that Goethe's turn toward the ideal of Hellenic harmony was an attempt to correct the faults of the modern age. Ultimately, Schiller's

---

[19] Butler, *Tyranny of Greece over Germany*, 108.

[20] Goethe's sketch was not only considered a model essay for intellectual biographies, but as Butler also asserts, it inspired the critic Walter Pater's work on Winckelmann (Butler, *Tyranny of Greece over Germany*, 134).

[21] Goethe 18: 134; quoted (in translation) by Hatfield, *Aesthetic Paganism in German Literature*, 62.

impression of Goethe became the inspiration for his own concept of the naïve—which he associated with the Greeks—in his essay *On Naïve and Sentimental Poetry* (1795–6). Schiller, who had felt his ambitions increasingly stifled by this literary Leviathan he grudgingly admired, made a pilgrimage to Weimar in 1787 expressly to meet Goethe. Prior to that, and throughout the early 1780s, Schiller's own work is peppered with references to Greek mythology. His engagement with Goethe encouraged that enthusiasm. Over the course of the friendship they began in Weimar, Goethe and Schiller exchanged over a thousand letters, and until Schiller's death in 1805, the pair devoted all their creative efforts to imposing upon Germany their version of the Classical ideal and became the co-founders of Weimar Classicism.

While heretofore the legacy of Hellenic harmony had been established and transmitted primarily by art historians, critics, archaeologists, and literary figures, by the early 1790s, Schiller's discovery of Kant's work and his serious study of philosophy began to change the direction of this current. Schiller's understanding of the most crucial moves in Kant's critical analysis of the faculty of reason, such as the distinction between phenomena and noumena, and in his moral philosophy, chiefly the strict isolation of inclination from duty, heightened anxieties already present in his and Goethe's work. Kant's *Critique of Pure Reason* (1781/8) established epistemic boundaries that placed everything formerly identified as having genuine epistemic value (i.e., knowledge of what is 'real', of what is behind the appearances) beyond the reach of human cognition. Modern man suffered at once from *too much knowledge*; the result of the successful forward march of the sciences was a greater body of data than any one human being could hope to assimilate. And at the same time he suffered from having *not enough knowledge*; the legacy of the Copernican revolution in philosophy was, for many German thinkers, a heightened awareness and intensified longing for what human cognition could not possibly attain. Human beings were condemned to achieve at best a small and specialized understanding of things.

Schiller complained loudly of this condition:

Everlastingly chained to a single little fragment of the Whole, man himself develops into nothing but a fragment; everlastingly in his ear the monotonous sound of the wheel that he turns, he never develops the harmony of his being, and instead of putting the stamp of humanity upon his own nature, he becomes nothing more than the imprint of his occupation or of specialized knowledge.[22]

---

[22] Schiller, *Letters* 6: 35.

And Goethe painted this same picture in a different medium, a picture of a quintessentially modern world: 'a world disintegrating beneath an ever-increasing burden of knowledge and culture, . . . that no single human being could assimilate it and organize it into a whole'.[23] Goethe's hero Faust feels he is not at home in the world; that his desires to know outstrip his merely mortal capacities becomes one of the chief sources of what many Weimar Classicists saw as a singularly modern tragedy. Faust suffers from precisely the condition theorized in Kant's first *Critique*: the human mind is powerful enough to discover but never to surpass its limits. Man desires a knowledge that is unattainable for him but to which he continues to attach the highest value, and it causes him to suffer acutely. Faust, it might be said, is the first modern sacrifice to the incurable pathology Nietzsche would later diagnose as the ascetic ideal. As Nietzsche puts it in the *Genealogy of Morality*, Kant's commitment to the existence of truths that utterly outstrip our cognitive abilities, his decree that, ' "there *is* a realm of truth and being, but precisely *reason* is *excluded* from it!" ',[24] is the maximum expression in philosophical thought of this perverse ideal. Furthermore, it seems to guarantee precisely what Kant claims in the *Critique of Pure Reason* to want to avoid—the conclusion that human intellectual inquiry is doomed to frustration. Against the small and specialized knowledge available to one who is a mere 'fragment of the Whole', Goethe and Schiller upheld the noble simplicity, the *unity* of the Hellenic individual, both internally, in the sense that the Hellenic subject seemed to them to have greater self-awareness than the modern individual and to be more transparent to himself, and externally, insofar as they took the Hellenic subject to be part of a more cohesive and harmonious society.

Schiller's *Letters on the Aesthetic Education of Man* juxtapose this Hellenic ideal with a number of tensions still keenly felt in the legacy of the *Aufklärung* and in Kant's system: an increasing demand, for instance, that human beings set aside the passions to make room for reason, sacrifice inclination to follow duty, and turn away from 'nature' in the interests of 'civilization'. In the Sixth Letter, Schiller asks:

What individual Modern could sally forth and engage, man against man, with an individual Athenian for the prize of humanity? . . . Why was the individual Greek

[23]  Butler, *Tyranny of Greece over Germany*, 86.

[24]  Friedrich Nietzsche, *On the Genealogy of Morality*, trans. Maudemarie Clark and Alan J. Swensen (Indianapolis: Hackett, 1998), 3: 12. Cited by essay number, then section number. Kant is not mentioned by name in this well-known passage, but Nietzsche's thinly veiled reference to the absurdity of the thing in itself makes the allusion clear.

qualified to be the representative of his age, and why can no single Modern venture as much? Because it was from all-unifying Nature that the former, and from the all-dividing Intellect that the latter, received their respective forms.[25]

The modern individual felt himself assailed from within, by competition among a number of rationally defensible ends—the pursuit of his own desires, the advancement of the interests of the community and of individual others, and also from without, as the pace of modern life and the division of labor began increasingly to force upon the individual many different roles, leaving him with a struggle to define himself within his community and make sense of his place in the world. At the same time, the Christian distinction between the human and the divine, and more pointedly its denigration of the human and 'worldly', far from offering a comforting alternative to the fractured modern soul, only deepened its sense of alienation.

Goethe's work clearly captures the religious dimension of modern man's unfulfilled longing in his total isolation from a transcendent creator; the gods of Greece are by contrast immanent, more human, and more *humane*. Guided again by Winckelmann, whose attraction to the Greek ideal was surely in part an attraction to the sensual 'this-worldliness' of its sculptural representations, Goethe's Classicism displays his determination quite literally to resurrect these gods. The colossal mythical figures to whom he is most attracted—Prometheus, Faust—assert their greatness in their interactions with the Olympians. Their direct challenges to the gods are as inconceivable within the framework of a fully transcendent Christian metaphysics as they are unacceptable within the framework of its ethics. As one commentator notes, Goethe's literary canon expresses his 'conviction that the morality of the ancients was on the whole saner and more enlightened than Christian ethics'.[26] And Schiller's early literary effort, 'The Gods of Greece' (1788), written soon after his meeting with Goethe, conveys this same idea. Its tone of urgency and lamentation crystallizes perhaps better than any other contemporary work the attitude that Greek civilization is a lost ideal:

> Whilst the smiling Earth ye governed still,
> And with Rapture's soft and guiding hand
> Led the happy Nations at your will,
> Beauteous Beings from the Fable-land!
> Whilst your blissful worship smiled around,
> Ah! how diff'rent was it in that day!

---

[25] Schiller, *Letters* 6: 33.    [26] Hatfield, *Aesthetic Paganism in German Literature*, 68.

When the people still thy temples crowned,
Venus Amathusia!

. . .

Gloomy sternness and denial sad
Ne'er were in your service blest descried;
Each heart throbbed then with emotions glad,
For the Happy were with you allied.
Nothing then was Holy, save the Fair;
Of no rapture was the God ashamed,
When the modest Muse was blushing there,
When their sway the Graces claimed!

. . .

Beauteous World, where art thou gone? Oh! thou,
Nature's blooming youth, return once more!
Ah, but in Song's fairy region now
Lives thy fabled trace so dear of yore!
Cold and perished, sorrow now the plains,
Not one Godhead greets my longing sight;
Ah, the Shadow only now remains
Of you living Image bright!

All those lovely blossoms now are gone,
Scattered by the North-wind's piercing breath;
To enrich, amongst the whole, but ONE,
All this God-like world was doomed to death.
Sadly turn I to the stars on high—
Thou, Selene, canst not there be found!
Through the forest, through the waves I cry—
Ah, they echo back no sound![27]

The coming of Christ, the 'ONE', heralded by the 'piercing breath' of the cold northern wind, spells doom for the Olympic pantheon and substitutes for the inspiring and divine beauty ('the Fair') of Greek culture a considerably darker and more severe 'holiness', and the end of happiness. Man should be guided naturally toward the good, by the inner light of his feeling for beauty, Schiller thought, but the modern Christian had goodness imposed upon him from without, from above, and beauty (the aesthetic) was degraded along with everything worldly.

Kant's work directly threatened the two characteristics of human subjectivity that Winckelmann had argued were conducive to the greatness of the Hellenic

---

[27] *The Poems of Schiller, Complete*, trans. Henry D. Wireman (Philadelphia: I. G. Kohler, 1871), 64–9.

people and culture: harmony and freedom. The strict distinction between *inclination* and *duty* and Kant's insistence that an action motivated by fellow-feeling and human sympathy rather than by the recognition of its being rationally necessary has 'no true moral worth',[28] though not grounded in Christianity, were immediately recognized to have duplicated it in spirit. So the Greek ideal of a human life that is internally harmonious was appropriated to oppose the divided self left by Kantian ethics—a subject who is by nature constantly at war with himself over the satisfaction of duty or inclination, two irreconcilable forces. In addition, Weimar Classicism maintained the freedom Winckelmann discovered in the Hellenic subject, freedom in the sense of personal liberty, against the Kantian concept of freedom. The freedom that makes Kantian moral agency possible, namely autonomy, is as its etymology suggests merely another form of rule, obedience to which guarantees to put the subject in a state of perpetual conflict—a self divided against itself. For the *Goethezeit* Classicists, to look back to Greece was to look back to a time when freedom was not in tension with morality to begin with and therefore did not pose it any threat. This vision, clearly, wedded them to a conception of morality very different from the contemporary religious morality; hence Goethe's and Schiller's longing to resurrect the more humane gods of Greece.

For years, Schiller and his close contemporaries tried to effect change from 'within the system'—that is, to amend or modify Kant's philosophy so as to mitigate its apparently devastating spiritual and psychic effects. Thus Schiller says in the opening of his *Letters on the Aesthetic Education of Man* (1793–5), 'I shall not attempt to hide from you that it is for the most part Kantian principles on which the following theses will be based.'[29] But in presenting Kant's moral principles as the 'immemorial pronouncements of Common Reason', which must command universal assent once they are rightly understood, he introduces ideas with which Kant himself would never have agreed. For the dictates of Kantian morality are, on Schiller's account, nothing more than a highly technical formulation of the 'data of that moral *instinct* which Nature in her wisdom appointed Man's guardian until . . . he should have arrived at years of discretion'.[30] Kant makes it abundantly clear, however, in the *Critique of Practical Reason* and in the *Groundwork* as well, that he stands wholly opposed to any attempt to posit in human beings a 'moral sentiment' or

---

[28] Immanuel Kant, *Groundwork of the Metaphysics of Morals*, trans. Mary J. Gregor, in *Immanuel Kant: Practical Philosophy* (Cambridge: Cambridge University Press, 1996); AK 4: 398.

[29] Schiller, *Letters* 1: 3.    [30] Schiller, *Letters* 1: 5; emphasis added.

'instinct' that could possibly do the work of practical reason; even if there were such a faculty, and even if its results happened to agree with the issuances of the rational faculty, there would be nothing praiseworthy in following them. Without drawing attention to this important disagreement with Kant as such, however, Schiller continues:

> If, then, man is to retain his power of choice and yet, at the same time, be a reliable link in the chain of causality, this can only be brought about through both these motive forces, *inclination and duty*, producing completely identical results in the world of phenomena; . . . that is to say, through *impulse being sufficiently in harmony with reason* to qualify as universal legislator.[31]

With the same determination with which Winckelmann found 'quiet grandeur' in *Laocoon*, Schiller attempted to amend the Kantian system to make room for the inclinations and sentiments he thought modern man was being forced increasingly to deny. Against this background, it should be no surprise that Schiller turns explicitly to the Greeks for his example of a people that realized such harmony and 'wholeness'. In his *Letters* and elsewhere,[32] he developed his conception of the Greek individual and also the Greek state—the *polis*—as an ideal community, one that could actively promote and provide the cultural climate to facilitate the development of the whole man rather than keeping him 'everlastingly chained to a single little fragment of the Whole', so that 'he never develops the harmony of his being . . .'.[33] The *polis*, as we shall see, would become, especially for Hegel, an important model of the ideal political life and a model for the structure of the self.

# III. KANT

Schiller, then, describes the ideal moral agent as an individual whose aims are so harmoniously organized that happiness and morality may be realized together, and who is 'whole' in virtue of his not having sacrificed feeling to rationality or neglected himself in order to fulfill his obligation to his fellows. Anyone who asserts with the same forcefulness as Kant did, however, that *happiness* is utterly unsuitable as a ground of morality, that any attempt to ground morality on *feeling* or sentiment is necessarily contradictory, and that

---

[31] Schiller, *Letters* 4: 17; emphasis added.    [32] See in particular his essay 'On Dignity and Grace'.
[33] Schiller, *Letters* 6: 35.

a free will is determined by the moral law as recognized by reason alone, irrespective of *inclination*, must reject the Greek ideal as Schiller expresses it. Whether Kant himself developed his views, especially his ethical views, as a conscious rejection of this ideal, however, is a complicated question. Kant discusses ideas in antiquity relatively rarely in his major works. His references to the Greeks remain vague and sweeping; when they appear, they are more often than not to 'the ancients' in the generic, as in: 'The ancients revealed this error [of seeking an empirical object that can ground a moral law] openly by directing their moral investigation entirely to the determination of the concept of the *highest good* . . .'.[34] When Kant does appeal to particular thinkers or schools of thought (e.g. Plato, the Epicureans, or the Stoics), his references are usually only illustrative.

Given the paucity of references to the ancients, it has been suggested that what contact figures like Kant, and even Schiller and Goethe, actually had with Greek texts was 'of a very slight nature',[35] but this seems unlikely to be true. In the middle of the eighteenth century, classical philology was still something of a fledgling enterprise, but it began to grow, especially as the study and criticism of religious texts gained momentum. By the century's end, the work of Greek authors was fairly widely available and classicists began to insist on reading their works, especially those of Plato, in the original language. These circumstances, in fact, helped make it possible for Winckelmann in the 1750s to throw off the shackles of Aristotelian scholasticism and study the Greek authors for whom he had developed such a passion. During the next decade, Platonic themes began to emerge in the writing of many German thinkers, such as Herder, Hamann, and Wieland, and new translations and commentaries on Plato's work gained popularity, including Moses Mendelssohn's book *Phädon oder über die Unsterblichkeit der Seele* in 1767, with which Kant was clearly familiar—he devotes a section of the *Critique of Pure Reason* to a refutation of Mendelssohn's version of the *Phaedo* proof.[36] By the 1780s there was a

[34]  Immanuel Kant, *Critique of Practical Reason*, trans. Mary J. Gregor in *Immanuel Kant: Practical Philosophy* (Cambridge: Cambridge University Press, 1996); AK 5: 64.

[35]  Klaus Reich, 'Kant and Greek Ethics', *Mind* 48 (1939), 338–54, 446–63; p. 338. Reich argues for a substantial influence of Plato on the development of Kant's ethical philosophy, in spite of the slight contact he alleges. Somewhat quaintly, Reich suggests that geniuses of the likes of Kant and Goethe would have required less contact in order to produce great works that bear the stamp of influence by the Greeks (p. 339).

[36]  The book and its relation to Kant's own work are also discussed in correspondence between Kant and Mendelssohn, 1766. Cited in Reich, 'Kant and Greek Ethics', 345, who argues that it was his exposure to Mendelssohn's *Phaedo* that inspired Kant to turn his back on Epicureanism and Greek ethics in general.

wide variety of material available, and given its popularity in literature and its infiltration of the academy, it would have been difficult to avoid exposure to it.

And Kant does not consistently neglect these sources: clearly, he finds it useful sometimes in his mature works to compare and contrast his own views with those of ancient thinkers. In the first *Critique*, for example, a contrast between the 'merely sensual' Epicurus and the 'merely intellectual' Plato illustrates Kant's distinction between the methodological commitments of empiricism and dogmatism respectively.[37] Kant is critical of both trends, of course, so prima facie his comparison does not appear to favor one over the other. But when Kant turns his attention to matters of practical reason, in which whatever is merely sensual and appeals to pleasure as a criterion of ethical judgment is to be rejected, things are different. On this score, Kant does indicate that he thinks Plato gets something importantly right, and Epicurus something importantly wrong. When he touches on practical philosophy in the *Critique of Pure Reason*, Kant has no compunction about forming an alliance with Plato:

Plato found his ideas preeminently in everything that is practical, i.e., in what rests on freedom, which for its part stands under cognitions that are a proper product of reason. Whoever would draw the concepts of virtue from experience, . . . would make of virtue an ambiguous non-entity, changeable with time and circumstances, useless for any sort of rule. On the contrary, we are all aware that when someone is represented as a model of virtue, we always have *the true original* in our own mind alone, with which we compare this alleged model and according to which alone we estimate it.[38]

He embraces the usefulness of Platonic archetypes, 'true originals', when they clarify his considered position on morality—as he will put it in the second *Critique*, if a categorical imperative is to be possible at all, there must be something that grounds moral judgments a priori. In the passage quoted above, Kant claims baldly that, 'If we extract from its exaggerated expression, then, the philosopher's [Plato's] spiritual flight, which considers the physical copies in the world order, and then ascends to their architectonic connection according to ends, i.e. ideas, is an endeavor that deserves respect and imitation . . . '.[39] That is to say, if Plato were not in fact Plato, but Kant, he

---

[37] Immanuel Kant, *Critique of Pure Reason*, trans. and ed. Paul Guyer and Allen Wood (Cambridge: Cambridge University Press, 1998); *AK* A472/B500, A853/B881.

[38] *AK* A315/B371, emphasis added; the discussion of Plato extends from A312/B368 to A321/B377.

[39] *AK* A317–18/B374–75.

should be imitated. This imperative is about as far away from Winckelmann's own imperative to imitate the ancients as he could have imagined.

In his treatises on ethics, Kant maintains the comparative illustration between Plato as a rationalist and Epicurus as a sensualist. The *Groundwork*, for instance, retains the distinctly Platonic language and flavor of the passage quoted above when Kant claims:

Even the Holy One of the Gospel must first be compared with our ideal of moral perfection before he is cognized as such; even he says of himself, 'Why do you call me (whom you see) good? None is good (*the archetype of the good*) but God only (whom you do not see).' But whence have we the concept of God as the highest good? Solely from the *idea* of moral perfection that reason frames a priori and connects inseparably with the concept of a free will. ... [Examples] can never justify setting aside their *true original, which lies in reason*, and guiding oneself by examples.[40]

Epicurus is on the other hand the chief representative of hedonism, a wrong-headed and pernicious attempt to ground practical imperatives on empirical principles. Kant clearly takes Epicurus to have failed to distinguish between pleasure and happiness, and since he does not go to lengths to distinguish them himself, Kant tends to conflate hedonism and eudaimonism. In attacking the idea that pleasure could be a rationally defensible end, he rejects eudaimonism itself as utterly irreconcilable with genuine morality, and he makes this point emphatically in the *Critique of Practical Reason*:

*Happiness* is the state of a rational being in the world in the whole of whose existence *everything goes according to his wish and will*, and rests, therefore, on the harmony of nature with his whole end as well as with the essential determining ground of his will. Now the moral law as a law of freedom commands through determining grounds that are to be quite independent of nature and of its harmony with our faculty of desire. ... Consequently, there is not the least ground in the moral law for a necessary connection between the morality and the proportionate happiness of a being belonging to the world as part of it and hence dependent upon it, who for that reason cannot by his will be a cause of this nature and, as far as his happiness is concerned, cannot by his own powers make it harmonize thoroughly with his practical principles.[41]

We might think Kant would be more favorably inclined toward the Stoics: while the Epicureans 'assumed an altogether false principle of morals as supreme', he says, 'namely that of happiness. ... The Stoics, on the contrary, had chosen their supreme practical principle quite correctly, namely virtue, as

[40] *AK* iv. 408–9, emphasis added.    [41] *AK* v. 124.

the condition of the highest good . . . '.[42] But Kant's resistance to all versions of eudaimonism as he understands it, that is, to any ethical philosophy that identifies the highest good with a subjective state and not with the workings of rationality as such, runs deep enough to obscure any subtle distinctions between the two schools.[43]

On Kant's account of Stoic ethics, the happiness of the Stoic sage is the consequence of his contemplating the virtue he recognizes in himself. But if this end is in any way part of the motivational structure of Stoic action, as Kant apparently takes it to be, then it too is pathological. In sum, he says, 'if *eudaimonism* (the principle of happiness) is set up as the basic principle instead of *eleutheronomy* (the principle of the freedom of internal lawgiving), the result is the *euthanasia* (easy death) of all morals'.[44] Thus, where Kant does praise the Stoics for their emphasis on virtue rather than pleasure or feeling, he (again) praises only the elements of his own system as he finds them illustrated in Stoic thought. Elsewhere, he is perfectly ready to collapse the distinctions between their philosophy and the Epicurean in order to condemn what he himself opposes. In the end, even Kant's appreciation for the rationalism of Platonic philosophy extends only so far as it accords with his requirement that moral laws be grounded a priori; in these passages, he fails utterly to give Plato's own concern for the highest good, Plato's eudaimonism, its due.

At first blush, Kant's critical system seems to have developed independently of any conscious or direct influence by the Greeks. Yet, having seen something of the extent to which Hellenism had by this time taken hold in Germany, we cannot conclude that the resources available to Kant were inadequate to the task of understanding and engaging with the Greeks had he cared to do so. Kant was well aware of the Greek revival among his contemporaries (indeed, by at least 1770 it was impossible *not* to be familiar with Winckelmann's

---

[42] *AK* v. 126.

[43] For a more developed account of Kant's attitude toward the Stoics, see T. H. Irwin, 'Kant's Criticisms of Eudaemonism', in Stephen Engstrom and Jennifer Whiting (eds.), *Aristotle, Kant, and the Stoics* (Cambridge: Cambridge University Press, 1996). Irwin argues compellingly that Kant's critiques of Greek ethical philosophy labor under a crucial misunderstanding, or mischaracterization, of eudaemonism: 'Kant', he claims, 'clearly regards eudaemonism (in his sense of the term) as a type of hedonism' (p. 70). Kant attributes to all Greek moralists the view that eudaimonia is the highest good, accusing them all of failing to see that the good at which their systems aim 'is unavailable to agents who do not recognize some reason to follow moral requirements apart from the expected pleasure' (p. 69). Kant's failure to have achieved a more sophisticated view of ancient ethics is, Irwin thinks, responsible for his misplaced criticisms of the Stoics.

[44] Immanuel Kant, *The Metaphysics of Morals*, trans. Mary J. Gregor in *Immanuel Kant: Practical Philosophy* (Cambridge: Cambridge University Press, 1996); *AK* vi. 377–8.

vision of Greece and the enthusiastic following it had inspired). In light of his awareness of this trend, his own lack of engagement with it is so remarkable that Nicholas White, in his study of Greek ethics and its legacy in the modern age, has observed that it is difficult not to take Kant's silence about the Greeks as a 'studied neglect'.[45] But what would motivate such willful neglect? White suggests that what Winckelmann saw as an admirable unity and simplicity in the Greek view of subjectivity, Kant understood as betraying a lamentable primitivism. Thus, the Greek view is simply not worth the trouble of fleshing out.[46] But the charge of primitivism itself seems somehow so deeply uncharitable, so facile, that it is tempting to look for other explanations for Kant's attitude. We have looked at passages in which Kant advances interpretations that are selective in such a way as to be self-serving. Perhaps, then, as a way of underscoring the revolutionary nature of his own critical system, Kant's inattention to the ancients is best read as (1) an acknowledgment of the firmness of the Hellenes' grip on the German imagination and (2) an insistence upon shifting the terms of philosophical debate onto an entirely modern field. If this is accurate to Kant's hostile treatment of Greek ethics, however, then his attempt to erase the influence of the Greeks and redefine the terms of the debate must be deemed unsuccessful. His successors clung determinedly to the ideal of 'noble simplicity and quiet grandeur' to counteract the reduction of the individual human being to a merely serviceable, unfeeling part of a vast rationalistic machine.

# IV. THE REACTION TO KANT: IDEALISM

The appearance of Kant's critiques, of course, determined much of the philosophical agenda in Germany at the turn of the nineteenth century and thereafter. But the overwhelming success of the critical philosophy owes a debt to another intellectual watershed in the late eighteenth century, namely the so-called 'pantheism' controversy that erupted between Friedrich Jacobi

---

[45] Nicholas White, *The Individual and Conflict in Greek Ethics* (Oxford: Clarendon Press, 2002), 22 ff.

[46] 'It is something of an irony', White notes, 'that Kant should play any role at all in the history of modern reactions to Greek ethics, inasmuch as he devotes virtually no energy at all to discussing it—so patently inadequate does he take it to be. His importance to the historiography of Greek ethics consists almost entirely in the ways in which his opponents used Greek thinking to attack his doctrines' (*The Individual and Conflict in Greek Ethics*, 22–3).

(1743–1819) and Moses Mendelssohn (1729–86) in 1783. What began as a dispute between these two thinkers over Lessing's alleged Spinozism soon commanded the attention of a much wider audience. Frederick Beiser has argued that it was Reinhold's accessible presentation of Kant's system in his *Briefe über die kantische Philosophie* that helped make it such a sensation, but that it did so in part by making it relevant to what was already a vibrant dispute.[47] As Beiser points out, 'It is difficult to imagine a controversy whose cause was so incidental and whose effects were so great.'[48] The controversy threw a spotlight on a dilemma of particular urgency to the *Aufklärung*, parallel to the one we have already encountered between the rationalist and the empiricist approaches to history: Jacobi fretted that the unchecked activity of reason, far from supporting and justifying conventional morality and religious faith, would undermine both and could only end in atheism and nihilism. The only alternative seemed to be to abandon (or severely restrict) reason and embrace fideism, a move Mendelssohn resisted. But while this controversy may have pushed to the fore and provided a venue for the expression of anxieties about the nature and role of reason, these anxieties were already well-entrenched. We have seen in Winckelmann's *History* what might otherwise appear as a mere methodological confusion, between his thoroughgoing commitment to the existence of a rational principle governing the unfolding of history (his own sort of fideism) and his insistence on appropriating the empirical and methodological resources used with increasing success in the sciences. Winckelmann's work, which can legitimately claim something like a cult following among the major figures of late eighteenth- and early nineteenth-century German scholarship, appeared in 1764, not only anticipating but setting the stage for the controversy that brought down the *Aufklärung* and that persisted in so many forms over the next century.

This dilemma played itself out in creating a rift between (1) those philosophers who followed Kant in accepting the authority of reason and its capacity to discover foundational first principles on which the rest of our knowledge would be built, and (2) those who became deeply skeptical of its authority. The skepticism was invited: Kant was determined that knowledge should make room for faith, but as it appeared to many of his successors, he had done so in a way that made a deep skepticism inevitable. Those who took up the second

---

[47]  See Frederick Beiser, *The Fate of Reason* (Cambridge, MA: Harvard University Press, 1987), 45. Chapters 2 and 3 give an especially rich account of the controversy, its origins, and its philosophical significance.
[48]  Ibid. 44.

position and became suspicious of the authority of reason became known as the Romantics. For many of these thinkers, the same skepticism Hegel recognized as a threat became a weapon of antiquity rediscovered—hence Gottlob Ernst Schulze's (1761–1833) having adopted the pen name 'Aenesidemus' in homage to the Pyrrhonian tradition. Though Romanticism is often derided for having rejected reason altogether and for having given philosophy over to poetry, this is an unfortunate caricature.[49] Far from abandoning reason itself, the central figures especially in early German Romanticism (*Frühromantik*) used this skepticism to develop a sophisticated and, in their view, *genuinely* critical response to the Kantian demand that feeling and sentiment, which are natural to man, always give way to reason. We will turn to their views presently. Meanwhile, as we will see, the German Idealists took up the first position and attempted to vindicate reason's ability to discover first principles and to derive from them a complete philosophical system. G. W. F. Hegel, in particular, recognized as an obstacle to this project an especially virulent form of skepticism—one that originated not with Kant's system but in antiquity, and he viewed its defeat as an urgent problem.[50]

In the *Wissenschaftslehre*, Fichte had erected a new systematic philosophy in which the 'I' plays the role of self-evident foundation: 'Attend to yourself', he exhorts in its Introduction, 'turn your attention away from everything that surrounds you and towards your inner life; this is the first demand that philosophy makes of its disciple. Our concern is not with anything that lies outside you, but only with yourself.'[51] Fichte introduced his system as 'Kantian' in character. Like many of Kant's followers, he rejected as meaningless the idea of a transcendent domain of unknowable things-in-themselves. But methodologically, he followed Kant in adopting the commitment that philosophy discover and proceed from first principles. Schelling further radicalized the importance of conscious experience as the starting point, and the ground, for philosophical investigation by defending what became known

[49] Manfred Frank builds a case for this reading in lectures collected under the heading, *The Philosophical Foundations of Early German Romanticism*, trans. Elizabeth Millán-Zaibert (Albany: SUNY Press, 2004).

[50] Michael Forster has argued persuasively that the dialectical structure of historical change that Hegel presents in the *Phenomenology* is motivated by what Hegel sees as the urgency of answering a particularly virulent form of skepticism (Pyrrhonism) that threatened to emerge with the rejection of Kantianism *simpliciter*. See his *Hegel and Skepticism* (Cambridge, MA: Harvard University Press, 1989).

[51] J. G. Fichte, *Science of Knowledge*, ed. and trans. Peter Heath and John Lachs (Cambridge: Cambridge University Press, 1982), 6; (*Werke*, i. 422). For a detailed account of Fichte's view, see Frederick Neuhouser's *Fichte's Theory of Subjectivity* (Cambridge: Cambridge University Press, 1990).

as his 'philosophy of identity', his view that there is an underlying identity between the mind and the world. The structures of the mind that allow us to come to know the world must be built into nature itself, so that by investigating the former we can come to know the latter. Schelling's view is terrifically optimistic; but the optimism that human consciousness could come to know the absolute and that in doing so it could restore its sense of belonging in a world from which Kantian dualism and the Enlightenment threatened to alienate it altogether, finds its most confident expression in Hegel's *Phenomenology of Spirit* (1807).

Hegel shares with his predecessors Fichte and Schelling a deep commitment, inherited from Kant, to the unity of reason. But all three remained suspicious that the very dualisms we have observed in Kant's system would preclude his putting to rest the skeptical challenges facing philosophy. Recognizing that Kant's dualism had in some sense only driven the problem deeper, the post-Kantian Idealists became determined to discover a monistic principle that could serve as an adequate foundation for philosophical reasoning. Each turned to an investigation of conscious experience as appropriately basic. Contra Fichte, Hegel argued that the nature of the *subject* cannot be understood apart from its *objects*, which meant that the radical turn inward advocated in the *Wissenschaftslehre* was a fundamental methodological error. Ultimately, the Hegel of the *Phenomenology* diagnoses Fichte's inward turn as a partial but important cause of modern alienation. It is not unusual to read the *Phenomenology* as a sort of homecoming narrative, as the story of how 'Consciousness' has become estranged from itself and how it can achieve complete self-awareness only by overcoming this alienation.[52] Hegel's account of the original estrangement has all the ingredients of a biblical fall from grace, or of a 'Paradise Lost'. Now, with some understanding of Winckelmann's Greece and the tenacity with which his idealization of it held on in the late eighteenth and nineteenth centuries in Germany, it is easier to see how Hegel came to identify that 'happy state' of grace with the 'Ethical Life' of Greek culture, a life he himself describes in the *Phenomenology* in distinctly Winckelmannian terms—'beautiful harmony and tranquil equilibrium'.[53]

In this work and in the *Philosophy of History*, Hegel's explanations of the decline and ultimate collapse of Greek culture and with it 'the realm of ethical

---

[52] G.W.F. Hegel, *Phenomenology of Spirit*, trans. A. V. Miller (Oxford: Oxford University Press, 1977), §36. Hereafter, '*PS*'.

[53] *PS* §476.

life'[54] offer a vivid contrast to the condition in which modern Spirit finds itself. He identifies as an important cause of this unhappy condition the withdrawal of the individual from the community. In Greek life, the *polis* is a genuine whole, and individual happiness is realized in the unity among citizens and in the type of self-knowledge that unity affords:

The *labor* of the individual for his own needs is just as much a satisfaction of the needs of others as of his own, and the satisfaction of his own needs he obtains only through the labor of others. As the *individual* in his individual work already *unconsciously* performs a *universal* work, so again he also performs the universal work as his *conscious* object; the whole becomes, as a whole, his own work, for which he sacrifices himself and precisely in so doing receives back from it his own self. ... This unity of being-for-another or making oneself a Thing, and of being-for-self, this universal Substance, speaks its *universal language* in the customs and laws of its nation. But this existent unchangeable essence is the expression of the very individuality which seems opposed to it. ... In the universal Spirit, therefore, each has only the certainty of himself, of finding in the actual world nothing but himself; he is as certain of the others as he is of himself. ... The wisest men of antiquity have therefore declared that wisdom and virtue consist in living in accordance with the customs of one's nation.[55]

Hegel was not entirely uncritical of this picture. In Greek ethical life as he depicts it, there is harmony and agreement in the community on matters of practical reason; ethical norms are enforced by the community. Without grounds for distinguishing between what is 'individual' and what is 'universal', these prescriptions are not burdens imposed by an alien, external, or transcendent source. They are not felt as impositions upon inclination, as duty is in Kant's ethical system. However, the harmony Hegel identifies in this period is sustained, he thinks, by the disposition of each individual to defer somewhat unreflectively to the community. Hence the idyll attained in the Greek ethical life is tainted by *naïveté*. The contrast between antiquity and modernity in terms of such *naïveté* finds precedents both in Schiller, whose essay *On Naïve and Sentimental Poetry* draws the same contrast, and in Kant, whose ethical thought strongly suggests that the failure of the Greeks to have developed a successful and systematic ethics can be attributed to their primitive, monistic conception of moral agency.

This criticism makes it impossible for Hegel to advocate a 'return' to the ethical realm as realized by his Greeks; to some extent, the individualistic turn away from this ideal taken by Hegel's immediate predecessors was inevitable, on the account offered in the *Phenomenology* and elsewhere. Nevertheless,

---

[54] *PS* §349.　　[55] *PS* §351–2.

some part of the Greek ideal must be recovered if the alienation Hegel diagnoses in modernity is to be overcome. We have seen that Hegel identifies the beginning of this alienation with the demise of Greek ethical life, but the restoration of Hellenic harmony, to whatever extent it is possible, will require an understanding of the *causes* of that demise. For Hegel, each of the historical moments he considers is characterized by a unique form of cognition. Greek ethical life is characterized by the type of certainty he attributes to individuals in the passage quoted above: 'In the universal Spirit, therefore, each has only the certainty of himself, of finding in the actual world nothing but himself; he is as certain of the others as he is of himself.'[56] The 'certainty' the Greek citizen has of himself is not the result of his having 'turned his attention away from everything that surrounds him and towards his inner life', as Fichte put it; it is, rather, that Reason at this stage in history lacks the conceptual complexity to make the distinctions (e.g. between 'self' and 'other') necessary for entertaining doubt at all. Hence, the individual 'is as certain of the others as he is of himself'. The *naïveté* of this form of cognition is shattered by the arrival of skepticism; first, in the form of the Greek Sophists,[57] and later, in the form of the aporetic methods of the Hellenistic skeptics, the sophistication of which Hegel praised earlier in *The Relation of Skepticism to Philosophy*.

The *Phenomenology* assigns a central role to skepticism in antiquity and its intellectual preconditions in explaining the collapse of the 'beautiful harmony and tranquil equilibrium' of Greek culture.[58] 'In Skepticism', Hegel posits, 'the wholly unessential and non-independent character of this "other" becomes explicit *for consciousness*; the [abstract] thought becomes the concrete thinking which annihilates the being of the world in all its manifold determinateness';[59] skepticism, that is, is the beginning of the end for an ethical ideal under-written by a form of cognition that is capable of recognizing only unity. The

---

[56] Ibid.

[57] As he explains in the *Philosophy of History* [*Vorlesungen über die Philosophie der Geschichte*] (Stuttgart: Reclam, 1961), 375.

[58] A more extended defense of the centrality of Greek skepticism to the development of the Hegelian dialectic is not possible here; see the excellent discussion of this issue in Michael Forster's *Hegel and Skepticism* (Cambridge, MA: Harvard University Press, 1989). According to Forster, 'Hegel's understanding of the nature of ancient skepticism plays an important role within his philosophy of history, manifesting itself there in his conception of what he at one point refers to as "skeptical culture" (*skeptische Bildung*). Hegel sees the historical emergence of this skeptical culture as a key to understanding the collapse of the general form of cognition and the religious and ethical attitudes that characterized the pagan Greek city-states and their replacement by the general form of cognition and the religious attitudes characteristic of the ascendant Judeo-Christian tradition' (p. 49).

[59] *PS* §202.

restoration of unity, in any degree, demands that the skeptical challenge be met. Fortunately, as Hegel explains at length in *The Relation of Skepticism to Philosophy*, modern skepticism suffers from an internal instability and exhibits a less scrupulous methodology than the skepticism of the ancients—especially the 'genuine' skepticism of the Pyrrhonists.[60] Hegel's claim is that whereas the Pyrrhonist maintains coherence by not taking for granted any claim on which he purports to suspend judgment, the modern skeptic's methods are self-undermining. The attack on modern forms of skepticism in this work is directed primarily at the Romantic thinker Gottlob Schulze, mentioned above, whom Hegel takes dogmatically to have assumed the existence of an external reality, a reality behind the appearances, the nature of which he would then bring into question.[61] Schulze, like many *Frühromantik* philosophers, attempted to revive Greek skepticism to combat the thoroughgoing rationalism of Kant and of Absolute Idealism.

# V. THE REACTION TO KANT: *FRÜHROMANTIK*

The Romantic movement, of which Friedrich Schlegel (1772–1829) and his contemporaries both in Jena (including among others his brother August Wilhelm Schlegel (1767–1845), Friedrich Immanuel Niethammer (1766–1848), and Friedrich von Hardenberg (1772–1801), better known under the name 'Novalis') and elsewhere (Johann Christian Friedrich Hölderlin (1770–1843)) were the center, did in fact characterize philosophy in rather poetic terms as a 'longing for the infinite'. They agreed that its task is to strive after an adequate conception of reality, but many of them came to terms with the idea that this task is never-ending. This group, many of them students of Karl Leonard Reinhold (1757–1823), perhaps the most enthusiastic proponent of Kant's philosophy at the time, became highly critical of the idea that reason could achieve such a conception; indeed, they thought, Kant, to the extent that his critical philosophy was successful, had shown that it could not.

According to Friedrich Schlegel, then, it is aesthetic experience or the experience of beauty that gives us what cannot be captured by reason. Art, therefore, completes philosophy. But, as Schlegel went on to argue in various

---

[60] See G. W. F. Hegel, *The Relation of Skepticism to Philosophy*, in *Jenaer Schriften* (Frankfurt am Main: Suhrkamp, 1977), 237 ff.

[61] Ibid. 219–20.

contributions to *Das Athenäum*, the short-lived but influential journal he founded in Jena (1798–1800), art must be governed by objective rules; and for the determination of these, he returned quite consciously to Winckelmann's elucidation of 'Polyclitus' rules, the perfect rules of art' and his presentation of Greece as an example of the unity between art and life.[62] With this vision of life as a guide, Schlegel went on to advocate a radical program to romanticize art, nature, science, and life. Like Schiller's concept of 'aesthetic education', the Romantic program for *Bildung* was ambitious and inclusive: a plan for the reconstruction of modern society on the model of the Greek *polis*, in which the community would flourish *because* the conditions for *individual* freedom and flourishing had been established. Early German Romanticism was no narrow literary movement; collectively, its proponents aimed at a political and social ideal that was staunchly individualistic, and that emphasized freedom and creative expression as a human necessity. They embraced the 'critical' philosophical spirit of the age, but argued that Kant had gone too far in his insistence on the authority of reason at the expense of feeling, especially in the form of aesthetic experience.

The 'Jena constellation' to which Schlegel was so central also included Friedrich Heinrich Jacobi and Novalis, both of whom rejected 'unconditioned' first principles as either dispensable or unattainable. Jacobi, for instance, observed in his book on Spinoza that propositions (i.e. Kantian judgments), if justified, are always justified by some other proposition (i.e. they are always 'conditioned').[63] But this, he argued, leads inevitably to infinite regress, or else to what the Greek skeptics would have called the Mode of Hypothesis, in which we simply stipulate some proposition as a starting point. According to Jacobi and also Novalis, that starting point could be nothing other than a *feeling*. Thus, 'To believe means: to take a fact to be certain without anything further, where no additional light would be shed upon the fact through an additional grounding of it—where a grounding is neither possible nor necessary.' Novalis recapitulates this position succinctly with the words: 'What I don't know, but I feel..., I believe'.[64] The Romantics, in this sense also, manifested the 'critical' spirit of

---

[62] For further discussion, see Frederick C. Beiser's *The Romantic Imperative: The Concept of Early German Romanticism* (Cambridge, MA: Harvard University Press, 2003), esp. ch. 1.

[63] F. H. Jacobi from the seventh *Beilage* of his *Spinoza Büchlein*; discussed in Frank, *The Philosophical Foundations of Early German Romanticism*, 34.

[64] Ibid. 23–37, argues at length for the characterization of German Romanticism as a principled skepticism rather than a rejection of reason. For the quote from Novalis, see *Novalis Schriften*, 5 vols., ed. Paul Kluckhohn and Richard Samuel (Stuttgart: Kohlhammer, 1960–98); ii. 105, ll. 1–3, 11–13.

the age (as a type of skepticism), and on this score charged Kant with not having gone far enough! Not far enough, that is, to have submitted to criticism the lingering dogmatism in his own system—the residue of Platonic rationalism.

# VI. THE LATE NINETEENTH CENTURY: NIETZSCHE AND HEIDEGGER

By the late nineteenth century, those who became critical of Idealism in all its forms were thinkers who had cut their teeth on classical philology. Doxographical lectures began to be standard academic fare in Germany by the middle of that century, as scholars like August Boeckh (1785–1867), a colleague of Hegel's at the University of Berlin who (though more an encyclopedist than a philosopher) inspired a generation of scholars enthusiastic about antiquity, gave classical texts regular exposure.[65] Ludwig Feuerbach's (1804–72) early infatuation with Hegel's work inspired him to study Stoic thought; and as a student, Karl Marx (1818–83) too studied Greek philosophy and produced a dissertation on the atomist philosophers Democritus and Epicurus. But the German thinker of the late nineteenth century best known for his engagement with the Greeks is surely Friedrich Nietzsche (1844–1900).

Nietzsche was trained as a classical philologist; he early on acquired a facility with classical languages that surpassed his fluency with modern foreign languages, wrote several articles as a student on Diogenes Laertius' *Lives of the Philosophers*, and maintained a life-long engagement with Greek philosophy. His complicated attitude toward the figure of Socrates is well known, and much has been made of his effusive praise of Heraclitus in his late as well as in his early texts. His early unpublished work includes an important set of lectures on the pre-Platonic philosophers and a number of essays devoted to Hellenistic thought; of these essays, *Philosophy in the Tragic Age of the Greeks* (1873) has probably attracted the most scholarly attention. Nietzsche's first major academic publication, *The Birth of Tragedy* (1872), opens with the claim that,

We will have gained much for the science of aesthetics, once we perceive not merely by logical inference, but with the immediate certainty of vision, that the continuous

---

[65] For an account of the rise of classical philology in the German academy, of its competing methodological traditions, and for a persuasive reading of Friedrich Nietzsche's place in this milieu, see James Whitman's 'Nietzsche in the Magisterial Tradition of German Classical Philology', *Journal of the History of Ideas* 47 (1986), 453–68.

development of art is bound up with the *Apollinian* and *Dionysian* duality. ... The terms Dionysian and Apollinian we borrow from the Greeks, who disclose to the discerning mind the profound mysteries of their view of art, not, to be sure, in concepts, but in the intensely clear figures of their gods.[66]

Like Winckelmann's *Reflections on the Imitation of Greek Works*, the reach of Nietzsche's *Birth of Tragedy* went far beyond its claim to be merely an investigation into aesthetic principles. Written during the most intense phase of Nietzsche's devotion to Richard Wagner, another devotee of Goethe to whom Nietzsche's preface is addressed, *The Birth of Tragedy* contains more than a trace of Goethe's 'pagan' influence. The aim of Nietzsche's philological method was to understand Greek culture by literally *reanimating* it, just as Goethe had aimed to do, 'not, to be sure, in concepts', or 'merely by logical inference', but 'with the immediate certainty of vision'. Prior to Nietzsche, few of the authors we have seen had drawn attention to the Dionysian element in Greek religion and art.

Prima facie, the wild frenzy of the Dionysian would seem anathema to the 'noble simplicity and quiet grandeur' so widely attributed to the Greeks, not to mention to the internal harmony ascribed to the Greek 'self'. But it is necessary to note, first, that Nietzsche treats the tension between the Apollinian and Dionysian elements primarily as a cultural phenomenon; individuals are generally dominated by one tendency or the other. And second, even in the arena of culture (at least a successful, flourishing culture), these two forces are not so much at war with one another as they are held in a state of dynamic tension. The result of this tension, like the tension of the strings on a well-tuned instrument, can be described, perfectly appropriately in the context of an aesthetic treatise, as a sort of 'harmony'. Nietzsche's metaphor here for the relationship of Apollinian to Dionysian is the 'duality of the sexes', which suggests the nature of the relationship is, first of all, entirely *natural*, but also *necessary* and *productive*. What it produces, when successful, is something aesthetically valuable. Nietzsche's occasionally disparaging remarks about 'romanticism' aside, the recovery of the Dionysian is in Nietzsche's hands the key to the recovery of the much sought-after wholeness and harmony of the Romantic tradition:

Under the charm of the Dionysian not only is the union between man and man reaffirmed, but nature which has become alienated, hostile, or subjugated, celebrates

---

[66] Friedrich Nietzsche, *The Birth of Tragedy*, trans. Walter Kaufmann in *Basic Writings of Nietzsche* (New York: Modern Library, 1966), §1. Hereafter '*BT*'.

once more her reconciliation with her lost son, man. . . . Now, with the gospel of universal harmony, each one feels himself not only united, reconciled, and fused with his neighbor, but as one with him, as if the veil of *māyā* had been torn aside and were now merely fluttering in tatters before the mysterious primordial unity. . . . [Man] is no longer an artist, he has become a work of art . . .[67]

Nietzsche's description and his reference to man as nature's 'lost son' vividly recaptures the longing of Schiller's 'Gods of Greece'; this same passage alludes indirectly to Schiller's lyric poem 'Ode to Joy' in its mention of Beethoven's Ninth Symphony. Nietzsche's debt to his 'great teacher', Arthur Schopenhauer, is of course in evidence here as well: Schopenhauer defended the view that aesthetic experience is the highest and the only truly valuable experience in an otherwise meaningless existence. But the idea that it is possible for a human being not simply to create art but to create *himself as art* resonates loudly with the 'romantic imperative' (*der romantische Imperativ*) introduced in the late 1790s by Friedrich Schlegel,[68] which was equally an exhortation for man to make of life and of himself something aesthetically beautiful.

Though he later moved away from many of the themes of *The Birth of Tragedy*, soon repudiating Schopenhauer's crypto-Kantian metaphysics and abandoning his friendship with Wagner, Nietzsche retained his own version of the 'romantic imperative', that life is best judged by aesthetic criteria, as envisioned by Schlegel.[69] Moreover, Nietzsche echoed the Romantic tradition in its criticism of Kant's system, even employing the strategies of the Greek skeptics in his attacks on Kant's metaphysical doctrines and in his scathing treatment of the asceticism in Kantian ethics.[70] As in the epistemology of Jacobi and Novalis, which was inspired by their contact with the methods of the Pyrrhonian skeptics, as we saw above, Nietzsche concludes that all human knowledge is situated or 'conditioned' by further principles, such that the very idea of a presuppositionless first principle or wholly objective starting point for inquiry

---

[67]  *BT* §1.        [68]  Friedrich Schlegel, *Kritische Ausgabe*, xvi. 134; fragment no. 586.

[69]  This theme persists in Nietzsche's many exhortations to 'give style to one's character', in his claims that man's aim as a self-creator would be to create something aesthetically pleasing, and in his insistence that the monstrosity of the ascetic ideal manifests itself physically. He observes, for instance, how the Christian determination to see the world as ugly has 'made' the world ugly. Alexander Nehamas, in *Nietzsche: Life as Literature* (Cambridge, MA: Harvard University Press, 1985), defends an extreme version of this reading, according to which Nietzsche sees reality as a text, a work of literature, and is committed to the idea that the human being can be the author of his own life. There is no doubt that this idea would be distinctly appealing to Schlegel, but it takes Nietzsche's commitment to the idea beyond what can be supported by the texts.

[70]  For a more extended defense of skeptical themes in Nietzsche's work, see my 'The Pyrrhonian Revival in Montaigne and Nietzsche', *The Journal of the History of Ideas*, 65/3 ( July 2004), 497–514.

is at best an unattainable ideal, and at worst a sheer absurdity. Nietzsche's celebrated 'perspectivism' is a reincarnation of precisely the view found in the early German Romantics, established on a Pyrrhonian model and marshaled against the dogmatic rashness of metaphysics and the asceticism of religious ideals.

Nietzsche at times derides the tradition of German Romanticism for its excesses, but his stated attitude is belied by his methodological and critical affinities with it, by his great admiration for its literary progenitor Goethe, and by his reverence for Hölderlin, who, though he never gained admittance into the 'Jena constellation', shared its 'longing for the infinite' and its commitment to the ideal of Hellenic harmony. Hölderlin, who knew Herder, Goethe, and Schiller, was the last of a living tradition of Winckelmannites. He produced a master's thesis on Winckelmann's *History of Art Among the Ancients*, and in the late 1790s and early 1800s produced a quite liberal translation of Sophocles' *Antigone* and some other essays on classical works, none of which were particularly well received by contemporary classicists. Schiller and Goethe, whom Hölderlin especially admired, generally treated him coolly, and between one another often derided him.[71] Thus Hölderlin, who descended into madness for the last forty years of his life, had little impact on his immediate contemporaries. His best work appeared only posthumously, in 1846.[72] Nietzsche was the first major thinker genuinely to appreciate Hölderlin's genius, and from the standpoint of the historiography of the Greek legacy in Germany, Hölderlin's poetry might be considered the penultimate link in the chain begun by Winckelmann in 1755. Nietzsche, then, would be the last, but for the emergence of an early twentieth-century thinker who identified himself even more conspicuously with the Greeks, namely Martin Heidegger (1889–1976).

Heidegger's philosophy is the pinnacle of the Romantic nostalgia for Hellenic harmony, and also its last gasp; after Nietzsche, Heidegger is perhaps Hölderlin's most prominent philosophical admirer. The stated goal of Heidegger's magnum opus *Being and Time* (1927) is to recover the question of the meaning of 'Being', something of which moderns at least since Descartes have lost sight. *Being and Time* is guided by its own 'fall from grace' narrative: the initial strides toward an adequate interpretation of Being were undertaken by 'the Greeks', but in the interim the conditions even for the raising of the

---

[71] Butler, *Tyranny of Greece over Germany*, 236, for example, recounts an anecdote in which the Hellenist J. H. Voss in 1804 wrote to a friend, 'Do read the fourth chorus of the *Antigone*; you should have seen Schiller laugh!'

[72] Ibid., 238.

question of what 'Being' means have been obscured. Like Hölderlin, Heidegger seems grimly determined to resurrect ancient Greece as a means of redeeming man from his unhappy state.

Heidegger's conspicuous admiration notwithstanding, however, through the lens of his work the Greeks remain in soft focus more than in the work of perhaps any German thinker since Winckelmann. The fantastic *naïveté* of Winckelmann's Hellenic ideal was made possible in part by his treatment of 'the Greeks' as an homogeneous group, an unfortunate simplification that found its way into the hands of his successors for many years. In the early part of the nineteenth century, the development of classical philology helped to correct this oversimplification, by increasing the general accessibility and promoting the importance of primary texts. As it made more and more subtle accounts of the differences among a rich variety of ancient traditions possible, it raised expectations for the depth and thoroughness of those accounts. Heidegger, on the contemporary end of this inheritance, should reflect these advances clearly. Indeed, he committed himself to the painstaking study of many ancient texts, especially pedagogically—he would devote entire semester seminars to the study of works as short as Plato's *Phaedo*. But his philological efforts, as we see them in *Being in Time*, for example, are more than anything a signature of his philosophical commitments. In the Introduction II to *Being and Time*, for instance, he declares that,

Everyone who is acquainted with the middle ages sees that Descartes is 'dependent' upon medieval scholasticism and employs its terminology. . . . The full extent of this cannot be estimated until both the meaning and the limitations of the ancient ontology have been exhibited in terms of an orientation directed towards the question of Being. . . . When this is done, it will be manifest that the ancient way of interpreting the Being of entities is oriented towards the 'world' or 'Nature' in the widest sense, and that it is indeed in terms of 'time' that its understanding of Being is obtained. The outward evidence for this . . . is the treatment of the meaning of Being as παρό υσία or όυσία, which signifies, in ontologico-Temporal terms, 'presence'. Entities are grasped in their Being as 'presence'; this means that they are understood with regard to a definite mode of time—the 'Present'.[73]

Here, Heidegger illustrates the difference between the understanding of Being prior to as opposed to after the 'Fall' he posits. But the 'ancient way', as the 'medieval way', is presented in the generic, irrespective of important differences among thinkers or schools. Moreover, as an instance of a general

---

[73] Martin Heidegger, *Being and Time*, trans. John Macquarrie and Edward Robinson (San Francisco: Harper & Row, 1962), 46–7.

methodological strategy in *Being and Time* and elsewhere, Heidegger baldly makes claim to a derivation from ὀυσία to παρόυσία, introducing it as evidence of a conceptual connection he would have us make between *existence* and *presence*. The existential import and psychological insight of *Being and Time* is beyond reproach, but for all of Heidegger's ostensive engagement with the Greeks, his treatment of them is a significant departure from the tradition of scholarly engagement with Hellenistic philosophy as it emerged in Germany from the middle of the eighteenth century. It may be entirely appropriate that this tradition ends with the work of a thinker who, very much in the spirit of Winckelmann, was determined to find in Greek thought more than anything else a palliative for the modern condition.

## VII. The Myth of Hellenic Harmony

The German love affair with the Greeks having persisted for so long, and its influence having been at once so ubiquitous and so diffuse, it is difficult to draw genuinely satisfying and appropriately synoptic conclusions about it. Better, in one sense, to let Goethe's dictum serve as a reminder of the many and various uses to which ancient ideas were put over the period we have been considering—that insofar as these figures were 'Greeks', they were so each in his own way. Nevertheless, it was also taken as part of Goethe's claim that each *ought* to be a Greek, and as we have seen, that imperative—and the seriousness with which it was received—is the common thread in this long tradition. The admiration for the Hellenic ideal cut across the most central philosophical divisions of the post-Enlightenment era and was able make more tangible what was at stake and provide a common touchstone for these debates. But perhaps most importantly, since its inception in Winckelmann's work, the Hellenic ideal of the free spirit who embodies 'noble simplicity and quiet grandeur' exercised a powerful normative force on German thinkers: it came to be accepted as part of the task of philosophy that it have something to say about what counts as the best sort of life for *modern* individuals and how it might be achieved. Winckelmann's original vision became the regulative ideal for this project: the credit must go to Winckelmann for having established Hellenism as a sort of highest good, the modern eudaimonia. And as in antiquity, major schools of thought broke with one another over their analyses of the concept, what they took its content to be, and the best means of achieving it. In this way, the contact with the Greeks lent modern German thought its own decidedly eudaimonistic orientation.

Ironically, however, the overwhelming success of this ideal depended in no small part on its being something of a caricature. In the words of one commentator, the German philosophical imagination had been decisively conquered 'by the mythical inhabitants of a Greece that never was on sea or land'.[74] His valuable scholarly achievement notwithstanding, the depth of Winckelmann's commitment to find harmony and freedom in the Hellenic individual allowed for a sometimes indiscriminate mixing of observations from Greek authors, from the pre-classical through the Hellenistic. His reading and reconstruction were at some points highly selective; and this selectivity was in no way peculiar to Winckelmann. If we look back at the Weimar classicists' enchantment with Greece, it is important to note that their fascination with Hellenism and their commitment to Winckelmann's ideal generally came about *prior to* their contact with the original sources.

Schiller is a vivid case in point here: his early writings made liberal use of allusions to Greek mythology, but his references came at several removes from the sources and were at this stage of his career more accurate as indicators of contemporary fashion than of Schiller's intellectual appreciation. He did not know Greek at the time, and there is little evidence that he had read any of the relevant plays or other ancient works. References to ancient mythology in poems such as 'Group in the Tartarus' and 'Elysium' in Schiller's *Anthology*, for instance, border on pastiche, and they bear the distinctive stamp of Winckelmann's description of *Laocoon*, which Schiller may have known only via Lessing's treatise.[75] It was only Schiller's contact in Weimar with Goethe, and even earlier with Goethe's friend Christoph Martin Wieland (1733–1813), that inspired a passion for Greek thought that motivated Schiller to study

---

[74] Butler, *Tyranny of Greece over Germany*, 80.

[75] This observation is commonplace in the scholarship on Schiller's early work, but takes a particularly scathing form in Butler's *Tyranny of Greece over Germany*: 'Schiller's pantheon was crowded with a throng of meaningless Graeco-Roman-Anacreontic divinities...on the whole the pseudo-Greek influence was superficial in the extreme; and Greek mythology and the Greek conception of fate had less than no effect on Schiller's early dramas in spite of a classical reference here and there. He may have owed something to Plutarch during this period, but demonstrably nothing whatsoever to the Greek dramatists, whom he had not read at school, and did not read in Stuttgart, Mannheim, Bauerbach, Leipzig or Dresden. He was acquainted with Homer, notably with Bürger's versions of some passages, and gave his own verse-rendering of Hector's farewell to Andromache which Amalia sang in *The Robbers*; but Homer, whilst occasionally supplementing his knowledge of Virgil's and Ovid's gods and heroes, in no way nourished his genius, either in his plays or in his poems, where indeed the decadent Renaissance deities are rampant' (Butler, *Tyranny of Greece over Germany*, 163; see also Hatfield, *Aesthetic Paganism in German Literature*, 139).

Homer in earnest and finally (in 1788) to learn the language.[76] In Schiller's case and many others, it was the adoption of the Hellenic ideal *as ideal* that motivated the study of the sources, and not the other way around.

In short, the Greeks could be all things to all people, but only as long as a modicum of vagueness remained in the history. Goethe once confessed in a letter that, 'he could never have written [*Iphigenia*] . . . had he not been then relatively ignorant of the historical Greeks'.[77] It is tempting to say the same of *Being and Time*, except that we know Heidegger to have been in better possession of the relevant facts about Greek history, language, and culture. The sweeping generalizations and misty, romantic paeans to Greece turned out to be unsustainable in the face of more rigorous inquiry, which is why the nostalgic qualities of Heidegger's work sit so uneasily with its philosophical sophistication. What ultimately destroyed the viability of Greece as an ideal, finally in the twentieth century, was just that which dispelled the ignorance and destroyed the illusion itself—the progress of modern scholarship.

---

[76]  See Schiller's letter to Körner of 28 August 1788.
[77]  Goethe xxii. 642; quoted (in translation) by Hatfield, *Aesthetic Paganism in German Literature*, 22.

# CHAPTER 18

# POLITICAL, MORAL, AND CRITICAL THEORY

## ON THE PRACTICAL PHILOSOPHY OF THE FRANKFURT SCHOOL

JAMES GORDON FINLAYSON

'What exists is bad. Something else must take its place.'

Louis Auguste Blanqui

## INTRODUCTION: FRANKFURT SCHOOL CRITICAL THEORY

'CRITICAL THEORY' is now part of the lingua franca of academic discourse in literary and cultural studies, art history, intellectual history, sociology, and not least in social and political philosophy. Yet, for all that, it is not easy to say accurately what it is. Even the label 'the Frankfurt School' can be misleading, for it was never the official name of an institution. Rather it was the retrospectively adopted label for a sub-tradition of German social theory, comprising the work of various theorists from different disciplines working in the Frankfurt-based Institut für Sozialforschung (Institute for Social Research) from the 1930s onwards, and publishing in its journal, the *Zeitschrift für Sozialforschung*, until it ceased publication in 1941. This group of thinkers is often divided into three generations.[1] The label 'Frankfurt School critical theory' is a collective noun for the thought of various thinkers spanning these three 'generations'. Naturally the ideas of each of these thinkers changed over the years.[2] Even Adorno's thought, which remained remarkably stable over the course of his life, underwent important developments.[3] Critical

---

[1] The division of Frankfurt School theorists into generations, with Horkheimer, Adorno, and Marcuse deemed as first-generation theorists, Jürgen Habermas a second-generation theorist, and Axel Honneth a third-generation theorist, is also potentially misleading. The real first generation at the Institut under the directorship of Carl Grünberg comprised thinkers such as Karl August Wittvogel, Richard Sorge, Henryk Grossmann, Friedrich Pollock, and Felix Weil. See Martin Jay, *The Dialectical Imagination* (London: Heinemann, 1973); and Rolf Wiggershaus, *The Frankfurt School*, (Cambridge: Polity, 1994). Habermas, who is closely associated with the Frankfurt School, was only at the Institut for a short period in the late 1950s. So the 'school' and its members must not be identified too closely with the Institut für Sozialforschung and its members.

[2] Habermas remarks that his 'research programme has remained the *same* since about 1970'. See Jürgen Habermas, *Justification and Application* (Cambridge: Polity, 1993), 149. Habermas's early work is similar in approach to that of the first generation of Frankfurt School thinkers. In the 1970s, inspired by pragmatism and speech-act theory, Habermas went back to the drawing board. His mature theory as expounded in *Theory of Communication*, his various writings on discourse ethics, and *Between Facts and Norms*, form part of this same basic research programme. There have, of course, been a lot of developments within that programme. For a brief overview, see James Gordon Finlayson, *Habermas: A Very Short Introduction* (Oxford: Oxford University Press, 2005).

[3] Consider the way in which Adorno uses the concept of 'immanent critique' in his Hegel studies and in *Against Epistemology* (*Metakritik der Erkenntnislehre*) which was eventually published 1956, but for which much of the preparatory work had been done when Adorno was a graduate student at Merton College, Oxford in the mid-1930s. In these texts Adorno endorses 'immanent critique' and rejects 'transcendent critique' on the grounds that the latter 'sympathizes with authority in its very form'. Adorno, *Hegel: Three Studies*, trans. Shierry Weber Nicholsen (Cambridge, MA: MIT Press, 1993), 146; *Theodor W. Adorno: Gesammelte Schriften*, ed. R. Tiedemann (Frankfurt am Main: Suhrkamp, 1997), v. 14–15 and 374 (henceforth GS). This early view is prima facie hard to square with his later remark in 'Cultural Criticism and Society' (1949) that, '[t]o insist on the choice between immanence and transcendence is a relapse into the traditional logic which was the object of Hegel's polemic against Kant' (Adorno, *Prisms*, trans. Samuel and Shierry Weber (Cambridge MA: MIT Press, 1981), 31; Adorno, GS x/1. 25). Later still, in *Negative Dialectics* (1967), Adorno more or less equates the context of immanence with the context of delusion, and in the final sections of the book there is a rehabilitation of transcendent metaphysics, albeit in the moment of its fall. To take just two remarks of many: 'Dialectics is the self-consciousness of the objective context of delusion (*Verblendungszusammenhang*): it is not already to have escaped it. Objectively, its aim is to break out of this context from within' and 'No light falls on people and things, in which transcendence is not reflected' (Adorno, *Negative Dialectics*,

theory is thus a multifarious and dynamic body of thought, and it is hard to make general statements about its relation to practical philosophy without shoehorning it into one-size-fits-all judgments. To avoid so doing I shall indicate wherever possible whose critical theory is at issue and at what phase in its development.

Frankfurt School critical theory is a particular kind of *Gesellschaftskritik* or social criticism, the practical aims of which are essential to and inseparable from it. Indeed, as distinct from social theory or sociology, critical theory is, in the eyes of its architects and practitioners, a kind of *practice*. Yet critical theory is still very much philosophy. One might think, then, that critical theory must be closely related to 'practical philosophy', a term by which we generally understand (i) normative ethical theory, (ii) normative political theory, and (iii) prudence or practical wisdom. In fact, its relation to the three main areas of practical philosophy is strained and not at all straightforward. The two major objections that have been levelled at the critical theory of Horkheimer and Adorno were that it had no politics, and that it suffered from a 'normative deficit' or the absence of normative foundations. These objections called the practical aspirations of critical theory seriously into question. Furthermore, critical theory from early on had an almost entirely negative view of instrumental reasoning. This raises the question of what kind of practical upshot Frankfurt School critical theory can have, absent all political, moral, and prudential considerations?

# 1. WHAT IS A *CRITICAL* THEORY OF SOCIETY?

To answer this question we must have a better understanding of what critical theory is. Nietzsche observed that only what has no history can be defined, and critical theory has a history.[4] Still, we can characterize critical theory

---

trans. E. B. Ashton (London: Routledge, 1973), 406 and 404–5; Adorno, GS vi. 398 and 396). This has led one critic to argue that Adorno is advancing 'the concept of transcendent critique' and to deny that Adorno's social criticism is immanent criticism. See Andrew Buchwalter, 'Hegel, Adorno and the Concept of Transcendent Critique', *Philosophy and Social Criticism* 12/4 (1987), 297–328.

[4] Friedrich Nietzsche, 'Zur Genealogie der Moral', in Friedrich Nietzsche, *Kritische Studienausgabe*, v, ed. G. Colli and M. Montinari (Munich: Deutsche Taschenbuch Verlag GmbH, 1999), 317. *On the Genealogy of Morals*, ed. K. Ansell-Pearson (Cambridge: Cambridge University Press, 1994), 57. On the historical development of first-generation critical theory see Helmut Dubiel, *Theory and Politics: Studies in the Development of Critical Theory*, trans. B. Gregg (Cambridge, MA: MIT Press, 1985). On the history of the Frankfurt School see Wiggershaus, *The Frankfurt School*.

adequately for our purposes by pointing out its salient features and then by giving an historical account of how it came to have these. In 'Traditional and Critical Theory', an essay of 1937 that later acquired the status of a canonical text, Horkheimer attempted to distinguish 'critical theory' from what he called 'traditional theory'.

## 1.1  Traditional and Critical Theory

'Traditional theory' is a very wide term encompassing a whole range of different kinds of theory from rationalist metaphysics, empiricism and natural science, through to formal systems of mathematics and logic. In Horkheimer's view all traditional theory shares some significant general features: it aims to be a unified, systematic, and complete body of knowledge consisting of laws or propositions standing over and against a realm of independent facts it purports to mirror. Traditional theory is ordered into different specialist domains that Horkheimer saw as a reflection of the intellectual division of labour. Traditional theorists work within these given disciplinary boundaries. Finally, traditional theory stands apparently disconnected from the society which gave rise to it, and divorced from the context of meanings and actions that characterize human life within it.

Horkheimer was less interested in calling into question the validity of the various kinds of knowledge he brings under the umbrella term 'traditional theory' than he was in challenging what he saw as the 'positivist' dogma that the only valid kind of knowledge was that provided by the natural sciences.[5] Instead of naturalizing epistemology (by making natural science the model of all knowledge) as some positivists and later Quine undertook to do, Horkheimer's intention was to humanize it, or at least some of it. Thus, his criticism of traditional theory can be understood as part of a wider movement, including the hermeneutic tradition of Wilhelm Dilthey and European phenomenology, that set out to explicate and vindicate the specific nature of the historical, human, and the social sciences.[6]

Critical theory, argued Horkheimer, is, in contrast to traditional theory, inherently interdisciplinary. It draws on a range of different disciplines and

---

[5] In this respect it is more helpful to see critical theory as a dialectical transformation of certain parts of traditional theory rather than as a simple alternative to it.

[6] Husserl was working on *The Crisis of the European Sciences* in 1937, the year in which 'Traditional and Critical Theory' appeared in the *Zeitschrift*.

challenges the boundaries within which they operate. Moreover, critical theory stands in a self-conscious relation to the society around it. It is self-reflective about its own status and social function, and this self-reflectiveness is built into the theory. Where traditional theory purports to mirror a domain of unchanging, independently existing facts, critical theory is aware of the social and historical context in which knowledge arises, and which always already determines the objects of knowledge. In the case of traditional theory knower and known, perceiver and perceived, are taken to be entirely independent; in the case of critical theory they are not. It is because there is a concealed or forgotten constitutive relation between human activity and social reality, Horkheimer claimed, that critical theory can take upon itself the practical aim of the transformation of social reality.

## 1.2  The Practical Aims of Critical Theory

For Horkheimer critical theory is a particular kind of 'human activity' or 'critical attitude' (*kritisches Verhalten*) aimed at emancipation.[7] He mentions various practical aims, the main ones being the achievement of 'reasonable conditions of life', 'social transformation', and 'the elimination (*Aufhebung*) of social injustice'.[8] These can be called *remedial* aims since they have to do with how to reform, improve, or transform society for the better. Not all the practical aims of critical theory are remedial. Critical theory also has *diagnostic* aims. The diagnostic aim of critical theory can be stated relatively simply: it is to discover and to give an account of *what is wrong with* a society, its institutions, its practices and its economic organization, to show in what respects it is not *as it ought to be*.

---

[7]  Max Horkheimer, 'Traditional and Critical Theory', in his *Critical Theory: Selected Essays* (New York: Herder and Herder, 1972), 206–7 (henceforth CT); *Max Horkheimer. Kritische Theorie: eine Dokumentation*, ed. A. Schmidt, ii (Frankfurt am Main, Fischer Verlag, 1968), 155–7 (in two volumes, henceforth KT i and ii).

[8]  In 'Traditional and Critical Theory' Horkheimer refers to three such interests: the 'interest in reasonable conditions', the 'interest in social transformation', and the 'interest in the elimination (*Aufhebung*) of social injustice' (Horkheimer, CT 199, 241, 243; KT ii. 147, 189, 190). As Herbert Schnädelbach points out, in the original 1937 article in the *Zeitschrift* Horkheimer talks not of the 'interest in the elimination (*Aufhebung*) of social injustice' but of the 'interest in the overcoming of class domination'. This marks a noticeable shift from a Marxist conception critical theory's aim in 1937 to a more explicitly moral (and less openly Marxist) aim in 1968. See *Zeitschrift für Sozialforschung* 6 (1937), 292; Herbert Schnädelbach, 'Max Horkheimer and the Moral Philosophy of German Idealism', in S. Benhabib, W. Bonss, and J. McCole (eds.), *On Max Horkheimer* (Cambridge, MA: MIT Press, 1993), 305.

Critical theory can thus be provisionally characterized as a philosophical theory of society with two kinds of practical aim: diagnostic and remedial. Both of these aims are closely linked, just as they are in medicine, from which the term 'diagnosis' is borrowed: without a proper diagnosis there would be no question of a remedy. Similarly, the aim of critical theory is not simply to identify and correctly describe what is wrong, but to put it right. Of course different critical theorists, in response to changing historical and social circumstances, offered different diagnoses and remedies. They also had different conceptions of the relation between the diagnostic and remedial aims of the theory. Roughly, what distinguished early critical theory from its later variants is that it had more faith in its ability to fulfil its remedial aims, whilst later critical theory (everything from 1944 onward), for a variety of different reasons, came to focus more on the diagnostic aim.

In a series of recent articles on the legacy of critical theory, Axel Honneth has put forward the thesis that the diagnosis of what is wrong with society, or, to continue the medical language, the diagnosis of 'social pathology', is a necessary minimal aim of any theory critical theory. True, numerous other social and political thinkers, not just Frankfurt School theorists, offer theories that are *critical* in this minimal sense. For example, the Anglo-American analytic tradition of political philosophy is *critical* in this sense. John Rawls famously wrote that, '[j]ustice is the first virtue of social institutions, as truth is of systems of thought.' [9] He asks the question, is the basic structure of society just? This has practical implications because 'laws and institutions, no matter how efficient and well-arranged must be reformed or abolished if they are unjust'.[10] This is not to deny the correctness of Honneth's thesis, which is not trying to capture what is distinctive about Frankfurt School critical theory, but rather to show what is necessary to it. It claims to identify a general feature common to all Frankfurt School critical theory, from the work of Horkheimer in the 1930s, through that of Horkheimer, Adorno, and Marcuse after the war, right up to and including the work of Habermas and Honneth himself.[11]

Diagnostic and remedial aims are common to all kinds of social criticism, for example those voiced by protest groups, social movements, dissidents,

---

[9]  John Rawls, *Theory of Justice* (Oxford: Oxford University Press, 1973), 3.
[10]  Ibid.
[11]  Recall that the first-generation theorists Adorno, Horkheimer and Marcuse produced a lot of work, over a long period (from the 1930s to the 1970s) in which their ideas developed considerably. It is not as easy as it might seem to capture features common to all of it.

etc. These may not take the form of *theory*, but of literature, poetry, civil disobedience, or unrest instead. As Michael Walzer puts it, '[t]he special role of the critic is to describe what is wrong in ways that suggest a remedy.'[12] Not all social critics are also social theorists. What is characteristic of the Frankfurt School critical theorist is the role that social theory (not just philosophy, but also sociology, social psychology, and psychoanalysis) plays in the articulation of their criticism.

## 1.3  Critique and Criticism

Our initial characterization of critical theory is drawn from a consideration of Horkheimer's essay 'Traditional and Critical Theory'. The history of critical theory does not begin with the minting of the concept 'critical theory', of course, and if we want properly to understand the nature of critical theory and its practical aims, as well as the specific form of criticism the Frankfurt theorists put in play, we must trace the history of two other concepts, criticism/critique and reason/rationality.

It is a habit of twentieth-Century German philosophy to seek a partially obscured meaning of a term hidden in its etymological origins and then work forward to its present meaning. In truth not much is to be gained by looking at the etymology of the word 'criticism', which stems from the Greek adjective κριτικός, formed from the verb κρίνω, meaning to separate, distinguish, discriminate, adjudicate, judge and decide, apart from the fact that the verb to criticize still means in some contexts to discriminate and to judge.[13] It is more helpful to look at the modern, specifically philosophical concept of criticism that emerged in Germany in the seventeenth and eighteenth centuries. Prior to Kant, the word 'Kritik', which in German just meant criticism and had no technical connotations, had been mainly used in the context of textual criticism. Criticism referred to the practice of restoring, completing, and where possible authenticating (usually ancient) manuscripts.[14] In the *Critique of Pure Reason* (1781) Kant gave the term 'critique' its primary modern sense

---

[12]  Michael Walzer, *The Company of Critics* (London: Peter Halban, 1989), 10.
[13]  Liddell and Scott, *Intermediate Greek–English Lexicon* (Oxford: Clarendon Press, 1985), 450.
[14]  The first occurrence of the term in the German language dates back to a passage from Stolle's *Kurze Anleitung zur Historie der Gelehrtheit* (1718) excerpted by Kant in his Logic: 'Die Critic heißt insgemein eine Kunst, die alten Autors zu verstehen (oder verständlich zu machen), was sie geschrieben, von dem was man ihnen untergeschoben, oder verfälscht hat, zu unterscheiden, und das verdorbene auszubessern oder zu ersetzen' (Kant, *Handschriftliche Nachlaß*. Logik. Immanuel Kant, *Werke*, ed. Königlich Preussischen Akademie der Wissenschaften (Berlin: Georg Reimer, 1911) xvi.

of theoretical self-reflection: a critique in this new sense, as attested by the subjective and objective genitive in the title, is a self-examination of reason by reason. Kant's first *Critique* set itself both negative and positive tasks: negatively, it was to limit and thus to suspend the claims of transcendent dogmatic metaphysics, for example, that of St Anselm, to be able to deduce the existence of God entirely a priori.[15] Positively, it was to establish (contra Hume's scepticism about induction) the a priori credentials of the synthetic propositions of natural science and to vindicate the principles of pure reason.

Critical theory is a descendant of Kantian critique in so far as it too understands itself as a form of rational self-reflection, a reflection on reason by reason, but this is about as far as the parallel goes. For one thing, Kant thinks of the critique of pure reason as a kind of meta-theory, distinct from the synthetic a priori knowledge and analytic a priori knowledge on which it reflects, whereas critical theory is primarily a kind of critical practice, albeit a self-reflective one. For another, Kant conceived reason as a faculty of mind and as a realm of pure, a priori ideas and principles, and viewed rationality as the proper exercise of this faculty when brought to bear on judgement and human action.[16]

Viewed historically, Kant's first *Critique* was, however, more than just a book on epistemology and metaphysics. There was a larger practical and cultural agenda to the work, the lineaments of which can be discerned in the political and judicial metaphors in which Kant couches his project in the Prefaces and in the Transcendental Doctrine of Method.[17] Kant's *Critique of*

---

170, Anm. 10 (henceforth AA)). See O. Brunner, W. Conze, and R. Koselleck (eds.), *Geschichtliche Grundbegriffe: Historisches Lexikon zur politisch-sozialen Sprache in Deutschland*, (Stuttgart: Klett-Cotta, 1982), iii. 660.

[15] St Anselm, *Proslogion* 1, chs. 2–5, trans. M. J. Charlesworth (Oxford: Clarendon Press, 1965). Immanuel Kant, *Critique of Pure Reason*, trans. P. Guyer and A. Wood (Cambridge: Cambridge University Press, 1998), A592 ff., B620 (henceforth CPR). See also CPR Avii–xxii; Bviii–xliv.

[16] Kant's view is similar to the way in which rationality and irrationality are commonly understood in analytic philosophy, as formal and intrapersonal relations between a person's thought and actions. See, for example, T. M. Scanlon, *What we Owe to Each Other* (Cambridge, MA: Harvard University Press, 1998), 25: 'Rationality involves systematic connections between different aspects of a person's thought and behaviour.' David Pears prefers to speak of 'a proper use of information in the mind' (David Pears, *Motivated Irrationality* (Oxford: Oxford University Press, 1984), 7).

[17] See Onora O'Neill, 'Reason and Politics in the Kantian Enterprise', in *Constructions of Reason* (Cambridge: Cambridge University Press, 1989), 3–28; Willi Goetschel, *Kant's Writing as Critical Praxis* (Durham, NC: Duke University Press, 1994); and Katerina Deligiorgi, *Kant and the Culture of Enlightenment* (Albany: SUNY Press, 2005). On the political significance of the term 'critique' in the cultural and political context of the emergence of enlightenment amidst Central European absolutist rule, see R. Koselleck, *Kritik und Krise* (Frankfurt am Main: Suhrkamp, 1973). On the relation between critique' and public opinion (*Öffentlichkeit*) in the Enlightenment see Habermas, *Strukturwandel der*

*Pure Reason* was widely understood by both its detractors and admirers to have shown that human reason was the only true authority and thus to have issued a direct challenge to the dogmatic claims of religious and political powers.[18] In this respect Kantian critique is closely linked to the social and political project of *enlightenment*, a process that Kant himself described in his 1783 essay, 'An Answer to the Question: What is Enlightenment?' as the emancipation of a people from its state of *Unmündigkeit* (minority or tutelage) towards a state of *Mündigkeit*, i.e. autonomy, responsibility, and maturity.[19] In this context critique/criticism is less a doctrine of epistemological modesty, than a call to arms, a summons to all immature, dependent citizens and subjects to think for themselves, to use their own understanding, and a challenge to an (Enlightened) absolutist ruler to heed the views of citizens and subjects. As we can see from a famous footnote in the preface to the first edition of the *Critique of Pure Reason*, Kant's peculiar project of 'critique' is not separate from, but rather an example of, criticism in a much broader sense:

Our age is the true age of criticism, to which everything must submit. Religion through its holiness, and legislation through its majesty commonly seek to exempt themselves from it. But in this way they heap justified suspicion upon themselves, and cannot claim the genuine respect that reason grants only to what has been able to stand the test of free and public examination.[20]

Criticism in the broader sense, as the free public use of reason, has an important social and political function, namely to test the legitimacy or rightfulness of all claims to authority. Put in different terms, it is an instance of what A. O. Hirschman calls a voice mechanism, a channel of

---

*Öffentlichkeit: Untersuchungen zu einer Kategorie der bürgerlichen Gesellschaft* (Darmstadt and Neuwied: Luchterhand, 1962), translated as *Structural Transformation of the Public Sphere: An Inquiry into a Category of Bourgeois Society*, trans. T. Bürger and F. Lawrence (Cambridge, MA: MIT Press, 1989).

[18]   See, for example, Heinrich Heine, 'Zur Geschichte der Religion und Philosophie in Deutschland', in *Heine: Werke in fünf Bänden* (Weimar: 1958), v. 94–110. On the conservative theological backlash against the 'Kantian enragé' Carl Immanuel Diez, see also Dieter Henrich, *Hegel im Kontext* (Frankfurt am Main: Suhrkamp, 1971), 54 ff. This point is borne out in a line from Hegel's letter to Schelling in 1795: 'From the Kantian system and its highest completion, I expect a revolution in Germany . . . Heads will be reeling at this summit of all philosophy by which man is so greatly exalted' (*Hegel: The Letters*, trans. C. Butler and C. Seiler (Bloomington: Indiana University Press, 1984), 35).

[19]   In Kant, *Political Writings*, ed. H. B. Reiss, 2nd edn. (Cambridge: Cambridge University Press, 1991), 54–61; AA viii. 33–43. The most common translation for Kant's term *Unmündigkeit* namely 'immaturity', is probably the most misleading, because it is a biological term. Kant avoids using biological terms, such as *Unreife*, for the good reason that *Unmündigkeit* is not a biological category but a legal one. However, he also avoids using the legal term minority—*Minderjährigkeit*—which is a form of *Unmündigkeit* with a biological basis—since not all people who are *unmündig* are minors.

[20]   Kant, CPR A xi. See also A 738–9/B766–7.

information between the ruled and the rulers (in this case the Church and more importantly the State) which can serve as a vehicle of recuperation.[21] Kant is at pains to point out that philosophers, in their role as critics, pose no threat to an absolutist state like that of Prussia under the 'benevolent despot', Frederick II. On the contrary they are a benefit to it in so far as they address themselves 'in *respectful* tones to the state, which is thereby implored to take the rightful needs of the people to heart'.[22] Criticism thus provides rulers with information which will be useful for them in framing legislation in a republican manner, which is why Kant is so keen to safeguard the freedom of speech and to support and encourage the enlightenment of a people.[23] For Kant, to govern *in a republican manner* is to exercise power legitimately.[24] He makes a close connection between criticism and the principle of right, which forms the basis of all legitimate government and legislation.[25] The principle of right is contained in the idea of the original contract that *obliges* legislators to frame laws in accordance with the general will, and serves as the touchstone of legitimacy:

This is the test of the rightfulness of every public law. For if the law is such that a whole people could not possibly agree to it . . . it is unjust; but if it is at least *possible* that a people could agree to it, it is our duty to consider the law as just . . . .[26]

The broader notion of criticism that is in play in Kant's political writings is at once: (1) a vehicle of public education, (2) a criterion of the legitimacy of law,

---

[21] A. O. Hirschman, *Exit, Voice, and Loyalty: Responses to Decline in Firms, Organizations, and States* (Cambridge, MA: Harvard University Press, 1970) and *Essays in Trespassing: Economics to Politics and Beyond* (Cambridge: Cambridge University Press, 1981), 209–85.

[22] Kant, 'The Contest of the Faculties', in *Political Writings*, 186.

[23] 'To try to deny the citizen this freedom [of the pen—GF] . . . means withholding from the ruler all knowledge of those matters which, if he knew nothing about them, he would himself rectify, so that he is thereby put into a self-stultifying position. For his will issues commands to his subjects (as citizens) only insofar as he represents the general will of the people' (Kant, *Political Writings*, 85; AA viii. 304).

[24] One should not confuse what Kant conceives as governing in a republican manner with democracy. Everything that Kant writes about the democratic organization of states shows that he stands in a very long tradition of political theorists who are who are not in favour of democracy—understood as rule by the people—but against it. Of the three forms of sovereignty—autocracy, aristocracy, and democracy—Kant considers the last to be the least representative and the least rightful: Kant 'Perpetual Peace' in Kant, *Political Writings*, 100–2; AA viii. 352–4.

[25] '*Right* is the restriction of each individual's freedom so that it harmonises with the freedom of everyone else (in so far as this is possible within the terms of the general law)' (Kant, 'On the Common Saying: This may be true in theory, but does not apply in practice', in Kant, *Political Writings*, 73; AA viii. 290).

[26] Kant, 'On the Common Saying . . .', in *Political Writings*, 79; and 'An Answer to the Question: What is Enlightenment?', ibid. 57; AA viii. 296 and 40.

and (3) a useful diagnostic tool of governance for an absolutist ruler, provided he is minded to heed the respectful promptings of philosophers and to govern in a republican manner, i.e. to frame legislation in accordance with the will of the people.

## 1.4 Reason/Rationality

One important difference between first-generation Frankfurt School critical theorists and Kant is that the former all reject what they consider to be Kant's formal conception of reason and rationality in favour of a substantial conception of reason that is owed to Hegel. Unlike Kant, Hegel does not see reason as a faculty of the mind: reason is in the world; it is an animating principle of reality itself. According to Hegel's metaphysics, the idea of reason enters the world as *Geist* or spirit through the minds and actions of human beings, and as a result Hegel construes rationality as a predicate of the world. The rationality of the social world is also a historical achievement of spirit. According to Hegel's philosophy of history the process of the becoming-spiritual of the social world does not begin to complete itself until the dawning of the French Revolution, apropos of which Hegel makes the following observation:

The thought, the concept of justice validated itself *all at once*, and the old framework of injustice could offer no resistance. In the thought of justice, a constitution has now been established, and from now on everything is to be built on this basis. So long as the sun stood in the heavens and the planets circled around it, it went unnoticed that mankind stands on its head, i.e. on thought, and builds reality accordingly.[27]

The result or residue of this process of spiritualization is a state which Hegel calls the 'actuality' ((*Wirklichkeit*)) of reason. The famous *Doppelsatz* in the preface to his 1820 *Elements of the Philosophy of Right* illustrates what he means by this:

What is rational (*vernünftig*) is actual (*wirklich*), and what is actual is also rational.[28]

[27] 'Der Gedanke, der Begriff des Rechts machte sich mit *einem Male* geltend, und dagegen konnte das alte Gerüst des Unrechts keinen Widerstand leisten. Im Gedanken des Rechts ist also jetzt eine Verfassung errichtet worden, und auf diesem Grunde sollte nunmehr alles basiert sein. Solange die Sonne am Firmamente steht und die Planeten um sie herumkreisen, war das nicht gesehen worden, daß der Mensch sich auf den Kopf, d. i. auf den Gedanken stellt und die Wirklichkeit nach diesem erbaut' (G. W. F. *Werke: Hegel in 20 Bänden*, ed. Eva Moldenhauer and Karl Markus Michel (Frankfurt am Main: Surhkamp, 1986), xii. 529 (henceforth *Werke*)).

[28] Hegel, *Elements of the Philosophy of Right*, ed. Allen W. Wood, trans. H. B. Nisbet (Cambridge: Cambridge University Press, 1991), 20 (henceforth EPR); Hegel, *Werke*, vii. 24.

In the first place, institutions that are actual are real; they exist. But Hegel makes clear that the mere existence of something is not sufficient for its being actual. 'Actuality' designates social reality that exists for a reason, i.e. which has a demonstrable point that maintains it in existence.[29] Hegel contrasts this with 'mere being' or 'lazy existence' which has no such point.[30] According to Hegel, the continuing demonstrable reason for the existence of an institution also renders it intelligible, by revealing its point. This does not mean that the actuality of an institution is always transparent and open to view; it is often not. It is the task of the philosophy of right to lay bare the rationality of the social world, and, by bringing people to a deeper comprehension of their social world, to make them at home it.[31] This brings us to the third point,

[29] Hegel warns against the error of conflating 'actuality' and 'existence' in §6 of the *Encyclopaedia Logic*, which he wrote nearly a decade after the *Philosophy of Right* was first published. See Hegel, *Werke*, viii. 47–9; *Hegel: The Encyclopedia Logic*, trans. T. F. Geraets, W. A. Suchting, and H. S. Harris (Indianapolis: Hackett, 1991), 28–30.

[30] 'Dieses Gute, diese Vernunft in ihrer konkretesten Vorstellung ist Gott...Diesen will die Philosophie erfassen; denn nur was aus ihm vollführt ist, hat Wirklichkeit, was ihm nicht gemäß ist, ist nur faule Existenz' (Hegel, *Werke*, xii. 53). See also *The Encyclopedia Logic* §6, 29; Hegel, *Werke*, viii. 48. In his philosophy of right, Hegel gives example of institutions, for example the monasteries, that continue to exist even though they have long ago lost their point since the reasons why they came into existence no longer obtain, and of institutions like the Roman law that permitted a father to sell his children into slavery that were contrary to right even though they were consistent with Roman conceptions of paternal authority and matrimony (EPR, 29–30; Hegel, *Werke*, vii. 35–7).

[31] Frankfurt School thinkers frequently attack what they take to be the uncritical and apologetic conclusions of Hegel's philosophy of right in so far as it assigns to philosophy the task of effecting a reconciliation between individuals and the state, by demonstrating that they are, whether they realize it or not, at home in their social world. Adorno, for example, repeats an objection, famously levelled by Rudolf Haym in 1857, which accompanied the work from its publication in 1820. 'According to the distinction between abstract and real possibility only what has itself become actual is truly possible. Such philosophy marches with the stronger battalions. It accords with the judgement of a reality, which always buries underneath itself anything that could be otherwise' (Adorno, *Hegel*, 82–6; GS v. 320). Adorno here conflates the technical term 'actuality' with reality or existence. (Rudolf Haym, *Hegel und seine Zeit*, cited in *Materialien zu Hegels Rechtsphilosophie*, ed. M. Riedel, i (Frankfurt am Main: Suhrkamp, 1975.), 365–95.) Marcuse's view is that 'Hegel's work is reactionary in so far as the social order it reflects is so, and progressive in so far as it is progressive' (Marcuse, *Reason and Revolution* (London: Routledge & Kegan Paul, 1969; first publ. 1941), 178). The general attitude of the Frankfurt theorists towards Hegel's philosophy is that the radical implications of the dialectic, especially as demonstrated in the *Science of Logic* and the *Phenomenology of Spirit*—is obscured and distorted by Hegel's idealist and monistic metaphysics, and that this distortion gives rise to the apologetic tone of the *Philosophy of Right*. By contrast modern commentators, with the help of new critical editions of Hegel's lectures, now virtually all agree that his philosophy of right is not apologetic and quietistic, and certainly not a mere justification—or reflection—of what exists, indeed that it is compatible with, and was probably intended as, a qualified form of social criticism with the aim of furthering piecemeal reform. That said, however, nobody can accuse Hegel of having overemphasized the critical import of his work, and there is a lot of evidence of his deliberately having toned down and disguised the critical political content of his views in order to assuage or to confuse the censors. This was particularly true

that the actuality of an institution is something good in that it demonstrably satisfies people's deepest interests.

According to Hegel's substantial conception of reason, then, that the social world is rational implies both that it is intelligible and that it is good—in the sense that it is demonstrably in tune with the deepest interests of human beings.[32] Far from being something neutral and formal, rationality is a perfectionist notion.[33] We can see this perfectionism at work in Hegel's criticism of the position he calls 'morality' or 'the moral standpoint', which he associates with Kant, who conceives morality as the rational self-determination of the individual will.[34] From the moral standpoint each individual must calculate for himself what reason demands (for example, by asking whether her maxims are universalizable, or by asking what the sage would do) and then bring these demands to bear on the world by acting on upon them. In so doing the moral agent must abstract from his or her own interests, needs, and desires. In Hegel's estimation this mistaken view stems from Kant's formal, one-sided conception of reason. Kant reduces reason to a formal test of the universalizability of maxims only because he has screened out its social and institutional pre-conditions.

in the period immediately following the Carlsbad Decrees of 1819, when censorship was ratcheted up following the assassination of the reactionary poet August von Kotzbue by a student of J. F. Fries's, Karl Ludwig Sand. See *G. W. F. Hegel. Die Philosophie des Rechts*, ed. K-H. Ilting (Stuttgart: Klett-Cotta, 1983). The following amusing anecdote from Heine is also revealing. 'I often used to see him [Hegel] looking around anxiously as if in fear he might be understood. He was very fond of me, for he was sure I would never betray him. As a matter of fact, I then thought that he was very obsequious. Once when I grew impatient with him for saying: "All that is, is rational", he smiled strangely and remarked, "It may also be said that all that is rational must be." Then he looked about him hastily; but he was speedily reassured, for only Heinrich Beer had heard his words' (Heinrich Heine, *Self-Portrait and Other Prose Writings*, trans. F. Ewen (Secaucus: Citadel Press, 1948), 254–5).

[32] Robert Stern challenges the view put forward here, namely that Hegel has a substantial and implicitly perfectionist conception of rationality, in 'Hegel's *Doppelsatz*: A Neutral Reading', *Journal of the History of Philosophy* 44/2 (2006), 235–66. The interpretation I endorse is similar to that of Raymond Geuss. See 'Art and Theodicy', in Geuss, *Morality, Culture and History: Essays on German Philosophy* (Cambridge: Cambridge University Press, 1999), 78–84.

[33] Perfectionism is the view that some ways of life are good, and that there are matters of fact about what these are. Perfectionists make claims not just about kinds of lives, but about the forms of life or societies in which these lives are lived. A perfectionist need not hold that there is only one good way of life. There may be several competing good ways of living.

[34] Hegel is well known for having levelled some hard-hitting objections to what he called 'morality' or 'the moral standpoint', a term he reserved almost exclusively for Kant, Fichte, and, what is less well known, for the Stoics: 'Wir sagen statt Tugend Moralität, indem das, wonach ich mich in meinen Handlungen richten soll, nicht mein Wille sein soll, der zur Gewohnheit geworden ist wie in der Tugend: Moralität enthält wesentlich meine subjective Reflexion, meine Überzeugung, daß das, was ich tue, den allgemeinen, vernünftigen Willensbestimmungen, den allgemeinen Pflichten gemäß ist' (Hegel, *Werke*, xix. 284).

Hegel's substantial notion of reason arises as the sublation (*Aufhebung*), i.e. the simultaneous annulment, preservation, and transfiguration, of morality in (and into) ethical life.[35] Hegel maintains, with Kant, that 'welfare is not a good without right' but adds that 'right is not the good without welfare', thereby explicitly rejecting Kant's thesis that nothing is unconditionally good save the good will.[36] Morality, for Hegel, is not something separable from, and indifferent to, the happiness of individuals; the demands of morality (which are also demands of reason) have to be brought into a systematic harmony with individual and collective well-being. Human beings can be rational in this substantial sense, i.e. they can simultaneously aim at their own good and at the good of the community, only within a specific set of social institutions that shapes their entire outlook and existence. This is the implication of Hegel's thesis that the 'obligation... which is present in morality is fulfilled only in the ethical realm'.[37] The formal demands of reason must be, and to an extent already have been, translated into 'the substantial element of the concept' and into 'external existence', that is, incorporated into a whole network of institutions and practices—family, civil society, and the state.[38] As a consequence of this historically accomplished translation of reason into social substance, philosophy's proper task is, according to Hegel, simply that of recognizing the rational in the actual. To comprehend the rational substance of the social world as the objectification of spirit is to understand why institutions exist as they do, and to appreciate their point, namely that they promote the individual and collective good of the inhabitants and subjects of ethical life. When institutions are 'actual' in Hegel's sense, i.e. when they really do have a demonstrable point, and when society has a rational structure, the subjects who recognize this are 'free', in the sense that they are *at home* in and no longer estranged from their social world.[39]

[35] For a more nuanced discussion of this issue see Ludwig Siep, 'Was heisst: "Aufhebung der Moralität in Sittlichkeit" in Hegel's *Rechtsphilosophie*?', *Hegel-Studien* 17 (1982), 75–94.

[36] Hegel, EPR §130, 157–8; Hegel, *Werke*, vii. 243–4.

[37] Hegel, EPR §108, 137; Hegel, *Werke*, vii. 207.

[38] The best account of this is to be found in F. Neuhouser, *The Foundations of Hegel's Social Theory* (Cambridge, MA: Harvard University Press, 2000).

[39] 'The colourful canvas of the world is before me; I stand opposed to it and in this attitude I overcome (*aufhebe*) its opposition to me. "I" is as at home in the world, when it knows it; even more when it has comprehended it' (Hegel, EPR §4, 36). 'Ich ist in der Welt zu Hause wenn es sie kennt, noch mehr, wenn es sie begriffen hat' (Hegel, *Werke*, vii. 47).

# 1.5  Marx and Lukács: Immanent Critique and the Rational Society

We have traced the origins of a *perfectionist* idea of a rational society in Hegel. It is the idea of a society of free and equal citizens, which is institutionally *organized* in such a way that the individual good stands in a systematic harmony with the collective good.[40] The term 'critique/criticism', is not much used by the mature Hegel except to designate the philosophical positions of Kant and Fichte against which he argues. After Hegel, the term 'criticism' finds renewed currency. It is adopted by the Young Hegelians and Marx, and becomes a central concept of Hegelian Marxism.

In a famous passage from a letter to Arnold Ruge in 1843 Marx talks about 'the ruthless criticism of the existing order' and differentiates it from transcendent and moralizing criticism.[41] According to Marx, philosophy can level such criticism to the extent that it can descry a rational content, namely a good society in nascent form, inherent in the actually existing irrational society.

Reason has always existed, only not always in a rational form. The critic can therefore engage with every form of theoretical and practical consciousness and develop (*entwickeln*) true actuality from the forms of existing actuality *themselves* as their ought and final goal.... We do not, then, confront the world as doctrinaires with a new principle: here is the truth, kneel before it! We develop new principles for the world out of principles of the world.[42]

Here Marx assumes, first, that there is such a thing as a 'true reality' (i.e. a good or rational society) opposed to, yet germinating within, the criticized false reality; and, secondly that this nascent truth can be recognized for what

---

[40]  The idea that the political community can be understood as a living organism, and the related idea that the *polis* is a body, the parts of which relate to the whole in the same way in which the parts of the body relate to the whole, is of course a very old idea, which crops up in Aristotle, Menenius Agrippa, Hobbes, Rousseau, Kant, Schiller, and Hegel, among many others.

[41]  Marx, *Early Writings*, trans. R. Livingstone (London: Penguin, 1984), 207; Marx and Engels, *Werke*, i (Berlin: Dietz Verlag, 1956), 344.

[42]  Marx, *Early Writings*, 208 (translation amended). The German reads: 'Die Vernunft hat immer existiert, nur nicht immer in der vernünftigen Form. Der Kritiker kann also an jede Form des theoretischen und praktischen Bewußtseins anknüpfen und aus den *eigenen* Formen der existierenden Wirklichkeit die wahre Wirklichkeit als ihr Sollen und ihren Endzweck entwickeln.... Wir treten dann nicht der Welt doktrinär mit einem neuen Prinzip entgegen: Hier ist die Wahrheit, hier kniee nieder! Wir entwickeln der Welt aus den Prinzipien der Welt neue Prinzipien' (Marx and Engels, *Werke*, i. 345).

it is, even though it is inchoate and encrypted in an irrational form. Once these assumptions are granted social criticism can proceed immanently, that is without recourse to transcendent, ahistorical ideals. In essence, the task of the social critic that Marx envisages in this passage is not altogether different from the role of phenomenological observer in Hegel's *Phenomenology of Spirit*, who is supposed to add nothing of his own and whose role is one of 'merely looking on (*das reine Zusehen*)' as spirit unfolds itself; nor is it that different from the task Hegel assigns to philosophers (and philosophically enlightened citizens) in the *Philosophy of Right*, namely to recognize the rational in the actual.[43] The Marx of 1843, like Hegel, makes it look as if the task of the critic, that of 'developing new principles', is primarily a theoretical activity rather than a practical and social one.[44]

Somewhat later, György Lukács, in his 1919 essay 'Tactics and Ethics', was to develop this conception of immanent criticism.

Since the ultimate objective [i.e. the achievement of a communist society, GF] has been categorized, not as Utopia, *but as reality which has to be achieved*, positing it above and beyond the immediate advantage does not mean abstracting from reality or attempting to impose certain ideals on reality, but rather it entails the knowledge and transformation into action of those forces already at work *within* social reality—those forces, that is, which are directed towards the realization of the ultimate objective ... The Marxist theory of class struggle, which in this respect is wholly derived from Hegel's conceptual system, changes the transcendent objective into an immanent one; the class struggle of the proletariat is at once the objective itself and its realization.[45]

Lukács argued that the knowledge of the immanent, progressive, self-transforming tendencies of society must be translated into action. In *History and Class-Consciousness*, three years later, he advanced the view that the proletariat is in the unique position to instigate such action. The workers can and do become conscious of themselves as the subject-object of history, and thereby gain reliable knowledge of the whole society and of the progressive

---

[43] Hegel, Introduction to the *Phenomenology of Spirit*, trans. A. V. Miller (Oxford: Oxford University Press, 1977), 54; Hegel, *Werke*, iii. 77. See also Hegel, *Werke*, vii. §32Z, 86; Hegel, EPR, 61–2.

[44] This might seem strange from someone who only two years later, in the 11th thesis on Feuerbach, famously accused philosophers of only having interpreted the world, when the point was to change it (Marx and Engels, *Werke*, iii. 535). However, in this letter Marx still cleaves to Feuerbach's (Hegelian) method, and understands the task of criticism to be that of bringing man to a correct self-conscious understanding of his own political activity or, as he says: 'the self-clarification (critical philosophy) of the struggles and wishes of the age' (Marx, *Early Writings*, 209; Marx and Engels, *Werke*, i. 345).

[45] Lukács, *Political Writings, 1919–1929*, ed. and trans. R. Livingstone (London: New Left Books, 1972), 4–5.

historical tendency that they collectively constitute.[46] In so far as Lukács held that an act of becoming conscious could bring the rudiments of a true praxis to light, through the distorting veil of reified social relations and ideological forms of consciousness, he implies—like Marx before him—that the good society, the realization of which lies in the future, is already present or actual, albeit in an inchoate form.[47]

## 1.6 Horkheimer's Vision of the Rational Society

The conception of the immanent critique of society developed by the young Marx and Lukács fuses a notion of criticism originating in Kant with the perfectionist idea of the rational society stemming from Hegel. Horkheimer's critical theory of the 1930s is located squarely in this Hegelian-Marxist tradition of immanent criticism. Horkheimer maintains: (1) that the ideal of a 'rational society' is inherent in presently existing reality; (2) that it is a real, though not fully developed, potential; and (3) that it is recognizable as such by the social critic. In his materialist period (1930–7) Horkheimer develops a conception of social happiness that is clearly a descendant of the perfectionist notion whose history we have been tracing. For Horkheimer, happiness is predicated not just of individuals but of social wholes.[48] As a predicate of society it denotes an organized totality in which the individual interest harmonizes with the common interest. He maintains that at present (in the 1930s) happiness remains an ideal, a potential for a more humane society.

> In the future society . . . the life of the whole and of the individuals alike is produced not merely as a natural effect but as the consequence of rational designs that take account of the happiness of individuals in equal measure. In place of the blind mechanism of economic struggles, which presently condition happiness and—for the greater part of humanity—unhappiness, the purposive application of the immeasurable wealth of human and material forces of production emerges.[49]

---

[46] Lukács, 'Reification and the Consciousness of the Proletariat', in *History and Class-Consciousness* (London: Merlin Press, 1990), 2; *Geschichte und Klassenbewusstsein* (Darmstadt: Luchterhand, 1968), 60.

[47] Axel Honneth, *Verdinglichung* (Frankfurt am Main: Suhrkamp, 2005), 34.

[48] On happiness as a predicate of society, see Raymond Geuss, 'Happiness and Politics', in his *Outside Ethics* (Princeton: Princeton University Press, 2005), 97–111.

[49] Horkheimer, 'Materialism and Metaphysics', in *Between Philosophy and Social Science* (Cambridge, MA: MIT Press, 1993), 29 (henceforth BPS); Horkheimer, KT i. 88.

The ideal of social happiness provides critical theory with both diagnostic and remedial aims. Horkheimer argues that it is the *unplanned* and *irrational* nature of present social and economic relations that gives rise to inequality, injustice, and unhappiness, and that what is required is a socialist transformation of property relations and the implementation of a rationally planned economy.[50]

According to Horkheimer, the ideal of a rational society is encapsulated and expressed in the humanitarian principles of the enlightenment—justice, equality, and freedom. But these are not, he insisted, *moral* principles, metaphysical postulates or eternal values. They are the 'isolated features of the rational society as they are anticipated in morality' which emerge concretely out of the experience of the discrepancy between the actuality of human suffering and the real technological and economic potential for eliminating human misery.[51] At the same time, social happiness is not *merely* ideal; it is not wholly absent from existing society. Traces of it, anticipations of the rational society, exist already in the moral feelings of love, compassion, and solidarity, and the anthropological fact that humans cannot help wanting happiness.[52]

Horkheimer opposes the ideal inherent in moral sentiments to the bourgeois morality of Kant. He claims that in the bourgeois era the human psyche is stamped with the features of possessive individualism. However, motives of individual self-interest are not sufficient to cement society together. Hence, once religious traditions and hierarchies have ebbed away, other mechanisms are needed to provide a repository of altruistic motives and a commitment to the common good. Morality comes to fill the void, by trying to shore up a historically contingent set of behavioural norms and values with the illusory metaphysical backing of a transcendent order of reality.[53] Where Kant presents the universality and necessity of moral laws as indications of the a priori nature of morality, Horkheimer interprets these features

[50] On this see Dubiel, *Theory and Politics*, 42–4. This view survives in Horkheimer's 'Traditional and Critical Theory' in CT 188–252 and KT ii 137–200, and can also be seen in Marcuse's reply, 'Philosophy and Critical Theory', in *Negations* (London: Penguin Press, 1968).

[51] 'Materialism and Metaphysics', Horkheimer, CT 45 and KT i. 66. See also 'Materialism and Morality', in Max Horkheimer, BPS 37–8; KT i. 97–8.

[52] These moral feelings, and the associated 'claim to happiness' (*Glück*), Horkheimer thinks, do not stand in need of any further 'justification or grounding': KT i. 64 and 94. Of course while it might be an anthropological fact that each person desires his or her own happiness, it is by no means so obvious that each person desires the happiness of anyone else, or the happiness of everybody, and that the ideal of *social happiness* needs no justification (CT 44; BPS 34–5).

[53] Horkheimer, BPS, 14–22; CT, 22–24; Horkheimer, KT i. 71–6 and 42–5.

as relics of their religious origins.[54] He also portrays them as a psychic consequence of the suppression of the instincts that is functionally necessary to the integration of modern mass society.[55] On his view morality serves an ideological function: it counteracts the social solvent of individual self-interest, thus preserving the status quo, and thus acting as a brake on social progress.

Later, in 'Traditional and Critical Theory', he argues that human beings have a fundamental interest in emancipation which guides the experience and perception of 'the idea of a reasonable organisation of society that will meet the needs of the whole community (*der Allgemeinen*)', and that this interest is 'immanent in human labour'.[56] Horkheimer shares with most Hegelian-Marxists the assumption that the vision of the good society can be realized, under altered relations of production, through human labour. However, he rejects Lukács's view that the proletariat is in the best position to avail itself of this vision and to realize it. In his eyes, it is the critical theorist not the proletariat, who has reliable knowledge of the social whole and thus privileged access to the idea of the good society. This epistemic privilege is due to the inherent self-reflectiveness and interdisciplinarity of critical theory, which help it to overcome the intellectual division of labour. Yet Horkheimer does not propose a convincing alternative account of the agency of historical change, noting only that the 'interest in social transformation' is motivated by 'the experience of prevailing injustice' and that it needs to be 'guided and shaped' by the theory.[57]

## 2. CRITICAL THEORY AND *DIALECTIC* OF *ENLIGHTENMENT*

Adorno and Horkheimer's jointly authored *Dialectic of Enlightenment*, first published in 1944 and written during their enforced exile in America, marks a sea change in the development of critical theory. The change stems primarily

---

[54] 'The fear which moral prescriptions . . . still carry from their origins in religious authority is foreign to materialism.' Horkheimer, KT i. 91; BPS 32. See also Horkheimer, CT 18 and KT i. 39.
[55] Horkheimer, KT i. 92; BPS, 32.    [56] Ibid., CT 213; Horkheimer, KT ii. 162.
[57] Ibid., 199, 241, 243; KT ii. 47, 189, 190. NB: throughout his loose, though readable, translation of 'Traditional and Critical Theory' Matthew J. O'Connell translates the German word *Interesse* as 'concern'.

from their account of reason and rationality, which in turn radically alters their conception of the practical aims of critical theory.

## 2.1 The Critique of Instrumental Rationality

The *Dialectic of Enlightenment* contains an account of the prehistory of reason and rationality. At the heart of this account is the anthropological claim that reason is a tool or instrument for the purpose of subduing and taming external nature. With the aid of reason, human beings prevent their subjection to nature and overcome their fear of the unknown.[58] Adorno and Horkheimer add to this a historical thesis that the process of civilization and rationalization that culminates in the historical Enlightenment, privileges calculating, scientific, and technically exploitable knowledge above all others. Thus enlightenment betrays the essence of human reason as a form of domination and mastery: reason becomes 'a mere means (*Hilfsmittel*) of the all-inclusive economic apparatus. It serves as a general tool, useful for the manufacture of all other tools, rigidly directed towards its purpose, and as fatal as the precisely calculated business of material reproduction, whose result for human beings is beyond all calculation.' [59] At the same time reason betrays the essence of Enlightenment by failing to live up to its ideal of justice, equality, and happiness.

A little later, in *Eclipse of Reason*, Horkheimer distinguishes between objective and subjective reason. Objective reason becomes his term for the substantial and normatively rich notion of the rational society. Subjective reason is understood as a device or instrument by which the subject calculates the most efficient means to a given end. His view is that the former has atrophied while the latter has expanded, and that this is not just a theoretical development; for the decline of the metaphysical systems of Plato, Aristotle, and German Idealism and the growth of empiricism and positivism reflect an underlying social and economic process of the functionalization or instrumentalization of reason within the capitalist economy.[60] Indeed, not only

---

[58] 'The essence of enlightenment is the alternative the unavoidable outcome of which is domination. Human beings have always had to choose between their subjection by nature, or the subjection of nature by the self' (Adorno and Horkheimer, *Dialectic of Enlightenment*, trans. John Cumming (London: Verso, 1997), 32; Adorno, GS iii. 39).

[59] Adorno and Horkheimer, *Dialectic of Enlightenment*, 30; Adorno, GS iii. 47.

[60] Horkheimer, 'Zum Begriff der Vernunft' in *Max Horkheimer: Sozialphilosophische Studien* (Frankfurt am Main: Fischer Taschenbuch Verlag, 1972), 49. See also Horkheimer, *The Eclipse of Reason* (New York: Continuum, 1974; first publ. 1947), 4.

reason, but thought in general, has been caught in the grip of this process.[61] On this view, concepts themselves are degraded into means by which particulars are subsumed under ever more general concepts and laws for the purpose of regimenting nature into a world of stable and uniform objects that are predictable and amenable to manipulation and control. At the same time, according to Horkheimer and Adorno, the world has been denuded of intrinsically worthwhile ends; meaningful ways of living have gradually been replaced by worthless and trivial activities. In the course of capitalist society's development individual self-interest has become the overarching motive of human action, whilst the desires and needs of individuals have become more prone to manipulation and control by advertising, the media, and the culture industry, with the result that they eventually fit seamlessly with what the capitalist economy can supply. Subjects have come to want exactly those goods that are on offer. Not only do they accept current social and political reality as it is, they actively want more of the same. Their needs and desires come to exert a conservative pressure on what exists. In this way, fundamentally irrational institutions develop the ability to cloak themselves in the appearance of rationality, to supplant what Hegel called 'actuality' and thereby to block the path to emancipation. As Adorno puts it: 'This process of making oneself the same, of civilization, of fitting in, uses up all the energy which could make things different, until the point is reached at which what has been determined as universal humanity emerges as the barbarity which it is.'[62] When the self-interested behaviour of individual agents becomes functionally integrated by an economic system aiming at the increase in productive forces for its own sake, there arises what Adorno calls the *totally administered society*.

In the totally administered society the social and economic structure of capitalist society appears as a system of instrumental reason with nothing to put value in the system save the value of self-preservation. Adorno refers to this condition as 'universal fungibility'.[63] Self-preservation is a matter of mere survival through cunning adaptation to the demands of the system. In a dialectical irony, the self preserves itself only at the cost of emptying

---

[61] Horkheimer, *Eclipse of Reason*, 4. See also *Dialectic of Enlightenment*, 39: 'Even representation is only an instrument. In thought human beings distance themselves from nature, in order to consider how to dominate it. Like the thing, the material tool . . . the concept is the ideal tool, fit to do service for everything, wherever it can be applied' (Adorno, GS iii. 57).

[62] Adorno, 'Reflexionen zur Klassentheorie', GS xiii. 390.

[63] For example, *Dialectic of Enlightenment*, 10; GS iii. 26.

itself of meaning and vitality.[64] This process of draining lives of meaning, thus undermining the very point of living, is the theme announced in the Dedication of Adorno's *Minima Moralia*—'Our perspective of life has passed into an ideology which conceals the fact that there is life no longer'—and in the motto of the first part of the book—'Life does not live.'[65] The same thought is encapsulated in one of the most memorable aphorisms of that work: 'Es gibt kein richtiges Leben im falschen.'[66] It is not easy to convey in English the full significance of this sentence. Literally it means: 'There is no right living in the false (life)' or, put more idiomatically: 'The false life cannot be truly lived.' (By a 'false' life Adorno means one dominated by universal fungibility.) However, the sentence can also mean that there is no *proper living* in a false life, or that one cannot really live a false life. It is not just what Adorno calls the correct life (*das richtige Leben*), or the good life, that is no longer possible under current conditions, but *life itself*, in so far as life means more than mere survival. In the totally administered society self-preservation is the ultimate end of all activity, but the life that was worth preserving has withered away. The final irony is that the economic system that arose for the purpose of ensuring human survival ends up, through technological developments such as the atom bomb, threatening to obliterate human life from the face of the earth.[67]

---

[64]  Adorno, *Minima Moralia*, trans. E. F. N. Jephcott (London: Verso, 1974), 15; GS iv. 13. Adorno, *Notes to Literature I* (New York: Columbia University Press, 1991), 250–1; GS xi. 292–3.

[65]  Adorno, *Minima Moralia*, 20; GS iv. 21.

[66]  Jephcott's translation of this sentence, 'Wrong life cannot be lived rightly', makes it look as if Adorno is using the moral concepts 'right' and 'wrong', whereas, in fact, he eschews an openly moral vocabulary and deploys the terms 'richtig' and 'falsch' (right/false, correct/incorrect). There is no doubt an allusion to the good life here, for the Dedication opens with a remark about an age-old philosophical topic that has fallen into neglect: 'die Lehre vom richtigen Leben.' Yet 'correct living' also refers to something less than the good life. In similar vein Adorno consistently describes the social world as 'false' and 'untrue'. This indicates that Adorno's diagnosis that there can be no morally right action in a 'false' or 'untrue' world is not simply a first-order moral claim about the world. The view that life is false involves a complex set of social criticisms of morality, rather than a moral criticism of society. This is why, for example, Raymond Geuss argues that Adorno attempts to situate his philosophy *outside ethics*. See 'Outside Ethics', in Geuss, *Outside Ethics*, 40–67. For much the same reason Axel Honneth has argued that the authors of *Dialectic of Enlightenment* put forward a 'world-disclosing critique' that 'remains below the threshold at which moral judgments of the justice of the world are located' (Honneth, 'The Possibility of a Disclosing Critique of Society: The *Dialectic of Enlightenment* in Light of Current Debates in Social Criticism', *Constellations* 7 (2000), 122–5). In my view, as I argue below, Adorno is not successful, or at least not consistent, in this attempt to eschew morality, since he often ends up making claims about the social world that cannot but be interpreted as moral, broadly speaking.

[67]  Adorno, *Dialectic of Enlightenment*, 224; GS iii. 255; Adorno, *Negative Dialectics*, 320; GS vi. 314; Adorno, *Metaphysics: Concept and Problems* (Cambridge: Polity, 2000), 104.

## 2.2 Reason and the Remedy in the Evil

According to Horkheimer's original programme, critical theory harboured the optimistic assumption that through a transformation of the relations of production the creative power of human labour could be unlocked and guided in other directions with the help of the perfectionist ideal of the rational society. Marx's positive assessment of the technology-guided mastery of nature, and the expansion of the forces of production, remained part of this ideal, as did the desirability of rational social and economic planning. These were the envisaged vehicles of the realization of the rational society. As a direct consequence of their critique of instrumental reason, Horkheimer and Adorno came to reject the productivism of Marx and orthodox Marxism, and along with it the technocratic understanding of human labour and the desirability of rational economic and social planning. They saw no reason to think that increases in the forces of production would, under transformed (namely communist) relations of production, automatically lead to a better society. The knowledge of conditions in the Soviet Union only confirmed their view that such increases would at best lead to more production, to increases in the exploitation and domination of nature, to the complete control over people and things, that is, to totalitarianism, a far cry from the radical qualitative transformation of society and emancipation at which they aimed.[68] These developments of the theory stemmed from a deep change in their assessment of rationality: the very rationality that they had hitherto assumed was the solution now became the origin of the problem that was to be addressed. [69]

Deprived of the (in retrospect) somewhat naive appeal to a perfectionist ideal of a rational society immanent in human labour, Adorno and Horkheimer

---

[68] See also Adorno, *Negative Dialectics*, 306–7; GS vi. 301–2. Hannah Arendt's critique of Marx's belief in the redemptive power of labour is well known. See *The Human Condition* (Chicago: Chicago University Press, 1958), 1–7 and 79–136. Habermas's distinction between work and interaction, and his systematic critique of Marx for dogmatically assuming that social development (the development of normative moral structures) would follow the path of the dialectical development of the modes of production, follow the same line of thinking. He argues that Marxist theory has to supplement its analysis of the development modes of production with an analysis of the development of normative structures. Habermas, *Theory and Practice* (Cambridge: Polity, 1973), 142–70, and *Zur Rekonstruktion des Historischen Materialismus* (Frankfurt am Main: Suhrkamp, 1976), 144–200. An equally eloquent and cogent critique of Marx's productivism is to be found in Simone Weil's *Oppression and Liberty* (London: Routledge & Kegan Paul, 1958; (repr. 2002), 38–52.
[69] For example Horkheimer, KT ii. 161; CT 213. See Theunissen's brilliant analysis in his *Gesellschaft und Geschichte: Zur Kritik der kritischen Theorie* (Berlin: de Gruyter, 1969), 15, trans. G. Finlayson and P. Dews in *Habermas: A Critical Reader*, ed. P. Dews (Oxford: Blackwell, 1999), 250.

now faced serious questions not just about the content of the diagnostic and remedial aims of critical theory, but about the availability of its standard of criticism. The obvious response to their critique of instrumental reason would have been to relinquish the appeal to reason and to develop a conception of critique grounded in something other than reason. However, they reject what one might call this Romantic response. Rather than give up their faith in the emancipatory power of reason altogether and seek an alternative to it, they turn to an aporetic trope, namely that reason, which is the cause of the original evil, is also the remedy to it. This line of thought is prominent throughout Adorno's work. For example, in his essay on Hegel's concept of experience he embraces Hegel's idea

that the reified and rationalized society of the bourgeois era, the society in which a nature-dominating reason had come to fruition, could become a society worthy of human beings—not by regressing to older, irrational states prior to the division of labour, but only by applying rationality to itself, in other words, only through the healing awareness of the marks of unreason in its own reason, and the traces of the rational in the irrational as well.[70]

Adorno here alludes to the occurrence of 'the ancient topos: only the spear that inflicted the wound can heal it' in Richard Wagner's *Parsifal*.[71] This topos occurs again in *Negative Dialectics* where Adorno makes a similar claim about conceptual thought: 'Concepts alone can bring about what the concept prevents, cognition is a $\tau\rho\acute{\omega}\sigma\alpha\varsigma \ \acute{\iota}\acute{\alpha}\sigma\varepsilon\tau\alpha\iota$.'[72]

A similar claim is made about Enlightenment reason in *Dialectic of Enlightenment* where the authors cite the following lines from Hölderlin's ode *Patmos*: 'But where danger lies, the saving power grows also' (*Wo aber Gefahr is, wächst | das Rettende auch*)'.[73] Reason is the saving power because it is used to master external nature and to prevent man's subjection to it. It is also

---

[70] Adorno, *Hegel*, 74; Adorno, GS v. 313.

[71] The origins of the topos are recounted in a lost epic, the *Cypria*, part of the Trojan epic cycle. The story concerns King Telephus who is struck by Achilles' spear, during a siege mistakenly laid to an innocent polis, Teuthrania. 'The wounder will heal' is the cryptic pronouncement of the oracle to whom the Teuthranians turn in medical desperation. For an illuminating discussion of the trope in Hegel and Adorno, see Iain Macdonald, 'The Wounder Will Heal: Cognition and Reconciliation in Hegel and Adorno', *Philosophy Today* 44 (Supplement 2000), 132–9. For a discussion of the trope and its sources in the context of the work of Jean-Jacques Rousseau, see Jean Starobinski, 'La Lance d'Achille', in *Le Remède dans le mal. Critique et légitimation de l'artifice à l'âge des Lumières* (Paris: Gallimard, 1989), 165–208.

[72] 'Nur Begriffe können vollbringen, was der Begriff verhindert. Erkenntnis ist ein $\tau\rho\acute{\omega}\sigma\alpha\varsigma \ \acute{\iota}\acute{\alpha}\sigma\varepsilon\tau\alpha\iota$' (Adorno, *Negative Dialectics*, 53; GS vi. 62).

[73] *Dialectic of Enlightenment*, 47; Adorno, GS iii. 65. This citation is introduced as a comment on the fate of Odysseus. According to Adorno and Horkheimer, Odysseus uses his native cunning in order

the danger, 'for the substance that is dominated, suppressed, and dissolved by virtue of self-preservation, is none other than the very living thing ... that should be preserved'.[74] The authors draw lessons for twentieth-century society from the fate of Odysseus, who is presented as a prototype of the bourgeois individual:

Totalitarian capitalism has a technique of satisfying needs that, because of its reified form that is determined by domination and mastery, actually makes the satisfaction of needs impossible and leads to the extermination of humanity. This unreason (*Widervernünftigkeit*) of totalitarian capitalism is prototypically instantiated in the hero who escapes sacrifice by sacrificing himself.[75]

Another striking example of the thesis that reason is the remedy in the evil occurs in the preface:

The *aporia* which faced us in our work proved to be the first phenomenon for investigation: the self-destruction of enlightenment. We are wholly convinced—and therein lies our *petitio principii*— that social freedom is inseparable from enlightened thinking. Nevertheless, we believe that we have just as clearly recognised that the concept of this very way of thinking, no less than the actual historical forms—the institutions of society—with which it is interwoven, already contains the seed of the reversal universally apparent today.[76]

The thesis can be read in two different ways according to whether reason is construed as an allopathic or a homeopathic remedy. On the allopathic reading, reason contains different agents within it that can have contrary effects—that of poison and antidote. This reading is implicit in Horkheimer's distinction in *Eclipse of Reason* between objective and subjective reason, and also in interpretations of Adorno, where it is claimed that he embraces mimetic rationality as an *alternative* to Enlightenment reason, free from its fateful entwinement with domination and mastery. On the homeopathic reading, the remedy is provided by the very same agent that inflicted the wound—reason. Both these interpretations must be distinguished from the quaint providentialism that underlies some of Rousseau's pronouncements on *le remède dans le mal*.[77] However, the allopathic reading fails to capture

to preserve himself and to master external nature, but ends up losing his self and subjecting himself all the more to its demands.

[74]  *Dialectic of Enlightenment*, 54; Adorno, GS iii. 73.
[75]  Ibid. 55; Adorno, GS iii. 73.    [76]  Ibid. xiii; Adorno, GS iii. 13.
[77]  'Eternal providence, by placing salutary simples alongside noxious plants, and by endowing the substance of certain harmful animals with remedies for their wounds, has taught the sovereigns who are are it ministers to imitate its wisdom' (Rousseau, 'Discours sur Les Science et les Arts', in his *Oeuvres complètes* (Paris: Gallimard, 1961–9), iii. 26).

the *aporetic* structure of the dialectic and the point, which is evident from the original myth, that the healing and the wounding agent are in fact one and the same, albeit put to different uses on different occasions. Only the homeopathic reading does justice to this thought.[78]

The thesis that reason is the remedy in the evil raises a nasty question for critical theorists. If reason is both remedy and evil, why does not critical theory—as an instance of enlightened reason—misfire in just the same way as Odysseus' cunning is supposed to do? If it does misfire, it is not clear how it can provide a remedy. If it does not, then the thesis that reason is the remedy in the evil looks like another version of the early perfectionist ideal of reason. After all, the remedy is still supposed to be *contained in* reason itself; and the diagnosis of a capitalist society that is 'contrary to reason' is offered in the light of the ideal inherent in reason. Viewed in this light, the homeopathic construal of reason as the remedy in the evil looks implausibly optimistic. The next sentence of the passage from the preface cited above is: '[i]f enlightenment does not incorporate reflexion on this regressive moment, it seals its own fate.' But what if it does incorporate such reflection, as critical theory, according to Horkheimer's original understanding of it, is supposed to do? The implication appears to be that reflecting on the very course of reason's degeneration into a calculus of efficiency for the purpose of mastering external nature can somehow prevent or stall this fate, and with it the fate of rationalized, technocratic, administered society.[79] How can reflection—the reflection of the critical theorist—accomplish that much?

The notion of reflection in play here seems to be drawn from psychoanalysis, where the patient's reflecting on the original scene in which a pathological symptom such as a neurosis was formed could loosen its hold. According to Freud, insight into the aetiology of a neurosis can have therapeutic benefits. This is certainly how Horkheimer envisages reflection. 'The disease of reason is that reason was born from man's urge to dominate nature, and the "recovery" depends on insight into the nature of the original disease, not on a cure of the latest symptoms.'[80] However, even if it is true that

---

[78] The earliest suggestion I have found in the literature that Adorno makes use of the figure of innoculation or homeopathy is made by Michael Cahn. See Cahn, 'Subversive Mimesis', in Mihai Spariosu (ed.), *Mimesis in Contemporary Theory* (Philadelphia: John Benjamins' Publishing Company), 1984.

[79] See Horkheimer's *Eclipse of Reason*, 176. See also his 1951 essay 'Zum Begriff der Vernunft', in *Max Horkheimer: Sozialphilosophischer Studien*, 55–8.

[80] Horkheimer, *Eclipse of Reason*, 176.

therapeutic benefits flow from the patient's reflection on the formation of his own neurotic symptom, it is extremely doubtful whether any analogous benefits flow from the critical theorist's reflections on the nature of capitalist society. There are too many obvious disanalogies between the two cases: not least that society is not a subject writ large with the capacity to know itself, and that social theorists do not relate to the society they theorize about as the psychoanalyst relates to the analysand.[81] There is a weaker and more plausible claim here, namely that insight brought about by reflection on the original 'disease of reason', i.e. the insight won by a critical theory of society, is a necessary but not a sufficient condition of recovery (i.e. social transformation), but that does not really do justice to the thought that the remedy is *in* the evil.

# 3. THE POLITICS OF CRITICAL THEORY

## 3.1 Adorno, Horkheimer, and the Absent Politics of Critical Theory

We have followed the development of first-generation critical theory up to the point at which it takes on its mature and most influential form. We are now in a position to address the first significant criticism of critical theory, namely that after the war critical theory abandoned all its practical political commitments because of the theoretical cul-de-sac into which Adorno and Horkheimer had taken it. This is potentially a very damning objection, for, of all theories, a critical theory of society ought to have concrete political implications.

We should begin by recalling that critical theory has two kinds of practical aim, remedial and diagnostic. There is no question of critical theory's having abandoned its diagnostic aim, though it might be thought that, absent its remedial aims, any diagnostic aim it may still have is otiose. (What is the

---

[81] Habermas explores the analogy between psychoanalysis and critical theory, and tries to demonstrate a link between the cognitive and practical remedial effects of critique in *Knowledge and Human Interests* (Boston: Beacon Press, 1971); *Erkenntnis und Interesse* (Frankfurt am Main: Suhrkamp, 1968). However, as he soon came to realize, his theory fell foul of the objection raised here. See Habermas, *The Past as Future* (Cambridge: Polity, 1994), 101. For a qualified defence of his early idea that critical theory is based on an emancipatory interest, see *Autonomy and Solidarity: Interviews with Jürgen Habermas*, ed. P. Dews (London: Verso, 1992), 193.

point of a diagnosis without a remedy?) My view is that critical theory never gives up all its remedial aims, and therefore never retreats from politics altogether. What I have been calling remedial questions include questions about the institutional and administrative structure of a transformed, good society, about the means of social transformation, and about what individuals who are in the midst of the bad actually existing society should do in the here and now. The remedial aims of critical theory can be divided into two groups: the first concerns matters at the collective and institutional level, the second concerns the individual members of society. The first group of remedial aims are concerned with the transformation of society as a whole, its institutional structure, administrative arrangements, and organization. The second group are what I call therapeutic aims, which are concerned with the transformation of individuals. The two kinds of aim are closely interrelated, since one cannot change society without changing human beings. They are also in each case both negative and positive, according as they concern what must be destroyed and abolished and what has to be created or built in its place. This yields the following picture of the remedial aims of critical theory.

It is a commonplace that in the Marxist revolutionary and socialist traditions of social philosophy the debate about how the good society should be organized

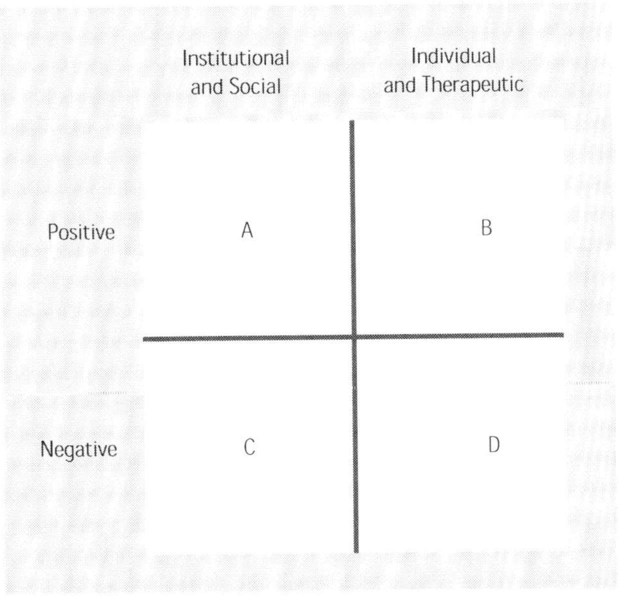

Fig. 1 The Remedial Aims of Critical Social Theory

and administered (A above) has never been prosecuted as assiduously as the debate on the more immediate questions of what should be abolished (C) and how.[82] The Frankfurt School theorists, particularly Adorno and Horkheimer after the war, were especially reticent on such questions. Nonetheless, the lineaments of the vision of the rational society to which they clung in spite of the critique of instrumental reason can be discerned: the improvement of social conditions, the elimination of misery, the achievement of a fair division of goods and opportunities, the creation of a more equal and just society and the establishment of social harmony (A).

After the war, however, Adorno and Horkheimer became convinced that existing capitalist society was so thoroughly compromised that these aims could not be attained through modifications of present society and the actualisation of potentials within it. Critical theory showed that what was required was a radical social transformation of, and break with, presently existing society. Radical or not, one has to be careful about dubbing this aim a 'revolution', a word that both Adorno and Horkheimer conspicuously avoid.[83] The remedial aims of critical theory were *revolutionary* only in the sense that they implied that what was needed was a total qualitative transformation of individual and collective life into something different from and discontinuous with presently existing society.[84] The term 'utopia' (which Adorno uses a lot) is less misleading than 'revolution' in this context, for 'utopia' refers to an end-state and not to the means or vehicle by which such an end is to be realized. In fact, for reasons we have just seen, Adorno's and Horkheimer's critical theory cannot be *revolutionary* in a common understanding of the term since it is not designed to help a revolutionary elite seize power, gain control of a territory, and appropriate the means of production.[85] On their view, any theory that was merely a means to an end, even a politically desirable one, was bound to misfire and to lead to just

---

[82] See Irving Howe, 'On the Moral Basis of Socialism', *Dissent* (Fall 1981), 491–5: 'A moral sentiment may be admirable but it does not, by itself, constitute a sufficient basis for politics. When in fact we examine the record of socialism, we find that it is precisely in the realm of proposals for its enactment that it has suffered from terrible vagueness and has been forced to make major retreats. An intellectual scandal has been its paucity of thought regarding the structural workings of socialist society; most Marxists in fact, have not thought it worth the trouble.'

[83] See n. 8 above.

[84] See Raymond Geuss, 'Dialectics and the Revolutionary Impulse', Fred Rush (ed.), in *The Cambridge Companion to Critical Theory* (Cambridge: Cambridge University Press, 2004), 103–39.

[85] Ibid. See also Horkheimer, *Critique of Instrumental Reason* (New York: Continuum, 1974), 81. 'Before they seized power the aim of Lenin and most of his friends was a society of freedom and justice, yet in reality they opened the way to a terroristic totalitarian bureaucracy.'

another form of domination and oppression. Consequently, they had almost nothing to say either about political and revolutionary strategy.

This constellation of views led to an impasse. Achieving the positive remedial aims of critical theory (A and B above) required the abolition of oppressive, unjust social structures and hierarchies, and the overturning of the various forces that maintained and solidified them (C and D above). Yet critical theory was virtually silent on how the negative task (C) should be carried out. It appeared that its positive remedial aims (A and B) could be achieved neither by reform nor by a revolution. Here was one set of reasons why Horkheimer and Adorno came to be so reticent about the remedial aims of critical theory (A and C).

As a consequence many critics and commentators, even sympathetic ones, have been quick to accuse Adorno and Horkheimer of retreating from *politics*. The most notorious formulation of this kind of objection was made by the Hungarian Marxist and literary critic György Lukács, who in 1962 penned an infamous slight:

A considerable part of the leading German intelligentsia, including Adorno, have taken up residence in the 'Grand Hotel Abyss' . . . 'a beautiful hotel, equipped with every comfort, on the edge of an abyss, of nothingness, of absurdity. And the daily contemplation of the abyss between excellent meals or artistic entertainments, can only heighten the enjoyment of the subtle comforts offered.'[86]

This remark has encouraged the caricature of Adorno as a mandarin aesthete, remote from the real-life concerns of actual people, whose lack of revolutionary politics was largely a matter of personal distaste. The caricature is unfair, however, particularly when construed as a personal attack on Adorno, since he was a highly active public intellectual, who took his responsibilities as a social and cultural critic, educator, and radio broadcaster very seriously. He always made strenuous efforts to reach his audience, and was not afraid either to tackle highly controversial and politically divisive questions such as Germany's relationship to its past, or to risk alienating his audience by taking an unpopular line.[87] In the 1960s Adorno did get involved in student politics albeit selectively and perhaps reluctantly. He attended meetings and spoke at a demonstration against the 'Emergency Laws'. He defended students' right

---

[86] Lukács, *The Theory of the Novel: A Historico-philosophical Essay on the Forms of Great Epic Literature*, trans. Anna Bostock (Cambridge, MA: MIT Press, 1971). The quotation is from Lukács, *Die Zerstörung der Vernunft* (Neuwied: Luchterhand, 1962), 219.

[87] See Henry Pickford, 'The Dialectic of Theory and Praxis: Late Adorno', in N. C. Gibson. and A. Rubin (eds.), *Adorno: A Critical Reader* (Oxford: Blackwell, 2002), 312–41.

to protest and went so far as publicly to condemn the state and the police over an infamous incident in November 1967 when a student, Benno Ohnesorg, was shot in the back by a policeman at a demonstration.[88]

Why, then, did the mud flung by Lukács and others stick? The answer is that there was a grain of truth in Lukács's remark—not the irrelevant fact that Adorno, as the son of a wealthy wine importer, probably was a connoisseur of fine wine as well as of art, but the fact that some of his arguments against the adventitious and arbitrary nature of practice look more like post-hoc rationalizations for doing just what he liked to do anyway—composing, listening to modern music, philosophizing, or reading Proust—and for not doing things he disliked, such as participating in organized politics, joining parties, going on demonstrations, etc.[89] Cynics raised their eyebrows to Adorno's view (one he no doubt sincerely espoused) that under present conditions a small number of carefully selected works of European, avant-garde music and literature represented the only source of unreified experience from which a true political practice might emerge, as it were, from the ruins of the present. For on this view, Adorno's *métier*, art theory and philosophically informed cultural criticism, represented the only politics worth pursuing, and his way of living the only 'right living' available.

However, Adorno was much more forthcoming about the individual and therapeutic aims of critical theory (B and D above) than he ever was about its social and institutional aims (A and C). Commentators have paid less attention to these aims than they deserve, for they are where the primary political and practical upshot of Adorno's conception of critical theory is located. I use the word 'therapeutic' here advisedly, not because the remedial aim I have in mind is in any way quietistic, but only because it is addressed, in the first instance, to individual behaviour, attitudes, and beliefs. In the best case, of course, the ultimate individual aim of critical theory is to abolish the subjective states of unhappiness, unfulfilment, and alienation experienced by members of society

---

[88] See Stefan Müller-Doohm, *Adorno: A Biography* (Cambridge: Polity, 2005), 449–53; and Espen Hammer, *Adorno and the Political* (London, Routledge, 2006), 18–26.

[89] Adorno was personally allergic to collectivism of any kind, steered clear of all political parties, and was extremely distrustful of any organization that required obedience to leadership, principle, or ideology. It was qualities such as these, together with his rejection of Marxism-Leninism, and his distrust of activism and instrumentalism, that helped eventually to bring him into conflict with the student movement, with whose aims—opposition to the state, the creation of a more just and humane society—he broadly sympathized. However, it was his engagement in student politics which gave rise to the conflict, not his aloofness. See Müller-Doohm, *Adorno*, 453–66; Hammer, *Adorno and the Political*, 22–6; and Simone Chambers, 'The Politics of Critical Theory', in Tom Huhn (ed.), *The Cambridge Companion to Adorno* (Cambridge: Cambridge University Press, 2004), 228.

(D) and replace them with something better, namely happiness, fulfilment, and an unalienated, meaningful life. And the best case would require the abolition of the existing reasons for those states of unhappiness, alienation, etc.—just the kind of wholesale institutional transformation of society that Adorno doubted was achievable under present conditions. There is, however, a second best: epistemic emancipation, the disillusioning or undeceiving of subjects about their condition and about the social conditions under which they live, the dispelling of beliefs and attitudes that unbeknownst to them contribute to their oppression.

Adorno was keen to point out the irony that this disillusioning process may bring to consciousness the reasons why unhappiness and alienation are in fact the appropriate response under the social circumstances. He came to think that the majority of people have been so assailed by social pressure to conform, so manipulated and duped by advertising and the culture industry that they are inclined to accept the world and their situation as it is. In short, people want the light entertainment, the glossy magazines, the soap operas, and the industrial hamburgers that are readily available to them. Critical theory cannot aim to fill unhappy lives with happiness for the simple reason that unhappiness and alienation are not the immediate problem. The immediate problem is that people are not unhappy or alienated, so that bringing them back to a state of well-founded and conscious unhappiness with the world and alienation from it would be a step forward.[90] (Here is another sense in which the therapeutic aim of critical theory is quite unlike other therapies.) This aim is theoretical, but it also has practical, political implications for the here and now. Critical theory aims at encouraging a self-transformation of individuals in anticipation of an eventual radical qualitative social and political transformation, i.e. in anticipation of what Adorno called 'utopia'.

---

[90] See, for example, Adorno, *Minima Moralia*, 39; Adorno, GS iv. 43. In its practical aspect Adorno's philosophy can be interestingly compared with the kind of care of the soul characteristic of Stoicism. The elimination of suffering, the attainment of true happiness through virtue, is for the Stoic, as for Adorno, compatible with empirical suffering—pain and misery—and with worldly unhappiness. Compare Hegel's remark on Stoicism, 'Die Stoiker sagten: Nur Tugend sei zu suchen; mit der Tugend ist aber für sich selbst Glückseligkeit gefunden ... diese Glückseligkeit ist die wahrhafte, unerschütterliche, wenn auch sonst der Mensch in Unglück ist' (Hegel, *Werke*, xix. 282), with the following sentence from *Negative Dialectics*: 'Conscious unhappiness (*unglückliches Bewußtsein*) is not a delusion of the mind's vanity, but something inherent in it; the one authentic dignity it has received in its separation from the body' (*Negative Dialectics*, 20; Adorno, GS vi. 203). Here the translator's inversion of *unglückliches Bewußtsein* in the English translation, though it loses the allusion to Hegel, expresses Adorno's thought perfectly.

It is therefore mistaken to think that after the war Adorno and Horkheimer simply abandoned the practical and political aims of critical theory. In spite of their reputation, they never gave up all its remedial aims, even if they drew back from the task of bringing about institutional and social change. In Adorno's view, critical theory still has very concrete remedial aims: namely to provoke subjects into adopting a variety of strategies of non-cooperation with and resistance to institutionalized forms of social unfreedom, and the myriad social pressures to conform or play along with prevailing norms and values.[91] The politics of critical theory may be a politics of the second best and of the time being, but it is a politics nonetheless. Moreover, Adorno came up with some very concrete practical suggestions about how this remedial aim could be achieved. In 'Democratic Leadership and Mass Manipulation' he suggested the distribution of pamphlets documenting the psychological techniques of fascist agitators which can act as 'vaccines against anti-democratic indoctrination'.[92] And in a 1969 radio interview on the topic of 'Education towards Maturity (Mündigkeit)', he suggested that sixth-form pupils could be taken to see commercial films and 'quite easily shown what a swindle they are and what lies they tell' and that they can in this way be 'immunized against' the illusions spawned by radio broadcasts and other light entertainments.[93] Critique, as Adorno envisages it here, is a transformative practice; the transformation it aims at is in the first instance a transformation of individuals. It offers a kind of individual 'therapy' or antidote to the pressure to conform, by encouraging Mündigkeit, a virtue the exercise of which would befit a 'right' politics were it available, thereby keeping alive the possibility of a truly democratic politics and its broader remedial aim.[94]

---

[91] Adorno also speaks of 'resistance against all that has been imposed on us, and what the world has made of us', of 'resistance against the bad', and of resistance 'against the innumerable externally imposed forms of morality' (Probleme der Moralphilosophie. Theodor W. Adorno: Nachgelassene Schriften IV, x (Frankfurt am Main: Suhrkamp, 1996), 248–54). For a detailed account of Adorno's ethics of resistance, see J. G. Finlayson, 'Adorno on the Ethical and the Ineffable', European Journal of Philosophy 10/1 (2002), 1–25.

[92] Adorno, GS xx/1. 278.

[93] Adorno, 'Erziehung zur Mündigkeit', in Theodor W. Adorno: Erziehung zur Mündigkeit (Frankfurt am Main: Suhrkamp, 1971), 145–6.

[94] Note that what I have called the therapeutic aim is not to reduce or avoid conflict and to promote acquiescence and acceptance of one's situation. On the contrary, Adorno wants to inculcate an ethos of vigilance and resistance to the myriad social pressures to conform, adjust, or fit in with current, but in Adorno's eyes devalued, distorted, and reified ways of living.

Critique and the prerequisite of democracy, political maturity (*Mündigkeit*) belong together. The person who speaks for himself is politically mature, because he has thought for himself and is not merely repeating someone else.[95]

For Adorno, democracy without mature ((*mündige*)) independent-minded citizens capable of making reasoned, discriminating, and informed decisions is a democracy in name only; a consensus manufactured by mass manipulation. [96]

## 3.2  Habermas and the Question of Politics

It is interesting to compare Horkheimer and Adorno with Habermas, who has criticized the critical theory of his predecessors for its political deficit. Habermas, one should remember, was of a different generation from his predecessors and had a very different experience of post-war West Germany (other significant differences are that he was not Jewish, and never forced into exile). Adorno and Horkheimer were deeply affected by their encounters first with Nazism, and then with McCarthyite America, which led to their developing not just a hypersensitivity to incipient traces of totalitarianism, but also, in Habermas's view, an insensitivity to the benefits of post-war social democratic institutions.[97] This led to a significant difference in their respective diagnoses. Habermas criticizes Adorno and Horkheimer for having a one-sided and unduly negative view of the Enlightenment and the various processes of rationalization and modernization that accompany it, as well as for an 'undervaluation of the traditions of democracy and of the constitutional state'.[98] He was deeply struck by the improbable success of the project of grafting constitutional democracy onto an alien tradition, under an Adenauer regime which was in many respects reluctant to acknowledge and break with its Nazi past. He argued that Marxist social theory up to and including Adorno's and Horkheimer's had badly underestimated the

---

[95]  Adorno, 'Kritik', GS x/2. 784. 'Critique' in *Adorno: Critical Models: Interventions and Catchwords*, trans. Henry W. Pickford (New York: Columbia University Press, 1998), 281.

[96]  Adorno, GS xx/1. 268: 'To apply the idea of a democracy in a merely formalistic way, to accept the will of the majority *per se*, without consideration for the *content* of democratic decisions, may ultimately lead to the complete perversion of democracy itself and ultimately to its abolition.' See also GS xx/1. 269.

[97]  As Habermas puts it 'the actual historical experience of the Federal Republic...was more or less impenetrable to them' ('Life-forms, Morality and the Task of the Philosopher', in Habermas, *Autonomy and Solidarity*, 197).

[98]  Habermas, *Autonomy and Solidarity*, 98.

resources in bourgeois political and legal institutions to solve the practical problems facing modern capitalist societies.[99] The differences between Habermas and the first generation of critical theorists lay not just in their estimation of the transformative potential of *democracy*; it lay in their respective views of political institutions as such. Whatever faith Adorno still had in democracy tended to be counteracted by his deep mistrust of all extant political institutions.[100] By contrast, from *On the Structural Transformation of the Public Sphere* (1962) right through to *Between Facts and Norms* (1992) Habermas's work has focused on the role of democratic institutions and public spheres of civil society in shaping autonomous, morally responsible citizens.[101]

Though Habermas puts much more emphasis on understanding the nature and function of modern democratic institutions, rather like Adorno he believes that social theory cannot take it upon itself 'to design just institutions'.[102] The resemblance between Habermas and Adorno on this point, however, conceals deeper differences in their positions, and in the considerations that underlie them. Habermas makes a distinction between social theory, undertaken from the third-person perspective of the theorist in his or her capacity as expert, and social criticism, an activity performed by participants in social practices and by democratic citizens. This difference in perspective gives rise to a difference in aims.[103] The practical aims of social theory are not the same as those of social criticism. On Habermas's view the

---

[99] 'Things got better with the re-introduction of democracy and . . . the rule of law' (*Autonomy and Solidarity*, 189). See also 'The Dialectics of Rationalization', ibid. 102.

[100] According to Habermas, 'Horkheimer and Adorno . . . found political institutions void of all traces of reason. For them, reason had become utopian in the literal sense of the word: it has lost all its locations and thus ushered in the whole problematic of negative dialectics' (*Autonomy and Solidarity*, 103). Peter Wagner has recently attempted to qualify this now widely accepted view, by showing that Adorno was 'indeed interested in political institutions'. See Wagner, 'Versuch das Endspiel zu verstehen. Kapitalismusanalyse als Gesellschaftstheorie', in Axel Honneth (ed.), *Dialektik der Freiheit: Frankfurter Adorno-Konferenz 2003* (Frankfurt am Main, Suhrkamp, 2003), 211. However, the counterevidence he adduces (two short unpublished essays and an article in English entitled 'Democratic Leadership and Mass Manipulation') is not only extremely slight, as he admits, but if anything supports the view that he contests. For even in these essays there is little in the way of concrete analysis and discussion of the nature and role of political institutions.

[101] Habermas, *Strukturwandel der Öffentlichkeit* (Darmstadt and Neuwied: Luchterhand, 1962), *Structural Transformation of the Public Sphere* (Cambridge MA: MIT Press, 1989); *Between Facts and Norms* (Cambridge: Polity, 1996), *Faktizität und Geltung* (Frankfurt am Main: Suhrkamp, 1992).

[102] 'Life-forms. Morality and the Task of the Philosopher', *Autonomy and Solidarity*, 200.

[103] This difference in perspective between theorist and participant is reflected in Habermas's own work, which is divided into two: his theoretical works aimed at an academic audience and his political and cultural interventions on specific issues aimed at a lay readership, which form a significant body of work collected under the title of *Kleine politische Schriften*. The one exception to this is his discussion

criticism of the social theorist aims to help participants in social practices 'clarify their understanding of themselves'. Beyond this the most that critical social theory can achieve is to indicate 'necessary conditions under which emancipated forms of life would be possible today'.[104] By contrast, social criticism, which is 'the common business of political discourses among citizens', *can* aim to bring about concrete institutional change. 'It is the attempt of participants to answer the question "what now?"—in these circumstances, for us particular people, what are or would be the best institutions?'[105] In the *Theory of Communicative Action* Habermas analyses the role played by new social movements such as environmentalism and feminism in indicating areas in need of reform, and in lobbying for social change in specific areas, while in his later political theory he analyses the role played by informal public spheres and civil society in channelling public reasons into democratic decision-making mechanisms. Philosophers can, to be sure, contribute in their role as public intellectuals to the processes of collective self-interpretation and self-clarification and opinion formation that take place in civil society, but their offerings have no expert weight or authority. They are, according to Habermas offered as 'advice' to the members of civil society.[106]

None of this has anything to do with the insidious dialectical connection between theory—indeed conceptual thought—and domination. Habermas's conclusions are evinced by a quite different diagnosis of modern society and its failings, and by a view of the aims of the social theorist that takes cognizance of the different perspectives of the critic qua social theorist and the critic qua participant in social practices and democratic institutions. He has more modest expectations of what can be expected from the critical social *theory*, and a more sanguine view of what can be expected from social agents and democratic citizens in modern democratic societies.

---

on the moral implications of gene technology in *The Future of Human Nature* (Cambridge: Polity, 2003), which falls into both categories. This is due I think to the nature of the topic, which is one of the few areas where public debate needs to be informed by the expert contributions of philosophers and physicians.

[104]  Habermas, *Autonomy and Solidarity*, 202, and 168.        [105]  Ibid. 200 ff.

[106]  Habermas, 'Noch einmal: Zum Verhältnis von Theorie und Praxis', in *Wahrheit und Rechtfertigung* (Frankfurt am Main: Suhrkamp, 1999), 319–34. See also *Autonomy and Solidarity*, 200–1, and 'Themes in Postmetaphysical Thinking', in *Postmetaphysical Thinking* (Cambridge: Polity; 1992), 28–57.

# 4. Morality and Critical Theory

## 4.1 The Problem of Normative Foundations

This brings us, finally, to the second major objection to critical theory. In the 1980s Jürgen Habermas was the first to locate what he called the problem of the 'normative foundations' of critical theory in Adorno and Horkheimer's *Dialectic of Enlightenment*.

From the beginning, critical theory laboured over the problem of giving an account of its own normative foundations (*normativen Grundlagen*); since Horkheimer and Adorno made their turn to the critique of instrumental reason early in the 1940s, this problem has become drastically apparent. [107]

Habermas develops several different lines of objection, all under the umbrella criticism that first-generation critical theory suffers from a 'normative deficit'. His own critical social theory is widely understood in the literature to have made good this deficit. Yet it is not easy to understand what exactly the problem is and how he purports to solve it. The difficulty stems from an ambiguity in the term 'normative', which occurs frequently in Habermas's conceptual vocabulary (viz. 'normative foundations or grounds', 'normative validity', 'normative rightness', etc.). At the one extreme, the adjective 'normative' is used exclusively in the context of morality. At the other extreme lie all kinds of non-moral rules: rules of logic, truth (on some accounts) rules of grammar and rules of discourse. In between these two poles there is a whole gamut of notions such as hypothetical imperatives (on most accounts), principles of universalizability or consistency in action, rules of etiquette, etc., all of which are 'normative' in that they can be formulated with the operator 'ought'. This ambiguity haunts much of Habermas's writing and is also rife throughout the secondary literature. [108]

---

[107] Jürgen Habermas, *Theory of Communicative Action*, i (Cambridge: Polity, 1984), 374.

[108] Rainer Forst's article is typical of the confusion that reigns here: 'As *normative* theory, Critical Theory ... argues for the integrity of a sphere of communicative, normative integration, as well as for the realization of the possibility of social and political discourse ... As normative theory, it claims the fallible truth of a reconstruction of the presuppositions of communicative action.' Forst uses the term 'normative' to mean something like 'wholesome' and 'integral', but also 'justified' and 'probably true'. Later in the same article he argues that Habermas's theory is normative in a moral sense by dint of positing 'certain standards of human moral agency'. Rainer Forst, 'Justice, Reason and Critique: Basic Concepts of Critical Theory', in David M. Rasmussen (ed.), *Handbook of Critical Theory* (Oxford: Blackwell, 1999), 143–7.

If that were not unhelpful enough, it is also often unclear what is meant by the term 'foundation' or 'grounds' (*Grundlage*). Habermas states that the *Dialectic of Enlightenment* lacks 'an account of its own normative grounds'. Does this mean that it lacks normative justification, i.e. reasons, arguments evidence, etc., or that it lacks a theory? If by 'normative' he means moral, then the claim is either that the normative conclusions of critical social theory need to be supported by moral arguments and reasons, or that they require a full-blown moral theory. Honneth, for example, appears to take the latter view, for he argues that it is with 'communicative ethics'—i.e. with a moral theory—that 'Habermas . . . has attempted to justify the normative claims of a critical social theory.'[109] I take the former view and understand Habermas's objection as follows. Adorno and Horkheimer's critical theory makes broadly moral claims, but cannot, for various reasons, avail itself of the substantive moral considerations that would justify these. Hence, either its conclusions are unsupported, or it is inconsistent. By 'broadly moral' I mean that they fall within the compass of the values and norms that govern peoples' beliefs and attitudes towards the life, character and actions of other social agents. 'Morality', as we have already seen, is often used by its detractors and supporters in a much narrower sense, to mean a morality of rule or principle that tells one what one ought to do and why, usually by establishing negative duties or prohibitions on certain actions.[110] On the narrower view moral obligations are characteristically taken to have a special importance and stringency, and priority over other values, and morality is held to be distinct from ethics or ethical life, and from conceptions of the good or the good life, and considerations of virtue.[111] However, it is natural and useful to use the term 'morality' in a broader and more inclusive sense, as I do here, which is not opposed to but inclusive of ethics and these other notions, and yet still to think of it as having a certain centrality, importance, and priority. For these are the very features in virtue of which broadly moral notions such as

---

[109] Honneth, *Critique of Power: Reflective Stages in a Critical Social Theory*, trans. K. Baynes (Cambridge MA: MIT Press, 1991), 282.

[110] This usage was invented by Hegel (see n. 34 above) but persists in more contemporary writers. Among the prominent recent critics of the moral standpoint are G. E. Anscombe, 'Modern Moral Philosophy', *Philosophy* 33 (1958), 1–19; Bernard Williams, *Ethics and the Limits of Philosophy* (London: Fontana Press, 1985), 74–196. Chapter 10 is entitled 'Morality the peculiar institution'. See also Geuss, 'Outside Ethics', in *Outside Ethics*, 40–67.

[111] This is also true of theorists who defend conceptions of the moral standpoint, prominent among whom are Kurt Baier, *The Moral Point of View* (New York: Random House, 1965; first publ. 1958); Scanlon, *What we Owe to Each Other*; and Jürgen Habermas, *Moral Consciousness and Communicative Action* (Cambridge, Polity, 1990).

'moral goodness', 'moral rightness', and 'moral value' are distinguishable from non-moral notions of value and goodness such as aesthetic values, economic goods, rules of etiquette, matters of taste, and such like.

I take it to be obvious, and now generally accepted, that Horkheimer and Adorno do make broadly moral claims. The claim, which they never hid, that the social world is not as it ought to be and should be changed, has to be understood in broadly moral terms.[112] For even when Adorno uses the vocabulary of 'false' and 'untrue' to describe existing society rather than the more familiar moral terms 'wrong', 'impermissible', 'bad', and so forth, he also employs more morally freighted terms, 'evil' (*böse*), 'bad' (*schlecht*), 'the bad' (*das Schlechte*), 'absolute evil', and 'radically evil'.[113] The textual evidence that first-generation critical theorists make broadly moral claims is overwhelming and incontrovertible, so I restrict myself to two examples.

In the condition of their unfreedom Hitler has imposed a new categorical imperative on human beings, namely: to order their thought and actions such that Auschwitz never reoccur, nothing similar ever happen.[114]

The only thing that can perhaps be said is, that the good life (*das richtige Leben*) today would consist in the shape of resistance against the forms of a false life (*eines falschen Lebens*), which has been seen through and critically dissected by the most progressive minds.[115]

If one does not interpret passages such as these, which are by no means exceptions, as having moral weight, one has missed their point. So critical theory must presuppose some broadly moral considerations or its conclusions are not justified.[116] This point should be handled carefully, for Adorno

---

[112] Jay Bernstein, in the first sentence of his long study on Adorno's ethics, puts the point thus: 'No reading of the works of T. W. Adorno can fail to be struck by the ethical intensity of his writing, sentence by sentence, word by word' (J. M. Bernstein, *Adorno: Disenchantment and Ethics* (Cambridge: Cambridge University Press, 2001), 1). The most comprehensive discussion of the various difficulties besetting Adorno's ethical thought and the different solutions that have been offered to them is provided by Fabian Freyenhagen, 'Adorno's Negativistic Ethics' (PhD thesis, Department of Philosophy, University of Sheffield, 2005).

[113] *Dialectic of Enlightenment*, 168; Adorno, GS iii. 192. See also *Hegel Three Studies*, 62; Adorno, GS v. 303.

[114] Adorno, *Negative Dialectics*, 365; Adorno, GS vi. 358. See also *Adorno: Critical Models*, 90–1 and 202–3; GSx/2., 555–73 and 674–91; Adorno, *Metaphysics: Concept and Problems*, 116.

[115] Adorno, *Probleme der Moralphilosophie*, 249.

[116] Cf. Giuseppe Tassone, 'Amoral Adorno: Negative Dialectics outside Ethics', *European Journal of Social Theory* 8/3 (2005), 251–67. In my view Tassone grossly overstates the point—Adorno is clearly not *amoral* in any sense of the word moral. Raymond Geuss makes the more nuanced point that Adorno does not appeal to morality in the narrow sense, but tries to position himself outside the standpoint from which it makes sense to ask characteristically (narrow) moral questions such as 'what

and Horkheimer obviously do not treat the claims of their social theory as deductions from listed premises. [117] However, if one takes the notion of justification in a wide sense, for example, the sense in which I can say that my reaction of moral indignation is justified by my merely seeing someone maltreating another person, then Adorno clearly does think that his theory is justified in this sense, since it 'answers to a world which is thoroughly false'. [118]

The trouble is that for various reasons, some of which we have already mentioned, Adorno and Horkheimer's view of morality is such as to make it impossible to understand their diagnosis of what is wrong with the social world along broadly moral lines. Why is this? The first-generation Frankfurt theorists inherited a battery of objections to Kantian morality from Schiller and Hegel among others, who attacked its dualist assumptions, and the view that rationality could be construed as the external imposition of rational form on a chaotic manifold of sentiments and inclinations. Drawing on Freud's notion of the superego, they argued that a Kantian morality of principles tended to supplant and to corrode the deep underlying affective ties to other people and things and to foster coldness and indifference in their place, giving rise to an attitude of obedience to and identification with authority. [119] Horkheimer was if anything more damning of rationalist morality than Adorno. [120] One of his more memorable lines is that Sade and Nietzsche incite the hatred of progressives because they trumpeted far and wide '[t]he impossibility of deriving from reason any principled argument against murder'. [121]

Adorno was probably more suspicious of ethical life than he was of a morality of principle. In his 1963 lectures on the *Problems of Moral Philosophy* he makes clear that, under current conditions, *Sittlichkeit*, ethical life or the morality of custom, rather than *Moralität*, the morality of principle, is the

---

ought I to do?' or 'what is the good life for man?' (See n. 62 above.) This is consistent with my claim that the claims of his social theory are moral in the broader sense of that term.

[117] Adorno rejected any kind of deductive reasoning as incipient ideology or mere tautology (Adorno, *Minima Moralia*, 70 and 80; GS iv. 79 and 90).

[118] 'Theorie und geistige Erfahrung bedürfen ihrer Wechselwirkung. Jene enthält nicht Antworten auf alle, sondern reagiert auf die bis innerste falsche Welt' (Adorno, GS vi, 41; *Negative Dialectics*, 31).

[119] See for example *Dialectic of Enlightenment*, 81–120; GS iii. 100–41. See also *Negative Dialectics*, 221–3 and 260–1, especially the section 'Reason, Ego, Superego', 270–4. 'Critique of the super-ego has to become a critique of the society that produced it: if criticism goes silent in the face of it, it kow-tows to the ruling social norm' (Adorno, GS vi. 221–2, 257–8, and 267–71).

[120] Compare Horkheimer's essays 'Materialismus und Moral' (KT i. 71–110) and 'Kants Philosophie und die Aufklärung', in Alfred Schmidt (ed.), *Zur Kritik der instrumentellen Vernunft* (Frankfurt am Main: Fischer Athenäum Verlag, 1967), with lectures 14 and 15 of Adorno's *Probleme der Moralphilosophie*.

[121] *Dialectic of Enlightenment*, 119; Adorno, GS iii. 140.

immediate danger.[122] Once ethical life stands in need of rational reassurance, it has hardened into a mere way of life, and because of the pressures it exerts on individuals to adapt and conform, ethical life, in Adorno's eyes, is less able to provide a source of resistance and criticism, and more likely to lead to totalitarianism than a morality of principle:

One can actually say that the horror perpetrated by Fascism is to a great extent nothing but an extension of traditional ethics (*Volksitten*), which has turned into something irrational and violent precisely because it has been divorced from reason.[123]

It is not just that culture, tradition, and ethical life failed to provide an effective basis for resistance to Nazism, rather, under specific historical conditions they provided the very soil in which it took root.

Adorno, then, condemns both morality and ethical life for not being able to provide any effective resistance to fascism and shows that, each in its own way contributed to the emergence of totalitarianism. Moreover, Adorno's and Horkheimer's thoroughgoing critique of instrumental reason implies that prudential considerations (doing what is best in the light of one's self-interest) cannot provide any reliable source of normativity. It also puts paid to Horkheimer's early consequentialist view that worth of an action is determined by whether or not it leads to the elimination of human suffering and oppression, and to the establishment of a rationally organized society and the 'happiness of life as a whole'.[124] Adorno and Horkheimer can appeal neither to morality nor to ethical life, neither to a Kantian 'ethics of conviction' (*Gesinnungsethik*) nor to a consequentialist 'ethics of responsibility' (*Verantwortungsethik*).[125] In short, they distance themselves from all the relevant considerations that might justify the broadly

---

[122] See Adorno's interpretation of Ibsen's *Wild Duck* in lecture 16 of *Probleme der Moralphilosophie*, 244–5: 'Infolgedessen läuft dann die ausgeführte Verantwortungsethik darauf hinaus, daß das, was ist—und was bei Hegel der Weltlauf heißt, den er ja gegen die Eitelkeit der protestierenden Innerlichkeit verteidigt—, gegen das Subjekt jeweils recht hat' (Adorno, *Probleme der Moralphilosophie*, 244–5).

[123] 'Man kann eigentlich sagen, daß das Grauen, das der Faschismus verübt hat, in einem sehr weitem Maße gar nichts anderes ist als eine Verlängerung von Volksitten, die eben dadurch, daß sie von der Vernunft sich abgelöst haben, dieses Widervernünftige und Gewalttätige angenommen haben . . .' (Adorno, *Probleme Der Moralphilosophie*, 33).

[124] Horkheimer, BPS 30. Horkheimer speaks of 'die Sorge um . . . das Glück des Lebens überhaupt' in the German original: KT i. 88.

[125] Max Weber introduced the distinction between *Gesinnungsethik* or 'ethics of conviction' and *Verantwortungsethik* or 'ethics of responsibility' in his 1919 lectures on 'The Profession and Vocation of Politics'. By *Gesinnungsethik* Weber has in mind primarily a Christian ethics but also (Kantian and Fichtean) deontological conceptions of morality: Weber, *Political Writings*, ed. P. Lassman and R. Spiers (Cambridge: Cambridge University Press, 2003). Adorno tends to switch between these two distinctions without paying attention to the differences. See Adorno, *Probleme der Moralphilosophie*, lecture 17,

moral conclusions of their critical theory. Thus they manoeuvre themselves into the dilemma described above: they cannot adduce the broadly moral considerations their conclusions require on pain of inconsistency; but if they do not, the claims of their critical theory remain unsupported.

## 4.2 Habermas's Discourse Ethics and the Normative Foundations of Social Theory

The problem of normative foundations has had a significant influence on the subsequent development of critical social theory. There is a widespread view in the literature that Habermas makes discourse ethics into a central component of his social theory in order to solve the normative problem. Discourse ethics makes good the normative deficit by providing critical theory with normative foundations. Honneth, for example, maintains that Habermas first establishes discourse ethics on the normative basis of the pragmatic presuppositions of communicative action, and then uses the latter 'to justify the normative claims of critical social theory'.[126] If the widespread view is correct, and if we understand normative here to mean 'broadly moral', then it follows that Habermas shifts Frankfurt School social theory away from the tradition of Hegelian-Marxism back to the kind of normative moral and political philosophy that predominates in the analytic tradition.

However, the widespread view is misleading in several respects. First, none of the universal pragmatic features of speech and action that Habermas reconstructs in his pragmatic theory of meaning and theory of communicative rationality, such as the rules of discourse, are normative in the *moral* sense. Second, Habermas's discourse ethics is not a straightforward normative moral theory. It does not purport to answer the question of what one ought to do and why by referring to valid moral norms. Rather it advances a defeasible reconstruction of the moral competence of modern social agents, and the rudiments of a theoretical justification of the moral standpoint. It does this by

---

pp. 248–62. In fact the two distinctions do not map onto one another, because whereas morality and *Gesinnungsethik* are roughly equivalent, Weber's term *Verantwortungsethik* is different from the term 'ethical life'. It refers rather to consequentialism, particularly in the domain of the political. The closest English equivalent to the distinction between *Gesinnungsethik* and *Verantwortungsethik* is therefore that between deontology and consequentialism.

[126] Honneth, *Critique of Power: Reflective Stages in a Critical Social Theory*, trans. K. Baynes (Cambridge, MA: MIT Press, 1991), 282.

providing a set of arguments that are supposed to establish principle (U).[127] Principle (U) only captures the procedure of moral discourse by which agents in the lifeworld determine the validity of moral norms for the purpose of solving conflicts of interest: it is not itself a substantive moral principle or valid moral norm. Discourse ethics therefore offers no normative support for whatever broadly moral conclusions critical social theory may draw. At best, it provides indirect theoretical justification for Habermas's social theory.[128] Finally, Habermas's social theory does not set out to criticize society in virtue of its degree of conformity to principle (U) or to any substantive moral principle. This is exactly what Habermas claims cannot be done by the social theorist. He explicitly rebukes Rawls for thinking that the theorist can criticize society by first designing 'the basic norms of a well-ordered society on the drafting table' and then checking society against it.[129]

If we understand normative, by contrast, to mean something less than moral, then there is some truth to the widespread view. Habermas attempts to solve the normative problem in two steps. First, he supplies critical social theory with normative grounds—in the form of discourse ethics, the theory of communicative rationality, and the pragmatic theory of meaning. Second, he modulates its conclusions so they are adequately supported by these grounds, which means the criticisms that it levels do not have moral weight. Consider Habermas's diagnostic thesis of the colonization of the lifeworld by the system, one example of which is the intrusion of markets into formerly non market-domains and the destruction and various distortions to which it leads. The colonization thesis does indeed give an account of what is *wrong with* capitalist society.[130] Briefly put, the consequence of colonization is that the systems of

---

[127] A recent formulation of (U) states that: 'a norm is valid if and only if the foreseeable consequences and side effects of its general observance for the interests and value-orientations of each individual could be freely accepted jointly by all concerned' (Habermas, *Die Einbeziehung des Anderen* (Frankfurt am Main: Suhrkamp, 1997), 60). I use this version because it is the first formulation that makes clear that (U) is a biconditional.

[128] If discourse ethics is correct, then, since it fits snugly with his social theory, it increases the likelihood that the latter is correct. It is true that, according to Habermas, the rules of discourse form one premise of an argument which is supposed to evince principle (U), the moral principle, by deduction (a deduction that incidentally neither Habermas nor anyone else has done successfully). But this is neither here nor there, since principle (U) is not a moral norm, and only a valid moral norm or set of substantive moral values could justify the broadly moral normative conclusions of social theory.

[129] Habermas, *The Past as Future*, 101; *Autonomy and Solidarity*, 202. See also *Die Einbeziehung des Anderen*, 65–95.

[130] In an earlier work Habermas develops the notion of 'systematically distorted communication', which he understands as speech that violates the pragmatic presuppositions of communication oriented towards reaching understanding. He then takes this as the basis of his explanation of social

money and power destabilize themselves and come into crisis by destroying the very environment on which their good functioning depends, namely the lifeworld, the repository of communication and discourse, and, among other things, the locus of the moral standpoint. The process of colonization is thus self-destabilizing and ultimately self-stultifying.[131] This is a *normative* diagnosis, for the underlying idea of malfunction is a normative notion, but it is not a broadly moral claim. The idea of a social pathology, on the analogy with medicine, is intended to offer a normative model of social criticism, robust enough to render intelligible the diagnostic claims that something is *wrong with* society, that it is not *as it ought to be*, whilst not trading illicitly on moral considerations.[132]

It is true that the programme of discourse ethics plays a central role in Habermas's mature social theory. However, this is not, pace Honneth and others, because a moral theory is needed to justify the normative claims of critical social theory. It is because Habermas offers a comprehensive theory of modern society, which on his view consists in multiple overlapping spheres of discourse (alongside the economy, the state, the administrative and legal system). Discourse ethics is central to this theory because of the central role that moral discourse plays in modern societies in the socialization of individuals, in the coordination of social action, and because of the internal relation between morality and the legitimacy of law.[133] The relation of Habermas's discourse ethics to his social theory is a complex one, reflecting differences in theoretical approach between him and his predecessors, in their respective diagnoses of modernity, and in their analysis of the social function of morality. Habermas does not think of universal, deontological morality as an internalized form of social repression, or as a manifestation of bourgeois ideology. He sees it chiefly as a response to the need to coordinate the actions

---

pathologies. Since the presuppositions of communication and the rules of discourse are normative but non-moral, it follows that a critical social theory advanced on this basis also does not make any broadly moral claims. 'Überlegung zur Kommunikationspathologie' (1974), in *Vorstudien und Ergänzungen zur Theorie des kommunikativen Handelns* (Frankfurt am Main: Suhrkamp, 1984), 226–73.

[131]  Clearly there are echoes here of the animus against instrumental rationality running through Adorno and Horkheimer's work.

[132]  No doubt this model of theoretical criticism raises difficulties of its own. For example, it presupposes standards of normal or non-pathological society, which have to be construed in terms of its proper functioning. This might itself be thought to be a weak form of perfectionism, in so far as it implies a picture of a well-functioning society, namely one where a flourishing lifeworld, replenished by communication and discourse, manages to coexist with systems such as markets and the state.

[133]  See Habermas, *Between Facts and Norms; Faktizität und Geltung*, 135–51.

of a plurality of agents in modern, large-scale societies, once the solidifying force of shared values and traditions has dissipated. He places Kantian morality in the context of the ontogenetic and phylogenetic development from conventional to post-conventional morality. On his view the emergence of a modern morality of principle represents a significant gain in complexity and problem solving capacity: it is a precondition of *Mündigkeit*, and of democratic citizenship. Whilst the various claims that Habermas makes *about morality* and its social role tend to be more positive than those of Adorno and Horkheimer—he sees morality as a resource that modern societies cannot do without—he abides by his view that the task of the social theorist is not to make moral criticisms of society.[134] He leaves that task to moral agents, to citizens, and to members of civil society, which is one reason why Habermas's most trenchant and vocal social criticism is to be found, not in his theoretical works, but in the many newspaper articles, talks, and interviews collected in his *Kleine politische Schriften*.[135]

---

[134] In *The Theory of Communicative Action* Habermas states that the task of a critical theory of society, once it is cleansed of the substantial conception of reason smuggled in under the guise of a philosophy of history, must forswear critical evaluation and normative (i.e. moral) judgments of 'totalities, forms of life and culture . . . as a whole' (Habermas, *The Theory of Communicative Action*, ii (Cambridge: Polity Press, 1987), 383; *Theorie des kommunikativen Handelns*, ii (Frankfurt am Main: Suhrkamp, 1988), 562).

[135] Thanks to Henry Pickford, Fabian Freyenhagen, James Furner, Fred Neuhouser, Michael Rosen, Lucy Allais, Andrew Chitty, Nicholas Joll, and Nigel Hope.

# CHAPTER 19

# THE HUMANISM DEBATE

## THOMAS BALDWIN

THE 'Humanism Debate' was an extended critical discussion of the relationship between ethical values and human nature. The most famous exchange in this debate was that between Sartre and Heidegger. On one side Sartre proclaimed in his 1945 lecture (Sartre 1946) that 'Existentialism is a Humanism'; on the other side Heidegger responded in his 1946 'Letter on Humanism' (Heidegger 1947) that it was necessary to 'speak against humanism'. But the debate was not confined to Sartre and Heidegger: its participants included many of the leading French and German philosophers of the twentieth century, too many to discuss here. As well as Sartre and Heidegger I shall discuss the contributions of Lukács, Merleau-Ponty, Foucault, and Derrida.

## §1 'HUMANISM'

Before looking at the details and ramifications of this debate it is worth saying a bit about the term 'humanism'. It is often said that this term (or rather *Humanismus*) was first introduced by the German educator F. F. Niethammer in 1808 to defend the study of Latin and Greek in schools; and Heidegger alludes to this position when he remarks that 'a *studium humanitatis*, which in a certain way reaches back to the ancients and thus also becomes a revival of Greek civilization, always adheres to historically understood humanism' (Heidegger 1947: 244). Those who make this connection with the ancient world invoke the 'humanists' of the Renaissance, such as Erasmus, who sought to revive the study of the values of the ancient world and the conception there of *homo humanus* who exemplified these values; and it is certainly from this study of the writings of the ancient world (the *literae humaniores*) that we get our conception of 'humane studies' or 'humanities'. But once one looks at historical dictionaries this classicist origin for the use of the term 'humanism' is called into question. For the term '*humanisme*' can be found in French from 1765 with the meaning 'love of humanity' (philanthropy), and use of the term at this time does not appear to bring with it any specifically classical allusion. Subsequently Comte's development of his 'religion of humanity' in the 1850s was especially influential as a form of 'humanism', and around this time the term is increasingly used in French and English to describe positions which emphasize the intrinsic value of humanity. Contemporary 'humanist' associations have their origins in the influence of Comte's work (the British 'Humanistic Religious Association' was founded in 1853). It is clear, too, that the 'humanism' of Sartre's lecture is to be understood in terms of this Comtean tradition, even though Sartre explicitly distances himself from Comte's 'religion of humanity'.

# §2 SARTRE, 'EXISTENTIALISM IS A HUMANISM'[1]

Sartre delivered this lecture in Paris in 1945, just after the end of the Second World War, and it was subsequently published in 1946. Although the lecture is not definitive of his philosophy, it is rightly renowned as a classic presentation and defence by Sartre of his existentialism, and it expresses his position at a particularly significant time, soon after he had completed his first major work of philosophy, *Being and Nothingness* (Sartre 1943) which was published

---

[1] It needs to be emphasized that in his title Sartre asserts that existentialism is a form of humanism; this positive claim is lost in the common (mis)translation of the title as 'Existentialism and Humanism'.

during the occupation of France, and before he had begun the engagement with Marxism which dominated his thought from the 1950s until the end of his life. As we shall see, however, it is a delicate matter to work out quite how the lecture, and, in particular, Sartre's espousal here of 'humanism', should be situated alongside his other works, both earlier and later.

Sartre begins the lecture by announcing that it is his purpose to defend existentialism against its critics: those Catholic critics who accuse it of offering nothing but a nihilistic counsel of despair and equally those communist critics who maintain that it provides no basis for affirming the solidarity of mankind. Against such critics, Sartre maintains that 'existentialism is a humanism' in the sense that it is a doctrine that renders human life possible (Sartre 1946: 24), and he ends the lecture precisely by affirming his 'existential humanism':

This is humanism, because we remind man that there is no legislator but himself; that he himself, thus abandoned, must decide for himself; also because we show that it is not by turning back upon himself, but always by seeking, beyond himself, an aim which is one of liberation, of some particular realisation, that man will realise himself precisely as human.    (Sartre 1946: 56)

It is not obvious what Sartre has in mind here. But the message of the lecture as a whole is that we realize our humanity by creatively projecting ourselves beyond established expectations and ways of life to new goals through 'experiments in living' (to borrow J. S. Mill's phrase) in which we explore new ways of being human.

We can get an initial understanding of Sartre's position from his philosophical novel *Nausea*, written in the 1930s. Sartre here begins by expressing the familiar disgust of French intellectuals at bourgeois life: the hero, Roquentin, is increasingly nauseated by his own alienated life as an unsuccessful historian and by that of the ordinary citizens whose meaningless lives are mercilessly described in grubby detail. But the tone of the book changes as Roquentin's nausea projects him into a state of metaphysical ecstasy in which familiar categories melt away and things float free from their names; and as the ecstasy fades he returns to the world as a new man, with a new hope that he will be able to justify his existence by creating a work of art—something 'beautiful and hard as steel' which 'would make people ashamed of their existence' (Sartre 1938: 252). We find here a structure that becomes increasingly familiar in Sartre's work: on the one hand there is a relentless critique of misconceptions that he takes to be characteristic of ordinary life; but, on the other hand, he offers the possibility of a different, better, life. In *Nausea*, it is art that is presented as offering this possibility, though Sartre's description of this clearly has an element of irony: is the reader really intended to suppose that Sartre, who is all too clearly the man behind Roquentin's mask, has managed to 'justify' his own existence by writing *Nausea*? But perhaps this element of irony is just the point. In *Being and Nothingness* Sartre remarks that 'Play (*Jeu*), like Kierkegaard's irony, releases subjectivity' (Sartre 1943: 580), namely the subjectivity of a subject who recognizes his own freedom and rejects the 'spirit of seriousness' that is characteristic of bourgeois values.

One of the aspects of bourgeois life of which Sartre expresses his contempt in *Nausea* is the Comtean humanism that was characteristic of French culture of the 1930s. Here is a small part of Roquentin's (Sartre's) scornful diatribe against the whole tribe of humanists:

the humanist philosopher who bends over his brothers like an elder brother who is conscious of his responsibilities; the humanist who loves men as they are, the one who loves them as they ought to be, the one who wants to save them with their consent, and the one who will save them in spite of themselves, . . . the one who loves man for his death, the one who loves man for his life, the happy humanist who always knows what to say to make people laugh, the gloomy humanist whom you usually meet at wakes. They all hate one another: as individuals, of course, not as men.   (Sartre 1938: 169)

Sartre alludes to this passage in his later lecture (Sartre 1946: 54). The mark of that kind of bad humanism, he claims, is that it 'upholds man as the end-in-himself and as the supreme value', and he contrasts it with his own existential humanism which holds that 'Man is all the time outside of himself: it is in projecting and losing himself beyond himself that he makes man to exist' (Sartre 1946: 54–5). The contrast is not drawn here as clearly as one would like, but it is something like this: the bad form of humanism holds that intrinsic value resides in certain human abilities or dispositions whose value can be identified in the context of a theory of human nature that is thought of as definitive. But, for Sartre, there cannot be any such definitive theory or account of human nature; for it is only through projects in which one makes oneself open to new possibilities that one achieves anything worthwhile and thereby 'makes man to exist', as he puts it. So although there is the possibility of a worthwhile life in which one realizes one's 'human' potential for self-creation ('There is this in common between art and morality, that in both we have to do with creation and invention'—Sartre 1946: 49), this kind of strenuous humanism is very different from the complacent celebration of human sensitivity or achievement that Sartre repudiates. One might still object that the contrast here is not as deep as Sartre presents it, in that what seems to be distinctive of Sartrean humanism is just that intrinsic value resides in the capacity for free self-creation unlike the capacities such as compassion or scientific understanding celebrated by other humanists. But Sartre will respond that this way of expressing his position misrepresents it, and this issue will be better understood when placed in the context of the philosophy developed in *Being and Nothingness*.

The central theme of Sartre's phenomenological ontology in *Being and Nothingness* is the relationship between consciousness and its objects. Consciousness is 'non-substantial', a 'pure appearance' which exists only to the degree to which it appears to itself (Sartre 1943: xxxii). As appearance, however, it is always the appearance of something other than itself, its 'object', which appears as something substantial, something which has 'being'. Thus, to reverse the book's title, the relationship between consciousness and its objects is a relationship between 'Nothingness and Being'. Sartre's account of this relationship builds on the claim that 'our being is immediately "in situation"' (Sartre 1943: 39); the objects of consciousness always appear in the light of our way of making sense of them as aspects of a situation or 'world' which is the way in which we choose to make sense of ourselves. Hence the relationship between consciousness and its objects is always a relationship between a self and its world (Sartre 1943: 104). Roquentin's ecstatic experience of things floating free from their names was, therefore, the fantasy of a consciousness which has lost its 'selfness' and thus its world. According to Sartre, this 'self' is chosen through 'an original projection of myself which stands as my choice of myself in the world' (Sartre 1943: 39); but the fact that we create ourselves by such a choice is normally hidden from us. Because our immediate, unreflective, consciousness is the appearance of things within a world, we normally think of ourselves by reference to the world which is in this way apparent to us. Hence we think of ourselves as objects within the world, albeit objects of a special kind that can initiate changes in it, but which are nonetheless subject to causal influences from it. For Sartre this conception of ourselves is deeply mistaken; in truth, we are each a 'nothingness', a stream of consciousness unified as a self for whom there is a world, but not an object within that world.

Along with this misconception of ourselves there is a similar realist misconception of values, to the effect that these are aspects of the world which, of themselves, impose demands upon us. It seems to us that 'Values are sown on my path as thousands of little real demands, like the signs which order us to keep off the grass'; but in truth 'Value derives its being from its exigency and not its exigency from its being' (Sartre 1943: 38). Indeed these misconceptions are at bottom the same, since, for Sartre, the choice of oneself is fundamentally a choice of an ideal which both unifies a life by giving meaning to it and situates it in a world by giving significance to phenomena. So the 'exigency' which gives being to one's values is the demand that comes from one's choice of the kind of person one aims to be. Since this choice is the fundamental exercise of freedom, 'It follows that my freedom is the unique foundation of values and that *nothing*, absolutely nothing, justifies me in adopting this or that particular value' (Sartre 1943: 38). By contrast, however, the realist about values fails, indeed refuses, to recognize that he has this kind of freedom and represents his values as capable of justification within an absolute theory,—religious, metaphysical, or even scientific, as the Comtean humanist believes. One form of this realist illusion is a belief in natural rights of man, and in *Nausea* Sartre ridicules the bourgeois leaders of Bouville depicted in the art gallery for their complacent belief that in their life they have performed the duties and enjoyed the rights appropriate for maintaining the moral order of the universe. But this realist illusion is, for Sartre, equally characteristic of the Marxist's 'spirit of seriousness' whereby it is supposed that the demands of morality are inherent within the historical dialectic so that a Marxist (such as Bruno in Sartre's 1945 trilogy of novels *The Roads to Freedom*) takes himself to be under an obligation to support the proletariat because this is what the Marxist science of society prescribes without realizing that in truth this obligation manifests his own free choice of values (Sartre 1943: 580). Much of *Being and Nothingness* is an exploration of the manifold ways in which this illusory realist faith that there is some absolute justification for values which would enable one to justify one's life permeates our ordinary consciousness and activities. Sartre thinks of it as a search for 'foundation', and writes that under this illusion:

Every human reality is a passion in that it projects losing itself so as to found being and by the same stroke to constitute the In-itself which escapes contingency by being its own foundation, the *Ens causa sui*, which religions call God. Thus the passion of man is the reverse of that of Christ, for man loses himself as man in order that God may be born. But the idea of God is contradictory and we lose ourselves in vain. Man is a useless passion. (Sartre 1943: 615)

Indeed, because such a life is 'useless', it leads to the nihilist conclusion that 'all human activities are equivalent . . . and that all are on principle doomed to failure. Thus it amounts to the same thing whether one gets drunk alone or is a leader of nations' (Sartre 1943: 627).

Despite appearances, however, it is not Sartre's view that absolutely all activities are 'doomed to failure'. That conclusion applies only to lives informed by the realist illusion that there is an absolute foundation for values. But what of a life freed from this realist illusion? For Sartre this insight is likely to induce 'anguish' since 'It is anguish before values which is the recognition of the ideality of values' (Sartre 1943: 38; it is important to grasp that the term 'ideality' here contrasts with 'reality'—Sartre's point is not that values are ideals, since the realist also accepts this); this anguish manifests our sense that as 'a being by whom values exist, I am unjustifiable. My freedom is anguished at being the foundation of values while itself without foundation' (Sartre 1943: 38). In the closing sentences of *Being and Nothingness* Sartre suggests that once one understands this anguish properly and internalizes the true 'ideality of values' a quite different kind of life becomes possible, a life which he proposes to discuss in a work explicitly about morality. Notoriously this work was never published, and we, his readers, are therefore left to reconstruct the substance of Sartre's intentions from a variety of sources, including his lecture *Existentialism is a humanism*. For it is clear that his existential humanism is precisely the thesis that, not only is this different kind of life possible, but also that it alone offers a way in which human life is not 'doomed to failure'. Before returning to this lecture for more details, however, it is worth noting a couple of other helpful texts.

The first is a passage from Sartre's wonderful *War Diaries* (Sartre 1983a), the diaries he kept during the phoney war of 1939–40 when he was serving in the French army. In these diaries, among many other things, Sartre sketches lines of thought which he goes on to develop in *Being and Nothingness* but he also sets down some points which do not appear so clearly there or elsewhere, including the following passage:

> But if human reality is for its own end, if morality is the law that regulates *through* the world the relationship between human reality and itself, the first consequence is that human reality is obliged to account only to itself for its morality. ... The second consequence is that there's no way to determine the prescriptions of that morality, except by determining the nature of human reality. We must take care here not to fall into the error which consists in deriving values from facts. For human reality is not a fact.  (Sartre 1983a: 108–9)

It is the last part of this which is revealing; for, one might say, the realist illusion of the Comtean humanist is that one can derive values from facts about human nature; whereas the existential humanist denies that human reality is a fact and precisely from this denial seeks to 'determine the prescriptions' of morality. The second passage comes from Sartre's discussion of Descartes' radically voluntarist thesis that truths of all kinds are dependent on God's will. Sartre argues that the freedom Descartes here attributed to God in fact belongs to man, and that the recognition of this freedom is the 'basis of humanism':

> It took two centuries of crisis—a crisis of Faith and a crisis of Science—for man to regain the creative freedom that Descartes placed in God, and for anyone finally to suspect the following truth, which is an essential basis of humanism: man is the being as a result of whose appearance a world exists.   (Sartre 1947a: 184)

These two texts indicate the fundamental direction of Sartre's line of thought. Human reality is not a 'fact' because facts concern states of affairs within the world, and so far from belonging within the world, human reality, or man, 'is the being as a result of whose appearance a world exists'. But how are we then to determine the prescriptions of morality from this conception of man? Sartre's belief is that the reflective assimilation of this way of thinking about our creative activity does have some implications for the way in which we should live. The claim, cited earlier that '*nothing*, absolutely nothing, justifies me in adopting this or that particular value' (Sartre 1943: 38) has to be understood as ruling out justifications which cite external 'facts' of the kind invoked by the realist, but as leaving open the possibility of justifications which arise from a reflective understanding of the truth of existential humanism, that 'my freedom is the unique foundation of values'. In effect the position here is Kantian: external, 'heteronomous', prescriptions are unjustifiable impositions, but an autonomous freedom which takes its own creative freedom as essential to its own possibilities can find there a basis for an authentic form of life which will also be a moral life. One element of this life, identified as such in *Existentialism and Humanism*, will be a refusal to engage in self-deception (Sartre 1946: 51), in particular concerning one's own responsibilities. One can see how this prescription emerges from Sartre's test, but what is much more contentious is his claim that because of my recognition that my own freedom is dependent upon that of others, and vice versa, 'I am obliged to will the liberty of others at the same time as mine' (Sartre 1946: 52). For it is not clear how this obligation arises, nor how it is consistent with other things Sartre says in *Being and Nothingness*. I want to leave this issue aside for the moment, however, since it is central to Lukács's critique of Sartre which I discuss below. Instead I want to look briefly at Sartre's *Notebooks for an Ethics* of 1947–8 (Sartre 1983b).[2]

---

[2]  Here too Sartre has been ill-served by his translator: Sartre's title is 'Cahiers pour une morale' and he writes consistently about morality ('une morale'). His translator seems to treat 'ethics' as a mere

These *Notebooks* are of course Sartre's preparatory sketches for the book, 'Une morale', which was supposed to follow *Being and Nothingness* and provide a positive account of his existential humanism. Since the notebooks are nearly six hundred pages long there is no question of providing a detailed discussion of them here. But there is one point which merits some attention. Towards the end, Sartre discusses at length the theme of the quasi-religious 'conversion' which is supposed to make possible 'the realm of morality'. This conversion is described as taking 'human freedom as the foundation of the world's being', and thereby giving 'a foundation to one's being by creating something outside oneself' (Sartre 1983b: 470). Manifestly, this theme of 'freedom as foundation' connects directly with *Existentialism is a Humanism*, and what is then notable is the way in which he develops this. First, he writes about 'the true relation between things and the authentic man, . . . which is neither identification nor appropriation: to lose oneself so that some reality may be' (Sartre 1983b: 495). As an example of this kind of 'losing oneself' he alludes to Antoine Saint-Exupéry's description of a flight over mountains: in this case 'my action suddenly makes the being of the mountains unfold, like a flower that blossoms, and I want this being with the very movement that brings it about that I choose myself' (Sartre 1983b: 487). Hence authenticity brings with it a kind of humility in relation to the world, the 'humility of finitude' (Sartre 1983b: 498). So the implication of an authentic understanding of humanism, of man as 'the being as a result of whose appearance a world exists', is not that man should arrogate to himself the divine role of creation, but instead that he should accept with humility the role of losing himself in the course of bringing being to things. This is not the way of losing oneself he had discussed in *Being and Nothingness* (see the passage from Sartre (1943: 615 cited earlier to the effect that 'Man is a useless passion'); the thought there was that we should 'lose' ourselves in finding or constructing a God-like absolute foundation for values. Here, by contrast, no such foundation is sought; instead we lose ourselves simply by being that whereby the contingent but wonderful value of things is made manifest.

The second way in which Sartre develops this theme concerns relationships between people. What Sartre says here overlaps with the point alluded to earlier but still to be discussed, that authentic freedom is supposed to bring with it a commitment to respecting the freedom of others; but what is again

---

terminological variant of 'morality' and uses the terms interchangeably to translate 'morale'. In truth, of course, ethics concerns a good deal more than morality.

notable here is the way in which Sartre emphasizes the revelatory aspect of our interdependence:

For example, the other *becomes* witty if I exist. He cannot be witty for himself. To be witty is to reveal a certain new, unexpected, humorous aspect of the world, filled with insight. But the one who *reveals* this aspect grasps only the *aspect*, he makes fun of the world.   (Sartre 1983b: 507)

In this respect, therefore, our relation with others is like our relation with the world: 'And as with regard to pure Being, I rejoice that the Other should become what he is through my passion' (Sartre 1983b: 507–8). But in this case there is also a difference: 'Yet I do not limit myself to conferring another dimension of being on him. I also make myself the guardian of his finitude. In my freedom his freedom finds safety: I am the one who watches his back' (Sartre 1983b: 508). This concern for another, however, is a concern for that particular person, and this, Sartre maintains, is characteristic of authenticity:

This project that the authentic man of action pursues is never 'the good of humanity', but rather in such and such particular circumstances, with such and such means, at such and such historical conjuncture, the liberation or the development of such and such concrete group.   (Sartre 1983b: 507)

This point, then, gives us a final mark of Sartre's existential humanism: whereas the Comtean humanist does indeed affect to worship 'the good of humanity', the Sartrean humanist's concern is directed towards those with whom he is actually engaged, those whose life in some way makes a difference to his own.

## §3 EXISTENTIALISM OR MARXISM

In 1947 Lukács published a Marxist critique of existentialism under the title *Existentialism or Marxism* (Lukács 1948). This includes a substantial discussion of Sartre's lecture in which Lukács criticizes Sartre's remarks in the lecture about the 'obligation to will the freedom of others'. Lukács notes that in *Being and Nothingness* Sartre had taken a very different position, to the effect that 'respect for the freedom of others is an empty word: if we could ever form the project of respecting this liberty, any attitude that we would take to the other would be a violation of that liberty which we were pretending to respect' (Sartre 1943: 409). Hence, Lukács concludes:

The contradiction is clear. Of course, it is not our business to control the orthodoxy of existentialism, and if this were only a concession made to facilitate the development of the doctrine, we would not press the point. But, in our opinion, this contradiction lies at the foundations of existentialism itself, in connection with its doctrines of ontological solipsism and irrationalism.    (Lukács 1948: 110–11)

It is clear that Lukács has identified an important issue here. His claim that this contradiction is not just a superficial mistake by Sartre but 'lies at the foundations of existentialism' poses a serious challenge to Sartre's existential humanism, and, Lukács infers, shows the superiority of his own 'Marxist humanism'. I shall discuss this Marxist humanism below; but first it is necessary to return to Sartre to assess Lukács's criticism.

If one goes back to *Being and Nothingness* and the account Sartre gives there of our fundamental relationships with others, the justice of Lukács's criticism is hard to dispute. Sartre's account starts from his fundamental conception of consciousness as a pure appearance, an intentional act which is nothing more than the appearance of things other than itself but which also differentiates itself from the things of which it is the appearance and thus does not occur within the world which appears to it. Sartre thus infers that there is an unbridgeable gulf between the way in which we are for ourselves, namely this elusive free consciousness to which a world appears, and the way in which we are for others, namely something which appears to them as having certain characteristics. For simply by being manifest to another person, as an 'object' in the world which is the correlate of their consciousness, our own elusive freedom is qualified by being interpreted in the light of their presumptions and projects. All objectification is alienation, and Sartre captures this alienation in a brief, chilling, dialogue:

'I swear to you that I will do it.'
'Maybe so. You tell me so. I want to believe you. It is indeed possible that you will do it.' (Sartre 1943: 265)

In the light of this approach to our understanding of each other, it is not surprising that Sartre concludes in *Being and Nothingness* that 'respect for the freedom of others is an empty word'. The issue, therefore, is whether there is any way for him to escape Lukács's charge of contradiction when in 'Existentialism is a Humanism' he writes of our 'obligation to will the freedom of others'. Sartre hints in *Being and Nothingness* that an alternative way of relating to others, arising from an 'ethics of deliverance and salvation', may be possible after 'a radical conversion' (Sartre 1943: 412 fn.), and it is clear in *Existentialism and Humanism* (and the *Notebooks for an Ethics*) that he connects such a conversion with the transformation to authentic existence whose possibility is celebrated in the lecture. But it is also clear that this thesis is problematic. It is easy to associate the attitudes characteristic of inauthentic existence, such as the spirit of seriousness, with a tendency to think of oneself primarily as one is for others, especially if one thinks of the situation of children who have little option but to think of themselves in this way. But this association would imply that authenticity comes with a kind of self-consciousness in which one liberates oneself from dependence upon others; and Sartre himself suggests this when he writes at this time, concerning Baudelaire: 'He saw that freedom led necessarily to absolute solitude and to a total responsibility' (Sartre 1947b: 66).

The only way to bring interdependence into this story would be to argue that the achievement of this kind of 'absolute solitude' requires a collective effort of liberation. Yet if our relations with others are fundamentally alienating, as Sartre argued in *Being and Nothingness*, it cannot be that it is precisely by joining with others that we liberate ourselves. In the *Notebooks for an Ethics*, as we saw above, Sartre does indeed affirm the possibility of authentic relationships with others which allow for a 'deeper recognition and reciprocal comprehension of freedoms' (Sartre 1983b: 414). But it remains unclear how this is possible since he still conceives of this possibility as a transformation which supervenes upon relationships which are fundamentally alienating:

All of History has to be comprehended as a function of that primitive alienation from which mankind cannot escape. Alienation is not oppression. It is the predominance of the Other in the pair Other and Same, the priority of the objective, and consequently the necessity of all behaviour and ideology to project itself into the element of the Other and to return to their promoters as alienated and alienating.    (Sartre 1983b: 413)

Contrary to the message of this passage, what is needed is a demonstration that the possibility of mutual recognition of interdependence was in fact available right from the start, within the basic structures of consciousness, and was only obstructed by the habits and misconceptions which are characteristic of the spirit of seriousness. It is an open question, which I shall not attempt to answer here, whether one can construct a demonstration of this kind while remaining faithful to Sartre's phenomenological ontology. Clearly any such demonstration would imply that the account of being-for-others set out in *Being and Nothingness* is crucially incomplete.

This conclusion leaves the assessment of Sartre's existential humanism incomplete. But what of existential humanism itself? Although this position is predominantly associated with Sartre, it is worth looking briefly to his contemporary, Maurice Merleau-Ponty, for an alternative approach to it. Merleau-Ponty never presented his own version of existential humanism in an essay on the subject comparable, say, to Sartre's lecture. But in a series of essays from 1946–7 in which he discusses the relationship between liberalism and Marxism, which he published as a single volume under the title *Humanism and Terror*, he endorses a 'humanism in extension' which, he says,

acknowledges in every man a power more precious than his productive capacity, not in virtue of being an organism endowed with such and such a talent, but as a being capable of self-determination and of situating himself in the world.    (Merleau-Ponty 1947: 176)

This is substantially the same as Sartre's existential humanism; and the connection with existentialism is explicit when, at the end of the same essay, Merleau-Ponty contrasts a 'bad existentialism' which 'exhausts itself in the description of the collision between reason and the contradictions of experience and terminates in the consciousness of defeat' (Merleau-Ponty 1947: 188) with a philosophy which recognizes that 'the human world is an open or unfinished system and the same radical contingency which threatens it with discord also rescues it from the inevitability of disorder and prevents us from despairing of it' (Merleau-Ponty 1947: 188).

What now needs attention is the way in which Merleau-Ponty seeks to avoid the impasse which is, arguably, the fate of Sartre's position. The key to this is that in his masterpiece, his *Phenomenology of Perception* (Merleau-Ponty 1945a), Merleau-Ponty rejects Sartre's fundamental conception of a consciousness which is just the pure appearance of things, and argues that what is fundamental to human life is not consciousness at all but behaviour which manifests a capacity for perception and action rooted in our embodiment. Despite this emphasis on the role of the body, however, Merleau-Ponty argues that our powers of perception and action are not the product of neural and other physiological systems that are independently explicable in causal scientific terms; instead he argues that there is here an original phenomenon, an 'operative intentionality', whereby perception and voluntary movement give meaning to things in a way which is antecedent to explicit conceptualization or representation in language and which thereby ensures that our life is fundamentally a way of 'being-in-the-world':

> We found beneath the intentionality of acts, or thetic intentionality, another kind which is the condition of the former's possibility; namely an operative intentionality already at work before any positing or any judgment... (Merleau-Ponty 1945a: 429)

With this thesis as his foundation Merleau-Ponty is then able in the final chapter of *Phenomenology of Perception* to develop an account of human freedom which differs radically from Sartre's. Where Sartre holds that our elusive, self-differentiating, freedom is an essential feature of every act of consciousness, and therefore that all talk of 'liberation' can amount only to reflective grasp of the significance of a freedom we already possess, Merleau-Ponty holds that personal freedom is a possibility for change that is always available to us but by no means always likely. Thus, in a characteristic passage he begins by setting out Sartre's view: 'I am free in relation to fatigue to precisely the extent that I am free in relation to my being in the world, free to make my way by transforming it' (Merleau-Ponty 1945a: 441). But he then continues by qualifying the position thus advanced: 'But here once more we must recognize a sort of sedimentation of our life: an attitude towards the world, when it has received frequent confirmation, acquires a favoured status for us' (Merleau-Ponty 1945a: 441). So although by means of a free act we can always 'blow away' such an attitude, 'having built our life upon an inferiority complex which has been operative for twenty years, it is not *probable* that we shall change' (Merleau-Ponty 1945a: 442).

One result of this difference is that Merleau-Ponty's existential humanism is not vulnerable to the charge of vacuousness in the way that Sartre's position is—Lukács complains that because, for Sartre 'my freedom is just any act (getting on a tram, lighting a cigarette, or not doing so)' his position 'deprives liberty itself of all meaning' (Lukács 1948: 112). Equally Merleau-Ponty argues that because the significance of much of our behaviour is unreflective and pre-personal, we do not confront each other as subjects inevitably opposed to each other; instead we live in a common world whose meaning is essentially intersubjective. Thus whereas Sartre exemplified the alienation that comes with objectification by the brief, chilling, dialogue quoted above, for Merleau-Ponty the experience of dialogue is exemplary of precisely the opposite point of view, the way in which our openness to each other enables us to develop a shared understanding:

In the experience of dialogue, there is constituted between the other person and myself a common ground; my thought and his are interwoven into a single fabric, my words and those of my interlocutor are called forth by the state of the discussion, and they are inserted into a shared operation of which neither of us is the creator. We have here a dual being, where the other is for me no longer a mere bit of behaviour in my transcendental field, or I in his; we are collaborators for each other in consummate reciprocity. Our perspectives merge with each other, and we co-exist through a common world.   (Merleau-Ponty 1945a: 354)

It is obvious, then, that Merleau-Ponty is not vulnerable to the objection which Lukács levels at Sartre concerning his commitment to further the freedom of others. For Merleau-Ponty, because our experience is fundamentally intersubjective it allows for interdependence from the start, as in the example of the dialogue in which 'we are collaborators in consummate reciprocity'. Hence there is no problem about his affirming this interdependence in the closing sentences of his *Phenomenology*:

I can miss being free only if I try to bypass my natural and social situation by refusing to take it up, in the first place, instead of assuming it in order to join up with the natural and human world. ... Shall I risk my life for so little? Shall I give up my freedom in order to save freedom? There is no theoretical reply to these questions. But there are these *things* which stand, irrefutable, there is before you this person whom you love, there are these men whose existence around you is that of slaves, and *your* freedom cannot be willed without leaving behind its singular relevance, and without willing freedom *for all*.   (Merleau-Ponty 1945a: 456)

In this way, therefore, Merleau-Ponty's remarks show how there can be an existential humanism which is freed from the difficulties inherent in Sartre's position. For Lukács, these difficulties sufficed to show the inadequacy of existential humanism as compared with Marxism; for Merleau-Ponty, by contrast, there is no essential opposition here. From one direction, he argues, Marxism needs to rid itself of materialist metaphysics and accommodate itself to the insights of existential phenomenology: 'a living Marxism should "save" and integrate existentialist research instead of stifling it' (Merleau-Ponty 1945b: 82). Equally, he argues, existentialism cannot be content with the kind of liberal humanism which rests content with the 'formal liberty' of individual rights and due process of law while concealing the exploitation of the weak by the strong. Instead, an existential commitment to freedom requires a willingness to engage with 'the practice of liberty, in the inevitably imperfect movement which joins us to others' (Merleau-Ponty 1947: xxiv), and this must lead to a willingness to join with Marxists in the struggle for 'actual' as opposed to 'formal' liberty: 'the proletariat by his mode of existence, and as a "man of universal history" is the inheritor of liberal humanism. ... Marxism is no immorality but rather the determination not to consider virtues and ethics only in the heart of each man but also in the coexistence of men' (Merleau-Ponty 1947: 125–6). So, for Merleau-Ponty, at least in 1947, an existential humanism should also be a Marxist humanism.

A few years later Merleau-Ponty was not so sure. In essays written in 1953–4, and collected in 1955 as *Adventures of the Dialectic* (Merleau-Ponty 1955), he reviewed sceptically the course of Marxist theory and communist political power during the first half of the twentieth century. In one of these essays he looked back at Lukács' ' "Western" Marxism' (the phrase comes from Merleau-Ponty himself), in particular at the position Lukács had propounded in his essay 'Reification and the Consciousness of the Proletariat' which he published in his collection *History and Class-Consciousness*. What is significant for us here is the fact that it is in this essay that Lukács explains what he takes to be distinctive of 'Marx's humanism' (Lukács 1923: 190). Lukács starts from the old Protagorean formula that 'man is the measure of all things', which he takes to be essential to any humanist position, and he gives this formula an epistemological interpretation, as implying that all knowledge reflects a human perspective. But, drawing on Marx's *Theses on Feuerbach*, Lukács transforms this relativist position into a dialectical one by taking it, first, that the human perspective is essentially one which draws upon the human capacity for action, or 'praxis' as Marx and Lukács call it, and, second, that the exercise of this capacity leads to changes in the circumstances of action, especially the methods and relations of production, which are then liable to alter the perspective of agents. So there is not just one human perspective, but a historical series of them whose order is 'dialectical'. But, he claims, there is one perspective which is privileged especially with respect to knowledge of social matters, namely that of the working class, or proletariat, since they alone experience the ways in which their own labour brings about changes in methods and relations of production. Through the changes in their own conditions of life they experience the fact '*history is the history of the unceasing overthrow of the objective forms that shape the life of man*' (Lukács 1923: 186; italics in the original); and as a result 'the proletariat is the identical subject-object of the historical process, i.e. the first subject in history that is (objectively) capable of an adequate social consciousness' (Lukács 1923: 199). Lukács finally takes it that this privileged perspective brings with it authority with respect to questions of moral and political action: 'Whether an action is functionally right or wrong is decided ultimately by the evolution of the proletarian class consciousness' (Lukács 1923: 199).

This conclusion shows how, for Lukács, Marxist humanism differs from the individualist existential humanism he later encountered in Sartre's lecture. Sartre in fact seems to have taken Lukács's criticisms very much to heart. For in his own later Marxist writings such as his *Critique of Dialectical Knowledge* the role of classes and other social groups is taken as fundamental and the significance of individual consciousness is correspondingly diminished. In Merleau-Ponty's case, by contrast, the intellectual direction runs in another direction. In *Humanism and Terror* he follows Lukács in affirming that 'the proletarian by his mode of existence, and as a "man of universal history" is the inheritor of liberal humanism' (Merleau-Ponty 1947: 125). But in *The Adventures of the Dialectic*, while acknowledging Lukács's originality and inspiration, he suggests that the dialectic has become stuck: the bureaucracy, rigidity, and downright oppression characteristic of the Soviet Union indicate that the Marxist theory of dialectical progress is called into question once a communist party has taken power and the proletariat has no obvious class enemy to confront. Hence he ends the book calling for 'a new liberalism' (Merleau-Ponty 1955: 225), which would appear to be an attempt to find a way of combining socialist values with liberal political institutions.

## §4 Heidegger, 'Letter on Humanism'

In 1946 Jean Beaufret, a French philosopher with a special interest in recent German philosophy, wrote to Heidegger and invited him to respond to some questions which arose from Sartre's lecture *Existentialism and Humanism*, which had just been published. Heidegger was at this time in a difficult situation since he had been prohibited from teaching by the French authorities in his part of occupied Germany and he therefore took this opportunity to reach out to French intellectual circles by responding at length to Beaufret's invitation with his 'Letter on Humanism' which was published in 1947.

In his 'Letter' Heidegger concentrates primarily on Beaufret's question concerning what humanism now means. Although Sartre's lecture provides the immediate context for this question, Beaufret may well have hoped that Heidegger would also reflect on the significance of the Second World War for the meaning of humanism. If so he will have been disappointed; for Heidegger uses the 'Letter' to provide an extended statement of his current philosophical position, concentrating on an explanation of why he is not a 'humanist' in the accepted sense of the term, and, in particular, why he is not a humanist in Sartre's sense. Indeed, a subsidiary theme of the 'Letter' is his dissociation of his philosophical position from that of Sartre, a task which he must have felt that he needed to undertake in the light of the fact that Sartre had explicitly associated him (Heidegger) with his own position in his lecture.

Heidegger's objection to humanism is that humanism is committed to a way of thinking which is 'metaphysical' in the sense that it takes for granted that humanity has a determinate 'essence' or 'nature' as a determinate kind of thing by reference to which fundamental questions about the value and significance of human life can be answered. What Heidegger objects to here is that these humanist accounts of the essence of humanity proceed without starting from the question which he takes to be fundamental, namely that of the relationship between humanity and 'being'; for, he maintains, first, that it is only in the light of an answer to this question that one can provide a correct account of the essence of humanity, and, second, that the correct account is one which undermines humanist positions since this essential relationship between humanity and 'being' precludes humanity having the kind of essence that humanists assume. The question that then confronts readers of Heidegger at this point is what it is that he means by his references to 'being' as such in remarks such as the following:

Accordingly, every humanism remains metaphysical. In defining the humanity of the human being, humanism not only does not ask about the relation of being to the essence of the human being; because of its metaphysical origin humanism even impedes the question by neither recognising nor understanding it.    (Heidegger 1947: 245)

Being as such is not 'a' being, an individuated thing of some kind, such as God (Heidegger 1947: 252); instead it is that which is presupposed in all ordinary thought and talk, but not normally thought or represented at all. Indeed Heidegger maintains that the kind of thinking which best captures the 'truth of being' is poetry, a kind of writing which is necessarily elusive and suggestive, rather than representational. Nonetheless I think that one can approach Heidegger's intentions by construing his references to being as references to a possibility, namely the possibility of there being anything, where this is conceived not as a 'cosmic ground' (Heidegger 1947: 252) such as the primordial Big Bang of physical theory, but as the 'ontological' possibility that things be so-and-so at all, which one might express as the possibility of truth. In putting forward this suggestion I realize that this suggestion is open to the criticism that, as with the approach of the 'humanists' Heidegger criticizes, it seeks to tame the wild question of being by putting a 'metaphysical' interpretation on it; but in response I would urge three points. First, Heidegger himself frequently acknowledges the close relationship between being and truth, and propounds his famous account of truth as the 'un-covering' of being in a way which is congenial to my suggestion. Second, Heidegger's approach to philosophy is recognizably Kantian in spirit in that he keeps asking about the fundamental conditions for the possibility of intentionality, reason, and so on. Hence it is not alien to this approach to construe his question of being as a question about a possibility which he takes to be fundamental,—the possibility of things being so-and-so. Third, as will emerge below, this approach has the virtue of fitting well with one of the central themes of the 'Letter', namely that language has a central role in making the connection between humanity and being.

Returning now to Heidegger's objection to humanism, Heidegger's complaint is that humanists take for granted a certain way of thinking about the possibility of truth, namely that truths are captured by statements which represent the states of affairs which make them true; and this assumption, he thinks, leads them to treat things of all kinds, including human beings, as things with properties which can be thus represented by true statements, and thus as things with a definite nature or essence. According to Heidegger this 'metaphysical' assumption is at best misleading; fundamentally, truth is not the correspondence of true statements with that which they represent but the activity of bringing aspects of the world out into the open and thereby 'un-covering' them. But, Heidegger claims, the metaphysical assumption about truth as representation entered 'Western philosophy' through the genius of Plato and has decisively shaped not only the development of natural science from Aristotle onwards but also the subsequent philosophical tradition which runs from Plato to Nietzsche (whose work Heidegger strangely regards as the culmination of this metaphysical tradition) and within which all existing humanisms are located. This association between humanism and the Greeks explains why, as I noted at the start (§1), he takes it that humanism always involves a more or less tacit reference to Greek civilization; indeed when the 'Letter on Humanism' was first published in 1947 it was accompanied by Heidegger's 1942 paper on 'Plato's Doctrine of Truth' in which Heidegger argues in detail that Plato's famous myth of the cave is to be understood as a way of introducing his theory of ideas as a representational paradigm for truth and knowledge; and Heidegger ends the paper with a brief statement of the thesis that 'the beginning of metaphysics in the thought of Plato is at the same time the beginning of "humanism"' (Heidegger 1942: 181)—precisely the thesis he then elaborated in the 'Letter'.

What remains to be clarified here is why a non-metaphysical way of approaching the question of being should be so important when humanism is at issue. Heidegger expresses the relationship between humanity and being by a biblical metaphor—'the human being is the shepherd of being' (Heidegger 1947: 252; cf. p. 260). What he means by this is that it is distinctive of human beings that it is within human life that the condition for the possibility of things being so-and-so, i.e. the possibility of truth, is realized. Heidegger calls our capacity for realizing the possibility of truth 'ek-sistence'. This odd word is a new spelling of the word 'existence' (*Existenz*) and its introduction indicates a significant revision in Heidegger's conception of human existence. I say more about this below, but staying for the moment with the position advanced in the 'Letter' Heidegger takes it that it is 'ek-sistence' which is truly essential to humanity: 'What the human being is—or, as it is called in the traditional language of metaphysics, the "essence' of the human being—lies in his ek-sistence' (Heidegger 1947: 247). The negative claim about other humanisms is, then, that because they have failed to capture man's essential 'ek-sistent' capacity to bring truth into 'the clearing of being', they have provided inadequate accounts of human life within which one cannot say what it is for someone to 'become free for his humanity and find his worth in it' (Heidegger 1947: 245); and the corresponding positive claim is that the key to humanity's ek-sistence is language, the 'house of being' (Heidegger 1947: 239), which not only provides for the ontological possibility of truth but also provides the only answers worth having to the questions about human freedom and value which traditional humanism has attempted unsuccessfully to address; for it is in virtue of the fact that language is the house of being that it is also 'the home in which man dwells' (Heidegger 1947: 245).

Much here stills remains to be clarified, insofar as this is possible, and discussed. But a couple of verbal points should be quickly set aside. First, it just has to be accepted that Heidegger's use of the term 'metaphysics' is somewhat idiosyncratic. In his 1929 inaugural lecture at Freiburg 'What is Metaphysics?' he had himself used the term 'metaphysics' approvingly to insist that 'metaphysics belongs to the "nature of the human being"' (Heidegger 1929: 96) because fundamental questions about 'the nothing' which transcend questions about the existence or not of particular beings or kinds can only be properly raised through experiences such as anxiety which are fundamental to human existence (Dasein, as he here calls it). In this usage, 'metaphysics' contrasts with 'science', so that his thesis is that scientific accounts of human nature are inadequate because they cannot encompass the metaphysical significance of experiences such as anxiety. But as his philosophical views changed during the early 1930s, in ways which I shall briefly discuss below, he came to use the term 'metaphysics' primarily for the kind of Platonic metaphysics of ideas which he took to be an essential precondition of scientific thought. Hence he thereafter expressed his own insistence on the importance of non-scientific, non-technological, ways of thinking, and especially on the importance of 'poetic' language as a way of bringing truth to being, precisely as an affirmation of a non-metaphysical way of thinking. The second verbal point is that in his 'Letter' Heidegger acknowledges that once he has expressed his own position as an account of the 'essence' of humanity, one might say that his position is not one which is 'against humanism' of all kinds, but involves instead an altogether new kind of humanism (Heidegger 1947: 263). In response, however, Heidegger indicates that his preference is to resist this move in order that the radical difference, as he sees it, between his own position, marked out as 'against' or 'beyond' humanism, and that of existing humanisms can be properly appreciated.

But is there really such a radical difference? A comparison here with Sartre is useful: Sartre, as we saw, contrasts his own existential humanism with previous humanisms, primarily for the reason that these other humanisms treated man as a kind of thing within the world with a specific nature that is to be celebrated or in other ways elaborated as a basis for addressing questions of value whereas his own existential humanism affirms that man is the being for which there is a world and that man's value precisely derives from this transcendental capacity. This sounds like Heidegger's contrast between metaphysical humanisms which treat man as 'a being' and his own non-metaphysical non-humanism which stresses man's essential ek-sistence whereby the truth of being is expressed and which in the 'Letter' he also describes as 'being-in-the-world' (Heidegger 1947: 266). But Heidegger is very insistent that Sartre's existential humanism is just another form of metaphysical humanism. The main explanation for this, I think, is to be found in the notorious passage in Sartre's lecture in which he represents himself as putting forward a definition of existentialism which Heidegger has also employed. Sartre writes:

All the same, [existentialism] can easily be defined.

The question is only complicated because there are two kinds of existentialists. There are, on the one hand, the Christians . . . ; and on the other the existential atheists, amongst whom we must place Heidegger as well as the French existentialists and myself. What they have in common is simply the fact that they believe that *existence* comes before *essence*—or, if you will, that we must begin from the subjective. (Sartre 1946: 26)

It is not difficult to understand why Heidegger was irritated by this passage and sought to dissociate himself from it. A small point is the description of him as an 'atheist': in fact, Heidegger's attitude to religion was much too complex to merit this description, which he rejected (Heidegger 1947: 266–7). A similar point is the description of him as an 'existentialist', which he always emphatically repudiated. But a much more substantive point concerns Sartre's use of the phrase 'existence comes before essence'. This phrase comes from *Being and Time* (Heidegger 1927: 68) but Sartre's use of it is rather different from Heidegger's. For Heidegger this phrase is a not very happy way of re-expressing the thesis he has just been making, that the essence of man (Dasein) is 'existence' (*Existenz*), which he explains in the following way: 'Dasein always understands itself in terms of its existence—in terms of a possibility of itself: to be itself or not itself. Dasein has either chosen these possibilities itself, or got itself into them, or grown up in them already' (Heidegger 1927: 33).

This is the thesis which I alluded to above when discussing the thesis of the 'Letter' that the essence of man is 'ek-sistence'. It is obvious that what sounds the same is in fact a very different claim, and I will come back to this difference below when discussing the relationship between *Being and Time* and the 'Letter'. But returning now to the relationship between Heidegger and Sartre, the emphasis on 'possibilities' is one that Sartre shares, though Sartre differs from Heidegger in holding that the possibilities that give us our personal identity are inescapably chosen, whereas for Heidegger this is only one way in which we acquire an identity defined in terms of possibilities for ourselves—it may also be that we have 'got into them' by chance or 'grown up in them' thanks to our parents and culture. What is more important here, however, is that although Sartre's phrase 'existence comes before essence' is supposed to identify the distinctive feature of human life as conceived by 'existentialists', he allows that the concept of existence employed here is not restricted to human beings, so that, for example, he can legitimately contrast human beings with functional objects such paper-knives by saying that for them 'essence comes before existence'. But since Heidegger holds that the kind of 'existence' that is characteristic of man (Dasein) is quite different from the generic existence of things such as knives, he takes it that Sartre's use of the phrase 'existence comes before essence' is quite different from his own use of it, and remains constrained by the metaphysical presumption that men and knives are essentially similar beings, things which exist within the world. So, he concludes, if existentialism is defined by reference to the use of this phrase, understood as Sartre seems to understand it, then he, Heidegger, is certainly not an existentialist, and Sartre's existential humanism remains metaphysical.

This critical reaction is fair enough, given Sartre's loose use of language in the lecture. But it is a bit disappointing since it is clear from *Being and Nothingness* that Sartre's conception of consciousness is in some respects close to Heidegger's conception of Dasein as presented in *Being and Time*, and in particular in respect of the thesis that consciousness, and thus man, so far from being a phenomenon that occurs within the world, is that being whose nihilating intentionality gives significance to things as a world. So the question that we need to address is whether Heidegger's 'Letter' indicates why this position, Sartre's actual position, might be construed as 'metaphysical' or in other ways unsatisfactory. In thinking about this we can go back again to the 'definition' of existentialism in Sartre's lecture, but now to his gloss on the phrase 'existence comes before essence' as 'we must begin from the subjective'. The reference here to subjectivity is characteristically Sartrean, and recurs in his definition of existential humanism in the lecture:

There is no other world except the human world, the world of human subjectivity. This relation of transcendence as constitutive of man (not in the sense that God is transcendent, but in the sense of self-surpassing) with subjectivity (in such a sense that man is not shut up in himself but forever present in a human world)—it is this we call existential humanism.    (Sartre 1946: 55)

So here there is no loose language, but a point which is central to Sartre's conception of consciousness as 'subjectivity itself' (Sartre 1943: xxxiii). Furthermore it is fair to say that this aspect of Sartre's philosophy is the result of his attachment to metaphysics, the metaphysics of subjectivity as expounded by Descartes, which is explicitly endorsed by Sartre in the lecture (Sartre 1946: 44) and *Being and Nothingness* (Sartre 1943: 73–4). Since, as we saw earlier in the discussion of Sartre, this aspect of his philosophy leads to deep difficulties, at this point Heidegger's critique of Sartre strikes home.

At this point, however, one should also recall that Sartre's Cartesian metaphysics is not an essential feature of existential humanism; Merleau-Ponty's humanism is precisely an existential humanism that lacks the metaphysics of consciousness and subjectivity. So, one may wonder, is it vulnerable to Heidegger's critique? This is, I think, a complex question which cannot be pursued here.[3] But it is worth considering briefly how things stand in relation to Heidegger's position in *Being and Time*: could one regard this as a non-metaphysical form of existential humanism? In the 'Letter', Heidegger refers back many times to *Being and Time* to indicate the continuity of his thought while also acknowledging that the position put forward there was in some respects unsatisfactory: 'in order to make the attempt at thinking recognisable and at the same time understandable for existing philosophy, it could at first be expressed only within the horizon of that existing philosophy and the use of its terms' (Heidegger 1947: 271). This enigmatic remark should be read alongside a comment in volume IV of the published text of Heidegger's 1940 lectures on Nietzsche, in which a brief discussion of *Being and Time* ends with the following remark:

Above all, however, the path taken terminates abruptly at a decisive point. The reason for the disruption is that the attempt and the path it chose confront the danger of unwillingly becoming merely another entrenchment of subjectivity; that the attempt itself hinders the decisive steps; that is, hinders an adequate exposition of them in their essential execution.   (Heidegger 1961: 141)

The editors of the volume indicate that the typescript of the lectures suggests that this passage was not in fact part of the 1940 lectures, but was added later,—perhaps, they suggest, at the time of the 'Letter' (Heidegger 1961: 140 fn.). So, one can ask, why this anxiety about 'subjectivity' in *Being and Time*? For there is no question but that in *Being and Time* Heidegger emphatically rejects the Cartesian metaphysics of subjective consciousness which Sartre retained (see, for example, Heidegger 1927: 87–90, and especially pp. 417–18). I am not sure what Heidegger had in mind, but there is a central theme of *Being and Time* which both invites the accusation of being a kind of subjectivism and which does not recur in the 'Letter', namely the discussion of authenticity.

Heidegger introduces the distinction between authentic and inauthentic modes of existence at the start of *Being and Time* (Heidegger 1927: 68), but the

---

[3] I think that in *Phenomenology of Perception* there is a strand of subjectivism which invites Heidegger's criticism; but one of the changes which Merleau-Ponty introduces into his position in *The Visible and the Invisible* removes the ground for this criticism. I discuss this issue in my essay 'Speaking and Spoken Speech', in T. Baldwin (ed.), *Reading Merleau-Ponty* (London: Routledge, 2007).

first sustained discussion of authenticity comes towards the end of Division One when he introduces the phenomenon of anxiety (*angst*). The significance of anxiety is that it reveals to us that we are 'not-at-home' in the world; in the passage that follows Heidegger discusses this by referring back to his discussion of 'being-in':

Being-in was defined as 'residing alongside . . .', 'Being-familiar with . . .'. This character of Being-in was then brought to view more concretely through the everyday publicness of the 'they', which brings tranquillized self-assurance—'Being-at-home', with all its obviousness—into the average everydayness of Dasein. On the other hand, as Dasein falls, anxiety brings it back from its absorption in the 'world'. Everyday familiarity collapses. Dasein has been individualised, but individualised *as* Being-in-the-world. Being-in enters into the existential 'mode' of the '*not-at-home*'. (Heidegger 1927: 233)

This is a difficult passage: although our existence is essentially being-in-the-world, anxiety makes clear to us that properly speaking we are 'not-at-home' in the world; as he puts it, '*From an existential-ontological point of view, the "not-at-home" must be conceived as the more primordial phenomenon*' (Heidegger 1927: 234; Heidegger's emphasis). But what is it to be 'in-the-world' but not 'at-home' in it? It is, I think, not to take one's goals and possibilities from those which are conventionally endorsed within the world, from the 'they'-world; instead, as Heidegger puts it here, 'Anxiety makes manifest in Dasein its *Being towards* its ownmost potentiality-for-Being—that is, its *Being-free-for* the freedom of choosing itself and taking hold of itself' (Heidegger 1927: 232). In this way, as Heidegger puts it, anxiety 'individualizes' each of us, thereby disclosing us to ourselves as '*solus ipse*'. This is a striking phrase and Heidegger then continues, manifesting, as one might put it, a degree of anxiety about what he has here let himself for:

But this existential 'solipsism' is so far from the displacement of putting an isolated subject-Thing into the innocuous emptiness of a worldless occurring, that in an extreme sense what it does is precisely bring Dasein face to face with its world as world, and thus bring it face to face with itself as Being-in-the-world.   (Heidegger 1927: 233)

One can see what Heidegger is driving at here—his conception of the individualization which is accomplished through anxiety and authentic choice of one's own way of fulfilling one's 'potentiality-for-being' is not a way of back-tracking on his anti-subjectivist emphasis on our essential being-in-the-world. Nonetheless the phrase 'existential solipsism' is very striking and indicative of what one might call an 'existential subjectivism'. After all, in his discussion of anxiety Heidegger explicitly refers to Kierkegaard (see Heidegger 1927: 235 fn. iv), and Kierkegaard explicitly affirms that in this area 'Truth is subjectivity' because we have each to find our own individual way to salvation through the experience of *angst*.

My suggestion, therefore, is that through his account of authenticity Heidegger introduces into *Being and Time* a secularized version of Kierkegaard's existential subjectivism. Indeed it is precisely this aspect of *Being and Time*, much enhanced in the first three chapters of Division Two of the book, which gives this book its existential content and its emotional force, as in the following passage: 'Along with the sober anxiety which brings us face to face with our individualised potentiality-for-Being, there goes an unshakeable joy in this possibility' (Heidegger 1927: 358). It is clear too that this was the aspect of Heidegger's position which primarily captured Sartre's attention (the character of Orestes in Sartre's play *The Flies* exactly exemplifies Heidegger's combination of 'sober anxiety' and 'unshakeable joy') and led him to associate Heidegger with his own existential humanism. As we have seen, that association was in many ways misleading; but, equally, the presence of this strand of existential subjectivism or humanism in *Being and Time* should be recognized. Whether it should be classified as 'metaphysical' or not by the terms of Heidegger's categorization of metaphysics is not, I think, very important, though the fact, acknowledged by Heidegger himself, that its roots lie in Kierkegaard's theology suggest to me that it should be so classified.

Finally, now, we can return to the 'Letter on Humanism' and use the salient differences between the position advanced here and that found in *Being and Time* to identify the distinctive character of his later non-metaphysical non-humanism. One difference is manifest from the very first page of the 'Letter', in the claim that 'Language is the house of being. In its home human beings dwell' (Heidegger 1947: 239). Although in *Being and Time* Heidegger recognizes that language is an essential feature of human life, it does not have the ontological significance there which it has in the 'Letter'. If anything in *Being and Time* is the 'house of being' it is Dasein itself, humanity; but, as we have seen, authentic Dasein is precisely 'not-at-home' in the world, so there is no straightforward way in which one might conceive of man finding a home in Dasein. Indeed the significance of 'being at home' is reversed: in *Being and Time* authentic Dasein is 'not-at-home', and realizes its individualized potentiality-for-being only through the 'anticipatory resoluteness' through which it confronts its own 'freedom towards death' (Heidegger 1927: 311). In the 'Letter', by contrast, Heidegger points critically to the 'homelessness' of modern man (Heidegger 1947: 258), which he associates with the 'devastation of language' (Heidegger 1947: 243) as it loses the capacity to express creative thought and becomes merely an instrument for technical control; and, equally, he expresses his hope that humanity may yet have a worthwhile future precisely through the possibility that men may yet be able to find a home in language. So, in effect, the existential humanism of *Being and Time* which is inherent in the conception of authenticity and the prospect of an 'individualised potentiality-for-being' is absent from the 'Letter'; the role of Dasein is largely taken over by language and the valency of the metaphor of 'being at home' is reversed. Heidegger then uses this metaphor to articulate the ethical content of his new non-metaphysical non-humanism, drawing characteristically on the fact that the root meaning of the Greek word 'ethos' is 'dwelling place'. The suggestion, then, is that we will be able to find an ethics when we are truly at home in language, that is when our language is one which enables us to think the truth of being: 'that thinking which thinks the truth of being as the primordial element of the human being, as one who eksists, is in itself originary ethics' (Heidegger 1947: 271).

This is Heidegger at his most enigmatic, but some points are clear. There is an unequivocal negative thesis, that it is not the business of philosophy to provide a 'code' of ethics, a determinate prescription as to how one should live: philosophers who attempt this 'overestimate philosophy' (Heidegger 1947: 276). The positive suggestion is that somehow from within the practice of using language in a creative way to bring truths to light one can find ways of living well, and indeed that there is no other legitimate way of achieving this:

Only so far as the human being, ek-sisting into the truth of being, belongs to being can there come from being itself the assignment of those directives that must become law and rule for human beings. ... Only such enjoining is capable of supporting and obligating. Otherwise all law remains merely something fabricated by human reason. (Heidegger 1947: 274)

It is difficult to know what to make of this: how can our being in the right, ek-sistent, relation to being enable us to live well? Since Heidegger holds that 'Language itself is poetry in the essential sense' (Heidegger 1950: 46) one suggestion here might be that we are to find value through activities which are like poetry and creative art, broadly conceived, and thus that Heidegger's thesis is similar to Nietzsche's thought that we are to live in a way which 'gives style' to our lives (*The Gay Science* §290). Although I think there is something to this, there is also a danger of setting up the romantic genius as an ethical ideal, and it is quite clear that this is not what Heidegger has in mind—he remarks that 'modern subjectivism . . . misinterprets creation as the product of the genius of the self-sovereign subject' (Heidegger 1950: 48). Thus we would do better here to think of the 'humility of finitude' which Sartre attempted to characterize in his *Notebooks on Ethics* (see §2 above).[4] But a full account of Heidegger's ethical position in the 'Letter' requires a much fuller discussion of his conception of being than I can provide here.[5] What I think one can confidently say is that the quietism of this ethical non-humanism which can be modelled on the 'inconspicuous furrows' that 'the farmer, slow of step, draws through the field' (Heidegger 1947: 276) will be very different from the 'unshakeable joy' of the authentic Dasein who projects his own individual potentiality-for-Being.

# §5 FOUCAULT: THE END OF MAN

Heidegger's 'Letter on Humanism' was seized upon by the post-war generation of younger French philosophers who wanted to escape from the shadow cast by Sartre's philosophy and turned to German philosophers, especially Husserl and Heidegger, to help create a space in which they could work creatively without deferring to Sartre. This influence is clearly apparent in Michel Foucault's work.

In his 1978 lecture 'What is Enlightenment?' Foucault follows Heidegger in maintaining that 'what is called humanism has always been obliged to lean on certain conceptions of man borrowed from religion, science or politics. Humanism serves to color and to justify the conceptions of man to which it is, after all, obliged to take recourse' (Foucault 1984: 44). But Foucault does not follow Heidegger when he goes on to contrast humanism with a principle which he takes from Kant and which he affirms—'the principle of a critique and a permanent creation of ourselves in our autonomy: that is, a principle that is at the heart of the historical consciousness that the Enlightenment has of itself' (Foucault 1984: 44). As he explains, however, the kind of critique

---

[4]  There is no explicit reference to Heidegger's 'Letter' in Sartre's *Notebooks*, but the dates are such that it seems likely that Sartre will have read Heidegger's 'Letter' while writing them.
[5]  One would need, for example, to give proper consideration to his remarks about 'healing' and 'strife', in particular to the thought that 'being itself is in strife' (Heidegger 1947: 272). I think there is something to be gained from such an investigation, but this is not the place for it.

he has in mind is not Kant's: whereas Kant used his critiques to explore the limits of possibility in order to be able to demonstrate the mistakes one makes in attempting to transgress them, Foucault seeks to explore limits to possibility which turn out to depend on contingent circumstances so that we can transgress them. He puts it thus at the end of the lecture:

I do not know whether it must be said today that the critical task still entails faith in Enlightenment; I continue to think that this work requires work on our limits, that is, a patient labour giving form to our impatience for liberty.    (Foucault 1984: 50)

Much of Foucault's work lay precisely in this field, of exploring the contingent historical practices which lie behind repressive social practices in respect of the insane, the ill, the 'delinquent', and the sexually 'deviant'; and always the implication of recognizing the contingencies was that things could and should be different, that we should find other, less repressive, ways of dealing with the phenomena which give rise to our familiar institutions, the asylum, the clinic, and the prison. I shall not, however, attempt to describe here Foucault's immensely impressive work in these fields; what I shall concentrate on is the development of his views about 'man', from his early critique of the human sciences to his later discussions of the constitution of moral subjectivity.

Foucault undertakes his critique of the human sciences, the sciences of 'labour, life and language'—i.e. economics, human biology, and historical linguistics—in his 1966 book *The Order of Things* (Foucault 1966). One of his aims here is to demonstrate that the human sciences do not really deserve the name of science because they deal with a subject matter—'man'—which has been historically constituted in 'Western culture' during the nineteenth century but which lacks an enduring objective rationale and has indeed, he suggests, now passed its period of worthwhile use. It is difficult to know quite what to make of this. Foucault contrasts natural sciences such as chemistry which, he says, 'present characteristics of objectivity and systematicity which make it possible to define them as sciences' with inquiries which 'do not answer to those criteria, that is, their form of coherence and their relation to their objects are determined by their positivity alone' (Foucault 1966: 365), amongst which he counts the 'human sciences'. Thus the idea here seems to be that because the concept of man employed in these sciences does not characterize an enduring objective phenomenon, but only a culturally constituted one, whatever knowledge these 'sciences' accumulate is dependent on cultural formations that are liable to disintegrate. Furthermore, Foucault argues, not only are they liable to disintegrate, they are actually doing so at present: we are reaching 'the end of man', whose concept will soon be erased 'like a face drawn in sand at the edge of the sea' (Foucault 1966: 387). Two themes seem to drive this sceptical thesis: one is that the concept of man employed in the human sciences is incoherent; the other that the phenomena (labour, life, and language) dealt with by the human sciences are much better dealt with in other ways. The first theme is developed in a series of arguments which largely revolve around the difficulty of maintaining a coherent perspective which treats man both as the subject of knowledge and as its object, as both subjective and objective. The difficulty here is familiar; but whether there is an insoluble aporia which should lead us to abandon the concept of something which can be both subject and object is disputable. Merleau-Ponty argues in *The Visible and the Invisible*, for example, that the 'reversibility' of the roles of subject and object is actually the essential feature of our being, exemplified both by our senses and by our living body (Merleau-Ponty 1964: 136–7). But Foucault seems more influenced by Heidegger, who would argue that instead of 'man' so conceived we need Dasein to get 'beyond' the subject/object dualism characteristic of modern 'metaphysics', or indeed, that we need to treat language as the primary phenomenon, the 'house of being'. This last point certainly chimes with the second theme of Foucault's argument, which is that the phenomena of labour, life, and language are much better handled through the resources of structuralist theory, at least in anthropology and linguistics, than by the traditional human sciences which start from assumptions about individual human subjects.

It is not clear that one should have to choose absolutely between an individualist perspective which looks to the intentions and beliefs of human subjects and a more generalized perspective which looks to intersubjective systems of meaning and dependence. The interpretation of a text, for example, would seem to require both perspectives. Foucault, however, is nothing if not consistent at this time in his anti-humanist repudiation of human subjectivity. In *The Order of Things* he cites the case of Mallarmé who 'was constantly effacing himself from his own language, to the point of not wishing to figure in it except as an executant in a pure ceremony of the Book in which the discourse would compose itself' (Foucault 1966: 306). Foucault presented himself as undertaking just such a 'pure ceremony' himself in a lecture he gave in 1969 under the title 'What is an Author?' (Foucault 1969). For he argues here that the author is simply he who, in our culture, performs certain 'functions' in relation to the appearance of a text; but one can conceive of cultures (e.g. those with oral traditions of song and poetry) where texts are not tied to authors, and, he suggests, our own culture is moving in that direction, so that we should no longer ask 'Who really spoke? . . . With what authenticity or originality?' (Foucault 1969: 119), but instead we might simply ask 'What are the modes of existence of this discourse?' and even (and this was the last sentence of the lecture) 'What difference does it make who is speaking?' (Foucault 1969: 120). We might well agree that from the point of view of assessing what is said, indeed, it should not make a difference who is speaking; but from the point of view of understanding what is said, it is hard to deny that it often does make a difference since we tailor our understanding of each other to our knowledge of each other's situation and experience.

A central theme of Foucault's anti-humanism was that there is no one fundamental 'human nature', but that varied forms of human subjectivity have been constituted by different cultural practices. One of the most interesting areas in which he explored this theme was that which he thought of as the constitution of 'moral' subjectivity in the context of sexual behaviour. He argued that in the ancient world sexual conduct was largely governed by 'aesthetic' values, concerning the kinds of pleasure whose enjoyment is consistent with a dignified life as opposed to those which are 'base' because in giving way to them one shows oneself to be unable to control one's appetites. But when Christianity became established, he argued, a different set of values, primarily concerning purity and the avoidance of sin, are introduced. Hence, he concludes in his 1983 interview in Berkeley:

Consequently, between paganism and Christianity, the opposition is not between tolerance and austerity, but between a form of austerity which is linked to an aesthetics of existence and other forms of austerity which are linked to the necessity of renouncing the self and deciphering its truth.   (Foucault 1983: 366)

A question to which this passage gives rise, as does Foucault's whole approach, is whether proper recognition of the malleability of human nature, a malleability which reaches into the constitution of the most intimate areas of life, conduces to a moral relativism which holds that there is nothing determinate to be said in favour of one type of practice as opposed to any other beyond its conformity to one prevailing set of cultural circumstances rather than another. But this question is no sooner posed than answered: Foucault remained true to the critical principle he enunciated in his lecture on the Enlightenment, the principle which offers to each of us the possibility of 'a permanent creation of ourselves in our autonomy' and commends 'the philosophical ethos appropriate to the critical ontology of ourselves as a historico-practical test of the limits that we may go beyond, and thus as work carried out by ourselves upon ourselves as free beings' (Foucault 1984: 47). But what is characteristic of Foucault's position is that he holds that current conceptions of human nature can tell us little that is useful about what would count as exercises of 'autonomy' and 'freedom'; instead we have to work out by his kind of patient genealogical inquiry which possibilities should in fact be available to us, and in this way extend our freedom. One can still ask, however, whether he has any test for the value of these possibilities. The answer given in his 1983 interview is this: 'From the idea that the self is not given to us, I think that there is only one practical consequence: we have to create ourselves as a work of art' (Foucault 1983: 351). This passage comes from a paragraph in which Foucault discusses and rejects Sartre's existential humanism. But Foucault's discussion shows that he misunderstands Sartre, attributing to him the view that authenticity requires of us that we be our 'true self', and contrasting that position with his own, according to which the test of authenticity is whether one's life is genuinely creative. As the discussion in §2 indicated, however, this position is in fact close to that of Sartre who remarks that 'There is this in common between art and morality, that in both we have to do with creation and invention' (Sartre 1946: 49). Thus so far from escaping from Sartre's shadow, and despite his sceptical anti-humanism, Foucault ends up affirming a position which is recognizable as a version of existential humanism.

# §6 DERRIDA: THE END OF HUMANISM

The philosopher who, more than anyone else, took to heart Heidegger's critique of humanism was Foucault's contemporary and adversary, Jacques Derrida. Derrida wrote far too much for me to attempt to show here the role of this theme in his work; so I shall content myself here with a discussion of its role in Derrida's early work in which he launches his conception of deconstruction, and then take a brief look at one of Derrida's later works in which a more complex position seems to be advanced.

In his 1968 lecture 'The Ends of Man' (Derrida 1972) Derrida begins by expounding the main theme of Heidegger's 'Letter', to the effect that the humanism propounded by Sartre is 'metaphysical' in a pejorative sense, and he proceeds to show how this bad humanism infected the interpretation of the German philosophers Hegel, Husserl, and Heidegger whose works set the intellectual context for mid-twentieth-century French philosophy, even giving rise to the translation of Heidegger's *Dasein* as *'la réalité humaine'* ('human reality'). Having set this out, however, Derrida proceeds to show that a kind of humanism is still to be found in the work of Hegel, Husserl, and even Heidegger through the special role they assign to 'man' in their philosophy. Derrida focuses particularly on Heidegger's 'Letter', on the special relationship between man and being such that through the capacity for 'ek-sistence' man is the distinctive shepherd of being. Derrida picks out one of Heidegger's ways of making this point: 'This way of being is proper (*eigen*) only to the human being' (Heidegger 1947: 247). Derrida emphasizes Heidegger's use here of the term '*eigen*', which is of course connected with the term standardly translated as 'authenticity'—*Eigentlicheit*. So the suggestion is that something of Heidegger's earlier conception of authenticity is carried forward into his 'Letter' in his conception of the proper relationship between man and being. Derrida then closes the lecture by wondering whether this thesis should still be accepted, that is whether we do still accept 'the co-belonging and co-propriety of the name of man and the name of Being' (Derrida 1972: 133). Using a term which is significant for him, and to which I shall return, he suggests that this thesis is now 'trembling', and he suggests that if we read Nietzsche, not as the last metaphysician, as Heidegger read him, but as the first post-metaphysical philosopher, we can begin to see what it might be to think of a form of life which finally moves 'beyond' humanism.

If we now go back to Derrida's 1967 masterpiece *Of Grammatology* we find again the talk of 'trembling' (Derrida 1967: 24), here used as a way of introducing the conception of deconstruction as a kind of subversive conceptual reconstruction from the inside. Derrida introduces deconstruction here precisely because he wants to deconstruct Heidegger's account of the 'proximity' of man to being by situating it alongside his own conception of '*différance*'. Derrida's thought here is difficult to grasp, but one can get some sense of it from the passage in which he makes this proposal:

To come to recognize, not within but on the horizon of the Heideggerian paths, and yet in them, that the meaning of being is not a transcendental or trans-epochal signified . . . but already . . . a determined signifying trace, is to affirm that within the decisive concept of ontico-ontological difference, *all is not to be thought at one go*; a being and being, ontic and ontological, 'ontico-ontological' are, in an original style, *derivative* with regard to difference; and with respect to what I shall later call differance, an economic concept designating the production of differing/deferring. (Derrida 1967: 23; Derrida's emphasis)

I shall say more below about 'differance', but the point to grasp now is that Derrida here proposes not to displace altogether Heidegger's account of being and the associated distinctions between beings ('ontic') and being itself ('ontological'), but to deconstruct it by showing how meaning, and thus being, are constituted through the work of differance, though not 'all at one go'.

What then is 'differance' and the 'production of differing/deferring'? Derrida holds that the possibility of meaning depends upon the use of systems of signs, or, more generally systems of 'traces', since the account is intended to apply to contents of any kind and not just linguistic meanings. He further argues that the systems which organize these traces are both synchronic, so that meaning is expressed through systematic 'differences' between different traces (one can think here of colour words whose meaning depends on their role within the network of different terms by which different colours are named), and also diachronic, so that meaning is also individuated through the 'deferred' use of similar tokens, or traces, in later contexts. Using the jargon of analytical philosophy one can approximate Derrida's conception of the 'originary' differance by thinking of it as the fusion of holism about meaning ('difference') with the rule-following considerations ('deferring'). Derrida then draws from this position three key implications. First: meaning, or content, requires systems of signs or traces. So the best model for language is as a kind of 'writing' that involves differential systems of traces which persist and can be used by many 'writers', rather than as a form of 'speech' whose meaning we are tempted to think of as constituted for the speaker by a one-off association between the spoken sound and his subjective idea. Second, once it is understood that meaning does not come 'all at one go', it follows that meanings, including the meaning of being, should not be thought of as 'present to consciousness' or even manifest 'in the clearing'; instead meaning here and now is inescapably dependent on what is 'absent', on the use of other signs and the use of the same sign on other occasions, what Derrida calls 'the presence-absence of the trace' which, he says, 'one should not even call its ambiguity but rather its play' (Derrida 1967: 71). Third, because it is through this 'play of presence-absence' that meaning is constituted, it cannot be made the object of a science (Derrida 1967: 57).

Derrida then uses these implications to elaborate his deconstructive criticism of Heidegger's residual humanism, his attachment to the thought that man is the 'proper' shepherd of being. Derrida puts the point clearly in the following passage:

To make enigmatic what one thinks one understands by the words 'proximity', 'immediacy', 'presence' (the proximate [*proche*], the own [*propre*], and the 'pre-' of presence), is my final intention in this book. This deconstruction of presence accomplishes itself through the deconstruction of consciousness, and therefore through the irreducible notion of the trace.    (Derrida 1967: 70)

Heidegger, of course, does not invoke 'consciousness' (perhaps Derrida has Sartre in mind at this point); but, as we saw in §4, the special role of man in relation to being, his 'proximity' to being, is central to the 'Letter'. So Derrida's 'final intention' has been to deconstruct the terms of Heidegger's residual humanism. But one should now ask what account of 'man', if any, Derrida himself has to offer. Not surprisingly it turns out to be precisely the vehicle, if one can so speak, of differance, or 'supplementarity', as Derrida calls it in the following passage:

Thus supplementarity makes possible all that constitutes that is proper (*propre*) to man: speech, society, passion etc. But what is this 'proper' to man? On the one hand, it is that of which the possibility must be thought before man, and outside of him. Man allows himself to be announced to himself after the fact of supplementarity, which is thus not an attribute—accidental or essential—of man. For, on the other hand, supplementarity, which *is nothing*, neither a presence nor an absence, is neither a substance nor an essence of man. It is precisely the play of presence and absence, the opening of this play that no metaphysical or ontological concept can comprehend. (Derrida 1967: 244)

So even for Derrida it still makes sense to ask about what is proper to man. The answer, however, is not the presence of being to man, but the play of presence and absence which alone makes possible 'speech, society, passion etc.' and thus human life.

I want to look finally at Derrida's much later (1992) discussion of some ethical themes in his book *The Gift of Death* (Derrida 1992). For this discussion indicates, to me at least, a significant development in Derrida's account of human life; and it also provides, as we shall see, ways of connecting this account with some of the existential themes that are present throughout the humanism debate. The initial context for such a connection is provided by the fact that Derrida here discusses Kierkegaard's famous book *Fear and Trembling*, which Sartre also discusses in his lecture. The topic of Kierkegaard's book is of course the Old Testament story of Abraham and Isaac, and the issue with which Kierkegaard wrestles is how one might come to think it right for Abraham to obey what he takes to be God's command and deliberately murder his only child, Isaac. For Kierkegaard we confront here a paradox, that Abraham's duty to God could justify 'suspension' of the most direct ethical principle that one should not kill the innocent, and he argues that this paradox can be resolved only through an understanding of the existential significance of religious faith. For Sartre the story has a different existential significance, namely that because we cannot discover authoritative priorities based on 'real' claims of value we have to take responsibility for our own moral choices. Even if Abraham decides to follow what he takes to be the command of God, he cannot avoid the responsibility for his action since it is he who has given this interpretation to his experience (Sartre 1946: 31).

What then of Derrida? The presence of the word 'trembling' in Kierkegaard's title prepares the reader to expect a position which will involve deconstruction; but this involvement will not emerge until the very end. According to Derrida Abraham's dilemma exemplifies the irreducible 'aporia of responsibility' (Derrida 1992: 61). On one side Abraham cannot escape the general ethical responsibility not to kill the innocent; on the other side Abraham owes an absolute, singular, responsibility to God. For Derrida there is no way in principle of escaping this aporia and Abraham's situation is not in principle different from that which we ourselves encounter all the time as we fulfil our ordinary ethical responsibilities while not attending to our responsibility to those innumerable silent others who have no formal call upon our attention but whose needs are just as pressing if not more so. Derrida writes:

By preferring my work, by giving it my time and attention, . . . I am perhaps fulfilling my duty. But I am sacrificing and betraying at every moment all my other obligations: my obligations to the other others whom I know or don't know . . .    (Derrida 1992: 69)

So far Derrida's position sounds broadly similar to Sartre's. But Derrida provides further descriptions of the two types of responsibility here which both connect this discussion back to his earlier work and move beyond it. First, Abraham's general ethical responsibility is described in terms which are clearly reminiscent of the position advanced in *Of Grammatology*. For in this case, where we can justify ourselves to others by language, there are principles which belong to a general ethical system. But Abraham's other type of responsibility, his singular absolute responsibility to God, is described in terms that are quite new; for here Abraham has to be 'silent' and there is no system to which this duty belongs (Derrida 1992: 61). This language appears,

I think, only in Derrida's later 'ethical' writings; and it is developed in *The Gift of Death* in a remarkable way. Derrida interprets Abraham's absolute responsibility to God in terms of 'a secret relationship' with oneself; for 'God is in me, he is the absolute "me" or "self", he is that structure of invisible interiority that is called, in Kierkegaard's sense, subjectivity' (Derrida 1992: 109). So Derrida here contrasts the theme of the inescapable generality of language which was predominant in *Of Grammatology* with a concern for singular 'subjectivity' that is new.

What is one to make of this? Has a humanist metaphysics of presence made a dramatic return in the context of Derrida's ethics? That cannot be right. I think the way to understand this later position is as a repetition, now within ethics, of 'the play of presence and absence'. For Derrida insists that the aporia of responsibility involves an 'insoluble and paradoxical contradiction' (Derrida 1992: 61) and this reminds one of his earlier thesis that 'The concept of the arche-trace . . . is in fact contradictory and not acceptable within the logic of identity' (Derrida 1967: 61). So the 'trembling' of Kierkegaard's title should be taken to indicate that we find here a play of singular presence and general absence. In setting this out, I should add that I am not myself persuaded that acceptance is the appropriate attitude to contradictions, either in logic or in ethics. But Derrida's position, as I have interpreted it here, does make possible a final move which is very attractive. The Kierkegaardian terms in which Derrida describes absolute singular responsibility, as a secret subjective relationship, are irresistibly suggestive of 'authenticity' and once that is seen, it is likewise easy to see how it is appropriate to regard our general ethical responsibility (especially as Derrida describes it) as a kind of inauthenticity. Once that connection is made, the account of our responsibilities as a play of presence and absence is transformed into the thought that our ethical life is an inescapable tension between the demands of authenticity and inauthenticity. So we end up here with a deconstruction of authenticity, and thereby, I believe, the correct conclusion to 'the humanism debate'.

Throughout much of this debate, as we have seen, the predominant theme was a contrast between a 'bad' 'metaphysical' humanism which draws on the values inherent in established practices and a preferred 'existential' 'non-metaphysical' humanism which looks to creative activities as a way of finding value in human life. One of the most striking aspects of Derrida's early work was the implication that this priority might be questioned. For even though existential humanism sought to be non-metaphysical it could easily be represented as guilty of the 'metaphysics of presence', in that it suggested that through free creative activity one fulfilled the essence of humanity and thereby brought oneself into the presence of being. Whereas, if what is proper to man is, instead, a play of presence and absence, and absence is interpreted in terms of a relationship to practices and systems which help to give meaning to one's life, then we get a different picture, whereby the value of life resides in the interplay between free agency and broader practices which give meaning to individual acts. In Derrida's early work the emphasis falls primarily on this latter point, on the way in which the 'differance' provided by linguistic systems and practices makes possible the meaning of individual speech-acts, and the 'supplementarity' of social structures and practices gives meaning to personal life. It is this emphasis which is redressed in later works such as *The Gift of Death* by identifying Abraham's absolute singular responsibility and contrasting this with the ordinary responsibility which arises from general ethical norms. But Derrida does not follow Kierkegaard in arguing for a suspension of the ethical in special situations such as that experienced by Abraham. Instead he holds that situations of this kind are a common feature of ordinary life and that we just have to find ways of managing the conflict between general moral demands and singular subjective responsibilities on a case-by-case basis.

This conclusion finally puts an end to the choice which frames much of the humanism debate, that in order to escape from inauthenticity, from the passive acceptance of the values inherent in one's situation, one needs to occupy a privileged position of personal authenticity in which one finds from within one's own subjective self-understanding a way of creating a life worth living. As we have seen, the standard complaint about this way of framing the choice has always been that there is not enough content to the conception of authenticity to substantiate the aspiration, attractive though it is, to derive from it alone a conception of a life worth living. The response to this complaint which I take from Derrida is that the choice here is a false one. We cannot make sense of 'authentic' personal responsibility except in the context of 'inauthentic' general ethical demands which constrain the content of our personal decisions. So the very idea of authenticity needs to be deconstructed by acknowledging the internal relationship between the values in play in ordinary inauthentic life and the requirements of personal authenticity. But deconstruction is not denial: here, as elsewhere, it signifies an internal critique which emphasizes the interdependence of alternatives which have previously been thought of as opposed. Thus the achievement of personal authenticity can still be thought of as an essential human potentiality, but it needs to be set alongside an equally essential human dependence on the ordinary relationships and conditions which provide the context for personal life. What is proper to man is the tension between the general and the personal, the interplay between the inauthentic and the authentic, if we continue to use these terms.

## References

(All page references in the text are to the page numbers of the specified English translations where a translation is specified)

DERRIDA, J. (1967) *De la grammatologie* (Paris: Minuit). Trans. G. Spivak, *Of Grammatology* (Baltimore: Johns Hopkins University Press, 1976).

—— (1972) 'Les Fins de l'homme', in *Marges de la philosophie* (Paris: Minuit). Trans. A. Bass, 'The Ends of Man', in *Margins of Philosophy* (Brighton: Harvester, 1982), 109–36.

—— (1992) 'Donner le mort', in *L'éthique du don, Jacques Derrida et la pensée du don* (Paris: Transition). Trans. D. Wills, *The Gift of Death* (Chicago: University of Chicago Press, 1995).

FOUCAULT, M. (1966) *Les Mots et les choses* (Paris: Gallimard). Trans. *The Order of Things* (London: Tavistock, 1970).

—— (1969) 'Qu'est-ce qu'un auteur', *Bulletin de la Societé Francaise de Philosophie* 63: 73–104. Trans. J. Harari, 'What is an Author?', in *The Foucault Reader*, P. Rabinow (New York: Random House, 1984; new edition, London: Penguin, 1991), 101–22.

—— (1983) 'On the Genealogy of Ethics: An Overview of Work in Progress', in *Michel Foucault: Beyond Structuralism and Hermeneutics*, 2nd edn. (Chicago: University of Chicago Press). Reprinted in *The Foucault Reader*, (ed.) P. Rabinow (New York: Random House, 1984). New edition (London: Penguin, 1991), 340–72.

—— (1984) 'What is Enlightenment', trans. C. Porter, in *The Foucault Reader*, ed. P. Rabinow (New York: Random House). New edition (London: Penguin, 1991), 32–50.

HEIDEGGER, M. (1927) *Sein und Zeit*, in *Jahrbuch für Phänomenologie und phänomenologische Forschung*, (ed.) E. Husserl. Trans. J. Macquarrie and E. Robinson, *Being and Time* (Oxford: Blackwell, 1962).

—— (1929) *Was ist Metaphysik* (Berlin: F. Cohen). Reprinted in *Wegmarken* (Frankfurt: Klostermann, 1967). Trans. D. F. Krell, 'What is Metaphysics?' in *Pathmarks*, (ed.) W. McNeill (Cambridge: Cambridge University Press, 1998), 82–96.

—— (1942) 'Platons Lehre von der Wahrheit', in *Geistige Überlieferung, das Zweite Jahrbuch* (Berlin: H. Küpper). Reprinted in *Wegmarken* (Frankfurt: Klostermann, 1967). Trans. T. Sheehan, 'Plato's Doctrine of Truth', in *Pathmarks*, (ed.) W. McNeill (Cambridge: Cambridge University Press, 1998), 155–82.

HEIDEGGER, M. (1947) *Brief über den Humanismus* (Bern: A. Francke). Reprinted in *Wegmarken* (Frankfurt: Klostermann, 1976). Trans. F. A. Capuzzi, 'Letter on Humanism', in *Pathmarks*, (ed.) W. McNeill (Cambridge: Cambridge University Press, 1998), 239–76.

—— (1950) 'Der Ursprung des Kunstwerkes', in *Holzwege* (Frankfurt: Klostermann). Trans. J. Young and K. Haynes, 'The Origin of the Work of Art', in *Off the Beaten Track* (Cambridge: Cambridge University Press, 2002), 1–56.

—— (1961) *Nietzsche Zweiter Band* (Pfullingen: Verlag Günther Neske). Trans. D. F. Krell, *Nietzsche Vol. IV* (New York: Harper & Row, 1982).

LUKÁCS, G. (1923) *Geschichte und Klassenbewusstsein* (Berlin: Malik-Verlag). Trans. R. Livingstone, *History and Class-Consciousness* (London: Merlin, 1971).

—— (1948) *Existentialisme ou marxisme* (Paris: Nagel). ( There is no English translation of this book so the translations are my own.)

MERLEAU-PONTY, M. (1945a) *Phénoménologie de la perception* (Paris: Gallimard). Trans. C. Smith, *Phenomenology of Perception* (London: Routledge, 1962).

—— (1945b) 'La querelle sur l'existentialisme', *Situations* I. Reprinted in *Sens et non-sens* (Paris: Nagel, 1948). Trans. H. Dreyfus and P. Dreyfus, 'The Battle over Existentialism', in *Sense and Non-sense* (Evanston IL: Northwestern University Press, 1964), 71–82.

—— (1947) *Humanisme et terreur* (Paris: Gallimard). Trans. J. O'Neill, *Humanism and Terror* (Boston MA: Beacon, 1969).

—— (1955) *Les Aventures de la dialectique* (Paris: Gallimard). Trans. J. O'Neill, *The Adventures of the Dialectic* (Evanston IL: Northwestern University Press, 1973).

—— (1964) *Le Visible et l'invisible* (Paris: Gallimard). Trans. A. Lingis, *The Visible and the Invisible* (Evanston IL: Northwestern University Press, 1968).

SARTRE, J-P. (1938) *La Nausée* (Paris: Gallimard). Trans. R. Baldick, *Nausea* (Harmondsworth: Penguin, 1965).

—— (1943) *L'Être et le néant* (Paris: Gallimard). Trans. H. Barnes, *Being and Nothingness* (London: Methuen, 1958). Translation reprinted 1969 with revised page numbers.

—— (1946) *L'Existentialisme est un humanisme* (Paris: Nagel). Trans. P. Mairet, *Existentialism and Humanism* (London: Methuen, 1948).

—— (1947a) 'La liberté cartésienne', *Situations* I. Trans. A. Michelson, 'Cartesian Freedom', in *Literary and Philosophical Essays* (London: Hutchinson, 1955), 169–88.

—— (1947b) *Baudelaire* (Paris: Gallimard). Trans. M. Turnell, *Baudelaire* (London: Hamish Hamilton, 1949).

—— (1983a) *Les carnets de le drôle de guerre* (Paris: Gallimard). Trans. Q. Hoare, *War Diaries* (London: Verso, 1984).

—— (1983b) *Cahiers pour une morale* (Paris: Gallimard). Trans. D. Pellauer, *Notebooks for an Ethics* (Chicago: University of Chicago Press, 1992).

# CHAPTER 20

# MORALITY CRITICS

## BRIAN LEITER

WHAT could be wrong with *morality*? Popular, including religious, thinking has long proceeded on the assumption that 'morality' as a system of norms deserves our allegiance and that 'moral conduct' should earn our praise and admiration. Modern philosophy has, on this (as on other matters) not been far away from the popular consensus. Hume 'discovered', happily, that 'by nature' human beings were disposed to have the sentiments and dispositions constitutive of sound morality; Kant sought to vindicate the deontological moral intuitions of the ordinary German peasant; while Sidgwick found that the 'unconscious' morality of the English 'peasants' was utilitarian, not deontological (and locked in hopeless conflict, alas, with egoistic considerations). Most of moral philosophy of the past one hundred years—from Habermas and the adherents of 'discourse ethics' (descendants of the Kantian project), to the proliferating Anglophone Kantians, to the earnest utilitarianisms of J. J. C. Smart, R. B. Brandt, Peter Singer, and others—has proceeded on the assumption that morality and a moral life are worth understanding because they are worth having and leading.

One striking feature of post-Kantian philosophy in Europe has been the emergence of *morality critics*, philosophers who, *contra* the popular consensus, dispute the value of morality and the moral life. Their views find a faint echo in the work of some Anglophone moral philosophers (Philippa Foot and Bernard Williams are the main exemplars), but, as we will see, the 'Continental' criticisms of morality generally cut far deeper and more radically.[1] Whereas the Anglophone skeptics take issue with, for example, the 'demandingness' of utilitarian moral theory, or the purported 'overridingness' of moral obligations as Kantians understand them, the Continental critics pitch their concerns less at the level of academic theory than at the level of social, political, and cultural life. These Continental morality critics object that morality *in practice* is an obstacle to *human flourishing* itself.

So understood, this attack on morality raises two immediate questions. First, the Continental morality critics are plainly not without *ethical* views of their own—namely, views, broadly, about the good life for (some or all) human beings—since it is on the basis of these views that they criticize 'morality'. Therefore, we need to understand the contours of the 'morality' to which these critics object—for ease of reference, we will call it 'morality in the pejorative sense' (MPS)—since it must be distinguished from the normative considerations that inform their critiques. We will refer to this as the 'Scope Problem' about morality criticism.

Second, we can usefully divide Continental critics of morality into two camps: those who see morality as a *direct* threat to human flourishing; and those who see morality as an *indirect* threat. In the first camp are those thinkers who see the individual's acceptance of morality *as such* as an obstacle to the individual's flourishing; in very different ways, Nietzsche and Freud are these kinds of morality critics. In the second camp are those philosophers who see morality as among the 'ideological' instruments that sustain socio-economic relations that are obstacles to individual flourishing. On this second account—most obviously represented by Marx and perhaps some of his descendants associated with the Frankfurt School[2]—it is not allegiance to morality *per se* that thwarts individual flourishing, but rather the role such allegiance plays in sustaining certain socio-economic relations, the latter of which constitute the *immediate* obstacle to flourishing. We will call the former 'Direct Morality Critics' and the latter 'Indirect Morality Critics.' (Foucault straddles both approaches, and so we will discuss him in a transitional section.) Unsurprisingly, answers to the Scope Problem will differ as between Direct and Indirect Morality Critics; they will also, as it happens, differ quite a bit among

---

[1] See generally, Brian Leiter, 'Nietzsche and the Morality Critics', *Ethics* 107 (1997), 250–85.
[2] For reasons of space, the discussion will focus mainly on Marx's views.

those I am calling the Direct Morality Critics because of how they conceive the connection between taking morality seriously and human flourishing. Although the ultimate plausibility and viability of both kinds of Morality Critiques will turn on empirical evidence from the human sciences, psychological evidence will loom larger for the Direct Morality Critics, while (broadly) socio-economic considerations will count in assessing Indirect Morality Criticism.

In Sections I and II, I sketch the broad contours of the two strands of Continental Morality Criticism, turning in the concluding Section III to a critical consideration of the plausibility and prospects of these lines of critique of morality. Continental Morality Critics (or at least some of them) pose a far more serious and worrisome challenge to morality than their Anglophone counterparts, I shall argue, one that demands attention in an era when the boundaries between philosophy and the empirical sciences are, happily, increasingly blurred.

# I. Direct Morality Critics: Nietzsche and Freud (and the Special Case of Foucault)

*Direct Morality Critics* claim that *acceptance* of MPS by the *individual* is a *causal* obstacle to the individual's *flourishing*. Each element here—*acceptance, individual, causal,* and *flourishing*—requires some preliminary elaboration before we turn to the particular arguments of the three paradigmatic Continental thinkers with whom we are concerned here, namely, Nietzsche, Freud, and in a more complicated way, Foucault.

## Acceptance

For Direct Morality Critics, what matters is that, at a minimum, someone *accepts* MPS, that is, takes the prescriptions and proscriptions characteristic of MPS to have normative authority (i.e. to provide overriding reasons for action). For Nietzsche and Freud, acceptance itself suffices: individuals need not act *in accordance with* the explicit normative demands of MPS, they need only believe that they provide overriding reasons for actions. MPS does its damage (about which more, below) simply in virtue of agents viewing it as authoritative, even if many or most of their conscious, intentional actions are not in accord with the normative demands of MPS. Whether Foucault requires an additional element beyond 'mere' acceptance is a matter to which we will return, below.

### Individual

For Direct Morality Critics, MPS wreaks its harm if the *individual* takes its normative authority seriously: even a Robinson Cruso would be damaged. Nietzsche, Freud, and Foucault, to be sure, all think that socio-historical conditions figure in the explanation of the dominance of MPS, but what is decisive in terms of the effect on individual flourishing is that the individual take MPS seriously (even if individuals take it seriously *only* because society in general does).[3] By contrast, Indirect Morality Critics will allow that MPS will harm human flourishing even for individuals who do not accept its normative authority. (Foucault's position, as we will see, straddles these two.)

### Causal

Direct Morality Critics bear the burden of specifying a psychological mechanism by which *individual acceptance* causes a failure to flourish. Nietzsche and Freud have fairly rich, if contestable, mechanistic stories, while Foucault's picture demands considerable supplementation if we are to understand the mechanisms at work.

### Flourishing

Because Morality Critics are worried about the effect of MPS on human *flourishing* they must have some (at least inchoate) conception of the human good (of what constitutes a good or flourishing life) *and* at the same time this conception of the good life for humans must be independent of the MPS that is the target of the critique. Freud presents the simplest case, in part because his conception of flourishing is so thin: *Lieben und Arbeiten* ('to love and to work') is its famous slogan (as reported by Erik Erikson). Foucault's is more ephemeral, as we shall see, though Freud shares with Foucault the hope that the ideal of flourishing is a universal one, available to anyone in

---

[3] Foucault, as we will see, does recognize scenarios in which MPS causes harm even to individuals who do not accept it.

the absence of MPS (among other obstacles, of course). Nietzsche's ideal of human flourishing, by contrast—exemplified by great human beings like Goethe—is not a universal ideal, since Nietzsche thinks it can only be realized by select 'higher' human beings.[4]

## A. Nietzsche

Nietzsche believes that all normative systems which perform something like the role we associate with 'morality' share certain structural characteristics, namely, that they have both *descriptive* and *normative* components, in the sense that: (a) they presuppose a particular descriptive account of human agency, meaning that for the normative claims comprising the system to have intelligible application to human agents, particular metaphysical and empirical claims about agency must be true; and (b) they embrace norms which favor the interests of some people, perhaps at the expense of others.[5] A set of moral norms is an MPS for Nietzsche only if it:

(i) presupposes three *particular* descriptive claims about the nature of human agents (e.g. that they possess free will or that their selves, and their motivations, are relatively transparent) ('the Descriptive Component'); and/or

(ii) embrace norms that harm the 'highest men' while benefiting the 'lowest' ('the Normative Component').

For Nietzsche, to be sure, what ultimately defines MPS as against unobjectionable normative systems is the distinctive normative agenda (namely, (ii)). Thus, while Nietzsche criticizes at length the description of agency that is typically part and parcel of MPS, he also holds that '[i]t is *not* error as error that' he objects to fundamentally in MPS (EH IV:7):[6] that is, it is *not* the falsity of the descriptive account of agency presupposed by MPS, *per se*, that is the heart of the problem, but rather its distinctive normative commitments.

---

[4] See Brian Leiter, *Nietzsche on Morality* (London: Routledge, 2002), esp. pp. 115–25.

[5] This is an abbreviated version of the account in Leiter, *Nietzsche on Morality*, chs. 3 and 4.

[6] I will cite to Nietzsche's texts using the standard English-language acronyms: *The Birth of Tragedy* (BT), *Human, All-too-Human* (HAH), *Dawn* (D), *The Gay Science* (GS), *Thus Spoke Zarathustra* (Z), *Beyond Good and Evil* (BGE), *On the Genealogy of Morality* (GM), *Twilight of the Idols* (TI), *The Antichrist* (A), *Ecce Homo* (EH), and *The Will to Power* (WP). Translations, with occasional minor emendations, are by Walter Kaufmann and/or R. J. Hollingdale; in making emendations, I rely on the *Sämtliche Werke: Kritische Studienausgabe in 15 Bänden*, ed. G. Colli and M. Montinari (Berlin: de Gruyter, 1980). Roman numerals refer to major parts or chapters; Arabic numerals refer to sections, not pages.

Thus, strictly speaking, it is true that an MPS would be objectionable even if it did not involve a commitment to an untenable descriptive account of agency. Because Nietzsche's two most common—and closely related—specific targets are, however, Christian and Kantian morality, the critique of the descriptive component of MPS figures prominently in Nietzsche's writing. But our focus here shall be on the thesis that MPS thwarts the flourishing of 'higher men", since it this that aligns him most closely with the post-Kantian Continental tradition of 'morality critics'.

For Nietzsche, the worry is not that MPS is a threat to human flourishing *per se*, but rather that it is an obstacle to the flourishing of the highest specimens of humanity. 'When a decadent type of man ascended to the rank of the highest type [via MPS]', he says, 'this could only happen at *the expense of its countertype* [emphasis added], the type of man that is strong and sure of life' (EH III:5). This theme is sounded throughout Nietzsche's work. In a book of 1880, for example, he writes that, 'Our weak, unmanly social concepts of good and evil and their tremendous ascendancy over body and soul have finally weakened all bodies and souls and snapped the self-reliant, independent, unprejudiced men, the pillars of a *strong* civilization' (D 163). Similarly, in a posthumously published note of 1885, he remarks that 'men of great creativity, the really great men according to my understanding, will be sought in vain today' because 'nothing stands more malignantly in the way of their rise and evolution . . . than what in Europe today is called simply "morality"' (WP 957). In the preface to the *Genealogy*, Nietzsche sums up his basic concern particularly well:

What if a symptom of regression lurked in the 'good', likewise a danger, a seduction, a poison, a narcotic, through which the present lived *at the expense of the future*? Perhaps more comfortably, less dangerously, but at the same time in a meaner style, more basely?—So that morality itself were to blame if the *highest power and splendor* [*Mächtigkeit und Pracht*] possible to the type man was never in fact attained? So that morality itself was the danger of dangers? (GM Pref: 6)

So Nietzsche's fundamental objection to MPS is that it thwarts the development of human excellence, i.e. 'the highest power and splendor possible to the type man'. But what is the *content* of MPS? Throughout his writings, Nietzsche identifies a variety of normative positions with MPS:[7] versions

---

[7]  See See D 108, 132, 174; GS 116, 294, 328, 338, 345, 352, 377; Z I:4, II:8, III:1, 9, IV:13, 10; BGE 197, 198, 201–2, 225, 257; GM Pref:5, III: 11 ff.; TI II, V, IX:35, 37–8, 48; A: 7, 43; EH III:D-2, IV:4, 7–8; WP 752.

of MPS, for example, place a positive valence on happiness, altruism, and equality; conversely, MPS places a negative valence on suffering, on self-love or self-interest, and inequality. (I shall call the former a 'pro' attitude, the latter a 'con' attitude.) Note, of course, that these various possible normative components of MPS should be construed as *ideal-typical*: they single out for emphasis and criticism certain important features of larger and more complex normative views. Morality does not, of course, consist only of pro and con 'attitudes' or positive and negative valences, but rather particular prescriptive and proscriptive commands, suitable to the plethora of particular circumstances to which such these general attitudes and valences might be relevant. Yet Nietzsche is typically concerned with the underlying (ideal-typical) attitude—or 'spirit' of MPS—rather than the particular rules of conduct.

We may now state Nietzsche's critique of MPS more precisely. Let us call that which morality has a 'pro' attitude towards the 'Pro-Object'', while that which morality has a 'con' attitude towards is the 'Con-Object'. Keeping in mind that what seems to have *intrinsic* value for Nietzsche is human excellence or human greatness, we can say that Nietzsche's criticisms consist of two parts:

(a) With respect to the Pro-Object, Nietzsche argues either (i) that the Pro-Object has no *intrinsic* value (in the cases where MPS claims it does); or (ii) that it does not have any or not nearly as much *extrinsic* value as MPS treats it as having; and

(b) With respect to the Con-Object, Nietzsche argues *only* that the Con-Objects are *extrinsically* valuable for the cultivation of human excellence—and that this is obscured by the 'con' attitude endorsed by MPS.

What unifies, then, Nietzsche's seemingly disparate critical remarks—about altruism, happiness, pity, equality, Kantian respect for persons, utilitarianism, etc.—is that he thinks a culture in which such norms prevail as morality will be a culture which eliminates the conditions for the realization of human excellence—the latter requiring, on Nietzsche's view, concern with the self, suffering, a certain stoic indifference, a sense of hierarchy and difference, and the like. Indeed, when we turn to the *details* of Nietzsche's criticisms of these norms we find that, in fact, this is precisely what he argues. Let us consider two examples.

According to Nietzsche, the 'spirit' of MPS is that happiness is good, and suffering bad. What, one wonders, could be harmful about this sort of seemingly innocuous valuation? An early remark of Nietzsche's suggests an answer:

Are we not, with this tremendous objective of obliterating all the sharp edges of life, well on the way to turning mankind into *sand*? Sand! Small, soft, round, unending sand! Is that your ideal, you heralds of the sympathetic affections? (D 174)

In a later work, Nietzsche says—referring to hedonists and utilitarians—that, 'Well-being as you understand it—that is no goal, that seems to us an *end*, a state that soon makes man ridiculous and contemptible' (BGE 225). By the hedonistic doctrine of well-being, Nietzsche takes the utilitarians to have in mind '*English* happiness", namely, 'comfort and fashion' (BGE 228)—a construal which, if unfair to *some* utilitarians (like Mill), may do justice to our ordinary aspirations to happiness. In a similar vein, Nietzsche has Zarathustra dismiss 'wretched contentment' as an ideal (Z Pref:3), while also revealing that it was precisely 'the last men'—the 'most despicable men'—who 'invented happiness (*Glück]*' in the first place (Pref:5).

Thus, the first part of Nietzsche's objection is this: happiness is not an intrinsically valuable end; men who aim for it—directly or through cultivating the dispositions that lead to it—would be 'ridiculous and contemptible'. Note, of course, that Nietzsche allows that he himself and the 'free spirits' will be 'cheerful' or 'gay' (*fröhlich*)—they are, after all, the proponents of the 'gay science'. But the point is that such 'happiness' is not *criterial* of being a *higher* person, and thus it is not something that the higher person—in contrast to the adherent of MPS—aims for.

Why, though, would aiming for happiness make a person so unworthy of admiration? For Nietzsche, it is because *suffering* is positively necessary for the cultivation of human excellence, which is the only thing that warrants admiration. Nietzsche writes, for example, that:

The discipline of suffering, of *great* suffering—do you not know that only *this* discipline has created all enhancements of man so far? That tension of the soul in unhappiness which cultivates its strength, its shudders face to face with great ruin, its inventiveness and courage in enduring, persevering, interpreting, and exploiting suffering, and whatever has been granted to it of profundity, secret, mask, spirit, cunning, greatness—was it not granted to it through suffering, through the discipline of great suffering? (BGE 225; cf. BGE 270)

Now Nietzsche, of course, is not arguing here that—in contrast to the view of MPS—suffering is really *intrinsically* valuable (not even MPS claims that). The value of suffering, according to Nietzsche, is only extrinsic: suffering—'great' suffering—is a prerequisite of any great human achievement. As Nietzsche puts the point elsewhere: 'Only great pain is the ultimate liberator of the spirit. . . . I doubt that such pain makes us "better"; but I know that it makes us more profound' (GS Pref:3). Nietzsche's attack, then, conforms to the model sketched above: (i) he rejects the view that happiness is *intrinsically* valuable; and (ii) he thinks that the negative attitude of MPS toward suffering obscures its important extrinsic value.

In regard to (ii), it is worth recalling a biographical fact about Nietzsche: namely, that perhaps no philosopher in history knew suffering more intimately than he did. For many years, he endured excruciating headaches and nausea, lasting for days at a time, and during which he was bedridden and often alone. Yet notwithstanding his appallingly bad health throughout the 1880s, he produced in less than a decade the bulk of his remarkable philosophical corpus. In fact, he believed that his suffering contributed essentially to his work; here is a typical—admittedly hyperbolic—remark from *Ecce Homo*:

In the midst of the torments that go with an uninterrupted three-day migraine, accompanied by laborious vomiting of phlegm, I possessed a dialectician's clarity *par excellence* and thought through with very cold blood matters for which under healthier circumstances I am not mountain-climber, not subtle, not *cold* enough. (EH I:1)

Even as early as 1880, he writes in a letter that, 'My existence is a fearful burden. I would have thrown it off long ago if I had not been making the most instructive tests and experiments on mental and moral questions in precisely this condition of suffering and almost complete renunciation.'[8] Thus, on Nietzsche's picture of his own life, it was absolutely essential and invaluable that he suffered as he did: hence his willingness to will his life's eternal return, *including all its suffering*. We might add, too, that if Nietzsche had taken seriously MPS's evaluation of happiness and suffering, then he should not have been able to maintain his Dionysian attitude toward life; to the contrary, rather than will its repetition, he should have judged his life a failure because it involved so much hardship. Indeed, he explicitly stands that moral valuation on its head. 'Never have I felt happier with myself', he declares, 'than in the sickest and most painful periods of my life' (EH III:HAH-4).

Now it may perhaps be quite true—even uncontroversial—that great achievements (certainly great artistic achievements) seem to grow out of intense suffering—there is no shortage in the history of art and literature

---

[8]   Quoted in Ronald Hayman, *Nietzsche* (New York: Penguin, 1980), 219.

of such cases. But why should anyone think MPS is an obstacle to this phenomenon? I have dubbed this the 'Harm Puzzle'', namely, why should one think that the general moral prescription to alleviate suffering must stop the suffering of great artists, hence stop them from producing great art? One might think, in fact, that MPS could perfectly well allow an exception for those individuals whose own suffering is essential to the realization of central life projects. After all, a prescription to alleviate suffering does not arise in a vacuum: presumably it reflects a concern with promoting well-being, under some construal. But if some individuals—nascent Goethes, Nietzsches, and other geniuses—would be *better off* with a good dose of suffering, then why would MPS recommend otherwise? Why, then, should it be the case that MPS 'harms' potentially 'higher men'?

This challenge, however, misunderstands Nietzsche's point, which is not, we might say, about *theory* but about *culture*. (Indeed, Nietzsche claims that Christian morality has 'waged war unto death . . . against the *presupposition* of every elevation, every growth of culture' (A 43), and that what 'has been called morality' threatens to 'deprive existence ([*Dasein*] of its *great* character' (EH IV:4).) Nietzsche's claim is that when moral values dominate a culture, they exercise a subtle and pernicious effect on the attitudes of all members of that culture. If moral values emphasize the badness of suffering and the goodness of happiness, then individuals with the potential for great achievements will understand, evaluate, and perhaps even conduct their own lives in light of these moral norms. If, in fact, suffering is a precondition for these individuals to do anything great, and if they have internalized the norm that suffering must be alleviated, and that happiness is the ultimate goal, then we run the risk that, rather than—to put it crudely—suffer and create, they will instead waste their energies pursuing pleasure, lamenting their suffering and seeking to alleviate it. Moral values may not explicitly prohibit artists or other potentially 'excellent' persons from ever suffering; but the risk is that a culture—like ours—which has internalized the norms *against* suffering and *for* pleasure will be a culture in which potential artists—and other doers of great things—will, *in fact*, squander themselves in self-pity and the seeking of pleasure.

Nietzsche's response to the Harm Puzzle, then, turns on an empirical claim about what the *real effect* of MPS will be. That is, we can understand Nietzsche to argue as follows: the normative component of MPS is harmful not because its specific prescriptions and proscriptions explicitly require potentially excellent persons to forego that which allows them to flourish; that is, the claim is *not* that a conscientious application of the 'theory' of MPS is incompatible with the flourishing of higher men. Rather, Nietzsche's claim is that MPS *in practice* simply does not make such fine distinctions: under a regime of moral values—and importantly because of MPS's commitment to the idea that one morality is appropriate for all—potentially higher men will come to adopt such values as applicable to themselves as well. Thus, the normative component of MPS is harmful because, in reality, it will have the effect of leading potentially excellent persons to value what is in fact not conducive to their flourishing and devalue what is in fact essential to it.

We have seen, then, a paradigmatic example of Nietzsche's critique of MPS. His central objection to MPS is that it thwarts the development of human excellence. It does so insofar as an individual who is a nascent higher human being takes MPS norms seriously. The causal mechanism by which this harm is wrought is given by the speculative psychological story Nietzsche tells which has the structure seen in the case of norms favoring happiness and devaluing suffering: namely, nascent higher human beings who take MPS so seriously that they undertake actions inhospitable to their flourishing, or who are stricken by disabling self-doubt and guilt so that they fail to take actions necessary for their flourishing.

## B. Freud

Freud offers two famous accounts of the origin of moral conscience: in one, conscience arises through the internalization (or 'introjection') of the parental superegos as a way of resolving the Oedipal complex;[9] in the other, conscience arises as a result of the introjection of innate aggressive drives, whose taming is a necessary precondition for civilization.[10] Yet the two accounts are complementary once we recall that the superego—the locus of moral conscience—has a dual function for Freud, as the enforcer of moral standards and as the custodian of the 'ego ideal' to which we aspire. As John Deigh observes: 'The [enforcement] operations of conscience [for Freud] owe their motivational force to [internalized] aggressive instincts; the operations of the ego ideal owe theirs to sexual drives',[11] namely, those drives at issue in

---

[9]  See Sigmund Freud, 'The Dissection of the Psychical Personality', in *New Introductory Lectures on Psychoanalysis*, trans. J. Strachey (New York: Norton, 1965), 57

[10]  See Sigmund Freud, *Civilization and its Discontents*, trans. J. Strachey (New York: Norton, 1961), esp. pp. 78–9.

[11]  John Deigh, 'Freud, Naturalism, and Modern Moral Philosophy', in *The Sources of Moral Agency* (Cambridge: Cambridge University Press, 1996), 127.

the resolution of the Oedipal complex. The upshot, then, is that 'judgments of morality and value have motivational force that is traceable to these basic (aggressive and sexual] instincts'.[12]

Freud, however, differs from Marx and 'Marxish' writers in not grounding his critique of morality on the purported facts about its genesis: Freud tells us about the general etiology of moral beliefs and how they acquire their motivational force for the agent, but he does not think those facts count *against* morality.[13] What makes MPS a threat to human flourishing is not its genesis, *per se*, but its content: namely, when it proscribes instinctual gratifications out of proportion to the needs of civilization, and thus causes *gratuitous* unhappiness.

This line of argument is developed most systematically in two of Freud's later works, *The Future of an Illusion* (1927) and *Civilization and its Discontents* (1930), the latter less constructive and hopeful in its emphasis than the former. Humans, on Freud's picture, have two fundamental instincts, one for pleasure (and the avoidance of pain), the other for aggression.[14] The former disposes them quite naturally to enter into 'civilization'—into regulated and productive social interactions with others[15]—because civilization facilitates satisfaction of the pleasure instinct along two dimensions.[16] First, civilization can ameliorate and sometimes thwart altogether the human pain and suffering that flows from three sources: the human body; the external, or natural, world; and our relations with other human beings.[17] Civilization has not ended death or sickness, but it has dramatically postponed one and ameliorated the other.

---

[12] John Deigh, 'Freud, Naturalism, and Modern Moral Philosophy', in *The Sources of Moral Agency* (Cambridge: Cambridge University Press, 1996), 127.

[13] Freud's approach to religion is, in this regard, somewhat different. See Sigmund Freud, *The Future of an Illusion*, ed. and trans. J. Strachey (New York: Norton, 1961), esp. ch. 6. Religion, Freud claims, is an 'illusion', meaning 'a wish-fulfillment is a prominent factor in its motivation', but no claim is made about the truth or falsity of the illusion. But he notes that the discovery that religious beliefs are illusions 'also strongly influences our attitude to the question' about the truth of religion: '[O]ur attitude to the problem of religion will undergo a marked displacement. We shall tell ourselves that it would be very nice if there were a God who created the world and was a benevolent Providence, and if there were a moral order in the universe and an after-life; but it is a very striking fact that all this is exactly as we are bound to wish it to be' (ibid. 33).

[14] The latter is, of course, really the externalization of a 'death instinct', which, in conflict with the instinct for pleasure, turns outward, aiming for the 'death' of others rather than the self. The evidential grounds for positing a 'death instinct' seem shaky at best, whereas the prima facie plausibility of positing a basic aggressive tendency in human beings (or at least men) is apparent. For ease of exposition, I omit discussion of the 'death instinct' in the text.

[15] Freud describes civilization as 'the whole sum of the achievements and the regulations which distinguish our lives from those of our animal ancestors and which serve two purposes—namely to protect men against nature and to adjust our mutual relations' (ibid. 40). See also, *The Future of an Illusion*, 6.

[16] Ibid. 15.      [17] *Civilization and its Discontents*, 25.

Civilization cannot prevent earthquakes or tornados or tsunamis, but it can both create the institutions which provide adequate warnings so that humans can take safety precautions and make possible the construction of *habitats* that can weather some of these natural catastrophes and *institutions* (hospitals, fire departments, etc.) that can heal some of their consequences. Finally, civilization—partly through the force of law and partly through the force of norms of social interaction and cooperation it sustains—both makes it possible for our fellow humans to contribute to protecting us from the painful ravages of our own bodies and from the natural world, and, in addition, prevents them from becoming yet new instruments of pain by prohibiting, e.g. cannibalism, rape, robbery, assault, and so on.

But civilization's role in satisfying the pleasure instinct is not simply the negative one of facilitating avoidance of pain and suffering: for the laws, as well as the non-legal norms of social interaction and cooperation, of civilization also make possible the *direct* satisfaction of the pleasure instinct precisely by making possible 'the communal life of human beings'.[18] Thanks to civilization, humans, or at least a majority of humans, can achieve fairly frequent and extended sexual and other intimate gratifications, if not with the same person, then with a succession of persons. Pleasing copulation in the proverbial 'state of nature' is far more likely to be 'nasty, brutish, and short' than it need be in civilized society. More importantly, civilization makes possible the pursuit of inhibited libidinal aims—'evenly suspended, steadfast, affectionate feeling'—for one's fellow humans,[19] which is, again, a kind of attenuated satisfaction of the erotic instincts unavailable in pre-civilized contexts.

The dilemma, according to Freud, is that civilization, in doing all this work, must also impose significant instinctual frustrations as well. To confer its benefits—those already noted—civilization must also restrict discharge of aggressive instincts against one's fellows: with respect to one's 'neighbor', one is forbidden 'to exploit his capacity for work without compensation, to use him sexually without his consent, to seize his possessions, to humiliate him, to cause him pain, to torture and to kill him'.[20] Indeed, the fundamental internalization of the aggressive instinct that civilized life demands explains, Freud suggests (following, of course, Nietzsche), the human capacity for self-laceration with guilt. '[E]very piece of aggression whose satisfaction the subject gives up", says Freud, 'is taken over by the super-ego and increases the

---

[18] Ibid. 54.    [19] Ibid.    [20] Ibid. 65.

latter's aggressiveness (against the ego).'[21] As a result, 'the price we pay for our advance in civilization is a loss of happiness through the heightening of the sense of guilt'.[22]

Instinctual frustration is not confined in civilized society simply to the anti-social and aggressive instincts whose regular expression would shatter the social world; civilization is also frequently marked by norms restricting all kinds of gratifications of the sexual instinct, from the incest taboo, to (legal and moral) prohibitions on non-marital or non-monogamous relationships, to the various norms (again, legal and moral) that restrict or stigmatize alternative forms of sexual gratification (e.g. sodomy and masturbation).[23] These additional instinctual frustrations add a new coin to the realm of human misery, since some of the stigmatized (and thus unfulfilled) associated wishes (e.g. to sleep with the mother) manifest themselves in transmorgified forms as neurotic symptoms that impair the agent's ability 'to love and to work'—and sometimes much else.[24]

Instinctual frustration is, then, a source of unhappiness and suffering—both directly (e.g. by denying gratification of a sexual drive) and indirectly (e.g. by leading to neurosis or intensifying guilt)—even as civilization ameliorates other kinds of pain and suffering through its offices. The 'discontents' of civilization are, on the Freudian picture, precisely those whose grief from instinctual frustration overshadows (in reality, or otherwise) the benefits that accrue from participation in civilized life. But—and this is central to Freud's pessimistic vision in *Civilization and its Discontents*—we are all, to one extent or another, 'discontents' simply in virtue of being humans living in civilized society. Civilization simply cannot do away with 'discontents' given what humans are like and given the instinctual frustrations necessary for communal life.

Now, however, we can see the precise contours of a Freudian objection to morality (and to laws, to the extent that they track the objectionable moral content): for while civilization *requires* a great deal of instinctual frustration if it is to thwart or ameliorate the causes of human suffering,

---

[21] *Civilization and its Discontents*, 85.        [22] Ibid. 91.

[23] Ibid. 56–7. Instinctual frustration, bear in mind, begins very early, and reaches well beyond the paradigmatically aggressive and sexual. Small children, for example, take great pleasure in defecating when and where they want, and one of society's first and most dramatic restrictions is to put an end to that practice within the first few years of life.

[24] Neurotic symptoms, for Freud, are expressions of the instinctual energy originally attached to some repressed idea or wish. See the excellent discussion in Richard Wollheim, *Sigmund Freud* (Cambridge: Cambridge University Press, 1971), ch. 3.

as well as facilitate certain kinds of human pursuit of pleasure, there are many kinds of instinctual frustration that are *irrelevant* to the achievement of these objectives. Stamping out, or stigmatizing, masturbation, anal sex, and pre-marital copulation contributes little or nothing to preventing earthquakes, disease, and cannibalism—and, at the same time, may exacerbate neurotic suffering. In the Freudian 'utilitarian' calculation, the problem with MPS is that it imposes gratuitous instinctual frustration (and thus unhappiness) beyond what is necessary for any contribution to human well-being.

In *The Future of an Illusion*, Freud writes that,

The decisive question is whether and to what extent it is possible to lessen the burden of the instinctual sacrifices imposed on men, to reconcile men to those which must necessarily remain and to provide a compensation for them.[25]

He later issues a 'plea' for 'deriving (the 'precepts of civilization] from social necessity', at least when individuals are in the maturity of their faculties.[26]

Freud alludes to this theme in the later work, *Civilization and its Discontents*, when he refers to the view that,

[A] person becomes neurotic because he cannot tolerate the amount of frustration which society imposes on him in the service of its cultural ideals, and it was inferred from this that the abolition or reduction of those demands would result in a return to possibilities of happiness.[27]

But in this later work Freud now expresses more skepticism about the viability of this kind of trade-off, hinting that the threat to civilization of the aggressive instincts may be so great, that the 'unreasonable' demands of morality may be necessary to keep them in check.[28] While the tone of the later work is pessimistic, Freud's final verdict is unclear. It will fall to later writers influenced by Freud, like Herbert Marcuse,[29] to draw more explicitly the conclusion that bourgeois society demands excessive instinctual frustration relative to the needs of civilization, and that a relaxing of those demands holds out new possibilities for human happiness and flourishing.

As a morality critic, then, Freud is quite modest (certainly compared to Nietzsche, but also in some ways to Foucault), indeed, pleasingly liberal

---

[25] *The Future of an Illusion*, 7.       [26] Ibid. 41–2.       [27] *Civilization and its Discontents*, 36.

[28] See, e.g. the discussion of the unreasonable precept 'love thy neighbour as thyself' in *Civilization and its Discontents*, ch. 5.

[29] See Herbert Marcuse, *Eros and Civilization* (Boston: Beacon Press, 1955) and, in a somewhat wilder vein, Herbert Marcuse, *An Essay on Liberation* (Boston: Beacon Press, 1969).

and tolerant (notwithstanding some of his culturally specific attitudes about women and homosexuality). Morality thwarts flourishing insofar as the individual accepts moral demands for instinctual frustration that are, from a social point of view, unnecessary; and the causal mechanism through which this harm is inflicted is that described by Freudian psychoanalysis in explaining the genesis of neurosis.

## C. Foucault

Foucault, as we shall see, shares strategies with both the Direct and Indirect Morality Critics, and so provides a useful transition point between the two. For Foucault, the modern era is marked by the emergence of a new kind of power—what he ultimately calls 'bio-power'[30]—that differs from the classical, 'juridical' models of power, captured so well by John Austin's (early nineteenth-century) view of law (and, ergo, state power) as a command of the sovereign backed by a threat of sanction. 'We need to cut off the King's head', says Foucault, adding that 'in political theory that still has to be done.'[31] The agents of power and repression are no longer (or no longer *only*) the agents of the 'King' or the state, and so the exclusive questions of political theory should no longer concern the justifications for and limits upon the exercise of centralized power by 'the King'. Rather, in the era of bio-power, repression and regulation operate far more insidiously, for now it is the individual himself who is the agent of his or her own 'oppression' and discipline.

How are individuals co-opted for their own oppression? According to Foucault, it is through the *epistemic* (and consequent *practical*) authority that accrues to what I will call 'judgments of normality', namely, judgments about what constitute *normal* ways of being human: how much to eat, how to care for the body, what kind of sex to have, how to raise children, what constitutes a 'healthy' marriage, and so on. Of course, it appears that all societies, ancient and modern, have been suffused with 'judgments of normality', even if the particular norms, and their particular objects, have differed in various respects. Any student of Christianity or Islam or Judaism knows,

---

[30] In *The History of Sexuality*, i: *An Introduction*, trans. Robert Hurley (New York: Vintage Books, 1980), Foucault says he uses 'bio-power' to mark 'an explosion of numerous and diverse techniques for achieving the subjugation of bodies and the control of populations' which began in the seventeenth century. Ibid. 140.

[31] Michel Foucault, 'Truth and Power', in *Power/Knowledge*, ed. Colin Gordon (New York: Pantheon, 1980), 121.

for example, that the ancient and modern communities in each religious tradition are permeated to the core with 'judgments of normality' of the kinds just noted.

So what distinguishes 'judgments of normality' in the putatively 'modern' era of bio-power? It cannot be the emphasis on the regulation of the 'body' *per se*, since Foucault's own work—especially in the later volumes on *The History of Sexuality*[32]— makes clear how far back these concerns go.[33] Rather, Foucault's work suggests that what marks judgments of normality in the modern era is that their authority derives from 'the human sciences', that is, from claims about how one *ought* to be whose authority is, in the first instance, *epistemic* rather than moral or religious.[34]

Even this, however, does not yet suffice to distinguish the era of bio-power, since, for example, orthodox religious traditions typically ground their moral authority in a kind of *epistemic* authority (recall 'the truth will set you free'), such as access to the divine will in one form or another. What really distinguishes the claim of epistemic authority in the era of bio-power is that the human sciences claim a certain distinctively modern version of such authority: for they present themselves as grounded in claims about human beings that emerge from inquiries that adhere to the epistemic strictures of the natural sciences, strictures that emerged with the scientific revolution and triumphed (more or less) with the Enlightenment. The epistemic authority of judgments of normality in the era of bio-power derives from their purportedly *scientific* status, not, for example, their religious status.

The difficulty, in Foucault's view, is that the epistemic pretense of the human sciences is just that: *pretense*. What Foucault says about 'a science as "dubious" as psychiatry' is meant to apply more generally to the human sciences with which he is concerned: 'the epistemological profile of psychiatry is a low one and psychiatric practice is linked with a whole range of institutions, economic requirements, and political issues of social regulation.'[35] This remark is revealing about Foucault's argumentative strategy, namely, that he

---

[32] See esp. *The Uses of Pleasure* and *The Care of the Self*, both trans. Robert Hurley (New York: Vintage Books, 1988).

[33] Foucault certainly thinks, to be sure, that the techniques for regulating and 'disciplining' bodies have grown more sophisticated in the modern era. The classic study is, of course, his *Discipline and Punish*, trans. Alan Sheridan (New York: Pantheon, 1977).

[34] The best, and probably best-known, examples are *Madness and Civilization*, trans. Richard Howard (New York: Pantheon, 1965) and *Discipline and Punish*.

[35] 'Truth and Power', 109.

does not (as some writers have done)[36] engage in a frontal attack on the epistemic standing of particular human sciences, but rather explores their history to expose the influence of economic, political, and, importantly, moral considerations on their development. This does not, strictly speaking, show these sciences to make false claims; but it aims to raise (hopefully) debilitating doubts about the warrant for those claims.[37]

What links the epistemic pretensions of the human sciences, and their 'discoveries' about what 'normal' humans are like, to practical imperatives about *how one ought to live* is never clearly articulated by Foucault, but the structure of practical reasoning he (plausibly) supposes to be at work seems to be this: (1) agents want to maximize their flourishing (principle of prudential reason); (2) the human sciences illuminate how (normal) human beings flourish; (3) ergo, agents have prudential reasons to adjust their behavior to comport with the results of the human sciences. 'Flourish' here should be understood in a suitably broad sense to encompass many different senses of 'living well or happily', while the normality at issue in (2) is not simply descriptive (e.g. *statistical* normality), but fundamentally *normative*, meaning something akin to 'agents who flourish': the human sciences illuminate the 'facts' about what human beings do who 'live well'. The structure of practical reasoning described above, then, captures the truly pernicious aspect of the modern era of bio-power: as long as (2) is *taken to be true*, (3) necessarily follows given the plausible (and uncontested, at least by Foucault) assumption that the principle of prudential reason operates. Thus, insofar as the human sciences are accorded epistemic authority, individuals will 'police' and regulate themselves to conform to its findings and edicts.

---

[36] See, e.g. Adolf Grünbaum, *The Foundations of Psychoanalysis: A Philosophical Critique* (Berkeley: University of California Press, 1984); Dominic Murphy, *Psychiatry in the Scientific Image* (Cambridge, MA: MIT Press, 2006).

[37] See Brian Leiter, 'The Hermeneutics of Suspicion: Recovering Marx, Nietzsche, and Freud', in B. Leiter (ed.), *The Future for Philosophy* (Oxford: Clarendon Press, 2004), 103–5. Alas, Foucault is extremely unclear about the character and ultimate import of his skepticism about the human sciences. Often his position echoes Rudolf Carnap's on 'external' and 'internal' questions (in his famous paper on 'Empiricism, Semantics, and Ontology', in L. Linsky (ed.), *Semantics and the Philosophy of Language* (Urbana: University of Illinois Press, 1952)), as when Foucault says he is only interested in 'seeing historically how effects of truth are produced within discourses which in themselves are neither true or false' ('Truth and Power', 118). The 'external' question about whether, for example, psychiatric claims about human beings are true or false is a misguided, indeed unintelligible question. Foucault's willingness to exclude 'non-dubious' sciences like physics and chemistry from his critical analysis belies what I suspect is a rather deep affinity with the 'logical positivist' view of the sciences.

Notice that centralized state power (the 'juridical' model of power noted earlier) is hardly irrelevant on this story. As Foucault himself documents in *Madness and Civilization, The Birth of the Clinic, Discipline and Punish*, and elsewhere, the state in the modern era is distinguished by its profound and intimate interest in the character of the populations it rules—their health, their reproductive patterns, their productivity, and so on. As Foucault writes in an essay on 'The Politics of Health in the Eighteenth Century',[38] this period witnessed, '[T]he emergence of the health and physical well-being of the population in general as one of the essential objectives of political power. [The question becomes] how to raise the level of health of the social body as a whole.' In consequence, we see the state undertaking,

demographic estimates, the calculation of the pyramid of ages, different life expectations and levels of mortality, studies of the reciprocal growth of wealth and growth of population, various measures of incitement to marriage and procreation, the development of forms of education and professional training. ... The biological traits of a population become relevant factors for economic management, and it becomes necessary to organize around them an apparatus that will ensure not only their subjection but the constant increase of their utility.[39]

Indeed, in *Discipline and Punish*, Foucault says he is exploring 'the present scientifico-legal complex from which the power to punish derives its bases, justifications, and rules',[40] meaning that the state (as the force directly behind the 'legal' part of the complex) remains a central actor in this story of oppression in the era of bio-power.

Where in all this does a *critique of morality* enter? While the power of the human sciences derives from a claim to *epistemic* (not moral) authority, morality is implicated in three ways. First, the claim to epistemic authority becomes practically effective in virtue of a scheme of practical reasoning already described, a scheme which depends, fundamentally, upon an ethical imperative to treat the truth as practically decisive in realizing the agent's good;[41] the purported truths of the human sciences, in turn, simply provide the occasion for an instantiation of that imperative. Second, the purported truths of the human sciences (about how normal individuals 'flourish') are predicated on implicit and explicit moral views about what constitute

---

[38] *Power/Knowledge*, 277.     [39] Ibid. 278–9.     [40] *Discipline and Punish*, 23.
[41] This point obviously resonates with Nietzsche's concerns in the Third Essay of the *Genealogy*, though, despite his professed affection for Nietzsche, Foucault nowhere pursues anything like a critique of this practical principle to compare with Nietzsche's.

'normal' ways of being. Third, and finally, a consequence of the epistemic authority accorded particular human sciences is that their claims affect moral attitudes about their subject matters and, in particular, tend to implicate a conception of the self, both its nature and its (morally) proper governance.[42] Foucault, as a morality critic, wants to criticize and challenge each of these moral claims: he wants to argue against granting the claims of the human sciences practical authority over our lives (though not because he rejects the authority of *truth*, but because he rejects the idea that the human sciences have the requisite access to the truth); he wants to challenge the implicitly and explicitly moralized views of normality; and he wants to call attention to and raise questions about the moral attitudes, and the ethical conception of the self in particular, that emerges from the human sciences. The first challenge seems to me the most inchoate in Foucault, though like the other two it depends crucially on the challenge to the *epistemic* authority of the human sciences.

These concerns are perhaps most vividly illustrated in *Madness and Civilization* (notwithstanding some excesses of this early work) and volume one of *The History of Sexuality*, but they permeate all Foucault's works that involve an historical analysis of institutions.[43] Let us take *Madness and Civilization* as illustrative of Foucault's critical practice.[44] He begins by describing the medieval houses in which lepers were isolated, but his real point is that, 'What doubtless remained longer than leprosy, and would persist when the [leper] houses had been empty for years, were the values and images attached to the figure of the leper, as well as the meaning of his exclusion.'[45] The 'poor vagabonds, criminals, and "deranged minds"',[46] to whom Foucault soon turns, have their own 'values and images attached' to them and the 'meaning' of their exclusions must be decoded as well. As he puts it later: 'The asylum was substituted for the [leper] house, in the geography of haunted places as in the landscape of the moral universe.'[47] So one aim of Foucault's work is to

---

[42] These concerns are suggested, for example, by Foucault's remarks in one of the last interviews he gave before his death: 'Polemics, Politics, and Problematizations', in *The Foucault Reader*, 386–7.

[43] Foucault himself says that 'the prison was linked from its beginning to a project for the transformation of individuals', but in this respect it is no different from any of the other institutions to which he has turned his attention: 'The prison was meant to be an instrument, comparable with—and no less perfect than—the school, the barracks, or the hospital, acting with precision upon its individual subjects' ('Prison Talk', in *Power/Knowledge*, 39–40).

[44] In assessing the success of Foucault's critique, we will later examine *The History of Sexuality*.

[45] *Madness and Civilization*, 6.    [46] Ibid. 7.    [47] Ibid. 57.

bring out the *moral* status of those condemned and excluded on grounds that
were not always explicitly moral, or that blurred the line between the 'moral'
and 'non-moral' considerations.

For example, the Parisian 'Hôpital Général', which Foucault treats as representative of 'the great confinement' of the 1660s (when one out of every 100
Parisians was put away!),[48] had as its official mission 'preventing "mendicancy
and idleness as the source of all disorders" ',[49] so that the community, in effect,
'acquired an ethical power of segregation, which permitted it to eject, as into
another world, all forms of social uselessness'.[50] Foucault continues:

> [T]he relation between the practice of confinement and the insistence on work is
> not defined by economic considerations; far from it. A moral perception sustains
> and animates it... [T]he origin of poverty was [taken to be] neither scarcity nor
> unemployment, but 'the weakening of discipline and the relaxation of morals.' The
> edict [creating the Hôpital] was full of moral denunciations. ... Hence the Hôpital
> does not have the appearance of a mere refuge for those whom age, infirmity, or
> sickness keep from working; it will have not only the aspect of a forced labor camp,
> but also that of a moral institution responsible for punishing, for correcting a certain
> moral 'abeyance'. ... The Hôpital Général has an ethical status. ...
>
> [I]t is in this context that the obligation to work assumes its meaning as both
> ethical exercise and moral guarantee ... The prisoner who could and who would work
> would be released, not so much because he was again useful to society, but because
> he had again subscribed to the great ethical pact of human existence. ... [T]he very
> requirement of labor was instituted as an exercise in moral reform and constraint,
> which reveals, if not the ultimate meaning, at least the essential justification of the
> confinement.
>
> An important phenomenon, this invention of a site of constraint where morality
> castigates by means of administrative enforcement. ... [I]n this great confinement of
> the classical age, the essential thing—and the new event—is that men were confined
> in cities of pure morality. ...[51]

The subtext of this historical account is that the underlying *moral* rationale for
confinement is, itself, of dubious merit, but what really matters for Foucault
is that this socio-historical phenomenon was merely a prelude to the modern
era of 'scientific' psychiatry: in other words, this spectacle of moral policing
under the guise of a hospital (or medical care) was not a peculiarity of this
earlier era alone. Even purportedly great 'medical' reformers of the treatment
of mental illness in the late eighteenth century like Pinel of France were still
writing: 'How necessary it is, in order to forestall hypochondria, melancholia,

---

[48] Ibid. 38, 45.      [49] Ibid. 47.      [50] Ibid. 58.      [51] Ibid. 58–60.

or mania, to follow the immutable laws of morality!'[52] As Foucault explains, '[T]he asylum becomes, in Pinel's hands, an instrument of moral uniformity and of social denunciation', in which to 'guarantee bourgeois morality a universality of fact and permit it to be imposed as a law upon all forms of insanity'.[53] Foucault continues:

[W]hile Pinel...strongly asserted that his moral action was not necessarily linked to any scientific competence [unlike later practitioners of psychiatry], it was thought, and by the patient first of all, that it was in the esotericism of knowledge, that the doctor had found the power to unravel insanity; and increasingly the patient...would alienate himself in the physician, accepting entirely and in advance all his prestige, submitting from the very first to a will he experienced as magic, and to a science he regarded as prescience and divination. ...If we wanted to analyze the profound structures of objectivity in the knowledge and practice of nineteenth-century psychiatry from Pinel to Freud, we should have to show in fact that such objectivity was from the start a reification of a magical nature, which could only be accomplished with the complicity of the patient himself, and beginning from a transparent and clear moral practice, gradually forgotten as positivism imposed its myths of scientific objectivity; a practice forgotten in its origins and its meaning, but always used and always present. What we call psychiatric practice is a certain moral tactic contemporary with the end of the eighteenth century, preserved in the rites of asylum life, and overlaid by the myths of positivism.[54]

Only here, towards the end of Foucault's brilliantly evocative history and polemic, do we now see what Foucault the morality critic has exposed: namely, that moral considerations which are now of dubious merit have driven practices of confinement and regulation throughout the modern era, and they have done so right into the present, but under the guise of an epistemic (more precisely, scientistic) authority they have not really earned. The implicit invitation Foucault presents to the reader is to rethink and resist the conceptions of normality (of sanity and madness, of sexual normalcy and perversion, of criminality and law-abidingness, etc.) that permeate these systems of control.

If Foucault has an answer to the Scope Problem that confronts all morality critics, it is more suggested than explained. It appears that Foucault objects to those regimes of morality embedded in the judgments of normality whose practical authority derives from an undeserved claim of epistemic authority. But equally vague is the conception of *flourishing* that he values, the kind of

---

[52]  *Madness and Civilization*, 197.        [53]  Ibid. 259.        [54]  Ibid. 275–6.

flourishing that presumably grounds his indignation at the practical authority underwritten by such dubious epistemic credentials. As Michael Walzer, in a highly critical essay, put it: Foucault aims not 'for revolution but for local resistance'.[55] It is a characterization Foucault effectively endorses:

The role for theory today seems to me to be just this: not to formulate the global systematic theory which holds everything in place, but to analyse the specificity of mechanisms of power, to locate the connections and extensions, to build little by little strategic knowledge.[56]

'Strategic knowledge' is, in context, clearly knowledge that facilitates 'local resistance': against prisons, psychiatric establishments, the purveyors of sexual norms and stereotypes—precisely all those whom Foucault, in his actual political practice, resisted. What 'global systematic theory' explains how these all hang together remains somewhat elusive.

Like Direct Morality Critics, Foucault lays emphasis on the fact that individuals are complicit in their own oppression by *accepting* as practically decisive the purported truths of the human sciences. But insofar as the judgments of normality that emerge from the human sciences are given practical authority over people through institutions—through courts and administrative bodies that deem people mentally unfit, through psychiatrists who testify in court, and the like—individuals can be oppressed by them whether or not they hold them as individuals. Despite, then, his skepticism about juridical and centralized models of power (which he so often associates with Marxism), Foucault shares with Marxist morality critics the central idea that the flourishing of individuals is hostage to ideas and institutions beyond their control. It is to Marx and 'Marxish' morality criticism that we now turn.


## II. INDIRECT MORALITY CRITICS: MARX

What is importantly distinctive of the Marxist critique of morality is that the individual's acceptance of MPS is not, *per se*, harmful; the obstacle to flourishing arises from the role that *general* acceptance of MPS plays in

---

[55] Michael Walzer, 'The Politics of Michel Foucault', in D. Hoy (ed.), *Foucault: A Critical Reader* (Oxford: Blackwell, 1986), 55.

[56] 'Power and Strategies', in *Power/Knowledge*, 145.

sustaining socio-economic relations inhospitable to human flourishing. Thus, the structure of Marxist morality criticism runs as follows:

1. Capitalism is an obstacle to human flourishing.
2. An important causal mechanism that sustains capitalism is the ideological superstructure of society.
3. The ideological superstructure of society includes the morality that is generally accepted by people in the society.

So, on this account, the objection to morality is that it makes a causal contribution to sustaining a state of affairs that is an obstacle to human flourishing. The claims about causation here are, it is fair to say, somewhat elusive. On G. A. Cohen's influential (and plausible) reconstruction of the Marxist view,[57] the material conditions of society (i.e. the level of development of the technological and other productive forces) make (causally) possible a certain regime of property rights ('relations of production' in Marxist lingo), but, at the same time, the regime of property rights makes a causal contribution to developing the material conditions (the productive forces). The regime of property rights, in turn, makes possible a certain ideological superstructure—a dominant set of moral, political, and perhaps legal ideas[58]—which, at the same time, makes a causal contribution to the property rights regime by 'legitimizing' it, i.e. by representing and constituting it as legal, by portraying it as morally justified, and so on.

Since morality is only one part of the ideological superstructure (and not obviously the most important part), and since the latter's causal contribution is contingent on (1) the regime of property rights, which itself is contingent on (2) the level of development of the productive forces, it turns out that it is quite difficult to say what contribution MPS is actually making to sustaining socio-economic conditions inhospitable to human flourishing. These ambiguities about causal strength are an ineliminable part of the core

[57] G. A. Cohen, *Karl Marx's Theory of History: A Defence* (Princeton: Princeton University Press, 1978). The clearest statement of the doctrine of historical materialism as Cohen reconstructs it comes from the 1859 Preface to *A Contribution to the Critique of Political Economy*; later formulations rely more heavily on the 'history is the history of class struggle' formulation made famous in *The Communist Manifesto*. And Marx's actual practice of historical explanation—for example, in *The Eighteenth Brumaire of Napoleon Bonaparte*—seems much closer to this latter slogan than to the orthodox functionalism of the 1859 Preface. Peter Railton offers an elegant reconciliation of the two paradigms of historical materialism in 'Explanatory Asymmetry in Historical Materialism', *Ethics* 97/1 (1986), 233–9; cf. the discussion in Cohen, *Karl Marx's Theory of History*, 292–3.

[58] The regime of property rights is, itself, constituted by law, so not all of law can be part of the superstructure.

of Marx's historical materialism, but they also have as a consequence that Indirect Morality Criticism of the Marxist kind is far less damning than Direct Morality Criticism: first, because any individual's acceptance of morality as decisive in practical reasoning is untouched by the Marxist critique; and, second, because the causal role of morality in thwarting human flourishing is part of a lengthy causal chain, where the intervening forces may be far more decisive than morality itself.

In what follows, we shall examine (A) Marx's conception of human flourishing, (B) Marx's theory of ideology, and (C) how Marx's ethical views (those implicit in the conception of human flourishing) are invulnerable (if they are) to the criticisms inherent in his theory of ideology.

## A. Capitalism and Human Flourishing

That capitalism is an obstacle to human well-being is a consistent theme throughout Marx's career, but the most explicit philosophical treatment of the problem comes in the early discussion of 'alienation' (*Entfremdung*) from the *1844 Manuscripts*. Alienated individuals are not flourishing, and so if we understand what Marx means by alienation, we may illuminate his ideal of human flourishing.

Notwithstanding the connotations of the term 'alienation' in popular parlance, for Marx alienated individuals do not necessarily experience a characteristic phenomenology. Persons are alienated, for Marx, when their essential nature is thwarted from expression or realization. To be sure, typical psychological consequences may flow from this state of affairs obtaining, but they are not criterial of alienation: someone could be alienated without necessarily having a distinctive feeling or experience.

We learn from Marx's early essay 'On the Jewish Question' that part of our essential nature has to do with (1) our being dependent on cooperative work with others, and (2) being conscious of the truth of (1). But the picture is filled out in the *1844 Manuscripts* in important ways.[59] Crudely put, we might say that on Marx's view it is part of our essential nature that we achieve self-affirmation through productive activity ('free, conscious activity is man's species character', 76). 'Private property' (more precisely, capital) thwarts

---

[59] All references are by page number (in the text) to the translations in *The Marx-Engels Reader*, 2nd edn., ed. R. C. Tucker (New York: Norton, 1978).

the expression of this part of our nature. It is the task, then, of the *1844 Manuscripts* to explain these points.

In these early writings, Marx famously distinguishes between four kinds of alienation—from the product of one's labor, from productive activity, from species-being, and from other men (71–7)—though two themes are central. Men are alienated centrally when (1) their work is 'not the satisfaction of a need [but] merely a *means* to satisfy needs external to it' (e.g. to earn money to buy food and shelter) (74), which is to say that their labor is not 'free', that is 'free from physical need' (76) (evidence of that is that men abandon work 'like the plague' 'as soon as no physical or other compulsion exists', 74); and (2) they fail to recognize the central role of labor for the species man, that is, that 'the productive life is the life of the species' (76). From the account of alienation, we can infer, conversely, that on Marx's view an individual is flourishing when two fundamental conditions are satisfied: first, he labors *freely*, meaning that work is an end-in-itself, and not merely a means to 'earn a living'; and, second, he is conscious of the central role of free and spontaneous labor for men as such, and thus recognizes his kinship with all other men in this regard. Capitalism, and its system of private property (meaning property in the labor of others), must be abolished, since 'private property is...the product, the result, the necessary consequence, of *alienated labor*, of the external relation of the worker to nature and to himself' (79). Since communism 'annuls' private property its establishment is, in turn, a condition of human flourishing, i.e. non-alienation (82). As Marx puts it: '[C]ommunism...is the *genuine* resolution of the conflict between man and nature and between man and man—the true resolution of the strife between existence and essence, between objectification and self-confirmation, between freedom and necessity, between the individual and the species' (84).

## B. Morality as Ideology

All ideologies (in the pejorative sense with which we are concerned here) are forms of consciousness that are *false* in some respect.[60] In Marx's writing, two kinds of mistakes seem to be primarily at issue. First, ideologies involve a false belief that 'the particular interest of a subgroup is the general interest

---

[60] For a useful typology, see Raymond Geuss, *The Idea of a Critical Theory: Habermas and the Frankfurt School* (Cambridge: Cambridge University Press, 1981), 13–21.

of the group as a whole.'[61] Second, ideologies involve a mistake about their origin: agents think that the ideology arose because of its responsiveness to epistemically relevant considerations (e.g. evidence, reasons, etc.), when, in fact, it arose *only* because it was responsive to the interests of the dominant economic class in the existing economic system.[62] The two senses are obviously connected: by involving a mistake about the class-specific interest generating certain moral and political ideas, an ideology, at the same time, serves the interests of the economically dominant class by leading to general acceptance of the moral and political ideas that favor the dominant economic class by allowing them to be perceived (thanks to the mistake about their genesis) as arising from responsiveness to relevant epistemic considerations.[63] As Marx himself sums up the connection in *The German Ideology*: 'For each new class which puts itself in the place of one ruling before, it is compelled, merely in order to carry through its aim, to represent its interest as the common interest of all the members of society' (174). Its aim, in this context, is to continue to maximize the material wealth of its class.

Morality, as we noted earlier, is not alone in performing this ideological function of promoting the interests of the ruling economic class, while obscuring the origins of its beliefs: 'Law, morality, religion are to [the enlightened proletariat] so many bourgeois prejudices, behind which lurk in ambush just as many bourgeois interests' (482). This, of course, is why the precise contribution of morality to sustaining capitalism, and thus thwarting human flourishing, is hard to make precise. But whatever its precise causal contribution to sustaining capitalism, morality is clearly one component of the ideological superstructure of capitalist society on Marx's view.[64]

---

[61] Ibid. 14.

[62] Science may be in the interest of the ruling class, after all, but it is still responsive to epistemic norms, and so anyone with epistemic interests has reason to accept science. Ideologies, by contrast, have their genesis explained solely by their capacity to further the interests of the ruling class. See generally, Peter Railton, 'Marx and the Objectivity of Science', in R. Boyd et al. (eds.), *The Philosophy of Science* (Cambridge, MA: MIT Press, 1991).

[63] Since we are talking about 'moral and political ideas', epistemically relevant considerations can include moral considerations of various kinds, insofar as they are taken to be relevant to the justification of those ideas.

[64] Michael Rosen usefully examines Marx's critique in light of the Hegelian distinction between *Moralität* and *Sittlichkeit*, and Hegel's critique of the former, in 'The Marxist Critique of Morality and the Theory of Ideology', in E. Harcourt (ed.), *Morality, Reflection, and Ideology* (Oxford: Oxford University Press, 2000), but wrongly, I think, tries to map the philosophical import of Marx's critique of MPS on to that distinction. Only the *Sittlichkeit* of a communist society would be invulnerable, we will see, to Marx's worry about the ideological character of morality; under capitalism, the *Moralität/Sittlichkeit* distinction does not capture what is dangerous about MPS.

## C. Why Isn't Marx's View Itself Ideological?
   (The Scope Problem)

Why is Marx's conception of the good life (of human flourishing) not itself ideological? Put differently: why isn't the evaluative perspective that informs Marx's own critique of MPS—the morality that figures in the ideological superstructure that contributes causally to sustaining capitalism—not itself another ideology? Many commentators have been bothered by this issue.[65] Allen Wood, for example writes:

No reader of Marx could possibly deny that he makes 'value judgments' about capitalism, and Marx never attempts fastidiously to segregate his scientific analysis of capitalism from his angry condemnation of it. When Marx accuses capitalism of stunting human potentialities, stifling their development and preventing their actualization, he avails himself unashamedly of judgments about people's needs and interests, and even of a (recognizably Aristotelian) naturalistic framework of ideas concerning the nature of human well-being and fulfillment.

Judgments about what is good for people, what is in their interests, certainly are 'value judgments', but they are not necessarily *moral* judgments, since even if I care nothing about morality at all, I may still be interested in promoting the interests and well-being of myself and others whose welfare I happen to care about. It would be entirely consistent for Marx to reject morality and nevertheless advocate the abolition of capitalism on the ground that it frustrates human well-being, so long as his concern with human well-being is not based on any moral values or principles. Marx's attack on morality is not an attack on 'value judgments', but it is a rejection of specifically *moral* judgments, especially those involving the ideas of right and justice.[66]

Wood's version of the Scope Problem depends, however, on an arbitrary stipulation to the effect that broadly 'utilitarian' schemes of evaluation—schemes of evaluation based on how some action or socio-economic system affects human well-being—could not be *moral*, only those based on 'rights and justice' can be 'moral'. On that rendering, Marx's answer to the Scope Problem is simple: he rejects 'rights and justice' as ideological, but not his own evaluation of capitalism as an obstacle to human flourishing. That solves the Scope Problem by fiat, but not in a way that is philosophically interesting. For certainly one natural way of reading Marx, suggested by Wood's own formulation, is that Marx holds that (1) the criterion of right action and

---

[65] A helpful survey of much of the literature is Steven Lukes, *Marxism and Morality* (Oxford: Oxford University Press, 1985).

[66] Allen Wood, 'Marx against Morality', in Peter Singer (ed.), *A Companion to Ethics* (Oxford: Blackwell, 1991), 512.

justice is the maximization of well-being; and (2) the criterion of well-being is objective ('recognizably Aristotelian' as Wood puts it), i.e. it is based on a certain conception of human nature and the conditions for human flourishing. Capitalism, on this account, is morally objectionable because it fails to maximize well-being so understood.[67] We might gloss that, as Wood does, as being 'interested in promoting . . . the well-being of . . . others whose welfare I happen to care about', though it is not at all clear that Marx's view ought to be so described. The 'happen to care about' part is, I take it, what seems in tension with a genuinely *moral* concern, insofar as we think moral norms must be *categorical* rather than *hypothetical* imperatives: i.e. if there is a moral demand to promote the well-being of all, then we *ought* to promote their well-being (and criticize systems that thwart well-being) whether or not we have any antecedent desire for the well-being of those affected. But the 'happen to care about' comes from Wood, not Marx. Indeed, there seems no clear textual basis for saying what Marx thinks about the categoricity of moral demands. Instead, it seems precisely the kind of abstract theoretical issue his general pragmatism would lead him to eschew: establishing that the moral demand to promote well-being is categorical would not do one wit to bring about the downfall of capitalism after all!

Is there a Marxian answer to the Scope Problem that does not depend on stipulative definitions? Recall that a morality is ideological on Marx's account insofar as its acceptability depends on a mistake about its class-interest-specific genesis and character. It follows, then, that moral beliefs are non-ideological if either (1) they do not have a class-interest-specific genesis

---

[67] It is clearer that Marx has a conception of well-being or welfare than that he is committed to maximization of well-being as the criterion of right action or justice, though, for reasons of space, I shall have to put those interpretive issues to one side here. G. A. Cohen assumes, without textual evidence, that 'equality' is the animating moral ideal for Marx in his book *If You're an Egalitarian, How Come You're So Rich?* (Cambridge, MA: Harvard University Press, 2000). Now it is true, to be sure, that Marx is committed to equality in the same way Bentham (and every post-Enlightenment thinker) is: the well-being of *each* individual counts, and counts equally. But beyond this *banal* egalitarianism, it is not clear that equality is a significant moral norm for Marx—the way it was, say, for Mao (who thought that it was *good* to make people equal through leveling, which was plainly *not* Marx's view), or for Dworkin (equal concern and respect is the fundamental moral principle in liberal societies), or for Rawls (we only tolerate as much inequality in wealth as is in the interests of the worst-off). But take the famous Marxian slogan, 'To each according to his needs, from each according to his ability.' The first clause reflects a well-being, not an equality, view: each gets as much as they need to flourish. And the second clause *presupposes* unequal ability and thus contemplates vastly different contributions to production. *Huge* inequalities are a possible upshot here, and there is no *egalitarian* constraint on their realization, except perhaps that flowing from the role of species-being as part of the good life for humans.

(or, more precisely, their acceptability does not depend upon a mistake about this genesis), or (2) they are not class-interest-specific (or, more precisely, their acceptability does not depend upon a mistake about their character in this regard). Marx and Engels sometimes seem to focus on 'classlessness' (in both senses (1) and (2)) as the condition for morality being non-ideological. So, e.g., Engels speaks of 'a really human morality' as one that 'stands above class antagonisms' (726). Yet Marx equally often presents communism as itself in the interests of a specific class. He describes, for example, 'the proletarian movement', i.e. communism, as simply being 'in the interests of the vast majority' (482). 'The Communists fight . . . for the momentary interests of the working class' (489). Marx derides the German 'True' Socialists (though he might just as well have been thinking of Habermas) for thinking that socialism reflects 'the requirements of truth; not the interests of the proletariat, but the interests of Human Nature, of Man in general, who belongs to no class, has no reality, who exists only in the misty realm of philosophical fantasy' (494). And he derides Critical-Utopian Socialists for 'consider[ing] themselves far superior to all class antagonisms. They want to improve the condition of every member of society, even that of the most favored' (498).

Perhaps we can make sense of the apparent tensions in Marx's position in light of the following passage from *The Communist Manifesto*:

The theoretical conclusions of the Communists are in no way based on ideas or principles that have been invented, or discovered, by this or that would-be universal reformer. They merely express in general terms actual relations springing from the existing class struggle, from a historical movement under our very ideas.    (484)

Perhaps, then, Marx's view is that the ethical ideal animating communism is a class-interest-specific morality, just one in the interests of the vast majority, as opposed to the ruling class. But this morality is *not* ideological because its acceptability does not depend on its not being class-interest-specific—indeed, there is no mistake about its genesis either. 'The proletarian movement is the self-conscious, independent movement of the immense majority, in the interests of the immense majority' (482).

If the preceding is correct, it would follow that Marx's implicit 'utilitarianism' would not necessarily be the morality of a communist society. What such a morality would be is something that will simply have to be discovered in the course of historical developments, since, as Engels says, 'all moral theories have been . . . the product . . . of the economic conditions of society obtaining at the time' (726). Only under communist relations of production would individuals actually discover the morality appropriate to a non-class society. And such a morality would be non-ideological because there would be no economic classes in communist society, and thus no class-specific interests for any morality to serve.

# III. Assessing Continental Morality Critics

To take Continental Morality Critics seriously as philosophical critics of morality requires us to ask whether their critiques are sound. In this concluding section, I will not discuss Freud further, since his critique is the least radical and so much of the soundness of Freudian doubts about morality turns on what are now hotly contested issues about the epistemic *bona fides* of his general theory of the mind and human development.[68] But with respect to Nietzsche, Foucault, and Marx we may pose at least a few important critical questions that bear on the continuing interest of their critiques.

## A. Nietzsche

With respect to Nietzsche, the first critical worry is easy to state: is not the Nietzschean critique of morality simply hyperbolic? Surely if there is a culture of mediocrity and banality in ascendance, it is not primarily the work of morality, but perhaps of the free market, the leveling effects of which have been described by sociologists, historians, and philosophers. Indeed, the right

[68] Grünbaum's critique of Freud in *The Foundations of Psychoanalysis* (especially as popularized by Frederick Crews and others) is, alas, better known than the devastating critiques of Grünbaum by, among others, Arthur Fine and Mickey Forbes, 'Grünbaum on Freud: Three Grounds for Dissent', *Behavioral and Brain Sciences* 9 (1986), 237–8; Jim Hopkins, 'Epistemology and Depth Psychology: Critical Notes on *The Foundations of Psychoanalysis*', in P. Clark and C. Wright (eds.), *Mind, Psychoanalysis and Science* (Oxford: Blackwell, 1988); David Sachs, 'In Fairness to Freud', reprinted in J. Neu (ed.), *The Cambridge Companion to Freud* (Cambridge: Cambridge University Press, 1992); and Richard Wollheim, 'Desire, Belief, and Professor Grünbaum's Freud', in his *The Mind and its Depths* (Cambridge, Mass.: Harvard University Press, 1993). For recent experimental literature in support of Freudian hypotheses, see generally Drew Westen, 'The Scientific Legacy of Sigmund Freud: Toward a Psychodynamically Informed Psychological Science', *Psychological Bulletin* 124 (1998), 333–71; and for an excellent empirical case study of one particular Freudian hypothesis about reaction formation, see Henry E. Adams, Lester W. Wright, Jr., and Bethany A. Lohr, 'Is Homophobia Associated with Homosexual Arousal?', *Journal of Abnormal Psychology* 105 (1996), 440–5.

model for Nietzschean-style morality/culture critique is not the 'idealistic'-sounding Nietzsche described here, but rather the materialist Adorno of *Minima Moralia*, who traces cultural mediocrity to its capitalist roots.

Now while the early Nietzsche of 'Schopenhauer as Educator' did worry about the effects of capitalism, militaristic nationalism, and proto-fascism on the cultural conditions for the production of genius, the later Nietzsche seems all too ready to lay the blame for all cultural decline at the doorstep of MPS.[69] Nietzsche's challenge may be a novel and important one, but anyone who reads his repeated denouncements of morality cannot escape the feeling that he suffered from a certain explanatory tunnel-vision, with the result that, in some measure, his case against morality seems overstated.

Of course, one might want to say something much stronger: Nietzsche's point is not just hyperbolic, but perversely backward. For surely it is the *lack* of morality in social policy and public institutions—a lack which permits widespread poverty and despair to persist generation upon generation; that allows daily economic struggle and uncertainty to define the basic character of most people's lives—that is most responsible for a lack of human flourishing. Surely in a more moral society, with a genuine commitment to social justice and human equality, there would be far more Goethes, far more creativity and admirable human achievement. As Philippa Foot has sharply put it: 'How could one see the present dangers that the world is in as showing that there is too much pity and too little egoism around?'[70]

Here, again, though we must be careful in how we construe the Nietzschean point. Consider the Nietzsche who asks: 'Where has the last feeling of decency and self-respect gone when even our statesmen, an otherwise quite unembarrassed type of man, anti-Christians through and through in their deeds, still call themselves Christians today and attend communion?' (A 38). Clearly this Nietzsche is under no illusions about the extent to which public actors do not act morally. Indeed, Nietzsche continues in even more explicit terms: 'Every practice of every moment, every instinct, every valuation that is translated into *action* is today anti-Christian: what a *miscarriage of falseness* must modern man be, that he is *not ashamed* to be called a Christian in spite of all this!' (A 38). What, then, is going on here? If Nietzsche is not, contrary

---

[69] To be sure, Nietzsche also often 'blames' Christianity, but for Nietzsche Christianity was simply 'the most prodigal elaboration of the moral theme to which humanity has ever been subjected' (BT Pref:5).

[70] 'Nietzsche: The Revaluation of Values', in R. C. Solomon (ed.), *Nietzsche: A Collection of Critical Essays* (South Bend: University of Notre Dame Press, 1973), 168.

to Foot's suggestion, embracing the absurd view that there is too much pity and altruism in the world, what exactly is his critical point?

Nietzsche's paradigmatic worry seems to be the following: that a nascent creative genius will come to take the norms of MPS so seriously that he will fail to realize his genius. Rather than tolerate (even welcome) suffering, he will seek relief from hardship and devote himself to the pursuit of pleasure; rather than practice what Nietzsche calls 'severe self-love', and attend to himself in the ways requisite for productive creative work, he will embrace the ideology of altruism, and reject 'self-love' as improper; rather than learn how to look down on himself, to desire to overcome his present self and become something better, he will embrace the prevailing rhetoric of equality—captured nicely in the pop-psychology slogan 'I'm OK, you're OK'—and thus never learn to feel the contempt for self that might lead one to strive for something more. It is not, then, that Nietzsche thinks people *practice* too much altruism—after all, it is Nietzsche who notes that egoistic actions 'have hitherto been by far the most frequent actions' (D 148)—but rather that they *believe* too much in the value of altruism, equality, happiness, and the other norms of MPS. It is the prevalence of the MPS *ideology* that worries Nietzsche: for even if there is neither much altruism nor equality in the world, there is almost universal endorsement of the *value* of altruism and equality—even, notoriously (and as Nietzsche seemed well aware), by those who are its worst enemies in practice. Nietzsche's claim is that a culture which embraces the ideology of MPS—even if it does not act in accordance with this ideology—presents the real threat to the realization of human excellence, because it teaches potential higher types to disvalue what would be most conducive to their creativity and value what is irrelevant or perhaps even hostile to it.

Indeed, surely it is the individuals of great creativity and sensitivity who are far more likely to take seriously the ideology of MPS than the politicians whose hypocrisy Nietzsche derides in the remark quoted earlier. As Nietzsche observes at one point: 'What distinguishes the higher human beings from the lower is that the former see and hear immeasurably more, and see and hear more thoughtfully' (GS 301). But it is precisely this trait of the 'higher human beings' that makes them all the more susceptible to the deleterious effects of MPS: a thoughtless brute is hardly likely to worry about the morality of his acts—but nor is he likely to become a creative genius. But the higher types that Nietzsche worries about are both likely candidates for critical self-reflection in light of the norms of MPS and, at the same time, those for whom such norms are most harmful. Indeed, we might say that it is precisely Nietzsche's aim to help these higher human beings 'see and hear' something more: namely, that MPS values are really disadvantageous for them.

That Nietzsche's concern is with the prevalence of the MPS ideology—not the prevalence of actions in accord with MPS—and, in particular, with the effect of this ideology on the *self-conception* of potentially higher types is suggested in many places. In *Dawn*, he speaks of wanting to deprive egoistic actions of 'their bad conscience' (148). In *Beyond Good and Evil*, Nietzsche observes that in order to '[s]tand all valuations *on their head*', Christianity had to

cast suspicion on the joy in beauty, bend everything haughty . . . conquering, domineering, all the instincts characteristic of the highest and best-turned-out type of 'man', into unsureness, dilemma of conscience [*Gewissens-Noth*], self-destruction. . . . (BGE 62)

In *Twilight of the Idols*, he describes the 'man' 'improved' by MPS as,

a caricature of man, like a miscarriage: he had become a 'sinner', he was stuck in a cage, *imprisoned among all sorts of terrible concepts* [*schreckliche Begriffe*]. And there he lay, sick, miserable, malevolent against himself: full of hatred against the springs of life, full of suspicion against all that was still strong and happy.    (TI, VII:2, emphasis added)

In each case, we see that the thrust of the worry is that higher types will come to evaluate and think of themselves in terms of the *concepts* peculiar to MPS (and Christianity)—that they will become 'imprisoned among all sorts of terrible concepts'—with the result that they will be cast into self-doubt and a destructive self-loathing, and thus never realize the excellences of which they are capable.

Now one might want to respond on Foot's behalf, however, and insist that there is still something perverse about the Nietzschean complaint. Granted Nietzsche does not believe that most people are *actually* too altruistic and society *in practice* is too egalitarian; granted that Nietzsche's real worry is about the fact that we, as a moral culture, pay so much lip-service to the value of altruism, egalitarianism, and the rest—with the resultant deleterious effects on the self-conception and development of nascent Goethes. Yet surely it is still the case that if our society *really* were more altruistic and egalitarian more individuals would have the chance to flourish and do creative work. This is the core of the charge of perversity, and nothing said so far has exonerated Nietzsche from it.

In fact, it seems that it is precisely this moral optimism common, for example, to utilitarians and Marxists—this belief that a more moral society would produce more opportunity for more people to do creative work—that Nietzsche does, indeed, want to question. Nietzsche's illiberal attitudes in this regard are apparent; he says—to take but one example—that, 'We simply do not consider it desirable that a realm of justice and harmony [*Eintracht*] should be established on earth' (GS 377). It is bad enough for Nietzsche that MPS values have so far succeeded in saying, 'stubbornly and inexorably, 'I am morality itself, and nothing besides is morality' '(BGE 202); it could only be worse on his view if more and more of our actions were really brought into accord with these values. For Nietzsche wants to urge—contrary to the moral optimists—that in a way largely unappreciated and (perhaps) unintended a thoroughly *moral* culture undermines the conditions under which the most splendid human creativity is possible, and generates instead a society of Zarathustra's 'last men'. If we are trained always to think of happiness and comfort and safety and the needs of others, we shall cut ourselves off from the preconditions for creative excellence on the Nietzschean picture: suffering, hardship, danger, self-concern, and the rest.

Nietzsche's critique raises then the following general concern for any moral theory: namely, what would the culture that embraces the moral theory *actually* look like—and, in particular, would it be acceptable according to the standards of the theory itself? This would not constitute a direct criticism of the theory, but it surely constitutes a worry that any theory we might want to choose to live by should address. It might also help loosen our attachment to what Robert Nozick aptly calls 'normative sociology': 'the study of what the causes of problems *ought to be*'. Thus, says Nozick, 'We *want* one bad thing to be caused by another [bad thing].'[71] But if Nietzsche is right then we may have to confront the possibility that seemingly good things—like many of the norms of MPS—cause apparently 'bad' things, like the gradual disappearance of human excellence.

Whatever the philosophical and psychological merits of Nietzsche's *critique* of MPS, it seems increasingly apparent that his moral psychology is far more empirically plausible than either of the leading philosophical contenders as accounts of moral motivation and action, such as Aristotle's or Kant's. Since Joshua Knobe and I have made this case elsewhere at some length,[72] I will not belabor the point here.

---

[71] Robert Nozick, *Anarchy, State and Utopia* (New York: Basic Books, 1974), 247.

[72] Joshua Knobe and Brian Leiter, 'The Case for Nietzschean Moral Psychology', in B. Leiter and N. Sinhababu (eds.) *Nietzsche and Morality* (Oxford: Oxford University Press, 2007).

## B. Foucault

Foucault himself, it will be recalled, exempts from his critical gaze non-'dubious' sciences like physics and chemistry, focusing instead on those human sciences whose 'epistemological profile' is 'a low one'.[73] But even with respect to the latter, he does not argue, as some have done, for the 'lowness' of the epistemological profile; instead, he, calls attention to the influence of economic, political, and moral considerations on their development. Yet it is now surely a familiar point in post-Kuhnian philosophy of science that the influence of social and historical factors might be compatible with the epistemically special standing of the sciences.[74] And that possibility is potentially fatal to Foucault as a morality critic.

For recall that central to Foucault's critique is the role that the epistemic pretensions of the sciences play in a structure of practical reasoning which leads agents concerned with their flourishing to become the agents of their own oppression.[75] And the crucial bit of 'pretense' is, as we noted earlier, that the human sciences illuminate how (normal) human beings flourish. Recall that Foucault, unlike Nietzsche, does not contest the practical authority of truth (i.e., the claim of the truth to determine what *ought* to be done); he rather denies that the claims in question are true or have the epistemic warrant that we would expect true claims to have. So the entire Foucauldian edifice—at least insofar as it bears on morality criticism—turns on the epistemic status of the claims of the human sciences. And on this central point, Foucault has, surprisingly, almost nothing relevant to say. Perhaps *contemporary* medicine and contemporary psychiatry have identified *kinds*: in that case, Foucault's story is the story of bogus science of the past enlisted on behalf of moral and political objectives, a story whose general outlines have long been familiar, even if Foucault tells striking new aspects of it. On the epistemic standing of the *current* human sciences, all Foucault leaves us with is a suspicion, rather than an argument.[76]

---

[73] 'Truth and Power', 109.

[74] A classic articulation of this idea is Philip Kitcher, *The Advancement of Science* (New York: Oxford University Press, 1993), esp. ch. 5.

[75] See above p. 728.

[76] At least in the case of criminology, Foucault may have the resources for a response to this worry in *Discipline and Punish*. For one might read him there as arguing that because criminology is intertwined with disciplinary institutions that, in fact, *produce* criminals and delinquents by legitimizing certain disciplinary techniques, criminology creates the very subjects it purports to give us knowledge about. Criminology is dubious, then, precisely in the sense that its 'kinds' are in fact artifacts of its epistemic pretensions. If this is Foucault's argument, and if it could be generalized, then it might constitute a

The suspicion is, itself, sometimes undercut by Foucault's cavalier attitude towards the phenomena in question. Consider the following remarkable passage from *The History of Sexuality* about which Foucault's devoted followers rarely comment:

One day in 1867, a farm hand from the village of Lapcourt, who was somewhat simple-minded, employed here then there, depending on the season, living hand-to-mouth . . . was turned in to the authorities. At the border of a field, he had obtained a few caresses from a little girl, just as he had done before and seen done by the village urchins round about him. . . . So he was pointed out by the girl's parents to the mayor of the village, reported by the mayor to the gendarmes, led by the gendarmes to the judge, who indicted him and turned him over first to a doctor, then to two other experts. . . . What is the significant thing about this story? The pettiness of it all; the fact that this everyday occurrence in the life of village sexuality, these inconsequential bucolic pleasures, could become, from a certain time, the object not only of a collective intolerance but of a judicial action, a medical intervention, a careful clinical examination, and an entire theoretical elaboration.[77]

The same underlying events might, of course, be described rather differently: namely, that up until the time of this incident, pedophilia and child sexual abuse had been routinely tolerated—treated as an 'inconsequential bucolic pleasure'—but gradually people came to realize that 'simple-minded' men being masturbated by young girls was not such a good thing (not so 'inconsequential'), and thus the modern scientific study of pedophilia, and its harms, commenced. Why we should prefer Foucault's version to the alternative is unclear. Why not think that in the nineteenth century a certain psychological *type* was discovered, namely, the pedophile, and that the harms of pedophilia were also discovered, even if the nineteenth-century versions of these discoveries have been superseded by a century of investigation? Absent an answer to questions like this, Foucault's entire critique of morality is in danger.

To be sure, even if Foucault does not himself supply the arguments, the reasons for being skeptical about the epistemic claims of the human sciences have been well articulated by others. What Foucauldian morality criticism now requires, if it is to be of continued interest, is a systematic critique of the epistemic status of the conceptions of 'normality' at work in the contemporary human sciences, from psychiatry to criminology.

different explanation for how Foucault is attacking the epistemic status of the claims of the human sciences directly. (I am grateful to David Dudrick for discussion of this issue.)

[77]  *History of Sexuality*, 31.

## C. Marx and the Critique of Ideology

Central to the Marxist critique of MPS is, as we have seen, Marx's theory of ideology, since it is through the causal role of the ideological superstructure of society in sustaining capitalism that morality (as one part of that super-structure) makes a causal contribution to thwarting human flourishing. Is the Marxist theory of ideology, however, credible? Michael Rosen has recently argued powerfully that it is not.[78] The Marxist theory of ideology, on Rosen's (reasonable) rendering, is an answer to the question: 'Why do the many accept the rule of the few, even when it seems to be plainly against their interests to do so?' (1). The Marxist answer (as Rosen puts it) is that

1. they [the few] maintain themselves in virtue of false consciousness on the part of the citizens.
2. this false consciousness occurs in response to the needs of society.[79] (260)

Call the first 'the False Consciousness Thesis', and the second, 'the Society as Self-Maintaining System Thesis'. Rosen complains that the Society as Self-Maintaining System Thesis 'requires an ontological commitment that is not justified according to the explanatory standards of the natural sciences' (pp. 258–9). But it is a familiar point in post-Quinean philosophy of science that we are entitled to whatever ontology we need for the best explanation of the observable phenomena: if the Marxist theory of ideology is, *in fact*, the best explanation of the socio-economic phenomena, and the Marxist theory requires an ontology of societies as self-maintaining systems, then that is the ontology of the social world we get.

Rosen's real objection to the Marxist theory, then, is that 'there are alternative answers' (p. 259) to why the many accept the rule of the few, even when it is not in their interests, i.e. the Society as Self-Maintaining System is not, in fact, part of the *best* explanation of the phenomenon. Strictly speaking, of course, showing that there are 'alternative answers' won't suffice, since what we need to establish is that the alternatives are parts of *better* explanations for the phenomena. (Of course, Marxists too bear the burden of showing the theory of ideology is the *best* explanation.) Yet we need not confront that

---

[78] Michael Rosen, *On Voluntary Servitude: False Consciousness and the Theory of Ideology* (Cambridge, MA: Harvard University Press, 1996). All further references will be included in the body of the text by page number.

[79] On the rendering given earlier, ideology arises in response to the needs of the ruling class in society, though this difference in formulation does not, I think, mark a substantive difference with Rosen's approach.

issue, since it is not clear that Rosen actually adduces alternatives that are even *plausible* contenders. For example, Rosen suggests that the rule of the few might simply be the result of coordination problems confronting the many in overthrowing the few (pp. 260–2). Even putting aside doubts about the claims of rational choice theory which undergird the analysis of coordination problems,[80] the real problem here is that coordination problems don't explain the relevant phenomenon. The coordination problem explanation of why the few rule the many is that the many can't coordinate their behavior to overthrow the few, but the *actual* phenomenon the Marxist theory explains is that the many don't even see the need to overthrow the few, indeed, don't even see that the few rule the many!

Perhaps we may save the coordination problem explanation by supplementing it with appeal to the phenomenon of 'sour grapes': because the many can't overthrow the few, they end up believing that the few are *not* really dominating them, not really worth overthrowing. Rosen's general skepticism (pp. 265–6) about the explanatory power of the 'sour grapes' mechanism, however, seems especially warranted here: where, one wonders, is the evidence that the dominated classes recognize themselves as dominated by the *few*, only to turn away from that and decide the grapes are sour?

At another point, Rosen suggests that perhaps the False Consciousness Thesis is true, but the Society as Self-Maintaining System Thesis false (pp. 262–70). The difficulty, now, is to explain the former without recourse to the idea that it is 'in the interests' of society for the many to suffer from false consciousness. Rosen complains throughout that Marx 'gives no adequate suggestion regarding the mechanism by which' society's interests might bring about the truth of the False Consciousness Thesis (e.g. p. 274). While it is plainly true that Marx does not offer a detailed account of the mechanisms, it is equally clear that Rosen's treatment of the accounts Marx *does* offer are abrupt and uncharitable. So, for example, Marx famously proposed in *The Germany Ideology* that,

the class which is the ruling *material* force of a society is at the same time its ruling *intellectual* force. The class which has the means of material production at its disposal, has control at the same time over the means of mental production, so that thereby, generally speaking, the ideas of those who lack the means of mental production are subject to it.

[80] See Robert Paul Wolff, 'Methodological Individualism and Marx: Some Remarks on Elster, Game Theory, and Other Things', *Canadian Journal of Philosophy* 20 (1990), 469–86.

To this Rosen retorts that Marx here embraces,

a view of those who live under the domination of the ruling class as passive victims, taking their ideas from those who control the 'means of mental production' like obedient chicks, with no critical reflection on their part as to whether the ideas are either true or in their own rational interests. This, it seems, is an almost paranoid view. Why should one suppose that the ruling class is capable of promoting its own interests effectively, forming its ideas in response to those interests, whereas the dominated class simply accept whatever is served up to them? (pp. 182–3)

Although this passage is heavy on rhetoric (Marx is 'paranoid') and thin on argument (what is the actual *evidence* for thinking most people are not like 'obedient chicks'?), what really matters is that Rosen fails to consider obvious answers to his last question. The best reason to suppose that the ruling class is, in fact, effective in promoting its own interests, and the dominated class is not, is precisely that ideas favorable to the interests of the ruling class typically dominate, and without being recognized as such!

In the United States, for example, a majority of the population favors abolition of the estate tax—what the ideologues of the ruling class now call a 'death tax'—believing that it affects them, and that it results in the loss of family businesses and farms.[81] In fact, only 2 percent of the population pays the estate tax, and there is no documented case of families losing their farms or businesses as a result of the tax's operation. Examples like this—in which the majority have factually inaccurate beliefs, which are in the interests of those with money and power—could, of course, be multiplied. Does this just happen by accident?

Rosen would fairly demand, though, an explanation of why the ruling class is so good at identifying and promoting its interests, while the majority is not. But, again, there is an obvious answer: for isn't it generally quite easy to identify your short-term interests when the status quo is to your benefit? In such circumstances, you favor the status quo! In other words, if the status quo provides tangible benefits to the few—lots of money, prestige, and power—is it any surprise that the few are well-disposed to the status quo, and are particularly good at thinking of ways to tinker with the status quo (e.g. repeal the already minimal estate tax) to increase their money, prestige,

---

[81] 'Focus on Forms Masks Estate Tax Confusion', *New York Times* (April 8, 2001). As the economist Paul Krugman notes, a successful propaganda campaign resulted in the following bit of false consciousness by early 2003: '49 percent of Americans believed that most families had to pay the estate tax, while only 33 percent gave the right answer that only a few families had to pay' ('The Tax-Cut Con', *New York Times Magazine* (September 14, 2003), 59).

and power? (The few can then promote their interests for exactly the reasons Marx identifies: they own the means of mental production.)[82]

By contrast, it is far trickier for the many to assess what is in their interest, precisely because it requires a counterfactual thought-experiment, in addition to evaluating complex questions of socio-economic causation. More precisely, the many have to ascertain that (1) the status quo—the whole complex socio-economic order in which they find themselves—is not in their interests (this may be the easiest part); (2) there are alternatives to the status quo which would be more in their interest; and (3) it is worth the costs to make the transition to the alternatives—to give up on the bad situation one knows in order to make the leap in to a (theoretically) better unknown. Obstacles to the already difficult task of making determinations (1) and (2)—let alone (3)—will be especially plentiful, precisely because the few are strongly, and effectively (given their control of the means of mental production), committed to the denial of (1) and (2). Since Rosen fails to consider any possible Marxian fleshing-out of the bare-bones explanation of ideological dominance in works like *The German Ideology*, his criticisms of the Marxist theory of ideology ultimately ring hollow.

Even if we can deflect the more sophisticated criticisms of the Marxist theory of ideology, like Rosen's, this still leaves the most complex philosophical/empirical issue unresolved. For even granting that morality is part of the ideological superstructure of society, and even granting that ideology plays the causal role the Marxist theory of ideology supposes, the crucial claim for Marxist morality criticism is that the socio-economic system that ideology sustains—namely, capitalism—is an impediment to human flourishing. But is it?

Marx takes over from Hegel the idea that essential to human well-being is a kind of 'reconciliation' with the social world,[83] which, in Marx's hands, turns into a thesis about the centrality of recognizing one's 'species-being'. I am not aware of developments in empirical psychology in the last two hundred years that vindicate this emphasis. For independent philosophical reasons, it also seems dubious whether this could really be central to a person's good. After

---

[82] See, e.g. Edward Herman and Noam Chomsky, *Manufacturing Consent: The Political Economy of the Mass Media* (New York: Pantheon, 1988); Noam Chomsky, *Necessary Illusions: Thought Control in Democratic Societies* (Boston: South End Press, 1989); Ben Bagdikian, *The Media Monopoly* (Boston: Beacon, 1997); Robert McChesney, *Corporate Media and the Threat to Democracy* (New York: Seven Stories, 1997); Eric Alterman, *What Liberal Media?* (New York: Basic Books, 2003).

[83] See generally, Michael O. Hardimon, *Hegel's Social Philosophy: The Project of Reconciliation* (Cambridge: Cambridge University Press, 1994).

all, it seems central to the idea of a person's well-being that the individual, at least under appropriate circumstances, would *care* about his well-being, yet as Marx conceives it, human well-being (the state of non-alienation) is not dependent on the individual's psychological response to it (how the individual feels is not criterial of well-being on Marx's view). So it could be true that the ideological superstructure of society (including MPS) makes a causal contribution to sustaining capitalism, and it could be true that capitalism is an obstacle to human flourishing *as Marx understands it*, but it is not clear that Marx's conception of human flourishing is plausible. To be sure, capitalism may, in fact, be an obstacle to human flourishing, and MPS may make a causal contribution to that state of affairs, but the nature of human flourishing on this account would have to go beyond Marx's account.

## D.  Concluding Observations

Criticism of 'morality' is not unfamiliar in English-speaking philosophy over the last thirty years, but the criticisms have been of a quite different kind than those central to the Continental morality critics we have looked at here. For Anglo-American work has been critical only of particular *theories* of morality, but not of morality itself: that is, their target has been morality as more-or-less systematized, improved, and codified in some theoretical framework produced by a philosopher, as distinct from morality as an everyday cultural phenomenon, the stuff of common sense and common opinion, guiding the conduct of ordinary people. Even if the theory does capture what is *conceptually* central to morality as an everyday cultural phenomenon, a Continental morality critic may still worry about the effects of the unsystematic, uncodified, unimproved moral beliefs that comprise the daily life of the culture.

Admittedly, Anglophone philosophers often present themselves as critics of morality itself—in that sense they echo the Continental morality critics—but, on examination, it is clear that their targets are only specific philosophical theories of morality, consequentialist and deontological. The Bernard Williams of *Ethics and the Limits of Philosophy*[84] is illustrative in this regard, for he might seem, at first sight, a counter-example to this characterization. After all, Williams calls 'morality' 'the peculiar institution' and says this morality 'is not

---

[84]  Bernard Williams, *Ethics and the Limits of Philosophy* (Cambridge, MA: Harvard University Press, 1985). Cited hereafter in the text as ELP by page number.

an invention of philosophers...[but rather] the outlook, or, incoherently, part of the outlook, of almost all of us' (ELP, p. 174). He goes on to worry about the 'several natural ways in which' this morality's special notion of obligation 'can come to dominate a life altogether' (ELP, pp. 181–2). In passages like these, Williams seems to be objecting *not* that the best moral *theory* requires obligation to dominate life, but rather that once moral obligation is allowed to 'structure ethical thought' (ELP, p. 182) it has a 'natural' tendency to rule out all other considerations.

Yet appearances here are deceiving. While Williams plainly wants to align himself with Nietzsche as a critic of morality as a genuine cultural phenomenon—hence the rhetoric about 'the peculiar institution' and morality not being 'an invention of philosophers'—it is far from clear that the notion of moral obligation he discusses is anything other than a philosopher's 'invention', or, at best, such a severe systematic reworking of the ordinary notion as to be only a distant relative of the unsystematic, uncodified notion of obligation actually at work in our culture. Morality's purportedly threatening notion of 'obligation', for example, is constructed by Williams entirely from the works of Kant and Ross, with no gesture at showing what relation their philosophically refined notions of 'obligation' bear to those in play in ordinary life. Yet where is the evidence, one might ask, that real people treat 'moral obligation[s] [as] inescapable' (ELP, p. 177) and that they accept the idea that 'only an obligation can beat an obligation' (ELP, p. 180)? Surely the evidence is not in the way people actually live, in the way they actually honor—or, more often, breach—their moral obligations—a point Nietzsche well understood. What is the evidence that, in our relativistic culture, individuals think that 'moral obligation applies to people even if they do not want it to' (ELP, p. 178)? Even Williams, in leading up to the specter of morality dominating life, says that 'the thought can gain a footing (*I am not saying that it has to*) that I could be better employed than in doing something I am under no [moral] obligation to do, and, if I could be, then I ought to be' (ELP, p. 181, emphasis added). But surely this 'thought' might only gain a footing for Kant or Ross, or some other philosopher who followed out to its logical conclusion a deontological *theory*. It is a pure philosopher's fantasy to think that real people in the moral culture at large find themselves overwhelmed by this burdensome sense of moral obligation. Like other Anglophone critics of morality, Williams writes as though he is attacking 'morality', when what he is really attacking is 'morality' as conceived, systematized, and refined by philosophers. Such a critique may be a worthy endeavor, but it is very different from worrying about the 'dangers' of ordinary morality as understood—unsystematically and inchoately—by ordinary people. Nietzsche, Freud, Foucault, and Marx are simply not worried about this kind of *very* English academic understanding of morality.

All the Continental Morality Critics depend essentially on empirical claims about the social and cultural affects of MPS: the acceptance of the moral norms prevalent in our modern Western culture are inhospitable to the flourishing of extraordinary individuals (Nietzsche), to the 'happiness' of ordinary persons (Freud), to the good, unalienated life for human being (Marx), etc. Academic moral theory is simply not in the picture as a relevant causal consideration. If the Anglophone critics of morality are right, then we have failed in our attempts to produce an ethical theory that could tell us how to live both well *and* rightly. It is decidedly not an upshot of their critique, however, that, as a matter of fact, we cannot or do not live well: if utilitarianism, in theory, alienates us from our projects, in reality, it goes without saying that it has no such effect. In the culture at large, hardly anyone knows what utilitarianism is, let alone observes its strictures to the extremes that would lead one to worry that it 'demands too much'. With Continental Morality Critics things stand differently. If they are right, then we are supposed to be confronted with something very real: our untutored morality, the morality of ordinary men and women, the morality that infuses our culture, is, in fact, an obstacle to human flourishing. In its Continental incarnations, philosophy quickly crosses the line into psychology, cultural anthropology, and social critique—territory now occupied (regrettably) almost exclusively by literary theorists. Yet as the post-Quinean revolution in English-speaking philosophy has led Anglophone philosophers to become more attentive to the human sciences (for example, psychology and anthropology), the time now seems ripe to integrate the Continental critique of morality into the mainstream of moral theory.[85]

---

[85] I am indebted to John Deigh for useful discussion about Freud, to David Dudrick for helpful advice about Foucault, and to the graduate students in my seminars in Austin on 'Marx and Freud' and 'Nietzsche and Foucault' for helpful questions and insights, especially David Bernard, Jessica Berry, Christopher Raymond, Neil Sinhababu, and Ariela Tubert.

# Bibliography

## Frequently Referenced Primary Sources

Below is the bibliographical information, together with the most common acronym, for the primary sources most frequently referenced by contributors to this volume.

### Aristotle (384 bc—322 bc)

| | |
|---|---|
| *EN* | *Ethica Nicomachea; Nicomachean Ethics*, ed. L. Bywater (Oxford: Oxford Classical Texts, 1894, 1986) |
| *M* | *Metaphysics*, trans. and ed. W. D. Ross (Oxford: Oxford University Press, 1924) |
| *P* | *Poetics*, trans. and ed. D. W. Lucas (Oxford: Clarendon Press, 1968) |
| *PPA* | *Prior and Posterior Analytics*, trans. and ed. W. D. Ross (Oxford: Oxford University Press, 1957) |
| *Top.* | *Topica et Sophistici Elenchi; Topics* and *On Sophistical Refutations*, trans. and ed. W. D. Ross (Oxford: Oxford Classical Texts, 1958) |

### Jean-Jacques Rousseau (1712–1778)

| | |
|---|---|
| *CW* | *Collected Writings*, ed. Roger Masters and Christopher Kelly (Hanover, Pa.: University Press of New England, 1990) |
| *DPW* | *The Discourses and Other Early Political Writings*, ed. Victor Gourevitch (New York: Cambridge University Press, 1997) |
| *E* | *Emile* (1762), trans. Alan Bloom (New York: Basic Books, 1979) |
| *Œuvres* | *Œuvres Complètes*, ed. Bernard Gagnebin and Marcel Raymond (Paris: Paris Bibliothèque de la Pléiade, 1961–9) |
| *SC* | *The Social Contract and Other Later Political Writings*, ed. Victor Gourevitch (New York: Cambridge University Press, 1997) |

### Immanuel Kant (1724–1804)

| | |
|---|---|
| *AA* | *Gesammelte Schriften* (1900– ), ed. Deutsche Akademie der Wissenschaften (Berlin: Walter de Gruyter) |
| *A/B* | *Kritik der Reinen Vernunft* [A = 1781, B = 1787], trans. Paul Guyer and Allen W. Wood as *Critique of Pure Reason* (Cambridge: Cambridge University Press, 1998) |

| | |
|---|---|
| *Corr.* | *Correspondence*, trans. Arnulf Zweig (Cambridge: Cambridge University Press, 1999) |
| *DRS (UGR)* | 'Von dem ersten Grunde des Unterschiedes der Gegenden im Raume' (1768), in *AA*, pp. 375–83; trans. David Walford as 'Concerning the Ultimate Ground of the Differentiation of Regions in Space', in *TP*₁, pp. 361–72 |
| *KPW* | *Kant's Political Writings* (1970), ed. H. B. Reiss, 2nd enlarged edn. (Cambridge: Cambridge University Press, 1991) |
| *KW* | *Kants Werke*, Akademie Textausgabe, ed. Königlich Preußische Akademie der Wissenschaften (Berlin: Walter de Gruyter, 1968) |
| *PC* | *Philosophical Correspondence, 1759–99*, trans. and ed. A. Zweig (Chicago: University of Chicago Press, 1967) |
| *PP* | *Practical Philosophy* (1996), trans. and ed. Mary J. Gregor, with an Introduction by A. W. Wood (Cambridge: Cambridge University Press) |
| *RLR (RGV)* | *Religion Innerhalb der Grenzen der Blossen Vernunft* (1793), trans. T. M. Green and H. H. Hudson as *Religion within the Limits of Reason Alone* (New York: Harper Row, 1960) |
| *TP*₁ | *Theoretical Philosophy, 1755–1770*, trans. David Walford with Ralf Meerbote (Cambridge: Cambridge University Press, 1992) |
| *TP*₂ | *Theoretical Philosophy after 1781*, trans. Michael Friedman, Gary Hatfield, Henry Allison, and Peter Heath, ed. Henry Allison and Peter Heath (Cambridge: Cambridge University Press, 2002) |
| *Werke* | *Werke*, ed. Königlich Preußische Akademie der Wissenschaften (Berlin: Georg Reimer, 1911) |

## Johann Gottlieb Fichte (1762–1814)

| | |
|---|---|
| *EPW* | *Early Philosophical Writings*, trans. and ed. Daniel Breazeale (Ithaca, NY: Cornell University Press, 1988) |
| *FGA* | *Gesamtausgabe der Bayrischen Akademie der Wissenschaften*, ed. Reinhard Lauth and Hans Gliwitzky, with Josef Beeler, Erich Fuchs, Ives Radrizzani, and Peter K. Schneider (Stuttgart-Bad Canstatt: Frommann-Holzboog (1964–    ) |
| *FNR (GNR)* | *Grundlage des Naturrechts nach Prinzipien der Wissenschaftslehre* (1796–7), trans. Michael Baur as *Foundations of Natural Right*, ed. Frederick Neuhouser (Cambridge: Cambridge University Press, 2000) |
| *FTP* (*WLnm*) | *Wissenschaftslehre Nova Methodo* (1796/9), trans. and ed. by D. Breazeale as *Foundations of Transcendental Philosophy* (Ithaca, NY: Cornell University Press, 1992) |
| *PF* | *Philosophie der Freimaurerei: Briefe an Konstant* (1802/3), in *FGA*, i/8. 409–62; trans. Roscoe Pound as *Philosophy of Freemasonry:* |

*Letters to Constant*, in Roscoe Pound, *Masonic Addresses and Writings of Roscoe Pound* (New York: Macoy, 1953)

SE (SS)     *Das System der Sittenlehre nach den Prinzipien der Wissenschaftslehre* (1798), in *SW*, iv. 1–365; ed. and trans. Daniel Breazeale and Günter Zöller as *The System of Ethics* (Cambridge: Cambridge University Press, 2005)

SK     *Grundlage der Gesamten Wissenschaftslehre* (1794–5), trans. Peter Heath as *Foundations of the Entire Science of Knowledge*, in Peter Heath and John Lachs (eds.), *Fichte: Science of Knowledge* (Cambridge: Cambridge University Press, 1982)

SW     *Sämmtliche Werke* (1845–6), ed. Immanuel Hermann Fichte (Berlin: Veit; Hamburg: Meiner, 1971)

## Georg Wilhelm Friedrich Hegel (1770–1831)

Ae     *Vorlesungen über die Ästhetik*, in *HW*, xiii–xv; trans. T. M. Knox as *Aesthetics: Lectures on Fine Art*, 2 vols. (Oxford: Clarendon Press, 1975)

DFS     *Die Differenz des Fichteschen und Schellingschen Systems der Philosophie* (1801), trans. Walter Cerf and H. S. Harris as *The Difference between Fichte's and Schelling's Systems of Philosophy* (Albany, NY: SUNY Press, 1977)

EPS₁     *Enzyklopädie der philosophischen Wissenschaften, Erster Teil: Die Wissenschaft der Logik* (1830), in *HW*, viii; trans. William Wallace as *Hegel's Logic* (Oxford: Clarendon Press, 1975); trans. T. F. Geraets, W. A. Suchting, and H. S. Harris as *The Encyclopaedia Logic: Part One of the Encyclopaedia of the Philosophical Sciences* (Indianapolis: Hackett, 1991)

EPS₂     *Enzyklopädie der philosophischen Wissenschaften, Zweiter Teil: Die Naturphilosophie* (1830), in *HW*, ix; trans. Michael John Petry as *Hegel's Philosophy of Nature: Part Two of the Encyclopaedia of the Philosophical Sciences*, 3 vols (London: George Allen & Unwin, 1970)

EPS₃     *Enzyklopädie der philosophischen Wissenschaften, Dritter Teil: Die Philosophie des Geistes* (1830), in *HW*, x; trans. William Wallace and A. V. Miller as *Philosophy of Mind: Being Part Three of the Encyclopaedia of Philosophical Sciences* (Oxford: Oxford University Press, 1971)

FHR (VHR)     'Vorrede zu Hinrichs' Religionsphilosophie' (1822), in *HW*, xi. 41–66; trans. as 'Foreword to Hinrichs' Religion in its Inner Relation to Science', in Jon Stewart (ed.), *Miscellaneous Writings of G. W. F. Hegel* (Evanston, IL: Northwestern University Press, 2002)

FK (GW)     *Glauben und Wissen oder Reflexionsphilosophie der Subjektivität in der Vollständigkeit ihrer Formen als Kantische, Jacobische und*

|       | *Fichtesche Philosophie* (1803), trans. Walter Cerf and H. S. Harris as *Faith and Knowledge* (Albany, NY: SUNY Press, 1977) |
| GP | *Vorlesungen über die Geschichte der Philosophie* (1836), i–iii, in *HW*, xviii–xx |
| HW (*Werke*) | *Werke in 20 Bänden, Auf der Grundlage der Werke von 1832–1845,* Theorie-Werkausgabe, neu editiert, ed. Eva Moldenhauer and Karl Markus Michel (Frankfurt am Main: Suhrkamp, 1969–71, 1979, 1986) |
| Letters | *Hegel: The Letters*, trans. C. Butler and C. Seiler (Bloomington: Indiana University Press, 1984) |
| PG | *Vorlesungen über die Philosophie der Geschichte* (1837), in *HW*, xii; trans. H. B. Nisbet as *Lectures on the Philosophy of World History* (Cambridge: Cambridge University Press, 1975) |
| PR/EPR | *Grundlinien der Philosophie des Rechts* (1821); trans. H. B. Nisbet as *Elements of the Philosophy of Right*, ed. Allen W. Wood (Cambridge: Cambridge University Press, 1991) |
| PS (*PhS*) | *Phänomenologie des Geistes* (1806/7), in *HW*, iii; trans. A. V. Miller as *Hegel's Phenomenology of Spirit* (Oxford: Oxford University Press, 1977) |
| SL (*WL*) | *Wissenschaft der Logik* (1812–16), in *HW*, v–vi; trans. A. V. Miller as *Hegel's Science of Logic* (London: George Allen & Unwin, 1977) |
| VSP | *Verhältnis des Skeptizismus zur Philosophie* (1802), in *Jenaer Schriften*, in *HW*, ii |

## Karl Wilhelm Friedrich von Schlegel (1772–1829)

| KFSA | *Kritische Friedrich-Schlegel-Ausgabe*, ed. Ernst Behler et al. (Paderborn: Schöningh, 1958– ) |
| SPF | *Philosophical Fragments*, trans. Peter Firchow (Minneapolis: University of Minnesota Press, 1991) |

## Novalis (Georg Friedrich Philipp Freiherr von Hardenberg, 1772–1801)

| FS | *Fichte-Studien*, in *Schriften*, ii: *Das philosophische Werk I*, ed. Richard Samuel, Hans-Joaquim Mähl, and Gerhard Schulz (Stuttgart: Kohlhammer, 1981); trans. as *Fichte Studies*, ed. Jane Kneller (Cambridge: Cambridge University Press, 2003) |
| NS | *Schriften*, 5 vols., ed. Paul Kluckhohn and Richard Samuel (Stuttgart: Kohlhammer, 1960–98) |
| PW | *Philosophical Writings*, trans. and ed. Margaret Mahony Stoljar (Albany: State University of New York Press, 1997) |
| Werke | *Werke, Tagebücher und Briefe*, ed. Hans-Jachim Mähl and Richard Samuel (München: Hanser, 1978) |

## Friedrich Wilhelm Joseph Schelling (1775–1854)

FPSP (FDSP)
: *Fernere Darstellungen aus dem System der Philosophie* (1802), trans. Michael G. Vater as 'Further Presentations from the System of Philosophy', *Philosophical Forum* 32/4 (2001), 373–97

FSW
: *Schellings Werke, Nach der Originalausgabe in neuer Anordnung*, ed. Manfred Schröter (München: Beck, 1927– )

STI
: *System des transcendentalen Idealismus* (1800), FSW, ii. 327–634; *System of Transcendental Idealism*, trans. Peter Heath as *System of Transcendental Idealism* (Charlottesville: University Press of Virginia, 1978)

UHK (UMW)
: *Über das Unbedingte im menschlichen Wissen* (1795), ed. and trans. F. Marti as *The Unconditional in Human Knowledge: Four Early Essays, 1794–1796* (Lewisburg, PA: Bucknell University Press, 1980)

US (MAS)
: *Vorlesungen über die Methode des akademischen Studiums* (1803) trans. E. S. Morgan, ed. N. Guterman, *On University Studies* (Athens, OH: Ohio University Press, 1966)

Werke
: *Sämmtliche Werke* (1856–61), 14 vols., ed. K. F. A. Schelling (Stuttgart and Augsburg: J. G. Cotta; Darmstadt: Wissenschaftliche Buchgesellschaft, 1974–6)

## Friedrich Nietzsche (1844–1900)

A
: *Der Anti-Christ* (1888); *The Anti-Christ*, trans. R. J. Hollingdale in *Twilight of the Idols and The Anti-Christ* (New York: Penguin, 1968)

BGE
: *Beyond Good and Evil* (1886); *Jenseits von Gut und Böse*, trans. R. J. Hollingdale (New York: Penguin, 1973), trans. J. Norman (Cambridge: Cambridge University Press, 2002)

BT
: *Die Geburt der Tragödie* (1872); *The Birth of Tragedy*, in *Nietzsche's Werke: Kritische Gesamtausgabe*, ed. Giorgio Colli and Mazzino Montinari (Berlin: de Gruyter, 1972), Abt. 3, Bd. 1; trans. Walter Kaufmann in *The Birth of Tragedy, Out of the Spirit of Music and The Case of Wagner* (New York: Vintage Books, 1967)

D
: *Morgenröte: Gedanken Über die Moralischen Vorurteile* (1881); *Daybreak: Reflections on Moral Prejudices*, trans. R. J. Hollingdale (Cambridge: Cambridge University Press, 1997)

EH
: *Ecce Homo* (1888), trans. Walter Kaufmann in *On the Genealogy of Morals and Ecce Homo* (New York: Vintage Books, 1967)

GM
: *Zur Genealogie der Moral* (1887); *On the Genealogy of Morals*, trans. Walter Kaufmann in *On the Genealogy of Morals and Ecce Homo* (New York: Vintage Books, 1967), trans. Maudemarie Clark and Alan J. Swensen (Indianapolis: Hackett, 1998)

GS           *Die fröhliche Wissenschaft* (1882); *The Gay Science*, in *Nietzsche's Werke: Kritische Gesamtausgabe*, ed. Giorgio Colli and Mazzino Montinari (Berlin: de Gruyter, 1972), Abt. 5, Bd. 2; trans. Walter Kaufmann (New York: Vintage, 1974), trans. J. Naukhoff (Cambridge: Cambridge University Press, 2001)

HH           *Menschliches, Allzumenschliches* (1878); *Human, All Too Human*, trans. Marion Faber and Stephen Lehman (Lincoln: University of Nebraska Press, 1984)

KS           *Sämtliche Werke: Kritische Studienausgabe* (1980), ed. Gorgio Colli and Mazzino Montinari (Berlin: de Gruyter; München: Deutscher Taschenbuch Verlag, 1999)

PN           *The Portable Nietzsche*, ed. Walter Kaufmann (New York: Penguin, 1976)

TI           *Götzendämmerung* (1888); *Twilight of the Idols Twilight of the Idols*, trans. R. J. Hollingdale in *Twilight of the Idols and The Anti-Christ* (Harmondsworth: Penguin, 1968)

UM           *Unzeitgemäße Betrachtungen* (1873–6); *Untimely Meditations*, trans. R. Hollingdale, ed. D. Breazeale (Cambridge: Cambridge University Press, 1997)

WP           *Der Wille Zur Macht* (1883–8); *The Will to Power*, trans. Walter Kaufmann and R. J. Hollingdale (New York: Vintage Books, 1968)

Z            *Also Sprach Zarathustra* (1883–5); *Thus Spoke Zarathustra*, trans. R. J. Hollingdale (New York: Penguin, 1961)

References (except for *KS* and *PN*) are to sections and sub-sections, not pages.

## Edmund Husserl (1859–1938)

CM           *Cartesianische Meditationen* (1929), ed. E. Ströker (Hamburg: Felix Meiner, 1995), trans. D. Cairns as *Cartesian Meditations* (The Hague: Martinus Nijhoff, 1977)

Crisis       *Die Krisis der europäischen Wissenschaften und die transzendentale Phänomenologie* (1936), in *Husserliana* 6, ed. W. Biemel (The Hague: Martinus Nijhoff, 1954), trans. D. Carr as *The Crisis of the European Sciences and Transcendental Phenomenology* (Evanston, IL: Northwestern University Press, 1970)

EJ           *Erfahrung und Urteil* (1939), ed. Ludwig Landgrebe (Hamburg: Felix Meiner, 1985), trans. J. S. Churchill and K. Ameriks as *Experience and Judgment* (Evanston: Northwestern University Press, 1973)

FTL          *Formale und transzendentale Logik: Versuch einer Kritik der logischen Vernunft* (1929), (Tübingen: Max Niemeyer 1981), trans. D. Cairns as *Formal and Transcendental Logic* (The Hague: Martinus Nijhoff, 1969)

| | |
|---|---|
| *HUA 2* | *Husserliana*, ii: *Die Idee der Phänomenologie: Fünf Vorlesungen* (1907), ed. W. Biemel (The Hague: Martinus Nijhoff, 1950, 1973), 14; trans. W. P. Alston and G. Nakhnikian as *The Idea of Phenomenology* (The Hague: Martinus Nijhoff, 1966, 1973) |
| *HUA 8* | *Husserliana*, viii: *Erste Philosophie, Zweiter Teil: Theorie der phänomenologischen Reduktion (1923–1924)*, trans. in *First Philosophy, Second Part: Theory of Phenomenological Reduction*, ed. R. Boehm (The Hague: Martinus Nijhoff, 1959) |
| *HUA 23* | *Husserliana*, xxiii: *Phantasie, Bildbewusstsein, Erinnerung: Zur Phänomenologie der anschaulichen Vergegenwärtigungen—Texte aus dem Nachlaß (1898–1925)*, ed. E. Marbach (The Hague: Martinus Nijhoff, 1980) |
| *HUA 24* | *Husserliana*, xxiv: *Einleitung in die Logik und Erkenntnistheorie, Vorlesungen (1906–7)*, ed. Ullrich Melle, (Dordrecht: Martinus Nijhoff, 1984) |
| *HUA 26* | *Husserliana*, xxvi: *Vorlesungen über Bedeutungslehre. Sommersemester 1908*, ed. Ursula Panzer (Dordrecht: Martinus Nijhoff, 1987) |
| *Id 1* | *Ideen zu einer reinen Phänomenologie und phänomenologischen Philosophie, Erstes Buch* (1913), in *Jahrbuch für Philosophie und phänomenologische Forschung* 1, 1–323; (Tübingen: Max Niemeyer, 1980, 1993); trans. Fred Kersten as *Ideas Pertaining to a Pure Phenomenology and to a Phenomenological Philosophy, First Book* (Dordrecht: Kluwer, 1982) |
| *Id 2* | *Ideen zu einer reinen Phänomenologie und phänomenologischen Philosophie, Zweites Buch*, ed. M. Biemel (The Hague: Martinus Nijhoff, 1952); trans. R. Rojcewicz and A. Schuwer as *Ideas Pertaining to a Pure Phenomenology and a Phenomenological Philosophy, Second Book* (Dordrecht: Kluwer, 1989) |
| *LI* | *Logische Untersuchungen, Erster Teil: Prolegomena Zur reinen Logik* (1900; Tübingen: Max Niemeyer, 1980); *Logische Untersuchungen, Zweiter Teil: Untersuchungen zur Phänomenologie und Theorie der Erkenntnis* (1901; Tübingen: Niemeyer, 1921, 1980); trans. J. N. Findlay as *Logical Investigations*, 2 vols. (London: Routledge, 1970, 2001) |
| *PA* | *Philosophie der Arithmetik* (1891), trans. Dallas Willard as (2003) *Philosophy of Arithmetic* (Dordrecht: Kluwer) |
| *PRS (PSW)* | 'Philosophie als Strenge Wissenschaft' (1910–11), *Logos* 1, 289–341; trans. Quentin Lauer as 'Philosophy as Rigorous Science', in *Husserl: Shorter Works*, ed. P. McCormick, P. and F. Elliston (Notre Dame: University of Notre Dame Press, 1981) |
| *SW (AV)* | *Aufsätze und Vorträge (1911–1921)*, ed. T. Nenon and H. R. Sepp (Dordrecht: Martinus Nijhoff, 1987); trans. Q. Lauer as *Husserl:* |

|        | Shorter Works, ed. P. McCormick and F. Elliston (Notre Dame: University of Notre Dame Press, 1981) |
|--------|---|
| Time   | Zur Phänomenologie des Inneren Zeitbewussteins (1893–1917), in Jahrbuch für Philosophie und phänomenologische Forschung 9 (1928), 367–498; ed. R. Boehm (The Hague: Martinus Nijhoff, 1966); ed. Martin Heidegger (Tübingen: Max Niemeyer, 1980); trans. J. B. Brough as On the Phenomenology of the Consciousness of Internal Time (1893–1917) (Dordrecht: Kluwer, 1990) |
| TS     | Ding und Raum, Vorlesungen (1907), ed. U. Claesges (The Hague: Martinus Nijhoff, 1973), ed. K-H. Hahnengress and S. Rapic (Hamburg: Felix Meiner, 1991); trans. R. Rojcewicz as Thing and Space, Lectures of 1907 (Dordrecht: Kluwer, 1997) |

## Martin Heidegger (1889–1976)

| BPP (GP)  | Grundprobleme der Phänomenologie (1927), Marburg Lectures, Summer 1927, Gesamtausgabe 24, ed. F-W. von Herrmann (Frankfurt: Klostermann, 1975); trans. A. Hofstadter as The Basic Problems of Phenomenology (Bloomington: Indiana University Press, 1982; rev. edn., 1988) |
|-----------|---|
| BT (SZ)   | Sein und Zeit (Halle/Saale: Niemeyer, 1927); trans. John Macquarrie and Edward Robinson as Being and Time (New York: Harper & Row, 1962; Oxford: Basil Blackwell, 1962, 1967, 1978) |
| BW        | Basic Writings, ed. David Farrell Krell (New York: Harper Collins, 1977) |
| D         | 'Memorial Address' (1955), Gelassenheit (1959); trans. J. M. Anderson and E. H. Freund as Discourse on Thinking (San Francisco: Harper Row, 1971) |
| GM        | Die Grundbegriffe der Metaphysik: Welt, Endlichkeit, Einsamkeit, Gesamtausgabe 29/30 (1929), ed. Otto Saame und Ina Saame-Speidel (Frankfurt: Klostermann, 1983); trans. W. McNeill and N. Walker as The Fundamental Concepts of Metaphysics: World, Finitude, Solitude (Bloomington: Indiana University Press, 1995) |
| HCT (GZ)  | Prolegomena zur Geschichte des Zeitbegriffs; trans. Theodore Kisiel as History of the Concept of Time (Bloomington: Indiana University Press, 1985) |
| KPM       | Kant und das Problem der Metaphysik (1929), Fünfte Erweiterte Ausgabe (Frankfurt am Main: Klostermann, 1991); trans. Richard Taft as Kant and the Problem of Metaphysics, 5th enlarged edn. (Bloomington: Indiana University Press, 1997) |
| OBT       | Holzwege (1950), 6th rev. edn. (Frankfurt: Klostermann, 1980); trans. J. Young and K. Haynes as Off the Beaten Track (Cambridge: Cambridge University Press, 2002) |

| | |
|---|---|
| OHF | *Ontologie: Hermeneutik der Faktizität* (1923), *Gesamtausgabe 63*, ed. K. Bröcker-Oltmanns (Frankfurt: Klostermann, 1988); trans. J. van Buren as *Ontology: The Hermeneutics of Facticity* (Bloomington: Indiana University Press, 1999) |
| P (W) | *Wegmarken, Gesamtausgabe 9 (1919–58)*, ed. F-W. von Herrmann (Frankfurt: Klostermann, 1976), 5; ed. W. McNeill as *Pathmarks* (Cambridge: Cambridge University Press, 1998) |
| PLT | *Poetry, Language, Thought*, trans. A. Hofstadter (New York: Harper & Row, 1971) |
| PRL | *Phänomenologie des religiösen Lebens* (1918–22), *Gesamtausgabe 60*, ed. M. Jung, T. Regehly, and C. Strube (Frankfurt: Klostermann, 1995); trans. M. Fritsch and J. A. Gosett-Ferencei as *The Phenomenology of Religious Life* (Bloomington: Indiana University Press, 2004) |
| QCT | *The Question Concerning Technology and Other Essays*, trans. W. Lovitt (New York: Harper & Row, 1971) |
| SD | *Zur Sache des Denkens* (Tübingen: Niemeyer, 1969) |

## Max Horkheimer (1895–1973)

| | |
|---|---|
| BPSS | *Between Philosophy and Social Science: Selected Early Writing* (1968), trans. G. F. Hunter, M. Kramer, and J. Torpey (Cambridge, MA: MIT Press, 1993) |
| CIR (KIV) | *Zur Kritik der instrumentalen Vernunft* (Frankfurt am Main: Fischer, 1967); trans. M. J. O'Connell et al. as *Critique of Instrumental Reason* (New York: Continuum, 1974) |
| CT (KT) | *Kritische Theorie*, i–ii (Frankfurt am Main: Fischer Verlag, 1968); trans. M. J. O'Connell et al. as *Critical Theory: Selected Writings of Max Horkheimer* (New York: Continuum, 1972) |
| ER | *The Eclipse of Reason* (New York: Continuum, 1947, 1974) |
| HGS | *Gesammelte Schriften*, ed. G. Schmid-Noerr and A. Schmidt (Frankfurt am Main: Fischer, 1987 ff) |
| SPS | *Sozialphilosophische Studien* (Frankfurt am Main: Athenäum Fischer Taschenbuchverlag, 1972) |

## Theodor W. Adorno (1903–1969)

| | |
|---|---|
| AE | *Against Epistemology: A Metacritique; Studies in Husserl and the Phenomenological Antinomies* (1956), trans. W. Domingo (Cambridge, MA: MIT Press, 1982) |
| AGS | *Gesammelte Schriften*, ed. R. Tiedemann (Frankfurt am Main: Suhrkamp, 1970 ff, 1997) |
| AT (ÄT) | *Ästhetische Theorie* (Frankfurt am Main: Suhrkamp, 1970); trans. and ed. by R. Hullot-Kentor as *Aesthetic Theory* (Minneapolis: |

|       | University of Minnesota Press, 1997; London: Athlone Press, 1997) |
|-------|-------------------------------------------------------------------|
| B     | *Beethoven: The Philosophy of Music: Fragments and Texts* (1970), trans. Edmund F. N. Jephcott, ed. Rolf Tiedemann (Cambridge: Polity, 1998) |
| CM    | *Critical Models: Interventions and Catchwords* (1963), trans. Henry W. Pickford (New York: Columbia University Press, 1998) |
| EM    | *Erziehung zur Mündigkeit* (Frankfurt am Main: Suhrkamp, 1971) |
| H     | *Hegel: Three Studies* (1963), trans. Shierry Weber Nicholsen (Cambridge, MA: MIT Press, 1993) |
| MCP   | *Metaphysics: Concept and Problems* (1965), trans. Edmund F. N. Jephcott, ed. R. Tiedemann (Stanford: Stanford University Press, 2000) |
| MM    | *Minima Moralia: Reflections from Damaged Life* (Frankfurt am Main: Suhrkamp, 1951), trans. Edmund F. N. Jephcott (London: New Left Books, 1974) |
| ND    | *Negative Dialektik* (Frankfurt am Main: Suhrkamp, 1966), trans. E. B. Ashton as *Negative Dialectics* (London: Routledge, 1973) |
| NS    | *Nachgelassene Schriften* (Frankfurt am Main: Suhrkamp, 1996) |
| P     | *Prisms* (1955), trans. Samuel and Shierry Weber (Cambridge, MA: MIT Press, 1981) |
| PMM   | *Philosophy of Modern Music* (1949), trans. Anne G. Mitchell and Wesley V. Blomster (New York: Continuum, 2003) |
| PMP   | *Problems of Moral Philosophy* (1963), trans. R. Livingstone, ed. T. Schröder (Stanford: Stanford University Press, 2000) |

With Max Horkheimer:

| DE (DA) | *Die Dialektik der Aufklärung* (1944/7; Frankfurt am Main: Fischer, 1969); trans. Edmund F. N. Jephcott as *Dialectic of Enlightenment: Philosophical Fragments*, ed. G. S. Noerr (Stanford: Stanford University Press, 2002) |

With Herbert Marcuse:

| CGSM | 'Correspondence on the German Student Movement' (1969), *New Left Review* 1/233 (1999), 123–36 |

## Jean-Paul Sartre (1905–1980)

| BEM | *Between Existentialism and Marxism* (1959), trans. John Mathews (New York: Morrow Quill, 1979) |
| BN  | *L'Être et le néant: essai d'ontologie phénoménologique* (Paris: Gallimard, 1943), trans. H. E. Barnes as *Being and Nothingness: An Essay of Phenomenological Ontology* (New York: Philosophical Library, 1956; London: Methuen, 1958) |

| | |
|---|---|
| CDR | *Critique de la raison dialectique, précédé de questions de methode*, i: *Théorie des ensembles pratiques* (Paris: Gallimard, 1960), repr. in new annotated edn., 1985; first essay trans. H. E. Barnes as *Search for a Method* (New York: Knopf, 1963); main text trans. A. Sheridan-Smith as *Critique of Dialectical Reason*, ed. J. Rée (London: New Left Books, 1976) |
| EH | *L'Existentialisme est un humanisme* (Paris: Nagel, 1946) |
| IPPI | *L'Imaginaire: psychologie phénoménologique de l'imagination* (Paris: Gallimard, 1940), trans. Jonathan Webber as (2004), *The Imaginary: A Phenomenological Psychology of the Imagination* (London: Routledge) |
| NE | *Cahiers pour une morale* (Paris: Gallimard, 1983), trans. David Pellauer as *Notebooks for an Ethics* (Chicago: University of Chicago Press, 1992) |
| STE | *Esquisse d'une théorie des émotions* (Paris: Hermann, 1939), trans. Philip Mairet as (1962), *Sketch for a Theory of the Emotions* (London: Methuen) |
| TE | *The Transcendence of the Ego* (1957), trans. and ed. Forrest Williams and Robert Kirkpatrick (New York: Octagon Books, 1972) |
| WL | *Qu'est ce que la littérature?, Situations 2* (Paris: Gallimard, 1948), trans. Bernard Frechtman as *What is Literature?* (London: Methuen, 1986) |

## Jürgen Habermas (1929–)

| | |
|---|---|
| AS | *Autonomy and Solidarity: Interviews with Jürgen Habermas*, ed. Peter Dews (London: Verso, 1992) |
| EzD | *Erläuterungen zur Diskursethik* (Frankfurt am Main: Suhrkamp, 1991) |
| FHN (ZMN) | *Die Zukunft der menschlichen Natur: Auf dem Weg zu einer liberalen Eugenik?* (Frankfurt am Main: Suhrkamp, 2001), trans. Hella Beister and Max Pensky as *The Future of Human* Nature (Cambridge: Polity, 2003) |
| FN (FG) | *Faktizität und Geltung: Beiträge Zur Diskurstheorie des Rechts und des demokratischen Rechtsstaats* (Frankfurt am Main: Suhrkamp, 1992); trans. William Rehg as *Between Facts and Norms: Contributions to a Discourse Theory of Law and Democracy* (Cambridge: Polity, 1996) |
| IO (EA) | *Die Einbeziehung des Anderen: Studien zur politischen Theorie* (Frankfurt am Main: Suhrkamp, 1996), trans. Ciaran Cronin as *The Inclusion of the Other* (Cambridge, MA: MIT Press, 1998) |
| IPCA | 'From Kant's "Ideas" of Pure Reason to the "Idealizing" Presuppositions of Communicative Action', in W. Rehg and |

|        | J. Bohman (eds.), *Pluralism and the Pragmatic Turn: The Transformation of Critical Theory* (Cambridge, MA: MIT Press, 2001), 11–39 (first published as Part I of *KHDV*) |
|--------|---|
| JA | *Justification and Application*, trans. Ciaran Cronin (Cambridge: Polity, 1993) |
| KHDV | *Kommunikatives Handeln und detranszendentalisierte Vernunft* (Stuttgart: Reclam Verlag, 2001) |
| KHI | *Knowledge and Human Interests*, trans. J. Shapiro (Boston: Beacon, 1971) |
| KHI (EI) | *Erkenntnis und Interesse* (Frankfurt am Main: Suhrkamp, 1968), trans. J. Shapiro as *Knowledge and Human Interests* (Boston: Beacon Press, 1971) |
| KPS | *Kleine politische Schriften I–IV* (Frankfurt am Main: Suhrkamp, 1981) |
| MC (MkH) | *Moralbewußtsein und kommunikatives Handeln* (Frankfurt am Main: Suhrkamp, 1983); trans. Christian Lenhardt and Shierry Weber Nicholsen as *Moral Consciousness and Communicative Action* (Cambridge, MA: MIT Press, 1990) |
| PDM | *Der philosophische Diskurs der Moderne: Zwölf Vorlesungen* (Frankfurt am Main: Suhrkamp, 1985), trans. Frederick G. Lawrence as *The Philosophical Discourse of Modernity* (Cambridge, MA: MIT Press, 1987) |
| PF (VZ) | *Vergangenheit als Zukunft* (Zurich: Pendo, 1991), trans. Max Pensky as *The Past as Future* (Cambridge: Polity, 1994) |
| PPP | *Philosophisch-politische Profile* (Frankfurt am Main: Suhrkamp, 1981); trans by F. Lawrence as *Philosophical-Political Profiles* (Cambridge, MA: MIT Press, 1983) |
| PT (NmD) | *Nachmetaphysisches Denken: Philosophische Aufsätze* (Frankfurt am Main: Suhrkamp, 1988); trans. William Mark Hohengarten as *Post-metaphysical Thinking* (Cambridge, MA: MIT Press, 1992) |
| RHM | *Zur Rekonstruktion des historischen Materialismus* (Frankfurt am Main: Suhrkamp, 1976) |
| STPS (SÖ) | *Strukturwandel der Öffentlichkeit: Untersuchungen zu einer Kategorie der bürgerlichen Gesellschaft* (Darmstadt und Neuwied: Luchterhand, 1962), trans. T. Bürger and F. Lawrence as *The Structural Transformation of the Public Sphere: An Inquiry into a Category of Bourgeois Society* (Cambridge, MA: MIT Press, 1989) |
| TCA | *Theorie des kommunikativen Handelns*, i–ii (Frankfurt am Main: Suhrkamp, 1981); trans. Thomas McCarthy as *The Theory of Communicative Action*, 2 vols. (Boston: Beacon Press, 1984–7) |
| TP | *Theorie und Praxis: Sozialphilosophische Studien* (Neuwied: Luchterhand, 1963), trans. J. Viertel as *Theory and Practice* (Cambridge: Polity, 1973) |

| VE | *Vorstudien und Ergänzungen zur Theorie des kommunikativen Handelns* (Frankfurt am Main: Suhrkamp, 1984) |
| WR | *Wahrheit und Rechtfertigung* (Frankfurt am Main: Suhrkamp, 1999) |

## Other Works Referenced

ADAIR-TOTEFF, CHRISTOPHER (1994), 'The Neo-Kantian *Raum* Controversy', *British Journal of the History of Philosophy* 2/2, 131–48.

ADAMS, HENRY E., WRIGHT JR., LESTER W., and LOHR, BETHANY A. (1996), 'Is Homophobia Associated with Homosexual Arousal?', *Journal of Abnormal Psychology* 105, 440–5.

AERTSEN, JAN A. (1991), 'The Medieval Doctrine of the Transcendentals: The Current State of Research', *Bulletin de Philosophie Médiévale* 33, 130–47.

—— (1996), *Medieval Philosophy and the Transcendentals: The Case of Thomas Aquinas* (Leiden: Brill).

—— (1998), 'Transzendental, II', in Ritter, Joachim and Gründer, Karlfried (eds.), *Historisches Wörterbuch der Philosophie* (Darmstadt: Wissenschaftliche Buchgesellschaft), x. 1360–5.

AGAMBEN, GIORGIO (1998), *Homo Sacer: Sovereign Power and Bare Life*, trans. Daniel Heller-Roazen (Stanford: Stanford University Press).

—— (2005), *State of Exception*, trans. Kevin Attell (Chicago: University of Chicago Press).

ALEXANDER, H. G. (ed.) (1956), *The Leibniz–Clarke Correspondence* (Manchester: Manchester University Press).

ALLISON, HENRY (1983), *Kant's Transcendental Idealism* (New Haven: Yale University Press).

—— (1990), *Kant's Theory of Freedom* (New York: Cambridge University Press).

ALTERMAN, ERIC (2003), *What Liberal Media?* (New York: Basic Books).

ALTHUSSER, LOUIS (1993), *The Future Lasts a Long Time*, trans. Richard Veasey (London: Chatto & Windus).

—— (1995), *Sur la reproduction* (Paris: Presses Universitaires de France).

—— (1997), *The Spectre of Hegel: Early Writings*, (ed.) F. Matheron and G. M. Goshgarian (London: Verso).

—— (2003), *The Humanist Controversy and Other Texts*, trans. G. M. Goshgarian, ed. F. Matheron (London: Verso).

ANDERSON, JOEL AND HONNETH, AXEL (2005), 'Autonomy, Vulnerability, Recognition and Justice', in Christman and Anderson, eds. (2005), pp. 127–49.

ANDERSON, PERRY (1980), *Arguments within Western Marxism* (London: Verso).

—— (2005), *Spectrum: From Right to Left in the World of Ideas* (London: Verso).

ANSCOMBE, G. E. M. (1958), 'Modern Moral Philosophy', *Philosophy* 33, 1–19.

ANSELM, ST (1965), *Proslogion*, trans. M. J. Charlesworth (Oxford: Clarendon Press).

ARATO, ANDREW and BREINES, PAUL (1979), *The Young Lukács and the Origins of Western Marxism* (London: Pluto).

ARENDT, HANNAH (1958), *The Human Condition* (Chicago: Chicago University Press).

ARTHUR, CHRISTOPHER J. (2002), *The New Dialectic and Marx's Capital* (Leiden: Brill)

AUSTIN, J. L. (1955), *How to Do Things with Words* (Cambridge, MA: Harvard University Press).

BACHELARD, GASTON (1929), *La Valeur inductive de la relativité* (Paris: Vrin).

—— (1949), *Le Rationalisme appliqué* (Paris: Presses Universitaires de France).

—— (1951), *L'activité rationaliste de la physique contemporaine* (Paris: Presses Universitaires de France).

—— (1969), *The Psychoanalysis of Fire*, trans. G. C. Waterston (New York: Orion).

—— (1984), *The New Scientific Spirit*, trans. A Goldhammer (Boston: Beacon Press)

BACKHAUS, HANS-GEORG (2005), 'Some Aspects of Marx's Concept of Critique in the Context of his Economic-Philosophical Theory', in Bonefeld, Werner, and Psychopedis, Kosmas, (eds.) (2005), *Human Dignity: Social Autonomy and the Critique of Capitalism* (Aldershot: Ashgate), 13–30.

BADIOU, ALAIN (1988), *L'Etre et l'événement* (Paris: Seuil).

—— (1997), *Saint Paul, La Fondation de l'universalisme* (Paris: Presses Universitaires de France).

—— (1998), *D'un desastre obscur* (Paris: Editions de l'Aube).

—— (2000), *Deleuze: The Clamor of Being*, trans. Louise Burchill (Minneapolis: University of Minnesota Press).

—— (2001), *Ethics: An Essay on the Understanding of Evil* (London: Verso).

—— (2004), *Theoretical Writings*, trans. and ed. R. Brassier and A. Toscano (London: Continuum).

BAGDIKIAN, BEN (1997), *The Media Monopoly*, 5th edn. (Boston: Beacon Press).

BAIER, KURT (1965), *The Moral Point of View* (New York, Random House).

BALAKRISHNAN, GOPAL, (ed.) (2003), *Debating Empire* (London: Verso).

BALDWIN, T. (1988), 'Phenomenology, Solipsism and Egocentric Thought', *Proceedings of the Aristotelian Society*, Supp. vol. 62, 27–44.

BALIBAR, ÉTIENNE (1991), *Ecrits pour Althusser* (Paris: La Découverte).

BAMBACH, CHARLES (1995), *Heidegger, Dilthey, and the Crisis of Historicism* (Ithaca: Cornell University Press).

BARCLAY, LINDA (2000), 'Autonomy and the Social Self', in Mackenzie and Stoljar, (eds.) (2000: 52–71).

BARRY, BRIAN (2005), *Why Social Justice Matters* (Cambridge: Polity).

BAUGH, BRUCE (2003), *French Hegel: From Surrealism to Postmodernism* (New York and London: Routledge).

BEISER, FREDERICK C. (1987), *The Fate of Reason: German Philosophy from Kant to Fichte* (Cambridge, MA: Harvard University Press).

—— (2002), *German Idealism: The Struggle against Subjectivism, 1781–1801* (Cambridge, MA: Harvard University Press)

—— (2003), *The Romantic Imperative: The Concept of Early German Romanticism* (Cambridge, MA: Harvard University Press).

—— (2005), *Schiller as Philosopher: A Re-examination* (Oxford: Clarendon Press).

BELL, DAVID (1990), *Husserl* (London: Routledge).

BENHABIB, SEYLA (1986), *Critique, Norm, Utopia: A Study of the Foundations of Critical Theory* (New York: Columbia University Press).

BENNETT, JONATHAN (1974), *Kant's Dialectic* (Cambridge: Cambridge University Press).

BENNETT, MAX R. and HACKER, P. M. S. (2003), *Philosophical Foundations of Neuroscience* (Oxford: Blackwell).

BENSAïD, DANIEL (1995), *La Discordance Des Temps* (Paris: Editions de la Passion).

—— (2001), *Resistances* (Paris: Fayard).

—— (2002), *Marx for Our Times*, trans. Gregory Elliott (London: Verso).

—— (2003), *Un monde á changer* (Paris: Textuel).

BENSON, PAUL (2000), 'Feeling Crazy: Self-Worth and the Social Character of Responsibility', in Mackenzie and Stoljar, (eds.), pp. 72–93.

—— (2005), 'Taking Ownership: Authority and Voice in Autonomous Agency', in Christman and Anderson (eds.) pp. 101–26.

BERGSON, HENRI (1934), *La Pensée et le mouvant* (Paris: Libraire Félix Alcan).

—— (1944), *Creative Evolution*, trans. Arthur Mitchell (New York: Modern Library).

—— (1946), *The Creative Mind: An Introduction to Metaphysics*, trans. Mabelle L. Andison (New York: Philosophical Library).

—— (1988), *Matter and Memory*, trans. N. M. Paul and W. S. Winter (New York: Zone Books).

BERLIN, ISAIAH (1969), *Four Essays on Liberty* (New York: Oxford University Press).

BERMÚDEZ, JOSÉ L. (1994), 'Peacocke's Argument against the Autonomy of Nonconceptual Representational Content', *Mind and Language* 9, 402–18.

BERMÚDEZ, J. L., Marcel, Anthony and Eilan, Naomi (eds.) (1995), *The Body and the Self* (Cambridge, MA: MIT Press).

—— (1995), 'Nonconceptual Content: From Perceptual Experience to Subpersonal Computational States', *Mind and Language* 10, 333–67.

BERNSTEIN, JAY M. (1992), *The Fate of Art: Aesthetic Alienation from Kant to Derrida and Adorno* (Cambridge: Polity).

—— (1995), *Recovering Ethical Life: Jürgen Habermas and the Future of Critical Theory* (London: Routledge).

—— (2001), *Adorno: Disenchantment and Ethics* (Cambridge, Cambridge University Press).

BERRY, JESSICA N. (2004), 'The Pyrrhonian Revival in Montaigne and Nietzsche', *The Journal of the History of Ideas* 65/3 (July), 497–514.

BHASKAR, ROY (1978), *A Realist Theory of Science*, 2nd edn. (Hassocks: Harvester).

—— (1979), *The Possibility of Naturalism* (Brighton: Harvester).

BIDET, JACQUES (1999), *Théorie générale* (Paris: Presses Universitaires de France).

—— (2000), *Que faire du 'Capital'?*, 2nd edn. (Paris: Presses Universitaires de France).

BIEMEL, WALTER (1968), 'Der Briefwechsel Dilthey–Husserl', *Man and World* 1, 428–46.

BISCH-REICHENWALD AARS, KRISTIAN (1900), *Zur psychologischen Analyse der Welt* (Leipzig: Johann Ambrosius Barth).

BLATTNER, WILLIAM (1999), *Heidegger's Temporal Idealism* (Cambridge: Cambridge University Press).

BLOCK, NED (1995), 'On a Confusion about a Function of Consciousness', *Behavioral and Brain Sciences* 18, 227–47.

BLUMENBERG, HANS (1957), 'Das Licht als Metapher der Wahrheit', *Studium Generale* 10, 432–54.

—— (1966), *Die Legitimität der Neuzeit* (Frankfurt am Main: Suhrkamp), trans. Robert M. Wallace as *The Legitimacy of the Modern Age* (Cambridge, MA: MIT Press, 1985).

BOURDIEU, PIERRE (1996), *The Rules of Art*, trans. Susan Emanuel (Cambridge: Polity).

—— (2000), *Pascalian Meditations*, trans. Richard Nice (Cambridge: Polity).

—— (2001), *Science de la science et réflexivité* (Paris: Raisons D'Agir).

BOTTOMORE, TOM and GOODE, PATRICK (eds.) (1978), *Austro-Marxism* (Oxford: Clarendon Press).

BOWIE, ANDREW (1990a), *Aesthetics and Subjectivity: From Kant to Nietzsche* (Manchester: Manchester University Press).

—— (1990b), *Romanticism and Critical Theory: The Philosophy of German Literary Theory* (Manchester: Manchester University Press).

BOYD, RICHARD; GASPER, PHILIP, and TROUT, J. D. (eds.) 1991), *The Philosophy of Science* (Cambridge, MA: MIT Press).

BRANDOM, ROBERT B. (2002), *Tales of the Mighty Dead* (Cambridge, MA: Harvard University Press).

BRANISS, CHRISTIAN JOHANN (1848), *Die wissenschaftliche Aufgabe der Gegenwart als leitende Idee im akademischen Studium* (Breslau: Gosohorsky).

BRECKMAN, WARREN (1999), *Marx, the Young Hegelians, and the Origins of Radical Social Theory* (Cambridge: Cambridge University Press).

BREWER, BILL (1999), *Perception and Reason* (Oxford: Clarendon Press).

BRUNNER, OTTO, CONZE, WERNER, and KOSELLECK, REINHART (eds.) (1982), *Geschichtliche Grundbegriffe: Historische Lexikon zur politisch-sozialen Sprache in Deutschland* (Stuttgart: Klett-Cotta).

BUBNER, RÜDIGER (1989), *Ästhetische Erfahrung* (Frankfurt am Main: Suhrkamp).

BUCHWALTER, ANDREW (1987), 'Hegel, Adorno and the Concept of Transcendent Critique', *Philosophy and Social Criticism* 12, 297–328.

BUCK-MORSS, SUSAN (1977), *The Origin of Negative Dialectics: Theodor W. Adorno, Walter Benjamin, and the Frankfurt Institute* (New York: Free Press).

BUGENTHAL, DAPHNE B. (1986), 'Unmasking the "Polite Smile": Situational and Personal Determinants of Managed Affect in Adult-Child Interaction', *Personality and Social Psychology Bulletin* 12, 7–16.

BÜRGER, PETER (1983), *Zur Kritik der idealistischen Ästhetik* (Frankfurt am Main: Suhrkamp).

BUTLER, ELIZA M. (1958), *The Tyranny of Greece Over Germany*, 2nd edn. (Boston: Beacon Press).

CAHN, MICHAEL (1984), 'Subversive Mimesis', in Mihai Spariosu (ed.), *Mimesis in Contemporary Theory* (Philadelphia: John Benjamins' Publishing Company).

CALLINICOS, ALEX (1976), *Althusser's Marxism* (London: Pluto).

—— (1989a), *Against Postmodernism: A Marxist Critique* (Cambridge: Polity).

—— ed. (1989b), *Marxist Theory* (Oxford: Oxford University Press).

—— (1995), *Theories and Narratives* (Cambridge: Polity).

—— (1999), 'Social Theory Put to the Test of Practice: Pierre Bourdieu and Anthony Giddens', *New Left Review* 1/236, 287–95.

—— (2000), *Equality* (Cambridge: Polity).

—— (2001), 'Having Your Cake and Eating It', *Historical Materialism* 9, 169–95.

—— (2003a), 'Marxism and Anarchism', in T. Baldwin (ed.), *The Cambridge History of Philosophy, 1870–1945* (Cambridge: Cambridge University Press), 297–308.

—— (2003b), 'Western Marxism and Ideology Critique', in T. Baldwin (ed.), *The Cambridge History of Philosophy, 1870–1945* (Cambridge: Cambridge University Press), 685–91.

—— (2004), *Making History*, 2nd edn. (Leiden: Brill).

—— (2005), 'Against the New Dialectic', *Historical Materialism* 13/2, 41–59.

—— (2006), *The Resources of Critique* (Cambridge: Polity).

CAMPBELL, JOHN (1997), 'Sense, Reference and Selective Attention', *Proceedings of the Aristotelian Society*, Supp. vol. 71, 55–74.

—— (1998), 'Joint Attention and the First Person', in Anthony O'Hear (ed.), *Current Issues in Philosophy of Mind* (Cambridge: Cambridge University Press).

—— (2002), *Reference and Consciousness* (Oxford: Clarendon Press).

CAMUS, ALBERT (1942), *Le Mythe de Sisyphe*, trans. J. O'Brian as *The Myth of Sisyphus* (Harmondsworth: Penguin, 1975).

CANGUILHEM, GEORGES (1977a), *Idéologie et Rationalité* (Paris: Vrin).

—— (1977b), *La Formation du concept de reflex au XVIIe et XVIII siècle*, 2nd edn. (Paris: Vrin).

—— (1978), *On the Normal and the Pathological*, trans. C. R. Fawcett (Dordrecht: Reidel).

—— (1983), *Etudes d'histoire et de philosophie des sciences*, 5th edn. (Paris: Vrin).

CARMAN, TAYLOR (2003), *Heidegger's Analytic: Interpretation, Discourse, and Authenticity in 'Being and Time'* (Cambridge: Cambridge University Press).

CARNAP, RUDOLF (1952), 'Empiricism, Semantics, and Ontology', in Linsky, ed. (1952), 208–28.

—— (1956), *Meaning and Necessity*, 2nd edn. (Chicago: University of Chicago Press).

CARR, DAVID (1973–4), 'The "Fifth Meditation" and Husserl's Cartesianism', *Philosophy and Phenomenological Research* 34, 14–15.

CASSIRER, ERNST (1932), *Die Philosophie der Aufklärung* (Tübingen: Mohr).

—— (1970), *Rousseau, Kant and Goethe* (Princeton: Princeton University Press).

CHAMBERS, SIMONE (1996), *Reasonable Democracy: Jürgen Habermas and the Politics of Discourse* (Ithaca: Cornell University Press).

—— (2004), 'The Politics of Critical Theory', in Rush, (ed.) (2004a), 219–47.

CHENEY, DOROTHY L. and SEYFARTH, ROBERT M. (1990), *How Monkeys See the World* (Chicago: University of Chicago Press).

CHOMSKY, NOAM (1989), *Necessary Illusions: Thought Control in Democratic Societies* (Boston: South End Press).

CHRISTMAN, JOHN (ed.) (1989), *The Inner Citadel: Essays on Individual Autonomy* (New York: Oxford University Press).

—— (2004), 'Relational Autonomy, Liberal Individualism, and the Social Constitution of Selves', *Philosophical Studies* 117, 143–64.

CHRISTMAN, JOHN and JOEL ANDERSON (eds.) (2005), *Autonomy and the Challenge of Liberalism* (New York: Cambridge University Press).

CLAESGES, ULRICH (1964), *Edmund Husserls Theorie der Raumkonstitution* (The Hague: Martinus Nijhoff).

CLARK, PETER and WRIGHT, CRISPIN (eds.) (1988), *Mind, Psychoanalysis and Science* (Oxford: Blackwell).

CLIMACUS, JOHANNES (1992), *Concluding Unscientific Postscript*, trans. H. V. Hong and E. H. Hong (Princeton: Princeton University Press).

COHEN, GERALD A. (1995), *Self-Ownership, Freedom, and Equality* (Cambridge: Cambridge University Press).

—— (2000a), *If You're an Egalitarian, How Come You're So Rich?* (Cambridge, MA: Harvard University Press).

—— (2000b), *Karl Marx's Theory of History*, 2nd edn. (Oxford: Oxford University Press).

COHEN, HERMANN (1883), *Das Prinzip der Infinitesimalmethode und seine Geschichte. Einleitung mit kritischem Nachtrag zu F. A. Langes 'Geschichte des Materialismus'. Dritte Auslage* (1914), in *Hermann Cohen, Werke*, ed. Helmut Holzhey (Hildesheim: Olms, 1984), 5.

—— (1918), *Kants Theorie der Erfahrung*, 3rd edn., in *Hermann Cohen, Werke*, ed. Helmut Holzhey (Hildesheim: Olms, 1984), 1.1–2.

COHEN, JOSHUA (1986), 'Reflection on Rousseau: Autonomy and Democracy', *Philosophy and Public Affairs* 15, 275–97.

—— (1997), 'The Natural Goodness of Humanity', in Reath, Herman, and Korsgaard, eds. (1997), 102–39.

COLLIER, ANDREW (1994), *Critical Realism: An Introduction to the Philosophy of Roy Bhaskar* (London: Verso).

CRAIG, EDWARD (1986), *The Mind of God and the Works of Man* (Oxford: Oxford University Press).

CROWTHER, PAUL (1993), *Art and Embodiment: From Aesthetics to Self-Consciousness* (Oxford: Clarendon Press).

DANTO, ARTHUR C. and MORGENBESSER, SIDNEY EDS. (1960), *Philosophy of Science* (Cleveland and New York: Meridian Books).

DARJES, JOACHIM GEORG (1747), *Introductio in artem inueniendi, seu logicam theoretico-practicam, qua analytica atque dialectica in usum auditorum suorum methodo iis commoda proponuntur* (Jena).

DAVIDSON, DONALD (1984), 'On the Very Idea of a Conceptual Scheme', in his *Inquiries into Truth and Interpretation* (Oxford: Oxford University Press, 1984).

DE GAYNESFORD, MAXIMILIAN (1996), 'Humanism, Reflective Capacities, and Prejudice', in Mozaffar Qizilbash (ed.), *Impurity, Authenticity and Humanity* (Oxford: Arthur Rowe Ltd.), 109–16.

—— (1997), 'Critical Notice', *Ratio* 10, 91–6.

—— (2001), 'Bodily Organs and Organisation', in M. Bryden (ed.), *Deleuze and Religion* (London: Routledge), 87–98.

—— (2003), 'Kant and Strawson on the First Person', in Hans-Johann Glock (ed.), *Strawson and Kant* (Oxford: Oxford University Press), 155–67.

—— (2004), 'On Referring to Oneself', *Theoria* 70, 121–61.

DEIGH, JOHN (1996), *The Sources of Moral Agency* (Cambridge: Cambridge University Press).

DELEUZE, GILLES (1956), 'La Conception de la différence chez Bergson', *Les Etudes Bergsoniennes*, iv. 77–112; trans. Melissa McMahon as 'Bergson's Conception of Difference', in Mullarkey, John (ed.) (1999), *The New Bergson* (Manchester: Manchester University Press), 42–65.

—— (1968), *Spinoza et le Problème de l'expression* (Paris: Minuit).

—— (1983), *Nietzsche and Philosophy*, trans. H. Tomlinson (New York: Columbia University Press).

—— (1994), *Difference and Repetition*, trans. Paul Patton (London: Athlone Press).

DELEUZE, GILLES and GUATTARI, FÉLIX (1988), *A Thousand Plateaus: Capitalism and Schizophrenia*, trans. Brian Massumi (London: Athlone Press).

DELIGIORGI, KATERINA (2005), *Kant and the Culture of Enlightenment* (Albany: SUNY Press).

DENT, NICHOLAS (2005), *Rousseau* (London: Routledge).

DE PALMA, VITTORIO (2005), 'Ist Husserls Phänomenologie ein transzendentaler Idealismus?', *Husserl-Studien* 21, 183–206.

DERRIDA, JACQUES (1967a), *De la grammatologie*, trans. Gayatri Chakrovorty Spivak as *Of Grammatology* (Baltimore and London: Johns Hopkins University Press, 1976).

—— (1967b), *L'écriture et la différence*, trans. Alan Bass as *Writing and Difference* (Chicago: University of Chicago Press, 1978).

—— (1982), *Du droit á la philosophie*, trans. Alan Bass as *Margins of Philosophy* (Chicago: University of Chicago Press, 1982).

—— (1994), *Politiques de L'amitié*, trans. George Collins as *Politics of Friendship* (London: Verso, (1997).

DESCARTES, RENÉ (1632), *Le Monde*, trans. M. S. Mahoney as *The World* (New York: Abaris Books, (1980).

—— (1637), *Discours de la méthode pour bien conduir sa raison et chercher la vérité dans les sciences plus la Dioptrique, les Meteores, et la Geometrie, qui sont des essais de cette methode; Discourse on the Method for Properly Conducting Reason and Searching for Truth in the Sciences, as well as the Dioptrics, the Meteors, and the Geometry, which are Essays in this Method*, in *The Philosophical Writings of Descartes*, ed. and trans. J. Cottingham, R. Stoothoff, D. Murdoch, and A. Kenny (Cambridge: Cambridge University Press, 1984–91), vol. i.

—— (1641), *Meditationes de prima philosophia; Meditations on First Philosophy* in *The Philosophical Writings of Descartes*, ed. and trans. J. Cottingham, R. Stoothoff, D. Murdoch, and A. Kenny (Cambridge: Cambridge University Press, 1984–91), vol. ii.

—— (1644), *Principia philosophiae; Principles of Philosophy*, trans. V. R. Miller and R. P. Miller (Dordrecht: D. Reidel, 1983).

DEWEY, JOHN (1934), *Art as Experience* (New York: Minton, Balch & Co.).

DEWS, PETER (ed.) (1992), *Autonomy and Solidarity: Interviews with Jürgen Habermas* (London, Verso).

DILTHEY, WILHELM (1957), *Philosophy of Existence* (New York: Bookman Associates).

—— (1966), *Gesammelte Schriften*, ed. Bernhard Groethuysen (Göttingen: Vandenhoeck & Ruprecht).

—— (1979), *Selected Writings*, (ed.) H. P. Rickman (Cambridge: Cambridge University Press).

—— (1989), *Introduction to the Human Sciences* (Princeton: Princeton University Press).

—— (1996), *Hermeneutics and the Study of History* (Princeton: Princeton University Press).

—— (2002), *The Formation of the Historical World in the Human Sciences. Selected Works*, iii, (ed.) R. Makkreel and F. Rodi (Princeton: Princeton University Press).

DOSTAL, ROBERT J. (ed.) (2002), *The Cambridge Companion to Gadamer* (Cambridge: Cambridge University Press).

DREYFUS, HUBERT (1991), *Being-in-the-World: A Commentary on Heidegger's* Being and Time (Cambridge, MA: MIT Press).

DROYSEN, JOHANN GUSTAV (1937), *Historik: Vorlesungen über Enzyklopädie und Methodologie der Geschichte*, ed. Rudolf Hübner (Munich: Oldenbourg).

DRUMMOND, JOHN J. (1979–80), 'On Seeing a Material Thing in Space', *Philosophy and Phenomenological Research* 40, 19–32.

—— (1990), *Husserlian Intentionality and Non-foundational Realism: Noema and Object* (Dordrecht: Kluwer).

DUBIEL, HELMUT (1985), *Theory and Politics: Studies in the Development of Critical Theory*, trans. B. Gregg (Cambridge, MA: MIT Press).

DUMMETT, MICHAEL A. E. (1991), *Frege and Other Philosophers* (Oxford: Clarendon Press).

—— (1993), *Origins of Analytical Philosophy* (London: Duckworth).

DUMÉNIL, G. (1978), *Le Concept de loi économique dans 'Le Capital'* (Paris: Maspero).

DURKHEIM, ÉMILE (2003), *Les Formes élémentaires de la vie religieuse*, 5th edn. (Paris: Presses Universitaires de France).

DÜSING, KLAUS (1969), 'Spekulation und Reflexion: Zur Zusammenarbeit Schellings und Hegels in Jena', *Hegel-Studien* 5, 95–128.

DUSSEL, ENRIQUE (2001), *Towards an Unknown Marx*, trans. Yolanda Angulo, (ed.) Fred Moseley (London: Routledge).

EAGLETON, TERRY (1990), *The Ideology of the Aesthetic* (Oxford: Blackwell).

—— (1997), *Marx and Freedom* (London: Phoenix).

—— (2002), *Sweet Violence* (Oxford: Blackwell).

—— (2003), *After Theory* (London: Allen Lane).

EILAN, NAOMI (1998), 'Perceptual Intentionality: Attention and Consciousness', in O'Hear, Anthony (ed.) (1998), *Current Issues in Philosophy of Mind* (Cambridge: Cambridge University Press).

EKMAN, PAUL, HAGER, J. C., and FRIESEN, WALLACE V. (1981), 'The Symmetry of Emotional and Deliberate Facial Actions', *Psychophysiology* 18, 101–6.

EKMAN, PAUL and FRIESEN, WALLACE V. (1982), 'Felt, False and Miserable Smiles', *Journal of Nonverbal Behavior* 6, 238–52.

ELDRIDGE, RICHARD (1997), *Leading a Human Life: Wittgenstein, Intentionality, and Romanticism* (Chicago: University of Chicago Press).

—— (2001), *The Persistence of Romanticism: Essays in Philosophy and Literature* (Cambridge: Cambridge University Press).

ELLIOTT, GREGORY (1987), *Althusser: The Detour of Theory* (London: Verso).

—— (ed.) (1994), *Althusser: A Critical Reader* (Oxford: Blackwell).

ELSTER, JON (1985), *Making Sense of Marx* (Cambridge: Cambridge University Press).

ENGELS, FRIEDRICH (1886), 'Ludwig Feuerbach und der Ausgang der klassischen deutschen Philosophie', *Die Neue Zeit*, Vierter Jahrgang, Nr. 4–5; trans. as *Ludwig Feuerbach and the End of Classical German Philosophy*, in Karl Marx and Friedrich Engels (1949), *Selected Works*, iii (Moscow: Progress, 1970), 326–64.

ENGSTROM, STEPHEN (1988), 'Conditioned Autonomy', *Philosophy and Phenomenological Research* 58, 435–53.

—— (1992), 'The Concept of the Highest Good in Kant's Moral Philosophy', *Philosophy and Phenomenological Research* 52, 747–80.

ERDMANN, JOHANN EDUARD (1866), *Die deutsche Philosophie seit Hegels Tod*, trans. Williston S. Hough, *History of Philosophy*, iii (London: Swan Sonnenschein, 1890).

ERMATH, MICHAEL (1978), *Wilhelm Dilthey: The Critique of Historical Reason* (Chicago: University of Chicago Press).

ERNESTI, JOHANN AUGUST (1761), *Institutio Interpretis Novi Testamenti*, trans. C. H. Terrot as *Principles of Biblical Interpretation*, 2 vols. (Edinburgh: Thomas Clark, 1832–3).

EVANS, GARETH (1982), *The Varieties of Reference* (Oxford: Clarendon Press).

—— (1985), *Collected Papers*, (ed.) A. Phillips (Oxford: Oxford University Press).

FEUERBACH, LUDWIG (1839–46), 'Zur Kritik der Hegelschen Philosophie', in *Gesammelte Werke, Kleinere Schriften II (1839–1846)*, 43–5, (ed.), Werner Schuffenhauer, trans. Zawar Hanfi as *The Fiery Brook: Selected Writings of Ludwig Feuerbach*

(Garden City: Doubleday, 1972), 77–9; reprinted in Robert Stern (ed.), *G. W. F. Hegel: Critical Assessments*, 4 vols. (London: Routledge, 1993), i. 117–18.

FINE, ARTHUR and FORBES, MICKEY (1986), 'Grünbaum on Freud: Three Grounds for Dissent', *Behavioral and Brain Sciences* 9, 237–8.

FINLAYSON, JAMES GORDON, (1999), 'Habermas' Discourse Ethics and Hegel's Critique of Kant's Moral Theory', in P. Dews (ed.), *Habermas: A Critical Reader* (Oxford, Blackwell), 29–52.

—— (2002), 'Adorno on the Ethical and the Ineffable', *European Journal of Philosophy* 10/1, 1–25.

—— (2005), *Habermas: A Very Short Introduction* (Oxford: Oxford University Press).

FISCHER, KUNO (1865), *System der Logik und der Metaphysik oder Wissenschaftslehre*, 2nd edn. (Heidelberg: Basserman; Frankfurt am Main: Minerva, 1983).

FØLLESDAL, DAGFINN (1969), 'Husserl's Notion of the Noema', *Journal of Philosophy* 66, 680–7.

FORST, RAINER (1999), 'Justice, Reason and Critique: Basic Concepts of Critical Theory', in David M. Rasmussen (ed.), *Handbook of Critical Theory* (Oxford: Blackwell), 143–7.

—— (2005), 'Political Liberty: Integrating Five Conceptions of Autonomy', in Christman and Anderson (2005), pp. 226–41.

FORSTER, MICHAEL N. (1989), *Hegel and Skepticism* (Cambridge, MA: Harvard University Press).

—— (ed.) (2002a), *Herder: Philosophical Writings* (Cambridge: Cambridge University Press).

—— (2002b), 'Herder's Philosophy of Language, Interpretation, and Translation: Three Fundamental Principles', *The Review Metaphysics* 56, 323 ff.

—— (2002c), 'Friedrich Daniel Ernst Schleiermacher', in Edward N. Zalta (ed.), *The Stanford Encyclopedia of Philosophy (Winter 2002 Edition)*, online at<http://plato.stanford.edu/archives/win2002/entries/schleiermacher/>

—— (2003a), 'Gods, Animals, and Artists: Some Problem Cases in Herder's Philosophy of Language', *Inquiry* 46, 65–96.

—— (2003b), 'Hegel and Some (Near) Contemporaries: Narrow or Broad Expressivism?', in W. Welsch and K. Vieweg (eds.), *Das Interesse des Denkens: Hegel aus heutiger Sicht* (Munich: Wilhelm Fink).

—— (2004), *Wittgenstein on the Arbitrariness of Grammar* (Princeton: Princeton University Press).

—— (2005), 'Schleiermacher's Hermeneutics: Some Problems and Solutions', *The Harvard Review of Philosophy* 13/1.

—— (forthcoming a), 'Hegel and Hermeneutics', in F. Beiser (ed.), *The Cambridge Companion to Hegel*, 2nd edn. (Cambridge: Cambridge University Press).

—— (forthcoming b), 'A Wittgensteinian Anti-Platonism'

FOUCAULT, MICHEL (1965), *Madness and Civilisation*, trans. R. Howard (New York: Pantheon).

—— (1970), *The Order of Things* (London: Tavistock Publications).

—— (1971), 'Foucault Responds 2', *Diacritics* 1/2 (Winter 1971), 60.

—— (1975), *Discipline and Punish*, trans. Alan Sheridan (Harmondsworth: Penguin)

—— (1980a), *The History of Sexuality*, i: *An Introduction*, trans. Robert Hurley (New York: Vintage Books).

—— (1980b), *Power/Knowledge*, (ed.) Colin Gordon (New York: Pantheon).

—— (1984), *The Foucault Reader*, (ed.) Paul Rabinow (New York: Pantheon).

—— (1988a), *The Uses of Pleasure: The History of Sexuality*, ii, trans. R. Hurley (New York: Pantheon).

—— (1988b), *The Care of the Self: The History of Sexuality*, iii, trans. R. Hurley (New York: Pantheon).

—— (1998), *The Essential Works of Michel Foucault, 1954–1984*, ii: *Aesthetics, Method, and Epistemology*, (ed.) Paul Rabinow (Harmondsworth: Penguin).

FRANK, MANFRED (1985), *Das individuelle Allgemeine* (Frankfurt am Main: Suhrkamp).

—— (1997), *'Unendliche Annäherung': Die Anfänge der philosophischen Frühromantik* (Frankfurt am Main: Suhrkamp), trans. Elizabeth Millán-Zaibert as *The Philosophical Foundations of Early German Romanticism* (Albany: SUNY Press, 2004).

FRANKS, PAUL W. (1999), 'Transcendental Arguments, Reason and Scepticism: Contemporary Debates and the Origins of Post-Kantianism', in Stern, (ed.) (1999), 111–45.

—— (2005), *All or Nothing: Systematicity, Transcendental Arguments, and Skepticism in German Idealism* (Cambridge, MA: Harvard University Press).

FREGE, GOTTLOB (1894), 'Rezension von E. G. Husserl, *Philosophie der Arithmetik*. I', *Zeitschrift für Philosophie und philosophische Kritik* 103, 313–32.

—— (1956), 'The Thought', *Mind* 65, 289–311.

FREUD, SIGMUND (1900), *Die Traumdeutung*, trans. James Strachey as *The Interpretation of Dreams* (New York: Avon, 1965).

—— (1905), *Der Witz und seine Beziehung zum Unbewussten*, trans. Joyce Crick as *The Joke and its Relation to the Unconscious* (London: Penguin, 2002).

—— (1927), *Die Zukunft einer Illusion*, trans. James Strachey as *The Future of an Illusion* (New York: Norton, 1961).

—— (1930), *Das Unbehagen in der Kultur*, trans. James Stranchey as *Civilization and its Discontents* (New York: Norton, 1961).

—— (1933), *Neue Folgen der Vorlesungen zur Einführung in die Psychoanalyse*, trans. James Strachey as *New Introductory Lectures on Psychoanalysis* (New York: Norton, 1965).

FREYENHAGEN, FABIAN (2005), 'Adorno's Negativistic Ethics', Ph.D. thesis (Department of Philosophy, University of Sheffield).

FRIEDMAN, MARILYN (1997), 'Autonomy and Social Relationships', in Meyers, Diana (ed.), *Feminists Rethink the Self* (Boulder CO: Westview Press).

FRIEDMAN, MICHAEL (1999), *A Parting of the Ways: Carnap, Cassirer, Heidegger* (Chicago: Open Court)

FRIES, JAKOB FRIEDRICH (1967), *Sämtliche Schriften*, (ed.) Gert König and Lutz Geldsetzer (Aalen: Scientia Verlag).

FRÜCHTL, JOSEF (1986), *Mimesis: Konstellation des Zentralbegriffs bei Adorno* (Würzburg: Königshaus & Neumann).

GADAMER, HANS-GEORG (1990), *Wahrheit und Methode: Grundzüge einer philosophischen Hermeneutik*, 6. Auflage, *Gesammelte Werke*, i (Tübingen: Mohr), trans. Joel Weinsheimer and Donald G. Marshall as *Truth and Method*, 2nd rev. edn. (London: Sheed & Ward, 1993).

GAUS, GERALD (2005), 'The Place of Autonomy within Liberalism', in Christman and Anderson (2005), pp. 272–89.

GEIGER, MORITZ (1911), 'Das Bewusstsein von Gefühlen', *Münchner philosophische Abhandlungen, Festschrift for Theodor Lipps* (Leipzig: Johann Ambrosius Barth).

GENETTE, GÉRARD (1999), *The Aesthetic Relation*, trans. G. M. Goshgarian (Ithaca: Cornell University Press).

GERAS, NORMAN (1970), 'Essence and Appearance: Aspects of Fetishism in Marx's *Capital*', *New Left Review* 1/65, 69–85.

—— (1985), 'The Controversy about Marx and Justice', *New Left Review* 1/100, 47–85.

GEUSS, RAYMOND (1981), *The Idea of a Critical Theory: Habermas and the Frankfurt School* (Cambridge: Cambridge University Press).

—— (1999), *Morality, Culture and History: Essays on German Philosophy* (Cambridge, Cambridge University Press).

—— (2004), 'Dialectics and the Revolutionary Impulse', in Rush (2004a), 103–39.

—— (2005), *Outside Ethics* (Princeton: Princeton University Press).

GIBSON, JAMES J. (1979), *The Ecological Approach to Visual Perception* (Hillsdale: Lawrence Erlbaum).

GOETHE, JOHANN WOLFGANG (1948–54), *Gedenkausgabe der Werke, Briefe und Gespräche*, 24 vols., ed. Ernst Beutler (Zurich: Artemis).

GOETSCHEL, WILLI (1994), *Kant's Writing as Critical Praxis* (Durham, NC: Duke University Press).

GOLDMANN, LUCIEN (1948), *Introduction à la Philosophie de Kant* (Paris: Gallimard, 1967), trans. Robert Black as *Immanuel Kant* (London: New Left Books, 1971).

—— (1955), *Le Dieu caché* (Paris: Gallimard), trans. Philip Thody as *The Hidden God* (London: Routledge, 1964).

GRIFFIN, DONALD R. (1984), *Animal Thinking* (Cambridge, MA: Harvard University Press).

—— (2001), *Animal Minds* (Chicago: University of Chicago Press).

GRÜNBAUM, ADOLF (1984), *The Foundations of Psychoanalysis: A Philosophical Critique* (Berkeley: University of California Press).

GUIGNON, CHARLES (2004), 'Becoming a Self: The Role of Authenticity in *Being and Time*', in his Guignon (ed.), *The Existentialists* (Oxford: Rowman & Littlefield).

GURWITSCH, ARON (1964), *The Field of Consciousness* (Pittsburgh: Duquesne University Press).

GUTTING, GARY (1973), 'Conceptual Structures and Scientific Change', *Studies in History and Philosophy of Science* 4, 209–30.

—— (1989), *Michel Foucault's Archaeology of Scientific Reason* (Cambridge: Cambridge University Press)

—— (2001), *French Philosophy in the Twentieth Century* (Cambridge: Cambridge University Press).

—— (2003), 'Thomas Kuhn and French Philosophy of Science', in Nickles, Thomas (ed.), *Thomas Kuhn* (Cambridge: Cambridge University Press)

GUYER, PAUL (1990), 'Reason and Reflective Judgment: Kant on the Significance of Systematicity', *Noûs* 24, 17–44.

—— (2003), 'Kant on the Theory and Practice of Autonomy', *Social Philosophy and Policy* 20/2, 70–98.

HAACK, SUSAN (1993), *Evidence and Inquiry* (Oxford: Blackwell).

HAAR, MICHEL (1996), 'Critical Remarks on the Heideggerian Reading of Nietzsche', in Christopher Macann (ed.), *Critical Heidegger* (London: Routledge), 121–33.

HACKER, PETER M. S. (1987), *Appearance and Reality* (Oxford: Blackwell).

—— (2006) 'Passing by the Naturalistic Turn: On Quine's Cul-de-sac', *Philosophy* 81, 231–53.

HACKING, IAN (1975), *Why Does Language Matter to Philosophy?* (Cambridge: Cambridge University Press).

HALLWARD, PETER (2003), *Badiou: A Subject to Truth* (Minneapolis: University of Minnesota Press).

HAMMER, ESPEN (2006), *Adorno and the Political* (London: Routledge).

HAMMERMEISTER, KAI (2002), *The German Aesthetic Tradition* (Cambridge: Cambridge University Press).

HARDIMON, MICHAEL O. (1994), *Hegel's Social Philosophy: The Project of Reconciliation* (Cambridge: Cambridge University Press).

HARDT, MICHAEL and NEGRI, ANTONIO (2000), *Empire* (Cambridge, MA: Harvard University Press).

—— (2004), *Multitude: War and Democracy in the Age of Empire* (New York: Penguin).

HARTMANN, EDUARD VON (1907), *System der Philosophie im Grundriß 1: Grundriß der Erkenntnislehre* (Bad Sachsa im Harz: Hermann Haacke Verlagsbuchhandlung).

HARVEY, DAVID (2005), *A Short History of Neo-liberalism* (Oxford: Oxford University Press).

HATFIELD, GARY (1990), *The Natural and the Normative: Theories of Spatial Vision from Kant to Helmholtz* (Cambridge, MA: MIT Press).

HATFIELD, HENRY C. (1943), *Winckelmann and his German Critics* (New York: King's Crown Press).

—— (1964), *Aesthetic Paganism in German Literature* (Cambridge, MA: Harvard University Press).

HAYM, RUDOLF (1975), *Materialien zu Hegel's Rechtsphilosophie*, i, (ed.) M. Riedel (Frankfurt am Main: Suhrkamp).

HAYMAN, RONALD (1980), *Nietzsche* (New York: Penguin).

HEINE, HEINRICH (1834), 'Zur Geschichte der Religion und Philosophie in Deutsch-land', in *Heine: Werke in fünf Bänden* (Weimar: Aufbau Verlag, 1958), v. 94–110.

—— (1948), *Self-Portrait and Other Prose Writings*, trans. F. Ewen (Secaucus: Citadel Press).

HELMHOLTZ, HERMANN VON (1850–67), *Handbuch der physiologischen Optik* (Leipzig: Voss); trans. James P. C. Southall as *Helmholtz's Treatise on Physiological Optics* (Menasha, WI: Optical Society of America, 1924–5; Bristol: Thoemmes, 2000).

—— (1896), *Vorträge und Reden* (Braunschweig: Vieweg); partially trans. and ed. by David Cahan in *Science and Culture: Popular and Philosophical Essays* (Chicago, IL: University of Chicago Press, 1995).

HENRICH, DIETER (1971), *Hegel im Kontext* (Frankfurt am Main: Suhrkamp).

—— (1994), *The Unity of Reason* (Cambridge, MA: Harvard University Press).

—— (2001), *Versuch über Kunst und Leben: Subjektivität, Weltverstehen, Kunst* (Munich: Hanser).

HERDER, JOHANN GOTTFRIED (1768), *Über Thomas Abbts Schriften; On Thomas Abbt's Writings*, in *Philosophical Writings*, trans. and ed. Michael N. Foster (Cambridge: Cambridge University Press, 2002), 167–77.

—— (1769), *Kritische Wälder*, partially trans. and ed. Gregory Moore as *Critical Forests*, in *Johann Gottfried Herder: Selected Writings in Aesthetics* (Princeton: Princeton University Press, 2006).

—— (1772), *Abhandlung über den Ursprung der Sprache; Treatise on the Origin of Language*, in *Philosophical Writings*, trans. and ed. Michael N. Foster (Cambridge: Cambridge University Press, 2002), 65–164.

—— (1774), *Auch eine Philosophie der Geschichte der Menschheit*, in *Sämtliche Werke*, ed. Bernard Suphan (Berlin: Weidmann, 1891), vol. v; *This Too a Philosophy of History for the Formation of Humanity*, in *Philosophical Writings*, trans. and ed. Michael N. Foster (Cambridge: Cambridge University Press, 2002), 272–358.

—— (1778), *Von Erkennen und Empfindenden der menschlichen Seele; On the Cognition and Sensation of the Human Soul*, in *Philosophical Writings*, trans. and ed. Michael N. Foster (Cambridge: Cambridge University Press, 2002), 187–243.

—— (2002), *Philosophical Writings*, trans. and ed. Michael N. Foster (Cambridge: Cambridge University Press).

HERMAN, BARBARA (1981), 'On the Value of Acting from the Motive of Duty', *Philosophical Review* 90, 351–82.

HERMAN, EDWARD and CHOMSKY, NOAM (1988), *Manufacturing Consent: The Political Economy of the Mass Media* (New York: Pantheon).

HEUSSI, KARL (1932), *Die Krisis des Historismus* (Tübingen: Mohr).

HILMER, BRIGITTE (2002), 'Kunst als Spiegel der Philosophie', in Andrea Kern, and Ruth Sonderegger (eds.), *Falsche Gegensätze: Zeitgenössische Positionen zur philosophischen Ästhetik* (Frankfurt am Main: Suhrkamp).

HINSKE, NORBERT (1970), *Kants Weg zur Transzendentalphilosophie* (Stuttgart: Kohlhammer)

—— (1998– ), *Werke*, ed. Klaus Hammacher and Walter Jaeschke (Hamburg: Meiner).

HIRSCHMAN, ALBERT O. (1970), *Exit, Voice, and Loyalty: Responses to Decline in Firms, Organizations, and States* (Cambridge, MA: Harvard University Press).

—— (1981), *Essays in Trespassing: Economics to Politics and Beyond* (Cambridge: Cambridge University Press).

HÖLDERLIN, FRIEDRICH (1796), *Hyperion (Die Vorletzte Fassung)*, in *Sämtliche Werke: Große Stuttgarter Ausgabe*, iii, ed. Friedrich Beißner (Stuttgart: Kohlhammer, 1957), 235–52.

—— (1800), 'Über die Verfahrungsweise des poetischen Geistes', in *Sämtliche Werke: Große Stuttgarter Ausgabe*, iv, ed. Friedrich Beißner (Stuttgart: Kohlhammer, 1961), 241–65, trans. as 'Operations of Poetic Spirit', in *Essays and Letters on Theory*, trans. and ed. Thomas Pfau (Albany: State University of New York Press, 1988)

HOLLAND, EUGENE W. (1999), *Deleuze and Guattari's Anti-Oedipus: Introduction to Schizoanalysis* (London: Routledge).

HOLLOWAY, JOHN (2002), *Change the World without Taking Power* (London: Pluto).

HONNETH, AXEL (1991), *Critique of Power: Reflective Stages in a Critical Social Theory*, trans. K. Baynes (Cambridge, MA: MIT Press).

—— (1994), 'History and Interaction: On the Structuralist Interpretation of Historical Materlialism', in Elliott (ed.) (1994), pp. 73–103.

—— (1992) *Kampf um Anerkennung* (Frankfurt: Suhrkamp, 1992).

—— (1996), *The Struggle for Recognition*, trans. Joel Anderson (Cambridge, MA: MIT Press).

—— (2000) 'The Possibility of a Disclosing Critique of Society: The *Dialectic of Enlightenment* in Light of Current Debates in Social Criticism', *Constellations* 7, 122–5.

—— (2005), *Verdinglichung* (Frankfurt am Main: Suhrkamp).

HOPKINS, JIM (1988), 'Epistemology and Depth Psychology: Critical Notes on *The Foundations of Psychoanalysis*', in Clark and Wright, (eds.) (1988), 30–66.

HOWE, IRVING (1981), 'On the Moral Basis of Socialism', *Dissent* (Fall 1981), 491–5.

HOY, DAVID C. (ed.) (1986), *Foucault: A Critical Reader* (Oxford: Blackwell).

HOYNINGEN-HUENE, PAUL (1993), *Reconstructing Scientific Revolutions* (Chicago: University of Chicago Press).

HUME, DAVID (1739), *A Treatise of Human Nature*, 2nd edn., (ed.) L. A. Selby-Bigge and P. H. Nidditch (Oxford: Oxford University Press, 1978).

IGGERS, GEORG G. (1968), *German Conception of History* (Middletown, CN: Wesleyan University Press).

ILIENKOV, EVALD V. (1982), *The Dialectics of the Abstract and the Concrete in Marx's 'Capital'* (Moscow: Progress).

IRWIN, TERENCE (1996), 'Kant's Criticisms of Eudaimonism', in Stephen Engstrom and Jennifer Whiting (eds.), *Aristotle, Kant, and the Stoics* (Cambridge: Cambridge University Press), 63–101.

JACOBI, FRIEDRICH HEINRICH (1812–25), *Werke*, (ed.) C. J. Roth and J. F. Köppen (Leipzig: Fleischer; Darmstadt: Wissenschaftliche Buchgesellschaft, 1968).

—— (1994), *The Main Philosophical Writings and the Novel 'Allwill'*, trans. and ed. George di Giovanni (Montreal and Kingston: McGill-Queens University Press).

JAEGER, FRIEDRICH and RÜSEN, JÖRN (1992), *Geschichte des Historismus* (München: Beck).

JAKOBSON, ROMAN (1959), 'On Linguistic Aspects of Translation', in Lawrence Venuti (ed.), *The Translation Studies Reader* (London and New York: Routledge, 2000).

JAMES, SUSAN (1997), *Passion and Action: The Emotions in Seventeenth-Century Philosophy* (Oxford: Oxford University Press).

JAMESON, FREDERIC (1981), *The Political Unconscious: Narrative as a Socially Symbolic Act* (Ithaca, NY: Cornell University Press).

—— (1990), *Late Marxism: Adorno, or, the Persistence of the Dialectic* (London: Verso).

—— (1991), *Postmodernism, or the Cultural Logic of Late Capitalism* (Durham, NC: Duke University Press).

—— (1998), *The Cultural Turn: Selected Writings on the Postmodern, 1983–1998* (London: Verso).

JANAWAY, CHRISTOPHER (1991), 'Nietzsche, the Self, and Schopenhauer', in Keith Ansell-Pearson (ed.), *Nietzsche and Modern German Thought* (London: Routledge).

JARAUSCH, KONRAD (1986), 'The Institutionalization of History in 18th-Century Germany', in Hans Erich Bödeker et al. (eds.), *Aufklärung und Geschichte* (Göttingen: Vandanhoeck & Ruprecht), 25–48.

JAY, MARTIN (1973), *The Dialectical Imagination* (London: Heinemann)

JOHNSTON, DAVID KAY (2001), 'Focus on Forms Masks Estate Tax Confusion', *New York Times*, 8 April 2001.

KAPLAN, E. ANN and SPRINKER, MICHAEL (eds.) (1993), *The Althusserian Legacy* (London: Verso).

KENNY, ANTHONY (1968), *Descartes: A Study of his Philosophy* (New York: Random House).

KERN, I. (1964), *Husserl und Kant: Eine Untersuchung über Husserls Verhältnis zu Kant und zum Neukantianismus* (The Hague: Martinus Nijhoff).

KIERKEGAARD, SØREN (1841), *Om Begrebet Ironi*, trans. and ed. H. Hong and E. Hong as *The Concept of Irony* (Princeton: Princeton University Press, 1989).

—— (1909–48), *Papirer*, (ed.) P. A. Heiberg, V. Kuhr, and E. Torstling (Copenhagen: Gyldendal).

KIM, JAEGWON (1993), *Supervenience and Mind: Selected Philosophical Essays* (Cambridge: Cambridge University Press).

KITCHER, PHILIP (1993), *The Advancement of Science* (New York: Oxford University Press).

KNOBE, JOSHUA and LEITER, BRIAN (2007), 'The Case for Nietzschean Moral Psychology', in Leiter and Sinhababu, eds. (2007), pp. 83–109.

KÖHNKE, KLAUS C. (1986), *Entstehung und Aufstieg des Neukantianismus: Die deutsche Universitätsphilosophie zwischen Idealismus und Positivismus* (Frankfurt am Main:

Suhrkamp), partially trans. R. J. Hollingdale as *The Rise of Neo-Kantianism: German Academic Philosophy between Idealism and Positivism* (Cambridge: Cambridge University Press, 1991).

KOLAKOWSKI, LESZEK (1985), *Bergson* (Oxford: Oxford University Press).

KÖRNER, JOSEPH (1928), 'Friedrich Schlegels "Philosophie der Philologie" ', *Logos* 17, 1–72.

KOSELLECK, R. (1973), *Kritik und Krise* (Frankfurt am Main: Suhrkamp).

KOUVELAKIS, STATHIS (2000), 'La Politique dans ses limites, ou les paradoxes d'Alain Badiou', *Actuel Marx* 28.

—— (2003), *Philosophie et Revolution: De Kant à Marx* (Paris: Presses Universitaires de France); trans. G. M. Goshgarian as *Philosophy and Revolution: From Kant to Marx* (London: Verso).

KRUGMAN, PAUL (2003), 'The Tax-Cut Con', *New York Times Magazine*, 14 September 2003.

KUHN, THOMAS S. (1962), *The Structure of Scientific Revolutions* (Chicago: University of Chicago Press).

LABICA, GEORGES (1980), *Marxism and the Status of Philosophy* (Brighton: Harvester)

LACLAU, ERNESTO and MOUFFE, CHANTAL (1985), *Hegemony and Socialist Strategy* (London: Verso).

LACOUE-LABARTHE, PHILIPPE and NANCY, JEAN-LUC (1988), *The Literary Absolute: The Theory of Literature in German Romanticism*, trans. Philip Barnard and Cheryl Lester (Albany, NY: SUNY Press).

LANE, JEREMY F. (2000), *Pierre Bourdieu: A Critical Introduction* (London: Pluto).

LARMORE, CHARLES (1979), *Patterns of Moral Complexity* (Cambridge: Cambridge University Press).

LEAR, JONATHAN (2005), *Freud* (London: Routledge).

LECERCLE, JEAN-JACQUES (1999), 'Cantor, Lacan, Mao, Beckett, Même Combat: The Philosophy of Alain Badiou', *Radical Philosophy* 93, 6–13.

LEIBNIZ, GOTTFRIED WILHELM (1923– ), *Sämtliche Schriften und Briefe*, (ed.) Deutsche Akademie der Wissenschaften (Darmstadt: Reichl; Berlin: Akademie-Verlag 1990)

LEITER, BRIAN (1997), 'Nietzsche and the Morality Critics', *Ethics* 107/2, 250–85.

—— (2002), *Nietzsche on Morality* (London: Routledge).

—— (ed.) (2004), *The Future for Philosophy* (Oxford: Clarendon Press).

—— (2004), 'The Hermeneutics of Suspicion: Recovering Marx, Nietzsche, and Freud', in Leiter, (ed.) (2004), pp. 74–105.

LEITER, BRIAN and SINHABABU, NEIL (eds.) (2007), *Nietzsche and Morality* (Oxford: Oxford University Press).

LESSING, GOTTHOLD EPHRAIM (1989), *Werke und Briefe* (Frankfurt: Deutscher Klassiker Verlag).

LEVINS, RICHARD and LEWONTIN, RICHARD (1985), *The Dialectical Biologist* (Cambridge, MA: Harvard University Press).

LINSKY, LEONARD (ed.) (1952), *Semantics and the Philosophy of Language* (Urbana: University of Illinois Press).

LOCKE, JOHN (1690), *An Essay Concerning Human Understanding*, (ed.) P. H. Nidditch (Oxford: Oxford University Press, 1975).

LOTZE, RUDOLF HERMANN (1874), *Logik* (Leipzig: Hirzel), trans. Bernard Bosanquet as *Logic* (Oxford: Clarendon Press, 1884)

LOUX, MICHAEL J. (1978), *Substance and Attribute: A Study in Ontology* (Dordrecht: D. Reidel).

—— (1998a), *Metaphysics: A Contemporary Introduction* (London: Routledge).

—— (1998b), 'Beyond Substrata and Bundles: A Prolegomenon to a Substance Ontology', in Stephen Laurence and Cynthia Macdonald (eds.), *Contemporary Readings in the Foundations of Metaphysics* (Oxford: Blackwell), 233–47.

LOVEJOY, ARTHUR O. (1936), *The Great Chain of Being* (Cambridge, MA: Harvard University Press).

LOWE, E. JONATHAN (1989), *Kinds of Being: A Study of Individuation, Identity and the Logic of Sortal Terms* (Oxford: Blackwell).

—— (1999), 'Form without Matter', in David S. Oderberg (ed.), *Form and Matter: Themes in Contemporary Metaphysics* (Oxford: Blackwell), 1–21.

LOWITH, KARL (1994), *My Life in Germany before and after 1933* (Urbana: University of Illinois Press).

LÖWY, MICHAEL (1979), *Georg Lukács: From Romanticism to Bolshevism*, trans. Patrick Camiller (London: New Left Books).

LUKÁCS, GYÖRGY (1923), *Geschichte und Klassenbewusstsein*, trans. Rodney Livingstone as *History and Class Consciousness* (London: Merlin Press, 1971).

—— (1924), *Lenin: A Study in the Unity of his Thought*, trans. Nicholas Jacobs (New Delhi: Seagull Books, 2005).

—— (1938), *The Young Hegel: Studies in the Relations between Dialectics and Economics*, trans. Rodney Livingstone (Cambridge, MA: MIT Press, 1975).

—— (1954), *Die Zerstörung der Vernunft* (Neuwied: Luchterhand, 1962).

—— (1971), *The Theory of the Novel: A Historico-philosophical Essay on the Forms of Great Epic Literature*, trans. Anna Bostock (London: Merlin Press).

—— (1972), *Political Writings, 1919–1929*, ed. and trans. R. Livingstone (London: New Left Books).

—— (2000), *A Defence of 'History and Class Consciousness'*, trans. John Rees (London: Verso).

LUKES, STEVEN (1985), *Marxism and Morality* (Oxford: Clarendon Press).

MCCARTHY, THOMAS (1991), *Ideals and Illusions* (Cambridge, MA: The MIT Press).

MACHEREY, PIERRE (1979), *Hegel ou Spinoza?* (Paris: Minuit).

MCCHESNEY, ROBERT (1997), *Corporate Media and the Threat to Democracy* (New York: Seven Stories).

MACDONALD, IAIN (2000), 'The Wounder Will Heal: Cognition and Reconciliation in Hegel and Adorno', *Philosophy Today* 44 (Supplement), 132–9.

MCDOWELL, JOHN (1994), *Mind and World* (Cambridge, MA: Harvard University Press).

MACINTYRE, ALASDAIR (1981), *After Virtue* (London: Duckworth).

MACKENZIE, CATRIONA and STOLJAR, NATALIE (2000), *Relational Autonomy: Feminist Perspectives on Autonomy, Agency and the Social Self* (New York: Oxford University Press).

MACKIE, JOHN L. (1974), *The Cement of the Universe: A Study of Causation* (Oxford: Clarendon Press).

MAIMON, SALOMON (1975–6), *Gesammelte Werke*, (ed.) V. Verra (Hildesheim: Olms).

MALABOU, CATHERINE (1996), 'Who's Afraid of Hegelian Wolves?', in Paul Patton (ed.), *Deleuze: A Critical Reader* (Oxford: Blackwell).

MARCUSE, HERBERT (1941), *Reason and Revolution* (London: Routledge & Kegan Paul, 1969).

—— (1955), *Eros and Civilization* (Boston: Beacon Press).

—— (1968), *Negations* (London: Penguin Press).

—— (1969), *An Essay on Liberation* (Boston: Beacon Press).

MARTIN, GOTTFRIED (1961), 'Die deutsche ontologische Kant-Interpretation', in *Gesammelte Abhandlungen, Kant-Studien Ergänzungshefte* 81, 104–9.

MARTIN, MICHAEL G. F. (1998), 'Setting Things before the Mind', in A. O'Hear (ed.), *Current Issues in Philosophy of Mind* (Cambridge: Cambridge University Press).

MARX, KARL (1977), *Selected Writings*, (ed.) D. McLellan (Oxford: Oxford University Press).

—— (1984), *Early Writings*, trans. R. Livingstone (London: Penguin)

MARX, KARL and ENGELS, FRIEDRICH (1956–90), *Werke* (Berlin: Dietz Verlag).

—— (1970), *The German Ideology*, (ed.) C. J. Arthur (London: Lawrence & Wishart).

—— (1975–), *Collected Works*, 50 vols. (London: Lawrence & Wishart).

MAUS, INGEBORG (2002), 'Liberties and Popular Sovereignty: On Habermas's Reconstruction of the System of Rights', in R. von Schomberg, and K. Baynes (eds.), *Discourse and Democracy* (Albany: SUNY Press).

MEGILL, ALLAN (1985), *Prophets of Extremity: Nietzsche, Heidegger, Foucault, Derrida* (Berkeley: University of California Press).

MEINECKE, FRIEDRICH (1965a), *Die Entstehung des Historismus* (München: Oldenbourg).

—— (1965b), *Zur Theorie und Philosophie der Geschichte* (Stuttgart: Koehler).

MERLEAU-PONTY, MAURICE (1945), *Phénoménologie de la perception* (Paris: Gallimard), trans. Colin Smith as *Phenomenology of Perception* (London: Routledge, 1962).

—— (1948), *Sens et non-sens* (Paris: Nagel), trans. Hubert L. Dreyfus and Patricia Allen Dreyfus as *Sense and Non-sense* (Evanston, IL: Northwestern University Press, 1964).

—— (1955), *Les Aventures de la dialectique* (Paris: Gallimard), trans. Joseph Bien as *Adventures of the Dialectic* (London: Heinemann, 1974).

—— (1958), *Les Sciences de l'homme et la phénoménologie* (Paris: Centre de Documentation Universitaire), trans. John Wild as 'Phenomenology and the Sciences of Man', in *The Primacy of Perception*, (ed.) James Edie (Evanston: Northwestern University Press, 1964), 43–95.

MERLEAU-PONTY, MAURICE (1960), *Signes* (Paris: Gallimard), trans. Richard McCleary as *Signs* (Evanston: Northwestern University Press, 1964).

—— (1991), *Texts and Dialogues*, ed. Hugh J. Silverman and James Barry, Jr. (Atlantic Highlands, NJ: Humanities Press).

MEYERS, DIANA (1989), *Self, Society and Personal Choice* (New York: Columbia University Press).

MILL, JOHN STUART (1863), *Utilitarianism* (London: Fontana, 1962).

MOORE, ADRIAN W. (1997), *Points of View* (Oxford: Clarendon Press).

MOORE, GEORGE E. (1959), 'Certainty', in his *Philosophical Papers* (London, George, Allen & Unwin).

MÖSER, JUSTUS (1944–95), *Sämtliche Werke: Historisch-kritische Ausgabe*, (ed.) Akademie der Wissenschaften zu Göttingen (Osnabrück: Wenner).

MOULIER-BOUTANG, YANN (1992), *Louis Althusser: Une biographie* (Paris: Grasset).

MÜLLER, JOHANNES PETER (1826), *Zur vergleichenden Physiologie des Gesichtssinnes des Menschen und der Thiere* (Leipzig: Cnobloch).

—— (1834–40), *Handbuch des Physiologie des Menschen*, 2 vols. (Koblenz: Hölscher).

MULLIGAN, KEVIN and SMITH, BARRY (1986), 'A Husserlian Theory of Indexicality', *Grazer Philosophische Studien* 28, 133–63.

MURPHY, DOMINIC (2006), *Psychiatry in the Scientific Image* (Cambridge, MA: MIT Press).

NEGRI, ANTONIO (1979), *Marx beyond Marx*, trans. Harry Cleaver, Michael Ryan, and Maurizio Viano, ed. Jim Fleming (South Hadley, MA: Bergin & Garvey, 1984).

—— (1991), *The Savage Anomaly*, trans. Michael Hardt (Minneapolis: University of Minnesota Press).

—— (1997), *Le Pouvoir Constituant* (Paris: Presses Universitaires de France).

NEHAMAS, ALEXANDER (1985), *Nietzsche: Life as Literature* (Cambridge, MA: Harvard University Press).

NEISSER, U. (1967), *Cognitive Psychology* (New York: Appleton-Century-Crofts).

NELL, ONORA (1975), *Acting on Principle* (New York: Columbia University Press).

NEU, JEROME (ed.) (1992), *The Cambridge Companion to Freud* (Cambridge: Cambridge University Press).

NEUHOUSER, FREDERICK (1993), 'Freedom, Dependence and the General Will', *The Philosophical Review* 102, 363–95.

—— (2000), *The Foundations of Hegel's Social Theory* (Cambridge, MA: Harvard University Press).

NOZICK, ROBERT (1974), *Anarchy, State and Utopia* (New York: Basic Books).

OLAFSON, FREDERICK (1987), *Heidegger and the Philosophy of Mind* (New Haven: Yale University Press).

O'NEILL, ONORA (1989), *Constructions of Reason* (Cambridge: Cambridge University Press).

OSHANA, MARINA (1998), 'Personal Autonomy and Society', *The Journal of Social Philosophy* 29, 81–102.

O'SHAUGHNESSY, BRIAN (1980), *The Will: A Dual Aspect Theory*, 2 vols. (Cambridge: Cambridge University Press).

PARKINSON, G. H. R. (ed.) (1966), *Leibniz: Logical Papers* (Oxford: Clarendon Press).

PASSAVANT, PAUL A. and DEAN, JODI (eds.) (2004), *Empire's New Clothes* (New York: Routledge).

PASSMORE, JOHN (1991), *Serious Art: A Study of the Concept in all the Major Arts* (London: Duckworth).

PATSCH, HERMANN (1966), 'Friedrich Schlegels 'Philosophie der Philologie' und Schleiermachers frühe Entwürfe zur Hermeneutik—Zur Frühgeschichte der Romantischen Hermeneutik', *Zeitschrift für Theologie und Kirche* 63, 434–72.

PATTON, LYDIA (2004), 'Hermann Cohen's History and Philosophy of Science', PhD Dissertation (Montreal: McGill University).

PEACOCKE, CHRISTOPHER (1992), 'Scenarios, Concepts and Perception', in Tim Crane (ed.), *The Contents of Experience* (Cambridge: Cambridge University Press).

—— (2001), 'Phenomenology and Nonconceptual Content', *Philosophy and Phenomenological Research* 62, 609–17.

PEARS, DAVID (1984), *Motivated Irrationality* (Oxford: Oxford University Press).

PHILIPSE, HERMAN (1982), 'The Problem of Occasional Expressions in Edmund Husserl's Logical Investigations', *Journal of the British Society for Phenomenology* 13 (1982), 168–85.

—— (1994), 'Towards a Postmodern Conception of Metaphysics: On the Genealogy and Successor Disciplines of Modern Philosophy', *Metaphilosophy* 25, 1–44.

—— (1995), 'Transcendental Idealism', in Smith and Woodruff Smith eds. (1995), pp. 239–322.

—— (1998), *Heidegger's Philosophy of Being: A Critical Interpretation* (Princeton: Princeton University Press).

—— (1999a) 'Heidegger and Ethics', *Inquiry* 42, 439–74.

—— (1999b), 'Heidegger's Grand (Pascalian) Strategy: On the Problem of Reinterpreting the Existentialia', in *Metaphysics. The Proceedings of the Twentieth World Congress of Philosophy*, ii (Bowling Green, KV: Philosophy Documentation Center).

—— (2001), 'What is a Natural Conception of the World?', *International Journal of Philosophical Studies* 9, 385–99.

—— (2003), 'Heideggers philosophisch-religiöse (Pascalsche) Strategie: Über das Problem der Umdeutung der Existenzialien', *Zeitschrift für Philosophische Forschung* 57, 571–88.

PETTIT, PHILIP and SMITH, MICHAEL (1996), 'Freedom in Belief and Desire', *Journal of Philosophy* 93, 429–49.

PICKFORD, HENRY (2002), 'The Dialectic of Theory and Praxis: Late Adorno', in N. C. Gibson, and A. Rubin (eds.), *Adorno: A Critical Reader* (Oxford: Blackwell), 312–41.

PIPPIN, ROBERT (1989), *Hegel's Idealism: The Satisfactions of Self-Consciousness* (Cambridge: Cambridge University Press).

PIPPIN, ROBERT (1995), 'Hegel on the Rationality and Priority of Ethical Life', *Neue Hefte für Philosophie* 35, 95–126.

—— (1999), *Modernism as a Philosophical Problem*, 2nd edn. (New York: Blackwell).

—— (2005), *The Persistence of Subjectivity: On the Kantian Aftermath* (Cambridge: Cambridge University Press).

POELLNER, PETER (2003), 'Non-conceptual Content, Experience and the Self', *Journal of Consciousness Studies* 10/2, 32–57.

—— (2004), 'Self-Deception, Consciousness and Value: The Nietzschean Contribution', *Journal of Consciousness Studies* 11/10–11, 44–65.

—— (2007), 'Affect, Value and Objectivity', in Leiter and Sinhababu, eds. (2007), pp. 227–61.

POGGE, THOMAS W. (ed.) (2001), *Global Justice* (Oxford: Blackwell).

—— (2002), *World Poverty and Human Rights* (Cambridge: Polity).

POPPER, KARL R. (1957), *The Poverty of Historicism* (London: Routledge & Kegan Paul).

POTTS, ALEX (1994), *Flesh and the Ideal: Winckelmann and the Origins of Art History* (New Haven: Yale University Press).

PRANTL, CARL (1852), *Die gegenwärtige Aufgabe der Philosophie* (Munich: Akademie der Wissenschaften).

PRITCHARD, DUNCAN (2002), 'Recent Work on Radical Skepticism', *American Philosophical Quarterly* 39, 215–57.

QUINE, W. V. O. (1960), *Word and Object* (Cambridge, MA: MIT Press).

—— (1969), *Ontological Relativity and Other Essays* (New York: Columbia University Press).

—— (1990), *Pursuit of Truth* (Cambridge, MA: Harvard University Press).

—— (1995), *From Stimulus to Science* (Cambridge, MA: Harvard University Press).

RAILTON, PETER (1986), 'Explanatory Asymmetry in Historical Materialism', *Ethics* 97/1, 233–9.

—— (1991), 'Marx and the Objectivity of Science', in Boyd et al. (eds.) (1991), pp. 763–73.

—— (2003), *Facts, Values, Norms: Essays Towards a Morality of Consequence* (Cambridge: Cambridge University Press).

RANCIÈRE, JACQUES (1973), 'Le Concept De critique et la critique de l'économie politique dès les manuscrits de 1844 au Capital', in L. Althusser, et al. (eds.), *Lire le Capital*, 4 vols. (Paris: Presses Universitaires de France).

RANKE, LEOPOLD VON (1831–2), 'Idee der Universalhistorie', in *Vorlesungens-Einleitung: Aus Werk und Nachlass*, ed. Walther Fuchs and Theodor Schieder (Munich: Oldenbourg, 1975).

—— (1868–90), *Sämtliche Werke* (Leizig: Duncker & Humblot).

RATTANSI, ALI (ed.) (1989), *Ideology, Method and Marx* (London: Routledge).

RAWLS, JOHN (1973), *Theory of Justice* (Oxford: Oxford University Press).

RAYMOND, PIERRE (ed.) (1997), *Althusser philosophe* (Paris: Presses Universitaires de France).

REATH, ANDREWS, HERMAN, BARBARA, and KORSGAARD, CHRISTINE (eds.) (1997), *Reclaiming the History of Ethics* (New York: Cambridge University Press).

REDDING, PAUL (1999), *The Logic of Affect* (Ithaca, NY: Cornell University Press).

REES, JOHN (1998), *The Algebra of Revolution: The Dialectic and the Classical Marxist Tradition* (London: Routledge).

REICH, KLAUS (1939), 'Kant and Greek Ethics', *Mind* 48, 338–54, 446–63.

REILL, PETER HANNS (1975), *The German Enlightenment and Rise of Historicism* (Berkeley: University of California Press).

REINHOLD, KARL LEONHARD (1790–4), *Beiträge zur Berichtigung bisheriger Mißverständnisse der Philosophen*, 2 vols. (Jena: Mauke); 2nd edn., ed. Faustino Fabbianelli (Hamburg: Meiner, 2003).

RENAULT, EMMANUEL (1995), *Marx et L'idée de critique* (Paris: Presses Universitaires de France).

REYNOLDS, JACK and ROFFE, JON (eds.) (2004), *Understanding Derrida* (New York: Continuum).

RICHARDS, IVOR A. (1926), *The Principles of Literary Criticism*, 2nd edn. (London: Routledge).

RICKERT, HEINRICH (1899), *Kulturwissenschaft und Naturwissenschaft* (Tübingen: Mohr).

—— (1902), *Die Grenzen der naturwissenschaftlichen Begriffsbildung* (Tübingen: Mohr), trans. Guy Oakes as *The Limits of Concept Formation in Natural Science* (Cambridge: Cambridge University Press, 1986).

—— (1905), 'Die Probleme der Geschichtsphilosophie', in Wilhelm Windelband (ed.), *Die Philosophie im Beginn des zwanzigsten Jahrhunderts. Festschrift für Kuno Fischer* (Heidelberg: Carl Winter), 51–135.

—— (1909), 'Zwei Wege der Erkenntnistheorie', *Kant-Studien* 14, 169–228.

RICOEUR, PAUL (1970), *Freud and Philosophy: An Essay on Interpretation* (New Haven and London: Yale University Press).

RITTER, JOACHIM, GRÜNDER, KARLFRIEND, and GABRIEL, GOTTFRIED (eds.) (1971–2005), *Historisches Wörterbuch der Philosophie* (Basel: Schwabe).

ROBERTS, MARCUS (1996), *Analytical Marxism: A Critique* (London: Verso).

RORTY, RICHARD (1979), *Philosophy and the Mirror of Nature* (Princeton: Princeton University Press).

ROSDOLSKY, ROMAN (1977), *The Making of Marx's 'Capital'* (London: Pluto).

ROSE, STEVEN (1998), *Lifelines* (London: Penguin)

ROSEN, MICHAEL (1982), *Hegel's Dialectic and its Criticism* (Cambridge: Cambridge University Press).

—— (1996), *On Voluntary Servitude* (Cambridge: Polity).

—— (1999), 'From Kant to Fichte: a Reply to Franks', in Stern (ed.) (1999), pp. 147–54.

ROTHKO, MARK (2004), *The Artist's Reality: Philosophies of Art*, (ed.) Christopher Rothko (New Haven: Yale University Press).

ROWLANDS, MARK (2003), *Externalism* (Chesham: Acumen).

RUBIN, ISAAK ILLICH (1972), *Essays on Marx's Theory of Value*, trans. Miloš Samardžija and Fredy Perlman (Detroit: Black & Red).

RUSH, FRED (2000), 'Reason and Regulation in Kant', *Review of Metaphysics* 53, 837–62.

—— (2003), 'Romanticism and Benjamin's Critical Epistemology', in B. Hanssen and A. Benjamin (eds.), *Walter Benjamin and Romanticism* (London and New York: Continuum), 123–36.

—— (2004a), *The Cambridge Companion to Critical Theory* (Cambridge and New York: Cambridge University Press).

—— (2004b), 'Conceptual Foundations of Early Critical Theory', in Rush (ed.) (2004a), pp. 6–39.

—— (2005), 'Mikroanalyse, Genealogie, Konstellationsforschung', in M. Mulsow and M. Stamm (eds.), *Konstellationsforschung* (Frankfurt am Main: Suhrkamp), 149–72.

—— (2006), 'Irony and Romantic Subjectivity', in N. Kompridis (ed.), *Philosophical Romanticism* (London: Routledge), 173–95.

RUSSELL, BERTRAND (1962), *An Inquiry into Meaning and Truth* (Harmondsworth: Penguin).

RYLE, GILBERT (1954), *Dilemmas: The Tanner Lectures* (Cambridge: Cambridge University Press).

SAAD-FILHO, ALFREDO (2002), *The Value of Marx: Political Economy for Contemporary Capitalism* (London: Routledge).

SACHS, DAVID (1992), 'In Fairness to Freud', in Neu (ed.) (1992), pp. 309–38.

SACKS, MARK (2000), *Objectivity and Insight* (Oxford: Clarendon Press).

SAVAGE-RUMBAUGH, SUE, SHANKER, STUART G., and TAYLOR, TALBOT J. (1998), *Apes, Language, and the Human Mind* (Oxford: Oxford University Press).

SCANLON, THOMAS M. (1998), *What We Owe to Each Other* (Cambridge. MA: Harvard University Press).

SCHAEFFER, JEAN-MARIE (1992), *L'art de l'âge moderne* (Paris: Gallimard), trans. Steven Rendall as *Art of the Modern Age: Philosophy of Art from Kant to Heidegger* (Princeton: Princeton University Press, 2000).

SCHELER, MAX (1973), *Wesen und Formen der Sympathie*, 6th edn., in his *Gesammelte Werke*, vii, ed. Manfred S. Frings (Bern and Munich: Francke), trans. Peter Heath as *The Nature of Sympathy* (London: Routledge, 1979).

—— (1977), *Erkenntnis und Arbeit* (Frankfurt am Main: Vittorio Klostermann).

SCHILLER, FRIEDRICH (1871), *The Poems of Schiller, Complete*, trans. Henry D. Wireman (Philadelphia: I. G. Kohler).

—— (1962), *Über die ästhetische Erziehung des Menschen in einer Reihe von Briefen (1793–95)*, in *Schillers Werke: Nationalausgabe*, xx (Philosophische Schriften, Teil 1), ed. Benno von Wiese and Helmut Koopmann (Weimar: Böhlaus), 309–412; trans. Elizabeth M. Wilkinson and L. A. Willoughby as *On the Aesthetic Education of Man: In a Series of Letters* (Oxford: Clarendon Press, 1982)

—— (1977), *Briefe 1796–98*, in *Schillers Werke: Nationalausgabe*, xxix, (ed.) Norbert Oellers and Fritjhof Stock (Weimar: Böhlaus).

Schleiermacher, Friedrich Daniel Ernst (1830), *Der christliche Glaube nach den Grundsätzen der evangelischen Kirche im Zusammenhange dargestellt*, 2nd edn., in *Kritische Gesamtausgabe*, Abt. I, Bd. 13, Teilbde. 1–2, ed. Rolf Schäfer (Berlin: de Gruyter, 2003), trans. as *The Christian Faith*, (ed.) H. R. Mackintosh and J. S. Stewart (London: Continuum/T. & T. Clark, 1999).

—— (1838), *Hermeneutik und Kritik*, trans. as *Hermeneutics and Criticism*, (ed.) A. L. Willson (Cambridge: Cambridge University Press, 1998).

—— (1986), *Hermeneutics: The Handwritten Manuscripts*, (ed.) J. Duke and J. Forstman (Atlanta, GA: Scholars Press).

Schmitt, Carl (1985), *Political Theology* (Cambridge, MA: MIT Press).

Schnädelbach, Herbert (1974), *Geschichtsphilosophie nach Hegel* (Freiburg: Alber).

—— (1984), *Philosophy in Germany, 1831–1933* (Cambridge: Cambridge University Press).

—— (1993), 'Max Horkheimer and the Moral Philosophy of German Idealism', in S. Benhabib, W. Bonss, and J. McCole (eds.), *On Max Horkheimer* (Cambridge, MA: MIT Press).

Schneewind, Jerome (1998), *The Invention of Autonomy* (Cambridge: Cambridge University Press).

Schopenhauer, Arthur (1819), *Die Welt als Wille und Vorstellung*, in *Sämtliche Werke*, ed. Arthur Hübscher, ii (Wiesbaden: Brockhaus, 1949); trans. E. F. J. Payne as *The World as Will and Representation* (New York: Dover, 1969)

—— (1851), *Parerga and Paralipomena*, 2 vols., trans. E. F. J. Payne (Oxford: Clarendon Press, 1974).

Schulte-Sasse, Jochen (ed.) (1997), *Theory as Practice: An Anthology of German Romantic Writings* (Minneapolis: University of Minnesota Press).

Searle, John R. (1979), *Expression and Meaning: Studies in the Theory of Speech Acts* (Cambridge: Cambridge University Press).

—— (1983), *Intentionality* (Cambridge: Cambridge University Press).

Sellars, Wilfrid (1963), *Science, Perception, and Reality* (London: Routledge & Kegan Paul).

Sharpe, Matthew (2004), *Understanding Derrida*, (ed.) J. Reynolds and J. Roffe (New York: Continuum).

Siep, Ludwig (1982), 'Was heisst: "Aufhebung der Moralität in Sittlichkeit" in Hegel's Rechtsphilosophie?', *Hegel-Studien* 17, 75–94.

—— (1983), 'The "Aufhebung" of Morality in Ethical Life', in L. Stepelevich, and D. Lamb (eds.), *Hegel's Philosophy of Action* (Atlantic Highlands, NJ: Humanities Press), 137–55.

Simon, Ernst (1928), 'Ranke und Hegel', in *Beiheft der historischen Zeitschrift* 15 (Munich: Oldenbourg), 16–119.

Singer, Peter (ed.) (1991), *A Companion to Ethics* (Oxford: Blackwell).

Skinner, Quentin (1988), 'Meaning and Understanding in the History of Ideas', in J. Tully (ed.), *Meaning and Context: Quentin Skinner and his Critics* (Princeton: Princeton University Press).

Smith, A. David (2003), *Husserl and the 'Cartesian Meditations'* (London: Routledge).

SMITH, BARRY and SMITH, DAVID WOODRUFF, (eds.) (1995), *The Cambridge Companion to Husserl* (Cambridge: Cambridge University Press).

SMITH, DAVID WOODRUFF (1994), 'How to Husserl a Quine—and a Heidegger, Too', *Synthese* 98, 153–73.

SMITH, DAVID WOODRUFF and McINTYRE, RONALD (1982), *Husserl and Intentionality* (Dordrecht: Reidel).

SMITH, TONY (1990), *The Logic of Marx's 'Capital'* (Albany, NY: SUNY Press).

SOAMES, SCOTT (2003), *Philosophical Analysis in the Twentieth Century*, ii: *The Age of Meaning* (Princeton: Princeton University Press).

SOBER, ELLIOT (1993), *The Nature of Selection*, 2nd edn. (Chicago, IL: Chicago University Press).

SOKOLOWSKI, ROBERT (1970), *The Formation of Husserl's Concept of Constitution* (The Hague: Martinus Nijhoff).

SOLDATI, GIANFRANCO (1994), *Bedeutung und psychischer Gehalt: Zur sprachanalytischen Kritik von Husserls früher Phänomenologie* (Paderborn: Ferdinand Schöningh).

SOLOMON, ROBERT C. (ed.) (1973), *Nietzsche: A Collection of Critical Essays* (South Bend: University of Notre Dame Press).

SOTERIOU, MATTHEW (2005), 'The Subjective View of Experience and its Objective Commitments', *Proceedings of the Aristotelian Society* 105, 177–90.

SPRIGGE, TIMOTHY L. S. (1970), *Facts, Words and Beliefs* (London: Routledge).

STAROBINSKI, JEAN (1989), *Le Remède dans le mal, critique et légitimation de L'artifice á L'âge des Lumières* (Paris: Gallimard).

STEDMAN-JONES, GARETH (1971), 'The Marxism of the Early Lukács', *New Left Review* 1/70, 27–64.

STEIN, EDITH (1917), *Zum Problem der Einfühlung* (Munich: Kaffke, 1980).

STEINER, GEORGE (1989), *Real Presences: Is There Anything in What We Say?* (London: Faber & Faber).

STERN, ROBERT (ed.) (1999), *Transcendental Arguments: Problems and Prospects* (Oxford: Oxford University Press).

—— (2006), 'Hegel's *Doppelsatz*: A Neutral Reading', *Journal of the History of Philosophy* 44/2, 235–66.

STOLJAR, NATALIE (2000), 'Autonomy and the Feminist Intuition', in Mackenzie and Stoljar (2000), pp. 94–111.

STOLNITZ, JEROME (1992), 'On the Cognitive Triviality of Art', *British Journal of Aesthetics* 32, 191–200.

STRAWSON, GALEN (1994), *Mental Reality* (Cambridge, MA: MIT Press).

STRAWSON, PETER F. (1959), *Individuals* (London: Methuen).

—— (1966), *The Bounds of Sense* (London: Methuen).

—— (1977), *Logico-linguistic Papers* (Bristol: Methuen).

SULLIVAN, JOHN W. N. (1927), *Beethoven: His Spiritual Development* (London: Jonathan Cape).

TASSONE, GIUSEPPE (2005), 'Amoral Adorno: Negative Dialectics outside Ethics', *European Journal of Social Theory* 8/3, 251–67.

TAYLOR, CHARLES (1985), *Philosophy and the Human Sciences: Philosophical Papers 2* (Cambridge: Cambridge University Press).

—— (1989), *Sources of the Self* (Cambridge: Cambridge University Press).

TAYLOR, JAMES STACEY (ed.) (1995), *Personal Autonomy* (New York: Cambridge University Press).

THEUNISSEN, MICHAEL (1969), *Gesellschaft und Geschichte: Zur Kritik der kritischen Theorie* (Berlin: de Gruyter); trans. G. Finlayson and P. Dews as 'Society and History: A Critique of Critical Theory', in P. Dews (ed.), *Habermas: A Critical Reader* (Oxford: Blackwell, 1999), 241–71.

THOMPSON, EDWARD P. (1978), *The Poverty of Theory and Other Essays* (London: Merlin Press).

TRENDELENBURG, ADOLF (1840), *Logische Untersuchungen* (Leipzig: Hirzel).

—— (1867), *Historische Beiträge zur Philosophie* (Berlin: Bethge).

—— (1870), *Kuno Fischer und sein Kant* (Leipzig: Hirzel).

TROELTSCH, ERNST (1922a), *Der Historismus und seine Probleme* (Tübingen: Mohr).

—— (1922b), 'Die Krise des Historismus', *Die Neue Rundschau* 33, 572–90.

TUCKER, ROBERT C. (ed.) (1978), *The Marx-Engels Reader*, 2nd edn. (New York: W. W. Norton).

TUGENDHAT, ERNST (1970), *Der Wahrheitsbegriff bei Husserl und Heidegger* (Berlin: de Gruyter).

—— (1976), *Vorlesungen zur Einführung in die sprachanalytische Philosophie* (Frankfurt am Main: Suhrkamp); trans. P. A. Gorner as *Traditional and Analytical Philosophy* (Cambridge: Cambridge University Press, 1982).

—— (1986), *Self-Consciousness and Self-Determination* (Cambridge, MA: MIT Press).

VAIHINGER, HANS (1892), *Kommentar zu Kants Kritik der reinen Vernunft* (Berlin: Union Deutsche Verlagsgesellschaft)

VIRNO, PAOLO (2004), *The Grammar of the Multitude*, trans. Sylvère Lotringer (New York: Semiotexte).

VORLÄNDER, KARL (1975), *Geschichte der Philosophie* (Hamburg: Felix Meiner).

WAGNER, PETER (2003), 'Versuch das Endspiel zu Verstehen, Kapitalismusanalyse als Gesellschaftstheorie', in Axel Honneth (ed.), *Dialektik der Freiheit: Frankfurter Adorno-Konferenz 2003* (Frankfurt am Main: Suhrkamp).

WALZER, MICHAEL (1986), 'The Politics of Michel Foucault', in Hoy (ed.) (1986), pp. 51–8.

—— (1989), *The Company of Critics* (London: Peter Halban).

WEIL, SIMONE (1958), *Oppression and Liberty* (London: Routledge & Kegan Paul).

WELLMER, ALBRECHT (1984–5), 'Truth, Semblance and Reconciliation—Adorno's Aesthetic Redemption of Modernity', *Telos* 62, 89–115.

WELSHON, REX (2004), *The Philosophy of Nietzsche* (Montreal: McGill-Queen's University Press).

WESTEN, DREW (1998), 'The Scientific Legacy of Sigmund Freud: Toward a Psychodynamically Informed Psychological Science', *Psychological Bulletin* 124, 333–71.

WHITE, NICHOLAS (2002), *The Individual and Conflict in Greek Ethics* (Oxford: Clarendon Press).

WHITE, RICHARD (1997), *Nietzsche and the Problem of Sovereignty* (Urbana: University of Illinois Press).

WHITMAN, JAMES (1986), 'Nietzsche in the Magisterial Tradition of German Classical Philology', *Journal of the History of Ideas* 47, 453–68.

WIGGERSHAUS, ROLF (1994), *The Frankfurt School* (Cambridge: Polity).

WILDT, ANDREAS (1982), *Autonomie und Anerkennung, Hegels Moralitätskritik im Lichte seiner Fichte-Rezeption* (Stuttgart: Klett-Cotta).

WILLIAMS, BERNARD (1981), *Moral Luck* (New York: Cambridge University Press).

—— (1985), *Ethics and the Limits of Philosophy* (Cambridge, MA: Harvard University Press).

WILLIAMS, BERNARD and SMART, J. J. C. (1973), *Utilitarianism: For and Against* (New York: Cambridge University Press).

WILLSON, A. LESLIE (ed.) (1982), *German Romantic Criticism* (New York: Continuum).

WINCKELMANN, JOHANN JOACHIM (1755), *Gedanken über die Nachahmung der griechischen Werke in der Malerei und Bildhauerkunst*, trans. Elfriede Heyer and Roger C. Norton as (1987), *Reflections on the Imitation of Greek Works in Painting and Sculpture* (LaSalle, IL: Open Court).

—— (1764), *Geschichte der Kunst des Alterthums*, trans. Alexander Gode as *History of Ancient Art* (New York: Frederick Ungar, 1968).

WINDELBAND, WILHELM (1878–80), *Geschichte der neueren Philosophie*, 2 vols. (Leipzig: Breitkopf & Härtel).

—— (1883), *Präludien: Aufsätze und Reden zur Philosophie und ihrer Geschichte* (Tübingen: Mohr).

—— (1910), *Die Erneuerung des Hegelianismus*, Sitzungsberichte der Heidelberger Akademie der Wissenschaften, Philosophisch-Historische Klasse (Heidelberg: Winter).

WITTGENSTEIN, LUDWIG (1927), *Tractatus Logico-philosophicus*, trans. D. F. Pears and B. F. McGuinness (London: Routledge, 1961).

—— (1953), *Philosophical Investigations*, (ed.) G. E. M. Anscombe and R. Rhees, rev. trans. G. E. M. Anscombe, 3rd edn. (Oxford: Blackwell, 2001).

WOLF, SUSAN (1995), 'Freedom within Reason', in J. S. Taylor, ed. (1995), 258–75.

WOLFF, CHRISTIAN (1968), *Gesammelte Werke*, (ed.) Jean Ecole, H. W. Arndt, Ch. A. Corr, J. E. Hofmann, and M. Thomann (Hildesheim: Olms).

WOLFF, MICHAEL (1981), *Der Begriff des Widerspruchs: Eine Studie zur Dialektik Kants und Hegels* (Königstein: Hain-Athenäum).

WOLFF, ROBERT PAUL (1990), 'Methodological Individualism and Marx: Some Remarks on Elster, Game Theory, and Other Things', *Canadian Journal of Philosophy* 20, 469–86.

WOLLHEIM, RICHARD (1971), *Sigmund Freud* (Cambridge: Cambridge University Press).

—— (1993), *The Mind and its Depths* (Cambridge, MA: Harvard University Press).

Wood, Allen (1970), *Kant's Moral Religion* (Ithaca, NY: Cornell University Press).

—— (1990), *Hegel's Ethical Thought* (New York: Cambridge University Press).

—— (1991), 'Marx against Morality', in Singer, (ed.) (1991) 511–24.

Woodruff Smith, David: *see* Smith, David Woodruff, and Young, James O. (2001), *Art and Knowledge* (London: Routledge).

Young, Julian (1992), *Nietzsche's Philosophy of Art* (Cambridge: Cambridge University Press).

—— (1997), *Heidegger, Philosophy, Nazism* (Cambridge: Cambridge University Press).

—— (2002), *Heidegger's Later Philosophy* (Cambridge: Cambridge University Press).

—— (2003), *The Death of God and the Meaning of Life* (London: Routledge).

—— (2006), *Nietzsche's Philosophy of Religion* (Cambridge: Cambridge University Press).

Yovel, Yirmiyahu (1980), *Kant and the Philosophy of History* (Princeton: Princeton University Press).

Zahavi, Dan (1999), *Self-Awareness and Alterity* (Evanston: Northwestern University Press).

Žižek, Slavoj (1999), *The Ticklish Subject* (London: Verso).

Zuidervaart, Lambert (2004), *Artistic Truth: Aesthetics, Discourse, and Imaginative Disclosure* (Cambridge: Cambridge University Press).

# Index

Printed in Great Britain
by Amazon.co.uk, Ltd.,
Marston Gate.